Real-Time Data Analysis Exercises

Up-to-date macro data is a great way to engage in and understand the usefulness of macro variables and their impact on the economy. Real-Time Data Analysis exercises communicate directly with the Federal Reserve Bank of St. Louis's FRED site, so every time FRED posts new data, students see new data.

End-of-chapter exercises accompanied by the Real-Time Data Analysis icon 〰 include Real-Time Data versions in **MyEconLab**.

Select in-text figures labeled **MyEconLab** Real-Time Data update in the electronic version of the text using FRED data.

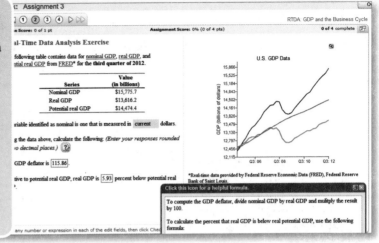

Current News Exercises

Posted weekly, we find the latest microeconomic and macroeconomic news stories, post them, and write auto-graded multi-part exercises that illustrate the economic way of thinking about the news.

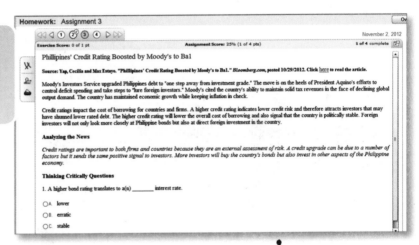

Interactive Homework Exercises

Participate in a fun and engaging activity that helps promote active learning and mastery of important economic concepts.

Pearson's experiments program is flexible and easy for instructors and students to use. For a complete list of available experiments, visit *www.myeconlab.com*.

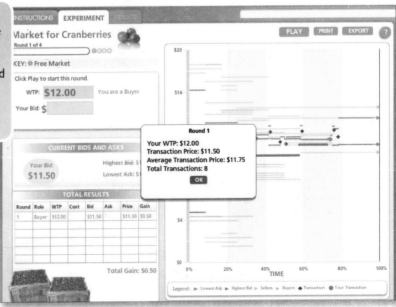

Featured Applications in This Book

Microeconomics

THEORY AND APPLICATIONS WITH CALCULUS

THIRD EDITION

THE PEARSON SERIES IN ECONOMICS

Abel/Bernanke/Croushore
*Macroeconomics**

Bade/Parkin
*Foundations of Economics**

Berck/Helfand
*The Economics of the
Environment*

Bierman/Fernandez
*Game Theory with Economic
Applications*

Blanchard
*Macroeconomics**

Blau/Ferber/Winkler
*The Economics of Women,
Men and Work*

**Boardman/Greenberg/Vining/
Weimer**
Cost-Benefit Analysis

Boyer
*Principles of Transportation
Economics*

Branson
*Macroeconomic Theory and
Policy*

Brock/Adams
*The Structure of American
Industry*

Bruce
*Public Finance and the
American Economy*

Carlton/Perloff
*Modern Industrial
Organization*

Case/Fair/Oster
*Principles of Economics**

Caves/Frankel/Jones
*World Trade and Payments:
An Introduction*

Chapman
*Environmental Economics:
Theory, Application, and
Policy*

Cooter/Ulen
Law & Economics

Downs
*An Economic Theory of
Democracy*

Ehrenberg/Smith
Modern Labor Economics

Farnham
Economics for Managers

Folland/Goodman/Stano
*The Economics of Health
and Health Care*

Fort
Sports Economics

Froyen
Macroeconomics

Fusfeld
The Age of the Economist

Gerber
*International Economics**

González-Rivera
*Forecasting for Economics and
Business*

Gordon
*Macroeconomics**

Greene
Econometric Analysis

Gregory
Essentials of Economics

Gregory/Stuart
*Russian and Soviet Economic
Performance and Structure*

Hartwick/Olewiler
*The Economics of Natural
Resource Use*

Heilbroner/Milberg
*The Making of the Economic
Society*

Heyne/Boettke/Prychitko
*The Economic Way of
Thinking*

Hoffman/Averett
*Women and the Economy:
Family, Work, and Pay*

Holt
*Markets, Games and Strategic
Behavior*

Hubbard/O'Brien
*Economics**

*Money, Banking, and the
Financial System**

Hubbard/O'Brien/Rafferty
*Macroeconomics**

Hughes/Cain
American Economic History

Husted/Melvin
International Economics

Jehle/Reny
Advanced Microeconomic Theory

Johnson-Lans
A Health Economics Primer

Keat/Young
Managerial Economics

Klein
*Mathematical Methods for
Economics*

Krugman/Obstfeld/Melitz
*International Economics:
Theory & Policy**

Laidler
The Demand for Money

Leeds/von Allmen
The Economics of Sports

Leeds/von Allmen/Schiming
*Economics**

Lipsey/Ragan/Storer
*Economics**

Lynn
*Economic Development:
Theory and Practice for a
Divided World*

Miller
*Economics Today**

*Understanding Modern
Economics*

Miller/Benjamin
*The Economics of Macro
Issues*

Miller/Benjamin/North
*The Economics of Public
Issues*

Mills/Hamilton
Urban Economics

Mishkin
*The Economics of Money,
Banking, and Financial Markets**

*The Economics of Money,
Banking, and Financial Markets,
Business School Edition**

*Macroeconomics: Policy and
Practice**

Murray
*Econometrics: A Modern
Introduction*

Nafziger
*The Economics of Developing
Countries*

O'Sullivan/Sheffrin/Perez
*Economics: Principles,
Applications and Tools**

Parkin
*Economics**

Perloff
*Microeconomics**

*Microeconomics: Theory and
Applications with Calculus**

Phelps
Health Economics

Pindyck/Rubinfeld
*Microeconomics**

**Riddell/Shackelford/Stamos/
Schneider**
*Economics: A Tool for Critically
Understanding Society*

Ritter/Silber/Udell
*Principles of Money, Banking
& Financial Markets**

Roberts
*The Choice: A Fable of Free
Trade and Protection*

Rohlf
*Introduction to Economic
Reasoning*

Ruffin/Gregory
Principles of Economics

Sargent
*Rational Expectations and
Inflation*

Sawyer/Sprinkle
International Economics

Scherer
*Industry Structure, Strategy,
and Public Policy*

Schiller
*The Economics of Poverty and
Discrimination*

Sherman
Market Regulation

Silberberg
Principles of Microeconomics

Stock/Watson
Introduction to Econometrics

Studenmund
*Using Econometrics: A Practical
Guide*

Tietenberg/Lewis
*Environmental and Natural
Resource Economics*

*Environmental Economics and
Policy*

Todaro/Smith
Economic Development

Waldman
Microeconomics

Waldman/Jensen
*Industrial Organization:
Theory and Practice*

**Walters/Walters/Appel/Calla-
han/Centanni/Maex/O'Neill**
*Econversations: Today's
Students Discuss Today's Issues*

Weil
Economic Growth

Williamson
Macroeconomics

*denotes MyEconLab titles   Visit **www.myeconlab.com** to learn more

Microeconomics

THEORY AND APPLICATIONS WITH CALCULUS

THIRD EDITION

JEFFREY M. PERLOFF

UNIVERSITY OF CALIFORNIA, BERKELEY

PEARSON

Boston   Columbus   Indianapolis   New York   San Francisco   Upper Saddle River
Amsterdam   Cape Town   Dubai   London   Madrid   Milan   Munich   Paris   Montreal   Toronto
Delhi   Mexico City   Sao Paulo   Sydney   Hong Kong   Seoul   Singapore   Taipei   Tokyo

For Lisa

Editor-in-Chief: Donna Battista
Executive Acquisitions Editor: Adrienne D'Ambrosio
Editorial Project Manager: Sarah Dumouchelle
Editorial Assistant: Elissa Senra-Sargent
Executive Marketing Manager: Lori DeShazo
Managing Editor: Jeff Holcomb
Senior Production Project Manager: Meredith Gertz
Senior Procurement Specialist: Carol Melville
Art Director and Cover Designer:
   Jonathan Boylan
Cover Image: Olga Lyubkina/Shutterstock
Image Manager: Rachel Youdelman
Photo Research: Integra Software Services, Ltd.
Text Permissions Project Supervisor: Jill C. Dougan

Text Permissions Research: Electronic Publishing Services
Director of Media: Susan Schoenberg
Content Leads, MyEconLab: Noel Lotz and
   Courtney Kamauf
Executive Media Producer: Melissa Honig
Project Management and Text Design: Gillian Hall,
   The Aardvark Group
Composition and Illustrations: Laserwords Maine
Copyeditor: Kathleen Cantwell
Proofreader: Holly McLean-Aldis
Indexer: John Lewis
Printer/Binder: RR Donnelley
Cover Printer: Lehigh Phoenix
Text Font: Sabon

Credits and acknowledgments borrowed from other sources and reproduced, with permission, in this textbook appear on the appropriate page within text or on page E-90.

Library of Congress Cataloging-in-Publication Data

Perloff, Jeffrey M.
   Microeconomics : theory & applications with calculus / Jeffrey Perloff.—3rd ed.
      p. cm.
   Includes bibliographical references and index.
   ISBN 978-0-13-301993-3
   1. Microeconomics. I. Title.
   HB172.P39 2014
   338.5—dc22

10 9 8 7 6 5 4 3 2 1

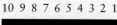

www.pearsonhighered.com

ISBN 10: 0-13-301993-4
ISBN 13: 978-0-13-301993-3

Brief Contents

Contents

Preface

This book is a new type of intermediate microeconomics textbook. Previously, the choice was between books that use calculus to present formal theory dryly and with few, if any, applications to the real world and books that include applications but present theory using algebra and graphs only. This book uses calculus, algebra, and graphs to present microeconomic theory based on actual examples and then uses the theory to analyze real-world problems. My purpose is to show that economic theory has practical, problem-solving uses and is not an empty academic exercise.

This book shows how individuals, policymakers, and firms use microeconomic tools to analyze and resolve problems. For example, students learn that:

- individuals can draw on microeconomic theories when deciding whether to invest and whether to sign a contract that pegs prices to the government's measure of inflation;
- policymakers (and voters) can employ microeconomics to predict the impact of taxes, regulations, and other measures before they are enacted;
- lawyers and judges use microeconomics in antitrust, discrimination, and contract cases; and
- firms apply microeconomic principles to produce at least cost and maximize profit, select strategies, decide whether to buy from a market or to produce internally, and write contracts to provide optimal incentives for employees.

My experience in teaching microeconomics for the departments of economics at the Massachusetts Institute of Technology; the University of Pennsylvania; the University of California, Berkeley; the Department of Agricultural and Resource Economics at Berkeley; and the Wharton Business School has convinced me that students prefer this emphasis on real-world issues.

Changes in the Third Edition

In the Third Edition, all chapters are moderately to substantially revised, 80% of the Applications are new or updated, and there are 24 new Solved Problems. Every chapter (after Chapter 1) contains a new Challenge feature (and the Challenge Solution) and has many new end-of-chapter exercises.

Revised Chapters

The presentation of theories is revised in many chapters. The major changes include the following:

Consumer Theory. The material on demand functions in Chapters 3 and 4 is reorganized between the chapters. In Chapter 3, the utility section is substantially rewritten and supplemented, particularly regarding the treatment of the marginal rate of substitution (*MRS*), the quasilinear utility function, and constrained consumer choice. The chapter now examines the five most common utility functions in detail (for example, see new Tables 3.1 and 3.2), and greatly expands its coverage of corner solutions. In Chapter 4, the section on systems of demand functions and income elasticities is significantly revised, and the treatment of Giffen goods is expanded. Chapter 5 updates the treatments of government policies such as taxes and food stamps. All three chapters have numerous new end-of-chapter exercises.

Behavioral Economics. This edition adds new material on behavioral economics. The biggest change is the addition of Section 13.4 on behavioral game theory.

Pricing. Chapter 12 on pricing and advertising is substantially reorganized and rewritten, with new section heads and modified terminology. It also presents new material on mixed bundling and sales.

Externalities. Chapter 17 on property rights, externalities, rivalry, and exclusion is substantially revised and reorganized, with added stress on the role of property rights; a new, simpler treatment of the Coase Theorem; and substantial changes to the sections covering the optimal provision of a public good, the benefits versus costs from controlling pollution, and the market for pollution.

Other Changes. Sections that are substantially rewritten or expanded include types of firms (Chapter 6); minimizing costs (Chapter 7); perfect competition (Chapter 8); the shut down decision (Chapter 8); entry and exit (Chapter 8); effects of government policies on supply and demand curves (Chapter 9); Pareto and other welfare concepts (Chapter 10); market power and welfare (Chapter 11); welfare effects of taxes (Chapter 11); sources of market power (Chapter 11); insurance (Chapter 17); lemons markets (Chapter 18); and efficiency wages (Chapter 19).

The material on monopsony previously in Chapter 15 is now in Chapter 11. Chapter 13 on game theory is reorganized and rewritten, and includes the new behavioral game theory section. Chapter 14 on oligopoly is substantially rewritten, reorganized, and shortened. Chapter 19 on contracts and moral hazard has a new section on checks on principals, while the former section on payments linked to production or profit is now in MyEconLab.

Applications

This edition has 113 Applications. Of these, 80% are new or updated: 40% are new and 40% are updated from the previous edition. Moreover, 60% of the Applications are international or concern countries other than the United States.

To make room for these new Applications, some Applications from the Second Edition are now in MyEconLab. With these additions, the book's online components have 199 Applications.

Solved Problems and Exercises

Solved Problems are very popular with students, so this edition increases the number of Solved Problems by 30% to 103. Every chapter (after Chapter 1) has a new or revised Solved Problem. In each of these chapters, some of these Solved Problems are linked to Applications.

The end-of-chapter exercises are changed in two ways. First, they are now organized by topics rather than divided into mathematical and graphical exercises. A mathematical exercise is indicated by an **M** at the end of the exercise. Second, this edition contains many new end-of-chapter exercises, including new mathematical problems and many exercises based on current topics such as Medicare, tainted candy from Asia, light bulb regulation, the Olympics, Kindle, oil spills, alcopops, and others.

Challenges

New to this edition are Challenges, which combine an Application and a Solved Problem. Each chapter (after Chapter 1) begins with a Challenge, which discusses a real-world issue and concludes with one or more questions based on that discussion. At the end of the chapter, a Challenge Solution answers these questions. The purpose of each of these Challenges indicates to students that the material in that chapter is useful in analyzing real-world problems.

How This Book Differs from Others

This book differs from most other microeconomics texts in four main ways. First, it uses a mixture of calculus, algebra, and graphs to define economic theory. Second, it integrates real-world examples throughout the exposition, in addition to offering extended Applications. Third, it places greater emphasis on modern theories—such as industrial organization theories, game theory, transaction cost theory, information theory, contract theory, and behavioral economics—that are useful in analyzing actual markets. Fourth, it employs a step-by-step approach that demonstrates how to use microeconomic theory to solve problems and analyze policy issues.

Calculus

Much of microeconomic theory is based on maximizing behavior. Calculus is particularly helpful in solving maximization problems, while graphs help illustrate how to maximize. This book combines calculus, algebra, graphs, and verbal arguments to make the theory as clear as possible.

Modern Theories

The first half of the book (Chapters 2–10) examines competitive markets and shows that competition has very desirable properties. The rest of the book (Chapters 11–19) concentrates on imperfectly competitive markets—in which firms have market power (the ability to profitably set price above the unit cost of production), firms and consumers are uncertain about the future and have limited information, or there are externalities and public goods.

This book goes beyond basic microeconomic theory and looks at theories and applications from many important contemporary fields of economics. Extensive coverage of problems from resource economics, labor economics, international trade, public finance, and industrial organization is featured throughout. The book uses behavioral economics to discuss consumer choice, bandwagon effects on monopoly pricing over time, and the importance of time-varying discounting in explaining procrastination and in avoiding environmental disasters.

This book differs from other microeconomics texts by using game theory throughout the second half rather than isolating the topic in a single chapter. The book introduces game theory in Chapter 13, analyzing both static games (such as the prisoners' dilemma) and multi-period games (such as collusion and preventing entry). Special attention is paid to auction strategies. Chapters 14, 16, 17, 18, and 19 employ game theory to analyze oligopoly behavior and many other topics. Unlike most texts, this book covers pure and mixed strategies and analyzes both normal-form and extensive-form games.

The last two chapters draw from modern contract theory to extensively analyze adverse selection and moral hazard, unlike other texts that mention these topics only in passing, if at all. The text covers lemons markets, signaling, shirking prevention, and revealing information (including through contract choice).

Widget-Free Economics

To convince students that economics is practical and useful—not just a textbook exercise—this book presents theories using examples of real people and real firms based on actual data rather than fictional analyses of widgets or other artificial examples. These real economic stories are integrated into the formal presentation of many economic theories, discussed in Applications, and analyzed in what-if policy discussions.

Integrated Real-World Examples. This book uses real-world examples throughout the narrative to illustrate many basic theories of microeconomics. Students learn the basic model of supply and demand using estimated supply-and-demand curves for Canadian processed pork and U.S. sweetheart roses. They analyze consumer choice by employing typical consumers' estimated indifference curves between beer and wine and students' indifference curves between live music and music tracks. They learn about production and cost functions using evidence from a U.S. furniture manufacturer. Students see monopoly theory applied to a patented pharmaceutical, Botox. They use oligopoly theories to analyze the rivalry between United Airlines and American Airlines on the Chicago–Los Angeles route and between Coke and Pepsi in the cola industry. They see Apple's monopoly pricing of iPads and learn about multimarket price discrimination through the use of data on how Warner Brothers sets prices for *Harry Potter and the Deathly Hallows Part 2* DVD across countries.

What-If Policy Analysis. This book uses economic models to probe the likely outcomes of changes in public policies. Students learn how to conduct what-if analyses of policies such as taxes, subsidies, barriers to entry, price floors and ceilings, quotas and tariffs, zoning, pollution controls, and licensing laws. The text analyzes the effects of taxes on virtually every type of market.

The book also reveals the limits of economic theory for policy analysis. For example, to illustrate why attention to actual institutions is important, the text uses three different models to show how the effects of minimum wages vary across types of markets and institutions. Similarly, the text illustrates that a minimum wage law that is harmful in a competitive market may be desirable in certain noncompetitive markets.

Applications. The text includes many Applications at the end of sections that illustrate the versatility of microeconomic theory. The Applications focus on such diverse topics as:

- the derivation of an isoquant for semiconductors, using actual data;
- why Apple stopped selling all iTunes songs for the same price;
- the amount by which recipients value Christmas presents relative to the cost to gift givers;
- how much Tiger Wood's scandal affected companies that hired him as a sponsor;
- whether buying flight insurance makes sense.

Step-by-Step Problem Solving

Many instructors report that their biggest challenge in teaching microeconomics is helping students learn to solve new problems. This book is based on the belief that the best way to teach this important skill is to demonstrate problem solving repeatedly and then to give students exercises to do on their own. Each chapter (after Chapter 1) provides several Solved Problems that show students how to answer qualitative and quantitative problems using a step-by-step approach. Rather than empty arithmetic exercises demanding no more of students than employing algebra or a memorized mathematical formula, the Solved Problems focus on important economic issues such as analyzing government policies and determining firms' optimal strategies.

One Solved Problem uses game theory to examine why Intel and AMD use different advertising strategies in the central processing unit (CPU) market. Another shows how a monopolistically competitive airline equilibrium would change if fixed costs (such as fees for landing slots) rise. Others examine why firms charge different prices at factory stores than elsewhere and when markets for lemons exist, among many other topics.

The Solved Problems illustrate how to approach the formal end-of-chapter exercises. Students can solve some of the exercises using graphs or verbal arguments, while others require math.

Alternative Organizations

Because instructors cover material in many different orders, the text is designed for maximum flexibility. The most common approach to teaching microeconomics is to cover some or all of the chapters in their given sequence. Common variants include:

- presenting uncertainty (Sections 16.1 through 16.3) immediately after consumer theory;
- covering competitive factor markets (Section 15.1) immediately after competition (Chapters 8 and 9);
- introducing game theory (Chapter 13) early in the course; and
- covering general equilibrium and welfare issues (Chapter 10) at the end of the course instead of immediately after the competitive model.

Instructors can present the material in Chapters 13–19 in various orders, although Section 16.4 should follow Chapter 15, and Chapter 19 should follow Chapter 18 if both are covered.

Many business school courses skip consumer theory (and possibly some aspects of supply and demand) to allow more time for the topics covered in the second half of the book. Business school faculty may want to place particular emphasis on game theory, strategies, oligopoly, and monopolistic competition (Chapters 13 and 14); capital markets (Chapter 15); uncertainty (Chapter 16); and modern contract theory (Chapters 18 and 19).

MyEconLab

MyEconLab's powerful assessment and tutorial system works hand-in-hand with the Third Edition of *Microeconomics: Theory and Applications with Calculus*.

Features for Instructors

MyEconLab includes comprehensive homework, quiz, test, and tutorial options, where instructors can manage all assessment needs in one program.

- Select end-of-chapter exercises, including algorithmic, draw-graph, and numerical, are available for assignment.
- Test Item File questions are available for homework assignment.

- The Custom Exercise Builder allows instructors the flexibility of creating their own problems for assignment.
- The powerful Gradebook records each student's performance and time spent on the tests, study plan, and homework and generates reports by student or chapter.
- Advanced Communication Tools enable students and instructors to communicate through email, discussion board, chat, and ClassLive.
- Customization options provide new and enhanced ways to share documents, add content, and rename menu items.
- Prebuilt courses offer a turn-key method for instructors to create a course that includes assignments by chapter.

Features for Students

MyEconLab puts students in control of their learning through a collection of testing, practice, and study tools. Students can study on their own, or they can complete assignments created by their instructor. In MyEconLab's structured environment, students practice what they learn, test their understanding, and pursue a personalized study plan generated from their performance on sample tests and quizzes. In Homework or Study Plan mode, students have access to a wealth of tutorial features, including the following:

- Two calculus appendices, the "Inequality Constraints Appendix" and the "Duality Appendix," are available in the Chapter Resources section.
- Additional Applications are available in the Chapter Resources section.
- Instant feedback on exercises taken directly from the text helps students understand and apply the concepts.
- Links to the eText promote reading of the text just when the student needs to revisit a concept or an explanation.
- Learning aids help students analyze a problem in small steps, much the same way an instructor would do during office hours.
- Enhanced Pearson eText, available within the online course materials and offline via an iPad/Android app, allows instructors and students to highlight, bookmark, and take notes.
- Temporary Access for students who are awaiting financial aid provides a 17-day grace period of temporary access.

Applications, Appendices, and Answers to Selected End-of-Chapter Exercises are also available on the Companion Website at **www.pearsonhighered.com/perloff**.

Experiments in MyEconLab

Experiments are a fun and engaging way to promote active learning and mastery of important economic concepts. Pearson's Experiment program is flexible and easy for instructors and students to use.

- Single-player experiments allow students to play against virtual players from anywhere at any time they have an Internet connection.
- Multiplayer experiments allow instructors to assign and manage a real-time experiment with their class.
- Pre- and post-questions for each experiment are available for assignment in MyEconLab.

For a complete list of available experiments, visit **www.myeconlab.com**.

Teaching Resources

Many useful teaching resources can be downloaded from the Instructor Resource Center, **www.pearsonhighered.com/perloff**, or the catalog page for *Microeconomics: Theory and Applications with Calculus*. The *Instructor's Resource Manual*, by Léonie Stone, State University of New York at Geneseo, has many useful and creative teaching ideas. It also offers additional Applications, as well as extra problems and answers, and it provides solutions for all of the end-of-chapter exercises.

The *Test Bank*, by Xin Fan, Hawaii Pacific University, features many different types of problems of varying levels of complexity, suitable for homework assignments and exams. The TestGen Files provide these test questions in a versatile, editable electronic format.

The book's PowerPoint® Presentation, written by James Dearden, Lehigh University, provides instructors with a set of comprehensive lecture slides. Embedded animated figures highlight the dynamic nature of microeconomics in action.

Acknowledgments

This book evolved from my earlier, less mathematical intermediate microeconomics textbook. I thank the many faculty members and students who helped me produce both books, as well as Jane Tufts, who provided invaluable editorial help on my earlier text. I was very lucky that Sylvia Mallory, who worked on the earlier book, was my development editor on the first edition of this book as well. Sylvia worked valiantly to improve my writing style and helped to shape and improve every aspect of the book's contents and appearance.

Denise Clinton, Digital Publisher, and Adrienne D'Ambrosio, my outstanding Executive Acquisitions Editor, worked closely with Sylvia and me in planning the book and were instrumental in every phase of the project. In this edition, Sarah Dumouchelle took over the role of Editorial Project Manager and has been invaluable. She worked closely with Adrienne D'Ambrosio and me in deciding how this edition would be modified.

I have an enormous debt of gratitude to my students at MIT, the University of Pennsylvania, and the University of California, Berkeley, who dealt patiently with my various approaches to teaching them microeconomics and made useful (and generally polite) suggestions. Peter Berck, Ethan Ligon, and Larry Karp, my colleagues at the University of California, Berkeley, made many useful suggestions. Guojun He, Yann Panassie, and Hugo Salgado were incredibly helpful in producing figures, researching many of the Applications, or making constructive comments on chapter drafts.

Many people were very generous in providing me with data, models, and examples for the various Applications and Solved Problems in this book, including among others Thomas Bauer (University of Bochum); Peter Berck (University of California, Berkeley); James Brander (University of British Columbia); Leemore Dafny (Northwestern University); Lucas Davis (University of California, Berkeley); James Dearden (Lehigh University); Farid Gasmi (Université des Sciences Sociales); Avi Goldfarb (University of Toronto); Claudia Goldin (Harvard University); Rachel Goodhue (University of California, Davis); William Greene (New York University); Nile Hatch (University of Illinois); Larry Karp (University of California, Berkeley); Ryan Kellogg (University of Michigan); Arthur Kennickell (Federal Reserve, Washington); Fahad Khalil (University of Washington); Lutz Killian (University of Michigan); J. Paul Leigh (University of California, Davis); Christopher Knittel (Massachusetts Institute of Technology); Jean-Jacques Laffont (deceased); Ulrike Malmendier (University of California, Berkeley); Karl D. Meilke (University of Guelph); Eric Muehlegger (Harvard University); Giancarlo Moschini (Iowa State University); Michael Roberts (North Carolina State University); Junichi Suzuki (University of Toronto); Catherine Tucker (MIT); Harald Uhlig (University of Chicago); Quang Vuong (Université des Sciences Sociales, Toulouse, and University of Southern California); and Joel Waldfogel (University of Minnesota).

I am grateful to the many teachers of microeconomics who spent untold hours reading and commenting on chapter drafts. Many of the best ideas in this book are due to the following individuals who provided valuable comments at various stages:

R. K. Anderson, *Texas A & M*
Richard Beil, *Auburn University*
Kenny Bell, *University of California, Berkeley*
Robert A. Berman, *American University*
Douglas Blair, *Rutgers University*
James Brander, *University of British Columbia*
Jurgen Brauer, *Augusta State University*
Margaret Bray, *London School of Economics*
Helle Bunzel, *Iowa State University*
Paul Calcott, *Victoria University of Wellington*
Lauren Calimeris, *University of Colorado at Boulder*
Anoshua Chaudhuri, *San Francisco State University*
Anthony Davies, *Duquesne University*
James Dearden, *Lehigh University*
Wayne Edwards, *University of Alaska, Anchorage*
Patrick M. Emerson, *Oregon State University*
Eduardo Faingold, *Yale University*
Rachael Goodhue, *University of California, Davis*
Ron Goettler, *Carnegie Mellon University, Doha, Qatar*
Thomas Gresik, *University of Notre Dame*
Barnali Gupta, *Miami University*
Per Svejstrup Hansen, *University of Southern Denmark*

Johnson Kakeu, *Georgia Institute of Technology*
Vijay Krishna, *University of North Carolina, Chapel Hill*
Stephen Lauermann, *University of Michigan*
Carrie A. Meyer, *George Mason University*
Joshua B. Miller, *University of Minnesota, Twin Cities*
Stephen M. Miller, *University of Nevada, Las Vegas*
Olivia Mitchell, *University of Pennsylvania*
Jeffery Miron, *Harvard University*
Shalah Mostashari, *Texas A&M University*
Alexandre Padilla, *Metropolitan State College of Denver*
Michael R. Ransom, *Brigham Young University*
Riccardo Scarpa, *University of Waikato, New Zealand*
Burkhard C. Schipper, *University of California, Davis*
Riccardo Scarpa, *University of Waikato*
Galina A. Schwartz, *University of California, Berkeley*
Steven Snyder, *Lehigh University*
Barry Sopher, *Rutgers University*
Etku Unver, *Boston College*
Ruth Uwaifo, *Georgia Institute of Technology*
Ron S. Warren, Jr., *University of Georgia*
Bruce Wydick, *University of California, San Francisco*

I am particularly grateful to Jim Brander of the University of British Columbia who has given me many deep and insightful comments on this book and with whom I am writing another, related book. One of my biggest debts is to Jim Dearden, who not only provided incisive comments on every aspect of my earlier textbook, but also wrote a number of the end-of-chapter exercises. I am very grateful to Ethan Ligon for co-authoring the Calculus Appendix, which follows the last chapter.

In addition, I thank Bob Solow, the world's finest economics teacher, who showed me how to simplify models without losing their essence. I've also learned a great deal over the years about economics and writing from my co-authors on other projects, especially Dennis Carlton (my co-author on *Modern Industrial Organization*), Jackie Persons, Steve Salop, Michael Wachter, Larry Karp, Peter Berck, Amos Golan, George Judge, Ximing Wu, and Dan Rubinfeld (whom I thank for still talking to me despite my decision to write microeconomics textbooks).

It was a pleasure to work with the good people at Pearson, who were incredibly helpful in producing this book. Meredith Gertz, Senior Production Project Manager, did her usual superlative job of supervising the production process and assembling the extended publishing team. Joe Vetere, Senior Technical Art Specialist, helped me prepare graphics. Gillian Hall has my sincere thanks for outstanding work in managing the design of the handsome interior and preparing the text for publication. My thanks to Jonathan Boylan for the cover design. I also want to acknowledge, with gratitude, the efforts of Melissa Honig in developing the Web site, Noel Lotz and Courtney Kamauf for their work on MyEconLab, and Lori DeShazo in marketing the entire program.

Finally, I thank my family, Jackie Persons and Lisa Perloff, for their great patience and support during the nearly endless writing process. And I apologize for misusing their names—and those of my other relatives and friends—in this book!

J.M.P.

Introduction

1

I've often wondered what goes into a hot dog. Now I know and I wish I didn't.
—William Zinsser

If each of us could get all the food, clothing, and toys we want without working, no one would study economics. Unfortunately, most of the good things in life are scarce—we can't all have as much as we want. Thus, scarcity is the mother of economics.

Microeconomics is the study of how individuals and firms make themselves as well off as possible in a world of scarcity, and the consequences of those individual decisions for markets and the entire economy. In studying microeconomics, we examine how individual consumers and firms make decisions and how the interaction of many individual decisions affects markets.

Microeconomics is often called *price theory* to emphasize the important role that prices play in determining market outcomes. Microeconomics explains how the actions of all buyers and sellers determine prices and how prices influence the decisions and actions of individual buyers and sellers.

---

1. **Microeconomics: The Allocation of Scarce Resources.** Microeconomics is the study of the allocation of scarce resources.

2. **Models.** Economists use models to make testable predictions.

3. **Uses of Microeconomic Models.** Individuals, governments, and firms use microeconomic models and predictions in decision making.

In this chapter, we discuss three main topics

1.1 Microeconomics: The Allocation of Scarce Resources

Individuals and firms allocate their limited resources to make themselves as well off as possible. Consumers select the mix of goods and services that makes them as happy as possible given their limited wealth. Firms decide which goods to produce, where to produce them, how much to produce to maximize their profits, and how to produce those levels of output at the lowest cost by using more or less of various inputs such as labor, capital, materials, and energy. The owners of a depletable natural resource such as oil decide when to use it. Government decision makers decide which goods and services the government will produce and whether to subsidize, tax, or regulate industries and consumers to benefit consumers, firms, or government employees.

Trade-Offs

People make trade-offs because they can't have everything. A society faces three key trade-offs:

1. **Which goods and services to produce.** If a society produces more cars, it must produce fewer of other goods and services, because there are only so many *resources*—workers, raw materials, capital, and energy—available to produce goods.
2. **How to produce.** To produce a given level of output, a firm must use more of one input if it uses less of another input. Cracker and cookie manufacturers switch between palm oil and coconut oil, depending on which is less expensive.
3. **Who gets the goods and services.** The more of society's goods and services you get, the less someone else gets.

Who Makes the Decisions

The government may make these three allocation decisions explicitly, or the final decisions may reflect the interaction of independent decisions by many individual consumers and firms. In the former Soviet Union, the government told manufacturers how many cars of each type to make and which inputs to use to make them. The government also decided which consumers would get cars.

In most other countries, how many cars of each type are produced and who gets them are determined by how much it costs to make cars of a particular quality in the least expensive way and how much consumers are willing to pay for them. More consumers would own a handcrafted Rolls-Royce and fewer would buy a mass-produced Toyota Camry if a Rolls were not 21 times more expensive than a Camry.

How Prices Determine Allocations

An Economist's Theory of Reincarnation: If you're good, you come back on a higher level. Cats come back as dogs, dogs come back as horses, and people—if they've been real good like George Washington—come back as money.

Prices link the decisions about *which goods and services to produce, how to produce them,* and *who gets them.* Prices influence the decisions of individual consumers and firms, and the interactions of these decisions by consumers, firms, and the government determine price.

Interactions between consumers and firms take place in a **market**, which is an exchange mechanism that allows buyers to trade with sellers. A market may be a town square where people go to trade food and clothing, or it may be an international telecommunications network over which people buy and sell financial securities. Typically, when we talk about a single market, we are referring to trade in a single good or a group of goods that are closely related, such as soft drinks, movies, novels, or automobiles.

Most of this book concerns how prices are determined within a market. We show that the organization of the market, especially the number of buyers and sellers in the market and the amount of information they have, helps determine whether the price equals the cost of production. We also show that if there is no market—and hence no market price—serious problems, such as high pollution levels, result.

Many American, Australian, British, Canadian, New Zealand, and Taiwanese jurisdictions are proposing a *Twinkie tax* on unhealthful fatty and sweet foods or a tax on sugary soft drinks to reduce obesity and cholesterol problems, particularly among children. One survey found that 45% of adults would support a 1¢ tax per pound of soft drinks, chips, and butter, with the revenues used to fund health education programs.

In recent years, many communities around the world debated (and some passed) new taxes on sugar-sweetened soft drinks. In 2012, Chicago debated increasing the beverage tax by 1¢ per ounce on soft drinks, energy drinks, and other sugary beverages. At least 25 states differentially tax soft drinks, candy, chewing gum, and snack foods such as potato chips. Today, many school districts throughout the United States ban soft drink vending machines. This ban discourages consumption, as would an extremely high tax. Britain's largest life insurance firm charges obese people higher premiums for life insurance policies.

New taxes will affect *which foods are produced*, as firms offer new low-fat and low-sugar products, and *how fast-foods are produced*, as manufacturers reformulate their products to lower their tax burden. These taxes will also influence *who gets these goods* as consumers, especially children, replace them with less expensive, untaxed products.[1]

1.2   Models

Everything should be made as simple as possible, but not simpler.
—Albert Einstein

To *explain* how individuals and firms allocate resources and how market prices are determined, economists use a **model**: a description of the relationship between two or more variables. Economists also use models to *predict* how a change in one variable will affect another variable.

According to an *income threshold model*, no one who has an income level below a threshold buys a particular consumer durable, which is a good that can be used for long periods, such as a refrigerator or car. The theory also holds that almost everyone whose income is above that threshold buys the durable.

If this theory is correct, we predict that, as most people's incomes rise above the threshold in less-developed countries, consumer durable purchases will increase from near zero to large numbers virtually overnight. This prediction is consistent with evidence from Malaysia, where the income threshold for buying a car is about $4,000.

In China, incomes are rising rapidly and are exceeding the threshold levels for many types of durable goods. As a result, many experts predicted that the greatest consumer durable goods sales boom in history would take place there over the next decade. Anticipating this boom, many companies greatly increased their investments in durable goods manufacturing plants in China. Annual foreign direct investments went from $916 million a year in 1983 to $116 billion in 2011. In expectation of this growth potential, even

---

[1]The sources for Applications are available at the back of the book.

traditional political opponents of the People's Republic—Taiwan, South Korea, and Russia—invested in China.

Li Rifu, a 46-year-old Chinese farmer and watch repairman, thought that buying a car would improve the odds that his 22- and 24-year-old sons would find girlfriends, marry, and produce grandchildren. Soon after Mr. Li purchased his Geely King Kong for the equivalent of $9,000, both sons met girlfriends, and his older son got married. Four-fifths of all new cars sold in China are bought by first-time customers. An influx of first-time buyers was responsible for China's ninefold increase in car sales from 2000 to 2009. By 2010, China became the second largest producer of automobiles in the world, trailing only Germany.

Simplifications by Assumption

We stated the income threshold model verbally, but we could have presented it graphically or mathematically. Regardless of how the model is described, an economic model is a simplification of reality that contains only reality's most important features. Without simplifications, it is difficult to make predictions because the real world is too complex to analyze fully.

By analogy, if the owner's manual accompanying a new DVD recorder had a diagram showing the relationships among all the parts in the DVD, the diagram would be overwhelming and useless. But a diagram that includes a photo of the buttons on the front of the machine, with labels describing the purpose of each, is useful and informative.

Economists make many *assumptions* to simplify their models.[2] When using the income threshold model to explain car-purchasing behavior in China, we assume that factors other than income, such as the vehicles' color choices, are irrelevant to the decision to buy cars. Therefore, we ignore the color of cars that are sold in China when we describe the relationship between average income and the number of cars that consumers want. If our assumption is correct, we make our auto market analysis simpler without losing important details by ignoring color. If we're wrong and these ignored issues are important, our predictions may be inaccurate.

Throughout this book, we start with strong assumptions to simplify our models. Later, we add complexities. For example, in most of the book, we assume that consumers know each firm's price for a product. In many markets, such as the New York Stock Exchange, this assumption is realistic. However, it is not realistic in other markets, such as the market for used automobiles, in which consumers do not know the prices that each firm charges. To devise an accurate model for markets in which consumers have limited information, in Chapter 18, we add consumer uncertainty about price into the model.

---

[2]An engineer, an economist, and a physicist are stranded on a deserted island with a can of beans but no can opener. How should they open the can? The engineer proposes hitting the can with a rock. The physicist suggests building a fire under the can to build up pressure and burst it open. The economist thinks for a while and then says, "Assume that we have a can opener …"

Testing Theories

Given a choice between two theories, take the one which is funnier.
—Blore's Razor

Economic *theory* is the development and use of a model to test *hypotheses*, which are predictions about cause and effect. We are interested in models that make clear, testable predictions, such as "If the price rises, the quantity demanded falls." A theory stating that "People's behaviors depend on their tastes, and their tastes change randomly at random intervals" is not very useful because it does not lead to testable predictions.

Economists test theories by checking whether predictions are correct. If a prediction does not come true, economists may reject the theory.[3] Economists use a model until it is refuted by evidence or until a better model is developed.

A good model makes sharp, clear predictions that are consistent with reality. Some very simple models make sharp predictions that are incorrect, and other, more complex models make ambiguous predictions—in which any outcome is possible— that are untestable. The skill in model building is to chart a middle ground.

The purpose of this book is to teach you how to think like an economist, in the sense that you can build testable theories using economic models or apply existing models to new situations. Although economists think alike, in that they develop and use testable models, they often disagree. One may present a logically consistent argument that prices will go up in the next quarter. Another economist, using a different but equally logical theory, may contend that prices will fall in that quarter. If the economists are reasonable, they agree that pure logic alone cannot resolve their dispute. Indeed, they agree that they'll have to use empirical evidence—facts about the real world—to determine which prediction is correct.

Maximizing Subject to Constraints

Although one economist's model may differ from another's, a key assumption in most microeconomic models is that individuals allocate their scarce resources so as to make themselves as well off as possible. Of all the affordable combinations of goods, consumers pick the bundle of goods that gives them the most possible enjoyment. Firms try to maximize their profits given limited resources and existing technology. That resources are limited plays a crucial role in these models. Were it not for scarcity, people could consume unlimited amounts of goods and services, and sellers could become rich beyond limit.

As we show throughout this book, the maximizing behavior of individuals and firms determines society's three main allocation decisions: which goods are produced, how they are produced, and who gets them. For example, diamond-studded pocket combs will be sold only if firms find it profitable to sell them. The firms will make and sell these combs only if consumers value the combs at least as much as it costs the firm to produce them. Consumers will buy the combs only if they get more pleasure from the combs than they would from other goods they could buy with the same resources.

---

[3]We can use evidence of whether a theory's predictions are correct to refute the theory but not to prove it. If a model's prediction is inconsistent with what actually happened, the model must be wrong, so we reject it. Even if the model's prediction is consistent with reality, however, the model's prediction may be correct for the wrong reason. Hence, we cannot prove that the model is correct— we can only fail to reject it.

Many of the models that we examine are based on maximizing an objective that is subject to a constraint. Consumers maximize their well-being subject to a budget constraint, which says that their resources limit how many goods they can buy. Firms maximize profits subject to technological and other constraints. Governments may try to maximize the welfare of consumers or firms subject to constraints imposed by limited resources and the behavior of consumers and firms. We cover the formal economic analysis of maximizing behavior in Chapters 2–19 and review the underlying mathematics in the Calculus Appendix at the end of the book.

Positive Versus Normative

Those are my principles. If you don't like them I have others. —Groucho Marx

The use of models of maximizing behavior sometimes leads to predictions that seem harsh or heartless. For instance, a World Bank economist predicted that if an African government used price controls to keep the price of food low during a drought, food shortages would occur and people would starve. The predicted outcome is awful, but the economist was not heartless. The economist was only making a scientific prediction about the relationship between cause and effect: Price controls (cause) lead to food shortages and starvation (effect).

Such a scientific prediction is known as a **positive statement**: a testable hypothesis about matters of fact such as cause and effect relations. *Positive* does not mean that we are certain about the truth of our statement; it indicates only that we can test whether it is true.

If the World Bank economist is correct, should the government control prices? If government policymakers believe the economist's predictions, they know that the low prices will help consumers who are able to buy as much food as they want, and hurt both the food sellers and those who are unable to buy as much food as they want, some of whom may die from malnutrition. As a result, the government's decision of whether to use price controls turns on whether the government cares more about the winners or the losers. In other words, to decide on its policy, the government makes a value judgment.

Instead of making a prediction and testing it and then making a value judgment to decide whether to use price controls, government policymakers could make a value judgment directly. The value judgment could be based on the belief that "because people *should* have prepared for the drought, the government should not try to help them by keeping food prices low" or "people should be protected against price gouging during a drought, so the government should use price controls."

These two statements are *not* scientific predictions. Each is a value judgment or **normative statement**: a conclusion as to whether something is good or bad. A normative statement cannot be tested because a value judgment cannot be refuted by evidence. It is a prescription rather than a prediction. A normative statement concerns what somebody believes should happen; a positive statement concerns what will happen.

Although a normative conclusion can be drawn without first conducting a positive analysis, a policy debate will be more informed if positive analyses are conducted first.[4] Suppose your normative belief is that the government should help

---

[4]Some economists draw the normative conclusion that, as social scientists, we economists should restrict ourselves to positive analyses. Others argue that we shouldn't give up our right to make value judgments just like the next person (who happens to be biased, prejudiced, and pigheaded, unlike us).

the poor. Should you vote for a candidate who advocates a higher minimum wage (a law that requires firms to pay wages at or above a specified level); a European-style welfare system (guaranteeing health care, housing, and other basic goods and services); an end to our current welfare system; a negative income tax (the less income a person receives, the more that person receives from the government); or job training programs? Positive economic analysis can be used to predict whether these programs will benefit poor people but *not* whether these programs are good or bad. Using these predictions and your value judgment, you decide for whom to vote.

Economists' emphasis on positive analysis has implications for what they study and even their use of language. For example, many economists stress that they study people's *wants* rather than their needs. Although people need certain minimum levels of food, shelter, and clothing to survive, most people in developed economies have enough money to buy goods well in excess of the minimum levels necessary to maintain life. Consequently, calling something a *need* in a wealthy country is often a value judgment. You almost certainly have been told by an elder that "you *need* a college education." That person was probably making a value judgment—"you *should* go to college"—rather than a scientific prediction that you will suffer terrible economic deprivation if you don't go to college. We can't test such value judgments, but we can test hypotheses such as "people with a college education earn substantially more than comparable people with only a high school education."

1.3   Uses of Microeconomic Models

Have you ever imagined a world without hypothetical situations? —Steven Wright

Because microeconomic models *explain* why economic decisions are made and allow us to make *predictions*, they can be very useful for individuals, governments, and firms in making decisions. Throughout this book, we consider examples of how microeconomics aids in actual decision making. Here, we briefly look at some uses by individuals and governments.

Individuals use microeconomics to make purchasing and other decisions. Examples include considering inflation when choosing whether to rent an apartment (Chapter 5); determining whether going to college is a good investment (Chapter 15); deciding whether to invest in stocks or invest in bonds (Chapter 16); determining whether to buy insurance (Chapter 16); and knowing whether you should pay a lawyer by the hour or a percentage of any winnings (Chapter 19).

Microeconomics can help citizens make voting decisions based on candidates' views on economic issues. Elected and appointed government officials use economic models in many ways. Recent administrations have placed increased emphasis on economic analysis. Economic and environmental impact studies are required before many projects can commence. The President's Council of Economic Advisers and other federal economists analyze and advise national government agencies on the likely economic effects of all major policies.

Indeed, often governments use microeconomic models to predict the probable impact of a policy. We show how to predict the likely impact of a tax on the tax revenues raised (Chapter 2), the effects of trade policies such as tariffs and quotas on markets (Chapter 9), and whether San Francisco would earn more by raising the price for cable car rides (Chapter 11). Governments also use economics to decide how best to prevent pollution and global warming (Chapter 17).

Decisions by firms reflect microeconomic analysis. Firms price discriminate (charge individuals different prices) or bundle goods to increase their profits (Chapter 12). Strategic decisions concerning pricing, setting quantities, advertising, or entering into a market can be predicted using game theory (Chapter 13). In particular, oligopolistic and monopolistically competitive markets, such as American Airlines and United Airlines competition on the Chicago–Los Angeles route, can be analyzed and predicted using game theory (Chapter 14). When a mining company should extract ore depends on interest rates (Chapter 15). Firms decide whether to offer employees deferred payments to ensure hard work (Chapter 19).

SUMMARY

1. **Microeconomics: The Allocation of Scarce Resources.** Microeconomics is the study of the allocation of scarce resources. Consumers, firms, and governments must make allocation decisions. A society faces three key trade-offs: which goods and services to produce, how to produce them, and who gets them. These decisions are interrelated and depend on the prices that consumers and firms face and on government actions. Market prices affect the decisions of individual consumers and firms, and the interaction of the decisions of individual consumers and firms determines market prices. The organization of the market, especially the number of firms in the market and the information consumers and firms have, plays an important role in determining whether the market price is equal to, or higher than the cost of producing an additional unit of output.

2. **Models.** Models based on economic theories are used to predict the future and to answer questions

about how some change, such as a tax increase, will affect various sectors of the economy. A good theory is simple to use and makes clear, testable predictions that are not refuted by evidence. Most microeconomic models are based on maximizing behavior. Economists use models to construct *positive* hypotheses concerning how a cause leads to an effect. These positive questions can be tested. In contrast, *normative* statements, which are value judgments, cannot be tested.

3. **Uses of Microeconomic Models.** Individuals, governments, and firms use microeconomic models and predictions to make decisions. For example, to maximize its profits, a firm needs to know consumers' decision-making criteria, the trade-offs between various ways of producing and marketing its product, government regulations, and other factors.

Supply
and Demand

Talk is cheap because supply exceeds demand.

Countries around the globe are debating whether to permit firms to grow or sell genetically modified (GM) foods, which have their DNA altered through genetic engineering rather than through conventional breeding.[1] The introduction of GM techniques can affect both the quantity of a crop farmer's supply and whether consumers want to buy that crop. Using GM techniques, farmers can produce more output at a given cost.

The first commercial GM food was Calgene's Flavr Savr tomato, which resisted rotting and could stay on the vine longer to ripen to full flavor. It was first marketed in 1994 without any special labeling. Other common GM crops include canola, corn, cotton, rice, soybean, and sugar cane.

In 2012, developing countries were expected to grow more GM crops than more affluent countries in that year. Twenty-nine countries grow GM food crops, which are mostly herbicide-resistant varieties of maize, soy and oilseed rape. However, more than 40% of this acreage is in the United States, while Brazil and Argentina grow much of the rest. GM cotton is primarily grown in China and India. European farmers are less likely to grow GM crops, where GM crops are grown on only 0.1% of the cultivable land.

Some scientists and consumer groups have raised safety concerns about GM crops. In the European Union (EU), Australia, and several other countries, governments have required labeling of GM products. Although Japan has not approved the cultivation of GM crops, it is the nation with the greatest GM food consumption and does not require labeling. According to some polls, 70% of consumers in Europe object to GM foods. Fears cause some consumers to refuse to buy a GM crop (or the entire crop if GM products cannot be distinguished). In some countries, certain GM foods have been banned. In 2008, the EU was forced to end its de facto ban on GM crop imports when the World Trade Organization ruled that the ban lacked scientific merit and hence violated international trade rules. In 2011, while most of the EU was banning planting GM crops, the European Court of Justice ruled that the EU's constituent countries could not independently ban genetically modified crops. Consumers in other countries, such as the United States, are less concerned about GM foods, though many jurisdictions were considering labeling requirements in 2012.

In yet other countries, consumers may not be aware of the use of GM seeds. In 2008, Vietnam announced that it was going to start using GM soybean, corn, and cotton seeds

---

[1]The sources for Applications and Challenges are available at the back of the book.

to lower food prices and reduce imports. By 2010, a study found that one-third of crops sampled in Vietnam were genetically modified (many imported). Vietnam's government has announced labeling regulations but has not yet explained how it will implement these regulations.

Whether a country approves GM crops turns on questions of safety and economics. Will the use of GM seeds lead to lower prices and more food sold? What happens to prices and quantities sold if many consumers refuse to buy GM crops? (We will return to these questions at the end of this chapter.)

To analyze questions concerning the price and quantity responses from introducing new products or technologies, imposing government regulations or taxes, or other events, economists may use the *supply-and-demand model*. When asked, "What is the most important thing you know about economics?" many people reply, "Supply equals demand." This statement is shorthand for one of the simplest yet most powerful models of economics. The supply-and-demand model describes how consumers and suppliers interact to determine the quantity of a good or service sold in a market and the price at which it is sold. To use the model, you need to determine three things: buyers' behavior, sellers' behavior, and their interaction.

After reading that grandiose claim, you might ask, "Is that all there is to economics? Can I become an expert economist that fast?" The answer to both questions, of course, is no. In addition, you need to learn the limits of this model and which other models to use when this one does not apply. (You must also learn the economists' secret handshake.)

Even with its limitations, the supply-and-demand model is the most widely used economic model. It provides a good description of how markets function, and it works particularly well in markets that have many buyers and sellers, such as most agriculture and labor markets. Like all good theories, the supply-and-demand model can be tested—and possibly proven false. But in markets where it is applicable, it allows us to make accurate predictions easily.

In this chapter, we examine eight main topics

1. **Demand.** The quantity of a good or service that consumers demand depends on price and other factors such as consumers' incomes and the prices of related goods.

2. **Supply.** The quantity of a good or service that firms supply depends on price and other factors such as the cost of inputs that firms use to produce the good or service.

3. **Market Equilibrium.** The interaction between consumers' demand curve and firms' supply curve determines the market price and quantity of a good or service that is bought and sold.

4. **Shocking the Equilibrium: Comparative Statics.** Changes in a factor that affect demand (such as consumers' incomes), supply (such as a rise in the price of inputs), or a new government policy (such as a new tax), alter the market or *equilibrium* price and quantity of a good.

5. **Elasticities.** Given estimates of summary statistics called elasticities, economists can forecast the effects of changes in taxes and other factors on market price and quantity.

6. **Effects of a Sales Tax.** How a sales tax increase affects the price and quantity of a good, and whether the tax falls more heavily on consumers or on suppliers, depend on the supply and demand curves.

7. **Quantity Supplied Need Not Equal Quantity Demanded.** If the government regulates the prices in a market, the quantity supplied might not equal the quantity demanded.

8. **When to Use the Supply-and-Demand Model.** The supply-and-demand model applies to competitive markets only.

2.1 Demand

The **quantity demanded** is the amount of a good that consumers are *willing* to buy at a given price during a specified period (such as a day or a year), holding constant the other factors that influence purchases. The quantity demanded of a good or service can exceed the quantity actually sold. For example, as a promotion, a local store might sell DVDs for $1 each today only. At that low price, you might want to buy 25 DVDs, but because the store has only 10 remaining, you can buy at most 10 DVDs. The quantity you demand is 25—it's the amount you want—even though the amount you actually buy is 10.

Potential consumers decide how much of a good or service to buy based on its price, which is expressed as an amount of money per unit of the good (for example, dollars per pound), and many other factors, including consumers' tastes, information, and income; prices of other goods; and government actions. Before concentrating on the role price plays in determining demand, let's look briefly at some of the other factors.

Consumers make purchases based on their *tastes*. Consumers do not purchase foods they dislike, works of art they don't appreciate, or clothes they think are unfashionable or uncomfortable. However, advertising can influence people's tastes.

Similarly, *information* (or misinformation) about the uses of a good affects consumers' decisions. A few years ago, when many consumers were convinced that oatmeal could lower their cholesterol level, they rushed to grocery stores and bought large quantities of oatmeal. (They even ate it until they remembered that they disliked the taste.)

The *prices of other goods* also affect consumers' purchase decisions. Before deciding to buy a pair of Levi's jeans, you might check the prices of other brands. If the price of a close *substitute*—a product that you think is similar or identical to the jeans you are considering purchasing—is much lower than the price of the Levi's, you might buy that other brand instead. Similarly, the price of a *complement*—a good that you like to consume at the same time as the product you are considering buying—could affect your decision. If you only eat pie with ice cream, the higher the price of ice cream, the less likely you are to buy pie.

People's incomes play a major role in determining what and how much of a good or service they purchase. A person who suddenly inherits great wealth might purchase a Mercedes and other luxury items, and may be less likely to buy do-it-yourself repair kits.

Government rules and regulations affect people's purchase decisions. Sales taxes increase the price that a consumer must spend on a good, and government-imposed limits on the use of a good can affect demand. For example, if a city government bans the use of skateboards on its streets, skateboard sales fall.[2]

---

[2]When a Mississippi woman attempted to sell her granddaughter for $2,000 and a car, state legislators were horrified to discover that they had no law on the books prohibiting the sale of children and quickly passed such a law. (Gordon, Mac "Legislators Make Child-Selling Illegal," *Jackson Free Press*, March 16, 2009.)

Other factors can also affect the demand for specific goods. Some people are more likely to buy a pair of $200 shoes if their friends do. The demand for small, dying evergreen trees is substantially higher in December than in other months.

Although many factors influence demand, economists usually concentrate on how a product's price affects the quantity demanded. To determine how a change in price affects the quantity demanded, economists must hold constant other factors, such as income and tastes, which affect the quantity demand.

The Demand Function

The **demand function** shows the correspondence between the quantity demanded, price, and other factors that influence purchases. For example, the demand function might be

$$Q = D(p, p_s, p_c, Y), \tag{2.1}$$

where Q is the quantity demanded of a particular good in a given time period; p is its price per unit of the good; p_s is the price per unit of a substitute good (a good that might be consumed instead of this good); p_c is the price per unit of a complementary good (a good that might be consumed jointly with this good, such as cream with coffee); and Y is consumers' income.

An example is the estimated demand function for processed pork in Canada,[3]

$$Q = 171 - 20p + 20p_b + 3p_c + 2Y, \tag{2.2}$$

where Q is the quantity of pork demanded in million kilograms (kg) of dressed cold pork carcass weight per year; p is the price of pork in Canadian dollars per kilogram; p_b is the price of beef (a substitute good) in dollars per kilogram; p_c is the price of chicken (another substitute good) in dollars per kilogram; and Y is the income of consumers in dollars per year. Other factors that are not explicitly listed in the demand function are assumed to be irrelevant (such as the price of llamas in Peru) or held constant (such as the price of fish).

Usually we're primarily interested in the relationship between the quantity demanded and the price of the good. That is, we want to know the relationship between the quantity demanded and price, holding all other factors constant. For example, we could set p_b, p_c, and Y at their averages over the period studied: $p_b = \$4$ per kg, $p_c = \$3\frac{1}{3}$ per kg, and $Y = \$12.5$ thousand. If we substitute these values for p_b, p_c, and Y in Equation 2.2, we can rewrite the quantity demanded as a function of only the price of pork:

$$Q = 171 - 20p + 20p_b + 3p_c + 2Y$$

$$= 171 - 20p + (20 \times 4) + (3 \times 3\tfrac{1}{3}) + (2 \times 12.5)$$

$$= 286 - 20p = D(p). \tag{2.3}$$

We can graphically show this relationship, $Q = D(p) = 286 - 20p$, between the quantity demanded and price. A **demand curve** is a plot of the demand function

---

[3]Because prices, quantities, and other factors change simultaneously over time, economists use statistical techniques to hold constant the effects of factors other than the price of the good so that they can determine how price affects the quantity demanded. (See the Regression Appendix at the end of the book.) Moschini and Meilke (1992) used such techniques to estimate the pork demand curve. In Equation 2.2, I've rounded their numbers slightly for simplicity. As with any estimate, their estimates are probably more accurate in the observed range of pork prices ($1 to $6 per kg) than at very high or very low prices.

that shows the quantity demanded at each possible price, holding constant the other factors that influence purchases. Figure 2.1 shows the estimated demand curve, D^1, for processed pork in Canada. (Although this demand curve is a straight line, demand curves can be smooth curves or wavy lines.) By convention, the vertical axis of the graph measures the price, p, per unit of the good, which in our pork example is dollars per kilogram (kg). The horizontal axis measures the quantity, Q, of the good, per physical measure of the good per time period, which in this case is million kg of dressed cold pork carcasses per year.

The demand curve, D^1, hits the price (vertical) axis at $14.30, indicating that no quantity is demanded when the price is $14.30 per kg or higher. Using Equation 2.3, if we set $Q = 286 - 20p = 0$, we find that the demand curve hits the price axis at $p = 286/20 = \$14.30$. The demand curve hits the horizontal quantity axis at 286 million kg—the amount of pork that consumers want if the price is zero. If we set the price equal to zero in Equation 2.3, we find that the quantity demanded is $Q = 286 - (20 \times 0) = 286$.[4] By plugging the particular values for p in the figure into the demand equation, we can determine the corresponding quantities. For example, if $p = \$3.30$, then $Q = 286 - (20 \times 3.30) = 220$.

A Change in a Product's Price Causes a Movement Along the Demand Curve. The demand curve in Figure 2.1 shows that if the price increases from $3.30 to $4.30, the quantity consumers demand decreases by 20 units, from 220 to 200. These changes in the quantity demanded in response to changes in price are *movements along the demand curve*. The demand curve is a concise summary of the answers to the question "What happens to the quantity demanded as the price changes, when all other factors are held constant?"

One of the most important empirical findings in economics is the **Law of Demand**: Consumers demand more of a good the lower its price, holding constant tastes, the

Figure 2.1 A Demand Curve

The estimated demand curve, D^1, for processed pork in Canada (Moschini and Meilke, 1992) shows the relationship between the quantity demanded per year and the price per kg. The downward slope of the demand curve shows that, holding other factors that influence demand constant, consumers demand less of a good when its price is high and more when the price is low. A change in price causes a *movement along the demand curve*.

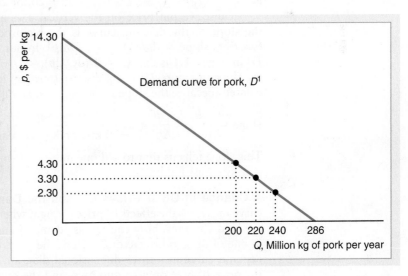

---

[4]Economists typically do not state the relevant physical and time period measures unless these measures are particularly useful in context. I'll generally follow this convention and refer to the price as, say, $3.30 (with the "per kg" understood) and the quantity as 220 (with the "million kg per year" understood).

prices of other goods, and other factors that influence the amount they consume.[5] One way to state the Law of Demand is that the demand curve slopes downward, as in Figure 2.1.

Because the derivative of the demand function with respect to price shows the *movement along the demand curve as we vary price*, another way to state the Law of Demand is that this derivative is negative: A higher price results in a lower quantity demanded. If the demand function is $Q = D(p)$, then the Law of Demand says that $dQ/dp < 0$, where dQ/dp is the derivative of the D function with respect to p. (Unless we state otherwise, we assume that all demand and other functions are continuous and differentiable everywhere.) The derivative of the quantity of pork demanded with respect to its price in Equation 2.3 is

$$\frac{dQ}{dp} = -20,$$

which is negative, so the Law of Demand holds. Given $dQ/dp = -20$, a small change in the price (measured in dollars per kg) causes a 20-times-larger fall in the quantity demanded (measured in million kg per year).

This derivative gives the change in the quantity demanded in response to an infinitesimal change in the price. In general, if we look at a discrete, relatively large increase in the price, the change in the quantity might not be proportional to the change for a small increase in the price. However, here the derivative is a constant that does not vary with the price, so the same derivative holds for large and small price changes.

For example, let the price increase from $p_1 = \$3.30$ to $p_2 = \$4.30$. That is, the change in the price $\Delta p = p_2 - p_1 = \$4.30 - \$3.30 = \$1$. (The Δ symbol, the Greek letter capital delta, means "change in" the following variable, so Δp means "change in price.") As Figure 2.1 shows, the corresponding quantities are $Q_1 = 220$ and $Q_2 = 200$. Thus, if $\Delta p = \$1$, the change in the quantity demanded is $\Delta Q = Q_2 - Q_1 = 200 - 220 = -20$, or 20 times the change in price.

Because we put price on the vertical axis and quantity on the horizontal axis, the slope of the demand curve is the reciprocal of the derivative of the demand function: slope $= dp/dQ = 1/(dQ/dp)$. In our example, the slope of demand curve D^1 in Figure 2.1 is $dp/dQ = 1/(dQ/dp) = 1/(-20) = -0.05$. We can also calculate the slope in Figure 2.1 using the rise-over-run formula and the numbers we just calculated (because the slope is the same for small and for large changes):

$$\text{slope} = \frac{\text{rise}}{\text{run}} = \frac{\Delta p}{\Delta Q} = \frac{\$1 \text{ per kg}}{-20 \text{ million kg per year}} = -\$0.05 \text{ per million kg per year.}$$

This slope tells us that to sell one more unit (million kg per year) of pork, the price (per kg) must fall by 5¢.

A Change in Other Prices Causes the Demand Curve to Shift. If a demand curve measures the effects of price changes when all other factors that affect demand are held constant, how can we use demand curves to show the effects of a change in one of these other factors, such as the price of beef? One solution is to draw the demand curve in a three-dimensional diagram with the price of pork on one axis, the price of beef on a second axis, and the quantity of pork on the third axis. But just thinking about drawing such a diagram probably makes your head hurt.

---

[5]In Chapter 4, we show that theory does not require that the Law of Demand holds; however, available empirical evidence strongly supports the Law of Demand.

Economists use a simpler approach to show how a change in a factor other than the price of a good affects its demand. A change in any factor other than the price of the good itself causes a *shift of the demand curve* rather than a *movement along the demand curve*.

If the price of beef rises and the price of pork remains constant, some people will switch from buying beef to buying pork. Suppose that the price of beef rises by 60¢ from $4.00 per kg to $4.60 per kg, but the price of chicken and income remain at their average levels. Using the demand function in Equation 2.2, we can calculate the new pork demand function relating the quantity demanded to only the price:[6]

$$Q = 298 - 20p. \tag{2.4}$$

Figure 2.2 shows that the higher price of beef causes the entire pork demand curve to shift 12 units to the right from D^1 (corresponding to the demand function in Equation 2.3) to D^2 (corresponding to the demand function in Equation 2.4).

Why does the demand function shift by 12 units? Using the demand function Equation 2.2, we find that the partial derivative of the quantity of pork demanded with respect to the price of beef is $\partial Q/\partial p_b = 20$. Thus, if the price of beef increases by 60¢, the quantity of pork demanded rises by $20 \times 0.6 = 12$ units, holding all other factors constant.

To properly analyze the effects of a change in some variable on the quantity demanded, we must distinguish between a *movement along a demand curve* and a *shift of a demand curve*. A change in the *price of a good* causes a *movement along its demand curve*. A change in *any other factor besides the price of the good* causes a *shift of the demand curve*.

Figure 2.2 A Shift of the Demand Curve

The demand curve for processed pork shifts to the right from D^1 to D^2 as the price of beef rises from $4 to $4.60. As a result of the increase in beef prices, more pork is demanded at any given price.

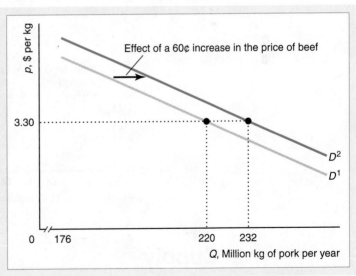

[6]Substituting $p_b = \$4.60$ into Equation 2.2 and using the same values as before for p_c and Y, we find that

$$Q = 171 - 20p + 20p_b + 3p_c + 2Y = 171 - 20p + (20 \times 4.60) + (3 \times 3\tfrac{1}{3}) + (2 \times 12.5)$$
$$= 298 - 20p.$$

Summing Demand Functions

If we know the demand curve for each of two consumers, how do we determine the total demand for the two consumers combined? The total quantity demanded at a given price is the sum of the quantity each consumer demands at that price.

We can use the demand functions to determine the total demand of several consumers. Suppose the demand function for Consumer 1 is $Q_1 = D^1(p)$, and the demand function for Consumer 2 is $Q_2 = D^2(p)$. At price p, Consumer 1 demands Q_1 units, Consumer 2 demands Q_2 units, and the total demand of both consumers is the sum of the quantities each demands separately:

$$Q = Q_1 + Q_2 = D^1(p) + D^2(p).$$

We can generalize this approach to look at the total demand for three or more consumers.

APPLICATION

Aggregating
the Demand for
Broadband Service

We illustrate how to combine individual demand curves to get a total demand curve graphically using estimated demand curves for broadband (high-speed) Internet service (Duffy-Deno, 2003). The following figure shows the demand curve for small firms (1 to 19 employees), the demand curve for larger firms, and the demand curve for all firms, which is the horizontal sum of the other two demand curves.

When the price per kilobyte per second (Kbps) of data transmitted is 40¢, the quantity demanded by small firms is $Q_s = 10$ (in millions of Kbps), and the quantity demanded by larger firms is $Q_l = 11.5$. Thus, the total quantity demanded at that price is $Q = Q_s + Q_l = 10 + 11.5 = 21.5$.

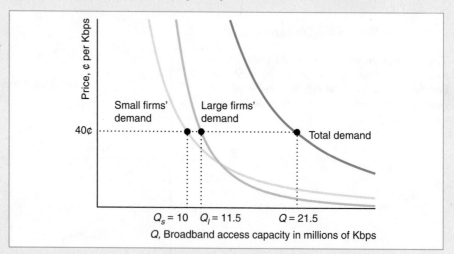

2.2 Supply

To determine the market price and quantity sold of a product, knowing how much consumers want is not enough. We also need to know how much firms want to supply at any given price.

The **quantity supplied** is the amount of a good that firms *want* to sell during a given period at a given price, holding constant other factors that influence firms' supply decisions, such as costs and government actions. Firms determine how much of a good to supply based on the price of that good and other factors, including the costs of production and government rules and regulations. Usually, we expect firms to supply more at a higher price. Before concentrating on the role price plays in determining supply, we'll briefly consider the role of some other factors.

Production cost affects how much of a good a firm wants to sell. As a firm's cost rises, it is willing to supply less of the good, all else the same. In the extreme case where the firm's cost exceeds what it can earn from selling the good, the firm sells nothing. Thus, factors that affect cost also affect supply. For example, a technological advance that allows a firm to produce a good at a lower cost causes the firm to supply more of that good, all else the same.

Government rules and regulations affect how much firms want to sell or are allowed to sell. Taxes and many government regulations—such as those covering pollution, sanitation, and health insurance—alter the costs of production. Other regulations affect when and how the product can be sold. For instance, the sale of cigarettes and liquor to children is prohibited. Also, most major cities around the world restrict the number of taxicabs.

The Supply Function

The **supply function** shows the correspondence between the quantity supplied, price, and other factors that influence the number of units offered for sale. Written generally (without specifying the functional form), the processed pork supply function is

$$Q = S(p, p_h),\tag{2.5}$$

where Q is the quantity of processed pork supplied per year, p is the price of processed pork per kg, and p_h is the price of hogs (the major input used to produce processed pork). The supply function, Equation 2.5, may be a function of other factors such as wages as well. By leaving out these other factors, we are implicitly holding them constant. Based on Moschini and Meilke (1992), the linear pork supply function in Canada is

$$Q = 178 + 40p - 60p_h,\tag{2.6}$$

where the quantity is in millions of kg of processed pork per year, and the prices are in Canadian dollars per kg of processed pork.

If we hold the price of hogs fixed at its typical value of $1.50 per kg, we can rewrite the supply function in Equation 2.6 as[7]

$$Q = 88 + 40p.\tag{2.7}$$

Because we hold fixed other variables that may affect the quantity supplied, such as costs and government rules, this supply function concisely answers the question "What happens to the quantity supplied as the price changes, holding all other factors constant?"

Corresponding to the supply function is a **supply curve**, which shows the quantity supplied at each possible price, holding constant the other factors that influence

[7]Substituting $p_h = \$1.50$ into Equation 2.6, we learn that
$$Q = 178 + 40p - 60p_h = 178 + 40p - (60 \times 1.50) = 88 + 40p.$$

firms' supply decisions. Figure 2.3 shows the supply curve, S^1, for processed pork that corresponds to the supply function, Equation 2.7. Because the supply function is linear, the corresponding supply curve is a straight line. As the price of processed pork increases from \$3.30 to \$5.30, holding other factors (the price of hogs) constant, the quantity of pork supplied increases from 220 to 300 million kg per year, which is a *movement along the supply curve.*

How much does an increase in the price affect the quantity supplied? By differentiating the supply function, Equation 2.7, with respect to price, we find that $dQ/dp = 40$. As this derivative is not a function of p, it holds for all price changes, both small and large. It shows that the quantity supplied increases by 40 units for each \$1 increase in price.

Because the derivative is positive, the supply curve S^1 slopes upward in Figure 2.3. Although the Law of Demand requires that the demand curve slope downward, there is *no* "Law of Supply" that requires the market supply curve to have a particular slope. The market supply curve can be upward sloping, vertical, horizontal, or downward sloping.

A change in a factor other than a product's price causes a *shift of the supply curve.* If the price of hogs increases by 25¢, the supply function becomes

$$Q = 73 + 40p. \tag{2.8}$$

By comparing this supply function to the original one in Equation 2.7, $Q = 88 + 40p$, we see that the supply curve, S^1, shifts 15 units to the left, to S^2 in Figure 2.4.

Alternatively, we can determine how far the supply curve shifts by partially differentiating the supply function Equation 2.6 with respect to the price of hogs: $\partial Q/\partial p_h = -60$. This partial derivative holds for all values of p_h and hence for both small and large changes in p_h. Thus, a 25¢ increase in the price of hogs causes a $-60 \times 0.25 = -15$ units change in the quantity of pork supplied at any price of pork.

Again, it is important to distinguish between a *movement along a supply curve* and a *shift of the supply curve.* When the price of pork changes, the change in the quantity supplied reflects a *movement along the supply curve.* When costs, government rules, or other variables that affect supply change, the entire *supply curve shifts.*

Figure 2.3 A Supply Curve

The estimated supply curve, S^1, for processed pork in Canada (Moschini and Meilke, 1992) shows the relationship between the quantity supplied per year and the price per kg, holding input prices and other factors that influence supply constant. The upward slope of this supply curve indicates that firms supply more of this good when its price is high and less when the price is low. An increase in the price of pork causes a *movement along the supply curve,* resulting in a larger quantity of pork supplied.

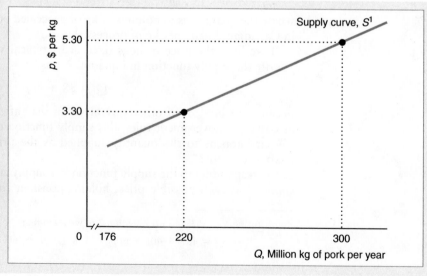

Figure 2.4 A Shift of a Supply Curve

An increase in the price of hogs from $1.50 to $1.75 per kg causes a *shift of the supply curve* from S^1 to S^2. At the price of processed pork of $3.30, the quantity supplied falls from 220 on S^1 to 205 on S^2.

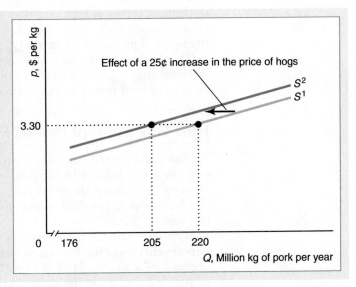

Summing Supply Functions

The total supply curve shows the total quantity of a product produced by all suppliers at each possible price. For example, the total supply curve of rice in Japan is the sum of the domestic and the foreign supply curves of rice.

Figure 2.5 shows the domestic supply curve, panel a, and foreign supply curve, panel b, of rice in Japan. The total supply curve, S in panel c, is the horizontal sum of the Japanese *domestic* supply curve, S^d, and the *foreign* supply curve, S^f. In the

Figure 2.5 Total Supply: The Sum of Domestic and Foreign Supply

If foreigners are allowed to sell their rice in Japan, the total Japanese supply of rice, S, is the horizontal sum of the domestic Japanese supply, S^d, and the imported foreign supply, S^f. With a ban on foreign imports, the foreign supply curve, $\bar{S}^f$, is zero at every price, so the total supply curve, $\bar{S}$, is the same as the domestic supply curve, S^d.

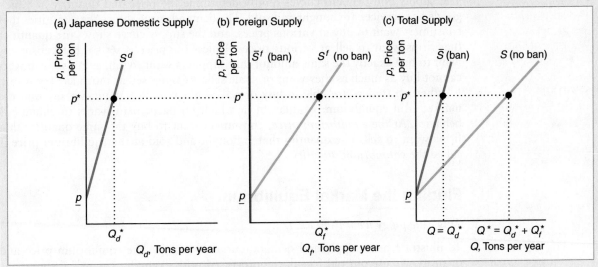

figure, the Japanese and foreign supplies are zero at any price equal to or less than p, so the total supply is zero. At prices above p, the Japanese and foreign supplies are positive, so the total supply is positive. For example, when the price is p^*, the quantity supplied by Japanese firms is Q_d^* panel a, the quantity supplied by foreign firms is Q_f^*, panel b, and the total quantity supplied is $Q^* = Q_d^* + Q_f^*$ panel c. Because the total supply curve is the horizontal sum of the domestic and foreign supply curves, the total supply curve is flatter than either of the other two supply curves.

How Government Import Policies Affect Supply Curves

We can use this approach for deriving the total supply curve to analyze the effect of government policies on the total supply curve. Traditionally, the Japanese government has banned the importation of foreign rice. We want to determine how much less rice is supplied at any given price to the Japanese market because of this ban.

Without a ban, the foreign supply curve is S^f in panel b of Figure 2.5. A ban on imports eliminates the foreign supply, so the foreign supply curve after the ban is imposed, $\overline{S}^f$ is a vertical line at $Q_f = 0$. The import ban has no effect on the domestic supply curve, S^d, so the supply curve is the same as in panel a.

Because the foreign supply with a ban, $\overline{S}^f$ in panel b, is zero at every price, the total supply with a ban, $\overline{S}$ in panel c, is the same as the Japanese domestic supply, S^d, at any given price. The total supply curve under the ban lies to the left of the total supply curve without a ban, S. Thus, the effect of the import ban is to rotate the total supply curve toward the vertical axis.

A limit that a government sets on the quantity of a foreign-produced good that may be imported is called a **quota**. By absolutely banning the importation of rice, the Japanese government sets a quota of zero on rice imports. Sometimes governments set positive quotas, $\overline{Q} > 0$. The foreign firms may supply as much as they want, Q_f, as long as they supply no more than the quota: $Q_f \le \overline{Q}$.

2.3 Market Equilibrium

The supply and demand curves jointly determine the price and quantity at which goods and services are bought and sold. The demand curve shows the quantities that consumers want to buy at various prices, and the supply curve shows the quantities that firms want to sell at various prices. Unless the price is set so that consumers want to buy exactly the same amount that suppliers want to sell, either some buyers cannot buy as much as they want or some sellers cannot sell as much as they want.

When all traders are able to buy or sell as much as they want, we say that the market is in **equilibrium**: a situation in which no participant wants to change its behavior. At the *equilibrium price*, consumers want to buy the same quantity that firms want to sell. The quantity that is bought and sold at the equilibrium price is called the *equilibrium quantity*.

Finding the Market Equilibrium

This little piggy went to market....

To illustrate how supply and demand curves determine the equilibrium price and quantity, we use our old friend, the processed pork example. Figure 2.6 shows the

Figure 2.6 Market Equilibrium

The intersection of the supply curve, *S*, and the demand curve, *D*, for processed pork determines the market equilibrium point, *e*, where $p = \$3.30$ per kg and $Q = 220$ million kg per year. At the lower price of $p = \$2.65$, the quantity supplied is only 194, whereas the quantity demanded is 233, so there is excess demand of 39. At $p = \$3.95$, a price higher than the equilibrium price, there is an excess supply of 39 because the quantity demanded, 207, is less than the quantity supplied, 246. When there is excess demand or supply, market forces drive the price back to the equilibrium price of $3.30.

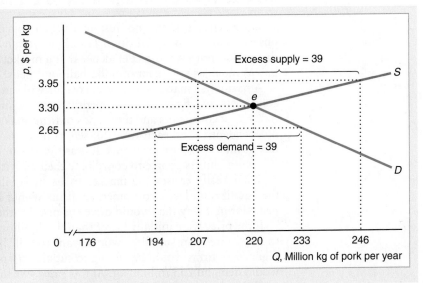

supply, *S*, and the demand, *D*, curves for pork. The supply and demand curves intersect at point *e*, the market equilibrium, where the equilibrium price is \$3.30 and the equilibrium quantity is 220 million kg per year, which is the quantity that firms want to sell and the quantity that consumers want to buy at the equilibrium price.

We can determine the market equilibrium for processed pork mathematically using the demand and supply functions, Equations 2.3 and 2.7. We use these two functions to solve for the equilibrium price at which the quantity demanded equals the quantity supplied (the equilibrium quantity).

The demand function in Equation 2.3 shows the relationship between the quantity of processed pork demanded, Q_d, and the price:

$$Q_d = 286 - 20p.$$

The supply function in Equation 2.3 describes the relationship between the quantity of processed pork supplied, Q_s, and the price:

$$Q_s = 88 + 40p.$$

We want to find the price at which $Q_d = Q_s = Q$, the equilibrium quantity. Because the left-hand sides of the two equations are equal in equilibrium, $Q_s = Q_d$, the right-hand sides of the two equations must be equal as well:

$$286 - 20p = 88 + 40p.$$

Adding $20p$ to both sides of this expression and subtracting 88 from both sides, we find that $198 = 60p$. Dividing both sides of this last expression by 60, we learn that the equilibrium price is $p = \$3.30$. We can determine the equilibrium quantity by substituting this equilibrium price, $p = \$3.30$, into either the supply or the demand equation:

$$Q_d = Q_s$$
$$286 - (20 \times 3.30) = 88 + (40 \times 3.30)$$
$$220 = 220.$$

Thus, the equilibrium quantity is 220 million kg.

Forces That Drive a Market to Equilibrium

A market equilibrium is not just an abstract concept or a theoretical possibility: We observe markets in equilibrium. The ability to buy as much as you want of a good at the market price is indirect evidence that a market is in equilibrium. You can usually buy as much as you want of milk, ballpoint pens, and many other goods.

Amazingly, a market equilibrium occurs without any explicit coordination between consumers and firms. In a competitive market such as that for agricultural goods, millions of consumers and thousands of firms make their buying and selling decisions independently. Yet, each firm can sell as much as it wants, and each consumer can buy as much as he or she wants. It is as though an unseen market force, like an *invisible hand*, directs people to coordinate their activities to achieve market equilibrium.

What really causes the market to be in equilibrium? If the price were not at the equilibrium level, consumers or firms would have an incentive to change their behavior in a way that would drive the price to the equilibrium level.[8]

If the price were initially lower than the equilibrium price, consumers would want to buy more than suppliers would want to sell. If the price of pork were $2.65 in Figure 2.6, firms would be willing to supply 194 million kg per year, but consumers would demand 233 million kg. At this price, the market would be in *disequilibrium*, meaning that the quantity demanded would not equal the quantity supplied. There would be **excess demand**—the amount by which the quantity demanded exceeds the quantity supplied at a specified price—of 39 (= 233 − 194) million kg per year at a price of $2.65.

Some consumers would be lucky enough to be able to buy the pork at $2.65. Other consumers would not find anyone willing to sell them pork at that price. What could they do? Some frustrated consumers might offer to pay suppliers more than $2.65. Alternatively, suppliers, noticing these disappointed consumers, might raise their prices. Such actions by consumers and producers would cause the market price to rise. At higher prices, the quantity that firms want to supply increases and the quantity that consumers want to buy decreases. The upward pressure on the price would continue until it reached the equilibrium price, $3.30, where there is no excess demand.

If, instead, the price were initially above the equilibrium level, suppliers would want to sell more than consumers would want to buy. For example, at a price of pork of $3.95, suppliers would want to sell 246 million kg per year but consumers would want to buy only 207 million, as the figure shows. At $3.95, the market would be in disequilibrium. There would be an **excess supply**—the amount by which the quantity supplied is greater than the quantity demanded at a specified price—of 39 (= 246 − 207) at a price of $3.95. Not all firms could sell as much as they wanted. Rather than incur storage costs (and possibly have their unsold pork spoil), firms would lower the price to attract additional customers. As long as the price remained above the equilibrium price, some firms would have unsold pork and would want to lower the price further. The price would fall until it reached the equilibrium level, $3.30, where there is no excess supply and hence no more pressure to lower the price further.[9]

---

[8]Our model of competitive market equilibrium, which occurs at a point in time, does not formally explain how dynamic adjustments occur. The following explanation, though plausible, is just one of a number of possible dynamic adjustment stories that economists have modeled.

[9]Not all markets reach equilibrium through the independent actions of many buyers or sellers. In institutionalized or formal markets, such as the Chicago Mercantile Exchange—where agricultural commodities, financial instruments, energy, and metals are traded—buyers and sellers meet at a single location (or on a single Web site). In these markets, certain individuals or firms, sometimes referred to as *market makers*, act to adjust the price and bring the market into equilibrium very quickly.

In summary, at any price other than the equilibrium price, either consumers or suppliers would be unable to trade as much as they want. These disappointed people would act to change the price, driving the price to the equilibrium level. The equilibrium price is called the *market clearing price* because it removes from the market all frustrated buyers and sellers: There is no excess demand or excess supply at the market clearing price.

2.4 Shocking the Equilibrium: Comparative Statics

If the variables we hold constant in the demand and supply functions do not change, an equilibrium would persist indefinitely because none of the participants in the market would apply pressure to change the price. However, the equilibrium changes if a shock occurs so that one of the variables we were holding constant changes, causing a shift in either the demand curve or the supply curve.

Comparative statics is the method economists use to analyze how variables controlled by consumers and firms—here, price and quantity—react to a change in *environmental variables* (also called *exogenous variables*) that they do not control. Such environmental variables include the prices of substitutes, the prices of substitutes and complements, the income level of consumers, and the prices of inputs. The term *comparative statics* literally refers to comparing a *static* equilibrium—an equilibrium at a point in time from before the change—to a static equilibrium after the change. (In contrast, economists may examine a dynamic model, in which the dynamic equilibrium adjusts over time.)

Comparative Statics with Discrete (Relatively Large) Changes

We can determine the comparative statics properties of an equilibrium by examining the effects of a discrete (relatively large) change in one environmental variable. We can do so by solving for the before- and after-equilibria and comparing them using mathematics or a graph. We illustrate this approach using our beloved pork example. Suppose all the environmental variables remain constant except the price of hogs, which increases by 25¢. It is now more expensive to produce pork because the price of a major input, hogs, has increased.

Because the price of hogs is not an argument to the demand function—a change in the price of an input does not affect consumers' desires—the demand curve does not shift. However, as we saw in Figure 2.4, the increase in the price of hogs causes the supply curve for pork to shift 15 units to the left from S^1 to S^2 at every possible price of pork.

Figure 2.7 reproduces this shift of the supply curve and adds the original demand curve. At the original equilibrium price of pork, $3.30, consumers still want to buy 220 million kg, but suppliers are now willing to supply only 205 million kg at that price, so there is excess demand of 15. Market pressure then forces the price of pork upward until it reaches the new equilibrium, e_2. At e_2, the new equilibrium price is $3.55, and the new equilibrium quantity is 215 million kg. Thus, the increase in the price of hogs causes the equilibrium price of processed pork to rise by 25¢ per kg, but the equilibrium quantity to fall by 5 million kg. Here the increase in the price of a factor causes a *shift of the supply curve* and a *movement along the demand curve*.

Figure 2.7 The Equilibrium Effect of a Shift of the Supply Curve

A 25¢ increase in the price of hogs causes the supply curve for processed pork to shift to the left from S^1 to S^2, driving the market equilibrium from e_1 to e_2, and the market equilibrium price from $3.30 to $3.55.

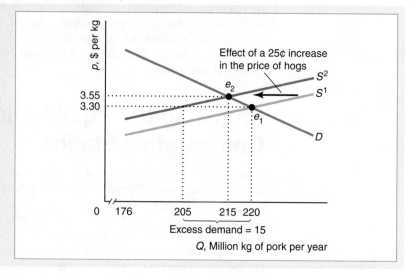

We can derive the same result by using equations to solve for the equilibrium before the change and after the discrete change in the price of hogs and by comparing the two equations. We have already solved for the original equilibrium, e_1, by setting the quantity in the demand function Equation 2.3 equal to the quantity in the supply function Equation 2.7. We obtain the new equilibrium, e_2, by equating the quantity in the demand function Equation 2.3 to that of the new supply function, with a 25¢ higher price of hogs, Equation 2.8:

$$286 - 20p = 73 + 40p.$$

Simplifying this expression, we find that the new equilibrium price is $p_2 = \$3.55$. Substituting that price into either the demand or the supply function, we learn that the new equilibrium quantity is $Q_2 = 215$, as Figure 2.7 shows. Thus, both methods show that an increase in the price of hogs causes the equilibrium price to rise and the equilibrium quantity to fall.

APPLICATION

Occupational Licensing

Licensing also affects labor markets, where the price is the wage or salary paid to a worker per day and the quantity is the number of workers (or hours they work). In the United States, more than 800 occupations require licenses issued by local, state, or federal government agencies, including acupuncturists, animal trainers, dietitians and nutritionists, doctors, electricians, embalmers, funeral directors, hairdressers, psychologists, real estate brokers, respiratory therapists, salespeople, teachers, and tree trimmers (but not economists).

During the early 1950s, fewer than 5% of U.S. workers were in occupations covered by licensing laws at the state level. Since then, the share of licensed workers has grown, rising to nearly 18% by the 1980s, at least 20% in 2000, and 29% in 2008. Licensing is more common in occupations that require extensive education: More than 40% of workers with a post-college education are required to have a license, compared to only 15% of those in which workers have less than a high school education.

To obtain a license in some occupations, you must pass a test, which is frequently designed by licensed members of the occupation. By making exams difficult, current members of the occupation can limit entry by new workers.

For example, only 42% of people taking the California State Bar Examination in February 2011 passed it, although all of them had law degrees. (The national rate for lawyers passing state bar exams in February 2011 was higher, but still only 60%.)

To the degree that testing is objective, licensing may raise the average quality of the workforce. However, too often its primary effect is to restrict the number of workers in an occupation. To analyze the effects of licensing, we can use a graph similar to Figure 2.7, where the wage is on the vertical axis and the number of workers per year is on the horizontal axis. Licensing shifts the occupational supply curve to the left, which reduces the equilibrium quantity of workers and raises the equilibrium wage. Kleiner and Krueger (2010) find that licensing raises occupational wages by 15% on average.

Comparative Statics with Small Changes

Alternatively, we can use calculus to determine the effect of a small change (as opposed to the discrete change we just used) in one environmental variable, holding the other such variables constant. Until now, we have used calculus to examine how an argument of a demand function affects the quantity demanded or how an argument of a supply function affects the quantity supplied. Now, however, we want to know how an environmental variable affects the equilibrium price and quantity that are determined by the intersection of the supply and demand curves.

Our first step is to characterize the equilibrium values as functions of the relevant environmental variables. Suppose that we hold constant all the environmental variables that affect demand so that the demand function is

$$Q = D(p). \tag{2.9}$$

One environmental variable, a, in the supply function changes, which causes the supply curve to shift. We write the supply function as

$$Q = S(p, a). \tag{2.10}$$

As before, we determine the equilibrium price by equating the quantities, Q, in Equations 2.9 and 2.10:

$$D(p) = S(p, a). \tag{2.11}$$

Equation 2.11 is an example of an *identity*. As a changes, p changes so that this equation continues to hold—the market remains in equilibrium. Thus, based on this equation, we can write the equilibrium price as an implicit function of the environmental variable: $p = p(a)$. That is, we can write the equilibrium condition in Equation 2.11 as

$$D(p(a)) = S(p(a), a). \tag{2.12}$$

We can characterize how the equilibrium price changes with a by differentiating the equilibrium condition Equation 2.12 with respect to a using the chain rule at the original equilibrium,[10]

$$\frac{dD(p(a))}{dp}\frac{dp}{da} = \frac{\partial S(p(a), a)}{\partial p}\frac{dp}{da} + \frac{\partial S(p(a), a)}{\partial a}. \tag{2.13}$$

---

[10]The chain rule is a formula for the derivative of the composite of two functions, such as $f(g(x))$. According to this rule, $df/dx = (df/dg)(dg/dx)$. See the Calculus Appendix at the end of the book.

Using algebra, we can rearrange Equation 2.13 as

$$\frac{dp}{da} = \frac{\dfrac{\partial S}{\partial a}}{\dfrac{dD}{dp} - \dfrac{\partial S}{\partial p}},$$ (2.14)

where we suppress the arguments of the functions for notational simplicity. Equation 2.14 shows the derivative of $p(a)$ with respect to a.

We know that $dD/dp < 0$ because of the Law of Demand. If the supply curve is upward sloping, then $\partial S/\partial p$ is positive, so the denominator of Equation 2.14, $dD/dp - \partial S/\partial p$, is negative. Thus, dp/da has the opposite sign as the numerator of Equation 2.14. If $\partial S/\partial a$ is negative, then dp/da is positive: As a increases, the equilibrium price rises. If $\partial S/\partial a$ is positive, an increase in a causes the equilibrium price to fall.

By using either the demand function or the supply function, we can use this result concerning the effect of a on the equilibrium price to determine the effect of a on the equilibrium quantity. For example, we can rewrite the demand function Equation 2.9 as

$$Q = D(p(a)).$$ (2.15)

Differentiating the demand function Equation 2.15 with respect to a using the chain rule, we find that

$$\frac{dQ}{da} = \frac{dD}{dp}\frac{dp}{da}.$$ (2.16)

Because $dD/dp < 0$ by the Law of Demand, the sign of dQ/da is the opposite of that of dp/da. That is, as a increases, the equilibrium price moves in the opposite direction of the equilibrium quantity. In Solved Problem 2.1, we use the pork example to illustrate this type of analysis.

SOLVED PROBLEM 2.1

How do the equilibrium price and quantity of pork vary as the price of hogs changes if the variables that affect demand are held constant at their typical values? Answer this comparative statics question using calculus. (*Hint*: This problem is of the same form as the more general one we just analyzed. In the pork market, the environmental variable that shifts supply, a, is p_h.)

Answer

1. *Solve for the equilibrium price of processed pork in terms of the price of hogs.* To obtain an expression for the equilibrium similar to Equation 2.14, we equate the right-hand sides of the demand function in Equation 2.3 and the supply function Equation 2.6 to obtain

$$286 - 20p = 178 + 40p - 60p_h, \text{ or}$$

$$p = 1.8 + p_h.$$ (2.17)

(As a check, when p_h equals its typical value, \$1.50, the equilibrium price of pork is $p = \$3.30$ according to Equation 2.17, which is consistent with our earlier calculations.)

2. *Use this equilibrium price equation to show how the equilibrium price changes as the price of hogs changes.* Differentiating the equilibrium price Equation 2.17 with respect to p_h gives an expression of the form of Equation 2.16:

$$\frac{dp}{dp_h} = 1. \qquad (2.18)$$

That is, as the price of hogs increases by 1¢, the equilibrium price of pork increases by 1¢. Because this condition holds for any value of p_h, it also holds for larger changes in the price of hogs. Thus, a 25¢ increase in the price of hogs causes a 25¢ increase in the equilibrium price of pork.

3. *Write the pork demand function as in Equation 2.15, and then differentiate it with respect to the price of hogs to show how the equilibrium quantity of pork varies with the price of hogs.* From the pork demand function, Equation 2.3, we can write the quantity demanded as

$$Q = D(p(p_h)) = 286 - 20p(p_h).$$

Differentiating this expression with respect to p_h using the chain rule, we obtain an expression in the form of Equation 2.16 with respect to p_h:

$$\frac{dQ}{dp_h} = \frac{dD}{dp}\frac{dp}{dp_h} = -20 \times 1 = -20. \qquad (2.19)$$

That is, as the price of hogs increases by \$1, the equilibrium quantity of processed pork falls by 20 units.[11]

Why the Shapes of Demand and Supply Curves Matter

The shapes and positions of the demand and supply curves determine by how much a shock affects the equilibrium price and quantity. We illustrate the importance of the shape of the demand curve by showing how our comparative statics results would change if the processed pork demand curve had a different shape. We continue to use the estimated supply curve of pork and examine what happens if the price of hogs increases by 25¢, causing the supply curve of pork to shift to the left from S^1 to S^2 in panel a of Figure 2.8. In the actual market, the shift of the supply curve causes a movement along the downward-sloping demand curve, D^1, so the equilibrium quantity falls from 220 to 215 million kg per year, and the equilibrium price rises from \$3.30 to \$3.55 per kg. The supply shock—an increase in the price of hogs—hurts consumers by increasing the equilibrium price of processed pork by 25¢ per kg. Consequently, customers buy less of it: 215 million kg instead of 220 million kg.

A supply shock would have different effects if the demand curve had a different shape. Suppose that the quantity demanded were not sensitive to a change in the price, so the same amount is demanded no matter what the price is, as the vertical demand curve D^2 in panel b shows. A 25¢ increase in the price of hogs again shifts the supply curve from S^1 to S^2. The equilibrium quantity does not change, but the price consumers pay rises by 37.5¢ to \$3.675. Thus, the amount consumers spend rises by more when the demand curve is vertical instead of downward sloping.

---

[11]Equation 2.19 holds for a small change in p_h. However, when supply and demand curves are linear, this equation holds for larger changes as well.

Figure 2.8 The Effect of a Shift of the Supply Curve, Depending on the Shape of the Demand Curve

A 25¢ increase in the price of hogs causes the supply curve for processed pork to shift to the left from S^1 to S^2. (a) Given the actual downward-sloping linear demand curve, the equilibrium price rises from $3.30 to $3.55, and the equilibrium quantity falls from 220 to 215. (b) If the demand curve were vertical, the supply shock would cause the price to rise to $3.675 while the quantity would remain unchanged. (c) If the demand curve were horizontal, the supply shock would not affect price but would cause quantity to fall to 205.

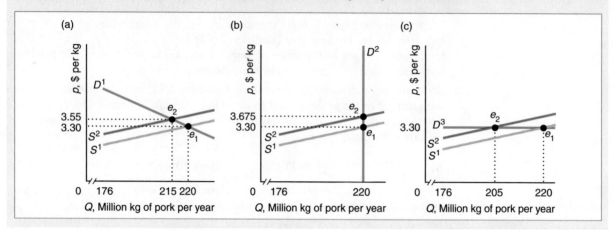

Now suppose that consumers are very sensitive to price changes, as the horizontal demand curve, D^3, in panel c shows. Consumers will buy virtually unlimited quantities of pork at $3.30 per kg (or less). However, if the price rises even slightly, they will stop buying pork altogether. With a horizontal demand curve, an increase in the price of hogs has *no* effect on the price consumers pay; however, the equilibrium quantity drops substantially to 205 million kg per year. Thus, how much the equilibrium quantity falls and how much the equilibrium price of processed pork rises when the price of hogs increases depend on the shape of the demand curve.

2.5 Elasticities

It is convenient to be able to summarize the responsiveness of one variable to a change in another variable using a summary statistic. In our last example, we wanted to know whether an increase in the price of a product causes a large or a small change in the quantity demanded (that is, whether the demand curve is relatively vertical or relatively horizontal at the current price). We can use summary statistics of the responsiveness of the quantity demanded and the quantity supplied to determine comparative statics properties of the equilibrium. Often, we have reasonable estimates of these summary statistics and can use them to predict what will happen to the equilibrium in a market—that is, to make comparative statics predictions. Later in this chapter, we will examine how the government can use these summary measures to predict how a tax on a product will affect the equilibrium price and quantity, and hence firms' revenues and the government's tax receipts.

Suppose that a variable z (for example, the quantity demanded or the quantity supplied) is a function of a variable x (say, the price of z) and possibly other variables such as y. We write this function as $z = f(x, y)$. For example, f could be the demand function, where z is the quantity demanded, x is the price, and y is income. We want a summary statistic that describes how much z changes as x changes, holding y

constant. An **elasticity** is the percentage change in one variable (here, z) in response to a given percentage change in another variable (here, x), holding other relevant variables (here, y) constant. The elasticity, E, of z with respect to x is

$$E = \frac{\text{percentage change in } z}{\text{percentage change in } x} = \frac{\Delta z/z}{\Delta x/x} = \frac{\partial z}{\partial x} \frac{x}{z}, \qquad (2.20)$$

where Δz is the change in z, so $\Delta z/z$ is the percentage change in z. If z changes by 3% when x changes by 1%, then the elasticity E is 3. Thus, the elasticity is a pure number (it has no units of measure).[12] As Δx goes to zero, $\Delta z/\Delta x$ goes to the partial derivative $\partial z/\partial x$. Economists usually calculate elasticities at this limit—that is, for infinitesimal changes in x.

Demand Elasticity

The **price elasticity of demand** (or simply the *demand elasticity* or *elasticity of demand*) is the percentage change in the quantity demanded, Q, in response to a given percentage change in the price, p, at a particular point on the demand curve. The price elasticity of demand (represented by ε, the Greek letter epsilon) is

$$\varepsilon = \frac{\text{percentage change in quantity demanded}}{\text{percentage change in price}} = \frac{\Delta Q/Q}{\Delta p/p} = \frac{\partial Q}{\partial p} \frac{p}{Q}, \qquad (2.21)$$

where $\partial Q/\partial p$ is the partial derivative of the demand function with respect to p (that is, holding constant other variables that affect the quantity demanded). For example, if $\varepsilon = -2$, then a 1% increase in the price results in a 2% decrease in the quantity demanded.

We can use Equation 2.21 to calculate the elasticity of demand for a linear demand function that holds fixed other variables that affect demand:

$$Q = a - bp,$$

where a is the quantity demanded when the price is zero, $Q = a - (b \times 0) = a$, and $-b$ is the ratio of the fall in the quantity relative to the rise in price: the derivative dQ/dp. The elasticity of demand is

$$\varepsilon = \frac{dQ}{dp} \frac{p}{Q} = -b\frac{p}{Q}. \qquad (2.22)$$

For the linear demand function for pork, $Q = a - bp = 286 - 20p$, at the initial equilibrium where $p = \$3.30$ and $Q = 220$, the elasticity of demand is

$$\varepsilon = b\frac{p}{Q} = -20 \times \frac{3.30}{220} = -0.3.$$

The negative sign on the elasticity of demand of pork illustrates the Law of Demand: Less quantity is demanded as the price rises.

The elasticity of demand concisely answers the question "How much does the quantity demanded of a product fall in response to a 1% increase in its price?" A 1% increase in price leads to an ε% change in the quantity demanded. For example, at the equilibrium, a 1% increase in the price of pork leads to a -0.3% fall in the

[12]Economists use the elasticity rather than the slope, $\partial z/\partial x$, as a summary statistic because the elasticity is a pure number, whereas the slope depends on the units of measurement. For example, if x is a price measured in pennies and we switch to measuring price using dollars, the slope changes, but the elasticity remains unchanged.

quantity of pork demanded. Thus, a price increase causes a less than proportionate fall in the quantity of pork demanded.

Elasticities Along the Demand Curve. The elasticity of demand varies along most demand curves. On downward-sloping linear demand curves that are neither vertical nor horizontal, the higher the price, the more negative the elasticity of demand. Consequently, even though the slope of the linear demand curve is constant, the elasticity varies along the curve. A 1% increase in the price causes a larger percentage fall in the quantity demanded near the top (left) of the demand curve than near the bottom (right).

Where a linear demand curve hits the quantity axis ($p = 0$ and $Q = a$), the elasticity of demand is $\varepsilon = -b \times (0/a) = 0$, according to Equation 2.22. The linear pork demand curve in Figure 2.9 illustrates this pattern. Where the price is zero, a 1% increase in price does not raise the price, so quantity demanded does not change. At a point where the elasticity of demand is zero, the demand curve is said to be *perfectly inelastic*. As a physical analogy, if you try to stretch an inelastic steel rod, the length does not change. The change in the price is the force pulling at demand; if the quantity demanded does not change in response to this force, the demand curve is perfectly inelastic.

For quantities between the midpoint of the linear demand curve and the lower end, where $Q = a$, the demand elasticity lies between 0 and -1: $0 > \varepsilon > -1$. A point along the demand curve where the elasticity is between 0 and -1 is *inelastic* (but not perfectly inelastic): A 1% increase in price leads to a fall in quantity of less than 1%. For example, at the original pork equilibrium, $\varepsilon = -0.3$, so a 1% increase in price causes quantity to fall by -0.3%.

At the midpoint of the linear demand curve, $p = a/(2b)$ and $Q = a/2$, so $\varepsilon = -bp/Q = -b[a/(2b)]/(a/2) = -1$.[13] Such an elasticity of demand is called a *unitary elasticity*.

At prices higher than at the midpoint of the demand curve, the elasticity of demand is less than negative one, $\varepsilon < -1$. In this range, the demand curve is called

Figure 2.9 The Demand Elasticity Varies Along a Linear Demand Curve

On a linear demand curve, such as the pork demand curve, the higher the price, the more elastic the demand curve (ε is larger in absolute value—a larger negative number). The demand curve is perfectly inelastic ($\varepsilon = 0$) where the demand curve hits the horizontal axis, is perfectly elastic where the demand curve hits the vertical axis, and has unitary elasticity ($\varepsilon = -1$) at the midpoint of the demand curve.

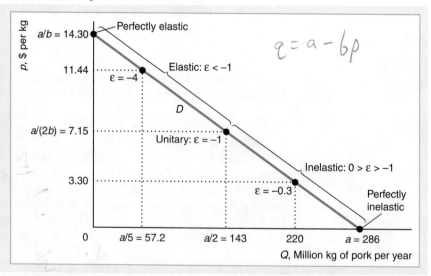

[13]The linear demand curve hits the price axis at $p = a/b$ and the quantity axis at $p = 0$. The midpoint occurs at $p = (a/b - 0)/2 = a/(2b)$, where the quantity is $Q = a - b[a/(2b)] = a/2$.

elastic: A 1% increase in price causes more than a 1% fall in quantity. A physical analogy is a rubber band that stretches substantially when you pull on it. In the figure where $Q = a/5$, the elasticity is -4, so a 1% increase in price causes a 4% drop in quantity.

As the price rises, the elasticity gets more and more negative, approaching negative infinity. Where the demand curve hits the price axis, it is *perfectly elastic*.[14] At the price a/b where $Q = 0$, a 1% decrease in p causes the quantity demanded to become positive, which is an infinite increase in quantity.

The elasticity of demand varies along most demand curves, not just downward-sloping linear ones. However, along a special type of demand curve, called a *constant-elasticity demand curve*, the elasticity is the same at every point along the curve. Constant-elasticity demand curves all have the exponential form

$$Q = Ap^{\varepsilon}, \tag{2.23}$$

where A is a positive constant and ε, a negative constant, is the elasticity at every point along this demand curve. By taking natural logarithms of both sides of Equation 2.23, we can rewrite this exponential demand curve as a log-linear demand curve:

$$\ln Q = \ln A + \varepsilon \ln p. \tag{2.24}$$

For example, in the application "Aggregating the Demand for Broadband Service" the estimated demand function for broadband services by large firms is $Q = 16p^{-0.296}$. Here, $A = 16$, and $\varepsilon = -0.296$ is the constant elasticity of demand. That is, the demand for broadband services by large firms is inelastic: $0 > \varepsilon > -1$. We can equivalently write this demand function as $\ln Q = \ln 16 - 0.296 \ln p \approx 2.773 - 0.296 \ln p$.

Figure 2.10 shows several constant-elasticity demand curves with different elasticities. Except for the vertical and the horizontal demand curves, the curves are convex to the origin (bend away from the origin). The two extreme cases of these constant-elasticity demand curves are the vertical and the horizontal demand curves. Along the demand curve that is horizontal at p^* in Figure 2.10, the elasticity is infinite everywhere. It is also a special case of a linear demand curve with a zero slope ($b = 0$). Along this demand curve, people are willing to buy as much as firms sell at any price less than or equal to p^*. If the price increases even slightly above p^*, however, demand falls to zero. Thus, a small increase in price causes an infinite drop in the quantity demanded, which means that the demand curve is perfectly elastic.

Why would a demand curve be horizontal? One reason is that consumers view one good as identical to another good and do not care which one they buy. Suppose that consumers view Washington State apples and Oregon apples as identical. They won't buy Washington apples if these apples sell for more than Oregon apples. Similarly, they won't buy Oregon apples if their price is higher than that of Washington apples. If the two prices are equal, consumers do not care which type of apple they buy. Thus, the demand curve for Oregon apples is horizontal at the price of Washington apples.

The other extreme case is the vertical demand curve, which is perfectly inelastic everywhere. Such a demand curve is also an extreme case of the linear demand curve with an infinite (vertical) slope. If the price goes up, the quantity

---

[14]The linear demand curve hits the price axis at $p = a/b$ and $Q = 0$, so the elasticity of demand is $-bp/0$. As the price approaches a/b, the elasticity approaches negative infinity, $-\infty$. An intuition for this result is provided by looking at a sequence where -1 divided by 0.1 is -10, -1 divided by 0.01 is -100, and so on. The smaller the number we divide by, the more negative the result, which goes to $-\infty$ in the limit.

Figure 2.10 Constant-Elasticity Demand Curves

These constant elasticity demand curves, $Q = Ap$, vary with respect to their elasticities. Curves with negative, finite elasticities are convex to the origin. The vertical, constant-elasticity demand curve is perfectly inelastic, while the horizontal curve is perfectly elastic.

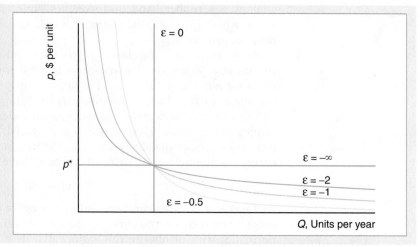

demanded is unchanged, $dQ/dp = 0$, so the elasticity of demand must be zero: $\varepsilon = (dQ/dp)(p/Q) = 0 \times (p/Q) = 0$.

A demand curve is vertical for *essential goods*—goods that people feel they must have and will pay anything to get. Because Sydney is a diabetic, his demand curve for insulin could be vertical at a day's dose, Q^*.[15]

SOLVED PROBLEM 2.2

Show that the price elasticity of demand is a constant ε if the demand function is exponential, $Q = Ap^\varepsilon$, or, equivalently, log-linear, $\ln Q = \ln A + \varepsilon \ln p$.

Answer

1. *Differentiate the exponential demand curve with respect to price to determine* dQ/dp, *and substitute that expression into the definition of the elasticity of demand.* Differentiating the demand curve $Q = Ap^\varepsilon$, we find that $dQ/dp = \varepsilon Ap^{\varepsilon-1}$. Substituting that expression into the elasticity definition, we learn that the elasticity is

$$\frac{dQ}{dp}\frac{p}{Q} = \varepsilon Ap^{\varepsilon-1}\frac{p}{Q} = \varepsilon Ap^{\varepsilon-1}\frac{p}{Ap^\varepsilon} = \varepsilon.$$

Because the elasticity is a constant that does not depend on the particular value of p, it is the same at every point along the demand curve.

2. *Differentiate the log-linear demand curve to determine* dQ/dp, *and substitute that expression into the definition of the elasticity of demand.* Differentiating the log-linear demand curve, $\ln Q = \ln A + \varepsilon \ln p$, with respect to p, we find that $d(\ln Q)/dp = (dQ/dp)/Q = \varepsilon/p$. Multiplying this equation by p, we again discover that the elasticity is constant:

$$\frac{dQ}{dp}\frac{p}{Q} = \varepsilon \frac{Q}{p}\frac{p}{Q} = \varepsilon.$$

---

[15]More realistically, he may have a maximum price, p^*, that he can afford to pay. Thus, his demand curve is vertical at Q^* up to p^* and horizontal at p^* to the left of Q^*.

Other Demand Elasticities. We refer to the price elasticity of demand as *the* elasticity of demand. However, there are other demand elasticities that show how the quantity demanded changes in response to changes in variables other than price that affect the quantity demanded. Two such demand elasticities are the income elasticity of demand and the cross-price elasticity of demand.

As people's incomes increase, their demand curves for products shift. If a demand curve shifts to the right, a larger quantity is demanded at any given price. If instead the demand curve shifts to the left, a smaller quantity is demanded at any given price.

We can measure how sensitive the quantity demanded at a given price is to income by using the **income elasticity of demand** (or *income elasticity*), which is the percentage change in the quantity demanded in response to a given percentage change in income, Y. The income elasticity of demand is

$$\xi = \frac{\text{percentage change in quantity demanded}}{\text{percentage change in income}} = \frac{\Delta Q/Q}{\Delta Y/Y} = \frac{\partial Q}{\partial Y}\frac{Y}{Q},$$

where ξ is the Greek letter xi. If the quantity demanded increases as income rises, the income elasticity of demand is positive. If the quantity demanded does not change as income rises, the income elasticity is zero. Finally, if the quantity demanded falls as income rises, the income elasticity is negative.

By partially differentiating the pork demand function, Equation 2.2, $Q = 171 - 20p + 20p_b + 3p_c + 2Y$, with respect to Y, we find that $\partial Q/\partial Y = 2$, so the income elasticity of demand for pork is $\xi = 2Y/Q$. At our original equilibrium, quantity $Q = 220$ and income $Y = 12.5$, so the income elasticity is $\xi = 2 \times (12.5/220) \approx 0.114$, or about one-ninth. The positive income elasticity shows that an increase in income causes the pork demand curve to shift to the right.

Income elasticities play an important role in our analysis of consumer behavior in Chapter 5. Typically, goods that consumers view as necessities, such as food, have income elasticities near zero. Goods that they consider luxuries generally have income elasticities greater than one.

The **cross-price elasticity of demand** is the percentage change in the quantity demanded in response to a given percentage change in the price of another good, p_o. The cross-price elasticity may be calculated as

$$\frac{\text{percentage change in quantity demanded}}{\text{percentage change in price of another good}} = \frac{\Delta Q/Q}{\Delta p_o/p_o} = \frac{\partial Q}{\partial p_o}\frac{p_o}{Q}.$$

When the cross-price elasticity is negative, the goods are complements. If the cross-price elasticity is negative, people buy less of one good when the price of the other, second good increases: The demand curve for the first good shifts to the left. For example, if people like cream in their coffee, as the price of cream rises, they consume less coffee, so the cross-price elasticity of the quantity of coffee with respect to the price of cream is negative.

If the cross-price elasticity is positive, the goods are substitutes.[16] As the price of the second good increases, people buy more of the first good. For example, the quantity demanded of pork increases when the price of beef, p_b, rises. By partially differentiating the pork demand function, Equation 2.2, $Q = 171 - 20p + 20p_b + 3p_c + 2Y$, with respect to the price of beef, we find that $\partial Q/\partial p_b = 20$. As a result, the cross-price elasticity between the price of beef and the quantity of pork is $20p_b/Q$. At the original equilibrium where $Q = 220$ million kg per year, and $p_b = \$4$ per kg, the cross-price elasticity is $20 \times (4/220) \approx 0.364$. As the price of beef rises by 1%, the quantity of pork demanded rises by a little more than one-third of 1%.

---

[16]*Jargon alert*: Graduate-level textbooks generally call these goods *gross substitutes* (and the goods in the previous example would be called *gross complements*).

Supply Elasticity

Just as we can use the elasticity of demand to summarize information about the responsiveness of the quantity demanded to price or other variables, we can use the elasticity of supply to summarize how responsive the quantity supplied of a product is to price changes or other variables. The **price elasticity of supply** (or *supply elasticity*) is the percentage change in the quantity supplied in response to a given percentage change in the price. The price elasticity of supply (η, the Greek letter eta) is

$$\eta = \frac{\text{percentage change in quantity supplied}}{\text{percentage change in price}} = \frac{\Delta Q/Q}{\Delta p/p} = \frac{\partial Q}{\partial p} \frac{p}{Q}, \quad (2.25)$$

where Q is the *quantity supplied*. If $\eta = 2$, a 1% increase in price leads to a 2% increase in the quantity supplied.

The definition of the price elasticity of supply, Equation 2.25, is very similar to the definition of the price elasticity of demand, Equation 2.21. The key distinction is that the elasticity of supply describes the movement along the *supply* curve as price changes, whereas the elasticity of demand describes the movement along the *demand* curve as price changes. That is, in the numerator, supply elasticity depends on the percentage change in the *quantity supplied*, whereas demand elasticity depends on the percentage change in the *quantity demanded*.

If the supply curve is upward sloping, $\partial p/\partial Q > 0$, the supply elasticity is positive: $\eta > 0$. If the supply curve slopes downward, the supply elasticity is negative: $\eta < 0$. For the pork supply function Equation 2.7, $Q = 88 + 40p$, the supply elasticity of pork at the original equilibrium, where $p = \$3.30$ and $Q = 220$, is

$$\eta = \frac{dQ}{dp} \frac{p}{Q} = 40 \times \frac{3.30}{220} = 0.6.$$

As the price of pork increases by 1%, the quantity supplied rises by slightly less than two-thirds of 1%.

The elasticity of supply varies along an upward-sloping supply curve. For example, because the elasticity of supply for the pork is $\eta = 40p/Q$, as the ratio p/Q rises, the supply elasticity rises.

At a point on a supply curve where the elasticity of supply is $\eta = 0$, we say that the supply curve is *perfectly inelastic*: The supply does not change as the price rises. If $0 < \eta < 1$, the supply curve is *inelastic* (but not perfectly inelastic): A 1% increase in the price causes a less than 1% rise in the quantity supplied. If $\eta > 1$, the supply curve is *elastic*. If η is infinite, the supply curve is *perfectly elastic*.

The supply elasticity does not vary along constant-elasticity supply functions, which are exponential or (equivalently) log-linear: $Q = Bp^{\eta}$ or $\ln Q = \ln B + \eta \ln p$. If η is a positive, finite number, the constant-elasticity supply curve starts at the origin, as Figure 2.11 shows. Two extreme examples of both constant-elasticity of supply curves and linear supply curves are the vertical supply curve and the horizontal supply curve.

A supply curve that is vertical at a quantity, Q^*, is perfectly inelastic. No matter what the price is, firms supply Q^*. An example of inelastic supply is a perishable item such as already-picked fresh fruit. If the perishable good is not sold, it quickly becomes worthless. Thus, the seller will accept any market price for the good.

A supply curve that is horizontal at a price, p^*, is perfectly elastic. Firms supply as much as the market wants—a potentially unlimited amount—if the price is p^* or above. Firms supply nothing at a price below p^*, which does not cover their cost of production.

Figure 2.11 Constant Elasticity Supply Curves

Constant elasticity supply curves, $Q = Bp^{\eta}$, with positive, finite elasticities start at the origin. They are concave to the horizontal axis if $1 < \eta < \infty$ and convex if $0 < \eta < 1$. The unitary elasticity supply curve is a straight line through the origin. The vertical constant elasticity supply curve is perfectly inelastic, while the horizontal curve is perfectly elastic.

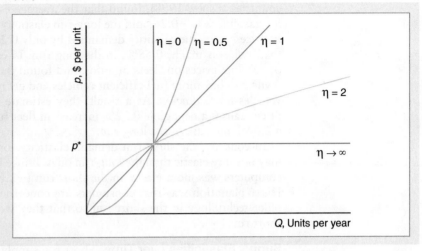

SOLVED PROBLEM 2.3

Show that the price elasticity of supply is 1 for a linear supply curve that starts at the origin.

Answer

1. *Write the formula for a linear supply curve that starts at the origin.* In general, a linear supply function is $Q = A + Bp$. For a linear supply curve to start at the origin ($p = 0$, $Q = 0$), when $p = 0$ then $Q = A$, so A, must be zero. Thus, the supply function is $Q = Bp$ (and $B > 0$).

2. *Calculate the supply elasticity based on this linear function by using the definition.* The supply elasticity is $\eta = (dQ/dp)(p/Q) = B(p/Q) = B(p/[bp]) = 1$, regardless of the slope of the line, B.

Comment: This supply function is a special case of the constant elasticity supply function where $Q = Bp^{\eta} = Bp^1$, so $\eta = 1$.

Long Run Versus Short Run

Typically, short-run demand or supply elasticities differ substantially from long-run elasticities. The duration of the short run depends on the planning horizon—how long it takes consumers or firms to adjust for a particular good.

Demand Elasticities over Time. Two factors that determine whether short-run demand elasticities are larger or smaller than long-run elasticities are the ease of substitution and storage opportunities. Often one can substitute between products in the long run but not in the short run.

For example, when oil prices rose rapidly in the 1970s and 1980s because the Organization of Petroleum Exporting Countries (OPEC) limited the supply of crude oil, most Western consumers could not greatly alter the amount of gasoline they demanded in the short run. Someone who drove 27 miles to and from work every day in a 1969 Chevy couldn't dramatically reduce the amount of gasoline he or she purchased right away. However in the long run, this person could buy a smaller car, get a job closer to home, join a carpool, or in other ways reduce the amount of gasoline purchased.

A survey of hundreds of estimates of gasoline demand elasticities across many countries (Espey, 1998), found that the average estimate of the short-run elasticity for gasoline was −0.26, and the long-run elasticity was −0.58. Thus, a 1% increase in price lowers the quantity demanded by only 0.26% in the short run but by more than twice as much, 0.58%, in the long run. Li et al. (2009) examined the effects of gasoline prices on fleets of autos, and found that high gasoline prices cause fleet owners to buy more fuel-efficient vehicles and get rid of older, less fuel-efficient used vehicles more quickly. As a result, they estimate that a 10% increase in gasoline prices causes a negligible 0.22% increase in fleet fuel economy in the short run, but a 2.04% increase in the long run.

In contrast, the short-run demand elasticity for goods that can be stored easily may be more elastic than the long-run ones. Prince (2008) found that the demand for computers was more elastic in the short run (−2.74) than in the long run (−2.17). His explanation was that consumers are concerned about being locked-in with an older technology in the short run so that they were more sensitive to price in the short run.

Supply Elasticities over Time.   Short-run supply curve elasticities may differ from long-run elasticities. If a manufacturing firm wants to increase production in the short run, it can do so by hiring workers to use its machines around the clock. However, how much it can expand its output is limited by the fixed size of its manufacturing plant and the number of machines it has. In the long run, however, the firm can build another plant and buy or build more equipment. Thus, we would expect a firm's long-run supply elasticity to be greater than it is in the short run.

Adelaja (1991) found that the short-run supply elasticity of milk is 0.36, whereas the long-run supply elasticity is 0.51. Thus, the long-run quantity response to a 1% increase in price is about 42% [= (0.51 − 0.36)/0.36] more than it is in the short run.

APPLICATION

Oil Drilling in the Arctic National Wildlife Refuge

We can use information about demand and supply elasticities to answer an important public policy question: Would selling oil from the Arctic National Wildlife Refuge (ANWR) substantially affect the price of oil? Established in 1980, the ANWR covers 20 million acres and is the largest of Alaska's 16 national wildlife refuges. It is believed to contain massive deposits of petroleum (about the amount consumed annually in the United States). For decades, a debate has raged over whether the ANWR's owners—the citizens of the United States—should keep it undeveloped or permit oil drilling.[17]

In the simplest form of this complex debate, President Obama has sided with environmentalists who stress that drilling would harm the wildlife refuge and pollute the environment. Mitt Romney, the 2012 Republican candidate for President, and the Republican Congress argue that extracting this oil would substantially reduce the price of petroleum (as well as decrease U.S. dependence on foreign oil and bring in large royalties). Recent spurts in the price of gasoline and the war in Iraq have heightened this intense debate.

---

[17]I am grateful to Robert Whaples, who wrote an earlier version of this analysis. In the following discussion, we assume for simplicity that the oil market is competitive, and we use current values for the prices and quantities of oil, even though drilling in the ANWR will not take place for at least a decade.

The effect of the sale of ANWR oil on the world price of oil is a key element in this debate. We can combine oil production information with supply and demand elasticities to estimate the price effects.

A number of studies estimate that the long-run elasticity of demand, ε, for oil is about -0.4 and the long-run supply elasticity, η, is about 0.3. Analysts agree less about how much ANWR oil will be produced. The Department of Energy's Energy Information Service (EIS) predicts that production from the ANWR would average about 800,000 barrels per day. That production would be about 1% of the worldwide oil production, which averaged about 84 million barrels per day from 2007 through early 2010 (and hit 90 million barrels in November 2011).

A report of the U.S. Department of Energy predicted that ANWR drilling could lower the price of oil by about 1%. Severin Borenstein, the director of the University of California Energy Institute, concluded that the ANWR might reduce oil prices by up to a few percentage points but that "drilling in ANWR will never noticeably affect gasoline prices."

In Solved Problem 2.4, we make our own calculation of the price effect of drilling in the ANWR. Here and in many of the solved problems in this book, you are asked to determine how a change in a variable or policy (such as permitting drilling in the ANWR) affects one or more variables (such as the world equilibrium price of oil).

SOLVED PROBLEM 2.4

What would be the effect of ANWR production on the world equilibrium price of oil given that $\varepsilon = -0.4$, $\eta = 0.3$, the pre-ANWR daily world production of oil is $Q_1 = 82$ million barrels per day, the pre-ANWR world price is $p_1 = \$100$ per barrel, and daily ANWR production is 0.8 million barrels per day?[18] We assume that the supply and demand curves are linear and that the introduction of ANWR oil would cause a parallel shift in the world supply curve to the right by 0.8 million barrels per day.

Answer

1. *Determine the long-run linear demand function that is consistent with pre-ANWR world output and price.* At the original equilibrium, e_1 in the figure, $p_1 = \$100$ and $Q_1 = 82$, and the elasticity of demand is $\varepsilon = (dQ/dp)(p_1/Q_1) = (dQ/dp)(100/82) = -0.4$. Using algebra, we find that dQ/dp equals $-0.4(82/100) = -0.328$, which is the inverse of the slope of the demand curve, D, in the figure. Knowing this slope and that demand equals 82 at \$100 per barrel, we can solve for the intercept because the quantity

---

[18]The price was about \$100 a barrel in mid 2012. From 2007 through 2012, the price of a barrel of oil fluctuated between about \$30 and \$140. The calculated percentage change in the price in Solved Problem 2.4 is not sensitive to the choice of the initial price of oil.

demanded rises by 0.328 for each dollar by which the price falls. The demand when the price is zero is $82 + (0.328 \times 100) = 114.8$. Thus, the equation for the demand curve is $Q = 114.8 - 0.328p$.

2. *Determine the long-run linear supply function that is consistent with pre-ANWR world output and price.* Where S^1 intercepts D at the original equilibrium, e_1, the elasticity of supply is $\eta = (dQ/dp)(p_1/Q_1) = (dQ/dp)(100/82) = 0.3$. Solving, we find that $dQ/dp = 0.3(82/100) = 0.246$. Because the quantity supplied falls by 0.246 for each dollar by which the price drops, the quantity supplied when the price is zero is $82 - (0.246 \times 100) = 57.4$. Thus, the equation for the pre-ANWR supply curve, S^1, in the figure, is $Q = 57.4 + 0.246p$.

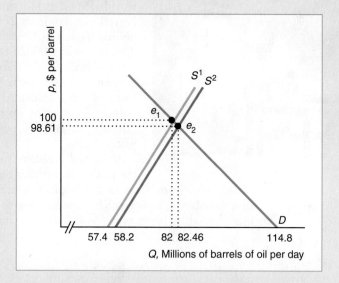

3. *Determine the post-ANWR long-run linear supply function.* The oil pumped from the ANWR would cause a parallel shift in the supply curve, moving S^1 to the right by 0.8 to S^2. That is, the slope remains the same, but the intercept on the quantity axis increases by 0.8. Thus, the supply function for S^2 is $Q = 58.2 + 0.246p$.

4. *Use the demand curve and the post-ANWR supply function to calculate the new equilibrium price and quantity.* The new equilibrium, e_2, occurs where S^2 intersects D. Setting the right-hand sides of the demand function and the post-ANWR supply function equal, we obtain an expression in the new price, p_2:

$$58.2 + 0.246p_2 = 114.8 - 0.328p_2.$$

We can solve this expression for the new equilibrium price: $p_2 \approx \$98.61$. That is, the price drops about $1.39, or approximately 1.4%. If we substitute this new price into either the demand curve or the post-ANWR supply curve, we find that the new equilibrium quantity is 82.46 million barrels per day. That is, equilibrium output rises by 0.46 million barrels per day (0.56%), which is only a little more than half of the predicted daily ANWR supply, because other suppliers will decrease their output slightly in response to the lower price.

Comment: Our estimate of a small drop in the world oil price if ANWR oil is sold would not change substantially if our estimates of the elasticities of supply and demand were moderately larger or smaller or if the equilibrium price of oil were higher or lower. The main reason for this result is that the ANWR output would be a very small portion of worldwide supply—the new supply curve would be only slightly to the right of the initial supply curve. Thus, drilling in the ANWR cannot insulate the American market from international events that roil the oil market. In contrast, a new war in the Persian Gulf could shift the worldwide supply curve to the left by 3 million barrels a day or more (nearly four times the ANWR production). Such a shock would cause the price of oil to soar whether we drill in the ANWR or not.

2.6 Effects of a Sales Tax

How much a tax affects the equilibrium price and quantity and how much of the tax falls on consumers depends on the elasticities of demand and supply. Knowing only the elasticities of demand and supply, we can make accurate predictions about the effects of a new tax and determine how much of the tax falls on consumers.

In this section, we examine three questions about the effects of a sales tax:

1. What effect does a sales tax have on a product's equilibrium price and quantity?
2. Is it true, as many people claim, that taxes assessed on producers are *passed along* to consumers? That is, do consumers pay for the entire tax, or do producers pay part of it?
3. Do the equilibrium price and quantity depend on whether the tax is assessed on consumers or on producers?

Two Types of Sales Taxes

Governments use two types of sales taxes. The most common sales tax is called an *ad valorem* tax by economists and *the* sales tax by real people. For every dollar that a consumer spends, the government keeps a fraction, α, which is the ad valorem tax rate. Japan's national sales tax is $\alpha = 5\%$. If a consumer in Japan buys a Nintendo Wii for ¥20,000,[19] the government collects $\alpha \times ¥20{,}000 = 5\% \times ¥20{,}000 = ¥1{,}000$ in taxes, and the seller receives $(1 - \alpha) \times ¥20{,}000 = ¥19{,}000$.[20]

The other type of sales tax is a *specific* or *unit* tax, where a specified dollar amount, τ, is collected per unit of output. For example, the federal government collects $\tau = 18.4¢$ on each gallon of gas sold in the United States.

Equilibrium Effects of a Specific Tax

To answer the three questions listed at the beginning of this section, we must extend the standard supply-and-demand analysis to include taxes. Let's start by assuming that the specific tax is assessed on firms at the time of sale. If the consumer pays p for a good, the government takes τ and the seller receives $p - \tau$.

---

[19]The symbol for Japan's currency, the yen, is ¥. In 2012, $1 \approx ¥82$.

[20]For specificity, we assume that the price firms receive is $p = (1 - \alpha)p^*$, where p^* is the price consumers pay, and α is the ad valorem tax rate on the price consumers pay. However, many governments (including the U.S. and Japanese governments) set the ad valorem sales tax, β, as an amount added to the price sellers charge, so consumers pay $p^* = (1 + \beta)p$. By setting α and β appropriately, the taxes are equivalent. Here, $p = p^*/(1 + \beta)$, so $(1 - \alpha) = 1/(1 + \beta)$. For example, if $\beta = \frac{1}{3}$ then $\alpha = \frac{1}{4}$.

Suppose that the government collects a specific tax of $\tau = \$1.05$ per kg of processed pork from pork producers. Because of the tax, suppliers keep only $p - \tau$ of price p that consumers pay. Thus, at every possible price paid by consumers, firms are willing to supply less than when they received the full amount consumers paid. Before the tax, firms were willing to supply 206 million kg per year at a price of \$2.95 as the pretax supply curve S^1 in Figure 2.12 shows. After the tax, firms receive only \$1.90 if consumers pay \$2.95, so they are no longer willing to supply a quantity of 206. For firms to be willing to supply a quantity of 206, they must receive \$2.95 after the tax, so consumers must pay \$4. By this reasoning, the after-tax supply curve, S^2, is $\tau = \$1.05$ above the original supply curve S^1 at every quantity, as the figure shows.

We can use this figure to illustrate the answer to our first question concerning the effects of the tax on the pork market equilibrium. *The specific tax causes the equilibrium price consumers pay to rise, and the equilibrium quantity to fall.*

The intersection of the pretax pork supply curve S^1 and the pork demand curve D in Figure 2.12 determines the pretax equilibrium, e_1. The equilibrium price is $p_1 = \$3.30$, and the equilibrium quantity is $Q_1 = 220$. The tax shifts the supply curve to S^2, so the after-tax equilibrium is e_2. At e_2, consumers pay $p_2 = \$4$, firms receive $p_2 - \$1.05 = \$2.95$, and $Q_2 = 206$. Thus, the tax causes the price that consumers pay to increase, $\Delta p = p_2 - p_1 = \$4 - \$3.30 = 70¢$, and the quantity to fall, $\Delta Q = Q_2 - Q_1 = 206 - 220 = -14$.

Although consumers and producers are worse off because of the tax, the government acquires new tax revenue of $T = \tau Q = \$1.05$ per kg $\times$ 206 million kg per year $= \$216.3$ million per year. The length of the shaded rectangle in the figure is $Q_2 = 206$ million kg per year, and its height is $\tau = \$1.05$ per kg, so the area of the rectangle equals the tax revenue. (The figure shows only part of the length of the rectangle because the horizontal axis starts at 176.)

How Specific Tax Effects Depend on Elasticities

We now turn to our second question: Who is hurt by the tax? To answer this comparative static question, we want to determine how the price that consumers pay and firms receive changes after the tax is imposed.

Figure 2.12 The Effect of a \$1.05 Specific Tax on the Pork Market Collected from Producers

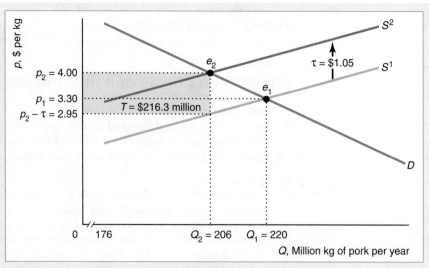

The specific tax of $\tau = \$1.05$ per kg collected from producers shifts the pretax pork supply curve from S^1 to the post-tax supply curve, S^2. The tax causes the equilibrium to shift from e_1 (determined by the intersection of S^1 and D) to e_2 (intersection of S^2 with D). The equilibrium price increases from \$3.30 to \$4. Two-thirds of the incidence of the tax falls on consumers, who spend 70¢ more per unit. Producers receive 35¢ less per unit after the tax. The government collects tax revenues of $T = \tau Q_2 = \$216.3$ million per year.

Because the government collects a specific or unit tax, τ, from sellers, sellers receive $p - \tau$ when consumers pay p. We can use this information to determine the effect of the tax on the equilibrium. In the new equilibrium, the price that consumers pay is determined by the equality between the demand function and the after-tax supply function,

$$D(p) = S(p - \tau).$$

Thus, the equilibrium price is an implicit function of the specific tax: $p = p(\tau)$. Consequently, the equilibrium condition is

$$D(p(\tau)) = S(p(\tau) - \tau). \tag{2.26}$$

We determine the effect a small tax has on the price by differentiating Equation 2.26 with respect to τ:

$$\frac{dD}{dp}\frac{dp}{d\tau} = \frac{dS}{dp}\frac{d(p(\tau) - \tau)}{d\tau} = \frac{dS}{dp}\left(\frac{dp}{d\tau} - 1\right).$$

Rearranging the terms, it follows that the change in the price that consumers pay with respect to the change in the tax is

$$\frac{dp}{d\tau} = \frac{\dfrac{dS}{dp}}{\dfrac{dS}{dp} - \dfrac{dD}{dp}}. \tag{2.27}$$

We know that $dD/dp < 0$ from the Law of Demand. If the supply curve slopes upward so that $dS/dp > 0$, then $dp/d\tau > 0$, as Figure 2.12 illustrates. The higher the tax, the greater the price consumers pay. If $dS/dp < 0$, the direction of change is ambiguous: It depends on the relative slopes of the supply and demand curves (the denominator).

By multiplying both the numerator and denominator of the right-hand side of Equation 2.27 by p/Q, we can express this derivative in terms of elasticities,

$$\frac{dp}{d\tau} = \frac{\dfrac{dS}{dp}\dfrac{p}{Q}}{\dfrac{dS}{dp}\dfrac{p}{Q} - \dfrac{dD}{dp}\dfrac{p}{Q}} = \frac{\eta}{\eta - \varepsilon}, \tag{2.28}$$

where the last equality follows because dS/dp and dD/dp are the changes in the quantities supplied and demanded as price changes, and the consumer and producer prices are identical when $\tau = 0$.[21] This expression holds for any size change in τ if both the demand and supply curves are linear. For most other shaped curves, the expression holds only for small changes.

We can now answer our second question: Who is hurt by the tax? The **incidence of a tax on consumers** is the share of the tax that falls on consumers. The incidence of the tax that falls on consumers is $dp/d\tau$, the amount by which the price to consumers rises as a fraction of the amount the tax increases. Firms receive $p - \tau$, so the

[21]To determine the effect on quantity, we can combine the price result from Equation 2.28 with information from either the demand or the supply function. Differentiating the demand function with respect to τ, we know that

$$\frac{dD}{dp}\frac{dp}{d\tau} = \frac{dD}{dp}\frac{\eta}{\eta - \varepsilon},$$

which is negative if the supply curve is upward sloping so that $\eta > 0$.

change in the price that firms receive as the tax changes is $d(p - \tau)/d\tau = dp/d\tau - 1$. The *incidence of the tax on firms* is the amount by which the price paid to firms falls: $1 - dp/d\tau$. The sum of the incidence of the tax to consumers and firms is $dp/d\tau + 1 - dp/d\tau = 1$. That is, the increase in the price consumers pay plus the drop in the price paid to firms equals the tax.

In the pork example, $\varepsilon = -0.3$ and $\eta = 0.6$, so the incidence of a specific tax on consumers is $dp/d\tau = \eta/(\eta - \varepsilon) = 0.6/[0.6 - (-0.3)] = 0.6/0.9 = \frac{2}{3}$, and the incidence of the tax on firms is $1 - \frac{2}{3} = \frac{1}{3}$.

Thus, a discrete change in the tax of $\Delta\tau = \tau - 0 = \$1.05$ causes the price that consumers pay to rise by $\Delta p = p_2 - p_1 = \$4.00 - \$3.30 = [\eta/(\eta - \varepsilon)]\Delta\tau = \frac{2}{3} \times \$1.05 = 70¢$, and the price to firms to fall by $\frac{1}{3} \times \$1.05 = 35¢$, as Figure 2.12 shows. The sum of the increase to consumers plus the loss to firms is $70¢ + 35¢ = \$1.05 = \tau$.

Equation 2.28 shows that, for a given supply elasticity, the more elastic the demand, the less the equilibrium price rises when a tax is imposed. Similarly, for a given demand elasticity, the smaller the supply elasticity, the smaller the increase in the equilibrium price that consumers pay when a tax is imposed. In the pork example, if the supply elasticity changed to $\eta = 0$ (a perfectly inelastic vertical supply curve) and ε remained -0.3, then $dp/d\tau = 0/[0 - (-0.3)] = 0$. Here, none of the incidence of the tax falls on consumers, so the entire incidence of the tax falls on firms.

SOLVED PROBLEM 2.5	If the supply curve is perfectly elastic and demand is linear and downward sloping, what is the effect of a \$1 specific tax collected from producers on equilibrium price and quantity, and what is the incidence on consumers? Why?

Answer

1. *Determine the equilibrium in the absence of a tax.* Before the tax, the perfectly elastic supply curve, S^1 in the graph, is horizontal at p_1. The downward-sloping linear demand curve, D, intersects S^1 at the pretax equilibrium, e_1, where the price is p_1 and the quantity is Q_1.

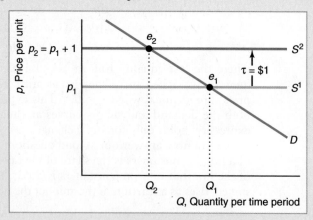

2. *Show how the tax shifts the supply curve and determine the new equilibrium.* A specific tax of \$1 shifts the pretax supply curve, S^1, upward by \$1 to S^2, which is horizontal at $p_1 + 1$. The intersection of D and S^2 determines the after-tax equilibrium, e_2, where the price consumers pay is $p_2 = p_1 + 1$, the price firms receive is $p_2 - 1 = p_1$, and the quantity is Q_2.

3. *Compare the before- and after-tax equilibria.* The specific tax causes the equilibrium quantity to fall from Q_1 to Q_2, the price firms receive to remain at p_1, and the equilibrium price consumers pay to rise from p_1 to $p_2 = p_1 + 1$. The entire incidence of the tax falls on consumers:

$$\frac{\Delta p}{\Delta \tau} = \frac{p_2 - p_1}{\Delta \tau} = \frac{\$1}{\$1} = 1.$$

(We can use Equation 2.28 to draw the same conclusion.)

4. *Explain why.* The reason consumers must absorb the entire tax is that firms will not supply the good at a price that is any lower than they received before the tax, p_1. Thus, the price must rise enough that the price suppliers receive after tax is unchanged. As consumers do not want to consume as much at a higher price, the equilibrium quantity falls.

APPLICATION

Subsidizing Ethanol

For many years, the U.S. government subsidized ethanol with the goal of replacing 15% of U.S. gasoline use with this biofuel, which is currently made from corn. The government used a variety of corn ethanol subsidies. According to a 2010 Rice University study, the government spent \$4 billion in 2008 to replace about 2% of the U.S. gasoline supply with ethanol at about \$1.95 per gallon on top of the gasoline retail price. Corn is also subsidized (lowering the cost of a key input). The two subsidies add about \$2.59 per gallon of ethanol.

A subsidy is a negative tax. Instead of the government taking money, it gives money. Thus, in contrast to a tax that results in an upward shift in the after-tax supply curve (as in Figure 2.12), a subsidy causes a downward shift in the supply curve. We can use the same incidence formula for a subsidy as for a tax because the subsidy is just a negative tax.

Taxpayers provided the subsidy. But what was the subsidy's incidence on ethanol consumers? That is, how much of the subsidy goes to purchasers of ethanol? According to Luchansky and Monks (2009), the supply elasticity of ethanol, η, is about 0.25, and the demand elasticity is about 2.9, so at the equilibrium, the supply curve is relatively inelastic (nearly the opposite of the situation in Solved Problem 2.5, where the supply curve is perfectly elastic), and the demand curve is relatively elastic. Using Equation 2.28, the consumer incidence was $\eta/(\eta - \varepsilon) = 0.25/(0.25 - [-2.9]) \approx 0.08$. In other words, almost none of the subsidy goes to consumers in the form of a lower price—producers captured nearly the entire subsidy. That may be in part why Congress allowed the explicit ethanol subsidy to expire in 2012 (though more subtle policies now benefit ethanol producers).

The Same Equilibrium No Matter Who Is Taxed

Our third question is, "Does the equilibrium or the incidence of the tax depend on whether the tax is collected from producers or consumers?" Surprisingly, in the supply-and-demand model, the equilibrium and the incidence of the tax are the same regardless of whether the government collects the tax from producers or from consumers.

We've already seen that firms are able to pass on some or all of the tax collected from them to consumers. We now show that, if the tax is collected from consumers, they can pass the producers' share back to the firms.

Suppose the specific tax $\tau = \$1.05$ on pork is collected from consumers rather than from producers. Because the government takes τ from each p that consumers spend, producers receive only $p - \tau$. Thus, the demand curve as seen by firms shifts downward by $1.05 from D to D^s in Figure 2.13.

The intersection of D^2 and S determines the after-tax equilibrium, where the equilibrium quantity is Q_2 and the price received by producers is $p_2 - \tau$. The price paid by consumers, p_2 (on the original demand curve D at Q_2), is τ above the price received by producers. We place the after-tax equilibrium, e_2, bullet on the market demand D in Figure 2.13 to show that it is the same as the e_2 in Figure 2.12.

Comparing Figure 2.13 to Figure 2.12, we see that the after-tax equilibrium is the same regardless of whether the tax is imposed on consumers or producers. The price to consumers rises by the same amount, $\Delta p = 70\cent$, and the incidence of the tax, $\Delta p / \Delta \tau = \frac{2}{3}$, is the same.

A specific tax, regardless of whether the tax is collected from consumers or producers, creates a *wedge* equal to the per-unit tax of τ between the price consumers pay, p, and the price producers receive, $p - \tau$. In short, regardless of whether firms or consumers pay the tax to the government, you can solve tax problems by shifting the supply curve, shifting the demand curve, or inserting a wedge between the supply and demand curves. All three approaches give the same answer.

The Similar Effects of Ad Valorem and Specific Taxes

In contrast to specific sales taxes, which are applied to relatively few goods, governments levy ad valorem taxes on a wide variety of goods. Most states apply ad valorem sales taxes to most goods and services, exempting only a few staples such

Figure 2.13 The Effects of a Specific Tax and an Ad Valorem Tax on Consumers

Without a tax, the demand curve is D and the supply curve is S. A specific tax of $\tau = \$1.05$ per kg collected from consumers shifts the demand curve to D^s, which is parallel to D. The new equilibrium is e_2 on the original demand curve D. If instead an ad valorem tax of $\alpha = 26.25\%$ is imposed, the demand curve facing firms is D^a. The gap between D and D^a, the per-unit tax, is larger at higher prices. The after-tax equilibrium is the same with both of these taxes.

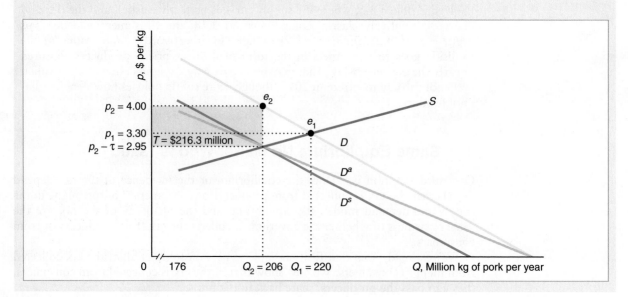

as food and medicine. There are 6,400 different ad valorem sales tax rates across the United States (Besley and Rosen, 1999), some of which are as high as 10.75% (in some areas of California).

Suppose that the government imposes an ad valorem tax of α, instead of a specific tax, on the price that consumers pay for processed pork. We already know that the equilibrium price is $4 with a specific tax of $1.05 per kg. At that price, an ad valorem tax of $\alpha = \$1.05/\$4 = 26.25\%$ raises the same amount of tax per unit as a $1.05 specific tax.

It is usually easiest to analyze the effects of an ad valorem tax by shifting the demand curve. Figure 2.13 shows how an ad valorem tax shifts the processed pork demand curve to D^a. At any given price p, the gap between D and D^a is αp, which is greater at high prices than at low prices. The gap is $1.05 ($= 0.2625 \times \$4$) per unit when the price is $4, and $2.10 when the price is $8.

Imposing an ad valorem tax causes the after-tax equilibrium quantity, Q_2, to fall below the original quantity, Q_1, and the after-tax price, p_2, to rise above the original price, p_1. The tax collected per unit of output is $\tau = \alpha p_2$. The incidence of the tax that falls on consumers is the change in price, $\Delta p = (p_2 - p_1)$, divided by the change in the per-unit tax, $\Delta \tau = \alpha p_2 - 0$, that is collected, $\Delta p/(\alpha p_2)$. The incidence of an ad valorem tax is generally shared between consumers and producers. Because the ad valorem tax of $\alpha = 26.25\%$ has exactly the same impact on the equilibrium pork price and raises the same amount of tax per unit as the $\tau = \$1.05$ specific tax, the incidence is the same for both types of taxes. (As with specific taxes, the incidence of the ad valorem tax depends on the elasticities of supply and demand, but we'll spare your having to go through that in detail.)

2.7 Quantity Supplied Need Not Equal Quantity Demanded

In a supply-and-demand model, the quantity supplied does not necessarily equal the quantity demanded because of the way we defined these two concepts. We defined the quantity supplied as the amount firms want to sell at a given price, holding constant other factors that affect supply, such as the price of inputs. We defined the quantity demanded as the quantity that consumers want to buy at a given price, if other factors that affect demand are held constant. The quantity that firms want to sell and the quantity that consumers want to buy at a given price need not equal the actual quantity that is bought and sold.

We could have defined the quantity supplied and the quantity demanded so that they must be equal. If we had defined the quantity supplied as the amount firms *actually* sell at a given price and the quantity demanded as the amount consumers *actually* buy, supply would have to equal demand in all markets because we *defined* the quantity demanded and the quantity supplied as the same quantity.

It is worth emphasizing this distinction because politicians, pundits, and the press are so often confused on this point. Someone who insists "demand *must* equal supply" must be defining demand and supply as the *actual* quantities sold. Because we define the quantities supplied and demanded in terms of people's *wants* and not *actual* quantities bought and sold, the statement that "supply equals demand" is a theory, not merely a definition.

According to our theory, the quantity supplied equals the quantity demanded at the intersection of the supply and demand curves if the government does not intervene. However, not all government interventions prevent markets from *clearing*: equilibrating the quantity supplied and the quantity demanded. For example, as we've seen, a government tax affects the equilibrium by shifting the supply curve or demand curve of a good but does not cause a gap between the quantity demanded and the quantity supplied. However, some government policies do more than merely shift the supply curve or demand curve.

For example, governments may directly control the prices of some products. For example, New York City limits the price or rent that property owners can charge for an apartment. If the price a government sets for a product differs from its market clearing price, either excess supply or excess demand results. We illustrate this result with two types of price control programs. The government may set a *price ceiling* at $\bar{p}$ so that the price at which goods are sold may be no higher than $\bar{p}$. When the government sets a *price floor* at $\bar{p}$, the price at which goods are sold may not fall below $\bar{p}$.

We can study the effects of such regulations using the supply-and-demand model. Despite the lack of equality between the quantity supplied and the quantity demanded, the supply-and-demand model is useful for analyzing price controls because it predicts the excess demand or excess supply that is observed.

Price Ceiling

A price ceiling legally limits the amount that can be charged for a product. The ceiling does not affect market outcomes if it is set above the equilibrium price that would be charged in the absence of the price control. For example, if the government says firms can charge no more than $\bar{p} = \$5$ per gallon of gas and firms are actually charging $p = \$3$, the government's price control policy is irrelevant. However, if the equilibrium price had been $6 per gallon, the price ceiling would limit the price in that market to only $5.

The U.S. government imposed price controls on gasoline several times. In the 1970s, OPEC reduced supplies of oil—which is converted into gasoline—to Western countries. As a result, the total supply curve for gasoline in the United States—the horizontal sum of domestic and OPEC supply curves—shifted to the left from S^1 to S^2 in Figure 2.14. Because of this shift, the equilibrium price of gasoline would have risen substantially, from p_1 to p_2. In an attempt to protect consumers by keeping gasoline prices from rising, the U.S. government set price ceilings on gasoline in 1973 and 1979.

The government told gas stations that they could charge no more than $\bar{p} = p_1$. Figure 2.14 shows the price ceiling as a solid horizontal line extending from the price axis at $\bar{p}$. The price control is binding because $p_2 > \bar{p}$. The observed price is the price ceiling. At $\bar{p}$, consumers *want* to buy $Q_d = Q_1$ gallons of gasoline, which is the equilibrium quantity they bought before OPEC acted. However, because of the price control, firms are willing to supply only Q_s gallons, which is determined by the intersection of the price control line with S^2. As a result, a binding price control causes excess demand of $Q_d - Q_s$.

Were it not for the price controls, market forces would drive up the market price to p_2, where the excess demand would be eliminated. The government's price ceiling prevents this adjustment from occurring, which causes a **shortage**, or persistent excess demand.

At the time the controls were implemented, some government officials falsely contended that the shortages were caused by OPEC's cutting off its supply of oil

Figure 2.14 The Effects of a Gasoline Price Ceiling

Supply shifts from S^1 to S^2. Under the government's price control program, gasoline stations may not charge a price above the price ceiling $\bar{p} = p_1$. At that price, producers are willing to supply only Q_s, which is less than the amount $Q_1 = Q_d$ that consumers want to buy. The result is excessive demand, or a shortage of $Q_d - Q_s$.

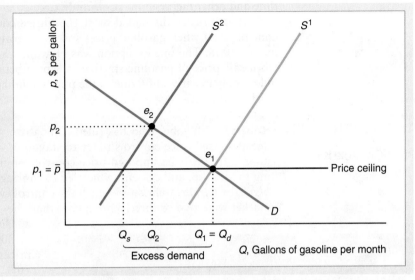

to the United States. Without the price controls, the new equilibrium would be e_2, where the equilibrium price, p_2, is greater than p_1, and the equilibrium, Q_2, is greater than the quantity sold under the control program, Q_s. However, there would have been no shortage.

The supply-and-demand model predicts that a binding price control results in equilibrium *with a shortage*. In this equilibrium, the quantity demanded does not equal the quantity supplied. The reason that we call this situation an equilibrium even though a shortage exists is that no consumers or firms want to act differently, *given the law*. Without a price control, consumers facing a shortage would try to get more output by offering to pay more, or firms would raise their prices. With an enforced price control, they know that they can't drive up the price, so they live with the shortage.

So what happens when there is a price shortage? Lucky consumers get to buy Q_s units at the low price of $\bar{p}$. Other potential customers are disappointed: They would like to buy at that price, but they cannot find anyone willing to sell gas to them. With enforced price controls, sellers use criteria other than price to allocate the scarce commodity. They may supply the commodity to their friends, long-term customers, or people of a certain race, gender, age, or religion. They may sell their goods on a first-come, first-served basis. Or they may limit everyone to only a few gallons.

Another possibility is for firms and customers to evade the price controls. A consumer could go to a gas station owner and say, "Let's not tell anyone, but I'll pay you twice the price the government sets if you'll sell me as much gas as I want." If enough customers and gas station owners behaved that way, no shortage would occur. A study of 92 major U.S. cities during the 1973 gasoline price control found no gasoline lines in 52 of the cities, where apparently the law was not enforced. However, in cities where the law was effective such as Chicago, Hartford, New York, Portland, and Tucson, potential customers waited in line at the pump for an hour or more.[22] Deacon and Sonstelie (1989) calculated that for every dollar

---

[22]See "Gas Lines," in the Supplemental Material to MyEconLab, Chapter Resources, Chapter 2 for a more detailed discussion of the effects of the 1973 and 1979 gasoline price controls.

consumers saved during the 1980 gasoline price controls, they lost $1.16 in waiting time and other factors.[23]

This experience dissuaded most U.S. jurisdictions from imposing gasoline price controls even when gasoline prices spiked following Hurricane Katrina in the summer of 2008. The one exception was Hawaii, which imposed price controls on the wholesale price of gasoline starting in September 2005, but suspended the controls indefinitely in early 2006 due to the public's unhappiness with the law.

APPLICATION

Price Controls Kill

Robert G. Mugabe, who has ruled Zimbabwe with an iron fist for nearly three decades, used price controls to try to stay in power by currying favor among the poor.[24] In 2001, he imposed price controls on many basic commodities, including food, soap, and cement, which led to shortages of these goods, and a thriving *black*, or *parallel, market* in which the controls were ignored. Prices on the black market were two or three times higher than the controlled prices.

He imposed more extreme controls in 2007. A government edict cut the prices of 26 essential items by up to 70%, and a subsequent edict imposed price controls on a much wider range of goods. Gangs of price inspectors patrolled shops and factories, imposing arbitrary price reductions. State-run newspapers exhorted citizens to turn in store owners whose prices exceeded the limits.

The Zimbabwean police reported that they arrested at least 4,000 businesspeople for not complying with the price controls. The government took over the nation's slaughterhouses after meat disappeared from stores, but in a typical week, butchers killed and dressed only 32 cows for the entire city of Bulawayo, with a population of 676,000 people.

Ordinary citizens initially greeted the price cuts with euphoria because they had been unable to buy even necessities because of hyperinflation and past price controls. Yet most ordinary citizens were unable to obtain much food because most of the cut-rate merchandise was snapped up by the police, soldiers, and members of Mr. Mugabe's governing party, who were tipped off prior to the price inspectors' rounds.

Manufacturing slowed to a crawl because firms could not buy raw materials and because the prices firms received were less than their costs of production.

---

[23]Some economists interpret this market as being in an equilibrium in which the effective price that consumers face is the actual price plus the value of the waiting time. Thus, the quantity demanded at the effective price equals the quantity supplied.

[24]Mr. Mugabe justified price controls as a means to deal with profiteering businesses that he said were part of a Western conspiracy to reimpose colonial rule. Actually, they were a vain attempt to slow the hyperinflation that resulted from his printing Zimbabwean money rapidly. Prices increased several billion times in 2008, and the government printed currency with a face value of 100 trillion Zimbabwe dollars.

Businesses laid off workers or reduced their hours, impoverishing the 15% or 20% of adult Zimbabweans who still had jobs. The 2007 price controls on manufacturing crippled this sector, forcing manufacturers to sell goods at roughly half of what it cost to produce them. By mid-2008, the output by Zimbabwe's manufacturing sector had fallen 27% compared to the previous year. Consequently, Zimbabweans died from starvation. Although we have no exact figures, according to the World Food Program, over five million Zimbabweans faced starvation in 2008.

Aid shipped into the country from international relief agencies and the two million Zimbabweans who have fled abroad have helped keep some people alive. In 2008, the World Food Program made an urgent appeal for $140 million in donations to feed Zimbabweans, stating that drought and political upheaval would soon exhaust the organization's stockpiles. Thankfully, Mr. Mugabe was forced to share power with opposition groups in 2009, and the price controls were lifted, which led to economic improvements.

Price Floor

Governments also commonly impose price floors. One of the most important examples of a price floor is the minimum wage in labor markets.

The minimum wage law forbids employers from paying less than a minimum wage, $\underline{w}$. Minimum wage laws date from 1894 in New Zealand, 1909 in the United Kingdom, and 1912 in Massachusetts. The Fair Labor Standards Act of 1938 set a federal U.S. minimum wage of 25¢. Today, the federal minimum wage is $7.25 an hour, but some states set a higher rate (Washington State's rate is $9.04 as of 2012). Effective October 2012, the UK minimum hourly wage is £6.08 for adult workers. The 2012 statutory monthly minimum wage ranges from the equivalent of 19€ in the Russian Federation to 485€ in Portugal, 1,398€ in France, and 1,801€ in Luxembourg.[25] If the minimum wage binds—exceeds the equilibrium wage, w^*—the minimum wage causes *unemployment*, which is a persistent excess supply of labor.[26]

For simplicity, suppose that there is a single labor market in which everyone is paid the same wage. Figure 2.15 shows the supply and demand curves for labor services (hours worked). Firms buy hours of labor service—they hire workers. The quantity measure on the horizontal axis is hours worked per year, and the price measure on the vertical axis is the wage per hour.

With no government intervention, the market equilibrium is e, where the wage is w^* and the number of hours worked is L^*. The minimum wage creates a price floor, a horizontal line, at $\underline{w}$. At that wage, the quantity demanded falls to L_d and the quantity supplied rises to L_s. As a result, there is an excess supply or unemployment of $L_s - L_d$. The minimum wage prevents market forces from eliminating the excess supply, so it leads to an equilibrium with unemployment. The original 1938 U.S. minimum wage law caused massive unemployment in the U.S. territory of Puerto Rico.

---

[25]The U.S. Department of Labor maintains at its Web site (**www.dol.gov**) an extensive history of the federal minimum wage law, labor markets, state minimum wage laws, and other information. For European minimum wages, see **www.fedee.com/minwage.html**. See **www.direct.gov.uk** for British rates.

[26]Where the minimum wage applies to only some labor markets (Chapter 10) or where only a single firm hires all the workers in a market (Chapter 15), a minimum wage might not cause unemployment. Card and Krueger (1995) provide evidence that recent rises in the minimum wage had negligible (at most) effects on employment in certain low-skill labor markets.

Figure 2.15 The Effects of a Minimum Wage

In the absence of a minimum wage, the equilibrium wage is w^*, and the equilibrium number of hours worked is L^*. A minimum wage, $\underline{w}$, set above w^*, leads to unemployment—persistent excess supply—because the quantity demanded, L_d, is less than the quantity supplied, L_s.

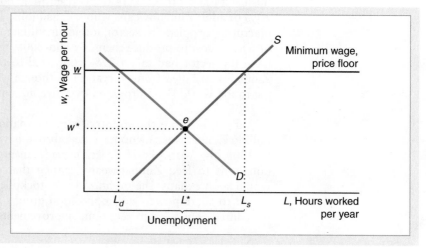

It is ironic that a law designed to help workers by raising their wages harms some of them by causing them to become unemployed. Minimum wage laws benefit only people who manage to remain employed.

2.8 When to Use the Supply-and-Demand Model

As we've seen, the supply-and-demand model can help us understand and predict real-world events in many markets. Through Chapter 10, we discuss *perfectly competitive* markets in which the supply-and-demand model is a powerful tool for predicting what will happen to market equilibrium if underlying conditions—tastes, incomes, and prices of inputs—change. A perfectly competitive market (Chapter 8) is one in which all firms and consumers are *price takers*: No market participant can affect the market price.

Perfectly competitive markets have five characteristics that result in price taking behavior:

1. There are many small buyers and sellers.
2. All firms produce identical products.
3. All market participants have full information about prices and product characteristics.
4. Transaction costs are negligible.
5. Firms can easily enter and exit the market.

When there are many firms and consumers in a market, no single firm or consumer is a large enough part of the market to affect the price. If you stop buying bread or if one of the many thousands of wheat farmers stops selling the wheat used to make the bread, the price of bread will not change.

In contrast, if there is only one seller of a good or service—a *monopoly* (Chapter 11)—that seller is a *price setter* and can affect the market price. Because demand curves slope downward, a monopoly can increase the price it receives by reducing the amount of a good it supplies. Firms are also price setters in an *oligopoly*—a market with only a small number of firms—or in markets in which they sell differentiated products, and consumers prefer one product to another (Chapter 14). In markets with price setters, the market price is usually higher than that predicted by the supply-and-demand model. That doesn't make the supply-and-demand model generally wrong. It means only that the supply-and-demand model does not apply to markets with a small number of sellers or buyers. In such markets, we use other models.

If consumers believe all firms produce identical products, consumers do not prefer one firm's good to another's. Thus, if one firm raises its price, consumers buy from the other firm. In contrast, if some consumers prefer Coke to Pepsi, Coke can charge more than Pepsi and not lose all its customers.

If consumers know the prices all firms charge and one firm raises its price, that firm's customers will buy from other firms. If consumers have less information about a product's quality than the firm that produces it, the firm can take advantage of consumers by selling them inferior-quality goods or by charging a much higher price than other firms charge. In such a market, the observed price may be higher than that predicted by the supply-and-demand model, the market may not exist at all (consumers and firms cannot reach agreements), or different firms may charge different prices for the same good (Chapter 18).

If it is cheap and easy for a buyer to find a seller and make a trade and if one firm raises its price, consumers can easily arrange to buy from another firm. That is, perfectly competitive markets typically have very low **transaction costs**: the expenses, over and above the price of the product, of finding a trading partner and making a trade for the product. These costs include the time and money spent gathering information about a product's quality and finding someone with whom to trade. Other transaction costs include the costs of writing and enforcing a contract, such as the cost of a lawyer's time. If transaction costs are very high, no trades at all might occur. In less extreme cases, individual trades may occur, but at a variety of prices.

The ability of firms to enter and exit a market freely leads to a large number of firms in a market and promotes price taking. Suppose a firm could raise its price and make a higher profit. If other firms could not enter the market, this firm would not be a price taker. However, if other firms can quickly and easily enter the market, the higher profit will encourage entry until the price is driven back to its original level.

Thus, the supply-and-demand model is not appropriate in markets in which there are one or a few sellers (such as the market for local water and sewage services); firms produce differentiated products (such as music CDs); consumers know less than sellers about the quality of products (such as used cars) or their prices; there are high transaction costs (such as nuclear turbine engines); or high entry and exit costs (such as aircraft manufacturing). Markets in which the supply-and-demand model has proved useful—markets with many firms and consumers and in which firms sell identical products—include agriculture, finance, labor, construction, services, wholesale, and retail.

CHALLENGE SOLUTION Quantities and Prices of Genetically Modified Foods	We conclude by returning to the Challenge posed at the beginning of the chapter where we asked about the effects on the price and quantity of a crop, such as corn, from the introduction of GM seeds. The supply curve shifts to the right because GM seeds produce more output than traditional seeds, holding all else constant. If consumers fear GM products, the demand curve for corn shifts to the left. We want to determine how the after-GM equilibrium compares to the before-GM equilibrium. When an event shifts both curves, the qualitative effect on the equilibrium price and quantity may be difficult to predict, even if we know the direction in which each curve shifts. Changes in the equilibrium price and

quantity depend on exactly how much the curves shift. In our analysis, we consider the possibility that the demand curve may shift only slightly in some countries where consumers don't mind GM products but substantially in others where many consumers fear GM products.

In the figure, the original, before-GM equilibrium, e_1, is determined by the intersection of the before-GM supply curve, S^1, and the before-GM demand curve, D^1, at price p_1 and quantity Q_1. Both panels a and b of the figure show this same equilibrium.

When GM seeds are introduced, the new supply curve, S^2, lies to the right of S^1. In panel a, the new demand curve, D^2, lies only slightly to the left of D^1, while in panel b, D^3 lies substantially to the left of D^1. In panel a, the new equilibrium e_2 is determined by the intersection of S^2 and D^2. In panel b, the new equilibrium e_3 reflects the intersection of S^2 and D^3.

The equilibrium price falls from p_1 to p_2 in panel a and to p_3 in panel b. However, the equilibrium quantity rises from Q_1 to Q_2 in panel a, but falls from Q_1 to Q_3 in panel b. Thus, when both curves shift, we can predict the direction of change of the equilibrium price, but cannot predict the change in the equilibrium quantity without knowing how much each curve shifts. Whether growers in a country decide to adopt GM seeds turns crucially on how resistant consumers are to these new products.

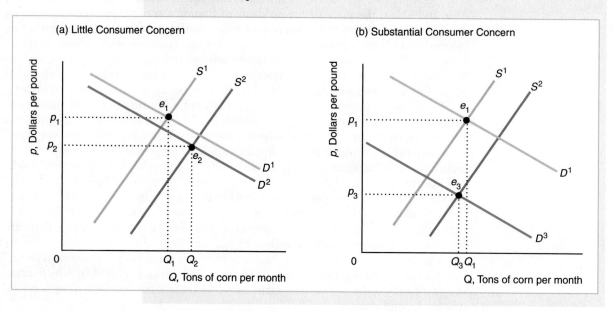

SUMMARY

1. Demand. The quantity of a good or service demanded by consumers depends on their tastes, the price of a good, the price of goods that are substitutes and complements, consumers' income, information, government regulations, and other factors. The *Law of Demand*—which is based on observation—says that *demand curves slope downward*. The higher the price, the less quantity is demanded, holding constant other factors that affect demand. A change in price causes a *movement along the demand curve*. A change in income, tastes, or another factor that affects demand other than price causes a *shift of the demand curve*. To derive a total demand curve, we horizontally sum the demand curves of individuals or types of consumers or countries. That is, we add the quantities demanded by each individual at a given price to determine the total quantity demanded.

2. **Supply.** The quantity of a good or service supplied by firms depends on the price, the firm's costs, government regulations, and other factors. The market supply curve need not slope upward but it usually does. A change in price causes a *movement along the supply curve*. A change in the price of an input or government regulation causes a *shift of the supply curve*. The total supply curve is the horizontal sum of the supply curves for individual firms.

3. **Market Equilibrium.** The intersection of the demand curve and the supply curve determines the equilibrium price and quantity in a market. Market forces—actions of consumers and firms—drive the price and quantity to the equilibrium levels if they are initially too low or too high.

4. **Shocking the Equilibrium: Comparative Statics.** A change in an underlying factor other than price causes a shift of the supply curve or the demand curve, which alters the equilibrium. Comparative statics is the method that economists use to analyze how variables controlled by consumers and firms—such as price and quantity—react to a change in *environmental variables* such as prices of substitutes and complements, income, and prices of inputs.

5. **Elasticities.** An elasticity is the percentage change in a variable in response to a given percentage change in another variable, holding all other relevant variables constant. The price elasticity of demand, ε, is the percentage change in the quantity demanded in response to a given percentage change in price: A 1% increase in price causes the quantity demanded to fall by ε%. Because demand curves slope downward according to the Law of Demand, the elasticity of demand is always negative. The price elasticity of supply, η, is

the percentage change in the quantity supplied in response to a given percentage change in price. Given estimated elasticities, we can forecast the comparative statics effects of a change in taxes or other variables that affect the equilibrium.

6. **Effects of a Sales Tax.** The two common types of sales taxes are ad valorem taxes, by which the government collects a fixed percentage of the price paid per unit, and specific taxes, by which the government collects a fixed amount of money per unit sold. Both types of sales taxes typically raise the equilibrium price and lower the equilibrium quantity. Also, both usually raise the price consumers pay and lower the price suppliers receive, so consumers do not bear the full burden or incidence of the tax. The effects on quantity, price, and the incidence of the tax that falls on consumers depend on the demand and supply elasticities. In competitive markets, the impact of a tax on equilibrium quantities, prices, and the incidence of the tax is unaffected by whether the tax is collected from consumers or producers.

7. **Quantity Supplied Need Not Equal Quantity Demanded.** The quantity supplied equals the quantity demanded in a competitive market if the government does not intervene. However, some government policies—such as price floors or ceilings—cause the quantity supplied to be greater or less than the quantity demanded, leading to persistent excesses or shortages.

8. **When to Use the Supply-and-Demand Model.** The supply-and-demand model is a powerful tool to explain what happens in a market or to make predictions about what will happen if an underlying factor in a market changes. However, this model is applicable only in competitive markets with many buyers and sellers, in which firms sell identical goods, participants have full information, transaction costs are low, and firms can easily enter and exit.

EXERCISES

If you ask me anything I don't know, I'm not going to answer. —Yogi Berra

■ = *exercise is available in* MyEconLab; * = *answer appears at the back of this book;* **M** = *mathematical problem.*

1. Demand

*1.1 Using the estimated demand function for processed pork in Canada, Equation 2.2, show how the quantity demanded, Q, at a given price changes as per capita income, Y, increases slightly (that is, calculate the partial derivative of the quantity demanded with respect to income). How much does Q change if income rises by $100 a year? **M**

*1.2 Suppose that the inverse demand function (where the demand curve is rearranged so that price is a function of quantity) for movies is $p = 120 - Q_1$ for college students and $p = 120 - 2Q_2$ for other town residents. What is the town's total demand function ($Q = Q_1 + Q_2$ as a function of p)? Use a diagram to illustrate your answer. (*Hint:* By looking at your diagram, you'll see that the total demand function has a kink, so care must be used in writing the total demand function.) **M**

1.3 In the application "Aggregating the Demand for Broadband Service" (based on Duffy-Deno, 2003), the demand function is $Q_s = 5.97p^{-0.563}$ for small firms and $Q_l = 8.77p^{-0.296}$ for larger firms, where price is in cents per kilobyte per second and quantity is in millions of kilobytes per second (Kbps). What is the total demand function for all firms? If the price for broadband service is 40¢ per Kbps, what is the equilibrium quantity demanded by small firms, large firms, and all firms? **M**

2. Supply

2.1 Given the pork supply function in Equation 2.6, how does the supply function that is only a function of price, Equation 2.7, change if the price of hogs doubles to $3 per kg? **M**

2.2 If the U.S. supply function of corn is $Q_a = 10 + 10p$ and the supply function of the rest of the world is $Q_r = 5 + 20p$, what is the world supply function? (*Hint*: Note that there is a kink in the world supply function.)

*2.3 Between 1971 and 2006, the United States from time to time imposed quotas or other restrictions on importing steel. A quota says that no more than $\overline{Q} > 0$ units of steel can be imported into the country. Suppose both the domestic supply curve of steel, S^d, and the foreign supply curve of steel for sale in the United States, S^f, are upward-sloping straight lines. How did a quota set by the United States on foreign steel imports of $\overline{Q}$ affect the total American supply curve for steel (domestic and foreign supply combined)?

3. Market Equilibrium

*3.1 Use a supply-and-demand diagram to explain the statement "Talk is cheap because supply exceeds demand." At what price is this comparison being made?

3.2 If the demand function is $Q = 110 - 20p$, and the supply function is $Q = 20 + 10p$, what are the equilibrium price and quantity? **M**

*3.3 Green, Howitt, and Russo (2005) estimate the supply and demand curves for California processing tomatoes. The supply function is $\ln Q = 0.2 + 0.55 \ln p$, where Q is the quantity of processing tomatoes in millions of tons per year and p is the price in dollars per ton. The demand function is $\ln Q = 2.6 - 0.2 \ln p + 0.15 \ln p_t$, where p_t is the price of tomato paste (which is what processing tomatoes are used to produce) in dollars

per ton. In 2002, $p_t = 110$. What is the demand function for processing tomatoes, where the quantity is solely a function of the price of processing tomatoes? Solve for the equilibrium price and the quantity of processing tomatoes (rounded to two digits after the decimal point). Draw the supply and demand curves (note that they are not straight lines), and label the equilibrium and axes appropriately. **M**

4. Shocking the Equilibrium: Comparative Statics

4.1 The 9/11 terrorist attacks caused the U.S. airline travel demand curve to shift left by an estimated 30% (Ito and Lee, 2005). Use a supply-and-demand diagram to show the likely effect on price and quantity (assuming that the market is competitive). Indicate the magnitude of the likely equilibrium price and quantity effects—for example, would you expect equilibrium quantity to change by about 30%? Show how the answer depends on the shape and location of the supply and demand curves.

4.2 Ethanol, a fuel, is made from corn. Ethanol production increased more than 8.5 times from 1,630 million gallons in 2000 to 13,900 million gallons in 2011 (www.ethanolrfa.org/pages/statistics). Use a supply-and-demand diagram to show the effect of this increased use of corn for producing ethanol on the price of corn and the consumption of corn as food.

*4.3 The supply function is $Q = 20 + 3p - 20r$, and the demand function is $Q = 220 - 2p$, where r is the rental cost of capital. How do the equilibrium price and quantity vary with r? (*Hint*: See Solved Problem 2.1.) **M**

4.4 Using calculus, determine the effect of an increase in the price of beef, p_b, from $4 to $4.60 on the equilibrium price and quantity in the Canadian pork example. (*Hint*: Conduct an analysis that differs from that in Solved Problem 2.1 in that the shock is to the demand curve rather than to the supply curve.) Illustrate your comparative statics analysis in a figure. **M**

4.5 Due to a recession that lowered incomes, the 2008 market prices for last-minute rentals of U.S. beachfront properties were lower than usual. Suppose that the inverse demand function for renting a beachfront property in Ocean City, New Jersey, during the first week of August is $p = 1,000 - Q + Y/20$, where Y is the median annual income of the people involved in this market, Q is quantity, and p is the rental price. The inverse supply function is $p = Q/2 + Y/40$.

a. Derive the equilibrium price, p, and quantity, Q, in terms of Y.

b. Use a supply-and-demand analysis to show the effect of decreased income on the equilibrium price of rental homes. That is, find dp/dY. Does a decrease in median income lead to a decrease in the equilibrium rental price? (*Hint*: See Solved Problem 2.1.) **M**

4.6 Lewit and Coate (1982) estimated that the price elasticity of demand for cigarettes is −0.42. Suppose that the daily market demand for cigarettes in New York City is $Q = 20{,}000p^{-0.42}$ and that the inverse market supply curve of cigarettes in the city is $p = 1.5p_w$, where p_w is the wholesale price of cigarettes. (That is, the inverse market supply curve is a horizontal line at a price, p, equal to $1.5p_w$. Retailers sell cigarettes if they receive a price that is 50% higher than what they pay for the cigarettes so as to cover their other costs.)

a. Assume that the New York retail market for cigarettes is competitive. Calculate the equilibrium price and quantity of cigarettes as a function of the wholesale price. Let Q^* represent the equilibrium quantity. Find dQ^*/dp_w.

b. Now suppose that New York City and State each impose a $1.50 specific tax on each pack of cigarettes, for a total of $3.00 per pack on all cigarettes possessed for sale or use in New York City. The retailers pay the tax. Using both math and a graph, show how the introduction of the tax shifts the market supply curve. How does the introduction of the tax affect the equilibrium retail price and quantity of cigarettes?

c. With the specific tax in place, calculate the equilibrium price and quantity of cigarettes as a function of wholesale price. How does the presence of the quantity tax affect dQ^*/dp_w? **M**

*4.7 Given the answer to Exercise 2.3, what effect does a U.S. quota on steel of $\overline{Q} > 0$ have on the equilibrium in the U.S. steel market? (*Hint*: The answer depends on whether the quota *binds*: is low enough to affect the equilibrium.)

4.8 Suppose the demand function for carpenters is $Q = 100 - w$, and the supply curve is $Q = 10 + 2w - T$, where Q is the number of carpenters, w is the wage, and T is the test score required to pass the licensing exam. By how much do the equilibrium quantity and wage vary as T increases?

5. Elasticities

5.1 The U.S. Tobacco Settlement Agreement between the major tobacco companies and 46 states caused the price of cigarettes to jump 45¢ (21%) in November 1998. Levy and Meara (2006) find only a 2.65% drop in prenatal smoking 15 months later. What is the elasticity of demand for prenatal smokers? **M**

5.2 Calculate the elasticity of demand, if the demand function is

a. $Q = 120 - 2p + 4Y$, at the point where $p = 10$, $Q = 20$,

b. $Q = 10p^{-2}$. (*Hint*: See Solved Problem 2.2.) **M**

5.3 In the application "Aggregating the Demand for Broadband Service" (based on Duffy-Deno, 2003), the demand function is $Q_s = 5.97p^{-0.563}$ for small firms and $Q_l = 8.77p^{-0.296}$ for larger ones. As the graph in the application shows, the two demand functions cross. What are the elasticities of demand for small and large firms where they cross? Explain. (*Hint*: This problem can be answered without doing any calculations. See Solved Problem 2.2.) **M**

5.4 When the U.S. government announced that a domestic mad cow was found in December 2003, analysts estimated that domestic supplies would increase in the short run by 10.4% as many other countries barred U.S. beef. An estimate of the price elasticity of beef demand is −0.626 (Henderson, 2003). Assuming that only the domestic supply curve shifted, how much would you expect the price to change? (*Note*: The U.S. price fell by about 15% in the first month, but that probably reflected shifts in both supply and demand curves.) **M**

5.5 According to Borjas (2003), immigration to the United States increased the labor supply of working men by 11.0% from 1980 to 2000, and reduced the wage of the average native worker by 3.2%. From these results, can we make any inferences about the elasticity of supply or demand? Which curve (or curves) changed, and why? Draw a supply-and-demand diagram and label the axes to illustrate what happened.

5.6 Keeler et al. (2004) estimate that the U.S. Tobacco Settlement between major tobacco companies and 46 states caused the price of cigarettes to jump by 45¢ per pack (21%) and overall per capita cigarette consumption to fall by 8.3%. What is the elasticity of demand for cigarettes? Is cigarette demand elastic or inelastic? **M**

5.7 In a commentary piece on the rising cost of health insurance ("Healthy, Wealthy, and Wise," *Wall Street Journal*, May 4, 2004, A20), economists John Cogan, Glenn Hubbard, and Daniel Kessler stated, "Each percentage-point rise in health-insurance costs increases the number of uninsured by 300,000 people." Assuming that their claim is correct, demonstrate that the price elasticity of demand for health insurance depends on the number of people who are insured. What is the price elasticity if 200 million people are insured? What is the price elasticity if 220 million people are insured? **M**

*5.8 Calculate the price and cross-price elasticities of demand for coconut oil. The coconut oil demand function (Buschena and Perloff, 1991) is $Q = 1,200 - 9.5p + 16.2p_p + 0.2Y$, where Q is the quantity of coconut oil demanded in thousands of metric tons per year, p is the price of coconut oil in cents per pound, p_p is the price of palm oil in cents per pound, and Y is the income of consumers. Assume that p is initially 45¢ per pound, p_p is 31¢ per pound, and Q is 1,275 thousand metric tons per year. **M**

5.9 Show that the supply elasticity of a linear supply curve that cuts the price axis is greater than 1 (elastic), and the coefficient of elasticity of any linear supply curve that cuts the quantity axis is less than 1 (inelastic). (*Hint:* See Solved Problem 2.3.) **M**

5.10 Solved Problem 2.4 claims that a new war in the Persian Gulf could shift the world oil supply curve to the left by 3 million barrels a day or more, causing the world price of oil to soar regardless of whether we drill in the ANWR. How accurate is this claim? Use the same type of analysis as in the solved problem to calculate how much such a shock would cause the price to rise with and without the ANWR production. **M**

6. Effects of a Sales Tax

6.1 What effect does a $1 specific tax have on equilibrium price and quantity, and what is the incidence on consumers, if the following is true:

a. The demand curve is perfectly inelastic.

b. The demand curve is perfectly elastic.

c. The supply curve is perfectly inelastic.

d. The supply curve is perfectly elastic.

e. The demand curve is perfectly elastic and the supply curve is perfectly inelastic.

Use graphs and math to explain your answers. (*Hint:* See Solved Problem 2.5.) **M**

6.2 On July 1, 1965, the federal ad valorem taxes on many goods and services were eliminated. Comparing prices before and after this change, we can determine how much the price fell in response to the tax's elimination. When the tax was in place, the tax per unit on a good that sold for p was αp. If the price fell by αp when the tax was eliminated, consumers must have been bearing the full incidence of the tax. Consequently, consumers got the full benefit of removing the tax from those goods. The entire

amount of the tax cut was passed on to consumers for all commodities and services that were studied for which the taxes were collected at the retail level (except admissions and club dues) and for most commodities for which excise taxes were imposed at the manufacturer level, including face powder, sterling silverware, wristwatches, and handbags (Brownlee and Perry, 1967). List the conditions (in terms of the elasticities or shapes of supply or demand curves) that are consistent with 100% pass-through of the taxes. Use graphs to illustrate your answer.

6.3 Essentially none of the savings from removing the federal ad valorem tax were passed on to consumers for motion picture admissions and club dues (Brownlee and Perry, 1967; see Exercise 6.2). List the conditions (in terms of the elasticities or shapes of supply or demand curves) that are consistent with 0% pass-through of the taxes. Use graphs to illustrate your answer. **M**

*6.4 Do you care whether a 15¢ tax per gallon of milk is collected from milk producers or from consumers at the store? Why or why not?

6.5 Green et al. (2005) estimate that for almonds, the demand elasticity is −0.47 and the long-run supply elasticity is 12.0. The corresponding elasticities are −0.68 and 0.73 for cotton and −0.26 and 0.64 for processing tomatoes. If the government were to apply a specific tax to each of these commodities, what would be the consumer tax incidence for each of these commodities? **M**

6.6 A subsidy is a negative tax through which the government gives people money instead of taking it from them. If the government applied a $1.05 specific subsidy instead of a specific tax in Figure 2.12, what would happen to the equilibrium price and quantity? Use the demand function and the after-subsidy supply function to solve for the new equilibrium values. What is the incidence of the subsidy on consumers? **M**

6.7 Canada provided a 35% subsidy of the wage of employees of video game manufacturers in 2011. ("Video game makers say subsidies are vital," *CBC News*, June 4, 2011.)

a. What is the effect of a wage subsidy of the equilibrium wage and quantity of workers?

b. What happens when the wage subsidy rate falls?

c. What is the incidence of the subsidy?

*6.8 Use calculus to show that an increase in a specific sales tax τ reduces quantity less and tax revenue more, the less elastic the demand curve. (*Hint:* The quantity demanded depends on its price, which in turn depends on the specific tax, $Q(p(\tau))$, and tax revenue is $R = p(\tau)Q(p(\tau))$.) **M**

7. Quantity Supplied Need Not Equal Quantity Demanded

7.1 After Hurricane Katrina damaged a substantial portion of the nation's oil-refining capacity in 2005, the price of gasoline shot up around the country. In 2006, many state and federal elected officials called for price controls. Had they been imposed, what effect would price controls have had? Who would have benefited, and who would have been harmed by the controls? Use a supply-and-demand diagram to illustrate your answers.

7.2 The Thai government actively intervenes in markets (Limsamarnphun, Nophakhun, "Govt Imposes Price Controls in Response to Complaints," *The Nation*, May 12, 2012).

   a. The government increased the daily minimum wage by 40% to Bt300 (300 bahts ≈ $9.63). Show the effect of a higher minimum wage on the number of workers demanded, the supply of workers, and unemployment if the law is applied to the entire labor market.

   b. Show how the increase in the minimum wage and higher rental fees at major shopping malls and retail outlets affected the supply curve of ready-to-eat meals. Explain why the equilibrium price of a meal rose to Bt40 from Bt30.

   c. In response to complaints from citizens about higher prices of meals, the government imposed price controls on 10 popular meals. Show the effect of these price controls in the market for meals.

   d. What is the likely effect of the price controls on meals on the labor market?

*7.3 Usury laws place a ceiling on interest rates that lenders such as banks can charge borrowers. Low-income households in states with usury laws have significantly lower levels of consumer credit (loans) than comparable households in states without usury laws (Villegas, 1989). Why? (*Hint*: The interest rate is the price of a loan, and the amount of the loan is the quantity.)

*7.4 An increase in the minimum wage could raise the total wage payment, $W = wL(w)$, where w is the minimum wage and $L(w)$ is the demand function for labor, despite the fall in demand for labor services. Show that whether the wage payments rise or fall depends on the elasticity of demand of labor. **M**

8. When to Use the Supply-and-Demand Model

8.1 Are predictions using the supply-and-demand model likely to be reliable in each of the following markets? Why or why not?

   a. Apples

   b. Convenience stores

   c. Electronic games (a market dominated by three firms)

   d. Used cars

9. Challenge

9.1 In the Challenge Solution, we could predict the change in the equilibrium price of crops but not the quantity when GM seeds are introduced. Are there any conditions on the shapes of the supply and demand curves (or their elasticities) such that we could predict the effect on quantity?

*9.2 Soon after the United States revealed the discovery of a single mad cow in December 2003, more than 40 countries slapped an embargo on U.S. beef. In addition, some U.S. consumers stopped eating beef. In the three weeks after the discovery, the quantity sold increased by 43% during the last week of October 2003, and the U.S. price in January 2004 fell by about 15%. Use supply-and-demand diagrams to explain why these events occurred.

3

A Consumer's Constrained Choice

If this is coffee, please bring me some tea; but if this is tea, please bring me some coffee. —Abraham Lincoln

CHALLENGE

Why Americans Buy E-Books and Germans Do Not

Are you reading this book electronically? E-books are appearing everywhere in the English-speaking world. Thanks to the popularity of the Kindle, iPad, and other e-book readers, by the end of 2011, e-books accounted for 16% of trade books sold in the United States and 11% in the United Kingdom. E-books sold well in Australia and Canada as well. In contrast, in Germany, only about 1% of books sold are e-books.

Why are e-books more successful in the United States than in Germany? Jürgen Harth of the German Publishers and Booksellers Association attributed the difference to tastes or what he called a "cultural issue." More than others, Germans love printed books—after all, printing was invented in Germany. As Harth said, "On just about every corner there's a bookshop. That's the big difference between Germany and the United States."

An alternative explanation concerns government regulations and taxes that affect prices in Germany. Even if Germans and Americans have the same tastes, Americans are more likely to buy e-books because they are relatively less expensive than printed books in the United States but not in Germany. Unlike in the United States, where publishers and booksellers can choose what prices to set, Germany regulates book prices. To protect small booksellers, its fixed-price system requires all booksellers to charge the same price. In addition, printed books are taxed at 7%, whereas e-books are subject to a 19% tax.[1] Must we appeal to differences in tastes to explain why Germans and Americans read different types of books, or can taxes and price differences explain this difference?

Microeconomics provides powerful insights into the myriad questions and choices facing consumers. In addition to the e-book question, we can address questions such as the following: How can we use information about consumers' allocations of their budgets across various goods in the past to predict how a price change will affect their demands for goods today? Are consumers better off receiving cash or a comparable amount in food stamps? Should people buy insurance or save their money? Work at home or in the marketplace? Have children? Invest in bonds or in stocks?

To answer these and other questions about how consumers allocate their income over many goods, we use a model that lets us look at an individual's decision making when faced with limited income and market-determined prices. This model allows us to derive the market demand curve that we used in our supply-and-demand model and to make a variety of predictions about consumers' responses to changes in prices and income.

---

[1]The United Kingdom has a similar difference in tax rates.

Our model of consumer behavior is based on the following premises:

- Individual *tastes* or *preferences* determine the amount of pleasure people derive from the goods and services they consume.
- Consumers face *constraints*, or limits, on their choices.
- Consumers *maximize* their well-being or pleasure from consumption subject to the budget and other constraints they face.

Consumers spend their money on the bundle of products that gives them the most pleasure. If you love music and don't have much of a sweet tooth, you probably spend a lot of your money on concerts and music downloads and relatively little on candy.[2] By contrast, your chocoholic friend with the tin ear might spend a great deal of money on Hershey's Kisses and very little on music downloads.

All consumers must choose which goods to buy because their limited incomes prevent them from buying everything that catches their fancy. In addition, government rules restrict what they can buy: Young consumers cannot buy alcohol or cigarettes legally, and laws prohibit people of all ages from buying crack cocaine and other recreational drugs (although, of course, enforcement is imperfect). Therefore, consumers buy the goods that give them the most pleasure, subject to the constraints that they cannot spend more money than they have nor can they spend it in ways forbidden by the government.

When conducting *positive* economic analyses (Chapter 1) designed to explain behavior rather than to judge it (*normative* statements), economists assume that *the consumer is the boss*. If your brother gets pleasure from smoking, economists wouldn't argue with him that it's bad for him any more than they'd tell your sister, who likes reading Stephen King novels, that she should read Adam Smith's *Wealth of Nations* instead.[3] Accepting each consumer's tastes is not the same as condoning how people behave. Economists want to predict behavior. They want to know, for example, whether your brother will smoke more next year if the price of cigarettes decreases 10%. The following prediction is unlikely to be correct: "He shouldn't smoke; therefore, we predict he'll stop smoking next year." A prediction based on your brother's actual tastes is more likely to be correct: "Given that he likes cigarettes, he is likely to smoke more of them next year if the price falls."

In this chapter, we examine five main topics	1. **Preferences.** We use five properties of preferences to predict which combinations, or bundle, of goods an individual prefers to other combinations.
	2. **Utility.** Economists summarize a consumer's preferences using a utility function, which assigns a numerical value to each possible bundle of goods, reflecting the consumer's relative ranking of the bundles.
	3. **Budget Constraint.** Prices, income, and government restrictions limit a consumer's ability to make purchases by determining the rate at which a consumer can trade one good for another.
	4. **Constrained Consumer Choice.** Consumers maximize their pleasure from consuming various possible bundles of goods given their income, which limits the amount of goods they can purchase.
	5. **Behavioral Economics.** Experiments indicate that people sometimes deviate from rational, utility-maximizing behavior.

---

[2]Microeconomics is the study of trade-offs: Should you save your money or buy that Superman *Action Comics* Number 1 you always wanted? Indeed, an anagram for *microeconomics* is *income or comics*.

[3]As the ancient Romans put it: "De gustibus non est disputandum"—there is no disputing about (accounting for) tastes. Or, as it was put in the movie *Grand Hotel* (1932), "Have caviar if you like, but it tastes like herring to me."

3.1 Preferences

Do not do unto others as you would that they would do unto you. Their tastes may not be the same. —George Bernard Shaw

We start our analysis of consumer behavior by examining consumer preferences. Using four assumptions, we can make many predictions about people's preferences. Once we know about consumers' preferences, we can add information about the constraints that consumers face so that we can answer many questions, such as the ones posed at the beginning of the chapter, or derive demand curves, as we do in Chapter 4.

As a consumer, you choose among many goods. Should you have ice cream or cake for dessert? Should you spend most of your money on a large apartment or rent a single room and use the money you save to pay for trips and concerts? In short, you must allocate your money to buy a *bundle* of goods (*market basket*, or combination of goods).

How do consumers choose the bundle of goods they buy? One possibility is that consumers behave randomly and blindly choose one good or another without any thought. However, consumers appear to make systematic choices. For example, you probably buy the same specific items, more or less, each time you go to the grocery store.

To explain consumer behavior, economists *assume* that consumers have a set of tastes or preferences that they use to guide them in choosing between goods. These tastes differ substantially among individuals. Three out of four European men prefer colored underwear, while three out of four American men prefer white underwear.[4] Let's start by specifying the underlying assumptions in the economist's model of consumer behavior.

Properties of Consumer Preferences

I have forced myself to contradict myself in order to avoid conforming to my own taste. —Marcel Duchamp, Dada artist

A consumer chooses between bundles of goods by ranking them as to the pleasure the consumer gets from consuming each. We summarize a consumer's ranking using a *preference relation* $\succsim$. If the consumer likes Bundle a at least as much as Bundle b, we say that the consumer *weakly prefers* a to b, which we write as $a \succsim b$.

Given this weak preference relation, we can derive two other relations. If the consumer weakly prefers Bundle a to b, $a \succsim b$, but the consumer does not weakly prefer b to a, then we say that the consumer *strictly prefers* a to b—would definitely choose a rather than b if given a choice—which we write as $a > b$.

If the consumer weakly prefers a to b and weakly prefers b to a—that is $a \succsim b$ and $b \succsim a$—then we say that the consumer is *indifferent* between the bundles, or likes the two bundles equally, which we write as $a \sim b$.

We make three assumptions about the properties of consumers' preferences. For brevity, we refer to these properties as *completeness*, *transitivity*, and *more is better*.

Completeness. The completeness property holds that, when facing a choice between any two bundles of goods, Bundles a and b, a consumer can rank them so that one and only one of the following relationships is true: $a \succsim b$, $b \succsim a$, or both relationships hold so that $a \sim b$. This property rules out the possibility that the consumer cannot decide which bundle is preferable.

---

[4]Boyd, L. M., "The Grab Bag," *San Francisco Examiner*, September 11, 1994, p. 5.

Transitivity

It would be very difficult to predict behavior if consumers' rankings of bundles were not logically consistent. The transitivity property eliminates the possibility of certain types of illogical behavior. According to this property, a consumer's preferences over bundles is consistent in the sense that, if the consumer *weakly prefers a* to *b*, $a \succsim b$, and weakly prefers *b* to *c*, $b \succsim c$, then the consumer also weakly prefers *a* to *c*, $a \succsim c$.

If your sister told you that she preferred a scoop of ice cream to a piece of cake, a piece of cake to a candy bar, and a candy bar to a scoop of ice cream, you'd probably think she'd lost her mind. At the very least, you wouldn't know which dessert to serve her.

If completeness and transitivity hold, then the preference relation $\succsim$ is said to be *rational*. That is, the consumer has well-defined preferences between any pair of alternatives.

More Is Better. The more-is-better property states that, all else the same, more of a commodity is better than less of it.[5] Indeed, economists define a **good** as a commodity for which more is preferred to less, at least at some levels of consumption. In contrast, a **bad** is something for which less is preferred to more, such as pollution. Other than in Chapter 17, we concentrate on goods.

Although the completeness and transitivity properties are crucial to the analysis that follows, the more-is-better property is included to simplify the analysis; our most important results would follow even without this property.

So why do economists assume that the more-is-better property holds? The most compelling reason is that it appears to be true for most people. Another reason is that if consumers can freely dispose of excess goods, consumers can be no worse off with extra goods. (We examine a third reason later in the chapter: We observe consumers buying goods only when this condition is met.)

APPLICATION

You Can't Have Too Much Money

Do people become satiated? Can people be so rich that they can buy everything they want so that additional income does not increase their feelings of well-being?

Using recent data from as many as 131 countries, Stevenson and Wolfers (2008) find a strong positive relationship between average levels of self-reported feelings of happiness or satisfaction and income per capita within and across countries. Moreover, they find no evidence of a satiation point beyond which wealthier countries have no further increases in subjective well-being.[6]

In a 2011 Harris poll, the share of Americans surveyed with annual incomes below $35,000 describing themselves as very happy was 33% compared to 37% for those earning $100,000 or more a year. (Strangely, those earning between $75,000 and $99,999 were the least likely to report being very happy, 29%.)

Less scientific, but perhaps more compelling, is a survey of wealthy U.S. citizens who were asked, "How much wealth do you need to live comfortably?" On

---

[5]*Jargon alert*: Economists call this property *nonsatiation* or *monotonicity*.

[6]According to polls taken from 2005 to 2011, the 11 countries with the happiest citizens were (in order) Denmark, Finland, Norway, Netherlands, Canada, Switzerland, Sweden, New Zealand, Australia, Ireland, and the United States. These countries are relatively wealthy. The countries with the unhappiest people were Togo (ranked last), Benin, and the Central African Republic, which are all very poor.

average, those with a net worth of over $1 million said that they needed $2.4 million to live comfortably, those with at least $5 million in net worth said that they need $10.4 million, and those with at least $10 million wanted $18.1 million. Apparently, most people never have enough.[7]

Preference Maps

Surprisingly, with just these three properties, we can tell a lot about a consumer's preferences. One of the simplest ways to summarize information about a consumer's preferences is to create a graphical interpretation—a map—of them. For simplicity, we concentrate on choices between only two goods, but the model can be generalized to handle any number of goods.

Each semester, Lisa, who lives for fast food, decides how many pizzas and burritos to eat. The various bundles of pizzas and burritos she might consume are shown in panel a of Figure 3.1, with (individual-size) pizzas per semester, q_1, on the horizontal axis and burritos per semester, q_2, on the vertical axis.

At Bundle e, for example, Lisa consumes 25 pizzas and 15 burritos per semester. According to the more-is-better property, all the bundles that lie above and to the right (area A) are preferred to Bundle e because they contain at least as much of both pizzas and burritos as Bundle e. Thus, Bundle f (30 pizzas and 20 burritos) in that region is preferred to e. By the same reasoning, Lisa prefers e to all the bundles that lie in area B, below and to the left of e, such as Bundle d (15 pizzas and 10 burritos).

From panel a, we do not know whether Lisa prefers Bundle e to bundles such as b (30 pizzas and 10 burritos) in the area D, which is the region below and to the right of e, or c (15 pizzas and 25 burritos) in area C, which is the region above and to the left of Bundle e. We can't use the more-is-better property to determine which bundle she prefers because each of these bundles contains more of one good and less of the other than e does. To be able to state with certainty whether Lisa prefers particular bundles in areas C or D to Bundle e, we have to know more about her tastes for pizza and burritos.

Indifference Curves

Suppose we asked Lisa to identify all the bundles that give her the same amount of pleasure as consuming Bundle e. In panel b of Figure 3.1, we use her answers to draw curve I^1 through all bundles she likes as much as she likes e. Curve I^1 is an **indifference curve**: the set of all bundles of goods that a consumer views as being equally desirable.

---

[7]When teaching microeconomics to Wharton MBAs, I told them about my cousin who had just joined a commune in Oregon. His worldly possessions consisted of a tent, a Franklin stove, enough food to live on, and a few clothes. He said that he didn't need any other goods—that he was *satiated*. A few years later, one of these students bumped into me on the street and said, "Professor, I don't remember your name or much of anything you taught me in your course, but I can't stop thinking about your cousin. Is it really true that he doesn't want *anything* else? His very existence is a repudiation of my whole way of life." Actually, my cousin had given up his ascetic life and was engaged in telemarketing, but I, for noble pedagogical reasons, responded, "Of course he still lives that way—you can't expect everyone to have the tastes of an MBA."

Figure 3.1 Bundles of Pizzas and Burritos Lisa Might Consume

(a) Lisa prefers more to less, so she prefers Bundle *e* to any bundle in area *B*, including *d*. Similarly, she prefers any bundle in area *A*, such as *f*, to *e*. (b) The indifference curve, I^1, shows a set of bundles (including *c*, *e*, and *a*)

among which she is indifferent. (c) The three indifference curves, I^1, I^2, and I^3, are part of Lisa's preference map, which summarizes her preferences.

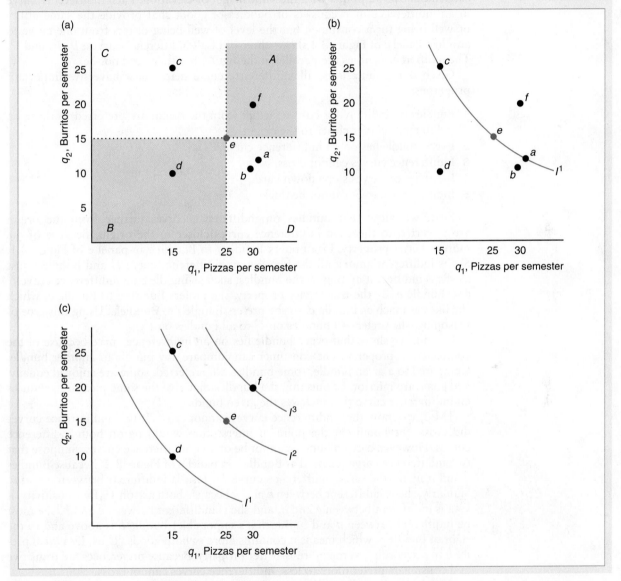

Indifference curve I^1 includes Bundles *c*, *e*, and *a*, so Lisa is indifferent about consuming Bundles *c*, *e*, and *a*. From this indifference curve, we also know that Lisa prefers *e* (25 pizzas and 15 burritos) to *b* (30 pizzas and 10 burritos). How do we know that? Bundle *b* lies below and to the left of Bundle *a*, so Bundle *a* is preferred to Bundle *b* according to the more-is-better property. Both Bundles *a* and *e* are on indifference curve I^1, so Lisa likes Bundle *e* as much as Bundle *a*. Because Lisa is indifferent between *e* and *a*, and she prefers *a* to *b*, she must prefer *e* to *b* by transitivity.

If we asked Lisa many, many questions, we could, in principle, draw an entire set of indifference curves through every possible bundle of burritos and pizzas. Lisa's preferences are summarized in an **indifference map**, or *preference map*, which is a complete set of indifference curves that summarize a consumer's tastes. We call it a *map* because it uses the same principle as a topographical or contour map, in which each line shows all points with the same height or elevation. Each indifference curve in an indifference map consists of bundles of goods that provide the same utility or well-being for a consumer, but the level of well-being differs from one curve to another. Panel c of Figure 3.1 shows three of Lisa's indifference curves: I^1, I^2, and I^3. The indifference curves are parallel in the figure, but they need not be.

Given our assumptions, all indifference curve maps must have five important properties:

1. Bundles on indifference curves farther from the origin are preferred to those on indifference curves closer to the origin.
2. Every bundle lies on an indifference curve.
3. Indifference curves cannot cross.
4. Indifference curves slope downward.
5. Indifference curves cannot be thick.

First, we show that bundles on indifference curves farther from the origin are preferred to those on indifference curves closer to the origin. Because of the more-is-better property, Lisa prefers Bundle f to Bundle e in panel c of Figure 3.1. She is indifferent among all the bundles on indifference curve I^3 and Bundle f, just as she is indifferent among all the bundles, such as Bundle c on indifference curve I^2 and Bundle e. By the transitivity property, she prefers Bundle f to Bundle e, which she likes as much as Bundle c, so she prefers Bundle f to Bundle c. Using this type of reasoning, she prefers all bundles on I^3 to all bundles on I^2.

Second, we show that every bundle lies on an indifference curve because of the completeness property: The consumer can compare any bundle to another bundle. Compared to a given bundle, some bundles are preferred, some are enjoyed equally, and some are inferior. Connecting the bundles that give the same pleasure produces an indifference curve that includes the given bundle.

Third, we show that indifference curves cannot cross. If two indifference curves did cross, the bundle at the point of intersection would be on both indifference curves. However, a given bundle cannot be on two indifference curves. Suppose that two indifference curves crossed at Bundle e in panel a of Figure 3.2. Because Bundles e and a lie on the same indifference curve I^1, Lisa is indifferent between e and a. Similarly, she is indifferent between e and b because both are on I^2. By transitivity, if Lisa is indifferent between e and a, and she is indifferent between e and b, she must be indifferent between a and b. But that's impossible! Bundle b is above and to the right of Bundle a, which means it contains more of both goods. Thus, Lisa *must* prefer b to a according to the more-is-better property. Because preferences are transitive and consumers prefer more to less, indifference curves cannot cross.

Fourth, we show that indifference curves must be downward sloping. Suppose, to the contrary, that an indifference curve sloped upward, as in panel b of Figure 3.2. The consumer is indifferent between Bundles a and b because both lie on the same indifference curve, I. But the consumer prefers b to a by the more-is-better property: Bundle a lies strictly below and to the left of Bundle b. Because of this contradiction—the consumer cannot be indifferent between a and b *and* strictly prefer b to a—indifference curves cannot be upward sloping. For example, if Lisa views pizza and burritos as goods, she cannot be indifferent between a bundle of one pizza and one burrito and another bundle with two of each.

Figure 3.2 Impossible Indifference Curves

(a) Suppose that the indifference curves cross at Bundle e. Lisa is indifferent between e and a on indifference curve I^0 and between e and b on I^1. If Lisa is indifferent between e and a, and she is indifferent between e and b, she must be indifferent between a and b due to transitivity. But b has more of both pizzas and burritos than a, so she *must* prefer a to b. Because of this contradiction, indifference curves cannot cross. (b) Suppose that indifference curve I slopes upward. The consumer is indifferent between b and a because they lie on I, but prefers b to a by the more-is-better assumption. Because of this contradiction, indifference curves cannot be upward sloping. (c) Suppose that indifference curve I is thick enough to contain both a and b. The consumer is indifferent between a and b because both are on I. However, the consumer prefers b to a by the more-is-better assumption because b lies above and to the right of a. Because of this contradiction, indifference curves cannot be thick.

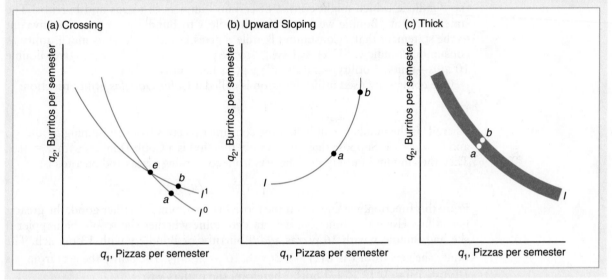

SOLVED PROBLEM 3.1

Can indifference curves be thick?

Answer

Draw an indifference curve that is at least two bundles thick, and show that a preference property is violated. Panel c of Figure 3.2 shows a thick indifference curve, I, with two bundles, a and b, identified. Bundle b lies above and to the right of a: Bundle b has more of both burritos and pizzas. Thus, because of the more-is-better property, Bundle b must be strictly preferred to Bundle a. But the consumer must be indifferent between a and b because both bundles are on the same indifference curve. Because both relationships between a and b cannot be true, there is a contradiction. Consequently, indifference curves cannot be thick. (We illustrate this point by drawing indifference curves with very thin lines in our figures.)

3.2 Utility

Underlying our model of consumer behavior is the belief that consumers can compare various bundles of goods and decide which bundle gives them the greatest pleasure. We can summarize a consumer's preferences by assigning a numerical value to each possible bundle to reflect the consumer's relative ranking of these bundles.

Following the terminology of Jeremy Bentham, John Stuart Mill, and other nineteenth-century British utilitarian economist-philosophers, economists apply the term **utility** to this set of numerical values that reflect the relative rankings of various bundles of goods.

Utility Function

The **utility function** is the relationship between utility measures and every possible bundle of goods. If we know the utility function, we can summarize the information in indifference maps succinctly. A utility function $U(x)$ assigns a numerical value to the Bundle x, which might consist of certain numbers of pizzas and burritos. The statement that "Bonnie weakly prefers Bundle x to Bundle y," $x \succsim y$, is equivalent to the statement that "Consuming Bundle x gives Bonnie at least as much utility as consuming Bundle y," $U(x) \geq U(y)$.[8] Bonnie prefers x to y if Bundle x gives Bonnie 10 *utils*—units of utility—and Bundle y gives her 8 utils.

One commonly used utility function is called a *Cobb-Douglas* utility function:[9]

$$U = q_1^a q_2^{1-a}, \tag{3.1}$$

where U is the number of utils that the consumer receives from consuming q_1 and q_2, and $0 < a < 1$. Suppose that Lisa's utility function is a Cobb-Douglas with $a = 0.5$. Then the amount of utility that she gets from consuming pizzas and burritos is

$$U = q_1^{0.5} q_2^{0.5} = \sqrt{q_1 q_2}.$$

From this function, we know that the more Lisa consumes of either good, the greater her utility. Using this function, we can determine whether she would be happier if she had Bundle x with 16 pizzas and 9 burritos or Bundle y with 13 of each. The utility she gets from x is $U(x) = 12 (= \sqrt{16 \times 9})$ utils. The utility she gets from y is $U(y) = 13 (= \sqrt{13 \times 13})$ utils. Therefore, she prefers y to x.

The utility function is a concept that economists use to help them think about consumer behavior; utility functions do not exist in any fundamental sense. For example, if you asked your mother, who is trying to decide whether to go to a movie or a play, what her utility function is, she would be puzzled—unless, of course, she is an economist. But if you asked her enough questions about which goods she would choose under various circumstances, you could construct a function that accurately summarizes her preferences. For example, by questioning people about which goods they would choose, Rousseas and Hart (1951) constructed indifference curves for eggs and bacon, and MacCrimmon and Toda (1969) constructed indifference curves for French pastries and money (which can be used to buy all other goods).

Ordinal Preferences

Typically, consumers can easily answer questions about whether they prefer one bundle to another, such as "Do you prefer a bundle with one scoop of ice cream and two pieces of cake to a bundle with two scoops of ice cream and one piece of

---

[8]A utility function represents a preference relation $\succsim$ only if the preference relation is rational (which we have assumed)—that is, it is complete and transitive. A proof is based on the idea that, because the utility function over real numbers includes any possible bundle and is transitive, the preference relation must also be complete and transitive.

[9]This functional form is named after Charles W. Cobb, a mathematician, and Paul H. Douglas, an economist and U.S. senator, who popularized it.

cake?" However, they have difficulty answering questions about how much more they prefer one bundle to another because they don't have a measure to describe how their pleasure from two goods or bundles differs. Therefore, we may know a consumer's rank ordering of bundles, but we are unlikely to know by how much more that consumer prefers one bundle to another.

If we know only consumers' relative rankings of bundles but not how much more they prefer one bundle to another, our measure of pleasure is an *ordinal* measure rather than a *cardinal* measure. An ordinal measure is one that tells us the relative ranking of two things but does not tell us how much more one rank is valued than another. If a professor assigns letter grades only to an exam, we know that a student who receives a grade of A did better than a student who receives a B, but we can't say how much better from that ordinal scale. Nor can we tell whether the difference in performance between an A student and a B student is greater or less than the difference between a B student and a C student.

A cardinal measure is one by which absolute comparisons between ranks may be made. Money is a cardinal measure. If you have $100 and your brother has $50, we know not only that you have more money than your brother but also that you have exactly twice as much money as he does.

In most of the book, we consider only ordinal utility. However, we use cardinal utility in our analysis of uncertainty in Chapter 16, and in a couple of other cases. If we use an ordinal utility measure, we should not put any weight on the absolute differences between the utility number associated with one bundle and that associated with another. We care only about the relative utility or ranking of the two bundles.

Because preference rankings are ordinal and not cardinal, many utility functions can correspond to a particular preference map. Suppose we know that Bill prefers Bundle x to Bundle y. A utility function that assigned 5 to x and 6 to y would be consistent with Bill's preference ranking. However, if we double all the numbers in this utility function, we would obtain a different utility function that assigned 10 to x and 12 to y. Both of these utility functions are consistent with Bill's preference ordering.

In general, given a utility function that is consistent with a consumer's preference ranking, we can transform that utility function into an unlimited number of other utility functions that are consistent with that ordering. Let $U(q_1, q_2)$ be the original utility function that assigns numerical values corresponding to any given combination of q_1 and q_2. Let F be an *increasing function* (in jargon, a *positive monotonic transformation*) such that if $x > y$, then $F(x) > F(y)$. By applying this transformation to the original utility function, we obtain a new function, $V(q_1, q_2) = F(U(q_1, q_2))$, which is a utility function with the same ordinal-ranking properties as $U(q_1, q_2)$. As an example, suppose that the transformation is linear: $F(x) = a + bx$, where $b > 0$. Then, $(q_1, q_2) = a + bU(q_1, q_2)$. The rank ordering is the same for these utility functions because $V(q_1, q_2) = a + bU(q_1, q_2) > V(q_1^*, q_2^*) = a + bU(q_1^*, q_2^*)$ if and only if $U(q_1, q_2) > U(q_1^*, q_2^*)$.

Thus, when we talk about utility numbers, we need to remember that these numbers are not unique and that we assign little meaning to the absolute numbers. We care only whether one bundle's utility value is greater than that of another.[10]

---

[10]The Cobb-Douglas utility function can be written generally as $U = Aq_1^c q_2^d$. However, we can always transform that utility function into the simpler one in Equation 3.1 through a positive monotonic transformation: $q_1^a q_2^{1-a} = F(Aq_1^c q_2^d)$, where $F(x) = x^{1/(c+d)}/A$, so that $a = c/(c + d)$.

Utility and Indifference Curves

An indifference curve consists of all those bundles that correspond to a particular utility measure. If a consumer's utility function is $U(q_1, q_2)$, then the expression for one of the corresponding indifference curves is

$$\overline{U} = U(q_1, q_2). \tag{3.2}$$

This expression determines all those bundles of q_1 and q_2 that give the consumer $\overline{U}$ utils of pleasure.

For example, if Lisa's utility function is $U = \sqrt{q_1 q_2}$, then her indifference curve $4 = \overline{U} = \sqrt{q_1 q_2}$ includes any (q_1, q_2) bundles such that $q_1 q_2 = 16$, including the bundles (4, 4), (2, 8), (8, 2), (1, 16), and (16, 1).

A three-dimensional diagram, Figure 3.3, shows how Lisa's utility varies with the amounts of pizza, q_1, and burritos, q_2, that she consumes. Panel a shows this relationship from a straight-ahead view, while panel b shows the same relationship looking at it from one side The figure measures q_1 on one axis on the "floor" of the diagram, q_2 on the other axis on the floor of the diagram, and $U(q_1, q_2)$ on the vertical axis. For example, in the figure, Bundle *a* lies on the floor of the diagram and contains two pizzas and two burritos. Directly above it on the utility surface or *hill*

Figure 3.3 The Relationship Between the Utility Function and Indifference Curves

Both panels a and b show Lisa's utility, $U(q_1, q_2)$ as a function of the amount of pizza, q_1, and burritos, q_2, that she consumes. The figure measures q_1 along one axis on the floor of the diagram, and q_2 along the other axis on the floor. Utility is measured on the vertical axis. As q_1, q_2, or both increase, she has more utility: She is on a higher point on the diagram. If we take all the points, the curve I^*, that are at a given height—given level of utility—on the utility surface and project those points down onto the floor of the diagram, we obtain the indifference curve I.

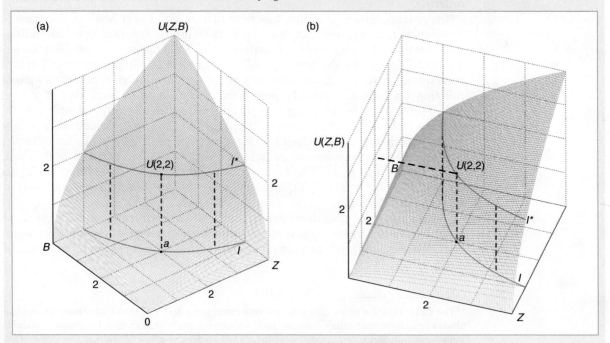

of happiness is a point labeled $U(2, 2)$. The vertical height of this point shows how much utility Lisa gets from consuming Bundle *a*. In the figure, $U(q_1, q_2) = \sqrt{q_1 q_2}$, so this height is $U(2, 2) = \sqrt{2 \times 2} = 2$. Because she prefers more to less, her utility rises as q_1 increases, q_2 increases, or both goods increase. That is, Lisa's hill of happiness rises as she consumes more of either or both goods.

What is the relationship between Lisa's utility function and one of her indifference curves—those combinations of q_1 and q_2 that give Lisa a particular level of utility? Imagine that the hill of happiness is made of clay. If you cut the hill at a particular level of utility, the height corresponding to Bundle *a*, $U(2, 2) = 2$, you get a smaller hill above the cut. The bottom edge of this hill—the edge where you cut— is the curve I^*. Now, suppose that you lower that smaller hill straight down onto the floor and trace the outside edge of this smaller hill. The outer edge of the hill on the two-dimensional floor is indifference curve *I*. Making other parallel cuts in the hill of happiness, placing the smaller hills on the floor, and tracing their outside edges, you can obtain a map of indifference curves on which each indifference curve reflects a different level of utility.

Willingness to Substitute Between Goods

Cornered   by Mike Baldwin

"We don't have poached eggs. How about an elephant tusk?"

How willing a consumer is to trade one good for another depends on the slope of the consumer's indifference curve, dq_2/dq_1, at the consumer's initial bundle of goods. Economists call the slope at a point on an indifference curve the **marginal rate of substitution** (*MRS*), because it is the maximum amount of one good that a consumer will sacrifice (trade) to obtain one more unit of another good.[11]

Lisa's *MRS* at Bundle *e* in Figure 3.4 is equal to the slope of the dashed line that is tangent to her indifference curve *I* at *e*. Because her indifference curve has a downward slope (and hence so does the line tangent to the indifference curve), her *MRS* at *e* is a negative number. The negative sign tells us that Lisa is willing to give up some pizza for more burritos and vice versa.

Although the *MRS* is defined as the slope at a particular bundle, we can illustrate the idea with a discrete change. If Lisa's $MRS = -2$, then she is indifferent between her current bundle and another bundle in which she gives up one unit of q_1 in exchange for two more units of q_2 (or gives up two units of q_2 for one more unit of q_1). For example, if Lisa's original Bundle *e* has nine pizzas and three burritos, she would be indifferent between that bundle and one in which she had eight (one fewer) pizzas and five (two additional) burritos.

The Relationship Between the Marginal Rate of Substitution and Marginal Utility. We can use calculus to determine the *MRS* at a point on Lisa's indifference curve in Equation 3.2. We show that the *MRS* depends on how much extra utility Lisa gets from a little more of each good. We call the extra utility that a consumer

---

[11]Sometimes it is difficult to guess whether other people think certain goods are close substitutes. For example, according to *Harper's Index*, 1994, flowers, perfume, and fire extinguishers rank 1, 2, and 3 among Mother's Day gifts that Americans consider "very appropriate."

Figure 3.4 Marginal Rate of Substitution

Lisa's marginal rate of substitution, $MRS = dq_2/dq_1$, at her initial bundle e is the slope of indifference curve I at that point. The marginal rate of substitution at e is the same as the slope of the line that is tangent to I at e. This indifference curve illustrates a diminishing marginal rate of substitution: The slope of the indifference curve becomes flatter as we move down and to the right along the curve (from Bundle f to e to g).

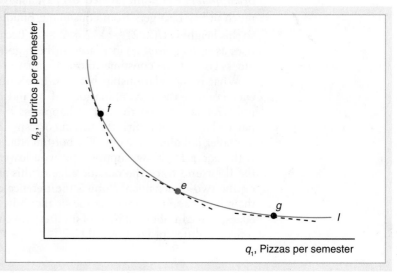

gets from consuming the last unit of a good the **marginal utility**. Given that Lisa's utility function is $U(q_1, q_2)$, the marginal utility she gets from a little more pizza, holding the quantity of burritos fixed, is

$$\text{marginal utility of pizza} = \frac{\partial U}{\partial q_1} = U_1.$$

Similarly, the marginal utility from more burritos is $U_2 = \partial U/\partial q_2$, where we hold the amount of pizza constant.

We can determine the MRS along an indifference curve by ascertaining the changes in q_1 and q_2 that leave her utility unchanged, keeping her on her original indifference curve, $\overline{U} = U(q_1, q_2)$. Let $q_2(q_1)$ be the implicit function that shows how much q_2 it takes to keep Lisa's utility at $\overline{U}$ given that she consumes q_1. We want to know how much q_2 must change if we increase q_1, dq_2/dq_1, given that we require her utility to remain constant. To answer this question, we use the chain rule to differentiate $\overline{U} = U(q_1, q_2(q_1))$ with respect to q_1, noting that because $\overline{U}$ is a constant, $d\overline{U}/dq_1 = 0$:

$$\frac{d\overline{U}}{dq_1} = 0 = \frac{\partial U(q_1, q_2(q_1))}{\partial q_1} + \frac{\partial U(q_1, q_2(q_1))}{\partial q_2}\frac{dq_2}{dq_1} = U_1 + U_2\frac{dq_2}{dq_1}. \quad (3.3)$$

The intuition behind Equation 3.3 is that as we move down and to the right along the indifference curve in Figure 3.4, we increase the amount of q_1 slightly, which increases Lisa's utility by U_1, so we must decrease her consumption of q_2 to hold her utility constant and keep her on the $\overline{U}$ indifference curve. Her decrease in utility from reducing q_2 in response to the increase in q_1 is $U_2(dq_2/dq_1)$, which is negative because dq_2/dq_1 is negative.

Rearranging the terms in Equation 3.3, we find that her marginal rate of substitution is

$$MRS = \frac{dq_2}{dq_1} = -\frac{\partial U/\partial q_1}{\partial U/\partial q_2} = -\frac{U_1}{U_2}. \quad (3.4)$$

Thus, the slope of her indifference curve is the negative of the ratio of her marginal utilities.

SOLVED PROBLEM 3.2

Jackie has a Cobb-Douglas utility function, $U = q_1^a q_2^{1-a}$, where q_1 is the number of tracks of recorded music she buys a year, and q_2 is the number of live music events she attends. What is her marginal rate of substitution?

Answer

1. *Determine the marginal utility Jackie gets from extra music tracks and the marginal utility she derives from more live music.* Her marginal utility from extra tracks is

$$U_1 = \frac{\partial U}{\partial q_1} = a q_1^{a-1} q_2^{1-a} = a\frac{U(q_1, q_2)}{q_1},$$

and her marginal utility from extra live music is

$$U_2 = (1 - a) q_1^a q_2^{-a} = (1 - a)\frac{U(q_1, q_2)}{q_2}.$$

2. *Express her marginal rate of substitution in terms of her marginal utilities.* Using Equation 3.4, we find that her marginal rate of substitution is

$$MRS = \frac{dq_2}{dq_1} = -\frac{U_1}{U_2} = -\frac{aU/q_1}{(1-a)U/q_2} = -\frac{a}{1-a}\frac{q_2}{q_1}. \tag{3.5}$$

APPLICATION

MRS Between Recorded Tracks and Live Music

In 2008, a typical 14- to 24-year old British consumer bought 24 music tracks, q_1, per quarter and consumed 18 units of live music, q_2, per quarter.[12] We estimate this average consumer's Cobb-Douglas utility function as

$$U = q_1^{0.4} q_2^{0.6}. \tag{3.6}$$

That is, in the Cobb-Douglas utility function Equation 3.1, $a = 0.4$.

Using our analysis in Solved Problem 3.2, given that Jackie's Cobb-Douglas utility function is that of the typical consumer, we can determine her marginal rate of substitution by substituting $q_1 = 24$, $q_2 = 18$, and $a = 0.4$ into Equation 3.5:

$$MRS = -\frac{a}{1-a}\frac{q_2}{q_1} = -\frac{0.4}{0.6}\frac{18}{24} = -0.5.$$

Diminishing Marginal Rate of Substitution. The marginal rate of substitution varies along a typical indifference curve that is convex to the origin, as is Lisa's indifference curve in Figure 3.4. As we move down and to the right along this indifference curve, the slope or *MRS* of the indifference curve becomes smaller in absolute value: Lisa will give up fewer burritos to obtain one pizza. This willingness to trade fewer burritos for one more pizza as we move down and to the right along the indifference curve reflects a *diminishing marginal rate of substitution*: The *MRS* approaches zero—becomes flatter or less sloped—as we move from Bundle *f* to *e* and then to *g* in the figure.

---

[12]A unit of live music is the amount that can be purchased for £1 (that is, it does not correspond to a full concert or a performance in a pub).

We can illustrate the diminishing marginal rate of substitution given that Lisa's has a Cobb-Douglas utility function where $a = 0.5$: $U = q_1^{0.5}q_2^{0.5}$. We know that this utility function has an $MRS = -q_2/q_1$ by setting $a = 0.5$ in Equation 3.4. On the indifference curve $4 = \bar{U} = q_1^{0.5}q_2^{0.5}$, two of the (q_1, q_2) bundles are $(2, 8)$ and $(4, 4)$. The MRS is $-8/2 = -4$ at $(2, 8)$ and $-4/4 = -1$ at $(4, 4)$. Thus, at $(2, 8)$, where Lisa has a relatively large amount of q_2 compared to q_1, Lisa is willing to give up four units of q_2 to get one more unit of q_1. However at $(4, 4)$, where Lisa has relatively less q_2, she is only willing to trade a unit of q_2 for a unit of q_1.

Curvature of Indifference Curves

The marginal rate of substitution varies along our typical convex indifference curve. How the marginal rate of substitution varies along an indifference curve depends on the underlying utility function. Table 3.1 uses Equation 3.4 to determine the MRS for five types of utility functions.

The indifference curves corresponding to these utility functions range between straight lines, where the MRS is a constant, to right-angle indifference curves, where no substitution is possible. Convex indifference curves lie between these extremes.[13]

Straight Line Indifference Curve. One extreme case of an indifference curve is a straight line, which occurs when two goods are **perfect substitutes**: goods that a consumer is completely indifferent as to which to consume. Because Ben cannot taste any difference between Coca-Cola and Pepsi-Cola, he views them as perfect substitutes: He is indifferent between having one additional can of Coke and one

Table 3.1 The Marginal Rate of Substitution (MRS) for Five Utility Functions

Utility Function	$U(q_1, q_2)$	$U_1 = \dfrac{\partial U(q_1, q_2)}{\partial q_1}$	$U_2 = \dfrac{\partial U(q_1, q_2)}{\partial q_2}$	$MRS = -\dfrac{U_1}{U_2}$
Perfect substitutes	$iq_1 + jq_2$	i	j	$-\dfrac{i}{j}$
Perfect complements	$\min(iq_1, jq_2)$	0	0	0
Cobb-Douglas	$q_1^a q_2^{1-a}$	$a\dfrac{U(q_1, q_2)}{q_1}$	$(1-a)\dfrac{U(q_1, q_2)}{q_2}$	$-\dfrac{a}{1-a}\dfrac{q_2}{q_1}$
Constant Elasticity of Substitution (CES)	$(q_1^\rho + q_2^\rho)^{1/\rho}$	$(q_1^\rho + q_2^\rho)^{(1-\rho)/\rho}q_1^{\rho-1}$	$(q_1^\rho + q_2^\rho)^{(1-\rho)/\rho}q_2^{\rho-1}$	$-\left(\dfrac{q_1}{q_2}\right)^{\rho-1}$
Quasilinear	$u(q_1) + q_2$	$\dfrac{du(q_1)}{dq_1}$	1	$-\dfrac{du(q_1)}{dq_1}$

Notes: $i > 0, j > 0, 0 < a < 1, \rho \neq 0$, and $\rho < 1$. We are evaluating the prefect complements' indifference curve at its right-angle corner, where it is not differentiable, hence the formula $MRS = -U_1/U_2$ is not well-defined. We arbitrarily say that the $MRS = 0$ because no substitution is possible.

---

[13]It is difficult to imagine that Lisa's indifference curves are *concave* to the origin. If her indifference curve were strictly concave, Lisa would be willing to give up more burritos to get one more pizza, the fewer the burritos she has.

additional can of Pepsi. His indifference curves for these two goods are straight, parallel lines with a slope of -1 everywhere along the curve, as in panel a of Figure 3.5, so his *MRS* is -1 at every point along these indifference curves. We can draw the same conclusion by noting that Ben's marginal utility from each good is identical, so his $MRS = -U_1/U_2 = -1$.

The slope of indifference curves of perfect substitutes need not always be -1; it can be any constant rate. For example, Amos knows from reading the labels that Clorox bleach is twice as strong as a generic brand. As a result, Amos is indifferent between one cup of Clorox and two cups of the generic bleach. His utility function over Clorox, q_1, and the generic bleach, q_2, is

$$U(q_1, q_2) = iq_1 + jq_2, \tag{3.7}$$

where both goods are measured in cups, $i = 2$, and $j = 1$. His indifference curves are straight lines. Because $U_1 = i$ and $U_2 = j$, his marginal rate of substitution is the same everywhere along this indifference curve: $MRS = -U_1/U_2 = -i/j = -2$.

Right Angle Indifference Curve. The other extreme case of an indifference curve occurs when two goods are **perfect complements**: goods that a consumer is interested in consuming only in fixed proportions. Maureen doesn't like apple pie, q_1, by itself or vanilla ice cream, q_2, by itself but she loves apple pie à la mode, a slice of pie with a scoop of vanilla ice cream on top. Her utility function is

$$U(q_1, q_2) = \min(iq_1, jq_2), \tag{3.8}$$

where $i = j = 1$ and the *min* function says that the utility equals the smaller of the two arguments, iq_1 or jq_2.

Her indifference curves have right angles in panel b of Figure 3.5. If she has only one piece of pie, she gets as much pleasure from it and one scoop of ice cream,

Figure 3.5 Perfect Substitutes, Perfect Complements, Imperfect Substitutes

(a) Ben views Coke and Pepsi as perfect substitutes. His indifference curves are straight, parallel lines with a marginal rate of substitution (slope) of -1. Ben is willing to exchange one can of Coke for one can of Pepsi. (b) Maureen likes pie à la mode but does not like pie or ice cream by itself: She views ice cream and pie as perfect complements. She will not substitute between the two; she consumes them only in equal quantities. (c) Lisa views burritos and pizza as imperfect substitutes. Her indifference curve lies between the extreme cases of perfect substitutes and perfect complements.

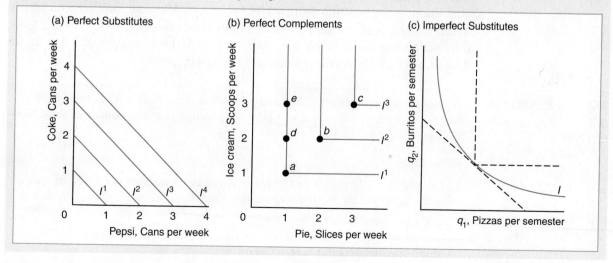

Bundle a, as from one piece and two scoops, Bundle d, or one piece and three scoops, Bundle e. The marginal utility is zero for each good, because increasing that good while holding the other one constant does not increase Maureen's utility. If she were at b, she would be unwilling to give up an extra slice of pie to get, say, two extra scoops of ice cream, as at point e. She wouldn't eat the extra scoops because she would not have pieces of pie to go with the ice cream. The only condition in which she doesn't have an excess of either good is when $iq_1 = jq_2$, or $q_2/q_1 = i/j$. She only consumes bundles like a, b, and c, where pie and ice cream are in equal proportions.

We cannot use Equation 3.4 to calculate her MRS because her utility function is nondifferentiable. We arbitrarily say that her $MRS = 0$ because she is unwilling to substitute more of one good for less of another.

Convex Indifference Curve. The standard-shaped, convex indifference curve in panel c of Figure 3.5 lies between these two extreme examples. Convex indifference curves show that a consumer views two goods as imperfect substitutes. A consumer with a Cobb-Douglas utility function, Equation 3.1, has convex indifference curves similar to that in panel c. That curve approaches the axes but does not hit them.

Another utility function that has convex indifference curves is the *constant elasticity of substitution* (CES) utility function[14]

$$U(q_1, q_2) = \left(q_1^\rho + q_2^\rho \right)^{1/\rho},$$

where $\rho \neq 0$ and $\rho < 1$. [If $\rho = 1$, then this utility function is a perfect substitutes utility function $U(q_1, q_2) = q_1 + q_2$.]

The marginal utility from q_i is $U_i = \left(q_1^\rho + q_2^\rho \right)^{(1-\rho)/\rho} q_i^{\rho-1}$, so the $MRS = -U_1/U_2 = -(q_1/q_2)^{\rho-1}$. For example, if $\rho = 0.5$, then the $MRS = -(q_1/q_2)^{-0.5} = -(q_2/q_1)^{0.5}$.

A third utility function that has convex indifference curves is the *quasilinear utility function*,

$$U(q_1, q_2) = u(q_1) + q_2, \tag{3.9}$$

where $u(q_1)$ is an increasing function of q_1, $du(q_1)/dq_1 > 0$, and $d^2u(q_1)/dq_1^2 \leq 0$. This utility function is called *quasilinear* because it is linear in one argument, q_2, but not necessarily in the other, q_1. [If $u(q_1) = q_1$, so both terms are linear, then this special case of the quasilinear utility function is the perfect substitutes utility function, $U(q_1, q_2) = q_1 + q_2$.]

An example is $u(q_1) = 4q_1^{0.5}$, which has the properties that $du(q_1)/dq_1 = 2q_1^{-0.5} > 0$, and $d^2u(q_1)/dq_1^2 = -q_1^{-0.5} < 0$. Figure 3.6 shows two indifference curves for the quasilinear utility function $U(q_1, q_2) = 4q_1^{0.5} + q_2$. Along an indifference curve in which utility is held constant at $\overline{U}$, the indifference curve is $\overline{U} = 4q_1^{0.5} + q_2$. Thus, this indifference curve hits the q_2-axis at $q_2 = \overline{U}$ because $q_1 = q_1^{0.5} = 0$ at the q_2-axis. Similarly, it hits the q_1-axis at $q_1 = (\overline{U}/4)^2$.

SOLVED PROBLEM **3.3**	A consumer has a quasilinear utility function, Equation 3.9, $U = u(q_1) + q_2$, where $du(q_1)/dq_1 > 0$ and $d^2u(q_1)/dq_1^2 < 0$. Show that the consumer's indifference curves are parallel and convex.

Answer

1. *Use the formula for an indifference curve to show that the slope at any q_1 is the same for all indifference curves, and thus the indifference curves must*

---

[14] We discuss the reason for this name in Chapter 6.

Figure 3.6 Quasilinear Preferences

The indifference curves I^1 and I^2 corresponding to the quasilinear utility function $U(q_1, q_2) = 4q_1^{0.5} + q_2$ are parallel. Each indifference curve has the same slope at a given q_1.

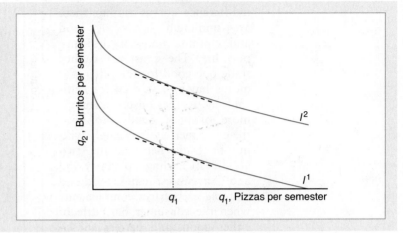

be parallel. At every point on an indifference curve, $\overline{U} = u(q_1) + q_2$. By rearranging this indifference curve equation, we find that the height of this indifference curve at a given q_1 is $q_2 = \overline{U} - u(q_1)$. By differentiating this expression with respect to q_1, we find that the slope of this indifference curve is $dq_2/dq_1 = d[\overline{U} - u(q_1)]/dq_1 = -du(q_1)/dq_1$. Because this expression is not a function of q_2, the slope for a given q_1 is independent of q_2 (the height of the indifference curve). Thus, the slope at q_1 must be the same on both the indifference curve in Figure 3.6. Because the indifference curves have the same slopes for each given q_1 and differ only in where they hit the q_2-axis, the indifference curves are parallel.

2. *Show that the indifference curves are convex by demonstrating that the derivative of the slope of the indifference curve with respect to q_1 is positive.* We just derived that the slope of the indifference curve is $dq_2/dq_1 = -du(q_1)/dq_1$. If we differentiate it again with respect to q_1, we find that the change in the slope of the indifference curve as q_1 increases is $d^2q_2/dq_1^2 = -d^2u(q_1)/dq_1^2$. Because $d^2u(q_1)/dq_1^2 < 0$, we know that $d^2q_2/dq_1^2 > 0$. The negative slope of an indifference curve becomes flatter as q_1 increases, which shows that the indifference curve is convex: It bends away from the origin. That is, the indifference curve has a diminishing marginal rate of substitution.

APPLICATION

Indifference Curves Between Food and Clothing

Using the estimates of Eastwood and Craven (1981), the figure shows the indifference curves of the average U.S. consumer between food consumed at home and clothing. The food and clothing measures are weighted averages of various goods. At relatively low quantities of food and clothing, the indifference curves, such as I^1, are nearly right angles: perfect complements. As we move away from the origin, the indifference curves become flatter—closer to perfect substitutes.

One interpretation of these indifference curves is that there are minimum levels of food and clothing necessary to support life. The consumer cannot trade one good for the other if it means having less than the critical level. As the consumer obtains more of both goods, however, the consumer is increasingly willing to trade between the two goods. According to Eastwood and Craven's estimates, food and clothing are perfect complements when the consumer has little of either good, and perfect substitutes when the consumer has large quantities of both goods.

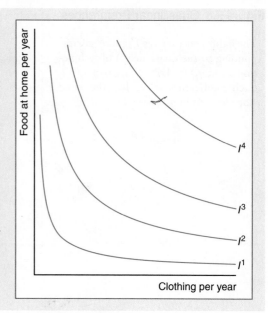

3.3 Budget Constraint

You can't have everything. . . . Where would you put it? —Steven Wright

Knowing an individual's preferences is only the first step in analyzing that person's consumption behavior. Consumers maximize their well-being subject to constraints. The most important constraint most of us face in deciding what to consume is our personal budget constraint.

If we cannot save and borrow, our budget is the income we receive in a given period. If we can save and borrow, we can save money early in life to consume later, such as when we retire; or we can borrow money when we are young and repay those sums later. Savings is, in effect, a good that consumers can buy. For simplicity, we assume that each consumer has a fixed amount of money to spend now, so we can use the terms *budget* and *income* interchangeably.

For graphical simplicity, we assume that consumers spend their money on only two goods. If Lisa spends all her budget, Y, on pizza and burritos, then

$$p_1 q_1 + p_2 q_2 = Y, \tag{3.10}$$

where $p_1 q_1$ is the amount she spends on pizza and $p_2 q_2$ is the amount she spends on burritos. Equation 3.10 is her **budget line**, or *budget constraint*: the bundles of goods that can be bought if a consumer's entire budget is spent on those goods at given prices. In Figure 3.7, we plot Lisa's budget line in pizza-burrito space, just as we did with her indifference curves. How many burritos can Lisa buy? Using algebra, we can rewrite her budget constraint, Equation 3.10, as

$$q_2 = \frac{Y - p_1 q_1}{p_2}. \tag{3.11}$$

According to Equation 3.11, she can buy more burritos with a higher income ($dq_2/dY = 1/p_2 > 0$), the purchase of fewer pizzas ($dq_2/dq_1 = -p_1/p_2 < 0$), or a lower

Figure 3.7 Budget Constraint

If $Y = \$50$, $p_1 = \$1$, and $p_2 = \$2$, Lisa can buy any bundle in the opportunity set—the shaded area—including points on the *budget line* L, which has a slope of $-\frac{1}{2}$.

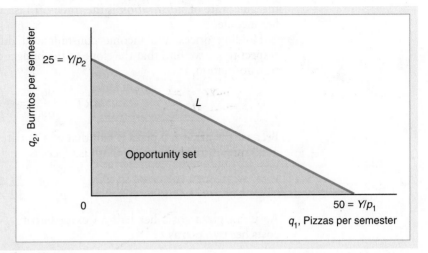

price of burritos or pizzas $[dq_2/dp_2 = -(Y - p_1q_1)/p_2^2 = -q_2/p_2 < 0, dq_2/dp_1 = -q_1/p_2 < 0]$. For example, if she has \$1 more of income (Y), she can buy $1/p_2$ more burritos.

If $p_1 = \$1$, $p_2 = \$2$, and $Y = \$50$, Equation 3.11 is

$$q_2 = \frac{\$50 - (\$1 \times q_1)}{\$2} = 25 - \frac{1}{2}q_1.$$

This equation is plotted in Figure 3.7. The budget line in the figure shows the combinations of burritos and pizzas that Lisa can buy if she spends all of her \$50 on these two goods. As this equation shows, every two pizzas cost Lisa one burrito. How many burritos can she buy if she spends all her money on burritos? By setting $q_1 = 0$ in Equation 3.11, we find that $q_2 = Y/p_2 = \$50/\$2 = 25$. Similarly, if she spends all her money on pizzas, $q_2 = 0$ and $q_1 = Y/p_1 = \$50/\$1 = 50$.

The budget constraint in Figure 3.7 is a smooth, continuous line. The continuous line shows that Lisa can buy fractional numbers of burritos and pizzas. Is that true? Do you know of a restaurant that will sell you a quarter of a burrito? Probably not. Why, then, don't we draw the opportunity set and the budget constraint as points (bundles) of whole numbers of burritos and pizzas? The reason is that Lisa can buy a burrito at a *rate* of one-half per period. If Lisa buys one burrito every other week, she buys an average of one-half burrito every week. Thus, it is plausible that she could purchase fractional amounts over time, and this diagram reflects her behavior over a semester.

Lisa could, of course, buy any bundle that costs less than \$50. An **opportunity set** consists of all the bundles a consumer can buy, including all the bundles inside the budget constraint and on the budget constraint (all those bundles of positive q_1 and q_2 such that $p_1q_1 + p_2q_2 \leq Y$). Lisa's opportunity set is the shaded area in the figure. For example, she could buy 10 burritos and 15 pizzas for \$35, which falls inside her budget constraint. However, she can obtain more of the two foods by spending all of her budget and picking a bundle on the budget line rather than a bundle below the line.

We call the slope of the budget line the **marginal rate of transformation** (*MRT*): the trade-off the market imposes on the consumer in terms of the amount of one good the consumer must give up to obtain more of the other good. The marginal rate of *transformation* is the rate at which Lisa is able to trade burritos for pizzas in the marketplace when the prices she pays and her income are fixed. In contrast, the marginal rate of *substitution* is the trade-off Lisa would *want* to make regardless of her income.

Holding prices and income constant and differentiating Equation 3.11 with respect to q_1, we find that the slope of the budget constraint, or the marginal rate of transformation, is

$$MRT = \frac{dq_2}{dq_1} = -\frac{p_1}{p_2}. \tag{3.12}$$

Because the price of a pizza is half that of a burrito ($p_1 = \$1$ and $p_2 = \$2$), the marginal rate of transformation that Lisa faces is

$$MRT = -\frac{p_1}{p_2} = -\frac{\$1}{\$2} = -\frac{1}{2}.$$

An extra pizza costs her half an extra burrito—or, equivalently, an extra burrito costs her two pizzas.

3.4   Constrained Consumer Choice

My problem lies in reconciling my gross habits with my net income. —Errol Flynn

Were it not for budget constraints, consumers who prefer more to less would consume unlimited amounts of at least some goods. Well, they can't have it all! Instead, consumers maximize their well-being subject to their budget constraints. To complete our analysis of consumer behavior, we have to determine the bundle of goods that maximizes an individual's well-being subject to the person's budget constraint.

Because Lisa enjoys consuming two goods only, she spends her entire budget on them.[15] That is, she chooses a bundle on the budget constraint rather than inside her opportunity set, where she would have money left over after buying the two goods. To spend her entire budget on these two goods, she must buy a positive amount of one or both of the goods.

An optimal bundle that has positive quantities of both goods so that it lies between the ends of the budget line is called an *interior solution*. If the consumer only buys one of the goods, the optimal bundle is at one end of the budget line, where the budget line forms a corner with one of the axes, so it is called a *corner solution*. We start our analysis by finding interior solutions using graphical and calculus methods. Then we address corner solutions.

Finding an Interior Solution Using Graphs

Veni, vidi, Visa. (We came, we saw, we went shopping.) —Jan Barrett

First, we use graphical methods to demonstrate that Lisa's optimal bundle must be on the budget line. Then, we show how to find the optimal bundle.

Figure 3.8 illustrates that Lisa's optimal bundle must be on the budget line. Bundles that lie on indifference curves above the constraint, such as those on I^3, are not in

---

[15]We examine the two-good case for graphic simplicity. Although it is difficult to use graphs to analyze behavior if consumers derive positive marginal utility from more than two goods, it is straightforward to do so using calculus.

Figure 3.8 Interior Solution

Lisa's optimal bundle is *e* (10 burritos and 30 pizzas) on indifference curve I^2. Indifference curve I^2 is tangent to her budget line *L* at *e*. Bundle *e* is the bundle on the highest indifference curve (highest utility) that she can afford. Any bundle that is preferred to *e* (such as points on indifference curve I^3) lies outside of her opportunity set, so she cannot afford them. Bundles inside the opportunity set, such as *d*, are less desirable than *e* because they represent less of one or both goods.

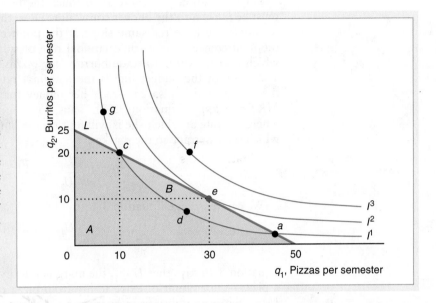

her opportunity set (area *A* + *B*). Although Lisa prefers Bundle *f* on indifference curve I^3 to Bundle *e* on I^2, she cannot afford to purchase *f*. Even though Lisa could buy a bundle inside the budget line *L*, she does not want to, because more is better than less: For any bundle inside the constraint (such as *d* on I^1), there is another bundle on the constraint with more of at least one of the two goods, and hence she prefers that bundle. Therefore, the optimal bundle must lie on the budget line.[16]

Bundles that lie on indifference curves that cross the budget line—such as I^1, which crosses the constraint at *a* and *c*—are less desirable than certain other bundles on the constraint. Only some of the bundles on indifference curve I^1 lie within the opportunity set: Lisa can afford to purchase Bundles *a* and *c* and all the points on I^1 between them, such as *d*. Because I^1 crosses the budget line, the bundles between *a* and *c* on I^1 lie strictly inside the constraint, so there are affordable bundles in area *B* that are preferable to these bundles—that contain more of one or both good. In particular, Lisa prefers Bundle *e* to *d* because *e* has more of both pizza and burritos than *d*. Because of transitivity, *e* is preferred to *a*, *c*, and all the other bundles on I^1—even those, like *g*, that Lisa can't afford. Thus, the optimal bundle—the *consumer's optimum*—must lie on the budget line and be on an indifference curve that does not cross it. If Lisa is consuming this bundle, she has no incentive to change her behavior by substituting one good for another.

Bundle *e* on indifference curve I^2 is the optimum bundle. *The optimal bundle is on the highest indifference curve that touches the budget line,* so it is the bundle that gives Lisa the highest utility subject to her budget constraint.

In this figure, the optimal bundle lies in the interior of the budget line away from the corners. Lisa prefers consuming a balanced diet, *e*, of 10 burritos and 30 pizzas, to eating only one type of food.

---

[16]Given that both goods are consumed in positive quantities and their prices are positive, more of either good must be preferred to less at her optimal bundle. Suppose that the opposite were true, and that Lisa prefers fewer burritos to more. Because burritos cost her money, she could increase her well-being by reducing the quantity of burritos she consumes (and increasing her consumption of pizza) until she consumes no burritos—a scenario that violates our assumption that she consumes positive quantities of both goods.

For the indifference curve I^2 to touch the budget constraint but not cross it, it must be *tangent* to the budget constraint. Thus, the budget constraint and the indifference curve have the same slope at the point e where they touch. The slope of the indifference curve is the marginal rate of substitution. It measures the rate at which Lisa is *willing* to trade burritos for pizzas: $MRS = -U_1/U_2$ (Equation 3.4). The slope of the budget line is the marginal rate of transformation. It measures the rate at which Lisa *can* trade her money for burritos or pizza in the market: $MRT = -p_1/p_2$ (Equation 3.12). Thus, Lisa's utility is maximized at the bundle where the rate at which she is willing to trade burritos for pizzas equals the rate at which she can trade in the market:

$$MRS = -\frac{U_1}{U_2} = -\frac{p_1}{p_2} = MRT. \tag{3.13}$$

We can rearrange Equation 3.13 to obtain

$$\frac{U_1}{p_1} = \frac{U_2}{p_2}. \tag{3.14}$$

Equation 3.14 says that U_1/p_1, the marginal utility of pizzas divided by the price of a pizza—the amount of extra utility from pizza per dollar spent on pizza—equals U_2/p_2, the extra utility from burritos per dollar spent on burritos. Thus, Lisa's utility is maximized if the last dollar she spends on pizzas gets her as much extra utility as the last dollar she spends on burritos. If the last dollar spent on pizzas gave Lisa more extra utility than the last dollar spent on burritos, Lisa could increase her happiness by spending more on pizzas and less on burritos.

Thus, to find the interior solution in Figure 3.8, we can use either of two equivalent conditions:

1. *Highest indifference curve rule*: The optimal bundle is on the highest indifference curve that touches the constraint.
2. *Tangency rule*: The optimal bundle is the point where an indifference curve is tangent to the budget line. Equivalently, $MRS = MRT$ (Equation 3.13) and $U_1/p_1 = U_2/p_2$ (Equation 3.14).

SOLVED PROBLEM 3.4

Maureen loves apple pie à la mode but she doesn't like apple pie, q_1, by itself or vanilla ice cream, q_2, by itself. That is, she views apple pie and ice cream as perfect complements. Show that the highest indifference curve rule can be used to find Maureen's optimal bundle, but that the tangency rule does not work. How many slices of pie and ice cream does she buy given that her income is Y?

Answer

1. *Use the highest indifference curve rule to find her optimal bundle in the figure.* Given budget line L^1, Maureen's optimal bundle is b because it is on the highest indifference curve that touches the budget line. Maureen can afford to buy Bundles a and b, but not c. She prefers b to a, because b contains more slices of apple pie à la mode.
2. *Show that the indifference curve is not tangent to the budget line at the optimal bundle.* At the optimal bundle, the budget line L^1 has a negative slope (its MRT is negative). Because the budget line hits the indifference curve at its right-angle corner—where no substitution is possible and there is no

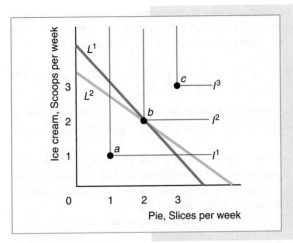

well-defined slope—the budget line cannot be tangent to the indifference curve. Indeed, if the budget line were L^2, b would remain Maureen's optimal bundle, even though L^2 has a different slope than L^1.

3. *Derive her optimal bundle using her budget constraint.* She buys q slices of apple pie à la mode by buying $q_1 = q$ slices of apple pie and $q_2 = q$ scoops of ice cream. The cost of one unit of apple pie à la mode is the sum of the price of a slice of apple pie, p_1, and the price of a scoop of ice cream, p_2. Thus, given that she spends all her income on apple pie à la mode, she buys $q = q_1 = q_2 = Y/(p_1 + p_2)$ units of each.

The highest indifference curve rules can always be used to find either interior or corner solutions. The tangency rule only applies for interior solutions where the indifference curve has the usual shape: it is a downward sloping, smooth curve that is convex to the origin.

Finding an Interior Solution Using Calculus

The individual choice of garnishment of a burger can be an important point to the consumer in this day when individualism is an increasingly important thing to people. —Donald N. Smith, president of Burger King

We have just shown how to use a graphical approach to determine which affordable bundle gives a consumer the highest possible level of utility. We now express this choice problem mathematically, and use calculus to find the optimal bundle.

Lisa's objective is to maximize her utility, $U(q_1, q_2)$, subject to (s.t.) her budget constraint:

$$\max_{q_1, q_2} U(q_1, q_2)$$
$$\text{s.t.} \quad Y = p_1q_1 + p_2q_2 \tag{3.15}$$

In this mathematical formulation of the problem, 3.15, the "max" term said to maximize her utility function by choice of her *control variables*—those variables that she chooses—q_1 and q_2, which appear under the max term. We assume that Lisa has no control over the prices she faces, p_1 and p_2, or her income, Y.

Because this problem is a constrained maximization—contains the "subject to" provision—we cannot use the standard unconstrained maximization calculus approach. However, we can transform this problem into an unconstrained problem that we know how to solve. If we know that Lisa buys both goods, we can use either the substitution method or the Lagrangian method.

Substitution Method. First, we can substitute the budget constraint into the utility function. Using algebra, we can rewrite the budget constraint as $q_1 = (Y - p_2q_2)/p_1$. If we substitute this expression for q_1 in the utility function, $U(q_1, q_2)$, we can rewrite Lisa's problem as

$$\max_{q_2} U\left(\frac{Y - p_2q_2}{p_1}, q_2\right). \tag{3.16}$$

Problem 3.16 is an unconstrained problem, so we can use standard maximization techniques to solve it. The first-order condition is obtained by setting the derivative of the utility function with respect to the only remaining control variable q_2 equal to zero:

$$\frac{dU}{dq_2} = \frac{\partial U}{\partial q_1}\frac{dq_1}{dq_2} + \frac{\partial U}{\partial q_2} = \left(-\frac{p_2}{p_1}\right)\frac{\partial U}{\partial q_1} + \frac{\partial U}{\partial q_2} = \left(-\frac{p_2}{p_1}\right)U_1 + U_2 = 0, \quad (3.17)$$

where $\partial U/\partial q_1 = U_1$ is the partial derivative of the utility function with respect to q_1 (the first argument) and dq_1/dq_2 is the derivative of $q_1 = (Y - p_2 q_2)/p_1$ with respect to q_2.

To be sure that we have a maximum, we need to check that the second-order condition holds (see the Calculus Appendix). This condition holds if the utility function is quasiconcave, which implies that the indifference curves are convex to the origin: The *MRS* is diminishing as we move down and to the right along the curve.

By rearranging these terms in Equation 3.17, we get the same condition for an optimum that we obtained using a graphical approach, Equation 3.13, which is that the marginal rate of substitution equals the marginal rate of transformation:[17]

$$MRS = -\frac{U_1}{U_2} = -\frac{p_1}{p_2} = MRT.$$

By rearranging these terms, we obtain the same expression as in Equation 3.14: $U_1/p_1 = U_2/p_2$.

If we combine the *MRS = MRT* condition with the budget constraint, we have two equations in two unknowns, q_1 and q_2, so we can solve for the optimal q_1 and q_2 as functions of prices, p_1 and p_2, and income, Y.

SOLVED PROBLEM 3.5

Michael has a constant elasticity of substitution (CES) utility function, $U(q_1, q_2) = (q_1^\rho + q_2^\rho)^{\frac{1}{\rho}}$, where $\rho \neq 0$ and $\rho \leq 1$.[18] Given that Michael's $\rho < 1$, what are his optimal values of q_1 and q_2 in terms of his income and the prices of the two goods?

Answer

1. *Substitute the income constraint into Michael's utility function to eliminate one control variable.* Michael's constrained utility maximization problem is

$$\max_{q_1, q_2} U(q_1, q_2) = (q_1^\rho + q_2^\rho)^{\frac{1}{\rho}}$$
$$\text{s.t.} \quad Y = p_1 q_1 + p_2 q_2.$$

We can rewrite Michael's budget constraint as $q_2 = (Y - p_1 q_1)/p_2$. Substituting this expression into his utility function, we can express Michael's utility maximization problem as:

$$\max_{q_1} U\left(q_1, \frac{Y - p_1 q_1}{p_2}\right) = \left(q_1^\rho + \left[\frac{Y - p_1 q_1}{p_2}\right]^\rho\right)^{1/\rho}.$$

By making this substitution, we have converted a constrained maximization problem with two control variables into an unconstrained problem with one control variable, q_1.

---

[17]Had we substituted for q_2 instead of for q_1 (which you should do to make sure that you understand how to solve this type of problem), we would have obtained the same condition.

[18]In Chapter 6, we discuss why this functional form has this name and that the Cobb-Douglas, perfect substitute, and perfect complement functional forms are special cases of the CES.

2. *Use the standard, unconstrained maximization approach to determine the optimal value for q_1.* To obtain the first-order condition, we use the chain rule and set the derivative of the utility function with respect to q_1 equal to zero:

$$\frac{1}{\rho}\left(q_1^\rho + \left[\frac{Y - p_1 q_1}{p_2}\right]^\rho\right)^{\frac{1-\rho}{\rho}}\left(\rho q_1^{\rho-1} + \rho\left[\frac{Y - p_1 q_1}{p_2}\right]^{\rho-1}\left[-\frac{p_1}{p_2}\right]\right) = 0.$$

Using algebra, we can solve this equation for Michael's optimal q_1 as a function of his income and the prices:[19]

$$q_1 = \frac{Y p_1^\sigma}{p_1^{\sigma+1} + p_2^{\sigma+1}}, \tag{3.18}$$

where $\sigma = 1/[\rho - 1]$. By repeating this analysis, substituting for q_1 instead of for q_2, we derive a similar expression for his optimal q_2:

$$q_2 = \frac{Y p_2^\sigma}{p_1^{\sigma+1} + p_2^{\sigma+1}}. \tag{3.19}$$

Thus, the utility-maximizing q_1 and q_2 are functions of his income and the prices.

Lagrangian Method. Another way to solve this constrained maximization problem is to use the Lagrangian method. The Lagrangian expression that corresponds to Problem 3.16 is

$$\mathcal{L} = U(q_1, q_2) + \lambda(Y - p_1 q_1 - p_2 q_2), \tag{3.20}$$

where λ (the Greek letter lambda) is the Lagrange multiplier. For values of q_1 and q_2 such that the constraint holds, $Y - p_1 q_1 - p_2 q_2 = 0$, so the functions $\mathcal{L}$ and U have the same values. Thus, if we look only at values of q_1 and q_2 for which the constraint holds, finding the constrained maximum value of U is the same as finding the critical value of $\mathcal{L}$.

The first-order conditions to find the critical value of q_1, q_2, and λ for an interior maximization are

$$\frac{\partial \mathcal{L}}{\partial q_1} = \frac{\partial U}{\partial q_1} - \lambda p_1 = U_1 - \lambda p_1 = 0. \tag{3.21}$$

$$\frac{\partial \mathcal{L}}{\partial q_2} = U_2 - \lambda p_2 = 0, \tag{3.22}$$

$$\frac{\partial \mathcal{L}}{\partial \lambda} = Y - p_1 q_1 - p_2 q_2 = 0. \tag{3.23}$$

---

[19]The term at the beginning of the first-order-condition,

$$\frac{1}{\rho}\left(q_1^\rho + \left[\frac{Y - p_1 q_1}{p_2}\right]^\rho\right)^{\frac{1-\rho}{\rho}},$$

is strictly positive because Michael buys a nonnegative amount of both goods, $q_1 \geq 0$ and $q_2 = [Y - p_1 q_1]/p_2 \geq 0$, and a positive amount of at least one of them. Thus, we can divide both sides of the equation by this term, and are left with $\rho q_1^{\rho-1} + \rho[(Y - p_1 q_1)/p_2]^{\rho-1}[-p_1/p_2] = 0$. Next, we divide both sides of this equation by ρ, move the second term to the right-hand-side of the equation, and divide both sides by $[(Y - p_1 q_1)/p_2]^{\rho-1}$ to get $(p_2 q_2/[Y - p_1 q_1])^{\rho-1} = p_1/p_2$. By exponentiating both sides by $1/[\rho - 1]$ and rearranging terms, we obtain Equation 3.18.

At the optimal levels of q_1, q_2, and λ, Equation 3.21 shows that the marginal utility of pizza, $U_1 = \partial U / \partial q_1$, equals its price times λ. Equation 3.22 provides an analogous condition for burritos. Equation 3.23 restates the budget constraint.

These three first-order conditions can be solved for the optimal values of q_1, q_2, and λ. Again, we should check that we have a maximum (see the Calculus Appendix at the end of the book).

What is λ? If we solve both Equations 3.21 and 3.22 for λ and then equate these expressions, we find that

$$\lambda = \frac{U_1}{p_1} = \frac{U_2}{p_2}. \tag{3.24}$$

That is, the optimal value of the Lagrangian multiplier, λ, equals the marginal utility of each good divided by its price, U_i/p_i, which is the extra utility one gets from the last dollar spent on that good.[20] Equation 3.24 is the same as Equation 3.14, which we derived using a graphical argument.

SOLVED PROBLEM 3.6

Julia has a Cobb-Douglas utility function, $U(q_1, q_2) = q_1^a q_2^{1-a}$. Use the Lagrangian method to find her optimal values of q_1 and q_2 in terms of her income and the prices.

Answer

1. *Show Julia's Lagrangian function and her first-order conditions.* Julia's Lagrangian function is $\mathcal{L} = q_1^a q_2^{1-a} + \lambda(Y - p_1 q_1 - p_2 q_2)$. The first-order conditions for her to maximize her utility subject to the constraint are

$$\frac{\partial \mathcal{L}}{\partial q_1} = U_1 - \lambda p_1 = a q_1^{a-1} q_2^{1-a} - \lambda p_1 = a \frac{U}{q_1} - \lambda p_1 = 0, \tag{3.25}$$

$$\frac{\partial \mathcal{L}}{\partial q_2} = U_2 - \lambda p_2 = (1-a) q_1^a q_2^{-a} - \lambda p_2 = (1-a)\frac{U}{q_2} - \lambda p_2 = 0, \tag{3.26}$$

$$\frac{\partial \mathcal{L}}{\partial \lambda} = Y - p_1 q_1 - p_2 q_2 = 0. \tag{3.27}$$

2. *Solve these three first-order equations for q_1 and q_2.* By equating the right-hand sides of the first two conditions, we obtain an equation that depends on q_1 and q_2 but not on λ:

$$(1-a)p_1 q_1 = a p_2 q_2. \tag{3.28}$$

The budget constraint, Equation 3.27, and the optimality condition, Equation 3.28, are two equations in q_1 and q_2. Rearranging the budget constraint, we know that $p_2 q_2 = Y - p_1 q_1$. By substituting this expression for $p_2 q_2$ into Equation 3.28, we can rewrite this expression as $(1-a)p_1 q_1 = a(Y - p_1 q_1)$. By rearranging terms, we find that

$$q_1 = a \frac{Y}{p_1}. \tag{3.29}$$

---

[20]More generally, the Lagrangian multiplier is often referred to as a *shadow value* that reflects the marginal rate of change in the objective function as the constraint is relaxed (see the Calculus Appendix at the end of the book).

Similarly, by substituting $p_1 q_1 = Y - p_2 q_2$ into Equation 3.26 and rearranging, we find that

$$q_2 = (1 - a)\frac{Y}{p_2}. \tag{3.30}$$

Thus, we can use our knowledge of the form of the utility function to solve the expression for the q_1 and q_2 that maximize utility in terms of income, prices, and the utility function parameter a.

SOLVED PROBLEM 3.7

Given that Julia has a Cobb-Douglas utility function $U = q_1^a q_2^{1-a}$, what share of her budget does she spend on q_1 and q_2 in terms of her income, prices, and the positive constant a?

Answer

Use Equations 3.29 and 3.30 to determine her budget shares. The share of her budget that Julia spends on pizza, s_1, is her expenditure on pizza, $p_1 q_1$, divided by her budget, Y, or $s_1 = p_1 q_1/Y$. By multiplying both sides of Equation 3.29, $q_1 = aY/p_1$, by p_1, we find that $s_1 = p_1 q_1/Y = a$. Thus, a is both her budget share of pizza and the exponent on the units of pizza in her utility function. Similarly, from Equation 3.30, we find that her budget share of burritos is $s_2 = p_2 q_2/Y = 1 - a$.

Comment: The Cobb-Douglas functional form was derived to have this property. If an individual has a Cobb-Douglas utility function, we can estimate a solely from information about the individual's budget shares. That is how we obtained our estimate of Jackie's Cobb-Douglas utility function for recorded tracks and live music.

APPLICATION

Utility Maximization for Recorded Tracks and Live Music

We return to our typical consumer, Jackie, who has an estimated Cobb-Douglas utility function of $U = q_1^{0.4} q_2^{0.6}$ for music tracks, q_1, and live music, q_2. The average price of a track from iTunes, Amazon, Rhapsody, and other vendors was about $p_1 = £0.5$ in 2008, and we arbitrarily set the price of live music, p_2, at £1 per unit (so the units do not correspond to a concert or a club visit). Jackie's budget constraint for purchasing these entertainment goods is

$$p_1 q_1 + p_2 q_2 = 0.5q_1 + q_2 = 30 = Y,$$

given that Jackie, like the average 14- to 24-year-old British consumer, spends £30 on music per quarter.

Using Equations 3.29 and 3.30 from Solved Problem 3.6, we can solve for Jackie's optimal numbers of tracks and units of live music:

$$q_1 = 0.4\frac{Y}{p_1} = 0.4 \times \frac{30}{0.5} = 24,$$

$$q_2 = 0.6\frac{Y}{p_2} = 0.6 \times \frac{30}{1} = 18.$$

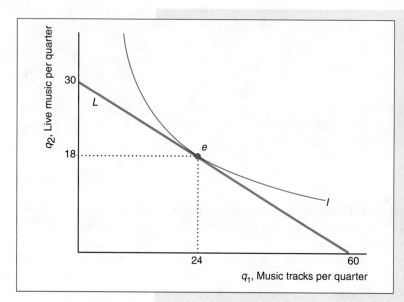

These quantities are the average quarterly purchases for a British youth in 2008. The figure shows that the optimal bundle is e where the indifference curve I is tangent to the budget line L.

We can use the result in Solved Problem 3.7 to confirm that the budget shares equal the exponents in Jackie's utility function. The share of Jackie's budget devoted to tracks is $p_1 q_1 / Y = (0.5 \times 24)/30 = 0.4$, which is the exponent on recorded tracks in her utility function. Similarly, the budget share she allocates to live music is $p_2 q_2 / Y = (1 \times 18)/30 = 0.6$, which is the live music exponent.

Finding Corner Solutions

So far, we have concentrated on utility functions where only an interior solution is possible. However, for some utility functions, we may have either a corner or an interior solution.

If a utility function's indifference curves do not hit the axes, a consumer's optimal bundle must be in the interior of the budget constraint. If a consumer has a perfect complements utility function or Cobb-Douglas utility function, the indifference curves do not hit the axes, so the optimal bundle lies in the interior, as Table 3.2 shows. Similarly, the indifference curves have this property if the consumer has a constant elasticity of substitution (CES) utility function, $U(q_1, q_2) = (q_1^\rho + q_2^\rho)^{\frac{1}{\rho}}$, where $\rho < 1$. However, if $\rho = 1$ in the CES utility function, then the utility function is $U(q_1, q_2) = q_1 + q_2$, which is a perfect substitutes utility function.

Perfect Substitutes Utility Function. Because a perfect substitutes utility function has straight line indifference curves that hit the axes, the optimal bundle may be at a corner or in the interior of the budget line. To illustrate why, we consider Ben's choice. Ben views Coca-Cola, q_1, and Pepsi Cola, q_2, as perfect substitutes, so his

Table 3.2   Type of Solution for Five Utility Functions

Utility Function	$U(q_1, q_2)$	Type of Solution
Perfect complements	$\min(iq_1, jq_2)$	interior
Cobb-Douglas	$q_1^a q_2^{1-a}$	interior
Constant Elasticity of Substitution	$(q_1^\rho + q_2^\rho)^{1/\rho}$	interior
Perfect substitutes	$iq_1 + jq_2$	interior or corner
Quasilinear	$u(q_1) + q_2$	interior or corner

Notes: $i > 0, j > 0, 0 < a < 1, \rho \neq 0$, and $\rho < 1$.

utility function is $U(q_1, q_2) = q_1 + q_2$. Figure 3.9 shows three straight-line indifference curves that correspond to this utility function.

The price of a 12-ounce can of Coke is p_1, and the price of a 12-ounce can of Pepsi is p_2. If $p_1 < p_2$, Ben gets more extra utility from the last dollar spent on Coke, $U_1/p_1 = 1/p_1$, then he gets from Pepsi, $U_2/p_2 = 1/p_2$, so he spends his entire income on Coke, $q_1 = Y/p_1$, and buys no Pepsi, $q_2 = 0$.

Figure 3.9 illustrates Ben's decision. Because Coke is less expensive than Pepsi, his budget line, L, is flatter than his indifference curves, I^1, I^2, and I^3. He can afford to buy Bundle a on indifference curve I^1 or Bundle b on indifference curve I^2, but he cannot afford any bundle on I^3 because it is everywhere above his budget constraint. We can find Ben's optimal bundle using the highest indifference curve rule: Ben's optimal bundle is b because it is on the highest indifference curve, I^2, that touches the budget constraint.

At the optimal Bundle b, the slope of the indifference curve, $MRS = -1$, does not equal the slope of the budget line, $MRT = -p_1/p_2 > -1$. Thus, we cannot find the optimal bundle at a corner using the tangency rule.

By symmetry, if $p_1 > p_2$, Ben chooses $q_1 = 0$ and $q_2 = Y/p_2$. If the prices are identical, $p_1 = p_2 = p$, he is indifferent as to which good to buy. Both his budget line and his indifference curves have the same slope, -1, so one of his indifference curves lies on top of the budget line. He is willing to buy any bundle on that budget line, in the interior or at either corner. All we can say is that $q_1 + q_2 = Y/p$.

Quasilinear Utility Function. Similarly, if a consumer has a quasilinear utility function, the indifference curves hit the axes, so either an interior or corner solution is possible. For example, Spenser has a quasilinear utility function $U(q_1, q_2) = 4q_1^{0.5} + q_2$.

We use a two-step procedure to determine the optimal bundle.[21] We first check to see if there is an interior solution using the tangency condition and the budget constraint. If we find that these conditions imply that he wants to buy positive quantities of both goods, we have found an interior solution. Otherwise, we have to determine a corner solution as a second step.

Figure 3.9 Corner Solution with Perfect Substitutes Utility Function

Ben views Coke and Pepsi as perfect substitutes, so his indifference curves are straight lines with a slope of -1. Because Coke is less expensive than Pepsi, his budget line, L, is flatter than his indifference curves. Although he can afford to buy bundle a on indifference curve I^1, his optimal bundle is b, because it is on the highest indifference curve, I^2, that touches the budget constraint.

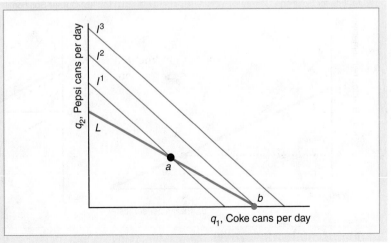

---

[21]A more direct approach to solving the consumer-maximization problem allowing for a corner solution is to use a Kuhn-Tucker analysis, which is discussed in the Calculus Appendix.

At an interior solution, such as panel a of Figure 3.10 shows, his indifference curve I is tangent to his budget line L, so that the $MRS = MRT = -p_1/p_2$. As we showed earlier, his marginal utility of q_1 is $U_1 = 2q_1^{-0.5}$ and his marginal utility of $q_2 = 1$, so his $MRS = -U_1/U_2 = -2q_1^{-0.5}$. Using algebra, we can use this tangency condition, $-2q_1^{-0.5} = -p_1/p_2$, to show that $q_1 = 4(p_2/p_1)^2$. Because q_1 does not depend on Y, Spenser buys the same quantity of q_1 regardless of his income, given that we have an interior solution where the tangency condition holds.[22]

By substituting this value of q_1 into the budget constraint, we can solve for q_2. We can write his budget constraint as $q_2 = Y/p_2 - (p_1q_1)/p_2$. Thus, $q_2 = Y/p_2 - (p_1 \times [4(p_2/p_1)^2])/p_2 = Y/p_2 - 4(p_2/p_1)$.

If the prices are $p_1 = p_2 = 1$, the tangency condition is $q_1 = 4(p_2/p_1)^2 = 4 \times (1/1)^2 = 4$. Substituting this value into the budget constraint, $q_2 = Y/p_2 - 4(p_2/p_1) = Y - 4$. Thus, if $Y > 4$, we have an interior solution where both quantities are positive. Panel a of Figure 3.10 shows an interior solution where Spenser's income is $Y = 6$. At the optimal Bundle e, where his indifference curve I is tangent to his budget line L, he buys $q_1 = 4$, and $q_2 = 6 - 4 = 2$.

At incomes below $Y = 4$, we do not have an interior solution—a tangency at positive levels of q_1 and q_2—as we illustrate in panel b of Figure 3.10. We first show that the only possibly point of tangency involves a negative quantity of one good. Then we determine the corner solution.

For example, if $Y = 2$, the formula we derived assuming that we were at a point of tangency tell us that $q_2 = 2 - 4 = -2$, which is not plausible. We illustrate this result in panel b, where we show two indifference curves. We draw I^1 for only nonnegative quantities of the two goods. However, we use the indifference curve

Figure 3.10 Interior or Corner Solution with Quasilinear Utility

Spenser has a quasilinear utility function $U(q_1, q_2) = 4 + q_2$. (a) When his income is greater than 4, he has an interior solution at e, where q_1 and q_2 are positive. His indifference curve I is tangent to his budget line L, so that his $MRS = MRT$. (b) At a lower income, he has a corner solution at

b, where he spends all his income on q_1. The only possible point of tangency, a, involves a negative quantity of q_2, which is not plausible. Loosely speaking, Spenser views q_1 as a necessity and q_2 as a luxury.

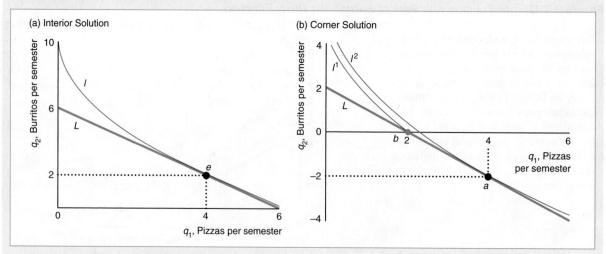

(a) Interior Solution

(b) Corner Solution

[22]Solved Problem 3.3 provides the intuition for this result. At any given q_1, the slope of the quasi-linear utility's indifference curve is the same. Thus, if we have a tangency with a low Y at a given q_1, we must have a tangency with a higher Y at that same quantity.

formula to extend I^2 to show what it would look like at negative values of q_2. By extending the indifference curve I^2 and the budget line L into the area below the horizontal axis where q_2 is negative, we show that the point of tangency a occurs at $q_1 = 4$ and $q_2 = -2$, which is implausible.

If we don't have an interior solution, we must have a corner solution. How do we know which good he buys? We know that if we are not at an interior (tangency) solution, then the marginal utility from the last dollar spent on each of the two goods are not equal: $U_1/p_1 \neq U_2/p_2$. Spenser prefers to buy only q_1 if $U_1/p_1 > U_2/p_2$. Given that both prices equal one, this condition holds if $U_1 = 2q_1^{-0.5} > U_2 = 1$. When $q_1 < 4$, $U_1 > U_2$. For example, when $q_1 = 2$, $U_1 \approx 1.41$, which is greater than $U_2 = 1$. Because the marginal utility of q_1 exceeds that of q_2 at low levels of q_1, if Spenser is going to have to give up one of the goods due to a lack of money, he'll give up q_2 and spend all his money on q_1. Thus, $q_1 = Y/p_1 = 2/1 = 2$, and $q_2 = 0$, which is the corner point b on indifference curve I^1 in panel b.

To summarize, if his income is low, Spenser spends all his money on q_1, buying $q_1 = Y/p_1 = Y$, which is a corner solution. If he has enough income for an interior solution, he buys a fixed amount of $q_1 = 4(p_2/p_1)^2 = 4$ and spends all his extra money on q_2 as his income rises. Loosely speaking, Spenser views q_1 as a necessity and q_2 as a luxury.

Optimal Bundles on Convex Sections of Indifference Curves. Earlier, based on introspection, we argued that most indifference curves are convex to the origin. Now that we know how to determine a consumer's optimal bundle, we can give a more compelling explanation about why we assume that indifference curves are convex. We can show that if indifference curves are smooth, optimal bundles lie either on convex sections of indifference curves or at the point where the budget constraint hits an axis.

Suppose that indifference curves were strictly concave to the origin as in panel a of Figure 3.11. Indifference curve I^1 is tangent to the budget line L at d, but Bundle d is not optimal. Bundle e on the corner between the budget constraint L and the burrito axis is on a higher indifference curve, I^2, than d. If a consumer had strictly concave indifference curves, the consumer would buy only one good—here, burritos. Thus, if consumers are to buy more than a single good, indifference curves must have convex sections.

If indifference curves have both concave and convex sections as in panel b of Figure 3.11, the optimal bundle lies in a convex section or at a corner. Bundle d, where a concave section of indifference curve I^1 is tangent to the budget line L, cannot be an optimal bundle. Here, e is the optimal bundle. It is tangent to the budget constraint in the convex portion of the higher indifference curve, I^2. Thus, if a consumer buys positive quantities of two goods, the indifference curve is convex and tangent to the budget line at the optimal bundle.

Minimizing Expenditure

Earlier, we showed how Lisa chooses quantities of goods so as to maximize her utility subject to a budget constraint. In a related or *dual* constrained minimization problem, Lisa wants to find that combination of goods that achieves a particular level of utility for the least expenditure.[23]

In Figure 3.8, we showed that, given the budget constraint that she faced, Lisa maximized her utility by picking a bundle of $q_1 = 30$ and $q_2 = 10$. She did that by choosing the highest indifference curve, I^2, that touched the budget constraint so that the indifference curve was tangent to the budget line.

---

[23]For a formal calculus presentation, see "Duality" in MyEconLab, Chapter Resources, Calculus Appendix.

Figure 3.11 Optimal Bundles on Convex Sections of Indifference Curves

(a) If indifference curves are strictly concave to the origin, the optimal bundle is at a corner (on one of the axes, where the consumer buys only one good). Indifference curve I^1 is tangent to the budget line L at Bundle d, but Bundle e is superior because it lies on a higher indifference curve, I^2. (b) If indifference curves have both concave and convex sections, a bundle such as d, which is tangent to the budget line L in the concave portion of indifference curve I^1, cannot be an optimal bundle because there must be a preferable bundle, here Bundle e, in the convex portion of a higher indifference curve I^2 (or at a corner).

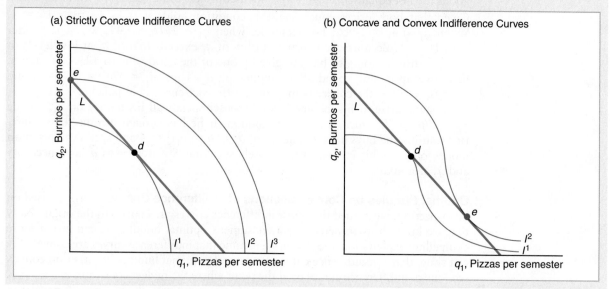

Now, let's consider the alternative problem in which we ask how Lisa can make the lowest possible expenditure to maintain her utility at a particular level, $\overline{U}$, which corresponds to indifference curve I^2. Figure 3.12 shows three possible budget lines corresponding to budgets or expenditures of E_1, E_2, and E_3. The lowest of these budget lines with expenditure E_1 lies below I_2, so Lisa cannot achieve the level of utility on I_2 for such a small expenditure. Both the other budget lines cross I_2; however, the budget line with expenditure E_2 is the least expensive way for her to stay on I_2. The rule for minimizing expenditure while achieving a given level of utility is to choose the lowest expenditure such that the budget line touches—is tangent to—the relevant indifference curve.

The slope of all the expenditure or budget lines is $-p_2/p_1$ (see Equation 3.11), which depends only on the market prices and not on income or expenditure. Thus, the point of tangency in Figure 3.12 is the same as in Figure 3.8. Lisa purchases $q_1 = 30$ and $q_2 = 10$ because that is the bundle that minimizes her expenditure conditional on staying on I^2.

Thus, solving either of the two problems—maximizing utility subject to a budget constraint or minimizing the expenditure subject to maintaining a given level of utility—yields the same optimal values for this problem. It is sometimes more useful to use the expenditure-minimizing approach because expenditures are observable and utility levels are not.

We can use calculus to solve the expenditure-minimizing problem. Lisa's objective is to minimize her expenditure, E, subject to the constraint that she hold her utility constant at $\overline{U} = U(q_1, q_2)$:

$$\min_{q_1, q_2} E = p_1 q_1 + p_2 q_2$$
$$\text{s.t. } \overline{U} = U(q_1, q_2). \tag{3.31}$$

Figure 3.12 Minimizing the Expenditure

The lowest expenditure that Lisa can make that will keep her on indifference curve I^2 is E_2. She buys 30 pizzas and 10 burritos.

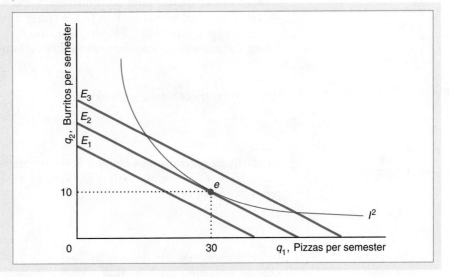

The solution of this problem is an expression of the minimum expenditure as a function of the prices and the specified utility level:

$$E = E(p_1, p_2, \overline{U}). \tag{3.32}$$

We call this expression the **expenditure function**: the relationship showing the minimal expenditures necessary to achieve a specific utility level for a given set of prices.

SOLVED PROBLEM 3.8

Given that Julia has a Cobb-Douglas utility function $U = q_1^a q_2^{1-a}$, what is her expenditure function?

Answer

1. *Show Julia's Lagrangian function and derive her first-order conditions.* Julia's Lagrangian function is $\mathcal{L} = p_1 q_1 + p_2 q_2 + \lambda(\overline{U} - q_1^a q_2^{1-a})$. The first-order conditions for her to minimize her expenditure subject to remaining on a given indifference curve are obtained by differentiating the Lagrangian function with respect to q_1, q_2, and λ, and setting each derivative equal to zero:

$$\frac{\partial \mathcal{L}}{\partial q_1} = p_1 - \lambda a q_1^{a-1} q_2^{1-a} = p_1 - \lambda a \frac{U}{q_1} = 0, \tag{3.33}$$

$$\frac{\partial \mathcal{L}}{\partial q_2} = p_2 - \lambda(1 - a)q_1^a q_2^{-a} = p_2 - \lambda(1 - a)\frac{U}{q_2} = 0, \tag{3.34}$$

$$\frac{\partial \mathcal{L}}{\partial \lambda} = \overline{U} - q_1^a q_2^{1-a} = 0. \tag{3.35}$$

2. *Solve these three first-order equations for q_1 and q_2.* By equating the right-hand sides of the first two conditions, we obtain an equation that depends on q_1 and q_2, but not on λ:

$$p_1 q_1/(aU) = p_2 q_2/[(1 - a)U], \text{ or}$$
$$(1 - a)p_1 q_1 = a p_2 q_2. \tag{3.36}$$

This condition is the same as Equation 3.28, which we derived in Solved Problem 3.6 when we maximized Julia's utility subject to the budget constraint.

Rearranging Equation 3.36, we learn that $p_2 q_2 = p_1 q_1 (1 - a)/a$. By substituting this expression into the expenditure definition, we find that

$$E = p_1 q_1 + p_2 q_2 = p_1 q_1 + p_1 q_1 (1 - a)/a = p_1 q_1/a.$$

Rearranging these terms, we find that

$$q_1 = a \frac{E}{p_1}. \tag{3.37}$$

Similarly, by rearranging Equation 3.36 to obtain $p_1 q_1 = p_2 q_2 a/(1 - a)$, substituting that expression into the expenditure definition, and rearranging terms, we learn that

$$q_2 = (1 - a) \frac{E}{p_2}. \tag{3.38}$$

By substituting the expressions in Equations 3.37 and 3.38 into the indifference curve expression, Equation 3.35, we observe that

$$\overline{U} = q_1^a q_2^{1-a} = \left(a \frac{E}{p_1} \right)^a \left([1 - a] \frac{E}{p_2} \right)^{1-a} = E \left(\frac{a}{p_1} \right)^a \left(\frac{1 - a}{p_2} \right)^{1-a}. \tag{3.39}$$

Solving this expression for E, we can write the expenditure function as

$$E = \overline{U} \left(\frac{p_1}{a} \right)^a \left(\frac{p_2}{1 - a} \right)^{1-a}. \tag{3.40}$$

Equation 3.40 shows the minimum expenditure necessary to achieve utility level $\overline{U}$ given the prices p_1 and p_2. For example, if $a = 1 - a = 0.5$, then

$$E = \overline{U}(p_1/0.5)^{0.5}(p_2/0.5)^{0.5} = 2\overline{U}(p_1 p_2)^{0.5}.$$

3.5   Behavioral Economics

So far, we have assumed that consumers are rational, maximizing individuals. A new field of study, **behavioral economics**, adds insights from psychology and empirical research on human cognition and emotional biases to the rational economic model to better predict economic decision making.[24] We discuss three applications of behavioral economics in this section: tests of transitivity, the endowment effect, and salience. Later in the book, we examine whether a consumer is influenced by the purchasing behavior of others (Chapter 11), whether individuals bid optimally in auctions (Chapter 13), why many people lack self-control (Chapter 16), and the psychology of decision making under uncertainty (Chapter 17).

Tests of Transitivity

In our presentation of the basic consumer choice model at the beginning of this chapter, we assumed that consumers make transitive choices. But do consumers actually make transitive choices?

---

[24]The introductory chapter of Camerer et al. (2004) and DellaVigna (2009) are excellent surveys of the major papers in this field and heavily influenced the following discussion.

A number of studies of both humans and animals show that preferences usually are transitive. Weinstein (1968) used an experiment to determine how frequently people give intransitive responses. None of the subjects knew the purpose of the experiment. They were given choices between 10 goods, offered in pairs, in every possible combination. To ensure that the monetary value of the items would not affect people's calculations, they were told that all of the goods had a value of $3. Weinstein found that 93.5% of the responses of adults—people over 18 years old—were transitive. However, only 79.2% of children ages 9 through 12 gave transitive responses.

Psychologists have also tested for transitivity using preferences for colors, photos of faces, and so forth. Bradbury and Ross (1990) found that, given a choice of three colors, nearly half of 4- to 5-year-olds gave intransitive responses, compared to 15% of 11- to 13-year-olds, and 5% of adults. Bradbury and Ross showed that novelty (a preference for a new color) is responsible for most intransitive responses, and that this effect is especially strong in children.

Based on these results, one might conclude that it is appropriate to assume that adults exhibit transitivity for most economic decisions but that the theory should be modified when applied to children or when novel goods are introduced.

Economists normally argue that rational people should be allowed to make their own consumption choices so as to maximize their well-being. However, some people argue that children's lack of transitivity or rationality provides a justification for political and economic restrictions and protections placed on young people. For example, many governments effectively prevent youths from drinking.[25]

Endowment Effect

Experiments show that people have a tendency to stick with the bundle of goods that they currently possess. One important reason for this tendency is called the **endowment effect**, which occurs when people place a higher value on a good if they own it than they do if they are considering buying it.

Normally we assume that an individual can buy or sell goods at the market price. Rather than rely on income to buy some mix of two goods, an individual who was *endowed* with several units of one good could sell some of them and use that money to buy units of another good.

We assume that a consumer's endowment does not affect the indifference map. In a classic buying and selling experiment, Kahneman et al. (1990) challenged this assumption. In an undergraduate law and economics class at Cornell University, 44 students were divided randomly into two groups. Members of one group were each given a coffee mug, which was available for sale at the student store for $6. Those students *endowed* with a mug were told that they could sell it and were asked the minimum price that they would accept for it. The subjects in the other group, who did not receive a mug, were asked how much they would pay to buy the mug. Given the standard assumptions of our model and that the subjects were chosen randomly, we would expect no difference between the selling and buying prices. However, the median selling price was $5.75 and the median buying price was $2.25, so sellers wanted more than twice what buyers would pay. This type of experiment has been repeated with many variations and typically an endowment effect is found.

However, some economists believe that this result has to do with how the experiment is designed. Plott and Zeiler (2005) argued that if you take adequate care to

---

[25]U.S. federal law prevents drinking before the age of 21, but most other countries set the minimum drinking age between 16 and 18. It is 16 in Belgium, Denmark, and France; 18 in Australia, Sweden, and the United Kingdom; and 18 or 19 in Canada. A justification for limiting drinking is given by Carpenter and Dobkin (2009). They find that when U.S. youths may start drinking alcohol legally at age 21, there is a 21% increase in the number of days on which they drink, which results in a 9% increase in their mortality rate.

train the subjects in the procedures and make sure they understand them, the result didn't hold. List (2003) examined the actual behavior of sports memorabilia collectors and found that amateurs who do not trade frequently exhibited an endowment effect, unlike professionals and amateurs who traded extensively. Thus, experience may minimize or eliminate the endowment effect, and people who buy goods for resale may be less likely to become attached to these goods.

Others accept the results and have considered how to modify the standard model to reflect the endowment effect (Knetsch, 1992). One implication of these experimental results is that people will only trade away from their endowments if prices change substantially. This resistance to trade could be captured by having a kink in the indifference curve at the endowment bundle. (We showed indifference curves with a kink at a 90° angle in panel b of Figure 3.5.) A kinked indifference curve could have an angle greater than 90° and be curved at points other than at the kink. If the indifference curve has a kink, the consumer does not shift to a new bundle in response to a small price change but does shift if the price change is large.

APPLICATION	*Why aren't you signed up for the 401K? I'd never be able to run that far.* —Dilbert
How You Ask the Question Matters	One practical implication of the endowment effect is that consumers' behavior may differ depending on how a choice is *framed* or posed to them. Many workers are offered the choice of enrolling in their firm's voluntary tax-deferred retirement plan, called a 401(k) plan. The firm can pose the choice in two ways: It can automatically sign up employees for the program and let them opt out if they want, or it can tell employees that to participate in the program they must sign up (opt in).

These two approaches might seem identical, but the behaviors they lead to are not. Madrian and Shea (2001, 2002) found that well over twice as many workers participate if they are automatically enrolled (but may opt out) than if they must opt in: 86% versus 37%. In short, inertia matters.

Because of this type of evidence, federal law was changed in 2006 and 2007 to make it easier for employers to enroll their employees in their 401(k) plans automatically. According to AON Hewitt, the share of large firms that automatically enroll new hires in 401(k) plans was 67% in 2012, up from 58% in 2007. Participation in defined contribution retirement plans in large companies rose from 67% in 2005 to 76% in 2010, due to the increased use of automatic enrollment.

Salience

Except in the last two chapters of this book, we examine economic theories that are based on the assumption that decision makers are aware of all relevant information. In this chapter, we assume that consumers know their own income or endowment, the relevant prices, and their own tastes, and hence they make informed decisions.

Behavioral economists and psychologists have demonstrated that people are more likely to consider information if it is presented in a way that grabs their attention or if it takes relatively little thought or calculation to understand. Economists use the term *salience*, in the sense of *striking* or *obvious*, to describe this idea.

For example, *tax salience* is the awareness of a tax. If a store's posted price includes the sales tax, consumers observe a change in the price as the tax rises. On the other hand, if a store posts the pre-tax price and collects the tax at the cash register, consumers are less likely to be aware that the post-tax price increases when the tax rate increases. Chetty et al. (2009) compare consumers' response to a rise in an ad valorem sales tax on beer that is included in the posted price to an increase in a general ad valorem sales tax that is collected at the cash register but not reflected in the posted beer price. Both means of collecting the tax have the same effect on the final price, so both should have the same effect on purchases if consumers pay attention.[26] However, a 10% increase in the posted price, which includes the sales tax, reduces beer consumption by 9%, whereas a 10% increase in the price due to an increased sales tax that is collected at the register reduces consumption by only 2%. Chetty et al. also conducted an experiment in which they posted tax-inclusive prices for 750 products in a grocery store and found that demand for these products fell by about 8% relative to control products in the store and comparable products at nearby stores.

One explanation for why a tax has no effect on consumer behavior is consumer ignorance. For example, Furnham (2005) found that even by the age of 14 or 15, British youths do not fully understand the nature and purpose of taxes. Similarly, unless the tax-inclusive price is posted, many consumers ignore or are unaware of taxes.

An alternative explanation for ignoring taxes is **bounded rationality**: People have a limited capacity to anticipate, solve complex problems, or enumerate all options. To avoid having to perform hundreds of calculations when making purchasing decisions at a grocery store, many people choose not to calculate the tax-inclusive price. However, when post-tax price information is easily available to them, consumers use it. One way to modify the standard model is to assume that people incur a cost to making calculations—such as the time taken or the mental strain—and that deciding whether to incur this cost is part of their rational decision-making process.

People incur this calculation cost only if they think the gain from a better choice of goods exceeds the cost. More people pay attention to a tax when the tax rate is high or when their demand for the good is elastic (sensitive to price changes). Similarly, some people are more likely to pay attention to taxes when making large, one-time purchases—such as buying a computer or car—rather than small, repeated purchases—such as soap or batteries.

Tax salience has important implications for tax policy. In Chapter 2, we showed that the tax incidence on consumers is the same regardless of whether the tax is collected from consumers or sellers (where we implicitly assumed that everyone was aware of the tax). However, if consumers are inattentive to taxes, they're more likely to bear the tax burden. If a tax on consumers rises and consumers don't notice, their demand for the good is relatively inelastic, causing consumers to bear more of the tax incidence (see Equation 2.28). In contrast, if the tax is placed on sellers, and the sellers want to pass on at least some of the tax to consumers, they raise their prices, which consumers observe.

CHALLENGE SOLUTION Why Americans Buy E-Books and Germans Do Not	Why do Germans largely ignore e-books, while many Americans are quickly switching to this new technology? While it's possible that this difference is due to different tastes in the two countries, there's evidence that attitudes toward e-books is similar in the two countries. For example, according to surveys, 59% of Americans and 56% of Germans report that they have no interest in e-books. Price differences provide a better explanation. Moreover, suppose that Max, a German, and Bob, a Yank, are avid readers with identical incomes and tastes. Each is indifferent between reading a novel in a traditional book or using an e-reader so that their indifference curves have a slope of −1, as the red line in the figure illustrates. We can use an indifference curve–budget line analysis to explain why Max buys printed books while Bob chooses electronic ones. In both countries, the pre-tax price of e-books is lower than that of printed books. In the United States, the after-tax price of e-books remains lower, so Bob's budget line L^B is flatter than his indifference curve. However, because the German

---

[26]The final price consumers pay is $p^* = p(1 + \beta)(1 + \alpha)$, where p is the pretax price, α is the general sales tax, and β is the excise tax on beer.

tax system sets a lower rate for printed books than for e-books, the after-tax price of e-books is higher in Germany, so Max's budget line L^M is steeper than his indifference curve. Thus, as the figure shows, Bob maximizes his utility by spending his entire book budget on e-books. He chooses the Bundle e_B where his indifference curve I hits his budget line L^B on the e-book axis. In contrast, Max spends his entire book budget on printed books, at point e_M.

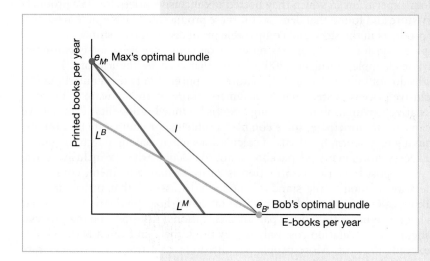

If Bob and Max viewed the two types of books as imperfect substitutes and had the usual convex indifference curves, they would each buy a mix of e-books and printed books. However, because of the relatively lower price of e-books in the United States, Bob would buy relatively more e-books.

SUMMARY

Consumers maximize their utility (well-being) subject to constraints based on their incomes and the prices of goods.

1. **Preferences.** To predict consumers' responses to changes in these constraints, economists use a theory about individuals' preferences. One way of summarizing consumer preferences is with an indifference map. An indifference curve consists of all bundles of goods that give the consumer a particular level of utility. Based on observations of consumer behavior, economists assume that consumers' preferences have three properties: completeness, transitivity, and more-is-better. Given these three assumptions, indifference curves have the following properties:

   ■ Consumers get more pleasure from bundles on indifference curves the farther the curves are from the origin.

   ■ Indifference curves cannot cross.

   ■ Every bundle lies on an indifference curve

   ■ Indifference curves cannot be thick.

   ■ Indifference curves slope downward.

   ■ Consumers are observed purchasing positive quantities of all relevant goods only where their indifference curves are convex to the origin.

   We also assume that consumers' preferences are continuous, and we use this assumption in our utility function analysis.

2. **Utility.** *Utility* is the set of numerical values that reflect the relative rankings of bundles of goods. Utility is an ordinal measure: By comparing the utility a consumer gets from each of two bundles, we know that the consumer prefers the bundle with the higher utility, but we can't tell by how much the consumer prefers that bundle. The utility function is unique only up to a positive monotonic transformation. The marginal utility from a good is the extra utility a person gets from consuming one more unit of it, holding the consumption of all other goods constant. The rate at which a consumer is willing to substitute one good for another, the marginal rate of substitution (*MRS*), depends on the relative amounts of marginal utility the consumer gets from each of the two goods.

3. **Budget Constraint.** The amount of goods consumers can buy at given prices is limited by their incomes. The greater their incomes and the lower the prices of goods, the better off consumers are. The rate at which they can exchange one good for another in the market, the marginal rate of transformation (*MRT*), depends on the relative prices of the two goods.

4. **Constrained Consumer Choice.** Each person picks an affordable bundle of goods to consume so as to maximize his or her pleasure. If an individual consumes both Good 1 and Good 2 (an interior solution) and has the usual shape indifference curves, the

individual's utility is maximized when the following equivalent conditions hold:

- The consumer buys the bundle of goods that is on the highest obtainable indifference curve.
- The indifference curve between the two goods is tangent to the budget constraint.
- The consumer's marginal rate of substitution (the slope of the indifference curve) equals the marginal rate of transformation (the slope of the budget line).
- The last dollar spent on Good 1 gives the consumer as much extra utility as the last dollar spent on Good 2.

However, consumers do not buy some of all possible goods, so their optimal bundles are corner solutions. At a corner, the last dollar spent on a good that is actually purchased gives a consumer more extra utility than would a dollar's worth of a good the consumer chose not to buy.

We can use our model in which a consumer maximizes his or her utility subject to a budget constraint to predict the consumer's optimal choice of goods as a function of the consumer's income and market prices.

5. Behavioral Economics. Using insights from psychology and empirical research on human cognition and emotional biases, economists are starting to modify the rational economic model to better predict economic decision making. While adults tend to make transitive choices, children are less likely to do so, especially when novelty is involved. Consequently, some people would argue that the ability of children to make economic choices should be limited. Consumers exhibit an endowment effect if they place a higher value on a good that they own than on the same good if that they are considering buying it. Such consumers are less sensitive to price changes and hence less likely to trade goods, as predicted by the standard consumer choice model. Many consumers fail to pay attention to sales taxes unless they are included in the product's final price, and thus ignore them when making purchasing decisions.

EXERCISES

■ = *exercise is available on* MyEconLab; * = *answer appears at the back of this book;* **M** = *mathematical problem.*

1. Preferences

1.1 Explain why economists assume that the more-is-better property holds. Give as many reasons as you can.

1.2 Can an indifference curve be downward sloping in one section, but then bend backward so that it forms a "hook" at the end of the indifference curve? (*Hint*: Look at Solved Problem 3.1.)

1.3 Explain why economists believe that indifference curves are convex. Give as many reasons as you can.

1.4 Don is altruistic. Show the possible shape of his indifference curves between charitable contributions and all other goods. Does this indifference curve violate any of our assumptions? Why or why not?

*1.5 Arthur spends his income on bread and chocolate. He views chocolate as a good but is neutral about bread, in that he doesn't care if he consumes it or not. Draw his indifference map.

2. Utility

2.1 Miguel considers tickets to the Houston Grand Opera and to Houston Astros baseball games to be perfect substitutes. Show his preference map. What is his utility function?

*2.2 Sofia will consume hot dogs only with whipped cream. Show her preference map. What is her utility function?

2.3 Fiona requires a minimum level of consumption, a *threshold*, to derive additional utility: $U(X, Z)$ is 0 if $X + Z \leq 5$ and is $X + Z$ otherwise. Draw Fiona's indifference curves. Which of our preference assumptions does this example violate?

*2.4 Tiffany's constant elasticity of substitution (CES) utility function is $U(q_1, q_2) = (q_1^\rho + q_2^\rho)^{1/\rho}$. Show that there is a positive monotonic transformation such that there is an equivalent utility function (one with the same preference ordering) $U(q_1, q_2) = q_1^\rho + q_2^\rho$. **M**

*2.5 Suppose we calculate the *MRS* at a particular bundle for a consumer whose utility function is $U(q_1, q_2)$. If we use a positive monotonic transformation, F, to obtain a new utility function, $V(q_1, q_2) = F(U(q_1, q_2))$, then this new utility function contains the same information about the consumer's rankings of bundles. Prove that the *MRS* is the same as with the original utility function. **M**

*2.6 What is the *MRS* for the CES utility function (which is slightly different from the one in the text), $U(q_1, q_2) = (aq_1^\rho + [1 - a]q_2^\rho)^{1/\rho}$? (*Hint*: Look at Solved Problem 3.2.) **M**

2.7 If José Maria's utility function is $U(q_1, q_2) = q_1 + Aq_1^a q_2^b + q_2$, what is his marginal utility from q_2? What is his marginal rate of substitution between these two goods? (*Hint:* Look at Solved Problem 3.2.) **M**

2.8 Phil's quasilinear utility function is $U(q_1, q_2) = \ln q_1 + q_2$. Show that his *MRS* is the same on all of his indifference curves at a given q_1. (*Hint:* Look at Solved Problem 3.3.) **M**

3. Budget Constraint

*3.1 What is the effect of a 50% income tax on Dale's budget line and opportunity set?

3.2 What happens to a consumer's optimal choice of goods if all prices and the consumer's income double? (*Hint:* What happens to the intercepts of the budget constraint?)

*3.3 Governments frequently limit how much of a good a consumer can buy. During emergencies, governments may ration "essential" goods such as water, food, and gasoline rather than let their prices rise. Suppose that the government rations water, setting quotas on how much a consumer can purchase. If a consumer can afford to buy 12,000 gallons a month but the government restricts purchases to no more than 10,000 gallons a month, how do the consumer's budget line and opportunity set change?

3.4 What happens to the budget line if the government applies a specific tax of $1 per gallon on gasoline but does not tax other goods? What happens to the budget line if the tax applies only to purchases of gasoline in excess of 10 gallons per week?

4. Constrained Consumer Choice

4.1 Suppose that Boston consumers pay twice as much for avocados as they pay for tangerines, whereas San Diego consumers pay half as much for avocados as they pay for tangerines. Assuming that consumers maximize their utility, which city's consumers have a higher marginal rate of substitution of avocados for tangerines? Explain your answer.

4.2 Elise consumes cans of anchovies, q_1, and boxes of biscuits, q_2. Each of her indifference curves reflects strictly diminishing marginal rates of substitution. Where $q_1 = 2$ and $q_2 = 2$, her marginal rate of substitution between cans of anchovies and boxes of biscuits equals -1. Will she prefer a bundle with three cans of anchovies and a box of biscuits to a bundle with two of each? Why? **M**

*4.3 Andy purchases only two goods, apples (q_1) and kumquats (q_2). He has an income of $40 and can buy apples at $2 per pound and kumquats at $4 per pound. His utility function is $U(q_1, q_2) = 3q_1 + 5q_2$. What is his marginal utility for apples, and what is his marginal utility for kumquats? What bundle of apples and kumquats should he purchase to maximize his utility? Why? **M**

4.4 Mark consumes only cookies and books. At his current consumption bundle, his marginal utility from books is 10 and from cookies is 5. Each book costs $10, and each cookie costs $2. Is he maximizing his utility? Explain. If he is not, how can he increase his utility while keeping his total expenditure constant? **M**

4.5 Some of the largest import tariffs, the tax on imported goods, are on shoes. Strangely, the higher the tariff, the cheaper the shoes. The highest U.S. tariff, 67%, is on a pair of $3 canvas sneakers, whereas the tariff on $12 sneakers is 37%, while $300 Italian leather imports have no tariff. (Adam Davidson, "U.S. Tariffs on Shoes Favor Well-Heeled Buyers," National Public Radio, June 12, 2007.) Laura buys either inexpensive, canvas sneakers ($3 before the tariff) or more expensive gym shoes ($12 before the tariff) for her children. Use an indifference curve-budget line analysis to show how imposing the unequal tariffs affects the bundle of shoes she buys compared to what she would have bought in the absence of tariffs. Can you confidently predict whether she'll buy relatively more expensive gym shoes after the tariff? Why or why not?

4.6 Helen views raspberries and blackberries as perfect complements. Initially, she buys five pints of each this month. Suppose that the price of raspberries falls while the price of blackberries rises such that the bundle of five pints of each lies on her budget line. Does her optimal bundle change? Explain. (*Hint:* See Solved Problem 3.4.)

4.7 Use indifference curve-budget line diagrams to illustrate the results in Table 3.2 for each of these utility functions.

4.8 For the utility function $U(q_1, q_2) = q_1^\rho + q_2^\rho$, solve for the optimal q_1 and q_2. (*Hint:* See Solved Problem 3.5.) **M**

4.9 The application "Indifference Curves Between Food and Clothing" postulates that there are minimum levels of food and clothing necessary to support life. Suppose that the amount of food one has is F, the minimum level to sustain life is $\underline{F}$, the amount of clothing one has is C, and the minimum necessary is $\underline{C}$. We can then modify the Cobb-Douglas utility function to reflect these minimum levels: $U(C, F) = (C - \underline{C})^a (F - \underline{F})^{1-\alpha}$, where $C \geq \underline{C}$ and $F \geq \underline{F}$. Using the approach similar to that in Solved Problem 3.6, derive the optimal amounts of food and clothing as a function of prices and a person's income. To do so, introduce the idea of *extra income*, Y^*, which is the income remaining after paying for the minimum levels of food and clothing: $Y^* = Y - p_C \underline{C} - p_F \underline{F}$. Show that the optimal quantity of clothing is $C = \underline{C} + aI^*/p_C$ and that the optimal quantity of food is $F = \underline{F} + (1 - a)I^*/p_F$.

Derive formulas for the share of income devoted to each good. **M**

4.10 A function $f(X, Y)$ is homogeneous of degree γ if, when we multiply each argument by a constant α, $f(\alpha X, \alpha Y) = \alpha^\gamma f(X, Y)$. Thus, if a function is homogeneous of degree zero, $f(\alpha X, \alpha Y) = \alpha^0 f(X, Y) = f(X, Y)$, because $\alpha^0 = 1$. Show that the optimality conditions for the Cobb-Douglas utility function in Solved Problem 3.6 are homogeneous of degree zero. Explain why that result is consistent with the intuition that if we double all prices and income the optimal bundle does not change. **M**

4.11 Diogo's utility function is $U(q_1, q_2) = q_1^{0.75} q_2^{0.25}$, where q_1 is chocolate candy and q_2 is slices of pie. If the price of a chocolate bar, p_1, is \$1, the price of a slice of pie, p_2, is \$2, and Y is \$80, what is Diogo's optimal bundle? (*Hint*: See Solved Problem 3.6.) **M**

4.12 In 2005, Americans bought 9.1 million home radios for \$202 million and 3.8 million home-theater-in-a-box units for \$730 million (*TWICE*, March 27, 2006, **www.twice.com/article/CA6319031.html**). Suppose that the average consumer has a Cobb-Douglas utility function and buys these two goods only. Given the results in Solved Problem 3.7, estimate a plausible Cobb-Douglas utility function such that the consumer would allocate income in the proportions actually observed. **M**

4.13 According to a 2010 survey of British students (**www.leedsuniversityunion.org.uk/helpandadvice/money/costofliving**), a typical student had a budget of £18.8 per week to spend on mobile telephones, Internet access, and music. That student spent about 45% on phones, 28% on Internet access, and 27% on music. Estimate the student's Cobb-Douglas utility function for these three goods. (*Hint*: See Solved Problem 3.7.) **M**

*4.14 David's utility function is $U = q_1 + 2q_2$. Describe his optimal bundle in terms of the prices of q_1 and q_2. **M**

*4.15 Vasco likes spare ribs, q_1, and fried chicken, q_2. His utility function is $U = 10q_1^2 q_2$. His weekly income is \$90, which he spends on ribs and chicken only.

a. If he pays \$10 for a slab of ribs and \$5 for a chicken, what is his optimal consumption bundle? Show his budget line, indifference curve, and optimal bundle, e_1, in a diagram.

b. Suppose the price of chicken doubles to \$10. How does his optimal consumption of chicken and ribs change? Show his new budget line and optimal bundle, e_2, in your diagram. **M**

4.16 Ann's utility function is $U = q_1 q_2 / (q_1 + q_2)$. Solve for her optimal values of q_1 and q_2 as a function of p_1, p_2, and Y. **M**

4.17 Wolf's utility function is $U = aq_1^{0.5} + q_2$. For given prices and income, show how whether he has an interior or corner solution depends on a. **M**

4.18 Given that Kip's utility function is $U(q_c, q_m) = q_c^{0.5} + q_m^{0.5}$, what is his expenditure function? (*Hint*: See Solved Problem 3.8.) **M**

5. Behavioral Economics

5.1 Illustrate the logic of the endowment effect using a kinked indifference curve. Let the angle be greater than 90°. Suppose that the prices change, so the slope of the budget line through the endowment changes.

a. Use the diagram to explain why an individual whose endowment point is at the kink will only trade from the endowment point if the price change is substantial.

b. What rules can we use to determine the optimal bundle? Can we use all the conditions that we derived for determining an interior solution?

6. Challenge

6.1 Use a graph to show how the analysis changes in the Challenge if Max and Bob view e-books and printed books as imperfect substitutes.

*6.2 In previous years, gasoline was less expensive in the United States than in Canada, but now, due to a change in taxes, gasoline costs less in Canada than in the United States. How will the gasoline-purchasing behavior of a Canadian who lives near the border and can easily buy gasoline in either country change? Your answer should include an indifference curve-budget line diagram.

6.3 Einav et al. (2012) found that people who live in high sales tax locations are much more likely than other consumers to purchase goods over the Internet because Internet purchases are generally exempt from the sales tax if the firm is located in another state. They found that a 1% increase in a state's sales tax increases online purchases by that state's residents by just under 2%. Is the explanation for this result similar to that in the Challenge Solution? Why or Why not?

6.4 Salvo and Huse (2012) found that roughly one-fifth of flexible-fuel (cars that can run on a mix of ethanol and gasoline) car owners choose gasoline when the price of gas is 20% above that of ethanol (in energy-adjusted terms) and, similarly, one-fifth of motorists choose ethanol when ethanol is 20% more expensive than gasoline. What can you say about these people's tastes?

4

Demand

I have enough money to last me the rest of my life, unless I buy something.
—Jackie Mason

CHALLENGE

Paying Employees to Relocate

When Google wants to transfer an employee from its Washington, D.C. office to its London branch, it must decide how much compensation to offer the worker to move. International firms are increasingly relocating workers throughout their home countries and internationally. For example, KPMG, an international accounting and consulting firm, has a goal of having 25% to 30% of its professional staff gain international experience. In 2010, it had about 5,000 of its 120,000 global employees on foreign assignment.

As you might expect, workers are not always enthusiastic about relocating. In a survey by Runzheimer International, 79% of relocation managers responded that they confronted resistance from employees who were asked to relocate to high-cost locations. A survey of some of their employees found that 81% objected to moving because of fear of a lowered standard of living.

One possible approach to enticing employees to relocate is for the firm to assess the goods and services consumed by employees in the original location and then pay those employees enough to allow them to consume essentially the same items in the new location. According to a survey by Organization Resource Counselors, Inc., 79% of international firms reported that they provided their workers with enough income abroad to maintain their home lifestyle.

At the end of the chapter, you will be asked : Do firms' standard compensation packages overcompensate workers by paying them more than is necessary to induce them to move to a new location? To answer that question, you will need to determine the firm's optimal compensation.

In Chapter 3, we introduced consumer theory, which explains how consumers make choices when faced with constraints. We begin this chapter by using consumer theory to determine the shape of a demand curve for a good by varying the good's price, holding other prices and income constant. Firms use information about the shape of demand curves when setting prices: How much can Apple profitably raise its price for the iPhone above its cost of producing it? Governments also use this information to predict the impact of policies such as taxes and price controls: If the government cuts the income tax rate, will tax revenues rise or fall?

Then, we apply consumer theory to show how an increase in people's incomes causes a demand curve to shift. Firms use information about the relationship between income and demand to predict which less-developed countries will substantially increase their demand for the firms' products when incomes rise.

Next, we discover that an increase in the price of a good has two effects on demand. First, consumers buy less of the now relatively more expensive good even if they are compensated with cash for the price increase. Second, holding consumers' incomes constant, an increase in price forces them to buy less of at least some goods.

We use the analysis of these two demand effects of a price increase to show why the government's measure of inflation, the Consumer Price Index (CPI), overestimates the amount of inflation. If you signed a long-term lease for an apartment in which your rent payments increase over time in proportion to the change in the CPI, you lose and your landlord gains from the bias.

Finally, having determined that we can infer how a consumer will behave based on the person's preferences, we use a *revealed preference* approach to show the opposite: that we can infer what a consumer's preferences are if we know the consumer's behavior. Using revealed preference, we can demonstrate that consumers substitute away from a good when its price rises.

In this chapter, we examine five main topics	1. **Deriving Demand Curves.** We use consumer theory to derive demand curves, showing how a change in a product's price causes a movement along its demand curve.
	2. **Effects of an Increase in Income.** We use consumer theory to determine how an increase in consumers' incomes results in their buying more of some or all goods.
	3. **Effects of a Price Increase.** A change in price has two effects on demand, one relating to a change in relative prices and the other concerning a change in consumers' opportunities.
	4. **Cost-of-Living Adjustment.** Using the analysis of the two effects of price changes, we show that the CPI overestimates the rate of inflation.
	5. **Revealed Preference.** Observing a consumer's choice at various prices allows us to infer what the consumer's preferences are and show that the consumer substitutes away from a good when its price increases.

4.1 Deriving Demand Curves

If people's tastes, their incomes, and the prices of other goods are held constant, an increase in the price of a good causes a *movement along the demand curve* for the good (Chapter 2). We use consumer theory to show how a consumer's choice changes as the price changes, thereby tracing out the demand curve.

System of Demand Functions

In Chapter 3, we used calculus to maximize the utility of a consumer subject to a budget constraint. We solved for the optimal quantities of sets of goods that the consumer chooses as functions of prices and the consumer's income. In doing so, we derived the consumer's system of demand functions for the goods.

For example, Lisa chooses between pizzas, q_1, and burritos, q_2, so her demand functions for pizza, q_1, and burritos, q_2, are of the form

$$q_1 = D_1(p_1, p_2, Y),$$
$$q_2 = D_2(p_1, p_2, Y),$$

where p_1 is the price of pizza, p_2 is the price of burritos, and Y is her income. We can trace out the demand function for one good by varying its price while holding other prices and income constant.

In Chapter 3, we illustrated this approach with five utility functions where a consumer chooses between two goods. Table 4.1 summarizes what we know about their demand functions. For the first three utility functions in the table—perfect complements, constant elasticity of substitution (where $\rho < 1$), and

Table 4.1   Demand Functions for Five Utility Functions

			Demand Functions	
Utility Function	$U(q_1, q_2)$	Solution	q_1	q_2
Perfect complements	$\min(q_1, q_2)$	interior	$Y/(p_1 + p_2)$	$Y/(p_1 + p_2)$
CES, $\rho \neq 0, \rho < 1, \sigma = 1/(\rho - 1)$	$(q_1^\rho + q_2^\rho)^{\frac{1}{\rho}}$	interior	$q_1 = \dfrac{Yp_1^\sigma}{p_1^{\sigma+1} + p_2^{\sigma+1}}$	$q_2 = \dfrac{Yp_2^\sigma}{p_1^{\sigma+1} + p_2^{\sigma+1}}$
Cobb-Douglas	$q_1^a q_2^{1-a}$	interior	aY/p_1	$(1 - a)Y/p_2$
Perfect substitutes, $p_1 = p_2 = p$	$q_1 + q_2$	interior	$q_1 + q_2 = Y/p$	
$\quad p_1 < p_2$		corner	Y/p_1	0
$\quad p_1 > p_2$		corner	0	Y/p_2
Quasilinear,	$aq_1^{0.5} + q_2$			
$\quad Y > a^2 p_2/[4p_1]$		interior	$\left(\dfrac{a}{2}\dfrac{p_2}{p_1}\right)^2$	$\dfrac{Y}{p_2} - \dfrac{a^2}{4}\dfrac{p_2}{p_1}$
$\quad Y \leq a^2 p_2/[4p_1]$		corner	Y/p_1	0

Cobb-Douglas—we have an interior solution where the consumer buys both goods. Here, the demand curves for both goods are strictly positive. The other two utility functions—perfect substitutes and quasilinear—may have either an interior solution or a corner solution, where the consumer buys only one of the goods.

We solved for the demand functions for perfect complements utility function, $U(q_1, q_2) = \min(q_1, q_2)$, in Solved Problem 3.4 and for the constant elasticity of substitution (CES) utility function, $U(q_1, q_2) = (q_1^\rho + q_2^\rho)^{\frac{1}{\rho}}$, in Solved Problem 3.5. For both these utility functions, the demand functions for q_1 and q_2 depend on both prices and income, as Table 4.1 shows.

In contrast, for the Cobb-Douglas utility function, $U(q_1, q_2) = q_1^a q_2^{1-a}$, the demand functions depend on the consumer's income and each good's own price, but not on the price of the other good. In Solved Problem 3.5, we derived the Cobb-Douglas demand functions, Equations 3.29 and 3.30, $q_1 = aY/p_1$ and $q_2 = (1 - a)Y/p_2$. Panel a of Figure 4.1 shows the demand curve for q_1, which we plot by holding Y fixed and varying p_1. The demand curve asymptotically approaches the quantity axis.

The demand curves for the perfect substitutes utility function, $U(q_1, q_2) = q_1 + q_2$, which has straight-line indifference curves, do not change smoothly with a good's price. In Chapter 3, we examined Ben's optimal choice between Coke and Pepsi, which he views as perfect substitutes. If the price of Coke, p_1, is above that of Pepsi, p_2, the demand for Coke is zero (corner solution), as panel b of Figure 4.1 shows. If the two prices are equal, $p_1 = p_2 = p$, then Ben buys Y/p cans of either Coke or Pepsi (interior solution), so the demand curve is horizontal and ranges between 0 and Y/p cans. Finally, if $p_1 < p_2$, Ben spends all his income on Coke, buying $q_1 = Y/p_1$ cans. Thus, in the corner solution where Coke is relatively cheap, the Coke demand curve has the same shape as the Cobb-Douglas demand curve.

A quasilinear utility function, $U(q_1, q_2) = u(q_1) + q_2$, can also have an interior or corner solution. In Chapter 3, we considered a particular example, $4q_1^{0.5} + q_2$. In Table 4.1, we slightly generalize this example to $aq_1^{0.5} + q_2$. If the consumer's income is low, $Y \leq a^2 p_2/[4p_1]$, the consumer buys none of q_2 (corner solution) and $q_1 = Y/p_1$.

Figure 4.1 Cobb-Douglas and Perfect Substitute Demand Curves

(a) The Cobb-Douglas demand curve for $q_1 = aY/p_1$ is a smooth curve that approaches the horizontal, q_1-axis as p_1 becomes small. (b) Ben demands no cans of Coca-Cola when the price of Coke, p_1, is greater than the price of Pepsi, p_2. When the two prices are equal, he wants a total number of cans equal to $Y/p_1 = Y/p_2$, but he is indifferent as to how many are Coke and how many are Pepsi. If $p_1 < p_2$, he only buys Coke, and his demand curve is $q_1 = Y/p_1$.

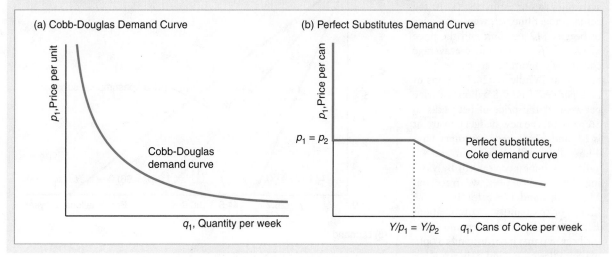

At higher incomes, the consumer buys a fixed amount of $q_1 = [(a/2)(p_2/p_1)]^2$, which is independent of Y, and spends the rest on $q_2 = Y/p_2 - (a^2/4)(p_2/p_1)$.

Graphical Interpretation

We can derive the demand curves graphically. If we increase the price of a product while holding other prices, the consumer's tastes, and income constant, we cause the consumer's budget constraint to rotate, prompting the consumer to choose a new optimal bundle. This change in the quantity demanded is the information we need to draw the demand curve.

We start by estimating a utility function between wine and beer, using data for U.S. consumers.[1] Panel a of Figure 4.2 shows three of the corresponding estimated indifference curves for the average U.S. consumer, whom we call Mimi.[2] These indifference curves are convex to the origin because Mimi views beer and wine as imperfect substitutes (Chapter 3).

The vertical axis in panel a measures the number of gallons of wine Mimi consumes each year, and the horizontal axis measures the number of gallons of beer she drinks each year. Mimi spends $Y = \$419$ per year on beer and wine. The price of beer, p_b, is \$12 per unit, and the price of wine, p_w, is \$35 per unit. The slope of her budget line, L^1, is $-p_b/p_w = -12/35 \approx \frac{1}{3}$. At those prices, Mimi consumes Bundle

---

[1]We estimated the utility function that underlies Figure 4.2 using an almost ideal demand system, which is a more flexible, functional form than the Cobb-Douglas, and which includes the Cobb-Douglas as a special case.

[2]My mother, Mimi, wanted the most degenerate character in the book named after her. I hope that you do not consume as much beer or wine as the typical American in this example. ("One reason I don't drink is that I want to know when I am having a good time."—Nancy, Lady Astor)

Figure 4.2 Deriving Mimi's Demand Curve

If the price of beer falls, holding the price of wine, the budget, and tastes constant, the typical American consumer, Mimi, buys more beer, according to our estimates. (a) At the actual budget line, L^1, where the price of beer is $12 per unit and the price of wine is $35 per unit, the average consumer's indifference curve I^1 is tangent at Bundle e_1, 26.7 gallons of beer per year and 2.8 gallons of wine per year. If the price of beer falls to $6 per unit, the new budget constraint is L^2, and the average consumer buys 44.5 gallons of beer per year and 4.3 gallons of wine per year. (b) By varying the price of beer, we trace out Mimi's demand curve for beer. The beer price-quantity combinations E_1, E_2, and E_3 on the demand curve for beer in panel b correspond to optimal bundles e_1, e_2, and e_3 in panel a.

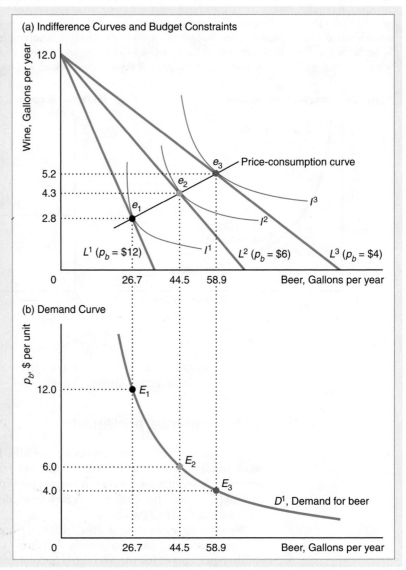

e_1, 26.7 gallons of beer per year and 2.8 gallons of wine per year, a combination that is determined by the tangency of indifference curve I^1 and budget line L^1.[3]

If the price of beer is reduced by half to $6 per unit and the price of wine and her budget remain constant, Mimi's budget line rotates outward to L^2. If she were to spend all her money on wine, she could buy the same $12(\approx 419/35)$ gallons of wine per year as before, so the intercept on the vertical axis of L^2 is the same as

---

[3]These figures are the U.S. average annual per capita consumption of wine and beer. These numbers are surprisingly high given that they reflect an average of teetotalers and (apparently very heavy) drinkers. According to the World Health Organization statistics for 2011, the consumption of liters of pure alcohol per capita by people 15 years and older was 9.4 in the United States compared to 0.3 in Saudi Arabia, 2.9 in Israel, 5.9 in China, 7.8 in Norway, 8.0 in Japan, 9.8 in Canada, 9.6 in New Zealand, 10.0 in Australia and the Netherlands, 10.3 in Sweden, 12.8 in Germany, 13.7 in France, 11.6 in Spain, 13.4 in the United Kingdom, 14.4 in Ireland, and 15.0 in Lithuania.

for L^1. However, if she were to spend all her money on beer, she could buy twice as much as before (70 instead of 35 gallons of beer), so L^2 hits the horizontal axis twice as far from the origin as L^1. As a result, L^2 has a flatter slope than L^1, about $-\frac{1}{6}(\approx -6/35)$.

Because beer is now relatively less expensive, Mimi drinks relatively more beer. She chooses Bundle e_2, 44.5 gallons of beer per year and 4.3 gallons of wine per year, where her indifference curve I^2 is tangent to L^2. If the price of beer falls to \$4 per unit, Mimi consumes Bundle e_3, 58.9 gallons of beer per year and 5.2 gallons of wine per year. The lower the price of beer, the happier Mimi is because she can consume more on the same budget: She is on a higher indifference curve (or perhaps just higher).

Panel a also shows the *price-consumption curve*, which is the line through the optimal bundles, such as e_1, e_2, and e_3, that Mimi would consume at each price of beer, when the price of wine and Mimi's budget are held constant. Because the price-consumption curve is upward sloping, we know that Mimi's consumption of both beer and wine increases as the price of beer falls.

We can use the same information in the price-consumption curve to draw Mimi's demand curve, D^1, for beer in panel b. Corresponding to each possible price of beer on the vertical axis of panel b, we record on the horizontal axis the quantity of beer demanded by Mimi from the price-consumption curve.

Points E_1, E_2, and E_3 on the demand curve in panel b correspond to Bundles e_1, e_2, and e_3 on the price-consumption curve in panel a. Both e_1 and E_1 show that when the price of beer is \$12, Mimi demands 26.7 gallons of beer per year. When the price falls to \$6 per unit, Mimi increases her consumption to 44.5 gallons of beer, point E_2. The demand curve for beer is downward sloping, as predicted by the Law of Demand.

We can use the relationship between the points in panels a and b to show that Mimi's utility is lower at point E_1 on D^1 than at point E_2. Point E_1 corresponds to Bundle e_1 on indifference curve I^1, whereas E_2 corresponds to Bundle e_2 on indifference curve I^2, which is farther from the origin than I^1, so Mimi's utility is higher at E_2 than at E_1. Mimi is better off at E_2 than at E_1 because the price of beer is lower at E_2, so she can buy more goods with the same budget.

APPLICATION

Quitting Smoking

I phoned my dad to tell him I had stopped smoking. He called me a quitter.
—Steven Pearl

Tobacco use, one of the biggest public health threats the world has ever faced, killed 100 million people in the twentieth century. In 2012, the U.S. Center for Disease Control (CDC) reported that cigarette smoking and secondhand smoke are responsible for one in every five deaths each year in the United States. Half of all smokers die of tobacco-related causes. Worldwide, tobacco kills 5.4 million people a year.

Of the more than one billion smokers in the world, over 80% live in low- and middle-income countries. One way to get people—particularly poor people—to quit smoking is to raise the price of tobacco relative to the prices of other goods (thereby changing the slope of the budget constraints that individuals face). In poorer countries, smokers are giving up cigarettes to buy cell phones. As cell phones have recently become affordable in many poorer countries, the price ratio of cell phones to tobacco has fallen substantially.

According to Labonne and Chase (2008), in 2003, before cell phones were common, 42% of households in the Philippine villages they studied used tobacco, and 2% of total village income was spent on tobacco. After the price of cell phones fell, ownership of the phones quadrupled from 2003 to 2006. As consumers spent more on mobile phones, tobacco use fell by one-third in households in which at least one member had smoked (so that consumption fell by one-fifth for the entire population). That is, if we put cell phones on the horizontal axis and tobacco on the vertical axis and lower the price of cell phones, the price-consumption curve is downward sloping (unlike that in Figure 4.2).

Cigarette taxes are often used to increase the price of cigarettes relative to other goods. At least 163 countries tax cigarettes to raise tax revenue and to discourage smoking. Lower-income and younger populations are more likely than others to quit smoking if the price increases. Colman and Remler (2008) estimated that price elasticities of demand for cigarettes among low-, middle-, and high-income groups are −0.37, −0.35, and −0.20, respectively. Several economic studies estimated that the price elasticity of demand is between −0.3 and −0.6 for the general U.S. population and between −0.6 and −0.7 for children. When the after-tax price of cigarettes in Canada increased 158% from 1979 to 1991 (after adjusting for inflation), teenage smoking dropped by 61% and overall smoking fell by 38%.

But what happens to those who continue to smoke heavily? To pay for their now more expensive habit, they have to reduce their expenditures on other goods, such as housing and food. Busch et al. (2004) found that among the poor, a 10% increase in the price of cigarettes causes smoking families to cut back on cigarettes by 9%, alcohol and transportation by 11%, food by 17%, and health care by 12%. Among the poor, smoking families allocate 36% of their expenditures to housing compared to 40% for nonsmokers. Thus, to continue to smoke, these people cut back on many basic goods. That is, if we put tobacco on the horizontal axis and all other goods on the vertical axis, the price-consumption curve is upward sloping, so that as the price of tobacco rises, the consumer buys less of both tobacco and all other goods.

4.2 Effects of an Increase in Income

It is better to be nouveau riche than never to have been riche at all.

An increase in an individual's income, holding tastes and prices constant, causes a *shift of the demand curve*. An increase in income causes a parallel shift of the budget constraint away from the origin, prompting a consumer to choose a new optimal bundle with more of some or all of the goods.

How Income Changes Shift Demand Curves

We illustrate the relationship between the quantity demanded and income by examining how Mimi's behavior changes when her income rises while the prices of beer and wine remain constant. Figure 4.3 shows three ways of looking at the relationship between income and the quantity demanded. All three diagrams have the same horizontal axis: the quantity of beer consumed per year. In the consumer theory diagram, panel a, the vertical axis is the quantity of wine consumed per year. In the demand curve diagram, panel b, the vertical axis is the price of beer per unit. In panel c, which directly shows the relationship between income and the quantity of beer demanded, the vertical axis is Mimi's budget, Y.

A rise in Mimi's income causes a parallel shift out of the budget constraint in panel a, which increases Mimi's opportunity set. Her budget constraint L^1 at her original income, $Y = \$419$, is tangent to her indifference curve I^1 at e_1.

Figure 4.3 Effect of a Budget Increase

As the annual budget for wine and beer, Y, increases from \$419 to \$628 and then to \$837, holding prices constant, the typical consumer buys more of both products, as the upward slope of the income-consumption curve illustrates (a). That the typical consumer buys more beer as income increases is shown by the outward shift of the demand curve for beer (b) and the upward slope of the Engel curve for beer (c).

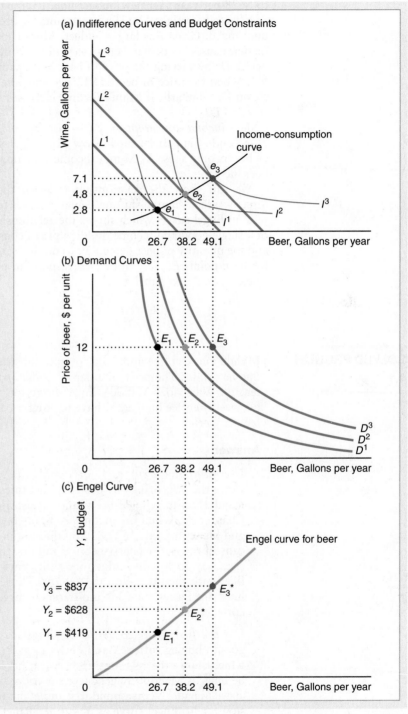

As before, Mimi's demand curve for beer is D^1 in panel b. Point E_1 on D^1, which corresponds to point e_1 in panel a, shows how much beer, 26.7 gallons per year, Mimi consumes when the price of beer is \$12 per unit and the price of wine is \$35 per unit.

Now suppose that Mimi's beer and wine budget, Y, increases by roughly 50% to $628 per year. Her new budget line, L^2 in panel a, is farther from the origin but parallel to her original budget constraint, L^1, because the prices of beer and wine are unchanged. Given this larger budget, Mimi chooses Bundle e_2. The increase in her income causes her demand curve to shift to D^2 in panel b. Holding Y at $628, we can derive D^2 by varying the price of beer in the same way that we derived D^1 in Figure 4.2. When the price of beer is $12 per unit, she buys 38.2 gallons of beer per year, E_2 on D^2. Similarly, if Mimi's income increases to $837 per year, her demand curve shifts to D^3.

The *income-consumption curve* (or *income-expansion path*) through Bundles e_1, e_2, and e_3 in panel a shows how Mimi's consumption of beer and wine increases as her income rises. As Mimi's income goes up, her consumption of both wine and beer increases.

We can show the relationship between the quantity demanded and income directly rather than by shifting demand curves to illustrate the effect. In panel c, we plot an **Engel curve**, which shows the relationship between the quantity demanded of a single good and income, holding prices constant. Income is on the vertical axis, and the quantity of beer demanded is on the horizontal axis. On Mimi's Engel curve for beer, points E_1^*, E_2^*, and E_3^* correspond to points E_1, E_2, and E_3 in panel b and to e_1, e_2, and e_3 in panel a.

SOLVED PROBLEM 4.1	Mahdu views coffee and tea as perfect substitutes: He is indifferent as to which one he drinks. The price of a cup of coffee, p_1, is less than the price of a cup of tea, p_2. What does Mahdu's Engel curve for coffee look like? How much does his weekly coffee budget, Y, have to rise for Mahdu to buy one more cup of coffee per week?

Answer

1. *Use indifference curves to derive Mahdu's optimal choice.* Because Mahdu views the two drinks as perfect substitutes, his indifference curves, such as I and I^* in panel a of the graph, are straight lines with a slope of -1 (see Chapter 3). When his income is Y, his budget line hits the tea axis at Y/p_2 and his coffee axis at Y/p_1. Mahdu maximizes his utility by consuming Y/p_1 cans of the less expensive coffee and no tea (corner solution). As his income rises, say, to Y^*, his budget line shifts outward and is parallel to the original line, with the same slope of $-p_1/p_2$. Thus, at each income level, his budget lines are flatter than his indifference curves, so his equilibria lie along the coffee axis.

2. *Use the first figure to derive his Engel curve.* Because his entire budget, Y, goes to buying coffee, Mahdu buys $q_1 = Y/p_1$ cups of coffee. This expression, which shows the relationship between his income and the quantity of coffee he buys, is Mahdu's Engel curve for coffee. The points E and E^* on the Engel curve in panel b correspond to e and e^* in panel a. We can rewrite this expression for his Engel curve as $Y = p_1 q_1$. Panel b shows that the Engel curve is a straight line. As q_1 increases by one cup (the "run"), Y increases by p_1 (the "rise"), so the slope of this Engel curve is $p_1 (= \text{rise/run} = p_1/1)$. Because his entire drink budget goes to buy coffee, his income needs to rise by only p_1 for him to buy one more cup of coffee per week.

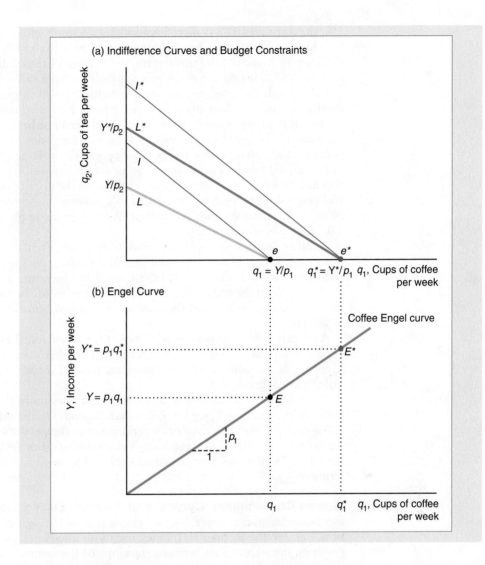

(a) Indifference Curves and Budget Constraints

(b) Engel Curve

Consumer Theory and Income Elasticities

Income elasticities tell us how much the quantity demanded of a product changes as income increases. We can use income elasticities to summarize the shape of the Engel curve or the shape of the income-consumption curve. Such knowledge is useful. For example, firms use income elasticities to predict the impact that a change in the income tax will have on the demand for their goods.

Income Elasticity. The *income elasticity of demand* (or *income elasticity*) is the percentage change in the quantity demanded of a product in response to a given percentage change in income, Y (Chapter 2):

$$\xi = \frac{\text{percentage change in quantity demanded}}{\text{percentage change in income}} = \frac{\Delta Q/Q}{\Delta Y/Y} = \frac{\partial Q}{\partial Y}\frac{Y}{Q},$$

where ξ is the Greek letter xi.

Mimi's income elasticity of beer, ξ_b, is 0.88 and that of wine, ξ_w, is 1.38 (based on our estimates for the average American consumer). When her income goes up by

1%, she consumes 0.88% more beer and 1.38% more wine. Similarly, as her income falls by 1%, she reduces her consumption of beer by 0.88% and wine by 1.38%. Contrary to frequent (and unsubstantiated) claims in the media, during a recession, average Americans do not drink more as their incomes fall—they drink less.

Some goods have negative income elasticities: $\xi < 0$. A good is called an **inferior good** if less of it is demanded as income rises. No value judgment is intended by the use of the term *inferior*. An inferior good need not be defective or of low quality. Some of the better-known examples of inferior goods are starchy foods such as potatoes and cassava, which very poor people eat in large quantities because they cannot afford meats or other foods. Some economists—apparently seriously—claim that human meat is an inferior good: Only when the price of other foods is very high and people are starving will they turn to cannibalism. Bezmen and Depken (2006) estimate that pirated goods are inferior: A 1% increase in per-capita income leads to a 0.25% reduction in piracy.

Another strange example concerns treating children as a consumption good. Even though people can't buy children in a market, people can decide how many children to have. Guinnane (2011) surveyed the literature and reported that most studies find that the income elasticity for the number of children in a family is negative but close to zero. Thus, the number of children demanded is not very sensitive to income.

A good is called a **normal good** if more of it is demanded as income rises. Thus, a good is a normal good if its income elasticity is greater than or equal to zero: $\xi \geq 0$. Most goods, including beer and wine, have positive income elasticities and thus are called normal goods.

If the quantity demanded of a normal good rises more than in proportion to a person's income, $\xi > 1$, we say it is a *luxury good*. On the other hand, if the quantity demanded rises less than or in proportion to the person's income ($0 \leq \xi \leq 1$), we say it is a *necessity*. Because Mimi's income elasticities are 0.88 for beer but 1.38 for wine, Mimi views beer as a necessity and wine as a luxury according to this terminology.

Income-Consumption Curves and Income Elasticities. The shape of the income-consumption curve for two goods tells us the sign of their income elasticities: whether the income elasticities for those goods are positive or negative. To illustrate the relationship between the slope of the income-consumption curve and the sign of income elasticities, we examine Peter's choices of food and housing. Peter purchases Bundle e in Figure 4.4 when his budget constraint is L^1. When his income increases so that his budget constraint is L^2, he selects a bundle on L^2. Which bundle he buys depends on his tastes—his indifference curves.

The horizontal and vertical dotted lines through e divide the new budget line, L^2, into three sections. The section where the new optimal bundle is located determines Peter's income elasticities of food and clothing.

Suppose that Peter's indifference curve is tangent to L^2 at a point in the upper-left section of L^2 (to the left of the vertical dotted line that goes through e) such as a. If Peter's income-consumption curve is ICC^1, which goes from e through a, he buys more housing and less food as his income rises, so housing is a normal good for Peter and food is an inferior good. (Although we draw these possible ICC curves as straight lines for simplicity, they could be curves.)

If instead the new optimal bundle is located in the middle section of L^2 (above the horizontal dotted line and to the right of the vertical dotted line), such as at b, his income-consumption curve ICC^2 through e and b is upward sloping. He buys more of both goods as his income rises, so both food and housing are normal goods.

Figure 4.4 Income-Consumption Curves and Income Elasticities

At the initial income, the budget constraint is L^1 and the optimal bundle is e. After income rises, the new constraint is L^2. With an upward-sloping income-consumption curve such as ICC^2, both goods are normal. With an income-consumption curve such as ICC^1, which goes through the upper-left section of L^2 (to the left of the vertical dotted line through e), housing is normal and food is inferior. With an income-consumption curve such as ICC^3, which cuts L^2 in the lower-right section (below the horizontal dotted line through e), food is normal and housing is inferior.

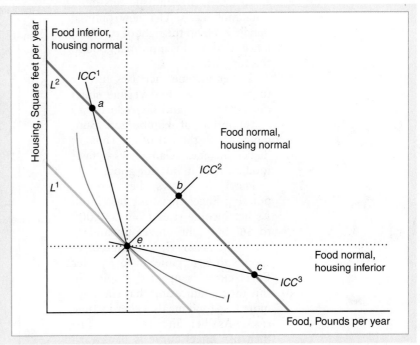

Finally, suppose that his new optimal bundle is in the bottom-right segment of L^2 (below the horizontal dotted line). If his new optimal bundle is c, his income-consumption curve ICC^3 slopes downward from e through c. As his income rises, Peter consumes more food and less housing, so food is a normal good and housing is an inferior good.

APPLICATION

Fast-Food Engel Curve

Is a meal at a fast-food restaurant a normal or inferior good? This question is important because, as incomes have risen over the last quarter century, Americans have spent a larger share of their income on fast food, which has been blamed for increased obesity. However, a number of studies find that obesity falls with income, which suggests that a fast-food meal may be an inferior good, at least at high incomes.

Kim and Leigh (2011) estimated the demand for fast-food restaurant visits as a function of prices, income, and various socioeconomic variables such as age, family size, and whether the family received food stamps (which lowers the price of supermarket food relative to restaurant food). They find that fast-food restaurant visits increase with income up to $60,000, and then decrease as income rises more.[4]

The figure derives the Engel curve for Gail, a typical consumer, based on their estimates. Panel a shows that Gail spends her money on fast-food meals (horizontal axis, where Y is measured in thousands) and all other goods (vertical axis). As Gail's income increases from $30,000 to $60,000, her budget line shifts outward, from

[4]In contrast, they find that full-service restaurant visits increase with income at least up to $95,000.

L^1 to L^2. As a result, she eats more restaurant meals: Her new optimal bundle e_2 lies to the right of e_1. Thus, a fast-food meal is a normal good in this range.

As her income increases further to \$90,000, her budget line shifts outward to L^3, and she reduces her consumption of hamburger: Bundle e_3 lies to the left of e_2. Thus, at higher incomes, Gail views a fast-food meal as an inferior good.

Panel b shows her corresponding Engel curve for fast food. As her income rises from \$30,000 to \$60,000, she moves up and to the right from E_1 (which corresponds to e_1 in panel a) to E_2. Her Engel curve is upward sloping in this range, indicating that she buys more fast-food meals as her income rises. As her income rises further, her Engel curve is backward bending.

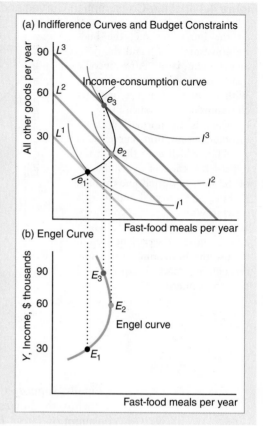

Some Goods Must Be Normal. It is impossible for all goods to be inferior, as Figure 4.4 illustrates. At his original income, Peter faces budget constraint L^1 and buys the combination of food and housing e. When his income goes up, his budget constraint shifts outward to L^2. Depending on his tastes (the shape of his indifference curves), he may buy more housing and less food, such as Bundle a; more of both, such as b; or more food and less housing, such as c. Therefore, either both goods are normal or one good is normal and the other is inferior.

If both goods were inferior, Peter would buy less of both goods as his income rises—which makes no sense. Were he to buy less of both, he would be buying a bundle that lies inside his original budget constraint, L^1. Even at his original, relatively low income, he could have purchased that bundle but chose not to, buying e instead.[5]

Weighted Income Elasticities. We just argued using graphical and verbal reasoning that a consumer cannot view all goods as inferior. We can derive a stronger result: The weighted sum of a consumer's income elasticities equals one. Firms and governments use this result to make predictions about income effects.

[5]Even if an individual does not buy more of the usual goods and services, that person may put the extra money into savings. We can use the consumer theory model to treat savings as a good if we allow for multiple periods. Empirical studies find that savings is a normal good.

We start with the consumer's budget constraint where there are n goods consumed, p_i is the price, and q_i is the quantity for Good i:

$$p_1 q_1 + p_2 q_2 + \cdots + p_n q_n = Y.$$

By differentiating this equation with respect to income, we obtain

$$p_1 \frac{dq_1}{dY} + p_2 \frac{dq_2}{dY} + \cdots + p_n \frac{dq_n}{dY} = 1.$$

Multiplying and dividing each term by $q_i Y$, we can rewrite this equation as

$$\frac{p_1 q_1}{Y} \frac{dq_1}{dY} \frac{Y}{q_1} + \frac{p_2 q_2}{Y} \frac{dq_2}{dY} \frac{Y}{q_2} + \cdots + \frac{p_n q_n}{Y} \frac{dq_n}{dY} \frac{Y}{q_n} = 1.$$

If we define the budget share of Good i as $\theta_i = p_i q_i / Y$ and note that the income elasticities are $\xi_i = (dq_i/dY)(Y/q_i)$, we can rewrite this expression to show that the weighted sum of the income elasticities equals one:

$$\theta_1 \xi_1 + \theta_2 \xi_2 + \cdots + \theta_n \xi_n = 1. \tag{4.1}$$

We can use this formula to make predictions about income elasticities. If we know the budget share of a good and a little bit about the income elasticities of some goods, we can calculate bounds on other, unknown income elasticities. Being able to obtain bounds on income elasticities is very useful to governments and firms. For example, over the last couple of decades, many Western manufacturing firms, learning that Chinese incomes were rising rapidly, have tried to estimate the income elasticities for their products among Chinese consumers to decide whether to enter the Chinese market.

SOLVED PROBLEM 4.2

A firm is considering building a plant in a developing country to sell manufactured goods in that country. The firm expects incomes to start rising soon and wants to know the income elasticity for goods other than food. The firm knows that the budget share spent on food is θ and that food is a necessity (its income elasticity, ξ_f, is between 0 and 1). The firm wants to know "How large could the income elasticity of all other goods, ξ_o, be? How small could it be?" What were the bounds on ξ_o for Chinese urban consumers whose θ was 60% in 1983? What are the bounds today when θ is 37%?[6]

Answer

1. *Write Equation 4.1 in terms of ξ_f, ξ_o, and θ, and then use algebra to rewrite this expression with the income elasticity of other goods on the left-hand side.* By substituting ξ_f, ξ_o, and θ into Equation 4.1, we find that $\theta \xi_f + (1 - \theta)\xi_o = 1$. We can rewrite this expression with the income elasticity of other goods—the number we want to estimate—on the left-hand side:

$$\xi_o = \frac{1 - \theta \xi_f}{1 - \theta}. \tag{4.2}$$

[6]State Statistical Bureau, *Statistical Yearbook of China*, State Statistical Bureau Publishing House, Beijing, China, various years.

2. *Use Equation 4.2 and the bounds on ξ_f to derive bounds on ξ_o.* Because $\xi_o = (1 - \theta\xi_f)/(1 - \theta)$, ξ_o is smaller the larger is ξ_f. Given that food is a necessity, the largest ξ_o can be is $1/(1 - \theta)$, where $\xi_f = 0$. The smallest it can be is $\xi_o = 1$, which occurs if $\xi_f = 1$. [*Note:* If ξ_f equals one, $\xi_o = (1 - \theta)/(1 - \theta) = 1$ regardless of food's budget share, θ.]

3. *Substitute for the two Chinese values of ω to determine the upper bounds.* The upper bound for ξ_o was $1/(1 - \theta) = 1/0.4 = 2.5$ in 1983 and $1/0.63 \approx 1.59$ now.

Comment: The upper bound on the income elasticity of nonfood goods in the United States is lower than in China because the share of consumption of food in the United States is smaller. The U.S. share of expenditures on food was 22% for welfare recipients and 14% for others in 2001–2002 (Paszkiewicz, 2005). Thus, the upper bound on ξ_o was about 1.28 for welfare recipients and 1.16 for others. From Equation 4.2, $\xi_o = (1 - \theta\xi_f)/(1 - \theta) \approx 1.16 - 0.16\xi_f$ for nonwelfare recipients. Most estimates of the U.S. ξ_f range between 0.4 and 0.9, so ξ_o must range from about 1.02 to 1.10 for this group.

4.3 Effects of a Price Increase

Holding tastes, other prices, and income constant, an increase in a price of a good has two effects on an individual's demand. One is the **substitution effect**: the change in the quantity of a good that a consumer demands when the good's price rises, holding other prices and the consumer's utility constant. If the consumer's utility is held constant as the price of the good increases, the consumer *substitutes* other goods that are now relatively cheaper for this now more expensive good.

The other effect is the **income effect**: the change in the quantity of a good a consumer demands because of a change in income, holding prices constant. An increase in price reduces a consumer's buying power, effectively reducing the consumer's *income* or opportunity set and causing the consumer to buy less of at least some goods. A doubling of the price of all the goods the consumer buys is equivalent to a drop in the consumer's income to half its original level. Even a rise in the price of only one good reduces a consumer's ability to buy the same amount of all goods previously purchased. For example, when the price of food increases in a poor country in which half or more of the population's income is spent on food, the effective purchasing power of the population falls substantially.

When the price of a product rises, the total change in the quantity purchased is the sum of the substitution effect and the income effect. When economists estimate the effect of a product's price change on the quantity an individual demands, they decompose the combined effect into the two separate components. By doing so, they gain extra information that they can use to answer questions about whether inflation measures are accurate, whether an increase in tax rates will raise tax revenue, and what the effects are of government policies that compensate some consumers. For example, President Jimmy Carter, when advocating a tax on gasoline, and President Bill Clinton, when calling for an energy tax, proposed compensating poor consumers to offset the harms from the tax. We can use our knowledge of the substitution and income effects from energy price changes to evaluate the effect of these policies.

Income and Substitution Effects with a Normal Good

To illustrate the substitution and income effects, we return to Jackie's choice between music tracks and live music based on our estimate of the average person's Cobb-Douglas utility function (see the Application "*MRS* Between Recorded Tracks and Live Music" in Chapter 3). The price of a unit of live music is $p_2 = £1$, and the price of downloading a music track is $p_1 = £0.5$. Now, suppose that the price of music tracks rises to £1, causing Jackie's budget constraint to rotate inward from L^1 to L^2 in Figure 4.5. The new budget constraint, L^2, is twice as steep ($-p_1/p_2 = -1/1 = -1$) as $L^1 (-0.5/1 = -0.5)$.

Because of the price increase, Jackie's opportunity set is smaller, so she must choose between fewer bundles of music tracks and live music than she could at the lower price. The area between the two budget constraints reflects the decrease in her opportunity set owing to the increase in the price of music tracks.

We determined that Jackie's demand functions for music tracks (songs), q_1, and live music, q_2, Equations 3.29 and 3.30, are

$$q_1 = 0.4\frac{Y}{p_1}, \tag{4.3}$$

$$q_2 = 0.6\frac{Y}{p_2}. \tag{4.4}$$

At the original price of tracks and with an entertainment budget of £30 per quarter, Jackie chooses Bundle e_1, $q_1 = 0.4 \times 30/0.5 = 24$ tracks and $q_2 = 0.6 \times 30/1 = 18$ units of live music per quarter, where her indifference curve I^1 is tangent to her budget constraint L^1. When the price of tracks rises, Jackie's new optimal bundle is e_2 (where she buys $q_1 = 0.4 \times 30/1 = 12$ tracks), which occurs where her indifference curve I^2 is tangent to L^2.

The increase in the amount of q_1 that she consumes as she moves from e_1 to e_2 is the *total effect* from the rise in the price: She buys 12(= 24 − 12) fewer tracks per quarter. In the figure, the red arrow pointing to the left labeled *Total*

Figure 4.5 Substitution and Income Effects with Normal Goods

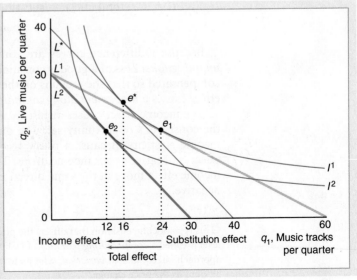

An increase in the price of music tracks from £0.5 to £1 causes Jackie's budget line to rotate from L^1 to L^2. The imaginary budget line L^* has the same slope as L^2 and is tangent to indifference curve I^1. The shift of the optimal bundle from e_1 to e_2 is the *total effect* of the price change. The total effect can be decomposed into the *substitution effect*—the movement from e_1 to e^*—and the *income effect*—the movement from e^* to e_2.

effect shows this decrease. We can break the total effect into a substitution effect and an income effect.

As the price increases, Jackie's opportunity set shrinks even though her income is unchanged. If, as a thought experiment, we compensate her for this loss by giving her extra income, we can determine her substitution effect. The substitution effect is the change in the quantity demanded from a *compensated change in the price* of music tracks, which occurs when we increase Jackie's income by enough to offset the rise in price so that her utility stays constant.[7] To determine the substitution effect, we draw an imaginary budget constraint, L^*, that is parallel to L^2 and tangent to Jackie's original indifference curve, I^1. This imaginary budget constraint, L^*, has the same slope, -1, as L^2 because both curves are based on the new, higher price of tracks. For L^* to be tangent to I^1, we need to increase Jackie's budget from £30 to £40 to offset the harm from the higher price of music tracks. If Jackie's budget constraint were L^*, she would choose Bundle e^*, where she buys $q_1 = 0.4 \times 40/1 = 16$ tracks.

Thus, if the price of tracks rises relative to that of live music *and* we hold Jackie's utility constant by raising her income to compensate her, Jackie's optimal bundle shifts from e_1 to e^*. The corresponding change in q_1 is the *substitution effect*. She buys 8 (= 24 − 16) fewer tracks per quarter, as the green arrow pointing to the left labeled *Substitution effect* illustrates.

Jackie also faces an income effect because the increase in price of tracks shrinks her opportunity set, so that she must buy a bundle on a lower indifference curve. As a thought experiment, we can ask how much we would have to lower her income while holding prices constant at the new level for her to choose a bundle on this new, lower indifference curve. The *income effect* is the change in the quantity of a good a consumer demands because of a change in income, holding prices constant. The parallel shift of the budget constraint from L^* to L^2 captures this effective decrease in income. The change in q_1 due to the movement from e^* to e_2 is the *income effect*, as the brown arrow pointing to the left labeled *Income effect* shows. Holding prices constant, as her budget decreases from £40 to £30, Jackie consumes 4 (= 16 − 12) fewer tracks per quarter.

The *total effect* from the price change is the *sum of the substitution and income effects*, as the arrows show. Jackie's total effect (in tracks per quarter) from a rise in the price of tracks is

$$\text{total effect} = \text{substitution effect} + \text{income effect}$$
$$-12 = -8 + (-4).$$

Because indifference curves are convex to the origin, *the substitution effect is unambiguous*: Less of a good is consumed when its price rises given that consumer is compensated so that she remains on the original indifference curve. The substitution effect causes a *movement along an indifference curve*.

The income effect causes a shift to another indifference curve due to a change in the consumer's opportunity set. The direction of the income effect depends on the income elasticity. Because a music track is a normal good for Jackie, her income effect is negative as her income drops. Thus, both Jackie's substitution effect and her income effect move in the same direction, so the total effect of the price rise must be negative.

---

[7]This type of compensation that offsets the price change to hold her utility constant at the original level is called a *compensating variation*. In Chapter 5, we compare this approach to the alternative approach, an *equivalent variation*, where the income adjustment harms the consumer by the same amount as the price change.

SOLVED PROBLEM 4.3

Next to its plant, a manufacturer of dinner plates has an outlet store that sells first-quality plates (perfect plates) and second-quality plates (slightly blemished plates). The outlet store sells a relatively large share of second-quality plates (or seconds). At its regular retail stores elsewhere, the firm sells many more first-quality plates than second-quality plates. Why? (Assume that consumers' tastes with respect to plates are the same everywhere, the income effects are very small, and there is a cost, s, of shipping each plate from the factory to the firm's other stores.)

Answer

1. *Determine how the relative prices of plates differ between the two types of stores.* The slope of the budget line that consumers face at the factory outlet store is $-p_1/p_2$, where p_1 is the price of first-quality plates, and p_2 is the price of seconds. It costs the same, s, to ship a first-quality plate as a second because they weigh the same and must be handled similarly. At its retail stores elsewhere, the firm adds the cost of shipping to the price it charges at its factory outlet store, so the price of a first-quality plate is $p_1 + s$ and the price of a second is $p_2 + s$. As a result, the slope of the budget line that consumers face at the retail stores is $-(p_1 + s)/(p_2 + s)$. The seconds are relatively less expensive at the factory outlet than they are at the other stores. For example, if $p_1 = \$2$, $p_2 = \$1$, and $s = \$1$ per plate, the slope of the budget line is -2 at the outlet store and $-3/2$ elsewhere. Thus, a first-quality plate costs twice as much as a second at the outlet store but only 1.5 times as much elsewhere.

2. *Use the relative price difference to explain why relatively more seconds are bought at the factory outlet.* Holding a consumer's income and tastes fixed, if the price of seconds rises relative to that of firsts (as we go from the factory outlet to the other retail shops), most consumers will buy relatively more firsts. The substitution effect is unambiguous: Were they compensated so that their utilities were held constant, consumers would unambiguously substitute firsts for seconds. It is possible that the income effect could go in the other direction (if plates are an inferior good); however, as most consumers spend relatively little of their total budgets on plates, the income effect is presumably small relative to the substitution effect. Thus, we expect relatively fewer seconds to be bought at the retail stores than at the factory outlet.

APPLICATION

Shipping the Good Stuff Away

According to the economic theory discussed in Solved Problem 4.3, we expect that the relatively larger the share is of higher-quality goods shipped, the greater the per-unit shipping fee will be. Is this theory true, and is the effect large? To answer these questions, Hummels and Skiba (2004) examined shipments between 6,000 country pairs for more than 5,000 goods. They found that doubling per-unit shipping costs results in a 70% to 143% increase in the average price of a good (excluding the cost of shipping) as a larger share of top-quality products is shipped.

The greater the distance between the trading countries, the higher was the cost of shipping. Hummels and Skiba speculate that the relatively high quality of Japanese goods is due to that country's relatively great distance from major importers.

Income and Substitution Effects with an Inferior Good

If a good is inferior, the income effect and the substitution effect move in opposite directions. For most inferior goods, the income effect is smaller than the substitution effect. As a result, the total effect moves in the same direction as the substitution effect, but the total effect is smaller. However, for a **Giffen good**, a decrease in its price causes the quantity demanded to fall because the income effect more than offsets the substitution effect.[8]

Jensen and Miller (2008) found that rice is a Giffen good in Hunan, China. Because rice is a Giffen good for Ximing, a fall in the rice price saves him money that he spends on other goods. Indeed, he decides to increase his spending on other goods even further by buying less rice. Thus, his demand curve for this Giffen good has an *upward* slope.

However, in Chapter 2, I claimed that the Law of Demand says that demand curves slope downward: Quantity demanded falls as the price rises. You're no doubt wondering how I'm going to worm my way out of this contradiction. I have two explanations. The first is that I claimed that the Law of Demand is an empirical regularity, not a theoretical necessity. Although it's theoretically possible for a demand curve to slope upward, other than the Hunan rice example, economists have found few, if any, real-world Giffen goods.[9] My second explanation is that the Law of Demand must hold theoretically for compensated demand curves, as we show in the next section.

SOLVED PROBLEM 4.4

Ximing spends his money on rice, a Giffen good, and all other goods. Show that when the price of rice falls, Ximing buys less rice. Decompose this total effect of a price change on his rice consumption into a substitution effect and an income effect.

Answer

1. *Determine Ximing's original optimal bundle e_1, using the tangency between his original budget line and one of his indifference curves.* In the figure, his original budget line L^1 is tangent to his indifference curve I^1 at e_1.

2. *Show how the optimal bundle changes from a drop in the price of rice.* As the price of rice drops, his new budget line L^2 becomes flatter, rotating around the original budget line's intercept on the vertical axis. The tangency between L^2 and indifference curve I^2 occurs at e_2, where Ximing consumes less rice than before because rice is a Giffen good.

3. *Draw a new, hypothetical budget line L^* based on the new price but that keeps Ximing on the original indifference curve.* Ximing's opportunity set grows when the rice price falls. To keep him on his original indifference curve, his income would have to fall by enough so that his new budget line L^2 shifts down to L^*, which is tangent to his original indifference curve I^1 at e^*.

[8]Robert Giffen, a nineteenth-century British economist, argued that poor people in Ireland increased their consumption of potatoes when the price rose because of a potato blight. However, more recent studies of the Irish potato famine dispute this observation.

[9]However, Battalio, Kagel, and Kogut (1991) showed in an experiment that quinine water is a Giffen good for lab rats.

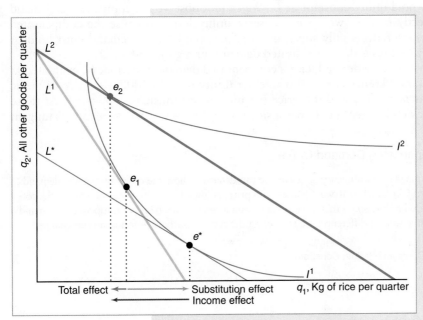

4. *Identify the substitution and income effects.* The substitution effect is the change in q_1 from the movement from e_1 to e^*: Ximing buys more rice when the price of rice drops but he remains on his original indifference curve. The movement from e^* to e_2 determines the income effect: Ximing buys less rice as his income increases holding prices constant. The total effect, the movement from e_1 to e_2, is the sum of the positive substitution effect and the negative income effect. Ximing buys less rice because the income effect is larger than the substitution effect.

Compensated Demand Curve

So far, the demand curves that we have derived graphically and mathematically allow a consumer's utility to vary as the price of the good increases. For example, a consumer's utility falls if the price of one of the goods rises. Consequently, the consumer's demand curve reflects both the substitution and income effects as the price of the product changes.

As panel a of Figure 4.2 illustrates, Mimi chooses a bundle on a lower indifference curve as the price of beer rises, so her utility level falls. Along her demand curve for beer, we hold other prices, income, and her tastes constant, while allowing her utility to vary. We can observe this type of demand curve by seeing how the purchases of a product change as its price increases. It is called *the* demand curve, the Marshallian demand curve (after Alfred Marshall, who popularized this approach), or the *uncompensated demand curve*. (Unless otherwise noted, when we talk about a demand curve, we mean the uncompensated demand curve.)

Alternatively, we could derive a *compensated demand curve*, which shows how the quantity demanded changes as the price rises, holding utility constant, so that the change in the quantity demanded reflects only the pure substitution effect from a price change. It is called the compensated demand curve because we would have to compensate an individual—give the individual extra income—as the price rises so as to hold the individual's utility constant. The compensated demand curve is also called the Hicksian demand curve, after John Hicks, who introduced the idea.

The compensated demand function for the first good is

$$q_1 = H(p_1, p_2, \overline{U}), \tag{4.5}$$

where we hold utility constant at $\overline{U}$. We cannot observe the compensated demand curve directly because we do not observe utility levels. Because the compensated demand curve reflects only substitution effects, the Law of Demand must hold: A price increase causes the compensated demand for a good to fall.

In Figure 4.6, we derive Jackie's compensated demand function, H, evaluated at her initial indifference curve, I, where her utility is $\overline{U}$. In 2008, the price of music tracks was $p_1 = £0.5$ and the price per unit of live music was $p_2 = £1$. At those prices, Jackie's budget line, L, has a slope of $-p_1/p_2 = -0.5/1 = -\frac{1}{2}$ and is tangent

Figure 4.6 Deriving Jackie's Compensated Demand Curve

Initially, Jackie's optimal bundle is determined by the tangency of budget line L and indifference curve I in panel a. If we vary the price of music tracks but change her budget so that the new line (segments) are tangent to the same indifference curve, we can determine how the quantity that she demands varies with price, holding her utility constant. Hence, the corresponding quantities in panel b on her compensated demand curve reflect the pure substitution effect of a price change.

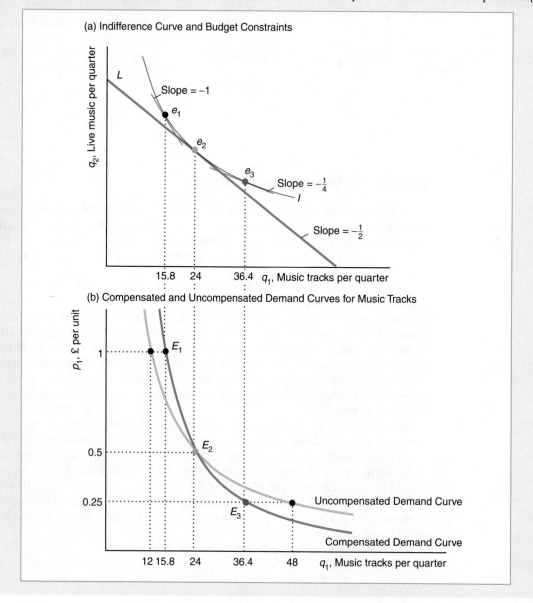

to *I* at e_2 in panel a. At this optimal bundle, she buys 24 tracks. The corresponding point E_2 on her compensated demand curve in panel b shows that she buys 24 tracks when they cost £0.5 each.

The two thin blue line segments in panel a show portions of other budget lines where we change p_1 and adjust Jackie's income to keep her on indifference curve *I*. At the budget line segment in the upper left, the price of tracks is £1, so Jackie's budget line's slope is −1. Her budget is increased enough that her new budget line is tangent to the original indifference curve, *I*, at e_1. This optimal bundle corresponds to E_1 on her compensated demand curve in panel b. Similarly, when p_1 is £0.25, we decrease her budget so that this budget line is tangent to her original indifference curve at e_3, which corresponds to E_3 on her compensated demand curve.

Panel b also shows Jackie's uncompensated demand curve: Equation 4.3, $q_1 = 0.4Y/p_1$. Her compensated and uncompensated demand curves *must* cross at the original price, $p_1 = £0.5$, where the original budget line, *L*, is tangent to *I* along which utility is $\overline{U}$. At that price, and only at that price, both demand curves are derived using the same budget line. The compensated demand curve is steeper than the uncompensated curve around this common point. The compensated demand curve is relatively steep because it reflects only the substitution effect. The uncompensated demand curve is flatter because the (normal good) income effect reinforces the substitution effect.

One way to derive the compensated demand curve is to use the expenditure function, Equation 3.32,

$$E = E(p_1, p_2, \overline{U}),$$

where *E* is the smallest expenditure that allows the consumer to achieve utility level $\overline{U}$, given market prices. If we differentiate the expenditure function with respect to the price of the first good, we obtain the compensated demand function for that good:[10]

$$\frac{\partial E}{\partial p_1} = H(p_1, p_2, \overline{U}) = q_1. \tag{4.6}$$

One informal explanation for Equation 4.6 is that if p_1 increases by \$1 on each of the q_1 units that the consumer buys, then the minimum amount the consumer must spend to keep his or her utility constant must increase by $\$q_1$. This expression can also be interpreted as the pure substitution effect on the quantity demanded because we are holding the consumer's utility constant as we change the price.

---

[10]This result is called Shephard's lemma. As we showed in Solved Problem 3.8, we can use the Lagrangian method to derive the expenditure function, where we want to minimize $E = p_1 q_1 + p_2 q_2$ subject to $\overline{U} = U(q_1, q_2)$. The Lagrangian equation is $\mathscr{L} = p_1 q_1 + p_2 q_2 + \lambda[\overline{U} - U(q_1, q_2)]$. According to the envelope theorem (see the Calculus Appendix), at the optimum,

$$\frac{\partial E}{\partial p_1} = \frac{\partial \mathscr{L}}{\partial p_1} = q_1,$$

which is Equation 4.6. It shows that the derivative of the expenditure function with respect to p_1 is q_1, the quantity that the consumer demands.

SOLVED PROBLEM 4.5

A consumer has a Cobb-Douglas utility function $U = q_1^a q_1^{1-a}$. Derive the compensated demand function for good q_1. Given that $a = 0.4$ in Jackie's utility function, what is her compensated demand function for music tracks, q_1?

Answer

1. *Write the formula for the expenditure function for this Cobb-Douglas utility function.* We derived this expenditure function in Solved Problem 3.7:

$$E = \overline{U}\left(\frac{p_1}{a}\right)^a \left(\frac{p_2}{1-a}\right)^{1-a}. \tag{4.7}$$

2. *Differentiate the expenditure function in Equation 4.7 with respect to p_1 to obtain the compensated demand function for q_1, making use of Equation 4.6.* The compensated demand function is

$$q_1 = \frac{\partial E}{\partial p_1} = \overline{U}\left(\frac{a}{1-a}\frac{p_2}{p_1}\right)^{1-a}. \tag{4.8}$$

3. *Substitute Jackie's value of a in Equation 4.7 to obtain her expenditure function, and in Equation 4.8 to obtain her compensated demand function for tracks.* Given that her $a = 0.4$, Jackie's expenditure function is

$$E = \overline{U}\left(\frac{p_1}{0.4}\right)^{0.4}\left(\frac{p_2}{0.6}\right)^{0.6} \approx 1.96\overline{U}p_1^{0.4}p_2^{0.6}, \tag{4.9}$$

and her compensated demand function for tracks is

$$q_1 = \overline{U}\left(\frac{0.4}{0.6}\frac{p_2}{p_1}\right)^{0.6} \approx 0.784\overline{U}\left(\frac{p_2}{p_1}\right)^{0.6}. \tag{4.10}$$

Comment: We showed above that when Jackie's quarterly budget is $Y = £30$ and she faces prices of $p_1 = £0.5$ and $p_2 = £1$, she chooses $q_1 = 24$ and $q_2 = 18$. The corresponding indifference curve is $\overline{U} = 24^{0.4}18^{0.6} \approx 20.2$. Thus, at the initial prices, her compensated demand for tracks, Equation 4.10, is $q_1 \approx 0.784 \times 20.2(1/0.5)^{0.6} \approx 24$, which is reassuring because the compensated and uncompensated demand curves must cross at the initial prices.

Slutsky Equation

We have shown graphically that the total effect from a price change can be decomposed into a substitution effect and an income effect. That same relationship can be derived mathematically. We can use this relationship in a variety of ways. For example, we can apply it to determine how likely a good is to be a Giffen good based on whether the consumer spends a relatively large or small share of the budget on this good. We can also use the relationship to determine the effect of government policies that compensate some consumers.

The usual price elasticity of demand, ε, captures the total effect of a price change—that is, the change along an uncompensated demand curve. We can break this price elasticity of demand into two terms involving elasticities that capture the substitution and income effects. We measure the substitution effect using the pure *substitution elasticity of demand*, ε^*, which is the percentage that the quantity demanded falls for a given percentage increase in price if we compensate the consumer to keep the consumer's utility constant. That is, ε^* is the elasticity of the compensated demand curve. The income effect is the income elasticity, ξ, times the share of the budget spent on that good, θ. This relationship among the price elasticity of demand, ε, the substitution elasticity of demand, ε^*, and the income elasticity of demand, ξ, is the *Slutsky equation* (named after its discoverer, the Russian economist Eugene Slutsky):[11]

$$\text{total effect} = \text{substitution effect} + \text{income effect}$$
$$\varepsilon = \varepsilon^* + (-\theta\xi). \tag{4.11}$$

If a consumer spends little on a good, a change in its price does not affect the person's total budget significantly. For example, if the price of garlic triples, your purchasing power will hardly be affected (unless perhaps you are a vampire slayer). Thus, the total effect, ε, for garlic hardly differs from the substitution effect, ε^*, because the price change has little effect on the consumer's income.

In Mimi's original optimal bundle, e_1 in Figure 4.2, where the price of beer was \$12 and Mimi bought 26.7 gallons of beer per year, Mimi spent about three-quarters of her \$419 beverage budget on beer: $\theta = 0.76 = (12 \times 26.7)/419$. Her income elasticity is $\xi = 0.88$, her price elasticity is $\varepsilon = -0.76$, and her substitution price elasticity is $\varepsilon^* = -0.09$. Thus, Mimi's Slutsky equation is

$$\varepsilon = \varepsilon^* - \theta\xi$$
$$-0.76 \approx -0.09 - (0.76 \times 0.88).$$

Because beer is a normal good for Mimi, the income effect reinforces the substitution effect. Indeed, the size of the total change, $\varepsilon = -0.76$, is due more to the income effect, $-\theta\xi = -0.67$, than to the substitution effect, $\varepsilon^* = -0.09$. If the price of beer rises by 1% but Mimi is given just enough extra income so that her utility remains constant, Mimi would reduce her consumption of beer by less than a tenth of a percent (substitution effect). Without compensation, Mimi reduces her consumption of beer by about three-quarters of a percent (total effect).

Similarly, in Jackie's original optimum, e_1 in Figure 4.5, the price of a track was £0.5, and Jackie bought 24 tracks per year. She spent $\theta = 0.4$ share of her budget on tracks (see Solved Problem 3.6). Her uncompensated demand function,

---

[11]When we derived the compensated demand function, H, we noted that it equals the uncompensated demand function, D, at the initial optimum where utility is $\overline{U}$.

$$q_1 = H(p_1, p_2, \overline{U}) = D(p_1, p_2, Y) = D(p_1, p_2, E(p_1, p_2, \overline{U})),$$

and Y equals the minimum expenditure needed to achieve that level of utility, as given by the expenditure function. If we differentiate with respect to p_1, we find that

$$\frac{\partial H}{\partial p_1} = \frac{\partial D}{\partial p_1} + \frac{\partial D}{\partial E}\frac{\partial E}{\partial p_1} = \frac{\partial D}{\partial p_1} + \frac{\partial D}{\partial E}q_1.$$

where we know that $\partial E/\partial p_1 = q_1$ from Equation 4.6. Rearranging terms and multiplying all terms by p_1/q_1, and the last term by Y/Y, we obtain

$$\frac{\partial D}{\partial p_1}\frac{p_1}{\partial p_1} = \frac{\partial H}{\partial p_1}\frac{p_1}{q_1} - q_1\frac{\partial D}{\partial E}\frac{p_1}{q_1}\frac{E}{E}.$$

This last expression is the Slutsky Equation 4.11, where $\varepsilon = (\partial D/\partial p_1)(p_1/q_1)$, $\varepsilon^* = (\partial H/\partial p_1)(p_1/q_1)$, $\theta = p_1 q_1/E$, and $\xi = (\partial D/\partial E)(p_1/E)$.

Equation 4.3, is $q_1 = 0.4Y/p_1$, so her price elasticity of demand is $\varepsilon = -1$, and her income elasticity is $\xi = 1$.[12] Her compensated demand function, Equation 4.10, is $q_1 = 0.784\overline{U}\,(p_2/p_1)^{0.6} = 0.784\overline{U}p_2^{0.6}p_1^{-0.6}$. Because it is a constant elasticity demand function where the exponent on p_1 is -0.6, we know that $\varepsilon^* = -0.6$. Thus, her Slutsky equation is

$$\varepsilon = \varepsilon^* - \theta\xi$$
$$-1 = -0.6 - (0.4 \times 1).$$

For a Giffen good to have an upward-sloping demand curve, ε must be positive. The substitution elasticity, ε^*, is always negative: Consumers buy less of a good when its price increases, holding utility constant. Thus, for a good to be a Giffen good and have an upward-sloping demand curve, the income effect, $-\theta\xi$, must be positive and large relative to the substitution effect. The income effect is more likely to be a large positive number if the good is very inferior (that is, ξ is a large negative number, which is not common) and the budget share, θ, is large (closer to one than to zero). One reason we don't see upward-sloping demand curves is that the goods on which consumers spend a large share of their budget, such as housing, are usually normal goods rather than inferior goods.

4.4 Cost-of-Living Adjustment

In spite of the cost of living, it's still popular. —Kathleen Norris

By knowing both the substitution and income effects, we can answer questions that we could not answer if we knew only the total effect of a price change. One particularly important use of consumer theory is to analyze how accurately the government measures inflation.

Many long-term contracts and government programs include *cost-of-living adjustments* (COLAs), which raise prices or incomes in proportion to an index of inflation. Not only business contracts, but also rental contracts, alimony payments, salaries, pensions, and Social Security payments, are frequently adjusted in this manner over time. We will use consumer theory to show that the cost-of-living measure that governments commonly use overestimates how the true cost of living changes over time. Because of this overestimation, you overpay your landlord if the rent on your apartment rises with this measure.

Inflation Indexes

The prices of most goods rise over time. We call the increase in the overall price level *inflation*.

The actual price of a good is called the *nominal price*. The price adjusted for inflation is the *real price*. Because the overall level of prices rises over time, nominal prices usually increase more rapidly than real prices. For example, the nominal price of a McDonald's hamburger rose from 15¢ in 1955 to 95¢ in 2012, over a six-fold increase. However, the real price of the burger fell because the prices of other goods rose more rapidly than that of the burger.

---

[12]We can equivalently write the demand curve as $\ln q_1 = \ln(0.4) + \ln Y - \ln p_1$, which is a constant-elasticity demand curve. We can find the price elasticity using the method in Solved Problem 2.2. Similarly, differentiating with respect to Y, we find that $(dq_1/dY)/q_1 = 1/Y$. Rearranging terms, we learn that $\xi = (dq_1/dY)(Y/q_1) = 1$.

How do we adjust for inflation to calculate the real price? Governments measure the cost of a standard bundle of goods, or market basket, to compare prices over time. This measure is called the Consumer Price Index (CPI). Each month, the government reports how much it costs to buy the bundle of goods that an average consumer purchased in a *base* year (with the base year changing every few years).

By comparing the cost of buying this bundle over time, we can determine how much the overall price level has increased. In the United States, the CPI was 26.7 in April 1955 and 229.1 in July 2012.[13] The cost of buying the bundle of goods increased 858% ($\approx$ 229.1/26.7) over this period.

We can use the CPI to calculate the real price of a McDonald's hamburger over time. In terms of 2012 dollars, the real price of the hamburger in 1955 was

$$\frac{\text{CPI for 2012}}{\text{CPI for 1955}} \times \text{price of a burger} = \frac{229.1}{26.7} \times 15\text{¢} = \$1.29.$$

If you could have purchased the hamburger in 1955 with 2012 dollars—which are worth less than 1955 dollars—the hamburger would have cost $1.29. The real price in 2012 dollars (and the nominal price) of the hamburger in 2012 was only 95¢. Thus, the real price fell by about 26%. If we compared the real prices in both years using 1955 dollars, we would reach the same conclusion that the real price of hamburgers fell by about 26%.

The government collects data on the quantities and prices of 364 individual goods and services, such as housing, dental services, watch and jewelry repairs, college tuition fees, taxi fares, women's hairpieces and wigs, hearing aids, slipcovers and decorative pillows, bananas, pork sausage, and funeral expenses. These prices rise at different rates. If the government merely reported all these price increases separately, most of us would find this information overwhelming. It is much more convenient to use a single summary statistic, the CPI, which tells us how prices rose *on average*.

We can use an example with only two goods, clothing and food, to show how the CPI is calculated. In the first year, consumers buy C_1 units of clothing and F_1 units of food at prices p_C^1 and p_F^1. We use this bundle of goods, C_1 and F_1, as our base bundle for comparison. In the second year, consumers buy C_2 and F_2 units at prices p_C^2 and p_F^2.

The government knows from its survey of prices that the price of clothing in the second year is p_C^2/p_C^1 times as large as the price the previous year. Similarly, the price of food is p_F^2/p_F^1 times as large as the price the previous year. For example, if the price of clothing were $1 in the first year and $2 in the second year, the price of clothing in the second year would be $\frac{2}{1} = 2$ times, or 100%, larger than in the first year.

One way we can average the price increases of each good is to weight them equally. But do we really want to do that? Do we want to give as much weight to the price increase for skateboards as to the price increase for cars? An alternative approach is to assign a larger weight to the price change of goods with relatively large budget shares. In constructing its averages, the CPI weights using budget shares.[14]

---

[13]The number 229.1 is not an actual dollar amount. Rather, it is the actual dollar cost of buying the bundle divided by a constant. That constant was chosen so that the average expenditure in the period 1982–1984 was 100.

[14]This discussion of the CPI is simplified in many ways. Sophisticated adjustments are made to the CPI that are ignored here, including repeated updating of the base year (chaining). See Pollak (1989) and Diewert and Nakamura (1993).

The CPI for the first year is the amount of income it took to buy the market basket that was actually purchased that year:

$$Y_1 = p_C^1 C_1 + p_F^1 F_1. \tag{4.12}$$

The cost of buying the first year's bundle in the second year is

$$Y_2 = p_C^2 C_1 + p_F^2 F_1. \tag{4.13}$$

That is, in the second year, we use the prices for the second year but the quantities from the first year.

To calculate the rate of inflation, we determine how much more income it took to buy the first year's bundle in the second year, which is the ratio of Equation 4.13 to Equation 4.12:

$$\frac{Y_2}{Y_1} = \frac{p_C^2 C_1 + p_F^2 F_1}{p_C^1 C_1 + p_F^1 F_1}.$$

For example, from July 2011 to July 2012, the U.S. CPI rose by $1.014 \approx Y_2/Y_1$ from $Y_1 = 225.9$ to $Y_2 = 229.1$. Thus, it cost on average 1.4% more in July 2012 than in July 2011 to buy the same bundle of goods.

The ratio Y_2/Y_1 reflects how much prices rise on average. By multiplying and dividing the first term in the numerator by p_C^1 and multiplying and dividing the second term by p_F^1, we find that this index is equivalent to

$$\frac{Y_2}{Y_1} = \frac{\left(\dfrac{p_C^2}{p_C^1}\right)p_C^1 C_1 + \left(\dfrac{p_F^2}{p_F^1}\right)p_F^1 F_1}{Y_1} = \left(\frac{p_C^2}{p_C^1}\right)\theta_C + \left(\frac{p_F^2}{p_F^1}\right)\theta_F,$$

where $\theta_C = p_C^1 C_1/Y_1$ and $\theta_F = p_F^1 F_1/Y_1$ are the budget shares of clothing and food in the first, or base, year. The CPI is a *weighted average* of the price increase for each good, p_C^2/p_C^1 and p_F^2/p_F^1, where the weights are each good's budget share in the base year, θ_C and θ_F.

Effects of Inflation Adjustments

A CPI adjustment of prices in a long-term contract overcompensates for inflation. We use an example involving an employment contract to illustrate the difference between using the CPI to adjust a long-term contract and using a true cost-of-living adjustment, which holds utility constant.

CPI Adjustment. Klaas signed a long-term contract when he was hired. According to the COLA clause in his contract, his employer increases his salary each year by the same percentage that the CPI increases. If the CPI this year is 5% higher than last year, Klaas' salary rises automatically by 5%.

Klaas spends all his money on clothing and food. His budget constraint in the first year is $Y_1 = p_C^1 C + p_F^1 F$, which we rewrite as

$$C = \frac{Y_1}{p_C^1} - \frac{p_F^1}{p_C^1} F.$$

The intercept of the budget constraint, L^1, on the vertical (clothing) axis in Figure 4.7 is Y_1/p_C^1, and the slope of the constraint is $-p_F^1/p_C^1$. The tangency of his indifference curve I^1 and the budget constraint L^1 determine his optimal consumption bundle in the first year, e_1, where he purchases C_1 and F_1.

Figure 4.7 CPI Adjustment

In the first year, when Klaas has an income of Y_1, his optimal bundle is e_1, where indifference curve I^1 is tangent to his budget constraint, L^1. In the second year, the price of clothing rises more than the price of food. Because his salary increases in proportion to the CPI, his second-year budget constraint, L^2, goes through e_1, so he can buy the same bundle as in the first year. His new optimal bundle, however, is e_2, where I^2 is tangent to L^2. The CPI adjustment overcompensates Klaas for the increase in prices: He is better off in the second year because his utility is greater on I^2 than on I^1. With a smaller true cost-of-living adjustment, Klaas' budget constraint, L^*, is tangent to I^1 at e^*.

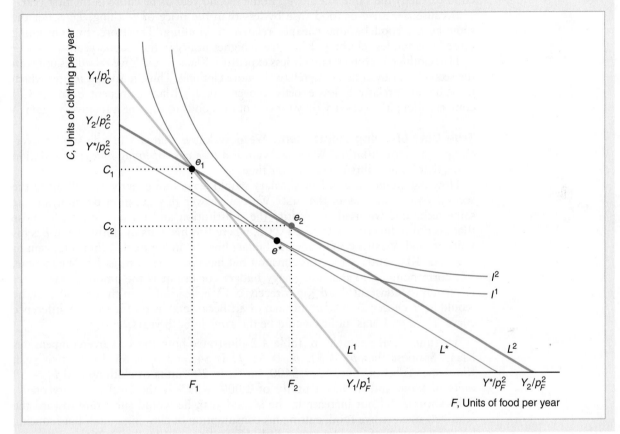

In the second year, his salary rises with the CPI to Y_2, so his budget constraint in that year, L^2, is

$$C = \frac{Y_2}{p_C^2} - \frac{p_F^2}{p_C^2}F.$$

The new constraint, L^2, has a flatter slope, $-p_F^1/p_C^2$ than L^1 because the price of clothing rose more than the price of food. The new constraint goes through the original optimal bundle, e_1, because by increasing his salary according to the CPI, the firm ensures that Klaas can buy the same bundle of goods in the second year that he bought in the first year.

He *can* buy the same bundle, but *does* he? The answer is no. His optimal bundle in the second year is e_2, where indifference curve I^2 is tangent to his new budget constraint, L^2. The movement from e_1 to e_2 is the *total effect* from the changes in the real prices of clothing and food. *This adjustment to his income does not keep him on his original indifference curve, I^1.*

Indeed, Klaas is better off in the second year than in the first. The CPI adjustment *overcompensates* him for the change in inflation in the sense that his utility increases.

Klaas is better off because the prices of clothing and food did not increase by the same amount. Suppose that the price of clothing and food had both increased by *exactly* the same amount. After a CPI adjustment, Klaas' budget constraint in the second year, L^2, would be exactly the same as in the first year, L^1, so he would choose exactly the same bundle, e_1, in the second year as he chose in the first year.

Because the price of food rose by less than the price of clothing, L^2 is not the same as L^1. Food became cheaper relative to clothing. Therefore, by consuming more food and less clothing, Klaas has a higher utility in the second year.

Had clothing become relatively less expensive, Klaas would have raised his utility in the second year by consuming relatively more clothing. Thus, it doesn't matter which good becomes relatively less expensive over time for Klaas to benefit from the CPI compensation; it's necessary only for one of the goods to become a relative bargain.

True Cost-of-Living Adjustment. We now know that a CPI adjustment over-compensates for inflation. What we want is a *true cost-of-living index*: an inflation index that holds utility constant over time.

How big an increase in Klaas' salary would leave him exactly as well off in the second year as he was in the first? We can answer this question by applying the same technique we used to identify the substitution and income effects. Suppose that his utility function is $U = 20\sqrt{CF}$, where C is his units of clothing and F is his units of food. We draw an imaginary budget line, L^* in Figure 4.7, that is tangent to I^1 so that Klaas' utility remains constant but has the same slope as L^2. The income, Y^*, corresponding to that imaginary budget constraint is the amount that leaves Klaas' utility constant. Had Klaas received Y^* instead of Y_2 in the second year, he would have chosen Bundle e^* instead of e_2. Because e^* is on the same indifference curve, I^1, as e_1, Klaas' utility would be the same in both years.

The numerical example in Table 4.2 illustrates how the CPI overcompensates Klaas. Suppose that p_C^1 is \$1, p_C^2 is \$2, p_F^1 is \$4, and p_F^2 is \$5. In the first year, Klaas spends his income, $Y_1 = \$400$, on $C_1 = 200$ units of clothing and $F_1 = 50$ units of food, and he has a utility of 2,000, which is the level of utility on I^1. If his income did not increase in the second year, he would substitute toward the relatively inexpensive food, cutting his consumption of clothing in half but reducing his consumption of food by only a fifth. His utility would fall to 1,265.

If his second-year income increases in proportion to the CPI, he can buy the same bundle, e_1, in the second year as in the first. His second-year income is

Table 4.2 Cost-of-Living Adjustments

	p_C	p_F	Income, Y	Clothing	Food	Utility, U
First year	\$1	\$4	\$400	200	50	2,000
Second year	\$2	\$5				
No adjustment			\$400	100	40	1,265
CPI adjustment			\$650	162.5	65	2,055
True COLA			\$632.50	158.1	63.2	2,000

$Y_2 = \$650(= p_C^2 C_1 + p_F^2 F_1 = \$2 \times 200 + \$5 \times 50)$. However, instead of buying the same bundle, he can substitute toward the relatively inexpensive food, buying less clothing than in the first year. This bundle is depicted by e_2. His utility then rises from 2,000 to approximately 2,055 (the level of utility on I^2). Clearly, Klaas is better off if his income increases to Y_2. In other words, the CPI adjustment overcompensates him.

How much would his income have to rise to leave him *only* as well off as he was in the first year? If his second-year income is $Y^* \approx \$632.50$, by substituting toward food and the Bundle e^* he can achieve the same level of utility, 2,000, as in the first year.

We can use the income that just compensates Klaas for the price changes, Y^*, to construct a true cost-of-living index. In our numerical example, the true cost-of-living index rose 58.1% [$\approx (632.50 - 400)/400$], while the CPI rose 62.5% [$= (650 - 400)/400$].

Size of the CPI Substitution Bias. We have just demonstrated that the CPI has an *upward bias* in the sense that an individual's utility rises if we increase the person's income by the same percentage by which the CPI rises. If we make the CPI adjustment, we are implicitly assuming—incorrectly—that consumers do not substitute toward relatively inexpensive goods when prices change, but they keep buying the same bundle of goods over time. We call this overcompensation a *substitution bias*.[15]

The CPI calculates the increase in prices as Y_2/Y_1. We can rewrite this expression as

$$\frac{Y_2}{Y_1} = \frac{Y^*}{Y_1} \frac{Y_2}{Y^*}.$$

The first term to the right of the equal sign, Y^*/Y_1, is the increase in the true cost of living. The second term, Y_2/Y^*, reflects the substitution bias in the CPI. It is greater than one because $Y_2 > Y^*$. In the example in Table 4.2, $Y_2/Y^* = 650/632.50 \approx 1.028$, so the CPI overestimates the increase in the cost of living by about 2.8%.

There is no substitution bias if all prices increase at the same rate so that relative prices remain constant. The faster some prices rise relative to others, the more pronounced the upward bias caused by the substitution that occurs toward less expensive goods.

APPLICATION

Fixing the CPI
Substitution Bias

Several studies estimate that, due to the substitution bias, the CPI inflation rate is about half a percentage point too high per year. What can be done to correct this bias? One approach is to estimate utility functions for individuals and use those data to calculate a true cost-of-living index. However, given the wide variety of tastes across individuals, as well as various technical estimation problems, this approach is not practical.

A second method is to use a *Paasche* index, which weights prices using the current quantities of goods purchased. In contrast, the CPI (which is also called a *Laspeyres* index) uses quantities from the earlier, base period. A Paasche index is likely to overstate the degree of substitution and thus to understate the change in the cost-of-living index. Hence, replacing the traditional Laspeyres index with the Paasche would merely replace an overestimate with an underestimate of the rate of inflation.

---

[15]The CPI has other biases as well. For example, Bils (2009) argues that CPI measures for consumer durables largely capture shifts to newer product models that display higher prices, rather than a price increase for a given set of goods. He estimates that as much as two-thirds of the price increase for new models is due to quality growth. Consequently, the CPI inflation for durables may have been overstated by almost two percentage points per year.

A third, compromise approach is to take an average of the Laspeyres and Paasche indexes because the true cost-of-living index lies between these two biased indexes. The most widely touted average is the *Fisher* index, which is the geometric mean of the Laspeyres and Paasche indexes (the square root of their product).[16]

Not everyone agrees that averaging the Laspeyres and Paasche indexes would be an improvement. For example, if people do not substitute, the CPI (Laspeyres) index is correct and the Fisher index, based on the geometric average, underestimates the rate of inflation.

Nonetheless, in recent years, the Bureau of Labor Statistics (BLS), which calculates the CPI, has made several adjustments to its CPI methodology, including using averaging. Starting in 1999, the BLS replaced the Laspeyres index with a Fisher approach to calculate almost all of its 200 basic indexes (such as "ice cream and related products") within the CPI. It still uses the Laspeyres approach for a few of the categories in which it does not expect much substitution, such as utilities (electricity, gas, cable television, and telephones), medical care, and housing, and it uses the Laspeyres method to combine the basic indexes to obtain the final CPI.

Now, the BLS updates the CPI weights (the market basket shares of consumption) every two years instead of only every decade or so, as the Bureau had done before 2002. More frequent updating reduces the substitution bias in a Laspeyres index because market basket shares are frozen for a shorter period. According to the BLS, had it used updated weights between 1989 and 1997, the CPI would have increased by only 31.9% rather than the reported 33.9%. The BLS believes that this change reduces the rate of increase in the CPI by approximately 0.2 percentage points per year.

Overestimating the rate of inflation has important implications for U.S. society because union agreements, Social Security, various retirement plans, welfare, and many other programs include CPI-based cost-of-living adjustments. According to one estimate, the bias in the CPI alone makes it the fourth-largest "federal program" after Social Security, health care, and defense. For example, the U.S. Postal Service (USPS) has a CPI-based COLA in its union contracts. In 2012, a typical mail carrier earned about $54,000 a year, so the estimated substitution bias of half a percent a year cost the USPS nearly $270 per employee. Because the USPS had about 546,000 employees in 2012, the total cost of this bias was about $147 million.

4.5 Revealed Preference

We have seen that we can predict a consumer's purchasing behavior if we know that person's preferences. We can also do the opposite: We can infer a consumer's preferences from observing the consumer's buying behavior. If we observe a consumer's choice at many different prices and income levels, we can derive the consumer's indifference curves using the *theory of revealed preference* (Samuelson, 1947). We can also use this theory to demonstrate the substitution effect. Economists can use this approach to estimate demand curves merely by observing the choices consumers make over time.

---

[16]If we use the Fisher index, we are implicitly assuming that there is a unitary elasticity of substitution among goods so that the share of consumer expenditures on each item remains constant as relative prices change (in contrast to the Laspeyres approach, where we assume that the quantities remain fixed).

Recovering Preferences

The basic assumption of the theory of revealed preference is that a consumer chooses bundles to maximize utility subject to a budget constraint: The consumer chooses the best bundle that the consumer can afford. We also assume that the consumer's indifference curve is convex to the origin so that the consumer picks a unique bundle on any budget constraint.

If such a consumer chooses a more expensive bundle of goods, *a*, over a less expensive bundle, *b*, then we say that the consumer *prefers* Bundle *a* to *b*. In panel a of Figure 4.8, when Linda's budget constraint is L^1, she chooses Bundle *a*, showing that she prefers *a* to *b*, which costs less than *a* because it lies strictly within her opportunity set.

If the consumer prefers Bundle *a* to *b* and Bundle *b* to *c*, then the consumer must prefer Bundle *a* to *c* because the consumer's preferences are transitive. In panel a, Linda chooses Bundle *a* over *b* when the budget line is L^1, and she picks Bundle *b* over *c* when the constraint is L^2; so, by transitivity, Linda prefers *a* to *c*. We say that Bundle *a* is *revealed to be preferred* to Bundle *c* if Linda chooses *a* over *c* directly, or if we learn indirectly that Linda prefers *a* to *b* and *b* to *c*.

We know that Linda prefers *a* to any other bundle in the shaded area, labeled "Worse Bundles," by a sequence of direct or indirect comparisons. Due to the more-is-better property (Chapter 3), Linda prefers bundles in the area above and to the right of *a*. Thus, the indifference curve through *a* must lie within the white area between the worse and better bundles.

If we learn that Linda chooses *d* when faced with budget line L^3 and *e* given line L^4 as panel b shows, we can expand her *better bundle* area. We know that her indifference curve through *a* must lie within the white area between the better and worse

Figure 4.8 Revealed Preference

(a) Linda chooses Bundle *a* on budget constraint L^1, so she prefers it to *b*, which costs less. On L^2, she chooses *b*, so she prefers it to *c*, which costs less. Thus, due to transitivity, Linda prefers *a* to *c* or any other of the *worse bundles*. She prefers the bundles in the shaded area above

and to the right of *a* according to the more-is-better property. (b) With more budget lines and choices, we learn more about the *better bundles*. Linda's indifference curve through *a* must lie in the white area between the worse and better bundles.

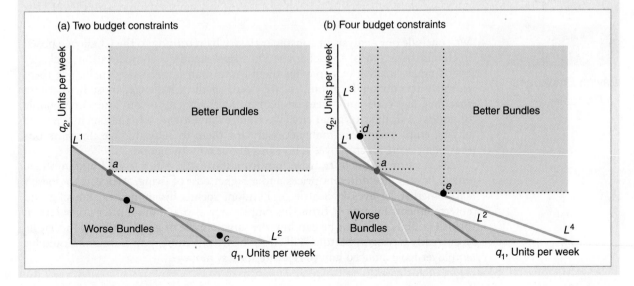

bundle areas. Thus, if we observe a large number of choices, we can determine the shape of her indifference curves, which summarizes her preferences.

Substitution Effect

One of the clearest and most important results from consumer theory is that the substitution effect is negative: The Law of Demand holds for compensated demand curves. This result stems from utility maximization, given that indifference curves are convex to the origin. The theory of revealed preference provides an alternative justification without appealing to unobservable indifference curves or utility functions.

Suppose that Steven is indifferent between Bundle a, which consists of M_a music tracks and C_a candy bars, and Bundle b, with M_b tracks and C_b candy bars. That is, the bundles are on the same indifference curve.

The price of candy bars, C, remains fixed at p_C, but the price of songs changes. We observe that when the price for M is p_M^a, Steven chooses Bundle a—that is, a is revealed to be preferred to b. Similarly, when the price is p_M^b, he chooses b over a.

Because Steven is indifferent between the two bundles, the cost of the chosen bundle must be less than or equal to that of the other bundle. Thus, if he chooses a when the price is p_M^a, then $p_M^a M_a + p_C C_a \leq p_M^a M_b + p_C C_b$, or

$$p_M^a(M_a - M_b) + p_C(C_a - C_b) \leq 0. \qquad (4.14)$$

And, if he chooses b when the price is p_M^b, then $p_M^b M_b + p_C C_b \leq p_M^b M_a + p_C C_a$, or

$$p_M^b(M_b - M_a) + p_C(C_b - C_a) \leq 0. \qquad (4.15)$$

Adding Equations 4.14 and 4.15, we learn that

$$(p_M^a - p_M^b)(M_a - M_b) \leq 0. \qquad (4.16)$$

Equation 4.16 shows that the product of the difference in prices times the difference in quantities of music purchased is nonpositive. That result can be true only if the price and the quantity move in opposite directions: When the price rises, the quantity falls. Thus, we are able to derive the substitution effect result without using utility functions or making any assumption about the curvature of indifference curves.

CHALLENGE SOLUTION

Paying Employees to Relocate

We conclude our analysis of consumer theory by returning to the Challenge posed in the introduction of this chapter: Do firms' standard compensation packages overcompensate workers, paying them more than is necessary to induce them to move to another location? As we noted in the Challenge, most firms claim that they pay their employees enough in their new city to buy the same bundle of goods as in their original city. We want to investigate whether such firms are paying employees more than necessary for them to relocate. We illustrate our reasoning using an employee who cares about only two goods.

Alexx's firm wants to transfer him from its Seattle office to its London office, where he will face different prices and a higher cost of living. Alexx, who doesn't care whether he lives in Seattle or London, spends his money on housing and entertainment. Like most firms, his employer will pay him an after-tax salary in British pounds such that he can buy the same bundle of goods in London that he is currently buying in Seattle. Will Alexx benefit by moving to London? Could his employer have induced him to relocate for less money?

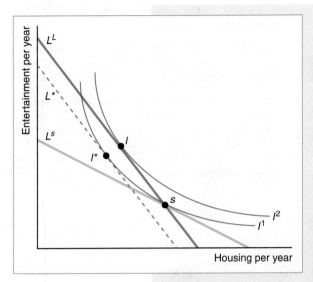

Alexx's optimal bundle, s, in Seattle is determined by the tangency of his indifference curve I^1 and his Seattle budget line L^S in the figure. In 2011, on average, it cost 53% more to live in London than in Seattle. If the prices of all goods are exactly 53% higher in London than in Seattle, the relative costs of housing and entertainment is the same in both cities. In that case, if Alexx's firm raises his income by 53%, his budget line does not change and he buys the same bundle, s, and his level of utility is unchanged.

However, relative prices are not the same in both cities. Controlling for quality, housing is relatively more expensive, and entertainment—concerts, theater, museums, zoos—is relatively less expensive in London than in Seattle. Thus, if Alexx's firm adjusts his income so that he can buy the same bundle, s, in London as he did in Seattle, his new budget line in London, L^L, must go through s but have a different slope. Because entertainment is relatively less expensive than housing in London compared to Seattle, if Alexx spends all his money on entertainment, he can buy more in London than in Seattle. Similarly, if he spends all his money on housing, he can buy less in London than in Seattle. As a result, L^L hits the vertical axis at a higher point than the L^S line and cuts the L^S line at Bundle s.

Alexx's new optimal bundle, l, is determined by the tangency of I^2 and L^L. Thus, because relative prices are different in London and Seattle, Alexx is better off with the transfer after receiving the firm's 53% higher salary. He was on I^1 and is now on I^2. Alexx could buy his original bundle, s, but chooses to substitute toward entertainment, which is relatively inexpensive in London, thereby raising his utility.

Consequently, his firm could have induced him to move for less compensation. If the firm lowers his income, the London budget line he faces will be closer to the origin but will have the same slope as L^L. The firm can lower his income until his lower-income London budget line, L^*, is tangent to his Seattle indifference curve, I^1, at Bundle l^*. Alexx still substitutes toward the relatively less expensive entertainment in London, but he is only as well off as he was in Seattle (he remains on the same indifference curve as when he lived in Seattle). Thus, his firm can induce Alexx to transfer to London for less than what the firm would have to pay so that Alexx could buy his original Seattle consumption bundle in London.

SUMMARY

1. **Deriving Demand Curves.** We can derive an individual demand curve using the information about the consumer's tastes, which are summarized in an indifference or preference map. Varying the price of one good, holding other prices and income constant, we find how the quantity demanded of a good varies with its price, which is the information we need to draw the demand curve. Consumers' tastes, which are captured by the indifference curves, determine the shape of the demand curve.

2. **Effects of an Increase in Income.** A consumer's demand curve shifts as the consumer's income rises. By varying income while holding prices constant, we determine how quantity demanded shifts with income, which is the information we need to show how the consumer's demand curve shifts. An Engel curve summarizes the relationship between income and quantity demanded, holding prices constant.

3. **Effects of a Price Increase.** An increase in the price of a good causes both a substitution effect and an income effect. The substitution effect is the amount by which a consumer's demand for a good falls because of a price increase if we compensate the consumer with enough extra income so that the consumer's

utility does not change. The direction of the substitution effect is unambiguous: A compensated rise in a good's price always causes consumers to buy less of the good. Without compensation, an increase in price rise reduces the consumer's opportunity set: The consumer can now buy less than before with the same income, which harms the consumer. Suppose instead that the prices are held constant, but the consumer's income is reduced by an amount that harms the consumer by as much as the price increase. The income effect is the change in the quantity demanded due to such an income adjustment. The income effect is negative if a good is normal (the income elasticity

is positive), and positive if the good is inferior (the income elasticity is negative).

4. **Cost-of-Living Adjustment.** The government's major index of inflation, the Consumer Price Index (CPI), overestimates inflation by ignoring the substitution effect.

5. **Revealed Preference.** If we observe a consumer's choice at various prices and income levels, we can infer the consumer's preferences: the shape of the consumer's indifference curves. We can also use the theory of revealed preference to show that a consumer substitutes away from a good as its price rises.

EXERCISES

■ = *exercise is available on* MyEconLab; * = *answer appears at the back of this book;* **M** = *mathematical problem.*

1. Deriving Demand Curves

1.1 Manufactured diamonds have become as big and virtually indistinguishable from the best natural diamonds (Dan Mitchell, "Fake Gems, Genuine Appeal," *New York Times*, June 21, 2008). Suppose consumers change from believing that manufactured diamonds, q_1, were imperfect substitutes for natural diamonds, q_2, to perfect substitutes, so that their utility function becomes $U(q_1, q_2) = q_1 + q_2$. What effect will that have on the demand for manufactured diamonds? Derive the new demand curve for manufactured diamonds and draw it. **M**

1.2 How would your answer to Exercise 1.1 change if $U = \ln(q_1 + q_2)$ so that consumers have diminishing marginal utility of diamonds? **M**

1.3 Derive Ryan's demand curve for q_1, given his CES utility function is $U = q_1^\rho + q_2^\rho$. **M**

1.4 David consumes two things: gasoline (G) and bread (B). David's utility function is $U(q_1, q_2) = 10q_1^{0.25}q_2^{0.75}$.

a. Derive David's demand curve for gasoline.

b. If the price of gasoline rises, how much does David reduce his consumption of gasoline, $\partial q_1/\partial p_1$?

c. For David, how does $\partial q_1/\partial p_1$ depend on his income? That is, how does David's change in gasoline consumption due to an increase in the price of gasoline depend on his income level? To answer these questions, find the cross-partial derivative, $\partial^2 q_1/(\partial p_1 \partial Y)$. **M**

1.5 If Philip's utility function is $U = 2q_1^{0.5} + q_2$, what are his demand functions for the two goods? **M**

1.6 Draw a figure to illustrate the Application "Quitting Smoking." That is, show why as the price of cell phones drops, less tobacco is consumed. (*Hint*: Draw a figure like panel a of Figure 4.2 with cell phones on the horizontal axis and tobacco on the vertical axis. However, unlike in Figure 4.2, the price-consumption curve should slope downward.)

*1.7 In 2005, a typical U.S. owner of a home theater (a television and a DVD player) bought 12 music CDs (q_1) per year and 6 Top-20 movie DVDs (q_2) per year. The average price of a CD was about $p_1 = \$15$, the average price of a DVD was roughly $p_2 = \$20$, and the typical consumer spent \$300 on these entertainment goods.[17] Based on these data, we estimate a typical consumer's Cobb-Douglas utility function is $U = q_1^{0.6}q_2^{0.4}$. Redraw Figure 4.2 based on this utility function. Explain the shape of the price-consumption curve. **M**

2. Effects of an Increase in Income

2.1 Have your folks given you cash or promised to leave you money after they're gone? If so, they may think of such gifts as a good. They decide whether to spend their money on fun, food, drink, cars, or give money to you. Hmmm. Altonji and Villanueva (2007) estimated that, for every extra dollar of expected lifetime resources, parents give their adult offspring between 2¢ and 3¢ in bequests and about 3¢ in transfers.

---

[17]We estimated the Cobb-Douglas utility function using budget share information and obtained prices and quantities from **www.leesmovieinfo.net**, the *New York Times*, and **ce.org**.

Those gifts are about one-fifth of what they give their children under 18 and spend on their college education. Illustrate how an increase in your parents' income affects their allocations between bequests to you and all other goods ("fun") in two related graphs, where one shows an income-consumption curve and the other shows an Engel curve for bequests.

*2.2 Guerdon always puts half a sliced banana, q_1, on his bowl of cereal, q_2—the two goods are perfect complements. What is his utility function? Derive his demand curve for bananas graphically and mathematically. (*Hint*: See Solved Problem 4.1.) **M**

2.3 According to the U.S. Consumer Expenditure Survey for 2008, Americans with incomes below $20,000 spend about 39% of their income on housing. What are the limits on their income elasticities of housing if all other goods are collectively normal? Given that they spend about 0.2% on books and other reading material, what are the limits on their income elasticities for reading matter if all other goods are collectively normal? (*Hint*: See Solved Problem 4.2.) **M**

*2.4 Given the estimated Cobb-Douglas utility function in Exercise 1.7, $U = q_1^{0.6} q_2^{0.4}$, for CDs, q_1, and DVDs, q_2, derive a typical consumer's Engel curve for movie DVDs. Illustrate in a figure. **M**

2.5 Derive the income elasticity of demand for individuals with (a) Cobb-Douglas, (b) perfect substitutes, and (c) perfect complements utility functions. **M**

2.6 Ryan has a constant elasticity of substitution utility function $U = q_1^\rho + q_2^\rho$. Derive his Engel curve. **M**

2.7 Sally's utility function is $U(q_1, q_2) = 4q_1^{0.5} + q_2$. Derive her Engel curve. **M**

3. Effects of a Price Increase

3.1 Under what conditions does the income effect reinforce the substitution effect? Under what conditions does it have an offsetting effect? If the income effect more than offsets the substitution effect for a good, what do we call that good? In a figure, illustrate that the income effect can more than offset the substitution effect (a Giffen good).

*3.2 Don spends his money on food and operas. Food is an inferior good for Don. Does he view an opera performance as an inferior or a normal good? Why? In a diagram, show a possible income-consumption curve for Don.

3.3 Pat eats eggs and toast for breakfast and insists on having three pieces of toast for every two eggs he eats. Derive his utility function. If the price of eggs increases but we compensate Pat to make him just as "happy" as he was before the price change, what

happens to his consumption of eggs? Draw a graph and explain your diagram. Does the change in his consumption reflect a substitution or an income effect?

3.4 Are relatively more high-quality navel oranges sold in California or in New York? Why? (*Hint*: See Solved Problem 4.3.)

*3.5 Draw a figure to illustrate the answer given in Solved Problem 4.3. Use math and a figure to show whether applying an ad valorem tax rather than a specific tax changes the analysis.

3.6 Lucy views Bayer aspirin and Tylenol as perfect substitutes. Initially the aspirin is cheaper. However, a price increase makes aspirin more expensive than Tylenol. Show the substitution, income, and total effect of this price change in a diagram.

*3.7 Philip's quasilinear utility function is $U = 4q_1^{0.5} + q_2$. His budget for these goods is $Y = 10$. Originally, the prices are $p_1 = p_2 = 1$. However, the price of the first good rises to $p_1 = 2$. Discuss the substitution, income, and total effect on the demand for q_1. **M**

3.8 Remy views ice cream and fudge sauce as perfect complements. Is it possible that either of these goods or both of them are Giffen goods? (*Hint*: See Solved Problem 4.4.)

*3.9 Sylvia's utility function is $U(q_1, q_2) = \min(q_1, jq_2)$. Derive her compensated (Hicksian) demand and expenditure functions. **M**

3.10 Bill's utility function is $U = 0.5 \ln q_1 + 0.5 \ln q_2$. What is his compensated demand function for q_1? (*Hint*: See Solved Problem 4.5.) **M**

3.11 Sylvan's utility function is $U(q_1, q_2) = q_1 + 2q_2$. Derive his compensated (Hicksian) demand and expenditure functions. **M**

4. Cost-of-Living Adjustment

*4.1 Alix consumes only coffee and coffee cake and only consumes them together (they are perfect complements). If we calculate a CPI using only these two goods, by how much will this CPI differ from the true cost-of-living index?

4.2 Jean views coffee and cream as perfect complements. In the first year, Jean picks an optimal bundle of coffee and cream, e_1. In the second year, inflation occurs, the prices of coffee and cream change by different amounts, and Jean receives a cost-of-living adjustment (COLA) based on the consumer price index (CPI) for these two goods. After the price changes and she receives the COLA, her new optimal bundle is e_2. Show the two equilibria in a figure. Is she better off, worse off, or equally well off at e_2 compared to e_1? Explain.

4.3 Ann's only income is her annual college scholarship, which she spends exclusively on gallons of ice cream and books. Last year, when ice cream cost $10 and used books cost $20, Ann spent her $250 scholarship on 5 gallons of ice cream and 10 books. This year, the price of ice cream rose to $15 and the price of books increased to $25. So that Ann can afford the same bundle of ice cream and books that she bought last year, her college raised her scholarship to $325. Ann has the usual-shaped indifference curves. Will Ann change the amount of ice cream and books that she buys this year? If so, explain how and why. Will Ann be better off, as well off, or worse off this year than last year? Why?

4.4 The *Economist* magazine publishes the Big Mac Index, which is based on the price of a Big Mac at McDonald's in various countries over time. Under what circumstances would people find this index to be as useful as or more useful than the consumer price index in measuring how their true cost of living changes over time?

4.5 During his first year at school, Guojun buys eight new college textbooks at a cost of $50 each. Used books cost $30 each. When the bookstore announces a 20% price increase in new texts and a 10% increase in used texts for the next year, Guojun's father offers him $80 extra. Is Guojun better off, the same, or worse off after the price change? Why?

4.6 Use a graph to illustrate that the Paasche cost-of-living index (see the Application "Fixing the CPI Substitution Bias") underestimates the rate of inflation when compared to the true cost-of-living index.

4.7 Cynthia buys gasoline and other goods. The government considers imposing a lump-sum tax, $+$ dollars per person, or a specific tax on gasoline of τ dollars per gallon. If $+$ and τ are such that either tax will raise the same amount of tax revenue from Cynthia, which tax does she prefer and why? Show your answer using a graph or calculus. **M**

5. Revealed Preferences

5.1 Remy spends her weekly income of $30 on chocolate, q_1, and shampoo, q_2. Initially, when the prices

are $p_1 = \$2 = p_2$, she buys $q_1 = 10$ and $q_2 = 5$. After the prices change to $p_1 = \$1$ and $p_2 = \$3$, she purchases $q_1 = 6$ and $q_2 = 8$. Draw her budget lines and choices in a diagram. Use a revealed preference argument to discuss whether or not she is maximizing her utility before and after the price changes.

5.2 Analyze the problem in Exercise 5.1 making use of Equation 4.16. **M**

5.3 Felix chooses between clothing, q_1, and food, q_2. His initial income is $1,000 a month, $p_1 = 100$, and $p_2 = 10$. At his initial bundle, he consumes $q_1 = 2$ and $q_2 = 80$. Later, his income rises to $1,200 and the price of clothing rises to $p_1 = 150$, but the price of food does not change. As a result, he reduces his consumption of clothing to one unit. Using a revealed preference reasoning (that is, knowing nothing about his indifference curves), can you determine how he ranks the two bundles?

6. Challenge

6.1 In the Challenge Solution, suppose that housing was relatively less expensive and entertainment was relatively more expensive in London than in Seattle, so that the L^L budget line cuts the L^S budget line from below rather than from above as in the Challenge Solution's figure. Show that the conclusion that Alexx is better off after his move still holds. Explain the logic behind the following statement: "The analysis holds as long as the relative prices differ in the two cities. Whether one price or the other is relatively higher in London than in Seattle is irrelevant to the analysis."

6.2 Jim's utility function is $U(q_1, q_2) = \min(q_1, q_2)$. The price of each good is $1, and his monthly income is $4,000. His firm wants him to relocate to another city where the price of q_2 is $2, but the price of q_1 and his income remain constant. Obviously, Jim would be worse off due to the move. What would be his equivalent variation or compensating variation? **M**

6.3 Jane's utility function is $U(q_1, q_2) = q_1 + q_2$. The price of each good is $1, and her monthly income is $4,000. Her firm wants her to relocate to another city where the price of q_2 is $2, but the price of q_1 and her income remain constant. What would be her equivalent variation or compensating variation? **M**

Consumer Welfare and Policy Analysis

5

The welfare of the people is the ultimate law. —Cicero

Child-care subsidies are common throughout the world. The United States and the United Kingdom spend 0.6% of GDP on child care, compared to 0.2% in Canada and Ireland, 0.3% in Japan, 0.4% in Australia and New Zealand, 1% in Norway, 1.2% in France and Sweden, and 1.6% in Denmark (Currie and Gahvari, 2008).

The increased employment of mothers outside the home has led to a steep rise in child care over the past several decades. In the United States today, nearly seven out of ten mothers work outside the home—more than twice the rate in 1970. Eight out of ten employed mothers with children under age six are likely to have some form of non-parental child-care arrangement. Six out of ten children under the age of six are in child care, as are 45% of children under age one.

Child care is a major burden for the poor, and the expense may prevent poor mothers from working. Paying for child care for children under the age of five absorbed 25% of the earnings for families with annual incomes under $14,400, but only 6% for families with incomes of $54,000 or more. Government child-care subsidies increase the probability that a single mother will work at a standard job by 7% (Tekin, 2007). As one would expect, the subsidies have larger impacts on welfare recipients than on wealthier mothers.

In large part to help poor families obtain child care so that the parents can work, the U.S. Child Care and Development Fund (CCDF) provided $5.2 billion to states in 2012. Child-care programs vary substantially across states in their generosity and in the form of the subsidy.[1] Most states provide an ad valorem or a specific subsidy (see Chapter 2) to lower the hourly rate that a poor family pays for child care.

Rather than subsidizing the price of child care, the government could provide an unrestricted lump-sum payment that could be spent on child care or on all other goods, such as food and housing. Canada provides such lump-sum payments.

For a given government expenditure, does a price subsidy or a lump-sum subsidy provide greater benefit to recipients? Which option increases the demand for child-care services by more? Which one inflicts less cost on other consumers of child care?

---

[1]For example, in 2009, for a family with two children to be eligible for a subsidy the family's maximum income was $4,515 in California and $2,863 in Louisiana. The maximum subsidy for a toddler was $254 per week in California and $92.50 per week in Louisiana. The family's fee for child care ranged between 20% and 60% of the cost of care in Louisiana, between 2% and 10% in Maine, and between $0 and $495 per month in Minnesota.

To answer these types of questions, first we will use consumer theory to develop various measures of consumer welfare. Then we will examine how several types of government policies affect consumer well-being. Finally, we will use consumer theory to study individuals' labor supply and analyze the impact of income taxes.

In this chapter, we examine five main topics

1. **Consumer Welfare.** The degree to which a consumer is helped or harmed by a change in the equilibrium price can be measured by using information from a consumer's demand curve or utility function.

2. **Expenditure Function and Consumer Welfare.** We can use the expenditure function to calculate how much more money we would have to give a consumer to offset the harm from a price increase.

3. **Market Consumer Surplus.** The market consumer surplus—the sum of the welfare effect across all consumers—can be measured using the market demand curve.

4. **Effects of Government Policies on Consumer Welfare.** We use our consumer welfare measures to determine the degree to which consumers are helped or harmed by quotas, food stamps, and child-care subsidies.

5. **Deriving Labor Supply Curves.** We derive a worker's labor supply curve using the individual's demand curve for leisure. We use the labor supply curve to determine how a reduction in the income tax rate affects consumer welfare, the supply of labor, and tax revenues.

5.1 Consumer Welfare

Economists and policymakers want to know how much consumers are helped or harmed by shocks that affect the equilibrium price and quantity of goods and services. Prices change when new inventions reduce costs or when a government imposes a tax or subsidy. Quantities change when a government sets a quota. To determine how these changes affect consumers, we need a measure of consumers' welfare.

If we knew a consumer's utility function, we could directly answer the question of how government actions, natural disasters, and other events affect consumers' welfare. If the price of beef increases, the budget line of someone who eats beef rotates inward, so the consumer is on a lower indifference curve at the new equilibrium. If we knew the levels of utility associated with the original indifference curve and the new indifference curve, we could measure the impact of the tax in terms of the change in the consumer's utility level.

However, this approach is not practical for a couple of reasons. First, we rarely know individuals' utility functions. Second, even if we had utility measures for various consumers, we would have no obvious way to compare the measures. One person might say that he gets 1,000 utils (units of utility) of pleasure from the same bundle that another consumer says gives her 872 utils. The first person is not necessarily happier—he may just be using a different scale.

As a result, we *measure consumer welfare in terms of dollars.* Instead of asking the question "How many utils would you lose if your daily commute increased by 15 minutes?" we could ask, "How much would you pay to avoid having your daily commute grow a quarter of an hour longer?" or "How much would it cost you in forgone earnings if your daily commute were 15 minutes longer?" It is more practical to compare dollars rather than utils across people.

Consumer welfare from a good is the benefit a consumer gets from consuming that good in excess of its cost. How much pleasure do you get from a good above and beyond its price? If you buy a good for exactly what it's worth to you, you are indifferent between making that transaction and not making it. Frequently, however, you buy things that are worth more to you than what they cost. Imagine that you've played tennis in the hot sun and are very thirsty. You can buy a soft drink from a vending machine for 75¢, but you'd be willing to pay much more because you are so thirsty. As a result, you're much better off making this purchase than not.

In this section, we first examine *consumer surplus*, which is the most widely used measure of consumer welfare. Consumer surplus is relatively easy to calculate using the uncompensated demand function and approximates the true value of a consumer's welfare. We then discuss approaches that provide exact values using compensated demand functions and examine how close consumer surplus comes to the exact values.

Willingness to Pay

If we can measure how much more you'd be willing to pay than you actually paid for a product, we'd know how much you gained from the transaction. Luckily, the demand curve contains the information we need to make this measurement. For convenience in most of the following discussion, we use the equivalent *inverse demand function*, which rearranges the demand function, $Q = D(p)$, so as to express a product's price as a function of the quantity of it demanded, $p = p(Q)$. For example, if the demand function is $Q = a - bp$, then the inverse demand function is $p = a/b - Q/b$.

To develop a welfare measure based on the inverse demand curve, we need to know what information is contained in an inverse demand curve. The inverse demand curve reflects a consumer's *marginal willingness to pay*: the maximum amount a consumer will spend for an extra unit. The consumer's marginal willingness to pay for a product is the *marginal value* the consumer places buying one more unit.

David's inverse demand curve for magazines per week in panel a of Figure 5.1 indicates his marginal willingness to pay for various numbers of magazines. David places a marginal value of $5 on the first magazine. As a result, if the price of a magazine is $5, David buys one magazine, point *a* on the demand curve. His marginal willingness to buy a second magazine is $4, so if the price falls to $4, he buys two magazines, *b*. His marginal willingness to buy three magazines is $3, so if the price of magazines is $3, he buys three magazines, *c*.

Consumer Surplus. The monetary difference between the maximum amount that a consumer is willing to pay for the quantity of the good purchased and what the good actually costs is called **consumer surplus** (CS). Consumer surplus is a dollar-value measure of the extra pleasure the consumer receives from the transaction beyond its price.

Measuring Consumer Surplus. David's consumer surplus from each additional magazine is his marginal willingness to pay minus what he pays to obtain the magazine. His marginal willingness to pay for the first magazine, $5, is area $CS_1 + E_1$. If the price is $3, his expenditure to obtain the magazine is area $E_1 = \$3$. Thus, his consumer surplus on the first magazine is area $CS_1 = (CS_1 + E_1) - E_1 = \$5 - \$3 = \$2$. Because his marginal willingness to pay for the second magazine is $4, his consumer surplus for the second magazine is the smaller area, $CS_2 = \$1$. His marginal

Figure 5.1 Consumer Surplus

(a) David's inverse demand curve for magazines has a step-like shape. When the price is $3, he buys three magazines, point *c*. David's marginal value for the first magazine is $5, areas $CS_1 + E_1$, and his expenditure is $3, area E_1, so his consumer surplus is $CS_1 = \$2$. His consumer surplus is $1 for the second magazine, area CS_2, and is $0 for the third (he is indifferent between buying and not buying it).

Thus, his total consumer surplus is the blue shaded area $CS_1 + CS_2 + CS_3 = \$3$, and his total expenditure is the tan shaded area $E_1 + E_2 + E_3 = \$9$. (b) Steven's willingness to pay for trading cards is the height of his smooth inverse demand curve. At price p_1, Steven's expenditure is $E(= p_1q_1)$, his consumer surplus is CS, and the total value he places on consuming q_1 trading cards per year is $CS + E$.

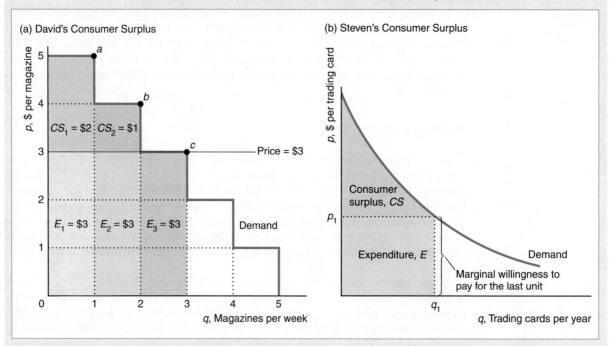

willingness to pay for the third magazine is $3, which equals what he must pay to obtain it, so his consumer surplus is zero, $CS_3 = \$0$. He is indifferent between buying and not buying the third magazine.

At a price of $3, David buys three magazines. His total consumer surplus from the three magazines he buys is the sum of the consumer surplus he gets from each of these magazines: $CS_1 + CS_2 + CS_3 = \$2 + \$1 + \$0 = \$3$. This total consumer surplus of $3 is the extra amount that David is willing to spend for the right to buy three magazines at $3 each. David is unwilling to buy a fourth magazine unless the price drops to $2 or less. If David's mother gives him a fourth magazine as a gift, the marginal value that David puts on that fourth magazine, $2, is less than what it cost his mother, $3.

Thus, an individual's consumer surplus is

- the extra value that a consumer gets from buying the desired number of units of a good in excess of the amount paid,
- the amount that a consumer would be willing to pay for the right to buy as many units as desired at the specified price, and
- the area under the consumer's inverse demand curve and above the market price up to the quantity of the product the consumer buys.

We can determine the consumer surplus associated with smooth inverse demand curves in the same way as we did with David's unusual stair-like inverse demand curve. Steven has a smooth inverse demand curve for baseball trading cards, panel b of Figure 5.1. The height of this inverse demand curve measures his willingness to pay for one more card. This willingness varies with the number of cards he buys in a year. The total value he places on obtaining q_1 cards per year is the area under the inverse demand curve up to q_1, the areas CS and E. Area E is his actual expenditure on q_1 cards. Because the price is p_1, his expenditure is $p_1 q_1$. Steven's consumer surplus from consuming q_1 trading cards is the value of consuming those cards, areas CS and E, minus his actual expenditures E to obtain them, or CS. Thus, his consumer surplus, CS, is the area under the inverse demand curve and above the horizontal line at the price p_1 up to the quantity he buys, q_1.

Just as we measure the consumer surplus for an individual by using that individual's inverse demand curve, we measure the consumer surplus of all consumers in a market by using the market inverse demand curve. *Market consumer surplus is the area under the market inverse demand curve above the market price up to the quantity consumers buy.*

To summarize, individual and market consumer surplus are practical and convenient measures of consumer welfare. Using consumer surplus has two advantages over using utility to discuss the welfare of consumers. First, the dollar-denominated consumer surplus of several individuals can be easily compared or combined, whereas the utility of various individuals cannot be easily compared or combined. Second, it is relatively easy to measure consumer surplus, whereas it is difficult to get a meaningful measure of utility directly. To calculate consumer surplus, all we have to do is measure the area under an inverse demand curve.

APPLICATION

Willingness to Pay and Consumer Surplus on eBay

People differ in their willingness to pay for a given item. We can determine willingness to pay of individuals for a 238 AD Roman coin—a sesterce (originally equivalent in value to four asses) of the image of Emperor Balbinus—by how much they bid in an eBay auction. On its Web site, eBay correctly argues (as we show in Chapter 13) that an individual's best strategy is to bid his or her *willingness to pay*: the maximum value that the bidder places on the item. From what eBay reports, we know the maximum bid of each person except the winner, who paid the second-highest amount bid plus an increment.[2]

In the figure, the bids for the coin are arranged from highest to lowest. Because each bar on the graph indicates the bid for one coin, the figure shows how many units could have been sold to this group of bidders at various prices. That is, it is the market inverse demand curve.

Bapna et al. (2008) set up a Web site, **www.Cniper.com** (no longer active), that automatically bid on eBay at the last moment (a process called sniping). To use the site, an individual had to specify a maximum willingness to pay, so that the authors knew the top bidder's willingness to pay. Bapna et al. found that the median consumer surplus was \$4 on goods that cost \$14 on average. They estimated the CS and the expenditures, E, for all eBay buyers and calculated that $CS/E = 30\%$. That is, bidders' consumer surplus gain is 30% of their expenditures.

---

[2]The increment depends on the size of the bid. It is \$1 for the bids between \$25 and \$100 and \$25 for bids between \$1,000 and \$2,499.99.

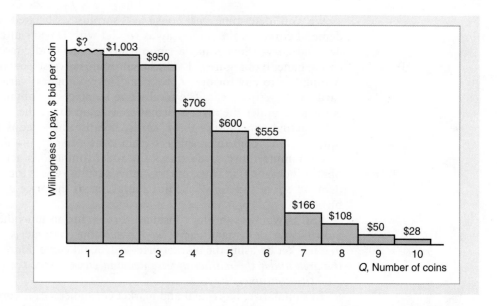

Effect of a Price Change on Consumer Surplus. If the price of a good rises, purchasers of that good lose consumer surplus. To illustrate this loss, we return to Jackie's estimated Cobb-Douglas utility, $U = q_1^{0.4}q_1^{0.6}$, between music tracks, q_1, and live music, q_2 (Chapters 3 and 4). In Chapter 3, we showed that her uncompensated demand curve for tracks is $q_1 = 0.4Y/p_1 = 12/p_1$ given that her music budget per quarter is $Y = £30$. At the initial price of tracks $p_1 = £0.5$, she bought $q_1 = 12/0.5 = 24$ song tracks.

Suppose that a government tax or an iTunes price increase causes the price of tracks to double to £1. Jackie now buys $q_1 = 12/1 = 12$ tracks. As Figure 5.2

Figure 5.2 A Change in Consumer Surplus

As the price increases from £0.5 to £1, Jackie loses consumer surplus equal to areas $A + B$.

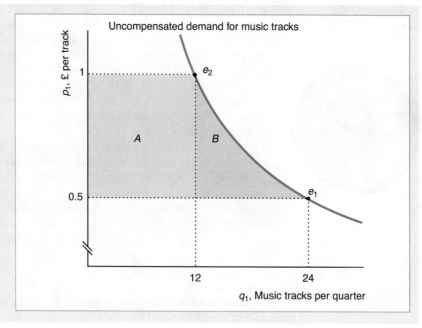

illustrates, she loses the amount of consumer surplus (ΔCS) equal to area $A + B$: the area between £0.5 and £1 on the price axis to the left of her uncompensated demand curve. Due to the price increase, she now buys 12 tracks for which she pays £0.5(= £1 − £0.5) more than originally, so area $A = £6 = £0.5 \times 12$. In addition, she loses surplus from no longer consuming 12(= 24 − 12) of the original 24 tracks, area B.[3]

SOLVED PROBLEM 5.1

What is the exact change in Jackie's consumer surplus, $A + B$, in Figure 5.2? How large is area B?

Answer

1. *State Jackie's uncompensated demand function of music tracks given her initial budget.* From Chapters 3 and 4, we know that her demand function for tracks is $q_1 = 12/p_1$.

2. *Integrate between £0.5 and £1 to the left of Jackie's uncompensated demand curve for tracks.* Her lost consumer surplus is

$$\Delta CS = -\int_{0.5}^{1} \frac{12}{p_1} dp_1 = -12 \ln p_1 \Big|_{0.5}^{1}$$

$$= -12 (\ln 1 - \ln 0.5) \approx -12 \times 0.69 \approx -8.28,$$

where we put a minus sign in front of the integrated area because the price increased, causing a loss of consumer surplus.

3. *Determine the size of area B residually.* Because areas $A + B = $ £8.28 and $A = £6 (= [£1 − £0.5] \times 12)$, area B is £2.28 (= £8.28 − £6).

Comment: A 100% increase in price causes Jackie's consumer surplus to fall by £8.28, which is 69% of the £12 she spends on tracks.

5.2 Expenditure Function and Consumer Welfare

Our desired consumer surplus measure is the income that we would need to give a consumer to offset the harm of an increase in price. That is, it is the extra income we would have to provide so that the consumer's utility would not change. Equivalently, this measure is the dollar value of the change in utility in the absence of compensation.

We have measured the effect of a price increase by a change in consumer surplus using an uncompensated demand curve, which provides an inexact measure of consumer welfare. It is an inexact measure because an uncompensated demand curve does not hold a consumer's utility constant as the price changes. Along an

---

[3]If we replace the curved demand curve with a straight line, we slightly overestimate area B as the area of a triangle: $\frac{1}{2} \times £0.5 \times 12 = £3$. We calculate the exact amount in Solved Problem 5.1.

uncompensated demand curve, as the price rises, the change in the quantity that the consumer buys reflects both a substitution and an income effect (Chapter 4). Economists frequently use the uncompensated demand curve to calculate consumer surplus because they usually have estimates of only the uncompensated demand curve.

However, if economists have an estimated compensated demand curve, they can calculate the pure income effect measure. Indeed, a compensated demand curve is constructed to answer the question of how much less of a product a consumer would purchase in response to a price increase if the consumer is given extra income to offset the price increase so as to hold the consumer's utility constant. That is, along a compensated demand curve, as the price rises, the change in the quantity demanded by the consumer reflects a pure substitution effect. The corresponding amount of income compensation is the measure we seek.

Luckily, we already have a means to calculate the relevant income compensation: the expenditure function (Equation 3.32), which is the minimal expenditure necessary to achieve a specific utility level, $\overline{U}$, for a given set of prices,

$$E = E(p_1, p_2, \overline{U}). \tag{5.1}$$

The expenditure function contains the same information as the compensated demand curve.

In Chapter 4, we showed that the compensated demand function for q_1 is the partial derivative of the expenditure function with respect to p_1: The compensated demand function is $\partial E(p_1, p_2, \overline{U})/\partial p_1$. Thus, if we integrate with respect to price to the left of the compensated demand function, we get the expenditure function.

We can calculate the consumer welfare loss of a price increase from p_1 to p_1^* as the difference between the expenditures at these two prices:

$$\text{welfare change} = E(p_1, p_2, \overline{U}) - E(p_1^*, p_2, \overline{U}). \tag{5.2}$$

In Equation 5.2, an increase in the price causes a drop in welfare.

However, to use this approach, we must decide which level of utility, $\overline{U}$, to use. We could use the level of utility corresponding to the original indifference curve or the level on the indifference curve of the optimal bundle after the price change. We call the first of these measures the *compensating variation* and the second one the *equivalent variation*.

The **compensating variation** (*CV*) is the amount of money one would have to give a consumer to offset completely the harm from a price increase—to keep the consumer on the original indifference curve. This measure of the welfare harm of a price increase is called the compensating variation because we give money to the consumer; that is, we compensate the consumer.

The **equivalent variation** (*EV*) is the amount of money one would have to take from a consumer to harm the consumer by as much as the price increase. This measure is the same, or equivalent, harm as that due to the price increase: It moves the consumer to the new, lower indifference curve.

Indifference Curve Analysis

We can use indifference curves to determine *CV* and *EV* effects of an increase in price. Again, we use the example based on Jackie's estimated utility function, in which she chooses between music tracks and live music. Initially, Jackie pays $p_1 = £0.5$ for each music track and $p_2 = £1$ for each unit of live music. In Figure 5.3, her original budget constraint is L^a and has a slope of $-p_1/p_2 = -p_1 = -0.5$. The budget

Figure 5.3 Compensating Variation and Equivalent Variation

At the initial price, Jackie's budget constraint, L^a, is tangent to her initial indifference curve I at a, where she buys 24 tracks. After the price of tracks doubles, her new budget constraint, L^b, is tangent to her indifference curve I^* at b, where she buys 12 tracks. Because the price of a unit of live music is £1, L^b hits the vertical axis at Y. If Jackie were given CV extra income to offset the price increase, her budget line would be L^{CV} (which is parallel to L^b), and she would be tangent to her original indifference curve, I, at point c. The budget line L^{CV} hits the vertical axis at $Y + CV$, so the difference between where this budget line and the L^b line strike the vertical axis equals CV. Similarly, at the original price, if we removed income equal to EV, her budget line would shift down to L^{EV}, and Jackie would choose bundle d on I^*. Thus, taking EV away harms her as much as the price increase. The gap between where L^b and L^{EV} touch the vertical axis equals EV.

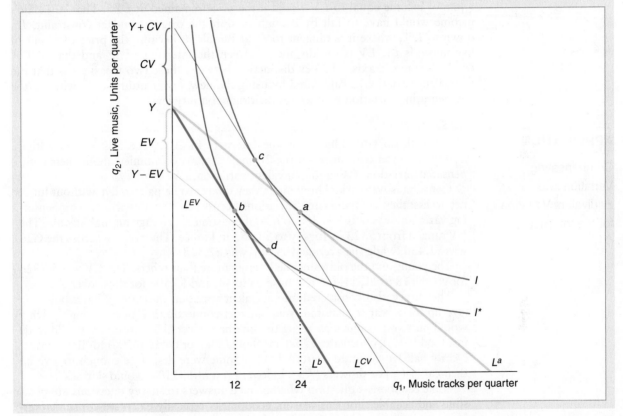

constraint is tangent to indifference curve I at her optimal bundle, a, where she buys 24 tracks.

Now, the price of tracks doubles to $p_1^* = £1$, so that Jackie's budget line rotates to L^b and has a slope of -1. The new budget line is tangent to indifference curve I^* at her new optimal bundle, b, where she buys 12 tracks. Jackie is harmed by the price increase: She is on a lower indifference curve I^* (utility level $\overline{U}^*$) instead of on I (utility level $\overline{U}$).

Compensating Variation. The amount of money that would fully compensate Jackie for a price increase is the compensating variation, CV. Suppose that after the price of tracks increases to £1, Jackie is given enough extra income, CV, so that her utility remains at $\overline{U}$. At this new income, $Y + CV$, Jackie's budget line is L^{CV}, which has the same slope, -1, as L^b. After the price changes and she receives this income compensation, she buys Bundle c.

How large is CV? Because the price of a unit of live music is £1 per unit, the before-compensation budget line, L^b, hits the live music axis at $Y = £30$, and the after-compensation budget line, L^{CV}, hits at $Y + CV$. Thus, the gap between the two intercepts is CV.

This analysis is the same one we engaged in to determine the substitution and income effects of a price change in Chapter 4. The compensating variation measure is the income (CV) involved in the income effect (the movement from b to c).

Equivalent Variation. The amount of income that, if taken from Jackie, would lower her utility by the same amount as the price increase for tracks from £0.5 to £1 is the equivalent variation, EV. The increase in price harms Jackie by as much as a loss of income equal to EV would if the price remained at £0.5. That is, Jackie's income would have to fall by enough to shift the original budget constraint, L^a, down to L^{EV}, where it is tangent to I^* at Bundle d. Because the price of a unit of live music is £1, EV is the distance between the intercept of L^a and that of L^{EV} on the live music axis. The key distinction between these two measures is that the equivalent variation is calculated by using the new, lower utility level, whereas the compensating variation is based on the original utility level.

APPLICATION

Compensating Variation and Equivalent Variation for the Internet

How much do you value using the Internet? In 2012, the Boston Consulting Group surveyed consumers in the 20 major world economies about their compensated variation, CV, and equivalent variation, EV.

Consumers were asked how much they'd have to be paid to live without Internet access: their compensating variation. Across the 20 countries, the compensating variation was between 3% to 6% of consumers' average annual income. The CV ranged from $323 in Turkey to $4,453 in France. The average across the G20 was $1,430, while the average U.S. CV was $2,528.

The young and the old value the Internet more than others. The CV was $2,926 for youths 18 to 21, $1,456 for those 35 to 44, and $3,506 for those over 55.

The survey also considered an equivalent variation measure: What would you give up for a year to maintain your Internet connection? That is, giving up what would hurt you as much as losing the Internet? Most U.S. consumers would trade fast food (83%), chocolate (77%), alcohol (73%), or coffee (69%) for the Internet. Nearly half would forgo exercise (43%). Some were desperate enough to give up their car (10%) or showers (7%). Indeed over a fifth (21%) would skip sex.[4]

Some economists question whether such answers to survey questions are plausible and reliable. For this reason, economists typically calculate consumer surplus, conjectural variation, and equivalent variation by using estimated inverse demand curves, which are based on actual observed behavior.

Comparing the Three Welfare Measures

Economists usually think of the change in consumer surplus as an approximation of the compensating variation and equivalent variation measures. Which consumer welfare measure is larger depends on the sign of the product's income elasticity. If the good is a normal good (as a music track is for Jackie), $|CV| > |\Delta CS| > |EV|$. If the good is an inferior good, $|CV| < |\Delta CS| < |EV|$.

[4]Most of these percentages are similar in the United Kingdom and France, where 21% of Brits would give up cars, 17% showers, and 25% sex; while 23% of French consumers would give up cars, 5% showers, and 16% sex.

An Example. We illustrate the relative size of the three measures based on our earlier example using Jackie's estimated Cobb-Douglas utility, in which a government tax causes the price of music tracks, p_1, to double from £0.5 to £1, so that now she buys 12, not 24 tracks per quarter.

In Figure 5.4, her lost consumer surplus, ΔCS, is areas $A + B$: the area between £0.5 and £1 on the price axis to the left of her uncompensated demand curve. Her compensating variation is $A + B + C$, which is the area between £0.5 and £1 to the left of the compensated demand curve corresponding to the original utility level, H^{CV}. This amount of money is just large enough to offset the harm of the higher price, so that Jackie will remain on her initial indifference curve. Finally, her equivalent variation is A, which is the area between £0.5 and £1 to the left of the compensated demand curve, corresponding to the new, lower utility level, H^{EV}. Losing this amount of money would harm Jackie as much as would the price increase. We can calculate CV and EV as the change in Jackie's expenditure function as the price rises, holding the price of a unit of live music constant at $p_2 = £1$.[5] Substituting this price into Equation 4.9, we know that Jackie's expenditure function is

$$E = \overline{U}\left(\frac{p_1}{0.4}\right)^{0.4}\left(\frac{p_2}{0.6}\right)^{0.6} \approx 1.96\overline{U}p_1^{0.4}p_2^{0.6} = 1.96\overline{U}p_1^{0.4}. \tag{5.3}$$

At Jackie's initial optimum, where $q_1 = 24$ and $q_2 = 18$, her utility is $\overline{U} = 24^{0.4}18^{0.6} \approx 20.20$. Thus, the expenditure function at the original equilibrium

Figure 5.4 Comparing CV, EV, and ΔCS

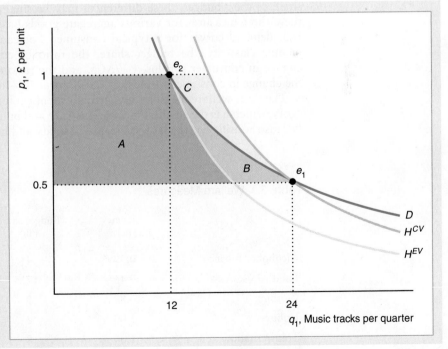

When the price rises from £0.5 to £1, Jackie loses consumer surplus, ΔCS, equal to $A + B$. Using her compensated demand curve at her initial utility level, H^{CV}, an increase of income or compensating variation, CV, equal to area $A + B + C$ would offset the harm from the price increase. Based on her compensated demand curve at the new utility level, H^{EV}, Jackie's loss from the price increase is equal to a loss of income of EV = area A.

---

[5]We would get the same answer if we integrate to the left of the relevant compensated demand curve, as we did with the uncompensated demand curve to get our consumer surplus measure.

is $E \approx 39.59p_1^{0.4}$. At her new optimum after the price change, where $q_1 = 12$ and $q_2 = 18$, the utility level $\overline{U}^* = 12^{0.4}18^{0.6} \approx 15.31$, so the new expenditure function is $E^* \approx 30.01p_1^{0.4}$. Thus,

$$CV = E(0.5) - E(1) = 39.59(0.5^{0.4} - 1^{0.4}) \approx 39.59 \times (-0.24) \approx -8.63, \quad (5.4)$$

$$EV = E^*(0.5) - E^*(1) = 30.01(0.5^{0.4} - 1^{0.4}) \approx 30.01 \times (-0.24) \approx -7.20. \quad (5.5)$$

As Figure 5.4 shows, Jackie's equivalent variation, $EV = A + B + C = -£7.20$, is a smaller loss (in absolute value) than her consumer surplus loss, $\Delta CS = A + B = -£8.28$, which is a smaller loss than her compensating variation, $CV = C = -£8.63$.

Differences Between the Three Measures. Although in principle, the three measures of welfare could differ substantially, for many goods they do not differ much for small changes in price. According to the Slutsky equation (Equation 4.11),

$$\varepsilon = \varepsilon^* - \theta\xi,$$

the uncompensated elasticity of demand, ε, equals the compensated elasticity of demand (pure substitution elasticity), ε^*, minus the budget share of the good, θ, times the income elasticity, ξ. The smaller the income elasticity or the smaller the budget share, the closer the substitution elasticity is to the total elasticity, and the closer the compensated and uncompensated demand curves are. Thus, the smaller the income elasticity or budget share, the closer the three welfare measures are to each other.

Because the budget shares of most goods are small, the three measures are often very close. Even for an aggregate good on which consumers spend a relatively large share of their budget, these differences may be small. Table 5.1 gives estimates of these three measures for various aggregate goods based on an estimated system of U.S. demand curves for a typical consumer. For each good, the table shows the income elasticity, the budget share, the ratio of compensating variation to the change in consumer surplus, $CV/\Delta CS$, and the ratio of the equivalent variation to the change in consumer surplus, $EV/\Delta CS$, for a 50% increase in price.

The three welfare measures are virtually identical for the alcohol and tobacco category, which has the smallest income elasticity and budget share of any of the goods. Because housing has the largest income elasticity and budget share, it has a relatively

Table 5.1 Welfare Measures

	Income Elasticity, ξ	Budget Share (%)	$\dfrac{EV}{\Delta CS}$	$\dfrac{CV}{\Delta CS}$
Alcohol & tobacco	0.39	4	99%	100.4%
Food	0.46	17	97	103
Clothing	0.88	8	97	102
Utilities	1.00	4	98	101
Transportation	1.04	8	97	103
Medical	1.37	9	95	104
Housing	1.38	15	93	107

Source: Calculations based on Blanciforti (1982).

large gap between the measures. However, even for housing, the difference between the change in uncompensated consumer surplus and either of the compensating consumer surplus measures is only 7%.

Willig (1976) showed theoretically that the three measures vary little for small price changes regardless of the size of the income effect. Indeed, for the seven goods in the table, if the price change were only 10%—instead of the 50% in the table— the differences between *CV* or *EV* and ΔCS are a small fraction of a percentage point for all goods except housing, where the difference is only about 1%.

Thus, the three measures of the welfare effect of a small price change give very similar answers even for aggregate goods. As a result, economists frequently use the change in consumer surplus, which is relatively easy to calculate because it is based on the uncompensated demand curve.

SOLVED PROBLEM 5.2

Lucy has a quasilinear utility function, Equation 3.9, $U(q_1, q_2) = u(q_1) + q_2$. When she maximizes her utility subject to her budget constraint, she chooses to consume both goods (an interior solution). The price of the second good, p_2, equals one. The price of q_1 increases from $\underline{p}_1$ to $\overline{p}_1$. Show that her compensating variation, *CV*, equals her equivalent variation, *EV*, and equals the change in her consumer surplus, ΔCS.

Answer

1. *Discuss Lucy's demand function for q_1 and write her utility function in terms of her expenditures.* From Chapter 4, we know that Lucy's demand for q_1 is a function of its price, $q_1(p_1)$. We can rewrite Lucy's expenditure function, $E = p_1 q_1 + q_2$, as $q_2 = E - p_1 q_1$. Substituting this expression into her utility function, we can write her utility as $u(q_1) + E - p_1 q_1$.

2. *Calculate the compensating variation at the two prices.* At $\underline{p}_1$, Lucy demands $\underline{q}_1 = q_1(\underline{p}_1)$ and her utility is $u(\underline{q}_1) + E - \underline{p}_1 \underline{q}_1$. At $\overline{p}_1$, $\overline{q}_1 = q_1(\overline{p}_1)$ and $u(\overline{q}_1) + E - \overline{p}_1 \overline{q}_1$. The compensating variation, *CV*, is the amount of extra money that she needs to receive if her utility is to remain constant despite the increase in price: $u(\underline{q}_1) + E - \underline{p}_1 \underline{q}_1 = u(\overline{q}_1) + E + CV - \overline{p}_1 \overline{q}_1$. Solving the equation for *CV*, we find that

$$CV = u(\underline{q}_1) - u(\overline{q}_1) + \overline{p}_1 \overline{q}_1 - \underline{p}_1 \underline{q}_1.$$

3. *Calculate the equivalent variation at the two prices and compare it to the compensating variation.* By similar reasoning, her equivalent variation, *EV*, is the amount that would have to be taken from her at the original price to lower her utility to that at the higher price. It is determined by $u(\underline{q}_1) + E - EV - \underline{p}_1 \underline{q}_1 = u(\overline{q}_1) + E - \overline{p}_1 \overline{q}_1$. Solving for *EV*, we learn that

$$EV = u(\underline{q}_1) - u(\overline{q}_1) + \overline{p}_1 \overline{q}_1 - \underline{p}_1 \underline{q}_1.$$

Thus, for a quasilinear utility function, $CV = EV$.

4. *Show that her consumer surplus equals the other two measures.* Because ΔCS lies between *EV* and *CV*, if $EV = CV$, then $EV = CV = \Delta CS$.

Comment: We noted earlier that $|CV| > |\Delta CS| > |EV|$ for a normal good (positive income effect) and that $|CV| < |\Delta CS| < |EV|$ for an inferior good (negative income effect). With a quasilinear utility function, the first goods has no income effect, so $|CV| = |\Delta CS| = |EV|$.

5.3 Market Consumer Surplus

A change in total consumer surplus captures the effects of a shock on all consumers in a market. Because the market demand curve is the (horizontal) sum of the individual demand curves, the market consumer surplus is the sum of each individual's consumer surplus.

We first measure the effect of a price increase on the market consumer surplus using an estimated market demand curve for sweetheart and hybrid tea roses sold in the United States.[6] We then discuss in which markets consumers are likely to suffer the greatest loss of consumer surplus due to a price increase.

Loss of Market Consumer Surplus from a Higher Price

Suppose that a new tax causes the (wholesale) price of roses to rise from the original equilibrium price of 30¢ to 32¢ per rose stem, which reflects a movement along the market inverse demand curve in Figure 5.5. The consumer surplus is area $A + B + C = \$173.74$ million per year at a price of 30¢, but it is only area $A = \$149.64$ million at a price of 32¢.[7] Thus, the loss in consumer surplus from the increase in the price is $B + C = \$24.1$ million per year.

Figure 5.5 A Fall in Market Consumer Surplus as the Price of Roses Rises

As the price of roses rises 2¢ per stem from 30¢ per stem, the quantity demanded decreases from 1.25 to 1.16 billion stems per year. The loss in market consumer surplus from the higher price, areas B and C, is $24.1 million per year.

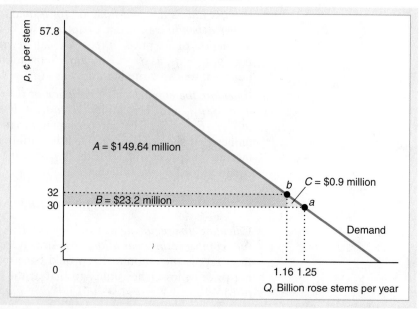

---

[6]This model was estimated using data from the *Statistical Abstract of the United States*, *Floriculture Crops*, *Floriculture and Environmental Horticulture Products*, and **usda.mannlib.cornell.edu**. The prices are in real 1991 dollars.

[7]The height of triangle A is 25.8¢ = 57.8¢ − 32¢ per stem, and the base is 1.16 billion stems per year, so its area is $\frac{1}{2} \times \$0.258 \times 1.16$ billion = \$149.64 million per year. The area of rectangle B is $\$0.02 \times 1.16$ billion = \$23.2 million. The area of triangle C is $\frac{1}{2} \times \$0.02 \times 0.09$ billion = \$0.9 million.

Markets in Which Consumer Surplus Losses Are Large

In general, as the price of a good increases, consumer surplus falls more (1) the greater the initial revenue spent on the good and (2) the less elastic the demand curve at the equilibrium.[8] More is spent on a good when its demand curve is farther to the right, so that areas like *A*, *B*, and *C* in Figure 5.5 are larger. The larger *B* + *C* is, the greater the drop in consumer surplus from a given percentage increase in price. Similarly, the less elastic a demand curve is (the closer it is to vertical), the less willing consumers are to give up the good, so consumers do not cut their consumption much as the price increases, and hence suffer a greater consumer surplus loss.

Higher prices cause a greater loss of consumer surplus in some markets than in others. Consumers would benefit if policymakers, before imposing a tax, considered in which market the tax would be likely to harm consumers the most.

We can use estimates of demand curves to predict for which good a price increase causes the greatest loss of consumer surplus. Table 5.2 shows the consumer surplus loss in billions of 2008 dollars from a 10% increase in the price of various goods. The table shows that the loss in consumer surplus is larger, the larger the initial revenue (price times quantity) that is spent on a good. A 10% increase in price causes a $149 billion loss of consumer surplus if the increase is imposed on medical

Table 5.2 The Effect of a 10% Price Increase on Consumer Surplus
(Revenue and Consumer Surplus in Billions of 2008 Dollars)

	Revenue	Elasticity of Demand, ε	Change in Consumer Surplus, ΔCS
Medical	1,554	−0.604	−151
Housing	1,543	−0.633	−149
Food	669	−0.245	−66
Clothing	338	−0.405	−33
Transportation	301	−0.461	−29
Utilities	308	−0.448	−30
Alcohol & tobacco	192	−0.162	−19

Sources: Revenues are from National Income and Product Accounts (NIPA), **www.bea.gov**; elasticities are based on Blanciforti (1982).

---

[8]If the demand curve is linear, as in Figure 5.5, the lost consumer surplus is area *B* + *C*. If *Q* is the initial quantity, 1.25, then the new quantity is $Q + \Delta Q$, 1.16 (where $\Delta Q = -0.09$), so area *B* is a rectangle, of $(Q + \Delta Q)\Delta p$, with length $Q + \Delta Q$ and height Δp. Similarly, area *C* is a triangle, $-\frac{1}{2}\Delta Q \Delta p$, of length $-\Delta Q$ and height Δp. For small changes in price, we can approximate any demand curve with a straight line, so $\Delta CS = (Q + \Delta Q)\Delta p - \frac{1}{2}\Delta Q \Delta p = (Q + \frac{1}{2}\Delta Q)\Delta p$ is a reasonable approximation of the true change in consumer surplus (a rectangle plus a triangle). We can rewrite this expression for ΔCS as

$$\Delta p\left(Q + \frac{1}{2}\Delta Q\right) = Q\Delta p\left[1 + \frac{1}{2}\left(\frac{\Delta Q}{Q}\frac{p}{\Delta p}\right)\frac{\Delta p}{p}\right] = (pQ)\frac{\Delta p}{p}\left(1 + \frac{1}{2}\varepsilon\frac{\Delta p}{p}\right) = Rx\left(1 + \frac{1}{2}\varepsilon x\right),$$

where $x = \Delta p/p$ is the percentage increase in the price, $R(= pQ)$ is the initial revenue from the sale of good *Q*, and ε is the elasticity of demand. This equation is used to calculate the last column in Table 5.2.

services where annual revenue is $1,554 billion, but only a $19 loss of consumer surplus if the increase is imposed on alcohol and tobacco where annual revenue is $192 billion.

At first glance, the relationship between elasticities of demand and the loss in consumer surplus in Table 5.2 looks backward: A given percent change in prices has a larger effect on consumer surplus for the relatively elastic demand curves. However, this relationship is coincidental: The large-revenue goods happen to have relatively elastic demand curves. The effect of a price change depends on both revenue and the demand elasticity. In this table, the relative size of the revenues is more important than the relative elasticities.

However, if we could hold the revenue constant and vary the elasticity, we would find that the consumer surplus lost from a price increase is larger as the demand curve becomes less elastic. If the demand curve for alcohol and tobacco were 10 times more elastic, -1.62, while the revenue stayed the same (so that the demand curve were flatter at the initial price and quantity), the consumer surplus loss would be nearly $1.2 billion less.

5.4 Effects of Government Policies on Consumer Welfare

The various consumer welfare measures are used to answer questions about the effect on consumers of government programs and other events that shift consumers' budget constraints. If the government imposes a quota, which reduces the number of units that a consumer buys, or provides a consumer with a certain amount of a good (such as food), the government creates a kink in the consumer's budget constraint. In contrast, if the government subsidizes the price of a good (such as a child-care subsidy) or provides cash to the consumer, it causes a rotation or a parallel shift of the budget line.

Quotas

Consumers' welfare is reduced if they cannot buy as many units of a good as they want. As a promotion, firms often sell a good at an unusually low price but limit the number of units that one can purchase. Governments, too, frequently limit how much of a good one can buy by setting a quota.

During emergencies, for example, governments sometimes ration "essential" goods such as water, food, energy, and flu vaccines rather than let these goods' prices rise. In the last few years, water quotas were imposed in areas of the United Kingdom, Fiji, China, Cyprus, Australia, and the United States (California, Georgia, North Carolina, Massachusetts, Oklahoma, and Texas). In recent years, legislation was proposed in the United States, Britain, and other countries to limit energy use. Under the Tradable Energy Quotas proposed by the United Kingdom, individuals would be issued a "carbon card" from which points would be deducted every time the cardholder purchased fossil fuel—for example, when filling up a gas tank or flying. Also, in recent years, many nations have rationed bird, swine, and other flu vaccines.

To illustrate the effect of a quota, we return to Jackie's choice between music tracks and live music. As Figure 5.6 shows, before the quota is imposed, Jackie's downward-sloping budget constraint consists of two line segments, L^1 and L^2. Her optimal bundle e_1, where she purchases 24 tracks and 18 units of live music per quarter, occurs where L^2 is tangent to I^1.

Figure 5.6 The Equivalent Variation of a Quota

Originally, Jackie faces a budget constraint consisting of the line segments L^1 and L^2 and buys 24 song tracks and 18 units of live music at e_1 on indifference curve I^1. When a quota limits purchases of tracks to 12 per quarter (vertical line at 12), the L^2 segment is no longer available and the shaded triangle, A, is lost from the opportunity set. The best that Jackie can do now is to purchase e_2 on indifference curve I^2. Suppose that Jackie did not face a quota but lost an amount of income equal to EV that caused her budget constraint to shift down to L^3, which is tangent to indifference curve I^2 at e_3. Thus, the effect on her utility of losing EV amount of income—shifting her from I^1 to I^2—is equivalent to the effect of the quota.

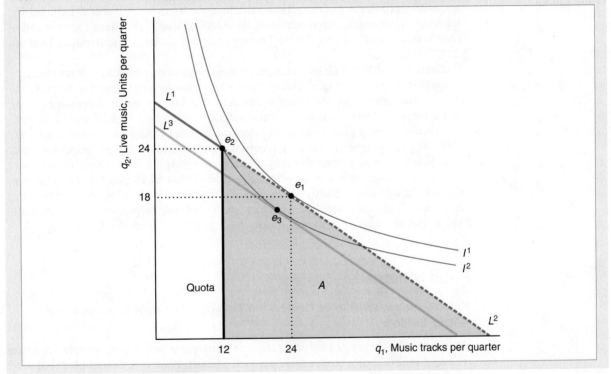

Now suppose that a government (or her mother) limits Jackie's purchases to no more than 12 tracks per quarter. Her new budget constraint is the same as the original for fewer than 12 tracks, L^1, and is vertical at 12 tracks. She loses part of the original opportunity set: the shaded triangle, area A, determined by the vertical line at 12 tracks, L^2, and the horizontal axis. Now, her best option is to purchase Bundle e_2—12 tracks and 24 units of live music—which is the point where the highest indifference curve, I^2, touches the new constraint. However, I^2 is not tangent to the budget constraint. Thus, with a quota, a consumer could have an interior solution in which she buys some of all the goods, but the tangency condition does not hold because the limit causes a kink in the budget constraint (as in the corner solution in Chapter 3).

The quota harms Jackie because she is now on indifference curve I^2, which is below her original indifference curve, I^1. To determine by how much she is harmed, we can calculate the equivalent variation: the amount of money we would have to take from Jackie to harm her as much as the quota does. We draw a budget line, L^3, that is parallel to L^2 but that just barely touches I^2. The difference between the expenditure on the original budget line and the new expenditure is Jackie's equivalent variation.

As we know, Jackie's original expenditure is £30. We can use her expenditure function, Equation 5.3, $E \approx 1.96\overline{U}p_1^{0.4}$, to determine the expenditure on L^3. Substituting $p_1 = £0.5$ and her utility on I^2 at e_2, $\overline{U} = 12^{0.4}24^{0.6} \approx 18.19$, into her expenditure function, we find that her expenditure on L^3 is about £27. Thus, Jackie's equivalent variation is £3(= £30 − £27).

APPLICATION Water Quota	Starting in 2001, a major drought, the "Big Dry," reduced the amount of water in storage throughout much of Southeast Australia. Australian state governments and water utilities imposed quotas to reduce the amount of water demanded by banning various outdoor water uses. At least 75% of Australians faced mandatory water restrictions in 2008. The government declared the drought over in 2012. Grafton and Ward (2008) compared the consumer surplus loss from restricting water use rather than allowing the price to rise so as to clear the market. To achieve the same reduction in the water demanded on the original demand curve, the price would have had to rise substantially from $1.01 to $2.35 per kiloliter. (Of course, raising price instead of imposing a quota would have created a hardship for poor people unless they received compensating financial help.) Grafton and Ward estimated that the loss in consumer surplus from using mandatory water restrictions rather than price adjustments was $235 million. The loss per household was about $150, which was slightly less than half the average Sydney household's annual water bill. This loss occurs because consumers who were willing to pay more to use water outdoors were prevented from doing so.

Food Stamps

I've known what it is to be hungry, but I always went right to a restaurant.
—Ring Lardner

We can use the theory of consumer choice to analyze whether poor people are better off receiving food or a comparable amount of cash. Poor U.S. households that meet income, asset, and employment eligibility requirements may receive coupons—food stamps—that they can use to purchase food from retail stores.

The U.S. Food Stamp Plan started in 1939. The modern version, the Food Stamp Program, was permanently funded starting in 1964. In 2008, it was renamed the Supplemental Nutrition Assistance Program (SNAP). SNAP is one of the nation's largest social welfare programs, with nearly 45 million people (one in seven U.S. residents) receiving food stamps at a cost of $78 billion in 2011. This rapidly growing program's expenditures have roughly doubled between 2000 and 2012. The share of food-at-home spending funded by SNAP is between 10% and 16% overall and 50% for low-income households (Beatty and Tuttle, 2012).

According to a 2008 U.S. Department of Agriculture report, 11.1% of U.S. households worry about having enough money to buy food, and 4.1% report that they suffer from inadequate food at some point during the year. In 2012, the Congressional Budget Office reported that three-quarters of households receiving SNAP benefits included a child, a person age 60 or older, or a disabled person. By the time they reach 20 years of age, half of all Americans and 90% of black children have received food stamps at least briefly.[9]

---

[9]According to Professor Mark Rank (DeParle, Jason, and Gebeloff, Robert, "The Safety Net: Food Stamp Use Soars, and Stigma Fades," *New York Times*, November 29, 2009).

Since the food stamp programs started, economists, nutritionists, and policymakers have debated "cashing out" food stamps by providing checks or cash instead of coupons that can be spent only on food. Legally, food stamps may not be sold, though a black market for them exists. Because of technological advances in electronic fund transfers, switching from food stamps to a cash program would lower administrative costs and reduce losses due to fraud and theft.

Would a switch to a comparable cash subsidy increase the well-being of food stamp recipients? Would the recipients spend less on food and more on other goods?

Poor people who receive cash have more choices than those who receive a comparable amount of food stamps. Only food can be obtained with food stamps. With cash, either food or other goods can be purchased. As a result, a cash grant increases a recipient's opportunity set by more than do food stamps of the same value.

In Figure 5.7, we made both the price of a unit of food and the price of all other goods $1 by choosing the units for each such that $1 buys one unit of each. Felicity has a monthly income of Y, so her budget line hits both axes at Y. Her opportunity set is area A.

If Felicity receives a subsidy of $100 in cash per month, her new monthly income is $Y + \$100$.[10] Her new budget constraint with cash hits both axes at $Y + 100$ and is parallel to the original budget constraint. Her opportunity set increases by $B + C$ to $A + B + C$.

If instead, Felicity receives $100 worth of food stamps, her food stamp budget constraint has a kink. Because the food stamps can be spent only on food, the budget constraint shifts 100 units to the right for any quantity of other goods up to Y units. For example, if Felicity buys only food, now $Y + 100$ units of food can be purchased. If she buys only other goods with the original Y income, she can get Y units of other goods plus 100 units of food. Because the food stamps cannot be turned into other goods, Felicity can't buy $Y + 100$ units of other goods, as she could under a cash transfer program. The food stamps opportunity set is area

Figure 5.7 Food Stamps Versus Cash

The lighter line shows the original budget line of an individual with Y income per month. The heavier line shows the budget constraint with $100 worth of food stamps. The budget constraint with a grant of $100 in cash is a line between $Y + 100$ on both axes. The opportunity set increases by area B with food stamps but by $B + C$ with cash. An individual with these indifference curves consumes Bundle d (with less than 100 units of food) with no subsidy, e (Y units of all other goods and 100 units of food) with food stamps, and f (more than Y units of all other goods and less than 100 units of food) with a cash subsidy. This individual's utility is greater with a cash subsidy than with food stamps.

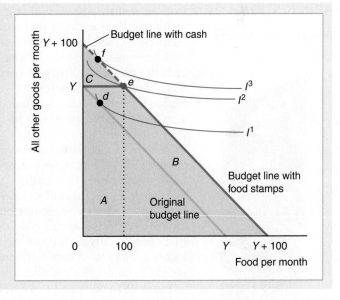

[10]The maximum possible monthly SNAP benefit for an individual was $200 in 2012 and the average benefit in 2010 was $152 (**www.cbpp.org/cms/index.cfm?fa=view&id=2226**, April 18, 2012).

$A + B$, which is larger than the pre-subsidy opportunity set by B. The opportunity set with food stamps is smaller than with the cash transfer program by C.

Felicity benefits as much from cash or an equivalent amount of food stamps if she would have spent at least $100 on food if given cash. In other words, she is indifferent between cash and food stamps if her indifference curve is tangent to the downward-sloping section of the food stamp budget constraint. Here, the equivalent variation is $100.

Conversely, if she would not spend at least $100 on food if given cash, she prefers receiving cash to food stamps. Given that she has the indifference curves in Figure 5.7, she prefers cash to food stamps. She chooses Bundle *e* (*Y* units of all other goods and 100 units of food) if she receives food stamps, but Bundle *f* (more than *Y* units of all other goods and less than 100 units of food) if she is given cash. She is on a higher indifference curve, I^2 rather than I^1, if given cash rather than food stamps. If we draw a budget line with the same slope as the original one (-1) that is tangent to I^2, we can calculate the equivalent variation as the difference between the expenditure on that budget line and the original one. The equivalent variation is less than $100.

Given that recipients are as well off or better off receiving cash as they are receiving food stamps, why do we have programs that provide food stamps instead of programs that provide cash? The introduction to a report by the U.S. Department of Agriculture's Food and Nutrition Service, which administers the food stamp program (Fasciano et al., 1993, p. 6), offers this explanation:

> *From the perspective of recipient households, cash is more efficient than coupons in that it permits each household to allocate its resources as it sees fit. . . . But in a more general sense, recipients' welfare clearly depends on public support for the program. And what evidence we have suggests that taxpayers are more comfortable providing in-kind, rather than cash, benefits and may consequently be more generous in their support of a coupon-based program. Thus, the question of which benefit form best promotes the welfare of financially needy households is more complex than it might appear.*

APPLICATION

Food Stamps Versus Cash

Consumer theory predicts that if recipients of food stamps received cash instead of stamps, their utility would remain the same or rise and some recipients would consume less food and more of other goods.

Whitmore (2002) found that a sizable minority of food stamp recipients would be better off if they were given cash instead of an equivalent value in food stamps. She estimated that between 20% and 30% of food stamp recipients would spend less on food than their food stamp benefit amount if they received cash instead of stamps, and therefore would be better off with cash. Of those who would trade their food stamps for cash, the average food stamp recipient values the stamps at 80% of their face value (although the average price on the underground market is only 65%). Thus, across all such recipients, $500 million is wasted by giving food stamps rather than cash.

Hoynes and Schanzenbach (2009) found that food stamps result in a decrease in out-of-pocket expenditures on food and an increase in overall food expenditures. For those households that would prefer cash to food stamps—those that spend relatively little of their income on food—food stamps cause them to increase their food consumption by about 22%, compared to 15% for other recipients, and 18% overall.

However, a more recent study, Beatty and Tuttle (2012), concluded that households spend more on food out of extra food stamps than out of extra cash. They found that recipients spent 36% of additional food stamp benefits on food.

5.5 Deriving Labor Supply Curves

So far, we've used consumer theory to examine consumers' demand behavior. Perhaps surprisingly, we can also apply the consumer theory model to derive a person's supply curve of labor. We do so by using consumer theory to obtain the person's demand curve for leisure time and then using that demand curve to derive the supply curve, which shows the hours the individual wants to work as a function of the wage. We then use our labor supply model to analyze how a change in the income tax rate affects the supply of labor and the revenue that the government collects.

Labor-Leisure Choice

The human race is faced with a cruel choice: work or daytime television.

People choose between working to earn money to buy goods and services and consuming *leisure*: all their time spent not working for pay. In addition to sleeping, eating, and playing, leisure—or more accurately nonwork, N—includes time spent cooking meals and fixing things around the house.

Hugo spends his total income, Y, on various goods. For simplicity, we assume that the price of these goods is $1 per unit, so he buys Y goods. His utility, U, depends on how many goods, Y, and how much leisure, N, he consumes:

$$U = U(Y, N). \tag{5.6}$$

He faces an hours-worked constraint and an income constraint. The number of hours he works per day, H, equals 24 minus the hours he spends on leisure:

$$H = 24 - N. \tag{5.7}$$

The total income, Y, that Hugo has to spend on goods equals his earned income—his wage times the number of hours he works, wH—and his unearned income, Y^*, such as income from an inheritance or a gift from his parents:

$$Y = wH + Y^*. \tag{5.8}$$

Using consumer theory, we can determine Hugo's demand curve for leisure once we know the price of leisure. What does your time cost you if you watch TV, go to school, or do anything other than work for an hour? It costs you the wage, w, you could have earned from an hour's work: The price of leisure is forgone earnings. The higher your wage, the more an hour of leisure costs you. Taking an afternoon off costs a lawyer who earns $250 an hour much more than it costs a fast food server who earns the minimum wage.

Panel a of Figure 5.8 shows Hugo's choice between leisure and goods. The vertical axis shows how many goods, Y, Hugo buys. The horizontal axis shows both hours of leisure, N, which are measured from left to right, and hours of work, H, which are measured from right to left. Hugo maximizes his utility given the *two* constraints he faces. First, he faces a time constraint, which is a vertical line at 24 hours of leisure. Because a day has only 24 hours, all the money in the world won't buy him more times. Second, Hugo faces a budget constraint. Because Hugo has no unearned income, his initial budget constraint, L^1, is $Y = w_1 H = w_1(24 - N)$. The slope of his budget constraint is $-w_1$, because each extra hour of leisure he consumes costs him w_1 goods.

Hugo picks his optimal hours of leisure, $N_1 = 16$, so he is on the highest indifference curve, I^1, that touches his budget constraint. He works $H_1 = 24 - N_1 = 8$ hours per day and earns an income of $Y_1 = w_1 H_1 = 8w_1$.

Figure 5.8 The Demand Curve for Leisure

(a) Hugo chooses between leisure, N, and other goods, Y, subject to a time constraint (the vertical line at 24 hours) and a budget constraint, L^1, which is $Y = w_1 H = w_1 \times (24 - N)$, and has a slope of $-w_1$. The tangency of his indifference curve I^1 with his budget constraint L^1 determines his optimal bundle, e_1, where he has $N_1 = 16$ hours of leisure and works $H_1 = 24 - N_1 = 8$ hours. If his wage rises from w_1 to w_2, Hugo shifts from optimal bundle e_1 to e_2. (b) Bundles e_1 and e_2 correspond to E_1 and E_2 on his leisure demand curve.

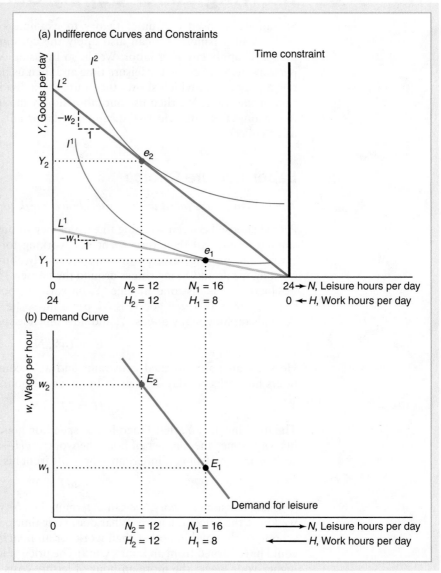

We derive Hugo's demand curve for leisure using the same method by which we derived Mimi's demand curve for beer in Chapter 4. We raise the price of leisure—the wage—in panel a of Figure 5.8 to trace Hugo's demand curve for leisure in panel b. As the wage increases from w_1 to w_2, leisure becomes more expensive, and Hugo demands less of it.

We can also solve this problem using calculus. Hugo maximizes his utility, Equation 5.6, subject to the time constraint, Equation 5.7, and the income constraint, Equation 5.8. Although we can analyze this problem using Lagrangian techniques, it is easier to do so by substitution. By substituting Equations 5.7 and 5.8 into 5.6, we can convert this constrained problem into an unconstrained maximization problem, where Hugo maximizes his utility through his choice of how many hours to work per day:

$$\max_{H} U = U(Y, N) = U(wH, 24 - H). \tag{5.9}$$

By using the chain rule of differentiation, we find that the first-order condition for an interior maximum to the problem in Equation 5.9 is

$$\frac{\partial U}{\partial Y}\frac{dY}{dH} + \frac{\partial U}{\partial N}\frac{dN}{dH} = U_Y w - U_N = 0, \tag{5.10}$$

where $U_Y = \partial U/\partial Y$ is the marginal utility of goods or income and $U_N = \partial U/\partial N$ is the marginal utility of leisure.[11] That is, Hugo sets his marginal rate of substitution of income for leisure, $MRS = -U_N/U_Y$, equal to his marginal rate of transformation of income for leisure, $MRT = -w$, in the market:

$$MRS = \frac{U_N}{U_Y} = -w = MRT. \tag{5.11}$$

Equivalently, the last dollar's worth of leisure, U_N/w, equals the marginal utility from the last dollar's worth of goods, U_Y.

By subtracting Hugo's demand for leisure at each wage—his demand curve for leisure in panel a of Figure 5.9—from 24, we construct his labor supply curve—the hours he is willing to work as a function of the wage, $H(w)$—in panel b. His supply

Figure 5.9 The Labor Supply Curve

(a) Hugo's demand for leisure is downward sloping. (b) At any given wage, the number of hours that Hugo works, h, and the number of hours of leisure, n, that he consumes add to 24. Thus, his supply curve for hours worked, which equals 24 hours minus the number of hours of leisure he demands, is upward sloping.

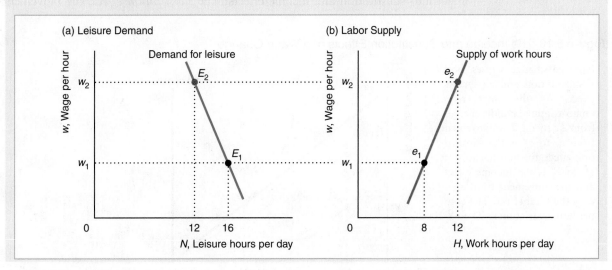

<hr />

[11]The second-order condition for an interior maximum is

$$\frac{\partial^2 U}{\partial Y^2}w^2 - 2\frac{\partial^2 U}{\partial Y \partial N}w + \frac{\partial^2 U}{\partial N^2} < 0.$$

curve for hours worked is the mirror image of the demand curve for leisure: For every extra hour of leisure that Hugo consumes, he works one hour less.

SOLVED PROBLEM 5.3

If Sofia has a Cobb-Douglas utility function, $U = (wH)^a(24 - H)^{1-a}$, what is her labor supply function? What is her supply function if $a = \frac{1}{3}$?

Answer

1. *To find the values that maximize her utility, set the derivative of Sofia's utility function with respect to H equal to zero.* This first-order condition is $aw(wH)^{a-1}(24 - H)^{1-a} - (1 - a)(wH)^a(24 - H)^{-a} = 0$. Simplifying, we find that $H = 24a$. Thus, Sofia works a fixed number of hours regardless of the wage.

2. *Substitute in the value $a = \frac{1}{3}$ to obtain the specific hours-worked function.* Given that $a = \frac{1}{3}$, she works $H = 8$ hours a day whether the wage is 50¢ or $50 per hour.

Income and Substitution Effects

An increase in the wage causes both income and substitution effects, which alter an individual's demand for leisure and supply of hours worked. The *total effect* of an increase in Hugo's wage from w_1 to w_2 is the movement from e_1 to e_2 in Figure 5.10. Hugo works $H_2 - H_1$ fewer hours and consumes $N_2 - N_1$ more hours of leisure.

By drawing an imaginary budget constraint, L^*, that is tangent to Hugo's original indifference curve and has the slope of the new wage, we can divide the total effect into substitution and income effects. The *substitution effect*, the movement

Figure 5.10 The Income and Substitution Effects of a Wage Change

A wage change causes both a substitution and an income effect. As the wage rises, Hugo's optimal bundle changes from e_1 to e_2. The movement from e_1 to e^* is the substitution effect, the movement from e^* to e_2 is the income effect, and the movement from e_1 to e_2 is the total effect. The compensating variation is $Y^* - Y_2$.

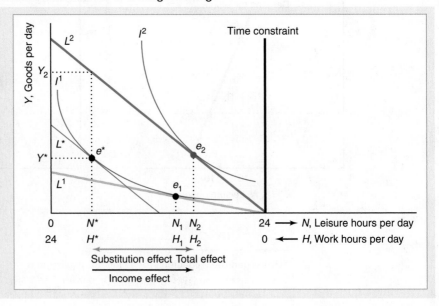

from e_1 to e^*, must be negative: A compensating wage increase causes Hugo to consume fewer hours of leisure, N^*, and to work more hours, H^*. As his wage rises, if Hugo works the same number of hours as before, he has a higher income. The *income effect* is the movement from e^* to e_2. The figure shows that his income effect is positive—he consumes more leisure as his income rises—because he views leisure as a normal good.

When leisure is a normal good, the substitution and income effects work in opposite directions. Which effect dominates depends on the relative size of the two effects. In Figure 5.10, Hugo's income effect dominates the substitution effect, so the total effect for leisure is positive: $N_2 > N_1$. Given that the total number of hours in a day is fixed, if Hugo consumes more leisure when his wage rises, then he must work fewer hours. That is, he is in a backward-bending section of his supply curve (his supply curve has the opposite slope of the one in panel b of Figure 5.9). Alternatively, if Hugo viewed leisure as an inferior good, both his substitution effect and income effect would work in the same direction, so that an increase in the wage would cause his hours of leisure to fall and his work hours to rise (as in Figure 5.9).

In Figure 5.10, by removing $Y^* - Y_2$ income from Hugo, we could offset the benefit of the wage increase by keeping him on indifference curve I^1. Thus, $Y^* - Y_2$ is the compensating variation.[12]

SOLVED PROBLEM 5.4

Enrico receives a no-strings-attached scholarship that pays him an extra Y^* per day. How does this scholarship affect the number of hours he wants to work? Does his utility increase?

Answer

1. *Show his consumer equilibrium without unearned income.* When Enrico had no unearned income, his budget constraint, L^1 in the graphs, hit the hours-leisure axis at 0 hours and had a slope of $-w$.

2. *Show how the unearned income affects his budget constraint.* The extra income causes a parallel upward shift of Y^*. His new budget constraint, L^2, has the same slope as before because his wage does not change. The extra income cannot buy Enrico more time, of course, so L^2 cannot extend to the right of the time constraint. As a result, L^2 is vertical at 0 hours up to Y^*: His income is Y^* if he works no hours. Above Y^*, L^2 slants toward the goods axis with a slope of $-w$.

3. *Show that the relative position of the new to the original equilibrium depends on his tastes.* The change in the number of hours he works depends on Enrico's tastes. Panels a and b show two possible sets of indifference curves. In both diagrams, when facing budget constraint L^1, Enrico chooses to work H_1 hours. In panel a, leisure is a normal good, so as his income rises, Enrico consumes more leisure: He moves from Bundle e_1 to Bundle e_2. In panel b, he views leisure as an inferior good and consumes fewer hours of leisure than at first: He moves from e_1 to e_3. (Another possibility is that the number of hours he works is unaffected by the extra unearned income.)

---

[12]See "Leisure-Income Choices of Textile Workers" in MyEconLab, Chapter Resources, Chapter 5 for an example of substitution and income effects based on estimated utility functions of workers.

4. *Discuss how his utility changes.* Regardless of his tastes, Enrico has more income in the new equilibrium and is on a higher indifference curve after receiving the scholarship. In short, he believes that more money is better than less.

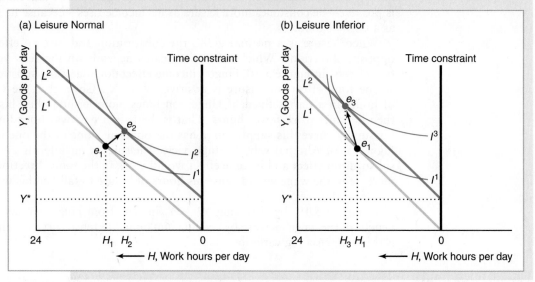

Shape of the Labor Supply Curve

Whether the labor supply curve slopes upward, bends backward, or has sections with both properties depends on the income elasticity of leisure. Suppose that a worker views leisure as an inferior good at low wages and a normal good at high wages. As the wage increases, the worker's demand for leisure first falls and then rises, and the hours supplied to the market first rise and then fall. (Alternatively, the labor supply curve may slope upward and then backward even if leisure is normal at all wages: At low wages, the substitution effect—working more hours—dominates the income effect—working fewer hours—while the opposite occurs at higher wages.)

The budget line rotates upward from L^1 to L^2 as the wage rises in panel a of Figure 5.11. Because leisure is an inferior good at low incomes, in the new optimal bundle, e_2, this worker consumes less leisure and buys more goods than at the original bundle, e_1.

At higher incomes, however, leisure is a normal good. At an even higher wage, the new equilibrium is e_3 on budget line L^3, where the quantity of leisure demanded is higher and the number of hours worked is lower. Thus, the corresponding supply curve for labor slopes upward at low wages and bends backward at higher wages in panel b.

Do labor supply curves slope upward or backward? Economic theory alone cannot answer this question, as both forward-sloping and backward-bending supply curves are *theoretically* possible. Empirical research is necessary to resolve this question.

Most studies (see the survey in Keane, 2011) find that the labor supply curves for British and American men are relatively vertical because the income and the substitution effects are offsetting or both small. Similar results are found in other countries such as Japan (Kuroda and Yamamoto, 2008) and the Netherlands

Figure 5.11 A Labor Supply Curve That Slopes Upward and Then Bends Backward

At low incomes, an increase in the wage causes the worker to work more hours: the movement from e_1 to e_2 in panel a or from E_1 to E_2 in panel b. At higher incomes, an increase in the wage causes the worker to work fewer hours: the movement from e_2 to e_3 or from E_2 to E_3.

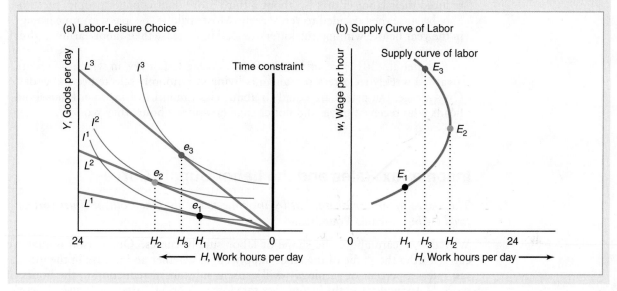

(Evers et al., 2008). Keane's average across all studies of males' pure substitution wage elasticity is about 0.31 (although most of the estimates are below 0.15). Most studies (see Keane's survey) find that females' labor supply curves are more steeply sloped, with most long-run wage elasticity estimates ranging from 1.25 to 5.6.

APPLICATION

Working After Winning the Lottery

Would you stop working if you won a lottery jackpot or inherited a large sum of money? Economists want to know how unearned income affects the amount of labor people are willing to supply because this question plays a crucial role in many government debates on taxes and welfare. For example, some legislators oppose negative income tax and welfare programs because they claim that giving money to poor people will induce them to stop working. Is that assertion true?

We could answer this question if we could observe the behavior of a large group of people, only some of whom were randomly selected to receive varying but large amounts of unearned income each year for decades. Governments conduct such experiments by running lotteries.

Imbens et al. (2001) compared the winners of major prizes to others who played the Massachusetts Megabucks lottery. Major prizes ranged from $22,000 to $9.7 million, with average winnings of $1.1 million, and were paid in yearly installments over two decades.

The average winner received $55,200 in prize money per year and chose to work slightly fewer hours so that his or her labor earnings fell by $1,877 per year. That is, winners increased their consumption and savings but did not substantially decrease their work hours.

On average, for every dollar of unearned income, winners reduced their work effort and hence their labor earnings by 11¢]. Men and women, big and very big winners, and people of all education levels behaved the same way. However, the behavior of winners differed by age and income groups. People ages 55 to 65 reduced their labor efforts by about a third more than younger people, presumably because they decided to retire early. Most striking, people with no earnings in the year before winning the lottery tended to increase their labor earnings after winning.

Kuhn et al. (2011) examined the Dutch Postcode Lottery, in which prizes are awarded weekly to lottery participants living in randomly selected postal codes. On average, the prizes are equal to about eight months of income. Household heads who received prizes did not change how many hours they worked.

Income Tax Rates and the Labor Supply Curve

The wages of sin are death, but by the time taxes are taken out, it's just sort of a tired feeling. —Paula Poundstone

Why do we care about the shape of labor supply curves? One reason is that we can tell from the shape of the labor supply curve whether an increase in the income tax rate—a percent of earnings—will cause a substantial reduction in the hours of work.[13] An increase in the income tax rate lowers workers' after-tax wages. If workers' supply curves are backward bending, a small increase in the tax rate increases hours worked (reducing leisure hours), boosts production, and increases the tax revenue collected. On the other hand, if people's supply curves are upward sloping, a small increase in the wage tax rate reduces hours worked, decreases production, and may lower the tax revenue collected.

Although they have been unwilling to emulate Lady Godiva's tax-fighting technique—allegedly, her husband, Leofric, the Earl of Mercia, agreed to her request to eliminate taxes if she rode naked through the Coventry marketplace—various U.S. presidents have advocated tax cuts. Presidents John Kennedy, Ronald Reagan, and George W. Bush argued that cutting the *marginal tax rate*—the percentage of the last dollar earned that the government takes in taxes—would induce people to work longer and produce more, both desirable effects. President Reagan predicted that the government's tax receipts would increase due to the additional work.

Because tax rates have changed substantially over time, we have a natural experiment to test this hypothesis. The Kennedy tax cuts lowered the top federal personal marginal tax rate from 91% to 70%. Due to the Reagan tax cuts, the maximum rate fell to 50% in 1982–1986, 38.5% in 1987, and 28% in 1988–1990. The rate rose to 31% in 1991–1992 and to 39.6% in 1993–2000. The Bush tax cuts reduced this rate to 38.6% for 2001–2003, 37.6% for 2004–2005, and 35% since 2006. (President Obama's 2012 proposal would expand two tax cuts for the working poor, but raise the top rate to 39.6%.)

---

[13]Although taxes are ancient, the modern income tax was introduced in 1798 by William Pitt the Younger: The British assessed 10% on annual incomes above £60 to finance the war with Napoleon. The U.S. Congress followed suit in 1861, collecting 3% on annual incomes over $800 to pay for the Civil War.

Many other countries' central governments have also lowered their top marginal tax rates in recent years. The top U.K. rate fell sharply during the Thatcher administration from 83% to 60% in 1979 and to 40% in 1988. It rose to 50% in 2010, and is scheduled to fall to 45% in April, 2013. Japan's top rate fell from 75% in 1983 to 60% in 1987, 50% in 1988, and to 37% in 1999, but it rose to 40% in 2007. In 1988, Canada raised the marginal tax rates for the two lowest income groups and lowered them for those falling into the top nine brackets.

Of more concern to individuals than the federal marginal tax rate is the tax rate that includes taxes collected by all levels of government. According to the Organization for Economic Cooperation and Development (OECD), the top all-inclusive marginal tax rate in 2011 was 15.0% in the Czech Republic, 30.0% in Mexico, 33.0% in New Zealand, 41.92% in the United States (on average across the states), 46.4% in Canada, 46.5% in Australia, 50.0% in Japan and the United Kingdom, 52.2% in Denmark, 53.7% in Belgium, and 56.6% in Sweden.

If the tax does not affect the pretax wage, the effect of imposing a tax rate of $\alpha = 25\% = 0.25$ is to reduce the effective wage from w to $(1 - \alpha)w = 0.75w$.[14] The tax reduces the after-tax wage by 25%, so a worker's budget constraint rotates downward, similar to rotating the budget constraint downward from L^2 to L^1, in Figure 5.11.

As we discussed, if the budget constraint rotates downward, the hours of work may increase or decrease, depending on whether a person considers leisure to be a normal or an inferior good. The worker in panel b of Figure 5.11 has a labor supply curve that at first slopes upward and then bends backward. If the worker's wage is very high, the worker is in the backward-bending section of the labor supply curve.

If so, the relationship between the marginal tax rate, α, and tax revenue, $\alpha w H$, is bell-shaped, as in Figure 5.12. This figure is the estimated U.S. tax revenue curve (Trabandt and Uhlig, 2011). At the marginal rate for the typical person, $\alpha = 28\%$, the government collects 100% of the amount of tax revenue it's currently collecting. At a zero tax rate, a small increase in the tax rate *must* increase the tax revenue because no revenue was collected when the tax rate was zero. However, if the tax rate rises a little more, the tax revenue collected must rise even higher, for two reasons: First, the government collects a larger percentage of every dollar earned because the tax rate is higher. Second, employees work more hours as the tax rate rises because workers are in the backward-bending sections of their labor supply curves.

As the marginal rate increases, tax revenue rises until the marginal rate reaches $\alpha^* = 63\%$, where the U.S. tax revenue would be 130% of its current level.[15] If the marginal tax rate increases more, workers are in the upward-sloping sections of their labor supply curves, so an increase in the tax rate reduces the number of hours worked. When the tax rate rises high enough, the reduction in hours worked more than offsets the gain from the higher rate, so the tax revenue falls.

---

[14]Under a progressive income tax system, the marginal tax rate increases with income, and the marginal tax rate is greater than the average tax rate. Suppose that the marginal tax rate is 20% on the first $10,000 earned and 30% on the second $10,000. Someone who earns $20,000 pays a tax of $2,000 (= 0.2 × $10,000) on the first $10,000 of earnings and $3,000 on the next $10,000. That taxpayer's average tax rate is 25% (= [$2,000 + $3,000]/$20,000). In 2012, the U.S. marginal tax rate on a single person with a taxable income of $50,000 was 25%, while the average rate was 17.06%. For simplicity, in the following analysis, we assume that the marginal tax rate is a constant, α, so the average tax rate is also α.

[15]On average for 14 European Union countries, α is also less than α^*, but raising the rate to α^* would raise European tax revenue by only 8% (Trabandt and Uhlig, 2011).

Figure 5.12 The Relationship of U.S. Tax Revenue to the Marginal Tax Rate

This curve shows how U.S. income tax revenue varies with the marginal income tax rate, τ, according to Trabandt and Uhlig (2011). The typical person pays $\alpha = 28\%$, which corresponds to 100% of the current tax revenue that the government collects. The tax revenue would be maximized at 130% of its current level if the marginal rate were set at $\alpha^* = 63\%$. For rates below α^*, an increase in the marginal rate raises larger tax revenue. However at rates above α^*, an increase in the marginal rate decreases tax revenue.

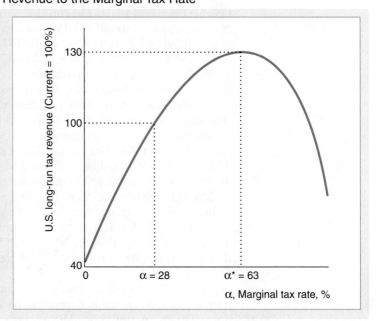

It makes little sense for a government to operate at very high marginal tax rates in the downward-sloping portion of this bell-shaped curve. The government could get more output *and* more tax revenue by cutting the marginal tax rate.

What is the effect on the tax revenue collected when the income tax rate increases? To answer this question, we let α be the constant marginal income tax rate and w be the worker's wage, so that for every w a worker is paid, the government receives αw. (We ignore unearned income and the possibility that the tax rate varies with income.)

Suppose the government collects τ share of the wage. If w is the worker's wage, then the government takes αw, and the worker's after-tax wage is $\omega = (1 - \alpha)w$. The government's tax revenue, T, is

$$T = \alpha w H[(1 - \alpha)w] = \alpha w H(\omega), \qquad (5.12)$$

where $H(\omega)$ is the hours of labor that a worker supplies given the after-tax wage ω.

By differentiating Equation 5.12 with respect to α, we can show how revenue changes as the tax rate increases:

$$\frac{dT}{d\tau} = wH(\omega) - \alpha w^2 \frac{dH}{d\omega}. \qquad (5.13)$$

Thus, a change in the tax rate has two effects. First, the government collects more revenue because of the higher tax rate: A one-unit increase in α causes the tax revenue to increase by $wH(\omega)$, the amount that the worker earns. Second, the change in the tax alters the hours worked. As the rate goes up, before-tax labor earnings, $wH(\omega)$, decrease if the labor supply is upward sloping, $dH/d\omega > 0$, which reduces the tax revenue by $\alpha w^2 dH/d\omega$.

The government can raise the amount of tax revenue collected by lowering the tax rate if the economy is on the downward-sloping part of the tax-revenue curve to the right of α^* in Figure 5.12. In Equation 5.13, for the tax revenue to decrease when the tax rate increases (or to rise when the tax rate decreases), we need $dT/d\alpha = wH - \alpha w^2 dH/d\omega < 0$. Using algebra, we can rewrite this condition as

$$\frac{1}{\alpha} < \frac{dH}{d\omega}\frac{w}{H(\omega)}.$$

If we multiply both sides of this expression by $(1 - \alpha)$, we obtain the condition that

$$\frac{1 - \alpha}{\alpha} < \frac{dH}{d\omega}\frac{\omega}{H(\omega)} = \eta, \qquad (5.14)$$

where $\eta = [dH/d\omega][\omega/H(\omega)]$ is the elasticity of supply of work hours with respect to after-tax wages, ω.

Thus, for the tax revenue the government collects to fall from a small increase in the tax rate, the elasticity of supply of labor must be greater than $(1 - \alpha)/\alpha$. In the United States in 2012, a single person earning between \$35,350 to \$85,650 had a marginal tax rate of $\alpha = 25\%$. For a small increase in this rate to lower the tax revenue collected, such a person's η had to be greater than 3 ($= 0.75/0.25$), which was not likely. In the past, some countries had very high tax rates where this condition could hold. For example, if $\alpha = 90\%$, the condition is met if the elasticity of supply is greater than $\frac{1}{9}$.

We now return to the questions raised in the Challenge at the beginning of the chapter: For a given government expenditure, does a child-care price subsidy or lump-sum subsidy provide greater benefit to recipients? Which increases the demand for child-care services by more? Which inflicts less cost on other consumers of child care?

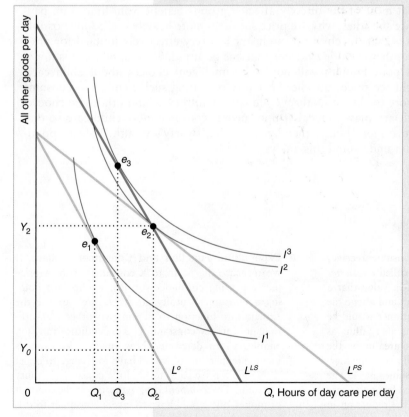

To determine which program benefits recipients more, we employ a model of consumer choice. The figure shows a poor family that chooses between hours of child care per day (Q) and all other goods per day. Given that the price of all other goods is \$1 per unit, the expenditure on all other goods is the income, Y, not spent on child care. The family's original budget constraint is L^o. The family chooses Bundle e_1 on indifference curve I^1, where the family consumes Q_1 hours of child-care services.

If the government gives a child-care price subsidy, the new budget line, L^{PS}, rotates out along the child-care axis. Now the family consumes Bundle e_2 on (higher) indifference curve I^2. The family consumes more hours of child care, Q_2, because child care is now less expensive and it is a normal good.

One way to measure the value of the subsidy the family receives is to calculate how many *other goods* the family could buy before and after the subsidy. If the family consumes Q_2 hours of child care, the family could have consumed Y_o other goods with the original budget constraint and Y_2 with the price-subsidy budget constraint. Given that Y_2 is the family's remaining income after paying for child care, the family buys Y_2 units of all other goods. Thus, the value to the family of the child-care price subsidy is $Y_2 - Y_o$.

If, instead of receiving a child-care price subsidy, the family were to receive a lump-sum payment of $Y_2 - Y_o$. taxpayers' costs for the two programs would be the same. The family's budget constraint after receiving a lump-sum payment, L^{LS}, has the same slope as the original one, L^o, because the relative prices of child care and all other goods are unchanged from their original levels. This budget constraint must go through e_2 because the family has just enough money to buy that bundle. However, given this budget constraint, the family would be better off if it buys Bundle e_3 on indifference curve I^3 (the reasoning is the same as that in the Chapter 4 Challenge Solution and the Consumer Price Index analysis in Figure 4.7). The family consumes less child care with the lump-sum subsidy than with the price subsidy, Q_3 rather than Q_2, but more than it originally did, Q_1.

Poor families prefer the lump-sum payment to the price subsidy because indifference curve I^3 is above I^2. Taxpayers are indifferent between the two programs because they both cost the same. The child-care industry prefers the price subsidy because the demand curve for its service is farther to the right: At any given price, more child care is demanded by poor families who receive a price subsidy rather than a lump-sum subsidy.

Given that most of the directly affected groups benefit from lump-sum payments to price subsidies, why are price subsidies more heavily used? One possible explanation is that the child-care industry has very effectively lobbied for price subsidies, but there is little evidence that has occurred. Second, politicians might believe that poor families will not make intelligent choices about child care, so they might see price subsidies as a way of getting such families to consume relatively more (or better-quality) child care than they would otherwise choose. Third, politicians may prefer that poor people consume more child care so that they can work more hours, thereby increasing society's wealth. Fourth, politicians may not understand this analysis.

SUMMARY

1. **Consumer Welfare.** The pleasure a consumer receives from a good in excess of its cost is called *consumer surplus*. Consumer surplus is the extra value that a consumer gets from a transaction over and above the amount paid, the amount that a consumer would be willing to pay for the right to buy as many units as desired at the specified price, and the area under the consumer's inverse demand curve and above the market price up to the quantity the consumer buys. The degree to which consumers are harmed by an increase in a product's price is measured by the reduction in consumer surplus.

2. **Expenditure Function and Consumer Welfare.** If we measure the harm to a consumer from a price increase using consumer surplus, we are not holding a consumer's utility constant. We can use the expenditure function to obtain two other measures that hold utility constant. The expenditure function enables us to determine how much a consumer's income (expenditure) would have to change to offset a change in price so as to hold the consumer's utility constant. The *compensating variation* is the amount of money one would have to give a consumer to offset completely the harm from a price increase—to

keep the consumer on the original indifference curve. The *equivalent variation* is the amount of money one would have to take from a consumer to harm the consumer by as much as the price increase would. For small price changes, the three measures of the effect of a price increase on a consumer's well-being—the change in consumer surplus, the compensating variation, and the equivalent variation—are typically close. The smaller the income elasticity or the smaller the budget share of the good, the smaller the differences between these three measures.

3. **Market Consumer Surplus.** The market consumer surplus—the sum of the welfare effect across all consumers—is the area under the market inverse demand curve above the market price. The more revenue that is spent on the good and the less elastic the demand curve is, the larger the market consumer surplus.

4. **Effects of Government Policies on Consumer Welfare.** A government quota on the consumption of a good, food stamps, or a child-care price subsidy creates a kink in a consumer's budget constraint, which affects how much consumers purchase and their well-being. Many, but not all, consumers would be better off if the government gave them an amount of money equal to the value of the food stamps or the child-care subsidy instead of these subsidies.

5. **Deriving Labor Supply Curves.** Using consumer theory, we can derive a person's daily demand curve for leisure (time spent on activities other than work), which shows how hours of leisure vary with the wage rate, which is the price of leisure. The number of hours that a person works equals 24 minus that person's leisure hours, so we can determine a person's daily labor supply curve from that person's demand curve for leisure. The labor supply curve is upward sloping if leisure is an inferior good and backward bending if it is a normal good. Whether a cut in the income tax rate will cause government tax revenue to rise or fall depends on the shape of the labor supply curve.

EXERCISES

■ = *exercise is available on* MyEconLab; * = *answer appears at the back of this book;* **M** = *mathematical problem.*

1. Consumer Welfare

*1.1 If the inverse demand function for toasters is $p = 60 - q$, what is the consumer surplus if the price is 30? **M**

1.2 If the inverse demand function for radios is $p = a - bq$, what is the consumer surplus if the price is $a/2$? **M**

1.3 According to Hong and Wolak (2008), a 5% postal price increase, such as the one in 2006, reduces postal revenue by $215 million and lowers consumer surplus by $333 million. Illustrate these results in a figure similar to that of Figure 5.2, and indicate the dollar amounts of areas A and B in the figure.

*1.4 Use the facts in Exercise 1.3:

  a. Hong and Wolak estimate that the elasticity of demand for postal services is -1.6. Assume that there is a constant elasticity of demand function, $Q = Xp^{-1.6}$, where X is a constant. In 2006, the price of a first-class stamp went from 37¢ to 39¢. Given the information in the problem about the effect of the price increase on revenue, calculate X.

  b. Calculate the size of the triangle corresponding to the lost consumer surplus (area B in Exercise 1.1). *Note*: You will get a slightly larger total surplus loss than the amount estimated by Hong and Wolak because they estimated a slightly different demand function. (*Hint*: See Solved Problem 5.1.) **M**

2. Expenditure Function and Consumer Welfare

2.1 In the application "Compensating Variation and Equivalent Variation for the Internet," people are asked how much they would have to be paid not to use the Internet or what else they'd have to give up to keep using it. What are these measures called? Graph what is being measured. Is there a better way to determine the equivalent variation?

*2.2 Redraw Figure 5.4 for an inferior good. Use your diagram to compare the relative sizes of CV, ΔCS, and EV.

2.3 Suppose that Lucy's quasilinear utility function in Solved Problem 5.2 is $U(q_1, q_2) = 2q_1^{0.5} + q_2$, $\underline{p}_1 = 2$, $p_2 = 4$, $\overline{p}_1 = 4$, $\underline{q}_1 = q_1(\underline{p}_1) = 4$, $\overline{q}_1 = q_1(\overline{p}_1) = 1$. Compare her CV, EV, and ΔCS. **M**

2.4 Marvin has a Cobb-Douglas utility function, $U = q_1^{0.5}q_2^{0.5}$, his income is $Y = 100$, and, initially he faces prices of $p_1 = 1$ and $p_2 = 2$. If p_1 increases to 2, what are his CV, ΔCS, and EV? (*Hint*: See Solved Problem 5.2.) **M**

2.5 The local swimming pool charges nonmembers $10 per visit. If you join the pool, you can swim for $5 per visit, but you have to pay an annual fee of F. Use an indifference curve diagram to find the value of F such that you are indifferent between joining and not joining. Suppose that the pool charged you exactly F. Would you go to the pool more or fewer times than if you did not join? For simplicity, assume that the price of all other goods is $1.

3. Market Consumer Surplus

3.1 Compare the welfare effects on a consumer between a lump-sum tax and an ad valorem (percentage) tax on all goods that raise the same amount of tax revenue. **M**

3.2 Use the numbers for the alcohol and tobacco category from Table 5.2 to draw a figure that illustrates the roles that the revenue and the elasticity of demand play in determining the loss of consumer surplus due to an increase in price. Indicate how the various areas of your figure correspond to the equation derived in footnote 8. **M**

3.3 Suppose that the inverse market demand for an upcoming Bruce Springsteen concert at Philadelphia's 20,000-seat Wachovia Center is $p = 1,000 - 0.04Q$. Mr. Springsteen is concerned about the well-being of his fans. He considers whether to auction the tickets to the concert. The auction works as follows: An auctioneer orders the bids from highest to lowest, and the price of each ticket equals the $20,000^{th}$ highest bid. The tickets go to the highest bidders. In the auction, assume that each person bids his or her willingness to pay.

a. What is the price of the tickets? What is the market consumer surplus?

b. Instead, suppose that Mr. Springsteen, for the benefit of his fans, decides to sell each ticket for $100. Based on the demand function, 22,500 people are willing to pay $100 or more. So, not everyone who wants to see the concert at the $100 price can purchase a ticket. Of these 22,500 people, suppose that all of the 20,000 people who acquire a ticket have a lower willingness to pay than all of the 2,500 people who do not. What is the consumer surplus?

c. Suppose Bruce Springsteen's objective in choosing whether to auction the tickets or to set a price of $100 is to maximize the market consumer surplus. Which does he choose: an auction or a $100 ticket price? **M**

*3.4 Two linear demand curves go through the initial equilibrium, e_1. One demand curve is less elastic than the other at e_1. For which demand curve will a price increase cause the larger consumer surplus loss?

4. Effects of Government Policies on Consumer Welfare

4.1 Max chooses between water and all other goods. If he spends all his money on water, he can buy 12,000 gallons per week. At current prices, his optimal

bundle is e_1. Show in a diagram. During a drought, the government limits the number of gallons per week that he may purchase to 10,000. Using diagrams, discuss under which conditions his new optimal bundle, e_2, will be the same as e_1. If the two bundles differ, can you state where e_2 must be located?

4.2 Ralph usually buys one pizza and two colas from the local pizzeria. The pizzeria announces a special: All pizzas after the first one are half price. Show the original and new budget constraints. What can you say about the bundle Ralph will choose when faced with the new constraint?

4.3 Since 1979, low-income recipients have been given food stamps without charge. However before 1979, people bought food stamps at a subsidized rate. For example, to get $1 worth of food stamps, a household paid about 20¢ (the exact amount varied by household characteristics and other factors). Show the budget constraint facing an individual if that individual is allowed to buy up to $100 per month in food stamps at 20¢ per each $1 coupon. Compare this constraint to the original budget constraint (original income is Y) with no assistance and the budget constraint if the individual receives $100 of food stamps for free.

4.4 Is a poor person more likely to benefit from $100 a month worth of food stamps (that can be used only to buy food) or $100 a month worth of clothing stamps (that can be used only to buy clothing)? Why?

4.5 If a relatively wealthy person spends more on food than a poor person before receiving food stamps, is the wealthy person less likely than the poor person to have a tangency at a point such as *f* in Figure 5.7?

4.6 Federal housing assistance programs provide allowances that can be spent only on housing. Several empirical studies find that recipients increase their non-housing expenditures by 10% to 20% (Harkness and Newman, 2003). Show that recipients might—but do not necessarily—increase their spending on non-housing, depending on their tastes.

4.7 Federal housing ($44 billion in 2011) and food stamp subsidy ($78 billion in 2011) programs are two of the largest in-kind transfer programs for the poor. Many poor people are eligible for both programs: 30% of housing assistance recipients also used food stamps, and 38% of FSP participants also received housing assistance (Harkness and Newman, 2003). Suppose Jill's income is $500 a month, which she spends on food and housing. The prices of food and housing are each $1 per unit. Draw her budget line. If she receives $100 in food stamps and $200 in a housing subsidy (which she can spend only on housing), how do her budget line and opportunity set change?

4.8 Educational vouchers are increasingly used in various parts of the United States. Suppose that the government offers poor people $5,000 education vouchers that can be used only to pay for education. Doreen would be better off with $5,000 in cash than with the educational voucher. In a graph, determine the cash value, V, Doreen places on the education voucher (that is, the amount of cash that would leave her as well off as with the voucher). Show how much education and "all other goods" she would consume with the educational voucher versus the cash payment of V.

5. Deriving Labor Supply Curves

5.1 Under a welfare plan, poor people are given a lump-sum payment of L. If they accept this welfare payment, they must pay a high marginal tax rate, $\alpha = \frac{1}{2}$, on anything they earn. If they do not accept the welfare payment, they do not have to pay a tax on their earnings. Show that whether an individual accepts welfare depends on the individual's tastes.

5.2 If an individual's labor supply curve slopes forward at low wages and bends backward at high wages, is leisure a Giffen good? If so, is leisure a Giffen good at high or low wage rates?

5.3 Bessie, who can currently work as many hours as she wants at a wage of w, chooses to work 10 hours a day. Her boss decides to limit the number of hours that she can work to 8 hours per day. Show how her budget constraint and choice of hours change. Is she unambiguously worse off as a result of this change? Why or why not?

5.4 Originally when he could work as many hours as he wanted at a wage w, Roy chose to work seven hours a day. The employer now offers him w for the first eight hours in a day and an over-time wage of $1.5w$ for every hour he works beyond a minimum of eight hours. Show how his budget constraint changes. Will he necessarily choose to work more than seven hours a day? Would your answer be different if he originally chose to work eight hours?

5.5 Jerome moonlights: He holds down two jobs. The higher-paying job pays w, but he can work at most eight hours. The other job pays w^*, but he can work as many hours as he wants. Show how Jerome determines how many total hours to work. Now suppose that the job with no restriction on hours was the higher paying job. How do Jerome's budget constraint and behavior change?

5.6 Taxes during the fourteenth century were very progressive. The 1377 poll tax on the Duke of Lancaster was 520 times that on a peasant. A poll tax is a lump-sum (fixed amount) tax per person, which is independent of the hours a person works or earns. Use a graph to show the effect of a poll tax on the labor-leisure decision. Does knowing that the tax was progressive tell us whether a nobleman or a peasant—assuming they have identical tastes—worked more hours?

5.7 Today, most developed countries have progressive income taxes. Under such a taxation program, is the marginal tax higher than, equal to, or lower than the average tax?

*5.8 Several political leaders, including some past presidential candidates, have proposed a flat income tax, where the marginal tax rate is constant. As of 2009, 24 countries—including 20 formerly centrally planned economies of Central and Eastern Europe and Eurasia—switched to a flat personal income tax rate (Duncan and Peter, 2009). Show that if each person is allowed a "personal deduction" where the first $10,000 earned by the person is untaxed, the flat tax can be a *progressive* tax in which rich people pay a higher average tax rate than poor people.

5.9 Inheritance taxes are older than income taxes. Caesar Augustus instituted a 5% tax on all inheritances (except gifts to children and spouses) to provide retirement funds for the military. During the last couple of decades, congressional Republicans and Democrats have vociferously debated the wisdom of cutting income taxes and inheritance taxes (which the Republicans call the death tax) to stimulate the economy by inducing people to work harder. Presumably, the government cares about a tax's effect on work effort and tax revenues.

a. George views leisure as a normal good. He works at a job that pays w an hour. Use a labor-leisure analysis to compare the effects on the hours he works from a marginal tax rate on his wage, α, or a lump-sum tax (a tax collected regardless of the number of hours he works), T. If the per-hour tax is used, he works 10 hours and earns $(1 - \alpha)10w$. The government sets $T = \alpha 10w$, so that it collects the same amount of money from either tax.

b. Now suppose that the government wants to raise a given amount of revenue through taxation by imposing either an inheritance tax or an income (wage) tax. Which is likely to reduce George's hours of work more, and why? (*Hint*: See Solved Problem 5.4.)

*5.10 Prescott (2004) argued that U.S. employees work 50% more than do German, French, and Italian employees because European employees face lower marginal tax rates. Assuming that workers in all four countries have the same tastes toward leisure and goods, must it necessarily be true that U.S. employees work longer hours? Use graphs to illustrate your answer, and explain why it is true or is not true. Does Prescott's evidence indicate anything about the relative sizes of the substitution and income effects? Why or why not?

*5.11 Originally, Julia could work as many hours as she wanted at a wage of w. She chose to work 12 hours per day. Then, her employer told her that, in the future, she may work as many hours as she wants up to a maximum of 8 hours (and she can find no additional part-time job). How does her optimal choice between leisure and goods change? Does this change hurt her?

5.12 Using calculus, show the effect of a change in the wage on the amount of leisure that an individual wants to consume. **M**

5.13 Suppose that Joe's wage varies with the hours he works: $w(H) = aH, a > 0$. Use both a graph and calculus to show how the number of hours he chooses to work depends on his tastes. **M**

5.14 Derive Sarah's labor supply function given that she has a quasilinear utility function, $U = Y^{0.5} + 2N$ and her income is $Y = wH$. What is the slope of her labor supply curve with respect to a change in the wage? (*Hint*: See Solved Problem 5.3.) **M**

5.15 Joe won $365,000 a year for life in the state lottery. Use a labor-leisure choice analysis to answer the following:

a. Show how Joe's lottery winnings affect the position of his budget line.

b. Joe's utility function for goods per day (Y) and hours of leisure per day (N) is $U = Y + 240N^{0.5}$. After winning the lottery, does Joe continue to work the same number of hours each day? What is the income effect of Joe's lottery gains on the amount of goods he buys per day? **M**

6. Challenge

6.1 Governments generally limit the amount of the subsidy. For example, in Yukon, Canada, the 2012 maximum subsidy for an infant is $625 per month. In 2009, a family's maximum child-care subsidy was 85% of the cost of care in Nevada and 70% in Louisiana, $72.50 per week in Alabama, 10% of gross income in Maine, and $153 per month plus $5 per month for each extra child in Mississippi. A binding limit on the subsidy creates a kink in the budget constraint. Show how a limit changes the analysis in the Challenge Solution.

*6.2 How do parents who do not receive subsidies feel about the two child-care programs analyzed in the Challenge Solution figure? (*Hint*: Use a supply-and-demand analysis.)

*6.3 How could the government set a smaller lump-sum subsidy that would make poor parents as well off as with the hourly child-care subsidy yet cost the government less? Given the tastes shown in the Challenge Solution figure, what would be the effect on the number of hours of child-care service that these parents buy? Are you calculating a compensating variation or an equivalent variation (given that the original family is initially at e_1 in the figure)?

6.4 U.S., Canadian, and many other governments limit the amount of a child-care subsidy that a family may receive. How does such a limit affect the Challenge Solution analysis?

Firms and Production

6

Hard work never killed anybody, but why take a chance? —Charlie McCarthy

CHALLENGE

Labor Productivity During Recessions

A few years ago, the American Licorice Company plant manager, John Nelson, made $10 million in capital investments when loans were easy to come by. The firm expected that these investments would lower costs and help the plant thrive in tough times, as in 2008–2011.

The factory produces 150,000 pounds of Red Vines licorice a day. The company's red licorice outsells its black ten to one. Both types are manufactured in the same plant. The manufacturing process starts by combining flour and corn syrup (for red licorice) or molasses (for black licorice) to form a slurry in giant vats. The temperature is raised to 200° for several hours. Flavors are introduced and a dye is added for red licorice. Next, the mixture is drained from the vats into barrels and cooled overnight, after which it is extruded through a machine to form long strands. Other machines punch an airhole through the center of the strands. Finally, the strands are twisted and cut.

The firm uses two approaches to dry the licorice strands. At one station, three workers take the black licorice strands off a conveyor belt, place them onto tall racks, and then roll the racks into sauna-like drying rooms. At an adjacent station, one worker monitors an automated system that transports the many trays of red licorice strands into a drying room the size of a high school gym. The trays slowly wind their way along a mile-long path through the 180° room and emerge at the other end ready for packaging. This automated drying process was part of the firm's $10 million in capital investment, and allowed the company to cut its labor force from 450 to 240 workers. (Similarly, a temporary reduction in the work force occurred in 2012 when some of the firm's workers went on strike.)

Food manufacturers are usually less affected by recessions than are firms in other industries. Nonetheless, during major economic downturns, the demand curve for licorice may shift to the left, and Mr. Nelson must consider whether to reduce production by laying off some of his workers. He needs to decide how many workers to layoff. To make this decision, he faces a managerial problem: How much will the output produced per worker rise or fall with each additional layoff?

This chapter examines the nature of firms and how they choose their inputs to produce efficiently. Chapter 7 considers how firms choose the least costly among all possible efficient production processes. Then, Chapter 8 combines this information about costs with information about revenues to determine how firms select the output level that maximizes profit.

The main lesson of this chapter and the next is that firms are not black boxes that mysteriously transform inputs (such as labor, capital, and material) into outputs. Economic theory explains how firms make decisions about production processes, types of inputs to use, and the volume of output to produce.

In this chapter, we examine six main topics	

1. **The Ownership and Management of Firms.** Decisions must be made about how a firm is owned and managed.

2. **Production.** A firm converts inputs into outputs using one of possibly many available technologies.

3. **Short-Run Production: One Variable and One Fixed Input.** In the short run, only some inputs can be varied, so the firm changes its output by adjusting its variable inputs.

4. **Long-Run Production: Two Variable Inputs.** The firm has more flexibility in how it produces and how it changes its output level in the long run, when all factors can be varied.

5. **Returns to Scale.** How the ratio of output to input varies with the size of the firm is an important factor in determining a firm's size.

6. **Productivity and Technical Change.** The amount of output that can be produced with a given quantity of inputs varies across firms and over time.

6.1 The Ownership and Management of Firms

A **firm** is an organization that converts *inputs* such as labor, materials, and capital into *outputs*, the goods and services that it sells. U.S. Steel combines iron ore, machinery, and labor to create steel. A local restaurant buys raw food, cooks it, and serves it. A landscape designer hires gardeners, rents machines, buys trees and shrubs, transports them to a customer's home, and supervises the project.

Private, Public, and Nonprofit Firms

Atheism is a non-prophet organization. —George Carlin

Firms and organizations that pursue economic activity fit into three broad categories: the private sector, the public sector, and the nonprofit sector. The *private sector*, sometimes referred to as the *for-profit private sector*, consists of firms owned by individuals or other non-governmental entities and whose owners try to earn a profit. Throughout this book, we concentrate on these firms. In almost every country, this sector contributes the most to the gross domestic product (GDP, a measure of a country's total output).

The *public sector* consists of firms and organizations that are owned by governments or government agencies. For example, the National Railroad Passenger Corporation (Amtrak) is owned primarily by the U.S. government. The armed forces and the court system are also part of the public sector, as are most schools, colleges, and universities.

The government produces less than one-fifth of the total GDP in most developed countries, including Switzerland (9%), the United States (12%), Ireland (12%), Canada (13%), Australia (16%), and the United Kingdom (17%).[1] The government's share is higher in some developed countries that provide many government services or maintain a relatively large army including Iceland (20%), the Netherlands (21%), Sweden (22%), and Israel (24%). The government's share varies substantially in less-developed countries, ranging from very low levels in Nigeria (4%) to very high levels in Eritrea (94%). Strikingly, a number of former communist countries such as Albania (20%) and China (28%) now have public sectors of comparable relative size to developed countries and hence must rely primarily on the private sector for economic activity.

The *nonprofit sector* consists of organizations that are neither government-owned nor intended to earn a profit, but typically pursue social or public interest objectives. Well-known examples include Greenpeace, Alcoholics Anonymous, and the Salvation Army, along with many other charitable, educational, health, and religious organizations.

According to the 2012 *U.S. Statistical Abstract*, the private sector created 75% of the U.S. gross domestic product, the government sector was responsible for 12%, and the nonprofits and households produced the remaining 13%.

Sometimes all three sectors play an important role in the same industry. For example, in the United States, Canada, the United Kingdom, and in many other countries, for-profit, nonprofit, and government-owned hospitals coexist. Enterprises that are partially owned by government and partially owned by private interests are referred to as *mixed enterprises* or *public-private partnerships*.

The Ownership of For-Profit Firms

The legal structure of a firm determines who is liable for its debts. Within the private sector, there are three primary legal forms of organization: a sole proprietorship, a general partnership, or a corporation.

Sole proprietorships are firms owned by an individual who is personally liable for the firm's debts.

General partnerships (often called *partnerships*) are businesses jointly owned and controlled by two or more people who are personally liable for the firm's debts. The owners operate under a partnership agreement. In most legal jurisdictions, if any partner leaves, the partnership agreement ends and a new partnership agreement is created if the firm is to continue operations.

Corporations are owned by *shareholders* in proportion to the number of shares or amount of stock they hold. The shareholders elect a board of directors to represent them. In turn, the board of directors usually hires managers to oversee the firm's operations. Some corporations are very small and have a single shareholder; others are very large and have thousands of shareholders. The legal name of a corporation often includes the term Incorporated (Inc.) or Limited (Ltd) to indicate its corporate status.

A fundamental characteristic of corporations is that the owners are not personally liable for the firm's debts; they have **limited liability:** The personal assets of corporate owners cannot be taken to pay a corporation's debts even if it goes into

---

[1]The data in this paragraph are from Heston et al. (2006) and the U.S. Statistical Abstract for 2012. Western governments' shares increased markedly (but presumably temporarily) during the Great Recession starting in 2007, when they bought part or all of a number of private firms to keep them from going bankrupt.

bankruptcy. Because corporations have limited liability, the most that shareholders can lose is the amount they paid for their stock, which typically becomes worthless if the corporation declares bankruptcy.[2]

The purpose of limiting liability was to allow firms to raise funds and grow beyond what was possible when owners risked personal assets on any firm in which they invested. According to the 2012 *U.S. Statistical Abstract*, U.S. corporations are responsible for 81% business receipts and 58% of net business income even though they are only 18% of all nonfarm firms. Nonfarm sole proprietorships are 72% of firms but make only 4% of the sales revenue and earn 15% of net income. Partnerships are 10% of firms, account for 15% of revenue, and make 27% of net income.

The Management of Firms

In a small firm, the owner usually manages the firm's operations. In larger firms, typically corporations and larger partnerships, a manager or a management team usually runs the company. In such firms, owners, managers, and lower-level supervisors are all decision makers.

As revelations about Enron, WorldCom, American International Group (AIG), MF Global, and JP Morgan Chase illustrate, various decision makers may have conflicting objectives. What is in the best interest of the owners may not be in the best interest of managers or other employees. For example, a manager may want a fancy office, a company car, a corporate jet, and other perks, but an owner would likely oppose those drains on profit.

The owner replaces the manager if the manager pursues personal objectives rather than the firm's objectives. In a corporation, the board of directors is responsible for ensuring that the manager stays on track. If the manager and the board of directors are ineffective, the shareholders can fire both or change certain policies through votes at the corporation's annual shareholders' meeting. Until Chapter 19, we'll ignore the potential conflict between managers and owners and assume that the owner *is* the manager of the firm and makes all the decisions.

What Owners Want

Economists usually assume that a firm's owners try to maximize profit. Presumably, most people invest in a firm to make money—lots of money, they hope. They want the firm to earn a positive profit rather than suffer a loss (a negative profit). A firm's **profit**, π, is the difference between its revenue, R, which is what it earns from selling a good, and its cost, C, which is what it pays for labor, materials, and other inputs:

$$\pi = R - C. \tag{6.1}$$

Typically, revenue is p, the price, times q, the firm's quantity: $R = pq$. (For simplicity, we will assume that the firm produces only one product.)

In reality, some owners have other objectives, such as running as large a firm as possible, owing a fancy building, or keeping risks low. However, Chapter 8 shows that a firm in a highly competitive market is likely to be driven out of business if it doesn't maximize its profit.

---

[2]Recently, the United States (1996), the United Kingdom (2000), and other countries have allowed any sole proprietorship, partnership, or corporation to register as a *limited liability company* (LLC). Thus, all firms—not just corporations—can now obtain limited liability.

To maximize its profit, a firm must produce as efficiently as possible. A firm engages in **efficient production** (achieves **technological efficiency**) if it cannot produce its current level of output with fewer inputs, given its existing knowledge about technology and how to organize production. Equivalently, a firm produces efficiently if, given the quantity of inputs used, no more output can be produced using existing knowledge.

If a firm does not produce efficiently, it cannot maximize its profit—so efficient production is a *necessary condition* for maximizing profit. Even if a firm efficiently produces a given level of output, it will not maximize its profit if that output level is too high or too low or if it uses an excessively expensive production process. Thus, efficient production alone is not a *sufficient condition* to ensure that a firm maximizes its profit.

A firm may use engineers and other experts to determine the most efficient ways to produce using a known method or technology. However, this knowledge does not indicate which of the many technologies, each of which uses different combinations of inputs, allows for production at the lowest cost or with the highest possible profit. How to produce at the lowest cost is an economic decision typically made by the firm's manager (see Chapter 7).

6.2 Production

A firm uses a *technology* or *production process* to transform *inputs* or *factors of production* into *outputs*. Firms use many types of inputs, most of which fall into three broad categories:

1. **Capital services (K):** use of long-lived inputs such as land, buildings (such as factories and stores), and equipment (such as machines and trucks)
2. **Labor services (L):** hours of work provided by managers, skilled workers (such as architects, economists, engineers, and plumbers), and less-skilled workers (such as custodians, construction laborers, and assembly-line workers)
3. **Materials (M):** natural resources and raw goods (such as oil, water, and wheat) and processed products (such as aluminum, plastic, paper, and steel) that are typically consumed in producing, or incorporated in making, the final product

For brevity, we typically refer to *capital services* as *capital* and *labor services* as *labor*. The output can be a *service* such as an automobile tune-up by a mechanic, or a *physical product* such as a computer chip or a potato chip.

Production Functions

Firms can transform inputs into outputs in many different ways. Candy manufacturing companies differ in the skills of their workforce and the amount of equipment they use. While all employ a chef, a manager, and relatively unskilled workers, some candy firms also use skilled technicians and modern equipment. In small candy companies, the relatively unskilled workers shape the candy, decorate it, package it, and box it by hand. In slightly larger firms, these same-level workers use conveyor belts and other industrial equipment. In modern large-scale plants, the relatively unskilled laborers work with robots and other state-of-the-art machines maintained by skilled technicians. Before deciding which production process to use, a firm must consider its options.

The various ways that a firm can transform inputs into output are summarized in the **production function**: the relationship between the quantities of inputs used and the *maximum* quantity of output that can be produced, given current knowledge about technology and organization. The production function for a firm that uses labor and capital only is

$$q = f(L, K), \tag{6.2}$$

where q units of output (wrapped candy bars) are produced using L units of labor services (days of work by relatively unskilled assembly-line workers) and K units of capital (the number of conveyor belts).

The production function shows only the *maximum* amount of output that can be produced from given levels of labor and capital, because the production function includes efficient production processes only. A profit-maximizing firm is not interested in production processes that are inefficient and wasteful: Why would the firm want to use two workers to do a job that one worker can perform as efficiently?

Time and the Variability of Inputs

A firm can more easily adjust its inputs in the long run than in the short run. Typically, a firm can vary the amount of materials and relatively unskilled labor it uses comparatively quickly. However, it needs more time to find and hire skilled workers, order new equipment, or build a new manufacturing plant.

The more time a firm has to adjust its inputs, the more factors of production it can alter. The **short run** is a period so brief that at least one factor of production cannot be varied practically. A factor that a firm cannot vary practically in the short run is called a **fixed input**. In contrast, a **variable input** is a factor of production whose quantity the firm can change readily during the relevant period. The **long run** is a long enough period that all inputs can be varied. In the long run all factors of production are variable inputs—no inputs are fixed.

Suppose that one day a painting company has more work than its crew can handle. Even if it wanted to, the firm does not have time to buy or rent an extra truck and buy another compressor to run a power sprayer; these inputs are fixed in the short run. To complete the day's work, the firm uses its only truck to drop off a temporary worker, equipped with only a brush and a can of paint, at the last job. However in the long run, the firm can adjust all its inputs. If the firm wants to paint more houses every day, it can hire more full-time workers, purchase a second truck, get another compressor to run a power sprayer, and buy a computer to track its projects.

The time it takes for all inputs to be variable depends on the factors a firm uses. For a janitorial service whose only major input is workers, the long run is a brief period. In contrast, an automobile manufacturer may need many years to build a new manufacturing plant or design and construct a new type of machine. A pistachio farmer needs about a decade before newly planted trees yield a substantial crop of nuts.

For many firms over a short period, say a month, materials and often labor are variable inputs. However, labor is not always a variable input. Finding additional highly skilled workers may take substantial time. Similarly, capital may be a variable or a fixed input. A firm can rent small capital assets (trucks and personal computers) quickly, but it may take years to obtain larger capital assets (buildings and large specialized pieces of equipment).

To illustrate the greater flexibility a firm has in the long run than in the short run, we examine the production function in Equation 6.2, in which output is a function of only labor and capital. We first look at the short-run and then at the long-run production process.

6.3 Short-Run Production: One Variable and One Fixed Input

In the short run, we assume that capital is a fixed input and that labor is a variable input, so the firm can increase output only by increasing the amount of labor it uses. In the short run, the firm's production function is

$$q = (L, \overline{K}), \tag{6.3}$$

where q is output, L is workers, and $\overline{K}$ is the fixed number of units of capital. The short-run production function is also referred to as the **total product of labor**—the amount of output (or *total product*) that a given amount of labor can produce holding the quantity of other inputs fixed.

The exact relationship between *output* or *total product* and *labor* is given in Equation 6.3. The **marginal product of labor** (MP_L) is the change in total output resulting from using an extra unit of labor, holding other factors (capital) constant. The marginal product of labor is the partial derivative of the production function with respect to labor,

$$MP_L = \frac{\partial q}{\partial L} = \frac{\partial f(L, K)}{\partial L}.$$

The **average product of labor** (AP_L) is the ratio of output to the number of workers used to produce that output,[3]

$$AP_L = \frac{q}{L}.$$

SOLVED PROBLEM 6.1

A computer assembly firm's production function is $q = 0.1LK + 3L^2K - 0.1L^3K$. What is its short-run production function if capital is fixed at $\overline{K} = 10$? Give the formulas for its marginal product of labor and its average product of labor. Draw two figures, one above the other. In the top figure, show the relationship between output (total product) and labor. In the bottom figure, show the MP_L and AP_L curves. Is this production function valid for all values of labor?

Answer

1. *Write the formula for the short-run production function by replacing K in the production function with its fixed short-run value.* To obtain a production function in the form of Equation 6.3, set capital in the production function equal to 10:

$$q = 0.1L(10) + 3L^2(10) - 0.1L^3(10) = L + 30L^2 - L^3.$$

2. *Determine the MP_L by differentiating the short-run production function with respect to labor.* The marginal product of labor is[4]

$$MP_L = \frac{dq}{dL} = \frac{d(L + 30L^2 - L^3)}{dL} = 1 + 60L - 3L^2.$$

---

[3]*Jargon alert*: Some economists call the MP_L the marginal physical product of labor and the AP_L the average physical product of labor.

[4]Because the short-run production function is solely a function of labor, $MP_L = dq/dL$. An alternative way to derive the MP_L is to differentiate the production function with respect to labor and then set capital equal to 10: $MP_L = \partial q/\partial L = \partial(0.1LK + 3L^2K - 0.1L^3K)/\partial L = 0.1K + 6LK - 0.3L^2K$. Evaluating at $\overline{K} = 10$, we obtain $MP_L = 1 + 60L - 3L^2$.

3. *Determine the AP_L by dividing the short-run production function by labor.* The average product of labor is

$$AP_L = \frac{q}{L} = \frac{L + 30L^2 - L^3}{L} = 1 + 30L - L^2.$$

4. *Draw the requested figures by plotting the short-run production function, MP_L, and AP_L equations.* Figure 6.1 shows how the total product of labor, marginal product of labor, and average product of labor vary with the number of workers.

5. *Show that the production function equation does not hold for all values of labor by noting that, beyond a certain level, extra workers lower output.* In the figure, the total product curve to the right of $L = 20$ is a dashed line, indicating that this section is not part of the true production function. Because output falls—the curve decreases—as the firm uses more than 20 workers, a rational firm would never use more than 20 workers. From the definition of a production function, we want the maximum quantity of output that can be produced from the given inputs, so if the firm had more than 20 workers, it could increase its output by sending the extra employees home. (The portions of the MP_L and AP_L curves beyond 20 workers also appear as dashed lines because they correspond to irrelevant sections of the short-run production function equation.)

Interpretation of Graphs

Figure 6.1 shows how the total product of labor (computers assembled), the average product of labor, and the marginal product of labor vary with the number of workers. The figures are smooth curves because the firm can hire a "fraction of a worker" by employing a worker for a fraction of a day. The total product of labor curve in panel a shows that output rises with labor until the firm employs 20 workers.

Panel b illustrates how the average product of labor and the marginal product of labor vary with the number of workers. By lining up the two panels vertically, we can show the relationships between the total product of labor, marginal product of labor, and average product of labor curves.

In most production processes—and as Figure 6.1 shows—the average product of labor first rises and then falls as labor increases. For example, the AP_L curve may initially rise because it helps to have more than two hands when assembling a computer. One worker holds a part in place while another worker bolts it down. As a result, output increases more than in proportion to labor, so the average product of labor rises. Similarly, output may initially rise more than in proportion to labor because of greater specialization of activities. With greater specialization, workers are assigned to tasks at which they are particularly adept, and time is saved by not having workers move from one task to another.

However, as the number of workers rises further, output may not increase by as much per worker because workers have to wait to use a particular piece of equipment or because they get in each other's way. In Figure 6.1, as the number of workers exceeds 15, total output increases less than in proportion to labor, so the average product falls.

The three curves are geometrically related. First, we use panel b to illustrate the relationship between the average and marginal product of labor curves. Then, we use panels a and b to show the relationship between the total product of labor curve and the other two curves.

Figure 6.1 Production Relationships with Variable Labor

(a) The short-run total product of labor curve, $q = L + 30L^2 - L^3$, shows how much output, q, can be assembled with 10 units of capital, which is fixed in the short run. Where extra workers reduce the amount of output produced, the total product of labor curve is a dashed line, which indicates that such production is inefficient production and not part of the production function. The slope of the line from the origin to point B is the average product of labor for 15 workers. (b) The marginal product of labor, MP_L, equals the average product of labor, AP_L, at the peak of the average product curve where the firm employs 15 workers.

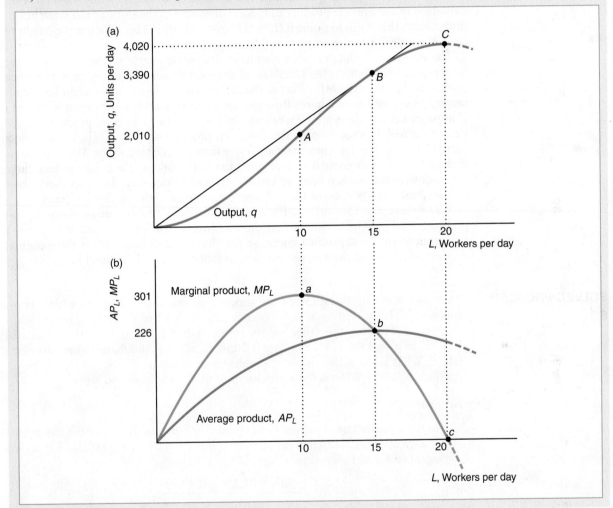

The average product of labor curve slopes upward where the marginal product of labor curve is above it and slopes downward where the marginal product curve is below it. If an extra worker adds more output—that worker's marginal product—than the average product of the initial workers, the extra worker raises the average product. As panel b shows, when there are fewer than 15 workers, the marginal product curve is above the average product curve, so the average product curve is upward sloping.

Similarly, if the marginal product of labor for a new worker is less than the former average product of labor, then the average product of labor falls. In the figure, the average product of labor falls beyond 15 workers. Because the average product of labor curve rises when the marginal product of labor curve is above it, and the average product of labor falls when the marginal product of labor is below it, the average product of labor curve reaches a peak, point *b* in panel b, where the marginal product of labor curve crosses it.[5]

We can determine the average product of labor curve, shown in panel b of Figure 6.1, using the total product of labor curve, shown in panel a. The AP_L for *L* workers equals the slope of a straight line from the origin to a point on the total product of labor curve for *L* workers in panel a. The slope ("rise over run") of this line equals output ("rise") divided by the number of workers ("run"), which is the definition of the average product of labor. For example, the slope of the straight line drawn from the origin to point *B* ($L = 15$, $q = 3{,}390$) is 226, which is the height of the AP_L curve in panel b when $L = 15$.

The marginal product of labor also has a geometric interpretation in terms of the total product of labor curve. The slope of the total product of labor curve at a given point, d*q*/d*L*, equals the MP_L. That is, the MP_L equals the slope of a straight line that is tangent to the total output curve for a given number of workers. For example, at point *C* in panel a where there are 20 workers, the line tangent to the total product curve is flat, so the MP_L is zero: A little extra labor has no effect on output. The total product curve is upward sloping when there are fewer than 20 workers, so the MP_L is positive. If the firm is foolish enough to hire more than 20 workers, the total product curve slopes downward (dashed line), so the MP_L would be negative: Extra workers lower output. Again, this portion of the MP_L curve is not part of the production function.

When there are 15 workers, the average product of labor equals the marginal product of labor. The reason is that the line from the origin to point *B* in panel a is tangent to the total product curve, so the slope of that line, 226, is the marginal product of labor and the average product of labor at point *b* in panel b.

SOLVED PROBLEM 6.2

Tian and Wan (2000) estimated the production function for rice in China as a function of labor, fertilizer, and other inputs such as seed, draft animals, and equipment. Holding the other inputs besides labor fixed, the total product of labor is $\ln q = 4.63 + 1.29 \ln L - 0.2(\ln L)^2$. What is the marginal product of labor? What is the relationship of the marginal product of labor to the average product of labor? What is the elasticity of output with respect to labor?

Answer

1. *Totally differentiate the short-run production function to obtain the marginal product of labor.* Differentiating $\ln q = 4.63 + 1.29 \ln L - 0.2(\ln L)^2$ with respect to *q* and *L*, we obtain

$$\frac{dq/dL}{q} = \frac{1.29 - 0.4 \ln L}{L}.$$

---

[5]We can use calculus to prove that the MP_L curve intersects the AP_L at its peak. Because capital is fixed, we can write the production function solely in terms of labor: $q = f(L)$. In the figure, $MP_L = dq/dL = df/dL > 0$. and $d^2f/dL^2 < 0$. A necessary condition to identify the amount of labor where the average product of labor curve, $AP_L = q/L = f(L)/L$, reaches a maximum is that the derivative of AP_L with respect to *L* equals zero:

$$\frac{dAP_L}{dL} = \left(\frac{dq}{dL} - \frac{q}{L}\right)\frac{1}{L} = 0.$$

(At the *L* determined by this first-order condition, AP_L is maximized if the second-order condition is negative: $d^2AP_L/dL^2 = d^2f/dL^2 < 0$.) From the necessary condition, $MP_L = dq/dL = q/L = AP_L$, at the peak of the AP_L curve.

By rearranging terms, we find that the

$$MP_L = dq/dL = (q/L)(1.29 - 0.4 \ln L).$$

2. *Determine the relationship between MP_L and AP_L using the expression for MP_L.* Using the definition for $AP_L = q/L$, we can rewrite the expression we derived for the marginal product of labor as $MP_L = AP_L(1.29 - 0.4 \ln L)$, so the MP_L is $(1.29 - 0.4 \ln L)$ times as large as is the AP_L. Equivalently, $MP_L/AP_L = 1.29 - 0.4 \ln L$.

3. *Show that the elasticity of output with respect to labor is the ratio of the marginal product of labor to the average product of labor and make use of the equation relating the MP_L to the AP_L.* Given the general definition of an elasticity, the elasticity of output produced with respect to labor is (dq/dL) (L/q). By substituting into this expression the definitions of $MP_L = dq/dL$ and $AP_L = q/L$, we find that the elasticity of output with respect to labor is $(dq/dL)(L/q) = MP_L/AP_L = 1.29 - 0.4 \ln L$.

Law of Diminishing Marginal Returns

Next to *supply equals demand*, probably the most commonly used phrase of economic jargon is the *law of diminishing marginal returns*. This "law" determines the shapes of the total product and marginal product of labor curves as a firm uses more and more labor. As with the "law" of supply and demand, this "law" is not theoretically necessary, but it is an empirical regularity.

The *law of diminishing marginal returns* (or *diminishing marginal product*) holds that *if a firm keeps increasing an input, holding all other inputs and technology constant, the corresponding increases in output will eventually become smaller.* That is, if only one input is increased, *the marginal product of that input will eventually diminish.* The marginal product of labor diminishes if $\partial MP_L/\partial L = \partial(\partial q/\partial L)/\partial L = \partial^2 q/\partial L^2 = \partial^2 f(L, K)/\partial L^2 < 0$. That is, the marginal product falls with increased labor if the second partial derivative of the production function with respect to labor is negative.

Panel b of Figure 6.1 illustrates diminishing marginal product of labor. At low levels of labor, the marginal product of labor rises with the number of workers. However, when the number of workers exceeds 10, each additional worker reduces the marginal product of labor.

Unfortunately, when attempting to cite this empirical regularity, many people overstate it. Instead of talking about "diminishing *marginal* returns," they talk about "diminishing returns." These phrases have different meanings. Where there are "diminishing marginal returns," the MP_L curve is falling—beyond 10 workers in panel b of Figure 6.1—but it may be positive, as the solid MP_L curve between 10 and 20 workers shows. With "diminishing returns," extra labor causes *output* to fall. Total returns diminish for more than 20 workers, and consequently the MP_L is negative, as the dashed MP_L line in panel b shows.

Thus, saying that there are diminishing returns is much stronger than saying that there are diminishing marginal returns. We often observe successful firms producing with diminishing marginal returns to labor, but we never see a well-run firm operating with diminishing total returns. Such a firm could produce more output by using fewer inputs.

A second common misinterpretation of this law is the claim that marginal products must fall as we increase an input without requiring that technology and other inputs remain constant. If we increase labor while simultaneously increasing other factors or adopting superior technologies, the marginal product of labor may rise indefinitely. Thomas Malthus provided the most famous example of this fallacy (as well as the reason economics is referred to as the "dismal science").

APPLICATION

Malthus and the Green Revolution

In 1798, Thomas Malthus—a clergyman and professor of modern history and political economy—predicted that population (if unchecked) would grow more rapidly than food production because the quantity of land was fixed. The problem, he believed, was that the fixed amount of land would lead to diminishing marginal product of labor, so output would rise less than in proportion to the increase in farm workers. Malthus grimly concluded that mass starvation would result. Brander and Taylor (1998) argued that such a disaster may have occurred on Easter Island around 500 years ago.

Today the earth supports a population about seven times greater than when Malthus made his predictions. Why haven't most of us starved to death? The simple explanation is that substantial technological progress has occurred in agriculture.

Two hundred years ago, most of the world's population had to work in agriculture. Today, less than 2% of the U.S. population works in agriculture. Over the last century, food production grew substantially faster than the population in most developed countries. For example, since World War II, the U.S. population doubled but U.S. food production tripled.

In 1850, it took more than 80 hours of labor to produce 100 bushels of corn. Introducing mechanical power cut the required labor in half. Labor hours were again cut in half by the introduction of hybrid seed and chemical fertilizers, and then in half again by the advent of herbicides and pesticides. Biotechnology, with the 1996 introduction of herbicide-tolerant and insect-resistant crops, has reduced the labor required to produce 100 bushels of corn to about two hours. Today, the output of a U.S. farm worker is 215% of that of a worker 50 years ago.

Of course, the risk of starvation is more severe in developing countries. Luckily, one man decided to defeat the threat of Malthusian disaster personally. Do you know anyone who saved a life? A hundred lives? Do you know the name of the man who probably saved the most lives in history? According to some estimates, during the second half of the twentieth century, Norman Borlaug and his fellow scientists prevented a *billion deaths* with their *green revolution*, which used modified seeds, tractors, irrigation, soil treatments, fertilizer, and various other ideas to increase production. Thanks to these innovations, wheat, rice, and corn production increased significantly in many low-income countries. In the late 1960s, Dr. Borlaug and his colleagues brought the techniques they developed in Mexico to India and Pakistan to reduce the risk of mass starvation there. The results were stunning. In 1968, Pakistan's wheat crop soared to 146% of the 1965 pre-green revolution crop. By 1970, it was 183% of the 1965 crop.

However, as Dr. Borlaug noted in his Nobel Prize speech, superior science is not the complete answer to preventing starvation. A sound economic system is needed as well.

It is the lack of a sound economic system that has doomed many Africans. Per capita food production has fallen in Sub-Saharan Africa over the past two decades and widespread starvation has plagued some African countries in recent

years. In 2012, the United Nations reported that hunger is the world's number one health risk, one in seven people in the world go to bed hungry, and one in four children in developing countries is underweight. Nearly half of all children under five in Southern Asia (India, Pakistan, Bangladesh and nearby countries) and 28% in Sub-Saharan Africa are underweight, and 15 million children die of hunger each year.

Although droughts have contributed, these tragedies are primarily due to political problems such as wars and the breakdown of economic production and distribution systems. Further, "neo-Malthusians" point to other areas of concern, emphasizing the role of global climate change in disrupting food production, and claiming that current methods of food production are not sustainable in view of environmental damage and continuing rapid population growth in many parts of the world. If these economic and political problems cannot be solved, Malthus may prove to be right for the wrong reason.

6.4 Long-Run Production: Two Variable Inputs

Eternity is a terrible thought. I mean, where's it going to end? —Tom Stoppard

We started our analysis of production functions by looking at a short-run production function in which one input, capital, is fixed, and the other, labor, is variable. In the long run, however, both of these inputs are variable. With both factors variable, a firm can produce a given level of output by using a great deal of labor and very little capital, a great deal of capital and very little labor, or moderate amounts of each. That is, the firm can substitute one input for another while continuing to produce the same level of output, in much the same way that a consumer can maintain a given level of utility by substituting one good for another.

Typically, a firm can produce in various ways, some of which require more labor than others. For example, a lumberyard can produce 200 planks an hour with 10 workers using handsaws, or 4 workers using handheld power saws, or 2 workers using bench power saws.

We can illustrate the basic idea using a Cobb-Douglas production function,

$$q = AL^aK^b, \tag{6.4}$$

where A, a, and b are constants.[6] If we redefine a unit of output as $1/A$, we can write the production function as $q = L^aK^b$, which is the form we generally use. Hsieh (1995) estimated that using a Cobb-Douglas production function for a U.S. firm producing electronics and other electrical equipment,

$$q = L^{0.5}K^{0.5}, \tag{6.5}$$

---

[6]The Cobb-Douglas production function (named after its inventors, Charles W. Cobb, a mathematician, and Paul H. Douglas, an economist and U.S. senator) is the most commonly used production function. The Cobb-Douglas production function has the same functional form as the Cobb-Douglas utility function, which we studied in Chapters 3 through 5. Unlike in those chapters, we do not require that $b = 1 - a$ in this chapter.

where L is labor (workers) per day and K is capital services per day. From inspection, there are many combinations of labor and capital that will produce the same level of output.

Isoquants

We can summarize the possible combinations of inputs that will produce a given level of output using an **isoquant**, which is a curve that shows the efficient combinations of labor and capital that can produce a single (*iso*) level of output (*quant*ity). If the production function is $q = f(L, K)$, then the equation for an isoquant where output is held constant at $\bar{q}$ is

$$\bar{q} = f(L, K) \tag{6.6}$$

For our particular production function, Equation 6.5, the isoquant is $\bar{q} = L^{0.5}K^{0.5}$.

Figure 6.2 shows an isoquant for $q = 6$, $q = 9$, and $q = 12$, which are three of the many possible isoquants. The isoquants show a firm's flexibility in producing a given level of output. These isoquants are smooth curves because the firm can use fractional units of each input.

Many combinations of labor and capital, (L, K), will produce 6 units of output, including (1, 36), (2, 18), (3, 12), (4, 9), (6, 6), (9, 4), (12, 3), (18, 2), and (36, 1). Figure 6.2 shows some of these combinations as points *a* through *f* on the $q = 6$ isoquant.

Properties of Isoquants. Isoquants have most of the same properties as indifference curves. The main difference is that an isoquant holds quantity constant, whereas an indifference curve holds utility constant. The quantities associated with isoquants have cardinal properties (for example, an output of 12 is twice as much as an output of 6), while the utilities associated with indifference curves have only ordinal properties (for example, 12 utils are associated with more pleasure than 6, but not necessarily twice as much pleasure).

We now consider four major properties of isoquants. Most of these properties result from efficient production by firms.

First, *the farther an isoquant is from the origin, the greater the level of output.* That is, the more inputs a firm uses, the more output it gets if it produces efficiently. At point *e* in Figure 6.2, the electronics firm is producing 6 units·of output with 12 workers and 3 units of capital. If the firm holds the number of workers constant and adds 9 more units of capital, it produces at point *g*. Point *g* must be on an isoquant with a higher level of output—here, 12 units—if the firm is producing efficiently and not wasting the extra labor.

Second, *isoquants do not cross.* Such intersections are inconsistent with the requirement that the firm always produces efficiently. For example, if the $q = 15$ and $q = 20$ isoquants crossed, the firm could produce at either output level with the same combination of labor and capital. The firm must be producing inefficiently if it produces $q = 15$ when it could produce $q = 20$. Thus, that labor-capital combination should not lie on the $q = 15$ isoquant, which should include only efficient combinations of inputs. So, efficiency requires that isoquants do not cross.

Third, *isoquants slope downward.* If an isoquant sloped upward, the firm could produce the same level of output with relatively few inputs or relatively many inputs. Producing with relatively many inputs would be inefficient. Consequently, because isoquants show only efficient production, an upward-sloping isoquant is impossible.

Figure 6.2 Family of Isoquants for a U.S. Electronics Manufacturing Firm

These isoquants for a U.S. firm producing electronics and other electrical equipment (Hsieh, 1995) show the combinations of labor and capital that produce various levels of output. Isoquants farther from the origin correspond to higher levels of output. Points *a*, *b*, *c*, *d*, *e*, and *f* are various combinations of labor and capital that the firm can use to produce *q* = 6 units of output. If the firm holds capital constant at 12 and increases labor from 3 (point *b*) to 12 (point *g*), the firm shifts from operating on the *q* = 6 isoquant to producing on the *q* = 12 isoquant.

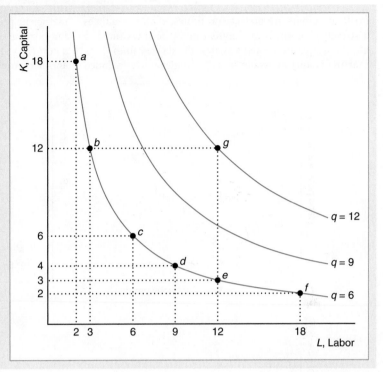

Fourth, *isoquants must be thin*. This result follows from virtually the same argument we just used to show that isoquants slope downward.

Shape of Isoquants. The curvature of an isoquant shows how readily a firm can substitute one input for another. The two extreme cases are production processes in which inputs are perfect substitutes and those in which inputs cannot be substituted for each other.

If the inputs are perfect substitutes, each isoquant is a straight line. Suppose either potatoes from Maine, *x*, or potatoes from Idaho, *y*, both of which are measured in pounds per day, can be used to produce potato salad, *q*, measured in pounds. This technology has a *linear production function*,

$$q = x + y.$$

A pound of potato salad can be produced by using one pound of Idaho potatoes and no Maine potatoes, one pound of Maine potatoes and no Idaho potatoes, or a half pound of each. The isoquant for *q* = one pound of potato salad is $1 = x + y$, or $y = 1 - x$. The slope of this straight-line isoquant is −1. Panel a of Figure 6.3 shows the *q* = 1, 2, and 3 isoquants.

Sometimes it is impossible to substitute one input for the other: Inputs must be used in fixed proportions. Such a technology is called a *fixed-proportions production function*. For example, the inputs needed to produce a 12-ounce box of cereal, *q*, are cereal (12-ounce units per day), *g*, and cardboard boxes (boxes per day), *b*. This fixed-proportions production function is

$$q = \min(g, b),$$

Figure 6.3 Substitutability of Inputs

(a) If the inputs are perfect substitutes, each isoquant is a straight line. (b) If the inputs cannot be substituted at all, the isoquants are right angles (the dashed lines show that the isoquants would be right angles if we included inefficient production). (c) Typical isoquants lie between the extreme cases of straight lines and right angles. Along a curved isoquant, the ability to substitute one input for another varies.

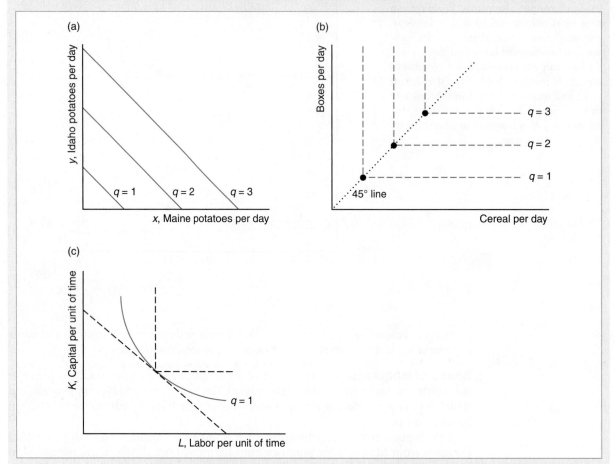

where the min function means "the minimum number of g or b." For example, if the firm has $g = 4$ units of cereal and $b = 3$ boxes, it can produce only $q = 3$ boxes of cereal. Thus, in panel b of Figure 6.3, the only efficient points of production are the large dots along the 45° line, where the firm uses equal quantities of both inputs. Dashed lines show that the isoquants would be right angles if isoquants could include inefficient production processes.

Other production processes allow imperfect substitution between inputs. These isoquants are convex (so the middle of the isoquant is closer to the origin than it would be if the isoquant were a straight line). They do not have the same slope at every point, unlike the straight-line isoquants. Most isoquants are smooth, slope downward, curve away from the origin, and lie between the extreme cases of straight lines (perfect substitutes) and right angles (nonsubstitutes), as panel c of Figure 6.3 illustrates.

APPLICATION

A Semiconductor Integrated Circuit Isoquant

We can show why isoquants curve away from the origin by deriving an isoquant for semiconductor integrated circuits (ICs, or "chips"). ICs—the "brains" of computers and other electronic devices—are made by building up layers of conductive and insulating materials on silicon wafers. Each wafer contains many ICs, which are subsequently cut into individual chips, called *dice*.

Semiconductor manufacturers ("fabs") buy the silicon wafers and then use labor and capital to produce the chips. A semiconductor IC's several layers of conductive and insulating materials are arranged in patterns that define the function of the chip.

During the manufacture of ICs, a track moves a wafer into a machine, where the wafer is spun and a light-sensitive liquid called photoresist is applied to its whole surface. Next, the photoresist is hardened. Then, the wafer advances along the track to a point where photolithography is used to define patterns in the photoresist. In photolithography, light transfers a pattern from a template, called a photomask, to the photoresist, which is then "developed" like film, creating a pattern by removing the resist from certain areas. A subsequent process can then add to or etch away those areas not protected by the resist.

In a repetition of this entire procedure, additional layers are created on the wafer. Because the conducting and insulating patterns in each layer interact with those in the previous layers, the patterns must line up correctly.

To align layers properly, firms use combinations of labor and equipment. In the least capital-intensive technology, employees use machines called *aligners*. Operators use microscopes and line up the layers by hand, and then expose the entire surface. An operator running an aligner can produce 250 layers, or 25 ten-layer chips per day.

A second, more capital-intensive technology uses machines called *steppers*. The stepper picks a spot on the wafer, automatically aligns the layers, and then exposes that area to light. Then the machine moves—*steps* to other sections—lining up and exposing each area in turn until the entire surface has been aligned and exposed. This technology requires less labor: A single worker can run two steppers and produce 500 layers, or 50 ten-layer chips per day.

A third, even more capital-intensive technology uses a stepper with wafer-handling equipment, which reduces the amount of labor even more. By linking the tracks directly to a stepper and automating the chip transfer process, human handling can be greatly reduced. A single worker can run four steppers with wafer-handling equipment and produce 1,000 layers, or 100 ten-layer chips per day.

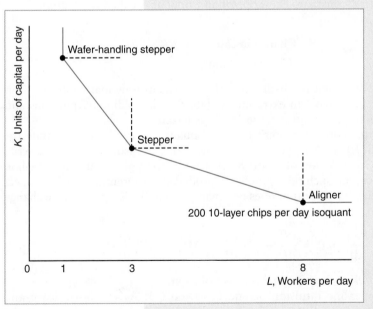

Only steppers can be used if the chip requires line widths of one micrometer or less. We show an isoquant for producing 200 ten-layer chips with lines that are more than one micrometer wide, for which any of the three technologies can be used.

All of these technologies use labor and capital in fixed proportions. Producing 200 chips takes 8 workers and 8 aligners, 3 workers and 6 steppers, or 1 worker and 4 steppers with wafer-handling capabilities. The accompanying graph shows the three right-angle isoquants corresponding to each of these technologies.

Some fabs, however, employ a combination of these technologies; some workers use one type of machine while others use different types. A fab that implements this process can produce using intermediate combinations of labor and capital, as the solid-line, kinked isoquant illustrates. A fab would *not* use a combination of the aligner and the wafer-handling stepper technologies because those combinations are less efficient than using the plain stepper (the line connecting the aligner and wafer-handling stepper technologies is farther from the origin than the lines between those technologies and the plain stepper technology).

New processes are constantly being invented. As they are introduced, the isoquant will have more and more kinks (one for each new process) and will begin to resemble the usual smooth-shaped isoquants.

Substituting Inputs

The slope of an isoquant shows the ability of a firm to replace one input with another while holding output constant. The slope of an isoquant is called the *marginal rate of technical substitution*:

$$MRTS = \frac{\text{Change in capital}}{\text{Change in labor}} = \frac{\Delta K}{\Delta L} = \frac{dK}{dL}.$$

The **marginal rate of technical substitution** (*MRTS*) tells us how many units of capital the firm can replace with an extra unit of labor while holding output constant. Because isoquants slope downward, the *MRTS* is negative.

To determine the slope at a point on an isoquant, we totally differentiate the isoquant, $\bar{q} = f(L, K)$, with respect to L and K. Along the isoquant, we can write capital as an implicit function of labor: $K(L)$. That is, for a given quantity of labor, there is a level of capital such that $\bar{q}$ units are produced. Differentiating with respect to labor (and realizing that output does not change along the isoquant as we change labor), we have

$$\frac{d\bar{q}}{dL} = 0 = \frac{\partial f}{\partial L} + \frac{\partial f}{\partial K}\frac{dK}{dL} = MP_L + MP_k\frac{dK}{dL}, \tag{6.7}$$

where $MP_K = \partial f/\partial K$ is the marginal product of capital.

There is an appealing intuition behind Equation 6.7. As we move down and to the right along an isoquant (such as the ones in Figure 6.2), we increase the amount of labor slightly, so we must decrease the amount of capital to stay on the same isoquant. A little extra labor produces MP_L amount of extra output, the marginal product of labor. For example, if the MP_L is 2 and the firm hires one extra worker, its output rises by 2 units. Similarly, a little extra capital increases output by MP_K, so the change in output due to the drop in capital in response to the increase in labor is $MP_K \times dK/dL$. If we are to stay on the same isoquant—that is, hold output constant—these two effects must offset each other: $MP_L = -MP_K \times dK/dL$.

By rearranging Equation 6.7, we find that the marginal rate of technical substitution, which is the change in capital relative to the change in labor, equals the negative of the ratio of the marginal products:

$$MRTS = \frac{dK}{dL} = -\frac{MP_L}{MP_k}.$$ (6.8)

SOLVED PROBLEM 6.3

What is the marginal rate of technical substitution for a general Cobb-Douglas production function, Equation 6.4, $q = AL^aK^b$?

Answer

1. *Calculate the marginal products of labor and capital by differentiating the Cobb-Douglas production function first with respect to labor and then with respect to capital.* The marginal product of labor is $MP_L = \partial q/\partial L = aAL^{a-1}K^b = aq/L$, and the marginal product of capital is $MP_K = \partial q/\partial K = bAL^aK^{b-1} = bq/K$.

2. *Substitute the expression for MP_L and MP_K into Equation 6.8 to determine the MRTS.* Making the indicated substitutions,

$$MRTS = -\frac{MP_L}{MP_K} = -\frac{a\dfrac{q}{L}}{b\dfrac{q}{K}} = -\frac{a}{b}\frac{K}{L}.$$ (6.9)

Thus, the *MRTS* for a Cobb-Douglas production function is a constant, $-a/b$, times the capital-labor ratio, K/L.

Diminishing Marginal Rates of Technical Substitution

We can illustrate how the *MRTS* changes along an isoquant using the estimated $q = 6 = L^{0.5}K^{0.5}$ isoquant for an electronics firm from Figure 6.2, which is reproduced in Figure 6.4. Setting $a = b = 0.5$ in Equation 6.9, we find that the slope along this isoquant is $MRTS = -K/L$.

At point c in Figure 6.4, where $K = 12$ and $L = 3$, the $MRTS = -4$. The dashed line that is tangent to the isoquant at that point has the same slope. In contrast, the $MRTS = -1$ at d ($K = 6, L = 6$), and the $MRTS = -0.25$ at e ($K = 3, L = 12$). Thus, as we move down and to the right along this curved isoquant, the slope becomes flatter—the slope gets closer to zero—because the ratio K/L grows closer to zero.

The curvature of the isoquant away from the origin reflects *diminishing marginal rates of technical substitution*. The more labor the firm has, the harder it is to replace the remaining capital with labor, so the *MRTS* falls as the isoquant becomes flatter.

In the special case in which isoquants are straight lines, isoquants do not exhibit diminishing marginal rates of technical substitution because neither input becomes more valuable in the production process: The inputs remain perfect substitutes. In our earlier example of producing potato salad, the *MRTS* is -1 at every point along the isoquant: one pound of Idaho potatoes always can be replaced by one pound of Maine potatoes. In the other special case of fixed proportions, where isoquants are right angles (or, perhaps more accurately, single points), no substitution is possible.

Figure 6.4 How the Marginal Rate of Technical Substitution Varies Along an Isoquant

Moving from point *c* to *d*, a U.S. electronics firm (Hsieh, 1995) can produce the same amount of output, $q = 6$, using six fewer units of capital, $\Delta K = -6$, if it uses three more workers. The slope of the isoquant, the *MRTS*, at a point is the same as the slope of the dashed tangent line. The *MRTS* goes from -4 at point *c* to -1 at *d* to -0.25 at *e*. Thus, as we move down and to the right, the isoquant becomes flatter: The slope gets closer to zero. Because it curves away from the origin, this isoquant exhibits a diminishing marginal rate of technical substitution: With each extra worker, the firm reduces capital by a smaller amount as the ratio of capital to labor falls.

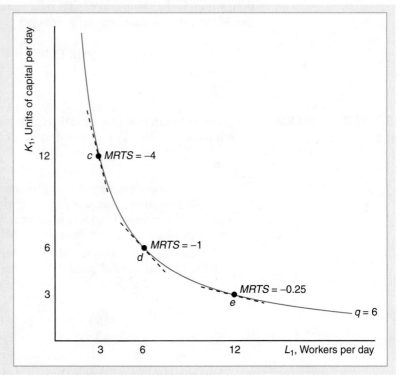

The Elasticity of Substitution

We've just seen that the marginal rate of technical substitution, the slope of the isoquant at a single point, varies as we move along a curved isoquant. It is useful to have a measure of this curvature, which reflects the ease with which a firm can substitute capital for labor. The best-known measure of the ease of substitution is the **elasticity of substitution**, σ (the Greek letter sigma), which is the percentage change in the capital-labor ratio divided by the percentage change in the *MRTS*:

$$\sigma = \frac{\dfrac{\mathrm{d}(K/L)}{K/L}}{\dfrac{\mathrm{d}MRTS}{MRTS}} = \frac{\mathrm{d}(K/L)}{\mathrm{d}MRTS}\frac{MRTS}{K/L}. \tag{6.10}$$

This measure tells us how the input factor ratio changes as the slope of the isoquant changes. If the elasticity is large—a small change in the slope results in a big increase in the factor ratio—the isoquant is relatively flat. As the elasticity falls, the isoquant becomes more curved. As we move along the isoquant, both K/L and the absolute value of the *MRTS* change in the same direction (see Figure 6.4), so the elasticity is positive.

Both the factor ratio, K/L, and the absolute value of the *MRTS*, $|MRTS|$, are positive numbers, so the logarithm of each is meaningful. It is often helpful to write the elasticity of substitution as a logarithmic derivative:[7]

$$\sigma = \frac{\mathrm{d}\ln(K/L)}{\mathrm{d}\ln|MRTS|}. \tag{6.11}$$

---

[7]By totally differentiating, we find that d ln (K/L) = d$(K/L)/(K/L)$ and d ln$|MRTS|$= d$MRTS/MRTS$, so [d ln(K/L)]/[d ln$|MRTS|$] = [d(K/L)/d$MRTS$][$MRTS/(K/L)$] = σ.

Constant Elasticity of Substitution Production Function. In general, the elasticity of substitution varies along an isoquant. An exception is the *constant elasticity of substitution* (CES) production function,

$$q = (aL^\rho + bK^\rho)^{\frac{d}{\rho}}, \qquad (6.12)$$

where ρ is a positive constant. For simplicity, we assume that $a = b = d = 1$, so

$$q = (L^\rho + K^\rho)^{\frac{1}{\rho}}, \qquad (6.13)$$

The marginal rate of technical substitution for a CES isoquant is[8]

$$MRTS = -\left(\frac{L}{K}\right)^{\rho-1}. \qquad (6.14)$$

That is, the *MRTS* varies with the labor-capital ratio. At every point on a CES isoquant, the constant elasticity of substitutions is[9]

$$\sigma = \frac{1}{1-\rho}. \qquad (6.15)$$

The linear, fixed-proportion, and Cobb-Douglas production functions are special cases of the constant elasticity production function.

Linear Production Function. Setting $\rho = 1$ in Equation 6.13, we get the linear production function $q = L + K$. At every point along a linear isoquant, the elasticity of substitution, $\sigma = 1/(1 - \rho) = 1/0$, is infinite: The two inputs are perfect substitutes.

Fixed-Proportion Production Function. As ρ approaches negative infinity, this production function approaches the fixed-proportion production function, which has right-angle isoquants (or, more accurately, single-point isoquants).[10] The elasticity of substitution is $\sigma = 1/(-\infty)$, which approaches zero: Substitution between the inputs is impossible.

Cobb-Douglas Production Function. As ρ approaches zero, a CES isoquant approaches a Cobb-Douglas isoquant, and hence the CES production function approaches a Cobb-Douglas production function.[11] According to Equation 6.14 for the CES production function, $MRTS = -(L/K)^{\rho-1}$. In the limit as ρ approaches zero, $MRTS = -K/L$. (We obtain the same result by setting $a = b$ in Equation 6.9.) The elasticity of substitution is $\sigma = 1/(1 - \rho) = 1/1 = 1$ at every point along a Cobb-Douglas isoquant.

---

[8]Using the chain rule, we know that the $MP_L = (1/\rho)(L^\rho + K^\rho)^{1/\rho-1}\rho L^{\rho-1} = (L^\rho + K^\rho)^{1/\rho-1}L^{\rho-1}$. Similarly, the $MP_K = (L^\rho + K^\rho)^{1/\rho-1}K^{\rho-1}$. Thus, the $MRTS = -MP_L/MP_K = -(L/K)^{\rho-1}$.

[9]From the *MRTS* Equation 6.14, we know that $K/L = |MRTS|^{1/(1-\rho)}$. Taking logarithms of both sides of this expression, we find that $\ln(K/L) = [1/(1 - \rho)]\ln|MRTS|$. We use the logarithmic derivative of the elasticity of substitution, Equation 6.11, to show that $\sigma = (d \ln K/L)/(d \ln|MRTS|) = 1/(1 - \rho)$.

[10]As ρ approaches $-\infty$ the CES isoquant approaches the right-angle, fixed-proportions isoquant. According to Equation 6.15, the $MRTS = -(L/K)^{-\infty}$. Thus, the *MRTS* is zero if $L > K$, and the *MRTS* goes to infinity if $K > L$.

[11]Balistreri et al. (2003) used a CES production function to estimate substitution elasticities for 28 industries that cover the entire U.S. economy and found that the estimated CES substitution elasticity did not differ significantly from the Cobb-Douglas elasticity in 20 of the 28 industries.

What is the elasticity of substitution for the general Cobb-Douglas production function, Equation 6.4, $q = AL^aK^b$? (*Comment*: We just showed that the elasticity of substitution is one for a Cobb-Douglas production function where $a = b$. We want to know if that result holds for the more general Cobb-Douglas production function.)

Answer

1. *Using the formula for the marginal rate of technical substitution, determine* d(K/L)/dMRTS *and* MRTS/(K/L), *which appear in the elasticity of substitution formula.* The marginal rate of technical substitution of a general Cobb-Douglas production function, Equation 6.9, is $MRTS = -(a/b)(K/L)$. Rearranging these terms,

$$\frac{K}{L} = -\frac{b}{a}MRTS. \tag{6.16}$$

Differentiating Equation 6.16 with respect to *MRTS*, we find that d(K/L)/dMRTS = $-b/a$. By rearranging the terms in Equation 6.16, we also know that MRTS/(K/L) = $-a/b$.

2. *Substitute the two expressions from Step 1 into the elasticity of substitution formula and simplify.* The elasticity of substitution for a Cobb-Douglas production function is

$$\sigma = \frac{d(K/L)}{dMRTS}\frac{MRTS}{K/L} = \left(-\frac{b}{a}\right)\left(-\frac{a}{b}\right) = 1. \tag{6.17}$$

6.5 Returns to Scale

So far, we have examined the effects of increasing one input while holding the other input constant (the shift from one isoquant to another), or decreasing the other input by an offsetting amount (the movement along an isoquant). We now turn to the question of *how much output changes if a firm increases all its inputs proportionately.* The answer to this question helps a firm determine its *scale* or size in the long run.

In the long run, a firm can increase its output by building a second plant and staffing it with the same number of workers as in the first plant. The firm's decision about whether to build a second plant partly depends on whether its output increases less than in proportion, in proportion, or more than in proportion to its inputs.

Constant, Increasing, and Decreasing Returns to Scale

If, when all inputs are increased by a certain percentage, output increases by that same percentage, the production function is said to exhibit **constant returns to scale** (*CRS*). A firm's production process has constant returns to scale if, when the firm doubles its inputs—for example, builds an identical second plant and uses the same amount of labor and equipment as in the first plant—it doubles its output: $f(2L, 2K) = 2f(L, K)$. [More generally, a production function is homogeneous of degree γ if $f(xL, xK) = x^\gamma f(L, K)$, where x is a positive constant. Thus, constant returns to scale is homogeneity of degree one.]

We can check whether the linear potato salad production function has constant returns to scale. If a firm uses x_1 pounds of Idaho potatoes and y_1 pounds of Maine potatoes, it produces $q_1 = x_1 + y_1$ pounds of potato salad. If it doubles both inputs, using $x_2 = 2x_1$ Idaho potatoes and $y_2 = 2y_1$ Maine potatoes, it doubles its output:

$$q_2 = x_2 + y_2 = 2x_1 + 2y_1 = 2q_1.$$

Thus, the potato salad production function exhibits constant returns to scale.

If output rises more than in proportion to an equal percentage increase in all inputs, the production function is said to exhibit **increasing returns to scale** (*IRS*). A technology exhibits increasing returns to scale if doubling inputs more than doubles the output: $f(2L, 2K) > 2f(L, K)$.

Why might a production function have increasing returns to scale? One reason is that although a firm could duplicate its small factory and double its output, it might be able to more than double its output by building a single large plant, which may allow for greater specialization of labor or capital. In the two smaller plants, workers must perform many unrelated tasks such as operating, maintaining, and fixing machines. In the single large plant, some workers may specialize in maintaining and fixing machines, thereby increasing efficiency. Similarly, a firm may use specialized equipment in a large plant but not in a small one.

If output rises less than in proportion to an equal percentage increase in all inputs, the production function exhibits **decreasing returns to scale** (*DRS*). A technology exhibits decreasing returns to scale if doubling inputs causes output to rise less than in proportion: $f(2L, 2K) < 2f(L, K)$.

One reason for decreasing returns to scale is that the difficulty of organizing, coordinating, and integrating activities increases with firm size. An owner may be able to manage one plant well but may have trouble running two plants. In some sense, the owner's difficulties in running a larger firm may reflect our failure to consider some factor such as management in our production function. When the firm increases the various inputs, it does not increase the management input in proportion. Therefore, the decreasing returns to scale is really due to a fixed input. Another reason is that large teams of workers may not function as well as small teams in which each individual has greater personal responsibility.

SOLVED PROBLEM 6.5

Under what conditions does a general Cobb-Douglas production function, $q = AL^aK^b$, exhibit decreasing, constant, or increasing returns to scale?

Answer

1. *Show how output changes if both inputs are doubled.* If the firm initially uses L and K amounts of inputs, it produces $q_1 = AL^aK^b$. After the firm doubles the amount of both labor and capital, it produces

$$q_2 = A(2L)^a(2K)^b = 2^{a+b}AL^aK^b. \tag{6.18}$$

That is, q_2 is 2^{a+b} times q_1. If we define $\gamma = a + b$, then Equation 6.18 tells us that

$$q_2 = 2^\gamma q_1. \tag{6.19}$$

Thus, if the inputs double, output increases by 2^γ.

2. *Give a rule for determining the returns to scale.* If we set $\gamma = 1$ in Equation 6.19, we find that $q_2 = 2^1 q_1 = 2q_1$. That is, output doubles when

the inputs double, so the Cobb-Douglas production function has constant returns to scale. If $\gamma < 1$, then $q_2 = 2^\gamma q_1 < 2q_1$ because $2^\gamma < 2$ if $\gamma < 1$. That is, when input doubles, output increases less than in proportion, so this Cobb-Douglas production function exhibits decreasing returns to scale. Finally, the Cobb-Douglas production function has increasing returns to scale if $\gamma > 1$ so that $q_2 > 2q_1$. Thus, the rule for determining returns to scale for a Cobb-Douglas production function is that the returns to scale are decreasing if $\gamma < 1$, constant if $\gamma = 1$, and increasing if $\gamma > 1$.

Comment: Thus, γ is a measure of the returns to scale. It is a *scale elasticity*: If all inputs increase by 1%, output increases by γ%.

APPLICATION

Returns to Scale in U.S. Manufacturing

Increasing, constant, and decreasing returns to scale are commonly observed. The table shows estimates of Cobb-Douglas production functions and rates of returns in various U.S. manufacturing industries (based on Hsieh, 1995).

The table shows that the estimated returns to scale measure for a tobacco firm is $\gamma = 0.51$: A 1% increase in the inputs causes output to rise by 0.51%. Because output rises less than in proportion to the inputs, the tobacco production function exhibits decreasing returns to scale. In contrast, firms that manufacture primary metals have increasing returns to scale production functions, in which a 1% increase in all inputs causes output to rise by 1.24%.

The accompanying graphs use isoquants to illustrate the returns to scale for the electronics, tobacco, and primary metal firms. We measure the units of labor, capital, and output so that, for all three firms, 100 units of labor and 100 units of capital produce 100 units of output on the $q = 100$ isoquant in the three panels. For the constant returns to scale electronics firm, panel a, if both labor and capital are doubled from 100 to 200 units, output doubles to 200 ($= 100 \times 2^1$, multiplying the original output by the rate of increase using Equation 6.19).

	Labor, a	Capital, b	Scale, $\gamma = a + b$
Decreasing Returns to Scale			
Tobacco products	0.18	0.33	0.51
Food and kindred products	0.43	0.48	0.91
Transportation equipment	0.44	0.48	0.92
Constant Returns to Scale			
Apparel and other textile products	0.70	0.31	1.01
Furniture and fixtures	0.62	0.40	1.02
Electronic and other electric equipment	0.49	0.53	1.02
Increasing Returns to Scale			
Paper and allied products	0.44	0.65	1.09
Petroleum and coal products	0.30	0.88	1.18
Primary metal	0.51	0.73	1.24

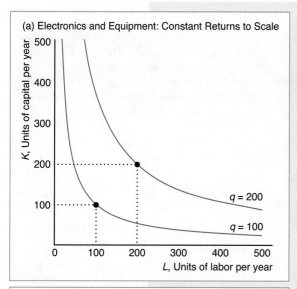

(a) Electronics and Equipment: Constant Returns to Scale

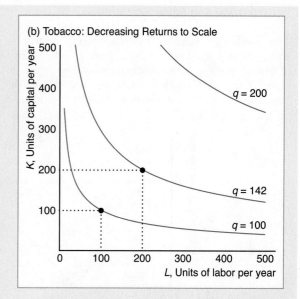

(b) Tobacco: Decreasing Returns to Scale

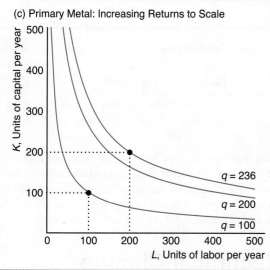

(c) Primary Metal: Increasing Returns to Scale

That same doubling of inputs causes output to rise to only 142($\approx 100 \times 2^{0.51}$) for the tobacco firm, panel b. Because output rises less than in proportion to inputs, the production function exhibits decreasing returns to scale. If the primary metal firm doubles its inputs, panel c, its output more than doubles, to 236($\approx 100 \times 2^{1.24}$) so the production function has increasing returns to scale.

These graphs illustrate that the spacing of the isoquant determines the returns to scale. The closer the $q = 100$ and $q = 200$ isoquants, the greater the returns to scale.

The returns to scale in these industries are estimated to be the same at all levels of output. A production function's returns to scale may vary, however, as the scale of the firm changes.

Varying Returns to Scale

Many production functions have increasing returns to scale for small amounts of output, constant returns for moderate amounts of output, and decreasing returns for large amounts of output. With a small firm, increasing labor and capital may produce gains from cooperation between workers and greater specialization of workers and equipment—*returns to specialization*—so there are increasing returns to scale. As the firm grows, returns to scale are eventually exhausted. With no more returns to specialization, the production process exhibits constant returns to scale. If the firm continues to grow, managing the staff becomes more difficult, so the firm suffers from decreasing returns to scale.

Figure 6.5 shows such a pattern. Again, the spacing of the isoquants reflects the returns to scale. Initially, the firm has one worker and one piece of equipment, point a, and produces one unit of output on the $q = 1$ isoquant. If the firm doubles its inputs, it produces at b, where $L = 2$ and $K = 2$, which lies on the dashed line through the

Figure 6.5 Varying Scale Economies

This production function exhibits varying returns to scale. Initially, the firm uses one worker and one unit of capital, point *a*. It repeatedly doubles these inputs to points *b*, *c*, and *d*, which lie along the dashed line. The first time the inputs are doubled, *a* to *b*, output more than doubles from $q = 1$ to $q = 3$, so the production function has increasing returns to scale. The next doubling, *b* to *c*, causes a proportionate increase in output, constant returns to scale. At the last doubling, from *c* to *d*, the production function exhibits decreasing returns to scale.

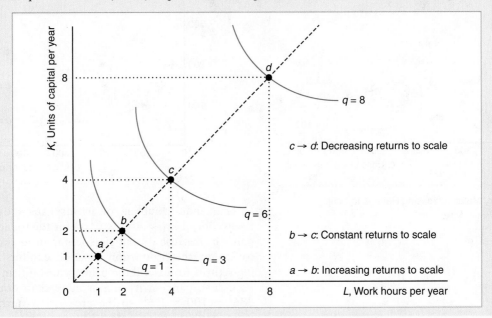

origin and point *a*. Output more than doubles to $q = 3$, so the production function exhibits increasing returns to scale in this range. Another doubling of inputs to *c* causes output to double to $q = 6$, so the production function has constant returns to scale in this range. Another doubling of inputs to *d* causes output to increase by only one-third, to $q = 8$, so the production function has decreasing returns to scale in this range.

6.6 Productivity and Technical Change

Because firms may use different technologies and different methods of organizing production, the amount of output that one firm produces from a given amount of inputs may differ from that produced by another. Moreover, after a technical or managerial innovation, a firm can produce more today from a given amount of inputs than it could in the past.

Relative Productivity

This chapter has assumed that firms produce efficiently. A firm must produce efficiently to maximize its profit. However, even if each firm in a market produces as efficiently as possible, firms may not be equally *productive*. One firm may be able to produce more than another from a given amount of inputs.

A firm may be more productive than another if its management knows a better way to organize production or if it has access to a new invention. Union-mandated work rules, racial or gender discrimination, government regulations, or other institutional restrictions that affect only certain firms may lower the relative productivity of those firms.

Differences in productivity across markets may be due to differences in the degree of competition. In competitive markets, where many firms can enter and exit easily, less productive firms lose money and are driven out of business, so the firms that actually continue to produce are equally productive (see Chapter 8). In a less competitive market with few firms and no possibility of entry by new ones, a less productive firm may be able to survive, so firms with varying levels of productivity are observed.

APPLICATION U.S. Electric Generation Efficiency	Prior to the mid-1990s, more than 90% of U.S. electricity was produced and sold to consumers by investor-owned utility monopolies that were subject to government price regulations. Beginning in the mid-1990s, some states mandated that electric production be *restructured*. In those states, the utility monopoly was forced to sell its electric generation plants to several other firms. These new firms sold the electricity they generated to the utility monopoly, which delivered the electricity to final consumers. Because they expected these new electric generator firms to compete with each other, state legislators hoped that this increased competition would result in greater production efficiency. Fabrizio, Rose, and Wolfram (2007) found that, in anticipation of greater competition, the generation plant operators in states that restructured reduced their labor and non-fuel expenses by 3% to 5% (holding output constant) relative to investor-owned utility monopoly plants in states that did not restructure. When compared to plants run by government- and cooperatively owned utility monopolies that were not exposed to restructuring incentives, these gains were even greater: 6% in labor and 13% in non-fuel expenses. Thus, restructuring, which led to greater competition, resulted in increased productivity.

Innovations

Maximum number of miles that Ford's most fuel-efficient 2003 car could drive on a gallon of gas: 36. Maximum number its 1912 Model T could: 35. —Harper's Index 2003

In its production process, a firm tries to use the best available technological and managerial knowledge. **Technical progress** is an advance in knowledge that allows more output to be produced with the same level of inputs. The invention of new products is a form of technical progress. The use of robotic arms increases the number of automobiles produced with a given amount of labor and raw materials. Better *management* or *organization of the production process* similarly allows the firm to produce more output from given levels of inputs.

Technical Progress. A technological innovation changes the production process. Last year, a firm produced

$$q_1 = f(L, K)$$

units of output using L units of labor services and K units of capital service. Due to a new invention employed by the firm, this year's production function differs from last year's, so the firm produces 10% more output with the same inputs:

$$q_2 = 1.1 f(L, K).$$

This firm has experienced *neutral technical change*, in which it can produce more output using the same ratio of inputs. For example, a technical innovation in the form of a new printing press allows more output to be produced using the same ratio of inputs as before: one worker to one printing press.

200   CHAPTER 6   *Firms and Production*

Many empirical studies find that systematic neutral technical progress occurs over time. In these studies, the production function is

$$q = A(t)f(L, K),\qquad(6.20)$$

where $A(t)$ is a function of time, t, that shows how much output grows over time for any given mix of inputs. For example, the annual rate at which computer and related goods output grew for given levels of inputs was 0.9% in the United Kingdom, 1.0% in Canada, 1.3% in the United States, 1.4% in France, and 1.5% in Australia.[12] Given that the U.S. annual growth rate is 1.3%, the U.S. computer production function, Equation 6.20, is $q = 1.013^t f(L, K)$, where t increases by 1 unit each year.

Non-neutral technical changes are innovations that alter the proportion in which inputs are used. Technological progress could be *capital saving*, where relatively less capital is used relative to other inputs. For example, the development of cell phones allowed firms to eliminate enough landline phones, fax machines, and computers to lower the capital-labor ratio for its sales or repair workers while increasing output.

Alternatively, technological progress may be *labor saving*. Basker (2012) found that the introduction of barcode scanners in grocery stores increased the average product of labor by 4.5% on average across stores. Amazon bought Kiva Systems in 2012 with the intention of using its robots to move items in Amazon's warehouses, replacing some workers. Robots help doctors perform surgery quicker and reduce patients' recovery times.

Organizational Change. Organizational change may also alter the production function and increase the amount of output produced by a given amount of inputs. In 1904, King C. Gillette used automated production techniques to produce a new type of razor blade that could be sold for 5¢—a fraction of the price charged by rivals—allowing working men to shave daily.

In the early 1900s, Henry Ford revolutionized mass production through two organizational innovations. First, he introduced interchangeable parts, which cut the time required to install parts because workers no longer had to file or machine individually made parts to get them to fit. Second, Ford introduced a conveyor belt and an assembly line to his production process. Before Ford, workers walked around the car, and each worker performed many assembly activities. In Ford's plant, each worker specialized in a single activity such as attaching the right rear fender to the chassis. A conveyor belt moved the car at a constant speed from worker to worker along the assembly line. Because his workers gained proficiency from specializing in only a few activities, and because the conveyor belts reduced the number of movements workers had to make, Ford could produce more automobiles with the same number of workers. In 1908, the Ford Model T sold for $850, when rival vehicles sold for $2,000. By the early 1920s, Ford had increased production from fewer than 1,000 cars per year to 2 million cars per year.

APPLICATION

Tata Nano's Technical and Organizational Innovations

In 2009, the automotive world was stunned when India's new Tata Motors started selling the Nano, its tiny, fuel-efficient four-passenger car. With a base price of less than $2,500, it is by far the world's least expensive car. The next cheapest car in India, the Maruti 800, sold for about $4,800.

The Nano's dramatically lower price is not the result of amazing new inventions; it is due to organizational innovations that led to simplifications and the use of less expensive materials and procedures. Although Tata Motors filed for 34 patents related to the design of the Nano (compared to the roughly 280 patents awarded to General Motors annually), most of these patents are for mundane

[12]OECD Productivity Database, December 17, 2004.

items such as the two-cylinder engine's balance shaft and the configuration of the transmission gears.

Instead of relying on innovations, Tata reorganized both production and distribution to lower costs. It reduced manufacturing costs at every stage of the process with a no-frills design, decreased vehicle weight, and made other major production improvements.

The Nano has a single windshield wiper, one side-view mirror, no power steering, a simplified door-opening lever, three nuts on the wheels instead of the customary four, and a trunk that does not open from the outside—it is accessed by folding down the rear seats. The Nano has smaller overall dimensions than the Maruti, but about 20% more seating capacity because of design decisions, such as putting the wheels at the extreme edges of the car. The Nano is much lighter than comparable models due to the reduced amount of steel, the use of lightweight steel, and the use of aluminum in the engine. The ribbed roof structure is not only a style element but also a strength structure, which is necessary because the design uses thin-gauge sheet metal. Because the engine is in the rear, the driveshaft doesn't need complex joints as in a front-engine car with front-wheel drive. To cut costs further, the company reduced the number of tools needed to make the components and thereby increased the life of the dies used by three times the norm. In consultation with their suppliers, Tata's engineers determined how many useful parts the design required, which helped them identify functions that could be integrated in parts.

Tata's plant can produce 250,000 Nanos per year and benefits from economies of scale. However, Tata's major organizational innovation was its open distribution and remote assembly. The Nano's modular design enables an experienced mechanic to assemble the car in a workshop. Therefore, Tata Motors can distribute a complete knock-down (CKD) kit to be assembled and serviced by local assembly hubs and entrepreneurs closer to consumers. The cost of transporting these kits, produced at a central manufacturing plant, is charged directly to the customer. This approach is expected to speed up the distribution process, particularly in the more remote locations of India. The car has been a great success selling more than 8,500 cars in May 2012.

CHALLENGE SOLUTION

Labor Productivity During Recessions

During a recession, a manager of the American Licorice Company has to reduce output and decides to lay off workers. Will the firm's labor productivity—average product of labor—go up and improve the firm's situation, or go down and harm it?

Layoffs have the positive effect of freeing up machines to be used by remaining workers. However, if layoffs force the remaining employees to perform a wide variety of tasks, the firm will lose the benefits from specialization. When there are many workers, the advantage of freeing up machines is important and increased multitasking is unlikely to be a problem. When there are only a few workers, freeing up more machines does not help much (some machines might stand idle some of the time), while multitasking becomes a more serious problem.

Holding capital constant, a change in the number of workers affects a firm's average product of labor. Labor productivity could rise or fall. For example, in panel b of Figure 6.1, the average product of labor rises with labor up to 15 workers per day and then falls as the number of workers increases. Equivalently, the average product of labor falls if the firm initially has 15 or fewer workers and lays off one person, but rises if the firm starts with more than 15 workers and lays off one.

For some production functions, layoffs always raise labor productivity because the AP_L curve is downward sloping everywhere. For such a production function, the positive effect of freeing up capital always dominates any negative effect of layoffs on the average product of labor. For example layoffs raise the AP_L for any Cobb-Douglas production function, $q = AL^\alpha K^\beta$, where α is less than one. The average product of labor is $AP_L = q/L = AL^\alpha K^\beta/L = AL^{\alpha-1}K^\beta$. By partially differentiating this expression with respect to labor, we find that the change in the AP_L as the amount of labor rises is $\partial AP_L/\partial L = (\alpha - 1)AL^{\alpha-2}K^\beta$, which is negative if $\alpha < 1$. All the estimated production functions listed in the application "Returns to Scale in U.S. Manufacturing" have this property. Thus, for such production functions, as labor falls, the average product of labor rises.

Let's return to our licorice manufacturer. According to Hsieh (1995), the Cobb-Douglas production function for food and kindred product plants is $q = AL^{0.43}K^{0.48}$, so $\alpha = 0.43$ is less than 1 and the AP_L curve slopes downward at every quantity: $\partial AP_L/\partial L = (-0.57)AL^{-1.57}K^{0.48} < 0$.

We can illustrate how much the AP_L rises with a layoff for this particular production function. If $A = 1$ and $L = K = 10$ initially, then the firm's output is $q = 10^{0.43} \times 10^{0.48} \approx 8.13$, and its average product of labor is $AP_L = q/L \approx 8.13/10 = 0.813$. If the number of workers is reduced by one, then output falls to $q = 9^{0.43} \times 10^{0.48} \approx 7.77$, and the average product of labor rises to $AP_L \approx 7.77/9 \approx 0.863$. That is, a 10% reduction in labor causes output to *fall* by 4.4%, but causes the average product of labor to *rise* by 6.2%. The firm's output falls less than 10% because each remaining worker is more productive.

Until recently, most large Japanese firms did not lay off workers during downturns. Thus, in contrast to U.S. firms, their average product of labor fell during recessions because their output fell while labor remained constant. Similarly, European firms show 30% less employment volatility over time than do U.S. firms at least in part because European firms that fire workers are subject to a tax (Veracierto, 2008). Consequently, with other factors held constant in the short run, recessions might be more damaging to the profit of a Japanese or European firm than to the profit of a comparable U.S. firm. However, retaining *good* workers over short-run downturns might be a good long-run policy.

SUMMARY

1. **The Ownership and Management of Firms.** Firms can be sole proprietorships, partnerships, or corporations. In small firms (particularly sole proprietorships and partnerships), the owners usually run the company. In large firms (such as most corporations), the owners hire managers to run the firms. Owners want to maximize profits. If managers have different objectives than owners, owners must keep a close watch to ensure that profits are maximized.

2. **Production.** Inputs, or factors of production—labor, capital, and materials—are combined to produce output using the current state of knowledge about technology and management. To maximize profits, a firm must produce as efficiently as possible: It must get the maximum amount of output from the inputs

it uses, given existing knowledge. A firm may have access to many efficient production processes that use different combinations of inputs to produce a given level of output. New technologies or new forms of organization can increase the amount of output that can be produced from a given combination of inputs. A production function shows how much output can be produced efficiently from various levels of inputs. A firm can vary all its inputs in the long run but only some of its inputs in the short run.

3. **Short-Run Production: One Variable and One Fixed Input.** In the short run, a firm cannot adjust the quantity of some inputs, such as capital. The firm varies its output by adjusting its variable inputs, such as labor. If all factors are fixed except labor, and

a firm that was using very little labor increases its labor, its output may rise more than in proportion to the increase in labor because of greater specialization of workers. Eventually, however, as more workers are hired, the workers get in each other's way or wait to share equipment, so output increases by smaller and smaller amounts. This phenomenon is described by the law of diminishing marginal returns: The marginal product of an input—the extra output from the last unit of input—eventually decreases as more of that input is used, holding other inputs fixed.

4. **Long-Run Production: Two Variable Inputs.** In the long run, when all inputs are variable, firms can substitute between inputs. An isoquant shows the combinations of inputs that can produce a given level of output. The marginal rate of technical substitution is the slope of the isoquant. Usually, the more of one input the firm uses, the more difficult it is to substitute that input for another input. That is, there are diminishing marginal rates of technical substitution as the firm uses more of one input. The elasticity of substitution reflects the ease of replacing one input with another in the production process, or, equivalently, the curvature of an isoquant.

5. **Returns to Scale.** If, when a firm increases all inputs in proportion, its output increases by the same proportion, the production process exhibits constant returns to scale. If output increases less than in proportion to inputs, the production process has decreasing returns to scale; if it increases more than in proportion, it has increasing returns to scale. All these types of returns to scale are commonly observed in various industries. Many production processes first exhibit increasing, then constant, and finally decreasing returns to scale as the size of the firm increases.

6. **Productivity and Technical Change.** Although all firms in an industry produce efficiently, given what they know and what institutional and other constraints they face, some firms may be more productive than others: They can produce more output from a given bundle of inputs. Due to innovations such as technical progress and new methods of organizing production, firms can produce more today than they could in the past from the same bundle of inputs. Such innovations change the production function.

EXERCISES

■ = *exercise is available in* MyEconLab; * = *answer appears at the back of this book;* **M** = *mathematical problem.*

1. The Ownership and Management of Firms

1.1 What types of firms would not normally try to maximize profit?

1.2 What types of organization allow owners of a firm to obtain the advantages of limited liability?

2. Production

2.1 With respect to production functions, how long is the *short run*?

3. Short-Run Production: One Variable and One Fixed Input

*3.1 If each extra worker produces an extra unit of output, how do the total product of labor, the average product of labor, and the marginal product of labor vary with the number of workers?

3.2 Each extra worker produces an extra unit of output, up to six workers. After six, no additional output is produced. Draw the total product of labor, average product of labor, and marginal product of labor curves.

3.3 In the short run, a firm cannot vary its capital, $\overline{K} = 2$, but it can vary its labor, L. It produces output q. Explain why the firm will or will not experience diminishing marginal returns to labor in the short run if its production function is $q = 10L + K$. (See Solved Problem 6.1.) **M**

*3.4 Suppose that the Cobb-Douglas production function is $q = L^{0.75}K^{0.25}$.

a. What is the average product of labor, holding capital fixed?

b. What is the marginal product of labor?

c. What are the AP_L and MP_L when $\overline{K} = 16$? (See Solved Problem 6.1.) **M**

3.5 If the Cobb-Douglas production function is $q = L^{0.75}K^{0.25}$, and $\overline{K} = 16$, what is the elasticity of output with respect to labor? (See Solved Problem 6.2.) **M**

4. Long-Run Production: Two Variable Inputs

4.1 What are the differences between an isoquant and an indifference curve?

4.2 Why must isoquants be thin?

4.3 Suppose that a firm has a fixed-proportions production function in which 1 unit of output is produced using one worker and 2 units of capital. If the firm has an extra worker and no more capital, it still can produce only 1 unit of output. Similarly, 1 more unit of capital produces no extra output.

a. Draw the isoquants for this production function.

b. Draw the total product of labor, average product of labor, and marginal product of labor curves (you will probably want to use two diagrams) for this production function.

*4.4 To produce a recorded CD, $q = 1$, a firm uses one blank disc, $D = 1$, and the services of a recording machine, $M = 1$, for one hour. Draw an isoquant for this production process. Explain the reason for its shape.

4.5 What is the production function if L and K are perfect substitutes and each unit of q requires 1 unit of L or 1 unit of K (or a combination of these inputs that equals 1)? **M**

4.6 The production function at Ginko's Copy Shop is $q = 1,000 \times \min(L, 3K)$, where q is the number of copies per hour, q, L is the number of workers, and K is the number of copy machines. As an example, if $L = 4$ and $K = 1$, then $\min(L, 3K) = 3$, and $q = 3,000$.

a. Draw the isoquants for this production function.

b. Draw the total product of labor, average product of labor, and marginal product of labor curves for this production function for some fixed level of capital.

4.7 Why might we expect the law of diminishing marginal product to hold?

*4.8 At $L = 4$ and $K = 4$, the marginal product of labor is 2 and the marginal product of capital is 3. What is the marginal rate of technical substitution? **M**

*4.9 Mark launders his white clothes using the production function $q = B + 0.5G$, where B is the number of cups of Clorox bleach and G is the number of cups of generic bleach that is half as potent. Draw an isoquant. What are the marginal products of B and G? What is the marginal rate of technical substitution at each point on an isoquant?

4.10 Alfred's Print Shop can use any one of three fixed-proportion technologies. Each involves one printer and one worker. Describe the possible shapes of the firm's isoquant. (*Hint*: Review the discussion in the application "A Semiconductor Integrated Circuit Isoquant.")

4.11 Draw a circle in a diagram with labor services on one axis and capital services on the other. This circle represents all the combinations of labor and capital that produce 100 units of output. Now, draw the isoquant for 100 units of output. (*Hint*: Remember that the isoquant includes only the efficient combinations of labor and capital.)

4.12 Michelle's business produces ceramic cups using labor, clay, and a kiln. She can manufacture 25 cups a day with one worker and 35 cups with two workers. Does her production process illustrate *diminishing returns to scale* or *diminishing marginal returns to scale*? Give a plausible explanation for why output does not increase proportionately with the number of workers.

4.13 By studying, Will can produce a higher grade, G_W, on an upcoming economics exam. His production function depends on the number of hours he studies marginal analysis problems, A, and the number of hours he studies supply and demand problems, R. Specifically, $G_W = 2.5A^{0.36}R^{0.64}$. His roommate David's grade production function is $G_D = 2.5A^{0.25}R^{0.75}$.

a. What is Will's marginal productivity from studying supply and demand problems? What is David's?

b. What is Will's marginal rate of technical substitution between studying the two types of problems? What is David's?

c. Is it possible that Will and David have different marginal productivity functions but the same marginal rate of technical substitution functions? Explain. **M**

4.14 Show that the CES production function $q = (aL^\rho + bK^\rho)^{1/\rho}$ can be written as $q = B(\rho)[cL^\rho + (1 - c) \times K^\rho]^{1/\rho}$. **M**

4.15 What is the *MRTS* of the CES production function $q = (aL^\rho + bK^\rho)^{d/\rho}$? (See Solved Problem 6.3.) **M**

4.16 What is the elasticity of substitution, σ, of the CES production function $q = (aL^\rho + bK^\rho)^{d/\rho}$? (See Solved Problem 6.4.) **M**

5. Returns to Scale

5.1 To speed relief to isolated South Asian communities that were devastated by the December 2004 tsunami, the U.S. Navy doubled the number of helicopters from 45 to 90 soon after the first ship arrived. Navy Admiral Thomas Fargo, head of the U.S. Pacific Command, was asked if doubling the number of helicopters would "produce twice as much [relief]." He replied, "Maybe pretty close to twice as much." (Vicky O'Hara, *All Things Considered*, National Public Radio, NPR, January 4, 2005). Identify the inputs and outputs and describe the production process. Is the admiral discussing a production process with nearly constant returns to scale, or is he referring to another property of the production process?

5.2 Show in a diagram that a production function can have diminishing marginal returns to a factor and constant returns to scale.

5.3 Under what conditions do the following production functions exhibit decreasing, constant, or increasing returns to scale?

a. $q = L + K$, a linear production function,

b. $q = AL^aK^b$, a general Cobb-Douglas production function,

c. $q = L + L^aK^b + K$,

d. $q = (aL^\rho + [1 - a]K^\rho)^{d/\rho}$, a CES production function. (See Solved Problem 6.5) **M**

*5.4 The production function for the automotive and parts industry is $q = L^{0.27}K^{0.16}M^{0.61}$, where M is energy and materials (based loosely on Klein, 2003). What kind of returns to scale does this production function exhibit? What is the marginal product of energy and materials? (See Solved Problem 6.5) **M**

5.5 As asserted in the comment to Solved Problem 6.5, show that γ is a scale elasticity. **M**

5.6 Is it possible that a firm's production function exhibits increasing returns to scale while exhibiting diminishing marginal productivity of each of its inputs? To answer this question, calculate the marginal productivities of capital and labor for the production of electronics and equipment, tobacco, and primary metal using the information listed in the application "Returns to Scale in U.S. Manufacturing." **M**

5.7 A production function is said to be homogeneous of degree γ if $f(xL, xK) = x^\gamma f(L, K)$, where x is a positive constant. That is, the production function has the same returns to scale for every combination of inputs. For such a production function, show that the marginal product of labor and marginal product of capital functions are homogeneous of degree $\gamma - 1$. **M**

5.8 Show that with a constant returns to scale production function, the *MRTS* between labor and capital depends only on the K/L ratio and not on the scale of production. (*Hint*: Use your result from Exercise 5.7.) **M**

5.9 Prove Euler's theorem that, if $f(L, K)$ is homogeneous of degree γ (see Exercise 5.7), then $L(\partial f/\partial L) + K(\partial f/\partial K) = \gamma f(L, K)$. Given this result, what can you conclude if a production function has constant returns to scale? Express your results in terms of the marginal products of labor and capital. **M**

6. Productivity and Technical Change

6.1 Until the mid-eighteenth century, when spinning became mechanized, cotton was an expensive and relatively unimportant textile (Virginia

Postrel, "What Separates Rich Nations from Poor Nations?" *New York Times*, January 1, 2004). Where it used to take an Indian hand-spinner 50,000 hours to hand-spin 100 pounds of cotton, an operator of a 1760s-era hand-operated cotton mule spinning machine could produce 100 pounds of stronger thread in 300 hours. After 1825, when the self-acting mule spinner automated the process, the time dropped to 135 hours, and cotton became an inexpensive, common cloth. Was this technological progress neutral? In a figure, show how these technological changes affected isoquants.

6.2 In a manufacturing plant, workers use a specialized machine to produce belts. A new labor-saving machine is invented. With the new machine, the firm can use fewer workers and still produce the same number of belts as it did using the old machine. In the long run, both labor and capital (the machine) are variable. From what you know, what is the effect of this invention on the AP_L, MP_L, and returns to scale? If you require more information to answer this question, specify what else you need to know.

6.3 Does it follow that, because we observe that the average product of labor is higher for Firm 1 than for Firm 2, Firm 1 is more productive in the sense that it can produce more output from a given amount of inputs? Why or why not?

*6.4 Firm 1 and Firm 2 use the same type of production function, but Firm 1 is only 90% as productive as Firm 2. That is, the production function of Firm 2 is $q_2 = f(L, K)$, and the production function of Firm 1 is $q_1 = 0.9f(L, K)$. At a particular level of inputs, how does the marginal product of labor differ between the firms? **M**

7. Challenge

7.1 If a firm lays off workers during a recession, how will the firm's marginal product of labor change?

*7.2 During recessions, American firms lay off a larger proportion of their workers than Japanese firms do. (It has been claimed that Japanese firms continue to produce at high levels and store the output or sell it at relatively low prices during recessions.) Assuming that the production function remains unchanged over a period that is long enough to include many recessions and expansions, would you expect the average product of labor to be higher in Japan or in the United States? Why?

7.3 For the CES production function $q = (aL^\rho + [1 - a]K^\rho)^{d/\rho}$, does $\partial AP_L/\partial L$ have an unambiguous sign? **M**

7

Costs

People want economy and they will pay any price to get it.
—Lee Iacocca (former CEO of Chrysler)

CHALLENGE

Technology Choice at Home Versus Abroad

A manager of a semiconductor manufacturing firm, who can choose from many different production technologies, must determine whether the firm should use the same technology in its foreign plant that it uses in its domestic plant. U.S. semiconductor manufacturing firms have been moving much of their production abroad since 1961, when Fairchild Semiconductor built a plant in Hong Kong. According to the Semiconductor Industry Association, worldwide semiconductor billings from the Americas dropped from 66% in 1976, to 34% in 1998, and to 17% in 2011.

Firms are moving their production abroad because of lower taxes, lower labor costs, and capital grants. Capital grants are funds provided by a foreign government to a firm to induce them to produce in that country. Such grants can reduce the cost of owning and operating an overseas semiconductor fabrication facility by as much as 25% compared to the costs of a U.S.-based plant. (However, in 2012, China, Thailand, and other Asian countries substantially raised their minimum wages, which reduces the incentive of U.S. firms to move production there.)

The semiconductor manufacturer can produce a chip using sophisticated equipment and relatively few workers or many workers and less complex equipment. In the United States, firms use a relatively capital-intensive technology, because doing so minimizes their cost of producing a given level of output. Will that same technology be cost minimizing if they move their production abroad?

A firm uses a two-step procedure to determine how to produce a certain amount of output efficiently. It first determines which production processes are *technologically efficient* so that it can produce the desired level of output with the least amount of inputs. As we saw in Chapter 6, the firm uses engineering and other information to determine its production function, which summarizes the many technologically efficient production processes available.

The firm's second step is to select the technologically efficient production process that is also **economically efficient**, minimizing the cost of producing a specified amount of output. To determine which process minimizes its cost of production, the firm uses information about the production function and the cost of inputs.

By reducing its cost of producing a given level of output, a firm can increase its profit. Any profit-maximizing competitive, monopolistic, or oligopolistic firm minimizes its cost of production.

In this chapter, we examine five main topics

1. **Measuring Costs.** Economists count both explicit costs and implicit (opportunity) costs.

2. **Short-Run Costs.** To minimize its costs in the short run, a firm can adjust its variable factors (such as labor), but it cannot adjust its fixed factors (such as capital).

3. **Long-Run Costs.** To minimize its costs in the long run, a firm can adjust all its inputs because all inputs are variable.

4. **Lower Costs in the Long Run.** Long-run cost is as low or lower than short-run cost because the firm has more flexibility in the long run, technological progress occurs, and workers and managers learn from experience.

5. **Cost of Producing Multiple Goods.** If a firm produces several goods simultaneously, the cost of each may depend on the quantity of all the goods it produces.

Businesspeople and economists need to understand the relationship between the costs of inputs and production to determine the most cost-efficient way to produce. Economists have an additional reason for wanting to understand costs. As we will see in later chapters, the relationship between output and costs plays an important role in determining the nature of a market—how many firms are in the market and how high price is relative to cost.

7.1 Measuring Costs

How much would it cost you to stand at the wrong end of a shooting gallery?
—S. J. Perelman

To show how a firm's cost varies with its output, we first have to measure costs. Businesspeople and economists often measure costs differently. Economists include all relevant costs. To run a firm profitably, a manager must think like an economist and consider all relevant costs. However, this same manager may direct the firm's accountant or bookkeeper to measure costs in ways that are more consistent with tax laws and other laws so as to make the firm's financial statements look good to stockholders or to minimize the firm's taxes.[1]

To produce a particular amount of output, a firm incurs costs for the required inputs such as labor, capital, energy, and materials. A firm's manager (or accountant) determines the cost of labor, capital, energy, and materials by multiplying the price of the factor by the number of units used. If workers earn $20 per hour and work 100 hours per day, then the firm's cost of labor is $20 \times 100 = \$2,000$ per day. The manager can easily calculate these *explicit costs*, which are its direct,

---

[1]See "Tax Rules" in MyEconLab, Chapter Resources, Chapter 7.

out-of-pocket payments for inputs to its production process within a given period. While calculating explicit costs is straightforward, some costs are *implicit* in that they reflect only a forgone opportunity rather than an explicit, current expenditure. Properly taking account of forgone opportunities requires particularly careful attention when dealing with durable capital goods as past expenditures for an input may be irrelevant to current cost calculations if that input has no current, alternative use.

Opportunity Costs

An economist is a person who, when invited to give a talk at a banquet, tells the audience there's no such thing as a free lunch.

The **economic cost** or **opportunity cost** of a resource is the value of the best alternative use of that resource. Explicit costs are opportunity costs. If a firm purchases an input in a market and uses that input immediately, the input's opportunity cost is the amount the firm pays for it, the market price. After all, if the firm does not use the input in its production process, its best alternative would be to sell it to someone else at the market price. The concept of an opportunity cost becomes particularly useful when the firm uses an input that is not available for purchase in a market or that was purchased in a market in the past.

A key example of such an opportunity cost is the value of a manager's time. For example, Maoyong owns and manages a firm. He pays himself only a small monthly salary of $1,000 because he also receives the firm's profit. However, Maoyong could work for another firm and earn $11,000 a month. Thus, the opportunity cost of his time is $11,000—from his best alternative use of his time—not the $1,000 he actually pays himself.

The classic example of an implicit opportunity cost is captured in the phrase "There's no such thing as a free lunch." Suppose that your parents offer to take you to lunch tomorrow. You know that they will pay for the meal, but you also know that this lunch will not truly be free. Your opportunity cost for the lunch is the best alternative use of your time. Presumably, the best alternative use of your time is studying this textbook, but other possible alternatives include working at a job or watching TV. Often, such an opportunity cost is substantial. (What are you giving up to study opportunity costs?)

APPLICATION

The Opportunity Cost of an MBA

During the sharp economic downturn in 2008–2010, did applications to MBA programs fall, hold steady, or take off like tech stocks during the first Internet bubble? Knowledge of opportunity costs helps us answer this question.

For many potential students, the biggest cost of attending an MBA program is the opportunity cost of giving up a well-paying job. Someone who leaves a job that pays $5,000 per month to attend an MBA program is, in effect, incurring a $5,000-per-month opportunity cost, in addition to the tuition and cost of textbooks (although this one is well worth the money).

Thus, it is not surprising that MBA applications rise in bad economic times when outside opportunities decline. People thinking of going back to school face a reduced opportunity cost of entering an MBA program if they think they may be laid off or not promoted during an economic downturn. As Stacey Kole, deputy dean for the MBA program at the University of Chicago Graduate School of Business observed, "When there's a go-go economy, fewer people decide to go back to school. When things go south the opportunity cost of leaving work is lower."

In 2008, when U.S. unemployment rose sharply and the economy was in poor shape, the number of people seeking admission to MBA programs shot up substantially. The number of applicants to MBA programs for the class of 2008–2009 increased over the previous year by 79% in the United States, 77% in the United Kingdom, and 69% in other European countries. Applicants increased substantially for 2009–2010 as well in Canada and Europe. However, as economic conditions improved, global applications were unchanged in 2010 and fell slightly in 2011.

SOLVED PROBLEM 7.1

Meredith's firm sends her to a conference for managers and has paid her registration fee. Included in the registration fee is admission to a class on how to price derivative securities such as options. She is considering attending, but her most attractive alternative opportunity is to attend a talk by Warren Buffett about his investment strategies, which is scheduled at the same time. Although she would be willing to pay $100 to hear his talk, the cost of a ticket is only $40. Given that there are no other costs involved in attending either event, what is Meredith's opportunity cost of attending the derivatives talk?

Answer

To calculate her opportunity cost, determine the benefit that Meredith would forgo by attending the derivatives class. Because she incurs no additional fee to attend the derivatives talk, Meredith's opportunity cost is the forgone benefit of hearing the Buffett speech. Because she values hearing the Buffett speech at $100, but only has to pay $40, her net benefit from hearing that talk is $60 (= $100 − $40). Thus, her opportunity cost of attending the derivatives talk is $60.

Capital Costs

Determining the opportunity cost of capital, such as land or equipment, requires special considerations. Capital is a **durable good**: a product that is usable for a long period, typically for many years. Two problems may arise in measuring the cost of capital. The first is how to allocate the initial purchase cost over time. The second is what to do if the value of the capital changes over time.

We can avoid these two measurement problems if capital is rented instead of purchased. For example, suppose a firm can rent a small pick-up truck for $400 a month or buy it outright for $20,000. If the firm rents the truck, the rental payment is the relevant opportunity cost per month. The truck is rented month-to-month, so the firm does not have to worry about how to allocate the purchase cost of a truck over time. Moreover, the rental rate will adjust if the cost of trucks changes over time. Thus, if the firm can rent capital for short periods, it calculates the cost of this capital in the same way that it calculates the cost of nondurable inputs such as labor services or materials.

The firm faces a more complex problem in determining the opportunity cost of the truck if it purchases the truck. The firm's accountant may *expense* the truck's purchase price by treating the full $20,000 as a cost at the time that the truck is purchased, or the accountant may *amortize* the cost by spreading the $20,000 over the life of the truck, following rules set by an accounting organization or by a relevant government authority such as the Internal Revenue Service (IRS).

A manager who wants to make sound decisions does not expense or amortize the truck using such rules. The true opportunity cost of using a truck that the firm owns is the amount that the firm could earn if it rented the truck to others. That is, regardless of whether the firm rents or buys the truck, the manager views the opportunity cost of this capital good as the rental rate for a given period. If the value of an older truck is less than that of a newer one, the rental rate for the truck falls over time.

But what if there is no rental market for trucks available to the firm? It is still important to determine an appropriate opportunity cost. Suppose that the firm has two choices: It can choose not to buy the truck and keep the truck's purchase price of $20,000, or it can use the truck for a year and sell it for $17,000 at the end of the year. If the firm does not purchase the truck, it will deposit the $20,000 in a bank account that pays 5% per year, so the firm will have $21,000 at the end of the year. Thus, the opportunity cost of capital of using the truck for a year is $21,000 − $17,000 = $4,000.[2] This $4,000 opportunity cost equals the $3,000 depreciation of the truck (= $20,000 − $17,000) plus the $1,000 in forgone interest that the firm could have earned over the year if the firm had invested the $20,000.

Because the values of trucks, machines, and other equipment decline over time, their rental rates fall, so the firm's opportunity costs decline. In contrast, the value of some land, buildings, and other forms of capital may rise over time. To maximize profit, a firm must properly measure the opportunity cost of a piece of capital even if its value rises over time. If a beauty parlor buys a building when similar buildings in the area rent for $1,000 per month, the opportunity cost of using the building is $1,000 a month. If land values increase so that rents in the area rise to $2,000 per month, the beauty parlor's opportunity cost of its building rises to $2,000 per month.

Sunk Costs

An opportunity cost is not always easy to observe but should always be considered when deciding how much to produce. In contrast, a **sunk cost**—a past expenditure that cannot be recovered—though easily observed, is not relevant to a manager when deciding how much to produce now. A sunk expenditure is not an opportunity cost.[3]

If a firm buys a forklift for $25,000 and can resell it for the same price, it is not a sunk expenditure, and the opportunity cost of the forklift is $25,000. If instead the firm buys a specialized piece of equipment for $25,000 and cannot resell it, then the original expenditure is a sunk cost. Because this equipment has no alternative use and cannot be resold, its opportunity cost is zero, and it should not be included in

---

[2]The firm would also pay for gasoline, insurance, licensing fees, and other operating costs, but these items would all be expensed as operating costs and would not appear in the firm's accounts as capital costs.

[3]Nonetheless, a sunk cost paid for a specialized input should still be deducted from income before paying taxes even if that cost is sunk, and must therefore appear in financial accounts.

the firm's current cost calculations. If the specialized equipment that originally cost $25,000 can be resold for $10,000, then only $15,000 of the original expenditure is a sunk cost, and the opportunity cost is $10,000.

To illustrate why a sunk cost should not influence a manager's current decisions, consider a firm that paid $300,000 for a piece of land for which the market value has fallen to $200,000. Now, the land's true opportunity cost is $200,000. The $100,000 difference between the $300,000 purchase price and the current market value of $200,000 is a sunk cost that has already been incurred and cannot be recovered. The land is worth $240,000 to the firm if it builds a plant on this parcel. Is it worth carrying out production on this land or should the land be sold for its market value of $200,000? If the firm uses the original purchase price in its decision-making process, the firm will falsely conclude that using the land for production will result in a $60,000 loss: the $240,000 value of using the land minus the purchase price of $300,000. Instead, the firm should use the land because it is worth $40,000 more as a production facility than if the firm sells the land for $200,000, its next best alternative. Thus, the firm should use the land's opportunity cost to make its decisions and ignore the land's sunk cost. In short, "There's no use crying over spilt milk."

7.2 Short-Run Costs

To make profit-maximizing decisions, a firm needs to know how its cost varies with output. A firm's cost rises as it increases its output. The short run is the period over which some inputs, such as labor, can be varied, while other inputs, such as capital, are fixed (Chapter 6). In contrast, the firm can vary all its inputs in the long run. For simplicity in our graphs, we concentrate on firms that use only two inputs: labor and capital. We focus on the case in which labor is the only variable input in the short run, and both labor and capital are variable in the long run. However, we can generalize our analysis to examine a firm that uses any number of inputs.

We start by examining various measures of cost, which we use to show the distinction between short-run and long-run costs. Then we show how the shapes of the short-run cost curves are related to the firm's production function.

Short-Run Cost Measures

We start by using a numerical example to illustrate the basic cost concepts. We then examine the graphic relationship between these concepts.

Fixed Cost, Variable Cost, and Total Cost. To produce a given level of output in the short run, a firm incurs costs for both its fixed and variable inputs. A **fixed cost** (F) is a cost that does not vary with the level of output. Fixed costs, which include expenditures on land, office space, production facilities, and other *overhead* expenses, cannot be avoided by reducing output and must be incurred as long as the firm stays in business.

Fixed costs are often sunk costs, but not always. For example, a restaurant rents space for $2,000 per month on a month-to-month lease. This rent does not vary with the number of meals served (its output level), so it is a fixed cost. Because the restaurant has already paid this month's rent, this fixed cost is also a sunk cost:

The restaurant cannot recover the $2,000 even if it goes out of business. Next month, if the restaurant stays open, it will have to pay the $2,000 rent. If the lease is a month-to-month rental agreement, this fixed cost of $2,000 is an *avoidable cost*, not a sunk cost. The restaurant can shut down, cancel its rental agreement, and avoid paying this fixed cost. Therefore, in planning for next month, the restaurant should treat the $2,000 rent as a fixed cost but not as a sunk cost. Thus, the fixed cost of $2,000 per month is a fixed cost in both the short run (this month) and the long run, but it is a sunk cost only in the short run.

A firm's **variable cost** (*VC*) is the production expense that changes with the quantity of output produced. The variable cost is the cost of the variable inputs—the inputs the firm can adjust to alter its output level, such as labor and materials.

A firm's **cost** (or **total cost,** *C*) is the sum of a firm's variable cost and fixed cost:

$$C = VC + F.$$

Because variable cost changes with the level of output, total cost also varies with the level of output.

To decide how much to produce, a firm uses measures of marginal and average costs. We derive four such measures using the fixed cost, the variable cost, and the total cost.

Marginal Cost. A firm's **marginal cost** (*MC*) is the amount by which a firm's cost changes if it produces one more unit of output. The marginal cost is

$$MC = \frac{dC(q)}{dq}. \tag{7.1}$$

Because only variable cost changes with output, we can also define marginal cost as the change in variable cost from a small increase in output, $MC = dVC(q)/dq$, where $VC(q)$ is the firm's variable cost function. Chapter 8 will show that a firm uses its marginal cost to decide whether changing its output level pays off.

Average Cost. Firms use three average cost measures. The **average fixed cost** (*AFC*) is the fixed cost divided by the units of output produced: $AFC = F/q$. The average fixed cost falls as output rises because the fixed cost is spread over more units: $dAFC/dq = -F/q^2 < 0$. The *AFC* curve approaches zero as the output level grows large.

The **average variable cost** (*AVC*) is the variable cost divided by the units of output produced: $AVC = VC/q$. Because the variable cost increases with output, the average variable cost may either increase or decrease as output rises. As Chapter 8 shows, a firm uses the average variable cost to determine whether to shut down operations when demand is low.

The **average cost** (*AC*)—or average total cost—is the total cost divided by the units of output produced: $AC = C/q$. Because total cost equals variable cost plus fixed cost, $C = VC + F$, when we divide both sides of the equation by q, we learn that

$$AC = \frac{C}{q} = \frac{VC}{q} + \frac{F}{q} = AVC + AFC. \tag{7.2}$$

That is, the average cost is the sum of the average variable cost and the average fixed cost. A firm uses its average cost to determine if it is making a profit.

SOLVED PROBLEM 7.2

A manufacturing plant has a short-run cost function of $C(q) = 100q - 4q^2 + 0.2q^3 + 450$. What is the firm's short-run fixed cost and variable cost function? Derive the formulas for its marginal cost, average variable cost, average fixed cost, and average cost. Draw two figures, one above the other. In the top figure, show the fixed cost, variable cost, and total cost curves. In the bottom figure, show the corresponding marginal cost curve and three average cost curves.

Answer

1. *Identify the fixed cost as the part of the short-run cost function that does not vary with output, q, and the remaining part of the cost function as the variable cost function.* The fixed cost is $F = 450$, the only part that does not vary with q. The variable cost function, $VC(q) = 100q - 4q^2 + 0.2q^3$, is the part of the cost function that varies with q.

2. *Determine the marginal cost by differentiating the short-run cost function (or variable cost function) with respect to output.* Differentiating, we find that

$$MC = \frac{dC(q)}{dq}$$

$$= \frac{d(100q - 4q^2 + 0.2q^3 + 450)}{dq}$$

$$= 100 - 8q + 0.6q^2.$$

3. *Calculate the three average cost functions using their definitions.*

$$AVC = \frac{V(q)}{q}$$

$$= \frac{100q - 4q^2 + 0.2q^3}{q}$$

$$= 100 - 4q + 0.2q^2,$$

$$AFC = \frac{F}{q} = \frac{450}{q},$$

$$AC = \frac{C(q)}{q}$$

$$= \frac{100q - 4q^2 + 0.2q^3 + 450}{q}$$

$$= 100 - 4q + 0.2q^2 + \frac{450}{q}$$

$$= AVC + AFC.$$

4. *Use these cost, marginal cost, and average cost functions to plot the specified figures.* Figure 7.1 shows these curves.

Figure 7.1 Short-Run Cost Curves

(a) Because the total cost differs from the variable cost by the fixed cost, $F = \$450$, the cost curve, C, is parallel to the variable cost curve, VC. (b) The marginal cost curve, MC, cuts the average variable cost, AVC, and average cost, AC, curves at their minimums. The height of the AC curve at point a equals the slope of the line from the origin to the cost curve at A. The height of the AVC at b equals the slope of the line from the origin to the variable cost curve at B. The height of the marginal cost is the slope of either the C or VC curve at that quantity.

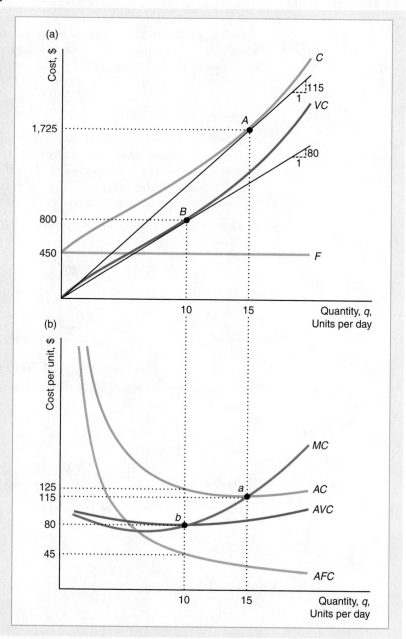

Short-Run Cost Curves

We illustrate the relationship between output and the various cost measures using the example in Solved Problem 7.2. Panel a of Figure 7.1 shows the variable cost, fixed cost, and total cost curves. The fixed cost, which does not vary with output, is a horizontal line at $450. The variable cost curve is zero when output is zero and rises as output increases. The total cost curve, which is the vertical sum of the variable cost curve and the fixed cost line, is $450 higher than the variable cost curve at every output level, so the variable cost and total cost curves are parallel.

Panel b shows the average fixed cost, average variable cost, average cost, and marginal cost curves. The average fixed cost curve falls as output increases. It approaches zero as output gets larger because the fixed cost is spread over many units of output. The average cost curve is the vertical sum of the average fixed cost and average variable cost curves. For example, at 10 units of output, the average variable cost is $80 and the average fixed cost is $45, so the average cost is $125.

The marginal cost curve cuts the U-shaped average cost and the average variable cost curves at their minimums.[4] The average cost (or average variable cost) curve rises where it lies below the marginal cost curve and falls where it lies above the marginal cost curve, so the marginal cost curve must cut the average cost curve at its minimum (by similar reasoning to that used in Chapter 6, where we discussed average and marginal products).

Production Functions and the Shape of Cost Curves

The production function determines the shape of a firm's cost curves. It shows the amount of inputs needed to produce a given level of output. The firm calculates its cost by multiplying the quantity of each input by its price and then summing.

If a firm produces output using capital and labor and its capital is fixed in the short run, the firm's variable cost is its cost of labor. Its labor cost is the wage per hour, w, times the number of hours of labor, L, so that its variable cost (labor cost) is $VC = wL$.

If input prices are constant, the production function determines the shape of the variable cost curve. We can write the short-run production function as $q = f(L, \overline{K}) = g(L)$ because capital does not vary. By inverting, we know that the amount of labor we need to produce any given amount of output is $L = g^{-1}(q)$. If the wage of labor is w, the variable cost function is $V(q) = wL = wg^{-1}(q)$. Similarly, the cost function is $C(q) = V(q) + F = wg^{-1}(q) + F$.

In the short run, when the firm's capital is fixed, the only way the firm can increase its output is to use more labor. If the firm increases its labor enough, it reaches the point of *diminishing marginal returns to labor*, where each extra worker increases output by a smaller amount. Because the variable cost function is the inverse of the short-run production function, its properties are determined by the short-run production function. If the production function exhibits diminishing marginal returns, then the variable cost rises more than in proportion as output increases.

Because the production function determines the shape of the variable cost curve, it also determines the shape of the marginal, average variable, and average cost curves. We now examine the shape of each of these cost curves in detail, because firms rely more on these per-unit cost measures than on total variable cost to make decisions about labor and capital.

---

[4]To determine the output level q where the average cost curve, $AC(q)$, reaches its minimum, we set the derivative of average cost with respect to q equal to zero:

$$\frac{dAC(q)}{dq} = \frac{d[C(q)/q]}{dq} = \left[\frac{dC(q)}{dq} - \frac{C(q)}{q}\right]\frac{1}{q} = 0.$$

This condition holds at the output q where $dC(q)/dq = C(q)/q$, or $MC = AC$. If the second-order condition holds at the same level for q, the average cost curve reaches its minimum at that quantity. The second-order condition requires that the average cost curve be falling to the left of this quantity and rising to the right. Similarly, $dAVC/dq = d[VC(q)/q]/dq = [dVC/dq - VC(q)/q](1/q) = 0$, so $MC = AVC$ at the minimum of the average variable cost curve.

Shape of the Marginal Cost Curve. The marginal cost is the change in variable cost as output increases by one unit: $MC = dVC/dq$. In the short run, capital is fixed, so the only way a firm can produce more output is to use extra labor. The extra labor required to produce one more unit of output is $dL/dq = 1/MP_L$. The extra labor costs the firm w per unit, so the firm's cost rises by $w(dL/dq)$. As a result, the firm's marginal cost is

$$MC = \frac{dV(q)}{dq} = w\frac{dL}{dq}.$$

The marginal cost equals the wage times the extra labor necessary to produce one more unit of output.

How do we know how much extra labor is needed to produce one more unit of output? This information comes from the production function. The marginal product of labor—the amount of extra output produced by another unit of labor, holding other inputs fixed—is $MP_L = dq/dL$. Thus, the extra labor needed to produce one more unit of output, dL/dq, is $1/MP_L$, so the firm's marginal cost is

$$MC = \frac{w}{MP_L}. \tag{7.3}$$

According to Equation 7.3, the marginal cost equals the wage divided by the marginal product of labor. If it takes four extra hours of labor services to produce one more unit of output, the marginal product of an hour of labor is $\frac{1}{4}$. Given a wage of $5 an hour, the marginal cost of one more unit of output is $5 divided by $\frac{1}{4}$ or $20.

Equation 7.3 shows that the marginal cost moves in the opposite direction to that of the marginal product of labor. At low levels of labor, the marginal product of labor commonly rises with additional workers who may help the original workers to collectively make better use of the firm's equipment (Chapter 6). As the marginal product of labor rises, the marginal cost falls.

Eventually, however, as the number of workers increases, workers must share the fixed amount of equipment and may get in each other's way. Consequently, the marginal cost curve slopes upward due to diminishing marginal returns to labor. As a result, the marginal cost first falls and then rises, as panel b of Figure 7.1 illustrates.

Shape of the Average Cost Curve. Because diminishing marginal returns to labor affect the shape of the variable cost curve, they also determine the shape of the average variable cost curve. The average variable cost is the variable cost divided by output: $AVC = VC/q$. For a firm that has labor as its only variable input, variable cost is wL, so average variable cost is

$$AVC = \frac{VC}{q} = \frac{wL}{q}.$$

Because the average product of labor is q/L, average variable cost is the wage divided by the average product of labor:

$$AVC = \frac{w}{AP_L}. \tag{7.4}$$

With a constant wage, the average variable cost moves in the opposite direction to that of the average product of labor in Equation 7.4. As we saw in Chapter 6, the average product of labor tends to rise and then fall, so the average cost tends to fall and then rise, as panel b of Figure 7.1 shows.

The average cost curve is the vertical sum of the average variable cost curve and the average fixed cost curve, as in panel b. If the average variable cost curve is U-shaped, adding the strictly falling average fixed cost makes the average cost fall more steeply than the average variable cost curve at low output levels. At high output levels, the average cost and average variable cost curves differ by ever-smaller amounts, as the average fixed cost, F/q, approaches zero. Thus, the average cost curve is also U-shaped.

APPLICATION

Short-Run Cost Curves for a Japanese Beer Manufacturer

We can derive the various short-run cost curves for a typical Japanese beer manufacturer using its estimated Cobb-Douglas production function (based on Flath, 2011)

$$q = 1.52L^{0.6}K^{0.4}. \tag{7.5}$$

We assume that the firm's capital is fixed at $\overline{K} = 100$ units in the short run.

Given that the rental rate of a unit of capital is \$8, the fixed cost, F, is \$800, the average fixed cost is

$$AFC = F/q = 800/q.$$

An increase in output reduces the AFC, $dAFC/dq = -800/q_2 < 0$, so the AVC slopes down and approaches the horizontal axis in the figure.

We can use the production function to derive the variable cost. Because capital is fixed in the short run, the short-run production function is solely a function of labor:

$$q = 1.52L^{0.6}100^{0.4} \approx 9.59L^{0.6}.$$

Rearranging this expression, we can write the number of workers, L, needed to produce q units of output, as a function solely of output:

$$L(q) = \left(\frac{q}{9.59}\right)^{\frac{1}{0.6}} = \left(\frac{1}{9.59}\right)^{1.67}q^{1.67} \approx 0.023q^{1.67}.$$

Now that we know how labor and output are related, we can calculate variable cost directly. The only variable input is labor, so if the wage is \$24, the firm's variable cost is

$$VC(q) = wL(q) = 24L(q).$$

Substituting for $L(q)$ from the previous equation into this variable cost equation, we learn how variable cost varies with output:

$$VC(q) = 24L(q) = 24(0.023q^{1.67}) \approx 0.55q^{1.67}.$$

Using this expression for variable cost, we can construct the other cost measures. Thus, to construct all the cost measures of the beer firm, we need only the production function and the prices of the inputs.

The average variable cost is $AVC = VC/q = 0.55q^{0.67}$. To obtain the equation for marginal cost as a function of output, we differentiate the variable cost, $VC(q)$, with respect to output:

$$MC(q) = \frac{dVC(q)}{dq} \approx \frac{d(0.55q^{1.67})}{dq} = 1.67 \times 0.55q^{0.67} \approx 0.92q^{0.67}.$$

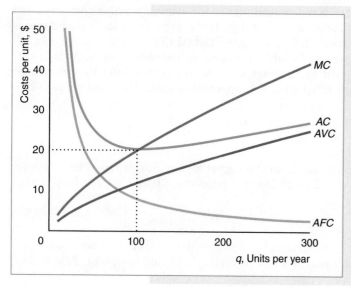

Total   cost   is $C = FC + VC = 800 + 0.55q^{1.67}$. Average cost is $AC = C/q = AFC + AVC = 800/q + 0.55q^{0.67}$.

As the figure shows, the short-run average cost curve for a Japanese beer manufacturer is U-shaped, because the AC is the vertical sum of the strictly falling AFC and the strictly increasing AVC. The firm's marginal cost curve lies above the rising average variable cost curve for all positive quantities of output and cuts the average cost curve at its minimum at $q = 100$.

Effects of Taxes on Costs

Taxes applied to a firm shift some or all of the marginal and average cost curves. For example, suppose that the government collects a specific tax of $10 per unit of output. This specific tax, which varies with output, affects the firm's variable cost but not its fixed cost. As a result, it affects the firm's average cost, average variable cost, and marginal cost curves but not its average fixed cost curve.

At every quantity, the average variable cost and the average cost rise by the full amount of the tax. Thus, the firm's after-tax average variable cost, AVC^a, is its average variable cost of production—the before-tax average variable cost, AVC^b—plus the tax per unit, $10: AVC^a = AVC^b + \$10$.

The average cost equals the average variable cost plus the average fixed cost. For example, in the last application, the Japanese beer firm's before-tax average cost is $AC^b = AVC + AFC = 0.55q^{0.67} + 800/q$. Because the tax increases average variable cost by $10 and does not affect the average fixed cost, average cost increases by $10: $AC^a = AC^b + 10 = 0.55q^{0.67} + 800/q + 10$. The tax also increases the firm's marginal cost by $10 per unit. The beer manufacturer's pre-tax marginal cost is $MC^b = 0.92q^{0.67}$, so its after-tax marginal cost is $MC^a = 0.92q^{0.67} + 10$.

Figure 7.2 shows these shifts in the marginal and average cost curves. The new marginal cost curve and average cost curve are parallel to the old ones: $10 higher at each quantity. At first, it may not look like the shift of the average cost curve is parallel, but you can convince yourself that it is a parallel shift by using a ruler.

Similarly, we can analyze the effect of a franchise tax on costs. A franchise tax—also called a business license fee—is a lump sum that a firm pays for the right to operate a business. For example, a tax of $800 per year is levied "for the privilege of doing business in California." The 2008 license fee was $326,000 to sell hot dogs in front of New York City's Metropolitan Museum of Art. These taxes do not vary with output, so they affect firms' fixed costs only—not their variable costs.

Figure 7.2 Effect of a Specific Tax on a Japanese Beer Manufacturer's Cost Curves

A specific tax of $10 per unit shifts both the marginal cost and average cost curves upward by $10. Because of the parallel upward shift of the average cost curve, the minimum of both the before-tax average cost curve, AC^b, and the after-tax average cost curve, AC^a, occurs at the same output, 100 units.

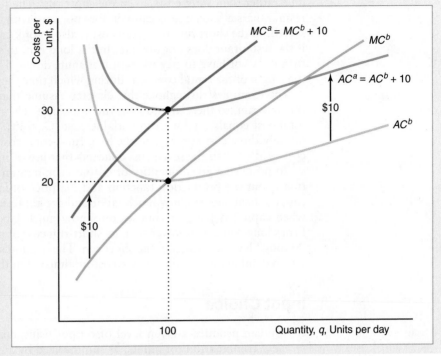

Short-Run Cost Summary

We have examined three cost-level curves—total cost, fixed cost, and variable cost—and four cost-per-unit curves—average cost, average fixed cost, average variable cost, and marginal cost. Understanding the shapes of these curves and the relationships among them is crucial to understanding the analysis of a firm's behavior in the rest of this book. The following basic concepts capture most of what you need to know about the relationships among the curves and their shapes:

- In the short run, the cost associated with inputs that cannot be adjusted is fixed, while the cost from inputs that can be adjusted is variable.
- Given constant input prices, the shapes of the cost, variable cost, marginal cost, and average cost curves are determined by the production function.
- Where a variable input has diminishing marginal returns, the variable cost and cost curves become relatively steep as output increases, so the average cost, average variable cost, and marginal cost curves rise with output.
- Both the average cost curve and the average variable cost curve fall at quantities where the marginal cost curve is below them and rise where the marginal cost is above them, so the marginal cost curve cuts both of these average cost curves at their minimum points.

7.3 Long-Run Costs

In the long run, a firm adjusts all its inputs to keep its cost of production as low as possible. The firm can change its plant size, design and build new equipment, and otherwise adjust inputs that were fixed in the short run.

Although firms may incur fixed costs in the long run, these fixed costs are *avoidable* rather than *sunk* costs, as in the short run. The rent of F per month paid by a restaurant is a fixed cost because it does not vary with the number of meals (output) served. In the short run, this fixed cost is also a sunk cost: The firm must pay F even if the restaurant does not operate. In the long run, this fixed cost is avoidable: The firm does not have to pay the rent if it shuts down. The long run is determined by the length of the rental contract, during which time the firm is obligated to pay rent.

The examples throughout this chapter assume that all inputs can be varied in the long run, so there are no long-run fixed costs ($F = 0$). As a result, the long-run total cost equals the long-run variable cost: $C = VC$. Thus, our firm concentrates on only three cost concepts in the long run—total cost, average cost, and marginal cost—rather than the seven cost concepts that it uses in the short run.

To produce a given quantity of output at minimum cost, our firm uses information about the production function and the price of labor and capital. In the long run, the firm chooses how much labor and capital to use, whereas in the short run, when capital is fixed, it chooses only how much labor to use. Consequently, the firm's long-run cost is lower than its short-run cost of production if it has to use the "wrong" level of capital in the short run. This section shows how a firm determines which combinations of inputs are cost-minimizing in the long run.

Input Choice

A firm can produce a given level of output using many different *technologically efficient* combinations of inputs, as summarized by an isoquant (Chapter 6). From among the technologically efficient combinations of inputs, a firm wants to choose the particular bundle with the lowest cost of production, which is the *economically efficient* combination of inputs. To do so, the firm combines information about technology from the isoquant with information about the cost of labor and capital.

We now show how information about cost can be summarized in an *isocost line*. Then we show how a firm can combine the information in isoquant and isocost lines to determine the economically efficient combination of inputs.

Isocost Line. The cost of producing a given level of output depends on the price of labor and capital. The firm hires L hours of labor services at a wage of w per hour, so its labor cost is wL. The firm rents K hours of machine services at a rental rate of r per hour, so its capital cost is rK. (If the firm owns the capital, r is the implicit rental rate.) The firm's total cost is the sum of its labor and capital costs:

$$C = wL + rK. \tag{7.6}$$

The firm can hire as much labor and capital as it wants at these constant input prices.

The firm can use many combinations of labor and capital that cost the same amount. These combinations of labor and capital are plotted on an **isocost line**, which indicates all the combinations of inputs that require the same (*iso*) total expenditure (*cost*). Along an isocost line, cost is fixed at a particular level, $\overline{C}$, so by setting cost at $\overline{C}$ in Equation 7.6, we can write the equation for the $\overline{C}$ isocost line as

$$\overline{C} = wL + rK. \tag{7.7}$$

Figure 7.3 shows three isocost lines for the Japanese beer manufacturer where the fixed cost is $\overline{C} = \$1,000$, $\$2,000$, or $\$3,000$; $w = \$24$ per hour; and $r = \$8$ per hour.

Figure 7.3 Cost Minimization

The beer manufacturer minimizes its cost of producing 100 units of output by producing at x ($L = 50$ and $K = 100$). This cost-minimizing combination of inputs is determined by the tangency between the $q = 100$ isoquant and the lowest isocost line, \$2,000, that touches that isoquant. At x, the isocost is tangent to the isoquant, so the slope of the isocost, $-w/r = -3$, equals the slope of the isoquant, which is the negative of the marginal rate of technical substitution. That is, the rate at which the firm can trade capital for labor in the input markets equals the rate at which it can substitute capital for labor in the production process.

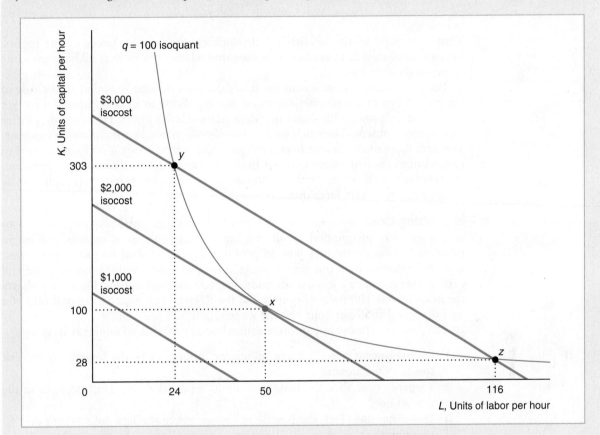

Using algebra, we can rewrite Equation 7.7 to show how much capital the firm can buy if it spends a total of $\overline{C}$ and purchases L units of labor:

$$K = \frac{\overline{C}}{r} - \frac{w}{r}L. \qquad (7.8)$$

The equation for the isocost lines in the figure is $K = \overline{C}/8 - (24/8)L = \overline{C}/8 - 3L$. We can use Equation 7.8 to derive three properties of isocost lines.

First, the point where the isocost lines hit the capital and labor axes depends on the firm's cost, $\overline{C}$, and the input prices. The $\overline{C}$ isocost line intersects the capital axis where the firm uses only capital. Setting $L = 0$ in Equation 7.8, we find that the firm buys $K = \overline{C}/r$ units of capital. Similarly, the intersection of the isocost line with the labor axis is at $\overline{C}/w$, which is the amount of labor the firm hires if it uses only labor.

Second, isocosts that are farther from the origin have higher costs than those closer to the origin. Because the isocost lines intersect the capital axis at $\overline{C}/r$ and the labor axis at $\overline{C}/w$, an increase in the cost shifts these intersections with the axes proportionately outward.

Third, the slope of each isocost line is the same. By differentiating Equation 7.8, we find that the slope of any isocost line is

$$\frac{dK}{dL} = -\frac{w}{r}.$$

Thus, the slope of the isocost line depends on the relative prices of the inputs. Because all isocost lines are based on the same relative prices, they all have the same slope, so they are parallel.

The role of the isocost line in the firm's decision making is similar to the role of the budget line in a consumer's decision making. Both an isocost line and a budget line are straight lines with slopes that depend on relative prices. However, they differ in an important way. The single budget line is determined by the consumer's income. The firm faces many isocost lines, each of which corresponds to a different level of expenditures the firm might make. A firm may incur a relatively low cost by producing relatively little output with few inputs, or it may incur a relatively high cost by producing a relatively large quantity.

Minimizing Cost. By combining the information about costs contained in the isocost lines with information about efficient production that is summarized by an isoquant, a firm determines how to produce a given level of output at the lowest cost. We examine how our beer manufacturer picks the combination of labor and capital that minimizes its cost of producing 100 units of output. Figure 7.3 shows the isoquant for 100 units of output and the isocost lines where the rental rate of a unit of capital is $8 per hour and the wage rate is $24 per hour.

The firm can choose any of three equivalent approaches to minimize its cost:

1. **Lowest-isocost rule.** Pick the bundle of inputs where the lowest isocost line touches the isoquant.
2. **Tangency rule.** Pick the bundle of inputs where the isoquant is tangent to the isocost line.
3. **Last-dollar rule.** Pick the bundle of inputs where the last dollar spent on one input gives as much extra output as the last dollar spent on any other input.

Using the *lowest-isocost rule*, the firm minimizes its cost by using the combination of inputs on the isoquant that lies on the lowest isocost line to touch the isoquant. The lowest possible isoquant that will allow the beer manufacturer to produce 100 units of output is tangent to the $2,000 isocost line. This isocost line touches the isoquant at the bundle of inputs x, where the firm uses $L = 50$ workers and $K = 100$ units of capital.

How do we know that x is the least costly way to produce 100 units of output? We need to demonstrate that other practical combinations of inputs produce fewer than 100 units or produce 100 units at greater cost.

If the firm spent less than $2,000, it could not produce 100 units of output. Each combination of inputs on the $1,000 isocost line lies below the isoquant, so the firm cannot produce 100 units of output for $1,000.

The firm can produce 100 units of output using other combinations of inputs besides x, but using these other bundles of inputs is more expensive. For example, the firm can produce 100 units of output using the combinations y ($L = 24$, $K = 303$) or z ($L = 116$, $K = 28$). Both these combinations, however, cost the firm $3,000.

If an isocost line crosses the isoquant twice, as the $3,000 isocost line does, there must be another lower isocost line that also touches the isoquant. The lowest possible isocost line to touch the isoquant, the $2,000 isocost line, is tangent to the isoquant at a single bundle, x. Thus, the firm may use the *tangency rule*: The firm chooses the input bundle where the relevant isoquant is tangent to an isocost line to produce a given level of output at the lowest cost.

We can interpret this tangency or cost minimization condition in two ways. At the point of tangency, the slope of the isoquant equals the slope of the isocost. As we saw in Chapter 6, the slope of the isoquant is the marginal rate of technical substitution (*MRTS*). The slope of the isocost is the negative of the ratio of the wage to the cost of capital, $-w/r$. Thus, to minimize its cost of producing a given level of output, a firm chooses its inputs so that the marginal rate of technical substitution equals the negative of the relative input prices:

$$MRTS = -\frac{w}{r}. \tag{7.9}$$

The firm chooses inputs so that the rate at which it can substitute capital for labor in the production process, the *MRTS*, exactly equals the rate at which it can trade capital for labor in input markets, $-w/r$.

Equation 6.8 shows that, for a Cobb-Douglas production function, $MRTS = -(a/b)(K/L)$. Because the beer manufacturer's Cobb-Douglas production function, Equation 7.5, is $q = 1.52L^{0.6}K^{0.4}$, its marginal rate of technical substitution is $-(0.6/0.4)K/L = -1.5K/L$. At $K = 100$ and $L = 50$, its *MRTS* is -3, which equals the negative of the ratio of its input prices, $-w/r = -24/8 = -3$. In contrast, at y the isocost cuts the isoquant so that the slopes are not equal. At y, the *MRTS* is -18.9375, so the isoquant is steeper than the isocost line, -3. Because the slopes are not equal at y, the firm can produce the same output at lower cost. As the figure shows, the cost of producing at y is $3,000, whereas the cost of producing at x is only $2,000.

We can interpret the condition in Equation 7.9 in another way. The marginal rate of technical substitution equals the negative of the ratio of the marginal product of labor to that of capital: $MRTS = -MP_L/MP_K$ (Equation 6.8). Thus, the cost-minimizing condition in Equation 7.9 is (taking the absolute value of both sides)

$$\frac{MP_L}{MP_K} = \frac{w}{r}. \tag{7.10}$$

Equation 7.10 may be rewritten as

$$\frac{MP_L}{w} = \frac{MP_K}{r}. \tag{7.11}$$

Equation 7.11 is the *last-dollar rule*: Cost is minimized if inputs are chosen so that the last dollar spent on labor adds as much extra output as the last dollar spent on capital.

To summarize, the firm can use three equivalent rules to determine the lowest-cost combination of inputs that will produce a given level of output when isoquants are smooth: the lowest-isocost rule; the tangency rule, Equations 7.9 and 7.10; and the last-dollar rule, Equation 7.11. If the isoquant is not smooth, the lowest-cost method of production cannot be determined by using the tangency rule or the last-dollar rule. The lowest-isocost rule always works, even when isoquants are not smooth.

SOLVED PROBLEM 7.3

Using the estimated Japanese beer manufacturer's production function, Equation 7.5, $q = 1.52L^{0.6}K^{0.4}$, calculate the extra output produced by spending the last dollar on either labor or capital at points x and y in Figure 7.3. Show whether the last-dollar rule, Equation 7.11, holds at either of these points.

Answer

1. *Determine the general formula for the extra output from the last dollar spent on labor of capital.* The marginal products of products of labor and capital are $MP_L = 0.6 \times 1.52L^{0.6-1}K^{0.4} = 0.6q/L$ and $MP_K = 0.4q/K$.

2. *Calculate the extra output from the last dollar expenditures at point x and check whether the last-dollar rule holds.* At point $x(L = 50, K = 100)$, the beer firm's marginal product of labor is 1.2 ($= 0.6 \times 100/50$) and its marginal product of capital is 0.4 ($= 0.4 \times 100/100$). The last dollar spent on labor results in $MP/w = 1.2/24 = 0.05$ more units of output. Spending its last dollar on capital, the firm produces $MP_K/r = 0.4/8 = 0.05$ extra output. Therefore, the last dollar rule, Equation 7.11, holds at x: spending one more dollar on labor results in as much extra output as spending the same amount on capital. Thus, the firm is minimizing its cost of producing 100 units of output by producing at x.

3. *Repeat the analysis at point y.* If the firm produces at $y(L = 24, K = 303)$, where it uses more capital and less labor, its MP_L is 2.5 ($= 0.6 \times 100/24$) and its MP_K is approximately 0.13 ($\approx 0.4 \times 100/303$). As a result, the last dollar spent on labor produces $MP_L/w = 2.5/24 \approx 0.1$ more units of output, whereas the last dollar spent on capital produces substantially less extra output, $MP_K/r \approx 0.13/303 \approx 0.017$, so the last-dollar rule does not hold.

Comment: At y, if the firm shifts \$1 from capital to labor, output falls by 0.017 due to the reduction in capital, but output increases by 0.1 due to the additional labor, for a net gain of 0.083 more output at the same cost. The firm should shift even more resources from capital to labor—thereby increasing the marginal product of capital and decreasing the marginal product of labor—until Equation 7.11 holds with equality at point x.

Using Calculus to Minimize Cost. Formally, the firm minimizes its cost, Equation 7.6, subject to the information about the production function that is contained in the isoquant expression: $\bar{q} = F(L, K)$. The corresponding Lagrangian problem is

$$\min_{L, K, \lambda} \mathcal{L} = wL + rK + \lambda[\bar{q} - f(L, K)]. \qquad (7.12)$$

Assuming that we have an interior solution where both L and K are positive, the first-order conditions are

$$\frac{\partial \mathcal{L}}{\partial L} = w - \lambda \frac{\partial f}{\partial L} = 0, \qquad (7.13)$$

$$\frac{\partial \mathcal{L}}{\partial K} = r - \lambda \frac{\partial f}{\partial K} = 0, \qquad (7.14)$$

$$\frac{\partial \mathcal{L}}{\partial \lambda} = \bar{q} - f(L, K) = 0. \qquad (7.15)$$

Dividing Equation 7.13 by Equation 7.14 and rearranging terms, we obtain the same expression as in Equation 7.10:

$$\frac{w}{r} = \frac{\dfrac{\partial f}{\partial L}}{\dfrac{\partial f}{\partial K}} = \frac{MP_L}{MP_K}. \qquad (7.16)$$

That is, we find that cost is minimized where the factor-price ratio equals the ratio of the marginal products.[5]

SOLVED PROBLEM 7.4

Use calculus to derive the cost minimizing capital-labor ratio for a constant elasticity of substitution (CES) production function, Equation 6.13, $q = (L^\rho + K^\rho)^{1/\rho}$. Then, given that $\rho = 0.5$, $w = r = 1$, and $q = 4$, solve for the cost minimizing L and K.

Answer

1. *Write the Lagrangian expression for this cost minimization problem.*

$$\mathcal{L} = wL + rK + \lambda\left(q - [L^\rho + K^\rho]^{\frac{1}{\rho}}\right).$$

2. *Set the derivatives of the Lagrangian with respect to L, K, and λ equal to zero, so as to obtain the first-order conditions.* The first-order conditions, which correspond to Equations 7.13–7.15, are

$$\frac{\partial \mathcal{L}}{\partial L} = w - \lambda \frac{1}{\rho}(L^\rho + K^\rho)^{\frac{1-\rho}{\rho}}\rho L^{\rho-1} = w - \lambda(L^\rho + K^\rho)^{\frac{1-\rho}{\rho}}L^{\rho-1} = 0, \quad (7.17)$$

$$\frac{\partial \mathcal{L}}{\partial K} = r - \lambda(L^\rho + K^\rho)^{\frac{1-\rho}{\rho}}K^{\rho-1} = 0, \qquad (7.18)$$

$$\frac{\partial \mathcal{L}}{\partial \lambda} = q - (L^\rho + K^\rho)^{\frac{1}{\rho}} = 0. \qquad (7.19)$$

3. *Divide Equation 7.17 by Equation 7.18* This ratio of first-order conditions, which corresponds to Equation 7.16, is

$$\frac{w}{r} = \frac{MP_L}{MP_K} = \frac{L^{\rho-1}}{K^{\rho-1}} = \left(\frac{L}{K}\right)^{\rho-1} = \left(\frac{K}{L}\right)^{\sigma}, \qquad (7.20)$$

where the last equality uses the definition of the elasticity of substitution, Equation 6.15, $\sigma = 1/(1 - \rho)$. If $\rho \to 0$, $\sigma \to 1$, so that the production function is Cobb-Douglas (Chapter 6), this condition is $w/r = K/L$. That is, a change in the factor-price ratio, w/r, has a proportional effect on the capital-labor ratio, K/L. The capital-labor ratio change is less than proportional if $\sigma < 1$, and more than proportional if $\sigma > 1$.

---

[5]Using Equations 7.13, 7.14, and 7.16, we find that $\lambda = w/MP_L = r/MP_K$. That is, the Lagrangian multiplier, λ, equals the ratio of the input price to the marginal product for each factor. As we already know, the input price divided by the factor's marginal product equals the marginal cost. Thus, the Lagrangian multiplier equals the marginal cost of production: It measures how much the cost increases if we produce one more unit of output.

4. *Given that* $\rho = 0.5$, $w = r = 1$, *and* $q = 4$, *solve Equation 7.19 and 7.20 for the cost minimizing L and K.* Substituting $w = r = 1$, into Equation 7.20, we find that $1 = (K/L)^2$, or $K/L = 1$, or $K = L$. Substituting $K = L$ and $q = 16$ into Equation 7.19, we discover that $4 = (2L^{0.5})^2$, or $2 = 2L^{0.5}$, or $L = 1 = K$.

Maximizing Output. An equivalent or *dual* problem to minimizing the cost of producing a given quantity of output is maximizing output for a given level of cost. (In a similar pair of problems in Chapter 3, we examined how firms maximize utility for a given budget constraint and minimize expenditure for a given level of utility.) Here, the Lagrangian problem is

$$\min_{L, K, \lambda} \mathcal{L} = f(L, K) + \lambda(\overline{C} - wL - rK). \tag{7.21}$$

Assuming that we have an interior solution where both L and K are positive, the first-order conditions are

$$\frac{\partial \mathcal{L}}{\partial L} = \frac{\partial f}{\partial L} - \lambda w = 0, \tag{7.22}$$

$$\frac{\partial \mathcal{L}}{\partial K} = \frac{\partial f}{\partial K} - \lambda r = 0, \tag{7.23}$$

$$\frac{\partial \mathcal{L}}{\partial \lambda} = \overline{C} - wL - rK = 0. \tag{7.24}$$

By examining the ratio of the first two conditions, Equations 7.22 and 7.23, we obtain the same condition as when we minimized cost by holding output constant: $MP_L/MP_K = (\partial f/\partial L)/(\partial f/\partial K) = w/r$. That is, at the output maximum, the slope of the isoquant equals the slope of the isocost line. Figure 7.4 shows that the firm

Figure 7.4 Output Maximization

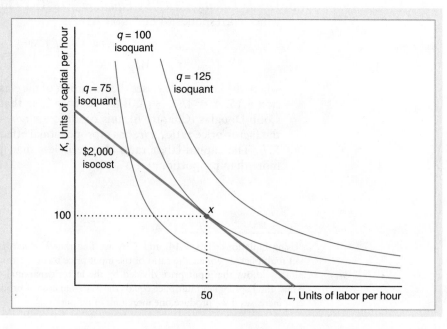

The beer manufacturer maximizes its production at a cost of $2,000 by producing 100 units of output at x using $L = 50$ and $K = 100$. The $q = 100$ isoquant is the highest one that touches the $2,000 isocost line. The firm operates where the $q = 100$ isoquant is tangent to the $2,000 isocost line.

maximizes its output for a given level of cost by operating where the highest feasible isoquant, $q = 100$, is tangent to the $2,000 isocost line.

Factor Price Changes. Once the beer manufacturer determines the lowest-cost combination of inputs to produce a given level of output, it uses that method as long as the input prices remain constant. How should the firm change its behavior if the cost of one of the factors changes?

Suppose that the wage falls from $24 to $8 but the rental rate of capital stays constant at $8. Because of the wage decrease, the new isocost line in Figure 7.5 has a flatter slope, $-w/r = -8/8 = -1$, than the original isocost line, $-w/r = -24/8 = -3$. The change in the wage does not affect technological efficiency, so it does not affect the isoquant. The relatively steep original isocost line is tangent to the 100-unit isoquant at point x ($L = 50, K = 100$), while the new, flatter isocost line is tangent to the isoquant at v ($L = 77, K = 52$). Because labor is now relatively less expensive, the firm uses more labor and less capital as labor becomes relatively less expensive. Moreover, the firm's cost of producing 100 units falls from $2,000 to $1,032 as a result of the decrease in the wage. This example illustrates that a change in the relative prices of inputs affects the combination of inputs that a firm selects and its cost of production.

Formally, we know from Equation 7.10 that the ratio of the factor prices equals the ratio of the marginal products: $w/r = MP_L/MP_K$. As we have already determined, this expression is $w/r = 1.5K/L$ for the beer manufacturer. Holding r fixed for a small change in w, the change in the factor ratio is $d(K/L)/dw = 1/(1.5r)$. For the beer manufacturer, where $r = 8$, $d(K/L)/dw = 1/12 \approx 0.083$. Because this derivative is positive, a small change in the wage leads to a higher capital-labor ratio because the firm substitutes some relatively less expensive capital for labor.

Figure 7.5 Change in Factor Price

Originally the wage was $24 and the rental rate of capital was $8, so the lowest isocost line ($2,000) was tangent to the $q = 100$ isoquant at x ($L = 50, K = 100$). When the wage fell to $8, the isocost lines became flatter: Labor became relatively less expensive than capital. The slope of the isocost lines falls from $-w/r = -24/8 = -3$ to $-8/8 = -1$. The new lowest isocost line ($1,032) is tangent at v ($L = 77, K = 52$). Thus, when the wage falls, the firm uses more labor and less capital to produce a given level of output, and the cost of production falls from $2,000 to $1,032.

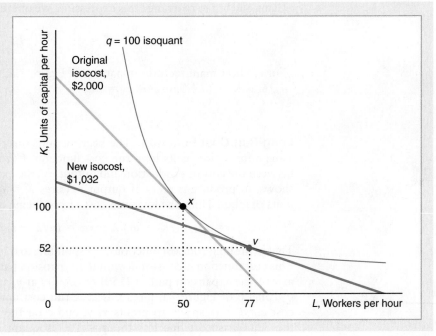

How Long-Run Cost Varies with Output

We now know how a firm determines the cost-minimizing combination of inputs for any given level of output. By repeating this analysis for different output levels, the firm determines how its cost varies with output.

Expansion Path. Panel a of Figure 7.6 shows the relationship between the lowest-cost factor combinations and various levels of output for the beer manufacturer when input prices are held constant at $w = \$24$ and $r = \$8$. The curve through the tangency points is the long-run **expansion path**: the cost-minimizing combination of labor and capital for each output level. The lowest-cost method of producing 100 units of output is to use the labor and capital combination x ($L = 50$ and $K = 100$), which lies on the \$2,000 isocost line. Similarly, the lowest-cost way to produce 200 units is to use z, which lies on the \$4,000 isocost line. The expansion path for the beer manufacturer is a straight line through the origin and x, y, and z, which has a slope of 2: At any given output level, the firm uses twice as much capital as labor. (In general, the expansion path need not be a straight line but can curve up or down as input use increases.)

SOLVED PROBLEM **7.5**	What is the expansion path function for a constant-returns-to-scale Cobb-Douglas production function $q = AL^aK^{1-a}$? What is the path for the estimated beer manufacturer, which has a production function of $q = 1.52L^{0.6}K^{0.4}$? **Answer** *Use the tangency condition between the isocost and the isoquant that determines the cost-minimizing factor ratio to derive the expansion path.* Because the marginal product of labor is $MP_L = aq/L$ and the marginal product of capital is $MP_K = (1-a)q/K$, the tangency condition is $$\frac{w}{r} = \frac{aq/L}{(1-a)q/K} = \frac{a}{1-a}\frac{K}{L}.$$ Using algebra to rearrange this expression, we obtain the expansion path formula: $$K = \frac{(1-a)}{a}\frac{w}{r}L. \qquad (7.25)$$ For the beer manufacturer in panel a of Figure 7.6, the expansion path, Equation 7.26, is $K = (0.4/0.6)(24/8)L = 2L$.

Long-Run Cost Function. The beer manufacturer's expansion path contains the same information as its long-run cost function, $C(q)$, which shows the relationship between the cost of production and output. As the expansion path plot in Figure 7.6 shows, to produce q units of output requires $K = q$ units of capital and $L = q/2$ units of labor. Thus, the long-run cost of producing q units of output is

$$C(q) = wL + rK = wq/2 + rq = (w/2 + r)q = (24/2 + 8)q = 20q.$$

That is, the long-run cost function corresponding to this expansion path is $C(q) = 20q$. This cost function is consistent with the expansion path in panel a: $C(100) = \$2,000$ at x on the expansion path, $C(150) = \$3,000$ at y, and $C(200) = \$4,000$ at z.

Panel b of Figure 7.6 plots this long-run cost curve. Points X, Y, and Z on the cost curve correspond to points x, y, and z on the expansion path. For example, the \$2,000 isocost line hits the $q = 100$ isoquant at x, which is the lowest-cost

Figure 7.6 Expansion Path and Long-Run Cost Curve

(a) The curve through the tangency points between iso-cost lines and isoquants, such as x, y, and z, is called the expansion path. The points on the expansion path are the cost-minimizing combinations of labor and capital for each output level. (b) The beer manufacturer's expansion path shows the same relationship between long-run cost and output as the long-run cost curve.

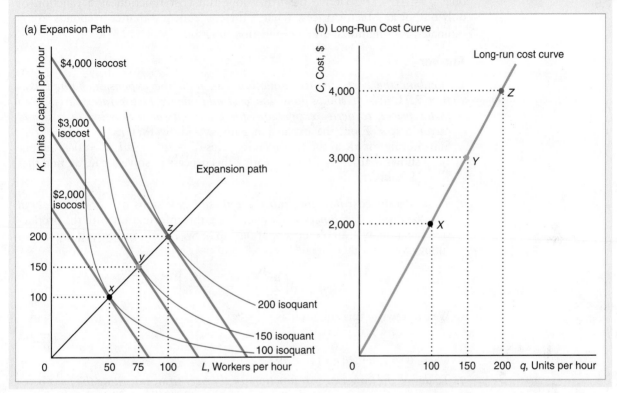

combination of labor and capital that can produce 100 units of output. Similarly, X on the long-run cost curve is at $2,000 and 100 units of output. Consistent with the expansion path, the cost curve shows that as output doubles, cost doubles.

Solving for the cost function from the production function is not always easy. However, a cost function is relatively simple to derive from the production function if the production function is homogeneous of degree γ so that $q = f(xL^*, xK^*) = x^\gamma f(L^*, K^*)$, where x is a positive constant and L^* and K^* are particular values of labor and capital. That is, the production function has the same returns to scale for any given combination of inputs. Important examples of such production functions include the Cobb-Douglas ($q = AL^aK^b$, $\gamma = a + b$), constant elasticity of substitution (CES), linear, and fixed-proportions production functions (see Chapter 6).

Because a firm's cost Equation 7.6 is $C = wL + rK$, were we to double the inputs, we would double the cost. More generally, if we multiplied each output by x, the new cost would be $C = (wL^* + rK^*)x = \theta x$, where $\theta = wL^* + rK^*$. Solving the production function for x, we know that $x = q^{1/\gamma}$. Substituting that expression in the cost identity, we find that the cost function for any homogeneous production function of degree γ is $C = \theta q^{1/\gamma}$. The constant in this cost function depends on factor prices and two constants, L^* and K^*. We would prefer to express the constant in terms of only the factor prices and parameters. We can do so by noting that the firm chooses the cost-minimizing combination of labor and capital, as summarized in the expansion path equation, as we illustrate in Solved Problem 7.6.

SOLVED PROBLEM 7.6

A firm has a Cobb-Douglas production function that is homogeneous of degree one: $q = AL^a K^{1-a}$. Derive the firm's long-run cost function as a function of only output and factor prices. What is the cost function that corresponds to the estimated beer manufacturer's production function $q = 1.52L^{0.6}K^{0.4}$?

Answer

1. *Combine the cost identity, Equation 7.6, with the expansion path, Equation 7.21, which shows how the cost-minimizing factor ratio varies with factor prices, to derive expressions for the inputs as a function of cost and factor prices.* From the expansion path, we know that $rK = wL(1 - a)/a$. Substituting for rK in the cost identity gives $C = wL + wL(1 - a)/a$. Simplifying shows that $L = aC/w$. Repeating this process to solve for K, we find that $K = (1 - a)C/r$.

2. *To derive the cost function, substitute these expressions of labor and capital into the production function.* By combining this information with the production function, we can obtain a relationship between cost and output. By substituting, we find that

$$q = A\left(\frac{aC}{w}\right)^a \left[\frac{(1 - a)C}{r}\right]^{1-a}.$$

We can rewrite this equation as

$$C = \theta q, \tag{7.26}$$

where $\theta = w^a r^{1-a}/[Aa^a(1 - a)^{1-a}]$.

3. *To derive the long-run cost function for the beer firm, substitute the parameter values into $C = \theta q$.* For the beer firm, $C = [24^{0.6}8^{0.4}/(1.52 \times 0.6^{0.6}0.4^{0.4})]q \approx 20q$.

The Shape of Long-Run Cost Curves

The shapes of the average cost and marginal cost curves depend on the shape of the long-run cost curve. The relationships among total, marginal, and average costs are the same for both the long-run and short-run cost functions. For example, if the long-run average cost curve is U-shaped, the long-run marginal cost curve cuts it at its minimum.

The long-run average cost curve may be U-shaped, but the reason for this shape differs from those given for the short-run average cost curve. A key explanation for why the short-run average cost initially slopes downward is that the average fixed cost curve is downward sloping: Spreading the fixed cost over more units of output lowers the average fixed cost per unit. Because there are no fixed costs in the long run, fixed costs cannot explain the initial downward slope of the long-run average cost curve.

A major reason why the short-run average cost curve slopes upward at higher levels of output is diminishing marginal returns. In the long run, however, all factors can be varied, so diminishing marginal returns do not explain the upward slope of a long-run average cost curve.

As with the short-run curves, the shape of the long-run curves is determined by the production function relationship between output and inputs. In the long run, returns to scale play a major role in determining the shape of the average cost curve and the other cost curves. As we discussed in Chapter 6, increasing all inputs in proportion may cause output to increase more than in proportion (increasing returns to scale) at low levels of output, in proportion (constant returns to scale) at intermediate levels of output, and less than in proportion (decreasing returns to scale) at high levels of output. If a production function has this returns-to-scale pattern and the prices of inputs are constant, the long-run average cost curve must be U-shaped.

A cost function is said to exhibit **economies of scale** if the average cost of production falls as output expands. We would expect economies of scale in the range where the production function has increasing returns to scale: Doubling inputs more than doubles output, so average cost falls with higher output.

With constant returns to scale, doubling the inputs causes output to double as well, so the average cost remains constant. If an increase in output has no effect on average cost—the average cost curve is flat—there are *no economies of scale*. In the range where the production function has constant returns to scale, the average cost remains constant, so the cost function has *no economies of scale*. Finally, in the range where the production function has decreasing returns to scale, average cost increases. A firm suffers from **diseconomies of scale** if average cost rises when output increases.

Average cost curves can have many different shapes. Perfectly competitive firms typically show U-shaped average cost curves. Average cost curves in noncompetitive markets may be U-shaped, L-shaped (average cost at first falls rapidly and then levels off as output increases), everywhere downward sloping, everywhere upward sloping, or take other shapes altogether. The shape of the average cost curve indicates whether the production process results in economies or diseconomies of scale.

Table 7.1 summarizes the shapes of average cost curves of firms in various Canadian manufacturing industries (as estimated by Robidoux and Lester, 1992). The table shows that U-shaped average cost curves are the exception rather than the rule in Canadian manufacturing and that nearly one-third of these average cost curves are L-shaped. Cement firms provide an example of such a cost curve.

Some of the L-shaped average cost curves may be part of a U-shaped curve with long, flat bottoms, where we don't observe any firm producing enough to exhibit diseconomies of scale.

Table 7.1   Shape of Average Cost Curves in Canadian Manufacturing

Scale Economies	Share of Manufacturing Industries, %	
Economies of scale: Initially downward-sloping *AC*	57	
Everywhere downward-sloping *AC*		18
L-shaped *AC* (downward sloping, then flat)		31
U-shaped *AC*		8
No economies of scale: Flat *AC*	23	
Diseconomies of scale: Upward-sloping *AC*	14	

Source: Robidoux and Lester (1992).

Over the years, the typical factory has grown in size to take advantage of economies of scale to keep costs down. However, three-dimensional (3D) printing may reverse this trend by making it as cheap to manufacture one item as it is a thousand.

With 3D printing, an employee gives instructions—essentially a blueprint—to the machine, presses print, and the machine builds the object from the ground up, either by depositing material from a nozzle, or by selectively solidifying a thin layer of plastic or metal dust using drops of glue or a tightly focused beam. The final product can be a tool, a panel for an airplane, or a work of art.

Until recently, 3D printers were primarily used to create prototypes in the aerospace, medical, and automotive industries. Then, the final products were produced using conventional manufacturing techniques. However, costs have fallen to the point where manufacturing using 3D printers is starting to be cost effective.

Moreover, new uses seem virtually unlimited. For example, in 2012, scientists at the University of Glasgow demonstrated that 3D printing can be used to create existing and new chemical compounds.

Many scientists and firms believe that 3D printing eventually will eliminate the need for factories and may eliminate the manufacturing advantage of low-wage countries. Eventually, as the cost of printing drops, these machines may be used to produce small, highly customized batches as end-users need them.

Estimating Cost Curves Versus Introspection

Economists use statistical methods to estimate a cost function. However, we can sometimes infer the shape through casual observation and deductive reasoning.

For example, in the good old days, the Good Humor Company sent out herds of ice cream trucks to purvey its products. It seems likely that the company's production process had fixed proportions and constant returns to scale: If it wanted to sell more, Good Humor dispatched another truck and another driver. Drivers and trucks are almost certainly nonsubstitutable inputs (the isoquants are right angles). If the cost of a driver is w per day, the rental cost is r per day, and q is the quantity of ice cream sold per day, then the cost function is $C = (w + r)q$.

Such deductive reasoning can lead one astray, as I once discovered. A water heater manufacturing firm provided me with many years of data on the inputs it used and the amount of output it produced. I also talked to the company's engineers about the production process and toured the plant (which resembled a scene from Dante's *Inferno*, with deafening noise levels and flames).

A water heater consists of an outside cylinder of metal, a liner, an electronic control unit, hundreds of tiny parts, and a couple of rods that slow corrosion. Workers cut out the metal for the cylinder, weld it together, and add the other parts. "OK," I said to myself, "this production process must be one of fixed proportions because the firm needs one of each input to produce a water heater. How could you substitute a cylinder for an electronic control unit? Or substitute labor for metal?"

I then used statistical techniques to estimate the production and cost functions. Following the usual procedure, I did not assume that I knew the exact form of the functions. Rather, I allowed the data to "tell" me the type of production and cost functions. To my surprise, the estimates indicated that the production process was not one of fixed proportions. Rather, the firm could readily substitute between labor and capital.

"Surely I've made a mistake," I said to the plant manager after describing these results.

"No," he said, "that's correct. There's a great deal of substitutability between labor and metal."

"How can they be substitutes?"

"Easy," he said. "We can use a lot of labor and waste very little metal by cutting out exactly what we want and being very careful. Or we can use relatively little labor, cut quickly, and waste more metal. When the cost of labor is relatively high, we waste more metal. When the cost of metal is relatively high, we cut more carefully." This practice, as the manager explained, minimizes the firm's cost.

7.4   Lower Costs in the Long Run

In its long-term planning, a firm selects a plant size and makes other investments to minimize its long-run cost based on how many units it produces. Once it chooses its plant size and equipment, these inputs are fixed in the short run. Thus, the firm's long-run decisions determine its short-run cost. Because the firm cannot vary its capital in the short run but can in the long run, its short-run cost is at least as high as long-run cost and is higher if the "wrong" level of capital is used in the short run.

Long-Run Average Cost as the Envelope of Short-Run Average Cost Curves

Because the firm can adjust its capital level optimally in the long run, the long-run average cost is always equal to or less than the short-run average cost. Panel a of Figure 7.7 shows a firm with a U-shaped long-run average cost curve. Suppose initially that the firm has only three possible plant sizes. The firm's short-run average cost curve is $SRAC^1$ for the smallest possible plant. The average cost of producing q_1 units of output using this plant, point a on $SRAC^1$, is \$10. If instead the firm used the next larger plant size, its cost of producing q_1 units of output, point b on $SRAC^2$, would be \$12. Thus, if the firm knows that it will produce only q_1 units of output, it minimizes its average cost by using the smaller plant. Its average cost of producing q_2 is lower on the $SRAC^2$ curve, point e, than on the $SRAC^1$ curve, point d.

In the long run, the firm chooses the plant size that minimizes its cost of production, so it selects the plant size with the lowest average cost for each possible output level. At q_1, it opts for the small plant, whereas at q_2, it uses the medium plant. Therefore, the long-run average cost curve is the solid, scalloped section of the three short-run cost curves.

But if there are many possible plant sizes, the long-run average curve, $LRAC$, is smooth and U-shaped. The $LRAC$ includes one point from each possible short-run average cost curve. This point, however, is not necessarily the minimum point from a short-run curve. For example, the $LRAC$ includes point a on $SRAC^1$ and not the curve's minimum point, c. A small plant operating at minimum average cost cannot produce at as low an average cost as a slightly larger plant that takes advantage of economies of scale.

Figure 7.7 Long-Run Average Cost as the Envelope of Short-Run Average Cost Curves

(a) If there are only three possible plant sizes, with short-run average costs $SRAC^1$, $SRAC^2$, and $SRAC^3$, the long-run average cost curve is the solid, scalloped portion of the three short-run curves. $LRAC$ is a smooth, U-shaped long-run average cost curve if there are many possible short-run average cost curves. (b) Because the beer firm's production function has constant returns to scale, its long-run average cost and marginal cost curves are horizontal.

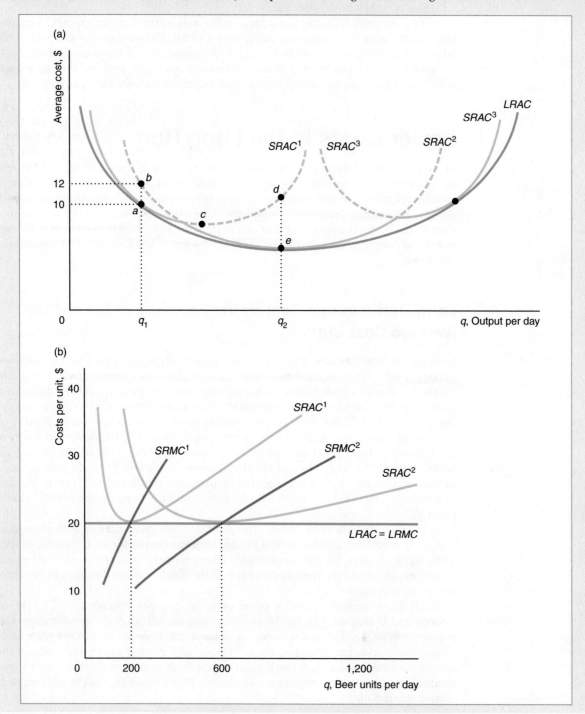

Panel b of Figure 7.7 shows the relationship between short-run and long-run average cost curves for the beer manufacturer. Because this production function has constant returns to scale, doubling both inputs doubles output, so the long-run average cost, $LRAC$, is constant at $20, as we saw earlier. If capital is fixed at 200 units, the firm's short-run average cost curve is $SRAC^1$. If the firm produces 200 units of output, its short-run and long-run average costs are equal. At any other output, its short-run cost is higher than its long-run cost.

The short-run marginal cost curves, $SRMC^1$ and $SRMC^2$, are upward sloping and equal the corresponding U-shaped short-run average cost curves, $SRAC^1$ and $SRAC^2$, only at their minimum points of $20. In contrast, because the long-run average cost is horizontal at $20, the long-run marginal cost curve, $LRMC$, is horizontal at $20. Thus, the long-run marginal cost curve is not the envelope of the short-run marginal cost curves.

APPLICATION

Choosing an Inkjet or Laser Printer

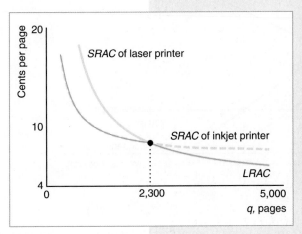

In 2012, you can buy a personal laser printer for $100 or an inkjet printer for $30 that prints 16 pages a minute at 1,200 dots per inch. If you buy the inkjet, you save $70 right off the bat. However, the laser printer costs less per page to operate. The cost of ink and paper is about 4¢ per page for a laser compared to about 7¢ per page for an inkjet. The average cost per page of operating a laser is $100/q + 0.04$, where q is the number of pages, while the average cost for an inkjet is $30/q + 0.07$. Thus, the average cost per page is lower with the inkjet until q reaches 2,300 pages, and thereafter the laser is less expensive per page.

The graph shows the short-run average cost curves for the laser printer and the inkjet printer. The inkjet printer is the lower-cost choice if you're printing fewer than 2,300 pages, and the laser printer is if you're printing more.

So, should you buy the laser printer? If you print more than 2,300 pages over its lifetime, the laser is less expensive to operate than the inkjet. If the printers last two years and you print 23 or more pages per week, then the laser printer is cost effective.

Short-Run and Long-Run Expansion Paths

Long-run cost is lower than short-run cost because a firm has more flexibility in the long run. To show the advantage of flexibility, we can compare the short-run and long-run expansion paths, which correspond to the short-run and long-run cost curves.

The beer manufacturer has greater flexibility in the long run. The tangency of the firm's isoquants and isocost lines determines the long-run expansion path in Figure 7.8. The firm expands output by increasing both its labor and capital, so its long-run expansion path is upward sloping. To increase its output from 100 to 200 units (that is, move from x to z), the firm doubles its capital from 100 to 200 units and its labor from 50 to 100 workers. As a result, its cost increases from $2,000 to $4,000.

In the short run, the firm cannot increase its capital, which is fixed at 100 units. The firm can increase its output only by using more labor, so its short-run expansion path is horizontal at $K = 100$. To expand its output from 100 to 200 units (move

Figure 7.8 Long-Run and Short-Run Expansion Paths

In the long run, the beer manufacturer increases its output by using more of both inputs, so its long-run expansion path is upward sloping. In the short run, the firm cannot vary its capital, so its short-run expansion path is horizontal at the fixed level of output. That is, it increases its output by increasing the amount of labor it uses. Expanding output from 100 to 200 raises the beer firm's long-run cost from $2,000 to $4,000 but raises its short-run cost from $2,000 to $4,616.

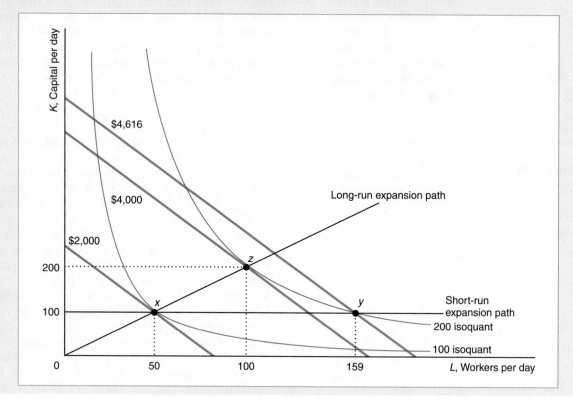

from x to y), the firm must increase its labor from 50 to 159 workers, and its cost rises from $2,000 to $4,616. Doubling output increases long-run cost by a factor of 2 and short-run cost by approximately 2.3.

How Learning by Doing Lowers Costs

Long-run cost is lower than short-run cost for three reasons. First, firms have more flexibility in the long run. Second, technological progress (Chapter 6) may lower cost over time. Third, the firm may benefit from **learning by doing**: The productive skills and knowledge of better ways to produce that workers and managers gain from experience. Workers who are given a new task may perform it slowly the first few times, but their speed increases with practice. Over time, managers may learn how to organize production more efficiently, determine which workers to assign to which tasks, and discover where inventories need to be increased and where they can be reduced. Engineers may optimize product designs by experimenting with various production methods. For these and other reasons, the average cost of production tends to fall over time, and the effect is particularly strong with new products.

Learning by doing might be a function of the time elapsed since a particular product or production process is introduced. More commonly, learning is a function of *cumulative output*: Workers become increasingly adept the more often they perform a task. We summarize the relationship between average costs and cumulative output by a **learning curve**. The learning curve for Intel central processing units (CPUs) in panel a of Figure 7.9 shows that Intel's average cost fell very rapidly with the first few million units of cumulative output, but then dropped relatively slowly with additional units (Salgado, 2008).

If a firm operates in the economies-of-scale section of its average cost curve, expanding output lowers its cost for two reasons: Its average cost falls today due to economies of scale, and for any given level of output, its average cost will be lower in the next period because of learning by doing.

In panel b of Figure 7.9, the firm currently produces q_1 units of output at point A on average cost curve AC^1. If it expands its output to q_2, its average cost falls in this

Figure 7.9 Learning by Doing

(a) As Intel produces more cumulative central processing units (CPUs), the average cost of production per unit falls (Salgado, 2008). The horizontal axis measures the cumulative production. (b) In the short run, extra production reduces a firm's average cost owing to economies of scale: Because $q_1 < q_2 < q_3$, A is higher than B, which is higher than C. In the long run, extra production reduces average cost as a result of learning by doing. To produce q_2 this period costs B on AC^1, but to produce that same output in the next period would cost only b on AC^2. If the firm produces q_3 instead of q_2 in this period, its average cost in the next period is AC^3 instead of AC^2 due to additional learning by doing. Thus, extra output in this period lowers the firm's cost in two ways: It lowers average cost in this period due to economies of scale and lowers average cost for any given output level in the next period due to learning by doing.

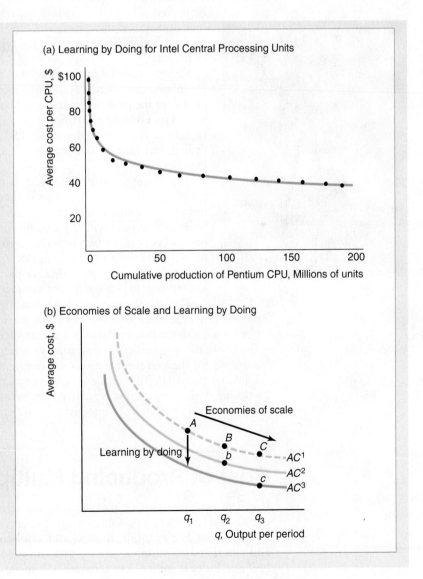

(a) Learning by Doing for Intel Central Processing Units

(b) Economies of Scale and Learning by Doing

period to point *B* due to economies of scale. Learning by doing in this period results in a lower average cost, AC^2, in the next period. If the firm continues to produce q_2 units of output in the next period, its average cost will fall to point *b* on AC^2.

If instead of expanding output to q_2 in Period 1, the firm expands to q_3, its average cost is even lower in Period 1 ($\bar{C}$ on AC^1) due to even greater economies of scale. Moreover, its average cost curve, AC^3, in Period 2 is even lower due to the extra experience gained from producing more output in Period 1. If the firm continues to produce q_3 in Period 2, its average cost is *c* on AC^3. Thus, all else being the same, if learning by doing depends on cumulative output, firms have an incentive to produce more in the short run than they otherwise would to lower their costs in the future.

APPLICATION

Learning by Drilling

Learning by doing can substantially reduce the cost of drilling oil wells. Two types of firms work together to drill oil wells. Oil production companies such as ExxonMobil and Chevron perform the technical design and planning of wells to be drilled. The actual drilling is performed by drilling companies that own and staff drilling rigs. The time it takes to drill a well varies across fields, which differ in terms of the types of soil and rocks and the depth of the oil.

Kellogg (2011) found that the more experience firms have—the cumulative number of wells that the oil production firm drilled in the field over the past two years—the less time it takes them to drill another well. His estimated learning curve shows that drilling time decreases rapidly at first, falling by about 15% after the first 25 wells have been drilled, but that drilling time does not fall much more with additional experience.

This decrease in drilling time is the sum of the benefits from two types of experience. The time it takes to drill a well falls as the production company drills (1) more wells in the field, and (2) drills more wells in that field with a particular drilling company. The second effect occurs because the two firms learn to work better together in a particular field. Because neither firm can apply its learning with a particular partner to its work with another partner, production companies prefer to continue to work with the same drilling rig firms over time.

The reduction in drilling time from a production firm's average stand-alone experience over the past two years is 6.4% or 1.5 fewer days to drill a well. This time savings reduces the cost of drilling a well by about $16,300. The relationship-specific learning from experience due to working with a drilling company for the average duration over two years reduces drilling time per well by 3.8%, or about $9,700 per well. On average, the reduction in drilling time from working with one rig crew regularly is twice as much as from working with rigs that frequently switch from one production firm to another.

7.5 Cost of Producing Multiple Goods

If a firm produces two or more goods, the cost of one good may depend on the output level of the other. Outputs are linked if a single input is used to produce both of them. For example, mutton and wool come from sheep, cattle provide beef and hides, and oil supplies heating fuel and gasoline. It is less expensive to produce beef and hides together than separately. If the goods are produced together, a single steer yields one unit of beef and one hide. If beef and hides are produced separately (throwing away the unused good), the same amount of output requires two steers and more labor.

We say that there are **economies of scope** if it is less expensive to produce goods jointly than separately (Panzar and Willig, 1977, 1981). A measure of the degree to which there are economies of *scope* (*SC*) is

$$SC = \frac{C(q_1, 0) + C(0, q_2) - C(q_1, q_2)}{C(q_1, q_2)},$$

where $C(q_1, 0)$ is the cost of producing q_1 units of the first good by itself, $C(0, q_2)$ is the cost of producing q_2 units of the second good, and $C(q_1, q_2)$ is the cost of producing both goods together. If the cost of producing the two goods separately, $C(q_1, 0) + C(0, q_2)$, is the same as the cost of producing them together, $C(q_1, q_2)$, then *SC* is zero. If it is cheaper to produce the goods jointly, *SC* is positive. If *SC* is negative, there are *diseconomies* of scope, and the two goods should be produced separately.

To illustrate this idea, suppose that Laura spends one day collecting mushrooms and wild strawberries in the woods. Her **production possibility frontier**—the maximum amount of outputs (mushrooms and strawberries) that can be produced from a fixed amount of input (Laura's effort during one day)—is PPF^1 in Figure 7.10. The production possibility frontier summarizes the trade-off Laura faces: She picks fewer mushrooms if she collects more strawberries in a day.

If Laura spends all day collecting only mushrooms, she picks eight pints; if she spends all day picking strawberries, she collects six pints. If she picks some of each, however, she can harvest more total pints: six pints of mushrooms and four pints of strawberries. The product possibility frontier is concave (the middle of the curve is farther from the origin than it would be if it were a straight line) because of the diminishing marginal returns to collecting only one of the two goods. If she collects only mushrooms, she must walk past wild strawberries without picking them. As a result, she has to walk farther if she collects only mushrooms than if she picks both. Thus, there are economies of scope in jointly collecting mushrooms and strawberries.

Figure 7.10 Joint Production

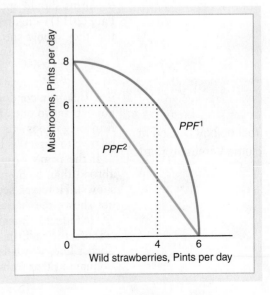

If there are economies of scope, the production possibility frontier bows away from the origin, PPF^1. If instead the production possibility frontier is a straight line, PPF^2, the cost of producing both goods does not fall if they are produced together.

If instead the production possibility frontier were a straight line, the cost of producing the two goods jointly would not be lower. Suppose, for example, that mushrooms grow in one section of the woods and strawberries in another section. In that case, Laura can collect only mushrooms without passing any strawberries. That production possibility frontier is a straight line, PPF^2 in Figure 7.10. By allocating her time between the two sections of the woods, Laura can collect any combination of mushrooms and strawberries by spending part of her day in one section of the woods and part in the other.

APPLICATION

Economies of Scope

Empirical studies show that some processes have economies of scope, others have none, and some have diseconomies of scope. In Japan, there are substantial economies of scope in producing and transmitting electricity, $SC = 0.2$ (Ida and Kuwahara, 2004), and in broadcasting for television and radio, $SC = 0.12$ (Asai, 2006). Growitsch and Wetzel (2009) found that there are economies of scope from combining passenger and freight services for the majority of 54 railway firms from 27 European countries. Yatchew (2000) concluded that there are scope economies in distributing electricity and other utilities in Ontario, Canada. Kong et al. (2009) found that Chinese airports exhibit substantial economies of scope.

In Switzerland, some utility firms provide gas, electric, and water, while others provide only one or two of these utilities. Farsi et al. (2008) estimated that most firms have scope economies. The SC ranges between 0.04 and 0.15 for the median size firm, but scope economies could reach 20% to 30% of total costs for small firms, which may help explain why only some firms provide multiple utilities.

Friedlaender, Winston, and Wang (1983) found that for American automobile manufacturers, it is 25% less expensive ($SC = 0.25$) to produce large cars together with small cars and trucks than to produce large cars separately and small cars and trucks together. However, there are no economies of scope from producing trucks together with small and large cars. Producing trucks separately from cars is efficient.

Cummins et al. (2010) tested whether U.S. insurance firms do better by selling both life-health and property-liability insurance or specializing and found that the firms should specialize due to diseconomies of scope. Similarly, Cohen and Paul (2011) estimated that drug treatment centers have diseconomies of scope so that they should specialize in either outpatient or inpatient treatment.

CHALLENGE SOLUTION

Technology Choice at Home Versus Abroad

If a U.S. semiconductor manufacturing firm shifts production from the firm's home plant to one abroad, should it use the same mix of inputs as at home? The firm may choose to use a different technology because the firm's cost of labor relative to capital is lower abroad than in the United States.

If the firm's isoquant is smooth, the firm uses a different bundle of inputs abroad than at home given that the relative factor prices differ (as Figure 7.5 shows). However, semiconductor manufacturers have kinked isoquants. The figure shows the isoquant that we examined in Chapter 6 in the Application A Semiconductor Integrated Circuit Isoquant. In its U.S. plant, the semiconductor manufacturing firm uses a wafer-handling stepper technology because the C^1 isocost line, which is the lowest isocost line that touches the isoquant, hits the isoquant at that technology.

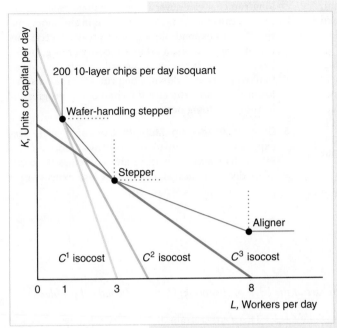

The firm's cost of both inputs is less abroad than in the United States, and its cost of labor is relatively less than the cost of capital at its foreign plant than at its U.S. plant. The slope of its isocost line is $-w/r$, where w is the wage and r is the rental cost of the manufacturing equipment. The smaller w is relative to r, the less steeply sloped is its isocost curve. Thus, the firm's foreign isocost line is flatter than its domestic C^1 isocost line.

If the firm's isoquant were smooth, the firm would certainly use a different technology at its foreign plant than in its home plant. However, its isoquant has kinks, so a small change in the relative input prices does not necessarily lead to a change in production technology. The firm could face either the C^2 or C^3 isocost curves, both of which are flatter than the C^1 isocost. If the firm faces the C^2 isocost line, which is only slightly flatter than the C^1 isocost, the firm still uses the capital-intensive wafer-handling stepper technology in its foreign plant. However, if the firm faces the much flatter C^3 isocost line, which hits the isoquant at the stepper technology, it switches technologies. (If the isocost line were even flatter, it could hit the isoquant at the aligner technology.)

Even if the wage change is small so that the firm's isocost is C^2 and the firm does not switch technologies abroad, the firm's cost will be lower abroad with the same technology because C^2 is less than C^1. However, if the wage is low enough that it can shift to a more labor-intensive technology, its costs will be even lower: C^3 is less than C^2.

Thus, whether the firm uses a different technology in its foreign plant than in its domestic plant turns on the relative factor prices in the two locations and whether the firm's isoquant is smooth. If the isoquant is smooth, even a slight difference in relative factor prices will induce the firm to shift along the isoquant and use a different technology with a different capital-labor ratio. However, if the isoquant has kinks, the firm will use a different technology only if the relative factor prices differ substantially.

SUMMARY

From all available technologically efficient production processes, a firm chooses the one that is economically efficient. The economically efficient production process is the technologically efficient process for which the cost of producing a given quantity of output is lowest, or the one that produces the most output for a given cost.

1. **Measuring Costs.** The economic or opportunity cost of a good is the value of its next best alternative use. Economic cost includes both explicit and implicit costs.

2. **Short-Run Costs.** In the short run, a firm can vary the costs of the factors that are adjustable, but the costs of other factors are fixed. The firm's average fixed cost falls as its output rises. If a firm has a short-run average cost curve that is U-shaped, its marginal cost curve lies below the average cost curve when average cost is falling and above the average cost curve when it is rising, so the marginal cost curve cuts the average cost curve at its minimum.

3. **Long-Run Costs.** In the long run, all factors can be varied, so all costs are variable. As a result, average cost and average variable cost are identical. A firm chooses the best combination of inputs to minimize its cost. To produce a given output level, it chooses

the lowest isocost line to touch the relevant isoquant, which is tangent to the isoquant. Equivalently, to minimize cost, the firm adjusts inputs until the last dollar spent on any input increases output by as much as the last dollar spent on any other input. If the firm calculates the cost of producing every possible output level given current input prices, it knows its cost function: Cost is a function of the input prices and the output level. If the firm's average cost falls as output expands, its cost function exhibits economies of scale. If the firm's average cost rises as output expands, it exhibits diseconomies of scale.

4. **Lower Costs in the Long Run.** The firm can always do in the long run what it does in the short run, so its long-run cost can never be greater than its short-run cost. Because some factors are fixed in the short run, the firm, to expand output, must greatly increase its use of other factors, a relatively costly choice. In the long run, the firm can adjust all factors, a process that keeps its cost down. Long-run cost may also be lower than short-run cost if technological progress or learning by doing occurs.

5. **Cost of Producing Multiple Goods.** If it is less expensive for a firm to produce two goods jointly rather than separately, there are economies of scope. With diseconomies of scope, it is less expensive to produce the goods separately.

EXERCISES

■ = *exercise is available on* MyEconLab; * = *answer appears at the back of this book;* **M** = *mathematical problem.*

1. Measuring Costs

1.1 You have a ticket to go to a concert by one of your favorite groups, the Hives, which you cannot resell. However, you can buy a ticket for $30 to attend a talk by Steven Colbert, at the same time as the concert. You are willing to pay up to $90 to hear Colbert. Given that there are no other costs involved in attending either event, what is your opportunity cost of attending the Hives concert? (*Hint*: See Solved Problem 7.1.)

1.2 Many corporations allow CEOs to use their firm's corporate jet for personal travel. The Internal Revenue Service (IRS) requires that the firm report personal use of its corporate jet as taxable executive income, and the Securities and Exchange Commission (SEC) requires that publicly traded corporations report the value of this benefit to shareholders. A firm may use any one of three valuation techniques. The IRS values a CEO's personal flight at or below the price of a first-class ticket. The SEC values the flight at the "incremental" cost of the flight: the additional costs to the corporation of the flight. The third alternative is the market value of chartering an aircraft. Of the three methods, the first-class ticket is least expensive and the chartered flight is most expensive.

a. What factors (such as fuel) determine the marginal explicit cost to a corporation of an executive's personal flight? Does any one of the three valuation methods correctly determine the marginal explicit cost?

b. What is the marginal opportunity cost to the corporation of an executive's personal flight?

*1.3 "There are certain fixed costs when you own a plane," former tennis star Andre Agassi explained, "so the more you fly it, the more economic sense it makes. . . . The first flight after I bought it, I took some friends to Palm Springs for lunch." (Ostler, Scott, "Andre Even Flies like a Champ," *San Francisco Chronicle,* February 8, 1993, C1.) Discuss whether Agassi's analysis is reasonable.

2. Short-Run Costs

2.1 A firm's short-run cost function is $C(q) = 200q - 6q^2 + 0.3q^3 + 400$. Determine the fixed cost, F; the variable cost function, AVC; the average cost, AC; the marginal cost, MC; and the average fixed-cost, AFC. (*Hint*: See Solved Problem 7.2.) **M**

2.2 Give the formulas for and plot AFC, MC, AVC, and AC if the cost function is

a. $C = 10 + 10q$,

b. $C = 10 + q^2$,

c. $C = 10 + 10q - 4q^2 + q^3$. (*Hint*: See Solved Problem 7.2.) **M**

2.3 A firm's cost curve is $C = F + 10q - bq^2 + q^3$, where $b > 0$.

a. For what values of b are cost, average cost, and average variable cost positive? (From now on, assume that all these measures of cost are positive at every output level.)

b. What is the shape of the AC curve? At what output level is the AC minimized?

c. At what output levels does the MC curve cross the AC and the AVC curves?

d. Use calculus to show that the MC curve must cross the AVC at its minimum point. **M**

2.4 The only variable input a janitorial service firm uses to clean offices is workers who are paid a wage, w, of $8 an hour. Each worker can clean four offices in an hour. Use math to determine the variable cost, the average variable cost, and the marginal cost of cleaning one more office. Draw a diagram similar to Figure 7.1 to show the variable cost, average variable cost, and marginal cost curves.

*2.5 A firm builds wooden shipping crates. How does the cost of producing a 1-cubic-foot crate (each side is 1 foot square) compare to the cost of building an 8-cubic-foot crate if wood costs $1 per square foot and the firm has no labor or other costs? More generally, how does cost vary with volume?

2.6 Gail works in a flower shop, where she produces 10 floral arrangements per hour. She is paid $10 an hour for the first eight hours she works and $15 an hour for each additional hour. What is the firm's cost function? What are its AC, AVC, and MC functions? Draw the AC, AVC, and MC curves. **M**

2.7 In 1796, Gottfried Christoph Härtel, a German music publisher, calculated the cost of printing music using an engraved plate technology and used these estimated cost functions to make production decisions. Härtel figured that the fixed cost of printing a musical page—the cost of engraving the plates—was 900 pfennigs. The marginal cost of each additional copy of the page was 5 pfennigs (Scherer, 2001).

a. Graph the total cost, average total cost, average variable cost, and marginal cost functions.

b. Is there a cost advantage to having only one music publisher print a given composition? Why?

c. Härtel used his data to do the following type of analysis: Suppose he expected to sell exactly 300 copies of a composition at 15 pfennigs per page. What is the highest price the publisher would be willing to pay the composer per page of the composition if he wants to at least break even? **M**

2.8 A U.S. chemical firm has a production function of $q = 10L^{0.32}K^{0.56}$ (Hsieh, 1995). It faces factor prices of $w = 10$ and $r = 20$. What are its short-run marginal and average variable cost curves? **M**

2.9 A glass manufacturer's production function is $q = 10L^{0.5}K^{0.5}$ (Hsieh, 1995). Suppose that its wage, w, is $1 per hour and the rental cost of capital, r, is $4.

a. Draw an accurate figure showing how the glass firm minimizes its cost of production.

b. What is the equation of the (long-run) expansion path for a glass firm? Illustrate in a graph.

c. Derive the long-run total cost curve equation as a function of q.

2.10 A firm has two plants that produce identical output. The cost functions are $C_1 = 10q - 4q^2 + q^3$ and $C_2 = 10q - 2q^2 + q^3$.

a. At what output level does the average cost curve of each plant reach its minimum?

b. If the firm wants to produce four units of output, how much should it produce in each plant? **M**

2.11 The estimated short-run cost function of a Japanese beer manufacturer is $C(q) = 0.55q^{1.67} + 800/q$ (see the application Short-Run Cost Curves for a Japanese Beer Manufacturer). At what positive quantity does the average cost function reach its minimum? If a $400 lump-sum tax is applied to the firm, at what positive quantity is the after-tax average cost minimized? **M**

*2.12 What is the effect of a lump-sum franchise tax $\mathscr{L}$ on the quantity at which a firm's after-tax average cost curve reaches its minimum, given that the firm's before-tax average cost curve is U-shaped?

3. Long-Run Costs

*3.1 What is the long-run cost function if the production function is $q = L + K$? **M**

*3.2 A bottling company uses two inputs to produce bottles of the soft drink Sludge: bottling machines, K, and workers, L. The isoquants have the usual smooth shape. The machine costs $1,000 per day to run, and the workers earn $200 per day. At the current level of production, the marginal product of the machine is an additional 200 bottles per day, and the marginal product of labor is 50 more bottles per day. Is this firm producing at minimum cost? If it is minimizing cost, explain why. If it is not minimizing cost, explain how the firm should change the ratio of inputs it uses to lower its cost. (*Hint*: See Solved Problem 7.3.) **M**

3.3 In 2003, Circuit City Stores, Inc., replaced skilled sales representatives who earned up to $54,000 per year with relatively unskilled workers who earned $14 to $18 per hour (Carlos Tejada and Gary McWilliams, "New Recipe for Cost Savings: Replace Highly Paid Workers," *Wall Street Journal*, June 11, 2003). Suppose that sales representatives sold one specific Sony high-definition TV model. Let q represent the number of TVs sold per hour, s the number of skilled sales representatives per hour, and u the number of unskilled representatives per hour. Working eight hours per day, each skilled worker sold six TVs per day, and each unskilled worker sold four. The wage rate of the skilled workers was $w_s = \$26$ per hour, and the wage rate of the unskilled workers was $w_u = \$16$ per hour.

a. Show the isoquant for $q = 4$ with both skilled and unskilled sales representatives. Are they substitutes?

b. Draw the isocost line for $C = \$104$ per hour.

c. Using an isocost-isoquant diagram, identify the cost-minimizing number of skilled and unskilled reps to sell $q = 4$ TVs per hour.

*3.4 You have 60 minutes to complete an exam with two questions. You want to maximize your score. Toward the end of the exam, the more time you spend on either question, the fewer extra points per minute you get for that question. How should you allocate your time between the two questions? (*Hint:* Think about producing an output of a score on the exam using inputs of time spent on each of the problems. Then use an equation similar to Equation 7.11.)

3.5 Suppose that the government subsidizes the cost of workers by paying for 25% of the wage (the rate offered by the U.S. government in the late 1970s under the New Jobs Tax Credit program). What effect does this subsidy have on the firm's choice of labor and capital to produce a given level of output?

*3.6 The all-American baseball is made using cork from Portugal, rubber from Malaysia, yarn from Australia, and leather from France, and it is stitched (108 stitches exactly) by workers in Costa Rica. To assemble a baseball takes one unit of each of these inputs. Ultimately, the finished product must be shipped to its final destination—say, Cooperstown, New York. The materials used cost the same in any location. Labor costs are lower in Costa Rica than in a possible alternative manufacturing site in Georgia, but shipping costs from Costa Rica are higher. Would you expect the production function to exhibit decreasing, increasing, or constant returns to scale? What is the cost function? What can you conclude about shipping costs if it is less expensive to produce baseballs in Costa Rica than in Georgia?

3.7 A firm has a Cobb-Douglas production function, $Q = AL^aK^b$, where $a + b < 1$. What properties does its cost function have? (*Hint:* Compare this cost function to that of the Japanese beer manufacturer.) **M**

3.8 Replace the production function in Solved Problem 7.4 with a Cobb-Douglas $q = AL^aK^b$, and use calculus to find the cost minimizing capital-labor ratio. **M**

3.9 Derive the long-run cost function for the constant elasticity of substitution production function $q = (L^\rho + K^\rho)^{1/\rho}$. (*Hint:* See Solved Problem 7.4.) **M**

3.10 For a Cobb-Douglas production function, how does the expansion path change if the wage increases while the rental rate of capital stays the same? (*Hint:* See Solved Problem 7.5.) **M**

3.11 The Bouncing Ball Ping Pong Company sells table tennis sets, which include two paddles and one net. What is the firm's long-run expansion path if it incurs no costs other than what it pays for paddles and nets, which it buys at market prices? How does its expansion path depend on the relative prices of paddles and nets? (*Hint:* See Solved Problem 7.5.)

3.12 Suppose that your firm's production function has constant returns to scale. What is the long-run expansion path?

3.13 A production function is homogeneous of degree γ and involves three inputs, L, K, and M (materials). The corresponding factor prices are w, r, and e. Derive the long-run cost curve. **M**

3.14 In Solved Problem 7.6, Equation 7.26 gives the long-run cost function of a firm with a constant-returns-to-scale Cobb-Douglas production function. Show how, for a given output level, cost changes as the wage, w, increases. Explain why. **M**

3.15 A water heater manufacturer produces q water heaters per day, q, using L workers and S square feet of sheet metal per day, using a constant elasticity of substitution production function, $q = (L^{-2} + S^{-2}/40)^{-0.5}$. The hourly wage rate is $\$20$, and the price per square foot of sheet metal is 50¢.

a. What is the marginal product of labor? What is the marginal product of capital?

b. What is the expansion path equation? Draw the expansion path.

c. Derive the long-run cost function.

d. Suppose the price of sheet metal decreases to 25¢. Draw the new expansion path. Discuss the magnitude of the shift in the expansion path due to this price decrease. **M**

3.16 California's State Board of Equalization imposed a higher tax on "alcopops," flavored beers containing more than 0.5% alcohol-based flavorings, such as vanilla extract (Guy L. Smith, "On Regulation of 'Alcopops,'" *San Francisco Chronicle*, April 10, 2009). Such beers are taxed as distilled spirits at $\$3.30$ a gallon rather than as beer at 20¢ a gallon. In response, manufacturers reformulated their beverages to avoid the tax. By early 2009, instead of collecting a predicted $\$38$ million a year in new taxes, the state collected only about $\$9,000$. Use an isocost-isoquant diagram to explain the firms' response. (*Hint*: Alcohol-based flavors and other flavors may be close to perfect substitutes.)

4. Lower Costs in the Long Run

4.1 A U-shaped long-run average cost curve is the envelope of U-shaped short-run average cost curves. On what part of the curve (downward sloping, flat, or upward sloping) does a short-run curve touch the long-run curve? (*Hint*: Your answer should depend on where the two curves touch on the long-run curve.)

*4.2 A firm's average cost is $AC = \alpha q^\beta$, where $\alpha > 0$. How can you interpret α? (*Hint*: Suppose that $q = 1$.) What sign must β have if this cost function reflects learning by doing? What happens to average cost as q increases? Draw the average cost curve as a function of output for particular values of α and β. **M**

5. Cost of Producing Multiple Goods

5.1 What can you say about Laura's economies of scope if her time is valued at $5 an hour and her production possibility frontier is PPF^1 in Figure 7.10?

6. Challenge

*6.1 In the Challenge Solution, show that for some wage and rental cost of capital the firm is indifferent between using the wafer-handling stepper technology and the stepper technology. How does this wage/cost-of-capital ratio compare to those in the C^2 and C^3 isocosts?

6.2 If it manufactures at home, a firm faces input prices for labor and capital of $\hat{w}$ and $\hat{r}$ and produces $\hat{q}$ units of output using $\hat{L}$ units of labor and $\hat{K}$ units of capital. Abroad, the wage and cost of capital are half as much as at home. If the firm manufactures abroad, will it change the amount of labor and capital it uses to produce $\hat{q}$? What happens to its cost of producing $\hat{q}$? **M**

*6.3 A U.S. electronics firm is considering moving its production to a plant in Asia. Its estimated production function is $q = L^{0.5}K^{0.5}$ (based on Hsieh, 1995). In the United States, $w = 10 = r$. At its

Asian plant, the firm will pay a 10% lower wage and a 10% higher cost of capital: $w^* = 10/1.1$ and $r^* = 1.1 \times 10 = 11$. What are L and K, and what is the cost of producing $q = 100$ units in both countries? What would be the cost of production in Asia if the firm had to use the same factor quantities as in the United States? **M**

6.4 A U.S. apparel manufacturer is considering moving its production abroad. Its production function is $q = L^{0.7}K^{0.3}$ (based on Hsieh, 1995). In the United States, $w = 7$ and $r = 3$. At its Asian plant, the firm will pay a 50% lower wage and a 50% higher cost of capital: $w = 7/1.5$ and $r = 3 \times 1.5$. What are L and K, and what is the cost of producing $q = 100$ units in both countries? What would be the cost of production in Asia if the firm had to use the same factor quantities as in the United States? **M**

6.5 Rosenberg (2004) reports the invention of a new machine that serves as a mobile station for receiving and accumulating packed flats of strawberries close to where they are picked, reducing workers' time and the burden of carrying full flats of strawberries. A machine-assisted crew of 15 pickers produces as much output, q^*, as that of an unaided crew of 25 workers. In a 6-day, 50-hour workweek, the machine replaces 500 worker hours. At an hourly wage cost of $10, a machine saves $5,000 per week in labor costs, or $130,000 over a 26-week harvesting season. The cost of machine operation and maintenance expressed as a daily rental is $200, or $1,200 for a 6-day week. Thus, the net savings equal $3,800 per week, or $98,800 for 26 weeks.

a. Draw the q^* isoquant assuming that only two technologies are available (pure labor and labor-machine). Label the isoquant and axes as thoroughly as possible.

b. Add an isocost line to show which technology the firm chooses. (Be sure to measure wage and rental costs on a comparable time basis.)

c. Draw the corresponding cost curves (with and without the machine), assuming constant returns to scale, and label the curves and the axes as thoroughly as possible. **M**

8

Competitive Firms and Markets

The love of money is the root of all virtue. —George Bernard Shaw

Businesses complain constantly about the cost and red tape that government regulations impose on them. The very competitive U.S. trucking industry has a particular beef. In recent years, federal and state fees have increased substantially and truckers have had to adhere to many new regulations.

The Federal Motor Carrier Safety Administration (FMCSA) and the state transportation agencies in 41 states administer interstate trucking licenses through the Unified Carrier Registration Agreement. Before going into the interstate trucking business, a firm needs a U.S. Department of Transportation number and must participate in the New Entrant Safety Assurance Process, which raised the standard of compliance starting in 2009. To pass the new entrant safety audit, a carrier must now meet 16 safety regulations and comply with the Americans with Disabilities Act and certain household goods-related requirements. A trucker must also maintain minimum insurance coverage, pay registration fees, and follow policies that differ across states before the FMCSA will grant permission to operate. The registration process is so complex and time-consuming that firms pay substantial amounts to brokers who expedite the application process and take care of state licensing requirements.

According to its Web site in 2012, the FMCSA has 27 types of driver regulations, 16 types of vehicle regulations, 42 types of company regulations, 4 types of hazardous materials regulations, and 14 types of other regulatory guidance. Of course, they may have added some additional rules while I wrote this last sentence.[1]

For a large truck, the annual federal interstate registration fee can exceed $8,000. During the 2007–2010 financial crisis, many states raised their annual fee from a few hundred to several thousand dollars per truck. In 2012, Congress debated requiring each truck to install "electronic on-board recorders," which would document its travel time and distance and cost $1,500. There are many additional fees and costly regulations that a trucker or firm must meet to operate. These largely lump-sum costs—which are not related to the number of miles driven—have increased substantially in recent years.

What effect do these new fixed costs have on the trucking industry's market price and quantity? Are individual firms providing more or fewer trucking services? Does the number of firms in the market rise or fall? (As we'll discuss at the end of the chapter, the answer to one of these questions is surprising.)

---

[1]Indeed, the first time I checked after writing that sentence, I found that they have added a new rule forbidding truckers from texting while driving. (Of course, many of these rules and regulations help protect society and truckers in particular.)

To answer questions like these, we need to combine our understanding of demand curves with knowledge about firm and market supply curves to predict industry price, quantity, and profits. We start our analysis of firm behavior by addressing the fundamental question "How much should a firm produce?" To pick a level of output that maximizes its profit, a firm must consider its cost function and how much it can sell at a given price. The amount the firm thinks it can sell depends in turn on the market demand of consumers and the firm's beliefs about how other firms in the market will behave. The behavior of firms depends on the **market structure**: the number of firms in the market, the ease with which firms can enter and leave the market, and the ability of firms to differentiate their products from those of their rivals.

In this chapter, we look at **perfect competition**: a market structure in which buyers and sellers are price takers. That is, neither firms nor consumers can sell or buy except at the market price. If a firm were to try to charge more than the market price, it would be unable to sell any of its output because consumers would buy the good at a lower price from other firms in the market. The market price summarizes everything that a firm needs to know about the demand of consumers *and* the behavior of its rivals. Thus, a competitive firm can ignore the specific behavior of individual rivals when deciding how much to produce.[2]

In this chapter, we examine four main topics

1. **Perfect Competition.** A perfectly competitive firm is a price taker, and as such, it faces a horizontal demand curve.

2. **Profit Maximization.** To maximize profit, any firm must make two decisions: what output level maximizes its profit (or minimizes its loss) and whether to produce at all.

3. **Competition in the Short Run.** In the short run, variable costs determine a profit-maximizing, competitive firm's supply curve, the market supply curve, and, with the market demand curve, the competitive equilibrium.

4. **Competition in the Long Run.** Firm supply, market supply, and competitive equilibrium are different in the long run than in the short run because firms can vary inputs that were fixed in the short run and new firms can enter the market.

8.1 Perfect Competition

Perfect competition is a common market structure with very desirable properties, so it is useful to compare other market structures to competition. In this section, we examine the properties of competitive firms and markets.

Price Taking

When most people talk about "competitive firms," they mean firms that are rivals for the same customers. By this interpretation, any market with more than one firm is competitive. However, to an economist, only some of these multifirm markets are competitive.

Economists say that a market is perfectly competitive if each firm in the market is a price taker that cannot significantly affect the market price for its output or the prices at which it buys inputs. Why would a competitive firm be a price taker?

[2]In contrast, in a market with a small number of firms, each firm must consider the behavior of each of its rivals, as we discuss in Chapters 13 and 14.

It has no choice. The firm *has* to be a price taker if it faces a demand curve that is horizontal at the market price. If the demand curve is horizontal at the market price, the firm can sell as much as it wants at that price, so it has no incentive to lower its price. Similarly, the firm cannot increase the price at which it sells by restricting its output because it faces an infinitely elastic demand (see Chapter 2): A small increase in price results in its demand falling to zero.

Why a Firm's Demand Curve Is Horizontal

Firms are likely to be price takers in markets that have some or all of the following properties:

- The market contains a large number of small firms and consumers.
- Firms sell identical products.
- Buyers and sellers have full information about the prices charged by all firms.
- Transaction costs—the expenses of finding a trading partner and completing the trade beyond the price paid for the good or service—are low.
- Firms can freely enter and exit the market.

Large Number of Small Firms and Consumers. If there are many small firms in a market, no one firm can raise or lower the market price. The more firms in a market, the less any one firm's output affects the market output and hence the market price.

For example, the 107,000 U.S. soybean farmers are price takers. If a typical grower drops out of the market, market supply falls by only 1/107,000 = 0.00093%, so the market price would not be noticeably affected. A soybean farm can sell any feasible output it produces at the prevailing market equilibrium price. In other words, *the firm's demand curve is a horizontal line at the market price.*

Similarly, perfect competition requires that buyers be price takers as well. For example, if firms have to sell to a single buyer—for example, producers of advanced weapons are allowed to sell only to their government—then the buyer sets the price.

Identical Products. Firms in a perfectly competitive market sell *identical* or *homogeneous* products. Consumers do not ask which farm grew a Granny Smith apple because they view all Granny Smith apples as essentially identical. If the products of all firms are identical, it is difficult for a single firm to raise its price above the going price charged by other firms.

In contrast, in the automobile market—which is not perfectly competitive—the characteristics of a BMW and a Honda Civic differ substantially. These products are *differentiated* or *heterogeneous*. Competition from Civics would not in itself be a very strong force preventing BMW from raising its price.

Full Information. Because buyers know that different firms produce identical products and know the prices charged by all firms, it is very difficult for any one firm to unilaterally raise its price above the market equilibrium price. If it did, consumers would simply switch to a different firm.

Negligible Transaction Costs. Perfectly competitive markets have very low transaction costs. Buyers and sellers do not have to spend much time and money finding each other or hiring lawyers to write contracts to execute a trade. If transaction costs are low, it is easy for a customer to buy from a rival firm if the customer's usual supplier raises its price.

In contrast, if transaction costs are high, customers might absorb a price increase from a traditional supplier. For example, because some consumers prefer to buy milk at a local convenience store rather than travel several miles to a supermarket, the convenience store can charge slightly more than the supermarket without losing all its customers.

In some perfectly competitive markets, many small buyers and sellers are brought together in a single room, so transaction costs are virtually zero. For example, transaction costs are very low at FloraHolland's daily flower auctions in the Netherlands, which attract 7,000 suppliers and 4,500 buyers from around the world. There are 125,000 auction transactions every day, with 12 billion cut flowers and 1.3 billion plants trading in a year.

Free Entry and Exit. The ability of firms to enter and exit a market freely leads to a large number of firms in a market and promotes price taking. Suppose a firm can raise its price and increase its profit. If other firms are not able to enter the market, the firm will not be a price taker. However, if other firms can quickly and easily enter the market, the higher profit will encourage entry until the price is driven back to the original level. Free exit is also important: If firms can freely enter a market but cannot exit easily if prices decline, they might be reluctant to enter the market in response to a short-run profit opportunity in the first place.[3]

Perfect Competition in the Chicago Commodity Exchange

The Chicago Commodity Exchange, where buyers and sellers can trade wheat and other commodities, has the various characteristics of perfect competition including a very large number of buyers and sellers, who are price takers. Anyone can be a buyer or seller. Indeed, a trader might buy wheat in the morning and sell it in the afternoon. They trade virtually *identical products*. Buyers and sellers have *full information* about products and prices, which is posted for everyone to see. Market participants waste no time finding someone who wants to trade and they can easily place buy or sell orders in person, over the telephone, or electronically without paperwork, so *transaction costs are negligible*. Finally, *buyers and sellers can easily enter this market and trade wheat*. These characteristics lead to an abundance of buyers and sellers and to price-taking behavior by these market participants.

Deviations from Perfect Competition

Many markets possess some but not all the characteristics of perfect competition, but are still highly competitive so that buyers and sellers are, for all practical purposes, price takers. For example, a government may limit entry into a market but if there are still many buyers and sellers, they may be price takers. Many cities use zoning laws to limit the number of certain types of stores or motels, yet these cities still have many firms. Other cities impose moderately large transaction costs on entrants by requiring them to buy licenses, post bonds, and deal with a slow moving city bureaucracy, yet a significant number of firms enter the market. Similarly, even if only some customers have full information, that may be sufficient to prevent firms from deviating significantly from price taking. For example, tourists do not know the prices at various stores, but locals do and they use their knowledge to prevent one store from charging unusually high prices.

Economists use the terms *competition* and *competitive* more restrictively than do real people. To an economist, a competitive firm is a price taker. In contrast, when

---

[3]For example, some governments require that firms give workers six months warning before they exit a market.

most people talk about competitive firms, they mean that firms are rivals for the same customers. Even in an oligopolistic market—one with only a few firms—the firms compete for the same customers so they are competitive in this broader sense. From now on, we will use the terms *competition* and *competitive* to refer to all markets in which no buyer or seller can significantly affect the market price—they are price takers—even if the market is not perfectly competitive.

Derivation of a Competitive Firm's Demand Curve

Are the demand curves faced by individual competitive firms actually flat? To answer this question, we use a modified supply-and-demand diagram to derive the demand curve for an individual firm.

An individual firm faces a **residual demand curve**: the market demand that is not met by other sellers at any given price. The firm's residual demand function, $D^r(p)$, shows the quantity demanded from the firm at price p. A firm sells only to people who have not already purchased the good from another seller. We can determine how much demand is left for a particular firm at each possible price using the market demand curve and the supply curve for all *other* firms in the market. The quantity the market demands is a function of the price: $Q = D(p)$. The supply curve of the other firms is $S^o(p)$. The residual demand function equals the market demand function, $D(p)$, minus the supply function of all other firms:

$$D^r(p) = D(p) - S^o(p). \qquad (8.1)$$

At prices so high that the amount supplied by other firms, $S^o(p)$, is greater than the quantity demanded by the market, $D(p)$, the residual quantity demanded, $D^r(p)$, is zero.

In Figure 8.1, we derive the residual demand for a Canadian manufacturing firm that produces metal chairs. Panel b shows the market demand curve, D, and the

Figure 8.1 Residual Demand Curve

The residual demand curve, $D^r(p)$, faced by a single office furniture manufacturing firm is the market demand, $D(p)$, minus the supply of the other firms in the market, $S^o(p)$. The residual demand curve is much flatter than the market demand curve.

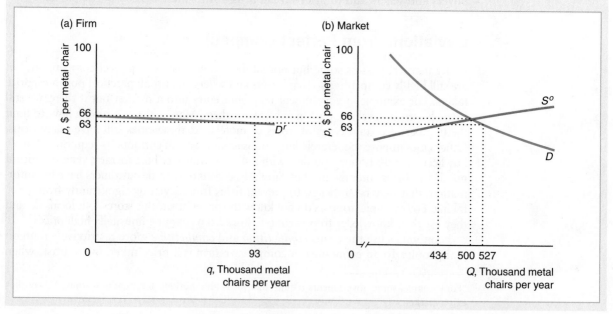

supply of all but one manufacturing firm, S^o.[4] At $p = \$66$ per chair, the supply of other firms, 500 units (where a unit is 1,000 metal chairs) per year, equals the market demand (panel b), so the residual quantity demanded of the remaining firm (panel a) is zero.

At prices below \$66, the other chair firms are not willing to supply as much as the market demands. At $p = \$63$, for example, the market demand is 527 units, but other firms want to supply only 434 units. As a result, the residual quantity demanded from the individual firm at $p = \$63$ is 93 ($= 527 - 434$) units. Thus, the residual demand curve at any given price is the horizontal difference between the market demand curve and the supply curve of the other firms.

The residual demand curve that the firm faces in panel a is much flatter than the market demand curve in panel b. As a result, the elasticity of the residual demand curve is much higher than the market elasticity.

If there are n identical firms in the market, the elasticity of demand, ε_i, facing Firm i is

$$\varepsilon_i = n\varepsilon - (n - 1)\eta_o, \tag{8.2}$$

where ε is the market elasticity of demand (a negative number), η_o is the elasticity of supply of each of the other firms (typically a positive number), and $n - 1$ is the number of other firms.[5]

There are $n = 78$ firms manufacturing metal chairs in Canada. If they are identical, the elasticity of demand facing a single firm is

$$\varepsilon_i = n\varepsilon - (n - 1)\eta_o = [78 \times (-1.1)] - (77 \times 3.1) = -85.8 - 238.7 = -324.5.$$

That is, a typical firm faces a residual demand elasticity, $\varepsilon_i = -324.5$, that's nearly 300 times the market elasticity, -1.1. If a firm raises its price by one-tenth of a percent, the quantity it can sell falls by nearly one-third. Therefore, the competitive model assumption that this firm faces a horizontal demand curve with an infinite price elasticity is not much of an exaggeration.

As Equation 8.2 shows, a firm's residual demand curve is more elastic the more firms, n, are in the market, the more elastic the market demand, ε, and the larger the elasticity of supply of the other firms, η_o. If the supply curve slopes upward, the residual demand elasticity, ε_i, must be at least as elastic as $n\varepsilon$ (because the

---

[4]The figure uses constant elasticity demand and supply curves (Chapter 2). The elasticity of supply is based on the estimated cost function from Robidoux and Lester (1988) for Canadian office furniture manufacturers. I estimate that the market elasticity of demand is $\varepsilon = -1.1$, using data from *Statistics Canada, Office Furniture Manufacturers*.

[5]To derive Equation 8.2, we start by differentiating the residual demand function, Equation 8.1, with respect to p:

$$\frac{dD^r}{dp} = \frac{dD}{dp} - \frac{dS^o}{dp}.$$

Because the n firms in the market are identical, each firm produces $q = Q/n$, where Q is total output. The output produced by the other firms is $Q_o = (n - 1)q$. Multiplying both sides of the previous expression by p/q and multiplying and dividing the first term on the right-hand side by Q/Q and the second term by Q_o/Q_o, this expression may be rewritten as

$$\frac{dD^r}{dp}\frac{p}{q} = \frac{dD}{dp}\frac{p}{Q}\frac{Q}{q} - \frac{dS^o}{dp}\frac{p}{Q_o}\frac{Q_o}{q},$$

where $q = D^r(p)$, $Q = D(p)$, and $Q_o = S^o(p)$. This expression can be rewritten as Equation 8.2 by noting that $Q/q = n$, $Q_o/q = (n - 1)$, $(dD^r/dp)(p/q) = \varepsilon_i$, $(dD/dp)(p/Q) = \varepsilon$, and $(dS^o/dp)(p/Q_o) = \eta_o$.

second term makes the estimate only more elastic), so using $n\varepsilon$ as an approximation is conservative. For example, even though the market elasticity of demand for soybeans is very inelastic at about -0.2, because there are roughly 107,000 soybean farms, the residual demand facing a single farm must be at least $n\varepsilon = 107{,}000 \times (-0.2) = -21{,}400$, which is extremely elastic.

Why Perfect Competition Is Important

Perfectly competitive markets are important for two reasons. First, many markets can be reasonably described as competitive. Many agricultural and other commodity markets, stock exchanges, retail and wholesale, building construction, and other types of markets have many or all of the properties of a perfectly competitive market. The competitive supply-and-demand model works well enough in these markets that it accurately predicts the effects of changes in taxes, costs, incomes, and other factors on market equilibrium.

Second, a perfectly competitive market has many desirable properties. Economists use this model as the ideal against which real-world markets are compared. Throughout the rest of this book, we consider that society as a whole is worse off if the properties of the perfectly competitive market fail to hold. From this point on, for brevity, we use the phrase *competitive market* to mean a *perfectly competitive market* unless we explicitly note an imperfection.

8.2 Profit Maximization

"Too caustic?" To hell with the cost. If it's a good picture, we'll make it.
—Samuel Goldwyn

Economists usually assume that *all* firms—not just competitive firms—want to maximize their profits. One reason is that many businesspeople say that their objective is to maximize profits. A second reason is that a firm—especially a competitive firm—that does not maximize profit is likely to lose money and be driven out of business. In this section, we examine how any type of firm—not just a competitive firm—maximizes its profit.

Profit

A firm's *profit*, π, is the difference between its revenues, R, and its cost, C:

$$\pi = R - C.$$

If profit is negative, $\pi < 0$, the firm suffers a *loss*.

Measuring a firm's revenue sales is straightforward: Revenue is price times quantity. Measuring cost is more challenging. From the economic point of view, the correct measure of cost is the *opportunity cost* or *economic cost*: the value of the best alternative use of any input the firm employs. As discussed in Chapter 7, the full opportunity cost of inputs used might exceed the explicit or out-of-pocket costs recorded in financial accounting statements. This distinction is important because a firm may make a serious mistake if it incorrectly measures profit by ignoring some relevant opportunity costs.

We always refer to *profit* or **economic profit** as revenue minus opportunity (economic) cost. For tax or other reasons, *business profit* may differ. For example, if a firm uses only explicit cost, then its reported profit may be larger than its economic profit.

A couple of examples illustrate the difference between the two profit measures and the importance of this distinction. Suppose you start your own firm.[6] You have to pay explicit costs such as workers' wages and the price of materials. Like many owners, you do not pay yourself a salary. Instead, you take home a business profit based on explicit costs only of $20,000 per year.

Economists (well-known spoilsports) argue that your profit is less than $20,000. Economic profit equals your business profit minus any additional opportunity cost. Suppose that instead of running your own business, you could have earned $25,000 a year working for someone else. The opportunity cost of your time working for your business is $25,000—your forgone salary. So even though your firm made a business profit of $20,000, your economic loss (negative economic profit) is $5,000. Put another way, the price of being your own boss is $5,000.

By looking at only the explicit cost and ignoring opportunity cost, you conclude that running your business is profitable. However, if you consider economic profit, you realize that working for others maximizes your income.

Similarly, when a firm decides whether to invest in a new venture, it must consider the next best alternative use of its funds. A firm considering setting up a new branch in Tucson must evaluate all the alternatives: placing the branch in Santa Fe, depositing the money it would otherwise spend on the new branch in the bank where it earns interest, and so on. If the best alternative use of the money is to put it in the bank and earn $10,000 per year in interest, the firm should build the new branch in Tucson only if it expects to make $10,000 or more per year in business profit. That is, the firm should create a Tucson branch only if its economic profit from the new branch is zero or greater. If its economic profit is zero, then it is earning the same return on its investment as it would from putting the money into its next best alternative, the bank.

Two Steps to Maximizing Profit

Any firm (not just a competitive firm) uses a two-step process to maximize profit. Because both revenue and cost vary with output, a firm's profit varies with its output level. Its profit function is

$$\pi(q) = R(q) - C(q), \tag{8.3}$$

where $R(q)$ is its revenue function and $C(q)$ is its cost function. To maximize its profit, a firm must answer two questions:

1. **Output decision:** If the firm produces, what output level, q^*, maximizes its profit or minimizes its loss?
2. **Shutdown decision:** Is it more profitable to produce q^* or to shut down and produce no output?

We use the profit curve in Figure 8.2 to illustrate these two basic decisions. This firm makes losses at very low and very high output levels and makes positive profits at moderate output levels. The profit curve first rises and then falls, reaching a maximum profit of π^* when its output is q^*. Because the firm makes a positive profit at that output, it chooses to produce q^* units of output.

Output Rules. A firm can use one of three equivalent rules to choose how much output to produce. All types of firms maximize profit using the same rules.

---

[6]Michael Dell started a mail-order computer company while he was in college. Today, his company is the world's largest personal computer company. In 2010, *Forbes* estimated Mr. Dell's wealth at $13.5 billion.

Figure 8.2 Maximizing Profit

By setting its output at q^*, the firm maximizes its profit at π^*, where $d\pi/dq = 0$.

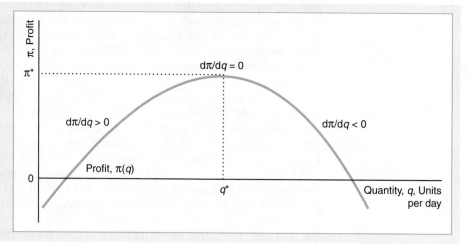

The most straightforward rule is:

Output Rule 1: *The firm sets its output where its profit is maximized.*
The profit curve in Figure 8.2 reaches its maximum, π^*, at output q^*. If the firm knows its entire profit curve, it can immediately set its output to maximize its profit.

Even if the firm does not know the exact shape of its profit curve, it may be able to find the maximum by experimenting. The firm starts by slightly increasing its output. If profit increases, the firm increases the output more. The firm keeps increasing output until its profit does not change. At that output, the firm is at the peak of the profit curve. If profit falls when the firm first increases its output, the firm tries decreasing its output. It keeps decreasing its output until it reaches the peak of the profit curve.

What the firm is doing is experimentally determining the slope of the profit curve. The slope of the profit curve is the firm's **marginal profit**: the change in the profit the firm gets from selling one more unit of output, $d\pi/dq$. In the figure, the marginal profit or slope is positive when output is less than q^*, zero when output is q^*, and negative when output is greater than q^*. Thus,

Output Rule 2: *A firm sets its output where its marginal profit is zero.*
We obtain this result formally using the first-order condition for a profit maximum. We set the derivative of the profit function, Equation 8.3, with respect to quantity equal to zero:

$$\frac{d\pi(q^*)}{dq} = 0. \tag{8.4}$$

Equation 8.4 states that a necessary condition for profit to be maximized is that the quantity be set at q^* where the firm's marginal profit with respect to quantity equals zero.

Equation 8.4 is a necessary condition for profit to be maximized. Sufficiency requires, in addition, that the second-order condition hold:

$$\frac{d^2\pi(q^*)}{dq^2} < 0. \tag{8.5}$$

That is, for profit to be maximized at q^*, when we increase the output beyond q^*, the marginal profit must decline.

Because profit is a function of revenue and cost, we can state this last condition in one additional way. We can obtain another necessary condition for profit maximization by setting the derivative of $\pi(q) = R(q) - C(q)$ with respect to output equal to zero:

$$\frac{d\pi(q^*)}{dq} = \frac{dR(q^*)}{dq} - \frac{dC(q^*)}{dq} = MR(q^*) - MC(q^*) = 0. \qquad (8.6)$$

The derivative of cost with respect to output, $dC(q)/dq = MC(q)$, is its marginal cost (Chapter 7). The firm's **marginal revenue**, MR, is the change in revenue it gains from selling one more unit of output: dR/dq. Equation 8.6 shows that a necessary condition for profit to be maximized is that the firm set its quantity at q^* where the difference between the firm's marginal revenue and marginal cost is zero. Thus, a third, equivalent rule is

Output Rule 3: *A firm sets its output where its marginal revenue equals its marginal cost,*

$$MR(q^*) = MC(q^*). \qquad (8.7)$$

For profit to be maximized at q^*, the second-order condition must hold:

$$\frac{d^2\pi(q^*)}{dq^2} = \frac{d^2R(q^*)}{dq^2} - \frac{d^2C(q^*)}{dq^2} = \frac{dMR(q^*)}{dq} = \frac{dMC(q^*)}{dq} < 0. \qquad (8.8)$$

That is, for profit to be maximized at q^*, the slope of the marginal revenue curve, dMR/dq, must be less than the slope of the marginal cost curve, dMC/dq.

Shutdown Rules. The firm chooses to produce q^* if it can make a profit. But even if the firm maximizes its profit at q^*, it does not necessarily follow that the firm is making a positive profit. If the firm makes a loss, does it shut down? Surprisingly, the answer is "It depends." The general rule, which holds for all types of firms in both the short and long run, is

Shutdown Rule 1: *The firm shuts down only if it can reduce its loss by doing so.*
In the short run, the firm has variable costs, such as labor and materials, as well as fixed plant and equipment costs (Chapter 7). If the fixed cost is a *sunk* cost, this expense cannot be avoided by stopping operations—the firm pays this cost whether it shuts down or not. By shutting down, the firm stops receiving revenue and stops paying avoidable costs, but it is still stuck with its fixed cost. Thus, it pays for the firm to shut down only if its revenue is less than its avoidable cost.

Suppose that the firm's revenue is $R = \$2,000$, its variable cost is $VC = \$1,000$, and its fixed cost is $F = \$3,000$, which is the price it paid for a machine that it cannot resell or use for any other purpose. This firm is making a short-run loss:

$$\pi = R - VC - F = \$2,000 - \$1,000 - \$3,000 = -\$2,000.$$

If the firm shuts down, it still has to pay its fixed cost of $3,000, and hence it loses $2,000. Because its fixed cost is sunk, the firm should ignore it when making its shutdown decision. Ignoring the fixed cost, the firm sees that its $2,000 revenue exceeds its $1,000 avoidable, variable cost by $1,000, so it does not shut down. The extra $1,000 can be used to offset some of the fixed cost.

However, if its revenue is only $500, it cannot cover the $1,000 avoidable, variable cost, and loses $500. Adding this $500 loss to the $3,000 it must pay in fixed cost, the firm's total loss is $3,500. Because the firm can reduce its loss from $3,500 to $3,000 by ceasing operations, it shuts down. (Remember the shutdown rule: The firm shuts down only if it can reduce its loss by doing so.)

In conclusion, the firm compares its revenue to its variable cost only when deciding whether to stop operating. Because the fixed cost is *sunk*—the expense cannot be avoided by stopping operations (Chapter 7)—the firm pays this cost whether it shuts down or not. Thus, the sunk fixed cost is irrelevant to the shutdown decision.

We usually assume that fixed cost is *sunk* (Chapter 7). However, if a firm can sell its capital for as much as it paid, its fixed cost is *avoidable* and should be taken into account when the firm is considering whether to shut down. A firm with a fully avoidable fixed cost always shuts down if it makes a short-run loss. If a firm buys a specialized piece of machinery for $1,000 that can be used only for its business but can be sold for scrap metal for $100, then $100 of the fixed cost is avoidable and $900 is sunk. Only the avoidable portion of a fixed cost is relevant for the shutdown decision.

In the long run, all costs are avoidable because the firm can eliminate them all by shutting down. Thus, in the long run, where the firm can avoid all losses by not operating, it pays to shut down if the firm faces any loss at all. As a result, we can restate the shutdown rule, which holds for all types of firms in both the short run and the long run, as

Shutdown Rule 2: *The firm shuts down only if its revenue is less than its avoidable cost.*

8.3   Competition in the Short Run

Having considered how firms maximize profit in general, we now examine the profit-maximizing behavior of competitive firms, paying careful attention to firms' shutdown decisions. In this section, we focus on the short run.

Short-Run Competitive Profit Maximization

A competitive firm, like other firms, first determines the output at which it maximizes its profit (or minimizes its loss). Second, it decides whether to produce or to shut down.

Short-Run Output Decision. We've already seen that *any* firm maximizes its profit at the output where its marginal profit is zero or, equivalently, where its marginal cost equals its marginal revenue. *Because it faces a horizontal demand curve, a competitive firm can sell as many units of output as it wants at the market price, p.* Thus, a competitive firm's revenue, $R(q) = pq$, increases by p if it sells one more unit of output, so its marginal revenue equals the market price: $MR = \mathrm{d}(pq)/\mathrm{d}q = p$. A competitive firm maximizes its profit by choosing its output such that

$$\frac{\mathrm{d}\pi(q^*)}{\mathrm{d}q} = \frac{\mathrm{d}pq^*}{\mathrm{d}q} - \frac{\mathrm{d}C(q^*)}{\mathrm{d}q} = p - MC(q^*) = 0. \qquad (8.9)$$

That is, because a competitive firm's marginal revenue equals the market price, a profit-maximizing competitive firm produces the amount of output q^* at which its *marginal cost equals the market price:* $MC(q^*) = p$.

For the quantity determined by Equation 8.9 to maximize profit, the second-order condition must hold: $\mathrm{d}^2\pi(q^*)/\mathrm{d}q^2 = \mathrm{d}p/\mathrm{d}q - \mathrm{d}MC(q^*)/\mathrm{d}q < 0$. Because the firm's marginal revenue, p, does not vary with q, $\mathrm{d}p/\mathrm{d}q = 0$. Thus, the second-order condition, which requires that the second derivative of the cost function with respect to quantity evaluated at the profit-maximizing quantity be negative, holds if the first derivative of the marginal cost function is positive:

$$\frac{\mathrm{d}MC(q^*)}{\mathrm{d}q} > 0. \qquad (8.10)$$

Equation 8.10 requires that the marginal cost curve be upward sloping at q^*.

To illustrate how a competitive firm maximizes its profit, we examine a typical Canadian lime manufacturing firm (based on the estimates of the variable cost function by Robidoux and Lester, 1988). Lime is a nonmetallic mineral used in mortars, plasters, cements, bleaching powders, steel, paper, glass, and other products. The lime plant's estimated cost curve, C, in panel a of Figure 8.3 rises less rapidly with output

Figure 8.3 How a Competitive Firm Maximizes Profit

(a) A competitive lime manufacturing firm produces 284 units of lime so as to maximize its profit at $\pi^* = \$426,000$ (Robidoux and Lester, 1988). (b) The firm's profit is maximized where its marginal revenue, MR, which is the market price $p = \$8$, equals its marginal cost, MC.

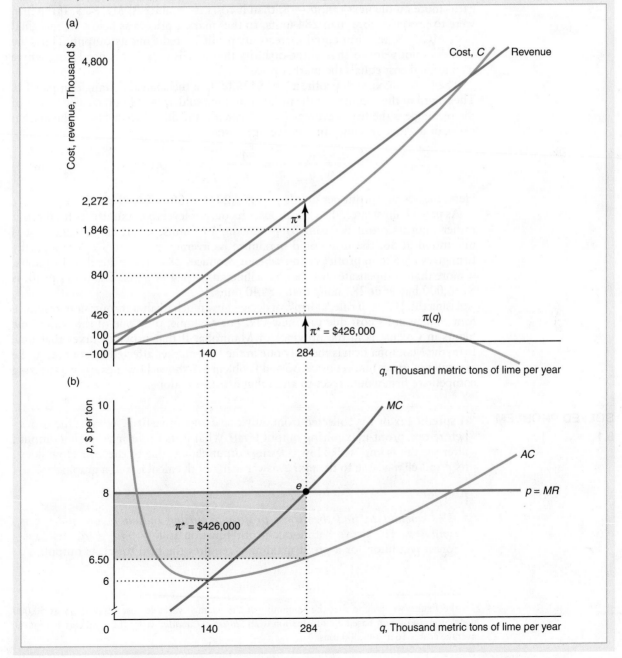

at low quantities than at higher quantities.[7] If the market price of lime is $p = 8$, the competitive firm faces a horizontal demand curve at 8 (in panel b), so the revenue curve, $R = pq = 8q$, in panel a is an upward-sloping straight line with a slope of 8.

By producing 284 units (where a unit is 1,000 metric tons), the firm maximizes its profit at $\pi^* = \$426,000$, which is the height of the profit curve and the difference between the revenue and cost curves at that quantity in panel a. At the competitive firm's profit-maximizing output, determined by Equation 8.9, its marginal cost equals the market price of $8 at point e in panel b.

Point e is the competitive firm's equilibrium. Were the firm to produce less than the equilibrium quantity, 284 units, the market price would be above its marginal cost. As a result, the firm could increase its profit by expanding output because it earns more on the next ton, $p = 8$, than it costs to produce it, $MC < 8$. If the firm were to produce more than 284 units, so that market price was below its marginal cost, $MC > 8$, the firm could increase its profit by reducing its output. Thus, the firm does not want to change the quantity that it sells only if it is producing where its marginal cost equals the market price.

The firm's maximum profit, $\pi^* = \$426,000$, is the shaded rectangle in panel b. The length of the rectangle is the number of units sold, $q = 284$ units. The height of the rectangle is the firm's average profit, which is the difference between the market price, or average revenue, and its average cost:

$$\frac{\pi}{q} = \frac{R}{q} - \frac{C}{q} = \frac{pq}{q} - \frac{C}{q} = p - AC. \tag{8.11}$$

Here, the average profit per unit is $p - AC(284) = \$8 - \$6.50 = \$1.50$.

As panel b illustrates, the firm chooses its output level to maximize its total profit rather than its profit per ton. By producing 140 units, where its average cost is minimized at $6, the firm could maximize its average profit at $2. Although the firm gives up 50¢ in profit per ton when it produces 284 units instead of 140 units, it more than compensates for that by selling an extra 144 units. The firm's profit is $146,000 higher at 284 units than at 140 units.

Using the $MC = p$ rule, a firm can decide how much to alter its output in response to a change in its cost due to a new tax. For example, only one of the many lime plants in Canada is in the province of Manitoba. If that province taxes that lime firm, the Manitoba firm is the only one in the lime market affected by the tax, so the tax will not affect market price. Solved Problem 8.1 shows how a profit-maximizing competitive firm would react to a tax that affected it alone.

SOLVED PROBLEM 8.1

A specific tax of τ is collected from only one competitive firm. What is the firm's before-tax, profit-maximizing output level? What is its profit-maximizing output after the tax is imposed? How does its output change due to the tax? How does its profit change due to the tax? Answer using both calculus and a graph.

Answer

1. *Use calculus to find the firm's profit-maximizing output before the tax is imposed.* The firm's before-tax profit function is $\pi = pq - C(q)$. Its first-order condition for a profit maximum requires the firm to set its output, q_1,

[7]In the figure, we assume that the minimum of the average variable cost curve is $5 at 50,000 metric tons of output. Based on information from *Statistics Canada*, we set the fixed cost so that the average cost is $6 at 140,000 tons.

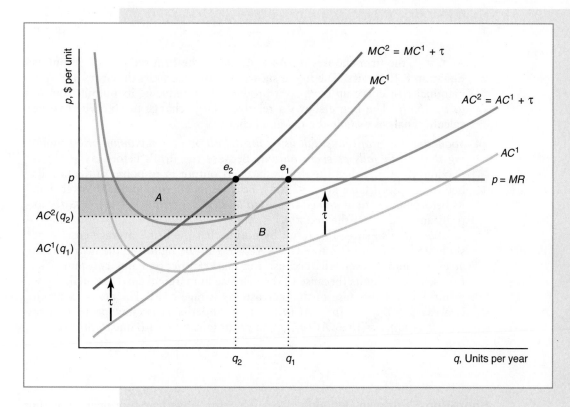

where $d\pi(q_1)/dq = p - dC(q_1)/dq = 0$, or $p = MC(q_1)$. As the figure shows, the firm maximizes its profit at e_1, where its MC^1 marginal cost curve crosses the market price line.

2. *Use calculus to find the firm's profit-maximizing output after the tax is imposed.* The after-tax profit is $\bar{\pi} = pq - C(q) - \tau q$. The firm maximizes its profit at q_2 where

$$\frac{d\bar{\pi}(q_2)}{dq} = p - \frac{dC(q_2)}{dq} - \tau = 0, \tag{8.12}$$

or $p = MC(q_2) + \tau$. (If $\tau = 0$, we obtain the same result as in our before-tax analysis.) The figure shows that the firm's after-tax marginal cost curve shifts from MC^1 to $MC^2 = MC^1 + \tau$. Because the firm is a price taker and the tax is applied to only this one firm, its marginal revenue before and after the tax is the market price, p. In the figure, the firm's new maximum is at e_2.

3. *Use comparative statics to determine how a change in the tax rate affects output.* Given the first-order condition, Equation 8.12, we can write the optimal quantity as a function of the tax rate: $q(\tau)$. Differentiating this first-order condition with respect to τ, we obtain

$$-\frac{d^2C}{dq^2}\frac{dq}{d\tau} - 1 = -\frac{dMC}{dq}\frac{dq}{d\tau} - 1 = 0.$$

The second-order condition for a profit maximum, Equation 8.10, requires that dMC/dq be negative, so

$$\frac{dq}{d\tau} = -\frac{1}{dMC/dq} < 0. \tag{8.13}$$

At $\tau = 0$, the firm chooses q_1. As τ increases, the firm reduces its output as Equation 8.13 shows. The figure shows that the tax shifts the firm's after-tax marginal cost curve up by τ, so it produces less, reducing its output from q_1 to q_2. (*Note:* The figure shows a relatively large change in tax, whereas the calculus analysis examines a marginal change.)

4. *Show that the profit must fall using the definition of a maximum or by showing that profit falls at every output.* Because the firm's before-tax profit is maximized at q_1, when the firm reduces its output in response to the tax, its before-tax profit falls: $\pi(q_2) < \pi(q_1)$. Because its after-tax profit is lower than its before-tax profit at *any given output level*, $p(q_2) = \pi(q_2) - \tau q_2 < \pi(q_2)$, its profit must fall after the tax: $\bar{\pi}(q_2) < \pi(q_1)$.

   We can also show this result by noting that the firm's average cost curve shifts up by τ from AC^1 to $AC^2 = AC^1 + \tau$ in the figure, so the firm's profit at every output level falls because the market price remains constant. The firm sells fewer units (because of the increase in marginal cost) and makes less profit per unit (because of the increase in average cost). The after-tax profit is area $A = \bar{\pi}(q_2) = [p - AC(q_2) - \tau]q_2$, and the before-tax profit is area $A + B = \pi(q_1) = [p - AC(q_1)]q_1$, so profit falls by area B due to the tax.

Short-Run Shutdown Decision. Does the competitive lime firm operate or shut down? We look at three possibilities where the market price is (1) above the minimum average cost (AC), (2) less than the minimum average cost but at least equal to or above the minimum average variable cost, or (3) below the minimum average variable cost.

First, if the market price is above the firm's average cost at the quantity that it's producing, the firm makes a profit and so it operates. In panel b of Figure 8.3, the competitive lime firm's average cost curve reaches its minimum of $6 per ton at 140 units. Thus, if the market price is above $6, the firm makes a profit of $p - AC$ on each unit it sells and operates. In the figure, the market price is $8, and the firm makes a profit of $426,000.

Second, the tricky case is when the market price is less than the minimum average cost but at least as great as the minimum average variable cost. If the price is in this range, the firm makes a loss, but it reduces its loss by operating rather than shutting down.

Figure 8.4, which reproduces the cost curves from panel b of Figure 8.3, illustrates this case for the lime firm, where the average cost curve reaches a minimum of $6 at 140 units, while the average variable cost curve hits its minimum of $5 at 50 units. When the market price is between $5 and $6, the lime firm is making a loss because the price is less than the AC, but the firm does not shut down.

For example at the market price of $5.50 in the figure, the firm minimizes its loss by producing 100 units where the marginal cost curve crosses the price line. At 100 units, the average cost is $6.12, so the firm's loss is $-62¢ = p - AC(100) = \$5.50 - \$6.12$ on each ton that it sells.[8]

---

[8]A firm cannot "lose a little on every sale but make it up on volume."

Figure 8.4 The Short-Run Shutdown Decision

The competitive lime manufacturing plant operates if price is above the minimum of the average variable cost curve, point *a*, at $5. With a market price of $5.50, the firm produces 100 units because that price is above $AVC(100) = \$5.14$, so the firm more than covers its out-of-pocket, variable costs. At that price, the firm suffers a loss of area $A = \$62,000$ because the price is less than the average cost of $6.12. If it shuts down, its loss is its fixed cost, area $A + B = \$98,000$. Therefore, the firm does not shut down.

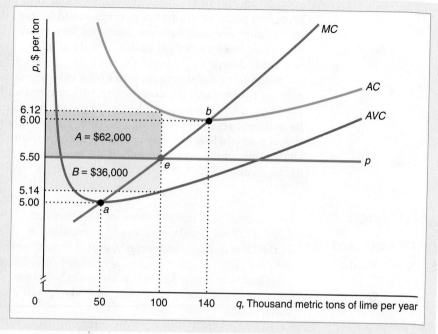

Why does the firm produce given that it is making a loss? The firm can gain by shutting down only if its revenue is less than its short-run variable cost:

$$pq < VC(q). \qquad (8.14)$$

By dividing both sides of Equation 8.14 by output, we can write this condition as

$$p < \frac{VC(q)}{q} = AVC. \qquad (8.15)$$

A competitive firm shuts down if the market price is less than the minimum of its short-run average variable cost curve.

If the firm shuts down in the short run it incurs a loss equal to its fixed cost of $98,000, which is the sum of the rectangle *A* and the rectangle *B*.[9] If the firm operates and produces $q = 100$ units, its average variable cost is $AVC = \$5.14$, which is less than the market price of $p = \$5.50$ per ton. It makes $36¢ = p - AVC = \$5.50 - \$5.14$ more on each ton than its average variable cost. The difference between the firm's revenue and its variable cost, $R - VC$, is the rectangle $B = \$36,000$, which has a length of 100 thousand tons and a height of 36¢. Thus, if the firm operates, it loses only $62,000 (rectangle *A*), which is less than its loss if it shuts down, $98,000. The firm makes a smaller loss by operating than by shutting down because its revenue more than covers its variable cost and hence helps to reduce the loss from the fixed cost.

[9]From Chapter 6, we know that the average cost is the sum of the average variable cost and the average fixed cost, $AC = AVC + F/q$. Thus, the gap between the average cost and the average variable cost curves at any given output is $AC - AVC = F/q$. Consequently, the height of the rectangle $A + B$ is $AC(100) - AVC(100) = F/100$, and the length of the rectangle is 100 units, so the area of the rectangle is F, or $98,000 = \$62,000 + \$36,000$.

Third, if the market price dips below the minimum of the average variable cost, $5 in Figure 8.4, then the firm should shut down in the short run. At any price less than the minimum average variable cost, the firm's revenue is less than its variable cost, so it makes a greater loss by operating than by shutting down because it loses money on each unit sold in addition to the fixed cost that it loses if it shuts down.

In summary, a competitive firm uses a two-step decision-making process to maximize its profit. First, the competitive firm determines the output that maximizes its profit or minimizes its loss when its marginal cost equals the market price (which is its marginal revenue): $p = MC$. Second, the firm chooses to produce that quantity unless it would lose more by operating than by shutting down. The competitive firm shuts down in the short run only if the market price is less than the minimum of its average variable cost, $p < AVC$.

APPLICATION

Oil, Oil Sands, and Oil Shale Shutdowns

Oil production starts and stops in the short run as the market price fluctuates. In 1998–1999 when oil prices were historically low, 74,000 of the 136,000 oil wells in the United States temporarily shut down or were permanently abandoned. At the time, Terry Smith, the general manager of Tidelands Oil Production Company, who had shut down 327 of his company's 834 wells, said that he would operate these wells again when the price rose above $10 a barrel—his minimum average variable cost.

Getting oil from oil wells is relatively easy. It is harder and more costly to obtain oil from other sources, so firms that use those alternative sources have a higher minimum average variable cost—higher shutdown points—and hence shutdown at a higher price than companies that pump oil from wells.

It might surprise you to know that Canada has the second-largest known oil reserves, 180 billion barrels, in the world, trailing only Saudi Arabia's 259 billion barrels, and far exceeding Iraq's third-place 113 billion. Yet you rarely hear about Canada's vast oil reserves because 97% of those reserves are in oil sands, which cover an area the size of Florida.

Oil sands are a mixture of heavy petroleum (bitumen), water, and sandstone. Extracting oil from oil sands is expensive and causes significant pollution in the production process. To liberate four barrels of crude oil from the sands, a processor must burn the equivalent of a fifth barrel. With the technology available in 2012, two tons of sand yielded only a single barrel (42 gallons) of oil.

The first large oil sands mining began in the 1960s, but because oil prices were often less than the $25-per-barrel average variable cost of recovering oil from the sands at that time, production was frequently shut down. In recent years, however, the combination of technological improvements in the production process and much higher oil prices lowered the average variable cost to $18 a barrel. That coupled with higher oil prices has led to continuous oil sands production without shutdowns. As of 2012 more than 50 oil companies have operations in the Canadian oil sands, including major international producers such as Exxon, BP (British Petroleum) and Royal Dutch Shell, major Canadian producers such as Suncor and Husky, and companies from China, Japan, and South Korea.

The huge amounts of oil hidden in oil sands may be dwarfed by those found in oil shale, which is sedimentary rock containing oil. According to current estimates, oil shale deposits in Colorado and neighboring areas in Utah and Wyoming contain 800 billion recoverable barrels, the equivalent of 40 years of U.S. oil consumption. The United States has between 1 and 2 trillion recoverable barrels from oil shale, which is at least four times Saudi Arabia's proven reserves of conventional crude oil.

A federal task force report concluded that the United States will be able to produce 3 million barrels of oil a day from oil shale and sands by 2035. Shell Oil reports that its average variable cost of extract oil from shale is $30 a barrel in Colorado. In recent years, the lowest price for world oil was $39 on December 12, 2008. Since then prices have risen significantly, reaching $100 per barrel in early 2011and remaining close to or above that level through mid 2012. Therefore, oil shale production has become profitable and extraction is occurring.

Short-Run Firm Supply Curve

We just analyzed how a competitive firm chooses its output for a given market price to maximize its profit. By repeating this analysis at different possible market prices, we can derive the firm's short-run supply curve, which shows how the quantity supplied by the competitive firm varies with the market price.

Tracing Out the Short-Run Supply Curve. As the market price increases from $p_1 = \$5$ to $p_2 = \$6$ to $p_3 = \$7$ to $p_4 = \$8$, the lime firm increases its output from 50 to 140 to 215 to 285 units per year, as Figure 8.5 shows. The

Figure 8.5 How the Profit-Maximizing Quantity Varies with Price

As the market price increases, the lime manufacturing firm produces more output. The change in the price traces out the marginal cost curve of the firm.

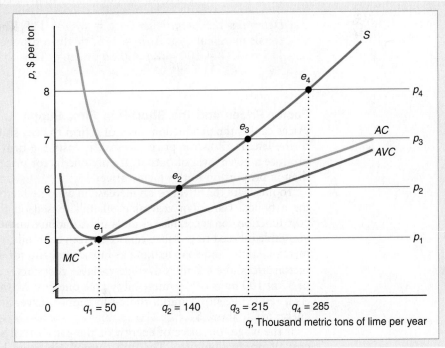

equilibrium at each market price, e_1 through e_4, is determined by the intersection of the relevant demand curve—market price line—and the firm's marginal cost curve. That is, as the market price increases, the equilibria trace out the marginal cost curve.

If the price falls below the firm's minimum average variable cost of $5, the firm shuts down. Thus, the competitive firm's short-run supply curve is its marginal cost curve above its minimum average variable cost.

The firm's short-run supply curve, S, is a thick line in the figure. At prices above $5, the short-run supply curve is the same as the marginal cost curve. The supply is zero when price is less than the minimum of the AVC curve of $5. (From now on, for simplicity, the graphs will not show the supply curve at prices below the minimum AVC.)

SOLVED PROBLEM 8.2

Given that a competitive firm's short-run cost function is $C(q) = 100q - 4q^2 + 0.2q^3 + 450$, what is the firm's short-run supply curve? If the price is $p = 115$, how much output does the firm supply?

Answer

1. *Determine the firm's supply curve by calculating for which output levels the firm's marginal cost is greater than its minimum average variable cost.* The firm's supply curve is its marginal cost above its minimum average variable cost. From Solved Problem 7.2, we know that $MC(q) = dC(q)/dq 100 - 8q + 0.6q^2$ and $AVC(q) = VC(q)/q = 100 - 4q + 0.2q^2$. We also know that the marginal cost cuts the average variable cost at its minimum (Chapter 7), so we can determine the q where the AVC reaches its minimum by equating the AVC and MC functions: $AVC = 100 - 4\underline{q} + 0.2\underline{q}^2 = 100 - 8\underline{q} + 0.6\underline{q}^2 = MC$. Solving, the minimum is $\underline{q} = 10$, as Figure 7.1 illustrates. Thus, the supply curve is the MC curve for output greater than or equal to 10.

2. *Determine the quantity where $p = MC = 115$.* The firm operates where price equals marginal cost. At $p = 115$, the firm produces the quantity q such that $115 = MC = 100 - 8q + 0.6q^2$, or $q = 15$.

Factor Prices and the Short-Run Firm Supply Curve. An increase in factor prices causes the production costs of a firm to rise, shifting the firm's supply curve to the left. If all factor prices double, it costs the firm twice as much as before to produce a given level of output. If only one factor price rises, its total cost rises less than in proportion to this factor price.

To illustrate the effect of an increase in a single factor price on supply, we examine a typical Canadian vegetable oil mill (based on the estimates of the variable cost function for vegetable oil mills by Robidoux and Lester, 1988). This firm uses vegetable oil seed to produce canola and soybean oils, which customers use in commercial baking and soap making as lubricants, and for other purposes. At the initial factor prices, the oil mill's average variable cost curve, AVC^1, reaches its minimum of $7 at 100 units of vegetable oil (where one unit is 100 metric tons), in Figure 8.6. As a result, the firm's initial short-run supply curve, S^1, is the initial marginal cost curve, MC^1, above $7.

If the wage, the price of energy, or the price of oil seeds increases, the oil mill's cost of production rises. The mill cannot substitute between oil seeds and other

Figure 8.6 Effect of an Increase in the Cost of Materials on the Vegetable Oil Supply Curve

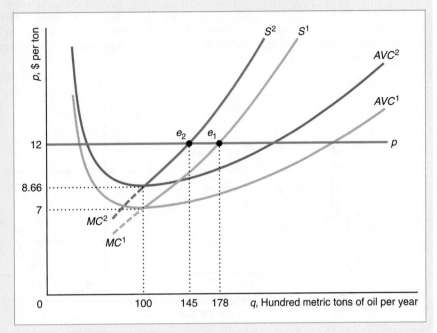

Materials are 95% of variable costs, so when the price of materials rises by 25%, variable costs rise by 23.75% (95% of 25%). As a result, the supply curve of a vegetable oil mill shifts upward from S^1 to S^2. If the market price is $12, the quantity supplied falls from 178 to 145 units.

factors of production. The cost of oil seeds is 95% of the variable cost. Thus, if the price of raw materials increases by 25%, variable cost rises by 95% × 25%, or 23.75%. This increase in the price of oil seeds causes the marginal cost curve to shift from MC^1 to MC^2 and the average variable cost curve to shift from AVC^1 to AVC^2 in the figure. As a result, the mill's short-run supply curve shifts upward from S^1 to S^2. The price increase causes the shutdown price to rise from $7 per unit to $8.66. At a market price of $12 per unit, at the original factor prices, the mill produces 178 units. After the increase in the price of vegetable oil seeds, the mill produces only 145 units if the market price remains constant.

Short-Run Market Supply Curve

The market supply curve is the horizontal sum of the supply curves of all the individual firms in the market (see Chapter 2). In the short run, the maximum number of firms in a market, n, is fixed because new firms need time to enter the market. If all the firms in a competitive market are identical, each firm's supply curve is identical, so the market supply at any price is n times the supply of an individual firm. Where firms have different shutdown prices, the market supply reflects a different number of firms at various prices even in the short run. We examine competitive markets first with firms that have identical costs and then with firms that have different costs.

Short-Run Market Supply with Identical Firms. To illustrate how to construct a short-run market supply curve, we suppose that the lime manufacturing market has $n = 5$ competitive firms with identical cost curves. Panel a of Figure 8.7 plots the short-run supply curve, S^1, of a typical firm—the MC curve above the minimum AVC—where the horizontal axis shows the firm's output, q, per year. Panel b

Figure 8.7 Short-Run Market Supply with Five Identical Lime Firms

(a) The short-run supply curve, S^1, for a typical lime manufacturing firm is its MC above the minimum of its AVC.
(b) The market supply curve, S^5, is the horizontal sum of
the supply curves of each of the five identical firms. The
curve S^4 shows what the market supply curve would be if
there were only four firms in the market.

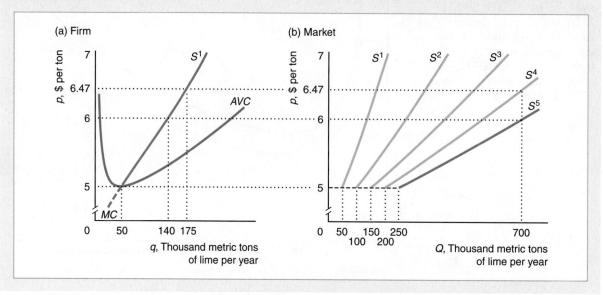

illustrates the competitive market supply curve, the dark line S^5, where the horizontal axis is market output, Q, per year. The price axis is the same in the two panels.

If the market price is less than $5 per ton, no firm supplies any output, so the
market supply is zero. At $5, each firm is willing to supply $q = 50$ units, as in panel
a. Consequently, the market supply is $Q = 5q = 250$ units in panel b. At $6 per
ton, each firm supplies 140 units, so the market supply is 700 (= 5×140) units.

Suppose, however, that there were fewer than five firms in the short run. The
light-colored lines in panel b show the market supply curves for various other numbers of firms. The market supply curve is S^1 if there is one price-taking firm, S^2 with
two firms, S^3 with three firms, and S^4 with four firms. The market supply curve
flattens as the number of firms in the market increases because the market supply
curve is the horizontal sum of more and more upward-sloping firm supply curves.
As the number of firms grows very large, the market supply curve approaches a
horizontal line at $5. Thus, *the more identical firms producing at a given price, the
flatter (more elastic) the short-run market supply curve at that price.* As a result, the
more firms in the market, the less the price has to increase for the short-run market
supply to increase substantially. Consumers pay $6 per ton to obtain 700 units of
lime if there are five firms but must pay $6.47 per ton to obtain that amount with
only four firms.

Short-Run Market Supply with Firms That Differ. If the firms in a competitive
market have different minimum average variable costs, not all firms produce at
every price, a situation that affects the shape of the short-run market supply curve.
Suppose that the only two firms in the lime market are our typical lime firm with a
supply curve of S^1 and another firm with a higher marginal and minimum average
cost with the supply curve of S^2 in Figure 8.8. The first firm produces if the market
price is at least $5, whereas the second firm does not produce unless the price is

Figure 8.8 Short-Run Market Supply with Two Different Lime Firms

The supply curve S^1 is the same as for the typical lime firm in Figure 8.7. A second firm has an MC that lies to the left of the original firm's cost curve and a higher minimum AVC. Thus, its supply curve, S^2, lies above and to the left of the original firm's supply curve, S^1. The market supply curve, S, is the horizontal sum of the two supply curves. When prices are high enough for both firms to produce, at \$6 and above, the market supply curve is flatter than the supply curve of either individual firm.

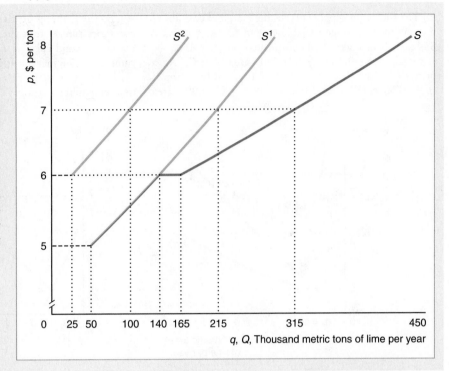

\$6 or more. At \$5, the first firm produces 50 units, so the quantity on the market supply curve, S, is 50 units. Between \$5 and \$6, only the first firm produces, so the market supply, S, is the same as the first firm's supply, S^1. If the price is \$6 or more, both firms produce, so the market supply curve is the horizontal summation of their two individual supply curves. For example, at \$7, the first firm produces 215 units, and the second firm supplies 100 units, so the market supply is 315 units.

As with the identical firms, where both firms produce, the market supply curve is flatter than that of either firm. Because the second firm does not produce at as low a price as the first firm, the short-run market supply curve has a steeper slope (less elastic supply) at relatively low prices than it would if the firms were identical.

Where firms differ, only the low-cost firm supplies goods at relatively low prices. As the price rises, the other, higher-cost firm starts supplying, creating a stair-like market supply curve. The more suppliers there are with differing costs, the more steps there are in the market supply curve. As price rises and more firms supply goods, the market supply curve flattens, so it takes a smaller increase in price to increase supply by a given amount. Stated another way, the more firms differ in costs, the steeper the market supply curve at low prices. Differences in costs are one explanation for why some market supply curves are upward sloping.

Short-Run Competitive Equilibrium

By combining the short-run market supply curve and the market demand curve, we can determine the short-run competitive equilibrium. We examine first how to determine the equilibrium in the lime market and then how the equilibrium changes when firms are taxed.

Figure 8.9 Short-Run Competitive Equilibrium in the Lime Market

(a) The short-run supply curve is the marginal cost above the minimum average variable cost of $5. At a price of $5, each firm makes a short-run loss of $(p - AC)q = (\$5 - \$6.97) \times 50{,}000 = -\$98{,}500$, area $A + C$. At a price of $7, the short-run profit of a typical lime firm is $(p - AC)q = (\$7 - \$6.20) \times 215{,}000 = \$172{,}000$, area

$A + B$. (b) If there are five firms in the lime market in the short run so that the market supply is S, and the market demand curve is D^1, then the short-run equilibrium is E_1, the market price is $7, and market output is $Q_1 = 1{,}075$ units. If the demand curve shifts to D^2, the market equilibrium is $p = \$5$ and $Q_2 = 250$ units.

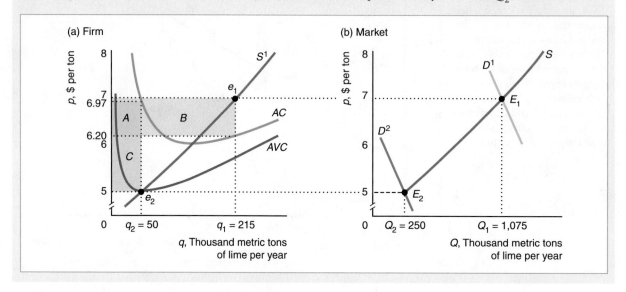

Suppose that there were five identical firms in the short-run equilibrium for the lime manufacturing industry. Panel a of Figure 8.9 shows the short-run cost curves and the supply curve, S^1, for a typical firm, and panel b shows the corresponding short-run competitive market supply curve, S.

In panel b, the initial demand curve D^1 intersects the market supply curve at E_1, the market equilibrium. The equilibrium quantity is $Q_1 = 1{,}075$ units of lime per year, and the equilibrium market price is $7.

In panel a, each competitive firm faces a horizontal demand curve at the equilibrium price of $7. Each price-taking firm chooses its output where its marginal cost curve intersects the horizontal demand curve at e_1. Because each firm maximizes its profit at e_1, no firm wants to change its behavior, so e_1 is each firm's equilibrium. In panel a, each firm makes a short-run profit of area $A + B = \$172{,}000$, which is the average profit per ton, $p - AC = \$7 - \$6.20 = 80¢$, times the firm's output, $q_1 = 215$ units. The equilibrium market output, Q_1, is the number of firms, n, times the equilibrium output of each firm: $Q_1 = nq_1 = 5 \times 215$ units $= 1{,}075$ units (panel b).

Now suppose that the demand curve shifts to D^2. The new market equilibrium is E_2, where the price is only $5. At that price, each firm produces $q = 50$ units, and market output is $Q = 250$ units. In panel a, each firm loses $98,500, area $A + C$, because it makes an average per ton of $(p - AC) = (\$5 - \$6.97) = -\$1.97$ and it sells $q_2 = 50$ units. However, such a firm does not shut down because the price equals the firm's average variable cost, so the firm is able to cover its out-of-pocket expenses.

SOLVED PROBLEM 8.3

What is the effect on the short-run equilibrium of a specific tax of τ per unit that is collected from all n identical firms in a market? Does the consumer bear the full incidence of the tax (the share of the tax that falls on consumers)?

Answer

1. *Show how the tax shifts a typical firm's marginal cost and average cost curves and hence its supply curve.* In Solved Problem 8.1, we showed that such a tax causes the marginal cost curve, the average cost curve, and (hence) the minimum average cost of the firm to shift up by τ, as illustrated in panel a of the figure. As a result, the short-run supply curve of the firm, labeled $S^1 + \tau$, shifts up by τ from the pretax supply curve, S^1.

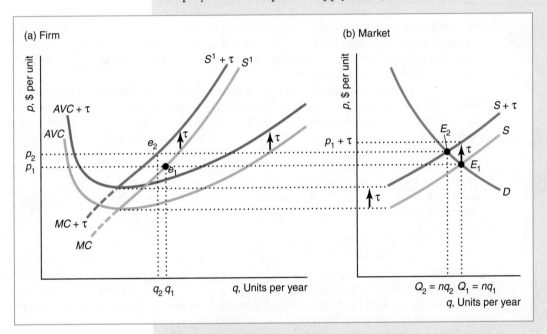

2. *Show how the market supply curve shifts.* The market supply curve is the sum of all the individual firm's supply curves, so it also shifts up by τ, from S to $S + \tau$ in panel b of the figure.

3. *Determine how the short-run market equilibrium changes.* The pre-tax short-run market equilibrium is E_1, where the downward-sloping market demand curve D intersects S in panel b. In that equilibrium, price is p_1 and quantity is Q_1, which equals n (the number of firms) times the quantity q_1 that a typical firm produces at p_1. The after-tax short-run market equilibrium, E_2, determined by the intersection of D and the after-tax supply curve, $S + \tau$, occurs at p_2 and Q_2. Because the after-tax price p_2 is above the after-tax minimum average variable cost, all the firms continue to produce, but they produce less than before: $q_2 < q_1$. Consequently, the equilibrium quantity falls from $Q_1 = nq_1$ to $Q_2 = nq_2$.

4. *Discuss the incidence of the tax.* The equilibrium price increases, but by less than the full amount of the tax: $p_2 < p_1 + \tau$. Because the supply curve slopes up and the demand curve slopes down, the incidence of the tax is shared between consumers and producers (Chapter 2).

8.4.   Competition in the Long Run

I think there is a world market for about five computers.
—Thomas J. Watson, IBM chairman, 1943

In the long run, competitive firms can vary inputs that were fixed in the short run, so the long-run firm and market supply curves differ from the short-run curves. After briefly looking at how a firm determines its long-run supply curve that maximizes its profit, we examine the relationship between short-run and long-run market supply curves and competitive equilibria.

Long-Run Competitive Profit Maximization

A firm's two profit-maximizing decisions—how much to produce and whether to produce at all—are simpler in the long run than in the short run. In the long run, typically all costs are variable, so the firm does not have to consider whether fixed costs are sunk or avoidable costs.

The firm chooses the quantity that maximizes its profit using the same rules as in the short run. The company will pick the quantity that maximizes long-run profit, which is the difference between revenue and long-run cost. Equivalently, it operates where long-run marginal profit is zero and where marginal revenue equals long-run marginal cost.

After determining the output level, q^*, that maximizes its profit or minimizes its loss, the firm decides whether to produce or shut down. The firm shuts down if its revenue is less than its avoidable or variable cost. In the long run, however, all costs are variable. As a result, in the long run, the firm shuts down if it would suffer an economic loss by continuing to operate.

Long-Run Firm Supply Curve

A firm's long-run supply curve is its long-run marginal cost curve above the minimum of its long-run average cost curve (because all costs are variable in the long run). The firm is free to choose its capital in the long run, so the firm's long-run supply curve may differ substantially from its short-run supply curve.

The firm chooses a plant size to maximize its long-run economic profit in light of its beliefs about the future. If its forecast is wrong, it may be stuck with a plant that is too small or too large for its chosen level of production in the short run. The firm corrects this mistake in plant size in the long run.

The firm in Figure 8.10 has different short- and long-run cost curves. In the short run, the firm uses a plant that is smaller than the optimal long-run size if the price is $35. The firm produces 50 units of output per year in the short run, where its short-run marginal cost, $SRMC$, equals the price, and makes a short-run profit equal to area A. The firm's short-run supply curve, S^{SR}, is its short-run marginal cost above the minimum, $20, of its short-run average variable cost, $SRAVC$.

If the firm expects the price to remain at $35, it builds a larger plant in the long run. Using the larger plant, the firm produces 110 units per year, where its long-run marginal cost, $LRMC$, equals the market price. It expects to make a long-run profit, area $A + B$, which is greater than its short-run profit by area B because it sells 60 more units, and its equilibrium long-run average cost, $LRAC = \$25$, is lower than its short-run average cost in equilibrium, $28.

The firm does not operate at a loss in the long run when all inputs are variable. It shuts down if the market price falls below the firm's minimum long-run average cost of $24. Thus, the competitive firm's long-run supply curve is its long-run marginal cost curve above $24.

Figure 8.10 The Short-Run and Long-Run Supply Curves

The firm's long-run supply curve, S^{LR}, is zero below its minimum average cost of $24 and equals the long-run marginal cost, *LRMC*, at higher prices. The firm produces more in the long run than in the short run, 110 units instead of 50 units, and earns a higher profit, area $A + B$, instead of just area A.

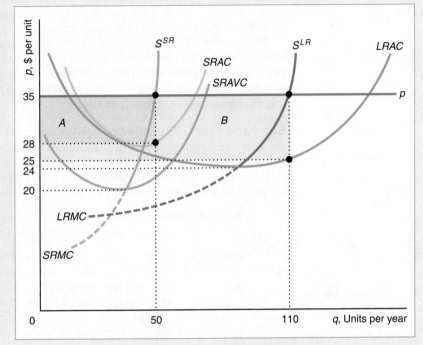

When a large number of firms initially built ethanol processing plants, they built relatively small ones. When the ethanol market took off in the first half decade of the twenty-first century, with the price reaching a peak of $4.23 a gallon in June 2006, many firms built larger plants or greatly increased their plant size. Then, with the more recent collapse of that market—the price fell below $3 and often below $1.50 from 2007 through 2012—many firms either closed their plants or reduced their size. The capacity of plants under construction or expansion went from 3,644 million gallons per year in 2005 to 5,635 in 2007, but since then the size has fallen to 1,432 in 2010 and 522 in 2011.

Long-Run Market Supply Curve

The competitive market supply curve is the horizontal sum of the supply curves of the individual firms in both the short run and the long run. Because the maximum number of firms in the market is fixed in the short run, we add the supply curves of a known number of firms to obtain the short-run market supply curve. The only way for the market to supply more output in the short run is for existing firms to produce more.

In the long run, firms can enter or leave the market. Thus, before we can add all the relevant firm supply curves to obtain the long-run market supply curve, we need to determine how many firms are in the market at each possible market price.

To construct the long-run market supply curve properly, we also have to determine how input prices vary with output. As the market expands or contracts substantially, changes in factor prices may shift firms' cost and supply curves. If so, we need to determine how such shifts in factor prices affect firm supply curves so that we can properly construct the market supply curve. The effect of changes in input prices is greater in the long run than in the short run because market output can change more dramatically in the long run.

We now look in detail at how entry and changing factor prices affect long-run market supply. We first derive the long-run market supply curve, assuming that the price of inputs remains constant as market output increases, so as to isolate the role of entry. We then examine how the market supply curve is affected if the price of inputs changes as market output rises.

Entry and Exit. The number of firms in a market in the long run is determined by the *entry* and *exit* of firms. In the United States, an estimated 198,000 new firms began operations and 167,000 firms exited in the fourth quarter of 2010.[10]

In the long run, each firm decides whether to enter or exit, depending on whether it can make a long-run profit. In a market with free entry and exit:

- A firm enters the market if it can make a long-run profit, $\pi > 0$.
- A firm exits the market to avoid a long-run loss, $\pi < 0$.

If firms in a market are making zero long-run profit, they are indifferent between staying in the market and exiting. We presume that if they are already in the market, they stay in the market when they are making zero long-run profit.

If the demand curve shifts to the right so that profit initially increases, entry occurs until the last firm to enter—the *marginal firm*—makes zero long-run profit. Similarly, when the demand curve shifts to the left, exit occurs until the marginal firm earns zero long-run profit.

In markets without barriers or fixed costs to entry, firms enter and exit freely. For example, many construction firms, which have no capital and provide only labor services, engage in *hit-and-run* entry and exit: They enter the market whenever they can make a profit and exit whenever they can't. These firms may enter and exit markets several times a year.

Entry or exit is typically easy in many agriculture, construction, wholesale and retail trade, transportation, and service industries, unless governments regulate them. Relatively few airline, trucking, or shipping firms serve a particular route, but they face extensive potential entry. Other firms can and will quickly enter and serve a route if a profit opportunity appears. Entrants shift their highly mobile equipment from less profitable routes to more profitable ones. A clear example is shipping firms, which move their vessels from one port to another as profit opportunities occur.

However, in many markets, firms face barriers to entry or must incur significant costs to enter. Entry and exit are relatively difficult in many manufacturing and mining industries as well as in government-regulated industries such as public utilities and insurance. Many city governments limit the number of cab drivers, creating an insurmountable barrier that prevents additional firms from entering. In some markets, a new firm considering entry must hire consultants to determine the profit opportunities, pay lawyers to write contracts, and incur other expenses. Typically, such costs of entry (or exit) are fixed costs.

Even if existing firms are making positive profits, no entry occurs in the short run if entering firms need time to find a location, build a new plant, and hire workers. In the long run, firms enter the market if they can make profits by so doing. The costs of entry are often lower, and hence the profits from entering are higher, if a

[10]www.bls.gov/web/cewbd/table11_1.txt (viewed June 17, 2012).

firm takes its time to enter. As a result, firms may enter markets long after profit opportunities first appear. In contrast, firms usually react faster to losses than to potential profits. We expect firms to shut down or exit the market quickly in the short run when price is below average variable cost.

APPLICATION Fast-Food Firms Entry in Russia	American fast-food restaurants are flooding into Russia. When McDonald's opened its first restaurant in Pushkin Square in 1990, workers greeted gigantic lines of customers. Today, it has 279 restaurants in Russia. For years, McDonald's faced little western competition, despite the popularity of western fast food. Belatedly recognizing the profit opportunities, other chains are flooding into Russia. Burger King opened 22 restaurants in just two years, Carl's Jr. has 17 restaurants in just two cities, Wendy's has 2 restaurants and plans to have 180 throughout Russia by 2020, Subway has about 200 shops under several franchisees, and Yum Brands (which owns KFC, Pizza Hut, and Taco Bell) has about 350 restaurants in Russia. Moscow is particularly ripe for entry by pizza restaurants. With a population of 13 million, it has only about 300 pizza restaurants. In contrast, Manhattan, with a population only about a tenth as large (1.6 million) has 4,000 pizza joints. Christopher Wynne, an American who is fluent in Russian and gained Russian expertise researching arms proliferation, left his original career to open pizza restaurants in Russia. He bought 51% of the Papa John's Russian franchise. Although he competes with the U.S. chains Sbarro and Domino's and a Russian chain, Pizza Fabrika, among others, he says, "I could succeed in my sleep there is so much opportunity here." In 2011, Mr. Wynne opened his twenty-fifth Papa John's outlet in Russia, doubling the number from the previous year. Nineteen of them are in Moscow. Each restaurant costs about $400,000 to open, but a restaurant can start earning an operating profit in three months. Mr. Wynne will continue opening outlets until the marginal restaurant earns zero economic profit.

Long-Run Market Supply with Identical Firms and Free Entry. The *long-run market supply curve is flat* at the minimum long-run average cost *if firms can freely enter and exit* the market, an unlimited number of *firms have identical costs*, and *input prices are constant*. This result follows from our reasoning about the short-run supply curve, in which we showed that the more firms there are in the market, the flatter the market supply curve. With many firms in the market in the long run, the market supply curve is effectively flat. (In the vegetable oil market "many" is 10 firms.)

The long-run supply curve of a typical vegetable oil mill, S^1 in panel a of Figure 8.11, is the long-run marginal cost curve above a minimum long-run average cost of $10. Because each firm shuts down if the market price is below $10, the long-run market supply curve is zero at a price below $10. If the price rises above $10, firms make positive profits, so new firms enter, expanding market output until profits are driven to zero, where price is again $10. The long-run market supply curve in panel b is a horizontal line at the minimum long-run average cost of the typical firm, $10. At a price of $10, each firm produces $q = 150$ units (where one unit equals 100 metric tons). Thus, the total output produced by n firms in the market is $Q = nq = n \times 150$ units. Extra market output is obtained by new firms entering the market.

Figure 8.11 Long-Run Firm and Market Supply with Identical Vegetable Oil Firms

(a) The long-run supply curve of a typical vegetable oil mill, S^1, is the long-run marginal cost curve above the minimum average cost of $10. (b) The long-run market supply curve is horizontal at the minimum of the long-run minimum average cost of a typical firm. Each firm produces 150 units, so market output is $150n$, where n is the number of firms.

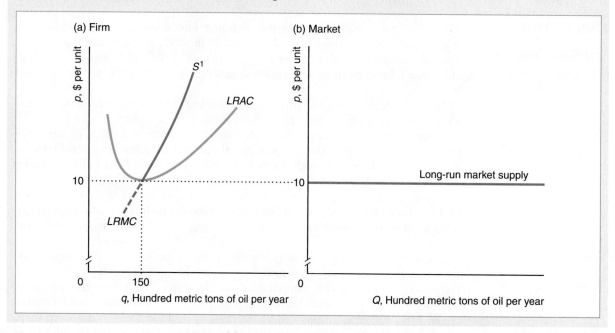

In summary, the long-run market supply curve is horizontal if the market has free entry and exit, an unlimited number of firms have identical costs, and input prices are constant. When these strong assumptions do not hold, the long-run market supply curve has a slope, as we now show.

Long-Run Market Supply When Entry Is Limited. If the number of firms in a market is limited in the long run, the market supply curve slopes upward. The number of firms is limited if the government restricts that number, if firms need a scarce resource, or if entry is costly. An example of a scarce resource is the limited number of lots on which a luxury Miami beachfront hotel can be built. High entry costs restrict the number of firms in a market because firms enter only if the long-run economic profit is greater than the cost of entering.

The only way to increase output if the number of firms is limited is for existing firms to produce more. Because individual firms' supply curves slope upward, the long-run market supply curve is also upward sloping. The reasoning is the same as in the short run, as panel b of Figure 8.7 illustrates, given that no more than five firms can enter. The market supply curve is the upward-sloping S^5 curve, which is the horizontal sum of the five firms' upward-sloping marginal cost curves above minimum average cost.

Long-Run Market Supply When Firms Differ. A second reason why some long-run market supply curves slope upward is that firms differ. Because firms with relatively low minimum long-run average costs are willing to enter the market at lower prices than others, an upward-sloping long-run market supply curve results. The long-run supply curve is upward sloping due to differences in costs across firms *only* if the amount that lower-cost firms can produce is limited. If there were an unlimited number of the lowest-cost firms, no higher-cost firm would produce. Effectively, then, the only firms producing in the market would have the same low costs of production.

APPLICATION

Upward-Sloping
Long-Run Supply
Curve for Cotton

Many countries produce cotton. Production costs differ among countries because of differences in the quality of land, rainfall, irrigation and labor costs, and other factors.

The length of each step-like segment of the long-run supply curve of cotton in the graph is the quantity produced by the named country. The amount that the low-cost countries can produce must be limited, or we would not observe production by the higher-cost countries.

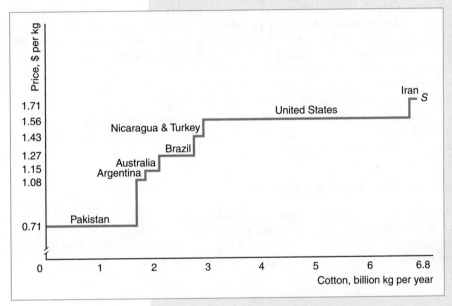

The height of each segment of the supply curve is the typical minimum average cost of production in that country. The average cost of production in Pakistan is less than half that in Iran. The supply curve has a step-like appearance because we are using an average of the estimated average cost in each country, which is a single number. If we knew the individual firms' supply curves in each of these countries, the market supply curve would have a smoother shape.

As the market price rises, the number of countries producing rises. At market prices below $1.08 per kilogram, only Pakistan produces. If the market price is below $1.50, the United States and Iran do not produce. If the price increases to $1.56, the United States supplies a large amount of cotton. In this range of the supply curve, supply is very elastic. For Iran to produce, the price has to rise to $1.71. Price increases in that range result in only a relatively small increase in supply. Thus, the supply curve is relatively inelastic at prices above $1.56.

Long-Run Market Supply When Input Prices Vary with Output. A third reason why market supply curves may slope is non-constant input prices. In markets where factor prices rise or fall when output increases, the long-run supply curve slopes even if firms have identical costs and can freely enter and exit.

If a relatively small share of the total quantity of a factor of production is used in a specific market, as that market's output expands, the price of the factor is unlikely to be affected. For example, dentists do not hire enough receptionists to affect the market wage for receptionists.

In contrast, if a very large share of a factor is used in one market, the price of that input is more likely to vary with that market's output. As jet plane manufacturers expand and buy more jet engines, the price of these engines rises because the jet plane manufacturers are the sole purchasers of these engines.

To produce more goods, firms must use more inputs. If the prices of some or all inputs rise when more inputs are purchased, the cost of producing the final good also rises. We call a market in which input prices rise with output an *increasing-cost market*. Few steelworkers have no fear of heights and are willing to construct tall buildings, so their supply curve is steeply upward sloping. As more skyscrapers are built at one time, the demand curve for these workers shifts to the right, driving up their wage.

We assume that all firms in a market have the same cost curves and that input prices rise as market output expands. We use the cost curves of a representative firm in panel a of Figure 8.12 to derive the upward-sloping market supply curve in panel b.

When input prices are relatively low, each identical firm has the same long-run marginal cost curve, MC^1, and average cost curve, AC^1, in panel a. A typical firm produces at minimum average cost, e_1, and sells q_1 units of output. The market supply is Q_1 in panel b when the market price is p_1. The n_1 firms collectively sell $Q_1 = n_1 q_1$ units of output, which is point E_1 on the market supply curve in panel b.

If the market demand curve shifts outward, the market price rises to p_2, new firms enter, and market output rises to Q_2, causing input prices to rise. As a result, the marginal cost curve shifts from MC^1 to MC^2, and the average cost curve rises from AC^1 to AC^2. The typical firm produces at a higher minimum average cost, e_2. At this higher price, there are n_2 firms in the market, so market output is $Q_2 = n_2 q_2$ at point E_2 on the market supply curve.

Figure 8.12 Long-Run Market Supply in an Increasing-Cost Market

At a relatively low market output, Q_1 in panel b, the firm's long-run marginal and average cost curves are MC^1 and AC^1 in panel a. At the higher market quantity Q_2, the cost curves shift upward to MC^2 and AC^2 as a result of the higher input prices. Given identical firms, each firm produces at minimum average cost, such as points e_1 and e_2. Long-run market supply, S, is upward sloping.

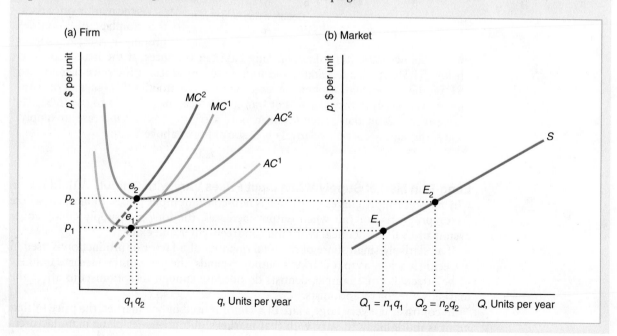

Thus, in both an increasing-cost market and a *constant-cost market*—where input prices remain constant as output increases—firms produce at minimum average cost in the long run. The difference is that the minimum average cost rises as market output increases in an increasing-cost market, whereas minimum average cost remains constant in a constant-cost market. In conclusion, *the long-run supply curve is upward sloping in an increasing-cost market and flat in a constant-cost market.*

In a decreasing-cost market, as market output rises, at least some factor prices fall. As a result, in a decreasing-cost market, the long-run market supply curve is downward sloping.

Increasing returns to scale may cause factor prices to fall. For example, when DVD drives were first introduced, relatively few were manufactured, and their cost of manufacturing was relatively high. Due to the high price of DVD drives and the lack of DVDs, there was much less demand for DVD drives than there is today. As demand for DVD drives increased, it became practical to automate more of the production process so that drives could be produced at a lower average cost. The resulting decrease in the price of these drives lowered the cost of personal computers.

To summarize, theory tells us that competitive long-run market supply curves may be flat, upward sloping, or downward sloping. If all firms are identical in a market in which firms can freely enter and input prices are constant, the long-run market supply curve is flat. If entry is limited, firms differ in costs, or input prices rise with output, the long-run supply curve is upward sloping. Finally, if input prices fall with market output, the long-run supply curve may be downward sloping.[11]

Long-Run Market Supply Curve with Trade. Cotton, oil, and many other goods are traded on world markets. The world equilibrium price and quantity for a good are determined by the intersection of the world supply curve—the horizontal sum of the supply curves of each producing country—and the world demand curve—the horizontal sum of the demand curves of each consuming country.

A country that imports a good has a supply curve that is the horizontal sum of its domestic industry's supply curve and the import supply curve. The domestic supply curve is the competitive long-run supply curve that we have just derived. However, we need to determine the import supply curve.

A country's import supply curve is the world's **residual supply curve**: the quantity that the market supplies that is not consumed by other demanders at any given price.[12] Because the country buys only that part of the world supply, $S(p)$, that is not consumed by any *other* demander elsewhere in the world, $D^o(p)$, its residual supply function, $S^r(p)$, is

$$S^r(p) = S(p) - D^o(p). \qquad (8.16)$$

At prices so low that $D^o(p)$ is greater than $S(p)$, the residual supply, $S^r(p)$, is zero.

In Figure 8.13, we derive Japan's residual supply curve for cotton in panel a using the world supply curve, S, and the demand curve of the rest of the world, D^o, in panel b. The scales differ for the quantity axes in the two panels. At a price of $850 per metric ton, the demand in other countries exhausts world supply (D^o intersects S at 32 million metric tons per year), so there is no residual supply for Japan. At a much higher price, $935, Japan's excess supply, 4 million metric tons, is the

---

[11]See "Slope of Long-Run Market Supply Curves" in MyEconLab, Chapter Resources, Chapter 8.

[12]*Jargon alert:* It is traditional to use the expression *excess supply* when discussing international trade and *residual supply* otherwise, though the terms are equivalent.

Figure 8.13 Excess or Residual Supply Curve

Japan's excess supply curve, S^r, for cotton is the horizontal difference between the world's supply curve, S, and the demand curve of the other countries in the world, D^o.

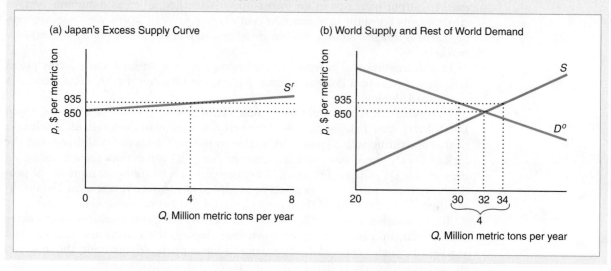

(a) Japan's Excess Supply Curve

(b) World Supply and Rest of World Demand

difference between the world supply, 30 million tons, and the quantity demanded elsewhere, 34 million tons. As the figure illustrates, the residual supply curve facing Japan is much closer to horizontal than the world supply curve.

The elasticity of residual supply, η_r, facing a given country is[13]

$$\eta_r = \frac{\eta}{\theta} - \frac{1-\theta}{\theta}\varepsilon_o,\qquad(8.17)$$

where η is the market supply elasticity, ε_o is the demand elasticity of the other countries, and $\theta = Q_r/Q$ is the importing country's share of the world's output.

If a country imports a small fraction of the world's supply, we expect it to face an almost perfectly elastic, horizontal residual supply curve. On the other hand, a relatively large consumer of the good might face an upward-sloping residual supply curve.

We can illustrate this difference for cotton, where $\eta = 0.5$ and $\varepsilon = -0.7$ (Green et al., 2005). The United States imports only $\theta = 0.1\%$ of the world's cotton, so its residual supply elasticity is

$$\eta_r = \frac{\eta}{0.001} - \frac{0.999}{0.001}\varepsilon_o$$

$$= 1,000\eta - 999\varepsilon_o$$

$$= (1,000 \times 0.5) - [999 \times (-0.)7] = 1,199.3,$$

which is 2,398.6 times more elastic than the world's supply elasticity. Canada's import share is 10 times larger, $\theta = 1\%$, so its residual supply elasticity is "only" 119.3. Nonetheless, its residual supply curve is nearly horizontal: A 1% increase in the price would induce imports to more than double, rising by 119.3%. Even Japan's $\theta = 2.5\%$ leads to a relatively elastic $\eta_r = 46.4$. In contrast, China imports 18.5% of the world's cotton, so its residual supply elasticity is 5.8. Even though its

[13]The derivation of this equation is similar to that of Equation 8.2.

residual supply elasticity is more than 11 times larger than the world's elasticity, it is still small enough for its excess supply curve to be upward sloping.

Thus, if a country is *small*—it imports a small share of the world's output—then it faces a horizontal import supply curve at the world equilibrium price. If its domestic supply curve lies strictly above the world price, then the country only imports and faces a horizontal supply curve. If some portion of its upward-sloping domestic supply curve lies below the world price, then its total supply curve is the same as the upward-sloping domestic supply curve up to the world price and is horizontal at the world price (Chapter 9 shows this type of supply curve for oil).

This analysis of trade applies to trade within a country too. The following application shows that it can be used to look at trade across geographic areas or jurisdictions such as states.

APPLICATION

Reformulated Gasoline Supply Curves

You can't buy the gasoline sold in Milwaukee in other parts of Wisconsin. Houston gas isn't the same as western Texas gas. California, Minnesota, Nevada, and most of America's biggest cities use one or more of at least 46 specialized blends—sometimes referred to as *boutique fuels*—while much of the rest of the country uses regular (generic) gasoline.

Because special blends are often designed to cut air pollution, they are more likely to be required by the U.S. Clean Air Act Amendments, state laws, or local ordinances in areas with serious pollution problems. For example, the objective of the federal Reformulated Fuels Program (RFG) is to reduce ground-level ozone-forming pollutants. It specifies both content criteria (such as benzene content limits) and emissions-based performance standards for refiners.

Only about 17.7 million barrels of crude oil could be processed per day by the 148 U.S. refineries in 2011 (with several slated to close in 2012), compared to the 18.6 million barrels that the then 324 refineries could process in 1981. Many of these remaining refineries produce regular gasoline, which is sold throughout most of the country. In states in which regular gasoline is used, wholesalers in one state ship gasoline across state lines in response to slightly higher prices in neighboring states. Consequently, the residual supply curve for regular gasoline for a given state is close to horizontal.

In contrast, gasoline is usually not imported into jurisdictions that require special blends. Few refiners produce any given special blend. Only 13 California refineries can produce California's special low-polluting blend of gasoline, California Reformulated Gasoline (CaRFG).[14] Because refineries require expensive upgrades to produce a new kind of gas, they generally do not switch from producing one type of gas to another type. Thus, even if the price of gasoline rises in California, wholesalers in other states do not send gasoline to California, because they cannot legally sell regular gasoline in California and it would cost too much to start producing CaRFG.

Consequently, unlike the nearly horizontal residual supply curve for regular gasoline, the reformulated gasoline residual supply curve is eventually upward sloping. At relatively small quantities, refineries can produce more gasoline without incurring higher costs, so the supply curve in this region is relatively flat. However, to produce much larger quantities of gasoline, refiners have to run their plants around the clock and convert a larger fraction of each gallon of oil into gasoline, incurring higher costs of production. Because of this higher cost, they are willing to sell larger quantities in this range only at a higher price, so the

---

[14]Auffhammer and Kellogg (2011) showed that California's regulation helps to reduce ground-level ozone, significantly improving air quality, but that current federal regulations are not effective.

supply curve slopes upward. When the refineries reach capacity, no matter how high the price gets, firms cannot produce more gasoline (at least until new refineries go online), so the supply curve becomes vertical.

California normally operates in the steeply upward-sloping section of its supply curve. At the end of the summer of 2009, when gas prices fell in the rest of the nation, California's gas price jumped an extra 30¢ per gallon relative to the average national price due to a series of production problems at its refineries.

Brown et al. (2008) found that when the RFG was first imposed, prices in regulated metropolitan areas increased by an average of 3¢ per gallon relative to unregulated areas—and the jump was over 7¢ in some cities such as Chicago—as the demand curve went from intersecting the supply curve in the flat section to intersecting it in the upward sloping section.

SOLVED PROBLEM 8.4

In the short run, what happens to the competitive market price of gasoline if the demand curve in a state shifts to the right as more people move to the state or start driving gas-hogging SUVs? In your answer, distinguish between areas in which regular gasoline is sold and jurisdictions that require special blends.

Answer

1. *Show the effect of a shift of the demand curve in areas that use regular gasoline.* In an area using regular gasoline, the supply curve is horizontal, as panel a of the figure shows. Thus, as the demand curve shifts to the right from D^1 to D^2, the equilibrium shifts along the supply curve from e_1 to e_2, and the price remains at p_1.

2. *Show the effects of both a small and large shift of the demand curve in a jurisdiction that uses a special blend.* The supply curve in panel b is drawn as described in the Application "Reformulated Gasoline Supply Curves." If the demand curve shifts slightly to the right from D^1 to D^2, the price remains unchanged at p_1 because the demand curve continues to intersect the supply curve in the flat region. However, if the demand curve shifts farther to the right to D^3, then the new intersection is in the upward-sloping section of the supply curve and the price increases to p_2. Consequently, unforeseen "jumps" in demand are more likely to cause a *price spike*—a large increase in price—in jurisdictions that use special blends.

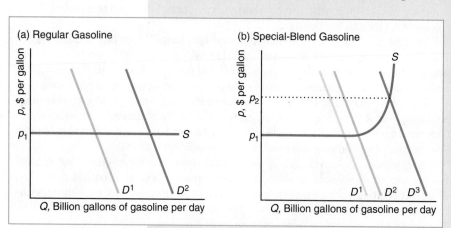

(a) Regular Gasoline — *p*, $ per gallon vs. *Q*, Billion gallons of gasoline per day; D^1, D^2, S, p_1

(b) Special-Blend Gasoline — *p*, $ per gallon vs. *Q*, Billion gallons of gasoline per day; D^1, D^2, D^3, S, p_1, p_2

Long-Run Competitive Equilibrium

The intersection of the long-run market supply and demand curves determines the long-run competitive equilibrium. With identical firms, constant input prices, and free entry and exit, the long-run competitive market supply is horizontal at minimum long-run average cost, so the equilibrium price equals long-run average cost. A shift in the demand curve affects only the equilibrium quantity and not the equilibrium price, which remains constant at the minimum long-run average cost.

The market supply curve is different in the short run than in the long run, so the long-run competitive equilibrium differs from the short-run equilibrium. The relationship between the short- and long-run equilibria depends on where the market demand curve crosses the short- and long-run market supply curves. Figure 8.14 illustrates this point using the short- and long-run supply curves for the vegetable oil mill market.

The short-run supply curve for a typical firm in panel a is the marginal cost curve above the minimum of the average variable cost, $7. At a price of $7, each firm produces 100 units, so the 20 firms in the market in the short run collectively supply $2,000 (= 20 \times 100)$ units of oil in panel b. At higher prices, the short-run market supply curve slopes upward because it is the horizontal summation of the firm's upward-sloping marginal cost curves.

We assume that the firms use the same size plant in the short run and the long run so that the minimum average cost is $10 in both the short run and the long run. Because all firms have the same costs and can enter freely, the long-run market supply curve is flat at the minimum average cost, $10, in panel b. At prices between $7 and $10, firms supply goods at a loss in the short run but not in the long run.

If the market demand curve is D^1, the short-run market equilibrium, F_1, lies below and to the right of the long-run market equilibrium, E_1. This relationship is reversed if the market demand curve is D^2.[15]

Figure 8.14 The Short-Run and Long-Run Equilibria for Vegetable Oil

(a) A typical vegetable oil mill is willing to produce 100 units of oil at a price of $7, 150 units at $10, or 165 units at $11. (b) The short-run market supply curve, S^{SR}, is the horizontal sum of 20 individual firms' short-run marginal cost curves above minimum average variable cost, $7. The long-run market supply curve, S^{LR}, is horizontal at the minimum average cost, $10. If the demand curve is D^1 in the short-run equilibrium, F_1, 20 firms sell 2,000 units of oil at $7. In the long-run equilibrium, E_1, 10 firms sell 1,500 units at $10. If demand is D^2, the short-run equilibrium is F_2 ($11; 3,300 units; 20 firms) and the long-run equilibrium is E_2 ($10; 3,600 units; 24 firms).

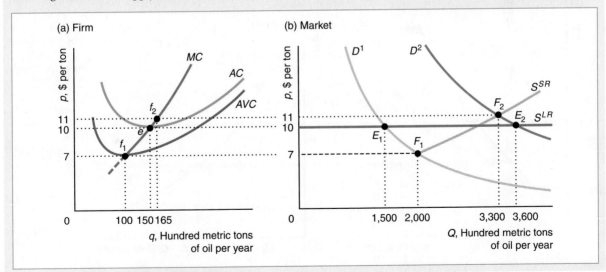

[15]Using data from *Statistics Canada*, I estimated that the elasticity of demand for vegetable oil is −0.8. Both D^1 and D^2 are constant −0.8 elasticity demand curves, but the demand at any price on D^2 is 2.4 times that on D^1.

In the short run, if the demand is as low as D^1, the market price in the short-run equilibrium, F_1, is \$7. At that price, each of the 20 firms produces 100 units, at f_1 in panel a. The firms lose money because the price of \$7 is below average cost at 100 units. These losses drive some of the firms out of the market in the long run, so market output falls and the market price rises. In the long-run equilibrium, E_1, price is \$10, and each firm produces 150 units, e, and breaks even. As the market demands only 1,500 units, only 10 (= 1,500/150) firms produce, so half the firms that produced in the short run exit the market.[16] Thus, with the D^1 demand curve, price rises and output falls in the long run.

If demand expands to D^2 in the short run, each of the 20 firms expands its output to 165 units, f_2, and the price rises to \$11, where the firms make profits: The price of \$11 is above the average cost at 165 units. These profits attract entry in the long run, and the price falls. In the long-run equilibrium, each firm produces 150 units, e, and 3,600 units are sold by the market, E_2, by 24 (= 3,600/150) firms. Thus, with the D^2 demand curve, price falls and output rises in the long run.

Because firms may enter and exit in the long run, taxes can have a counterintuitive effect on the competitive equilibrium. For example, as the following Challenge Solution shows, a lump-sum franchise tax causes the competitive equilibrium output of a firm to increase even though market output falls.

CHALLENGE SOLUTION

The Rising Cost of Keeping On Truckin'

We return to the Challenge questions about the effects of higher annual fees and other lump-sum costs on the trucking market price and quantity, the output of individual firms, and the number of trucking firms (assuming that the demand curve remains constant). Because firms may enter and exit this industry in the long run, such higher lump-sum costs can have a counterintuitive effect on the competitive equilibrium.

All trucks of a certain size are essentially identical, and trucks can easily enter and exit the industry (government regulations aside). Panel a of the figure shows a typical firm's cost curves and panel b shows the market equilibrium.

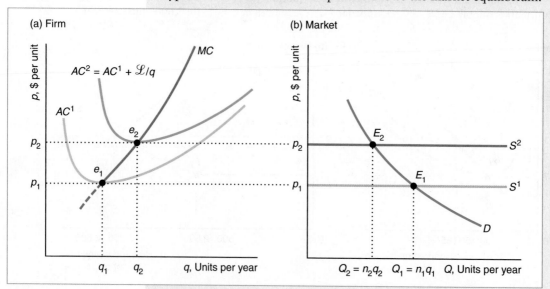

---

[16]Which firms leave? If the firms are identical, the theory says nothing about which ones leave and which ones stay. The firms that leave make zero economic profit, and those that stay make zero economic profit, so firms are indifferent as to whether to stay or exit.

The new, higher fees and other lump-sum costs raise the fixed cost of operating by $\mathcal{L}$. In panel a, a lump-sum, franchise tax shifts the typical firm's average cost curve upward from AC^1 to $AC^2 = AC^1 + \mathcal{L}/q$ but does not affect the marginal cost. As a result, the minimum average cost rises from e_1 to e_2.

Given that an unlimited number of identical truckers are willing to operate in this market, the long-run market supply is horizontal at minimum average cost. Thus, the market supply curve shifts upward in panel b by the same amount as the minimum average cost increases. Given a downward-sloping market demand curve D, the new equilibrium, E_2, has a lower quantity, $Q_2 < Q_1$, and higher price, $p_2 > p_1$, than the original equilibrium, E_1.

As the market price rises, the quantity that a firm produces rises from q_1 to q_2 in panel a. Because the marginal cost curve is upward sloping at the original equilibrium, when the average cost curve shifts up due to the higher fixed cost, the new minimum point on the average cost curve corresponds to a larger output than in the original equilibrium. Thus, any trucking firm still operating in the market produces at a larger volume.

Because the market quantity falls but each firm remaining in the market produces more, the number of firms in the market must fall. At the initial equilibrium, the number of firms was $n_1 = Q_1/q_1$. The new equilibrium number of firms, $n_2 = Q_2/q_2$, must be smaller than n_1 because $Q_2 < Q_1$ and $q_2 > q_1$. Therefore, an increase in fixed cost causes the market price and quantity to rise and the number of trucking firms to fall, as most people would have expected, but it has the surprising effect that it causes producing firms to increase the amount of services that they provide.

SUMMARY

1. **Perfect Competition.** Competitive firms are price takers that cannot influence market price. Markets are likely to be competitive if a large number of buyers and sellers transact in a market, all firms produce identical products, all market participants have full information about price and product characteristics, transaction costs are negligible, and firms can easily enter and exit the market. A competitive firm faces a horizontal demand curve at the market price.

2. **Profit Maximization.** Most firms maximize economic profit, which is revenue minus economic cost (explicit and implicit costs). Because business profit (which is revenue minus explicit cost) does not include implicit cost, economic profit tends to be less than business profit. A firm earning zero economic profit is making as much as it could if its resources were devoted to their best alternative uses. To maximize profit, all firms (not just competitive firms) must make two decisions. First, the firm must determine the quantity of output at which its profit is highest. Profit is maximized when marginal profit is zero or, equivalently, when marginal revenue equals marginal cost. Second, the firm must decide whether to produce at all.

3. **Competition in the Short Run.** Because a competitive firm is a price taker, its marginal revenue equals the market price. As a result, a competitive firm maximizes its profit by setting its output so that its short-run marginal cost equals the market price. The firm

shuts down if the market price is less than its minimum average variable cost. Thus, a profit-maximizing competitive firm's short-run supply curve is its marginal cost curve above its minimum average variable cost. The short-run market supply curve, which is the sum of the supply curves of the fixed number of firms producing in the short run, is flat at low output levels and upward sloping at larger levels. The short-run competitive equilibrium is determined by the intersection of the market demand curve and the short-run market supply curve. The effect of an increase in demand depends on whether demand intersects the market supply in the flat or upward-sloping section.

4. **Competition in the Long Run.** In the long run, a competitive firm sets its output where the market price equals its long-run marginal cost. It shuts down if the market price is less than the minimum of its long-run average cost because all costs are variable in the long run. Consequently, the competitive firm's supply curve is its long-run marginal cost above its minimum long-run average cost. The long-run supply curve of a firm may have a different slope than the short-run curve because the firm can vary its fixed factors in the long run. The long-run market supply curve is the horizontal sum of the supply curves of all the firms in the market. If all firms are identical, entry and exit are easy, and input prices are constant, the long-run market supply curve is flat at minimum

average cost. If firms differ, entry is difficult or costly, or input prices vary with output, the long-run market supply curve has an upward slope. The long-run market supply curve slopes upward if input prices

increase with output and slopes downward if input prices decrease with output. The long-run market equilibrium price and quantity are different from the short-run price and quantity.

EXERCISES

■ = *exercise is available on* MyEconLab; * = *answer appears at the back of this book;* **M** = *mathematical problem.*

1. Perfect Competition

1.1 A large city has nearly 500 restaurants, with new ones entering regularly as the population grows. The city decides to limit the number of restaurant licenses to 500. Which characteristics of this market are consistent with perfect competition and which are not? Is this restaurant market likely to be nearly perfectly competitive? Explain your answer.

1.2 Why would high transaction costs or imperfect information tend to prevent price-taking behavior?

2. Profit Maximization

2.1 Should a competitive firm ever produce when it is losing money? Why or why not?

2.2 Should a firm shut down (and why) if its revenue is $R = \$1,000$ per week and

 a. its variable cost is $VC = \$500$, and its sunk fixed cost is $F = \$600$?

 b. its variable cost is $VC = \$1,001$, and its sunk fixed cost $F = \$500$?

 c. its variable cost is $VC = \$500$, its fixed cost is 800, of which 600 is avoidable if it shuts down?

*2.3 A competitive firm's bookkeeper, upon reviewing the firm's books, finds that the company spent twice as much on its plant, a fixed cost, as the firm's manager had previously thought. Should the manager change the output level because of this new information? How does this new information affect profit?

2.4 Mercedes-Benz of San Francisco advertises on the radio that it has been owned and operated by the same family in the same location for 50 years (as of 2012). It then makes two claims: first, that it has lower overhead than other nearby auto dealers because it has owned this land for 50 years, and second, that it charges a lower price for its cars because of its lower overhead. Discuss the logic of these claims.

*2.5 A firm's profit function is $\pi(q) = R(q) - C(q) = 120q - (200 + 40q + 10q^2)$. What is the positive output level that maximizes the firm's profit (or minimizes its loss)? What is the firm's revenue, variable cost, and profit? Should it operate or shut down in the short run?

3. Competition in the Short Run

3.1 In Figure 8.3, why is the revenue curve a straight line in panel a? What is the slope of the revenue curve? What is the slope of the profit curve at the q where profit is maximized? What can you say about the slopes of the cost and revenue curves at the q where profit is maximized? Why is profit equal to the gold box in panel b?

3.2 The cost function for Acme Laundry is $C(q) = 10 + 10q + q^2$, where q is tons of laundry cleaned. What q should the firm choose to maximize its profit if the market price is p? How much does it produce if $p = 50$? **M**

3.3 If the cost function for John's Shoe Repair is $C(q) = 100 + 10q - q^2 + \frac{1}{3}q^3$, what is the firm's marginal cost function? What is its profit-maximizing condition if the market price is p? What is its supply curve? **M**

3.4 The government imposes a specific tax of $\tau = 2$ on laundry. Acme Laundry's pre-tax cost function is $C(q) = 10 + 10q + q^2$. How much should the firm produce to maximize its after-tax profit if the market price is p? How much does it produce if $p = 50$? (*Hint:* See Exercise 3.2 and Solved Problem 8.1.) **M**

3.5 If the pre-tax cost function for John's Shoe Repair is $C(q) = 100 + 10q - q^2 + \frac{1}{3}q^3$, and it faces a specific tax of $\tau = 10$, what is its profit-maximizing condition if the market price is p? Can you solve for a single, profit maximizing q in terms of p? (*Hint:* See Exercise 3.3 and Solved Problem 8.1.) **M**

3.6 If a specific subsidy (negative tax) of s is given to only one competitive firm, how should that firm change its output level to maximize its profit, and how does its maximum profit change? Use a graph to illustrate your answer. (*Hint:* See Solved Problem 8.1.)

3.7 What is the effect of an ad valorem tax of α (the share of the price that goes to the government) on a competitive firm's profit-maximizing output? (*Hint:* See Solved Problem 8.1.)

3.8 According to the Application "Oil, Oil Sands, and Oil Shale Shutdowns," due to technological advances, the minimum average variable cost of processing oil sands dropped from $25 a barrel in the 1960s to $18 today. In a figure, show how this change affects the supply curve of a typical competitive firm and the supply curve of all the firms producing oil from oil sands.

*3.9 For Red Delicious apple farmers in Washington, 2001 was a terrible year (Linda Ashton, "Bumper Crop a Bummer for Struggling Apple Farmers," *San Francisco Chronicle*, January 9, 2001, C7). The average price for Red Delicious apples was $10.61 per box, well below the shutdown level of $13.23. Many farmers did not pick the apples. Other farmers bulldozed their trees, getting out of the Red Delicious business for good, removing 25,000 acres from production. Why did some farmers choose not to pick apples, and others to bulldoze their trees? (*Hint*: Consider the average variable cost and expectations about future prices.)

3.10 When gasoline prices spike, producers consider using oil fields that once had been passed over because of the high costs of extracting oil.

a. In a figure, show what this statement implies about the shape of the oil extraction cost function.

b. Use the cost function you drew in part a to show how an increase in the market price of gasoline affects the amount of oil that a competitive firm extracts. Show the change in the firm's equilibrium profit.

*3.11 If a competitive firm's cost function is $C(q) = a + bq + cq^2 + dq^3$, where a, b, c, and d are constants, what is the firm's marginal cost function? What is the firm's profit-maximizing condition? (*Hint*: See Solved Problem 8.2.) **M**

3.12 A Christmas tree seller has a cost function $C = 6,860 + (p_T + t + 7/12)q + 37/27,000,000q^3$, where $p_T = 11.50 is the wholesale price of each tree and $t = 2.00 is the shipping price per tree. What is the seller's marginal cost function? What is the shutdown price? What is the seller's short-run supply function? If the seller's supply curve is $S(q, t)$, what is $\partial(q, t)/\partial t$? Evaluate it at $p_T = 11.50 and $t = 2.00. (*Hint*: See Solved Problem 8.2) **M**

*3.13 Many marginal cost curves are U-shaped. Consequently, the *MC* curve can equal price at two output levels. Which is the profit-maximizing output? Why?

3.14 Each of the 10 firms in a competitive market has a cost function of $C = 25 + q^2$. The market demand function is $Q = 120 - p$. Determine the equilibrium price, quantity per firm, and market quantity. **M**

3.15 Given the information in the previous exercise, what effect does a specific tax of $2.40 per unit have on the equilibrium price and quantities? (*Hint*: See Solved Problem 8.3.) **M**

4. Competition in the Long Run

4.1 Redraw Figure 8.10 to show the situation where the short-run plant size is too large, relative to the optimal long-run plant size.

*4.2 What is the effect on firm and market equilibrium of the U.S. law requiring a firm to give its workers six months' notice before it can shut down its plant?

4.3 Each firm in a competitive market has a cost function of $C = q + q^2 + q^3$. There are an unlimited number of potential firms in this market. The market demand function is $Q = 24 - p$. Determine the long-run equilibrium price, quantity per firm, market quantity, and number of firms. How do these values change if a tax of $1 per unit is collected from each firm? (*Hint*: See Solved Problem 8.3) **M**

4.4 The major oil spill in the Gulf of Mexico in 2010 caused the oil firm BP and the U.S. government to greatly increase purchases of boat services, various oil-absorbing materials, and other goods and services to minimize damage from the spill. Use side-by-side firm and market diagrams to show the effects (number of firms, price, output, profits) of such a shift in demand in one such industry in both the short run and the long run. Explain how your answer depends on whether the shift in demand is expected to be temporary or permanent.

*4.5 Derive the residual supply elasticity in Equation 8.17 using the definition of the residual demand function in Equation 8.16. What is the formula if there are n identical countries? **M**

*4.6 The federal specific tax on gasoline is 18.4¢ per gallon, and the average state specific tax is 20.2¢, ranging from 7.5¢ in Georgia to 25¢ in Connecticut. A statistical study (Chouinard and Perloff, 2004) finds that the incidence of the federal specific tax on consumers is substantially lower than that from state specific taxes. When the federal specific tax increases by 1¢, the retail price rises by about 0.5¢, so that retail consumers bear half the tax incidence. In contrast, when a state that uses regular gasoline increases its specific tax by 1¢, the retail price rises by nearly 1¢, so that the incidence of the tax falls almost entirely on consumers. (*Hint*: See Chapter 2 on tax incidence.)

a. What are the incidences of the federal and state specific gasoline taxes on firms?

b. Explain why the incidence on consumers differs between a federal and a state specific gasoline tax, assuming that the market is competitive. (*Hint*: Consider the residual supply curve facing a state compared to the supply curve facing the nation.)

c. Using the residual supply elasticity in Equation 8.17, estimate how much more elastic is the residual supply elasticity to one state than is the national supply elasticity. (For simplicity, assume that all 50 states are identical.) **M**

4.7 To reduce pollution, the California Air Resources Board in 1996 required the reformulation of gasoline sold in California. Since then, every few years, occasional disasters at California refineries have substantially cut the supply of gasoline and contributed to temporary large price increases. Environmentalists and California refiners (who had sunk large investments to produce the reformulated gasoline) opposed imports from other states, which would have kept prices down. To minimize fluctuations in prices in California, Severin Borenstein and Steven Stoft suggest setting a 15¢ surcharge on sellers of standard gasoline. In normal times, none of this gasoline would be sold, because it costs only 8¢ to 12¢ more to produce the California version. However, when disasters trigger a large shift in the supply curve of gasoline, firms could profitably import standard gasoline and keep the price in California from rising more than about 15¢ above prices in the rest of the United States. Use figures to evaluate Borenstein and Stoft's proposal. (*Hint*: See Solved Problem 8.4.)

4.8 Is the long-run supply curve for a good horizontal only if the long-run supply curves of all factors are horizontal? Explain.

4.9 Navel oranges are grown in California and Arizona. If Arizona starts collecting a specific tax per orange from its firms, what happens to the long-run market supply curve? (*Hint*: You may assume that all firms initially have the same costs. Your answer may depend on whether unlimited entry occurs.)

4.10 A 2010 law requires that people who buy food or alcohol in Washington, D.C., have to pay an extra nickel for every paper or plastic bag the store provides them. Does such a tax affect marginal cost (and of what good)? If so, by how much? How much of the tax is likely to be passed on to consumers?

4.11 In 2009, the voters of Oakland, California, passed a measure to tax medical cannabis (marijuana), effectively legalizing it. In 2010, the City Council adopted regulations permitting industrial-scale marijuana farms with no size limits but requiring each to pay a $211,000 per year fee.[17] One proposal calls for a 100,000 square foot farm, the size of two football fields. Prior to this legalization, only individuals could grow marijuana. These small farmers complained bitterly, arguing that the large firms would drive them out of the industry they helped to build due to economies of scale. Draw a figure to illustrate the situation. Under what conditions (such as relative costs, position of the demand curve, number of low-cost firms) will the smaller, higher-cost growers be driven out of business? (In 2012, the federal government brought an end to this business, at least for now.)

4.12 The Application "Upward-Sloping Long-Run Supply Curve for Cotton" shows a supply curve for cotton. Discuss the equilibrium if the world demand curve crosses this supply curve in either (a) a flat section labeled "Brazil" or (b) the vertical section to its right. What do farms in the United States do?

4.13 Cheap handheld video cameras have revolutionized the hard-core pornography market. Previously, making movies required expensive equipment and some technical expertise. Today, anyone with a couple hundred dollars and a moderately steady hand can buy and use a video camera to make a movie. Consequently, many new firms have entered the market, and the supply curve of porn movies has slithered substantially to the right. Whereas only 1,000 to 2,000 video porn titles were released annually in the United States from 1986 to 1991, that number grew to 10,300 in 1999 and to 13,588 by 2005.[18] Use a side-by-side diagram to illustrate how this technological innovation affected the long-run supply curve and the equilibrium in this market.

4.14 In late 2004 and early 2005, the price of raw coffee beans jumped as much as 50% from the previous year. In response, the price of roasted coffee rose about 14%. Similarly, in 2012, the price of raw beans fell by a third, yet the price of roasted coffee

---

[17]Matthai Kuruvila, "Oakland Allows Industrial-Scale Marijuana Farms," *San Francisco Chronicle*, July 21, 2010; Malia Wollan, "Oakland, Seeking Financial Lift, Approves Giant Marijuana Farms," *New York Times*, July 21, 2010.

[18]"Branded Flesh," *Economist*, August 14, 1999: 56; **internet-filter-review.toptenreviews.com/internet-pornography-statistics-pg9 .html** (viewed May 19, 2012).

fell by only a few percentage points. Why would the roasted coffee price change less than in proportion to the rise in the cost of raw beans?

5. Challenge

5.1 In the Challenge Solution, would it make a difference to the analysis whether the lump-sum costs such as registration fees are collected annually or only once when the firm starts operation? How would each of these franchise taxes affect the firm's long-run supply curve? Explain your answer.

5.2 Answer the Challenge for the short run rather than for the long run. (*Hint*: The answer depends on where the demand curve intersects the original short-run supply curve.)

5.3 The North American Free Trade Agreement provides for two-way, long-haul trucking across the U.S.-Mexican border. U.S. truckers have objected, arguing that the Mexican trucks don't have to meet the same environmental and safety standards as U.S. trucks. They are concerned that the combination of these lower fixed costs and lower Mexican wages will result in Mexican drivers taking business from them. Their complaints have delayed implementation of this agreement (except for a small pilot program during the Bush administration, which was ended during the Obama administration). What would be the short-run and long-run effects of allowing entry of Mexican drivers on market price and quantity and the number of U.S. truckers?

5.4 In a perfectly competitive market, all firms are identical, there is free entry and exit, and an unlimited number of potential entrants. Now, the government starts collecting a specific tax τ, how do the long-run market and firm equilibria change?

*5.5 The finding that the average real price of abortions has remained relatively constant over the last 25 years suggests that the supply curve is horizontal. Medoff (1997) estimated that the price elasticity of demand for abortions ranges from -0.70 to -0.99. By how much would the market price of abortions and the number of abortions change if a lump-sum tax is assessed on abortion clinics that raises their minimum average cost by 10%? Use a figure to illustrate your answer. **M**

*5.6 Answer the Challenge problem using calculus. (*Note*: This comparative statics problem is difficult because you will need to solve two or three equations simultaneously, and hence you may need to use matrix techniques.) **M**

9

Properties and Applications of the Competitive Model

No more good must be attempted than the public can bear.
—Thomas Jefferson

Cities around the world—including most major U.S., Canadian, and European cities—license and limit the number of taxicabs. Some cities regulate the number of cabs much more strictly than others. Tokyo has five times as many cabs as New York City, which has fewer licenses today than when licensing started in 1937. San Francisco, which severely limits cabs, has only a tenth as many cabs as Washington, D.C., which has fewer people but does not restrict the number of cabs. How restrictive is the licensing varies across cities: The number of residents per cab is 757 in Detroit, 748 in San Francisco, 538 in Dallas, 533 in Baltimore, 350 in Boston, 301 in New Orleans, and 203 in Honolulu.

Where cabs are strictly limited, like in New York City, the owner of a taxi license earns an unusually high operating profit. Moreover, owners of a license—called a medallion—can sell them for large sums of money. In 2012, the owner of a New York City cab medallion sold it for over $1.3 million. The value of all New York City taxi licenses is over $14 billion (much greater than the $2.6 billion insured value of the World Trade Center).

What effect does restrictive licensing have on taxi fares and cab company profits? What determines the value of a license? How much profit beyond the cost of the license can the acquiring firm expect? What are the effects of licensing on cab drivers and customers?

One of the major strengths of the competitive market model is that it can predict how government policies such as licensing, trade tariffs and quotas, global warming, and major cost-saving discoveries will affect consumers and producers. We start by examining the properties of a competitive market and then consider how government actions and other shocks affect the market and its properties.

We concentrate on two main properties of a competitive market. First, firms in a competitive equilibrium generally make zero (economic) profit in the long run. Second, competition maximizes a measure of societal welfare.

To many people, the term *welfare* refers to the government's payments to the poor. However, the term has an entirely different meaning for economists. Economists use *welfare* to refer to the well-being of various groups such as consumers and producers. They call an analysis of the impact of a change on various groups' well-being a study of *welfare economics*.

We introduced a measure of consumer well being, *consumer surplus* in Chapter 5. Here, we examine a similar concept for firms, *producer surplus*, which is closely related to profit and is used by economists to determine whether firms gain or lose when the equilibrium of a competitive market changes. The sum of producer surplus and consumer surplus equals the measure of welfare that we use in this chapter.

By predicting the effects of a proposed policy on consumer surplus, producer surplus, and welfare, economists can advise policymakers as to who will benefit, who will lose, and what the net effect of this policy likely will be. To decide whether to adopt a particular policy, policymakers may combine these predictions with their normative views (values), such as whether they are more interested in helping the group that gains or the group that loses.

In this chapter, we examine six main topics	1. **Zero Profit for Competitive Firms in the Long Run.** In the long-run competitive market equilibrium, profit-maximizing firms break even, so firms that do not try to maximize profits lose money and leave the market. 2. **Producer Surplus.** How much producers gain or lose from a change in the equilibrium price can be measured by producer surplus, which uses information from the marginal cost curve or the change in profit. 3. **Competition Maximizes Welfare.** Competition maximizes a measure of social welfare based on consumer surplus and producer surplus. 4. **Policies That Shift Supply Curves.** Government policies that shift supply curves to the left harm consumers and lower welfare in a competitive market. 5. **Policies That Create a Wedge Between Supply and Demand Curves.** Government policies such as taxes, price ceilings, price floors, and tariffs that create a wedge between the supply and demand curves reduce the equilibrium quantity, raise the equilibrium price to consumers, and therefore lower welfare. 6. **Comparing Both Types of Policies: Trade.** Policies that limit supply (such as quotas or bans on imports) or create a wedge between supply and demand (such as tariffs, which are taxes on imports) have different welfare effects when both policies reduce imports by equal amounts.

9.1 Zero Profit for Competitive Firms in the Long Run

Competitive firms earn zero profit in the long run whether or not entry is completely free. Consequently, competitive firms must maximize profit.

Zero Long-Run Profit with Free Entry

The long-run supply curve is horizontal if firms are free to enter the market, firms have identical cost, and input prices are constant. All firms in the market operate at minimum long-run average cost. That is, they are indifferent about whether or not to shut down because they are earning zero profit.

One implication of the shutdown rule is that firms are willing to operate in the long run even if they are making zero profit. This conclusion may seem strange unless you remember that we are talking about *economic profit*, which is revenue minus opportunity cost. Because opportunity cost includes the value of the next best investment, at a zero long-run economic profit, firms earn the normal business profit that they could gain by investing elsewhere in the economy.

For example, if a firm's owner had not built the plant the firm uses to produce, the owner could have spent that money on another business or put the money in a bank. The opportunity cost of the current plant, then, is the forgone profit from what the owner could have earned by investing the money elsewhere.

The five-year after-tax accounting return on capital across all firms is 10.5%, indicating that the typical firm earned a business profit of 10.5¢ for every dollar it invested in capital (*Forbes*). These firms were earning roughly zero economic profit but positive business profit.

Because business cost does not include all opportunity costs, business profit is larger than economic profit. Thus, a profit-maximizing firm may stay in business if it earns zero long-run economic profit but it shuts down if it earns zero long-run business profit.

Zero Long-Run Profit When Entry Is Limited

In some markets, firms cannot enter in response to long-run profit opportunities. The number of firms in these markets may be limited because the supply of an input is limited. For example, only so much land is suitable for mining uranium.

One might think that firms could make positive long-run economic profits in such markets; however, that's not true. The reason firms earn zero economic profits is that firms bidding for the scarce input drive up its price until their profits are zero.

Suppose that the number of acres suitable for growing tomatoes is limited. Figure 9.1 shows a typical farm's average cost curve if the rental cost of land is zero (the average cost curve includes only the farm's costs of labor, capital, materials, and energy—not land). At the market price p^*, the firm produces q^* bushels of tomatoes and makes a profit of π^*, the shaded rectangle in the figure.

Figure 9.1 Rent

If farmers did not have to pay rent for their farms, a farmer with relatively high-quality land would earn a positive long-run profit of π^*. Due to competitive bidding for this land, however, the rent equals π^*, so the landlord reaps all the benefits of the superior land, and the farmer earns a zero long-run economic profit.

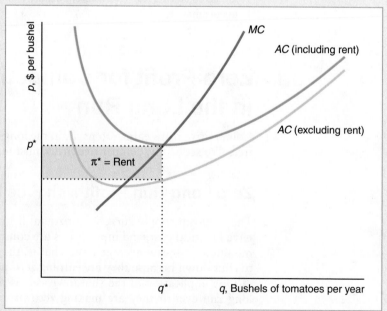

Thus, if the owner of the land does not charge rent, the farmer makes a profit. Unfortunately for the farmer, the landowner rents the land for π^*, so the farmer actually earns zero profit. Why does the landowner charge that much? The reason is that π^* is the opportunity cost of the land: The land is worth π^* to other potential farmers. These farmers will bid against each other to rent this land until the rent is driven up to π^*.

This rent is a fixed cost to the farmer because it does not vary with the amount of output. Thus, the rent affects the farm's average cost curve but not its marginal cost curve.

As a result, if the farm produces at all, it produces q^* where its marginal cost equals the market price, no matter what rent is charged. The higher average cost curve in the figure includes a rent equal to π^*. The minimum point of this average cost curve is p^* at q^* bushels of tomatoes, so the farmer earns zero economic profit.

If the demand curve shifts to the left so that the market price falls, the farmer suffers short-run losses. In the long run, the rental price of the land will fall enough that once again each farm earns zero economic profit.

Does it make a difference whether farmers own or rent the land? Not really. The opportunity cost to a farmer who owns superior land is the amount for which that land could be rented in a competitive land market. Thus, the economic profit of both owned and rented land is zero at the long-run equilibrium.

Good-quality land is not the only scarce resource. The price of any fixed factor will be bid up in a similar fashion until economic profit for the firm is zero in the long run. Similarly, the government may require that a firm have a license to operate and then limit the number of licenses available. The price of the license gets bid up by potential entrants, driving profit to zero. For example, the 2008 license fee was $326,000 a year for a hot dog stand on the north side of the steps of the Metropolitan Museum of Art in New York City.[1]

A scarce input—whether its fixed factor is a person with high ability or land—earns an extra opportunity value. This extra opportunity value is called a **rent**: a payment to the owner of an input beyond the minimum necessary for the factor to be supplied.

Bonnie manages a store for the salary of $40,000, the amount paid to a typical manager. Because she's a superior manager, however, the firm earns an economic profit of $50,000 a year. Other firms, seeing what a good job Bonnie is doing, offer her a higher salary. The bidding for her services drives her salary up to $90,000: her $40,000 base salary plus the $50,000 rent. After paying this rent to Bonnie, the store makes zero economic profit.

In short, if some firms in a market make short-run economic profits due to a scarce input, the other firms in the market bid for that input. This bidding drives up the price of the factor until all firms earn zero long-run profits. In such a market, the supply curve is flat because all firms have the same minimum long-run average cost.

---

[1]As a result of an auction the rate rose to $643,000 in 2009, but the new vendor was evicted for failure to pay the city in full. Since then, a dispute concerning the relevance of state veterans preference laws and city laws has left this fee in doubt. (In the hot dog stand photo, I'm the fellow in the blue shirt with the dopey expression.)

People with unusual abilities can earn staggering rents. For example, by the time Cher ended her four-year "Never Can Say Goodbye" tour at the Hollywood Bowl on April 30, 2005, she had sold nearly $200 million worth of tickets. Though no law stops anyone from trying to become a professional entertainer, most of us do not have enough talent and charisma to entice millions to pay to watch us perform.[2]

APPLICATION

Tiger Woods' Rents

Tiger Woods was leading a charmed life as the world's greatest golfer and an advertising star—earning $100 million a year in endorsements—when he and much of his endorsement career came to a crashing halt as he smashed his car in front of his home at about 2:30 A.M. on November 27, 2009. A series of revelations about his personal life that followed over the next few days further damaged his pristine public reputation, and several endorsers either suspended using him in their advertisements or dropped him altogether.

Knittel and Stango (2012) assessed the financial damage to these firms' shareholders using an event study approach in which they compared the stock prices of firms using Mr. Woods in their promotions relative to the stock market prices as a whole and those of close competitor firms. They examine the period between the crash and when Mr. Woods announced on December 11 that he was taking an "indefinite" leave from golf. Their results tell us about the rents that he was receiving.

They estimated that shareholders of companies endorsed by Mr. Woods lost $5 to $12 billion in wealth, which reflects stock investors' estimates of the damage from the end of effective endorsements over future years. Mr. Woods' five major sponsors—Accenture, Electronic Arts, Gatorade (PepsiCo), Gillette, and Nike—collectively lost between 2% and 3% of their aggregate market value after the accident. The losses were slightly higher for his main sports-related sponsors Electronic Arts, Gatorade, and Nike.

Mr. Woods' sports-related sponsors suffered more than his other sponsors. As Knittel and Stango point out, sponsorship from firms that are not sports-related, such as Accenture ("a global management consulting, technology services, and outsourcing company"), probably does not increase the overall value of the Tiger brand. Presumably, when Mr. Woods negotiated his original deal with Accenture, he captured all the excess profit generated for Accenture as a rent of about $20 million a year. Consequently, we would not expect Accenture to lose much from the end of their relationship with Mr. Woods, as Knittel and Stango's estimates show.

In contrast, partnering with sports-related firms such as Nike presumably increased the value of both the Nike and Tiger brands and created other financial opportunities for Mr. Woods. If so, Nike would likely have captured some of the profit generated by partnering with Tiger Woods above and beyond the $20 to $30 million Nike paid him annually. Consequently, the sports-related firms' shareholders suffered a sizable loss from Mr. Woods' fall from grace.

---

[2]However, the estates of major celebrities continue to collect rents even after they die. From Halloween 2010 to Halloween 2011, Michael Jackson earned $170 million, Elvis Presley $55 million, and Peanuts cartoonist Charles Schulz $25 million. Even Albert Einstein raked in $10 million from use of his image for products such as in Disney's Baby Einstein learning tools and a McDonald's happy meal promotion. (**Forbes.com**, October 25, 2011.)

The Need to Maximize Profit

The worst crime against working people is a company which fails to operate at a profit. —Samuel Gompers, first president of the American Federation of Labor

In a competitive market with identical firms and free entry, if most firms are profit-maximizing, profits are driven to zero at the long-run equilibrium. Any firm that does not maximize profit—that is, any firm that sets its output so that its marginal cost exceeds the market price or that fails to use the most cost-efficient methods of production—will lose money. Thus, *to survive in a competitive market, a firm must maximize its profit.*

9.2 Producer Surplus

Economists often use a measure that is closely related to profit when evaluating the effects of policies on firms' welfare. We developed a measure of consumer welfare—consumer surplus—in Chapter 5. A firm's gain from participating in the market is measured by its **producer surplus** (*PS*), which is the difference between the amount for which a good sells and the minimum amount necessary for the seller to be willing to produce the good. The minimum amount that a seller must receive to be willing to produce is the firm's avoidable production cost (the shutdown criterion discussed in Chapter 8).

Measuring Producer Surplus Using a Supply Curve

To determine a competitive firm's producer surplus, we use its supply curve: its marginal cost curve above its minimum average variable cost (Chapter 8). The firm's supply curve in panel a of Figure 9.2 looks like a staircase. The marginal cost of producing the first unit is $MC_1 = \$1$, which is the area below the marginal cost curve between 0 and 1. The marginal cost of producing the second unit is $MC_2 = \$2$, and so on. The variable cost, *VC*, of producing 4 units is the sum of the marginal costs for the first 4 units: $VC = MC_1 + MC_2 + MC_3 + MC_4 = \$1 + \$2 + \$3 + \$4 = \$10$.

If the market price, *p*, is \$4, the firm's revenue from the sale of the first unit exceeds its cost by $PS_1 = p - MC_1 = \$4 - \$1 = \$3$, which is its producer surplus on the first unit. The firm's producer surplus is \$2 on the second unit and \$1 on the third unit. On the fourth unit, the price equals marginal cost, so the firm just breaks even. As a result, the firm's total producer surplus, *PS*, from selling 4 units at \$4 each is the sum of its producer surplus on these 4 units: $PS = PS_1 + PS_2 + PS_3 + PS_4 = \$3 + \$2 + \$1 + \$0 = \$6.$[3]

Graphically, the total producer surplus is the area above the supply curve and below the market price up to the quantity actually produced. This same reasoning holds when the firm's supply curve is smooth, as in panel b.

---

[3]The firm is indifferent between producing the fourth unit or not. Its producer surplus would be the same if it produced only three units, because its marginal producer surplus from the fourth unit is zero.

Figure 9.2 Producer Surplus

(a) The firm's producer surplus, $6, is the area below the market price, $4, and above the marginal cost (supply curve) up to the quantity sold, 4. The area under the marginal cost curve up to the number of units actually produced is the variable cost of production. (b) The market producer surplus is the area above the supply curve and below the line at the market price, p^*, up to the quantity produced, Q^*. The area below the supply curve and to the left of the quantity produced by the market, Q^*, is the variable cost of producing that level of output.

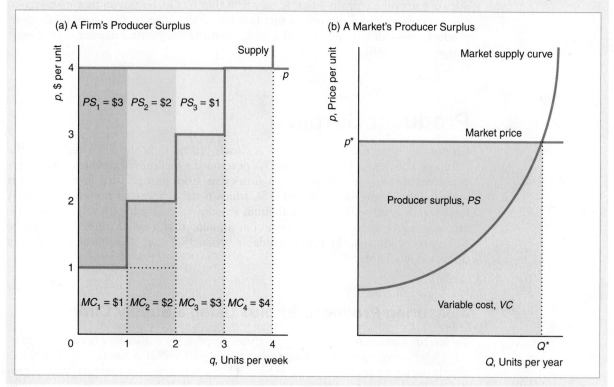

The producer surplus is found by integrating the difference between the firm's demand function—the straight line at p—and its marginal cost function, $MC(q)$, up to the quantity produced, q^* (here $q^* = 4$ units):[4]

$$PS = \int_0^{q^*} [p - MC(q)]dq = pq^* - VC(q^*) = R(q^*) - VC(q^*), \qquad (9.1)$$

where $R = pq^*$ is revenue. In panel a of Figure 9.2, revenue is $R = \$4 \times 4 = \$16$ and variable cost is $VC = \$10$, so producer surplus is $PS = \$6$.

Producer surplus is closely related to profit. Profit is revenue minus total cost, C, which equals variable cost plus fixed cost, F:

$$\pi = R - C = R - (VC + F). \qquad (9.2)$$

---

[4]The marginal cost can be obtained by differentiating with respect to output either the variable cost function, $VC(q)$, or the total cost function, $C(q) = VC(q) + F$, because F is a constant (Chapter 7). When we integrate under the marginal cost function, we obtain the variable cost function—that is, we cannot recover the constant fixed cost.

Thus, the difference between producer surplus, Equation 9.1, and profit, Equation 9.2, is fixed cost, $PS - \pi = F$. If the fixed cost is zero (as often occurs in the long run), producer surplus equals profit.[5]

Another interpretation of producer surplus is as a gain to trade. In the short run, if the firm produces and sells a good—that is, if the firm trades—it earns a profit of $\pi = R - VC - F$. If the firm shuts down—does not trade—it loses its fixed cost of $-F$. Thus, producer surplus equals the profit from trading minus the loss (fixed costs) it incurs from not trading:

$$PS = (R - VC - F) - (-F) = R - VC.$$

Using Producer Surplus

Even in the short run, we can use producer surplus to study the effects of any shock that does not affect the fixed cost of firms, such as a change in the price of a substitute or an input. Such shocks change profit by exactly the same amount as they change producer surplus because fixed costs do not change.

A major advantage of producer surplus is that we can use it to measure the effect of a shock on *all* the firms in a market without having to measure the profit of each firm separately. We can calculate market producer surplus using the market supply curve in the same way that we calculate a firm's producer surplus using its supply curve. The market producer surplus in panel b of Figure 9.2 is the area above the supply curve and below the market price line at p^* up to the quantity sold, Q^*. The market supply curve is the horizontal sum of the marginal cost curves of each of the firms (Chapter 8).

SOLVED PROBLEM 9.1

Green et al. (2005) estimate the inverse supply curve for California processed tomatoes as $p = 0.693Q^{1.82}$, where Q is the quantity of processing tomatoes in millions of tons per year and p is the price in dollars per ton. If the price falls from $60 (where the quantity supplied is about 11.6) to $50 (where the quantity supplied is approximately 10.5), how does producer surplus change? Illustrate in a figure. Show that you can obtain a good approximation using rectangles and triangles. (Round results to the nearest tenth.)

Answer

1. *Calculate the producer surplus at each price (or corresponding quantity) and take the difference to determine how producer surplus changes.* When the price is $60, the producer surplus is

$$PS_1 = \int_0^{11.6} (60 - 0.693Q^{1.82})dQ = 60Q - \frac{0.693}{2.82}Q^{2.82}\Big|_0^{11.6} \approx 449.3.$$

The producer surplus at the new price is

$$PS_2 = \int_0^{10.5} (50 - 0.693Q^{1.82})dQ \approx 338.7.$$

Thus, the change in producer surplus is $\Delta PS = PS_2 - PS_1 \approx 338.7 - 449.3 = -110.6$.

---

[5]Even though each competitive firm makes zero profit in the long run, owners of scarce resources used in that market may earn rents, as we discussed in Section 9.1. Thus, owners of scarce resources may receive positive producer surplus in the long run.

2. *At each price, the producer surplus is the area above the supply curve and below the price up to the quantity sold.* In the figure, area A corresponds to PS_2 because it is the area above the supply curve, below the price of \$50, up to the quantity 10.5. Similarly, PS_1 is the sum of areas A and B, so the loss in producer surplus, ΔPS, is area B.

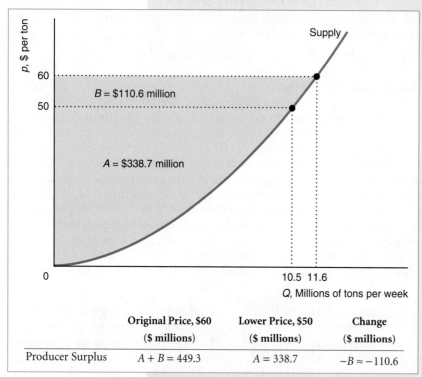

3. *Approximate area B as the sum of a rectangle and a triangle.* Area B consists of a rectangle with a height of 10 ($= 60 - 50$) and a length of 10.5 and a shape that's nearly a triangle with a height of 10 and a base of 1.1 ($= 11.6 - 10.5$). The sum of the areas of the rectangle and the triangle is $(10 \times 10.5) + (\frac{1}{2} \times 10 \times 1.1)$ $= 110.5$, which is close to the value, 110.6, that we obtained by integrating.

	Original Price, \$60 ($ millions)	Lower Price, \$50 ($ millions)	Change ($ millions)
Producer Surplus	$A + B = 449.3$	$A = 338.7$	$-B \approx -110.6$

9.3 Competition Maximizes Welfare

All is for the best in the best of all possible worlds. —Voltaire (*Candide*)

Perfect competition serves as an ideal or benchmark for other industries. This benchmark is widely used by economists and widely misused by politicians.

Most U.S. politicians have at one point or another in their careers stated (with a hand over their heart), "I believe in the free market." While I'm not about to bash free markets, I find this statement to be, at best, mysterious. What do the politicians mean by "believe in" and "free market?" Hopefully they realize that whether a free market is desirable is a scientific question rather than one of belief. Possibly, when they say they "believe in," they are making some claim that free markets are desirable for some unspecified reason. By "free market," they might mean a market without government regulation or intervention. I believe that this statement is a bad summary of what is probably the most important theoretical result in economics: *a perfectly competitive market maximizes an important measure of economic well-being.*[6]

---

[6]In 1776, Adam Smith, the father of modern economics, in his book *An Inquiry into the Nature and Causes of the Wealth of Nations*, was the first to observe that firms and consumers, acting independently in their self-interest, generate a desirable outcome. This insight is sometimes called the invisible hand theorem based on a phrase Smith used.

Measuring Welfare

How should we measure society's welfare? There are many reasonable answers to this question. One commonly used measure of the welfare of society, W, is the sum of consumer surplus (Chapter 5) plus producer surplus:

$$W = CS + PS.$$

This measure implicitly weights the well-being of consumers and producers equally. By using this measure, we are making a value judgment that the well-being of consumers and that of producers are equally important.

Not everyone agrees that society should try to maximize this measure of welfare. Groups of producers argue for legislation that benefits them even if it hurts consumers by more than the producers gain—as though only producer surplus matters. Similarly, some consumer advocates argue that we should care only about consumers, so social welfare should include only consumer surplus.

In this chapter, we use the consumer surplus plus producer surplus to measure welfare (and postpone a discussion of other welfare concepts until Chapter 10). One of the most striking results in economics is that competitive markets maximize this measure of welfare. If either less or more output than the competitive level is produced, welfare falls.

Why Producing Less Than the Competitive Output Lowers Welfare

Producing less than the competitive output lowers welfare. At the competitive equilibrium in Figure 9.3, e_1, where output is Q_1 and price is p_1, consumer surplus equals area $CS_1 = A + B + C$, producer surplus is $PS_1 = D + E$, and total welfare is $W_1 = A + B + C + D + E$. If output is reduced to Q_2 so that price rises to p_2 at e_2, consumer surplus is $CS_2 = A$, producer surplus is $PS_2 = B + D$, and welfare is $W_2 = A + B + D$.

The change in consumer surplus is

$$\Delta CS = CS_2 - CS_1 = A - (A + B + C) = -B - C.$$

Consumers lose B because they have to pay $p_2 - p_1$ more than they would at the competitive price for the Q_2 units they buy. Consumers lose C because they buy only Q_2 rather than Q_1 at the higher price.

The change in producer surplus is

$$\Delta PS = PS_2 - PS_1 = (B + D) - (D + E) = B - E.$$

Producers gain B because they now sell Q_2 units at p_2 rather than at p_1. They lose E because they sell $Q_2 - Q_1$ fewer units.

The change in welfare, is

$$
\begin{aligned}
\Delta W &= W_2 - W_1 \\
&= (CS_2 + PS_2) - (CS_1 + PS_1) \\
&= (CS_2 - CS_1) + (PS_2 - PS_1) = \Delta CS + \Delta PS \\
&= (-B - C) + (B - E) \\
&= -C - E.
\end{aligned}
$$

The area B is a transfer from consumers to producers—the extra amount consumers pay for the Q_2 units goes to the sellers—so it does not affect welfare. Welfare drops because consumers' loss of C and producers' loss of E benefit no one. This drop in

Figure 9.3 Why Reducing Output from the Competitive Level Lowers Welfare

Reducing output from the competitive level Q_1 to Q_2 causes price to increase from p_1 to p_2. Consumers suffer: Consumer surplus is now A, a fall of $\Delta CS = -B - C$. Producers may gain or lose: Producer surplus is now $B + D$, a change of $\Delta PS = B - E$. Overall, welfare falls by $\Delta W = -C - E$, which is a deadweight loss (DWL) to society.

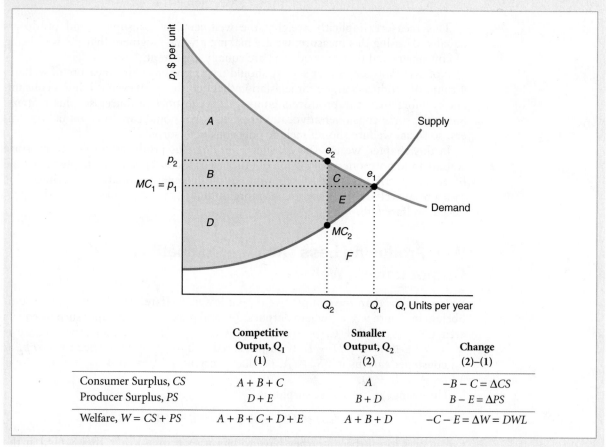

	Competitive Output, Q_1 (1)	Smaller Output, Q_2 (2)	Change (2)–(1)
Consumer Surplus, CS	$A + B + C$	A	$-B - C = \Delta CS$
Producer Surplus, PS	$D + E$	$B + D$	$B - E = \Delta PS$
Welfare, $W = CS + PS$	$A + B + C + D + E$	$A + B + D$	$-C - E = \Delta W = DWL$

welfare, $\Delta W = -C - E$, is a **deadweight loss** (DWL): the net reduction in welfare from a loss of surplus by one group that is not offset by a gain to another group.

The deadweight loss results because consumers value extra output by more than the marginal cost of producing it. At each output between Q_2 and Q_1, consumers' marginal willingness to pay for another unit—the height of the demand curve—is greater than the marginal cost of producing the next unit—the height of the supply curve. For example, at e_2, consumers value the next unit of output at p_2, which is much greater than the marginal cost, MC_2, of producing it. Increasing output from Q_2 to Q_1 raises firms' variable cost by area F, the area under the marginal cost (supply) curve between Q_2 and Q_1. Consumers value this extra output by the area under the demand curve between Q_2 and Q_1, area $C + E + F$. Thus, consumers value the extra output by $C + E$ more than it costs to produce it.

Society would be better off producing and consuming extra units of this good than spending the deadweight loss, $C + E$, on other goods. In short, *the deadweight loss is the opportunity cost of giving up some of this good to buy more of another good.*

Why Producing More Than the Competitive Output Lowers Welfare

Increasing output beyond the competitive level also decreases welfare because the cost of producing this extra output exceeds the value consumers place on it. Figure 9.4 shows the effect of increasing output from the competitive level Q_1 to Q_2 and letting the price fall to p_2, point e_2 on the demand curve, so that consumers buy the extra output.

Because price falls from p_1 to p_2, consumer surplus rises by

$$\Delta CS = C + D + E,$$

which is the area between p_2 and p_1 to the left of the demand curve. At the original price, p_1, producer surplus was $C + F$. The cost of producing the larger output is the area under the supply curve up to Q_2, $B + D + E + G + H$. The firms sell this quantity for only $p_2 Q_2$, area $F + G + H$. Thus, the new producer surplus is $F - B - D - E$. As a result, the increase in output causes producer surplus to fall by

$$\Delta PS = -B - C - D - E.$$

Because producers lose more than consumers gain, the deadweight loss is

$$\Delta W = \Delta CS + \Delta PS = (C + D + E) + (-B - C - D - E) = -B.$$

Figure 9.4 Why Increasing Output from the Competitive Level Lowers Welfare

Increasing output from the competitive level Q_1, to Q_2 lowers the price from p_1 to p_2. Consumer surplus rises by $C + D + E$, producer surplus falls by $B + C + D + E$, and welfare falls by B, which is a deadweight loss to society.

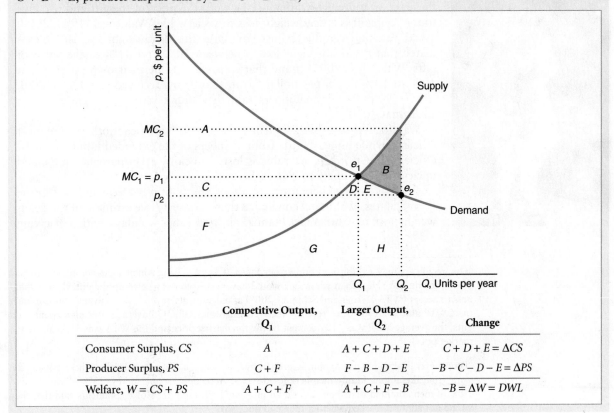

	Competitive Output, Q_1	Larger Output, Q_2	Change
Consumer Surplus, CS	A	$A + C + D + E$	$C + D + E = \Delta CS$
Producer Surplus, PS	$C + F$	$F - B - D - E$	$-B - C - D - E = \Delta PS$
Welfare, $W = CS + PS$	$A + C + F$	$A + C + F - B$	$-B = \Delta W = DWL$

A net loss occurs because consumers value the $Q_2 - Q_1$ extra output by only $E + H$, which is less than the extra cost, $B + E + H$, of producing it. The new price, p_2, is less than the marginal cost, MC_2, of producing Q_2. Too much output is being produced.

The reason that competition maximizes welfare is that price equals marginal cost at the competitive equilibrium. At the competitive equilibrium, demand equals supply, which ensures that price equals marginal cost. When price equals marginal cost, consumers value the last unit of output by exactly the amount that it costs to produce it. If consumers value the last unit by more than the marginal cost of production, welfare rises if more is produced. Similarly, if consumers value the last unit by less than its marginal cost, welfare is higher at a lower level of production.

A **market failure** is inefficient production or consumption, often because a price exceeds marginal cost. In the next application, we show that the surplus for the recipient of a gift is often less than the giver's cost, and hence gift giving is inefficient.

APPLICATION

The Deadweight Loss of Christmas Presents

Just how much did you enjoy the expensive woolen socks with the dancing purple teddy bears that your Aunt Fern gave you last Christmas? Often the cost of a gift exceeds the value that the recipient places on it.

Until the advent of gift cards, only 10% to 15% of holiday gifts were monetary. A gift of cash typically gives at least as much pleasure to the recipient as a gift that costs the same but can't be exchanged for cash. (So what if giving cash is tacky?) Of course, it's possible that a gift can give more pleasure to the recipient than it cost the giver—but how often does that happen to you?

An *efficient gift* is one that the recipient values as much as the gift costs the giver, or more. The difference between the price of the gift and its value to the recipient is a deadweight loss to society. Joel Waldfogel (1993, 2009) asked Yale undergraduates just how large this deadweight loss is. He estimated that the deadweight loss is between 10% and 33% of the value of gifts. Waldfogel (2005) found that consumers value their own purchases at 10% to 18% more, per dollar spent, than items received as gifts.[7] Indeed, only 65% of holiday shoppers said they didn't return a single gift after Christmas 2010.

Waldfogel found that gifts from friends and "significant others" are most efficient, while noncash gifts from members of the extended family are least efficient (one-third of the value is lost).[8] Luckily, grandparents, aunts, and uncles are most likely to give cash.

Given holiday expenditures of about $66 billion per year in 2007 in the United States, Waldfogel concluded that a conservative estimate of the deadweight loss of Christmas, Hanukkah, and other holidays with gift-giving

---

[7]Gift recipients may exhibit an endowment effect (Chapter 3) in which their willingness to pay (WTP) for the gift is less than what they would have to be offered to give up the gift, their willingness to accept (WTA). Bauer and Schmidt (2008) asked students at the Ruhr University in Germany their WTP and WTA for three recently received Christmas gifts. On average over all students and gifts, the average WTP was 11% percent below the market price and the WTA was 18% above the market price.

[8]People may deal with a disappointing present by "regifting" it. Some families have been passing the same fruitcake among family members for decades. According to one survey, 33% of women and 19% of men admitted that they pass on an unwanted gift (and 28% of respondents said that they would not admit it if asked whether they had done so).

rituals is about $12 billion. (And that's not counting about 2.8 billion hours spent shopping.)

The question remains why people don't give cash instead of presents. Indeed, 61% of Americans gave a gift card as a Christmas present. (A gift card is the equivalent of cash, though some can only be used in a particular store.) More than $30 billion in gift cards were purchased during the 2011 holiday season in the United States. If the reason others don't give cash or gift cards is that they get pleasure from picking the "perfect" gift, the deadweight loss that adjusts for the pleasure of the giver is lower than these calculations suggest. (Bah, humbug!)

9.4 Policies That Shift Supply Curves

I don't make jokes. I just watch the government and report the facts. —Will Rogers

One of the main reasons that economists developed welfare tools was to predict the impact of government programs that alter a competitive equilibrium. Virtually all government actions affect a competitive equilibrium in one of two ways. Some government policies shift the demand curve or the supply curve, such as a limit on the number of firms in a market. Others, such as sales taxes, create a wedge or gap between price and marginal cost so that they are not equal, even though they were in the original competitive equilibrium.

These government interventions move us from an unconstrained competitive equilibrium to a new, constrained competitive equilibrium. Because welfare was maximized at the initial competitive equilibrium, the examples of government-induced changes that we consider here lower welfare. In later chapters, we examine markets in which government intervention may raise welfare because welfare was not maximized initially.

Although government policies may cause either the supply curve or the demand curve to shift, we concentrate on policies that limit supply because they are used frequently and have clear-cut effects. If a government policy causes the supply curve to shift to the left, consumers make fewer purchases at a higher price and welfare falls. For example, if the supply curve in Figure 9.3 shifts to the left so that it hits the demand curve at e_2, then output falls from Q_1 to Q_2, the price rises from p_1 to p_2, and the drop in welfare is $-C - E$. The only "trick" in this analysis is that we use the original supply curve to evaluate producer surplus and welfare.[9]

During World War II, most of the nations involved limited the sales of consumer goods so that the nations' resources could be used for the war effort. Similarly, a government may cause a supply curve to shift to the left by restricting the number of firms in a market, such as by licensing taxicabs. We formally examine the effect of such policies in the Challenge Solution at the end of this chapter.

Entry Barrier. A government may also cause the supply curve to shift to the left by raising the cost of entry. If its cost will be greater than that of firms already in the market, a potential firm might not enter a market even if existing firms are making a profit. Any cost that falls only on potential entrants and not on current firms

---

[9]Welfare falls when governments restrict the consumption of competitive products that we all agree are *goods*, such as food and medical services. In contrast, if most of society wants to discourage the use of certain products, such as hallucinogenic drugs and poisons, policies that restrict consumption may increase some measures of society's welfare.

discourages entry. A long-run **barrier to entry** is an explicit restriction or a cost that applies only to potential new firms—existing firms are not subject to the restriction or do not bear the cost.

At the time they entered, incumbent firms had to pay many of the costs of entering a market that new entrants incur, such as the fixed costs of building plants, buying equipment, and advertising a new product. For example, the fixed cost to McDonald's and other fast-food chains of opening a new fast-food restaurant is about $2 million. These fixed costs are *costs of entry* but are *not* barriers to entry because they apply equally to incumbents and entrants. Costs incurred by both incumbents and entrants do not discourage potential firms from entering a market if existing firms are making money. Potential entrants know that they will do as well as existing firms once they begin operations, so they are willing to enter as long as profit opportunities exist.

Large sunk costs can be barriers to entry under two conditions. First, if capital markets do not work efficiently so that new firms have difficulty raising money, new firms may be unable to enter profitable markets. Second, if a firm must incur a large *sunk* cost, which increases the loss if it exits, the firm may be reluctant to enter a market in which it is uncertain of success.

Exit Restriction. U.S., European, and other governments have laws that delay how quickly some (typically large) firms can go out of business so as to give workers warnings about layoffs. Although these restrictions keep the number of firms in a market relatively high in the short run, they may reduce the number of firms in a market in the long run.

Why do exit restrictions limit the number of firms in a market? Suppose that you are considering starting a construction firm with no capital or other fixed factors. The firm's only input is labor. You know that there is relatively little demand for construction during business downturns and in the winter. To avoid paying workers when business is slack, you plan to shut down during those periods. Because you can avoid losses by shutting down during low-demand periods, you enter this market if your expected economic profits during good periods are zero or positive.

A law that requires you to give your workers six months' warning before laying them off prevents your firm from shutting down quickly. You know that you'll regularly suffer losses during business downturns because you'll have to pay your workers for up to six months during periods when you have nothing for them to do. Knowing that you'll incur these regular losses, you are less inclined to enter the market. Unless the economic profits during good periods are much higher than zero—high enough to offset your losses—you will not choose to enter the market. If exit barriers limit the number of firms, the same analysis that we used to examine entry barriers applies. Thus, exit barriers may raise prices, lower consumer surplus, and reduce welfare.

9.5 Policies That Create a Wedge Between Supply and Demand Curves

The most common government policies that create a wedge between supply and demand curves are sales taxes (or subsidies) and price controls. Because these policies create a gap between marginal cost and price, either too little or too much is produced. For example, a tax causes price to exceed marginal cost—that is, consumers value the good more than it costs to produce it—with the result that consumer surplus, producer surplus, and welfare fall (although tax revenue rises).

Welfare Effects of a Sales Tax

A new sales tax causes the price that consumers pay to rise (Chapter 2), resulting in a loss of consumer surplus, $\Delta CS < 0$, and the price that firms receive to fall, resulting in a drop in producer surplus, $\Delta PS < 0$. However, this tax provides the government with new tax revenue, $\Delta T = T > 0$, if tax revenue was zero before the new tax.

Assuming that the government does something useful with the tax revenue, we should include tax revenue in our definition of welfare:

$$W = CS + PS + T.$$

As a result, the change in welfare is

$$\Delta W = \Delta CS + \Delta PS + \Delta T.$$

Even when we include tax revenue in our welfare measure, a specific tax must lower welfare in, for example, the competitive market for tea roses. We show the welfare loss from a specific tax of $\tau = 11\cent$ per rose stem in Figure 9.5, which is based on estimated demand and supply curves.

Figure 9.5 Welfare Effects of a Specific Tax on Roses

The $\tau = 11\cent$ specific tax on roses creates an $11\cent$ per stem wedge between the price customers pay, $32\cent$, and the price producers receive, $21\cent$. Tax revenue is $T = \tau Q =$ $127.6 million per year. The deadweight loss to society is $C + E = \$4.95$ million per year.

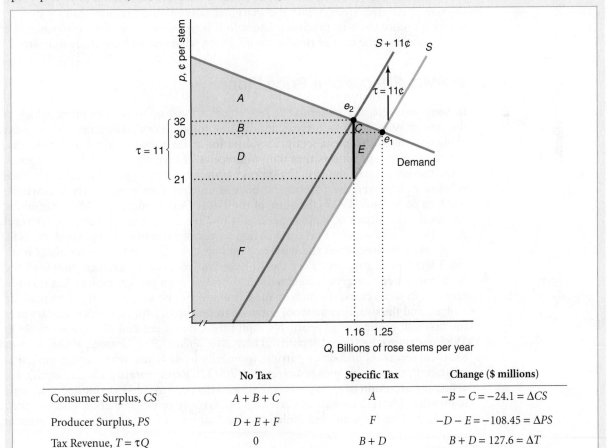

	No Tax	Specific Tax	Change ($ millions)
Consumer Surplus, CS	$A + B + C$	A	$-B - C = -24.1 = \Delta CS$
Producer Surplus, PS	$D + E + F$	F	$-D - E = -108.45 = \Delta PS$
Tax Revenue, $T = \tau Q$	0	$B + D$	$B + D = 127.6 = \Delta T$
Welfare, $W = CS + PS + T$	$A + B + C + D + E + F$	$A + B + D + F$	$-C - E = -4.95 = DWL$

Without the tax, the intersection of the demand curve, D, and the supply curve, S, determines the competitive equilibrium, e_1, at a price of 30¢ per stem and a quantity of 1.25 billion rose stems per year. Consumer surplus is $A + B + C$, producer surplus is $D + E + F$, tax revenue is zero, and there is no deadweight loss.

The specific tax shifts the effective supply curve up by 11¢, creating an 11¢ wedge or differential between the price consumers pay, 32¢, and the price producers receive, $32¢ - \tau = 21¢$. Equilibrium output falls from 1.25 to 1.16 billion stems per year.

The extra 2¢ per stem that buyers pay causes consumer surplus to fall by $B + C = \$24.1$ million per year, as we showed in Figure 5.5. Due to the 9¢ drop in the price firms receive, they lose producer surplus of $D + E = \$108.45$ million per year (Solved Problem 9.1). The government gains tax revenue of $\tau Q = 11¢$ per stem $\times$ 1.16 billion stems per year $= \$127.6$ million per year, area $B + D$.

The combined loss of consumer surplus and producer surplus is only partially offset by the government's gain in tax revenue, so welfare drops by

$$\Delta W = \Delta CS + \Delta PS + \Delta T = -\$24.1 - \$108.45 + \$127.6$$

$$= -\$4.95 \text{ million per year.}$$

This deadweight loss is area $C + E$.

Why does society suffer a deadweight loss? The reason is that the tax lowers output from the competitive level where welfare is maximized. An equivalent explanation for this inefficiency or loss to society is that the tax puts a wedge between price and marginal cost. At the new equilibrium, buyers are willing to pay $p = 32¢$ for one more rose stem, while the marginal cost to firms is only 21¢ $(= p - \tau)$. Shouldn't more roses be produced and sold if consumers are willing to pay nearly a third more than the cost of producing it? That's what our welfare study indicates.

Welfare Effects of a Price Floor

In some markets, the government sets a *price floor*, or minimum price, which is the lowest price a consumer can legally pay for the good. For example, in most countries, the government sets price floors for at least some agricultural products, which guarantee producers that they will receive at least a price of $\underline{p}$ for their good. If the market price is above $\underline{p}$, the support program is irrelevant. If the market price is below $\underline{p}$, however, the government buys as much output as necessary to drive the price up to $\underline{p}$. Since 1929 (the start of the Great Depression), the U.S. government has used price floors or similar programs to keep the prices of many agricultural products above the price that competition would determine in unregulated markets.

My favorite program is the wool and mohair subsidy. The U.S. government instituted wool price supports after the Korean War to ensure "strategic supplies" for uniforms. Later, Congress added mohair subsidies, even though mohair has no military use. In some years, the mohair subsidy exceeded the amount consumers paid for mohair, and the subsidies on wool and mohair reached a fifth of a billion dollars over the first half-century of support. No doubt the Clinton-era end of these subsidies in 1995 endangered national security. Thanks to Senator Phil Gramm, a well-known fiscal conservative, and other patriots (primarily from Texas, where much mohair is produced), the subsidy was resurrected in 2000.[10] Representative Lamar Smith took vehement exception to people who questioned the need to subsidize mohair: "Mohair is popular! I have a mohair sweater! It's my favorite one!" The 2006 budget called for $11 million for wool and mohair with a loan rate of $4.20 per pound. Again in

---

[10] As U.S. Representative Lynn Martin said, "No matter what your religion, you should try to become a government program, for then you will have everlasting life."

2011, the program was ended as a cost-cutting measure. However, the wool and mohair subsidy was restored in the 2012 budget at $7 million.

We now show the effect of a price support using estimated supply and demand curves for the soybean market (Holt, 1992). The intersection of the market demand curve and the market supply curve in Figure 9.6 determines the competitive equilibrium, e, in the absence of a price support program, where the equilibrium price is $p_1 = \$4.59$ per bushel and the equilibrium quantity is $Q_1 = 2.1$ billion bushels per year.[11]

With a price support on soybeans of $\underline{p} = \$5.00$ per bushel and the government's pledge to buy as much output as farmers want to sell, quantity sold is

Figure 9.6 Effect of Price Supports in Soybeans

Without government price supports, the equilibrium is e, where $p_1 = \$4.59$ per bushel and $Q_1 = 2.1$ billion bushels of soybeans per year (based on estimates in Holt, 1992). With the price support at $\underline{p} = \$5.00$ per bushel, output sold increases to Q_s and consumer purchases fall to Q_d, so the government must buy $Q_g = Q_s - Q_d$ at a cost of $1.283 billion per year. The deadweight loss is $C + F + G = \$1.226$ billion per year, not counting storage and administrative costs.

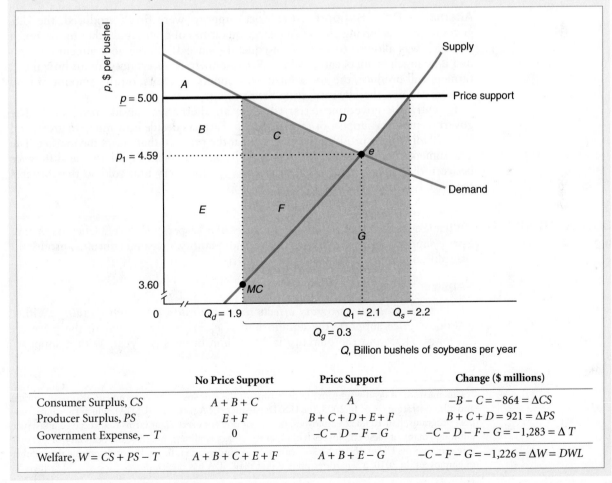

	No Price Support	Price Support	Change ($ millions)
Consumer Surplus, CS	$A + B + C$	A	$-B - C = -864 = \Delta CS$
Producer Surplus, PS	$E + F$	$B + C + D + E + F$	$B + C + D = 921 = \Delta PS$
Government Expense, $-T$	0	$-C - D - F - G$	$-C - D - F - G = -1{,}283 = \Delta T$
Welfare, $W = CS + PS - T$	$A + B + C + E + F$	$A + B + E - G$	$-C - F - G = -1{,}226 = \Delta W = DWL$

[11]The support or target price has increased slowly over time. It was $5.02 in 1985 and $6.00 in 2010–2012.

$Q_s = 2.2$ billion bushels. At $\underline{p}$, consumers buy less output, $Q_d = 1.9$ billion bushels, than the Q_1 they would have bought at the market-determined price p_1. As a result, consumer surplus falls by $B + C = \$864$ million. The government buys $Q_g = Q_s - Q_d \approx 0.3$ billion bushels per year, which is the excess supply, at a cost of $T = \underline{p} \times Q_g = C + D + F + G = \$1.283$ billion.

The government cannot resell the output domestically, because if it tried to do so, it would succeed only in driving down the price consumers pay. Instead, the government stores the output or sends it abroad.

Although farmers gain producer surplus of $B + C + D = \$921$ million, this program is an inefficient way to transfer money to them. Assuming that the government's purchases have no alternative use, the change in welfare is $\Delta W = \Delta CS + \Delta PS - T = -C - F - G = -\$1.226$ billion per year.[12] This deadweight loss reflects two distortions in this market:

1. **Excess production:** More output is produced than is consumed, so Q_g is stored, destroyed, or shipped abroad.
2. **Inefficiency in consumption:** At the quantity they actually buy, Q_d, consumers are willing to pay \$5 for the last bushel of soybeans, which is more than the marginal cost, $MC = \$3.60$, of producing that bushel.

Alternative Price Support. After price supports were first introduced, the U.S. government was buying and storing large quantities of grains and other foods, much of which was allowed to spoil. Consequently, since 1938, the government has limited how much farmers can produce. Because there is uncertainty about how much farmers will produce, the government sets quotas, or limits, on the amount of land farmers can use, thereby restricting their output.

Recently, the government started using an alternative subsidy program.[13] The government sets a support or target price, $\underline{p}$. Farmers decide how much to grow, and they sell all of their produce to consumers at the price, p, that clears the market. The government then gives the farmers a *deficiency* payment equal to the difference between the support and actual prices, $\underline{p} - p$, for every unit sold so that farmers receive the support price on their entire crop.

SOLVED PROBLEM 9.2

What are the effects in the soybean market of a \$5-per-bushel deficiency-payment price support on the equilibrium price and quantity, consumer surplus, producer surplus, and deadweight loss?

Answer

1. *Describe how the program affects the equilibrium price and quantity.* Without a price support, the equilibrium is e_1 in the figure, where the price is $p_1 = \$4.59$ and the quantity is 2.1 billion bushels per year. With a support

---

[12]This measure of deadweight loss underestimates the true loss. The government also pays storage and administration costs. In 2005, the U.S. Department of Agriculture (USDA), which runs farm support programs, had 109,832 employees, or one worker for every eight farms that received assistance (although many of these employees had other job responsibilities). In 2009, the Secretary of Agriculture said that the USDA computer software was so outdated that he could not determine the number of employees. In 2010, a senator estimated that the USDA has one employee for every 30 farmers.

[13]In the last few years, direct subsidies have been reduced, while subsidies for crop insurance have been greatly increased. President Obama's 2012 budget called for more, large cuts to agricultural subsidy programs and particularly to wealthy individuals. Whether these changes occur remains to be seen.

price of \$5 per bushel, the new equilibrium is e_2. Farmers produce at the quantity where the price support line hits their supply curve at 2.2 billion bushels. The equilibrium price is the height of the demand curve at 2.2 billion bushels, or approximately \$4.39 per bushel. Thus, the equilibrium price falls and the quantity increases.

2. *Show the welfare effects.* Because the price consumers pay drops from p_1 to p_2, consumer surplus rises by area $D + E$. Producers now receive $\underline{p}$ instead of p_1, so their producer surplus rises by $B + C$. Government payments are the difference between the support price, $\underline{p} = \$5$, and the price consumers pay, $p_2 = \$4.39$, times the number of units sold, 2.2 billion bushels per year, or the rectangle $B + C + D + E + F$. Because government expenditures exceed the gains to consumers and producers, welfare falls by the deadweight loss triangle F.[14]

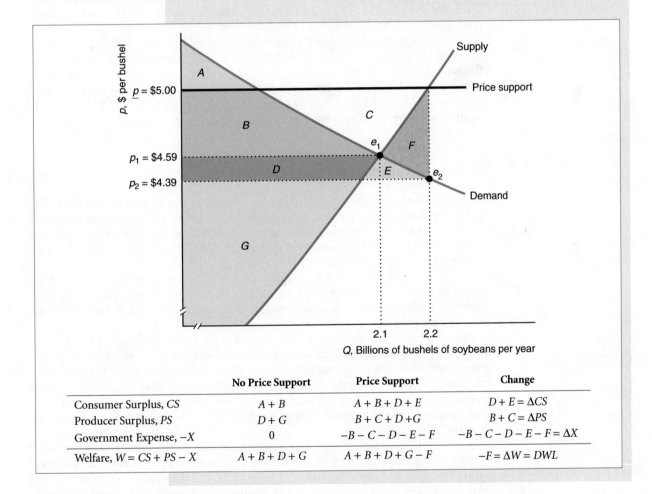

	No Price Support	Price Support	Change
Consumer Surplus, CS	$A + B$	$A + B + D + E$	$D + E = \Delta CS$
Producer Surplus, PS	$D + G$	$B + C + D + G$	$B + C = \Delta PS$
Government Expense, $-X$	0	$-B - C - D - E - F$	$-B - C - D - E - F = \Delta X$
Welfare, $W = CS + PS - X$	$A + B + D + G$	$A + B + D + G - F$	$-F = \Delta W = DWL$

---

[14]Compared to the soybean price support program in Figure 9.7, the deficiency payment approach results in a smaller deadweight loss (less than one-tenth of the original one) and lower government expenditures (though the expenditures need not be smaller in general).

APPLICATION

How Big Are Farm Subsidies and Who Gets Them?

Amount the EU paid to businessmen in Serbia–Montenegro for sugar subsidies before realizing that there was no sugar industry there: $1.2 million.
—Harper's Index, 2004

Virtually every country in the world showers its farmers with subsidies. Although government support to farmers has fallen in developed countries over the last decade, support remains high. Farmers in developed countries received $252 billion in direct agricultural producer support payments (subsidies) in 2011, including $74 billion in the European Union, $31 billion in the United States, $7 billion in Canada, and $5 billion in Japan.

These payments were a large percentage of actual farm sales in many countries, averaging 19% in developed countries. They ranged from 58% in Norway, 54% in Switzerland, 52% in Japan, 18% in the European Union, 14% in Canada, 8% in the United States, 1.5% in Australia, to only 1% in New Zealand.

Total U.S. agricultural support payments were $147 billion, or 1% of the U.S. gross domestic product. Each adult in the United States pays $650 a year to support agriculture. Did you get full value for your money?

The lion's share of American farm subsidies goes to large agricultural corporations, not to poor farmers. According to the Environmental Working Group, three-quarters of the payments go to the largest and wealthiest 10% of farm operations and landlords, while nearly two-thirds of farmers receive no direct payments. Indeed, 23 members of Congress receive payments, and $394 million went to absentee landlords who live in big cities.

Welfare Effects of a Price Ceiling

In some markets, the government sets a *price ceiling*: the highest price that a firm can legally charge. If the government sets the ceiling below the unregulated competitive price, consumers demand more than the unregulated equilibrium quantity and firms supply less than that quantity (Chapter 2). Producer surplus must fall because firms receive a lower price and sell fewer units.

As a result of the price ceiling, consumers buy the good at a lower price but are limited in how much they can buy by sellers. Because less is sold than at the pre-control equilibrium, there is a deadweight loss: Consumers value the good more than the marginal cost of producing extra units.

This measure of the deadweight loss may *underestimate* the true loss for two reasons. First, because consumers want to buy more units than are sold, they may spend additional time searching for a store with units for sale. This (often unsuccessful) search activity is wasteful and thus an additional deadweight loss to society. Deacon and Sonstelie (1989) calculated that for every $1 consumers saved from lower prices due to U.S. gasoline price controls in 1973, they lost $1.16 in waiting time and other factors.[15]

Second, when a price ceiling creates excess demand, the customers who are lucky enough to buy the good may not be the consumers who value it most. In a market without a price ceiling, all consumers who value the good more than the market price buy it, and those who value it less do not, so that those consumers who value it most buy the good. In contrast with a price control where the good is sold on a

---

[15]This type of wasteful search does not occur if the good is efficiently but inequitably distributed to people according to a discriminatory criteria such as race, gender, or attractiveness because people who are suffering discrimination know it is pointless to search.

first-come first-served basis, the consumers who reach the store first may not be the consumers with the highest willingness to pay. With a price control, if a lucky customer who buys a unit of the good has a willingness to pay of p_0, while someone who cannot buy it has a willingness to pay of $p_1 > p_0$, then the *allocative cost* to society of this unit being sold to the "wrong" consumer is $p_1 - p_0$.[16]

SOLVED PROBLEM 9.3	What is the effect on the equilibrium, consumer surplus, producer surplus, and welfare if the government sets a price ceiling, $\bar{p}$, below the unregulated competitive equilibrium price?

Answer

1. *Show the initial unregulated equilibrium.* The intersection of the demand curve and the supply curve determines the unregulated, competitive equilibrium e_1, where the equilibrium quantity is Q_1.

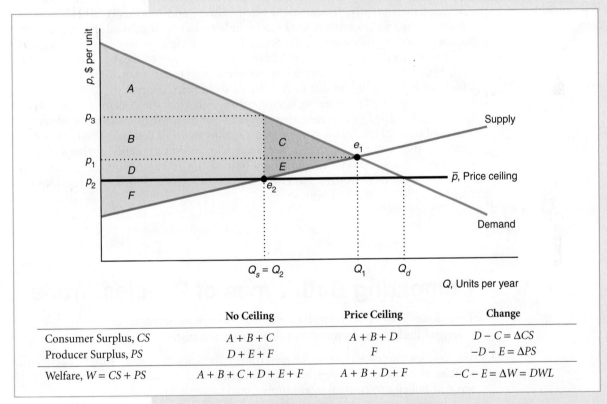

	No Ceiling	Price Ceiling	Change
Consumer Surplus, CS	$A + B + C$	$A + B + D$	$D - C = \Delta CS$
Producer Surplus, PS	$D + E + F$	F	$-D - E = \Delta PS$
Welfare, $W = CS + PS$	$A + B + C + D + E + F$	$A + B + D + F$	$-C - E = \Delta W = DWL$

2. *Show how the equilibrium changes with the price ceiling.* Because the price ceiling, $\bar{p}$, is set below the equilibrium price of p_1, the ceiling binds. At this lower price, consumer demand increases to Q_d while the quantity that firms are willing to supply falls to Q_s, so only $Q_s = Q_2$ units are sold at the new equilibrium, e_2. Thus, the price control causes the equilibrium quantity and price to fall, but consumers have excess demand of $Q_d - Q_s$.

---

[16]This allocative cost will be reduced or eliminated if there is a resale market where consumers who place a high value on the good can buy it from consumers who place a lower value on the good but were lucky enough to be able to buy it initially.

3. *Describe the welfare effects.* Because consumers are able to buy Q_s units at a lower price than before the controls, they gain area D. Consumers lose consumer surplus of C, however, because they can purchase only Q_s instead of Q_1 units of output. Thus, consumers gain net consumer surplus of $D - C$. Because they sell fewer units at a lower price, firms lose producer surplus $-D - E$. Part of this loss, D, is transferred to consumers in the form of lower prices, but the rest, E, is a loss to society. The deadweight loss to society—the change in welfare—is at least $\Delta W = \Delta CS + \Delta PS = -C - E$.

APPLICATION

The Social Cost of a Natural Gas Price Ceiling

From 1954 through 1989, U.S. federal law imposed a price ceiling on interstate sales of natural gas. The law did not apply to sales within states in the Southwest that produced the gas—primarily Louisiana, Oklahoma, New Mexico, and Texas. Consequently, consumers in the Midwest and Northeast, where most of the gas was used, were less likely to be able to buy as much natural gas as they wanted, unlike consumers in the Southwest. Because they could not buy natural gas, some consumers who would have otherwise done so did not install natural gas heating. As heating systems last for years, even today, many homes use dirtier fuels such as heating oil due to this decades-old price control.

By comparing consumer behavior before and after the control period, Davis and Kilian (2011) estimated that demand for natural gas exceeded observed sales of natural gas by an average of 19.4% from 1950 through 2000. They calculated that the allocative cost averaged $3.6 billion annually during this half century. This additional loss is nearly half of the estimated annual deadweight loss from the price control of $10.5 billion (MacAvoy, 2000). The total loss is $14.1 (= $10.5 + $3.6) billion.[17]

9.6.   Comparing Both Types of Policies: Trade

Traditionally, most of Australia's imports come from overseas.
—Keppel Enderbery, former Australian cabinet minister

We have examined examples of government policies that shift supply curves and policies that create a wedge between supply and demand. Governments use both types of policies to control international trade.

Allowing imports of foreign goods benefits the importing country. If a government reduces imports of a good, the domestic price rises; the profits increase for domestic firms that produce the good but domestic consumers are hurt. Our analysis will show that the loss to consumers exceeds the gain to producers.

---

[17]Consumers' share of the deadweight loss, area C in the figure in Solved Problem 9.3, is $9.3 billion annually; the sellers' share, area E, is $1.2 billion; so the entire deadweight loss is $10.5 billion. Consumers who are lucky enough to buy the gas gain area D = $6.9 billion from paying a lower price, which represents a transfer from sellers. Thus, altogether consumers lose $7.0 (= $9.3 + $4.6 − $6.9) billion and firms lose $8.1 (= $1.2 + $6.9) billion.

The government of the (potentially) importing country can use one of four trade policies:

1. **Allow free trade:** Any firm can sell in the importing country without restrictions.
2. **Ban all imports:** The government sets a quota of zero on imports.
3. **Set a positive quota:** The government limits imports to $\overline{Q}$.
4. **Set a tariff:** The government imposes a tax called a **tariff** (or a *duty*) only on imported goods.

We compare welfare under free trade to welfare under bans and quotas, which change the supply curve, and to welfare under tariffs, which create a wedge between supply and demand.

To illustrate the differences in welfare under these various policies, we examine the U.S. market for crude oil. We also assume, for the sake of simplicity, that transportation costs are zero and that the supply curve of the potentially imported good is horizontal at the world price p^*. Given these two assumptions, the importing country, the United States, can buy as much of this good as it wants at p^* per unit: It is a price taker in the world market because its demand is too small to influence the world price.

Free Trade Versus a Ban on Imports

No nation was ever ruined by trade. —Benjamin Franklin

Preventing imports raises the domestic market price. We now compare the equilibrium with and without free trade in the U.S. oil market.

The estimated U.S. daily demand function for oil is[18]

$$Q = D(p) = 35.4p^{-0.37}, \tag{9.3}$$

and the U.S. daily domestic supply function is

$$Q = S(p) = 3.35p^{0.33}. \tag{9.4}$$

Although the estimated U.S. domestic supply curve, S^a, in Figure 9.7 is upward sloping, the foreign supply curve is horizontal at the world price of $14.70. The total U.S. supply curve, S^1, is the horizontal sum of the domestic supply curve and the foreign supply curve. Thus, S^1 is the same as the upward-sloping domestic supply curve for prices below $14.70 and is horizontal at $14.70. Under free trade, the United States imports crude oil if its domestic price in the absence of imports would exceed the world price, $14.70 per barrel.

The free-trade equilibrium, e_1, is determined by the intersection of S^1 and the demand curve, where the U.S. price equals the world price, $14.70. Substituting $p = \$14.70$ into demand function in Equation 9.3, we find that the equilibrium quantity is about $13.1 \approx 35.4(14.70)^{-0.37}$ million barrels per day. At the equilibrium price of $14.70, domestic supply is about 8.2, so imports are $4.9 (= 13.1 - 8.2)$. U.S. consumer surplus is $A + B + C$, U.S. producer surplus is D, and U.S. welfare is $A + B + C + D$. Throughout our discussion of trade, we ignore welfare effects in other countries.

If imports are banned, the total U.S. supply curve, S^2, is the American domestic supply curve, S^a. The equilibrium is at e_2, where S^2 intersects the demand curve. The

---

[18]These short-run, constant-elasticity supply and demand equations for crude oil in 1988 are based on the short-run supply and demand elasticities reported by Anderson and Metzger (1991).

Figure 9.7 Loss from Eliminating Free Trade

Because the supply curve that foreigners face is horizontal at the world price of $14.70, the total U.S. supply curve of crude oil is S^1 when there is free trade. The free-trade equilibrium is e_1. With a ban on imports, the equilibrium e_2 occurs where the domestic supply curve, $S^a = S^2$, intersects D. The ban increases producer surplus by B = $132.5 million per day and decreases consumer surplus by $B + C$ = $163.7 million per day, so the deadweight loss is C = $31.2 million per day or $11.4 billion per year.

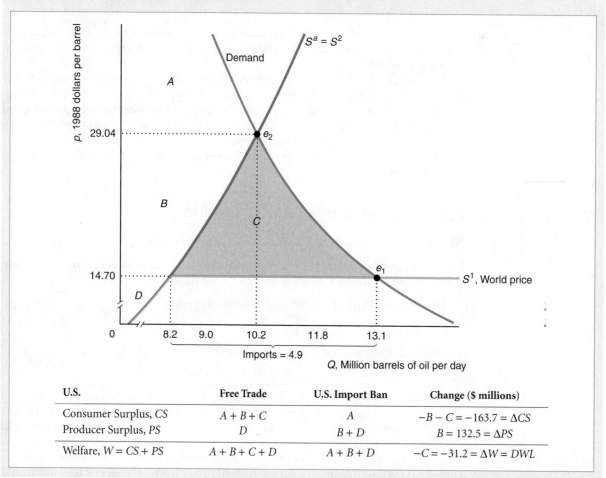

U.S.	Free Trade	U.S. Import Ban	Change ($ millions)
Consumer Surplus, CS	$A + B + C$	A	$-B - C = -163.7 = \Delta CS$
Producer Surplus, PS	D	$B + D$	$B = 132.5 = \Delta PS$
Welfare, $W = CS + PS$	$A + B + C + D$	$A + B + D$	$-C = -31.2 = \Delta W = DWL$

new equilibrium price is $29.04, and the new equilibrium quantity, 10.2 million barrels per day, is produced domestically.[19] Consumer surplus is A, producer surplus is $B + D$, and welfare is $A + B + D$.

The ban helps producers but harms consumers. Because of the higher price, domestic firms gain producer surplus of $\Delta PS = B$. The change in consumer surplus is $\Delta CS = -B - C$. Does the ban help the United States? The change in total welfare, ΔW, is the difference between the gain to producers and the loss to consumers, $\Delta W = \Delta PS + \Delta CS = -C$, so the ban hurts society.

---

[19]In equilibrium, the right-hand sides of Equations 9.3 and 9.4 are equal: $35.4p^{-0.37} = 3.35p^{0.33}$. By dividing both sides by $p^{-0.37}$ and 3.35, we find that $p^{0.7} \approx 10.57$. Raising both sides of this expression to the $1/0.7 = 1.43$ power shows that the no-trade equilibrium price is about $29.04. Substituting this price into Equation 9.3 or 9.4 gives us the equilibrium quantity, which is about 10.2.

SOLVED PROBLEM 9.4

Based on the estimates of the U.S. daily oil demand function in Equation 9.3 and the supply function in Equation 9.4, use calculus to determine the changes in producer surplus, consumer surplus, and welfare from eliminating free trade. (Round results to the nearest tenth.)

Answer

1. *Integrate with respect to price between the free-trade and no-trade prices to obtain the change in producer surplus.* If imports are banned, the gain in domestic producer surplus is the area to the left of the domestic supply curve between the free-trade price, $14.70, and the price with the ban in effect, $29.04, which is area B in Figure 9.7.[20] Integrating, we find that

$$\Delta PS = \int_{14.70}^{29.04} S(p)dp = \int_{14.70}^{29.04} 3.35p^{0.33}dp$$

$$= \frac{3.35}{1.33}p^{1.33}\Big|_{14.70}^{29.04} \approx 2.52(29.04^{1.33} - 14.70^{1.33}) \approx 132.5.$$

2. *Integrate with respect to price between the free-trade and no-trade prices to obtain the change in consumer surplus.* The lost consumer surplus is found by integrating to the left of the demand curve between the relevant prices:

$$\Delta CS = -\int_{14.70}^{29.04} D(p)dp = -\int_{14.70}^{29.04} 35.41p^{-0.37}dp = -163.7.$$

3. *To determine the change in welfare, sum the changes in consumer surplus and producer surplus.* The change in welfare is $\Delta W = \Delta CS + \Delta PS = -163.7 + 132.5 = -\$31.2$ million per day or $-\$11.4$ billion per year. This deadweight loss is 24% of the gain to producers: Consumers lose $1.24 for every $1 that producers gain from a ban.

Free Trade Versus a Tariff

TARIFF, n. A scale of taxes on imports, designed to protect the domestic producer against the greed of his customers. —Ambrose Bierce

There are two common types of tariffs: *specific tariffs* (τ dollars per unit) and *ad valorem tariffs* (α percent of the sales price). In recent years, tariffs have been applied throughout the world, most commonly to agricultural products.[21] American policy-makers have frequently debated the optimal tariff on crude oil as a way to raise revenue or to reduce dependence on foreign oil.

---

[20]Earlier we noted that we can also calculate the producer surplus by integrating below the price, above the supply (or marginal cost) function, up to the relevant quantity.

[21]After World War II, most trading nations signed the General Agreement on Tariffs and Trade (GATT), which limited their ability to subsidize exports or limit imports using quotas and tariffs. The rules prohibited most export subsidies and import quotas, except when imports threatened "market disruption" (a term that unfortunately was not defined). The GATT also required that any new tariff be offset by a reduction in other tariffs to compensate the exporting country. Modifications of the GATT and agreements negotiated by its successor, the World Trade Organization, have reduced or eliminated many tariffs.

You may be asking yourself, "Why should we study tariffs if we've already looked at taxes? Isn't a tariff just another tax?" Good point! Tariffs are just taxes. If only imported goods were sold, the effect of a tariff in the importing country would be the same as for a sales tax. We study tariffs separately because a tariff is applied only to imported goods, so it affects domestic and foreign producers differently.

Because tariffs apply only to imported goods, all else the same, they do not raise as much tax revenue or affect equilibrium quantities as much as taxes applied to all goods in a market. De Melo and Tarr (1992) found that almost five times more tax revenue would be generated by a 15% additional ad valorem tax on petroleum products ($34.6 billion) than by a 25% additional import tariff on oil and gas ($7.3 billion).

To illustrate the effect of a tariff, suppose that the government imposes a specific tariff of $\tau = \$5$ per barrel of crude oil. Given this tariff, firms will not import oil into the United States unless the U.S. price is at least $5 above the world price, $14.70. The tariff creates a wedge between the world price and the U.S. price. This tariff causes the total supply curve to shift from S^1 to S^3 in Figure 9.8. Given that the world's excess supply curve to the United States is horizontal at $14.70, a tariff shifts this supply curve upward so that it is horizontal at $19.70. As a result, the total U.S. supply curve with the tariff, S^3, equals the domestic supply curve for prices below $19.70 and is horizontal at $19.70.

The new equilibrium, e_3, occurs where S^3 intersects the demand curve. At this equilibrium, price is $19.70 and quantity is 11.8 million barrels of oil per day. At this higher price, domestic firms supply 9.0 million barrels, so imports are 2.8 ($= 11.8 - 9.0$).

The tariff *protects* American producers from foreign competition. The larger the tariff, the less oil is imported, and hence the higher the price that domestic firms can charge. (With a large enough tariff, nothing is imported, and the price rises to the no-trade level, $29.04.) With a tariff of $5, domestic firms' producer surplus increases by area $B = \$42.8$ million per day.

Because the price rises from $14.70 to $19.70, consumer surplus falls by $61.9 million per day. The government receives tariff revenues, T, equal to area $D = \$14$ million per day, which is $\tau = \$5$ times the quantity imported, 2.8.

The deadweight loss is $C + E = \$5.1$ million per day, or nearly $1.9 billion per year.[22] This deadweight loss equals almost 12% of the gain to producers. Consumers lose $1.45 for each $1 that domestic producers gain. Because the tariff does not completely eliminate imports, the welfare loss is smaller than it would be if all imports were banned.

We can interpret the two components of this deadweight loss. First, C is the loss from producing 9.0 million barrels per day instead of 8.2 million barrels per day. Domestic firms produce this extra output because the tariff drives up the price from $14.70 to $19.70. The cost of producing these extra 0.8 million barrels of oil per day domestically is $C + G$, the area under the domestic supply curve, S^a, between 8.2 and 9.0. Had Americans bought this oil at the world price, the cost would have been only $G = \$11.8$ million per day. Thus, C is the additional cost of producing the extra 0.8 million barrels of oil per day domestically instead of importing it.

Second, E is a *consumption distortion loss* from American consumers' buying too little oil, 11.8 instead of 13.1 million barrels, because the price rises from $14.70 to $19.70 owing to the tariff. American consumers value this extra output as $E + H$, the area under their demand curve between 11.8 and 13.1, whereas the value in international markets is only H, the area below the line at $14.70 between 11.8 and 13.1. Thus, E is the difference between the value at world prices and the value U.S. consumers place on this extra 1.3 million barrels per day.

---

[22]If the foreign supply is horizontal, welfare in the importing country must fall. However, if the foreign supply is upward sloping, welfare in the importing country may rise.

Figure 9.8 Effect of a Tariff (or Quota)

A tariff of $\tau = \$5$ per barrel of oil imported or a quota of $Q = 2.8$ drives the U.S. price of crude oil to $19.70, which is $5 more than the world price. Under the tariff, the equilibrium, e_3, is determined by the intersection of the S_3 total U.S. supply curve and the D demand curve. Under the quota, e_3 is determined by a quantity wedge of 2.8 million barrels per day between the quantity demanded, 9.0 million barrels per day, and the quantity supplied, 11.8 million barrels per day. Compared to free trade, producers gain $B = \$42.8$ million per day and consumers lose $B + C + D + E = \$61.9$ million per day from the tariff or quota. The deadweight loss under the quota is $C + D + E = \$19.1$ million per day. With a tariff, the government's tariff revenue increases by $D = \$14$ million a day, so the deadweight loss is only $C + E = \$5.1$ million per day.

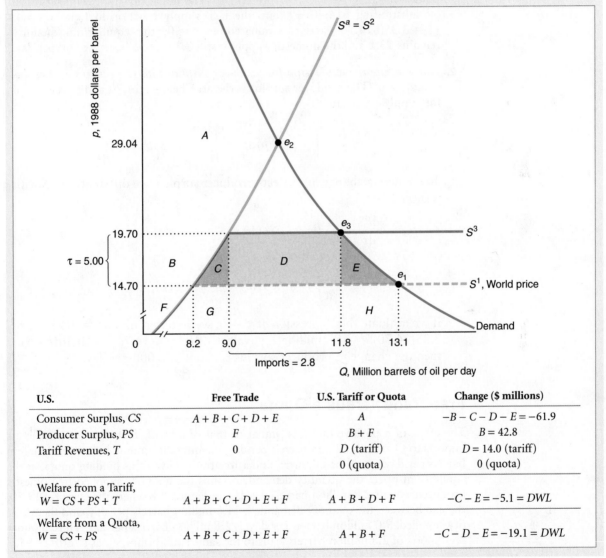

U.S.	Free Trade	U.S. Tariff or Quota	Change (\$ millions)
Consumer Surplus, CS	$A + B + C + D + E$	A	$-B - C - D - E = -61.9$
Producer Surplus, PS	F	$B + F$	$B = 42.8$
Tariff Revenues, T	0	D (tariff)	$D = 14.0$ (tariff)
		0 (quota)	0 (quota)
Welfare from a Tariff, $W = CS + PS + T$	$A + B + C + D + E + F$	$A + B + D + F$	$-C - E = -5.1 = DWL$
Welfare from a Quota, $W = CS + PS$	$A + B + C + D + E + F$	$A + B + F$	$-C - D - E = -19.1 = DWL$

SOLVED PROBLEM 9.5

Based on the estimates of the U.S. daily oil demand function in Equation 9.3 and supply function in Equation 9.4 and the preceding discussion, use calculus to determine the change in equilibrium quantity, the amount supplied by domestic firms, and their producer surplus from a marginal increase in a tariff, evaluated where the tariff is initially zero.

Answer

1. *Discuss the effect of the tariff on the U.S. equilibrium quantity and on the domestic supply of oil at the free-trade equilibrium.* Without the tariff, the U.S. supply curve of oil is horizontal at a price of $14.70 ($S^1$ in Figure 9.8), and the equilibrium is determined by the intersection of this horizontal supply curve with the demand curve. With a new, small tariff of τ, the U.S. supply curve is horizontal at $14.70 + \tau$, and the new equilibrium quantity is determined by substituting $p = 14.70 + \tau$ into the demand function in Equation 9.3: $Q = 35.4(14.70 + \tau)^{-0.67}$. The domestic supply is determined by substituting $14.70 + \tau$ into the U.S. supply function in Equation 9.4: $Q = 3.35(\$14.70 + \tau)^{0.33}$. Evaluated at $\tau = 0$, the equilibrium quantity remains 13.1 and the domestic supply is still 8.2 million barrels of oil per day.

2. *Differentiate the expression for producer surplus with respect to τ and evaluate at $\tau = 0$.* The producer surplus is the area below $14.70 and to the left of the supply curve (area $B + F$ in Figure 9.8):

$$PS = \int_0^{14.70+\tau} S(p)\,dp = \int_0^{14.70+\tau} 3.35p^{0.33}dp.$$

To see how a change in τ affects producer surplus, we differentiate PS with respect to τ:[23]

$$\frac{dPS}{d\tau} = \frac{d}{d\tau}\int_0^{14.70+\tau} S(p)dp = S(14.70 + \tau)$$

$$= \frac{d}{d\tau}\int_0^{14.70+\tau} 3.35p^{0.33}dp = 3.35(14.70 + \tau)^{0.33}.$$

If we evaluate this expression at $\tau = 0$, we find that $dPS/d\tau = S(14.70) = 3.35(14.70)^{0.33} \approx 8.2$ million. Equivalently, $dPS = S(14.70 + \tau)d\tau$. If $d\tau = 1\cent$, then the change in producer surplus is about $82,000 per day.

Free Trade Versus a Quota

The effect of a positive quota is similar to that of a tariff. If the government limits imports to $\overline{Q} = 2.8$ million barrels per day, the quota is binding because 4.9 million barrels per day would be imported under free trade. Given this binding quota, at the equilibrium price, the quantity demanded minus the quantity supplied by domestic producers equals 2.8 million barrels per day. In Figure 9.8 where the price is $19.70, the gap between the quantity demanded, 11.8 million barrels per day, and the quantity supplied, 9.0 million barrels per day, is 2.8 million barrels per day. Thus, a quota on imports of 2.8 million barrels leads to the same equilibrium, e_3, as a tariff of $5.

---

[23]We are using Leibniz's rule for differentiating a definite integral. According to Leibniz's rule,

$$\frac{d}{d\tau}\int_{a(\tau)}^{b(\tau)} f(\tau, p)dp = \int_{a(\tau)}^{b(\tau)} \frac{\partial f(\tau, p)}{\partial \tau}dp + f[\tau, b(\tau)]\frac{db(\tau)}{d(\tau)} - f[\tau, a(\tau)]\frac{da(\tau)}{d(\tau)}.$$

In our problem, neither a nor f are functions of τ and $db(\tau)/d\tau = d(14.70 + \tau)d\tau = 1$.

The gain to domestic producers, *B*, and the loss to consumers, *C* + *E*, are the same as those with a tariff. However, unlike with a tariff, the government does not receive any revenue when it uses a quota (unless the government sells import licenses). Area *D* may go to foreign exporters. As a result, the deadweight loss from the quota, $19.1 million per day, or $7.0 billion per year, is greater than under the tariff. This deadweight loss is nearly half (45%) of the gains to producers.

Thus, the importing country fares better using a tariff than setting a quota that reduces imports by the same amount. Consumers and domestic firms do as well under the two policies, but the government gains tariff revenues, *D*, only when the tariff is used.

Rent Seeking

Given that tariffs and quotas hurt the importing country, why do the Japanese, U.S., and other governments impose tariffs, quotas, or other trade barriers? The reason is that domestic producers stand to make large gains from such government actions; hence, it pays them to organize and lobby the government to enact these trade policies. Although consumers as a whole suffer large losses, the loss to any one consumer is usually small. Moreover, consumers rarely organize to lobby the government about trade issues. Thus, in most countries, producers are often able to convince (cajole, influence, or bribe) legislators or government officials to aid them, even though the loss to consumers exceeds the gain to domestic producers.

If domestic producers can talk the government into a tariff, quota, or other policy that reduces imports, they gain extra producer surplus (rents), such as area *B* in Figures 9.7 and 9.8. Economists call efforts and expenditures to gain a rent or a profit from government actions **rent seeking**. If producers or other interest groups bribe legislators to influence policy, the bribe is a transfer of income and hence does not increase deadweight loss (except to the degree that a harmful policy is chosen). However, if this rent-seeking behavior—such as hiring lobbyists and engaging in advertising to influence legislators—uses up resources, the deadweight loss from tariffs and quotas understates the true loss to society. The domestic producers may spend an amount up to the gain in producer surplus to influence the government.[24]

Indeed, some economists contend that the government revenues from tariffs are completely offset by administrative costs and rent-seeking behavior. If so—and if the tariffs and quotas do not affect world prices—the loss to society from tariffs and quotas equals the entire change in consumer surplus, such as area *B* + *C* in Figure 9.7 and area *B* + *C* + *D* + *E* in Figure 9.8.

Lopez and Pagoulatos (1994) estimated the deadweight loss and the additional losses due to rent-seeking activities in the United States in food and tobacco products. They estimated that the deadweight loss (in 2012 dollars) was $17.7 billion, which was 2.6% of the domestic consumption of these products. The largest deadweight losses were in milk products and sugar manufacturing, which primarily use import quotas to raise domestic prices. The gain in producer surplus is $63.9 billion, or 9.5% of domestic consumption. The government obtained $2.6 billion in tariff revenues, or 0.4% of consumption. If all of producer surplus and government revenues were expended in rent-seeking behavior and other wasteful activities, the total loss was $66.5 billion, or 12.5% of consumption, which is 4.75 times larger than the deadweight loss alone. In other words, the loss to society is somewhere between the deadweight loss of $17.7 billion and $84.2 billion.

---

[24]This argument was made in Tullock (1967) and Posner (1975). Fisher (1985) and Varian (1989) argued that the expenditure is typically less than the producer surplus.

Too bad the only people who know how to run the country are busy driving cabs and cutting hair. —George Burns

We can now answer the Challenge questions from the beginning of the chapter: What effect does restrictive licensing have on taxi fares and cab company profits? What determines the value of a license? How much profit beyond the cost of the license can the acquiring firm expect? What are the effects of licensing on cab drivers and customers?

By limiting the number of cabs, the government causes the supply curve of taxi rides to shift to the left or become more vertical.[25] As a result, the equilibrium price (taxi fare) rises and the equilibrium quantity falls. Consumers are harmed: They do not buy as much as they would at lower prices. Firms that are in the market when the limits are first imposed benefit from higher profits.

If the government did not limit entry, presumably a virtually unlimited number of potential taxi drivers with identical costs could enter the market freely. Panel a of the figure shows a typical taxi owner's marginal cost curve, MC, and average cost curve, AC^1. The MC curve slopes upward because a typical cabbie's opportunity cost of working more hours increases as the cabbie works longer hours (drives more customers). An outward shift of the demand curve is met by new firms entering, so the long-run supply curve of taxi rides, S^1 in panel b, is horizontal at the minimum of AC^1 (Chapter 8). For the market demand curve in the figure, the equilibrium is E_1 where the equilibrium price, p_1, equals the minimum of AC^1 of a typical cab. The total number of rides is $Q_1 = n_1 q_1$, where n_1 is the equilibrium number of cabs and q_1 is the number of rides per month provided by a typical cab.

Consumer surplus, $A + B + C$, is the area under the market demand curve above p_1 up to Q_1. There is no producer surplus because the supply curve is horizontal at the market price, which equals marginal and average cost. Thus, welfare is the same as consumer surplus.

The licensing law limits the number of license or medallions to operate cabs to $n_2 < n_1$. The market supply curve, S^2, is the horizontal sum of the marginal cost curves above the corresponding minimum average cost curves of the n_2 firms in the market. For the market to produce more than $n_2 q_1$ rides, the price must rise to induce the n_2 firms to supply more.

With the same demand curve as before, the equilibrium market price rises to p_2. At this higher price, each licensed cab firm produces more than before by operating longer hours, $q_2 > q_1$, but the total number of rides, $Q_2 = n_2 q_2$, falls because there are fewer cabs, n_2. Consumer surplus is A, producer surplus is B, and welfare is $A + B$.

Thus, because of the higher fares (prices) under a permit system, consumer surplus falls by $\Delta CS = -B - C$. The producer surplus of the lucky permit owners rises by $\Delta PS = B$. As a result, total welfare falls,

$$\Delta W = \Delta CS + \Delta PS = (-B - C) + B = -C,$$

which is a deadweight loss.

By preventing other potential cab firms from entering the market, limiting cab permits creates economic profit, the area labeled π in panel a, for permit owners. In

---

[25]There are two explanations for such regulation. First, using permits to limit the number of cabs raises the earnings of permit owners—usually taxi fleet owners—who lobby city officials for such restrictions. Second, some city officials contend that limiting cabs allows for better regulation of cabbies' behavior and protection of consumers. (However, it would seem possible that cities could directly regulate behavior and not restrict the number of cabs.)

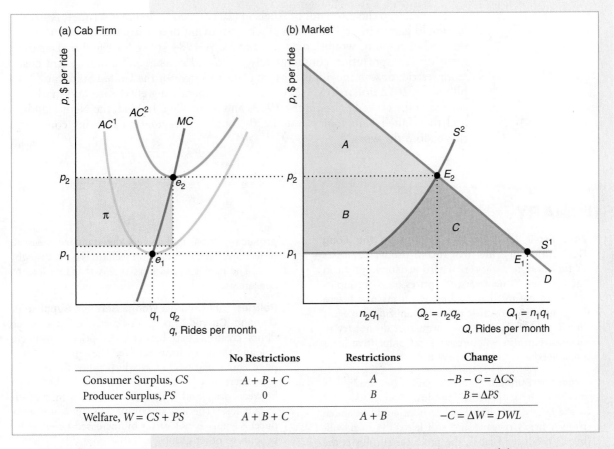

	No Restrictions	Restrictions	Change
Consumer Surplus, CS	$A + B + C$	A	$-B - C = \Delta CS$
Producer Surplus, PS	0	B	$B = \Delta PS$
Welfare, $W = CS + PS$	$A + B + C$	$A + B$	$-C = \Delta W = DWL$

many cities, these permits can be sold or rented, so the owner of the scarce resource, the license, can capture this unusual profit, or rent, by selling the license or medallion for enough to capture the current value of all future profits.

This value is created by the artificial scarcity of cabs. After Ireland's High Court relaxed a severe limit on taxis, the number of cabs in Dublin more than tripled from 2,722 to 8,609 and the value of a taxi license fell from I£90,000 to the new amount that the city charges for a license, I£5,000.

A cab driver pays a lump-sum fee to use the cab for each shift. This fee is similar to renting a car or other piece of capital. The higher the price of the license, the higher the fee. Thus, the new owner's average cost rises to AC^2. Because the fee is a fixed cost that is unrelated to output, it does not affect the marginal cost. Cab drivers earn zero economic profits because the market price, p_2, equals their average cost, the minimum of AC^2. The producer surplus, B, created by the limits on entry goes to the original owners of the permits rather than to the current cab drivers.

Despite the large returns to licenses in New York City, cab drivers do not make unusually high returns net of the license cost. New York cab drivers who lease medallions typically earn between $50 and $115 a day. In Boston, cabbies average 72 hours a week driving someone else's taxi to net maybe $550.

Thus, the original permit owners are the *only* ones who benefit from the restrictions, and their gains are less than the losses to others. If the government collected the rents each year in the form of an annual license, then these rents could be distributed to all citizens instead of to just a few lucky permit owners.

According to the estimates of Abelson (2010), people living in Sydney, Australia would gain $265 million annually by removing taxi restrictions, and most of that, $221 million, would go to consumers. A 1984 study for the U.S. Department of Transportation conservatively estimated consumers' annual extra cost from restrictions on the number of taxicabs throughout the United States at $2.3 billion (in 2012 dollars). Movements toward liberalizing entry into taxi markets started in the United States in the 1980s and in Sweden, Ireland, the Netherlands, and the United Kingdom in the 1990s, but tight regulation remains common throughout the world.

SUMMARY

1. **Zero Profit for Competitive Firms in the Long Run.** Although firms may make profits or losses in the short run, they earn zero economic profit in the long run. If necessary, the prices of scarce inputs adjust to ensure that competitive firms make zero long-run profit. Because profit-maximizing firms just break even in the long run, firms that do not try to maximize profits will lose money. Competitive firms must maximize profit to survive.

2. **Producer Surplus.** A firm's gain from trading is measured by its producer surplus. Producer surplus is the largest amount of money that could be taken from a firm's revenue and still leave the firm willing to produce. That is, the producer surplus is the amount that the firm is paid minus its variable cost of production, which is profit in the long run. It is the area below the price and above the supply curve up to the quantity that the firm sells. The effect of a change in price on a supplier is measured by the change in producer surplus.

3. **Competition Maximizes Welfare.** A standard measure of welfare is the sum of consumer surplus and producer surplus. The more price is above marginal cost, the lower is this measure of welfare. In the competitive equilibrium, in which price equals marginal cost, welfare is maximized.

4. **Policies That Shift Supply Curves.** Governments frequently limit the number of firms in a market directly by licensing them, or indirectly by raising the costs of entry to new firms or by raising the cost of exiting. A reduction in the number of firms in a competitive market raises price, hurts consumers, helps producing firms, and lowers the standard measure of welfare. This reduction in welfare is a deadweight loss: The gain to producers is less than the loss to consumers.

5. **Policies That Create a Wedge Between Supply and Demand Curves.** Taxes, price ceilings, and price floors create a gap between the price consumers pay and the price firms receive. These policies force price above marginal cost, which raises the price to consumers and lowers the amount sold. The wedge between price and marginal cost results in a deadweight loss: The loss of consumer surplus and producer surplus is not offset by increased taxes or by benefits to other groups.

6. **Comparing Both Types of Policies: Trade.** A government may use either a quantity restriction such as a quota, which shifts the supply curve, or a tariff, which creates a wedge, to reduce imports or achieve other goals. These policies may have different welfare implications. A tariff that reduces imports by the same amount as a quota has the same harms—a larger loss of consumer surplus than increased domestic producer surplus—but has a partially offsetting benefit—increased tariff revenues for the government. Rent-seeking activities are attempts by firms or individuals to influence a government to adopt a policy that favors them. By using up resources, rent seeking exacerbates the welfare loss beyond the deadweight loss caused by the policy itself. In a perfectly competitive market, government policies frequently lower welfare. As later chapters show, however, in markets that are not perfectly competitive, government policies may increase welfare.

EXERCISES

■ = *exercise is available on* MyEconLab; * = *answer appears at the back of this book;* **M** = *mathematical problem.*

1. Zero Profit for Competitive Firms in the Long Run

1.1 Only a limited amount of high-quality wine-growing land is available. The firms that farm the land are identical. Because the demand curve hits the market supply curve in its upward sloping section, the firms initially earn positive profit.

a. The owners of the land raise their rents to capture the profit. Show how the market supply curve changes (if at all).

b. Suppose some firms own the land and some rent. Do these firms behave differently in terms of their shutdown decision or in any other way?

1.2 The reputations of some of the world's most prestigious museums have been damaged by accusations that they obtained antiquities that were looted or stolen in violation of international laws and treaties aimed at halting illicit trade in art and antiquities (Ron Stodghill, "Do You Know Where That Art Has Been?" *New York Times*, March 18, 2007). A new wariness among private and public collectors to buy works whose provenance has not been rigorously established jeopardizes the business of even the most established dealers. Conversely, this fear has increased the value of antiquities that have a solid ownership history. The Aboutaam brothers, who are among the world's most powerful dealers of antiquities, back an international ban on trade in excavated antiquities. As Hicham Aboutaam said, "The more questionable works entering the antiquities market, the less their value and the larger the dark cloud that hangs over the field. That affects prices negatively. I think we could put an end to the new supply, and work comfortably with what we have."

a. What would be the effect of the ban on the current stock of antiquities for sale in the United States and Europe?

b. Would such a ban differentially affect established dealers and new dealers?

c. Why would established dealers back such a ban?

d. Discuss the implications of a ban using the concept of an economic rent.

1.3 Explain the reasoning in the Application "Tiger Woods' Rents" as to why Tiger Woods was able to capture essentially all the rents from some companies but not from others.

2. Producer Surplus

2.1 For a firm, how does the concept of *producer surplus* differ from that of *profit*?

2.2 If the supply curve is $q = 2 + 2p$, what is the producer surplus if the price is 10? (*Hint:* See Solved Problem 9.1.) **M**

2.3 If the supply function is $q = ap^\eta$, what is the producer surplus if price is p^*? (*Hint:* See Solved Problem 9.1.) **M**

3. How Competition Maximizes Welfare

3.1 If society cared only about the well-being of consumers so that it wanted to maximize consumer surplus, would a competitive market achieve that goal given that the government cannot force or bribe firms to produce more than the competitive level of output? How would your answer change if society cared only about maximizing producer surplus?

3.2 Suppose that the market demand for 32-oz. wide mouth Nalgene bottles is $Q = 50{,}000p^{-1.076}$, where Q is the quantity of bottles per week and p is the price per bottle. The market supply is $Q = 0.01p^{7.208}$. What is the equilibrium price and quantity? What is the consumer surplus? What is the producer surplus? **M**

3.3 Suppose that the inverse market demand for silicone replacement tips for Sony EX71 earbud headphones is $p = p_N - 0.1Q$, where p is the price per pair of replacement tips, p_N is the price of a new pair of headphones, and Q is the number of tips per week. Suppose that the inverse supply function of the replacement tips is $p = 2 + 0.012Q$.

a. Find the effect of a change in the price of a new pair of headphones on the equilibrium price of replacement tips at the equilibrium, dp/dp_N.

b. If $p_N = \$30$, what are the equilibrium p and Q? What is the consumer surplus? What is the producer surplus? **M**

3.4 The U.S. Department of Agriculture's (USDA) minimum general recommendation is five servings of fruits and vegetables a day. Jetter et al. (2004) estimated that if consumers followed that guideline, the equilibrium price and quantity of most fruits and vegetables would increase substantially. For example, the price of salad would rise 7.2%, output would increase 3.5%, and growers' revenues would jump 7.3% (presumably, health benefits would occur as well). Use a diagram to illustrate as many of these effects as possible and to show how consumer surplus and producer surplus change. Discuss how to calculate the consumer surplus (given that the USDA's recommendation shifts consumers' tastes or behavior).

3.5 Use an indifference curve diagram (gift goods on one axis and all other goods on the other) to illustrate that one is better off receiving cash than a gift. (*Hint*: See the discussion of gifts in this chapter and the discussion of food stamps in Chapter 5.) Relate your analysis to the Application "Deadweight Loss of Christmas Presents."

4. Policies That Shift Supply Curves

4.1 The government imposes a restriction on firms that shifts the supply curve in Figure 9.3 so that it intersects the demand curve at e_2. Discuss the effects on CS, PS, welfare, and DWL.

4.2 The park service wants to restrict the number of visitors to Yellowstone National Park to Q^*, which is fewer than the current volume. It considers two policies: (a) raising the price of admissions and (b) setting a quota. Compare the effects of these two policies on consumer surplus and welfare. Use a graph to show which policy is superior according to the welfare criterion.

5. Policies That Create a Wedge Between Supply and Demand Curves

5.1 If the inverse demand function for books is $p = 60 - q$ and the supply function is $q = p$, what is the initial equilibrium? What is the welfare effect of a specific tax of $\tau = \$2$ per unit on the equilibrium, CS, PS, welfare, and DWL? **M**

5.2 Suppose that the demand curve for wheat is $Q = 100 - 10p$ and that the supply curve is $Q = 10p$. What are the effects of a specific tax of $\tau = 1$ per unit on the equilibrium, government tax revenue, CS, PS, welfare, and DWL? **M**

5.3 The initial equilibrium is e, where the linear supply curve intersects the linear demand curve. Show the welfare effects of imposing a specific tax τ. Now suppose the demand curve becomes flatter, but still goes through point e, so that it is more elastic at e than originally. Discuss how the tax affects the equilibrium, CS, PS, welfare, and DWL differently than with the original demand curve.

5.4 Suppose that the demand curve for wheat is $Q = 100 - 10p$ and that the supply curve is $Q = 10p$. What are the effects of a subsidy (negative tax) of $s = 1$ per unit on the equilibrium, government subsidy cost, CS, PS, welfare, and DWL? **M**

*5.5 Suppose that the government gives rose producers a specific subsidy of $s = 11¢$ per stem. (Figure 9.5 shows the original demand and supply curves.) What is the effect of the subsidy on the equilibrium prices and quantity, consumer surplus, producer surplus, government expenditures, welfare, and deadweight loss?

5.6 What is the welfare effect of an ad valorem sales tax, α, assessed on each competitive firm in a market?

*5.7 What is the long-run welfare effect of a profit tax (the government collects a specified percentage of a firm's profit) assessed on each competitive firm in a market?

*5.8 What is the welfare effect of a lump-sum tax, $\mathcal{L}$, assessed on each competitive firm in a market? (*Hint*: See the Challenge Solution in Chapter 8.)

5.9 The United States not only subsidizes producers of cotton (in several ways, including a water subsidy and a price support) but also pays $1.7 billion to U.S. agribusiness and manufacturers to buy American cotton. It has paid $100 million each to Allenberg Cotton and Dunavant Enterprises and large amounts to more than 300 other firms (Elizabeth Becker, "U.S. Subsidizes Companies to Buy Subsidized Cotton," *New York Times*, November 4, 2003, C1, C2). Assume for simplicity that specific subsidies (dollars per unit) are used. Use a diagram to show how applying both subsidies changes the equilibrium from the no-subsidy case. Show who gains and who loses.

*5.10 Suppose that the demand curve for wheat is $q = 100 - 10p$ and the supply curve is $q = 10p$. The government imposes a price support at $p = 6$ using a deficiency payment program.

a. What is the quantity supplied, the price that clears the market, and the deficiency payment?

b. What effect does this program have on consumer surplus, producer surplus, welfare, and deadweight loss? (*Hint*: See Solved Problem 9.2.) **M**

5.11 Suppose that the demand curve for wheat is $Q = 100 - 10p$ and the supply curve is $Q = 10p$. The government imposes a price ceiling of $p = 3$.

a. Describe how the equilibrium changes.

b. What effect does this ceiling have on consumer surplus, producer surplus, and deadweight loss? **M**

5.12 The government wants to drive the price of soybeans above the equilibrium price, p_1, to p_2. It offers growers a payment of x to reduce their output from Q_1 (the equilibrium level) to Q_2, which is the quantity demanded by consumers at p_2. Show in a figure how large x must be for growers to reduce output to this level. What are the effects of this program on consumers, farmers, and total welfare? Compare this approach to (a) offering a price support of p_2, (b) offering a price support and a quota set at Q_1, and (c) offering a price support and a quota set at Q_2.

5.13 What were the welfare effects (who gained, who lost, what was the deadweight loss) of the gasoline price controls described in Chapter 2? Add the relevant areas to a drawing like Figure 2.14. (*Hint*: See Solved Problem 9.3.)

5.14 What are the welfare effects of a binding minimum wage? Use a graphical approach to show what happens if all workers are identical. Then describe in writing what is likely to happen to workers who differ by experience, education, age, gender, and race.

5.15 A mayor wants to help renters in her city. She considers two policies that will benefit renters equally. One policy is a *rent control*, which places a price ceiling, p, on rents. The other is a government housing subsidy of s dollars per month that lowers the amount renters pay (to p). Who benefits and who loses from these policies? Compare the effects of the two policies on the quantity of housing consumed, consumer surplus, producer surplus, government expenditure, and deadweight loss. Does the comparison of deadweight loss depend on the elasticities of supply and demand? (*Hint*: Consider extreme cases and see Solved Problem 9.3.) If so, how?

6. Comparing Both Types of Policies: Trade

6.1 Although 23 states barred the sale of self-service gasoline in 1968, most removed the bans by the mid-1970s. By 1992, self-service outlets sold nearly 80% of all U.S. gas, and only New Jersey and Oregon continued to ban self-service sales. Johnson and Romeo (2000) estimated that the ban in those two states raised the price of gasoline by approximately 3¢ to 5¢ per gallon. Why did the ban affect the price? Illustrate using a figure and explain. Show the welfare effects in your figure. Use a table to show who gains and who loses.

6.2 The U.S. Supreme Court ruled in May 2005 that people can buy wine directly from out-of-state vineyards. The Court held that state laws requiring people to buy directly from wine retailers within the state violate the Constitution's commerce clause.

a. Suppose the market for wine in New York is perfectly competitive both before and after the Supreme Court decision. Use the analysis of Section 9.6 to evaluate the effect of the Court's decision on the price of wine in New York.

b. Evaluate the increase in New York consumer surplus, producer surplus, and welfare.

6.3 Canada has 20% of the world's known freshwater resources, yet many Canadians believe that the country has little or none to spare. Over the years, U.S. and Canadian firms have struck deals to export bulk shipments of water to drought-afflicted U.S. cities and towns. Provincial leaders have blocked these deals in British Columbia and Ontario. Use graphs to show the likely outcome of such barriers to exports on the price and quantity of water used in Canada and in the United States if markets for water are competitive. Show the effects on consumer and producer surplus in both countries.

6.4 In Solved Problem 9.4, if the domestic demand curve is $Q = 20p^{-0.5}$, the domestic supply curve is $Q = 5p^{0.5}$, and the world price is 5, use calculus to determine the changes in producer surplus, consumer surplus, and welfare from eliminating free trade. **M**

*6.5 Based on the estimates of the U.S. daily oil demand function in Equation 9.3 and supply function in Equation 9.4, use calculus to determine the change in deadweight loss from a marginal increase in a tariff, evaluated where the tariff is initially zero. (*Hint*: You are being asked to determine how an area similar to that of $C + E$ in Figure 9.8 changes when a small tariff is initially applied. See Solved Problem 9.5.) **M**

6.6 The U.S. government claimed that China and Vietnam were dumping shrimp in the United States at a price below cost, and proposed duties as high as 112%. Suppose that China and Vietnam were subsidizing their shrimp fisheries. In a diagram, show who gains and who loses in the United States (compared to the equilibrium in which those nations do not subsidize their shrimp fisheries). The United States imposed a 10.17% antidumping duty (essentially a tariff) on shrimp from these and several other countries. Use your diagram to show how the large tariff would affect government revenues and the welfare of consumers and producers.

6.7 Show that if the importing country faces an upward-sloping foreign supply curve (excess supply curve), a tariff may raise welfare in the importing country.

6.8 Given that the world supply curve is horizontal at the world price for a given good, can a subsidy on imports raise welfare in the importing country? Explain your answer.

6.9 After Mexico signed the North American Free Trade Agreement (NAFTA) with the United States in 1994, corn imports from the United States doubled within a year, and today U.S. imports make up nearly one-third of the corn consumed in Mexico. According to Oxfam (2003), the price of Mexican corn has fallen more than 70% since NAFTA took effect. Part of the reason for this flow south of our border is that the U.S. government subsidizes corn production to the tune of $10 billion a year. According to Oxfam, the 2002 U.S. cost of production was $3.08 per bushel, but the export price was $2.69 per bushel, with the difference reflecting an export subsidy of 39¢ per bushel. The U.S. exported 5.3 metric tons. Use graphs to show the effect of such a subsidy on the welfare of various groups and on government expenditures in the United States and Mexico.

6.10 In the first quarter of 2012, the world price for raw sugar, 24¢ per pound, was about 70% of the domestic price, 34¢ per pound, because of quotas and tariffs on sugar imports. Consequently, American-made corn sweeteners can be profitably sold domestically. A decade ago, the U.S. Commerce Department estimated that the quotas and price support reduce American welfare by about $3 billion a year, so, each dollar of Archer Daniels Midland's profit from selling U.S. sugar costs Americans about $10. Model the effects of a quota on sugar in both the sugar and corn sweetener markets.

6.11 During the Napoleonic Wars, Britain blockaded North America, seizing U.S. vessels and cargo and impressing sailors. At President Thomas Jefferson's request, Congress imposed a nearly complete—perhaps 80%—embargo on international commerce from December 1807 to March 1809. Just before the embargo, exports were about 13% of the U.S. gross national product (GNP). Due to the embargo, U.S. consumers could not find acceptable substitutes for manufactured goods from Europe, and producers could not sell farm produce and other goods for

as much as in Europe. According to Irwin (2005), the welfare cost of the embargo was at least 8% of the GNP in 1807. Use graphs to show the effects of the embargo on a market for an exported good and one for an imported good. Show the change in equilibria and the welfare effects on consumers and firms.

6.12 A government is considering a quota and a tariff, both of which will reduce imports by the same amount. Why might the government prefer one of these policies to the other?

7. Challenge

7.1 In 2002, Los Angeles imposed a ban on new billboards. Owners of existing billboards did not oppose the ban. Why? What are the implications of the ban for producer surplus, consumer surplus, and welfare? Who are the producers and consumers in your analysis? How else does the ban affect welfare in Los Angeles? (*Hint*: The demand curve for billboards shifts to the right over time.)

7.2 There are many possible ways to limit the number of cabs in a city. The most common method is an explicit quota using a fixed number of medallions that are good forever and can be resold. One alternative is to charge a high license fee each year, which would reduce supply by as much as would a medallion or license that lasts only a year. A third option is to charge a daily tax on taxicabs. Using figures, compare and contrast the equilibrium under each of these approaches. Discuss who wins and who loses from each plan, considering consumers, drivers, the city, and (if relevant) medallion owners.

General Equilibrium and Economic Welfare

10

Capitalism is the astounding belief that the most wickedest of men will do the most wickedest of things for the greatest good of everyone.
—John Maynard Keynes

CHALLENGE

Anti-Price Gouging Laws

After a disaster strikes, prices tend to rise. For example, the average U.S. gasoline price increased by 46¢ per gallon after Hurricane Katrina in 2005 damaged most Gulf Coast oil refineries. Many state governments enforce anti-price gouging laws to prevent prices from rising, while prices may be free to adjust in neighboring states. For example, Louisiana's anti-price gouging law went into effect when Governor Bobby Jindal declared a state of emergency in response to the 2010 BP oil spill that endangered Louisiana's coast.

Rhode Island passed an anti-price gouging law in 2012, joining nearly 30 other states. Arkansas, California, Maine, New Jersey, Oklahoma, Oregon, and West Virginia set a "percentage increase cap limit" on how much price may be increased after a disaster, ranging from 10% to 25% of the price before the emergency. California passed its law in 1994 after the Northridge earthquake. Sixteen states prohibit "unconscionable" price increases. After Hurricane Katrina disrupted gasoline deliveries, then Massachusetts Governor Mitt Romney established a hotline for consumers to report evidence of price gouging. Connecticut, Georgia, Hawaii, Kentucky, Louisiana, Mississippi, and Utah have outright bans on price increases during an emergency. Georgia enacted its anti-price gouging statute after a 500-year flood in 1994. However, the Georgia state senate passed a bill in 2010 to remove its anti-price gouging legislation and allow gasoline prices to rise after an emergency. Other states do not have such laws.

Governments pass anti-price gouging laws because they're popular. After the post-Katrina gas price increases, an ABC News/Washington Post poll found that only 16% of respondents thought that the price increase was "justified," 72.7% thought that "oil companies and gas dealers are taking unfair advantage," 7.4% said both views were true, and the rest held another or no opinion.

In Chapter 2, we showed that a national price control causes shortages. However, does a binding price control that affects one state, but not a neighboring state, cause shortages? How does it affect prices and quantities sold in the two states? Which consumers benefit from these laws?

In addition to natural disasters, a change in government policies or other shocks often affect equilibrium price and quantity in more than one market. To determine the effects of such a change, we must examine the interrelationships among markets. In this chapter, we extend our analysis of equilibrium in a single market to equilibrium in all markets.

We also examine how a society decides whether a particular equilibrium (or change in equilibrium) in all markets is desirable. To do so, society must answer two questions: "Is the equilibrium efficient?" and "Is the equilibrium equitable?"

For an equilibrium to be efficient, both consumption and production must be efficient. Production is efficient only if it is impossible to produce more output at current cost given current knowledge (Chapter 6). Consumption is efficient only if goods cannot be reallocated among people so that at least someone is better off and no one is harmed. This chapter shows how we determine whether consumption is efficient.

Whether an equilibrium is efficient is a scientific question. It is possible that all members of society could agree on how to answer scientific questions concerning efficiency.

Deciding whether an equilibrium is equitable, however, involves making a value judgment as to whether each member of society has his or her fair or just share of all the goods and services. A common view in individualistic cultures is that each person is the best—and possibly, the only legitimate—judge of his or her own welfare. Nonetheless, to make social choices about events that affect more than one person, we must make interpersonal comparisons, through which we decide whether one person's gain is more or less important than another person's loss. For example, we showed that a price ceiling lowers a measure of total welfare when the value judgment that the well-being of consumers, consumer surplus, and the well-being of the owners of firms, producer surplus, are weighted equally (Chapter 9). People of goodwill—and others—may disagree greatly about questions of equity.

As a first step in studying welfare issues, many economists use a narrow value criterion due to the Italian economist Vilfredo Pareto to rank different allocations of goods and services for which no interpersonal comparisons need to be made. According to the **Pareto principle**, society should favor a change that benefits some people without harming others. Thus, according to this principle, if everyone shares in the extra surplus when a government policy eliminates a market failure, then the government should make this change.

A **Pareto improvement** is a change, such as a reallocation of goods between people, that helps at least one person without harming anyone else. An example of a Pareto improvement is an exchange when a baseball card collector trades cards with another collector. Both are better off and no one else is harmed by the exchange. Once all possible Pareto improvements have occurred, the outcome is **Pareto efficient** because any possible reallocation of goods and services would harm at least one person.[1]

Presumably, you agree that a government policy that makes all members of society better off is desirable. Do you also agree that a policy that makes some members better off without harming others is desirable? What about a policy that helps one group more than it hurts another? Or how about a policy that hurts another group more than it helps your group? It is unlikely that all members of society will agree on how to answer these questions—much less agree on the answers.

The efficiency and equity questions arise even in small social units such as a family. Suppose that your family has gathered in November and everyone wants pumpkin pie.

---

[1]Pareto efficiency is a more general concept than economic efficiency, which is based on maximization of welfare. If a market exhibits Pareto efficiency, the market is efficient: it maximizes welfare. Unlike the surplus concept, the Pareto concept can also be used in non-market situations. For example, if two people are happier after they marry, then that marriage is a Pareto improvement, even though we cannot reasonably define a related price or measure of consumer and producer surplus.

How much pie you bake will depend on the answer to efficiency and equity questions such as "How can we make the pie as large as possible with available resources?" and "How should we divide the pie?" It will probably be easier to agree about how to make the largest pie possible than about how to divide it equitably.

So far in this book (aside from Chapter 9's welfare analysis), we have used economic theory to answer the scientific efficiency question. We have concentrated on that question because the equity question requires a value judgment. (Strangely, most members of society seem to believe that economists are no better at making value judgments than anyone else.)

In this chapter, we examine five main topics	
	1. **General Equilibrium.** The welfare analysis in Chapter 9 (involving gains and losses in consumer and producer surplus) changes when a shift in government policy or another shock affects several markets at once.
	2. **Trading Between Two People.** When two people have goods but cannot produce more goods, both parties benefit from mutually agreeable trades.
	3. **Competitive Exchange.** The competitive equilibrium has two desirable properties: Any competitive equilibrium is Pareto efficient, and any Pareto-efficient allocation can be obtained by using competition given an appropriate income distribution.
	4. **Production and Trading.** The benefits from trade continue to hold when production is introduced.
	5. **Efficiency and Equity.** Because there are many Pareto-efficient allocations, a society uses its views about equity to choose among them.

10.1 General Equilibrium

So far, we have used a **partial-equilibrium analysis**: an examination of equilibrium and changes in equilibrium in one market in isolation. In a partial-equilibrium analysis in which we hold the prices and quantities of other goods fixed, we implicitly ignore the possibility that events in this market affect other markets' equilibrium prices and quantities.

When stated this baldly, partial-equilibrium analysis sounds foolish, but it need not be. Suppose that the government puts a specific tax on the price of hula hoops. If the tax is sizable, it will dramatically affect hula hoop sales. However, even a very large tax on hula hoops is unlikely to affect the markets for automobiles, doctors' services, or orange juice. It is even unlikely to affect the demand for other toys much. Thus, a partial-equilibrium analysis of the effect of such a tax should serve us well. Studying all markets simultaneously to analyze this tax would be unnecessary at best and confusing at worst.

Sometimes, however, we need to use a **general-equilibrium analysis**: the study of how equilibrium is determined in all markets simultaneously. For example, the discovery of a major oil deposit in a small country raises the income of its citizens, and the increased income affects all of that country's markets. Sometimes economists model many markets in an economy and solve for the general equilibrium in all of them simultaneously.

Frequently, economists look at equilibrium in several—but not all—markets simultaneously. We would expect a tax on comic books to affect the price of comic books, which in turn would affect the price of video games because video games are substitutes for comics. But we would not expect a tax on comics to have a measurable effect on the demand for washing machines. Therefore, it is reasonable to conduct a *multimarket analysis* of the effects of a tax on comics by looking only at the markets for comics, video games, and a few other closely related markets such as those for movies and trading cards. That is, a multimarket equilibrium analysis covers the relevant markets, but not all markets, as a general equilibrium analysis would.

Markets are closely related if an increase in the price in one market causes the demand or supply curve in another market to shift measurably. Suppose that a tax on coffee causes the price of coffee to increase. The rise in the price of coffee causes the demand curve for tea to shift outward (more tea is demanded at any given price of tea) because tea and coffee are substitutes. The price increase of coffee also causes the demand curve for cream to shift inward because coffee and cream are complements.

Similarly, supply curves in different markets may be related. If a farmer produces corn and soybeans, an increase in the price of corn will affect the relative amounts of both crops that the farmer chooses to produce.

Markets may also be linked if the output of one market is an input in another market. A shock that raises the price of computer chips will also raise the price of computers.

Thus, an event in one market may have a *spillover effect* on other, related markets for various reasons. Indeed, a single event may initiate a chain reaction of spillover effects that reverberates between markets.

Competitive Equilibrium in Two Interrelated Markets

Suppose that the demand functions for Good 1, Q_1, and Good 2, Q_2, depend on both prices, p_1 and p_2,

$$Q_1 = D_1(p_1, p_2),$$
$$Q_2 = D_2(p_1, p_2),$$

but that the supply function for each good depends only on the good's own price,

$$Q_1 = S_1(p_1),$$
$$Q_2 = S_2(p_2).$$

To determine the equilibrium p_1, p_2, Q_1, and Q_2, we solve these four equations in four unknowns simultaneously.

Doing so is straightforward with linear equations. Suppose that the demand functions are linear,

$$Q_1 = a_1 - b_1 p_1 + c_1 p_2, \tag{10.1}$$
$$Q_2 = a_2 - b_2 p_2 + c_2 p_1, \tag{10.2}$$

as are the supply functions,

$$Q_1 = d_1 + e_1 p_1, \tag{10.3}$$
$$Q_2 = d_2 + e_2 p_2, \tag{10.4}$$

where all the coefficients are positive numbers.

Equating the quantity demanded and supplied for both markets—setting the right-hand side of Equation 10.1 equal to the right-hand side of Equation 10.3, and similarly for Equations 10.2 and 10.4—we obtain

$$a_1 - b_1 p_1 + c_1 p_2 = d_1 + e_1 p_1, \tag{10.5}$$
$$a_2 - b_2 p_2 + c_2 p_1 = d_2 + e_2 p_2. \tag{10.6}$$

We now have two equations, 10.5 and 10.6, in two unknowns, p_1 and p_2, to solve. The solutions of these two equations are

$$p_1 = \frac{(b_2 + e_2)(a_1 - d_1) + c_1(a_2 - d_2)}{(b_1 + e_1)(b_2 + e_2) - c_1 c_2}, \tag{10.7}$$

$$p_2 = \frac{(b_1 + e_1)(a_2 - d_2) + c_2(a_1 - d_1)}{(b_1 + e_1)(b_2 + e_2) - c_1 c_2}. \tag{10.8}$$

Substituting these values for p_1 and p_2 in the demand functions 10.1 and 10.2 or in the supply functions 10.3 and 10.4, we obtain expressions for Q_1 and Q_2. Thus, by simultaneously solving the demand and supply curves for related markets, we can determine the equilibrium price and quantities in both markets.

APPLICATION

Partial-Equilibrium
Versus Multimarket-
Equilibrium Analysis
in Corn and Soybean
Markets

Consumers and producers substitute between corn and soybeans, so the demand and supply curves in these markets are related according to the estimates of Holt (1992). The quantity of corn demanded and the quantity of soybeans demanded depend on the price of corn, the price of soybeans, and other variables. Similarly, the quantities of corn and soybeans supplied depend on their relative prices.

A shock in one market affects both markets. Given actual supply and demand curves for corn and soybeans, the original equilibrium price of corn is $2.15 per bushel, and the quantity is 8.44 billion bushels per year; and the equilibrium price of soybeans is $4.12 per bushel, and the quantity is 2.07 billion bushels per year (see the first row of the table).[2] Now suppose that a scare about the safety of corn causes a parallel shift to the left of the foreign demand curve for American corn so that at the original price, the export of corn falls by 10%.

If we were conducting a partial-equilibrium analysis, we would examine the new corn equilibrium, where the new U.S. corn demand curve intersects the corn supply curve. The second row of the table shows the partial equilibrium effects on the corn equilibrium holding other prices (such as the price of soybeans) constant.

In a multimarket-equilibrium analysis, we consider how this shock to the corn market affects the soybean market, and how the changed soybean price in turn affects the corn market. The third row of the table shows the new multimarket equilibrium in both markets.

	Corn		Soybeans	
Equilibria	*Price*	*Quantity*	*Price*	*Quantity*
Original equilibria	2.15	8.44	4.12	2.07
New partial equilibrium	1.917	8.227		
New multimarket equilibria	1.905	8.263	3.82	2.05

---

[2]Until recently, the corn and soybean markets were subject to price controls (Chapter 9). However, we use the estimated demand and supply curves to determine what would happen in these markets without price controls.

Suppose that we were interested only in the effect of the shift in the foreign corn demand curve on the corn market. Could we rely on a partial-equilibrium analysis? According to a partial-equilibrium analysis, the price of corn falls 10.8% to $1.917. In contrast, in the multimarket-equilibrium analysis, the price falls 11.4% to $1.905, which is 1.2¢ less per bushel. That is, the partial-equilibrium analysis underestimates the price effect by 0.6 percentage point. Similarly, the fall in quantity is 2.5% according to the partial-equilibrium analysis and only 2.1% according to the multimarket-equilibrium analysis. Thus in this market, the biases from using a partial-equilibrium analysis are small.[3]

Minimum Wages with Incomplete Coverage

We used a partial-equilibrium analysis in Chapter 2 to examine the effects of a minimum wage law that holds throughout the entire labor market. The minimum wage causes the quantity of labor demanded to be less than the quantity of labor supplied. Workers who lose their jobs cannot find work elsewhere and are unemployed.

The story changes substantially, however, if the minimum wage law covers workers in only some sectors of the economy, as we show using a general-equilibrium analysis. This analysis is relevant because historically the U.S. minimum wage law has not covered all workers.

When a minimum wage is applied to a covered sector of the economy, the increase in the wage causes the quantity of labor demanded in that sector to fall. Workers who are displaced from jobs in the covered sector move to the uncovered sector, driving down the wage in that sector. When the U.S. minimum wage law was first passed in 1938, some economists joked that its purpose was to maintain family farms: The law drove workers out of manufacturing and other covered industries into the uncovered agricultural sector.

Figure 10.1 shows the effect of a minimum wage law when coverage is incomplete. The total demand curve, D in panel c, is the horizontal sum of the demand curve for labor services in the covered sector, D^c in panel a, and the demand curve in the uncovered sector, D^u in panel b. In the absence of a minimum wage law, the wage in both sectors is w_1, which is determined by the intersection of the total demand curve, D, and the total supply curve, S. At that wage, L_c^1 annual hours of work are hired in the covered sector, L_u^1 annual hours are hired in the uncovered sector, and $L_1 = L_c^1 + L_u^1$ total annual hours of work are performed.

If a minimum wage of $\underline{w}$ is set in the covered sector only, employment in that sector falls to L_c^2. To determine the wage and level of employment in the uncovered sector, we first need to determine how much labor service is available to that sector.

Anyone unable to find work in the covered sector goes to the uncovered sector. The supply curve of labor to the uncovered sector in panel b is a *residual supply curve*: the quantity the market supplies that is not met by demanders in other sectors

---

[3]For an example of where the bias from using a partial-equilibrium analysis instead of a multimarket or general-equilibrium analysis is large, see "Sin Taxes" in MyEconLab, Chapter Resources, Chapter 10.

Figure 10.1 Minimum Wage with Incomplete Coverage

In the absence of a minimum wage, the equilibrium wage is w_1. Applying a minimum wage, $\underline{w}$, to only one sector causes the quantity of labor services demanded in the covered sector to fall. The extra labor moves to the uncovered sector, driving the wage there down to w_2.

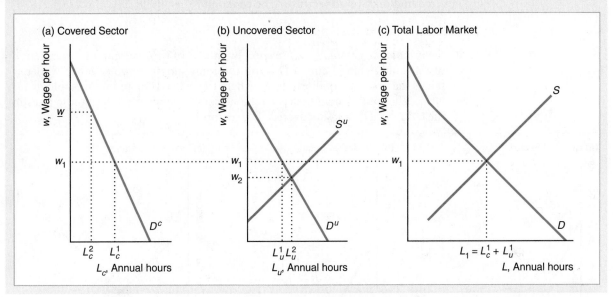

at any given wage (Chapter 8). With a binding minimum wage $\underline{w}$ in the covered sector, the residual supply function for the uncovered sector is

$$S^u(w) = S(w) - D^c(\underline{w}).$$

That is, the residual supply to the uncovered sector, $S^u(w)$, is the total supply, $S(w)$, at any given wage w minus the amount of labor used in the covered sector, $L_c^2 = D^c(\underline{w})$.

The intersection of D^u and S^u determines w_2, the new wage in the uncovered sector, and L_u^2, the new level of employment.[4] This general-equilibrium analysis shows that a minimum wage causes employment to drop in the covered sector, employment to rise (by a smaller amount) in the uncovered sector, and the wage in the uncovered sector to fall below the original competitive level. Thus, a minimum wage law with only partial coverage affects wage levels and employment levels in various sectors but need not create unemployment.

When the U.S. minimum wage was first passed in 1938, only 56% of workers were employed in covered firms. Today, many state minimum wages provide incomplete coverage.

More than 140 U.S. cities and counties enacted living-wage laws, a new type of minimum wage legislation where the minimum is high enough to allow a fully employed person to live above the poverty level in a given locale. Living-wage laws provide incomplete coverage, typically extending only to the employees of a government or to firms that contract with that government.

---

[4]This analysis is incomplete if the minimum wage causes the price of goods in the covered sector to rise relative to those in the uncovered sector, which in turn causes the demands for labor in those two sectors, D^c and D^u, to shift. Ignoring that possibility is reasonable if labor costs are a small fraction of total costs (hence the effect of the minimum wage is minimal on total costs) or if the demands for the final goods are relatively price insensitive.

SOLVED PROBLEM 10.1

After the government starts taxing the cost of labor by τ per hour in a covered sector only, the wage that workers in both the covered and the uncovered sectors receive is w, but the wage paid by firms in the covered sector is $w + \tau$. What effect does the subsidy have on wages, total employment, and employment in the covered and uncovered sectors of the economy?

Answer

1. *Determine the original equilibrium.* In panel c of the diagram, the intersection of the total demand curve, D^1, and the total supply curve of labor, S, determines the original equilibrium, e_1, where the wage is w_1 and total employment is L_1. The total demand curve is the horizontal sum of the demand curves in the covered, D_1^c, and uncovered, D^u, sectors.

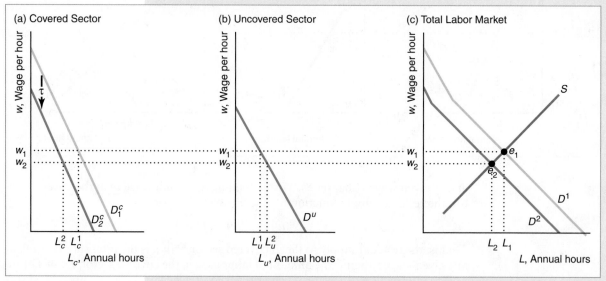

2. *Show the shift in the demand for labor in the covered sector and the resulting shift in the total demand curve.* The tax causes the demand curve for labor in the covered sector to shift downward from D_1^c to D_2^c in panel a. As a result, the total demand curve shifts inward to D^2 in panel c.

3. *Determine the equilibrium wage using the total demand and supply curves; then determine employment in the two sectors.* Workers shift between sectors until the new wage is equal in both sectors at w_2, which is determined by the intersection of the new total demand curve, D^2, and the total supply curve, S. Employment in the two sectors is L_2^c and L_2^u.

4. *Compare the equilibria.* The tax causes the wage, total employment, and employment in the covered sector to fall and employment in the uncovered sector to rise.

APPLICATION

Urban Flight

Philadelphia and some other cities tax wages, while suburban areas do not (or they set much lower rates). Philadelphia collects a wage tax from residents whether or not they work in the city and from nonresidents who work in the city. Unfortunately, this situation drives people and jobs from Philadelphia to the suburbs. To offset such job losses, the city has enacted a gradual wage tax reduction program. During the program's first five years, the wage tax on Philadelphia's workers declined slowly over time from a high of 4.96% in 1983 through 1995 to 3.928 in 2012.

A study conducted for Philadelphia estimated that if the city were to lower the wage tax by 0.4175 percentage points, 30,500 more people would work in the city. Local wage tax cuts are more effective than a federal cut because generally employees will not leave the country to avoid taxes, but they will consider moving to the burbs. Indeed, there has been much more growth on the suburban side of City Line Avenue, which runs along Philadelphia's border, than there was within city limits.

10.2 Trading Between Two People

In Chapter 9, we learned that tariffs, quotas, and other trade restrictions usually harm both importing and exporting nations because people who voluntarily trade benefit from that trade; otherwise, they would not have traded. In this section, we use a general-equilibrium model to show that free trade is Pareto efficient: After all voluntary trades have occurred, we cannot reallocate goods so as to make one person better off without harming another. Our analysis demonstrates that trade between two people is Pareto efficient and that the same property holds when many people trade in a competitive market.

Endowments

Suppose that Jane and Denise are neighbors in the wilds of Massachusetts. A nasty snowstorm hits, isolating them. They must trade with each other or consume only what they have at hand.

Collectively, they have 50 cords of firewood and 80 candy bars and no way of producing more of either good. Jane's **endowment**—her initial allocation of goods—is 30 cords of firewood and 20 candy bars. Denise's endowment is 20 ($= 50 - 30$) cords of firewood and 60 ($= 80 - 20$) candy bars. So Jane has relatively more wood, and Denise has relatively more candy.

We show these endowments in Figure 10.2. Panels a and b are typical indifference curve diagrams (Chapter 3) in which we measure cords of firewood on the vertical axis and candy bars on the horizontal axis. Jane's endowment is e_j (30 cords of wood and 20 candy bars) in panel a, and Denise's endowment is e_d in panel b. Both panels show the indifference curve through the endowment.

If we take Denise's diagram, rotate it, and put it on Jane's diagram, we obtain the box in panel c. This type of figure, called an *Edgeworth box* (after the English economist Francis Ysidro Edgeworth), illustrates trade between two people with fixed endowments of two goods. We use this Edgeworth box to illustrate a general-equilibrium model in which we examine simultaneous trade in firewood and in candy.

The height of the Edgeworth box represents 50 cords of firewood, and the length represents 80 candy bars, which are the combined endowments of Jane and Denise. Bundle e shows both endowments. Measuring from Jane's origin, 0_j, at the lower-left corner of the diagram, we see that Jane has 30 cords of wood and 20 candy bars at endowment e. Similarly, measuring from Denise's origin, 0_d, at the upper-right corner, we see that Denise has 60 candy bars and 20 cords of wood at e.

Figure 10.2 Endowments in an Edgeworth Box

(a) Jane's endowment is e_j; she has 20 candy bars and 30 cords of firewood. She is indifferent between that bundle and the others that lie on her indifference curve I_j^1. (b) Denise is indifferent between her endowment, e_d (60 candy bars and 20 cords of firewood), and the other bundles on I_d^1. (c) Their endowments are at e in the Edgeworth box formed by combining panels a and b. Jane prefers bundles in A and B to e. Denise prefers bundles in B and C to e. Thus, both prefer any bundle in area B to e.

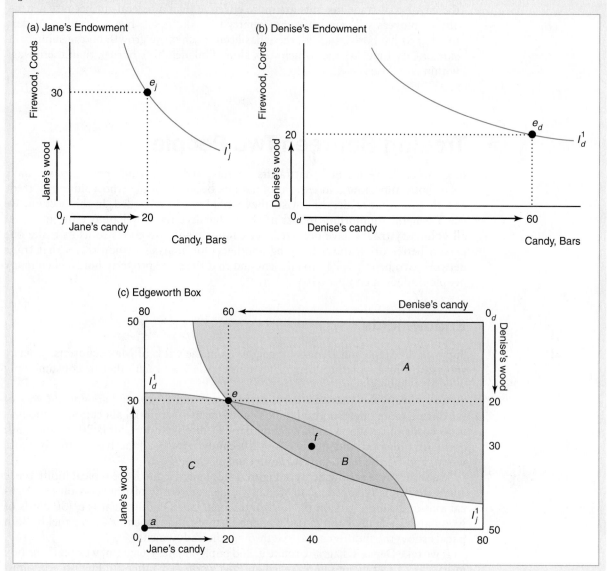

Mutually Beneficial Trades

Should Jane and Denise trade? The answer depends on their tastes, which are summarized by their indifference curves. We make four assumptions about their tastes and behavior:

1. **Utility maximization:** Each person *maximizes* her *utility*.
2. **Usual-shaped indifference curves:** Each person's indifference curves have the usual convex shape.

3. **Nonsatiation:** Each person has strictly positive *marginal utility* for each good, so each person wants as much of the good as possible (that is, neither person is ever satiated).

4. **No interdependence:** Neither person's utility depends on the other's consumption (that is, neither person derives pleasure or displeasure from the other's consumption), and neither person's consumption harms the other person (that is, one person's consumption of firewood does not cause smoke pollution that bothers the other person).

Figure 10.2 reflects these assumptions. In panel a, Jane's indifference curve, I_j^1, through her endowment point, e_j, is convex to her origin, 0_j. Jane is indifferent between e_j and any other bundle on I_j^1. She prefers bundles that lie above I_j^1 to e_j and prefers e_j to points that lie below I_j^1. Panel c also shows her indifference curve I_j^1. The bundles that Jane prefers to her endowment are in the shaded areas A and B, which lie above her indifference curve I_j^1.

Similarly, Denise's indifference curve, I_d^1, through her endowment is convex to her origin, 0_d, in the lower-left corner of panel b. This indifference curve, I_d^1, is still convex to 0_d in panel c, but 0_d is in the upper-right corner of the Edgeworth box. (It may help to rotate this book 180° when viewing Denise's indifference curves in an Edgeworth box. Then again, possibly many points will be clearer if you hold this book upside down.) The bundles Denise prefers to her endowment are in shaded areas B and C, which lie on the other side of her indifference curve I_d^1 from her origin 0_d (above I_d^1 if you turn this book upside down).

At endowment e in panel c, Jane and Denise can both benefit from a trade. Jane prefers bundles in A and B to e, and Denise prefers bundles in B and C to e, so *both* prefer bundles in area B to their endowment at e.

Suppose that they trade, reallocating goods from Bundle e to Bundle f. Jane gives up 10 cords of wood for 20 more candy bars, and Denise gives up 20 candy bars for 10 more cords of wood. As Figure 10.3 illustrates, both gain from such a trade. Jane's indifference curve I_j^2 through allocation f lies above her indifference curve I_j^1 through allocation e, so she is better off at f than at e. Similarly, Denise's indifference curve I_d^2 through f lies above (if you hold the book upside down) her indifference curve I_d^1 through e, so she also benefits from the trade.

Now that they've traded to Bundle f, do Jane and Denise want to make additional trades? To answer this question, we can repeat our analysis. Jane prefers all bundles above I_j^2, her indifference curve through f. Denise prefers all bundles above (when the book is held upside down) I_d^2 to f. However, there are no bundles that both prefer because I_j^2 and I_d^2 are tangent at f. Neither Jane nor Denise wants to trade from f to a bundle such as e, which is below both of their indifference curves. Jane would love to trade from f to c, which is on her higher indifference curve I_j^3, but such a trade would make Denise worse off because this bundle is on a lower indifference curve, I_d^1. Similarly, Denise prefers b to f, but Jane does not. Thus, *any* move from f harms at least one of them.

The reason no further trade is possible at a bundle like f is that Jane's marginal rate of substitution (the slope of her indifference curve), MRS_j, between wood and candy equals Denise's marginal rate of substitution, MRS_d. Jane's MRS_j is $-\frac{1}{2}$: She is willing to trade one cord of wood for two candy bars. Because Denise's indifference curve is tangent to Jane's, Denise's MRS_d must also be $-\frac{1}{2}$. When they both want to trade wood for candy at the same rate, they can't agree on additional trades.

In contrast, at a bundle such as e where their indifference curves are not tangent, MRS_j does not equal MRS_d. Denise's MRS_d is $-\frac{1}{3}$, and Jane's MRS_j is -2. Denise is willing to give up one cord of wood for three more candy bars or to sacrifice three candy bars for one more cord of wood. If Denise offers Jane three candy bars for one cord of wood, Jane will accept because she is willing to give up two cords of wood for one candy bar. This example illustrates that trades are possible where indifference curves intersect, because marginal rates of substitution are unequal.

Figure 10.3 Contract Curve

The contract curve contains all the Pareto-efficient allocations. Any bundle for which Jane's indifference curve is tangent to Denise's indifference curve lies on the contract curve, because no further trade is possible, so we can't reallocate goods to make one of them better off without harming the other. Starting at an endowment of *e*, Jane and Denise will trade to a bundle on the contract curve in area *B*: bundles between *b* and *c*. The table shows how they would trade to Bundle *f*.

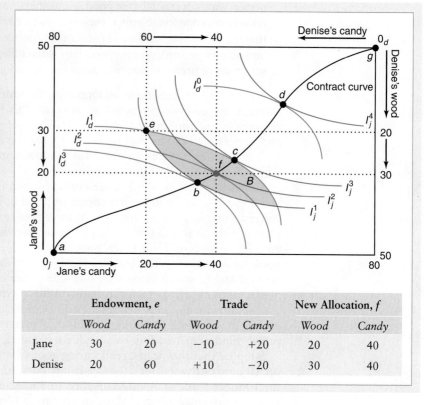

	Endowment, *e*		Trade		New Allocation, *f*	
	Wood	Candy	Wood	Candy	Wood	Candy
Jane	30	20	−10	+20	20	40
Denise	20	60	+10	−20	30	40

To summarize, we can make four equivalent statements about allocation *f*:

1. The indifference curves of the two parties are tangent at *f*.
2. The parties' marginal rates of substitution are equal at *f*.
3. No further mutually beneficial trades are possible at *f*.
4. The allocation at *f* is Pareto efficient: One party cannot be made better off without harming the other.

Indifference curves are also tangent at Bundles *b*, *c*, and *d*, so these allocations, like *f*, are Pareto efficient. By connecting all such bundles, we draw the **contract curve**: the set of all Pareto-efficient bundles. The reason for this name is that only at these points are the parties unwilling to engage in further trades, or contracts—these allocations are the final contracts. A move from any bundle on the contract curve must harm at least one person.

SOLVED PROBLEM 10.2

Are allocations *a* and *g* in Figure 10.3, where one person owns everything, part of the contract curve?

Answer

By showing that no mutually beneficial trades are possible at those points, demonstrate that those bundles are Pareto efficient. The allocation at which Jane has everything, *g*, is on the contract curve because no mutually beneficial trade is possible: Denise has no goods to trade with Jane. As a consequence, we cannot make Denise better off without taking goods from Jane. Similarly, when Denise has everything, *a*, we can make Jane better off only by taking wood or candy from Denise and giving it to Jane.

Deriving the Contract Curve

We can use calculus to derive the contract curve. We want to specify conditions where we make one individual as well off as possible without harming the other person.

Let Denise's utility function be $U_d(q_{d1}, q_{d2})$, where q_{d1} is the amount of candy and q_{d2} is the amount of wood belonging to Denise. Similarly, Jane's utility function is $U_j(q_{j1}, q_{j2})$. We want to determine the bundle that maximizes Jane's well-being, $U_j(q_{j1}, q_{j2})$, given that we hold Denise's utility constant at $\overline{U}_d = U_d(q_{d1}, q_{d2})$.

For example, in Figure 10.3, we take Denise's indifference curve I_d^2, along which her utility is $\overline{U}_d$, and ask what bundle places Jane on her highest indifference curve subject to Denise's being on I_d^2. That is, I_d^2 is the constraint (analogous to the budget line in earlier chapters) that Jane faces, and we pick a bundle on the highest one of Jane's indifference curves that touches I_d^2. As we already know, at Bundle *f*, Denise is on I_d^2 and Jane is on the highest feasible indifference curve, I_j^2.

Using a Lagrangian multiplier, λ, we can write the Lagrangian corresponding to the maximum problem as

$$\mathscr{L} = U_j(q_{j1}, q_{j2}) + \lambda[U_d(q_1 - q_{i1}, q_2 - q_{j2}) - \overline{U}_d], \qquad (10.9)$$

where $q_1 = q_{d1} + q_{j1}$ is the total amount of candy available and q_2 is the total amount of wood. The first-order conditions are

$$\frac{\partial \mathscr{L}}{\partial q_{i1}} = \frac{\partial U_j}{\partial q_{i1}} = \lambda \frac{\partial U_d}{\partial q_{i1}} = 0, \qquad (10.10)$$

$$\frac{\partial \mathscr{L}}{\partial q_{i2}} = \frac{\partial U_j}{\partial q_{i2}} = \lambda \frac{\partial U_d}{\partial q_{i2}} = 0, \qquad (10.11)$$

$$\frac{\partial \mathscr{L}}{\partial \lambda} = U_d(q_1 - q_{i1}, q_2 - q_{j2}) - \overline{U}_d = 0. \qquad (10.12)$$

If we equate the right-hand sides of Equations 10.10 and 10.11, we find that

$$MRS_j = \frac{\partial U_j / \partial q_{j1}}{\partial U_j / \partial q_{j2}} = \frac{\partial U_d / \partial q_{d1}}{\partial U_d / \partial q_{d2}} = MRS_d. \qquad (10.13)$$

That is, Jane's marginal rate of substitution equals Denise's marginal rate of substitution at an optimal bundle. In geometric terms, this condition says that Jane's indifference curve is tangent to Denise's indifference curve along the contract curve.

SOLVED PROBLEM 10.3

In a pure exchange economy with two goods, *G* and *H*, the two traders, Amos and Elise, have Cobb-Douglas utility functions. Amos' utility is $U_a = (G_a)^\alpha (H_a)^{1-\alpha}$, and Elise's is $U_e = (G_e)^\beta (H_e)^{1-\beta}$. Between them, Amos and Elise own 100 units of

G and 50 units of H. Thus, if Amos has G_a and H_a, Elise owns $G_e = 100 - G_a$ and $H_e = 50 - H_a$. Solve for their contract curve. Solve for the contract curve if $\alpha = \beta$.

Answer

1. *Use Equation 10.13 and the information about their endowments to determine the necessary condition for Amos and Elise's contract curve.* From Solved Problem 3.2, we know that Amos' marginal rate of substitution is $MRS_a = [\alpha/(1 - \alpha)]H_a/G_a$ and that Elise's is $MRS_e = [\beta/(1 - \beta)]H_e/G_e$. From Equation 10.13, we know that these marginal rates of substitution are equal along the contract curve: $MRS_a = MRS_e$. Equating the right-hand sides of the expressions for MRS_a and MRS_e and using the information about the endowments and some algebra, we can write the (quadratic) formula for the contract curve in terms of Amos' goods as

$$(\beta - \alpha)G_a H_a + \beta(\alpha - 1)50G_a + \alpha(1 - \beta)100\,H_a = 0.$$

2. *Substitute in $\alpha = \beta$ and solve.* If we set $\alpha = \beta$, then the contract curve is $(\beta^2 - \beta)50G_a + (\beta - \beta^2)100H_a = 0$. Dividing by $(\beta^2 - \beta)$ to obtain $50G_a - 100H_a = 0$, and using algebra, we conclude that the contract curve is a straight line: $G_a = 2H_a$.

Bargaining Ability

For every allocation off the contract curve, there are allocations on the contract curve that benefit at least one person. If they start at endowment e, Jane and Denise should trade until they reach a point on the contract curve between Bundles b and c in Figure 10.3. All the allocations in area B are better for one or both of them. However, if they trade to any allocation in B that is not on the contract curve, further beneficial trades are possible because their indifference curves intersect at that allocation.

Where will they end up on the contract curve between b and c? That depends on who is the better negotiator. Suppose Jane is. She knows that the more she gets, the worse off Denise will be and that Denise will not agree to any trade that makes her worse off than she is at e. Thus, the best trade Jane can make is one that leaves Denise only as well off as at e, which are the bundles on I_d^1. If Jane could pick any point she wanted along I_d^1, she would choose the bundle on her highest possible indifference curve, Bundle c, where I_j^3 is just tangent to I_d^1. After this trade, Denise is no better off than before, but Jane is much happier. By similar reasoning, if Denise is better at bargaining, the final allocation will be at b.

10.3   Competitive Exchange

Most trading throughout the world occurs without one-on-one bargaining between people. When you go to the store for a bottle of shampoo, you check its price and decide whether to buy it. You've probably never tried to bargain with the store clerk over the price of shampoo: You're a price taker in the shampoo market.

If we don't know much about how Jane and Denise bargain, all we can say is that they will trade to some allocation on the contract curve. However, if we know the exact trading process they use, we can apply that process to determine the final allocation. In particular, we can examine the competitive trading process to determine the competitive equilibrium in a pure exchange economy.

In Chapter 9, we used a partial-equilibrium approach to show that one measure of welfare, W, is maximized in a competitive market in which many voluntary trades occur. We now use a general-equilibrium model to show that a competitive market has two desirable properties:

1. **The competitive equilibrium is efficient:** Competition results in a Pareto-efficient allocation—no one can be made better off without making someone worse off—in all markets.
2. **Any efficient allocations can be achieved by competition:** Any possible efficient allocations can be obtained by competitive exchange given an appropriate initial allocation of goods.

Economists call these results the *First Theorem of Welfare Economics* and the *Second Theorem of Welfare Economics*, respectively. These results hold under fairly weak conditions.

Competitive Equilibrium

When two people trade, they are unlikely to view themselves as price takers. However, if there were many people with tastes and endowments like Jane's and many with tastes and endowments like Denise's, each person would be a price taker in the two goods. We can use an Edgeworth box to examine how such price takers would trade.

Because they can trade only two goods, each person needs to consider only the relative price of the two goods when deciding whether to trade. If the price of a cord of wood, p_w, is \$2, and the price of a candy bar, p_c, is \$1, then a candy bar costs half as much as a cord of wood: $p_c/p_w = \frac{1}{2}$. An individual can sell one cord of wood and use that money to buy two candy bars.

At the initial allocation, e, Jane has goods worth \$80 = (\$2 per cord × 30 cords of firewood) + (\$1 per candy bar × 20 candy bars). At these prices, Jane could keep her endowment or trade to an allocation with 40 cords of wood and no candy, 80 candy bars and no firewood, or any combination in between, as the price line (budget line) in panel a of Figure 10.4 shows. The price line is all the combinations of goods that Jane could get by trading, given her endowment. The price line goes through point e and has a slope of $-p_c/p_w = -\frac{1}{2}$.

Given the price line, what bundle of goods will Jane choose? She wants to maximize her utility by picking the bundle where one of her indifference curves, I_j^2, is tangent to her budget or price line. Denise wants to maximize her utility by choosing a bundle in the same way.

In a competitive market, prices adjust until the quantity supplied equals the quantity demanded. An auctioneer could help determine the equilibrium by calling out relative prices and asking how much is demanded and how much is offered for sale at those prices. If demand does not equal supply, then the auctioneer calls out another relative price. When demand equals supply, the transactions occur and the auction stops. At some ports, fishers sell their catch to fish wholesalers at daily auctions run in this manner.

Panel a of Figure 10.4 shows that, when candy costs half as much as wood, the quantity demanded of each good equals the quantity supplied. Jane (and every similar person) wants to sell 10 cords of wood and use that money to buy 20 additional candy bars. Similarly, Denise (and everyone like her) wants to sell 20 candy bars and

Figure 10.4 Competitive Equilibrium

The initial endowment is e. (a) If, along the price line facing Jane and Denise, $p_w = \$2$ and $p_c = \$1$, they trade to point f, where Jane's indifference curve, I_j^2, is tangent to the price line and to Denise's indifference curve, I_d^2. (b) No other price line results in an equilibrium. If $p_w = \$1.33$ and $p_c = \$1$, Denise wants to buy $12 \,(= 32 - 20)$ cords of firewood at these prices, but Jane wants to sell only $8 \,(= 30 - 22)$ cords. Similarly, Jane wants to buy $10 \,(= 30 - 20)$ candy bars, but Denise wants to sell $17 \,(= 60 - 43)$. Thus, these prices are not consistent with a competitive equilibrium.

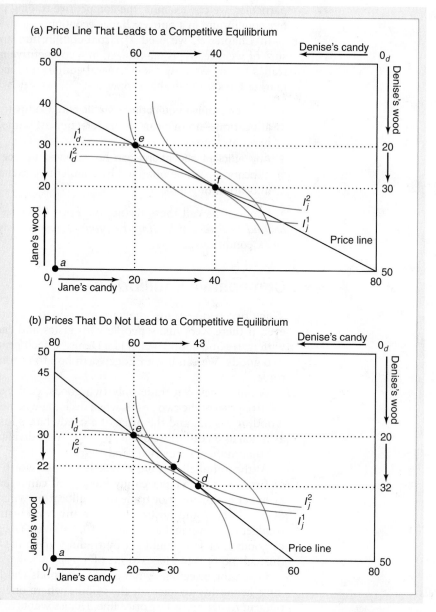

buy 10 cords of wood. Thus, the quantity of wood sold equals the quantity of wood bought, and the quantity of candy demanded equals the quantity of candy supplied. We can see in the figure that the quantities demanded equal the quantities supplied because the optimal bundle for both types of consumers is the same, Bundle f.

At any other price ratio, the quantity demanded of each good would not equal the quantity supplied. For example, if the price of candy remained constant at $p_c = \$1$ per bar but the price of wood fell to $p_w = \$1.33$ per cord, the price line would be steeper, with a slope of $-p_c/p_w = -1/1.33 = -3/4$ in panel b. At these prices, Jane wants to trade to Bundle j and Denise wants to trade to Bundle d. Because Jane wants to buy 10 extra candy bars but Denise wants to sell 17 extra candy bars, the quantity supplied does not equal the quantity demanded, so this price ratio does not result in a competitive equilibrium when the endowment is e.

SOLVED PROBLEM 10.4

Continuing with the example in Solved Problem 10.3—a pure exchange economy with two goods, $G = 100$ and $H = 50$, and two traders, Amos and Elise, with Cobb-Douglas utility functions $U_a = (G_a)^\alpha (H_a)^{1-\alpha}$ and $U_e = (G_e)^\beta (H_e)^{1-\beta}$, respectively—what are the competitive equilibrium prices? (*Note:* We can solve only for the relative prices. We normalize the price of H to equal 1 and solve for p, the price of G.)

Answer

1. *Determine their demand curves.* If Amos' endowment is G_a and H_a, then his income is $Y_a = pG_a + H_a$. Similarly, Elise's endowment is $G_e = 100 - G_a$ and $H_e = 50 - H_a$, so her income is $Y_e = p(100 - G_a) + (50 - H_a)$. Using Equations 3.29 and 3.30 for a Cobb-Douglas utility function, we know that Amos' demand functions are $G_a = \alpha Y_a / p$ and $H_a = (1 - \alpha)Y_a/1$. Similarly, Elise's demand functions are $G_e = \beta Y_e / p$ and $H_e = (1 - \beta)Y_e/1$.

2. *To determine the competitive equilibrium price, equate the demand and supply curves.* The sum of their demands for G equals the fixed supply: $G_a + G_e = 100$. Rearranging the terms in this expression and then substituting for G_e and H_e, we find that the equilibrium price of G is

$$p = \frac{\alpha H_a + \beta H_e}{100 - \alpha G_a + \beta G_e} = \frac{50\beta + (\alpha - \beta)H_a}{100(1 - \beta) + (\beta - \alpha)G_a}.$$

The Efficiency of Competition

In a competitive equilibrium, the indifference curves of both types of consumers are tangent at the same bundle on the price line. As a result, the slope (*MRS*) of each person's indifference curve equals the slope of the price line, so the slopes of the indifference curves are equal:

$$MRS_j = \frac{p_c}{p_w} = MRS_d. \tag{10.14}$$

The marginal rates of substitution are equal among consumers in the competitive equilibrium, so the competitive equilibrium must lie on the contract curve. Thus, we have demonstrated the First Theorem of Welfare Economics:

Any competitive equilibrium is Pareto efficient.

The intuition for this result is that people (who face the same prices) make all the voluntary trades they want in a competitive market. Because no additional voluntary trades can occur, there is no way to make someone better off without making someone else worse off in a competitive equilibrium. (If an involuntary trade occurs, at least one person is made worse off. A person who steals goods from another person—an involuntary exchange—gains at the expense of the victim.)

Obtaining Any Efficient Allocation Using Competition

Of the many possible Pareto-efficient allocations, the government may want to choose one. Can it achieve that allocation using the competitive market mechanism?

Our previous example illustrates that the competitive equilibrium depends on the endowment: the initial distribution of wealth. For example, if the initial endowment were *a* in panel a of Figure 10.4—where Denise has everything and Jane has nothing—the competitive equilibrium would be *a* because no trades would be possible.

Thus, for competition to lead to a particular allocation—say, *f*—the trading must start at an appropriate endowment. If the consumers' endowment is *f*, a Pareto-efficient point, their indifference curves are tangent at *f*, so no further trades occur. That is, *f* is a competitive equilibrium.

Many other endowments will also result in a competitive equilibrium at *f*. Panel a of Figure 10.4 shows that the resulting competitive equilibrium is *f* if the endowment is *e*. In that figure, a price line goes through both *e* and *f*. If the endowment is any bundle along this price line—not just *e* or *f*—then the competitive equilibrium is *f*, because only at *f* are the indifference curves tangent.

To summarize, any Pareto-efficient bundle *x* can be obtained as a competitive equilibrium if the initial endowment is *x*. That allocation can also be obtained as a competitive equilibrium if the endowment lies on a price line through *x*, where the slope of the price line equals the marginal rate of substitution of the indifference curves that are tangent at *x*. Thus, we have demonstrated the Second Theorem of Welfare Economics:

> *Any Pareto-efficient equilibrium can be obtained by competition given an appropriate endowment.*

The first welfare theorem tells us that society can achieve efficiency by allowing competition. The second welfare theorem adds that society can obtain the particular efficient allocation it prefers, based on its value judgments about equity, by appropriately redistributing endowments (income).

10.4 Production and Trading

So far our discussion has been based on a pure exchange economy with no production. We now examine an economy in which a fixed amount of a single input can be used to produce two different goods.

Comparative Advantage

Jane and Denise can produce candy or chop wood using their own labor. However, they differ as to how much of each good they can produce in a day.

Production Possibility Frontier. Jane can produce either three candy bars or six cords of firewood in a day. By splitting her time between the two activities, she can produce various combinations of the two goods. If *t* is the fraction of a day she spends making candy and $1 - t$ is the fraction she spends cutting wood, she produces $3t$ candy bars and $6(1 - t)$ cords of wood.

By varying *t* between 0 and 1, we trace out the line in panel a of Figure 10.5. This line is Jane's *production possibility frontier* (PPF^j; Chapter 7), which shows the maximum combinations of candy and wood that she can produce from a given amount of input. If Jane works all day using the best technology (such as a sharp ax), she achieves *efficiency in production* and produces combinations of goods on PPF^j. If she relaxes part of the day or does not use the best technology, she produces an inefficient combination of candy and wood that lies inside PPF^j.

Figure 10.5 Comparative Advantage and Production Possibility Frontiers

(a) Jane's production possibility frontier, PPF^j, shows that in a day, she can produce 6 cords of firewood or 3 candy bars or any combination of the two. Her marginal rate of transformation (MRT) is -2. (b) Denise's production possibility frontier, PPF^d, has an MRT of $\frac{1}{2}$. (c) Their joint production possibility frontier, PPF, has a kink at 6 cords of wood (produced by Jane) and 6 candy bars (produced by Denise) and is concave to the origin.

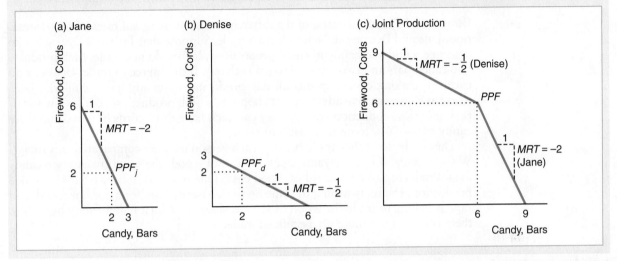

Marginal Rate of Transformation. The slope of the production possibility frontier is the *marginal rate of transformation* (MRT).[5] The marginal rate of transformation tells us how much more wood can be produced if the production of candy is reduced by one bar. Because Jane's PPF^j is a straight line with a slope of -2, her MRT is -2 at every allocation.

Denise can produce up to three cords of wood or six candy bars each day. Panel b shows her production possibility function, PPF^d, with an $MRT = -\frac{1}{2}$. Thus, with a day's work, Denise produce relatively more candy, and Jane can produce relatively more wood, as reflected by their differing marginal rates of transformation.

The marginal rate of transformation shows how much it costs to produce one good in terms of the forgone production of the other good. Someone with the ability to produce a good at a lower opportunity cost than someone else has a **comparative advantage** in producing that good. Denise has a comparative advantage in producing candy (she forgoes less in wood production to produce a given amount of candy), and Jane has a comparative advantage in producing wood.

By combining their outputs, they have the joint production possibility frontier PPF in panel c. If Denise and Jane spend all their time producing wood, Denise produces three cords and Jane produces six cords for a total of nine cords, which is where the joint PPF hits the wood axis. Similarly, if they both produce candy, together they can produce nine bars. If Denise specializes in making candy and Jane specializes in cutting wood, they produce six candy bars and six cords of wood, a combination that appears at the kink in the PPF.

If they choose to produce a relatively large quantity of candy and a relatively small amount of wood, Denise produces only candy and Jane produces some candy and some wood. Jane chops the wood because that is her comparative advantage.

---

[5]In Chapter 3, we called the slope of a consumer's budget line the marginal rate of transformation. For a price-taking consumer who obtains goods by buying them, the budget line plays the same role as the production possibility frontier for someone who produces the two goods.

The marginal rate of transformation in the lower portion of the *PPF* is Jane's, -2, because only she produces both candy and wood.

Similarly, if they produce little candy, Jane produces only wood and Denise produces some wood and some candy, so the marginal rate of transformation in the higher portion of the *PPF* is Denise's, $-\frac{1}{2}$. In short, the *PPF* has a kink at six cords of wood and six candy bars and is concave (bowed away from the origin).

Benefits of Trade. Because of the difference in their marginal rates of transformation, Jane and Denise can benefit from a trade. Suppose that Jane and Denise like to consume wood and candy in equal proportions. If they do not trade, each produces two candy bars and two cords of wood each day. If they agree to trade, Denise, who excels at making candy, spends all day producing six candy bars. Similarly, Jane, who has a comparative advantage at chopping wood, produces six cords of wood. If they split this production equally, they can each have three cords of wood and three candy bars—50% more than without trade.

They do better if they trade because each person uses her comparative advantage. Without trade, if Denise wants an extra cord of wood, she must give up two candy bars. Producing an extra cord of wood costs Jane only half a candy bar in forgone production. Denise is willing to trade up to two candy bars for a cord of wood, and Jane is willing to trade the wood as long as she gets at least half a candy bar. Thus, there is room for a mutually beneficial trade.

SOLVED PROBLEM 10.5

How does the joint production possibility frontier in panel c of Figure 10.5 change if Jane and Denise can also trade with Harvey, who can produce five cords of wood, five candy bars, or any linear combination of wood and candy in a day?

Answer

1. *Describe each person's individual production possibility frontier.* Panels a and b of Figure 10.5 show the production possibility frontiers of Jane and Denise. Harvey's production possibility frontier is a straight line that hits the firewood axis at five cords and the candy axis at five candy bars.

2. *Draw the joint PPF by starting at the quantity on the horizontal axis that is produced if everyone specializes in candy and then connecting the individual production possibility frontiers in order of comparative advantage in chopping wood.* If all three produce candy, they make 14 candy bars (on the horizontal axis of the accompanying graph). Jane has a comparative advantage at chopping wood over Harvey and Denise, and Harvey has a comparative advantage over Denise. Thus, Jane's production possibility frontier is the first frontier (starting at the lower right), then comes Harvey's, and then Denise's. The resulting *PPF* is concave to the origin. (If we change the order of the individual frontiers, the resulting *kinked line lies inside the PPF*. Thus, the new line cannot be the joint production possibility frontier, which shows the maximum possible production from the available labor inputs.)

The Number of Producers. When there are only two ways of producing wood and candy—Denise's and Jane's methods with different marginal rates of transformation—the joint production possibility frontier has a single kink (panel c of Figure 10.5). If another method of production with a different marginal rate of transformation—Harvey's—is added, the joint production possibility frontier has two kinks (as in Solved Problem 10.5).

If many people can produce candy and firewood with different marginal rates of transformation, the joint production possibility frontier has even more kinks. As the number of people becomes very large, the *PPF* becomes a smooth curve that is concave to the origin, as in Figure 10.6.

Because the *PPF* is concave, the marginal rate of transformation decreases (in absolute value) as we move up the *PPF*. The *PPF* has a flatter slope at *a*, where the $MRT = -\frac{1}{2}$, than at *b*, where the $MRT = -1$. At *a*, giving up a candy bar leads to half a cord more wood production. In contrast, at *b*, where relatively more candy is produced, giving up producing a candy bar frees enough resources that an additional cord of wood can be produced.

The marginal rate of transformation along this smooth *PPF* tells us about the marginal cost of producing one good relative to the marginal cost of producing the other good. The marginal rate of transformation equals the negative of the ratio of the marginal cost of producing candy, MC_c, and wood, MC_w (Equation 10.14):

$$MRS_j = \frac{p_c}{p_w} = MRS_d.$$

Suppose that at point *a* in Figure 10.6, a person's marginal cost of producing an extra candy bar is $1, and the marginal cost of producing an additional cord of firewood is $2. As a result, the person can produce one extra candy bar or half a cord of wood at a cost of $1. The marginal rate of transformation is the negative of the ratio of the marginal costs, $-(\$1/\$2) = -\frac{1}{2}$. To produce one more candy bar, the person must give up producing half a cord of wood.

Figure 10.6 Optimal Product Mix

The optimal product mix, *a*, could be determined by maximizing an individual's utility by picking the allocation for which an indifference curve is tangent to the production possibility frontier. It could also be determined by picking the allocation where the relative competitive price, p_c/p_p, equals the slope of the *PPF*.

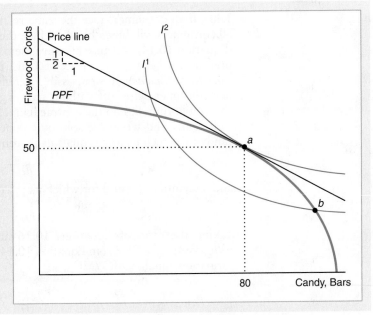

Efficient Product Mix

Which combination of products along the *PPF* does society choose? If a single person were to decide on the product mix, that person would pick the allocation of wood and candy along the *PPF* that maximized his or her utility. A person with the indifference curves in Figure 10.6 would pick Allocation *a*, which is the point where the *PPF* touches indifference curve I^2.

Because I^2 is tangent to the *PPF* at *a*, that person's marginal rate of substitution (the slope of indifference curve I^2) equals the marginal rate of transformation (the slope of the *PPF*). The marginal rate of substitution, *MRS*, tells us how much a consumer is willing to give up of one good to get another. The marginal rate of transformation, *MRT*, tells us how much of one good we need to give up to produce more of another good.

If the *MRS* does not equal the *MRT*, the consumer will be happier with a different product mix. At Allocation *b*, the indifference curve I^1 intersects the *PPF*, so the *MRS* does not equal the *MRT*. At *b*, the consumer is willing to give up one candy bar to get a third of a cord of wood ($MRS = -\frac{1}{3}$). but firms can produce one cord of wood for every candy bar not produced ($MRT = -1$). Thus at *b*, too little wood is being produced. If the firms increase wood production, the *MRS* will fall and the *MRT* will rise until they are equal at *a*, where $MRS = MRT = -\frac{1}{2}$.

We can extend this reasoning to look at the product mix choice of all consumers simultaneously. Each consumer's marginal rate of substitution must equal the economy's marginal rate of transformation, $MRS = MRT$, if the economy is to produce the optimal mix of goods for each consumer. How can we ensure that this condition holds for all consumers? One way is to use the competitive market.

Competition

Each price-taking consumer picks a bundle of goods so that the consumer's marginal rate of substitution equals the slope of the consumer's price line (the negative of the relative prices):

$$MRS = -\frac{p_c}{p_w}. \tag{10.15}$$

Thus, if all consumers face the same relative prices in the competitive equilibrium, all consumers will buy a bundle where their marginal rates of substitution are equal (Equation 10.14). Because all consumers have the same marginal rates of substitution, no further trades can occur. Thus, the competitive equilibrium achieves *consumption efficiency*: It is impossible to redistribute goods among consumers to make one consumer better off without harming another consumer. That is, the competitive equilibrium lies on the contract curve.

If candy and wood are sold by competitive firms, each firm sells a quantity of candy for which its price equals its marginal cost,

$$p_c = MC_c, \tag{10.16}$$

and a quantity of wood for which its price and marginal cost are equal,

$$p_w = MC_w. \tag{10.17}$$

Taking the ratio of Equations 10.16 and 10.17, we find that in competition, $p_c/p_w = MC_c/MC_w$. From Equation 10.14, we know that the marginal rate of transformation equals $-MC_c/MC_w$, so

$$MRT = -\frac{p_c}{p_w}. \tag{10.18}$$

We can illustrate why firms want to produce where Equation 10.18 holds. Suppose that a firm were producing at b in Figure 10.6, where its MRT is -1, and that $p_c = \$1$ and $p_w = \$2$, so $-p_c/p_w = \frac{1}{2}$. If the firm reduces its output by one candy bar, it loses $1 in candy sales but makes $2 more from selling the extra cord of wood, for a net gain of $1. Thus at b, where the $MRT < -p_c/p_w$, the firm should reduce its output of candy and increase its output of wood. In contrast, if the firm is producing at a, where the $MRT = -p_c/p_w = \frac{1}{2}$, it has no incentive to change its behavior: The gain from producing a little more wood exactly offsets the loss from producing a little less candy.

Combining Equations 10.3 and 10.6, we find that in the competitive equilibrium, the MRS equals the ratio of relative prices, which equal the MRT:

$$MRS = -\frac{p_c}{p_w} = MRT.$$

Because competition ensures that the MRS equals the MRT, a competitive equilibrium achieves an *efficient product mix*: The rate at which firms can transform one good into another equals the rate at which consumers are willing to substitute between the goods, as reflected by their willingness to pay for the two goods.

By combining the production possibility frontier and an Edgeworth box, we can show the competitive equilibrium in both production and consumption. Suppose that firms produce 50 cords of firewood and 80 candy bars at a in Figure 10.7. The size of the Edgeworth box—the maximum amount of wood and candy available to consumers—is determined by point a on the *PPF*.

Figure 10.7 Competitive Equilibrium

At the competitive equilibrium, the relative prices that firms and consumers face are the same (the price lines are parallel), so the $MRS = -p_c/p_w = MRT$.

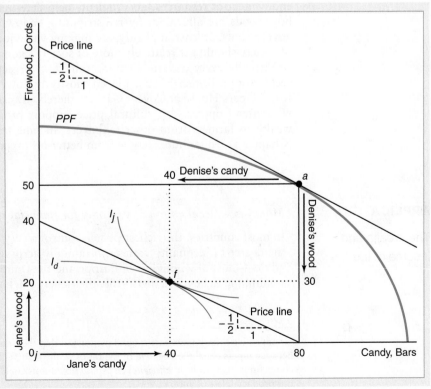

The prices consumers pay must equal the prices producers receive, so the price lines that consumers and producers face must have the same slope of $-p_c/p_w$. In equilibrium, the price lines are tangent to each consumer's indifference curve at f and to the *PPF* at a.

In this competitive equilibrium, supply equals demand in all markets. Consumers buy the mix of goods at f. Consumers like Jane, whose origin, 0_J, is at the lower-left corner, consume 20 cords of firewood and 40 candy bars. Consumers like Denise, whose origin is a at the upper right of the Edgeworth box, consume 30 ($= 50 - 20$) cords of firewood and 40 ($= 80 - 40$) candy bars.

The two key results concerning competition still hold in an economy with production. First, a competitive equilibrium is Pareto efficient, achieving efficiency in consumption and in output mix.[6] Second, any particular Pareto-efficient allocation between consumers can be obtained through competition, given that the government chooses an appropriate endowment.

10.5 Efficiency and Equity

How well various people in a society live depends on how the society deals with efficiency (the size of the pie) and equity (how the pie is divided). The actual outcome depends on individual choices and on government actions.

Role of the Government

By altering the efficiency with which goods are produced and distributed and the endowment of resources, governments help determine how much is produced and how goods are allocated. By redistributing endowments or by refusing to do so, governments, at least implicitly, are making value judgments about which members of society should get relatively more of society's goodies.

Virtually every government program, tax, or action redistributes wealth. Proceeds from a British lottery, played mostly by lower-income people, subsidize the Royal Opera House at Covent Garden, thereby transferring funds to the "rich toffs" who attend operas. Agricultural price support programs (Chapter 9) redistribute wealth to farmers from other taxpayers. Income taxes and food stamp programs (Chapter 5) redistribute income from better-off taxpayers to the poor.

APPLICATION	*Money is better than poverty, if only for financial reasons.* —Woody Allen
The Wealth and Income of the 1%	In most countries, the richest people control a very large share of the wealth, but the degree of inequality varies substantially across the world. The richest 1% of adults—most of whom live in Europe and the United States—own 40% of global wealth, the richest 2% own 51%, the richest 5% have 71%, and the richest 10%

---

[6]Competitive firms choose factor combinations so that their marginal rates of technical substitution between inputs equal the negative of the ratios of the relative factor prices (see Chapter 7). That is, competition also results in *efficiency in production*: Firms could not produce more of one good without producing less of another good.

account for 85% (Davies et al. 2007). In stark contrast, the bottom half of the world's adults own barely 1% of global assets.

If income were equally distributed, the ratio of the share of income held by the "richest" 10% to that of the "poorest" 10% would equal 1. Instead, according to United Nations statistics for 2008, the top 10% had 168 times the income of the bottom 10% in Bolivia, 72 times as much in Haiti, 25 times in Mexico, 16 times in the United States, 14 times in the United Kingdom, 9 times in Canada, and 5 times in Japan.

Since the United States was founded, changes in the economy have altered the share of the nation's wealth held by the richest 1% of Americans (see the figure). An array of social changes—sometimes occurring during or after wars and often codified into new laws—have greatly affected the distribution of wealth. For example, the emancipation of slaves in 1863 transferred vast wealth—the labor of the former slaves—from rich Southern landowners to the poor freed slaves.

The share of wealth—the total assets owned—held by the richest 1% generally increased until the Great Depression, declined through the mid-1970s, and has increased substantially since then. Thus, greatest wealth concentration occurred in 1929 during the Great Depression and today, following the Great Recession. A key cause of the recent increased concentration of wealth is that the top income tax rate fell from 70% to less than 30% at the beginning of the Reagan administration, shifting more of the tax burden to the middle class.

In 2007, U.S. wealth was roughly equally divided among the wealthiest 1% of people (33.8%), the next 9% (37.7%), and the bottom 90% (31.5%). The poorest half owned only 2.5% of the wealth. However just three years later in 2010, the distribution was even more substantially skewed: the wealthiest 1% had 34.5% of the wealth, the next 9% had 40%, the bottom 90% owned 25.5%, and the bottom half had only 1.1%. Indeed, one in four households had a zero or negative net worth. The wealthiest 1% of U.S. households had net worth that was 225 times greater than the median or typical household's net worth in 2009—the greatest ratio in history. According to Edward Wolff, the top 1% have $9 million or more in wealth.[7]

The income—current earnings—distribution is also highly skewed, but less than the wealth distribution. The top 1% of the income distribution received 21.3% percent of total income in 2009, the next 9% received 25.9%, and the remainder received 52.9%.[8] According to Emmanuel Saez, the top 1% earned $352,000 or more in 2010. In 2011, a typical S&P 500 chief executive officer (CEO) earned 380 times that of the average U.S. worker. The CEO earns more the first day of the year than a typical worker earns for the entire year.

---

[7]According to *Forbes*, the wealth of Bill Gates, the wealthiest American, was $61 billion in 2012 (down from $85 billion in 1999). Mexican Carlos Slim Helu and his family's wealth was $69 billion—the highest in the world.

[8]The U.S. federal government transfers 5% of total national household income from the rich to the poor: 2% using cash assistance such as general welfare programs and 3% using in-kind transfers such as food stamps and school lunch programs. Poor households receive 26% of their income from cash assistance and 18% from in-kind assistance. The United States government gives only 0.1% of its gross national product to poor nations. In contrast, Britain gives 0.26% and the Netherlands transfers 0.8%.

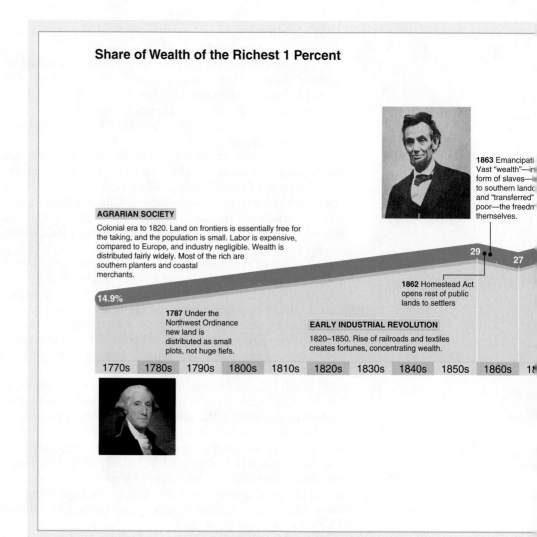

Share of Wealth of the Richest 1 Percent

1863 Emancipati
Vast "wealth"—in
form of slaves—i
to southern land
and "transferred"
poor—the freedm
themselves.

AGRARIAN SOCIETY

Colonial era to 1820. Land on frontiers is essentially free for
the taking, and the population is small. Labor is expensive,
compared to Europe, and industry negligible. Wealth is
distributed fairly widely. Most of the rich are
southern planters and coastal
merchants.

29

27

1862 Homestead Act
opens rest of public
lands to settlers

14.9%

1787 Under the
Northwest Ordinance
new land is
distributed as small
plots, not huge fiefs.

EARLY INDUSTRIAL REVOLUTION

1820–1850. Rise of railroads and textiles
creates fortunes, concentrating wealth.

1770s   1780s   1790s   1800s   1810s   1820s   1830s   1840s   1850s   1860s   18

Efficiency

Many economists and political leaders make the value judgment that governments
should use the Pareto principle, preferring allocations by which someone is made
better off if no one else is harmed. That is, they believe that governments should
allow voluntary trades, encourage competition, and otherwise try to prevent problems that reduce efficiency.

We can use the Pareto principle to rank allocations or government policies that
alter allocations. The Pareto criterion ranks allocation x over allocation y if some
people are better off at x and no one else is harmed. If that condition is met, we say
that x is *Pareto superior* to y.

The Pareto principle cannot always be used to compare allocations. Because there
are many possible Pareto-efficient allocations, however, a value judgment based on
interpersonal comparisons must be made to choose between the allocations. Issues
of interpersonal comparisons often occur when we evaluate various government
policies. If both allocation x and allocation y are Pareto efficient, we cannot use this

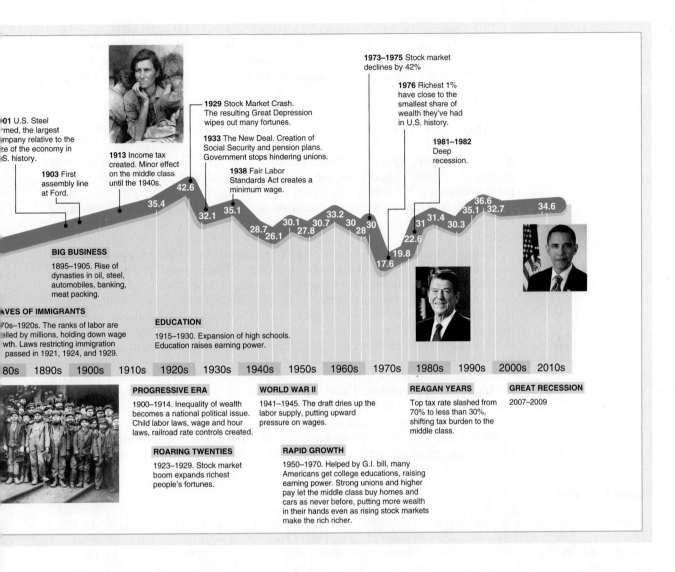

criterion to rank them. For example, if Denise has all the goods in x and Jane has all the goods in y, then we cannot rank these allocations using the Pareto rule.

Suppose that when a country ends a ban on imports and allows free trade, domestic consumers benefit by many times more than domestic producers suffer. Nonetheless, this policy change does not meet the Pareto efficiency criterion that someone be made better off without anyone suffering. However, the government could adopt a more complex policy that meets the Pareto criterion. Because consumers benefit by more than producers suffer, the government could take enough of the free-trade gains from consumers to compensate the producers so that no one is harmed and some people benefit.

The government rarely uses policies by which winners subsidize losers, however. If such subsidization does not occur, additional value judgments involving interpersonal comparisons must be made before deciding whether to adopt a policy.

We have been using a welfare measure, $W =$ consumer surplus + producer surplus, that equally weights benefits and losses to consumers and producers. On the basis of that particular interpersonal comparison criterion, if the gains to consumers outweigh the losses to producers, the policy change should be made.

Thus, calling for policy changes that lead to Pareto-superior allocations is a weaker rule than calling for policy changes that increase the welfare measure W. Any policy change that leads to a Pareto-superior allocation must increase W; however, some policy changes that increase W are not Pareto superior: There are both winners and losers.

Equity

If we are unwilling to use the Pareto principle or if that criterion does not allow us to rank the relevant allocations, we must make additional value judgments to rank these allocations. We can summarize these value judgments using a *social welfare function* that combines various consumers' utilities to provide a collective ranking of allocations. Loosely speaking, a social welfare function is a utility function for society.

We illustrate the use of a social welfare function using the pure exchange economy in which Jane and Denise trade wood and candy. There are many possible Pareto-efficient allocations along the contract curve in Figure 10.3. Jane and Denise's utility levels vary along the contract curve. Figure 10.8 shows the *utility possibility frontier* (*UPF*): the set of utility levels corresponding to the Pareto-efficient allocations along the contract curve. Point *a* in panel a corresponds to the end of the contract curve at which Denise has all the goods, and *c* corresponds to the allocation at which Jane has all the goods.

The curves labeled W^1, W^2, and W^3 in panel a are *isowelfare curves* based on the social welfare function. These curves are similar to indifference curves for individuals. They summarize all the allocations with identical levels of welfare. Society maximizes its welfare at point *b*.

Who decides on the welfare function? In most countries, government leaders make decisions about which allocations are most desirable. These officials may

Figure 10.8 Welfare Maximization

Society maximizes welfare by choosing the allocation for which the highest possible isowelfare curve touches the utility possibility frontier, *UPF*. (a) The isowelfare curves have the shape of a typical indifference curve. (b) The isowelfare lines have a slope of −1, indicating that the utilities of both people are treated equally at the margin.

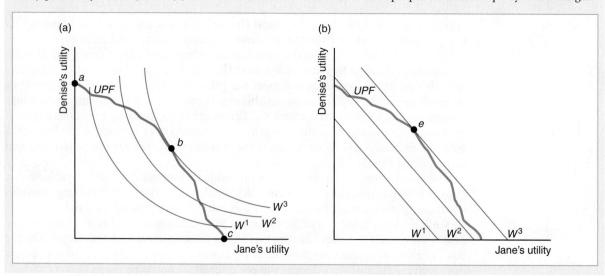

believe that transferring money from wealthy people to poor people raises welfare, or vice versa. When government officials choose a particular allocation, they are implicitly or explicitly judging which consumers are relatively deserving and hence should receive more goods than others.

Voting. In a democracy, important government policies that determine the allocation of goods are made by voting. Such democratic decision making is often difficult because people fundamentally disagree on how issues should be resolved and which groups of people should be favored.

In Chapter 3, we assumed that consumers could rank-order all bundles of goods in terms of their preferences (completeness) and that their rank over goods was transitive.[9] Suppose now that people have preferences over the allocations of goods among consumers. One possibility, as we assumed earlier, is that individuals care only about how many goods they receive—they do not care about how much others have. Another possibility is that because of envy, charity, pity, love, and other interpersonal feelings, individuals do care about how much everyone has.[10]

Let *a* be a particular allocation of goods that describes how much of each good an individual has. Each person can rank this allocation relative to Allocation *b*. For instance, individuals know whether they prefer an allocation by which everyone has equal amounts of all goods to another allocation by which people who work hard—or those of a particular skin, color, or religion—have relatively more goods than others.

Through voting, individuals express their rankings. One possible voting system requires that before the vote is taken, everyone agrees to be bound by the outcome in the sense that if a majority of people prefer Allocation *a* to Allocation *b*, then *a* is *socially preferred* to *b*.

Using majority voting to determine which allocations are preferred by society sounds reasonable, doesn't it? Such a system might work well. For example, if all individuals have the same transitive preferences, the social ordering has the same transitive ranking as that of each individual.

Unfortunately, sometimes voting does not work well, and the resulting social ordering of allocations is not transitive. To illustrate this possibility, suppose that three people have the transitive preferences in Table 10.1. Individual 1 prefers Allocation *a* to Allocation *b* to Allocation *c*. The other two individuals have different preferred orderings. Two out of three of these individuals prefer *a* to *b*; two out of three prefer *b* to *c*; and two out of three prefer *c* to *a*. Thus, voting leads to

Table 10.1 Preferences over Allocations of Three People

	Individual 1	Individual 2	Individual 3
First choice	*a*	*b*	*c*
Second choice	*b*	*c*	*a*
Third choice	*c*	*a*	*b*

---

[9]The transitivity (or *rationality*) assumption is that a consumer's preference over bundles is consistent in the sense that if the consumer weakly prefers Bundle *a* to Bundle *b* and weakly prefers Bundle *b* to Bundle *c*, then the consumer weakly prefers Bundle *a* to Bundle *c*.

[10]To an economist, love is nothing more than interdependent utility functions. Thus, it's a mystery how each successive generation of economists is produced.

nontransitive preferences, even though the preferences of each individual are transitive. As a result, there is no clearly defined socially preferred outcome. A majority of people prefers some other allocation to any particular allocation. Compared to Allocation *a*, a majority prefers *c*. Similarly, a majority prefers *b* over *c*, and a majority prefers *a* over *b*.

If people have this type of ranking of allocations, the chosen allocation will depend crucially on the order in which the vote is taken. Suppose that these three people first vote on whether they prefer *a* or *b* and then compare the winner to *c*. Because a majority prefers *a* to *b* in the first vote, they will compare *a* to *c* in the second vote, and *c* will be chosen. If instead they first compare *c* to *a* and the winner to *b*, then *b* will be chosen. Thus, the outcome depends on the political skill of various factions in determining the order of voting.

Similar problems arise with other types of voting schemes. Kenneth Arrow (1951), who received a Nobel Prize in economics in part for his work on social decision making, proved a startling and depressing result about democratic voting. This result is often referred to as Arrow's Impossibility Theorem. Arrow suggested that a socially desirable decision-making system, or social welfare function, should satisfy the following criteria:

- Social preferences should be complete (Chapter 3) and transitive, like individual preferences.
- If everyone prefers Allocation *a* to Allocation *b*, *a* should be socially preferred to *b*.
- Society's ranking of *a* and *b* should depend only on individuals' ordering of these two allocations, not on how they rank other alternatives.
- Dictatorship is not allowed; social preferences must not reflect the preferences of only a single individual.

Although each of these criteria seems reasonable—indeed, innocuous—Arrow proved that it is impossible to find a social decision-making rule that *always* satisfies all of these criteria. His result indicates that *democratic decision making* may fail—not that *democracy* must fail. After all, if everyone agrees on a ranking, these four criteria are satisfied.

If society is willing to give up one of these criteria, a democratic decision-making rule can guarantee that the other three criteria are met. For example, if we give up the third criterion, often referred to as the *independence of irrelevant alternatives*, certain complicated voting schemes in which individuals rank their preferences can meet the other criteria.

Social Welfare Functions.   How would you rank a given set of allocations if you were asked to vote? Philosophers, economists, newspaper columnists, politicians, radio talk-show hosts, and other deep thinkers have suggested various rules by which society might decide among various possible allocations. All these systems answer the question of which individuals' preferences should be given more weight in society's decision making. Determining how much weight to give to the preferences of various members of society is usually the key step in determining a social welfare function.

Probably the simplest and most egalitarian rule is that every member of society should receive exactly the same bundle of goods. If no further trading is allowed, this rule results in complete equality in the allocation of goods.

Jeremy Bentham (1748–1832) and his followers (including John Stuart Mill), the utilitarian philosophers, suggested that society should maximize the sum of the utilities of all members of society. Their social welfare function is the sum of the utilities of every member of society. The utilities of all people in society are given equal weight.[11] If U_i is the utility of Individual i and there are n people, the utilitarian welfare function is

$$W = U_1 + U_2 + \ldots + U_n.$$

However, this social welfare function may not lead to an egalitarian distribution of goods. Indeed, under this system, an allocation is judged superior, all else the same, if people who get the most pleasure from consuming certain goods are given more of those goods.

Panel b of Figure 10.8 shows some isowelfare lines corresponding to the utilitarian welfare function. These lines have a slope of -1 because the utilities of both parties are weighted equally. In the figure, welfare is maximized at e.

A generalization of the utilitarian approach assigns different weights to various individuals' utilities. If the weight assigned to Individual i is α_i, this generalized utilitarian welfare function is

$$W = \alpha_1 U_1 + \alpha_2 U_2 + \ldots + \alpha_n U_n.$$

Society could give greater weight to adults, hardworking people, or those who meet other criteria. Under South Africa's former apartheid system, the utilities of people with white skin were given more weight than those with other skin colors.

John Rawls (1971), a Harvard University philosopher, believed that society should maximize the well-being of the worst-off member of society, the person with the lowest level of utility. In the social welfare function, all the weight should be placed on the utility of the person with the lowest utility level. The Rawlsian welfare function is

$$W = \min (U_1, U_2, \ldots, U_n).$$

Rawls' rule leads to a relatively egalitarian distribution of goods.

One final rule, frequently espoused by various members of Congress and by wealthy landowners in less-developed countries, is to maintain the status quo. Proponents of this rule believe that the current allocation is the best possible allocation, and they argue against any reallocation of resources from one individual to another. Under this rule, the final allocation is likely to be very unequal. Why else would the wealthy want it?

All of these rules or social welfare functions reflect value judgments in which interpersonal comparisons are made. Because each reflects value judgments, we cannot compare them on scientific grounds.

Efficiency Versus Equity

Given a particular social welfare function, *society might prefer an inefficient allocation to an efficient one.* We can show this result by comparing two allocations. In Allocation *a*, you have everything and everyone else has nothing. This allocation is Pareto efficient: It is impossible to make others better off without harming you. In Allocation *b*, everyone has an equal amount of all goods. Allocation *b* is not Pareto efficient: I would be willing to trade all my zucchini for just about anything else. Despite Allocation *b*'s inefficiency, most people probably prefer *b* to *a*.

Although society might prefer an inefficient Allocation *b* to an efficient Allocation *a*, according to most social welfare functions, society would prefer some efficient

---

[11]It is difficult to compare utilities across individuals because the scaling of utilities across individuals is arbitrary (Chapter 3). A rule that avoids this utility comparison is to maximize a welfare measure that equally weights consumer surplus and producer surplus, which are denominated in dollars.

allocation to *b*. Suppose that Allocation *c* is the competitive equilibrium that would be obtained if people were allowed to trade starting from Endowment *b*, in which everyone has an equal share of all goods. By the utilitarian social welfare functions, Allocation *b* might be socially preferred to Allocation *a*, but Allocation *c* is certainly socially preferred to *b* (ruling out envy and similar interpersonal feelings). After all, if everyone is as well off or better off in Allocation *c* than in *b*, *c* must be better than *b* regardless of weights on individuals' utilities. According to the egalitarian rule, however, *b* is preferred to *c* because only strict equality matters. Thus by most, but not all, of the well-known social welfare functions, *there is an efficient allocation that is socially preferred to an inefficient allocation.*

Competitive equilibrium may not be very equitable even though it is Pareto efficient. Consequently, societies that believe in equity may tax the rich to give to the poor. If the money taken from the rich is given directly to the poor, society moves from one Pareto-efficient allocation to another.

Sometimes, however, in an attempt to achieve greater equity, efficiency is reduced. For example, advocates for the poor argue that providing public housing to the destitute leads to an allocation that is superior to the original competitive equilibrium. This reallocation is not efficient: The poor view themselves as better off receiving an amount of money equal to what the government spends on public housing. They could spend the money on the type of housing they like—rather than the type the government provides—or they could spend some of the money on food or other goods.[12]

Unfortunately, frequently there is a conflict between a society's goal of efficiency and its goal of achieving an equitable allocation. Even when the government redistributes money from one group to another, there are significant costs to this redistribution. If tax collectors and other government bureaucrats could be put to work producing rather than redistributing, total output would increase. Similarly, income taxes discourage some people from working as hard as they otherwise would (Chapter 5). Nonetheless, probably few people believe that the status quo is optimal and that the government should engage in no redistribution at all (although some legislators vote for tax laws as though they believe that we should redistribute from the poor to the rich).

Theory of the Second Best

Many politicians and media pundits—influenced by the basic logic of the argument that competition maximizes efficiency and our usual welfare measure—argue that we should eliminate any distortion (such as tariffs and quotas). However, care must be taken in making this argument. The argument holds if we eliminate *all* distortions, but it does not necessarily hold if we eliminate only some of them.

Consider a competitive economy with no distortions. It is a *first-best equilibrium* in which any distortion will reduce efficiency. If a single distortion arises—such as one caused by a ban on trade—and that distortion is eliminated, efficiency must rise as the economy reverts to the first-best equilibrium (see Chapter 9). Everyone can gain—welfare rises—if losers (such as producers who lose the benefits of a ban on trade) are compensated.

However, according to the Theory of the Second Best (Lipsey and Lancaster, 1956), if an economy has at least two market distortions, correcting one of them

---

[12]Letting the poor decide how to spend their income is efficient by our definition, even if they spend it on "sin goods" such as cigarettes, liquor, or illicit drugs. A similar argument was made regarding food stamps in Chapter 5.

may either increase or decrease welfare. For example, if a small country has a ban on trade and a subsidy on one good, permitting free trade may not raise efficiency.

Suppose that a wheat-producing country is a price taker on the world wheat market, where the world price is p_w. As we saw in Chapter 9, the country's total welfare is greater if it permits rather than bans free trade. Panel a of Figure 10.9 shows the gain to trade in the usual case. The domestic supply curve, S, is upward sloping, but the home country can import as much as it wants at the world price, p_w. In the free-trade equilibrium, e_1, the equilibrium quantity is Q_1 and the equilibrium price is the world price, p_w. With a ban on imports, the equilibrium is e_2, quantity falls to Q_2, and price rises to p_2. Consequently, the deadweight loss from the ban is area D.

Now suppose that the home government subsidizes its agricultural sector with a payment of s per unit of output. The subsidy creates a distortion: excess production (Chapter 9). The per-unit subsidy s causes the supply curve to shift down from S to S^* in panel b of Figure 10.9. If there is a ban on trade, the equilibrium is at e_3, with a larger quantity, Q_3, than in the original free-trade equilibrium and a lower consumer price, p_3. Because the true marginal cost (the height of the S curve at Q_3) is above the consumer price, there is deadweight loss.

If free trade is permitted, the Theory of the Second Best tells us that welfare does not necessarily rise, because the country still has the subsidy distortion. The free-trade equilibrium is e_4. Firms sell all their quantity, Q_4, at the world price, with Q_1 going to domestic consumers and $Q_4 - Q_1$ to consumers elsewhere.

Figure 10.9 Welfare Effect of Trade with and Without a Subsidy

Whether permitting trade raises welfare (consumer surplus plus producer surplus) depends on whether the economy has distortions. (a) If the only distortion is a trade ban, eliminating it must raise welfare. With free trade, the supply curve is the sum of the domestic supply curve and the world supply curve, which is horizontal at the world price, p_w. The equilibrium is e_1 where the supply curve intersects the domestic demand curve. In contrast, without trade, the equilibrium is e_2, where the domestic supply curve intersects the domestic demand curve. The deadweight loss from the ban is area D. (b) With a subsidy, the domestic supply curve shifts to S^*. The equilibrium with a trade ban is e_3 and the free-trade equilibrium is e_4. The gain to trade (ignoring the government's subsidy cost) is area $A + B$. The expansion of domestic output increases the government's subsidy cost by area $B + C$. Welfare falls because area C is greater than area A.

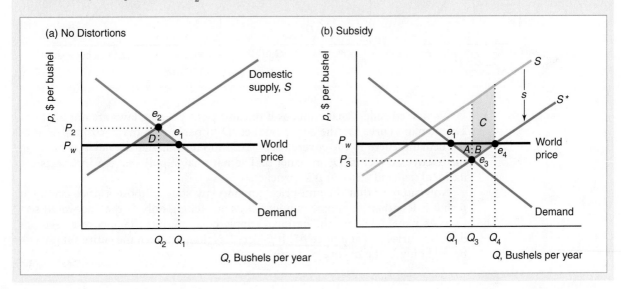

The private gain to trade—ignoring the government's cost of providing the subsidy—is area $A + B$ (see the discussion of Figure 9.9). However, the expansion of domestic output increases the government's cost of the subsidy by area $B + C$ (the height of this area is the distance between the two supply curves, which is the subsidy, s, and the length is the extra output sold). Thus, if area C is greater than area A, there is a net welfare loss from permitting trade. As the diagram is drawn, C is greater than A, so allowing trade lowers welfare, given that the subsidy is provided.

Does it follow from this argument that the country should prohibit free trade? No: To maximize efficiency, the country should allow free trade and eliminate the subsidy. However, unless winners compensate losers, not everyone will benefit.

CHALLENGE SOLUTION

Anti-Price Gouging Laws

We can use a multimarket model to analyze the Challenge questions about the effects of a binding price ceiling that applies to some states but not to others. The figure shows what happens if a binding price ceiling is imposed in the covered sector—those states that have anti-price gouging laws—and not in the uncovered sector—the other states.

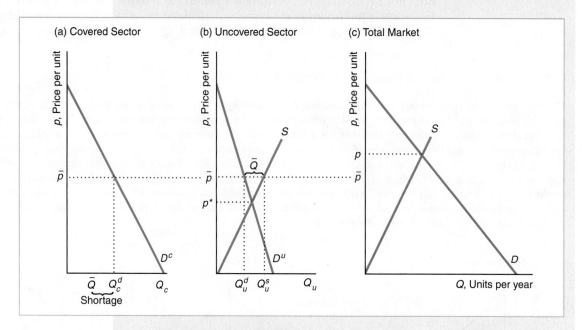

We first consider what happens if the anti-price gouging laws are not in effect. The demand curve for the entire market, D in panel c, is the horizontal sum of the demand curve in the covered sector, D^c in panel a, and the demand curve in the uncovered sector, D^u in panel b. The national supply curve S intersects the national demand curve at p in panel c.

Now suppose that the anti-price gouging law states impose a price ceiling at $\bar{p}$ that is less than p. Suppliers might consider selling only in the uncovered section. As panel b shows, the national supply curve, S, hits the uncovered sector's demand curve, D^u, at a price p^*. If $\bar{p}$ were less than p^*, then the entire supply will be sold only in the uncovered sector.

For example, in 2009 when West Virginia imposed anti-price gouging laws after flooding occurred in some parts of the state, Marathon Oil temporarily halted sales to independent gasoline retailers there. Similarly, the price controls in Zimbabwe (see the Chapter 2 Application "Price Controls Kill") caused Zimbabwean firms to stop selling in Zimbabwe and send their goods to neighboring countries.

However if p^* is less than $\bar{p}$, as in panel b, selling only in the uncovered sector is unattractive to suppliers. Instead, the suppliers sell at $\bar{p}$ in the uncovered sectors. At that price, uncovered sector consumers demand only Q_u^d, which is less than the Q_u^s that firms are willing to supply. The firms sell the excess beyond what is needed in the uncovered sector, $\bar{Q} = Q_u^s - Q_u^d$, in the covered sector. As panel a shows, $\bar{Q}$ is less than the quantity, Q_c^d, demanded at $\bar{p}$, so there is a shortage in the covered sector.

The anti-price gouging law lowers the price in both sectors to $\bar{p}$, which is less than the price p that would otherwise be charged. The consumers in the uncovered states do not suffer from a shortage, unlike the consumers in the covered states. Thus, anti-gouging laws unambiguously benefit residents of neighboring jurisdictions who can buy as much as they want at a lower price. Residents of jurisdictions with anti-gouging laws who can buy the good at a lower price benefit, but those who cannot buy the good at all are harmed. Firms are harmed because they sell the good at a price $\bar{p}$ that is less than the unregulated, competitive price p.

SUMMARY

1. **General Equilibrium.** A shock to one market may have a spillover effect in another market. In a general-equilibrium analysis, we consider the direct effects of a shock in one market and the spillover effects in other markets. In contrast, in a partial-equilibrium analysis, we look at one market only and ignore spillover effects. The partial-equilibrium and general-equilibrium effects can differ substantially.

2. **Trading Between Two People.** If people make all the trades they want, the resulting equilibrium will be Pareto efficient: That is, by moving from this equilibrium, we cannot make one person better off without harming another. At a Pareto-efficient equilibrium, the marginal rates of substitution between people are equal because their indifference curves are tangent.

3. **Competitive Exchange.** Competition, in which all traders are price takers, leads to an allocation in which the ratio of relative prices equals the marginal rates of substitution of each person. Thus, every competitive equilibrium is Pareto efficient. Moreover, any Pareto-efficient equilibrium can be obtained by competition, given an appropriate endowment.

4. **Production and Trading.** When one person can produce more of one good and another person can produce more of another good using the same inputs, trading can result in greater combined production.

5. **Efficiency and Equity.** The Pareto efficiency criterion reflects a value judgment that a change from one allocation to another is desirable if it makes someone better off without harming anyone else. This criterion does not allow all allocations to be ranked, because some people may be better off with one allocation and others may be better off with another. Nor does majority voting necessarily allow society to produce a consensus, transitive ordering of allocations. Economists, philosophers, and others have proposed many criteria for ranking allocations, as summarized in welfare functions. Society may use a welfare function to choose among Pareto-efficient (or other) allocations. If an economy suffers from multiple distortions, correcting only one of them may not raise welfare.

EXERCISES

■ = *exercise is available on* MyEconLab; * = *answer appears at the back of this book;* **M** = *mathematical problem.*

1. General Equilibrium

1.1 The demand functions for the only two goods in the economy are $Q_1 = 10 - 2p_1 + p_2$ and $Q_2 = 10 - 2p_2 + p_1$. There are five units of each good. Solve for the equilibrium: $p_1, p_2, Q_1,$ and Q_2. **M**

1.2 The demand functions for each of two goods depend on the prices of the goods, p_1 and p_2: $Q_1 = 15 - 3p_1 + p_2$ and $Q_2 = 6 - 2p_2 + p_1$. However, each supply curve depends only on its own price: $Q_1 = 2 + p_1$ and $Q_2 = 1 + p_2$. Solve for the equilibrium: $p_1, p_2, Q_1,$ and Q_2. **M**

1.3 The market demand for medical checkups per day is $Q_F = 25(198 + n_C/20,000 - p_F)$, where n_C is the number of patients per day who are at least 40 years old, and p_F is the price of a checkup. The market demand for the number of dental checkups per day, Q_T, is $Q_T = 100(150 - p_T)/3$, where p_T represents the price of a dental checkup. The long-run market supply of medical checkups is $Q_F = 50p_F - 10p_T$. The long-run market supply of dentists is $Q_T = 50p_T - 10p_F$. The supplies are linked because people decide on a medical and dental career based in part on relative earnings.

a. If $n_C = 40,000$, what is the equilibrium number of medical and dental checkups? What are the equilibrium prices? How would an increase in n_C affect the equilibrium prices? Determine dp_F/dn_C and dp_T/dn_C.

b. Suppose that, instead of determining the price of medical checkups by a market process, large health insurance companies set their reimbursement rates, effectively determining all medical prices. A medical doctor receives $35 per checkup from an insurance company, and a patient pays only $10. How many checkups do doctors offer collectively? What is the equilibrium quantity and price of dental checkups?

c. What is the effect of a shift from a competitive medical checkup market to insurance-company-dictated medical-doctor payments on the equilibrium salaries of dentists? **M**

1.4 The demand curve in Sector 1 of the labor market is $L_1 = a - bw$. The demand curve in Sector 2 is $L_2 = c - dw$. The supply curve of labor for the entire market is $L = e + fw$. In equilibrium, $L_1 + L_2 = L$.

a. Solve for the equilibrium with no minimum wage.

b. Solve for the equilibrium at which the minimum wage is $\underline{w}$ in Sector 1 ("the covered sector") only.

c. Solve for the equilibrium at which the minimum wage $\underline{w}$ applies to the entire labor market. **M**

1.5 Initially, all workers are paid a wage of w_1 per hour. The government taxes the cost of labor by t per hour only in the "covered" sector of the economy. That is, if the wage workers receive in the covered sector is w_2 per hour, firms pay $w_2 + t$ per hour. Show how the wages in the covered and uncovered sectors are determined in the post-tax equilibrium. Compared to the pre-tax equilibrium, what happens to total employment, L, employment in the covered sector, L_c, and employment in the uncovered sector, L_u?

1.6 Philadelphia collects an ad valorem tax of 3.928% on its residents' earnings (see the Application "Urban Flight"), unlike the surrounding areas. Show the effect of this tax on the equilibrium wage, total employment, employment in Philadelphia, and employment in the surrounding areas. (*Hint:* See Solved Problem 10.1.)

***1.7** What is the effect of a subsidy of s per hour on labor in only one sector of the economy on the equilibrium wage, total employment, and employment in the covered and uncovered sectors? (*Hint:* See Solved Problem 10.1.)

1.8 Suppose that the government gives a fixed subsidy of T per firm in one sector of the economy to encourage firms to hire more workers. What is the effect on the equilibrium wage, total employment, and employment in the covered and uncovered sectors?

1.9 Competitive firms in Africa sell their output only in Europe and the United States (which do not produce the good themselves). The industry's supply curve is upward sloping. Europe puts a tariff of t per unit on the good, but the United States does not. What is the effect of the tariff on the total quantity of the good sold, the quantity sold in Europe, the quantity sold in the United States, and equilibrium price(s)?

2. Trading Between Two People

2.1 Initially, Michael has 10 candy bars and 5 cookies, and Tony has 5 candy bars and 10 cookies. After trading, Michael has 12 candy bars and 3 cookies. In an Edgeworth box, label the initial allocation A and the new allocation B. Draw some indifference curves that are consistent with this trade being optimal for both Michael and Tony.

2.2 Explain why point e in Figure 10.3 is not on the contract curve. (*Hint*: See Solved Problem 10.2.)

2.3 The two people in a pure exchange economy have identical utility functions. Will they ever want to trade? Why or why not?

2.4 Two people trade two goods that they cannot produce. Suppose that one consumer's indifference curves are bowed away from the origin—the usual type of curves—but the other's are concave to the origin. In an Edgeworth box, show that a point of tangency between the two consumers' indifference curves is not a Pareto efficient bundle. (Identify another allocation that Pareto dominates.)

2.5 Adrienne and Stephen consume pizza, Z, and cola, C. Adrienne's utility function is $U_A = Z_A C_A$, and Stephen's is $U_A = Z_s^{0.5} C_s^{0.5}$. Their endowments are $Z_A = 10$, $C_A = 20$, $Z_S = 20$, and $C_S = 10$.

   a. What are the marginal rates of substitution for each person?

   b. What is the formula for the contract curve? Draw an Edgeworth box and indicate the contract curve. (*Hint*: See Solved Problem 10.3.) **M**

2.6 Continuing with Exercise 2.5, what are the competitive equilibrium prices, where one price is normalized to equal one? (*Hint*: See Solved Problem 10.4.) **M**

2.7 In a pure exchange economy with two goods, G and H, the two traders have Cobb-Douglas utility functions. Suppose that Tony's utility function is $U_t = G_t H_t$ and Margaret's utility function is $U_m = G_m (H_m)^2$. Between them, they own 100 units of G and 50 units of H. Solve for their contract curve. (*Hint*: See Solved Problem 10.4.) **M**

2.8 Continuing with Exercise 2.7, determine p, the competitive price of G, where the price of H is normalized to equal one. (*Hint*: See Solved Problem 10.4.) **M**

3. Competitive Exchange

3.1 In an Edgeworth box, illustrate that a Pareto-efficient equilibrium, point a, can be obtained by competition, given an appropriate endowment. Do so by identifying an initial endowment point, b, located somewhere other than at point a, such that the competitive equilibrium (resulting from competitive exchange) is a. Explain.

4. Production and Trading

*4.1 In panel c of Figure 10.5, the joint production possibility frontier is concave to the origin. When the two individual production possibility frontiers are combined, however, the resulting *PPF* could have

been drawn so that it was convex to the origin. How do we know which of these two ways of drawing the *PPF* to use?

*4.2. Pat and Chris can spend their non-leisure time working either in the marketplace or at home (preparing dinner, taking care of children, doing repairs). In the marketplace, Pat earns a higher wage, $w_p = \$20$, than Chris, $w_c = \$10$. Discuss how living together is likely to affect how much each of them works in the marketplace. In particular, discuss what effect marriage would have on their individual and combined budget constraints and their labor-leisure choices (see Chapter 5). In your discussion, take into account the theory of comparative advantage.

4.3 Suppose that Britain can produce 10 units of cloth or 5 units of food per day (or any linear combination) with available resources and that Greece can produce 2 units of food per day or 1 unit of cloth (or any combination). Britain has an *absolute advantage* over Greece in producing both goods. Does it still make sense for these countries to trade? Explain.

4.4 If Jane and Denise have identical, linear production possibility frontiers (see the Jane and Denise example in the text), are there gains to trade? Explain. (*Hint*: See Solved Problem 10.5.)

4.5 Modify Solved Problem 10.5 to show that the *PPF* more closely approximates a quarter of a circle if there are six people. One of these new people, Bill, can produce five cords of wood, or four candy bars, or any linear combination. The other, Helen, can produce four cords of wood, or five candy bars, or any linear combination.

4.6 Mexico and the United States can both produce food and toys. Mexico has 100 workers and the United States has 300 workers. If they do not trade, the United States consumes 10 units of food and 10 toys, and Mexico consumes 5 units of food and 1 toy. The following table shows how many workers are necessary to produce each good:

	Mexico	United States
Workers per pound of food	10	10
Workers per toy	50	20

   a. In the absence of trade, how many units of food and toys can the United States produce? How many can Mexico produce?

   b. Which country has a comparative advantage in producing food? In producing toys?

   c. Draw the production possibility for each country and show where the two produce without trade. Label the axes accurately.

d. Draw the production possibility frontier with trade.

e. Show that both countries can benefit from trade. (*Hint*: See Solved Problem 10.5.) **M**

5. Efficiency and Equity

5.1 A society consists of two people with utilities U_1 and U_2, and the social welfare function is $W = \alpha_1 U_1 + \alpha_2 U_2$. Draw a utility possibilities frontier similar to the ones in Figure 10.8. Use calculus to show that where social welfare is maximized, as α_1/α_2 increases, Person 1 benefits, and Person 2 is harmed. **M**

5.2 Give an example of a social welfare function that leads to the egalitarian allocation that everyone should be given exactly the same bundle of goods.

5.3 Suppose that society used the "opposite" of a Rawlsian welfare function: It tried to maximize the well-being of the best-off member of society. Write this welfare function. What allocation maximizes welfare in this society?

6. Challenge

6.1 Peaches are sold in a competitive market. There are two types of demanders: consumers who eat fresh peaches and canners. If the government places a binding price ceiling only on peaches sold directly to consumers, what happens to prices and quantities of peaches sold for each use?

6.2 A central city imposes a rent control law that places a binding ceiling on the rent that can be charged for an apartment. The suburbs of this city do not have rent control. What happens to the rental prices in the suburbs and to the equilibrium number of apartments in the total metropolitan area, in the city, and in the suburbs? (For simplicity, you may assume that people are indifferent as to whether they live in the city or in the suburbs.)

6.3 Initially, electricity is sold in New York and in other states at a competitive single price. Now suppose that New York restricts the quantity of electricity that its citizens can buy. Show what happens to the price of electricity and the quantities sold in New York and elsewhere.

6.4 A competitive industry with an upward-sloping supply curve sells Q_h of its product in its home country and Q_f in a foreign country, so the total quantity it sells is $Q = Q_h + Q_f$. No one else produces this product. There is no shipping cost. Determine the equilibrium price and quantity in each country. Now the foreign government imposes a binding quota, Q ($< Q_f$ at the original price). What happens to prices and quantities in both the home and the foreign market?

Monopoly and Monopsony

11

Monopoly: one parrot.

CHALLENGE

Pricing Apple's iPad

Apple started selling the iPad on April 3, 2010. The iPad was not the first tablet. Indeed, it wasn't Apple's first tablet: Apple sold another tablet, the Newton, from 1993–1998. But the iPad was the most elegant one, and the first one that many consumers wanted to own. Users interact with the iPad using Apple's multi-touch, finger-sensitive touchscreen (rather than a pressure-triggered stylus that most previous tablets used) and a virtual onscreen keyboard (rather than a physical one). Most importantly, the iPad offers an intuitive interface and is well integrated with Apple's iTunes music, eBooks, and various application programs.

People loved the original iPad. Even at $499 for the basic model, Apple had a virtual monopoly on high-end tablets in its first year. According to the research firm IDC, in 2010, Apple's market share of all tablets was 87%. Moreover, the other tablets available in 2010 were not viewed by most consumers as close substitutes. Apple reported that it sold 25 million iPads worldwide in its first full year, 2010–2011.

Within a year of iPad's introduction, over a hundred iPad wanna-be tablets were launched. To maintain its dominance, Apple replaced the original iPad with the feature-rich iPad 2 in 2011, added the enhanced iPad 3 in 2012, and cut the price of the iPad 2 by $100 in 2012.

Industry experts believe that Apple can produce tablets at far lower cost than most if not all of its competitors. Apple has formed strategic partnerships with other companies to buy large supplies of components, securing a lower price from suppliers than its competitors. Using its own patents, Apple avoids paying as many licensing fees as do other firms.

Copycat competitors with 10-inch screens have gained some market share from Apple. More basic tablets with smaller 7-inch screens that are little more than e-readers have sold a substantial number of units, so that the iPad's share of the total tablet market was 68% in the first quarter of 2012, but it still has a stranglehold on the high-end market.

In this chapter, we'll answer two questions about the iPad: How did Apple set the price for the iPad when it was essentially the only game in town? (See Solved Problem 11.2.) How did the presence of me-too rival products produced by firms with higher marginal costs affect Apple's pricing more recently? (See the Challenge Solution.)

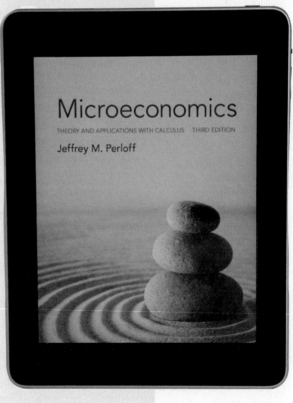

Microeconomics

THEORY AND APPLICATIONS WITH CALCULUS   THIRD EDITION

Jeffrey M. Perloff

A **monopoly** is the only supplier of a good for which there is no close substitute. Monopolies have been common since ancient times. In the fifth century BC, the Greek philosopher Thales gained control of most of the olive presses during a year of exceptionally productive harvests. Similarly, the ancient Egyptian pharaohs controlled the sale of food. In England, until Parliament limited the practice in 1624, kings granted monopoly rights called royal charters or patents to court favorites. Today, virtually every country grants a *patent*—an exclusive right to sell that lasts for a limited time—to an inventor of a new product, process, substance, or design. Until 1999, the U.S. government gave one company, Network Solutions, the right to be the sole registrar of Internet domain names.

Consumers hate monopolies because monopolies charge high prices. A monopoly can *set* its price—it is not a price taker like a competitive firm is. A monopoly's output is the market output, and the demand curve a monopoly faces is the market demand curve. Because the market demand curve is downward sloping, the monopoly doesn't lose all its sales if it raises its price, unlike a competitive firm. As a consequence, the monopoly sets its price above marginal cost to maximize its profit. Consumers buy less at this high monopoly price than they would at the competitive price, which equals marginal cost. As a result, welfare is lower than in a competitive market.

We also examine a **monopsony**: the only buyer of a good in a market. We show that a profit maximizing monopsony sets its price below the competitive level, which lowers welfare compared to a competitive market.

In this chapter, we examine seven main topics	1. **Monopoly Profit Maximization.** Like all firms, a monopoly maximizes its profit by setting its price or output so that its marginal revenue equals its marginal cost.
	2. **Market Power and Welfare.** How much the monopoly's price is above its marginal cost depends on the shape of the demand curve that the monopoly faces, and this gap between price and marginal cost lowers welfare relative to the competitive level.
	3. **Taxes and Monopoly.** Specific and ad valorem taxes increase the deadweight loss due to monopoly, may have consumer incidences in excess of 100%, and affect welfare differently from each other.
	4. **Causes of Monopolies.** Two major causes for a monopoly are a firm's cost advantage over other potential firms and government actions.
	5. **Government Actions That Reduce Market Power.** The welfare loss of a monopoly can be reduced or eliminated if the government regulates the price the monopoly charges or allows other firms to enter the market.
	6. **Monopoly Decisions over Time and Behavioral Economics.** If its current sales affect a monopoly's future demand curve, a monopoly that maximizes its long-run profit may choose not to maximize its short-run profit.
	7. **Monopsony.** A monopsony—a single buyer—maximizes its profit by paying a price below the competitive level, so welfare is lower than the competitive level.

11.1 Monopoly Profit Maximization

Competitive firms and monopolies alike maximize their profits using a two-step procedure (Chapter 8). First, the firm determines the output at which it makes the highest possible profit. Second, the firm decides whether to produce at that output level or to shut down, using the rules described in Chapter 8.

For a competitive firm, we distinguished between a lowercase q, which represented a firm's output, and an uppercase Q, which reflected the market quantity. Because a monopoly sells the entire market quantity, we use Q to indicate both the monopoly's quantity and the market quantity.

The Necessary Condition for Profit Maximization

A monopoly's first step is to pick its optimal output level. A monopoly, like any firm (Chapter 8), maximizes its profit by operating where its marginal revenue equals its marginal cost, as we now show formally.

A monopoly's profit function is $\pi(Q) = R(Q) - C(Q)$, where $R(Q)$ is its revenue function and $C(Q)$ is its cost function. The necessary condition for the monopoly to maximize its profit is found by choosing that output Q^* such that the derivative of its profit function with respect to output equals zero:

$$\frac{d^2\pi(Q^*)}{dQ} = \frac{dR(Q^*)}{dQ} - \frac{dC(Q^*)}{dQ} = 0, \tag{11.1}$$

where $dR/dQ = MR$ is its marginal revenue function (Chapter 8) and $dC/dQ = MC$ is its marginal cost function (Chapter 7). Thus, Equation 11.1 requires the monopoly to choose that output level Q^* such that *its marginal revenue equals its marginal cost*: $MR(Q^*) = MC(Q^*)$.

For profit to be maximized at Q^*, the second derivative of the profit function with respect to output must be negative:

$$\frac{d^2\pi(Q^*)}{dQ^2} = \frac{d^2R(Q^*)}{dQ^2} - \frac{d^2C(Q^*)}{dQ} < 0, \tag{11.2}$$

where d^2R/dQ^2 is the second derivative of the revenue function with respect to Q and d^2C/dQ^2 is the second derivative of the cost function. By definition, $d^2R/dQ^2 = dMR/dQ$ is the slope of its marginal revenue curve. Similarly, $d^2C/dQ^2 = dMC/dQ$ is the slope of the marginal cost curve. Thus, Equation 11.2 requires that, at the critical point Q^*, the slope of the marginal revenue curve be less than that of the marginal cost curve: $d^2R(Q^*)/dQ^2 < d^2C(Q^*)/dQ^2$ or $dMR(Q^*)/dQ < dMC(Q^*)/dQ$. Typically, this condition is met because the marginal cost curve is constant or increasing with output ($dMC/dQ \geq 0$) and the monopoly's marginal revenue curve is downward sloping ($dMR/dQ < 0$), as we will now show.

Marginal Revenue and the Demand Curves

A firm's marginal revenue curve depends on its demand curve. We will demonstrate that a monopoly's marginal revenue curve is downward sloping and lies below its demand curve at any positive quantity because its demand curve is downward sloping. The following reasoning applies to any firm that faces a downward-sloping demand curve—not just to a monopoly.

The monopoly's inverse demand function shows the price it receives for selling a given quantity: $p(Q)$. That price, $p(Q)$, is the monopoly's *average revenue* for a given quantity, Q. Its revenue function is its average revenue or price times the number of units it sells: $R(Q) = p(Q)Q$.

Using the product rule of differentiation, we can write the monopoly's marginal revenue function as

$$MR(Q) = \frac{dR(Q)}{dQ} = \frac{dp(Q)Q}{dQ} = p(Q)\frac{dQ}{dQ} + \frac{dp(Q)}{dQ}Q = p(Q) + \frac{dp(Q)}{dQ}. \tag{11.3}$$

The first term on the right-hand side of Equation 11.3, $p(Q)$, is the price or average revenue. The second term is the slope of the demand curve, $dp(Q)/dQ$, times the number of units sold, Q. Because the monopoly's inverse demand curve slopes downward, $dp(Q)/dQ < 0$, this second term is negative. (In contrast, a competitive firm's inverse demand curve has a slope of zero because it is horizontal, so the second term is zero, and the competitive firm's marginal revenue equals the market price, as we saw in Chapter 8.) Thus, at a given positive quantity, a monopoly's marginal revenue is less than its price or average revenue by $[dp(Q)/dQ]Q$. That is, *a monopoly's marginal revenue curve lies below its inverse demand curve at any positive quantity.*

Figure 11.1 illustrates the reason a monopoly's marginal revenue is less than its price. The monopoly, which is initially selling Q units at p_1, can increase the number of units it sells by one unit to $Q + 1$ by lowering its price to p_2.

The monopoly's initial revenue is $R_1 = p_1 Q = A + C$. When it sells the extra unit, its revenue is $R_2 = p_2(Q + 1) = A + B$. Thus, its marginal revenue from selling one additional unit is

$$MR = R_2 - R_1 = (A + B) - (A + C) = B - C.$$

The monopoly sells the extra unit of output at the new price, p_2, so it gains extra revenue from that last unit of $B = p_2 \times 1 = p_2$, which corresponds to the $p(Q)$ term in Equation 11.3. Because it had to lower its price, the monopoly loses the difference between the new price and the original price, $\Delta p = (p_2 - p_1)$, on the Q units it originally sold, $C = \Delta p \times Q$, which corresponds to the $(dp/dQ)Q$ term in Equation 11.3. Thus, the monopoly's marginal revenue, $B - C = p_2 - C$, is less than the price it charges by an amount equal to area C.

Figure 11.1 Average and Marginal Revenue

The demand curve shows the average revenue or price per unit of output sold. The monopoly's marginal revenue is less than the price p_2 by area C (the revenue lost due to a lower price on the Q units originally sold). The monopoly's initial revenue is $R_1 = p_1 Q = A + C$. If it sells one more unit, its revenue is $R_2 = p_2(Q + 1) = A + B = A + p_2$. Thus, its marginal revenue (if one extra unit is a very small increase in its output) is $MR = R_2 - R_1 = B - C = p_2 - C$, which is less than p_2.

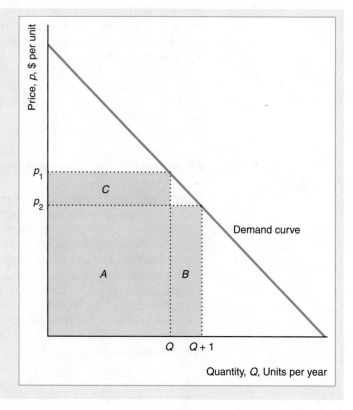

In general, the relationship between the marginal revenue and demand curves depends on the shape of the demand curve. For all linear demand curves, the relationship between the marginal revenue and demand curve is the same.

SOLVED PROBLEM 11.1	Show that if a monopoly's inverse demand curve is linear, its marginal revenue curve is also linear, has twice the slope of the inverse demand curve, intersects the vertical axis at the same point as the inverse demand curve, and intersects the horizontal axis at half the distance as does the inverse demand curve.

Answer

1. *Write a general formula for any downward-sloping linear inverse demand curve.* Any linear demand curve can be written as $p(Q) = a - bQ$, where a and b are positive constants.

2. *Derive the monopoly's revenue function and then derive its marginal revenue function by differentiating the revenue function with respect to its output.* The monopoly's revenue function is $R = p(Q)Q = aQ - bQ^2$. The marginal revenue function is the derivative of the revenue function with respect to quantity: $MR(Q) = dR/dQ = a - 2bQ$.

3. *Describe the properties of the marginal revenue function relative to those of the inverse demand function.* Both the marginal revenue function and the inverse demand functions are linear. Both hit the vertical (price) axis at a: $MR(0) = a - (2b \times 0) = a$ and $p(0) = a - (b \times 0) = a$. The slope of the marginal revenue curve, $dMR/dQ = -2b$, is twice the slope of the inverse demand curve $dp(Q)/dQ = -b$. Consequently, the MR curve hits the quantity axis at half the distance of the demand curve: $MR = 0 = a - 2bQ$, where $Q = a/(2b)$, and $p = 0 = a - bQ$, where $Q = a/b$.

Marginal Revenue Curve and the Price Elasticity of Demand

The marginal revenue at any given quantity depends on the inverse demand curve's height (the price) and the elasticity of demand. From Chapter 2, we know that the price elasticity of demand is $\varepsilon = (dQ/dp)/(p/Q) < 0$, which tells us the percentage by which quantity demanded falls as the price increases by 1%.

According to Equation 11.3, $MR = p + (dp/dQ)/Q$. By multiplying and dividing the second term by p, rearranging terms, and substituting using the definition of the elasticity of demand, we can write marginal revenue in terms of the elasticity of demand:

$$MR = p + \frac{dp}{dQ}Q = p + p\frac{dp}{dQ} = p\left[1 + \frac{1}{(dQ/dp)(p/Q)}\right] = p\left(1 + \frac{1}{\varepsilon}\right). \quad (11.4)$$

According to Equation 11.4, marginal revenue is closer to price as demand becomes more elastic. In the limit where $\varepsilon \to -\infty$, a monopoly faces a perfectly elastic demand curve (similar to that of a competitive firm), and its marginal revenue equals its price.

In Figure 11.2, we illustrate the relationship between the marginal revenue and the price elasticity of demand for a particular linear inverse demand function,

$$p(Q) = 24 - Q. \quad (11.5)$$

Figure 11.2 Elasticity of Demand and Total, Average, and Marginal Revenue

The demand curve (or the average revenue curve), $p = 24 - Q$, lies above the marginal revenue curve, $MR = 24 - 2Q$. Where the marginal revenue equals zero, $Q = 12$, and the elasticity of demand is $\varepsilon = -1$.

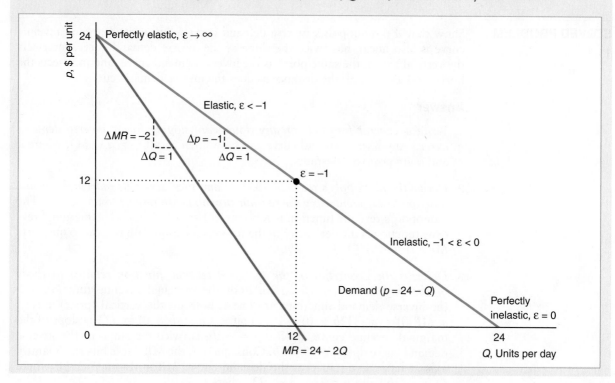

Its corresponding demand function is $Q(p) = 24 - p$. The slope of this demand function is $dQ/dp = -1$, so the elasticity of demand at a given output level is $\varepsilon = (dQ/dp)(p/Q) = -p/Q = -(24 - Q)/Q = 1 - 24/Q$.

From the results of Solved Problem 11.1, the monopoly's marginal revenue function is

$$MR(Q) = 24 - 2Q. \qquad (11.6)$$

Where the demand curve hits the price axis ($Q = 0$), the demand curve is perfectly elastic, so the marginal revenue equals price: $MR = p$. At the midpoint of any linear demand curve, the demand elasticity is unitary (see Chapter 2), $\varepsilon = -1$, so, using Equation 11.4, we know that the marginal revenue is zero:

$$MR = p[1 + 1/\varepsilon] = p[1 + 1/(-1)] = 0.$$

In our example at the midpoint of the demand curve where $Q = 12$, the elasticity is $\varepsilon = 1 - 24/12 = -1$, and the marginal revenue is $MR = 24 - (2 \times 12) = 0$. To the right of the midpoint of the demand curve, the demand curve is inelastic, $-1 \leq \varepsilon \leq 0$, so the marginal revenue is negative.

An Example of Monopoly Profit Maximization

In Chapter 8, we found that any type of firm maximizes its profit by selling its output such that its marginal cost equals its marginal revenue. We now examine how a monopoly maximizes its profit using an example with the linear inverse demand function in Equation 11.5, $p(Q) = 24 - Q$, and a quadratic short-run cost function,

$$C(Q) = VC(Q) + F = Q^2 + 12, \qquad (11.7)$$

where the monopoly's variable cost is $VC(Q) = Q^2$ and its fixed cost is $F = 12$ (see Chapter 7). The firm's marginal cost function is

$$MC(Q) = \frac{dC(Q)}{dQ} = 2Q. \qquad (11.8)$$

The average variable cost is $AVC = Q^2/Q = Q$, so it is a straight line through the origin with a slope of 1. The average cost is $AC = C/Q = (Q^2 + 12)/Q = Q + 12/Q$, which is U-shaped. Panel a of Figure 11.3 shows the MC, AVC, and AC curves.

Figure 11.3 Maximizing Profit

(a) At $Q = 6$, where marginal revenue, MR, equals marginal cost, MC, profit is maximized. The rectangle showing the maximum profit $60 is average profit per unit, $p - AC = \$18 - \$8 = \$10$, times six units. (b) Profit is maximized at a smaller quantity, $Q = 6$ (where marginal revenue equals marginal cost), than revenue is maximized, $Q = 12$ (where marginal revenue is zero).

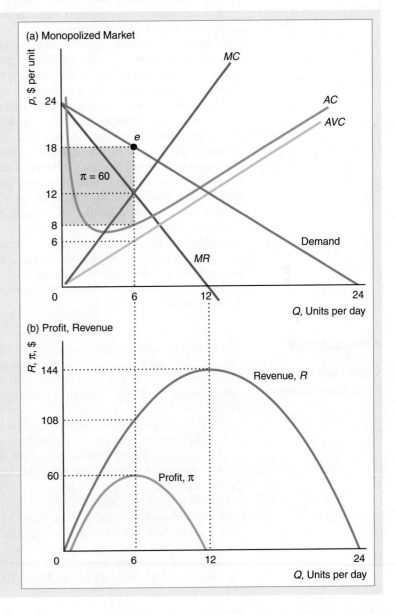

The Profit-Maximizing Output. The firm's highest possible profit is obtained by producing at the quantity Q^* where its marginal revenue equals its marginal cost function:

$$MR(Q^*) = 24 - 2Q^* = 2Q^* = MC(Q^*).$$

Solving this expression, we find that $Q^* = 6$. Panel a of Figure 11.3 shows that the monopoly's marginal revenue and marginal cost curves intersect at $Q^* = 6$.

Panel b shows the corresponding profit and revenue curves. The profit curve reaches its maximum at 6 units of output, where marginal profit—the slope of the profit curve—is zero. Because *marginal profit is marginal revenue minus marginal cost* (Chapter 8), marginal profit is zero where the marginal revenue curve intersects the marginal cost curve at 6 units in panel a. The height of the demand curve at the profit-maximizing quantity is $p = 18$. Thus, the monopoly maximizes its profit at point *e*, where it sells 6 units per day at a price of $18 per unit.

Why does the monopoly maximize its profit by producing 6 units where its marginal revenue equals its marginal cost? At smaller quantities, the monopoly's marginal revenue is greater than its marginal cost, so its marginal profit is positive. By increasing its output slightly, it raises its profit. Similarly, at quantities greater than 6 units, the monopoly's marginal cost is greater than its marginal revenue, so it can increase its profit by reducing its output slightly.

The profit-maximizing quantity is smaller than the revenue-maximizing quantity. The revenue curve reaches its maximum at $Q = 12$, where the slope of the revenue curve, the marginal revenue, is zero (panel a). In contrast, the profit curve reaches its maximum at $Q = 6$, where marginal revenue equals marginal cost. Because marginal cost is positive, marginal revenue must be positive when profit is maximized. Given that the marginal revenue curve has a negative slope, marginal revenue is positive at a smaller quantity than where it equals zero. Thus, the profit curve must reach a maximum at a smaller quantity, 6, than the revenue curve, 12.

As we already know, marginal revenue equals zero at the quantity where the demand curve has a unitary elasticity. Because a linear demand curve is more elastic at smaller quantities, *monopoly profit is maximized in the elastic portion of the demand curve.* (Here, profit is maximized at $Q = 6$ where the elasticity of demand is -3.) Equivalently, *a monopoly never operates in the inelastic portion of its demand curve.*

APPLICATION

Cable Cars and Profit Maximization

Since San Francisco's cable car system started operating in 1873, it has been one of the city's main tourist attractions. In mid-2005, the cash-strapped Municipal Railway raised the one-way fare by two-thirds from $3 to $5. Not surprisingly, the number of riders dropped substantially, and many residents called for a rate reduction.

The rate increase prompted many locals to switch to buses or other forms of transportation, but most tourists have a relatively inelastic demand curve for cable car rides. Frank Bernstein of Arizona, who visited San Francisco with his wife, two children, and mother-in-law, said that there was no way they would visit San Francisco without riding a cable car: "That's what you do when you're here." But the $50 cost for his family to ride a cable car from the Powell Street turnaround to Fisherman's Wharf and back "is a lot of money for our family. We'll do it once, but we won't do it again."

If the city ran the cable car system like a profit-maximizing monopoly, the decision to raise fares would be clearer. The 67% rate hike resulted in a 23% increase in revenue to $9,045,792 in the 2005–2006 fiscal year. For a reduction in rides

(output) to raise revenue, the city must have been operating in the inelastic portion of its demand curve ($\varepsilon > -1$) where $MR = p(1 + 1/\varepsilon) < 0$ prior to the fare increase. With fewer riders, costs stay constant or fall (if the city chooses to run fewer than its traditional 40 cars). Thus, its profit must increase.

However, the city may not be interested in maximizing its profit on the cable cars. Mayor Gavin Newsom said that having fewer riders "was my biggest fear when we raised the fare. I think we're right at the cusp of losing visitors who come to San Francisco and want to enjoy a ride on a cable car." The mayor believes that enjoyable and inexpensive cable car rides attract tourists to the city, thereby benefiting many local businesses.[1] Newsom observed, "Cable cars are so fundamental to the lifeblood of the city, and they represent so much more than the revenue they bring in." The mayor decided to continue to run the cable cars at a price below the profit-maximizing level. The fare stayed at $5 for six years, then rose to $6 in 2011 and has stayed there through 2012.

The Shutdown Decision. Should a profit-maximizing monopoly produce at the output level determined by its first-order condition, Q^*, or shut down? In the short run, the monopoly shuts down if the monopoly-optimal price is less than its average variable cost. In our short-run example in Figure 11.3, at the profit-maximizing output, the average variable cost is $AVC(6) = 6$, which is less than the price, $p(6) = 18$, so the firm chooses to produce. Equivalently, the firm's revenue, $R(6) = p(6)6 = (24 - 6)6 = 108$, exceeds its variable (or avoidable) cost, $VC(6) = 6^2 = 36$, so the firm chooses to produce.

Indeed, the monopoly makes a positive profit. Because its profit is $\pi = p(Q)Q - C(Q)$, its average profit is $\pi/Q = p(Q) - C(Q)/Q = p(Q) - AC$. Thus, its average profit (and hence its profit) is positive only if price is above the average cost. At $Q^* = 6$, its average cost, $AC(6) = 8$, is above its price, $p(6) = 18$. Its profit is $\pi = 60$, which is the shaded rectangle with a height equal to the average profit per unit, $p(6) - AC(6) = 18 - 8 = 10$, and a width of 6 units.

Choosing Price or Quantity

Unlike a competitive firm, a monopoly can adjust its price, so it has the choice of setting its price *or* its quantity to maximize its profit. (A competitive firm must set its quantity to maximize profit because it cannot affect market price.)

The monopoly is constrained by the market demand curve. Because the demand curve slopes downward, the monopoly faces a trade-off between a higher price and a lower quantity or a lower price and a higher quantity. The monopoly chooses the point on the demand curve that maximizes its profit. Unfortunately for the monopoly, it cannot set both its quantity and its price and thereby pick a point that is above the demand curve. If it could, the monopoly would choose an extremely high price and an extremely high output level and would become exceedingly wealthy.

---

[1]That is, the mayor believes that cable cars provide a positive externality; see Chapter 17.

If the monopoly sets its price, the demand curve determines how much output it sells. If the monopoly picks an output level, the demand curve determines the price. Because the monopoly wants to operate at the price and output at which its profit is maximized, it chooses the same profit-maximizing solution whether it sets the price or the output. In this chapter, we assume that the monopoly sets the quantity.

Effects of a Shift of the Demand Curve

Shifts in the demand curve or marginal cost curve affect the monopoly optimum and can have a wider variety of effects in a monopolized market than in a competitive market. In a competitive market, the effect of a shift in demand on a competitive firm's output depends only on the marginal cost curve (Chapter 8). In contrast, the effect of a shift in demand on a monopoly's output depends on the marginal cost curve and the demand curve.

A competitive firm's marginal cost curve tells us everything we need to know about the amount that the firm will supply at any given market price. The competitive firm's supply curve is its upward-sloping marginal cost curve above its minimum average variable cost. A competitive firm's supply behavior does not depend on the shape of the market demand curve because the firm always faces a horizontal residual demand curve at the market price. Thus, if you know a competitive firm's marginal cost curve, you can predict how much the firm will produce at any given market price.

In contrast, a monopoly's output decision depends on its marginal cost curve and its demand curve. Unlike a competitive firm, *a monopoly does not have a supply curve*. Knowing the monopoly's marginal cost curve is not sufficient for us to predict how much a monopoly will sell at any given price.

Figure 11.4 illustrates that the relationship between price and quantity is unique in a competitive market but not in a monopoly market. If the market is competitive, the initial equilibrium is e_1 in panel a, where the original demand curve D^1 intersects

Figure 11.4 Effects of a Shift of the Demand Curve

(a) A shift of the demand curve from D^1 to D^2 causes the competitive equilibrium to move from e_1 to e_2 along the supply curve (the horizontal sum of the marginal cost curves of all the competitive firms). Because the competitive equilibrium lies on the supply curve, each quantity corresponds to only one possible equilibrium price. (b) With a monopoly, this same shift of demand causes the monopoly optimum to change from E_1 to E_2. The monopoly quantity stays the same, but the monopoly price rises. Thus, a shift in demand does not map out a unique relationship between price and quantity in a monopolized market: The same quantity, $Q_1 = Q_2$, is associated with two different prices, p_1 and p_2.

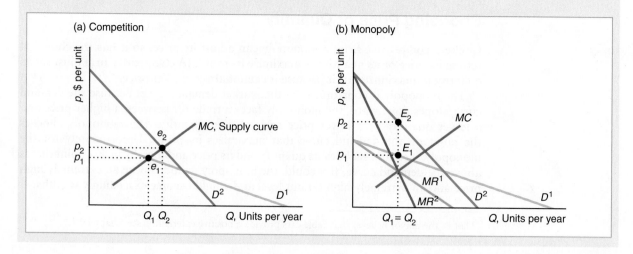

the supply curve, *MC*, which is the sum of the marginal cost curves of a large number of competitive firms. When the demand curve shifts to D^2, the new competitive equilibrium, e_2, has a higher price and quantity. A shift of the demand curve maps out competitive equilibria along the marginal cost curve, so for every equilibrium quantity, there is a single corresponding equilibrium price.

Panel b shows the corresponding situation with a monopoly. As demand shifts from D^1 to D^2, the monopoly optimum shifts from E_1 to E_2, so the price rises but the quantity stays constant, $Q_1 = Q_2$. Thus, *a given quantity can correspond to more than one monopoly-optimal price*. A shift in the demand curve may cause the monopoly-optimal price to stay constant and the quantity to change, or both price and quantity to change.

11.2 Market Power and Welfare

What determines how high a price a monopoly can charge? A monopoly has **market power**: the ability of a firm to charge a price above marginal cost and earn a positive profit. In this section, we examine the factors that determine how much above its marginal cost a monopoly sets its price and its effect on welfare.

Market Power and the Shape of the Demand Curve

The degree to which the monopoly raises its price above its marginal cost depends on the shape of the demand curve at the profit-maximizing quantity. If the monopoly faces a highly elastic—nearly flat—demand curve at the profit-maximizing quantity, it would lose substantial sales if it raised its price by even a small amount. Conversely, if the demand curve is not very elastic (is relatively steep) at that quantity, the monopoly would lose fewer sales from raising its price by the same amount.

We can derive the relationship between market power and the elasticity of demand at the profit-maximizing quantity using the expression for marginal revenue in Equation 11.4 and the firm's profit-maximizing condition that marginal revenue equals marginal cost:

$$MR = p\left(1 + \frac{1}{\varepsilon}\right) = MC. \tag{11.9}$$

By rearranging terms, we can rewrite Equation 11.9 as

$$\frac{p}{MC} = \frac{1}{1 + (1/\varepsilon)}. \tag{11.10}$$

According to Equation 11.10, the ratio of the price to marginal cost depends *only* on the elasticity of demand at the profit-maximizing quantity.

In our linear demand example in panel a of Figure 11.3, the elasticity of demand is $\varepsilon = -3$ at the monopoly optimum where $Q^* = 6$. As a result, the ratio of price to marginal cost is $p/MC = 1/[1 + 1/(-3)] = 1.5$, or $p = 1.5MC$. The profit-maximizing price, \$18, in panel a is 1.5 times the marginal cost of \$12.

Table 11.1 illustrates how the ratio of price to marginal cost varies with the elasticity of demand. When the elasticity is -1.01, which is only slightly elastic, the monopoly's profit-maximizing price is 101 times larger than its marginal cost: $p/MC = 1/[1 + 1/(-1.01)] \approx 101$. As the elasticity of demand approaches negative infinity (becomes perfectly elastic), $1/\varepsilon$ approaches zero, so the ratio of price to marginal cost shrinks to $p/MC = 1$.

Table 11.1   Elasticity of Demand, Price, and Marginal Cost

Elasticity of Demand, ε	Price/Marginal Cost Ratio, $p/MC = 1/[1 + (1/\varepsilon)]$	Lerner Index, $(p - MC)/p = -1/\varepsilon$
−1.01	101	0.99
−1.1	11	0.91
−2	2	0.50
−3	1.5	0.33
−5	1.25	0.20
−10	1.11	0.10
−100	1.01	0.01
−∞	1	0

(Left margin: more elastic ← → less elastic)

The table illustrates that not all monopolies can set high prices. A monopoly that faces a horizontal, perfectly elastic demand curve sets its price equal to its marginal cost—like a price-taking competitive firm does. If this monopoly were to raise its price, it would lose all its sales, so it maximizes its profit by setting its price equal to its marginal cost.

The more elastic the demand curve, the less a monopoly can raise its price without losing sales. All else the same, the more close substitutes for the monopoly's good there are, the more elastic the demand the monopoly faces. For example, Pearson has the monopoly right to produce and sell this textbook. However, many other publishers have the rights to produce and sell similar microeconomics textbooks (although you wouldn't like them as much). The demand Pearson faces is much more elastic than it would be if no substitutes were available. If you think this textbook is expensive, imagine the cost if no substitutes were published!

The Lerner Index

Another way to show how the elasticity of demand affects a monopoly's price relative to its marginal cost is to look at the firm's **Lerner Index** (or *price markup*): the ratio of the difference between price and marginal cost to the price: $(p - MC)/p$.[2] This measure is zero for a competitive firm because a competitive firm cannot raise its price above its marginal cost. The greater the difference between price and marginal cost, the larger the Lerner Index and the greater the monopoly's ability to set price above marginal cost.

If the firm is maximizing its profit, we can express the Lerner Index in terms of the elasticity of demand by rearranging Equation 11.10:

$$\frac{p - MC}{p} = -\frac{1}{\varepsilon}. \tag{11.11}$$

Because $MC \geq 0$ and $p \geq MC$, $0 \leq p - MC \leq p$ and the Lerner Index ranges from 0 to 1 for a profit-maximizing firm.[3] Equation 11.11 confirms that a competitive firm has a Lerner Index of zero because its demand curve is perfectly elastic. As Table 11.1 illustrates, the Lerner Index for a monopoly increases as the

---

[2]This index is named after its inventor, Abba Lerner.

[3]For the Lerner Index to be above 1, ε would have to be a negative fraction, indicating that the demand curve was inelastic at the monopoly optimum. However, a profit-maximizing monopoly never operates in the inelastic portion of its demand curve.

demand becomes less elastic. If $\varepsilon = -5$, the monopoly's markup or Lerner Index is $\frac{1}{5} = 0.2$; if $\varepsilon = -2$, the markup is $\frac{1}{2} = 0.5$; and if $\varepsilon = -1.01$, the markup is 0.99. Monopolies that face demand curves that are only slightly elastic set prices that are multiples of their marginal cost and have Lerner Indexes close to 1.

SOLVED PROBLEM 11.2

When the iPad was introduced, Apple's constant marginal cost of producing its top-of-the-line iPad was about $220, its fixed cost was $2,000 million (= $2 billion), and we estimate that its inverse demand function was $p = 770 - 11Q$, where Q is the millions of iPads purchased.[4] What was Apple's average cost function? Assuming that Apple was maximizing short-run monopoly profit, what was its marginal revenue function? What were its profit-maximizing price and quantity, profit, and Lerner Index? What was the elasticity of demand at the profit-maximizing level? Show Apple's profit-maximizing solution in a figure.

Answer

1. *Derive the average cost function using the information about Apple's marginal and fixed costs.* Given that Apple's marginal cost was constant, its average variable cost equaled its marginal cost, $200. Its average fixed cost was its fixed cost divided by the quantity produced, $2,000/Q$. Thus, its average cost was $AC = 200 + 2,000/Q$.

2. *Derive Apple's marginal revenue function using the information about its demand function.* Because the inverse demand function was $p = 770 - 11Q$, Apple's revenue function was $R = 770Q - 11Q^2$, so $MR = dR/dQ = 770 - 22Q$.

3. *Derive Apple's profit-maximizing price and quantity by equating the marginal revenue and marginal cost functions and solving.* Apple maximized its profit where

$$MR = 770 - 22Q = 220 = MC.$$

Solving this equation for the profit-maximizing output, we find that $Q = 25$ million iPads. By substituting this quantity into the inverse demand equation, we determine that the profit-maximizing price was $p = \$500$ per unit, as the figure shows.

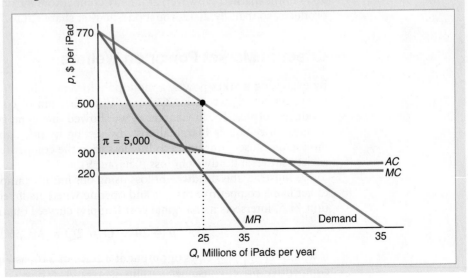

---

[4]See the Sources for "Pricing Apple's iPad," for details on these estimates.

4. *Calculate Apple's profit using the profit-maximizing price and quantity and the average cost.* The firm's profit was $\pi = (p - AC)Q = [500 - (220 + 2{,}000/25)]25 = \$5{,}000$ million $(= \$5$ billion$)$. The figure shows that the profit is a rectangle with a height of $(p - AC)$ and a length of Q.

5. *Determine the Lerner Index by substituting into the Lerner definition.* The iPad's Lerner Index is

$$\frac{p - MC}{p} = \frac{500 - 220}{500} = 0.56.$$

6. *Use Equation 11.11 to infer the elasticity.* According to that equation, a profit-maximizing monopoly operates where $(p - MC)/p = -1/\varepsilon$. Combining that equation with the Lerner Index from the previous step, we learn that $0.56 = -1/\varepsilon$, or $\varepsilon \approx -1.79$.

Sources of Market Power

What factors cause a monopoly to face a relatively elastic demand curve and hence have little market power? Ultimately, the elasticity of demand of the market demand curve depends on consumers' tastes and options. The more consumers want a good—the more willing they are to pay "virtually anything" for it—the less elastic is the demand curve.

Other things equal, the demand curve a firm (not necessarily a monopoly) faces becomes more elastic as (1) *better substitutes* for the firm's product are introduced, (2) *more firms* enter the market selling the same product, or (3) firms that provide the same service *locate closer* to this firm.

For example, when Apple introduced its iPod in 2001, it captured virtually the entire hard-disk music player market because its product was superior. It was a quarter of the size of its competitors, it was more elegant, had an intuitive interface, and used a high-speed FireWire interface to transfer files. By 2004, the iPod had 96% of the market. However, gradually competitors introduced comparable quality products, so that, by 2012, the iPod's market share fell to 72%.

Effect of Market Power on Welfare

By exercising market power, a monopoly lowers welfare relative to that of competition. As before, we define welfare, W, as the sum of consumer surplus, CS, and producer surplus, PS. In Chapter 9, we showed that competition maximizes welfare because price equals marginal cost. By setting its price above its marginal cost, a monopoly causes consumers to buy less than the competitive level of the good, and society suffers a deadweight loss (Chapter 9).

We illustrate this deadweight loss using our linear example. If the monopoly were to act like a competitive market and operate where its inverse demand curve, Equation 11.5, intersects its marginal cost (supply) curve, Equation 11.8,

$$p = 24 - Q = 2Q = MC,$$

it would sell $Q_c = 8$ units of output at a price of $16, as Figure 11.5 shows. At this competitive price, consumer surplus is area $A + B + C$ and producer surplus is area $D + E$.

Figure 11.5 Deadweight Loss of Monopoly

A competitive market would produce $Q_c = 8$ at $p_c = \$16$, where the demand curve intersects the marginal cost (supply) curve. A monopoly produces only $Q_m = 6$ at $p_m = \$18$, where the marginal revenue curve intersects the marginal cost curve. Under monopoly, consumer surplus is A, producer surplus is $B + D$, and the lost welfare or deadweight loss of monopoly is $-C - E$.

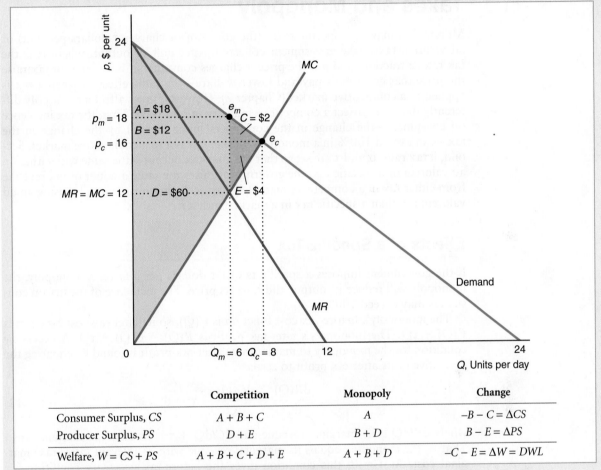

	Competition	Monopoly	Change
Consumer Surplus, CS	$A + B + C$	A	$-B - C = \Delta CS$
Producer Surplus, PS	$D + E$	$B + D$	$B - E = \Delta PS$
Welfare, $W = CS + PS$	$A + B + C + D + E$	$A + B + D$	$-C - E = \Delta W = DWL$

If the firm acts like a monopoly and operates where its marginal revenue equals its marginal cost, only 6 units are sold at the monopoly price of $18, and consumer surplus is only A. Part of the lost consumer surplus, B, goes to the monopoly; but the rest, C, is lost.

By charging the monopoly price of $18 instead of the competitive price of $16, the monopoly receives $2 more per unit and earns an extra profit of area $B = \$12$ on the $Q_m = 6$ units it sells. The monopoly loses area E, however, because it sells less than the competitive output. Consequently, the monopoly's producer surplus increases by $B - E$ over the competitive level. We know that its producer surplus increases, $B - E > 0$, because the monopoly had the option of producing at the competitive level and chose not to do so.

Social welfare with a monopoly is lower than with a competitive industry. The deadweight loss of monopoly is $-C - E$, which represents the consumer surplus and producer surplus lost because less than the competitive output is produced. As in the analysis of a tax in Chapter 9, the deadweight loss is due to the gap between price and marginal cost at the monopoly output. At $Q_m = 6$, the price, \$18, is above the marginal cost, \$12, so consumers are willing to pay more for the last unit of output than it costs to produce it.

11.3   Taxes and Monopoly

Monopolies may face specific taxes (the government charges τ dollars per unit) or ad valorem taxes (the government collects αp per unit of output, where α is the tax rate, a fraction, and p is the price it charges consumers). Both types of tax raise the price that consumers pay and lower welfare—the same effect as when a tax is applied to a competitive market (Chapter 2). However, taxes affect a monopoly differently than they affect a competitive industry in two ways. First, the tax incidence on consumers—the change in the consumers' price divided by the change in the tax—can exceed 100% in a monopoly market but not in a competitive market. Second, if tax rates α and τ are set so that the after-tax output is the same with either an ad valorem or a specific tax, the government raises the same amount of tax revenue from either tax in a competitive market (Chapter 2), but raises more by using an ad valorem tax than a specific tax in a market with a monopoly.

Effects of a Specific Tax

If the government imposes a specific tax of τ dollars per unit on a monopoly, the monopoly will reduce its output and raise its price. The incidence of the tax on consumers may exceed 100%.

The monopoly's before-tax cost function is $C(Q)$, so its after-tax cost function is $C(Q) + \tau Q$. The monopoly's after-tax profit is $R(Q) - C(Q) - \tau Q$. A necessary condition for the monopoly to maximize its after-tax profit is found by equating the derivative of its after-tax profit to zero:

$$\frac{dR(Q)}{dQ} - \frac{dC(Q)}{dQ} - \tau = 0, \qquad (11.12)$$

where dR/dQ is its marginal revenue and $dC/dQ + \tau$ is its after-tax marginal cost. That is, the monopoly equals its marginal revenue with its relevant (after-tax) marginal cost. At $\tau = 0$, this condition gives the before-tax necessary condition for profit maximization, Equation 11.1. The sufficient condition is the same as the before-tax Equation 11.2, $d^2R/dQ^2 - d^2C/dQ^2 < 0$, because $d\tau/dQ = 0$.

We can use comparative statics techniques to determine the effect of imposing a specific tax by asking how output changes as τ goes from zero to a small positive value. Based on the necessary condition, Equation 11.2, we can write the monopoly's optimal quantity as a function of the tax: $Q(\tau)$. Differentiating the necessary condition with respect to τ, we find that

$$\frac{d^2R}{dQ^2}\frac{dQ}{d\tau} - \frac{d^2C}{dQ^2}\frac{dQ}{d\tau} - 1 = 0,$$

or

$$\frac{dQ}{d\tau} = \frac{1}{\dfrac{d^2R}{dQ^2} - \dfrac{d^2C}{dQ^2}}. \qquad (11.13)$$

The denominator of the right-hand-side of Equation 11.13 is negative by the second-order condition, Equation 11.2, so $dQ/d\tau < 0$. That is, as the specific tax rises, the monopoly reduces its output. Because its demand curve is downward sloping, when the monopoly lowers its output, it raises its price by $dp(Q(\tau))/d\tau = (dp/dQ)(dQ/d\tau) > 0$.

In a competitive market, the incidence of a specific or ad valorem tax on consumers is less than or equal to 100% of the tax, and the incidence on consumers plus the incidence on suppliers is 100% (Chapter 2). In contrast in a monopoly market, the incidence of a specific tax falling on consumers can exceed 100%: The price consumers pay may rise by an amount greater than the tax.

To demonstrate this possibility, we suppose that a monopoly's marginal cost is constant at m and that its demand curve has a constant elasticity of ε, so its inverse demand function is $p = Q^{1/\varepsilon}$. Consequently, the monopoly's revenue function is $R = pQ = Q^{1+1/\varepsilon}$. The monopoly's marginal revenue is $MR = dQ^{1+1/\varepsilon}/dQ = (1 + 1/\varepsilon)Q^{1/\varepsilon}$.

To maximize its profit, the monopoly equates its after-tax marginal cost, $m + \tau$, with its marginal revenue function:

$$m + \tau = \left(1 + \frac{1}{\varepsilon}\right)Q^{1/\varepsilon}.$$

Solving this equation for the profit-maximizing output, the monopoly produces $Q = [(m + \tau)/(1 + 1/\varepsilon)]^\varepsilon$. The monopoly substitutes that value of Q into its inverse demand function, $p = Q^{1/\varepsilon}$, to choose the price it sets:

$$p = \frac{m + \tau}{1 + 1/\varepsilon}. \tag{11.14}$$

To determine the effect of a change in the tax on the price that consumers pay, we differentiate Equation 11.14 with respect to the tax: $dp/d\tau = 1/(1 + 1/\varepsilon)$. We know that $dp/d\tau$ is greater than one because a monopoly never operates in the inelastic portion of its demand curve so $\varepsilon < -1$. Thus, the incidence of the tax that falls on consumers exceeds 100%. However, for other types of demand curves, the tax incidence on consumers may be less than 100%, as the following solved problem shows.

SOLVED PROBLEM 11.3

If the government imposes a specific tax of $\tau = \$8$ per unit on the monopoly in the linear example in Figure 11.3, how does the monopoly change its profit-maximizing quantity and price? Use a figure to show how the tax affects tax revenue, consumer surplus, producer surplus, welfare, and deadweight loss. What is the incidence of the tax on consumers?

Answer

1. *Determine how imposing the tax affects the monopoly's optimum quantity by equating marginal revenue and after-tax marginal cost, and substitute the optimum quantity into the inverse demand function to find the profit-maximizing price.* Because the monopoly must pay the tax, its before-tax marginal cost, Equation 11.8, $2Q$, shifts to an after-tax marginal cost of $MC = 2Q + 8$.[5]

[5]As we discussed in Chapter 2, the government can impose a tax on the seller (here, the monopoly) or the buyers. Because the seller must pay this tax, the tax shifts the marginal cost curve, but not the demand or marginal revenue curves. In the next section, we assume that the tax is imposed on the buyers so that it shifts the demand marginal revenue curves and not the marginal cost curve.

The monopoly's marginal revenue, Equation 11.6, remains unchanged at $MR = 24 - 2Q$. The monopoly picks the output, Q^*, that equates its after-tax marginal cost and its marginal revenue: $2Q^* + 8 = 24 - 2Q^*$. Solving, we find that $Q^* = 4$. Because the monopoly's inverse demand function, Equation 11.5, is $p = 24 - Q$, it charges $p^* = 24 - 4 = 20$.

The graph shows that the intersection of the marginal revenue curve, MR, and the before-tax marginal cost curve, MC^1, determines the before-tax monopoly's optimum quantity, $Q_1 = 6$. At the before-tax optimum, e_1, the price is $p_1 = \$18$. The specific tax causes the monopoly's before-tax marginal cost curve, $MC^1 = 2Q$, to shift upward by \$8 to $MC^2 = MC^1 + 8 = 2Q + 8$. After the tax is applied, the monopoly operates where $MR = 24 - 2Q = 2Q + 8 = MC^2$. In the after-tax monopoly optimum, e_2, the quantity is $Q_2 = 4$ and the price is $p_2 = \$20$. Thus, output falls by $\Delta Q = 2$ units and the price increases by $\Delta p = \$2$.

2. *Show the change in tax revenue and the various welfare measures.* In the figure, area G is the tax revenue collected by the government, \$32, because its height is the distance between the two marginal cost curves, $\tau = \$8$, and its

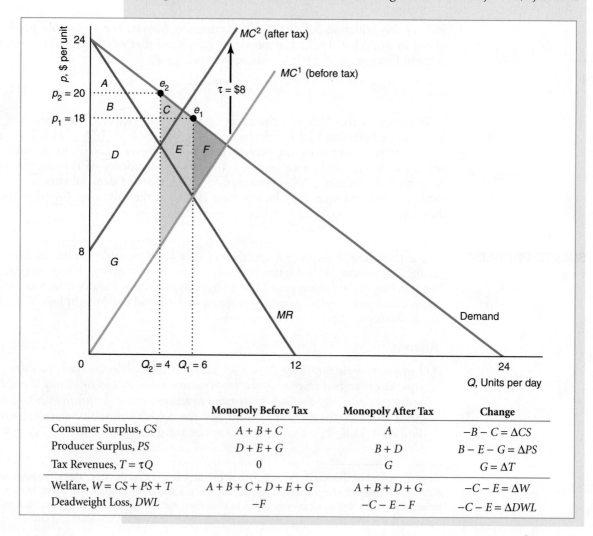

	Monopoly Before Tax	Monopoly After Tax	Change
Consumer Surplus, CS	$A + B + C$	A	$-B - C = \Delta CS$
Producer Surplus, PS	$D + E + G$	$B + D$	$B - E - G = \Delta PS$
Tax Revenues, $T = \tau Q$	0	G	$G = \Delta T$
Welfare, $W = CS + PS + T$	$A + B + C + D + E + G$	$A + B + D + G$	$-C - E = \Delta W$
Deadweight Loss, DWL	$-F$	$-C - E - F$	$-C - E = \Delta DWL$

length is the output the monopoly produces after the tax is imposed, $Q = 4$. The tax reduces consumer and producer surplus and increases the dead-weight loss. Consumer surplus falls by area $B + C$ from $A + B + C$ to A. The monopoly's producer surplus drops from $D + E + G$ to $B + D$, so its net decrease is $B - E - G$. We know that producer surplus falls because (a) the monopoly could have produced this reduced output level in the absence of the tax but did not because it was not the profit-maximizing output, so its before-tax profit falls, and (b) the monopoly must now pay taxes. The before-tax deadweight loss due to monopoly pricing was $-F$. The after-tax deadweight loss is $-C - E - F$, so the increase in deadweight loss (or loss in welfare) due to the tax is $-C - E$.

3. *Calculate the incidence of the tax.* Because the tax goes from \$0 to \$8, the change in the tax is $\Delta\tau = \$8$. The incidence of the tax on consumers is $\Delta p / \Delta\tau = \$2/\$8 = \frac{1}{4}$. That is, the monopoly absorbs \$6 of the tax and passes on only \$2.

Welfare Effects of Ad Valorem Versus Specific Taxes

Why do governments generally use ad valorem sales taxes rather than specific taxes? In a market with a monopoly, a government raises more tax revenue with an ad valorem tax α than with a specific tax τ when α and τ are set so that the after-tax output is the same with either tax, as we now show.[6]

In Figure 11.6, the before-tax market demand curve is D, and the corresponding marginal revenue is MR. The before-tax monopoly optimum is e_1. The MR curve intersects the MC curve at Q_1 units, which sell at a price of p_1.

We assume that the government imposes the tax on consumers rather than on the firm, so that the tax shifts the demand and marginal revenue curves rather than the marginal cost curve.[7] If the government imposes a specific tax τ, the monopoly's after-tax demand curve is D^s, which is the market demand curve D shifted down-ward by τ dollars. The corresponding marginal revenue curve, MR^s, intersects the marginal cost curve at Q_2. In this after-tax equilibrium, e_2, consumers pay p_2 and the monopoly receives $p_s = p_2 - \tau$ per unit. The government's revenue from the specific tax is area $A = \tau Q_2$.

If the government imposes an ad valorem tax α, the demand curve facing the monopoly is D^a. The gap between D^a and D, which is the tax per unit, αp, is greater at higher prices. By setting α appropriately, the corresponding marginal revenue curve, MR_a, intersects the marginal cost curve at Q_2, where consumers again pay p_2. Although the ad valorem tax reduces output by the same amount as the specific tax, the ad valorem tax raises more revenue, area $A + B = \alpha p_2 Q_2$.

Both sales taxes harm consumers by the same amount because they raise the price consumers pay from p_1 to p_2 and reduce the quantity purchased from Q_1 to Q_2. The ad valorem tax transfers more revenue from the monopoly to the government, so the government prefers the ad valorem tax and the monopoly prefers the specific tax.

---

[6]Chapter 2 shows that both taxes raise the same tax revenue in a competitive market. However, the taxes raise different amounts when applied to monopolies or other noncompetitive firms. See Delipalla and Keen (1992), Skeath and Trandel (1994), and Hamilton (1999).

[7]If instead the tax were imposed on the monopoly, we could capture the effect of a specific tax by shifting the marginal cost curve upward as in our answer to Solved Problem 11.3.

Figure 11.6 Ad Valorem Versus Specific Tax

A specific tax (τ) and an ad valorem tax (α) that reduce the monopoly output by the same amount (from Q_1 to Q_2) raise different amounts of tax revenues for the government. The tax revenue from the specific tax is area $A = \tau Q_2$. The tax revenue from the ad valorem tax is area $A + B = \alpha p_2 Q_2$.

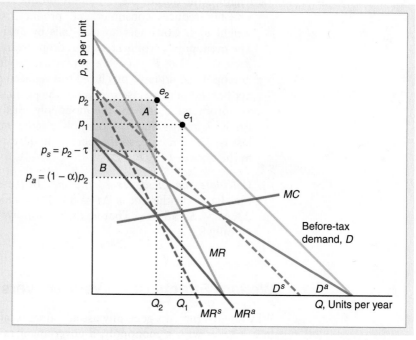

(Equivalently, if the government set τ and α so that they raised the same amount of tax revenue, the ad valorem tax would reduce output and consumer surplus less than the specific tax.) Amazingly, it makes sense for the government to employ an ad valorem tax, and most state and local governments use ad valorem taxes for most goods.[8]

11.4   Causes of Monopolies

I think it's wrong that only one company makes the game Monopoly.
—Steven Wright

Why are some markets monopolized? Two key reasons are that a firm has a cost advantage over other firms or a government created the monopoly.[9]

Cost Advantages

If a low-cost firm profitably sells at a price so low that potential competitors with higher costs would incur losses, no other firm enters the market. A firm can have a

---

[8]However, as Professor Stearns and his students at the University of Maryland informed me, the federal government uses a number of specific taxes (on alcohol, tobacco products, gasoline and other fuels, international air travel, tires, vaccines, ship passengers, and ozone-depleting chemicals) as well as ad valorem taxes (on telephone service, transportation of property by air, sport fishing equipment, bow and arrow components, gas-guzzling autos, foreign insurance, and firearms).

[9]In later chapters, we discuss three other means by which monopolies are created. First, the original firm in a market may use strategies that discourage other firms from entering the market (Chapter 13). Second, a merger into a single firm (Chapter 14) of all the firms in an industry creates a monopoly if new firms fail to enter the market. Third, firms may coordinate their activities and set their prices as a monopoly would (Chapter 14). Firms that act collectively in this way are called a *cartel*. In Section 11.6, we discuss how network externalities may lead to a monopoly.

cost advantage over potential rivals because it has an essential facility, it has a superior technology or organization, or it is a natural monopoly.

Essential Facility. A firm may have a lower cost than potential rivals if it controls an **essential facility**: a scarce resource that a rival needs to use to survive. For example, a firm that owns the only quarry in a region is the only firm that can profitably sell gravel to local construction firms. For example in 2012, Canadian pipeline giant Enbridge Inc. refused to allow the pipeline of a small Colorado firm to connect its highway of pipelines that bring Canadian oil sands crude oil into the United States.[10]

Superior Technology or Organization. A firm may have lower costs if it uses a superior technology or has a better way of organizing production. Henry Ford's methods of organizing production using assembly lines and standardization allowed him to produce cars at lower cost than rival firms until they copied his organizational techniques.

Natural Monopoly. One firm can produce the total market output at lower cost than several firms could if it is a **natural monopoly**. If the cost for any firm to produce q is $C(q)$, the condition for a natural monopoly is

$$C(Q) < C(q_1) + C(q_2) + \cdots + C(q_n), \tag{11.15}$$

where $Q = q_1 + q_2 + \cdots + q_n$ is the sum of the output of any $n \geq 2$ firms and where the condition holds for all output levels that could be demanded by the market. With a natural monopoly, it is more efficient to have only one firm produce than to have more than one firm produce.[11] Believing that they are natural monopolies, governments frequently grant monopoly rights to *public utilities* to provide essential goods or services such as water, gas, electric power, and mail delivery.

Suppose that a public utility has economies of scale (Chapter 7) at all levels of output, so its average cost curve falls as output increases for any observed level of output. If all potential firms have the same strictly declining average cost curve, this market has a natural monopoly, as we now consider.[12]

A company that supplies water to homes incurs a high fixed cost, F, to build a plant and connect houses to the plant. The firm's marginal cost, m, of supplying water is constant, so its marginal cost curve is horizontal and its average cost, $AC = m + F/Q$, declines as output rises. (The iPad cost function in Solved Problem 11.2 has this functional form.)

Figure 11.7 shows such marginal and average cost curves where $m = \$10$ and $F = \$60$. If the market output is 12 units per day, one firm produces that output at

---

[10]Northey, Hannah, "U.S. Producers Accuse Canadian Pipeline Company of Refusing to Carry Their Crude," *Greenwire*, July 12, 2012.

[11]A natural monopoly is the most efficient market structure only in the sense that the single firm produces at lowest cost. However, society's welfare may be greater with more firms producing at higher cost, because competition drives down the price from the monopoly level. One solution that allows society to maximize welfare is for the government to allow only one firm to produce but the government forces it to charge a price equal to marginal cost (as we discuss later in this chapter).

[12]A firm may be a natural monopoly even if its cost curve does not fall at all levels of output. If a U-shaped average cost curve reaches its minimum at 100 units of output, it may be less costly for only one firm to produce an output of 101 units even though its average cost curve is rising at that output. Thus, a cost function with economies of scale everywhere is a sufficient but not a necessary condition for a natural monopoly.

Figure 11.7 Natural Monopoly

This natural monopoly has a strictly declining average cost.

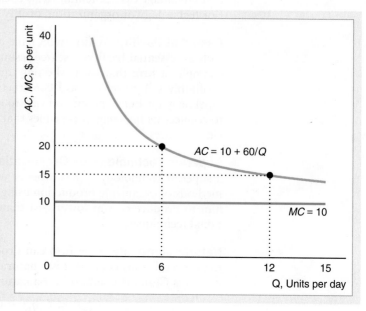

$AC = 10 + 60/Q$

$MC = 10$

Q, Units per day

an average cost of $15, or a total cost of $180 (= $15 × 12). If two firms each produce 6 units, the average cost is $20, and the cost of producing the market output is $240 (= $20 × 12), which is greater than the cost with a single firm.

    If the two firms were to divide the total production in any other way, their costs of production would still exceed the cost of a single firm (as Solved Problem 11.4 asks you to prove).[13] The reason is that the marginal cost per unit is the same no matter how many firms produce, but each additional firm adds a fixed cost, which raises the cost of producing a given quantity. If only one firm provides water, the cost of building a second plant and a second set of pipes is avoided.

SOLVED PROBLEM 11.4

A firm that delivers Q units of water to households has a total cost of $C(Q) = mQ + F$. If any entrant would have the same cost, does this market have a natural monopoly?

Answer

Determine whether costs rise if two firms produce a given quantity. Let q_1 be the output of Firm 1 and q_2 be the output of Firm 2. The combined cost of these firms producing $Q = q_1 + q_2$ is

$$C(q_1) + C(q_2) = (mq_1 + F) + (mq_2 + F) = m(q_1 + q_2) + 2F = mQ + 2F.$$

If a single firm produces Q, its cost is $C(Q) = mQ + F$. Thus the cost of producing any given Q is greater with two firms than with one firm, so this market has a natural monopoly.

---

[13]See "Electric Power Utilities" in MyEconLab, Chapter Resources, Chapter 11.

Government Actions That Create Monopolies

Governments create many monopolies. In some markets, governments establish a barrier to entry to potential competitors. In other markets, governments create monopolies explicitly. A government may own and manage a monopoly. In the United States, as in most other countries, the postal service is a government monopoly. Indeed, the U.S. Constitution explicitly grants the government the right to establish a postal service. Many local governments own and operate public utility monopolies that provide garbage collection, electricity, water, gas, phone services, and other utilities. Most national governments grant patents to the inventor of a new product that gives the patent holder monopoly rights for 20 years.

Barriers to Entry. By preventing other firms from entering a market, governments create monopolies. Governments typically create monopolies by making it difficult for new firms to obtain a license to operate, by granting a firm the rights to be a monopoly, or by auctioning the rights to be a monopoly.

Frequently, firms need government licenses to operate. If a government makes it difficult for new firms to obtain licenses, the first firm to become licensed can maintain its monopoly. Until recently, many U.S. cities required new hospitals or other inpatient establishments to demonstrate the need for a new facility by securing a certificate of need, which allowed them to enter the market.

Government grants of monopoly rights have been common for public utilities. Instead of running a public utility itself, a government gives a private company the monopoly rights to operate the utility. A government may capture some of the monopoly's profits by charging a high rent to the monopoly. Alternatively, government officials may capture the rents for monopoly rights through bribery.

Governments around the world have privatized many state-owned monopolies in the past several decades. By auctioning its monopolies to private firms, a government can capture the future value of monopoly earnings. Alternatively, a government could auction the rights to the firm that offers to charge the lowest price, so as to maximize social welfare.[14]

Patents. If a firm cannot prevent imitation by keeping its discovery secret, it may obtain government protection to prevent other firms from duplicating its discovery and entering the market. Virtually all countries provide such protection through a **patent**: an exclusive right granted to the inventor to sell a new and useful product, process, substance, or design for a fixed time. A patent grants an inventor the right to be the monopoly provider of the good for a number of years. (Similarly, a copyright gives its owner the exclusive production, publication, or sales rights to artistic, dramatic, literary, or musical works.)

The length of a patent varies across countries. The U.S. Constitution explicitly gives the government the right to grant authors and inventors exclusive rights to their writings (copyrights) and to their discoveries (patents) for limited periods of time. Traditionally, U.S. patents lasted 17 years from the date they were *granted*, but in 1995, the United States agreed to change its patent law as part of an international agreement. Now, U.S. patents last for 20 years after the date the inventor *files* for patent protection. The length of protection is likely to be shorter under the new rules because frequently it takes more than three years after filing to obtain final approval of a patent.

---

[14]*Jargon alert:* A low price auction is called a Demsetz auction by many economists.

A firm with a patent monopoly sets a high price, which results in deadweight loss. Why, then, do governments grant patent monopolies? The main reason is that inventive activity would fall if there were no patent monopolies or other incentives to inventors. The costs of developing a new drug or new computer chip are often hundreds of millions or even billions of dollars. If anyone could copy a new drug or computer chip and compete with the inventor, few individuals or firms would undertake the costly research. Thus, the government is explicitly trading-off the long-run benefits of additional inventions against the shorter-term harms of monopoly pricing during the period of patent protection.[15]

APPLICATION

Botox Patent Monopoly

Ophthalmologist Dr. Alan Scott turned the deadly poison botulinum toxin into a miracle drug to treat two eye conditions: strabismus, a condition in which the eyes are not properly aligned, and blepharospasm, an uncontrollable closure of the eyes. Strabismus affects about 4% of children and blepharospasm left about 25,000 Americans functionally blind before Scott's discovery. His patented drug, Botox, is sold by Allergan, Inc.

Dr. Scott has been amused to see several of the unintended beneficiaries of his research at the annual Academy Awards. Even before it was explicitly approved for cosmetic use, many doctors were injecting Botox into the facial muscles of actors, models, and others to smooth out their wrinkles. (The drug paralyzes the muscles, so those injected with it also lose their ability to frown or smile—and, some would say, act.) The treatment is only temporary, lasting up to 120 days, so repeated injections are necessary. In 2002, Allergan had expected to sell $400 million worth of Botox. However, in April of that year, the U.S. Food and Drug Administration approved the use of Botox for cosmetic purposes. The FDA ruling allows the company to advertise the drug widely.

Allergan sold $800 million worth of Botox in 2004 and expected sales of $1.8 billion in 2012. Allergan has a near-monopoly in the treatment of wrinkles, although plastic surgery, as well as collagen injections, Restylane, hyaluronic acid, and other fillers, provide limited competition. According to the American Society of Plastic Surgeons, between 2002 and 2004, the number of facelifts dropped 3% to about 114,000, while the number of Botox injections skyrocketed 166%. Indeed, Botox injections rose 388% from 2000 to 2005.

Dr. Scott can produce a vial of Botox in his lab for about $25. Allergan sells the potion to doctors for about $400. Assuming that the firm is setting its price to maximize its short-run profit, we can rearrange Equation 11.11 to determine the elasticity of demand for Botox:

$$\varepsilon = -\frac{p}{p - MC} = -\frac{400}{400 - 25} \approx -1.067.$$

Thus, the demand that Allergan faces is only slightly elastic: A 1% increase in price causes quantity to fall by slightly more than 1%.

If we assume that the demand curve is linear and given that the elasticity of demand is -1.067 at the 2002 monopoly optimum, e_m (1 million vials sold at

---

[15]Although patents may increase innovation, abuses of patent law may inhibit innovation. For example, *patent trolls* obtain minor patents that they use in lawsuits to block other more serious inventors unless they are paid a *ransom*. In addition, the large number of patents and patent holders in many areas, such as information technology and biotechnology, impose large transaction costs on potential inventors. Thus, while a well-designed patent system provides strong incentives for innovation, a poorly designed system can be counter-productive.

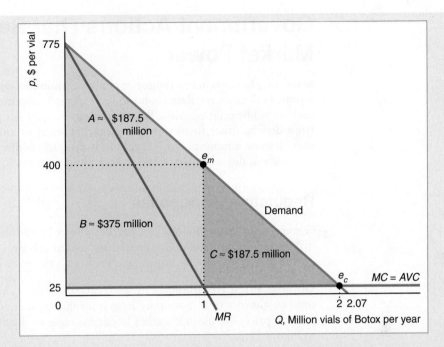

$400 each, producing revenue of $400 million), then Allergan's inverse demand function is[16]

$$p = 775 - 375Q.$$

This demand curve (see the graph) has a slope of -375 and hits the price axis at $775 and the quantity axis at about 2.07 million vials per year. Thus, its revenue is $R = 775Q - 375Q^2$, so its marginal revenue curve is

$$MR = dR/dQ = 775 - 750Q.$$

The MR curve strikes the price axis at $775 and has twice the slope, -750, of the demand curve.

The intersection of the marginal revenue and marginal cost curves,

$$MR = 775 - 750Q = 25 = MC,$$

determines the monopoly equilibrium at the profit-maximizing quantity of 1 million vials per year and at a price of $400 per vial.

Were the company to sell Botox at a price equal to its marginal cost of $25 (as a competitive industry would), consumer surplus would equal area $A + B + C$. The height of triangle $A + B + C$ is $750 = 775 - 25$, and its length is 2 million vials, so its area is $750 (= \frac{1}{2} \times 750 \times 2)$ million. At the higher monopoly price of $400, the consumer surplus is $A = \$187.5$ million. Compared to the competitive solution, e_c, buyers lose consumer surplus of $B + C = \$562.5$ million per year. Part of this loss, $B = \$375$ million per year, is transferred from consumers to Allergan. The rest, $C = \$187.5$ million per year, is the deadweight loss from monopoly pricing. Allergan's profit is its producer surplus, B, minus its fixed costs.

---

[16]The graph shows an inverse linear demand curve of the form $p = a - bQ$. Such a linear demand curve has an elasticity of $\varepsilon = -(1/b)(p/Q)$. Given that the elasticity of demand is $-400/375 = -(1/b)(400/1)$, where Q is measured in millions of vials, then $b = 375$. Solving $p = 400 = a - 375$, we find that $a = 775$.

11.5   Government Actions That Reduce Market Power

Some governments act to reduce or eliminate monopolies' market power. Many governments directly regulate monopolies, especially those created by the government, such as public utilities. Most Western countries have designed laws to prevent a firm from driving other firms out of the market so as to monopolize it. A government may destroy a monopoly by breaking it up into smaller, independent firms (as the government did with Alcoa, the former aluminum monopoly).

Regulating Monopolies

Governments limit monopolies' market power in various ways. For example, most utilities are subject to direct regulation. Alternatively, governments may limit the harms of a monopoly by imposing a ceiling on the price it can charge.

Optimal Price Regulation. In some markets, the government can eliminate the deadweight loss of a monopoly by requiring that it charge no more than the competitive price. We use our earlier linear example to illustrate this type of regulation in Figure 11.8.

If the government doesn't regulate the profit-maximizing monopoly, the monopoly optimum is e_m, at which 6 units are sold at the monopoly price of $18. Suppose that the government sets a ceiling price of $16, the price at which the marginal cost curve intersects the market demand curve. Because the monopoly cannot charge more than $16 per unit, the monopoly's regulated demand curve is horizontal at $16 (up to 8 units) and is the same as the market demand curve at lower prices. The marginal revenue curve corresponding to the regulated demand curve, MR^r, is horizontal where the regulated demand curve is horizontal (up to 8 units) and equals the marginal revenue curve, MR, corresponding to the market demand curve at larger quantities.

The regulated monopoly sets its output at 8 units, where MR^r equals its marginal cost, MC, and charges the maximum permitted price of $16. The regulated firm still makes a profit because its average cost is less than $16 at 8 units. The optimally regulated monopoly optimum, e_o, is the same as the competitive equilibrium, where marginal cost (supply) equals the market demand curve.[17] Thus, setting a price ceiling where the MC curve and market demand curve intersect eliminates the deadweight loss of monopoly.

How do we know that this regulation is optimal? The answer is that this regulated outcome is the same as would occur if this market were competitive, where welfare is maximized (Chapter 9). As the table accompanying Figure 11.8 shows, the deadweight loss of monopoly, $C + E$, is eliminated by this optimal regulation.

Nonoptimal Price Regulation. If the government sets the price ceiling at any point other than the optimal level, there is deadweight loss. Suppose that the government sets the regulated price below the optimal level, which is $16 in Figure 11.8. If it sets the price below the firm's minimum average cost, the firm shuts down, so the deadweight loss equals the sum of the consumer plus producer surplus under optimal regulation, $A + B + C + D + E$.

---

[17]The monopoly produces at e_o only if the regulated price is greater than its average variable cost. Here, the regulated price, $16, exceeds the average variable cost at 8 units of $8. Indeed, the firm makes a profit because the average cost at 8 units is $9.50.

Figure 11.8 Optimal Price Regulation

If the government sets a price ceiling at $16, where the monopoly's marginal cost curve hits the demand curve, the new demand curve that the monopoly faces has a kink at 8 units, and the corresponding marginal revenue curve, MR^r, "jumps" at that quantity. The regulated monopoly sets its output where $MR^r = MC$, selling the same quantity, 8 units, at the same price, $16, as a competitive industry would. The regulation eliminates the monopoly deadweight loss, $C + E$. Consumer surplus, $A + B + C$, and producer surplus, $D + E$, are the same as under competition.

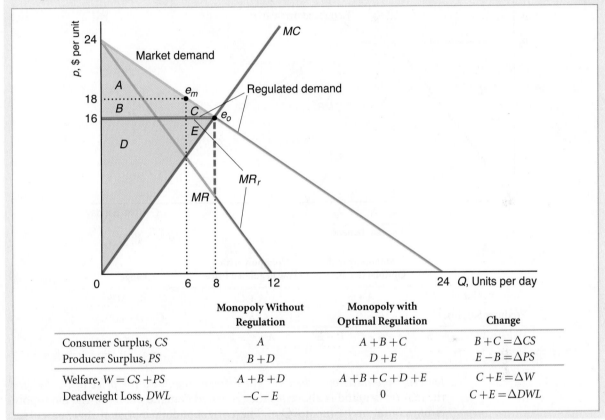

	Monopoly Without Regulation	Monopoly with Optimal Regulation	Change
Consumer Surplus, CS	A	$A + B + C$	$B + C = \Delta CS$
Producer Surplus, PS	$B + D$	$D + E$	$E - B = \Delta PS$
Welfare, $W = CS + PS$	$A + B + D$	$A + B + C + D + E$	$C + E = \Delta W$
Deadweight Loss, DWL	$-C - E$	0	$C + E = \Delta DWL$

If the government sets the price ceiling below the optimally regulated price but high enough that the firm does not shut down, consumers who are lucky enough to buy the good benefit because they can buy it at a lower price than they could with optimal regulation. As we show in the following solved problem, there is a deadweight loss because less output is sold than with optimal regulation.

SOLVED PROBLEM
11.5

Suppose that the government sets a price, p_2, that is below the socially optimal level, p_1, but above the monopoly's minimum average cost. How do the price, quantity sold, quantity demanded, and welfare under this regulation compare to those under optimal regulation?

Answer

1. *Describe the optimally regulated outcome.* With optimal regulation, e_1, the price is set at p_1, where the market demand curve intersects the monopoly's marginal cost curve on the accompanying graph. The optimally regulated monopoly sells Q_1 units.

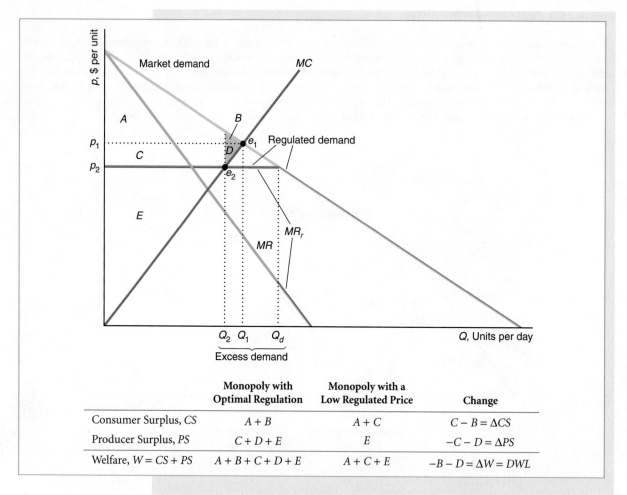

	Monopoly with Optimal Regulation	Monopoly with a Low Regulated Price	Change
Consumer Surplus, CS	$A + B$	$A + C$	$C - B = \Delta CS$
Producer Surplus, PS	$C + D + E$	E	$-C - D = \Delta PS$
Welfare, $W = CS + PS$	$A + B + C + D + E$	$A + C + E$	$-B - D = \Delta W = DWL$

2. *Describe the outcome when the government regulates the price at p_2.* Where the market demand is above p_2, the regulated demand curve for the monopoly is horizontal at p_2 (up to Q_d). The corresponding marginal revenue curve, MRr, is horizontal where the regulated demand curve is horizontal and equals the marginal revenue curve corresponding to the market demand curve, MR, where the regulated demand curve is downward sloping. The monopoly maximizes its profit by selling Q_2 units at p_2. The new regulated monopoly optimum is e_2, where MR^r intersects MC. The firm does not shut down when regulated as long as its average variable cost at Q_2 is less than p_2.

3. *Compare the outcomes.* The quantity that the monopoly sells falls from Q_1 to Q_2 when the government lowers its price ceiling from p_1 to p_2. At that lower price, consumers want to buy Q_d, so there is excess demand equal to $Q_d - Q_2$. Compared to optimal regulation, welfare is lower by at least $B + D$.

Comment: The welfare loss is greater if unlucky consumers waste time trying to buy the good unsuccessfully or if goods are not allocated optimally among consumers. A consumer who values the good at only p_2 may be lucky enough to buy it, while a consumer who values the good at p_1 or more may not be able to obtain it (Chapter 9).

Problems in Regulating. Governments often fail to regulate monopolies optimally for at least three reasons. First, due to limited information about the demand and marginal cost curves, governments may set a price ceiling above or below the competitive level.

Second, regulation may be ineffective when regulators are *captured*: influenced by the firms they regulate. Typically, this influence is more subtle than an outright bribe. Many American regulators worked in the industry before they became regulators and hence are sympathetic to those firms. For many other regulators, the reverse is true: They aspire to obtain good jobs in the industry eventually, so they do not want to offend potential employers. And some regulators, relying on industry experts for their information, may be misled or at least heavily influenced by the industry. U.S. Food and Drug Administration advisers voted 15 to 11 to recommend approval of four Bayer AG birth-control pills, but three of the advisers, who voted favorably, had ties to Bayer, serving as consultants, speakers, or researchers.[18] Arguing that these influences are inherent, some economists contend that price and other types of regulation are unlikely to result in efficiency.

Third, because regulators generally cannot subsidize the monopoly, they may be unable to set the price as low as they want because the firm may shut down. In a natural monopoly where the average cost curve is strictly above the marginal cost curve, if the regulator sets the price equal to the marginal cost so as to eliminate deadweight loss, the firm cannot afford to operate. If the regulators cannot subsidize the firm, they must raise the price to a level where the firm at least breaks even.

APPLICATION

Natural Gas
Regulation

Because U.S. natural gas monopolies are natural monopolies and regulators generally cannot subsidize them, the regulated price is set above marginal cost, so there is deadweight loss. The figure is based on the estimates of Davis and Muehlegger (2010).[19] If unregulated, this monopoly would sell 12.1 trillion cubic feet of natural gas per year, which is determined by the intersection of its marginal revenue and marginal cost curves. It would charge the corresponding price on the demand curve at point *a*. Its profit would equal the rectangle *A*, with a length equal to the quantity, 12.1 trillion cubic feet, and a height equal to the difference between the price at *a* and the corresponding average cost.

To eliminate deadweight loss, the government should set the price ceiling equal to the marginal cost of $5.78 per thousand cubic feet of natural gas so that the monopoly behaves like a price taker. The price ceiling or marginal cost curve hits the demand curve at *c* where the quantity is 24.2 billion cubic feet per year—double the unregulated quantity. At that quantity, the regulated utility would lose money. The regulated price, $5.78, is less than the average cost at that quantity of $7.78, so it would lose $2 on each thousand cubic feet it sells, or $48.2 billion in total. Thus, it will be willing to sell this quantity at this price only if the government subsidizes it.

Typically, it is politically infeasible for a government regulatory agency to subsidize a monopoly. On average, the natural gas regulatory agencies set the price at $7.88 per thousand cubic feet, where the demand curve intersects the average

[18]Burton, Thomas M., "FDA Panelists Had Ties to Bayer," *Wall Street Journal*, January 11, 2012.

[19]We use their most conservative estimate, the one that produces the smallest deadweight loss. We approximate their demand curve with a linear one that has the same price elasticity of demand of 0.2 at point *b*. This figure represents the aggregation of state-level monopolies to the national level.

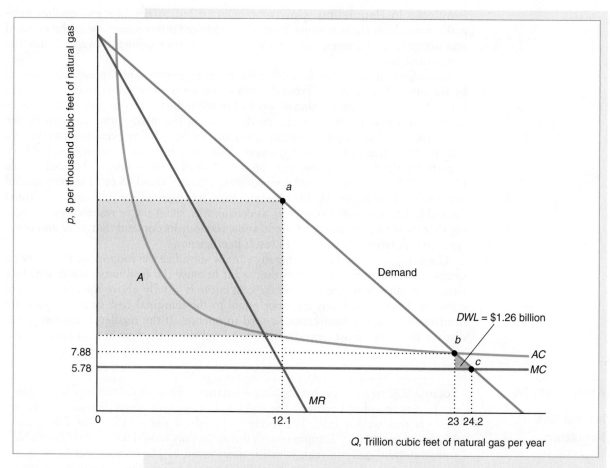

cost curve and the monopoly breaks even, point *b*. The monopoly sells 23 trillion cubic feet per year. The corresponding price, $7.88, is 36% above marginal cost, $5.78. Consequently, there is deadweight loss of $1.26 billion annually, which is the gray triangle in the figure. This deadweight loss is much smaller than it would be if the monopoly were unregulated.

Increasing Competition

Encouraging competition is an alternative to regulation as a means of reducing the harms of monopoly. When a government has created a monopoly by preventing entry, it can quickly reduce the monopoly's market power by allowing other firms to enter. As new firms enter the market, the former monopoly must lower its price to compete, so welfare rises.

Similarly, a government may end a ban on imports so that a domestic monopoly faces competition from foreign firms. If costs for the domestic firm are the same as costs for the foreign firms and there are many foreign firms, the former monopoly becomes just one of many competitive firms. As the market becomes competitive, consumers pay the competitive price, and the deadweight loss of monopoly is eliminated.

Globally, governments are increasing competition in previously monopolized markets. For example, many governments around the world forced former telephone and energy monopolies to compete.

Similarly, under pressure from the World Trade Organization, many countries are reducing or eliminating barriers that protected domestic monopolies. The entry of foreign competitive firms into a market can create a new, more competitive market structure.

11.6 Monopoly Decisions over Time and Behavioral Economics

We have examined how a monopoly behaves in the current period, ignoring the future. For many markets, this kind of analysis is appropriate. However, in some markets, today's decisions affect demand or cost in the future. In such markets, the monopoly may maximize its long-run profit by making a decision today that does not maximize its short-run profit. For example, frequently a firm introduces a product—such as a new candy bar—by initially charging a low price or by providing free samples so that customers learn about its quality and provide word-of-mouth advertising. We now consider an important reason why consumers' demand in the future may depend on a monopoly's actions in the present.

Network Externalities

The number of customers a firm has today may affect the demand curve it faces in the future. A good has a **network externality** if one person's demand depends on the consumption of a good by others.[20] If a good has a *positive* network externality, its value to a consumer grows as the number of units sold increases.

The telephone provides a classic example of a positive network externality. When the phone was introduced, potential adopters had no reason to get phone service unless their family and friends did. Why buy a phone if there's no one to call? For Bell's phone network to succeed, it had to achieve a *critical mass* of users—enough adopters that others wanted to join. Had it failed to achieve this critical mass, demand would have withered and the network would have died. Similarly, the market for fax machines grew very slowly until a critical mass was achieved when many end users owned them.

Direct Effect. Many industries exhibit positive network externalities where the customer gets a *direct* benefit from a larger network. The larger an ATM network (such as the Plus network), the greater the odds that you will find an ATM when you want one, so the more likely it is that you will want to use that network. The more people who use a particular computer operating system, the more attractive it is to someone who wants to exchange files or programs with other users.

Behavioral Economics. These examples of the direct effect of network externalities depend on the size of the network because customers want to interact with each other. However, sometimes consumer behavior depends on beliefs or tastes that can be explained by psychological and sociological theories. These explanations are the focus of a subfield of economics called *behavioral economics*.

---

[20]In Chapter 17, we discuss the more general case of an externality, which occurs when a person's well-being or a firm's production capability is directly affected by the actions of other consumers or firms rather than indirectly through changes in prices. The following discussion on network externalities is based on Liebenstein (1950), Rohlfs (1974), Katz and Shapiro (1994), Economides (1996), Shapiro and Varian (1999), and Rohlfs (2001).

One alternative explanation for a direct network externality effect is based on tastes. Harvey Liebenstein (1950) suggested that consumers sometimes want a good because "everyone else has it." A fad or other popularity-based explanation for a positive network externality is called a **bandwagon effect**: A person places greater value on a good as more and more people possess it.[21] The success of the iPod may be partially due to its early popularity. UGG boots may be another example of a bandwagon effect.

The opposite of the bandwagon effect (positive network externality), is a negative network externality called a **snob effect**: A person places greater value on a good as fewer and fewer people possess it. Some people prefer an original painting by an unknown artist to a lithograph by a star because no one else can possess that painting. (As Yogi Berra said, "Nobody goes there anymore; it's too crowded.")

Indirect Effect. In some markets, positive network externalities are indirect and stem from complementary goods that are offered when a product has a critical mass of users. Why buy a particular computer if software programs for it are not available? The more extra devices and software that work with a particular computer, the more people want to buy that computer; but these extra devices are available only if a critical mass of customers buys the computer. Similarly, the more people who drive diesel-powered cars, the more likely it is that gas stations will sell diesel fuel; and the more stations that sell the fuel, the more likely it is that someone will want to drive a diesel car. As a final example, once a critical mass of customers has broadband Internet service, more services will provide downloadable music and movies, and more high-definition Web pages will become available; and once those killer apps appear, more people will sign up for broadband service.

Network Externalities as an Explanation for Monopolies

Because of the need for a critical mass of customers in a market with a positive network externality, we frequently see only one large firm surviving. Visa's ad campaign tells consumers that Visa cards are accepted "everywhere you want to be," including places that "don't take American Express." One could view its ad campaign as an attempt to convince consumers that its card has a critical mass and therefore that everyone should switch to it.

The Windows operating system largely dominates the market—not because it is technically superior to Apple's operating system or Linux—but because it has a critical mass of users. Consequently, a developer can earn more producing software that works with Windows than with other operating systems; and the larger number of software programs makes Windows increasingly attractive to users.

But having obtained a monopoly, a firm does not necessarily keep it. History is filled with examples where one product knocks off another: "The king is dead; long live the king." Google replaced Yahoo! as the predominant search engine. Explorer displaced Netscape as the big-dog browser (and Chrome may be about to displace Explorer). Levi Strauss is no longer the fashion leader among the jeans set.

APPLICATION	In recent years, many people have argued that natural monopolies emerge after brief periods of Internet competition. A typical Web business requires a large up-front fixed cost—primarily for development and promotion—but has a relatively
Critical Mass and eBay	

---

[21]*Jargon alert*: Some economists use *bandwagon effect* to mean any positive network externality—not just those that are based on popularity.

low marginal cost. Thus, Internet start-ups typically have downward sloping average cost per user curves. Which of the actual or potential firms with decreasing average costs will dominate and become a natural monopoly?[22]

In the early years, eBay's online auction site, which started in 1995, faced competition from a variety of other Internet sites including one that the then mighty Yahoo! created in 1998. At the time, many commentators correctly predicted that whichever auction site first achieved a critical mass of users would drive the other sites out of business. Indeed, most of these alternative sites died or faded into obscurity. For example, Yahoo! Auctions closed its U.S. and Canada sections of the site in 2007, and its Singapore section in 2008 (although its Hong Kong, Taiwanese, and Japanese sites continue to operate).

Apparently the convenience of having one site where virtually all buyers and sellers congregate—which lowers buyers' search cost—and creating valuable reputations by having a feedback system (Brown and Morgan, 2006), more than compensates sellers for the lack of competition in sellers' fees. Brown and Morgan (2009) found that, prior to the demise of the Yahoo! auction site, the same type of items attracted an average of two additional bidders on eBay and, consequently, the prices on eBay were consistently 20% to 70% percent higher than Yahoo! prices.

Introductory Prices: A Two-Period Monopoly Model

A monopoly may be able to solve the chicken-and-egg problem of getting a critical mass for its product by initially selling the product at a low introductory price. By doing so, the firm maximizes its long-run profit but not its short-run profit.

Suppose that a monopoly sells its good—say, root-beer-scented jeans—for only two periods (after that, the demand goes to zero as a new craze hits the market). If the monopoly sells less than a critical quantity of output, Q, in the first period, its second-period demand curve lies close to the price axis. However, if the good is a success in the first period—selling at least Q units—the second-period demand curve shifts substantially to the right.

If the monopoly maximizes its short-run profit in the first period, it charges p^* and sells Q^* units, which is fewer than Q. To sell Q units, it would have to lower its first-period price to $\underline{p} < p^*$, which would reduce its first-period profit from π^* to $\underline{\pi}$.

In the second period, the monopoly maximizes its profit given its second-period demand curve. If the monopoly sold only Q^* units in the first period, it earns a relatively low second-period profit of π_l. However, if it sold Q units in the first period, it makes a relatively high second-period profit, π_h.

Should the monopoly charge a low introductory price in the first period? Its objective is to maximize its long-run profit: the sum of its profit in the two periods.[23] It maximizes its long-run profit by charging a low introductory price in the first period if the extra profit in the second period, $\pi_h - \pi_l$, from achieving a critical mass in the

---

[22]If Internet sites provide differentiated products (see Chapter 14), then several sites may coexist even though average costs are strictly decreasing. In 2007, commentators were predicting the emergence of natural monopolies in social networks such as MySpace. However, whether a single social network can dominate for long is debatable as the sites are differentiated. Even if MySpace or Facebook temporarily dominates other similar sites, it may eventually lose ground to Web businesses with newer models, such as Twitter.

[23]In Chapter 15, we discuss why firms place lower value on profit in the future than on profit today and how a firm can compare profit in the future to profit today. For now, we assume that the monopoly places equal value on profit in both periods.

first period is greater than its forgone profit in the first period, $\pi^* - \pi$. This policy must be profitable for some firms: A Google search found 8.9 million Web pages touting introductory prices.

11.7 Monopsony

In Chapter 11, we saw that a *monopoly*, a single *seller*, picks a point—a price and a quantity combination—on the market *demand curve* that maximizes its profit. A *monopsony*, a single *buyer* in a market, chooses a price-quantity combination from the industry *supply curve* that maximizes its profit. A monopsony is the mirror image of monopoly, and it exercises its market power by buying at a price *below* the price that competitive buyers would pay.

Because an American manufacturer of state-of-the-art weapon systems can legally sell only to the federal government, the government is a monopsony. U.S. professional baseball teams, which act collectively, are the only U.S. firms that hire professional baseball players.[24] In many fisheries there is only one, monopsonistic buyer of fish (or at most a small number of buyers, an *oligopsony*).

Monopsony Profit Maximization

Suppose that a firm is the sole employer in town—a monopsony in the local labor market. The firm uses only one factor, labor, L, to produce a final good. The value that the firm places on the last worker it hires is the marginal revenue product of that worker—the value of the extra output the worker produces—which is the height of the firm's labor demand curve for the number of workers the firm employs.

The firm has a downward-sloping demand curve in panel a of Figure 11.9. The firm faces an upward-sloping supply curve of labor: The higher its daily wage, w, the more people want to work for the firm. The firm's *marginal expenditure*—the additional cost of hiring one more worker—depends on the shape of the supply curve.

The supply curve shows the average expenditure, or wage, that the monopsony pays to hire a certain number of workers. For example, the monopsony's average expenditure or wage is \$20 if it hires $L = 20$ workers per day. If the monopsony wants to obtain one more worker, it must raise its wage because the supply curve is upward sloping. Because it pays all workers the same wage, the monopsony must also pay more to each worker that it was already employing. Thus, the monopsony's marginal expenditure on the last worker is greater than that worker's wage.

The monopsony's total expenditure is $E = w(L)L$, where $w(L)$ is the wage given by the market labor supply curve. Its marginal expenditure is

$$ME = w(L) + \frac{dw}{dL}L, \tag{11.16}$$

where $w(L)$ is the wage paid the additional worker and $L[dw(L)/dL]$ is the extra amount the monopsony pays the current workers. Because the supply curve is upward sloping, $dw(L)/dL > 0$, the marginal expenditure, ME, is greater than the average expenditure, $w(L)$.

---

[24]Baseball players belong to a union that acts collectively, like a monopoly, in an attempt to offset the monopsony market power of the baseball teams.

Figure 11.9 Monopsony

(a) The marginal expenditure curve—the monopsony's marginal cost of buying one more unit—lies above the upward-sloping market supply curve. The monopsony equilibrium, e_m, occurs where the marginal expenditure curve intersects the monopsony's demand curve. The monopsony buys fewer units at a lower price, $w_m = \$20$, than a competitive market, $w_c = \$30$, would. (b) The supply curve is more elastic at the optimum than in (a), so the value that the monopsony places on the last unit (which equals the marginal expenditure of $40) exceeds the price the monopsony pays, $w_m = \$30$, by less than in (a).

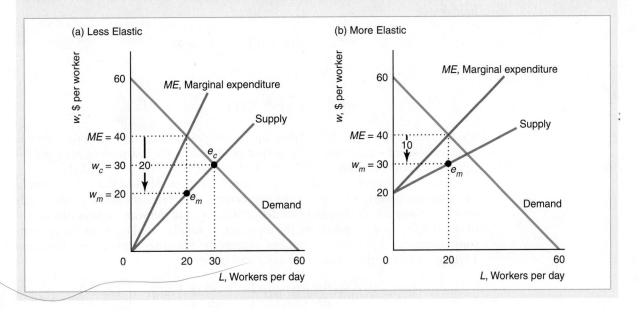

In contrast, if the firm were a competitive price taker in the labor market, it would face a supply curve that was horizontal at the market wage. Consequently, such a competitive firm's marginal expenditure to hire an additional worker would be the market wage.

Any profit-maximizing firm—a monopsony and a competitive firm alike—buys labor services up to the point at which the marginal value of the last unit of a factor equals the firm's marginal expenditure. If the last unit is worth more to the buyer than its marginal expenditure, the buyer purchases another unit. Similarly, if the last unit is less valuable than its marginal expenditure, the buyer purchases one less unit.

In the figure, the monopsony employs 20 units of the factor. The intersection of its marginal expenditure curve and its demand curve determines the monopsony equilibrium, e_m. The monopsony values the labor services of the last worker at $40 (the height of its demand curve), and its marginal expenditure at that unit (the height of its marginal expenditure curve) is $40. It pays only $20 (the height of the supply curve). In other words, the monopsony values the last unit at $20 more than it actually has to pay.

If the market in Figure 11.9 were competitive, the intersection of the market demand curve and the market supply curve would determine the competitive equilibrium at e_c, where buyers purchase 30 units at $p_c = \$30$ per unit. Thus, the monopsony hires fewer workers, 20 versus 30, than a competitive market would hire and pays a lower wage, $20 versus $30.

We can also use calculus to analyze the labor monopsony's behavior. For simplicity, we assume that the firm is a price taker in the output market. It chooses how much labor to hire to maximize its profit,

$$\pi = pQ(L) - w(L)L,$$

where $Q(L)$ is the production function, the amount of output produced using L hours of labor. The firm maximizes its profit by setting the derivative of profit with respect to labor equal to zero (assuming that the second-order condition holds):

$$p\frac{dQ}{dL} - w(L) - \frac{dw}{dL}L = 0,$$

or

$$MRP_L = p\frac{dQ}{dL} = w(L) + \frac{dw}{dL}L = ME. \qquad (11.17)$$

That is, the monopsony hires labor up to the point where the marginal revenue product of labor—the value of the output produced by the last worker, $p(dQ/dL)$—equals the marginal expenditure on the last worker, $ME = w + (dw/dL)L$.

Monopsony power is the ability of a single buyer to pay less than the competitive price profitably. The size of the gap between the value the monopsony places on the last worker (the height of its demand curve) and the wage it pays (the height of the supply curve) depends on the elasticity of supply of labor, η, at the monopsony optimum. Using algebra, we can express the marginal expenditure, Equation 11.16, in terms of the elasticity of supply of labor:

$$ME = w(L) + \frac{dw}{dL}L = w(L)\left(1 + \frac{dw}{dL}\frac{L}{w}\right) = w(L)\left(1 + \frac{1}{\eta}\right), \qquad (11.18)$$

The markup of the marginal expenditure (which equals the value to the monopsony) over the wage is inversely proportional to the elasticity of supply at the optimum: By rearranging the terms in Equation 11.18, we derive an expression analogous to the Lerner Index:

$$\frac{ME - w}{w} = \frac{1}{\eta}. \qquad (11.19)$$

Equation 11.19 shows that the percentage markup of the marginal expenditure (and the value to the monopsony) to the wage, $(ME - w)/w$, is inversely proportional to the elasticity of the supply of labor. Only if the firm is a price taker, so that η is infinite, does the wage equal the marginal expenditure.

By comparing panels a and b in Figure 11.9, we see that the less elastic the supply curve at the optimum, the greater the gap between marginal expenditure and the wage. At the monopsony optimum, the supply curve in panel b of Figure 11.9 is more elastic than the supply curve in panel a.[25] The gap between marginal expenditure and wage is greater in panel a, $ME - w = \$20$, than in panel b, $ME - w = \$10$. Similarly, the markup in panel a, $(ME - w)/w = 20/20 = 1$, is much greater than that in panel b, $(ME - w)/w = 10/30 = \frac{1}{3}$.

---

[25]The supply curve in panel a is $w = L$, while that in panel b is $w = 20 + \frac{1}{2}L$. The elasticity of supply, $\eta = (dL/dw)(w/L)$, at the optimum is $w/L = 20/20 = 1$ in panel a and $2w/L = 2 \times 30/20 = 3$ in panel b. Consequently, the supply curve at the optimum is three times as elastic in panel b as in panel a.

SOLVED PROBLEM 11.6

How does the equilibrium in a labor market with a monopsony employer change if a minimum wage is set at the competitive level?

Answer

1. *Determine the original monopsony equilibrium.* Given the supply curve in the graph, the marginal expenditure curve is ME^1. The intersection of ME^1 and the demand curve determines the monopsony equilibrium, e_1. The monopsony hires L_1 workers at a wage of w_1.

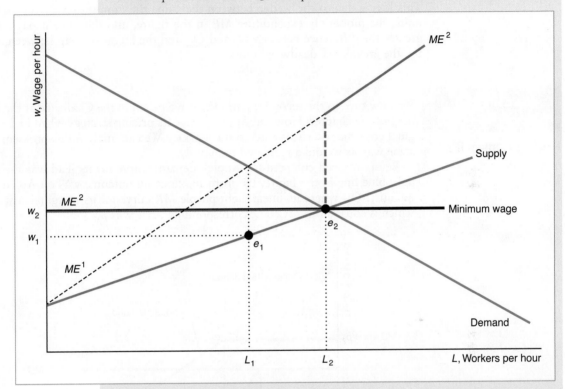

2. *Determine the effect of the minimum wage on the marginal expenditure curve.* The minimum wage makes the supply curve, as viewed by the monopsony, flat in the range where the minimum wage is above the original supply curve (fewer than L_2 workers). The new marginal expenditure curve, ME^2, is flat where the supply curve is flat. Where the supply curve is upward sloping, ME^2 is the same as ME^1.

3. *Determine the post-minimum-wage equilibrium.* The monopsony operates where its new marginal expenditure curve, ME^2, intersects the demand curve. With the minimum wage, the demand curve crosses the ME^2 curve at the end of the flat section. Thus, at the new equilibrium, e_2, the monopsony pays the minimum wage, w_2, and employs L_2 workers.

4. *Compare the equilibria.* The post-minimum-wage equilibrium is the same as the competitive equilibrium determined by the intersection of the demand and supply curves. Workers receive a higher wage, and more people are employed than in the monopsony equilibrium. Thus, imposing the minimum wage helps workers and hurts the monopsony.

Welfare Effects of Monopsony

By creating a wedge between the value to the monopsony and the value to the suppliers, the monopsony causes a welfare loss in comparison to a competitive market. In Figure 11.9, sellers lose producer surplus, $D + E$, because the monopsony price, p_m, for a good is below the competitive price, p_c. Area D is a transfer from the sellers to the monopsony and represents the savings of $p_c - p_m$ on the Q_m units the monopsony buys. The monopsony loses C because suppliers sell it less output, Q_m instead of Q_c, at the low price. Thus, the deadweight loss of monopsony is $C + E$. This loss is due to the wedge between the value the monopsony places on the Q_m units, the monopoly expenditure ME in the figure, and the price it pays, p_m. The greater the difference between Q_c and Q_m and the larger the gap between ME and p_m, the greater the deadweight loss.

**CHALLENGE
SOLUTION**

Pricing Apple's iPad

We now turn to the second question that we raised in the Challenge at the beginning of the chapter: How did Apple change its pricing strategy when higher marginal cost, me-too rivals entered the market? We can analyze this problem in the same way as we did a regulated monopoly.

Before it faced competitors, Apple's demand curve for its iPad was the linear, light-blue line in the figure. Its profit-maximizing outcome was e_1: Apple set its quantity, Q_1, where its linear, light-purple MR curve hit its marginal cost curve, which is constant at MC. The corresponding price was p_1.

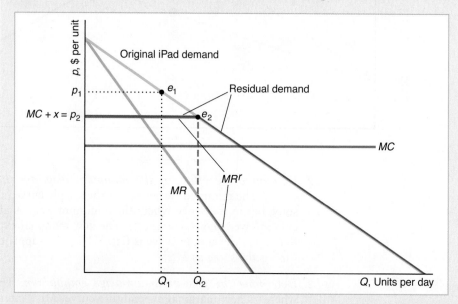

Now, many rival firms enter the market and produce near clones of the iPad. Each new firm has a higher marginal cost (at the minimum of their average cost curve), $MC + x$, than does Apple.

Economists refer to such a market as one in which a *dominant firm* faces a *competitive fringe*. The large number of identical, higher-cost rivals—the competitive fringe—act like (competitive) price takers so that their collective supply curve is horizontal at $p_2 = MC + x$. Apple is no longer a monopoly. It is a dominant firm that sells more than any of its rivals and acts like a price setter. Given that consumers view the rival products as equivalent to the iPad, Apple can no longer charge more than $p_2 = MC + x$, so its residual demand curve is the kinked, dark-blue line.[26] Apple still acts like a monopoly with respect to its residual demand curve (rather than to its original demand curve). Corresponding to Apple's residual demand curve is a kinked marginal revenue curve, MR^r, that crosses Apple's marginal cost line at Q_2. Apple maximizes its profit by selling Q_2 units for p_2 at e_2. That is, Apple sells more iPads at a lower price than before the other firms enter the market. Apple lowered its price of its basic iPad2 from $499 to $399 in 2012.

The presence of these high-cost competitors acts much as would a government price control to limit Apple's price. Indeed, the residual demand curve for the iPad in the figure is similar to that of the regulated monopoly in Figure 11.8.

SUMMARY

1. **Monopoly Profit Maximization.** Like any firm, a monopoly—a single seller—maximizes its profit by setting its output so that its marginal revenue equals its marginal cost. The monopoly makes a positive profit if its average cost is less than the price at the profit-maximizing output. Because a monopoly does not have a supply curve, the effect of a shift in demand on a monopoly's output depends on the shapes of both its marginal cost curve and its demand curve. As a monopoly's demand curve shifts, price and output may change in the same direction or in different directions.

2. **Market Power and Welfare.** Market power is the ability of a firm to charge a price above marginal cost and earn a positive profit. The more elastic the demand the monopoly faces at the quantity at which it maximizes its profit, the closer its price to its marginal cost and the closer the Lerner Index or price markup, $(p - MC)/p$, is to zero, which is the competitive level. Because a monopoly's price is above its marginal cost, too little output is produced, and society suffers a deadweight loss. The monopoly makes higher profit than it would if it acted as a price taker. Consumers are worse off, buying less output at a higher price.

3. **Taxes and Monopoly.** A specific or an ad valorem tax exacerbates the deadweight loss of a monopoly by further reducing sales and driving up the price

to consumers. Unlike in a competitive market, the tax incidence on consumers can exceed 100% in a monopoly market. In a monopoly, the welfare losses from an ad valorem tax are less than from a specific tax that reduces output by the same amount (unlike in a competitive market where both taxes reduce welfare by the same amount).

4. **Causes of Monopolies.** A firm may be a monopoly if it controls a key input, has superior knowledge about producing or distributing a good, or has substantial economies of scale. In markets with substantial economies of scale, the single seller is called a natural monopoly because total production costs would rise if more than one firm produced. Governments may establish government-owned-and-operated monopolies. They may also create private monopolies by establishing barriers to entry that prevent other firms from competing. Governments grant patents, which give inventors monopoly rights for a limited time.

5. **Government Actions That Reduce Market Power.** A government can eliminate the welfare harm of a monopoly by forcing the firm to set its price at the competitive level. If the government sets the price at a different level or otherwise regulates non-optimally, welfare at the regulated monopoly optimum is lower than in the competitive equilibrium. A government can eliminate or reduce the harms of monopoly by allowing or facilitating entry.

[26]The result would be the same if the rival firms had the same marginal cost as Apple, but consumers were willing to pay up to x more for the iPad than for a rival product.

6. Monopoly Decisions over Time and Behavioral Economics. If a good has a positive network externality so that its value to a consumer grows as the number of units sold increases, then current sales affect a monopoly's future demand curve. A monopoly may maximize its long-run profit—its profit over time—by setting a low introductory price in the first period that it sells the good and then later raising its price as its product's popularity ensures large future sales at a higher price. Consequently, the monopoly is not maximizing its short-run profit in the first period but is maximizing the sum of its profits over all periods.

7. Monopsony. A profit-maximizing monopsony—a single buyer—sets its price so that the marginal value to the monopsony equals the firm's marginal expenditure. Because the monopsony pays a price below the competitive level, fewer units are sold than in a competitive market, producers of factors are worse off, the monopsony earns higher profits than it would if it were a price taker, and society suffers a deadweight loss.

EXERCISES

■ = exercise *is available on* MyEconLab; * = *answer appears at the back of this book;* **M** = *mathematical problem.*

1. Monopoly Profit Maximization

1.1 If the inverse demand function is $p = 300 - 3Q$, what is the marginal revenue function? Draw the demand and marginal revenue curves. At what quantities do the demand and marginal revenue lines hit the quantity axis? (*Hint*: See Solved Problem 11.1.) **M**

1.2 If the inverse demand curve a monopoly faces is $p = 10Q^{-0.5}$, what is the firm's marginal revenue curve? (*Hint*: See Solved Problem 11.1.) **M**

1.3 Given that the inverse demand function is $p(Q) = a - bQ + (c/2)Q^2$, derive the marginal revenue function. Compare the corresponding marginal revenue curve to the linear one (where $c = 0$) and show how its curvature depends on whether c is positive or negative. (*Hint*: See Solved Problem 11.1.) **M**

*1.4 Show that the elasticity of demand is unitary at the midpoint of a linear inverse demand function and hence that a monopoly will not operate to the right of this midpoint. **M**

1.5 The inverse demand curve that a monopoly faces is $p = 100 - Q$. The firm's cost curve is $C(Q) = 10 + 5Q$. What is the firm's profit-maximizing quantity and price? How does your answer change if $C(Q) = 100 + 5Q$? **M**

1.6 The inverse demand curve that a monopoly faces is $p = 10Q^{-0.5}$. The firm's cost curve is $C(Q) = 5Q$. What is the profit-maximizing quantity and price? **M**

1.7 Suppose that the inverse demand function for a monopolist's product is $p = 9 - Q/20$. Its cost function is $C = 10 + 10Q - 4Q^2 + \frac{2}{3}Q^3$. Draw marginal revenue and marginal cost curves. At what outputs does marginal revenue equal marginal cost? What is the profit-maximizing output? Check the second-order condition, $d^2\pi/dQ^2$, at the monopoly optimum. **M**

1.8 If a monopoly's inverse demand curve is $p = 13 - Q$ and its cost function is $C = 25 + Q + 0.5Q^2$, what Q^* maximizes the monopoly's profit (or minimizes its loss)? At Q^*, what is the price and the profit? Should the monopoly operate or shut down? **M**

1.9 Given that a monopoly's marginal revenue curve is strictly downward sloping, use math and a graph (such as Figure 11.3) to show why a monopoly's revenue curve reaches its maximum at a larger quantity than does its profit curve. **M**

1.10 Suppose that the inverse demand for San Francisco cable car rides is $p = 10 - Q/1,000$, where p is the price per ride and Q is the number of rides per day. Suppose the objective of San Francisco's Municipal Authority (the cable car operator) is to maximize its revenues. What is the revenue maximizing price? Suppose that San Francisco calculates that the city's businesses benefit from tourists and residents riding on the city's cable cars at $4 per ride. If the city's objective is to maximize the sum of the cable car revenues and the economic impact, what is the optimal price? **M**

1.11 AT&T Inc., the large U.S. phone company and the one-time monopoly, left the payphone business because people were switching to wireless phones (Crayton Harrison, "AT&T to Disconnect Pay-Phone Business After 129 Years," **Bloomberg.com**, December 3, 2007). The number of wireless subscribers quadrupled in the past decade: 80% of U.S. phone users now have mobile phones. Consequently, the number of payphones fell from 2.6 million at the peak in 1998 to 1 million in 2006. (But where will Clark Kent go to change into Superman now?) Use graphs to explain why a monopoly exits in a market when its demand curve shifts to the left.

1.12 Show why a monopoly may operate in the upward- or downward-sloping section of its long-run average cost curve but a competitive firm operates only in the upward-sloping section.

1.13 Are major-league baseball clubs profit-maximizing monopolies? Some observers of this market contend that baseball club owners want to maximize attendance or revenue. Alexander (2001) said that one test of whether a firm is a profit-maximizing monopoly is to check whether it is operating in the elastic portion of its demand curve, which, according to his analysis, is true. Why is that a relevant test? What would the elasticity be if a baseball club were maximizing revenue?

2. Market Power and Welfare

2.1 Under what circumstances does a monopoly set its price equal to its marginal cost?

*2.2 In 2009, the price of Amazon's Kindle 2 was $359, while iSuppli estimated that its marginal cost was $159. What was Amazon's Lerner Index? What elasticity of demand did it face if it was engaging in short-run profit maximization? **M**

2.3 The U.S. Postal Service (USPS) has a constitutionally guaranteed monopoly on first-class mail. In 2012, it charged 44¢ for a stamp, which was not the profit-maximizing price—the USPS goal, allegedly, is to break even rather than to turn a profit. Following the postal services in Australia, Britain, Canada, Switzerland, and Ireland, the USPS allowed **Stamps.com** to sell a sheet of twenty 44¢ stamps with a photo of your dog, your mommy, or whatever image you want for $18.99 (that's 94.95¢ per stamp, or a 216% markup). **Stamps.com** keeps the extra beyond the 44¢ it pays the USPS. What is the firm's Lerner Index? If **Stamps.com** is a profit-maximizing monopoly, what elasticity of demand does it face for a customized stamp?

*2.4 When the iPod was introduced, Apple's constant marginal cost of producing its top-of-the-line iPod was $200 (iSuppli), its fixed cost was approximately $736 million, and I estimate that its inverse demand function was $p = 600 - 25Q$, where Q is units measured in millions. What was Apple's average cost function? Assuming that Apple was maximizing short-run monopoly profit, what was its marginal revenue function? What were its profit-maximizing price and quantity, profit, and Lerner Index? What was the elasticity of demand at the profit-maximizing level? Show Apple's profit-maximizing solution in a figure.

2.5 In addition to the hard-drive-based iPod, Apple produces a flash-based audio player. Its 512MB iPod Shuffle (which does not have a hard drive) sold for $99 in 2005. According to iSuppli, Apple's per-unit cost of manufacturing the Shuffle was $45.37. What was Apple's price/marginal cost ratio? What was its Lerner Index? If we assume (possibly incorrectly) that Apple acted like a short-run profit-maximizing monopoly in pricing its iPod Shuffle, what elasticity of demand did Apple believe it faced? **M**

2.6 Suppose that all iPod owners consider only two options for downloading music to their MP3 players: purchasing songs from iTunes or copying songs from friends. With these two options, suppose the weekly inverse market demand for the Rolling Stones' song "Satisfaction" is $p = 1.98 - 0.00198Q$. The marginal cost to Apple Inc. of downloading a song is zero.

a. What is Apple's optimal price of "Satisfaction"? How many downloads of "Satisfaction" does Apple sell each week?

b. Now suppose that Apple sells a version of the iPod equipped with software in which songs played on the iPod must be downloaded from iTunes. For this iPod, the inverse market demand for "Satisfaction" is $p = 2.58 - 0.0129Q$. What is Apple's optimal price of downloads of "Satisfaction" for this new player? How many downloads of "Satisfaction" does Apple sell each week? **M**

2.7 Draw an example of a monopoly with a linear demand curve and a constant marginal cost curve.

a. Show the profit-maximizing price and output, p^* and Q^*, and identify the areas of consumer surplus, producer surplus, and deadweight loss. Also show the quantity, Q_c, that would be produced if the monopoly were to act like a price taker.

b. Now suppose that the demand curve is a smooth concave-to-the-origin curve (which hits both axes) that is tangent to the original demand curve at the point (Q^*, p^*). Explain why this monopoly equilibrium is the same as with the linear demand curve. Show how much output the firm would produce if it acted like a price taker. Show how the welfare areas change.

c. How would your answer in part a change if the demand curve is a smooth convex-to-the-origin curve (which hits both axes) that is tangent to the original demand curve at the point (Q^*, p^*)?

2.8 Suppose that many similar price-taking consumers (such as Denise in Chapter 10) have a single good (candy bars). Jane has a monopoly in wood, so she can set prices. Assume that no production is possible. Using an Edgeworth box, illustrate the monopoly optimum and show that it does not lie on the contract curve (that is, it isn't Pareto efficient).

3. Taxes and Monopoly

3.1 If the inverse demand function facing a monopoly is $p(Q)$ and its cost function is $C(Q)$, show the effect of a specific tax, τ, on the monopoly's profit-maximizing output. How does imposing τ affect its profit? **M**

3.2 A monopoly with a constant marginal cost m has a profit-maximizing price of p_1. It faces a constant elasticity demand curve with elasticity ε. After the government applies a specific tax of $1, its price is p_2. What is the price change $p_2 - p_1$ in terms of ε? How much does the price rise if the demand elasticity is -2? (*Hint*: Use Equation 11.10.) **M**

3.3 In 1996, Florida voted on (and rejected) a 1¢-per-pound excise tax on refined cane sugar in the Florida Everglades Agricultural Area. Swinton and Thomas (2001) used linear supply and demand curves (based on elasticities estimated by Marks, 1993) to calculate the incidence from this tax given that the market is competitive. Their inverse demand curve was $p = 1.787 - 0.0004641Q$, and their inverse supply curve was $p = -0.4896 + 0.00020165Q$. Calculate the incidence of the tax that falls on consumers (Chapter 2) for a competitive market. If producers joined together to form a monopoly, and the supply curve is actually the monopoly's marginal cost curve, what is the incidence of the tax? (*Hint*: The incidence that falls on consumers is the difference between the equilibrium price with and without the tax divided by the tax. Show that the incidence is 70% in a competitive market and 41% with a monopoly. See Solved Problem 11.3.) **M**

*3.4 Only Indian tribes can run casinos in California. These casinos are spread around the state so that each is a monopoly in its local community. California Governor Arnold Schwarzenegger negotiated with the state's tribes, getting them to agree to transfer a fraction of their profits to the state in exchange for concessions (Dan Morain and Evan Halper, "Casino Deals Said to Be Near," *Los Angeles Times*, June 16, 2004, 1). In 2004, he first proposed that the state get 25% of casino profits and then he dropped the level to 15%. He announced a deal with two tribes at 10% in 2005. How does a profit tax affect a monopoly's output and price? How would a monopoly change its behavior if the profit tax were 10% rather than 25%? (*Hint*: You may assume that the profit tax refers to the tribe's economic profit.) **M**

3.5 What is the effect of a franchise (lump-sum) tax on a monopoly? (*Hint*: Consider the possibility that the firm may shut down.)

4. Causes of Monopolies

*4.1 Can a firm be a natural monopoly if it has a U-shaped average cost curve? Why or why not? (*Hint*: See Solved Problem 11.4.)

4.2 Can a firm operating in the upward-sloping portion of its average cost curve be a natural monopoly? Explain. (*Hint*: See Solved Problem 11.4.)

4.3 Based on the information in the Botox Patent Monopoly application, what would happen to the equilibrium price and quantity if the government had collected a specific tax of $75 per vial of Botox? What welfare effects would such a tax have? **M**

4.4 In the Botox Patent Monopoly application, consumer surplus, area A, equals the deadweight loss, area C. Show that this equality is a result of the linear demand and constant marginal cost assumptions. **M**

4.5 Once the copyright runs out on a book or musical composition, the work can legally be put on the Internet for anyone to download. U.S. copyright law protects the monopoly for 95 years after the original publication. But in Australia and Europe, the copyright holds for only 50 years. Thus, an Australian Web site can post *Gone With the Wind*, a 1936 novel, or Elvis Presley's 1954 single "That's All Right," while a U.S. site cannot. Obviously, this legal nicety won't stop American fans from downloading from Australian or European sites. Discuss how limiting the length of a copyright would affect the pricing used by the publisher of a novel.

5. Government Actions That Reduce Market Power

5.1 Describe the effects on output and welfare if the government regulates a monopoly so that it may not charge a price above $\bar{p}$, which lies between the unregulated monopoly price and the optimally regulated price (determined by the intersection of the firm's marginal cost and the market demand curve). (*Hint*: See Solved Problem 11.5.)

5.2 Based on the information in the Botox Patent Monopoly application, what would happen to the equilibrium price and quantity if the government had set a price ceiling of $200 per vial of Botox? What welfare effects would such a price ceiling have? (*Hint*: See Solved Problem 11.5.) **M**

5.3 A monopoly drug company produces a lifesaving medicine at a constant cost of $10 per dose. The demand for this medicine is perfectly inelastic at prices less than or equal to the $100 (per day) income of the 100 patients who need to take this drug daily. At a higher price, nothing is bought.

Show the equilibrium price and quantity and the consumer and producer surplus in a graph. Now the government imposes a price ceiling of $30. Show how the equilibrium, consumer surplus, and producer surplus change. What is the deadweight loss, if any, from this price control?

5.4 The price of wholesale milk dropped by 30.3% in 1999 when the Pennsylvania Milk Marketing Board lowered the regulated price. The price to consumers fell by substantially less than 30.3%. Why? (*Hint*: Show that a monopoly will not necessarily lower its price by the same percentage as its constant marginal cost drops.)

6. Monopoly Decisions over Time and Behavioral Economics

*6.1 A monopoly produces a good with a network externality at a constant marginal and average cost of $2. In the first period, its inverse demand curve is $p = 10 - Q$. In the second period, its demand is $p = 10 - Q$ unless it sells at least $Q = 8$ units in the first period. If it meets or exceeds this target, then the demand curve rotates out by β (that is, it sells β times as many units for any given price), so that its inverse demand curve is $p = 10 - Q/\beta$. The monopoly knows that it can sell no output after the second period. The monopoly's objective is to maximize the sum of its profits over the two periods. In the first period, should the monopoly set the output that maximizes its profit in that period? How does your answer depend on β? (*Hint*: See the discussion about introductory prices in Section 11.8.) **M**

6.2 A monopoly chocolate manufacturer faces two types of consumers. The larger group, the hoi polloi, loves desserts and has a relatively flat, linear demand curve for chocolate. The smaller group, the snobs, is interested in buying chocolate only if the hoi polloi do not buy it. Given that the hoi polloi do not buy the chocolate, the snobs have a relatively steep, linear demand curve. Show the monopoly's possible outcomes—high price and low quantity, or low price and high quantity—and explain the condition under which the monopoly chooses to cater to the snobs rather than to the hoi polloi.

7. Monopsony

7.1 Suppose that the original labor supply curve, S^1, for a monopsony shifts to the right to S^2 if the firm spends $1,000 in advertising. Under what condition

should the monopsony engage in this advertising? (*Hint*: See the analysis of monopoly advertising.)

7.2 What happens to the monopsony equilibrium if the minimum wage is set slightly above or below the competitive wage? (*Hint*: See Solved Problem 11.6.)

7.3 Can a monopsony exercise monopsony power—that is, profitably set its price below the competitive level—if the supply curve it faces is horizontal? Why or why not?

7.4 What effect does a price support have on a monopsony? In particular, describe the equilibrium if the price support is set at the price where the supply curve intersects the demand curve.

7.5 A monopsony faces a supply curve of $p = 10 + Q$. What is its marginal expenditure curve? If the monopsony has a demand curve of $p = 50 - Q$, what are the equilibrium quantity and price? How does this equilibrium differ from the competitive equilibrium? **M**

*7.6 For general functions, solve for the monopsony's first-order condition if it is also a monopoly in the product market. **M**

8. Challenge

8.1 A country has a monopoly that is protected by a specific tariff, τ, on imported goods. The monopoly's profit-maximizing price is p^*. The world price of the good is p_w, which is less than p^*. Because the price of imported goods with the tariff is $p_w + \tau$, no foreign goods are imported. Under WTO pressure the government removes the tariff so that the supply of foreign goods to the country's consumers is horizontal at p_w. Show how much the former monopoly produces and what price it charges. Show who gains and who loses from removing the tariff. (*Hint*: Look at the effect of government price regulation on a monopoly's demand curve in Section 11.7 or the figure in the Challenge Solution.)

8.2 Bleyer Industries Inc., the only U.S. manufacturer of plastic Easter eggs, once manufactured 250 million eggs each year. However, imports from China cut into its business. In 2005, Bleyer filed for bankruptcy because the Chinese firms could produce the eggs at much lower costs ("U.S. Plastic Egg Industry a Shell of Its Former Self," *San Francisco Chronicle*, January 14, 2005). Use graphs to show how a competitive import industry could drive a monopoly out of business.

12

Pricing and Advertising

Everything is worth what its purchaser will pay for it.
—Publilius Syrus (first century BC)

CHALLENGE

Sale Price

Because many firms use *sales*—temporarily setting the price below the usual price—some customers pay lower prices than others over time. Grocery stores are particularly likely to put products on sale frequently. In large U.S. supermarkets, a soft drink brand is on sale 94% of the time. Either Coke or Pepsi is on sale half the weeks in a year.

Heinz Ketchup controls up to 60% of the U.S. market, 70% of the Canadian market, and nearly 80% of the U.K market. In 2012, Heinz sold over 650 million bottles of Ketchup in more than 140 countries and had annual sales of more than $1.5 billion. When Heinz goes on sale, *switchers*—ketchup customers who normally buy whichever brand is least expensive—purchase Heinz rather than the low-price generic ketchup. How can Heinz's managers design a pattern of sales that maximizes Heinz's profit by obtaining extra sales from switchers without losing substantial sums by selling to its loyal customers at a discount price? Under what conditions does it pay for Heinz to have a policy of periodic sales?

Until now, we have examined how a monopoly (or other price-setting firm) chooses a single price given that it does not advertise. We need to extend this analysis because many price-setting firms set multiple prices and advertise. The analysis in this chapter helps to answer many real-world questions such as: Why do firms put products on sale periodically? Why are airlines' fares substantially less if you book in advance? Why do the spiritualists who live at the Wonewoc Spiritualist Camp give readings for $40 for half an hour, but charge seniors only $35 on Wednesdays?[1] Why are some goods, including computers and software, bundled and sold at a single price? To answer these questions, we need to examine how monopolies and other noncompetitive firms set prices.

In Chapter 11, we examined how a monopoly maximizes its profit when it uses **uniform pricing**: charging the same price for every unit sold of a particular good. However, it is possible for monopolies (and other firms with market power) to employ more sophisticated pricing methods.

We now show that a monopoly can increase its profits if it can use **nonuniform pricing**, where a firm charges consumers different prices for the same product or charges a single customer a price that depends on the number of units the customer buys. In this chapter, we analyze nonuniform pricing for monopolies, but similar principles apply to any firm with market power.

---

[1]www.msnbc.msn.com/id/20377308/wid/11915829, August 29, 2007.

As we saw in Chapter 11, a monopoly that sets a high single price sells only to the customers who value the good enough to buy it at the monopoly price, and those customers receive some consumer surplus. The monopoly does not sell the good to other customers who value the good at less than the single price, even if those consumers would be willing to pay more than the marginal cost of production. These lost sales cause *deadweight loss*, which is the forgone value of these potential sales in excess of the cost of producing the good.

A firm with market power can earn a higher profit using nonuniform pricing than by setting a uniform price for two reasons. First, the firm captures some or all of the single-price consumer surplus. Second, the firm converts at least some of the single-price deadweight loss into profit by charging a price below the uniform price to some customers who would not purchase at the single price level. A monopoly that uses nonuniform pricing can lower the price to these otherwise excluded consumers without lowering the price to consumers who are willing to pay high prices.

In this chapter, we examine several types of nonuniform pricing including price discrimination, two-part pricing, and bundling. The most common form of nonuniform pricing is **price discrimination**: charging consumers different prices for the same good based on individual characteristics of consumers, membership in an identifiable subgroup of consumers, or on the quantity purchased by the consumers. For example for a full-year combination print and online subscription, the *Wall Street Journal* charges $99.95 to students, who are price sensitive, and $155 to other subscribers, who are less price sensitive.

Some firms with market power use other forms of nonuniform pricing to increase profits. A firm may use *two-part pricing*, where it charges a customer one fee for the right to buy the good and an additional fee for each unit purchased. For example, members of health or golf clubs typically pay an annual fee to belong to the club and then pay an additional amount each time they use the facilities. Similarly, mobile phone users pay a monthly fee for phone service and then may incur an additional charge per minute of conversation or for each text message.

Another type of nonuniform pricing is called *bundling*, where several products are sold together as a package. For example, many restaurants provide full-course dinners for a fixed price that is less than the sum of the prices charged if the items (appetizer, main dish, and dessert) are ordered separately(à la carte).

A monopoly may also increase its profit by advertising. A monopoly (or another firm with market power) may advertise to shift its demand curve so as to raise its profit, taking into account the cost of advertising.

In this chapter, we examine seven main topics

1. **Conditions for Price Discrimination.** A firm can increase its profit by price discriminating if it has market power, can identify which customers are more price sensitive than others, and can prevent customers who pay low prices from reselling to those who pay high prices.

2. **Perfect Price Discrimination.** If a monopoly can charge the maximum that each customer is willing to pay for each unit of output, the monopoly captures all potential consumer surplus and sells the efficient (competitive) level of output.

3. **Group Price Discrimination.** Firms that cannot perfectly price discriminate may charge a group of consumers with relatively elastic demands a lower price than they charge other groups.

4. **Nonlinear Pricing.** Some firms profit by charging different prices for large purchases than they charge for small ones, which is a form of price discrimination.

5. **Two-Part Pricing.** By charging consumers a fee for the right to buy any number of units and a price per unit, firms earn higher profits than they do by charging a single price per unit.

6. **Tie-In Sales.** By requiring customers to buy a second good or service along with the first, firms make higher profits than they do by selling the goods or services separately.

7. **Advertising.** A monopoly advertises to shift its demand curve and to increase its profit.

12.1 Conditions for Price Discrimination

We start by studying the most common form of nonuniform pricing, *price discrimination*, where a firm charges various consumers different prices for a good.

Why Price Discrimination Pays

For almost any good or service, some consumers are willing to pay more than others. A firm that sets a single price faces a trade-off between charging consumers who really want the good as much as they are willing to pay and charging a sufficiently low price that the firm does not lose sales to less enthusiastic customers. As a result, the firm usually sets an intermediate price. A price-discriminating firm that varies its prices across customers avoids this trade-off.

A firm earns a higher profit from price discrimination than from uniform pricing for two reasons. First, a price-discriminating firm charges a higher price to customers who are willing to pay more than the uniform price, capturing some or all of their consumer surplus—the difference between what a good is worth to a consumer and what the consumer pays—under uniform pricing. Second, a price-discriminating firm sells to some people who are not willing to pay as much as the uniform price.

Which Firms Can Price Discriminate

Not all firms can price discriminate. For a firm to price discriminate successfully, three conditions must be met.

First, a firm must have *market power*, otherwise it cannot charge any consumer more than the competitive price. A monopoly, an oligopoly firm, a monopolistically competitive firm, or a cartel may be able to price discriminate. A competitive firm cannot price discriminate.

Second, for a firm to profitably charge various consumers different prices, the **reservation price**—the maximum amount a person is willing to pay for a unit of output—must *vary* across consumers, and a firm must be able to *identify* which consumers are willing to pay relatively more. A movie theater manager may know that senior citizens have a lower reservation price for admission than do other adults. Theater employees can identify senior citizens by observation or by checking their driver's licenses. Even if all customers are identical, a firm may be able to price discriminate over the number of units each purchases. If a firm knows how each individual's reservation price varies with the number of units, it can charge each customer a higher price for the first unit of a good than it charges for subsequent units.

Third, a firm must be able to *prevent or limit resale* from customers that the firm charges a relatively low price to those whom the firm wants to charge a relatively high price. Price discrimination is ineffective if resale is easy, because ease of reselling would inhibit the firm's ability to make higher-price sales. A movie theater owner can charge senior citizens a lower price than other adults because as soon as the seniors buy their tickets they enter the theater and don't have time to resell them.

Except for competitive firms, most firms have some market power, and many of those firms can identify which groups of customers have a relatively high reservation price. Usually, the biggest obstacle to price discrimination is a firm's inability to prevent resale. However in some markets, resale is inherently difficult or impossible, firms can take actions that prevent resale, or government actions or laws prevent resale.

APPLICATION

Disneyland Pricing

Disneyland, in southern California, is a well-run operation that rarely misses a trick when it comes to increasing its profit. (Indeed, Disneyland mints money: When you enter the park, you can exchange U.S. currency for Disney dollars, which can be spent only in the park.)[2]

In 2012, Disneyland charged out-of-state adults $199 for a three-day park hopper ticket, which admits one to Disneyland and Disney's California Adventure park, but charged southern Californians only $154. This policy of charging locals a discounted price makes sense if visitors are willing to pay more than locals and if Disneyland can prevent locals from selling discounted tickets to nonlocals. Imagine a Midwesterner who's never been to Disneyland and wants to visit. Travel accounts for most of the trip's cost, so an extra few dollars for entrance to the park makes little percentage difference in the total cost of the visit and hence does not greatly affect that person's decision whether to go. In contrast, for a local who has been to Disneyland many times and for whom the entrance price is a larger share of the total cost, a slightly higher entrance fee might prevent a visit.[3]

Charging both groups the same price is not in Disney's best interest. If Disney were to charge the higher price to everyone, many locals wouldn't visit the park. If Disney were to use the lower price for everyone, it would be charging nonresidents much less than they are willing to pay.

Preventing Resale

Resale is difficult or impossible for most *services* and when *transaction costs are high*. If Joe the plumber charges you less than he charges your neighbor for clearing a pipe, you cannot make a deal with your neighbor to resell this service. The higher the transaction costs a consumer must incur to resell a good, the less likely is a resale. Suppose that you are able to buy a jar of pickles for $1 less than the usual price. Could you practically buy and sell this jar to someone, or would the transaction costs be prohibitive? The more valuable a product or the more widely consumed it is, the more likely it is that transaction costs are low enough that resale occurs.

---

[2]According to **www.babycenter.com**, it costs $411,214 to raise a child from cradle through college. Parents can cut that total in half, however: They don't *have* to take their kids to Disneyland.

[3]In 2012, a Southern Californian couple, Jeff Reitz and Tonya Mickesh, were out of work, so they decided to cheer themselves up by using their annual passes to visit Disneyland 366 days that year (a leap year).

Some firms act to raise transaction costs or otherwise make resale difficult. Disneyland prevents resale by checking a purchaser's driver's license and requiring that the ticket be used for same-day entrance. If your college requires that someone with a student ticket shows a student ID card before being admitted to a sporting event, it would be difficult to resell your low-price tickets to nonstudents, whom your college charges a higher price. When students at some universities buy computers at lower-than-usual prices, they must sign a contract that forbids them to resell it.

Similarly, a firm can prevent resale by *vertically integrating*: participating in more than one successive stage of the production and distribution chain for a good or service. Alcoa, the former aluminum monopoly, wanted to sell aluminum ingots to producers of aluminum wire at a lower price than it set for producers of aluminum aircraft parts. If Alcoa did so, however, the wire producers could easily resell their ingots. By starting its own wire production firm, Alcoa prevented resale and was able to charge high prices to firms that manufactured aircraft parts (Perry, 1980).

Governments frequently establish policies to promote price discrimination and to bar resale. For example, U.S. federal and some state governments require that milk producers, under penalty of law, price discriminate by selling milk at a higher price for fresh use than for processing (cheese, ice cream), and forbid resale. Government *tariffs* (taxes on imports) limit resale by making it expensive to buy goods in a low-price country and resell them in a high-price country. In some cases, laws prevent such reselling explicitly. Under U.S. trade laws, certain brand-name perfumes may not be sold in the United States except by their manufacturers.

APPLICATION

Preventing Resale of Designer Bags

During the holiday season, stores often limit how many of the hottest items—such as this year's best-selling toy—a customer can buy. But it may surprise you that Web sites of luxury-goods retailers such as Saks Fifth Avenue, Neiman Marcus, and Bergdorf Goodman limit how many designer handbags one can buy: "Due to popular demand, a customer may order no more than three units of this item every 30 days."

Why wouldn't manufacturers and stores want to sell as many units as possible? How many customers can even afford more than three Prada Visone Hobo handbags at $4,950 each? The simple explanation is that the restriction has nothing to do with "popular demand." Instead, it's designed to prevent resale so as to enable manufacturers to price discriminate internationally. The handbag manufacturers pressure the U.S. retailers to limit sales to prevent anyone from buying large numbers of bags and reselling them in Europe or Asia where the same items in Prada and Gucci stores often cost 20% to 40% more. For example, the Prada Nappa Antique Tote sells for $1,280 at Saks Fifth Avenue in New York City, but sells for $1,570 on Prada's Swiss Web site. Current exchange rates makes such international resale even more attractive, which explains why Prada's online site allows shipments only to selected countries, expressly forbids resale, and limits purchases.

Not All Price Differences Are Price Discrimination

Not every seller who charges consumers different prices is price discriminating. Hotels charge newlyweds more for bridal suites. Is that price discrimination? Some hotel managers say no. They contend that honeymooners, more than other guests, steal mementos, so the price differential reflects an actual cost differential.

The 2012 price for 51 weekly issues of the *Economist* magazine for a year is $356 if you buy it at the newsstand, $127 for a standard subscription, and $77 for a college student subscription. The difference between the newsstand cost and the standard subscription cost reflects, at least in part, the higher cost of selling the magazine at a newsstand rather than mailing it directly to customers, so this price difference does not reflect pure price discrimination. But the price difference between the standard subscription rate and the college student rate reflects pure price discrimination because the two subscriptions are identical in every respect except the price.

Types of Price Discrimination

There are three main types of price discrimination. With **perfect price discrimination**—also called *first-degree price discrimination*—the firm sells each unit at the maximum amount each customer is willing to pay, so prices differ across customers, and a given customer may pay more for some units than for others.

With **group price discrimination** (*third-degree price discrimination*), the firm charges different groups of customers different prices but charges a given customer the same price for every unit sold. Typically, not all customers pay different prices—the firm sets different prices only for a few groups of customers. Because this type of discrimination is the most common, the term *price discrimination* is often used to mean *group price discrimination*.

With **nonlinear price discrimination** (*second-degree price discrimination*), the price varies with the quantity purchased, but all customers who buy a given quantity pay the same price. That is, the consumer's expenditure on an item does not rise linearly (proportionately) with the amount purchased, which it would if the price were a constant.

In addition to price discriminating, many firms use other, more complicated types of nonuniform pricing. Later in this chapter, we examine two other frequently used forms of nonlinear pricing: two-part pricing and tie-in sales.

12.2 Perfect Price Discrimination

A firm with market power that knows exactly how much each customer is willing to pay for each unit of its good and that can prevent resale, can charge each person his or her reservation price. Such an all-knowing firm can *perfectly price discriminate*. By selling each unit of its output to the customer who values it the most at the maximum price that person is willing to pay, the perfectly price-discriminating monopoly captures all possible consumer surplus. This type of discrimination might be called *individual price discrimination*.

Perfect price discrimination is rare because firms do not have perfect information about their customers. Nevertheless, it is useful to examine perfect price discrimination because it is the most efficient form of price discrimination and provides a benchmark against which we compare other types of nonuniform pricing.

We now show how a firm with full information about consumer reservation prices can use that information to perfectly price discriminate. Next, we compare the market outcomes (price, quantity, surplus) of a perfectly price-discriminating monopoly to those of perfectly competitive and uniform-price monopoly firms.

How a Firm Perfectly Price Discriminates

A firm with market power that can prevent resale and has full information about its customers' willingness to pay price discriminates by selling each unit at its reservation price—the maximum amount any consumer would pay for it.

Graphical Analysis

The maximum price for any unit of output is given by the height of the demand curve at that output level. In the demand curve facing a monopoly in Figure 12.1, the first customer is willing to pay $6 for a unit, the next is willing to pay $5, and so forth. A perfectly price-discriminating firm sells its first unit of output for $6. Having sold the first unit, the firm can get at most $5 for its second unit. The firm must drop its price by $1 for each successive unit it sells.

A perfectly price-discriminating monopoly's marginal revenue is the same as its price. As the figure shows, the firm's marginal revenue is $MR_1 = \$6$ on the first unit, $MR_2 = \$5$ on the second unit, and $MR_3 = \$4$ on the third unit. As a result, *the firm's marginal revenue curve is its demand curve.*

This firm has a constant marginal cost of $4 per unit. It pays for the firm to produce the first unit because the firm sells that unit for $6, so its marginal revenue exceeds its marginal cost by $2. Similarly, the firm certainly wants to sell the second unit for $5, which also exceeds its marginal cost. The firm breaks even when it sells the third unit for $4. The firm is unwilling to sell more than three units because its marginal cost would exceed its marginal revenue on successive units. Thus, like any profit-maximizing firm, a perfectly price-discriminating firm produces at point *e*, where its marginal revenue curve intersects its marginal cost curve. (If you find it upsetting that the firm is indifferent between producing two and three units, assume that the firm's marginal cost is $3.99, so it definitely wants to produce three units.)

This perfectly price-discriminating firm earns revenues of $MR_1 + MR_2 + MR_3 = \$6 + \$5 + \$4 = \$15$, which is the area under its marginal revenue curve up to

Figure 12.1 Perfect Price Discrimination

The monopoly can charge $6 for the first unit, $5 for the second, and $4 for the third, as the demand curve shows. Its marginal revenue is $MR_1 = \$6$ for the first unit, $MR_2 = \$5$ for the second, and $MR_3 = \$4$ for the third. Thus, the demand curve is also the marginal revenue curve. Because the firm's marginal and average cost is $4 per unit, it is unwilling to sell at a price below $4, so it sells three units, point *e*, and breaks even on the last unit.

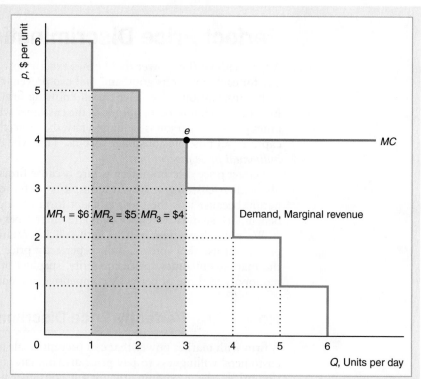

the number of units it sells, three. If the firm has no fixed cost, its cost of producing three units is $\$12 = \$4 \times 3$, so its profit is $\$3$.

Calculus Analysis

A perfectly price-discriminating monopoly charges each customer the reservation price $p = D(Q)$, where $D(Q)$ is the inverse demand function and Q is total output. The discriminating monopoly's revenue, R, is the area under the demand curve up to the quantity, Q, it sells,

$$R = \int_0^Q D(z)dz,$$

where z is a placeholder for quantity. Its objective is to maximize its profit through its choice of Q:

$$\max_Q \pi = \int_0^Q D(z)\,dz - C(Q). \tag{12.1}$$

Its first-order condition for a maximum is found by differentiating Equation 12.1 (using Leibniz's rule, Chapter 9, footnote 19) to obtain

$$\frac{d\pi}{dQ} = D(Q) - \frac{dC(Q)}{dQ} = 0. \tag{12.2}$$

According to Equation 12.2, the discriminating monopoly sells units up to the quantity, Q, where the reservation price for the last unit, $D(Q)$, equals its marginal cost, $dC(Q)/dQ$.

For this solution to maximize profits, the second-order condition must hold:

$$\frac{d^2\pi}{dQ^2} = \frac{dD(Q)}{dQ} - \frac{d^2C(Q)}{dQ^2} < 0.$$

Given that the demand curve has a negative slope, the second-order condition holds if the marginal cost curve is upper sloping, $d^2C(Q)/dQ^2 > 0$, or if the demand curve has a greater (absolute) slope than the marginal cost curve. The perfectly price-discriminating monopoly's profit is

$$\pi = \int_0^Q D(z)\,dz - C(Q).$$

SOLVED PROBLEM 12.1

Given that $D(Q) = a - bQ$, solve for the perfect price discrimination equilibrium. What quantity does a perfectly price discriminating monopoly sell if $a = 100$, $b = 1$, and marginal cost is constant at $MC = 10$?

Answer

1. *Write the profit function for this demand curve given that the monopoly price discriminates.* The profit function is

$$\pi = \int_0^Q (a - bz)\,dz - C(Q) = aQ - \frac{b}{2}Q^2 - C(Q). \tag{12.3}$$

2. *Solve for the optimal quantity by setting the derivative of profit in Equation 12.2 with respect to quantity equal to zero:* The first-order condition to maximize profit is:

$$a - bQ - \frac{dC(Q)}{dQ} = 0.$$

By rearranging terms, we find that $D(Q) = a - bQ = dC(Q)/dQ = MC$, as in Equation 12.2. Thus, the monopoly produces the quantity at which the demand curve hits the marginal cost curve. If $a = 100$, $b = 1$, and $MC = 10$, this condition is $100 - Q = 10$, or $Q = 90$.

Perfect Price Discrimination Is Efficient but Harms Some Consumers

Perfect price discrimination is efficient: It maximizes the sum of consumer surplus and producer surplus. Therefore, both perfect competition and perfect price discrimination maximize welfare. However *with perfect price discrimination, the entire surplus goes to the firm, whereas the surplus is shared under competition.*

If the market in Figure 12.2 is competitive, the intersection of the demand curve and the marginal cost curve, MC, determines the competitive equilibrium at e_c, where price is p_c and quantity is Q_c. Consumer surplus is $A + B + C$, producer surplus is $D + E$, and there is no deadweight loss. The market is efficient because the price, p_c, equals the marginal cost, MC_c.

With a single-price monopoly (which charges all customers the same price because it cannot distinguish among them), the intersection of the MC curve and the single-price monopoly's marginal revenue curve, MC_s, determines the output, Q_s.[4] The monopoly operates at e_s, where it charges p_s. The deadweight loss from monopoly is $C + E$. This efficiency loss is due to the monopoly's charging a price, p_s, that is above its marginal cost, MC_s, so less is sold than in a competitive market.

A perfectly price-discriminating firm sells each unit at its reservation price, which is the height of the demand curve. As a result, the firm's price-discriminating marginal revenue curve, MR_d, is the same as its demand curve. It sells the Q_d unit for p_c, where its marginal revenue curve, MR_d, intersects the marginal cost curve, MC, so it just covers its marginal cost on the last unit. The firm is unwilling to sell additional units because its marginal revenue would be less than the marginal cost of producing them.

A perfectly price-discriminating firm's producer surplus from the Q_d units it sells is the area below its demand curve and above its marginal cost curve, $A + B + C + D + E$. Its profit is the producer surplus minus any fixed cost. Consumers receive no consumer surplus because each consumer pays his or her reservation price. The perfectly price-discriminating firm's profit-maximizing solution has *no deadweight loss* because the last unit is sold at a price, p_c, that equals the marginal cost, MC_c, as in a competitive market. Thus, both a perfect price discrimination outcome and a competitive equilibrium are efficient.

The perfect price discrimination solution differs from the competitive equilibrium in two important ways. First, in the competitive equilibrium, everyone is charged a price equal to the equilibrium marginal cost, $p_c = MC_c$; however, in the perfect price

---

[4]We assume that if we convert a monopoly into a competitive industry, the industry's marginal cost curve—the lowest cost at which an additional unit can be produced by any firm—is the same as the monopoly MC curve. The industry MC curve is the industry supply curve (Chapter 8).

Figure 12.2 Competitive, Single-Price, and Perfect Discrimination Equilibria

In the competitive market equilibrium, e_c, price is p_c, quantity is Q_c, consumer surplus is $A + B + C$, producer surplus is $D + E$, and there is no deadweight loss. In the single-price monopoly equilibrium, e_s, price is p_s, quantity is Q_s, consumer surplus falls to A, producer surplus is $B + D$, and deadweight loss is $C + E$. In the perfect

discrimination equilibrium, the monopoly sells each unit at the customer's reservation price on the demand curve. It sells Q_d $(= Q_c)$ units, where the last unit is sold at its marginal cost. Customers have no consumer surplus, but there is no deadweight loss.

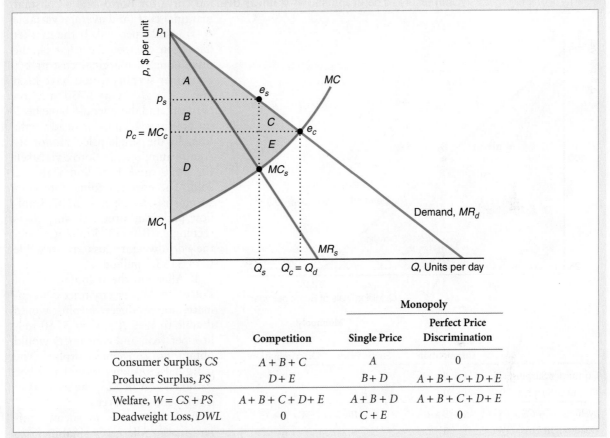

		Monopoly	
	Competition	Single Price	Perfect Price Discrimination
Consumer Surplus, CS	$A + B + C$	A	0
Producer Surplus, PS	$D + E$	$B + D$	$A + B + C + D + E$
Welfare, $W = CS + PS$	$A + B + C + D + E$	$A + B + D$	$A + B + C + D + E$
Deadweight Loss, DWL	0	$C + E$	0

discrimination equilibrium, only the last unit is sold at that price. The other units are sold at customers' reservation prices, which are greater than p_c. Second, consumers receive some net benefit (consumer surplus, $A + B + C$) in a competitive market, whereas a perfectly price-discriminating monopoly captures all the surplus or potential gains from trade. Thus, perfect price discrimination does not reduce efficiency—both output and welfare are the same as under competition—but it does redistribute income away from consumers. Consumers are much better off under competition.

Is a single-price or perfectly price-discriminating monopoly better for consumers? The perfect price discrimination equilibrium is more efficient than the single-price monopoly equilibrium because more output is produced. A single-price monopoly, however, takes less consumer surplus from consumers than a perfectly price-discriminating monopoly. Consumers who put a very high value on the good are better off with a single-price monopoly, where they have consumer surplus, than with perfect price discrimination, where they have none. Consumers with lower reservation prices who purchase from the perfectly price-discriminating monopoly but not from the single-price monopoly have no consumer surplus in either case. All the social gain from the extra output goes to the perfectly price-discriminating firm. Consumer surplus is greatest with competition, lower with single-price monopoly, and eliminated by perfect price discrimination.

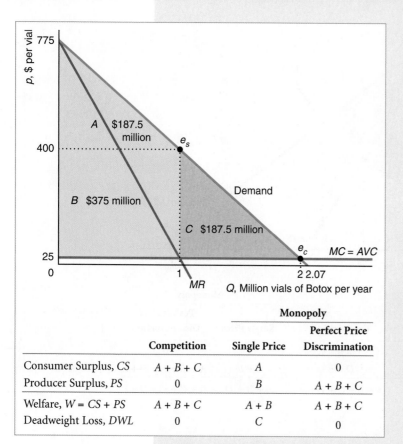

	Competition	Single Price	Perfect Price Discrimination
		Monopoly	
Consumer Surplus, *CS*	$A + B + C$	A	0
Producer Surplus, *PS*	0	B	$A + B + C$
Welfare, $W = CS + PS$	$A + B + C$	$A + B$	$A + B + C$
Deadweight Loss, *DWL*	0	C	0

APPLICATION

Botox Revisited

To show how perfect price discrimination differs from competition and single-price monopoly, we revisit the Application "Botox Patent Monopoly" in Chapter 11. The graph shows a linear demand curve for Botox and a constant marginal cost (and average variable cost) of $25 per vial. If the market had been competitive (that is, the price equaled marginal cost at e_c), consumer surplus would have been area $A + B + C = \$750$ million per year, and there would have been no producer surplus or deadweight loss. In the single-price monopoly equilibrium, e_s, the Botox vials sell for $400, and 1 million vials are sold. The corresponding consumer surplus is triangle $A = \$187.5$ million per year, producer surplus is rectangle $B = \$375$ million, and the deadweight loss is triangle $C = \$187.5$ million.

If Allergan, the manufacturer of Botox, could perfectly price discriminate, its producer surplus would double to $A + B + C = \$750$ million per year, and consumers would obtain no consumer surplus. The marginal consumer would pay the marginal cost of $25, the same as in a competitive market.

Both Allergan and society suffer from Allergan's inability to perfectly price discriminate. The profit of the single-price monopoly, $B = \$375$ million per day, is lower than that of a perfectly price-discriminating monopoly by $A + C = \$375$ million per year. Similarly, society's welfare under single-price monopoly is lower than from perfect price discrimination by the deadweight loss, C, of $187.5 million per year.

Transaction Costs and Perfect Price Discrimination

Some firms come close to perfect price discrimination. For example, the managers of the Suez Canal set tolls individually, considering many factors such as weather and each ship's alternative routes. However, many more firms set a single price or use another nonuniform pricing method.

Transaction costs are a major reason these firms do not perfectly price discriminate: It is too difficult or costly to gather information about each customer's price sensitivity. Recent advances in computer technologies, however, have lowered these costs, allowing hotels, car- and truck-rental companies, cruise lines, and airlines to price discriminate more often.

Private colleges request and receive financial information from students, which allows the schools to nearly perfectly price discriminate. The schools give partial scholarships as a means of reducing tuition to relatively poor students.

Many auto dealerships try to increase their profit by perfectly price discriminating, charging each customer the maximum the customer is willing to pay. These firms hire salespeople to ascertain potential customers' willingness to pay and to bargain with them. Even if firms cannot achieve perfect price discrimination, imperfect individual price discrimination can increase their profits significantly.

APPLICATION Google Uses Bidding for Ads to Price Discriminate	Google uses auctions to greatly reduce its transaction cost of determining a customer's willingness to pay for an ad on Google's Web site. When you query Google, paid advertising appears next to your search results. The ads that appear vary with your search term. By making searches for unusual topics easy and fast, Google helps firms reach difficult-to-find potential customers with targeted ads. For example, a lawyer specializing in toxic mold lawsuits can place an ad that is seen only by people who search for "toxic mold lawyer." Such focused advertising has higher payoff per view than traditional print and broadcast ads that reach much larger, non-targeted groups ("wasted eyeballs") and avoids the problem of finding addresses for direct mailing. Google uses auctions to price these ads. Advertisers are willing to bid higher to be listed first on Google's page. Goldfarb and Tucker (2008) found that how much lawyers will pay for context-based ads depends on the difficulty of making a match. Lawyers will pay more to advertise when there are fewer self-identified potential customers—fewer people searching for a particular phrase. They also found that lawyers bid more when there are fewer customers, and hence the need to target ads is greater. Some states have anti-ambulance-chaser regulations, which prohibit personal injury lawyers from directly contacting potential clients by snail mail, phone, or e-mail for a few months after an accident. In those states, the extra amount bid for ads linked to personal injury keywords rather than for other keywords such as "tax lawyer" is $1.01 (11%) more than in unregulated states. We're talking big bucks here: Trial lawyers earned $40 billion in 2004, which is 50% more than Microsoft or Intel and twice that of Coca-Cola. By taking advantage of advertisers' desire to reach small, difficult-to-find segments of the population and varying the price according to advertisers' willingness to pay, Google is essentially perfectly price discriminating.

12.3 Group Price Discrimination

Most firms have no practical way to estimate the reservation price for each of their customers. But many of these firms know which groups of customers are likely to have higher reservation prices on average than others. A firm engages in *group price discrimination* by dividing potential customers into two or more groups and setting different prices for each group. Consumer groups may differ by age (such as adults and children), by location (such as by country), or in other ways. All units of the good sold to customers within a group are sold at a single price. As with perfect (individual) price discrimination, to engage in group price discrimination, a firm must have market power, be able to identify groups with different reservation prices, and prevent resale.

For example, first-run movie theaters with market power charge seniors a lower ticket price than they charge younger adults because the elderly typically are not willing to pay as much to see a movie. By admitting seniors as soon as they prove their age and buy tickets, the theater prevents resale.

Group Price Discrimination with Two Groups

How does a firm set its prices if it sells to two (or more) groups of consumers with different demand curves and if resale between the two groups is impossible? Suppose that a monopoly can divide its customers into two (or more) groups—for example, consumers in two countries. It sells Q_1 to the first group and earns revenues of $R_1(Q_1)$, and it sells Q_2 units to the second group and earns $R_2(Q_2)$. Its cost of producing total output $Q = Q_1 + Q_2$ units is $C(Q)$. The monopoly can maximize its profit through its choice of prices or quantities to each group. We examine its problem when it chooses quantities:

$$\max_{Q_1, Q_2} \pi = R_1(Q_1) + R_2(Q_2) - C(Q_1 + Q_2). \tag{12.4}$$

The first-order conditions corresponding to Equation 12.4 are obtained by differentiating with respect to Q_1 and Q_2 and setting the partial derivative equal to zero:

$$\frac{\partial \pi}{\partial Q_1} = \frac{dR_1(Q_1)}{dQ_1} - \frac{dC(Q)}{dQ} \frac{\partial Q}{\partial Q_1} = 0, \tag{12.5}$$

$$\frac{\partial \pi}{\partial Q_2} = \frac{dR_2(Q_2)}{dQ_2} - \frac{dC(Q)}{dQ} \frac{\partial Q}{\partial Q_2} = 0. \tag{12.6}$$

Equation 12.5 says that the marginal revenue from sales to the first group, $MR^1 = dR_1(Q_1)/dQ_1$, should equal the marginal cost of producing the last unit of total output, $MC = dC(Q)/dQ$, because $\partial Q/\partial Q_1 = 1$. Similarly, Equation 12.6 shows that the marginal revenue from the second group, MR^2, should also equal the marginal cost. By combining Equations 12.5 and 12.6, we find that the two marginal revenues are equal where the monopoly is profit maximizing:

$$MR^1 = MC = MR^2. \tag{12.7}$$

DVD Example. We use a recent example to illustrate the basic idea. A copyright gives Warner Brothers the legal monopoly to produce and sell the *Harry Potter and the Deathly Hallows Part 2* DVD. Warner Brothers engaged in group price discrimination by charging different prices in the United States and the United Kingdom. Warner Brothers can ignore the problem of resale between the countries because the DVDs have incompatible formats.

The DVD was released during the holiday season of 2011 and sold $Q_A = 5.8$ million copies to American consumers at $p_A = \$29$ and $Q_B = 2.0$ million copies to British consumers at $p_B = \$39$ (£25).[5] How did Warner Brothers set p_A and p_B? Warner Brothers U.S. revenue is $R_A(Q_A) = p_A Q_A$ and its British revenue is $R_B(Q_B) = p_B Q_B$.

---

[5] Sources of information and data for this section (viewed July 10, 2012) include Amazon Web sites for each country, **warnerbros.com, www.ukfilmcouncil.org.uk, www.the-numbers.com/dvd/charts/ annual/2011.php**, and **www.bbc.co.uk/newsbeat/16444062**, January 6, 2012. We assume that the demand curves in each country are linear.

If Warner Brothers has the same constant marginal and average cost, m, in both countries, its profit (ignoring any sunk development cost and other fixed costs) from selling the DVD is $\pi_A = R_A(Q_A) - mQ_A$, where mQ_A is its cost of producing Q_A units. Warner Brothers wants to maximize its combined profit, π, which is the sum of its American and British profits, π_A and π_B:

$$\pi = \pi_A + \pi_B = [R_A(Q_A) - mQ_A] + [R_B(Q_B) - mQ_B].$$

The first-order conditions, which correspond to Equations 12.5 and 12.6, are $MR^A = dR_A/dQ_A = m$ and $MR^B = m$. Figure 12.3 shows our estimates of the linear demand curves in the two countries. In panel a, Warner Brothers maximized its U.S. profit by selling $Q_A = 5.8$ million DVDs, where its marginal revenue equaled its marginal cost $MR^A = m = 1$. It charged $p_A = \$39$. Similarly in panel b, the firm maximized its U.K. profit by selling $Q_B = 2.0$ million DVDS where $MR^B = m = \$1$. The corresponding price was $p_B = \$39$.

Prices and Elasticities. Because the monopoly equated the marginal revenue for each group to its common marginal cost, $MC = m$, the marginal revenues for the two countries are equal, $MR^A = m = MR^B$, as in Equation 12.7. We can use this equation to determine how the prices for the two groups vary with the price elasticities of demand at the profit-maximizing outputs.

Figure 12.3 Group Pricing of the *Harry Potter* DVD

Warner Brothers, the monopoly producer of the *Harry Potter and the Deathly Hallows Part 2* DVD, charges more in the United Kingdom, $p_B = \$39$ (£25), than in the United States, $p_A = \$29$, because demand is more elastic in the United States. Warner Brothers sets the quantity independently in each country where its relevant marginal revenue equals its common, constant marginal cost, $m = \$1$. As a result, it maximizes its profit by equating the two marginal revenues: $MR^A = 1 = MR^B$.

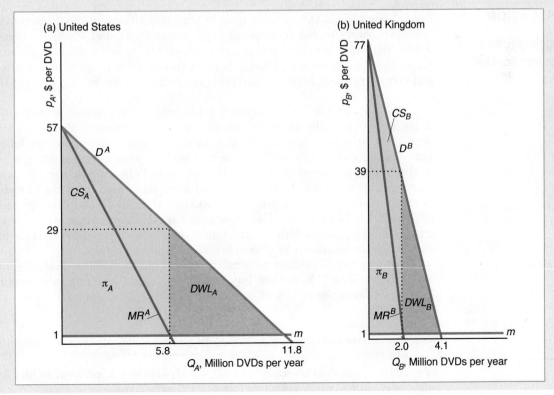

As we learned in Chapter 11, marginal revenue is a function of the price and the price elasticity of demand: $MR^A = p_A(1 + 1/\varepsilon_A)$, where ε_A is the price elasticity of demand for U.S. consumers, and $MR^B = p_B(1 + 1/\varepsilon_B)$, where ε_B is the price elasticity of demand for U.K. consumers. Rewriting the equation using these expressions for marginal revenue, we find that

$$MR^A = p_A\left(1 + \frac{1}{\varepsilon_A}\right) = m = p_B\left(1 + \frac{1}{\varepsilon_B}\right) = MR^B. \qquad (12.8)$$

By rearranging Equation 12.8, we learn that the ratio of prices in the two countries depends solely on demand elasticities in those countries:

$$\frac{p_B}{p_A} = \frac{1 + 1/\varepsilon_A}{1 + 1/\varepsilon_B}. \qquad (12.9)$$

We can illustrate these results using the DVD example. Given that $m = \$1$, $p_A = \$29$, and $p_B = \$39$ in Equation 12.8, Warner Brothers must believe that $\varepsilon_A = p_A/[m - p_A] = 29/[-28] \approx -1.0357$ and $\varepsilon_B = p_B/[m - p_B] = 39/[-38] \approx -1.0263$.[6] Substituting the prices and the demand elasticities into Equation 12.9, we determine that

$$\frac{p_B}{p_A} = \frac{\$39}{\$29} \approx 1.345 \approx \frac{1 + 1/(-1.0357)}{1 + 1/(-1.0263)} = \frac{1 + 1/\varepsilon_A}{1 + 1/\varepsilon_B}.$$

Thus, because Warner Brothers believed that the British demand curve is less elastic at its profit-maximizing prices than the U.S. demand curve ($\varepsilon_B \approx -1.0263$ is closer to zero than is $\varepsilon_A \approx -1.0357$), it charged British consumers 34% more than U.S. customers.[7]

APPLICATION Smuggling Prescription Drugs into the United States	Federal law forbids U.S. citizens from importing pharmaceuticals from Canada and other countries, but some people, city governments, and state governments openly flout this law. U.S. senior citizens have taken well-publicized bus trips across the Canadian and Mexican borders to buy their drugs at lower prices; and many Canadian, Mexican, and other Internet sites offer to ship drugs to U.S. customers.

A U.S. citizen's incentive to import is great, because the prices of many popular drugs are substantially lower in virtually every other country. Zoloft, an antidepressant, sells for one-third the U.S. price in Mexico and about one-half in Luxembourg and Austria. In 2012, the average U.S. price for statin drugs, which are prescribed to one-third of U.S. adults to control cholesterol, was more than four times greater than the U.K. price and more than three times the Canadian price. In recent years, drug prices in Canada, Europe, and Japan have averaged 60% to 70% of U.S. prices. The lower prices in other countries reflect price discrimination by pharmaceutical firms, more competition due to differences in patent laws, price regulation by governments, and other factors.

According to a Canadian pharmaceutical organization, 20 million U.S. citizens and 2 million U.K. citizens buy Canadian drugs by ordering them over the Internet. However, most U.S. citizens do not buy drugs from outside the country.

---

[6]We obtain the expression that $\varepsilon_i = p_i/(m - p_i)$ by rearranging the expression in Equation 12.8: $p_i(1 + 1/\varepsilon_i) = m$.

[7]By mid-2012, Amazon's U.S. price for the DVD was $7, while its U.K. price was $9.50, a British markup of about 36%, which is about the same as in the previous year.

A 2008 poll, found that only 11% of Americans reported ever having purchased pharmaceuticals outside of the United States. Thus, the U.S. ban, which is enforced by the federal government, appears to be relatively effective.

A 2008 poll found that 80% of Americans favored permitting importation of drugs, as European countries do. The Congressional Budget Office reported in 2011 that allowing drug imports from Canada and other selected countries would save U.S. consumers more than $19 billion a year. Nonetheless, attempts in Congress to change the law to allow imports have failed multiple times in the last couple of decades.

The main government objection to such a change in the law concerns the safety of imported drugs, although supplies from Canada, Europe, and Japan are very safe. Not surprisingly, U.S. pharmaceutical companies strongly oppose allowing drug imports. They fear that drugs they sell at lower prices in other countries will be imported into the United States, driving down their U.S. prices.

GlaxoSmithKline, Pfizer, and other drug companies have tried to reduce imports by refusing to sell to Canadian pharmacies that ship south of the border. Wyeth and AstraZeneca watch Canadian pharmacies and wholesale customers for spikes in sales volume that could indicate exports, and then restrict supplies to those pharmacies.

SOLVED PROBLEM 12.2

A monopoly drug producer with a constant marginal cost (and average cost) of $MC = 1$ sells in only two countries and faces a linear inverse demand curve of $p_1 = 6 - \frac{1}{2}Q_1$ in Country 1 and $p_2 = 9 - Q_2$ in Country 2. What price does the monopoly charge in each country with and without a ban against shipments between the countries?

Answer

If resale across borders is banned so that price discrimination is possible:

1. *Determine the profit-maximizing price that the monopoly sets in each country by setting the relevant marginal revenue equal to the marginal cost.* If the monopoly can price discriminate, it sets a monopoly price independently in each country. The marginal revenue curve is twice as steeply sloped as is the linear inverse demand curve (see Solved Problem 11.1), so the marginal revenue function in Country 1

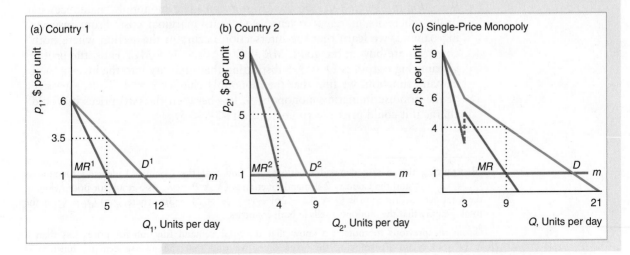

is $MR_1 = 6 - Q_1$, as panel a of the figure shows. The monopoly maximizes its profit where its marginal revenue function equals its marginal cost,

$$MR_1 = 6 - Q_1 = 1 = MC.$$

Solving, we find that its profit-maximizing output is $Q_1 = 5$. Substituting this expression back into the monopoly's inverse demand curve, we learn that its profit-maximizing price is $p_1 = 3.5$ as panel a illustrates. In Country 2, the inverse demand curve is $p_2 = 9 - Q_2$, so the monopoly chooses Q_2 such that $MR_2 = 9 - 2Q_2 = 1 = MC$. Thus, it maximizes its profit in Country 2 where $Q_2 = 4$ and $p_2 = 5$, as panel b shows.

If imports are permitted so that price discrimination is impossible:

2. *Derive the total demand curve.* If the monopoly cannot price discriminate, it charges the same price, p, in both countries. The monopoly faces the total demand curve in panel c, which is the horizontal sum of the demand curves for each of the two countries in panels a and b (Chapter 2). If the price is between 6 and 9, the quantity demanded is positive in only Country 2, so the total demand curve (panel c) is the same as Country 2's demand curve (panel b). If the price is less than 6 where both countries demand a positive quantity, the total demand curve (panel c) is the horizontal sum of the two individual countries' demand curves (panels a and b).[8] As panel c shows, the total demand curve has a kink at $p = 6$, because the quantity demanded in Country 1 is positive only below this price.

3. *Determine the marginal revenue curve corresponding to the total demand curve.* Because the total demand curve has a kink at $p = 6$, the corresponding marginal revenue curve has two sections. At prices above 6, the marginal revenue curve is the same as that of Country 2 in panel b. At prices below 6, where the total demand curve is the horizontal sum of the two countries' demand curves, the marginal revenue curve has twice the slope of the linear total inverse demand curve. The inverse total demand function is $p = 7 - \frac{1}{3}Q$, and the marginal revenue function is $MR = 7 - \frac{2}{3}Q$.[9] Panel c shows that the marginal revenue curve *jumps*—is discontinuous—at the quantity where the total demand curve has a kink.

4. *Solve for the single-price monopoly solution.* The monopoly maximizes its profit where its marginal revenue equals its marginal cost. From inspecting panel c, we learn that the intersection occurs in the section where both countries are buying the good: $MR = 7 - \frac{2}{3}Q = 1 = MC$. Thus, the profit-maximizing output is $Q = 9$. Substituting that quantity into the inverse total demand function, we find that the monopoly charges $p = 4$. Thus, the price of the nondiscriminating monopoly, 4, lies between the two prices it would charge if it could price discriminate: $3.50 < 4 < 5$.

---

[8] Rearranging the inverse demand functions, we find that the Country 1 demand function is $Q_1 = 12 - p_1$ and the Country 2 demand function is $Q_2 = 9 - p_2$. As a result for price below 6, the total demand function is $Q = (12 - 2p) + (9 - p) = 21 - 3p$, where $Q = Q_1 + Q_2$ is the total quantity that the monopoly sells in both countries.

[9] From the previous footnote, we know that the total demand function for prices less than 6 is $Q = 21 - 3p$. Rearranging this expression, we find that the inverse demand function is $p = 7 - \frac{1}{3}Q$. Because the marginal revenue function has twice as steep a slope, it is $MR = 7 - \frac{2}{3}Q$.

Identifying Groups

Firms use two approaches to divide customers into groups. One method is to divide buyers into groups based on *observable characteristics* of consumers that the firm believes are associated with relatively high or relatively low price elasticities. For example, movie theaters price discriminate using the age of customers. Similarly, some firms charge customers in one country higher prices than those in another country. In 2012, Windows 7 Home Premium edition sold for $166 in the United States, ¥499 ($78) in China, £110 ($171) in the United Kingdom, C$202($198) in Canada, €155 ($191) in France, and ¥19,362 ($243) in Japan. These differences are much greater than can be explained by shipping costs and reflect group price discrimination.

Another approach is to identify and divide consumers on the basis of their *actions*. The firm allows consumers to self-select the group to which they belong. For example, customers may be identified by their willingness to spend time to buy a good at a lower price. Firms price discriminate by taking advantage of the differing values that customers place on their time. For example, in the case of customers who are willing to spend time to obtain a bargain price, store owners might use queues (making people wait in line) and other time-intensive methods of selling goods. Because many high-wage people are unwilling to "waste their time shopping," store managers may run sales at which consumers who visit the store and pick up the good themselves get a low price, while high-wage consumers who order by phone or over the Internet pay a higher price. This type of price discrimination increases profit if people who put a high value on their time also have less elastic demands for the good.

APPLICATION

Buying Discounts

Firms use various approaches to induce consumers to indicate whether they have relatively high or low elasticities of demand. For each of these methods, consumers must incur some cost, such as their time, to receive a discount. Otherwise, all consumers would get the discount. By spending extra time to obtain a discount, price-sensitive consumers are able to differentiate themselves.

Coupons. Many firms use discount coupons to price discriminate. Through this device, firms divide customers into two groups: those who clip coupons and those who do not. People who are willing to spend their time clipping coupons buy cereals and other goods at lower prices than those who value their time more. A 2009 study by the Promotion Marketing Association Coupon Council found that consumers who spend 20 minutes per week clipping and organizing coupons could save up to $1,000 on an average annual grocery bill of $5,000 or more. More than three-quarters of U.S. consumers redeem coupons at least occasionally. In 2011, coupons with a face value of $470 billion were distributed by consumer package goods marketers to U.S. consumers. Of these, 3.5 billion coupons were redeemed for $4.6 billion.

The introduction of digital (for example, **EverSave.com** and **zavers.com**) coupons has made it easier for firms to target appropriate groups, but has lowered consumers' costs of using coupons, which means that a larger share of people use them. According to eMarketer, half of U.S. adults used online coupons in 2012. Digital coupons are more likely to be redeemed (15–20%) than are paper coupons (less than 1%).

Airline Tickets. By choosing between two different types of tickets, airline customers indicate whether they are likely to be business or recreational travelers. Airlines give customers a choice between high-price tickets with no strings attached and low-price fares that must be purchased long in advance.

Airlines know that many business travelers have little advance warning before they book a flight and have relatively inelastic demand curves. In contrast, vacation travelers can usually plan in advance and have relatively high elasticities of demand for air travel. The airlines' rules ensure that vacationers with relatively elastic demand obtain low fares while most business travelers with relatively inelastic demand buy high-price tickets (often more than four times higher than the plan-ahead rate). The average difference between the high and low price for passengers on the same U.S. route is 36% of an airline's average ticket price.

Reverse Auctions. Priceline.com and other online merchants use a name-your-own-price or "reverse" auction to identify price-sensitive customers. A customer enters a relatively low-price bid for a good or service, such as an airline ticket. Merchants decide whether or not to accept that bid. To prevent their less price-sensitive customers from using these methods, airlines force successful Priceline bidders to be flexible: to fly at off hours, to make one or more connections, and to accept any type of aircraft. Similarly, when bidding on groceries, a customer must list "one or two brands you like." As Jay Walker, Priceline's founder explained, "The manufacturers would rather not give you a discount, of course, but if you prove that you're willing to switch brands, they're willing to pay to keep you."

Rebates. Why do many firms offer a rebate of, say $5 instead of reducing the price on their product by $5? The reason is that a consumer must incur an extra, time-consuming step to receive the rebate. Thus, only those consumers who are price sensitive or place a low value on their time will actually apply for the rebate. According to a 2009 *Consumer Reports* survey, 47% of customers always or often apply for a rebate, 23% sometimes apply, 25% never apply, and 5% responded that the question was not applicable to them.

SOLVED PROBLEM 12.3

A monopoly producer with a constant marginal cost of $m = 20$ sells in two countries and can prevent reselling between the two countries. The inverse linear demand curve is $p_1 = 100 - Q_1$ in Country 1 and $p_2 = 100 - 2Q_2$ in Country 2. What price does the monopoly charge in each country? What quantity does it sell in each country? Does it price discriminate? Why or why not?

Answer

1. *Determine the profit-maximizing price and quantity that the monopoly sets in each country by setting the relevant marginal revenue equal to the marginal cost.* In Country 1, the inverse demand curve is $p_1 = 100 - Q_1$, so the revenue function is $R^1 = 100Q_1 - (Q_1)^2$, and hence the marginal revenue function is $MR^1 = dR^1/dQ_1 = 100 - 2Q_1$. It equates its marginal revenue to its marginal cost to determine its profit-maximizing quantity: $100 - 2Q_1 = 20$. Solving, the monopoly sets $Q_1 = 40$. Substituting this quantity into its inverse demand function, we learn that the monopoly's price is $p_1 = 100 - 40 = 60$. Similarly, in Country 2, the inverse demand curve is $p_2 = 100 - 2Q_2$, so the revenue function is $R^2 = 100Q_2 - 2(Q_2)^2$, and hence the marginal revenue function is $MR^2 = dR^2/dQ_2 = 100 - 4Q_2$. Equating marginal revenue and marginal cost, $100 - 4Q_2 = 20$, and solving, the monopoly sets $Q_2 = 20$ in Country 2. Its price is $p_2 = 100 - (2 \times 20) = 60$. Thus, the monopoly sells twice as much in Country 1 as in Country 2 but charges the same price in both countries.

2. *Explain, by solving for a general linear inverse demand function, why the monopoly does not price discriminate.* Although the firm has market power, can prevent reselling, and faces consumers in the two countries with different demand functions, it does not pay for the monopoly to price discriminate. Consider the monopoly's problem with a general linear inverse

demand function: $p = a - bQ$. Here, revenue is $R = aQ - bQ^2$, so $MR = dR/dQ = a - 2bQ$. Equating marginal revenue and marginal cost, $a - 2bQ = m$, and solving for Q, we find that $Q = (a - m)/(2b)$. Consequently, the price is $p = a - b(a - m)/(2b) = (a - m)/2$. Thus, the price depends only on the inverse demand function's intercept on the vertical axis, a, and not on its slope, b. Because both inverse demand functions in this example have the same vertical intercept—they differ only in their slopes—the monopoly sets the same equilibrium price in both countries. In equilibrium, the elasticity of demand is the same in both countries. Thus, while the monopoly could price discriminate, it chooses not to do so.

Welfare Effects of Group Price Discrimination

Group price discrimination results in inefficient production and consumption. As a result, welfare under group price discrimination is lower than it is under competition or perfect price discrimination. Welfare may be lower or higher with group price discrimination than with a single-price monopoly, however.

Group Price Discrimination Versus Competition

Consumer surplus is greater and more output is produced with competition (or perfect price discrimination) than with group price discrimination. In Figure 12.3, consumer surplus with group price discrimination is CS_A (for American consumers in panel a) and CS_B (for British consumers in panel b). Under competition, consumer surplus is the area below the demand curve and above the marginal cost curve: $CS_A + \pi_A + DWL_A$ in panel a and $CS_B + \pi_B + DWL_B$ in panel b.

Thus, group price discrimination transfers some of the competitive consumer surplus, π_1 and π_2, to the monopoly as additional profit and causes the deadweight loss, DWL_1 and DWL_2, of some of the rest of the competitive consumer surplus. The deadweight loss is due to the group price discriminating monopoly's charging prices above marginal cost, which results in reduced production from the optimal competitive level.

Group Price Discrimination Versus Single-Price Monopoly

From theory alone, it is impossible to tell whether welfare is higher if the monopoly uses group price discrimination or if it sets a single price. Both types of monopolies set price above marginal cost, so too little is produced relative to competition. Output may rise as the firm starts discriminating if groups that did not buy when the firm charged a single price start buying.

The closer the group price discriminating monopoly comes to perfect price discrimination (say, by dividing its customers into many groups rather than just two), the more output it produces, the less deadweight loss. However, unless a group price discriminating monopoly sells significantly more output than it would if it had to set a single price, welfare is likely to be lower with discrimination because of consumption inefficiency and time wasted shopping. These two inefficiencies do not occur with a monopoly that charges all consumers the same price. As a result, consumers place the same marginal value (the single sales price) on the good, so they have no incentive to trade with each other. Similarly, if everyone pays the same price, consumers have no incentive to search for lower prices.

12.4 Nonlinear Price Discrimination

Many firms are unable to determine which customers or groups of customers have the highest reservation prices. However, firms may know that most customers are willing to pay more for the first unit than for successive units: the typical customer's demand curve is downward sloping. Such firms can price discriminate by letting the price that each customer pays vary with the number of units purchased. The firm uses *nonlinear price discrimination* (second-degree price discrimination). Here, the price varies with quantity but each customer faces the same nonlinear pricing schedule.[10] To use nonlinear price discrimination, a firm must have market power and be able to prevent customers who buy at a low price from reselling to those who would otherwise pay a high price.

A 64-ounce bottle of V8 vegetable juice sells for $4.39 or 6.8¢ an ounce, while a 12-ounce bottle sells for $2.79 or 23¢ an ounce. This difference in the price per ounce reflects nonlinear price discrimination unless the price difference is due to cost differences (if making and filling a bottle is a very small share of the cost). This quantity discount results in customers who make large purchases paying more per unit than those who make small purchases.

Many utilities use *block-pricing* schedules, by which they charge one price for the first few units (a *block*) of usage and a different price for subsequent blocks. Both declining-block and increasing-block pricing are common.

The block-pricing monopoly in Figure 12.4 faces a linear demand curve for each (identical) customer. The demand curve hits the vertical axis at $90 and the horizontal axis at 90 units. The monopoly has a constant marginal and average cost of $m = \$30$. Panel a shows how this monopoly maximizes its profit if it can set two prices. The firm uses declining-block prices to maximize its profit.

The monopoly faces an inverse demand curve $p = 90 - Q$, and its marginal and average cost is $m = 30$. Consequently, the quantity-discounting utility's profit is

$$\pi = p(Q_1)Q_1 + p(Q_2)(Q_2 - Q_1) - mQ_2$$
$$= (90 - Q_1)Q_1 + (90 - Q_2)(Q_2 - Q_1) - 30Q_2,$$

where Q_1 is the largest quantity for which the first-block rate, $p_1 = 90 - Q_1$, is charged and Q_2 is the total quantity that a consumer purchases. The utility chooses Q_1 and Q_2 to maximize its profit. It sets the derivative of profit with respect to Q_1 equal to zero, $d\pi/dQ_1 = Q_2 - 2Q_1 = 0$, and the derivative of profit with respect to Q_2 equal to zero, $d\pi/dQ_2 = Q_1 - 2Q_2 + 60 = 0$. By solving these two equations simultaneously, the utility determines its profit-maximizing quantities, $Q_1 = 20$ and $Q_2 = 40$. The corresponding block prices are $p_1 = 90 - 20 = 70$ and $p_2 = 50$. That is, the monopoly charges a price of $70 on any quantity between 1 and 20— the first block—and $50 on any units beyond the first 20—the second block. (The point that determines the first block, $70 and 20 units, lies on the demand curve.) Given each consumer's demand curve, a consumer who decides to buy 40 units pays $1,400 (= \$70 \times 20$) for the first block and $1,000 (= \$50 \times 20$) for the second block.

If the monopoly can set only a single price (panel b), it produces where its marginal revenue equals its marginal cost, selling 30 units at $60 per unit. Thus, by using nonlinear pricing instead of using a single price, the utility sells more units, 40 instead of 30, and makes a higher profit, $B = \$1,200$ instead of $F = \$900$. With quantity discounting, consumer surplus is lower, $A + C = \$400$ instead of $E = \$450$; welfare (consumer surplus plus producer surplus) is higher, $A + B + C = \$1,600$ instead of $E + F = \$1,350$; and deadweight loss is lower, $D = \$200$ instead of $G = \$450$.

---

[10]A consumer's expenditure is a linear function of quantity only if the price is constant. If the price varies with quantity, then the expenditure is nonlinear.

Figure 12.4 Block Pricing

If this monopoly engages in block pricing with quantity discounting, it makes a larger profit (producer surplus) than it does if it sets a single price, and welfare is greater. (a) With block pricing, its profit is $B = \$1,200$ and welfare is $A + B + C = \$1,600$. (b) If it sets a single price (so that its marginal revenue equals its marginal cost), the monopoly's profit is $F = \$900$, and welfare is $E + F = \$1,350$.

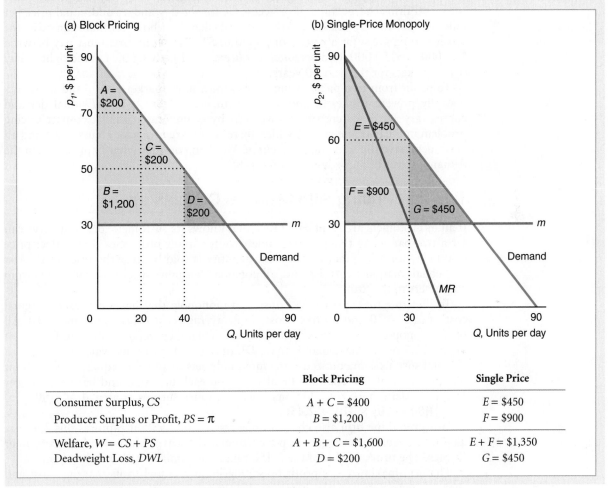

	Block Pricing	Single Price
Consumer Surplus, CS	$A + C = \$400$	$E = \$450$
Producer Surplus or Profit, $PS = \pi$	$B = \$1,200$	$F = \$900$
Welfare, $W = CS + PS$	$A + B + C = \$1,600$	$E + F = \$1,350$
Deadweight Loss, DWL	$D = \$200$	$G = \$450$

Thus, in this example, the firm and society are better off with quantity discounting, but consumers as a group suffer.

The more block prices that the monopoly can set, the closer the monopoly can get to perfect price discrimination. A deadweight loss results from the monopoly's setting a price above marginal cost so that too few units are sold. The more prices the monopoly sets, the lower the last price and hence the closer it is to marginal cost.

12.5 Two-Part Pricing

We now turn to another form of nonlinear pricing: *two-part pricings*. With two-part pricing, the average price per unit paid by a consumer varies with the number of units purchased by that consumer.

With **two-part pricing**, the firm charges each consumer a lump-sum *access fee* for the right to buy as many units of the good as the consumer wants at a per-unit *price*.[11] Thus, the overall payment consists of two prices: an access fee and a per-unit price. Because of the access fee, the average amount per unit that consumers pay is greater if they buy a small number of units than if they buy a larger number.

Two-part pricing is commonly used. Many fitness clubs charge a yearly access fee and a price per session. Many warehouse stores require that customers buy an annual membership before being allowed to buy goods at relatively low prices. Some car rental firms charge a rental or access fee for the day and an additional price per mile driven. To buy season tickets to the Dallas Cowboys football games in the lower seating areas (at a price from $590 to $1,250), a fan first must pay between $16,000 to $150,000 for a *personal seat license* (PSL), giving the fan the right to buy season tickets for the next 30 years.

To profit from two-part pricing, a firm must have market power and must successfully prevent resale. In addition, a firm must know how individual demand curves vary across its customers. We start by examining a firm's two-part pricing problem in the extreme case in which there is no variation across customers and all customers have the same demand curve. We then consider what happens when the demand curves of individual customers differ.

Two-Part Pricing with Identical Consumers

If all its customers are identical, a firm that knows its customers' demand curve can set a two-part price that has the same two important properties that perfect price discrimination has. First, the efficient quantity is sold because the price of the last unit equals marginal cost. Second, all potential consumer surplus is transferred from consumers to the firm.

To illustrate these points we consider a monopoly that has a constant marginal cost of $MC = 10$ and no fixed cost, so its average cost is also constant at 10. All of the monopoly's customers have the same demand curve, $q = 80 - p$. Panel a of Figure 12.5 shows the demand curve, D^1, of one such customer, Valerie.

Total surplus is maximized if the monopoly sets its price, p, equal to its constant marginal cost of 10. The firm breaks even on each unit sold and has no producer surplus. Valerie buys $q = 70$ units. Her consumer surplus is area $A = \frac{1}{2}(80 - p) q = \frac{1}{2}([80 - 10] \times 70) = 2,450$.

However, if the firm also charges an access fee of 2,450, it captures this 2,450 as its producer surplus or its profit per customer, and leaves Valerie with no consumer surplus. The firm's total profit is 2,450 times the number of identical customers.

The firm maximizes its profit by setting its price equal to its marginal cost and charging an access fee that captures the entire potential consumer surplus. If the firm were to charge a price above its marginal cost of 10, it would sell fewer units and make a smaller profit. In panel b of Figure 12.5, the firm charges $p = 20$. At that higher price, Valerie buys only 60 units, which is less than the 70 units that she buys at a price of 10 in panel a. The firm's profit from selling these 60 units is $B_1 = (20 - 10) \times 60 = 600$. For Valerie to agree to buy any units, the monopoly has to lower its access fee to 1,800 ($= \frac{1}{2} \times 60 \times 60$), the new potential consumer surplus, area A_1. The firm's total profit from Valerie is $A_1 + B_1 = 1,800 + 600 = 2,400$. This amount is less than the 2,450 ($= A$ in panel a) profit the firm earns if it sets price equal to marginal cost, 10, and charges the higher access fee. Area A in panel a equals $A_1 + B_1 + C_1$ in panel b. By charging a price above marginal cost, the firm loses C_1, which is the deadweight loss due to selling fewer units.

Similarly, if the firm were to charge a price below its marginal cost, it would also earn less profit. It would sell too many units and make a loss on each unit that it could not fully recapture by a higher access fee.

---

[11]*Jargon alert*: The prices used in two-part pricing are often referred to as *two-part tariffs*.

Figure 12.5 Two-Part Pricing with Identical Consumers

(a) Because all customers have the same individual demand curve as Valerie, D^1, the monopoly captures the entire potential consumer surplus using two-part pricing. The monopoly charges a per-unit fee price, p, equal to the marginal cost of 10, and an access fee, $\mathscr{L} = A = 2,450$, which is the blue triangle under the demand curve and above the per-unit price of $p = 10$. (b) Were the monopoly to set a price at 20, which is above its marginal cost,

it would earn less. It makes a profit of $B_1 = 600$ from the 10 it earns on the 60 units that Valerie buys at this higher price. However, the largest access fee the firm can make now is $\mathscr{L} = A_1 = 1,800$, so its total profit is 2,400, which is less than the 2,450 it makes if it sets its price equal to marginal cost. The difference is a deadweight loss of $C_1 = 50$, which is due to fewer units being sold at the higher price.

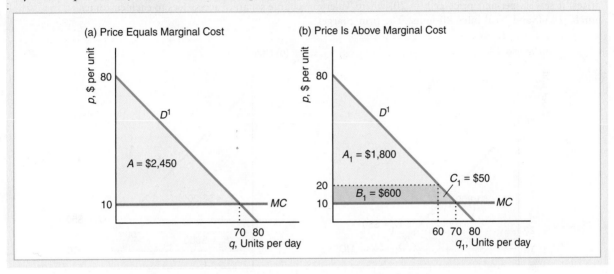

Two-Part Pricing with Differing Consumers

Two-part pricing is more complex if consumers have different demand curves. Suppose that the monopoly has two customers, Valerie, Consumer 1, and Neal, Consumer 2. Valerie's demand curve, $q_1 = 80 - p$, is D^1 in panel a of Figure 12.6 (which is the same as panel b of Figure 12.5), and Neal's demand curve, $q_2 = 100 - p$, is D^2 in panel b. The monopoly's marginal cost, $MC = m$, and average cost are constant at 10 per unit.

If the firm knows each customer's demand curve, can prevent resale, and can charge its customers different prices and access fees, it can capture the entire potential consumer surplus. The monopoly sets its price for both customers at $p = m = 10$ and sets its access fee equal to each customer's potential consumer surplus. At $p = 10$, Valerie buys 70 units (panel a), and Neal buys 90 units (panel b). If no access fee were charged, Valerie's consumer surplus, $CS_1 = \frac{1}{2}(80 - p)q_1 = \frac{1}{2}(80 - p)^2$, would equal the triangle below her demand curve and above the price line at 10, $A_1 + B_1 + C_1$, which is 2,450 ($= \frac{1}{2} \times 70 \times 70$). Similarly, Neal's consumer surplus, $CS_2 = \frac{1}{2}(100 - p)^2$, would be 4,050 ($= \frac{1}{2} \times 90 \times 90$), which is the triangle $A_2 + B_2 + C_2$. Thus, the monopoly charges a lump-sum access fee of $\mathscr{L}_1 = 2,450$ to Valerie and $\mathscr{L}_2 = 4,050$ to Neal, so that the customers receive no consumer surplus. The firm's total profit, $\mathscr{L}_1 + \mathscr{L}_2 = 2,450 + 4,050 = 6,500$, is the maximum possible profit, because the monopoly has captured the maximum potential consumer surplus from both customers.

Now suppose that the monopoly has to charge each consumer the same lump-sum fee, $\mathscr{L}$, and the same per-unit price, p. For example, because of legal restrictions, a telephone company charges all residential customers the same monthly fee and the same fee per call, even though the company knows that consumers' demands vary. As with group price discrimination, the monopoly does not capture the entire consumer surplus.

Figure 12.6 Two-Part Pricing with Differing Consumers

The monopoly faces two consumers. Valerie's demand curve is D^1 in panel a, and Neal's demand curve is D^2 in panel b. If the monopoly can set different prices and access fees for its two customers, it charges both a per-unit price of $p = 10$, which equals its marginal cost, and it charges an access fee of $\mathcal{L}_1 = 2,450 \ (= A_1 + B_1 + C_1)$ to Valerie and $\mathcal{L}_2 = 4,050 \ (= A_2 + B_2 + C_2)$ to Neal. If the monopoly cannot charge its customers different prices, it sets its per-unit price at $p = 20$, where Valerie purchases 60 and Neal buys 80 units. The firm charges both the same access fee of $\mathcal{L} = 1,800 = A_1$, which is Valerie's potential consumer surplus. The highest access fee that the firm could charge and have Neal buy is 3,200, but at that level, Valerie would not buy. By charging a price above its marginal cost, the firm captures $B_1 = 600$ from Valerie and $B_2 = 800$ from Neal. Thus, its total profit is $5,000 \ (= [2 \times 1,800] + 600 + 800)$, which is less than the $6,500 \ (= 2,450 + 4,050)$ it makes if it can charge separate access fees to each customer.

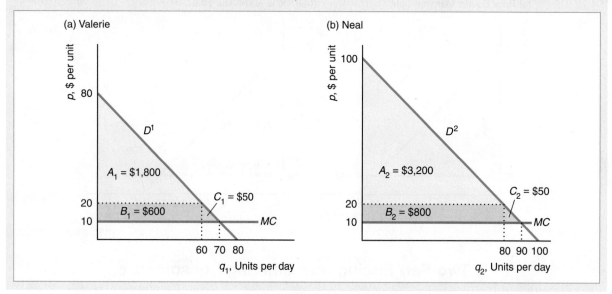

If the monopoly charges the lower fee, $\mathcal{L} = CS_1$, it sells to both consumers and its profit is

$$\pi = 2\mathcal{L} + (p - m)(q_1 + q_2) = (80 - p)^2 + (p - 10)(180 - 2p).$$

Setting the derivative of π with respect to p equal to zero, $-2(80 - p) + (180 - 2p) - 2(p - 10) = 0$, we find that the profit-maximizing price is $p = 20$. The monopoly charges a fee of $\mathcal{L} = CS_1 = \frac{1}{2}(80 - 20)^2 = 1,800$. Valerie buys 60 units, and Neal buys 80 units. The monopoly makes $(p - m) = (20 - 10) = 10$ on each unit, so it earns $B_1 + B_2 = 600 + 800 = 1,400$ from the units it sells. Its total profit is $5,000 = 2\mathcal{L} + B_1 + B_2 = (2 \times 1,800) + 1,400 = 5,000$.

If the monopoly charges the higher fee, $\mathcal{L} = CS_2$, it sells only to Consumer 2, and its profit is

$$\pi = \mathcal{L} + (p - m)q_2 = \frac{1}{2}(100 - p)^2 + (p - 10)(100 - p).$$

The monopoly's profit-maximizing price is $p = 10$, and its profit is $\mathcal{L} = CS_2 = 4,050$. Hence, the monopoly makes more by setting $\mathcal{L} = CS_1$ and selling to both customers at $p = 20$.

Thus, the monopoly maximizes its profit by setting the lower lump-sum fee and charging a price $p = 20$, which is above marginal cost. The monopoly earns less than if it could charge each customer a separate access fee: $5,000 < 6,500$. Valerie has no consumer surplus, but Neal enjoys a consumer surplus of $1,400 \ (= 3,200 - 1,800)$.

Why does the monopoly charge a price above marginal cost when using two-part pricing? By raising its price, the monopoly earns more per unit from both types of customers but lowers its customers' potential consumer surplus. Thus, if the monopoly can capture each customer's potential surplus by charging different lump-sum fees, it sets its price equal to marginal cost. However, if the monopoly cannot capture all the potential consumer surplus because it must charge everyone the same lump-sum fee, the increase in profit from Neal due to the higher price more than offsets the reduction in the lump-sum fee from Valerie.[12]

APPLICATION

Pricing iTunes

Prior to 2009, Apple's iTunes music store, the giant of music downloading, used *uniform pricing*, where it sold songs at 99¢ each. However, some of its competitors, such as Amazon MP3, did not use uniform pricing. Some record labels told Apple that they would not renew their contracts if Apple continued to use uniform pricing. Apparently responding to this pressure and the success of some of its competitors, Apple switched in 2009 to selling each song at one of three prices.

Did Apple's one-price-for-all-songs policy cost it substantial potential profit? How do consumer surplus and deadweight loss vary with pricing methods such as a single price, song-specific prices, price discrimination, and two-part pricing? To answer such questions, Shiller and Waldfogel (2011) surveyed nearly 1,000 students and determined each person's willingness to pay for each of 50 popular songs. Then they used this information to calculate optimal pricing under various pricing schemes.

First, under uniform pricing, the same price is charged for every song. Second, under variable pricing, each song sells at its individual profit-maximizing price. Third, Apple could use two-part pricing, charging a monthly or annual fee for access and then a fixed price for each download.

If we know the demand curve and the marginal cost, we can determine the consumer surplus (*CS*), the producer surplus (*PS*), or profit, and the deadweight loss (*DWL*) from each pricing regime. By dividing each of these surplus measures by the total available surplus—the area under the demand curve and above the marginal cost curve—we can determine the shares of *CS*, *PS*, and *DWL*. The following table shows Shiller and Waldfogel's estimates of the percentage shares of *CS*, *PS*, and *DWL* under each of the three pricing methods:

Pricing	PS	CS	DWL
Uniform	28	42	29
Variable	29	45	26
Two-part price	37	43	20

If these students have tastes similar to those of the general market, then Apple raised its profit by switching from uniform pricing to variable pricing (see the *PS* column in the table). However, these results suggest that it could do even better using two-part pricing. Deadweight loss decreases under either of the alternatives to uniform pricing. Consumers do best with variable pricing, but two-part pricing is also better for consumers than uniform pricing.

---

[12]If the monopoly lowers its price from 20 to the marginal cost of 10, it loses B_1 from Valerie, but it can raise its access from A_1 to $A_1 + B_1 + C_1$, so its total profit from Valerie increases by $C_1 = 50$. The access fee it collects from Neal also rises by $B_1 + C_1 = 650$, but its profit from unit sales falls by $B_2 = 800$, so its total profit decreases by 150. The loss from Neal, -150, more than offsets the gain from Valerie, 50. Thus, the monopoly makes 100 more by charging a price of 20 rather than 10.

12.6 Tie-In Sales

Another type of nonuniform pricing is a **tie-in sale**, in which customers can buy one product or service only if they agree to purchase another as well. There are two forms of tie-in sales.

The first type is a **requirement tie-in sale**, in which customers who buy one product from a firm are required to make all their purchases of another product from that firm. Some firms sell durable machines such as copiers under the condition that customers buy copier services and supplies from them in the future. Because the amount of services and supplies that each customer buys differs, the per-unit price of copiers varies across customers.

The second type of tie-in sale is **bundling** (or a *package tie-in sale*), in which two goods are combined so that customers cannot buy either good separately. For example, a Whirlpool refrigerator is sold with shelves, and a Hewlett-Packard inkjet printer comes with printer cartridges.

Most tie-in sales increase efficiency by lowering transaction costs. Indeed, tie-ins for efficiency purposes are so common that we hardly think about them. Presumably, no one would want to buy a shirt without buttons attached, so selling shirts with buttons lowers transaction costs. Because virtually everyone wants certain basic software, most companies sell computers with that software installed. Firms also often use tie-in sales to increase profits, as we now consider.

Requirement Tie-In Sales

Frequently, a firm cannot tell which customers are going to use its product the most and hence are willing to pay the most for it. These firms may be able to use a requirement tie-in sale to identify heavy users of the product and charge them more.

APPLICATION

IBM

In the 1930s, IBM increased its profit by using a requirement tie-in. IBM produced card punch machines, sorters, and tabulating machines (precursors of modern computers) that computed by using punched cards. Rather than selling its card punch machines, IBM leased them under the condition that the lease would terminate if any card not manufactured by IBM were used. (By leasing the equipment, IBM avoided resale problems and forced customers to buy its tabulating cards.) IBM charged customers more per card than other firms would have charged. If we think of the extra payment per card as part of the cost of using the machine, this requirement tie-in resulted in heavy users' paying more for the machines than others did. This tie-in was profitable because heavy users were willing to pay more.[13]

---

[13]The U.S. Supreme Court held that IBM's actions violated antitrust laws because they lessened competition in the (potential) market for tabulating cards. IBM's defense was that its requirement was designed to protect its reputation. IBM claimed that inferior tabulating cards might cause its machines to malfunction and that consumers would falsely blame IBM's equipment. The Court did not accept IBM's argument. The Court apparently did not understand—or at least care about—the price discrimination aspect of IBM's actions.

Bundling

Firms sometimes bundle even when there are no production advantages and transaction costs are small. Bundling allows firms to increase their profit by charging different prices to different consumers based on the consumers' willingness to pay. For example, a computer firm may sell a package including a computer and a printer for a single price even if there are no cost savings from selling these products together.

There are two common types of bundling. Some firms engage in *pure bundling*, in which only a package deal is offered, as when a cable company sells a bundle of Internet, phone, and television services for a single price but does not allow customers to purchase the individual services separately. Other firms use *mixed bundling*, in which the goods are available on a stand-alone basis in addition to being available as part of a bundle, such as a cable company that allows consumers to buy the bundle or the individual services they want.

Pure Bundling. Microsoft Works is a pure bundle. The primary components of this bundle are a word processing program and a spreadsheet program. These programs have fewer features than Microsoft's flagship Word and Excel programs and are not sold individually but only as a bundle.

Whether it pays for Microsoft to sell a bundle or sell the programs separately depends on how reservation prices for the components vary across customers. We use an example of a firm selling word processing and spreadsheet programs to illustrate two cases, one in which pure bundling produces a higher profit than selling the components separately, and one in which pure bundling is not profitable.

The marginal cost of producing an extra copy of either type of software is essentially zero, so the firm's revenue equals its profit. The firm must charge all customers the same price—it cannot price discriminate.

The firm has two customers, Alisha and Bob. The first two columns of Table 12.1 show the reservation prices for each consumer for the two products. Alisha's reservation price for the word processing program, 120, is greater than Bob's, 90; however, Alisha's reservation price for the spreadsheet program, 50, is less than Bob's, 70. The reservation prices are *negatively correlated*: the customer who has the higher reservation price for one product has the lower reservation price for the other product. The third column of the table shows each consumer's reservation price for the bundle, which is the sum of the reservations prices for the two underlying products.

If the firm sells the two products separately, it maximizes its profit by charging 90 for the word processor and selling to both consumers, so that its profit is 180, rather than charging 120 and selling only to Alisha. If it charges between 90 and 120, it still only sells to Alisha and earns less than if it charges 120. Similarly, the firm maximizes its profit by selling the spreadsheet program for 50 to both consumers, earning 100, rather than charging 70 and selling to only Bob. The firm's total profit from selling the programs separately is 280 (= 180 + 100).

Table 12.1 Negatively Correlated Reservation Prices

	Word Processor	Spreadsheet	Bundle
Alisha	120	50	170
Bob	90	70	160
Profit maximizing price	90	50	160
Units sold	2	2	2

If the firm sells the two products in a bundle, it maximizes its profit by charging 160, selling to both customers, and earning 320. This is a better outcome than charging 170 and selling only to Alisha. Pure bundling is more profitable for the firm because it earns 320 from selling the bundle and only 280 from selling the programs separately.

Pure bundling is more profitable because the firm captures more of the consumers' potential consumer surplus—their reservation prices. With separate prices, Alisha has consumer surplus of 30 (= 120 − 90) from the word processing program and none from the spreadsheet program. Bob receives no consumer surplus from the word processing program and 20 from the spreadsheet program. Thus, the total consumer surplus is 50. With pure bundling, Alisha gets 10 of consumer surplus and Bob gets none, so the total is only 10. Thus, the pure bundling approach captures 40 more potential consumer surplus than does pricing separately.

Whether pure bundling increases the firm's profit depends on the reservation prices. Table 12.2 shows the reservation prices for two different consumers, Carol and Dmitri. Carol has higher reservation prices for both products than does Dmitri. These reservation prices are *positively correlated*: A higher reservation price for one product is associated with a higher reservation price for the other product.

If the programs are sold separately, the firm charges 90 for the word processor, sells to both consumers, and earns 180. However, it makes more charging 90 for the spreadsheet program and selling only to Carol, than it does charging 40 for the spreadsheet, selling to both consumers, and earning 80. The firm's total profit if it prices separately is 270 (= 180 + 90).

If the firm uses pure bundling, it maximizes its profit by charging 130 for the bundle, selling to both customers, and making 260. Because the firm earns more selling the programs separately, 270, than when it bundles them, 260, pure bundling is not profitable in this example.

Table 12.2   Positively Correlated Reservation Prices

	Word Processor	Spreadsheet	Bundle
Carol	100	90	190
Dmitri	90	40	130
Profit maximizing price	90	90	130
Units Sold	2	1	2

Mixed Bundling. Restaurants, computer software firms, and many other companies commonly use mixed bundling, and allow consumers to buy the pure bundle or to buy any of the bundle's components separately. For example, Microsoft not only sells the Microsoft Office bundle, which includes Microsoft Word, Microsoft Excel, and various other programs, but it also sells the various programs individually. The following example illustrates that mixed bundling may be more profitable than pure bundling or only selling components separately because it captures more of the potential consumer surplus.

A firm that sells word processing and spreadsheet programs has four potential customers with the reservation prices in Table 12.3. Again, the firm's cost of production is zero, so maximizing its profit is equivalent to maximizing its revenue.

Aaron, a writer, places high value on the word processing program but has relatively little use for a spreadsheet program. Dorothy, an accountant, has the opposite pattern of preferences—placing a high value on having the spreadsheet program but little value on a word processing program. Brigitte and Charles have intermediate reservation prices. These reservation prices are negatively correlated: Customers

Table 12.3 Reservation Prices and Mixed Bundling

	Word Processor	Spreadsheet	Suite (Bundle)
Aaron	120	30	150
Brigitte	110	90	200
Charles	90	110	200
Dorothy	30	120	150

with a relatively high reservation price for one product have relatively low reservation prices for the other program. To determine its best pricing strategy, the firm calculates its profit by pricing the components separately, using pure bundling, and engaging in mixed bundling.

If the firm prices each program separately, it maximizes its profit by charging 90 for each product and selling each to three out of the four potential customers. It sells the word processing program to Aaron, Brigitte, and Charles. It sells the spreadsheet program to Brigitte, Charles, and Dorothy. Thus, it makes 270 (= 3 × 90) from each program or 540 total, which exceeds what it could earn by setting any other price per program.[14]

However, the firm can make a higher profit by engaging in pure bundling. It can charge 150 for the bundle, sell to all four consumers, and earn 600, 60 more than the 540 it makes from selling the programs separately.

With mixed bundling, the firm obtains an even larger profit. It charges 200 for the bundle and 120 for each product separately. The firm earns 400 from Brigitte and Charles, who buy the bundle. Aaron buys only the word processing program for 120, and Dorothy buys only the spreadsheet for another 120, so that the firm makes 240 from its individual program sales. Thus, its profit is 640 (= 400 + 240) from mixed bundling, which exceeds the 600 from pure bundling, and the 540 from individual sales. We could construct other examples with different numbers where selling the programs separately would dominate (such as where reservation prices are positively correlated as in Table 12.2) or where the pure bundle does best (as in Table 12.1).

12.7 Advertising

You can fool all the people all the time if the advertising is right and the budget is big enough. —Joseph E. Levine

In addition to setting its price or quantity, a monopoly has to make other decisions, one of the most important of which is how much to advertise to maximize its net profit. As we will show, the rule for setting the profit-maximizing amount of advertising is the same as that for setting the profit-maximizing amount of output: Set advertising or quantity where the marginal benefit (the extra gross profit from one more unit of advertising or the marginal revenue from one more unit of output) equals its marginal cost.

Advertising is only one way to promote a product. Other promotional activities include providing free samples and using sales agents. Some promotional tactics are

[14]If it sets a price of a program as low as 30, it sells both programs to all four customers, but makes only 240. If it charges 110 it sells each program to two customers and earns 440. If it charges 120, it makes a single sale of each program, so it earns 240.

subtle. For example, grocery stores place sugary breakfast cereals on lower shelves so they are at a child's eye level.[15]

A successful advertising or promotional campaign shifts the monopoly's demand curve by changing consumers' tastes or informing consumers about new products. The monopoly may be able to change the tastes of some consumers by telling them that a famous athlete or performer uses the product. Children and teenagers are frequently the targets of such advertising. If the advertising convinces some consumers that they can't live without the product, the monopoly's demand curve may shift outward and become less elastic at the new equilibrium, at which the firm charges a higher price for its product.

If the firm informs potential consumers about a new use for the product, demand at each price increases. For example in 1927, a Heinz advertisement suggested that putting its baked beans on toast was a good way to eat beans for breakfast as well as dinner. By so doing, it created a British national dish and shifted the demand curve for its product to the right.

Deciding Whether to Advertise

I have always believed that writing advertisements is the second most profitable form of writing. The first, of course, is ransom notes… —Philip Dusenberry

Even if advertising succeeds in shifting the demand curve, it may not pay for the firm to advertise. If advertising shifts the demand curve outward or makes it less elastic, the firm's *gross profit*, which ignores the cost of advertising, must rise. However, the firm undertakes this advertising campaign only if it expects its *net profit* (gross profit minus the cost of advertising) to increase.

To illustrate a monopoly's decision making, in Figure 12.7 we examine Coke's analysis of how much to advertise. For simplicity, we model Coke as a monopoly (by ignoring Pepsi and other brands). We use the estimated demand curve for Coke, which takes into account its advertising, from Gasmi, Laffont, and Vuong (1992). If Coke does not advertise, it faces the demand curve D^1. If Coke advertises at its current level, its demand curve shifts from D^1 to D^2.

Coke's marginal cost, MC, is constant and equals its average cost, AC, at $5 per unit (10 cases). Before advertising, Coke chooses its output, $Q_1 = 24$ million units, where its marginal cost equals its marginal revenue, MR^1, based on its demand curve, D^1. The profit-maximizing equilibrium is e_1, and the monopoly charges a price of $p_1 = \$11$. The monopoly's profit, π_1, is a box whose height is the difference between the price and the average cost, $6 (= \$11 - \$5)$ per unit, and whose length is the quantity, 24 units (tens of millions of cases of 12-ounce cans).

After its advertising campaign (involving dancing polar bears or whatever) shifts its demand curve to D^2, Coke chooses a higher quantity, $Q_2 = 28$, where the MR^2 and MC curves intersect. In this new equilibrium, e_2, Coke charges $p_2 = \$12$. Despite this higher price, Coke sells more Coke after advertising because of the outward shift of its demand curve.

As a consequence, Coke's gross profit rises more than 36%. Coke's new gross profit is the rectangle $\pi_1 + B$, where the height of the rectangle is the new price minus the average cost, $7, and the length is the quantity, 28. Thus, the benefit, B, to Coke from advertising at this level is the increase in its gross profit. If its cost of

---

[15]According to a survey of 27 supermarkets nationwide by the Center for Science in the Public Interest, the average position of 10 child-appealing brands (44% sugar) was on the next-to-bottom shelf, while the average position of 10 adult brands (10% sugar) was on the next-to-top shelf.

Figure 12.7 Advertising

Suppose that Coke were a monopoly. If it does not advertise, its demand curve is D^1. At its actual level of advertising, its demand curve is D^2. Advertising increases Coke's gross profit (ignoring the cost of advertising) from π_1 to $\pi_2 = \pi_1 + B$. Thus, if the cost of advertising is less than the benefits from advertising, B, Coke's net profit (gross profit minus the cost of advertising) rises.

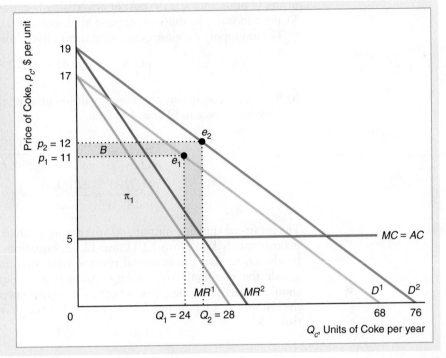

advertising is less than B, its net profit rises, and it pays for Coke to advertise at this level rather than not to advertise at all.

How Much to Advertise

The man who stops advertising to save money is like the man who stops the clock to save time.

In general, how much should a monopoly advertise to maximize its net profit? To answer this question, we consider what happens if the monopoly raises or lowers its advertising expenditures by $1, which is its marginal cost of an additional unit of advertising. If a monopoly spends an additional $1 on advertising and its gross profit rises by more than $1, its net profit rises, so the extra advertising pays. In contrast, the monopoly should reduce its advertising if the last dollar of advertising raises its gross profit by less than $1, causing its net profit to fall. Thus, the monopoly's level of advertising maximizes its net profit if the last dollar of advertising increases its gross profit by $1. In short, the rule for setting the profit-maximizing amount of advertising is the same as that for setting the profit-maximizing amount of output: Set advertising or quantity where the marginal benefit (the extra gross profit from one more unit of advertising or the marginal revenue from one more unit of output) equals its marginal cost.

Formally, to maximize its profit, a monopoly sets its quantity, Q, and level of advertising, A, to maximize its profit. Again, for simplicity, we assume that advertising affects only current sales, so that the inverse demand function the monopoly faces is $p = p(Q, A)$. That is, the price the monopoly charges to clear the market depends on how many units it sells and the amount of advertising. Consequently, the firm's revenue is $R = p(Q, A)Q = R(Q, A)$.

The firm's cost of production is $C(Q) + A$, where $C(Q)$ is the cost of manufacturing Q units and A is the cost of advertising because each unit of advertising costs $1 (by choosing the units of measure appropriately).

The monopoly maximizes its profit through its choice of quantity and advertising:

$$\max_{Q,A} \pi = R(Q, A) - C(Q) - A. \tag{12.10}$$

Its first-order conditions are found by differentiating the profit function in Equation 12.10 with respect to Q and A in turn:

$$\frac{\partial \pi(Q, A)}{\partial Q} = \frac{\partial R(Q, A)}{\partial Q} - \frac{dC(Q)}{dQ} = 0, \tag{12.11}$$

$$\frac{\partial \pi(Q, A)}{\partial A} = \frac{\partial R(Q, A)}{\partial A} - 1 = 0. \tag{12.12}$$

The profit-maximizing output and advertising levels are the Q^* and A^* that simultaneously satisfy Equations 12.11 and 12.12. Equation 12.11 says that output should be chosen so that the marginal revenue from one more unit of output, $\partial R/\partial Q$, equals the marginal cost, dC/dQ. According to Equation 12.12, the monopoly should advertise to the point where its marginal revenue or marginal benefit from the last unit of advertising, $\partial R/\partial A$, equals the marginal cost of the last unit of advertising, $1.

SOLVED PROBLEM 12.4

A monopoly's inverse demand function is $p = 100 - Q + 32A^{0.5}$, where Q is its quantity, p is its price, and A is the level of advertising. Its marginal cost of production is 10, and its cost of a unit of advertising is 1. What are the firm's profit-maximizing price, quantity, and level of advertising?

Answer

1. *Write the firm's profit function using its inverse demand function.* The monopoly's profit is

$$\pi = (100 - Q + 32A^{0.5})Q - 10Q - A = 90Q - Q^2 + 32A^{0.5}Q - A.$$

2. *Set the partial derivatives of the profit function with respect to Q and A to zero to obtain the equations that determine the profit maximizing levels, as in Equations 9.13 and 9.14.* The first-order conditions are

$$\frac{\partial \pi}{\partial Q} = 90 - 2Q + 32A^{0.5} = 0,$$

$$\frac{\partial \pi}{\partial A} = 16A^{-0.5} - 1 = 0.$$

3. *Solve this pair of equations in two unknowns, Q and A, for the profit maximizing levels.* We can rewrite the second equation as $A^{-0.5} = 1/16$, or $A = 4$. Substituting this value for A into the first equation yields $90 - 2Q + 32(4)^{0.5} = 0$, or $154 - 2Q = 0$, or $Q = 77$.

APPLICATION

Super Bowl
Commercials

Super Bowl commercials are the most expensive commercials on U.S. television. A 30-second spot during the Super Bowl averaged $3.5 million in 2012 (and is expected to cost $3.8 million in 2013). A high price for these commercials is not surprising because the cost of commercials generally increases with the number of viewers (*eyeballs* in industry jargon), and the Super Bowl is the most widely watched show, with over 111 million viewers in 2012. What is surprising is that Super Bowl advertising costs 2.5 times as much per viewer as other TV commercials.

However, a Super Bowl commercial is much more likely to influence viewers than commercials on other shows. The Super Bowl is not only a premier sports event, it showcases the most memorable commercials of the year, such as Apple's classic 1984 Macintosh ad, which is still discussed today. Indeed, many Super Bowl viewers are not even football fans—they watch to see these superior ads. Moreover, Super Bowl commercials receive extra exposure because these ads often *go viral* on the Internet.

Given that Super Bowl ads are more likely to be remembered by viewers, are these commercials worth the extra price? Obviously many advertisers believe so, as their demand for these ads has bid up the price. Kim (2011) found that immediately after a Super Bowl commercial airs, the advertising firm's stock value rises, which suggests that investors believe that Super Bowl commercials raise a firm's profits even given the high cost of the commercial. Ho, et al. (2009) found that, for the typical movie with a substantial advertising budget, a Super Bowl commercial raises theater revenues by more than the same expenditure on regular television advertising. However, for a movie that has a Super Bowl commercial, an additional expenditure on such commercials would exceed the additional revenues generated. Thus, these movie advertising managers appear to have made good decisions, spending close to the point where the marginal cost of a Super Bowl commercial equals the marginal benefit.

**CHALLENGE
SOLUTION**

Sale Price

By putting Heinz Ketchup on sale periodically, Heinz can price discriminate. To maximize its profit, how often should Heinz put its Ketchup on sale? Under what conditions does it pay for Heinz to have sales? To answer these questions, we study a simplified market in which Heinz competes with one other ketchup brand, which we refer to as generic ketchup.[16] Every *n* days, the typical consumer buys either Heinz or generic ketchup. (The number of days between purchases is determined by the storage space in consumers' homes and how frequently they eat ketchup.)

Switchers are price sensitive and buy the least expensive ketchup. They pay attention to price information and always know when Heinz is on sale.

Heinz considers holding periodic sales to capture switchers' purchases. The generic is sold at a competitive price equal to its marginal cost of production of $2.01 per unit. Suppose that Heinz's marginal cost is $MC = \$1$ per unit (due to its large scale) and that, if it only sold to its loyal customers, it would charge a monopoly price of $p = \$3$. Heinz's managers face a trade-off. If Heinz is

---

[16]The rest of the U.S. market consists primarily of Hunt ketchup (15%) and generic or house brands (22%). In the following discussion, we assume that customers who are loyal to Hunt or generic ketchup are unaffected by a Heinz sale, and hence ignore them.

infrequently on sale for less than the generic price, Heinz sells little to switchers. On the other hand, if Heinz is frequently on sale, it loses money on its sales to loyal customers.

We start by supposing that Heinz pricing policy is to charge a low, sales price, $2, once every n days. For the other $n - 1$ days, Heinz sells at the regular, non-sale (monopoly) price of $3, which is the monopoly price given the demand curve of the loyal customers. During a sale, the switchers buy enough Heinz to last them for n days until it's on sale again. Consequently, the switchers never buy the generic product. (Some other customers are loyal to the generic, so they buy it even when Heinz is on sale.)

If the loyal customers find that Heinz is on sale, which happens $1/n$ of all days, they buy n days worth at the sale price. Otherwise, they are willing to pay the regular price. If the other loyal customers were aware of this promotion pattern, they could get on a schedule such that they always bought on sale too, thereby making this strategy nonprofit maximizing. However, their shopping schedules are determined independently: They buy many goods and are not willing to distort their shopping patterns solely to buy this one good on sale.[17]

Could Heinz make more money by altering its promotion pattern? It does not want to place its good on sale more frequently because it would earn less from its loyal customers without making more sales to switchers. If it pays to hold sales at all, it does not want to have a sale less frequently because it would sell fewer units to switchers. During a promotion, Heinz wants to charge the highest price it can and yet still attract switchers, which is $2. If it sets a lower price, the quantity sold is unchanged, so its profit falls. If Heinz sets a sale price higher than $2, it loses all switchers.

Does it pay for Heinz to have sales? Whether it pays depends on the number of switchers, S, relative to the number of brand-loyal customers, B. If each customer buys one unit per day, then Heinz's profit per day if it sells only to loyals is $\pi = (p - MC)B = (3 - 1)B = 2B$, where $p = 3$ is Heinz's regular price and $MC = 1$ is its marginal and average cost. If Heinz uses the sale pricing scheme, its average profit per day is

$$\pi^* = 2B(n - 1)/n + (B + S)/n,$$

where the first term is the profit it makes, $2 per unit, selling B units to loyal customers for the fraction of days that Heinz is not on sale, $(n - 1)/n$, and the second term is the profit it makes, $1 per unit, selling B units to the loyal customers and S units to switchers for the fraction of days that it is on sale, $1/n$.

Thus, it pays to put Heinz on sale if $\pi < \pi^*$, or $2B < 2B(n - 1)/n + (B + S)/n$. Using algebra, we can simplify this expression to $B < S$. Thus, if there are more switchers than loyal customers, the sales policy is more profitable than selling at a uniform price to only loyal customers.

---

[17]We make this assumption for simplicity. In the real world, firms achieve a similar result by having random sales or by placing ads announcing sales where the ads are seen primarily by the switchers.

SUMMARY

1. **Conditions for Price Discrimination.** A firm can price discriminate if it has market power, knows which customers will pay more for each unit of output, and can prevent customers who pay low prices from reselling to those who pay high prices. A firm earns a higher profit from price discrimination than from uniform pricing because (a) the firm captures some or all of the consumer surplus of customers who are willing to pay more than the uniform price and (b) the firm sells to some people who would not buy at the uniform price.

2. **Perfect Price Discrimination.** To perfectly price discriminate, a firm must know the maximum amount each customer is willing to pay for each unit of output. If a firm charges customers the maximum that each is willing to pay for each unit of output, the monopoly captures all potential consumer surplus and sells the efficient (competitive) level of output. Compared to competition, total welfare is the same, consumers are worse off, and firms are better off under perfect price discrimination.

3. **Group Price Discrimination.** A firm that does not have enough information to perfectly price discriminate may know the relative elasticities of demand of groups of its customers. Such a profit-maximizing firm charges groups of consumers prices in proportion to their elasticities of demand, the group of consumers with the least elastic demand paying the highest price. Welfare is less under group price discrimination than under competition or perfect price discrimination but may be greater or less than that under single-price monopoly.

4. **Nonlinear Pricing.** Some firms charge customers different prices depending on how many units they purchase. If consumers who want more water have less elastic demands, a water utility can increase its profit by using declining-block pricing, in which the price for the first few gallons of water is higher than that for additional gallons.

5. **Two-Part Pricing.** By charging consumers one fee for the right to buy and a separate price per unit, firms may earn higher profits than if they charge only for each unit sold. If a firm knows its customers' demand curves, it can use two-part pricing (instead of perfect price discrimination) to capture the entire consumer surplus. Even if the firm does not know each customer's demand curve or cannot vary two-part pricing across customers, it can use two-part pricing to make a larger profit than it could get if it set a single price.

6. **Tie-In Sales.** A firm may increase its profit by using a tie-in sale that allows customers to buy one product only if they also purchase another product. In a requirement tie-in sale, customers who buy one good must make all of their purchases of another good or service from that firm. With bundling (a package tie-in sale), a firm sells only a bundle of two goods together. Prices differ across customers under both types of tie-in sales.

7. **Advertising.** A monopoly advertises or engages in other promotional activities to shift its demand curve to the right or to make it less elastic so as to raise its profit (taking account of its advertising expenses).

EXERCISES

■ = *exercise is available on* MyEconLab; * = *answer appears at the back of this book;* **M** = *mathematical problem.*

1. Conditions for Price Discrimination

1.1 As of 2012, the pharmaceutical companies Abbott Laboratories, AstraZeneca, Aventis Pharmaceuticals, Bristol-Myers Squibb Company, Eli Lilly, Glaxo-SmithKline, Janssen, Johnson & Johnson, Novartis, Ortho-McNeil, and Pfizer provide low-income, elderly people with a card guaranteeing them discounts on many prescription medicines. Why would these firms do that?

1.2 Alexx's monopoly currently sells its product at a single price. What conditions must be met so that he can profitably price discriminate?

*1.3 Spenser's Superior Stoves advertises a one-day sale on electric stoves. The ad specifies that no phone orders will be accepted and that the purchaser must transport the stove. Why does the firm include these restrictions?

*1.4 Many colleges provide students from low-income families with scholarships, subsidized loans, and other programs so that they pay lower tuitions than students from high-income families. Explain why universities behave this way.

1.5 Disneyland price discriminates by charging lower entry fees for children than for adults and for local residents than for other visitors. Why does it not have a resale problem?

1.6 The 2002 production run of 25,000 new Thunderbirds included only 2,000 cars for Canada. Yet potential buyers besieged Canadian Ford dealers. Many hoped to make a quick profit by reselling the cars in the United States. Reselling was relatively easy, and shipping costs were comparatively low. When the Thunderbird with the optional hardtop first became available at the end of 2001, Canadians paid C\$56,550 for the vehicle, while U.S. customers spent up to C\$73,000 in the United States. Why? Why did Ford require Canadian dealers to sign an agreement that prohibited moving vehicles to the United States?

1.7 On July 12, 2012, Hertz charged \$126.12 to rent a Nissan Altima for one day in New York City, but only \$55.49 a day in Miami. Is this price discrimination? Explain.

2. Perfect Price Discrimination

2.1 If a monopoly faces an inverse demand curve of $p = 90 - Q$, has a constant marginal and average cost of 30, and can perfectly price discriminate, what is its profit? What are the consumer surplus, welfare, and deadweight loss? How would these results change if the firm were a single-price monopoly? (*Hint*: See Solved Problem 12.1.) **M**

2.2 Using the information in the Application "Botox Revisited," determine how much Allergan loses by being a single-price monopoly rather than a perfectly price-discriminating monopoly. Explain.

2.3 See the Application "Google Uses Bidding for Ads to Price Discriminate," which discusses how advertisers on Google's Web site bid for the right for their ads to be posted when people search for certain phrases. Should a firm that provides local services (such as plumbing or pest control) expect to pay more or less for an ad in a small town or a large city? Why?

2.4 To promote her platinum-selling CD *Feels Like Home* in 2005, singer Norah Jones toured the country giving live performances. However, she sold an average of only two-thirds of the tickets available for each show, T^* (Robert Levine, "The Trick of Making a Hot Ticket Pay," *New York Times*, June 6, 2005, C1, C4). Suppose that the local promoter is the monopoly provider of each concert. Each concert hall has a fixed number of seats.

a. Assume that the promoter's cost is independent of the number of people who attend the concert (Ms. Jones received a guaranteed payment). Graph the promoter's marginal cost curve for the

concert hall, where the number of tickets sold is on the horizontal axis. Be sure to show T^*.

b. If the monopoly can charge a single market price, does the concert's failure to sell out prove that the monopoly set too high a price? Explain.

c. Would your answer in part b be the same if the monopoly can perfectly price discriminate? Use a graph to explain.

2.5 A firm is a natural monopoly (see Chapter 11). Its marginal cost curve is flat, and its average cost curve is downward sloping (because it has a fixed cost). The firm can perfectly price discriminate. Use a graph to show how much the monopoly produces, Q^*. Show graphically and mathematically that a monopoly might shut down if it can only set a single price but operate if it can perfectly price discriminate. **M**

3. Group Discrimination

3.1 A monopoly has a marginal cost of zero and faces two groups of consumers. At first, the monopoly could not prevent resale, so it maximized its profit by charging everyone the same price, $p = \$5$. No one from the first group chose to purchase. Now the monopoly can prevent resale, so it decides to price discriminate. Will total output expand? Why or why not? What happens to profit and consumer surplus?

3.2 A firm charges different prices to two groups. Would the firm ever operate where it was suffering a loss from its sales to the low-price group? Explain.

3.3 A monopoly sells in two countries, and resale between the countries is impossible. The demand curves in the two countries are $p_1 = 100 - Q_1$ and $p_2 = 120 - 2Q_2$. The monopoly's marginal cost is $m = 30$. Solve for the equilibrium price in each country. **M**

3.4 Hershey Park sells tickets at the gate and at local municipal offices. There are two groups of people. Suppose that the demand function for people who purchase tickets at the gate is $Q_G = 10,000 - 100p_G$ and that the demand function for people who purchase tickets at municipal offices is $Q_G = 9,000 - 100p_G$. The marginal cost of each patron is 5.

a. If Hershey Park cannot successfully segment the two markets, what are the profit-maximizing price and quantity? What is its maximum possible profit?

b. If the people who purchase tickets at one location would never consider purchasing them at the other and Hershey Park can successfully price discriminate, what are the profit-maximizing price and quantity? What is its maximum possible profit? **M**

*3.5 A patent gave Sony a legal monopoly to produce a robot dog called Aibo ("eye-BO"). The Chihuahua-sized robot could sit, beg, chase balls, dance, and play an electronic tune. When Sony started selling the toy in July 1999, it announced that it would sell 3,000 Aibo robots in Japan for about $2,000 each and a limited litter of 2,000 in the United States for about $2,500 each. Suppose that Sony's marginal cost of producing Aibos is $500. Its inverse demand curve was $p_J = 3,500 - \frac{1}{2}Q_J$ in Japan and $p_A = 4,500 - Q_A$ in the United States. Solve for the equilibrium prices and quantities (assuming that U.S. customers cannot buy robots from Japan). Show how the profit-maximizing price ratio depended on the elasticities of demand in the two countries. What are the deadweight losses in each country, and in which is the loss from monopoly pricing greater? **M**

*3.6 A monopoly sells its good in the U.S. and Japanese markets. The American inverse demand function is $p_A = 100 - Q_A$, and the Japanese inverse demand function is $p_J = 80 - 2Q_J$, where both prices, p_A and p_J, are measured in dollars. The firm's marginal cost of production is $m = 20$ in both countries. If the firm can prevent resale, what price will it charge in both markets? (*Hint*: The monopoly determines its optimal [monopoly] price in each country separately because customers cannot resell the good.) **M**

3.7 Universal Studios sold the *Mamma Mia!* DVD around the world. Universal charged $21.40 in Canada and $32 in Japan—more than the $20 it charged in the United States. Given that Universal had a constant marginal cost of $1, determine what the elasticities of demand must be in Canada and in Japan if Universal was profit maximizing. **M**

*3.8 Warner Home Entertainment sold the *Harry Potter and the Prisoner of Azkaban* two-DVD movie set in China for about $3, which was only one-fifth the U.S. price, and sold about 100,000 units. The price was extremely low in China because Chinese consumers are less wealthy and because (lower-quality) pirated versions were available in China for 72¢–$1.20, compared to the roughly $3 required to purchase the legal version (Jin Baicheng, "Powerful Ally Joins Government in War on Piracy," *China Daily*, March 11, 2005, 13). Assuming a marginal cost of $1, what is the Chinese elasticity of demand? Derive the demand function for China and illustrate Warner's policy in China using a figure similar to panel a in Figure 12.3. **M**

3.9 A monopoly sells its good in the United States, where the elasticity of demand is −2, and in Japan, where the elasticity of demand is −5. Its marginal cost is 10. At what price does the monopoly sell its good in each country if resale is impossible? **M**

3.10 How would the analysis in Solved Problem 12.2 change if $m = 7$ or if $m = 4$? (*Hint*: Where $m = 4$, the marginal cost curve crosses the *MR* curve three times—if we include the vertical section. The single-price monopoly will choose one of these three points where its profit is maximized.)

*3.11 A monopoly sells to n_1 consumers in Country 1 and n_2 in Country 2, where each person in Country 1 has a constant elasticity demand function of $q_1 = p^{\varepsilon_1}$ and every person in Country 2 has a demand function of $q_2 = p^{\varepsilon_2}$. Thus, the country demand functions are $Q_1 = n_1 p^{\varepsilon_1}$ and $Q_2 = n_2 p^{\varepsilon_2}$. Output can be manufactured at constant marginal cost m. What prices does the monopoly charge in the two countries if it can group price discriminate? If the monopoly cannot price discriminate, what price does it charge?

3.12 Show that the equilibrium elasticities in the two countries must be equal in Solved Problem 12.3. **M**

3.13 According to a report from the Foundation for Taxpayer and Consumer Rights, gasoline costs twice as much in Europe than in the United States because taxes are higher in Europe. However, the amount per gallon net of taxes that U.S. consumers pay is higher than that paid by Europeans. The report concludes that "U.S. motorists are essentially subsidizing European drivers, who pay more for taxes but substantially less into oil company profits" (Tom Doggett, "US Drivers Subsidize European Pump Prices," *Reuters*, August 31, 2006). Given that oil companies have market power and can price discriminate across countries, is it reasonable to conclude that U.S. consumers are subsidizing Europeans? Explain your answer.

3.14 Does a monopoly's ability to price discriminate between two groups of consumers depend on its marginal cost curve? Why or why not? [Consider two cases: (a) the marginal cost is so high that the monopoly is uninterested in selling to one group; (b) the marginal cost is low enough that the monopoly wants to sell to both groups.]

4. Nonlinear Price Discrimination

4.1 Are all the customers of the monopoly that uses block pricing in panel a of Figure 12.4 worse off than they would be if the firm set a single price (panel b)? Why or why not?

4.2 In panel b of Figure 12.4, the single-price monopoly faces a demand curve of $p = 90 - Q$ and a constant marginal (and average) cost of $m = \$30$. Find the profit-maximizing quantity (or price) using math. Determine the profit, consumer surplus, welfare, and deadweight loss. **M**

4.3 Suppose that the nonlinear price discriminating monopoly in panel a of Figure 12.4 can set three prices, depending on the quantity a consumer purchases. The firm's profit is

$$\pi = p_1 Q_1 + p_2(Q_2 - Q_1) + p_3(Q_3 - Q_2) - mQ_3,$$

where p_1 is the high price charged on the first Q_1 units (first block), p_2 is a lower price charged on the next $Q_2 - Q_1$ units, p_3 is the lowest price charged on the $Q_3 - Q_2$ remaining units, Q_3 is the total number of units actually purchased, and $m = \$30$ is the firm's constant marginal and average cost. Use calculus to determine the profit-maximizing p_1, p_2, and p_3. **M**

4.4 Consider the nonlinear price discrimination analysis in panel a of Figure 12.4.

a. Suppose that the monopoly can make consumers a take-it-or-leave-it offer. The monopoly sets a price, p^*, and a minimum quantity, Q^*, that a consumer must pay to be able to purchase any units at all. What price and minimum quantity should it set to achieve the same outcome as it would if it perfectly price discriminated?

b. Now suppose that the monopoly charges a price of $90 for the first 30 units and a price of $30 for subsequent units, but requires that a consumer buy at least 30 units to be allowed to buy any units. Compare this outcome to the one in part a and to the perfectly price-discriminating outcome. **M**

5. Two-Part Pricing

5.1 Using math, show why two-part pricing causes customers who purchase few units to pay more per unit than customers who buy more units. **M**

5.2 Knoebels Amusement Park in Elysburg, Pennsylvania, charges an access fee, $\mathscr{L}$, to enter its Crystal Pool. It also charges p per trip down the pool's water slides. Suppose that 400 teenagers visit the park, each of whom has a demand function of $q_1 = 5 - p$, and that 400 seniors also visit, each of whom has a demand function of $q_2 = 4 - p$. Knoebels' objective is to set $\mathscr{L}$ and p so as to maximize its profit given that it has no (non-sunk) cost and must charge both groups the same prices. What are the optimal $\mathscr{L}$ and p? **M**

5.3 Joe has just moved to a small town with only one golf course, the Northlands Golf Club. His inverse demand function is $p = 120 - 2q$, where q is the number of rounds of golf that he plays per year. The manager of the Northlands Club negotiates separately with each person who joins the club and can therefore charge individual prices. This manager has a good idea of what Joe's demand curve is and offers Joe a special deal, where Joe pays an annual membership fee and can play as many rounds as he wants at $20, which is the marginal cost his round imposes on the club. What membership fee would maximize profit for the club? The manager could have charged Joe a single price per round. How much extra profit does the club earn by using two-part pricing? **M**

5.4 Joe in Question 5.3 marries Susan, who is also an enthusiastic golfer. Susan wants to join the Northlands Club. The manager believes that Susan's inverse demand curve is $p = 100 - 2q$. The manager has a policy of offering each member of a married couple the same two-part prices, so he offers them both a new deal. What two-part pricing deal maximizes the club's profit? Will this new pricing have a higher or lower access fee and per unit fee than in Joe's original deal? How much more would the club make if it charges Susan and Joe separate prices? **M**

5.5 As described in the Application "Pricing iTunes," Shiller and Waldfogel (2011) estimated that if iTunes used two-part pricing charging an annual access fee and a low price per song, it would raise its profit by about 30% relative to what it would earn using uniform pricing or variable pricing. Assume that iTunes uses two-part pricing and assume that the marginal cost of an additional download is zero. How should iTunes set its profit-maximizing price per song if all consumers are identical? Illustrate profit-maximizing two-part pricing in a diagram for the identical consumer case. Explain why the actual profit-maximizing price per song is positive.

6. Tie-In Sales

6.1 A monopoly sells two products, of which consumers want only one. Assuming that it can prevent resale, can the monopoly increase its profit by bundling them, forcing consumers to buy both goods? Explain.

6.2 A computer hardware firm sells both laptop computers and printers. Through the magic of focus groups, their pricing team determines that they have an equal number of three types of customers, and that these customers' reservation prices are

	Laptop	Printer	Bundle
Customer A	$800	$100	$900
Customer B	$1,000	$50	$1,050
Customer C	$600	$150	$750

a. If the firm were to charge only individual prices (not use the bundle price), what prices should is set for its laptops and printers to maximize profit? Assuming for simplicity that the firm has only one customer of each type, how much does it earn in total?

b. After conducting a costly study, an outside consultant claims that the company could make more money from its customers if it sold laptops and printers together as a bundle instead of separately. Is the consultant right? Assume again that the firm has one customer of each type, how much does the firm earn in total from pure bundling?

c. Why does bundling pay or not pay?

6.3 The publisher Elsevier uses mixed-bundling pricing strategy. The publisher sells a university access to a bundle of 930 of its journals for $1.7 million for one year. It also offers the journals separately at individual prices. Because Elsevier offers the journals online (with password access), universities can track how often their students and faculty access journals and then cancel those journals that are seldom read. Suppose that a publisher offers a university only three journals—A, B, and C—at the unbundled, individual annual subscription prices of $p_A = \$1,600$, $p_B = \$800$, and $p_C = \$1,500$. Suppose a university's willingness to pay for each of the journals is $v_A = \$2,000$, $v_B = \$1,100$, and $v_C = \$1,400$.

a. If the publisher offers the journals only at the individual subscription prices, to which journals does the university subscribe?

b. Given these individual prices, what is the highest price that the university is willing to pay for the three journals bundled together?

c. Now suppose that the publisher offers the same deal to a second university with willingness to pay $v_A = \$1,800$, $v_B = \$100$, and $v_C = \$2,100$. With the two universities, calculate the revenue-maximizing individual and bundle prices. **M**

7. Advertising

7.1 Show how a monopoly would solve for its optimal price and advertising level if it sets price instead of quantity. **M**

7.2 The demand a monopoly faces is

$$p = 100 - Q + A^{0.5},$$

where Q is its quantity, p is its price, and A is its level of advertising. Its marginal cost of production is 10, and its cost of a unit of advertising is 1. What is the firm's profit equation? Solve for the firm's profit-maximizing price, quantity, and level of advertising. (*Hint*: See Solved Problem 12.4.) **M**

7.3 What is the monopoly's profit-maximizing output, Q, and level of advertising, A, if it faces a demand curve of $p = a - bQ + cA^\alpha$, its constant marginal cost of producing output is m, and the cost of a unit of advertising is $1? (*Hint*: See Solved Problem 12.4.) **M**

7.4 For every dollar spent on advertising pharmaceuticals, revenue increases by about $4.20 (CNN, December 17, 2004). If this number is accurate and the firms are operating rationally, what (if anything) can we infer about marginal production and distribution costs? **M**

7.5 Using a diagram similar to Figure 12.7 to illustrate the effect of social media on the demand for Super Bowl commercials. (*Hint*: See the Application "Super Bowl Commercials.")

8. Challenge

8.1 Each week, a department store places a different item of clothing on sale. Give an explanation based on price discrimination for why the store conducts such regular sales.

8.2 In the Challenge Solution, did the sales method achieve the same group price discrimination outcome that would be achieved if Heinz could set separate prices for loyal customers and for switchers? Why or why not?

13

Game Theory

A camper awakens to the growl of a hungry bear and sees his friend putting on a pair of running shoes. "You can't outrun a bear," scoffs the camper. His friend coolly replies, "I don't have to. I only have to outrun you!"

Intel and Advanced Micro Devices (AMD) dominate the central processing unit (CPU) market for personal computers, with 95% of total sales. Intel uses aggressive advertising—its very successful *Intel Inside* campaign—and charges relatively high prices, while AMD uses little advertising and relies on the appeal of its lower prices. Even though their products are comparable in quality, Intel controls more than three-quarters of the market.

According to Salgado's (2008) estimated demand functions, consumers are willing to pay a large premium for the Intel brand. He found that, if Intel increased its advertising by 10% (holding prices constant), the total market demand would increase by 1%, while Intel's relative share would rise by more than 3%. Demand for AMD products would therefore fall. Salgado's work indicates that the two firms' shares would be roughly equal if they advertised equally (regardless of the level).

From the start of the personal computer era, Intel has been the 800-pound gorilla in the CPU market. Intel was founded in 1968 and created the first commercial microprocessor chip in 1971. With the growth of the personal computer (PC) market, microchips became Intel's primary business. Intel engages in a variety of strategic actions to dissuade AMD and other firms from taking its customers, including aggressive advertising and lawsuits to protect its intellectual property. In 1991, Intel launched the Intel Inside® marketing and branding campaign. Intel offered to share costs for any manufacturer's PC print ads if they included the Intel logo. Not only did these funds reduce the computer manufacturers' costs, but also the logo was intended to assure consumers that their computers were powered by the latest technology. Within six months, 300 computer manufacturers had agreed to support the campaign. After the manufacturers' ads started to appear, Intel advertised globally to explain the significance of the logo to consumers. The Intel Inside campaign was one of the first successful attempts at *ingredient branding*.

Advanced Micro Devices (AMD) was founded in 1969, but didn't compete in the microchip market until 1975 when it started selling a reverse-engineered clone of the Intel 8080 microprocessor. In 1982, AMD and Intel signed a contract allowing AMD to be a licensed second-source manufacturer of Intel's 8086 and 8088 processors because IBM would use these chips in its PCs only if it had two microchip sources.

Why has Intel chosen to advertise aggressively while AMD engages in relatively little advertising? At the end of the chapter, we discuss a possible explanation: Intel was able to act first and thereby gain an advantage. (In contrast, in Solved Problem 13.1, we examine the possible outcomes if both firms acted simultaneously.)

In deciding how to price its products or how much to advertise, Procter and Gamble considers the pricing and advertising of its main rivals, Johnson and Johnson and Unilever. In such markets with a small number of firms, called an *oligopoly*, the firms know that their actions significantly affect each other's profit, so their actions depend on how they think their rivals will act. To understand how such oligopolistic firms interact, we employ **game theory**: a set of tools used by economists and others to analyze strategic decision-making.

Game theory has many practical applications. It is useful for analyzing how oligopolistic firms set prices, quantities, and advertising levels; for bargaining between unions and management or between the buyer and seller of a car; for interactions between polluters and those harmed by pollution; for transactions between the buyers and sellers of homes; for negotiations between parties with different amounts of information (such as between car owners and auto mechanics); for bidding in auctions; and for many other economic interactions. Game theory is also used by political scientists and military planners for avoiding or fighting wars, by biologists for analyzing evolutionary biology and ecology, and by philosophers, computer scientists, and many others.

In this chapter, we concentrate on how oligopolistic firms behave within a *game*. A **game** is an interaction between players (such as individuals or firms) in which players use strategies. A **strategy** is a battle plan that specifies the *actions* or *moves* that a player will make conditional on the information available at each move and for any possible contingency. For example, a firm may use a simple business strategy where it produces 100 units of output regardless of what a rival does. In such a case, the strategy consists of a single action—producing 100 units of output. However, a strategy can consist of a combination of actions or moves, possibly contingent on what a rival does. For example, a firm might decide to produce a small quantity as long as its rival produced a small amount in the previous period, and a large quantity otherwise.

Payoffs are the benefits received by players from a game's outcome, such as profits for firms or incomes or utilities for individuals. A *payoff function* specifies each player's payoff as a function of the strategies chosen by all players. We normally assume that players seek to maximize their payoffs. In essence, this assumption simply defines what we mean by payoffs. Payoffs include all relevant benefits experienced by the players. Therefore, rational players should try to obtain the highest payoffs they can.

The **rules of the game** include the *timing* of players' moves (such as whether one player moves first), the various actions that are possible at a particular point in the game, and possibly other specific aspects of how the game is played. A full description of a game normally includes a statement of the players, the rules of the game (including the possible actions or strategies), and the payoff function, along with a statement regarding the information available to the players.

We start by examining how firms interact strategically in a single period, and then turn to strategic interactions in games that last for more than one period. The single-period game is called a **static game**, in which each player acts only once and the players act simultaneously (or, at least, each player acts without knowing its rivals' actions). For example, each of two rival firms might make simultaneous one-time-only decisions about where to locate its new factory.

In a **dynamic game**, players move either repeatedly or sequentially. Therefore, dynamic games may be repeated games or sequential games. In a *repeated game*, a basic component game or *constituent game* is repeated, perhaps many times. Firms choose from the same set of possible actions again and again. In a *sequential game*, one player moves before another moves, possibly making alternating moves, as in chess or tic-tac-toe. A game is also sequential if players have a sequence of different decisions to make, even if moves are made simultaneously with a rival. For example, two firms might play a game in which they initially simultaneously choose how much capital to invest and then later simultaneously decide how much output to produce.

To analyze a game, we must know how much information participants have. We start by assuming that the relevant information is *common knowledge* to the players and then we relax that assumption. **Common knowledge** is a piece of information known by all players, and it is known by all players to be known by all players, and it is known to be known to be known, and so forth. In particular, we initially assume that players have **complete information**, a situation in which the strategies and payoffs of the game are *common knowledge*.

The information possessed by firms affects the outcome of a game. The outcome of a game in which a particular piece of information is known by all firms may differ from the outcome when some firms are uninformed. A firm may suffer a worse outcome if it does not know the potential payoffs of other firms.

In this chapter, we examine four main topics

1. **Static Games.** A static game is played once by players who act simultaneously and hence do not know how other players will act at the time they must make a decision.

2. **Dynamic Games.** In a dynamic game, players may have perfect information about previous moves, but imperfect information about current moves if players act simultaneously within each period.

3. **Auctions.** An auction is a game where bidders have incomplete information about the value that other bidders place on the auctioned good or service.

4. **Behavioral Game Theory.** Some people make biased decisions based on psychological factors rather than using a rational strategy.

13.1 Static Games

We begin by examining static games, in which the players choose their actions simultaneously, have complete information about the payoff function, and play the game once. Our example is a simplified version of the real-world competition between United Airlines and American Airlines on the Los Angeles–Chicago route (based on the estimates of Brander and Zhang, 1990), where we allow the firms to choose only one of two possible quantities.

The game has the following characteristics. The two *players* or firms are United and American. They play a *static game*—they compete only once. The *rules* of the game specify the possible actions or strategies that the firms can take and when they can take them. Each firm has only two possible *actions*: Each can fly either 48 thousand or 64 thousand passengers per quarter between Chicago and Los Angeles.[1] Other than announcing their output levels, the firms cannot communicate, so they cannot make side deals or otherwise coordinate their actions. Each firm's *strategy* is to take one of the two actions, choosing either a low output (48 thousand passengers per quarter) or a high output (64 thousand). The firms announce their actions or strategies *simultaneously*.

The firms have *complete information*: They are aware of the possible strategies and the corresponding payoff (profit) to each firm. However, their information is imperfect in one important respect. Because they choose their output levels simultaneously, neither airline knows what action its rival will take when it makes its output decision.

[1] We relax this assumption in Chapter 14 where we allow the firms to choose any output level, and call that game the Cournot game.

Normal-Form Games

We examine a **normal-form** representation of a static game of complete information, which specifies the players in the game, their possible strategies, and the payoff function that specifies the players' payoffs for each combination of strategies. The normal-form representation of this static game is the *payoff matrix (profit matrix)* in Table 13.1.

This payoff matrix shows the profits for each of the four possible combinations of the strategies that the firms may choose. For example, if American chooses a large quantity, $q_A = 64$ units per quarter, and United chooses a small quantity, $q_U = 48$ units per quarter, the firms' profits are in the cell in the lower-left corner of the profit matrix. That cell shows that American's profit is 5.1 ($5.1 million) per quarter in the upper-right corner, and United's profit is 3.8 ($3.8 million) per quarter in the lower-left corner. We now have a full description of the game, including a statement of the players, the rules, a list of the allowable actions or strategies, the payoffs, and the available information.

Because the firms choose their strategies simultaneously, each firm selects a strategy that maximizes its profit *given what it believes the other firm will do*. The firms are playing a *noncooperative game of imperfect information* in which each firm must choose an action before observing the simultaneous action by its rival. Thus, while the players have complete information about all players' payoffs, they have imperfect information about how the other will act.

We can predict the outcome of some games by using the insight that rational players will avoid strategies that are *dominated* by other strategies. First, we show that in some games we can predict a game's outcome if each firm has a single best strategy that dominates all others. Then, we show that in other games, by sequentially eliminating dominated strategies, we are left with a single outcome. Finally, we note that the outcome of a broader class of games can be precisely predicted based on each player's choosing a *best response* to the other players' actions—the response that produces the largest possible payoff.

Dominant Strategies.
[W]hen you have eliminated the impossible, whatever remains, however improbable, must be the truth. —Sherlock Holmes (Sir Arthur Conan Doyle)

We can precisely predict the outcome of any game in which every player has a **dominant strategy**: a strategy that produces a higher payoff than any other strategy the player can use for every possible combination of its rivals' strategies. When a

Table 13.1 Dominant Strategies in a Quantity Setting, Prisoners' Dilemma Game

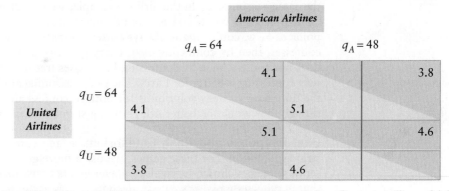

Note: Quantities are in thousands of passengers per quarter; (rounded) profits are in millions of dollars per quarter.

firm has a dominant strategy, a firm could have no belief about its rivals' choice of strategies that would cause it to choose one of its other, strictly *dominated strategies*.

Although firms do not always have dominant strategies, they have them in our airline game. American's managers can determine its dominant strategy using the following reasoning:

- *If United chooses the high-output strategy* ($q_U = 64$), *American's high-output strategy maximizes its profit*: Given United's strategy, American's profit is 4.1 ($4.1 million) with its high-output strategy ($q_A = 64$) and only 3.8 with its low-output strategy ($q_A = 48$). Thus, American is better off using a high-output strategy if United chooses its high-output strategy.
- *If United chooses the low-output strategy* ($q_U = 48$), *American's high-output strategy maximizes its profit*: Given United's strategy, American's profit is 5.1 with its high-output strategy and only 4.6 with its low-output strategy.
- *Thus, the high-output strategy is American's dominant strategy*: Whichever strategy United uses, American's profit is higher if it uses its high-output strategy. We show that American won't use its low-output strategy (because that strategy is dominated by the high-output strategy) by drawing a vertical, dark red line through American's low-output cell in Table 13.1.

By the same type of reasoning, United's high-output strategy is also a dominant strategy. We draw a horizontal, light red line through United's low-output strategy. Because the high-output strategy is a dominant strategy for both firms, we can predict that the outcome of this game is the pair of high-output strategies, $q_A = q_U = 64$. We show the resulting outcome—the cell in Table 13.1 where both firms use high-output strategies—by coloring that cell green.

A striking feature of this game is that the players choose strategies that do not maximize their joint profit. Each firm earns 4.6 if $q_A = q_U = 48$ rather than the 4.1 they actually earn by setting $q_A = q_U = 64$. In this type of game—called a **prisoners' dilemma** game—all players have dominant strategies that lead to a profit (or another payoff) that is inferior to what they could achieve if they cooperated and pursued alternative strategies.

The prisoners' dilemma takes its name from a classic cops-and-robbers example. The police arrest Larry and Duncan and put them in separate rooms so that they cannot talk to each other. An assistant district attorney (DA) tells Larry, "We have enough evidence to convict you both of a minor crime for which you will each serve a year in prison. If you confess and give evidence against your partner while he stays silent, we can convict him of a major crime for which he will serve five years and you will be released. If you both confess, you will each get two years."

Meanwhile, another assistant DA is proposing an identical offer to Duncan. By the same reasoning as in the airline example, we expect both Larry and Duncan to confess because confessing is a dominant strategy for each of them. From Larry's point of view, confessing is always better no matter what Duncan does. If Duncan confesses, then by confessing also, Larry gets two years instead of five. If Duncan does not confess, then by confessing Larry goes free instead of serving a year. Either way confessing is better for Larry. The same reasoning applies to Duncan. Therefore, the dominant strategy solution is for both to confess and get two years in jail, even though they would be better off, getting just one year in jail, if they both kept quiet.

Best Response and Nash Equilibrium. Many games do not have a dominant strategy solution. For these games, we use a more general approach. For any given set of strategies chosen by rivals, a player wants to use its **best response**: the strategy that maximizes a player's payoff given its beliefs about its rivals' strategies.

A dominant strategy is a strategy that is a best response to *all possible* strategies that a rival might use. Thus, a dominant strategy is a best response. However, even if a dominant strategy does not exist, each firm can determine its best response to *any possible* strategies chosen by its rivals.

The idea that players use best responses is the basis for the Nash equilibrium, a solution concept for games formally introduced by John Nash (1951). A set of strategies is a **Nash equilibrium** if, when all other players use these strategies, no player can obtain a higher payoff by choosing a different strategy. An appealing property of the Nash equilibrium is that it is self-enforcing: If each player uses a Nash equilibrium strategy, then no player would want to deviate by choosing another strategy. In other words, no player regrets its strategy choice when it learns the strategies chosen by the other players. Each player says "given the strategies chosen by my rivals, I made the best possible choice—I chose my best response."

The Nash equilibrium is the primary solution concept used by economists in analyzing games. It allows us to find solutions to more games than just those with a dominant strategy solution. If a game has a dominant strategy solution then that solution must also be a Nash equilibrium. However, a Nash equilibrium can be found for many games that do not have dominant strategy solutions.

To illustrate these points, we examine a more complex simultaneous-move game in which American and United can produce an output of 96, 64, or 48 (thousand passengers per quarter). This game has nine possible output combinations, as the 3 × 3 profit matrix in Table 13.2 shows. Neither American nor United has a single, dominant strategy, but we can find a Nash equilibrium by using a two-step procedure. First, we determine each firm's best response to any given strategy of the other firm. Second, we check whether there are any pairs of strategies (a cell in the profit table) that are best responses for both firms, so that the strategies in this cell are a Nash equilibrium.

We start by determining American's best response for each of United's possible actions. If United chooses $q_U = 96$ (thousand passengers per quarter), the first row of the table, then American's profit is 0 if it sets $q_A = 96$ (the first column), 2.0 if it chooses $q_A = 64$ (the second column), and 2.3 if it selects $q_A = 48$ (third column). Thus, American's best response if United sets $q_U = 96$ is to select $q_A = 48$. We indicate American's best response by coloring the upper triangle in the last (third column) cell in this row dark green. Similarly, if United sets $q_U = 64$ (second row), American's best response is to set $q_A = 64$, where it earns 4.1, so we color the upper triangle in the middle cell (second column) of the second row dark green. Finally, if United sets $q_U = 48$ (third row), American's best response is $q_A = 64$, where it earns 5.1, so we color the upper triangle in the middle cell of the third row dark green.

Table 13.2 Best Responses in a Quantity Setting, Prisoners' Dilemma Game

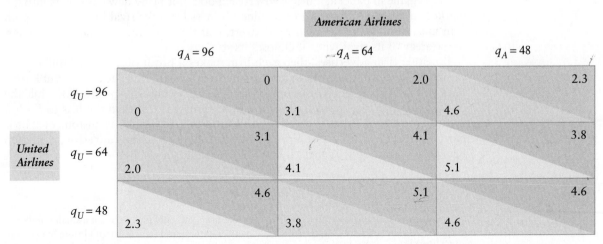

		American Airlines		
		$q_A = 96$	$q_A = 64$	$q_A = 48$
	$q_U = 96$	0 / 0	2.0 / 3.1	2.3 / 4.6
United Airlines	$q_U = 64$	3.1 / 2.0	4.1 / 4.1	3.8 / 5.1
	$q_U = 48$	4.6 / 2.3	5.1 / 3.8	4.6 / 4.6

Note: Quantities are in thousands of passengers per quarter; (rounded) profits are in millions of dollars per quarter.

We can use the same type of reasoning to determine United's best responses to each of American's strategies. If American chooses $q_A = 96$ (first column), then United's best response is $q_U = 48$ where its profit is 2.3, which we indicate by coloring the lower triangle light green in the lower left cell of the table. Similarly, we show that United's best response is $q_U = 64$, if American sets $q_A = 64$ or 48, which we show by coloring the relevant lower left triangles light green.

We now look for a Nash equilibrium, which is a pair of strategies where both firms are using a best-response strategy so that neither firm would want to change its strategy. There is only one cell in which both the upper and lower triangles are green: $q_A = q_U = 64$. Given that its rival uses this strategy, neither firm wants to deviate from its strategy. For example, if United continued to set $q_U = 64$, but American raised its quantity to 96, American's profit would fall from 4.1 to 3.8. Or, if American lowered its quantity to 48, its profit would fall to 3.1. Thus, American does not want to change its strategy.

Because no other cell has a pair of strategies that are best responses (green lower and upper triangles), at least one of the firms would want to change its strategy in each of these other cells. For example, at $q_A = q_U = 48$, either firm could raise its profit from 4.6 to 5.1 million by increasing its output to 64. At $q_A = 48$ and $q_U = 64$, American can raise its profit from 3.8 to 4.1 million by increasing its quantity to $q_A = 64$. Similarly, United would want to increase its output when $q_A = 64$ and $q_U = 48$. None of the other strategy combinations is a Nash equilibrium because at least one firm would want to deviate. Thus, we were able to find the single Nash equilibrium to this game by determining each firm's best responses.[2]

Failure to Maximize Joint Profits

The dominant-strategy analysis in Table 13.1 and the best-response analysis in Table 13.2 show that noncooperative firms may not reach the joint profit maximizing outcome. Whether players achieve the outcome that maximizes joint profit depends on the profit matrix. Table 13.3 shows an advertising game in which each firm can choose to advertise or not, with two possible profit matrices. In the first game, the rival doesn't benefit from advertising, and the Nash equilibrium does not maximize the collective profit to the firms. In contrast, in the second game where the rival benefits from advertising, the collective profit is maximized in the Nash equilibrium.

In the game in panel a, a firm's advertising does not bring new customers into the market but only has the effect of stealing business from the rival firm. Because each firm must decide whether or not to advertise at the same time, neither firm knows the strategy of its rival when it chooses its strategy.

If neither firm advertises, then each firm makes a profit of 2 (say, $2 million), as the upper-left cell of the profit matrix in panel a shows. If Firm 1 advertises but Firm 2 does not, then Firm 1 takes business from Firm 2 and raises its profit to 3, while the profit of Firm 2 is reduced to 0. The gain to Firm 1 is less than the loss to Firm 2 because the revenue that is transferred from Firm 2 to Firm 1 as customers shift is partially offset by the cost of Firm 2's advertising. If both firms advertise, then each firm gets a profit of 1, as the cell on the lower right shows.

---

[2]In these airline examples, we have assumed that the firms can only pick between a small number of output levels. However, in Chapter 14, we use game theory to find the Nash equilibrium in games in which the firms can choose any output level.

Table 13.3 Advertising Games: Prisoners' Dilemma or Joint Profit Maximizing Outcome?

(a) Advertising Only Takes Customers from Rivals

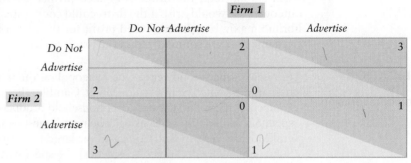

(b) Advertising Attracts New Customers to the Market

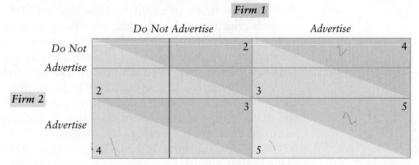

Advertising is a dominant strategy for both firms.[3] We use red lines to show that the firms do not use the dominated do-not-advertise strategies. The outcome in which both firms advertise is therefore a dominant strategy solution. Advertising for both firms is also a Nash equilibrium because each firm is choosing its best response to the other firm's strategy.

In this Nash equilibrium, each firm earns 1, which is less than the 2 it would make if neither firm advertised. Thus, *the sum of the firms' profits is not maximized in this simultaneous-choice one-period game.*

Many people are surprised when they see this result. Why don't the firms cooperate, refrain from advertising, and earn 2 instead of 1? This game is an example of a prisoners' dilemma: the game has a dominant strategy solution in which the players receive lower profits than they would get if the firms could cooperate. Each firm makes more money by advertising regardless of the strategy used by the other firm, even though their joint profit is maximized if neither advertises.

In the advertising game in panel b, advertising by a firm brings new customers to the market and consequently helps both firms. That is, each firm's advertising has a market expansion effect. If neither firm advertises, both earn 2. If only one firm advertises, its profit rises to 4, which is more than the 3 that the other firm makes. If both advertise, they are collectively better off than if only one advertises or neither

---

[3]Firm 1 goes through the following reasoning. "If my rival does not advertise, I get 2 if I do not advertise and I get 3 if I do advertise, so advertising is better. If my rival does advertise, I get 0 if I do not advertise and I get 1 if I do advertise, so advertising is still better." Regardless of what Firm 2 does, advertising is better for Firm 1, so advertising is a dominant strategy for Firm 1 (and not advertising is a dominated strategy). Firm 2 faces a symmetric problem and would also conclude that advertising is a dominant strategy.

advertises. Again, advertising is a dominant strategy for a firm because it earns more by advertising regardless of the strategy the other firm uses. This dominant strategy solution is a Nash equilibrium, but this game is not a prisoners' dilemma. In this Nash equilibrium, the firms' combined profits are maximized, which is the same outcome that would arise if the firms could cooperate. Thus, whether the Nash equilibrium maximizes the combined profit for the players depends on the properties of the game that are summarized in the profit matrix.

APPLICATION

Strategic Advertising

Firms with market power, such as oligopolies, often advertise.[4] The largest advertiser in the United States is Procter & Gamble, the producer of Crest toothpaste, Pampers diapers, and various other household products. In 2011, Procter & Gamble spent $2.9 billion on advertising. The next largest U.S. advertisers are AT&T, General Motors, Verizon, and Comcast. The largest advertisers based outside the United States are L'Oreal (France, cosmetics), Nestlé (Switzerland, foods) and Reckitt Benckiser (UK, cleaning products including Lysol, Dettol, Calgon, and Jet-Dry).

In oligopoly markets, firms consider the likely actions of their rivals when deciding how much to advertise. How much a firm should spend on advertising depends critically on whether the advertising helps or harms its rival.

For example, when a firm advertises to inform consumers about a new use for its product, its advertising may cause the quantity demanded for its own *and* rival brands to rise, as happened with toothpaste ads. Before World War I, only 26% of Americans brushed their teeth. By 1926, in part because of ads like those in Ipana's "pink toothbrush" campaign, which detailed the perils of bleeding gums, the share of Americans who brushed rose to 40%. Ipana's advertising helped all manufacturers of toothbrushes and toothpaste.

Although it's difficult to believe, starting in the 1970s, Wisk liquid detergent claimed that it solved a major social problem: ring around the collar.[5] Presumably, some consumers—even among those who were gullible enough to find this ad compelling—could generalize that applying other liquid detergents would work equally well.

Alternatively, a firm's advertising might increase demand for its product by taking customers away from other firms. A firm may use advertising to differentiate its products from those of rivals. The advertising may describe actual physical differences in the products or try to convince customers that essentially identical products differ. If a firm succeeds with this latter type of advertising, the products are sometimes described as *spuriously* differentiated.

A firm can raise its profit if it can convince consumers that its product is superior to other brands. From the 1930s through the early 1970s, *secret ingredients* were a mainstay of consumer advertising. These ingredients were given names combining letters and numbers to suggest that they were developed in laboratories rather than by Madison Avenue. Dial soap boasted that it contained AT-7. Rinso detergent had solium, Comet included Chlorinol, and Bufferin had di-alminate. Among the toothpastes, Colgate had Gardol, Gleem had GL-70, Crest had fluoristan, and Ipana had hexachlorophene and Durenamel.

About 30 years ago, secret ingredient claims fell out of favor, and manufacturers asserted that their brands contained *natural ingredients* such as baking soda and aloe. However, in the last few years, the secret ingredient approach has been reintroduced to differentiate brand-name products from generic competitors. Ads remind us that Clorets breath-freshening gum and mints contain Actizol. Cheer

[4]Under perfect competition, there is no reason for an individual firm to advertise as a firm can sell all it wishes at the going market price.

[5]www.youtube.com/watch?v=e3N_skYSGoY.

detergent touts an enzyme called Color Guard; Shade UVA Guard sunscreen lotion has Parasol 1789 and oxybenzone sun block agents; and Pond's Dramatic Results Skin Smoothing Capsules have Nutrium, "a miraculous oil-free complex."

Empirical evidence indicates that the impact of a firm's advertising on other firms varies across industries. The cola market is an example of the extreme case in which a firm's advertising brings few new customers into the market and primarily serves to steal business from rivals. Gasmi, Laffont, and Vuong (1992) reported that Coke or Pepsi's gain from advertising comes at the expense of its rivals; however, cola advertising has almost no effect on total market demand, as in panel a. Similarly, advertising by one brand of an erectile dysfunction drug increases its share and decreases that of its rivals (Davis and Markowitz, 2011).

At the other extreme is cigarette advertising. Roberts and Samuelson (1988) found that cigarette advertising increases the size of the market but does not change market shares substantially, as in panel b.[6]

Intermediate results include saltine crackers (Slade, 1995) and Canadian fast-foods, where advertising primarily increases general demand but has a small effect on market share (Richards and Padilla, 2009), and CPUs where Intel's advertising has a smaller effect on total market demand than on Intel's share (Salgado, 2008).

Multiple Equilibria

In accordance with our principles of free enterprise and healthy competition, I'm going to ask you two to fight to the death for it. —Monty Python

Many oligopoly games have more than one Nash equilibrium. We illustrate this possibility with an entry game. Two firms are each considering opening a gas station at a highway rest stop that has no gas stations. There's enough physical space for at most two gas stations. The profit matrix in Table 13.4 shows that there is enough demand for only one station to operate profitably. If both firms enter, each loses $1 (hundred thousand). Neither firm has a dominant strategy. Each firm's best action depends on what the other firm does.

By examining the firm's best responses, we can identify two Nash equilibria: Firm 1 *enters* and Firm 2 *does not enter*, or Firm 2 *enters* and Firm 1 *does not enter*. Each is a Nash equilibrium because neither firm wants to change its behavior. Given that Firm 2 does not enter, Firm 1 does not want to change its strategy from entering to staying out of the market. If it changed its behavior, it would go from earning $1 to

Table 13.4 Simultaneous Entry Game

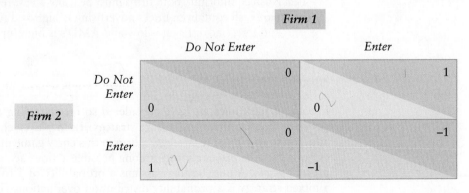

		Firm 1	
		Do Not Enter	Enter
Firm 2	Do Not Enter	0 / 0	0 / 1
	Enter	1 / 0	−1 / −1

---

[6]However, the Centers for Disease Control and Prevention's evidence suggests that advertising may shift the brand loyalty of youths.

earning $0. Similarly, given that Firm 1 enters, Firm 2 does not want to switch its behavior and enter because it would lose $1 instead of making $0. Where only Firm 2 enters is also a Nash equilibrium by the same type of reasoning.

How do the players know which (if any) Nash equilibrium will result? They *don't* know. It is difficult to see how the firms choose strategies unless they collude and can enforce their agreement. For example, the firm that enters could pay the other firm to stay out of the market. Without an enforceable collusive agreement, even discussions between the firms before they make decisions are unlikely to help. These pure Nash equilibria are unappealing because they call for identical firms to use different strategies.

SOLVED PROBLEM 13.1

Intel and AMD, the dominant central processing unit manufacturers, decide whether to set their advertising levels low or high. For now, we suppose that they play this game once, act simultaneously, and their profits are symmetric. If both choose low levels of advertising, Intel's profit, π_I, and AMD's profit, π_A, are each 2. If both choose high, each earns 3. If Intel's advertising is high and AMD's is low, $\pi_I = 8$ and $\pi_A = 4$. If Intel's advertising is low and AMD's is high, $\pi_I = 4$ and $\pi_A = 8$.

Answer

1. *Use a profit matrix to show the firms' best responses.* The payoff matrix shows the four possible pairs of strategies and the associated profits. If Intel chooses a low level of advertising (top row), AMD's profit is 2 if its advertising is low and 8 if it is high, so its best response is high, as indicated by the dark green triangle in the upper right of the top right cell. If Intel's advertising is high (bottom row), AMD's profit is 8 if its advertising is low and 3 if it is high, so its best response is low, as indicated by the dark green triangle in the upper right of the lower-left cell. Similarly, we use light green triangles in the lower left of cells to show Intel's best responses.

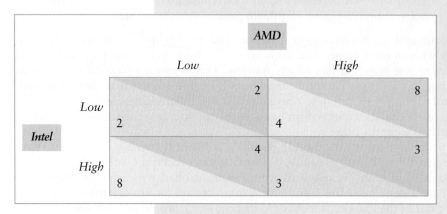

2. *Identify the Nash equilibria using the best-responses.* For a pair of strategies to be a Nash equilibrium, both firms must be using a best response. Thus, this game has two Nash equilibria: Intel's advertising is high and AMD's is low (lower-left cell) and Intel's advertising is low and AMD's is high (upper-right cell).

Mixed Strategies

In each of the games we have considered so far, including the entry game, we have assumed that the firms use a **pure strategy**: Each player chooses a single action. In addition to using a pure strategy, a firm in this entry game may employ a **mixed strategy** in which the player chooses among possible actions according to probabilities the player assigns. A pure strategy assigns a probability of 1 to a single action, whereas a mixed strategy is a probability distribution over actions. That is, a pure strategy is a rule telling the player what action to take, whereas a mixed strategy is a rule telling the player which dice to throw, coin to flip, or other method of choosing an action.

In the entry game, both firms may use the same mixed strategy. When both firms enter with a probability of one-half—say, if a flipped coin comes up heads—there is a Nash equilibrium in mixed strategies because neither firm wants to change its strategy, given that the other firm uses its Nash equilibrium mixed strategy.

If both firms use this mixed strategy, each of the four outcomes in the payoff matrix in Table 13.3 is equally likely. The probability that the outcome in a particular cell of the matrix occurs is the product of the probabilities that each player chooses the relevant action. The probability that a player chooses a given action is $\frac{1}{2}$, so the probability that both players will choose a given pair of actions is $\frac{1}{2} \times \frac{1}{2} = \frac{1}{4}$, because their actions are independent. Consequently, Firm 1 has a one-fourth chance of earning $1 (upper-right cell), a one-fourth chance of losing $1 (lower-right cell), and a one-half chance of earning $0 (upper-left and lower-left cells). Thus, Firm 1's expected profit— the firm's profit in each possible outcome times the probability of that outcome—is

$$\left(\$1 \times \frac{1}{4} \right) + \left(-\$1 \times \frac{1}{4} \right) + \left(\$0 \times \frac{1}{2} \right) = \$0.$$

Given that Firm 1 uses this mixed strategy, Firm 2 cannot achieve a higher expected profit by using a pure strategy. If Firm 2 uses the pure strategy of entering with probability 1, it earns $1 half the time and loses $1 the other half, so its expected profit is $0. If Firm 2 stays out with certainty, it earns $0 with certainty.

If Firm 2 believes that Firm 1 will use its equilibrium mixed strategy, Firm 2 is indifferent as to which pure strategy it uses (of the strategies that have a positive probability in that firm's mixed strategy). In contrast, if one of the actions in the equilibrium mixed strategy has a higher expected payoff than some other action, it would pay to increase the probability that Firm 2 takes the action with the higher expected payoff. However, if all of the pure strategies that have positive probability in a mixed strategy have the same expected payoff, then the expected payoff of the mixed strategy must also have that expected payoff. Thus, Firm 2 is indifferent as to whether it uses any of these pure strategies or any mixed strategy over these pure strategies.

In our example, why would a firm pick a mixed strategy where its probability of entering is one-half? In a symmetric game such as this one, we know that both players have the same probability of entering, θ. Moreover, for Firm 2 to use a mixed strategy, it must be indifferent between entering or not entering if Firm 1 enters with probability θ. Firm 2's payoff from entering is $[\theta \times (-1)] + [(1 - \theta) \times 1] = 1 - 2\theta$. Its payoff from not entering is $[\theta \times 0] + [(1 - \theta) \times 0] = 0$. Equating these two expected profits, $1 - 2\theta = 0$, and solving, we find that $\theta = \frac{1}{2}$ Thus, both firms using a mixed strategy where they enter with a probability of one-half is a Nash equilibrium.[7]

The entry game has two pure-strategy Nash equilibria—one firm employing the pure strategy of entering and the other firm pursuing the pure strategy of not entering—and a mixed-strategy Nash equilibrium. If Firm 1 decides to *enter* with a probability of $\frac{1}{2}$, Firm 2 is indifferent between choosing to enter with a probability of 1 (the pure strategy of *enter*), 0 (the pure strategy of *do not enter*), or any fraction in between these extremes. However, for the firms' strategies to constitute a mixed-strategy Nash equilibrium, both firms must choose to enter with a probability of one-half.

An important reason for introducing the concept of a mixed strategy is that some games have no pure-strategy Nash equilibria. However, Nash (1950) proved that every static game with a finite number of players and a finite number of actions has at least one Nash equilibrium, which may involve mixed strategies.

Some game theorists argue that mixed strategies are implausible because firms do not flip coins to choose strategies. One response is that firms may only appear to be

---

[7]"Solving for Mixed Strategies Using Calculus" in MyEconLab, Chapter Resources, Chapter 13 shows how to solve for this mixed-strategy equilibrium using calculus.

unpredictable. In this game with no dominant strategies, neither firm has a strong reason to believe that the other will choose a pure strategy. It may think about its rival's behavior as random. However, in actual games, a firm may use some information or reasoning that its rival does not observe so that it chooses a pure strategy. Another response is that a mixed strategy may be appealing in some games, such as the entry game, where a random strategy and symmetry between players are plausible.

APPLICATION

Tough Love

We can use game theory to explain many interactions between parents and their kids. In the United States, the term *boomerang generation* refers to young adults who return home after college, a first job, or the military to live with their parents. (In Japan, they're called *parasite singles*.)

The recent recession hit young people particularly hard. The U.S. unemployment rate for 20- to 24-year olds went from 8.5% in 2007 to 10.6% in 2008, then rose to 15.6% in 2009, and has stayed above 13% through 2012.

As a result, more adult children moved back with their parents after college. The share of 25- to 34-year-olds living in multigenerational households rose from 11% in 1980 to 20% in 2008 and 26% in 2010 (the highest it has been since the 1950s).[8] In the European Union, nearly half (46%) of young adults aged 18–34 lived with their parents in 2008.

In many parents' minds the question arises whether by supporting their kids, they discourage them from working. Rather than unconditionally supporting their children, would they help their kids more by engaging in tough love: kicking their kids out and making them support themselves? Solved Problem 13.2 addresses this question.

SOLVED PROBLEM 13.2

Mimi wants to support her son Jeff if he looks for work but not otherwise. Jeff wants to try to find a job only if Mimi will not support his life of indolence. Their payoff matrix is

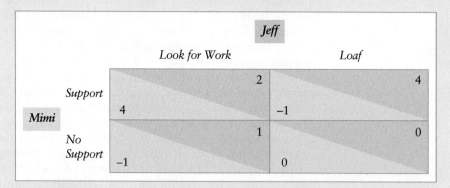

If Jeff and Mimi choose actions simultaneously, what are the pure- or mixed-strategy equilibria?

Answer

1. *Check whether any of the four possible pairs of pure strategies is a Nash equilibrium.* The four possible pure-strategy equilibria are support-look,

---

[8]A 2011 survey found that 59% of U.S. parents provide financial support to their adult children who are no longer in school. A 2012 British study reported that 80% of young adults received parental financial support.

support-loaf, no support-look, and no support-loaf. None of these pairs of pure strategies is a Nash equilibrium because one or the other player would want to change his or her strategy. The pair of strategies support-look is not a Nash equilibrium because, given that Mimi provides support, Jeff would have a higher payoff loafing, 4, than looking for work, 2. Support-loaf is not a Nash equilibrium because Mimi prefers not to support the bum, 0, to providing support, −1. We can reject no support-loaf because Jeff would prefer to look for work, 1, out of desperation rather than loaf, 0. Finally, no support-look is not a Nash equilibrium because Mimi would prefer to support her wonderful son, 4, rather than to feel guilty about not rewarding his search efforts, −1.

2. *By equating expected payoffs, determine the mixed-strategy equilibrium.* If Mimi provides support with probability θ_M, Jeff's expected payoff from looking for work is $2\theta_M + [1 \times (1 - \theta_M)] = 1 + \theta_M$, and his expected payoff from loafing is $4\theta_M + [0 \times (1 - \theta_M)] = 4\theta_M$. Thus, his expected payoffs are equal if $1 + \theta_M = 4\theta_M$, or $\theta_M = \frac{1}{3}$. If Jeff looks for work with probability θ_J, then Mimi's expected payoff from supporting him is $4\theta_J + [(-1) \times (1 - \theta_J)] = 5\theta_J - 1$, and her expected payoff from not supporting him is $-\theta_J + [0 \times (1 - \theta_J)] = -\theta_J$. By equating her expected payoffs, $5\theta_J - 1 = -\theta_J$, we determine that his mixed-strategy probability is $\theta_J = \frac{1}{6}$.

Comment: Although this game has no pure-strategy Nash equilibria, it does have a mixed-strategy Nash equilibrium.[9]

13.2 Dynamic Games

In static, normal-form games, players have imperfect information about how other players will act because everyone moves simultaneously and only once. In contrast, in *dynamic games*, players move sequentially or move simultaneously repeatedly over time, so a player has perfect information about other players' previous moves.

We consider two types of dynamic games. We start with a *repeated* or *multiperiod* game in which a single-period, simultaneous-move game, such as the airline prisoners' dilemma game, is repeated at least twice and possibly many times. Although the players move simultaneously in each period, they know about their rivals' moves in previous periods, so a rival's previous move may affect a player's current action. As a result, it is a dynamic game.

Then we turn to *sequential games*. We examine a *two-stage game*, which is played once and hence can be said to occur in a "single period." In the first stage, Player 1 moves. In the second stage, Player 2 moves and the game ends with the players' receiving payoffs based on their actions.

A major difference between static and dynamic games is that dynamic games require us to distinguish between strategies and actions. An *action* is a single move that a player makes at a specified time, such as choosing an output level or a price. A *strategy* is a battle plan that specifies the full set of actions that a player will make throughout the game and may involve actions that are conditional on prior actions of other players or on additional information available at a given time. For example, American's strategy might state that it will fly 64 thousand passengers between Chicago and Los Angeles this quarter if United flew 64 thousand last quarter, but that it will fly only 48 thousand this quarter if United flew 48 thousand last quarter.

[9]Do you understand mixed strategies? Try to defeat a computer at rock-paper-scissor: **www.nytimes.com/interactive/science/rock-paper-scissors.html?ref=science**. (*Hint*: the computer seems to use time to randomize, so its strategy isn't truly random—at least at first.)

This distinction between an action and a strategy is moot in a simultaneous-move static game, where an action and a strategy are effectively the same.

Repeated Game

The static games that we have been studying may be played repeatedly. In each period, there is a single stage: Both players move simultaneously. However, these are dynamic games because Player 1's move in period t precedes Player 2's move in period $t + 1$; hence, the earlier action may affect the later one. Such a repeated game is a *game of almost perfect information*: The players know all the moves from previous periods, but they do not know each other's moves within any one period because they all move simultaneously.

We showed that if American and United engage in a single-period prisoners' dilemma game, Table 13.1, the two firms produce more than they would if they colluded. Yet cartels do form. What's wrong with this theory, which says that cartels won't occur? One explanation is that markets last for many periods, and collusion is more likely to occur in a multi-period game than in a single-period game.

In a single-period game, one firm cannot punish the other firm for cheating on a cartel agreement. But if the firms meet period after period, a wayward firm can be punished by the other.

Suppose now that the airlines' single-period prisoners' dilemma game is repeated quarter after quarter. If they play a single-period game, each firm takes its rival's strategy as a given and assumes that it cannot affect that strategy. When the same game is played repeatedly, the firms may devise strategies for this period that depend on rivals' previous actions. For example, a firm may set a low output level for this period only if its rival set a low output level in the previous period.

In a repeated game, a firm can influence its rival's behavior by *signaling* and *threatening to punish*. For example, one airline firm could use a low-quantity strategy for a couple of periods to signal to the other firm its desire that the two firms cooperate and produce that low quantity in the future. If the other firm does not respond by lowering its output in future periods, the first firm suffers lower profits for a couple of periods only. However, if the other firm responds to this signal and lowers its quantity, both firms can profitably produce at the low quantity thereafter.

In addition to or instead of signaling, a firm can threaten to punish a rival for not restricting output. The profit matrix in Table 13.1 illustrates how firms can punish rivals to ensure collusion. Suppose that American announces or somehow indicates to United that it will use the following two-part strategy:

- American will produce the smaller quantity each period as long as United does the same.
- If United produces the larger quantity in period t, American will produce the larger quantity in period $t + 1$ and all subsequent periods.

If United believes that American will follow this strategy, United knows that it will make $4.6 million each period if it produces the lower quantity. Although United can make a higher profit, $5.1 million, in period t by producing the larger quantity, by doing so it lowers its potential profit to $4.1 million in each following period. Thus, United's best policy is to produce the lower quantity in each period unless it cares greatly about current profit and little about future profits. If United values future profits nearly as much as current ones, the one-period gain from deviating from the collusive output level will not compensate for the losses from reduced profits in future periods, which is the punishment American will impose. United presumably takes this threat by American seriously because American's best response is to produce the larger quantity if it believes it can't trust United to produce the smaller quantity.[10] Thus, if firms repeatedly play the same game *indefinitely*, they should find it easier to collude.

On the other hand, playing the same game many times does not necessarily help the firms cooperate. Suppose, for example, that the firms know that they are going to play the game for T periods. In the last period, they know that they're not going to play again, so they know they can cheat—produce a large quantity—without retribution. As a result, the last period is like a single-period game, and both firms produce the large quantity. That makes the $T - 1$ period the last interesting period. By the same reasoning, the firms will cheat in $T - 1$ because they know that they will both cheat in the last period and hence no additional punishment can be imposed. Continuing this type of argument, we conclude that maintaining an agreement to produce the small quantity will be difficult if the game has a known stopping point. If the players know that the game will end but aren't sure when, cheating is less likely to occur. Cooperation is therefore more likely in a game that will continue forever or one that will end at an uncertain time.

Sequential Game

In solving a problem of this sort, the grand thing is to be able to reason backward.
—Sherlock Holmes (Sir Arthur Conan Doyle)

In this section, we show how to represent these sequential games diagrammatically and how to predict their outcomes. Rather than use the normal form (payoff matrix), economists analyze dynamic games in their **extensive form**, which specifies the n players, the sequence in which they make their moves, the actions they can take at each move, the information that each player has about players' previous moves, and the payoff function over all possible strategies. In this section, we assume that players not only have complete information about the payoff function but also have perfect information about the play of the game to this point.

We illustrate a sequential-move or two-stage game using the airline example where American can choose its output level before United does. This game is called a *Stackelberg game*.[11] The striking result of this analysis is that when one player can move before the other, the outcome is different from that in a game where they have to move simultaneously. For simplicity, we assume that United and American can choose only output levels of 96, 64, and 48 thousand passengers per quarter.

Game Tree. The normal-form representation of this Stackelberg game, Table 13.2, does not capture the sequential nature of the firms' moves. To demonstrate the role of sequential moves, we use an *extensive-form diagram* or *game tree*, Figure 13.1, which shows the order of the firms' moves, each firm's possible actions at the time of its move, and the resulting profits at the end of the game.

In the figure, each box is a point of decision by one of the firms, called a *decision node*. The name in the decision node box indicates that it is that player's turn to move. The lines or *branches* extending out of the box represent a complete list of the possible actions that the player can make at that point in the game. On the left side of the figure, American, the leader, starts by picking one of the three output levels. In the middle of the figure, United, the follower, chooses one of the three quantities

---

[10]American does not have to punish United forever to induce it to cooperate. All it has to do is punish it for enough periods that it does not pay for United to deviate from the low-quantity strategy in any period.

[11]We discuss a generalized version of this game in Chapter 14.

after learning the output level American chose. The right side of the figure shows the profits that American and United earn, given that they sequentially took the actions to reach this final branch. For instance, if American selects 64 and then United chooses 96, American earns 2.0 ($2 million) profit per quarter and United earns 3.1.

Within this game are *subgames*. At a given stage, a subgame consists of all the subsequent decisions that players may make given the actions already taken. In the second stage where United makes a choice, there are three possible subgames. If in the first stage American chooses $q_A = 48$, the relevant subgame in Figure 13.1 is the top node in the second stage and its three branches. This game has four subgames. There are three subgames at the second stage where United makes a decision given each of American's three possible first-stage actions. There is an additional subgame at the time of the first-stage decision, which is the entire game.

Subgame Perfect Nash Equilibrium. To predict the outcome of this sequential game, we introduce a stronger version of the Nash equilibrium concept. A set of strategies forms a **subgame perfect Nash equilibrium** if the players' strategies are a Nash equilibrium in every subgame. As the entire dynamic game is a subgame, a subgame perfect Nash equilibrium is also a Nash equilibrium. In contrast, in a simultaneous-move game such as the static prisoners' dilemma, the only subgame is the game itself, so there is no important distinction between the Nash equilibrium and the subgame perfect Nash equilibrium.

Table 13.2 shows the normal-form representation of this game in which the Nash equilibrium to the simultaneous-move game is for each firm to choose 64. However, if the firms move sequentially, the subgame perfect Nash equilibrium results in a different outcome.

We can solve for the subgame perfect Nash equilibrium using **backward induction**, where we first determine the best response by the last player to move, next determine the best response for the player who made the next-to-last move, and then repeat the process until we reach the first move of the game. In our example, we work backward from the decision by the follower, United, to the decision by the leader, American, moving from the right to the left side of the game tree.

Figure 13.1 Airlines Game Tree

American, the leader firm, chooses its output level first. Given American's choice, United, the follower, picks an output level. The firms' profits that result from these decisions are shown on the right-hand side of the figure. Two red lines through an action line show that the firm rejects that action. The action that each firm chooses is indicated by a dark blue line.

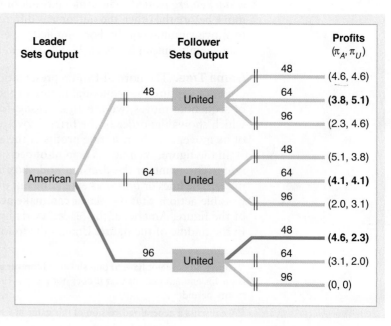

How should American, the leader, select its output in the first stage? For each possible quantity it can produce, American predicts what United will do and picks the output level that maximizes its own profit. Thus, to predict American's action in the first stage, American determines what United, the follower, will do in the second stage, given each possible output choice by American in the first stage. Using its conclusions about United's second-stage reaction, American makes its first-stage decision.

United, the follower, does not have a dominant strategy. The amount it chooses to produce depends on the quantity that American chose. If American chose 96, United's profit is 2.3 if its output is 48, 2.0 if it produces 64, and 0 if it picks a quantity of 96. Thus, if American chose 96, United's best response is 48. The double lines through the other two action lines show that United will not choose those actions.

Using the same reasoning, American determines how United will respond to each of American's possible actions, as the right-hand side of the figure illustrates. American predicts the following:

- If American chooses 48, United selects 64, so American's profit will be 3.8.
- If American chooses 64, United selects 64, so American's profit will be 4.1.
- If American chooses 96, United selects 48, so American's profit will be 4.6.

Thus, to maximize its profit, American chooses 96 in the first stage. United's strategy is to make its best response to American's first-stage action: United selects 64 if American chooses 48 or 64, and United picks 48 if American chooses 96. Thus, United responds in the second stage by selecting 48. In this subgame perfect Nash equilibrium, neither firm wants to change its strategy. Given that American Airlines sets its output at 96, United is using a strategy that maximizes its profit, $q_U = 48$, so it doesn't want to change. Similarly, given how United will respond to each possible American output level, American cannot make more profit than if it chooses 96.

The subgame perfect Nash equilibrium requires players to believe that their opponents will act optimally—in their own best interests. No player has an incentive to deviate from the equilibrium strategies. The reason for adding the requirement of subgame perfection is that we want to explain what will happen if a player does not follow the equilibrium path. For example, if American does not choose its equilibrium output in the first stage, subgame perfection requires that United will still follow the strategy that maximizes its profit in the second stage conditional on American's actual output choice.

Not all Nash equilibria are subgame perfect Nash equilibria. For example, suppose that American's strategy is to pick 96 in the first stage, and United's strategy is to choose 96 if American selects 48 or 64, and 48 if American chooses 96. The outcome is the same as the subgame perfect Nash equilibrium we just derived because American selects 96, United chooses 48, and neither firm wants to deviate.[12] Due to each firm's unwillingness to deviate, this set of strategies is a Nash equilibrium. However, this set of strategies is not a subgame perfect Nash equilibrium. Although this Nash equilibrium has the same equilibrium path as the subgame perfect Nash equilibrium, United's strategy differs out of the equilibrium path. If American had selected 48 (or 64), United's strategy would not result in a Nash equilibrium. United would receive a higher profit if it produced 64 rather than the 96 that this strategy requires. Therefore, this Nash equilibrium is not subgame perfect.

The subgame perfect Nash equilibrium differs from the simultaneous-move equilibrium in Table 13.2. If American can move first, its output is 96, which is 50% more than the 64 that it would fly if both firms move simultaneously. Similarly,

---

[12]Given United's strategy, American does not have any incentive to deviate. If American chooses 48 it will get 2.3 and if it chooses 64 it will get 2.0, both of which are less than 4.6 if it chooses 96. And given American's strategy, no change in United's strategy would raise its profit.

American earns 4.6 if it moves first, which is 15% more that the 4.1 it would earn if both firms move simultaneously. If United moves second, it selects a smaller quantity, 48, and earns a lower profit, 2.3, than it would if both firms move simultaneously, where it would fly 64 and earn 4.1. Thus, although United has more information in the sequential-move game than it does in the simultaneous-move game—it knows American's output level—it is worse off than if both firms chose their actions simultaneously.

Credibility. Why do the simultaneous-move and sequential-move games have different outcomes? Given the option to act first, American chooses a large output level to make it in United's best interest to pick a relatively small output level, 48. American benefits from moving first and choosing a relatively large quantity.

In the simultaneous-move game, why doesn't American announce that it will fly 96 thousand customers so as to induce United to pick a small quantity, 48? The answer is that when the firms move simultaneously, United doesn't believe American's warning that it will produce a large quantity, because it is not in American's best interest to produce that large a quantity of output. For a firm's announced strategy to be a **credible threat**, rivals must believe that the firm's strategy is rational in the sense that it is in the firm's best interest to use it.[13] If American chose the first-mover's equilibrium level of output, 96, and United produced the simultaneous-move equilibrium level, 64, American's profit would be lower than if it too chose the simultaneous-move level. Because American cannot be sure that United will believe its threat and reduce its output in the simultaneous-move game, American produces the simultaneous-move equilibrium output level, 64. In contrast, in the sequential-move game, because American moves first, its commitment to produce a large quantity is credible because it has already set that quantity.

The intuition for why commitment makes a threat credible is that of "burning bridges." If the general burns the bridge behind the army so that the troops can only advance and not retreat, the army becomes a more fearsome foe—like a cornered animal.[14] Similarly, by limiting its future options, a firm makes itself stronger.[15]

Not all firms can make credible threats, however, because not all firms can make commitments. Typically, for a threat to succeed, a firm must have an advantage that allows it to harm

Bizarro © 2008 Dan Piraro/King Features Syndicate

---

[13]You may have been in a restaurant and listened to an exasperated father trying to control his brat with such extreme threats as "If you don't behave, you'll have to sit in the car while we eat dinner" or "If you don't behave, you'll never watch television again." The kid, of course, does not view such threats as credible and continues to terrorize the restaurant—proving that the kid is a better game theorist than the father.

[14]"On hemmed-in ground, I would block any way of retreat. On desperate ground, I would proclaim to my soldiers the hopelessness of saving their lives." Sun Tzu, *On the Art of War*.

[15]Some psychologists use the idea of commitment to treat behavioral problems. A psychologist may advise an author with writer's block to set up an irreversible procedure whereby if the author's book is not finished by a certain date, the author's check for $10,000 will be sent to the group the author hates most in the world—be it the Nazi Party, the Ku Klux Klan, or the National Save the Skeets Foundation. Such an irreversible commitment encourages the author to complete the project by raising the cost of failure: We can imagine the author playing a game against the author's better self.

the other firm before that firm can retaliate. Identical firms that act simultaneously cannot credibly threaten each other. However, a firm may be able to make its threatened behavior believable if firms differ. An important difference is the ability of one firm to act before the other. For example, an incumbent firm could lobby for the passage of a law that forbids further entry.

Dynamic Entry Game. We can illustrate the use of laws as a form of commitment by using the entry game. In some markets, by moving first, a manger can act strategically to prevent potential rivals from entering the market. How can an *incumbent*, monopoly firm deter a (potential) *rival* from entering that market? Does it pay for the incumbent to take the actions that will deter entry?

The incumbent can prevent entry if it can make a creditable threat. However, a manager cannot deter entry merely by telling a potential rival, "Don't enter! This market ain't big enough for the two of us." The potential rival would merely laugh and suggest that the manager's firm exit if it doesn't want to share the market. The following examples demonstrate how, by acting first, a firm can make a credible threat that deters entry.

Suppose that a mall has a single shoe store, the incumbent firm. The incumbent may pay the mall's owner b to add a clause to its rental agreement that guarantees the incumbent the *exclusive right* to be the only shoe store in the mall. If this payment is made, the landlord agrees to rent the remaining space only to a restaurant, a toy store, or some other business that does not sell shoes. Should the shoe store pay?

The game tree, Figure 13.2, shows the two stages of the game involving the incumbent and its potential rival, another shoe store. In the first stage, the incumbent decides whether to pay b to prevent entry. In the second stage, the potential rival decides whether to enter. If it enters, it incurs a fixed fee of F to build its store in the mall.

The right side of the figure shows the incumbent's and the potential rival's profits (π_i, π_r) for each of the three possible outcomes. The outcome at the top of the figure shows that if the incumbent does not buy exclusivity and the potential rival does not enter, the incumbent earns the "monopoly" profit of $\pi_i = 10$ ($10 thousand) per month and its potential rival earns nothing, $\pi_r = 0$. The middle outcome shows that if the incumbent does not pay the exclusivity fee and the potential rival enters, the incumbent earns a duopoly profit of $\pi_i = 4$ and the rival earns the duopoly profit less its fixed cost, F, of entering, $\pi_r = 4 - F$. In the bottom outcome, the incumbent pays b for the exclusivity right so that it earns the monopoly profit less the exclusivity fee, $\pi_i = 10 - b$, and its potential rival earns nothing, $\pi_r = 0$.

Figure 13.2 Game Tree: Whether an Incumbent Pays to Prevent Entry

If the potential rival stays out of the mall, it makes no profit, $\pi_r = 0$, and the incumbent firm makes the monopoly profit, $\pi_i = 10$. If the potential rival enters, the incumbent earns the duopoly profit of 4 and the rival makes $4 - F$, where F is its fixed cost of entry. If the duopoly profit, 4, is less than F, entry does not occur. Otherwise, entry occurs unless the incumbent acts to deter entry by paying for exclusive rights to be the only firm in the mall. The incumbent pays the landlord only if $10 - b > 4$.

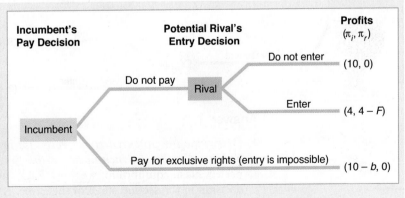

To solve for the subgame perfect Nash equilibrium, we work backwards, starting with the last decision, the potential rival's entry decision. The top portion of the game tree shows what happens if the incumbent does not pay the landlord to prevent entry. The potential rival enters if it earns more from entering, $\pi_r = 4 - F$, than if it stays out of the market, $\pi_r = 0$. That is, the potential rival enters if $F \leq 4$. In the bottom portion of the game tree where the incumbent pays b for an exclusive contract that prevents entry, the potential rival has no possible action.

Which of the three possible outcomes occurs depends on the parameters b (the incumbent's exclusivity fee) and F (the potential rival's fixed cost of entering the market):

- **Blockaded entry** ($F > 4$): The potential rival chooses not to enter even if the incumbent does not pay to have an exclusive contract, so $\pi_r = 0$. The incumbent avoids spending b and still earns the monopoly profit, $\pi_i = 10$.
- **Deterred entry** ($F \leq 4$, $b \leq 6$): Because $F \leq 4$, entry will occur unless the incumbent pays the exclusivity fee. The incumbent chooses to pay the exclusivity fee, b, because its profit from doing so, $\pi_i = 10 - b \geq 4$, which is at least as large as what it earns if it permits entry and earns the duopoly profit, $\pi_i = 4$. Because the rival does not enter, it earns nothing: $\pi_r = 0$.
- **Accommodated entry** ($F \leq 4$, $b > 6$): Entry will occur unless the incumbent pays the fee because the rival's fixed costs are less than or equal to 4. The incumbent does not pay for an exclusive contract. The exclusivity fee is so high that the incumbent earns more by allowing entry, $\pi_i = 4$, than it earns if it pays for exclusivity $\pi_i = 10 - b < 4$. Thus, the incumbent earns the duopoly profit, $\pi_i = 4$ and the rival makes $\pi_r = 4 - F$.

In short, the incumbent does not pay for an exclusive contract if the potential rival's cost of entry is prohibitively high ($F > 4$) or if the cost of the exclusive contract is too high ($b > 6$).

SOLVED PROBLEM 13.3

A firm invests in new equipment that lowers its marginal cost if the savings from lower production costs more than offset the cost of the investment. However, might an incumbent invest even when the investment does not lower its cost in response to potential entry? In the first stage of the game tree in the figure, the incumbent firm decides whether to invest in new robotic equipment, which will lower its marginal cost of production.

In the second stage, a potential rival decides whether to enter the market. Should this incumbent invest?

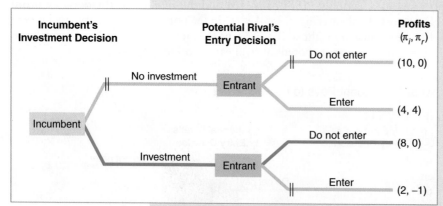

Answer

1. *Determine the potential rival's response in the second stage to each possible action taken by the incumbent in the first stage.* To solve for the subgame perfect Nash equilibrium, we work backwards from the potential rival's entry decision in the second stage of the game. If the incumbent does not invest, its rival enters because its profit from entering, $\pi_r = 4$, exceeds its zero profit if it

---

does not enter. If the incumbent does invest, its potential rival stays out of the market because entry would be unprofitable: $\pi_r = -1 < 0$.

2. *Determine the incumbent's decision given its potential rival's responses.* If the incumbent does not invest and the rival enters, the incumbent earns $\pi_i = 4$. If it invests and potential rival does not enter, the incumbent earns $\pi_i = 8$. Thus, the incumbent invests.

Comment: This investment would not pay if there were no threat of entry. Investing would cause the incumbent's profit to fall from $\pi_i = 10$ to 8.

APPLICATION

First Mover Advantages and Disadvantages

We've seen how the first firm that enters the market may gain an advantage over potential rivals by making a move before later entrants can. The first-mover firm may prevent entry by paying for exclusivity, committing to a large plant or new equipment, or in other ways.

Nonetheless, the first mover in a market is not always the big winner. There are at least three disadvantages of entering early rather than later. First, the first entrant has higher costs of entry due to having to enter quickly. Second, it has a greater chance of miscalculating demand. Third, later entrants may build on the pioneer's research to produce a superior product.

As the first of a new class of anti-ulcer drugs, Tagamet was extremely successful when it was introduced. However, the second entrant, Zantac, rapidly took the lion's share of the market. Zantac works similarly to Tagamet but has fewer side effects, could be taken less frequently when it was first introduced, and was promoted more effectively.

Recently, two groups of firms fought to determine the standard for the next generation of DVD players, featuring extended playing time and sharper images than previous models. One group led by Toshiba and NEC, with software from Microsoft, produced HD DVD discs. They were opposed by a group led by Sony that included Dell, Hewlett-Packard, Panasonic, Samsung, and Sharp, which championed Blu-ray technology. Toshiba, the main proponent of HD DVD, spent great sums of money to be the first to sell a next-generation DVD in 2006. It sold its initial HD DVD player for $499 even though it apparently contained nearly $700 worth of components, presumably to reinforce its first-to-market advantage by permeating the market with HD DVD units. In 2007, the backers of HD DVD reportedly paid Paramount and DreamWorks a combined $150 million to adopt their format. However, when most content producers sided with Blu-ray, Toshiba stopped producing HD DVD in 2008, conceding the market to the Blu-ray group.

Such examples of domination by a second entrant are unusual. Urban, Carter, and Gaskin (1986) examined 129 successful U.S. consumer products and found that the second entrant gained, on average, only three-quarters of the market share of the pioneer and that later entrants captured even smaller shares.

Two recent studies found similar results for mobile phone markets. Usero and Fernández (2009) examined European markets, and Jakopin and Klein (2012) studied 191 mobile network operators from 49 countries. Incumbents and first movers generally had larger market shares and were able to maintain their share advantage over time. Usero and Fernández found that followers were unlikely to erode the first mover's market share advantage by taking more aggressive market actions such as innovation and marketing, but they were able to gain market share through nonmarket actions such as litigation and complaints.

13.3 Auctions

To this point, we have examined games in which players have complete information about payoff functions. We now turn to an important game, the auction, in which players devise bidding strategies without knowing other players' payoff functions.

An **auction** is a sale in which a good or service is sold to the highest bidder. A substantial amount of exchange takes place through auctions. Government contracts are typically awarded using procurement auctions. In recent years, governments have auctioned portions of the airwaves for radio stations, mobile phones, and wireless Internet access and have used auctions to set up electricity and transport markets. Other goods commonly sold at auction are natural resources such as timber, as well as houses, cars, agricultural produce, horses, antiques, and art. In this section, we first consider the various types of auctions and then investigate how the rules of the auction influence buyers' strategies.

Elements of Auctions

Before deciding what strategy to use when bidding in an auction, one needs to know the rules of the game. Auctions have three key components: the number of units being sold, the format of the bidding, and the value that potential bidders place on the good.

Number of Units. Auctions can be used to sell one or many units of a good. In 2004, Google auctioned its initial public offering of many identical shares of stock at one time. In many other auctions, a single good—such as an original painting—is sold. For simplicity in this discussion, we concentrate on auctions where a single, indivisible item is sold.

Format. How auctions are conducted varies greatly. However, most approaches are variants of the *English auction*, the *Dutch auction*, or the *sealed-bid auction*.

- **English auction:** In the United States and Britain, almost everyone has seen an *English* or *ascending-bid auction*, at least in the movies. The auctioneer starts the bidding at the lowest price that is acceptable to the seller and then repeatedly encourages potential buyers to bid more than the previous highest bidder. The auction ends when no one is willing to bid more than the current highest bid by the time the auctioneer has called out "Going, going, gone!" The good is sold to the last bidder for the highest bid. Sotheby's and Christie's use English auctions to sell art and antiques.
- **Dutch auction:** A *Dutch auction* or *descending-bid auction* ends dramatically with the first "bid." The seller starts by asking if anyone wants to buy at a high price. The seller reduces the price by given increments until someone accepts the offered price and then buys at that price. Variants of Dutch auctions are often used to sell multiple goods simultaneously, such as in Google's initial public offering auction and the U.S. Treasury's sales of Treasury bills.
- **Sealed-bid auction:** In a *sealed-bid auction*, everyone submits a bid simultaneously without seeing the other bids (for example, by submitting each bid in a sealed envelope), and the highest bidder wins. The price the winner pays depends on whether it is a first-price auction or a second-price auction. In a *first-price auction*, the winner pays its own, highest bid. Governments often use this type of auction. In a *second-price auction*, the winner pays the amount bid by the second-highest bidder. Many online auction houses use a variant of the second-price auction.

For example, you bid on eBay by specifying the maximum amount you are willing to bid. If your maximum is greater than the maximum bid of other participants, eBay's computer places a bid on your behalf that is a small increment above the maximum bid of the second-highest bidder. This system differs from the traditional sealed-bid auction in that people can continue to bid until the official end of the auction, and potential bidders know the current bid price (but not the maximum that the highest bidder is willing to pay). Thus, eBay has some of the characteristics of an English auction.

Value. Auctioned goods are normally described as having a *private value* or a *common value*. Typically, this distinction turns on whether the good is unique.

- **Private value:** If each potential bidder places a different personal value on a good, we say that the good has a *private value*. Individual bidders know how much the good is worth to them but not how much other bidders value it. An archetypical example is an original work of art, which can be valued very differently by many people.
- **Common value:** Many auctions involve a good that has the same fundamental value to everyone, but no buyer knows exactly what that *common value* is. For example, in a timber auction, firms bid on all the trees in a given area. All firms know the current price of lumber; however, they do not know exactly how many board feet of lumber are contained in the trees.

In many actual auctions, goods have both private value and common value. For example, in the tree auction, bidding firms may differ not only in their estimates of the amount of lumber in the trees (common value), but also in their costs of harvesting (private value).

Bidding Strategies in Private-Value Auctions

A potential buyer's optimal strategy depends on the number of units, the format, and the type of values in an auction. For specificity, we examine auctions in which each bidder places a different private value on a single, indivisible good.

Second-Price Auction Strategies. According to eBay, if you choose to bid on an item in its second-price auction, you should "enter the maximum amount you are willing to spend."[16] Is eBay's advice correct?

In a traditional sealed-bid, second-price auction, bidding your highest value *weakly dominates* all other bidding strategies: The strategy of bidding your maximum value leaves you *as well off* as, or *better off* than, bidding any other value. The amount that you bid affects whether you win, but it does not affect how much you pay if you win, which equals the second-highest bid.

Suppose that you value a folk art carving at $100. If the highest amount that any other participant is willing to bid is $85 and you place a bid greater than $85, you will buy the carving for $85 and receive $15 (= $100 − $85) of consumer surplus. Other bidders pay nothing and gain no consumer surplus.

Should you ever bid more than your value? Suppose that you bid $120. There are three possibilities. First, if the highest bid of your rivals is greater than $120, then you do not buy the good and receive no consumer surplus. This outcome is the same as what you would have received if you had bid $100, so bidding higher than $100 does not benefit you.

Second, if the highest alternative bid is less than $100, then you win and receive the same consumer surplus that you would have received had you bid $100. Again, bidding higher does not affect the outcome.

---

[16]See pages.ebay.com/education/gettingstarted/bidding.html.

Third, if the highest bid by a rival were an amount between $100 and $120—say, $110—then bidding more than your maximum value causes you to win, but you purchase the good for more than you value it, so you receive negative consumer surplus: −$10 (= $100 − $110). In contrast, if you had bid your maximum value, you would not have won, and your consumer surplus would have been zero—which is better than losing $10. Thus, bidding more than your maximum value can never make you better off than bidding your maximum value, and you may suffer.

Should you ever bid less than your maximum value, say, $90? No, because you only lower the odds of winning without affecting the price that you pay if you do win. If the highest alternative bid is less than $90 or greater than your value, you receive the same consumer surplus by bidding $90 as you would by bidding $100. However, if the highest alternative bid lies between $90 and $100, you will lose the auction and give up positive consumer surplus by underbidding.

Thus, you do as well or better by bidding your value than by overbidding or underbidding. This argument does not turn on whether or not you know other bidders' valuation. If you know your own value but not other bidders' values, bidding your value is your best strategy. If everyone follows this strategy, the person who places the highest value on the good will win and will pay the second-highest value.

English Auction Strategy. Suppose instead that the seller uses an English auction to sell the carving to bidders with various private values. Your best strategy is to raise the current highest bid as long as your bid is less than the value you place on the good, $100. If the current bid is $85, you should increase your bid by the smallest permitted amount, say, $86, which is less than your value. If no one raises the bid further, you win and receive a positive surplus of $13. By the same reasoning, it always pays to increase your bid up to $100, where you receive zero surplus if you win.

However, it never pays to bid more than $100. The best outcome that you can hope for is to lose and receive zero surplus. Were you to win, you would have negative surplus.

If all participants bid up to their value, the winner will pay slightly more than the value of the second-highest bidder. Thus, the outcome is essentially the same as in the sealed-bid, second-price auction.

Equivalence of Auction Outcomes. For Dutch or first-price sealed-bid auctions, one can show that participants will *shave* their bids to less than their value. The basic intuition is that you do not know the values of the other bidders. Reducing your bid reduces the probability that you will win but increases your consumer surplus if you do win. Your optimal bid, which balances these two effects, is lower than your actual value. Your bid depends on your beliefs about the strategies of your rivals. It can be shown that the best strategy is to bid an amount that is equal to or slightly greater than what you expect will be the second-highest bid, given that your value is the highest.

The expected outcome is the same under each format for private-value auctions: The winner is the person with the highest value, and the winner pays roughly the second-highest value. According to the Revenue Equivalence Theorem (Klemperer, 2004), under certain plausible conditions we would expect the same revenue from any auction in which the winner is the person who places the highest value on the good.

Winner's Curse

The **winner's curse** is that the auction winner's bid exceeds the common-value item's value. Such overbidding occurs when there is uncertainty about the true value of the good. This phenomenon occurs in common-value auctions, but not in private-value auctions.

When the government auctions off timber on a plot of land, potential bidders may differ in their estimates of how many board feet of lumber are available on that land. The higher one's estimate, the more likely that one will make the winning bid. If the average bid is accurate, then the high bid is probably excessive. Thus, the winner's curse is paying too much.

Each bidder thinks, "I can minimize the likelihood of falling prey to the winner's curse by *shading* my bid: reducing the bid below my estimate. I know that if I win, I am probably overestimating the value of the good. The amount by which I should shade my bid depends on the number of other bidders, because the more bidders, the more likely that the winning bid is an overestimate."

Because intelligent bidders shade their bids, sellers generally receive more money with an English auction than with a sealed-bid auction. In an English auction, bidders revise their views about the object's value as they watch others bid.

APPLICATION

Bidder's Curse

What's the maximum you would bid for an item that you know that you can buy for a fixed price of p? No matter how much you value the good, it doesn't make sense to bid more than p. Yet, people commonly do that on eBay. Lee and Malmendier (2011) call bidding more than what should be one's valuation—here, the fixed price—*bidder's curse*.

They examined eBay auctions of a board game, Cashflow 101, a game that is supposed to help people better understand their finances. A search on eBay for Cashflow 101 not only listed the auctions but also the availability of the game for a fixed price. During the period studied, the game was continuously available for a fixed price on the eBay site (with identical or better quality and seller reputation and lower shipping cost).

Even if only a few buyers overbid, they affect the auction price and who wins. The auction price exceeded the fixed price in 42% of the auctions. The average overpayment was 10% of the fixed price. This overbidding was caused by a small number of bidders—only 17% bid above the fixed price. However, people who bid too much are disproportionately likely to win the auction and, hence, determine the winning price.

One possible behavioral economics explanation is that bidders paid limited attention to the fixed-price option. Lee and Malmendier found that overbidding was less likely the closer the fixed price appeared on the same screen to the auction and hence the more likely that bidders would notice the fixed-price listing.

Another explanation is lack of bidding experience. Garratt et al. (2012) conducted an experimental sealed-bid, second-price auction under "laboratory" settings. They found that inexperienced bidders—college students—were more likely to overbid than underbid. In contrast, experienced eBay bidders did not exhibit a systematic bias: They were just as likely to underbid as to overbid. That is, experienced bidders occasionally make random mistakes, but they do not systematically overbid as inexperienced people do.

13.4 Behavioral Game Theory

We normally assume that people are rational in the sense that they optimize using all available information. However, they may be subject to psychological biases and may have limited powers of calculation that causes them to act irrationally, as described in the Application "Bidder's Curse." Such possibilities are the domain of behavioral economics (Chapters 3 and 11), which seeks to augment the rational economic model so as to better understand and predict economic decision-making.

Another example of nonoptimal strategies occurs in *ultimatum games*. People often face an *ultimatum*, where one person (the *proposer*) makes a "take it or leave it" offer to another (the *responder*). No matter how long the parties have negotiated, once an ultimatum is issued, the responder has to accept or reject the offer with no opportunity to make a counter-offer. An ultimatum can be viewed as a sequential game in which the proposer moves first and the responder moves second.

APPLICATION	
GM's Ultimatum	In 2009, General Motors (GM) was struggling financially and planned to shut down about one-fourth of its dealerships in the United States and Canada.[17] Because GM was concerned that dealer opposition could cause delays and impose other costs, it offered dealers slated for closure an ultimatum. They would receive a (small) payment from GM if they did not oppose the restructuring plan.
	Dealers could accept the ultimatum and get something, or they could reject the offer, oppose the reorganization, and receive nothing. Although it was irrational, some dealers rejected the ultimatum and loudly complained that GM was "high-handed, oppressive, and patently unfair." In 2011, some terminated Canadian dealerships filed a class-action suit against GM of Canada.

An Experiment. The possibility that someone might turn down an offer even at some personal cost is important in business and personal negotiations. To gain insight into real decisions, Camerer (2003) conducted an ultimatum experiment.

A group of student participants meets in a computer lab. Each person is designated as either a proposer or a responder. Using the computers, each proposer is matched (anonymously) with one responder. The game is based on dividing $10. Each proposer makes an ultimatum offer to the responder of a particular amount. A responder who accepts receives the amount offered and the proposer gets the rest of the $10. If the responder rejects the offer, both players get nothing.

To find the rational, subgame perfect solution, we use backward induction. In the second stage, the responder should accept if the offer x is positive. Thus in the first stage, the proposer should offer the lowest possible positive amount.

However, such rational behavior is not a good predictor of actual outcomes. The lowest possible offer is rarely made and, when it is, it is usually rejected. Thus, a proposer who makes the mistake of expecting the responder to be fully rational is likely to receive nothing. The most common range for offers is between $3 and $4—far more than the "rational" minimum offer. Offers less than $2 are relatively rare and, when they do occur, are turned down about half the time.

One concern about such experiments is that the payoffs are small enough that not all participants take the game seriously. However, when the total amount to be divided was increased to $100, the results were essentially unchanged: The typical offer remained between 30% and 40% of the total. If anything, responders are even more likely to turn down lowball offers when the stakes are higher.

Reciprocity. Some responders who reject lowball offers feel the proposer is being greedy and would prefer to make a small sacrifice rather than reward such behavior. Some responders are angered by low offers, some feel insulted, and some feel that they should oppose "unfair" behavior. Most proposers anticipate such feelings and offer a significant amount to the responder, but almost always less than 50%.

---

[17]Schoenberger, Robert, "GM Sends Ultimatums to All Its 6000 US dealers," *Cleveland Plain Dealer*, June 2, 2009; and "GM Dealers Sue to Keep Doors Open," *Toronto Star*, November 27, 2009.

Apparently, most people accept that the advantage of moving first should provide some extra benefit to proposers, but not too much. Moreover, they believe in *reciprocity*. If others treat us well, we want to return the favor. If they treat us badly, we want to "get even" and will retaliate if the cost does not seem excessive. Thus, if a proposer makes a low offer, many responders are willing to give up something to punish the proposer, using "an eye for an eye" philosophy.

Eckel and Grossman (1996) found that men are more likely than women to punish if the personal cost is high in an ultimatum game. They speculate that this difference may explain gender patterns in wages and unemployment during downturns, where men are more likely to rigidly insist on a given wage than are women, who are more flexible.

CHALLENGE SOLUTION

Intel and AMD's Advertising Strategies

As we've seen, when one firm in a market acts before another, the first mover may gain an advantage large enough to discourage the second firm from entering the market. In a less extreme case, the original firm may gain a smaller advantage so that the second firm enters, but it produces less than the original firm (as in the airlines' Stackelberg model). We can use this insight to provide a possible explanation for the Challenge: In the market for CPUs for personal computers, why does Intel advertise substantially while AMD does not?

In Solved Problem 13.1, we examined a game where Intel and AMD act simultaneously and have symmetric profits (which is consistent with the estimates of Salgado, 2008). That game has two pure strategy equilibria. In each, one firm advertises at a low level while the other firm sets a high level. In Exercise 5.2, you are asked to show that there is also a mixed strategy equilibrium in which each firm sets its advertising low with probability $\frac{1}{7}$ (and has an expected profit of about 3.71).

In contrast, the game has a clear outcome given that Intel acted first, as actually happened. The game tree shows that Intel decides on how much to advertise before AMD can act. AMD then decides how much to advertise. We solve for the subgame-perfect, Nash equilibrium by working backwards. For the profits in this game, if Intel were to have a minimal advertising campaign, AMD makes more if it advertises a lot ($\pi_A = 8$) than if it too has a low level of advertising ($\pi_A = 2$). If Intel advertises heavily, AMD makes more with a low-level advertising campaign ($\pi_A = 4$) than with a high-level campaign ($\pi_A = 3$). Given how it expects AMD to behave, Intel intensively advertises because doing so produces a higher profit ($\pi_I = 8$) than does the lower level of advertising ($\pi_I = 4$).

Thus, because Intel acts first and can commit to advertising aggressively, it can place AMD in a position where it makes more with a low-key advertising campaign. Of course, the results might vary if the profits in the game tree differ, but this example provides a plausible explanation for why the firms use different strategies.

SUMMARY

1. **Static Games.** In a static game, such as the prisoners' dilemma game, players each make one move simultaneously. Economists use a normal-form representation or payoff matrix to analyze a static game. Typically, economists study static games in which players have complete information about the payoff function—the payoff to any player conditional on the actions all players take—but imperfect information about how their rivals behave because they act simultaneously. The set of players' strategies is a Nash equilibrium if, given that all other players use these strategies, no player can obtain a higher payoff by choosing a different strategy. Both pure-strategy and mixed-strategy Nash equilibria are possible in static games, and there may be multiple Nash equilibria for a given game. There is no guarantee that Nash equilibria in static games maximize the joint payoffs of all the players.

2. **Dynamic Games.** In dynamic games, a player considers the other players' previous moves when choosing a move. Players may use more complex strategies in dynamic games than in static games.

   In a repeated game, players replay a static game in which they move simultaneously within a period. The players have perfect information about other players' moves in previous periods but imperfect information within a period because the players move simultaneously. It is easier for players to maximize their joint payoff in a repeated game than in a single-period game.

   In sequential-move games, one player moves before the other player. Economists typically study sequential games of complete information about payoffs and perfect information about previous moves. The

first mover may have an advantage over the second mover, such as in a Stackelberg game. An incumbent with first-mover advantage prevents entry by making a *credible threat*. For example, in a Stackelberg game, the leader *commits* to producing so much output that it is in the follower's best interest to produce a relatively small amount of output. The best-known solution of a dynamic game is a subgame perfect Nash equilibrium, where the players' strategies are a Nash equilibrium in every subgame—the remaining game following a particular junction in the game.

3. **Auctions.** Auctions are games of incomplete information because bidders do not know the valuation others place on a good. Buyers' optimal strategies depend on the characteristics of an auction. Under fairly general conditions, if the auction rules result in a win by the person placing the highest value on a good that various bidders value differently, the expected price is the same in all auctions. For example, the expected price in various types of private-value auctions is the value of the good to the person who values it second highest. In auctions where everyone values the good the same, though they may differ in their estimates of that value, the successful bidder may suffer from the winner's curse—paying too much—unless bidders shade their bids to compensate for their overoptimistic estimation of the good's value.

4. **Behavioral Game Theory.** People may not use rational strategies because of psychological bias, lack of reasoning ability, or their belief that other managers will not use rational strategies. The ultimatum game illustrates that irrational strategies are commonly used in certain circumstances.

EXERCISES

■ = *exercise is available on* MyEconLab; * = *answer appears at the back of this book;* **M** = *mathematical problem.*

1. Static Games

*1.1 Show the payoff matrix and explain the reasoning in the prisoners' dilemma example where Larry and Duncan, possible criminals, will get one year in prison if neither talks; if one talks, one goes free and the other gets five years; and if both talk, both get two years. (*Note*: The payoffs are negative because they represent years in jail, which is a bad.)

1.2 Show that advertising is a dominant strategy for both firms in both panels of Table 13.3. Explain why that set of strategies is a Nash equilibrium.

*1.3 Two firms must simultaneously decide which quality to manufacture. The profit matrix (in tens of thousands of euros) is

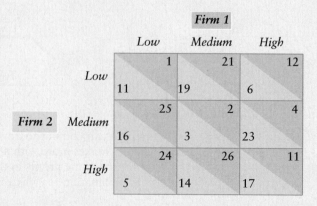

Identify all the Nash equilibria in this game. (See Solved Problem 13.1.)

1.4 Suppose Procter & Gamble (PG) and Johnson & Johnson (JNJ) are simultaneously considering new advertising campaigns. Each firm may choose a high, medium, or low level of advertising. What are each firm's best responses to its rival's strategies? Does either firm have a dominant strategy? What is the Nash equilibrium in this game? (See Solved Problem 13.1.)

PG

		High	Medium	Low
JNJ	High	1 / 1	2 / 3	3 / 5
	Medium	3 / 2	4 / 4	5 / 6
	Low	5 / 3	6 / 5	5 / 7

1.5 Lori employs Max. She wants him to work hard rather than to loaf. She considers offering him a bonus or not giving him one. All else the same, Max prefers to loaf. The payoff matrix is

Max

		Work	Loaf
Lori	Bonus	2 / 1	3 / −1
	No Bonus	−1 / 3	0 / 0

If they choose actions simultaneously, what are their strategies? (See Solved Problem 13.2.) **M**

1.6 The *Wall Street Journal* (Lippman, John, "The Producers: 'The Terminator' Is Back," March 8, 2002, A1) reported that Warner Brothers agreed to pay $50 million for its U.S. distribution rights, plus an additional $50 million in marketing costs, so that it could release *Terminator 3* (*T-3*) in the summer of 2003. It paid this large sum because it did not want another studio to release *T-3* on the same weekend in 2003 that Warner released its movie *Matrix 2*. Suppose that Warner had not purchased the distribution rights to *T-3* and that the film's producer retained the rights. Warner would have had to decide whether to release *Matrix 2* on the July 4 weekend or on the July 18 weekend. Simultaneously, *T-3*'s producer would have had to decide which of those two weekends to release its film. The payoff matrix (in millions of dollars) of the simultaneous-moves game would have been

Warner Bros.

		July 4	July 18
T-3 Producer	July 4	50 / 50	35 / 80
	July 18	90 / 30	20 / 20

a. What is the Nash equilibrium to this simultaneous-moves game?

b. Which release dates would have maximized the sum of the profits? Explain.

c. What is the greatest price Warner would have been willing to pay to purchase the distribution rights to *T-3*? What is the lowest price that *T-3*'s producer would have been willing to accept to sell the rights? Are there mutually beneficial prices at which the trade takes place?

d. If Warner purchased the distribution rights of *T-3*, when should it have released the film and when should it have released *Matrix 2*? Explain.

1.7 Suppose that two firms face the following payoff matrix:

Firm 1

		Low Price	High Price
Firm 2	Low Price	0 / 2	2 / 1
	High Price	7 / 0	6 / 6

Given these payoffs, Firm 2 wants to match Firm 1's price, but Firm 1 does not want to match Firm 2's price. What, if any, are the pure-strategy Nash equilibria of this game?

*1.8 What is the mixed-strategy Nash equilibrium for the game in Exercise 1.7? **M**

*1.9 Suppose that Toyota and GM are considering entering a new market for electric automobiles and that their profits (in millions of dollars) from entering or staying out of the market are

GM

		Enter	Do Not Enter
Toyota	Enter	10 \\ −40	250 \\ 0
	Do Not Enter	0 \\ 200	0 \\ 0

If the firms make their decisions simultaneously, which firms enter? How would your answer change if the U.S. government committed to paying GM a lump-sum subsidy of $50 million on the condition that it would produce this new type of car?

1.10 In the battle of the sexes game, the husband likes to go to the mountains on vacation, and the wife prefers the ocean, but they both prefer to take their vacations together.

Husband

		Mountains	Beach
Wife	Mountains	2 \\ 1	−1 \\ −1
	Beach	−1 \\ −1	1 \\ 2

What are the Nash equilibria? Discuss whether this game and equilibrium concept make sense for analyzing a couple's decisions. How might you change the game's rules so that it makes more sense? **M**

1.11 Takashi Hashiyama, president of the Japanese electronics firm Maspro Denkoh Corporation, was torn between commissioning Christie's or Sotheby's to auction the company's $20 million art collection, which

included a van Gogh, a Cézanne, and an early Picasso (Vogel, Carol, "Rock, Paper, Payoff," *New York Times*, April 29, 2005, A1, A24). He resolved the issue by having the two auction houses' representatives compete in the playground game of rock-paper-scissors. A rock (fist) breaks scissors (two extended fingers), scissors cut paper (flat hand), and paper smothers rock. At stake were several million dollars in commissions. Christie's won: scissors cut paper.

a. Show the profit or payoff matrix for this rock-paper-scissors game. (*Hint*: You may assume that the payoff is −1 if you lose, 0 if you tie, and 1 if you win.)

b. Sotheby's expert in Impressionist and modern art said, "[T]his is a game of chance, so we didn't really give it much thought. We had no strategy in mind." In contrast, the president of Christie's in Japan researched the psychology of the game and consulted with the 11-year-old twin daughters of the director of the Impressionist and modern art department. One of these girls said, "Everybody knows you always start with scissors. Rock is way too obvious, and scissors beats paper." The other opined, "Since they were beginners, scissors was definitely the safest." Evaluate these comments on strategy. What strategy would you recommend if you knew that your rival was consulting with 11-year-old girls? In general, what pure or mixed strategy would you have recommended, and why? **M**

1.12 Suppose that Panasonic and Zenith are the only two firms that can produce a new type of 3D TV. The payoff matrix shows the firms' profits (in millions of dollars):

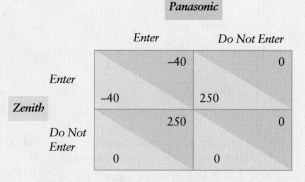

Panasonic

		Enter	Do Not Enter
Zenith	Enter	−40 \\ −40	250 \\ 0
	Do Not Enter	0 \\ 250	0 \\ 0

a. If both firms move simultaneously, does either firm have a dominant strategy? Explain.

b. What are the Nash equilibria given that both firms move simultaneously?

c. The U.S. government commits to paying Zenith a lump-sum subsidy of $50 million if it enters this market. What is the Nash equilibrium?

1.13 Two guys (suffering from testosterone poisoning) engage in the game of chicken. They drive toward each other in the middle of a road. As they approach the impact point, each has the option of continuing to drive down the middle of the road or to swerve. Both believe that if only one driver swerves, that driver loses face (payoff = 0) and the other gains in self-esteem (payoff = 2). If neither swerves, they are maimed or killed (payoff = −10). If both swerve, no harm is done to either (payoff = 1). Show the payoff matrix for the two drivers engaged in this game of chicken. Determine the Nash equilibria for this game. **M**

1.14 Modify the payoff matrix in the game of chicken in Exercise 1.13 so that the payoff is −2 if neither driver swerves. How does the equilibrium change? **M**

1.15 In the novel and film *The Princess Bride*, the villain Vizzini kidnaps the princess. In an attempt to rescue her, the hero, Westley, challenges Vizzini to a battle of wits. Consider this variation on the actual plot. (I do not want to reveal the story.) In the battle, Westley puts two identical glasses of wine behind his back, out of Vizzini's view, and adds iocane powder to one glass. Iocane is "odorless, tasteless, dissolves instantly in liquid, and is among the more deadly poisons known to man." Westley decides which glass to put on a table in front of Vizzini and which to put on the table in front of himself. Then, with Westley's back turned so that he cannot observe Vizzini's move, Vizzini decides whether to switch the two glasses. Assume the two simultaneously drink all the wine in their respective glasses. Assume also that each player's payoff from drinking the poisoned wine is −3 and the payoff from drinking the safe wine is +1. Write the payoff matrix for this simultaneous-moves game. Specify the possible Nash equilibria. Is there a pure-strategy Nash equilibrium? Is there a mixed-strategy Nash equilibrium? **M**

1.16 Suppose that you and a friend play a "matching pennies" game in which each of you uncovers a penny. If both pennies show heads or both show tails, you keep both. If one shows heads and the other shows tails, your friend keeps them. Show the payoff matrix. What, if any, is the pure-strategy Nash equilibrium to this game? Is there a mixed-strategy Nash equilibrium? If so, what is it? **M**

1.17 The 100-meter Olympic gold medalist and the 200-meter Olympic gold medalist have agreed to a 150-meter duel. Before the race, each athlete decides whether to improve his performance by taking anabolic steroids. Each athlete's payoff is 20 from winning the race, 10 from tying, and 0 from losing. Furthermore, each athlete's utility of taking steroids is −6. Model this scenario as a game in which the players simultaneously decide whether to take steroids.

a. What is the Nash equilibrium? Is the game a prisoners' dilemma? Explain.

b. Suppose that one athlete's utility of taking steroids is −12, while the other's remains at −6. What is the Nash equilibrium? Is the game a prisoners' dilemma? **M**

1.18 Acura and Volvo offer warranties on their automobiles, where w_A is the number of years of an Acura warranty and w_V is the number of years of a Volvo warranty. The revenue for Firm i, $i = A$ for Acura and V for Volvo, is $R_i = 27,000w_i/(w_A + w_V)$. Its cost of providing the warranty is $C_i = 2,000w_i$. Acura and Volvo participate in a warranty-setting game in which they simultaneously set warranties.

a. What is the profit function for each firm?

b. Suppose Acura and Volvo can set warranties in year lengths only, with a maximum of five years. Fill in a 5×5 payoff matrix with Acura's and Volvo's profits.

c. Determine the Nash equilibrium warranties.

d. Compare the Nash equilibrium warranties. If the two manufacturers offer the same warranty, explain why. If they offer different warranties, explain why.

e. Suppose Acura and Volvo collude in setting warranties. What warranties do they set?

f. Suppose Acura's cost of offering warranties decreases to $C_V = 1,000w_V$. What is the new Nash equilibrium? Explain the effect of the decrease in Volvo's cost function on the equilibrium warranties. **M**

2. Dynamic Games

2.1 Two firms are planning to sell 10 or 20 units of their goods and face the following profit matrix:

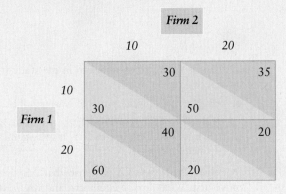

a. What is the Nash equilibrium if both firms make their decisions simultaneously?

b. How does your analysis change if the government imposes a lump-sum franchise tax of 40 on each firm (that is, the payoffs in the matrix are all reduced by 40). Explain how your analysis would change if the firms have an additional option of shutting down and avoiding the lump-sum tax rather than producing 10 or 20 units and paying the tax.

c. Draw the game tree if Firm 1 can decide first (and there is no tax). What is the outcome? Why?

d. Draw the game tree if Firm 2 can decide first. What is the outcome? Why?

2.2 In a repeated game, how does the outcome differ if firms know that the game will be (a) repeated indefinitely, (b) repeated a known, finite number of times, (c) repeated a finite number of times but the firms are unsure as to which period will be the last period?

*2.3 If the airline game in Table 13.1 is repeated, what happens if the players know the game will last five periods? What happens if the game is played indefinitely but one or both firms care only about current profit?

2.4 A small tourist town has two Italian restaurants, Romano's and Giardino's. Normally both restaurants prosper with no advertising. Romano's could take some of Giardino's customers by running radio ads and Giardino's could do the same thing. The one-month profit matrix (showing payoffs in thousands of dollars) is

Romano's

		Do Not Advertise	Advertise
Giardino's	Do Not Advertise	3 / 3	4 / 0
	Advertise	0 / 4	1 / 1

a. What is the Nash equilibrium in the static (one month) game?

b. Describe one or more possible Nash equilibria if the game is repeated indefinitely.

c. Are there multiple equilibria if the game is repeated indefinitely?

2.5 In Solved Problem 13.2, suppose that Mimi can move first. What are the equilibria, and why? Now repeat your analysis if Jeff can move first.

2.6. Solve for the Stackelberg subgame-perfect Nash equilibrium for the following game tree. What is the joint-profit maximizing outcome? Why is that not the outcome of this game?

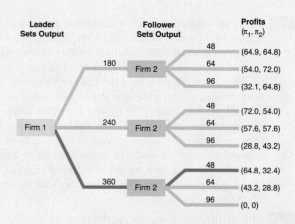

2.7 A thug wants the contents of a safe and is threatening the owner, the only person who knows the code, to open the safe. "I will kill you if you don't open the safe, and let you live if you do." Should the information holder believe the threat and open the safe? The table shows the value that each person places on the various possible outcomes.

	Thug	Safe's Owner
Open the safe, thug does not kill	4	3
Open the safe, thug kills	2	1
Do not open, thug kills	1	2
Do not open, thug does not kill	3	4

Such a game appears in many films, including *Die Hard*, *Crimson Tide*, and *The Maltese Falcon*.

a. Draw the game tree. Who moves first?

b. What is the equilibrium?

c. Does the safe's owner believe the thug's threat?

d. Does the safe's owner open the safe?

2.8 Levi Strauss and Wrangler are planning new generation jeans and must decide on the colors for their products. The possible colors are white, black, and violet. The payoff to each firm depends on the color it chooses and the color chosen by its rival, as the profit matrix shows:

Levi Strauss

		White	Black	Violet
Wrangler	White	10 / 10	30 / 20	40 / 30
	Black	20 / 30	0 / 0	35 / 15
	Violet	15 / 40	20 / 35	0 / 0

a. Given that the firms move simultaneously, identify any dominant strategies in this game, and find any pure strategy Nash equilibria.

b. Now suppose the firms move sequentially, with Wrangler moving first. Draw a game tree and identify any subgame perfect Nash equilibria in this sequential move game.

*2.9 A monopoly manufacturing plant currently uses many workers to pack its product into boxes. It can replace these workers with an expensive set of robotic arms. Although the robotic arms raise the monopoly's fixed cost substantially, they lower its marginal cost because it no longer has to hire as many workers. Buying the robotic arms raises its total cost: The monopoly can't sell enough boxes to make the machine pay for itself, given the market demand curve. Suppose the incumbent does not invest. If its rival does not enter, it earns $0 and the incumbent earns $900. If the rival enters, it earns $300 and the incumbent earns $400. Alternatively, the incumbent invests. If the rival does not enter, it earns $0 and the incumbent earns $500. If the rival enters, the rival loses $36 and the incumbent makes $132. Show the game tree. Should the monopoly buy the machine anyway? (See Solved Problem 13.3.)

*2.10 Suppose that an incumbent can commit to producing a large quantity of output before the potential entrant decides whether to enter. The incumbent chooses whether to commit to produce a small quantity or a large quantity. The rival then decides whether to enter. If the incumbent commits to the small output level and if the rival does not enter, the rival makes $0 and the incumbent makes $900. If it does enter, the rival makes $125 and the incumbent earns $450. If the incumbent commits to producing the large quantity, and the potential entrant stays out of the market, the potential entrant makes $0 and the incumbent makes $800. If the rival enters, the best the entrant can make is $0, the same amount it would earn if it didn't enter, but the incumbent earns only $400. Show the game tree. What is the subgame perfect Nash equilibrium? (See Solved Problem 13.3.)

*2.11 Before entry, the incumbent earns a monopoly profit of $\pi_m = \$10$ (million). If entry occurs, the incumbent and entrant each earn the duopoly profit, $\pi_d = \$3$. Suppose that the incumbent can induce the government to require all firms to install pollution-control devices that cost each firm $4. Show the game tree. Should the incumbent urge the government to require pollution-control devices? Why or why not? (See Solved Problem 13.3.)

2.12 Due to learning by doing (Chapter 7), the more that an incumbent firm produces in the first period, the lower its marginal cost in the second period. If a potential entrant expects the incumbent to produce a large quantity in the second period, it does not enter. Draw a game tree to illustrate why an incumbent would produce more in the first period than the single-period profit-maximizing level. Now change the payoffs in the tree to show a situation in which the firm does not increase production in the first period. (See Solved Problem 13.3.)

2.13 From the ninth century BC until the proliferation of gunpowder in the fifteenth century AD, the ultimate weapon of mass destruction was the catapult (Wilford, John Noble, "How Catapults Married Science, Politics and War," *New York Times*, February 24, 2004, D3). Hero of Alexandria pointed out in the first century AD that it was not enough to have catapults. You needed your potential enemies to know that you had catapults so that they would not attack you in the first place. As early as the fourth century BC, rulers set up what were essentially research and development laboratories to support military technology. However, unlike today, there was a conspicuous lack of secrecy. According to Alex Roland, a historian of technology at Duke University, "Rulers seemed to promote the technology for immediate payoff for themselves and had not yet worked through the notion that you ought to protect your investment with secrecy and restrictions. So engineers shopped their wares around, and information circulated freely among countries." Given this information, describe a ruler's optimal strategy with respect to catapult research, development, deployment, and public announcements. Should the strategy depend upon the country's wealth or size? What role does credibility of announcements play?

2.14 In 2007, Italy announced that an Italian journalist who had been held hostage for 15 days by the Taliban in Afghanistan had been ransomed for five Taliban prisoners. Governments in many nations denounced the act as a bad idea because it rewarded terrorism and encouraged more abductions. Use an extensive-form game tree to analyze the basic arguments. Can you draw any hard and fast conclusions about whether the Italians' actions were a good or bad idea? (*Hint*: Does your answer depend on the relative weight one puts on future costs and benefits relative to those today?)

3. Auctions

3.1 Suppose that Anna, Bill, and Cameron are the only people interested in the paintings of the Bucks County artist Walter Emerson Baum. His painting *Sellers Mill* is being auctioned by a second-price sealed-bid auction. Suppose Anna's value of the painting is $20,000, Bill's is $18,500, and Cameron's is $16,800. Each bidder's consumer surplus is $v_i - p$ if he or she wins the auction and 0 if he or she loses. The values are private. What is each bidder's optimal bid? Who wins the auction, and what price does he or she pay? **M**

3.2 At the end of performances of his Broadway play "Cyrano de Bergerac," Kevin Kline, who starred as Cyrano, the cavalier poet with a huge nose, auctioned his prosthetic proboscis, which he and his co-star, Jennifer Garner, autographed (**www .nytimes.com/2007/12/09/business/09suits.html**) to benefit Broadway Cares in its fight against AIDS. An English auction was used. One night, a television producer grabbed the nose for $1,400, while the next night it fetched $1,600. On other nights, it sold for $3,000 and $900. Why did the value fluctuate substantially from night to night? Which bidder's bid determined the sales price? How was the auction price affected by the audience's knowledge that the proceeds would go to charity?

4. Behavioral Game Theory

4.1 Draw a game tree that represents the ultimatum game in which the proposer is a first mover who decides how much to offer a responder and the responder then decides to accept or reject the offer. The total amount available is $50 if agreement is reached but both players get nothing if the responder rejects the offer.

4.2 A prisoners' dilemma game is played for a fixed number of periods. The fully rational solution is for each player to defect in each period. However, in experiments with students, players often cooperate for a significant number of periods if the total number of periods is fairly large (such as 10 or 20). What explanation can you give for this behavior?

5. Challenge

5.1 In the game between Intel and AMD in the Challenge Solution, suppose that each firm earns a profit of 9 if both firms advertise. What is the new subgame perfect Nash equilibrium outcome? Show in a game tree.

5.2 Derive the mixed strategy equilibrium if both Intel and AMD act simultaneously in the game in the Challenge Solution. What is the expected profit of each firm? (*Hint*: see Solved Problems 13.1 and 13.2 and the Challenge Solution.) **M**

Oligopoly and Monopolistic Competition

14

Anyone can win unless there happens to be a second entry. —George Ade

Governments consistently intervene in aircraft manufacturing markets. France, Germany, Spain, and the United Kingdom jointly own and heavily subsidize Airbus, which competes in the wide-body aircraft market with the U.S. firm Boeing. The U.S. government decries the European subsidies to Airbus while directing lucrative military contracts to Boeing, which the Europeans view as implicit subsidies.

In 1992, these governments signed a U.S.–EU agreement on trade in civil aircraft that limits government subsidies, including a maximum direct subsidy limit of 33% of development costs and various limits on variable costs. Irwin and Pavcnik (2004) found that aircraft prices increased by about 3.7% after the 1992 agreement. This price hike is consistent with a 5% increase in firms' marginal costs after the subsidy cuts.

Since then, Washington and the European Union have continued to trade counter-complaints in front of the World Trade Organization (WTO). Each repeatedly charges the other with illegally subsidizing its aircraft manufacturer. In 2010, the WTO ruled that Airbus received improper subsidies for its A380 superjumbo jet and several other aircraft, hurting Boeing. In 2012, the WTO ruled that Boeing and Airbus both received improper subsidies. Yet the cycle of subsidies, charges, agreements, and new subsidies continues…

If only one government subsidizes its firm, what is the effect on price and quantity in the aircraft manufacturing market (see Solved Problem 14.3)? What happens if both governments subsidize their firms (see the Challenge Solution)?

The major airlines within a country compete with relatively few other firms. Consequently, each firm's profit depends on its own actions and those of its rivals. Similarly, three firms—Nintendo, Microsoft, and Sony—dominate the $13 billion U.S. video game market, and each firm's profit depends on how its price stacks up to those of its rivals and whether its product has better features.

The airlines and the video game firms are each an **oligopoly**: a small group of firms in a market with substantial barriers to entry. Because relatively few firms compete in such a market, each can influence the price, and hence its actions affect rival

481

firms. The need to consider the behavior of rival firms makes an oligopoly firm's profit maximization decision more difficult than that of a monopoly or competitive firm. A monopoly has no rivals, and a competitive firm ignores the behavior of individual rivals—it considers only the market price and its own costs in choosing its profit-maximizing output.

An oligopoly firm that ignores or inaccurately predicts its rivals' behavior is likely to suffer a loss of profit. For example, as its rivals produce more cars, the price that Ford can get for its cars falls. If Ford underestimates how many cars Toyota and Honda will produce, Ford may produce too many automobiles and lose money.

Oligopolistic firms may act independently or coordinate their actions. If firms coordinate setting their prices or quantities, the firms are said to **collude**. A group of firms that collude is called a **cartel**. If all the firms in a market collude and behave like a monopoly, the members of a cartel collectively earn the monopoly profit—the maximum possible profit. Generally, collusion is illegal in most developed countries.

How do oligopolistic firms behave if they do not collude? Although there is only one model of competition and only one model of monopoly, there are many models of oligopolistic behavior that have many possible equilibrium prices and quantities.

The appropriate model depends on the characteristics of the market, including the type of *actions* firms take—such as set quantity or price—and whether firms act simultaneously or sequentially. We examine the three best-known oligopoly models in turn. In the *Cournot model*, firms simultaneously choose quantities without colluding. In the *Stackelberg model*, a leader firm chooses its quantity and then the follower firms independently choose their quantities. In the *Bertrand model*, firms simultaneously and independently choose prices.

To compare market outcomes within the various models, we must be able to characterize the oligopoly equilibrium. Because oligopolistic firms may take many possible actions (such as setting price or quantity or choosing an advertising level), the oligopoly equilibrium rule needs to refer to firms' behavior more generally than just setting output. Thus, we use the Nash equilibrium concept that we introduced in Chapter 13: a set of strategies is a *Nash equilibrium* if, when all other players use these strategies, no player can obtain a higher payoff by choosing a different strategy. In most models in this chapter, we use a special case of that definition that is appropriate for the single-period oligopoly models in which the only action that a firm can take is to set either its quantity or its price: A set of actions that the firms take is a *Nash equilibrium* if, holding the actions of all other firms constant, no firm can obtain a higher profit by choosing a different action.

If oligopolistic firms do not collude, they collectively earn less than the monopoly profit. Yet because there are relatively few firms in the market, oligopolistic firms that act independently may earn positive economic profits in the long run, unlike competitive firms.

In an oligopolistic market, one or more barriers to entry keep the number of firms small. In a market with no barriers to entry, firms enter the market until profits are driven to zero. In perfectly competitive markets, enough entry occurs that firms face a horizontal demand curve and are price takers. However, in other markets, even after entry has driven profits to zero, each firm faces a downward-sloping demand curve. Because of this slope, the firm can charge a price above its marginal cost, creating a *market failure*: inefficient (too little) consumption (Chapter 9). **Monopolistic competition** is a market structure in which firms have market power (the ability to raise price profitably above marginal cost) but no additional firm can enter and earn a positive profit.

In this chapter, we examine cartelized, oligopolistic, and monopolistically competitive markets in which firms set quantities or prices. As we saw in Chapter 11, the monopoly equilibrium is the same whether a monopoly sets price or quantity. In contrast, the oligopolistic and monopolistically competitive equilibria differ if firms set prices instead of quantities.

In this chapter, we examine six main topics	
	1. **Market Structures.** The number of firms, price, profits, and other properties of markets vary depending on whether the market is monopolistic, oligopolistic, monopolistically competitive, or competitive.
	2. **Cartels.** If firms successfully coordinate their actions, they can collectively behave like a monopoly.
	3. **Cournot Oligopoly Model.** In a Cournot model, in which firms simultaneously set their output levels without colluding, market output and firms' profits lie between the competitive and monopoly levels.
	4. **Stackelberg Oligopoly Model.** In a Stackelberg model, in which a *leader* firm chooses its output level before follower rival firms choose their output levels, market output is greater than if all firms choose their output simultaneously, and the leader makes a higher profit than the other firms.
	5. **Bertrand Oligopoly Model.** In a Bertrand model, in which firms simultaneously set their prices without colluding, the equilibrium depends critically on the degree of product differentiation.
	6. **Monopolistic Competition.** When firms can freely enter the market but face downward-sloping demand curves in equilibrium, firms charge prices above marginal cost but make no profit.

14.1 Market Structures

Markets differ according to the number of firms in the market, the ease with which firms may enter and leave the market, and the ability of firms in a market to differentiate their products from those of their rivals. Table 14.1 lists the characteristics and properties of monopoly, oligopoly, monopolistic competition, and competition. For each of these market structures, we assume that the firms face many price-taking buyers.

Competitive firms are price takers because they face horizontal demand curves; whereas monopolies, oligopolies, and monopolistically competitive firms are price setters because they face downward-sloping demand curves (row 1 of Table 14.1). All else the same, a monopoly sets a very high price, oligopolistic and monopolistically

Table 14.1 Properties of Monopoly, Oligopoly, Monopolistic Competition, and Competition

	Monopoly	Oligopoly	Monopolistic Competition	Competition
1. Ability to set price	Price setter	Price setter	Price setter	Price taker
2. Price level	very high	high	high	low
3. Market power	$p > MC$	$p > MC$	$p > MC$	$p = MC$
4. Entry conditions	No entry	Limited entry	Free entry	Free entry
5. Number of firms	1	Few	Few or many	Many
6. Long-run profit	≥ 0	≥ 0	0	0
7. Strategy dependent on individual rival firms' behavior	No (has no rivals)	Yes	Yes	No (cares about market price only)
8. Products	Single product	May be differentiated	May be differentiated	Undifferentiated
9. Example	Local natural gas utility	Automobile manufacturers	Plumbers in a small town	Apple farmers

competitive firms set high prices, and competitive firms receive a low price equal to the marginal cost of production (row 2). That is, except in competitive markets, price is above marginal cost (row 3), which creates market failures (too little output is sold).

A monopoly or an oligopoly does not fear entry (row 4) because of insurmountable barriers to entry such as government licenses and patents. In both competitive and monopolistically competitive markets, entry occurs until no new firm can profitably enter (so the marginal firm earns zero profit). These impediments to entry restrict the number of firms so that there is only one firm (*mono*) in a monopoly, and, usually, only a few (*oligo*) firms in an oligopoly, while there are a few or many firms in monopolistically competitive markets and many in competitive markets (row 5). Monopolistically competitive markets have fewer firms than perfectly competitive markets do. Because they have relatively few rivals and hence are large relative to the market, each monopolistically competitive firm faces a downward-sloping demand curve.

Oligopolistic and monopolistically competitive firms pay attention to rival firms' behavior, in contrast to monopolistic or competitive firms (row 7). A monopoly has no rivals. A competitive firm ignores the behavior of individual rivals in choosing its output because the market price tells the firm everything it needs to know about its competitors.

Oligopolistic and monopolistically competitive firms may produce differentiated products (row 8). For example, Camry and Taurus automobiles differ in size, weight, appearance, and other characteristics. In contrast, competitive apple farmers sell undifferentiated (homogeneous) products.

14.2 Cartels

People of the same trade seldom meet together, even for merriment and diversion, but the conversation ends in a conspiracy against the public, or some contrivance to raise prices. —Adam Smith, 1776

Oligopolistic firms have an incentive to collude so as to increase their profits. However, because firms can make even more money by cheating on the cartel, firms do not always collude successfully.

Why Cartels Succeed or Fail

As Adam Smith noted two centuries ago, firms have an incentive to form a cartel in which each firm reduces its output, which leads to higher prices and higher profits for individual firms and the firms collectively. Luckily for consumers' pocketbooks, cartels often fail because a government forbids them and because each firm in a cartel has an incentive to cheat on the cartel agreement by producing extra output. We now consider why cartels form, what laws prohibit cartels, why cartel members have an incentive to deviate from the cartel agreement, and why some cartels succeed and others fail.

Why Cartels Form. A cartel forms if members of the cartel believe that they can raise their profits by coordinating their actions. Although cartels usually involve oligopolies, cartels may form in a market that would otherwise be competitive.

If a competitive firm is maximizing its profit, why should joining a cartel increase its profit? The answer involves a subtle argument. When a competitive firm chooses its profit-maximizing output level, it considers how varying its output affects its profit only. The firm ignores the effect that changing its output level has on other firms' profits. A cartel, by contrast, considers how changes in any one firm's output affect the profits of all members of the cartel.

If a competitive firm lowers its output, it raises the market price very slightly—so slightly that the firm ignores the effect not only on other firms' profits but also on its own. If all the identical competitive firms in an industry lower their output by this same amount, however, the market price will change noticeably. Recognizing this effect of collective action, a cartel chooses to produce a smaller market output than is produced by a competitive market.

Figure 14.1 illustrates this difference between a competitive market and a cartel. There are n firms in this market, and no further entry is possible. Panel a shows the marginal and average cost curves of a typical firm. If all firms are price takers, the market supply curve, S, is the horizontal sum of the individual marginal cost curves above minimum average cost, as shown in panel b. At the competitive price, p_c, each price-taking firm produces q_c units of output (where MC intersects the line at p_c in panel a). The market output is $Q_c = nq_c$ (where S intersects the market demand curve in panel b).

Now suppose that the firms form a cartel. Should they reduce their output? At the competitive output, the cartel's marginal cost (which is the competitive industry supply curve, S in panel b) is greater than its marginal revenue, so the cartel's profit rises if it reduces output. The cartel's collective profit rises until output is reduced by enough that its marginal revenue equals its marginal cost at Q_m, the monopoly output. If the profit of the cartel increases, the profit of each of the n members of the cartel also increases. To achieve the cartel output level, each firm must reduce its output to $q_m = Q_m/n$, as panel a shows.

Figure 14.1 Competition Versus Cartel

(a) The marginal cost and average cost of one of the n firms in the market are shown. A competitive firm produces q_c units of output, whereas a cartel member produces $q_m < q_c$. At the cartel price, p_m, each cartel member has an incentive to increase its output from q_m to q^* (where the dotted line at p_m intersects the MC curve). (b) The competitive equilibrium, e_c, has more output and a lower price than the cartel equilibrium, e_m.

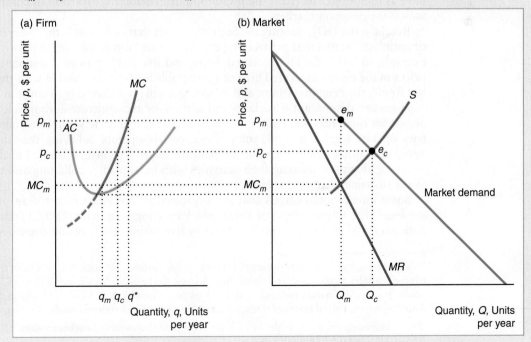

Why must the firms form a cartel to achieve these higher profits? A competitive firm produces q_c, where its marginal cost equals the market price. If only one firm reduces its output, it loses profit because it sells fewer units at essentially the same price. By getting all the firms to lower their output collectively, the cartel raises the market price and hence individual firms' profits. The less elastic the market demand curve faced by the potential cartel, all else the same, the higher the price the cartel sets (Chapter 11) and the greater the benefit from cartelizing. If the penalty for forming an illegal cartel is relatively low, some unscrupulous businesspeople may succumb to the lure of extra profits and join.

Laws Against Cartels. In the late nineteenth century, cartels (or, as they were called then, *trusts*) were legal and common in the United States. Oil, railroad, sugar, and tobacco trusts raised prices substantially above competitive levels.[1] In response to the trusts' high prices, the U.S. Congress passed the Sherman Antitrust Act in 1890 and the Federal Trade Commission Act of 1914, which prohibit firms from *explicitly* agreeing to take actions that reduce competition. In particular, cartels that are formed for the purpose of jointly setting price are strictly prohibited. By imposing penalties on firms caught colluding, these antitrust laws reduce the probability that cartels form. The Sherman Antitrust laws are enforced by the U.S. Department of Justice (DOJ), and the Federal Trade Commission Act is enforced by the Federal Trade Commission (FTC).

Virtually all industrialized nations have *antitrust laws*—or, as they are known in other countries, *competition policies*—that limit or forbid some or all cartels. Canada's Competition Act, a federal law that governs most business conduct, contains both criminal and civil provisions aimed at preventing anticompetitive practices. The EU has a competition policy, which, under the Treaty of the European Community (EC Treaty or Treaty of Rome) in 1957, gives it substantial powers to prevent actions that hinder competition. The first provision is Article 81 EC, which prohibits ". . . all agreements between undertakings, decisions by associations of undertakings and concerted practices which may affect trade between Member States and which have as their object or effect the prevention, restriction or distortion of competition within the common market . . ."

Recently, the DOJ, quoting the Supreme Court that collusion is the "supreme evil of antitrust," stated that prosecuting cartels was its "top enforcement priority." For example, in 2012, the DOJ accused Apple and five publishers of colluding to raise prices in the ebook market. Three of those publishers quickly settled with the DOJ, but Apple, the Penguin Group, and Macmillan will have their day in court in 2013.[2]

However, despite antitrust laws and actions by the antitrust authorities, cartels persist for three reasons. First, international cartels and cartels within certain countries operate legally. Second, some illegal cartels operate believing that they can avoid detection or that if caught the punishment will be insignificant. Third, some firms are able to coordinate their activities without explicitly colluding and thereby avoid violating competition laws.

Some international cartels that are organized by countries rather than by firms are legal. The Organization of Petroleum Exporting Countries (OPEC) is an international cartel that was formed in 1960 by five major oil-exporting countries: Iran,

---

[1]Nineteenth-century and early twentieth-century robber barons who made fortunes from these cartels include John Jacob Astor (real estate, fur), Andrew Carnegie (railroads, steel), Henry Clay Frick (steel), Jay Gould (finance, railroads), Mark Hopkins (railroads), J. P. Morgan (banking), John D. Rockefeller (oil), Leland Stanford (railroads), and Cornelius Vanderbilt (railroads, shipping).

[2]For an interesting comment on this lawsuit, see **www.publishersweekly.com/binary-data/ARTICLE_ ATTACHMENT/file/000/000/948-1.pdf**.

Iraq, Kuwait, Saudi Arabia, and Venezuela. In 1971, OPEC members agreed to take an active role in setting oil prices.

Many illegal cartels flout the competition laws in major industrial countries, believing that they are unlikely to get caught or that the punishments they face are so negligible that it pays to collude. Small fines fail to discourage cartel behavior. In a cartel case involving the $9 billion American carpet industry, a firm with $150 million in annual sales agreed with the U.S. Justice Department to plead guilty and pay a fine of $150,000. It is hard to imagine that a fine of one-tenth of 1% of annual sales significantly deters cartel behavior.

To determine guilt, American antitrust laws use evidence of conspiracy—such as explicit agreements—rather than the economic effect of monopoly. Charging monopoly-level prices is not necessarily illegal—only the "bad behavior" of explicitly agreeing to raise prices is against the law. As a result, some groups of firms charge monopoly-level prices without violating the competition laws. These firms may *tacitly collude* without meeting by signaling to each other through their actions. Although the firms' actions may not be illegal, they behave much like cartels. For example, MacAvoy (1995) concluded that the major U.S. long-distance telephone companies tacitly colluded; as a result, each firm's Lerner Index (Chapter 11), $(p - MC)/p$, exceeded 60%, which is well above the competitive level, 0%.[3]

In the last couple of decades, the European Commission has been pursuing competition (antitrust) cases under laws that are similar to U.S. statutes. Recently, the European Commission, the DOJ, and the FTC have become increasingly aggressive, prosecuting many more cases. Following the lead of the United States, which imposes both civil and criminal penalties, the British government introduced legislation in 2002 to criminalize certain cartel-related conduct. Similarly, Japan started in 2004 to pursue antitrust cases more aggressively. In recent years, the European Union, which uses only civil penalties, and the United States, which uses both criminal and civil penalties, have substantially increased fines.

APPLICATION

Catwalk Cartel

Being slender, rich, and beautiful doesn't make you immune to exploitation. Some of the world's most successful models charged 10 of New York's top modeling agencies—including Wilhelmina, Ford, Next, IMG, and Elite—with operating a sleazy cartel that cut their commissions by millions of dollars.

Carolyn Fears—a 5'11" redheaded former model who had earned up to $200,000 a year—initiated the private antitrust suit when she learned that her agency not only charged her a 20% commission every time she was booked, but also extracted a 20% commission from her employers (mostly magazines). Her class-action lawsuit alleged that the agencies collectively fixed commissions for Claudia Schiffer, Heidi Klum, Gisele Bundchen, and thousands of other models over many years.

The agencies had formed an industry group, International Model Managers Association, Inc. (IMMA), which held repeated meetings. Monique Pillard, an executive at Elite Model Management, fired off a memo concerning one IMMA meeting, in which she "made a point . . . that we are all committing suicide, if we do not stick together. Pauline's agreed with me but as usual, Bill Weinberg [of Wilhelmina] cautioned me about price fixing. . . . Ha! Ha! Ha! . . . the usual (expletive)." As the trial judge, Harold Baer, Jr., observed, while "Wilhelmina objects to the outward discussion of price fixing, it is plausible from Pillard's reaction that Wilhelmina's objection was to the dissemination of information, not to the underlying price-fixing agreement."

[3]See "Tacit Collusion in Long-Distance Service" in MyEconLab, Chapter Resources, Chapter 14.

The models argued that the association was little more than a front for helping agency heads monitor each other's pricing policies. Documents show that, shortly after association meetings, the agencies uniformly raised their commission rates from 10% to 15% and then to 20%. For example, at a meeting before the last increase, an Elite executive gave his competitors a heads-up—but had not informed his clients—that Elite planned to raise its commissions to 20%. He said that at Elite, "we were also favorable to letting everyone know as much as possible about our pricing policies."

In 2007, the models won their court case, having sued successfully under U.S. laws that prohibit price-fixing cartels. They received payments from the firms; for example, IMG paid the models $11 million. In 2011, the Competition Commission of Singapore fined a cartel consisting of 10 modeling agencies for price-fixing in a similar case.

Why Cartels Fail. Many cartels fail even without legal intervention. *Cartels fail if noncartel members can supply consumers with large quantities of goods.* For example, copper producers formed an international cartel that controlled only about a third of the noncommunist world's copper production and faced additional competition from firms that recycle copper from scrap materials. Because of this competition from noncartel members, the cartel was not successful in raising and keeping copper prices high.

In addition, *each member of a cartel has an incentive to cheat on the cartel agreement.* (As W. C. Fields said, "A thing worth having is a thing worth cheating for.") The owner of a firm may reason, "I joined the cartel to encourage others to reduce their output and increase profits for everyone. I can make more money, however, if I cheat on the cartel agreement by producing extra output. I can get away with cheating if the other firms can't tell who's producing the extra output because I'm just one of many firms and because I'll hardly affect the market price." By this reasoning, it is in each firm's best interest for all *other* firms to honor the cartel agreement—thus driving up the market price—while it ignores the agreement and makes extra profitable sales at the high price.

Figure 14.1 illustrates why firms want to cheat. At the cartel output, q_m in panel a, each cartel member's marginal cost is MC_m. The marginal revenue of a firm that violates the agreement is p_m because it is acting like a price taker with respect to the market price. Because the firm's marginal revenue (price) is above its marginal cost, the firm wants to increase its output. If the firm decides to violate the cartel agreement, it maximizes its profit by increasing its output to q^*, where its marginal cost equals p_m. As more and more firms leave the cartel, the cartel price falls. Eventually, if enough firms quit, the cartel collapses.

Maintaining Cartels

To keep firms from violating the cartel agreement, the cartel must be able to detect cheating and punish violators. Further, members of a cartel must keep their illegal behavior hidden from customers and government agencies.

Detection and Enforcement. Cartels use various techniques to detect cheating. Some cartels, for example, give members the right to inspect each other's books. Some rely on governments to report bids on government contracts so that cartel firms can learn if a member bids below the agreed-on price. Cartels may also divide the market by region or by customers, making it more likely that a firm that steals another firm's customers is detected, as in the case of a two-country mercury cartel (1928–1972) that allocated the Americas to Spain and Europe to Italy. Another option is for a cartel to turn to industry organizations that collect data on market share by firm. A cheating cartel's market share would rise, tipping off the other firms that it cheated.

Perhaps you have seen "low price" ads in which local retail stores guarantee to meet or beat the prices of competitors. These ads may in fact be a way for the firm to induce its customers to report cheating on a cartel agreement by other firms (Salop, 1986).

Various methods are used to enforce cartel agreements. For example, GE and Westinghouse, the two major sellers of large steam-turbine generators, included "most-favored-nation clauses" (more accurately, most-favored-customer clauses) in their contracts. These contracts stated that the seller would not offer a lower price to any other current or future buyer without offering the same price decrease to that buyer. This type of rebate clause creates a penalty for cheating on the cartel: If either company cheats by cutting prices, it has to lower prices to all previous buyers as well. Threats of violence are another means of enforcing a cartel agreement.

Government Support. Sometimes governments help create and enforce cartels, exempting them from antitrust laws. For example, U.S., European, and other governments signed an agreement in 1944 to establish a cartel to fix prices for international airline flights and prevent competition (which was struck down by the European Court of Justice in 2002).

Professional baseball teams have been exempted from some U.S. antitrust laws since 1922. As a result, they can use the courts to help enforce certain aspects of their cartel agreement. Major-league clubs are able to avoid competing for young athletes by means of a draft and contracts, limiting geographic competition between teams, jointly negotiating television and other rights, and through other collective actions.

Barriers to Entry. Barriers to entry that limit the number of firms help the cartel detect and punish cheating. The fewer the firms in a market, the more likely it is that other firms will know if a given firm cheats and the easier it is to impose penalties. Cartels with a large number of firms are relatively rare, except those involving professional associations. Hay and Kelley (1974) examined Department of Justice price-fixing cases from 1963 to 1972 and found that only 6.5% involved 50 or more conspirators, the average number of firms was 7.25, and 48% involved six or fewer firms.

When new firms enter their market, cartels frequently fail. For example, when only Italy and Spain sold mercury, they were able to establish and maintain a stable cartel. When a larger group of countries joined them, their attempts to cartelize the world mercury market repeatedly failed (MacKie-Mason and Pindyck, 1986).

Mergers. If antitrust or competition laws prevent firms from colluding, firms may try to merge instead. Consequently, many governments limit mergers so as to prevent all the firms in a market from combining and forming a monopoly.

U.S. laws restrict the ability of firms to merge if the effect would be anticompetitive. In recent years, the European Commission has been actively reviewing and blocking mergers. For example in 2011, the DOJ and the European Commission blocked a proposed merger between the world's two largest stock exchanges, the New York Stock Exchange and NASDAQ.

Would it be a good idea to ban all mergers? No, because some mergers result in more efficient production. Formerly separate firms may become more efficient because of greater scale, the sharing of trade secrets, or the closure of duplicative retail outlets. For example, when Chase and Chemical banks merged, they closed or combined seven Manhattan branches that were located within two blocks of other branches. Thus, whether a merger raises or lowers welfare depends on which of its two offsetting effects—reducing competition and increasing efficiency—is larger.

Since the 1990s, the hospital market has consolidated substantially through mergers, with an average of nearly 60 mergers per year in major metropolitan areas. Do prices fall because efficiency gains (such as reducing duplication of functions) or do they rise due to a reduction in competition?

Using a sample of U.S. hospitals, Dafny (2009) found that local hospital prices rise by about 40% after a merger, with the (apparently large) cost savings going to the hospitals rather than to the patients. Apparently, the price effects of hospital mergers vary substantially across hospitals. Haas-Wilson and Garmon (2011) studied a merger of two hospitals in Evanston, Illinois, and found that one hospital raised its prices by 20% but the other's prices remained constant. Tenn (2011) examined the Summit-Sutter mergers in Berkeley and Oakland, California, and found that Summit's prices increased between 28% and 44%. Brand et al. (2012) looked very carefully at one proposed hospital merger in Virginia and argued that it would raise prices by 4%.

14.3 Cournot Oligopoly Model

How do oligopoly firms behave if they do not collude? The French economist and mathematician Antoine-Augustin Cournot introduced the first formal model of oligopoly in 1838. Cournot explained how oligopoly firms behave if they simultaneously choose how much they produce.

The firms act independently and have imperfect information about their rivals, so each firm must choose its output level before knowing what the other firms will choose. The quantity that one firm produces directly affects the profits of the other firms because the market price depends on total output. Thus, in choosing its strategy to maximize its profit, each firm considers its beliefs about the output its rivals will sell. Cournot introduced an equilibrium concept that is the same as the Nash definition in which the action that firms take is to choose quantities.

To illustrate this model as simply as possible, we start by making four restrictive assumptions. First, we assume that the market lasts for only one period. Consequently, each firm chooses its quantity or price only once.

Second, we assume in this section that the firms act simultaneously. In our discussion of the Stackelberg model, we change this assumption so that one firm acts before the other.

Third, we initially assume that all firms are identical in the sense that they have the same cost functions and produce identical, *undifferentiated* products. Then, we show how the market outcomes change if costs differ or if consumers believe that the products differ across firms.

Fourth, we initially illustrate each of these oligopoly models for a **duopoly**: an oligopoly with two (*duo*) firms. Then, we examine the equilibrium changes as the number of firms increases.

The Duopoly Nash-Cournot Equilibrium

To illustrate the basic idea of the Cournot model, we start with a duopoly model. We examine the actual market where American Airlines and United Airlines compete for customers on flights between Chicago and Los Angeles.[4] The total

[4]This example is based on Brander and Zhang (1990). They reported data for economy and discount passengers taking direct flights between the two cities in the third quarter of 1985. In calculating the profits, we assume that Brander and Zhang's estimate of the firms' constant marginal cost is the same as the firms' relevant long-run average cost.

number of passengers flown by these two firms, Q, is the sum of the number of passengers flown on American, q_A, and those flown on United, q_U. No other companies can enter this market because they cannot obtain landing rights at both airports.[5]

How many passengers does each airline firm choose to carry? To answer this question, we determine the Nash equilibrium for this model. This Nash equilibrium, in which firms choose quantities, is also called a **Nash-Cournot equilibrium** (or a **Cournot equilibrium** or a **Nash-in-quantities equilibrium**): a set of quantities chosen by firms such that, holding the quantities of all other firms constant, no firm can obtain a higher profit by choosing a different quantity.

We studied this airline market in our normal-form game example in Chapter 13, where we assumed that the firms chose between two output levels only. That analysis illustrates a Nash-Cournot equilibrium. Here, we first generalize the analysis so that the firms can consider using any possible output level, and then we generalize the model to allow for a larger number of players, n. We determine each firm's *best-response* (Chapter 13)—the strategy that maximizes a player's payoff given its beliefs about its rivals' strategies—and use that information to solve for the Nash-Cournot equilibrium.

To determine the Nash-Cournot equilibrium, we must establish how each firm chooses its quantity. We start by using the total demand curve for the Chicago–Los Angeles route and a firm's belief about how much its rival will sell to determine its *residual demand curve*: the market demand that is not met by other sellers at any given price (Chapter 8). Next, we examine how a firm uses its residual demand curve to determine its best response: the output level that maximizes its profit given its belief about how much its rival will produce. Finally, we use the information contained in the firms' best-response functions to determine the Nash-Cournot equilibrium quantities.

The quantity that each firm chooses depends on the residual demand curve it faces and its marginal cost. American Airlines' profit-maximizing output depends on how many passengers it believes United will fly.

The estimated airline market demand function is linear,

$$Q = 339 - p, \tag{14.1}$$

where price, p, is the dollar cost of a one-way flight, and the total quantity of the two airlines combined, Q, is measured in thousands of passengers flying one way per quarter. Panels a and b of Figure 14.2 show that this market demand curve, D, is a straight line that hits the price axis at $339 and the quantity axis at 339 units (thousands of passengers) per quarter. Each airline has a constant marginal cost, MC, and an average cost, AC, of $147 per passenger per flight. Using only this information and our economic model, we can determine the Nash-Cournot equilibrium quantities for the two airlines.

Figure 14.2 illustrates two possibilities. If American Airlines were a monopoly, it wouldn't have to worry about United Airlines' actions. American's demand would be the market demand curve, D in panel a. To maximize its profit, American would set its output so that its marginal revenue curve, MR, intersected its marginal cost curve, MC, which is constant at $147 per passenger. Panel a shows that the monopoly output is 96 units (thousands of passengers) per quarter and that the monopoly price is $243 per passenger (one way).

---

[5]Existing airline firms have the right to buy, sell, or rent landing slots. However, by controlling landing slots, existing firms can make entry difficult.

Figure 14.2 American Airlines' Profit-Maximizing Output

(a) If American is a monopoly, it picks its profit-maximizing output, $q_A = 96$ units (thousand passengers) per quarter, so that its marginal revenue, MR, equals its marginal cost, MC. (b) If American believes that United will fly $q_U = 64$ units per quarter, its residual demand curve, D^r, is the market demand curve, D, minus q_U. American maximizes its profit at $q_A = 64$, where its marginal revenue, MR^r, equals MC.

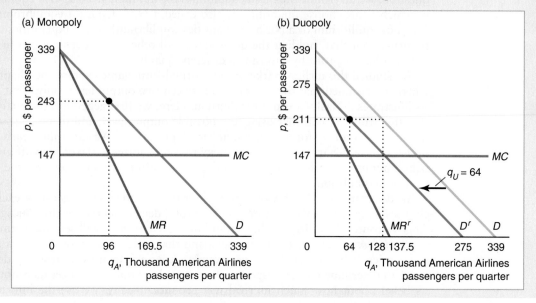

But because American competes with United, American must consider United's behavior when choosing its profit-maximizing output. American's demand is not the entire market demand. Rather, American is concerned with its residual demand curve. In general, if the market demand function is $D(p)$, and the supply of other firms is $S^o(p)$, then the residual demand function, $D^r(p)$, is

$$D^r(p) = D(p) - S^o(p).$$

Thus, if United flies q_U passengers regardless of the price, American transports only the residual demand, $Q = D(p) = 339 - p$ (Equation 14.1), minus the q_U passengers, so $q_A = Q - q_U$. The residual demand that American faces is

$$q_A = Q(p) - q_U = (339 - p) - q_U. \tag{14.2}$$

In panel b, American believes that United will fly $q_U = 64$, so American's residual demand curve, D^r, is the market demand curve, D, moved to the left by $q_U = 64$. For example, if the price is \$211, the total number of passengers who want to fly is $Q = 128$. If United transports $q_U = 64$, American flies $Q - q_U = 128 - 64 = 64 = q_A$.

What is American's best-response, profit-maximizing output if its managers believe that United will fly q_U passengers? *American can think of itself as having a monopoly with respect to the people who don't fly on United.* That is, American can think of itself as having a monopoly with respect to its residual demand curve, D^r. We will use our analysis based on the residual demand curve to derive American's *best-response function*, $q_A = B_A(q_U)$, which shows American's best-response or profit-maximizing output, q_A, as a function of United's output, q_U.[6]

---

[6]*Jargon alert*: Many economists refer to the best-response function as the reaction function.

To maximize its profit, American sets its output so that its marginal revenue corresponding to this residual demand, MR^r, equals its marginal cost. Thus, our first step is to determine American's marginal revenue. Rearranging the terms in Equation 14.2 shows that American's residual inverse demand function is

$$p = 339 - q_A - q_U. \tag{14.3}$$

Consequently, its revenue function based on its residual demand function is

$$R^r(q_A) = pq_A = (339 - q_A - q_U)q_A = 339q_A - (q_A)^2 - q_U q_A.$$

American views its revenue as a function solely of its own output, $R^r(q_A)$, because American treats United's quantity as a constant. Thus, American's marginal revenue with respect to its residual demand function is

$$MR^r = \frac{dR^r(q_A)}{dq_A} = 339 - 2q_A - q_U. \tag{14.4}$$

Equating its marginal revenue with its marginal cost, $147, American derives its best-response function, $MR^r = 339 - 2q_A - q_U = 147 = MC$, or

$$q_A = 96 - \frac{1}{2}q_U = B_A(q_U). \tag{14.5}$$

Figure 14.3 plots American Airlines' best-response function, Equation 14.5, which shows how many tickets American sells for each possible q_U. As the best-response curve shows, American sells the monopoly number of tickets, 96, if American thinks United will fly no passengers, $q_U = 0$. The negative slope of the best-response curve shows that American sells fewer tickets the more people American thinks that United will fly. American sells $q_A = 64$ if it thinks q_U will be 64. American shuts down, $q_A = 0$, if it thinks q_U will be 192 or more, because operating wouldn't be profitable.

Figure 14.3 American's and United's Best-Response Curves

The best-response curves show the output that each firm picks to maximize its profit, given its belief about its rival's output. The Nash-Cournot equilibrium occurs at the intersection of the best-response curves.

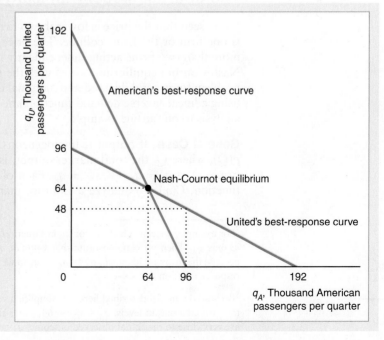

We can derive United's best-response function, $q_U = B_U(q_A)$, similarly. Given that the two firms have identical marginal costs and face the same market demand function, United's best-response function is the same as American's with the quantity subscripts reversed:

$$q_U = 96 - \frac{1}{2}q_A = B_U(q_A). \tag{14.6}$$

We obtain the Nash-Cournot equilibrium quantities by solving Equations 14.5 and 14.6 simultaneously for q_A and q_U.[7] This solution is the point where the firms' best-response curves intersect at $q_A = q_U = 64$. In a Nash-Cournot equilibrium, neither firm wants to change its output level given that the other firm is producing the equilibrium quantity. If American expects United to sell $q_U = 64$, American wants to sell $q_A = 64$. Because this point is on its best-response curve, American doesn't want to change its output from 64. Similarly, if United expects American to sell $q_A = 64$, United doesn't want to change q_U from 64. Thus, this pair of outputs is a Nash equilibrium: Given its correct belief about its rival's output, each firm is maximizing its profit, and neither firm wants to change its output.

Any pair of quantities other than the pair at an intersection of the best-response functions is *not* a Nash-Cournot equilibrium. If either firm is not on its best-response curve, it wants to change its output to increase its profit. For example, the output pair $q_A = 96$ and $q_U = 0$ is not a Nash-Cournot equilibrium. American is perfectly happy producing the monopoly output if United doesn't operate at all: American is on its best-response curve. United, however, would not be happy with this outcome because it is not on United's best-response curve. As its best-response curve shows, if it knows that American will sell $q_A = 96$, United maximizes its profit by selling $q_U = 48$. Only if $q_A = q_U = 64$ does neither firm want to change its action. Based on statistical tests, Brander and Zhang (1990) reported that they could not reject the hypothesis that the Cournot model is consistent with American's and United's behavior.[8]

The Cournot Model with Many Firms

We've seen that the price is lower if two firms set output independently than if there is one firm or the firms collude. The price to consumers is even lower if there are more than two firms acting independently in the market. We now examine how the Nash-Cournot equilibrium varies with the number of firms. We start by solving the problem for general demand and marginal cost functions for n firms. Then, we solve using a linear inverse demand function and a constant marginal cost and apply that analysis to our airline example.

General Case. If output is homogeneous, the market inverse demand function is $p(Q)$, where Q, the total market output, is the sum of the output of each of the n firms: $Q = q_1 + q_2 + \ldots + q_n$. Each of the n identical firms has the same cost function, $C(q_i)$. To analyze a Cournot market of identical firms, we first examine

---

[7]For example, we can substitute for q_U in Equation 14.5 using Equation 14.6 to obtain an equation in only q_A. Then we can substitute that value of q_A in Equation 14.6 to obtain q_U. Alternatively, because the firms are identical, $q_A = q_U = q$, so we can replace both q_A and q_U with q in either best-response function and solve for q.

[8]Because the model described here is a simplified version of the Brander and Zhang (1990) model, the predicted output levels, $q_A = q_U = 64$, differ slightly from theirs. Nonetheless, our predictions are very close to the actual observed outcome, $q_A = 65.9$ and $q_U = 62.7$.

the behavior of a representative firm. Firm 1 wants to maximize its profit through its choice of q_1:

$$\max_{q_1} \pi_1(q_1, q_2, \ldots, q_n) = q_1 p(q_1 + q_2 + \cdots + q_n) - C(q_1) = q_1 p(Q) - C(q_1). \quad (14.7)$$

Firm 1 views the outputs of the other firms as fixed, so $q_2, q_3, \ldots, q_n$ are constants. Firm 1's first-order condition is the partial derivative of its profit with respect to q_1 set equal to zero:[9]

$$\frac{\partial \pi}{\partial q_1} = p(Q) + q_1 \frac{dp(Q)}{dQ} \frac{\partial Q}{\partial q_1} - \frac{dC(q_1)}{dq_1} = 0. \quad (14.8)$$

Given that the other firms' outputs are constants, $dQ/dq_1 = d(q_1 + q_2 + \ldots + q_n)/dq_1 = dq_1/dq_1 = 1$. Making this substitution and rearranging terms, we see that the firm's first-order condition implies that Firm 1 equates is marginal revenue and its marginal cost:

$$MR = p(Q) + q_1 \frac{dp(Q)}{dQ} = \frac{dC(q_1)}{dq_1} = MC. \quad (14.9)$$

Equation 14.9 gives the firm's best-response function, allowing the firm to calculate its optimal q_1 for any given set of outputs of other firms. We can write Firm 1's best-response function as an implicit function of the other firm's output levels: $p(q_1 + q_2 + \cdots + q_n) + q_1(dp/dQ) - dC(q_1)/dq_1 = 0$. Thus, for any given set of $q_2, \ldots, q_n$, the firm can solve for the profit-maximizing q_1 using this expression.

Solving the best-response functions for all the firms simultaneously, we obtain the Nash-Cournot equilibrium quantities $q_1, q_2, \ldots, q_n$. Because all the firms are identical, in equilibrium $q_1 = q_2 = \cdots = q_n = q$.

The marginal revenue expression can be rewritten as $p[1 + (q/p)(dp/dQ)]$. Multiplying and dividing the last term by n, noting that $Q = nq$ (given that all firms are identical), and observing that the market elasticity of demand, ε, is defined as $(dQ/dp)(p/Q)$, we can rewrite the first-order conditions, such as Equation 14.9, as

$$MR = p\left(1 + \frac{1}{n\varepsilon}\right) = \frac{dC(q)}{dq} = MC. \quad (14.10)$$

In Equation 14.10, the firm's marginal revenue is expressed in terms of the elasticity of demand of its residual demand curve, $n\varepsilon$, which is the number of firms, n, times the market demand elasticity, ε. For example, if $n = 2$, the elasticity of demand of either firm's residual demand curve is twice as elastic as the market demand curve at the equilibrium.

We can rearrange Equation 14.10 to determine the Nash-Cournot equilibrium price:

$$p = \frac{MC}{\left(1 + \dfrac{1}{n\varepsilon}\right)}. \quad (14.11)$$

That is, the Nash-Cournot equilibrium price is above the MC by $1/(1 + [n\varepsilon]) > 1$.[10] Holding ε constant, the more firms there are, the more elastic is the residual demand

---

[9]We use a partial derivative to show that we are changing only q_1 and not the other outputs, $q_2, \ldots, q_n$. However, given that Firm 1 views those other outputs as constants so that the only variable in its profit function is q_1, we could use a derivative instead of a partial derivative.

[10]From the Law of Demand, we know that $\varepsilon < 0$, so $1/[n\varepsilon] < 0$. Given that each firm is operating in the elastic portion of its residual demand curve (using the same argument as we did in Chapter 11 to show that a monopoly would not operate in the inelastic portions of its demand curve), $n\varepsilon < -1$, so $1 > -1/[n\varepsilon]$. Thus, $1/(1 + [n\varepsilon]) > 1$.

curve, which causes the price to fall. For example, if the market elasticity ε is constant at -1, then $p = MC/(1 - \frac{1}{2}) = 2MC$ if $n = 2$, $p = MC/(1 - \frac{1}{3}) = 1.5MC$ if $n = 3$, and $p = MC/(1 - \frac{1}{4}) \approx 1.33MC$ if $n = 4$. As n grows without bound, the price approaches MC.

By further rearranging Equation 14.11, we obtain an expression for the Lerner Index, $(p - MC)/p$, in terms of the market demand elasticity and the number of firms:

$$\frac{p - MC}{p} = \frac{1}{n\varepsilon}. \tag{14.12}$$

The larger the Lerner Index, the greater the firm's market power. As Equation 14.12 shows, if we hold the market elasticity constant and increase the number of firms, the Lerner Index falls. As n approaches ∞, the elasticity facing any one firm approaches $-\infty$, so the Lerner Index approaches 0 and the market is competitive.

Linear Case. We cannot explicitly solve for a firm's best-response function or the Nash-Cournot equilibrium given general functional forms, but we can for specific functions, as we now show for the linear case. Suppose that the inverse market demand function is linear,

$$p = a - bQ,$$

and that each firm's marginal cost is m, a constant, and it has no fixed cost.

For this linear model, we can rewrite Firm 1's objective, Equation 14.7, as

$$\max_{q_1} \pi_1(q_1) = q_1[a - b(q_1 + q_2 + \cdots + q_n)] - mq_1. \tag{14.13}$$

Firm 1's first-order condition, Equation 14.9, to maximize its profit is

$$MR = a - b(2q_1 + q_2 + \cdots + q_n) = m = MC. \tag{14.14}$$

Because all firms have the same cost function, $q_2 = q_3 = \cdots = q_n \equiv q$ in equilibrium. Substituting these equalities into Equation 14.14, we find that the first firm's best-response function, B_1, is

$$q_1 = B_1(q_2, q_3, \ldots, q_n) = \frac{a - m}{2b} - \frac{n - 1}{2}q. \tag{14.15}$$

The right-hand sides of the other firms' best-response functions are identical.

All these best-response functions must hold simultaneously. The intersection of the best-response functions determines the Nash-Cournot equilibrium. Given that all the firms are identical, all choose the same output level in equilibrium. Thus, we can solve for the equilibrium by setting $q_1 = q$ in Equation 14.15 and rearranging terms to obtain

$$q = \frac{a - m}{(n + 1)b}. \tag{14.16}$$

Total market output, $Q = nq$, equals $n(a - m)/[(n + 1)b]$. The corresponding price is obtained by substituting this expression for market output into the demand function:

$$p = \frac{a + nm}{n + 1}. \tag{14.17}$$

Setting $n = 1$ in Equations 14.16 and 14.17 yields the monopoly quantity and price. As n becomes large, each firm's quantity approaches zero, total output approaches $(a - m)/b$, and price approaches m, which are the competitive levels.[11] The Lerner Index is

$$\frac{p - MC}{p} = \frac{a - m}{a + nm}. \tag{14.18}$$

As n grows large, the denominator in Equation 14.18 goes to infinity (∞), so the Lerner Index goes to 0 and there is no market power.

Airline Example. We can illustrate these results using our airline example, where $a = 339, b = 1, m = 147$, and $n = 2$. Suppose that additional airlines with an identical marginal cost of $m = \$147$ were to fly between Chicago and Los Angeles. Table 14.2 shows how the Nash-Cournot equilibrium price and the Lerner Index vary with the number of firms. Using the equations for the general linear model, we know that each firm's Nash-Cournot equilibrium quantity is $q = (339 - 147)/(n + 1) = 192/(n + 1)$ and the Nash-Cournot equilibrium price is $p = (339 + 147n)/(n + 1)$.

As we already know, if there were only one firm, it would produce the monopoly quantity, 96, at the monopoly price, \$243. We also know that each duopoly firm's output is 64, so market output is 128 and price is \$211. The duopoly market elasticity is $\varepsilon = -1.65$, so the residual demand elasticity that each duopoly firm faces is twice as large as the market elasticity, $2\varepsilon = -3.3$.

As the number of firms increases, each firm's output falls toward zero, but total output approaches 192, the quantity on the market demand curve where price equals the marginal cost of \$147. Although the market elasticity of demand falls as the number of firms grows, the residual demand curve for each firm becomes increasingly horizontal (perfectly elastic). As a result, the price approaches the marginal cost, \$147. Similarly, as the number of firms increases, the Lerner Index approaches the price-taking level of zero.

The table shows that having extra firms in the market benefits consumers. When the number of firms rises from 1 to 4, the price falls by a quarter and the Lerner Index is cut nearly in half. At 10 firms, the price is one-third less than the monopoly level, and the Lerner Index is one-quarter of the monopoly level.

Table 14.2 Nash-Cournot Equilibrium Varies with the Number of Firms

Number of Firms, n	Firm Output, q	Market Output, Q	Price, p	Market Elasticity, ε	Residual Demand Elasticity, $n\varepsilon$	Lerner Index, $(p - m)/p = -1/(n\varepsilon)$
1	96	96	243	−2.53	−2.53	0.40
2	64	128	211	−1.65	−3.30	0.30
3	48	144	195	−1.35	−4.06	0.25
4	38.4	154	185.40	−1.21	−4.83	0.21
5	32	160	179	−1.12	−5.59	0.18
10	17.5	175	164.45	−0.94	−9.42	0.11
50	3.8	188	150.76	−0.80	−40.05	0.02
100	1.9	190	148.90	−0.78	−78.33	0.01
200	1.0	191	147.96	−0.77	−154.89	0.01

---

[11]As the number of firms goes to infinity, the Nash-Cournot equilibrium goes to perfect competition only if average cost is nondecreasing (Ruffin, 1971).

The Cournot Model with Nonidentical Firms

For simplicity, we initially assumed that the firms were essentially identical: All firms had identical costs and produced identical products. However, costs often vary across firms, and firms often differentiate the products they produce from those of their rivals.

Unequal Costs. In the Cournot model, the firm sets its output so as to equate its marginal revenue to its marginal cost, as specified by its first-order condition. If firms' marginal costs vary, then so will the firms' first-order conditions and hence their best-response functions. In the resulting Nash-Cournot equilibrium, the relatively low-cost firm produces more, as Solved Problem 14.1 illustrates. However, as long as the products are not differentiated, the firms charge the same price.

SOLVED PROBLEM 14.1

If the inverse market demand function facing a duopoly is $p = a - bQ$, what are the Nash-Cournot equilibrium quantities if the marginal cost of Firm 1 is m and that of Firm 2 is $m + x$, where $x > 0$? Which firm produces more and which has the higher profit?

Answer

1. *Determine each firm's best-response function.* Firm 1's profit is the same as in Equation 14.13 where $n = 2$: $\pi_1 = [a - b(q_1 + q_2)]q_1 - mq_1$. Consequently, its best-response function is the same as Equation 14.15,

$$q_1 = \frac{a - m - bq_2}{2b}. \tag{14.19}$$

Firm 2's profit is the same as in Equation 14.13 except that m is replaced by $m + x$. That is, $\pi_2 = q_2[a - b(q_1 + q_2)] - (m + x)q_2$. Setting the derivative of Firm 2's profit with respect to q_2 (holding q_1 fixed) equal to zero, and rearranging terms, we find that the first-order condition for Firm 2 to maximize its profit is $MR_2 = a - b(2q_2 + q_1) = m + x = MC_2$. Rearranging this expression shows that Firm 2's best-response function is

$$q_2 = \frac{a - (m + x) - bq_1}{2b}. \tag{14.20}$$

2. *Use the best-response functions to solve for the Nash-Cournot equilibrium.* To determine the equilibrium, we solve Equations 14.19 and 14.20 simultaneously for q_1 and q_2:[12]

$$q_1 = \frac{a - m + x}{3b}, \tag{14.21}$$

$$q_2 = \frac{a - m - 2x}{3b}. \tag{14.22}$$

---

[12]By substituting the expression for q_1 from Equation 14.19 into Equation 14.20, we obtain

$$q_2 = \left[a - m - x - b\left(\frac{a - m - bq_2}{2b} \right) \right]/(2b).$$

Solving for q_2, we derive Equation 14.22. Substituting that expression into Equation 14.19 and simplifying, we get Equation 14.21.

3. *Use the Nash-Cournot equilibrium quantity equations to determine which firm produces more.* By inspection, $q_1 = [a - m + x]/[3b] > q_2 = [a - m - 2x]/[3b]$. As x increases, q_1 increases by $dq_1/dx = 1/[3b]$ and q_2 falls by $dq_2/dx = -2/[3b]$.

4. *Substitute the Nash-Cournot equilibrium quantity equations into the profit functions to determine which firm has a higher profit.* The low-cost firm has the higher profit. Using Equations 14.21 and 14.22, $q_1 + q_2 = (2a - 2m - x)/(3b)$. Substituting this expression and the expression for q_1 from Equation 14.21 into the profit function for Firm 1, we find that

$$\pi_1 = [a - m - b(q_1 + q_2)]q_1 = [a - m - (2a - 2m - x)/3](a - m + x)/(3b)$$
$$= (a - m + x)^2/[9b]$$

and, by similar reasoning, $\pi_2 = (a - m - 2x)^2/[9b]$. Thus,

$$\pi_1 = \frac{(a - m + x)^2}{9b} > \frac{(a - m - 2x)^2}{9b} = \pi_2.$$

APPLICATION

Air Ticket Prices and Rivalry

Because costs vary across competing airlines and consumers often prefer one airline to another, airlines have unequal market shares. The markup of price over marginal cost is much greater on routes in which one airline carries most of the passengers than it is on other routes. Unfortunately for consumers, a single firm is the only carrier or the dominant carrier on 58% of all U.S. domestic routes (Weiher et al., 2002).

The first column of the table identifies the market structure for U.S. air routes. The last column shows the share of routes. A single firm (monopoly) serves 18% of all routes. Duopolies control 19% of the routes, three-firm markets are 16%, four-firm markets are 13%, and five or more firms fly on 35% of the routes.

Although nearly two-thirds of all routes have three or more carriers, one or two firms dominate virtually all routes. We call a carrier a *dominant firm* if it has at least 60% of ticket sales by value but is not a monopoly. We call two carriers a *dominant pair* if they collectively have at least 60% of the market but neither firm is a dominant firm and three or more firms fly this route. All but 0.1% of routes have a monopoly (18%), a dominant firm (40%), or a dominant pair (42%).

The first row of the table shows that the price is slightly more than double (2.1 times) marginal cost on average across all U.S. routes and market structures. (This average price includes "free" frequent-flier tickets and other below-cost tickets.) The price is 3.3 times marginal cost for monopolies and 3.1 times marginal cost for dominant firms. In contrast, over the sample period, the average price is only 1.2 times marginal cost for dominant pairs.

The markup of price over marginal cost depends much more on whether there is a dominant firm or dominant pair than on the total number of firms in the market. If there is a dominant pair, whether there are four or five firms, the price is between 1.3 times marginal cost for a four-firm route and 1.4 times marginal cost for a route with five or more firms. If there is a dominant firm, price is 2.3 times marginal cost on duopoly routes, 1.9 times on three-firm routes, 2.2 times on four-firm routes, and 3.5 times on routes with five or more firms.

Type of Market	Lerner Index, $(p - MC)/p$	Share of All Routes (%)
All market types	0.52	100
Dominant firm	0.68	40
Dominant pair	0.17	42
One firm (monopoly)	0.70	18
Two firms (duopoly)	0.55	19
Dominant firm	0.57	14
No dominant firm	0.33	5
Three firms	0.44	16
Dominant firm	0.47	9
No dominant firm	0.23	7
Four firms	0.44	13
Dominant firm	0.55	6
Dominant pair	0.23	7
No dominant firm or pair	0.52	~0
Five or more firms	0.23	35
Dominant firm	0.71	11
Dominant pair	0.29	23
No dominant firm or pair	0.09	0.1

Thus, preventing a single firm from dominating a route may substantially lower prices. Even if two firms dominate the market, the markup of price over marginal cost is substantially lower than if a single firm dominates.

Differentiated Products. Firms differentiate their products to increase their profits. By differentiating its product from those of a rival, an oligopolistic firm can shift

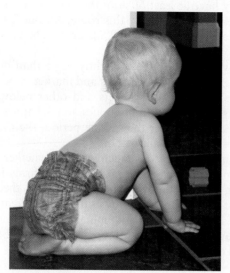

its demand curve to the right and make it less elastic. The less elastic the demand curve, the more that the firm can charge. Consumers are willing to pay more for a product that they perceive as being superior. Bayer charges more for its chemically identical aspirin than other brands because Bayer has convinced consumers that its product is safer or superior in some other way. Similarly Clorox's customers must believe that its product is superior in some way because they pay more for it than for the chemically identical bleach sold by its rivals.

One way to differentiate a product is to give it unique, "desirable" attributes, such as the Lexus car that parks itself. In 2010, Kimberly-Clark introduced a new Huggies disposable diaper with a printed denim pattern, including seams and back pockets, which boosted their sales 15%. A firm can differentiate its product by advertising, using colorful labels, and engaging in other promotional activities to convince consumers that its product is superior in some (possibly unspecified) way even though it is virtually identical to its rivals physically or chemically. Economists call this practice *spurious differentiation*.[13]

Even if the products are physically identical, if consumers think products differ, the Nash-Cournot quantities and prices will differ across firms. Each firm faces a different inverse demand function and hence charges a different price. For example, suppose that Firm 1's inverse demand function is $p_1 = a - b_1 q_1 - b_2 q_2$, where $b_1 > b_2$ if consumers believe that Good 1 is different from Good 2, and $b_1 = b_2 = b$ if the goods are identical. Given that consumers view the products as differentiated and Firm 2 faces a similar inverse demand function, we replace the single market demand with these individual demand functions in the Cournot model. Solved Problem 14.2 shows how to solve for the Nash-Cournot equilibrium in an actual market.

SOLVED PROBLEM 14.2

Intel and Advanced Micro Devices (AMD) are the only firms that produce central processing units (CPUs), which are the brains of personal computers. Both because the products differ physically and because Intel's *Intel Inside* advertising campaign has convinced some consumers of its superiority, customers view the CPUs as imperfect substitutes. Consequently, the two firms' inverse demand functions differ:

$$p_A = 197 - 15.1q_A - 0.3q_I, \tag{14.23}$$

$$p_I = 490 - 10q_I - 6q_A, \tag{14.24}$$

where price is dollars per CPU, quantity is in millions of CPUs, the subscript I indicates Intel, and the subscript A represents AMD.[14] Each firm faces a constant marginal cost of $m = \$40$ per unit. (We can ignore the firms' fixed costs because we know that the firms operate and the fixed costs do not affect the marginal costs.) Solve for the Nash-Cournot equilibrium quantities and prices.

Answer

1. *Determine each firm's best-response function.* Substituting the inverse demand equations 14.23 and 14.24 into the definition of profit and setting $m = 40$, we learn that the firms' profit functions are

$$\pi_A = (p_A - m)q_A = (157 - 15.1q_A - 0.3q_I)q_A, \tag{14.25}$$

$$\pi_I = (p_I - m)q_I = (450 - 10q_I - 6q_A)q_I. \tag{14.26}$$

The first-order conditions are $\partial\pi_A/\partial q_A = 157 - 30.2q_A - 0.3q_I$ and $\partial\pi_I/\partial q_I = 450 - 20q_I - 6q_A$. Rearranging these expressions, we obtain the best-response functions:

$$q_A = \frac{157 - 0.3q_I}{30.2}, \tag{14.27}$$

$$q_I = \frac{450 - 6q_A}{20}. \tag{14.28}$$

[13]The Cow Protection Department of the Rashtriya Swayamsevak Sangh (RSS), India's largest and oldest Hindu nationalist group announced that it was introducing a new, highly differentiated soft drink called gau jal, or "cow water," made from cow urine—a truly differentiated product. (Page, Jeremy, "India to Launch Cow Urine as Soft Drink," *Times Online*, February 11, 2009).

[14]I thank Hugo Salgado for estimating these inverse demand functions and providing evidence that this market is well described by a Nash-Cournot equilibrium.

2. *Use the best-response functions to solve for the Nash-Cournot equilibrium.* Solving the system of best-response functions 14.27 and 14.28, we find that the Nash-Cournot equilibrium quantities are $q_A \approx 5$ million CPUs, and $q_I \approx 21$ million CPUs. Substituting these values into the inverse demand functions, we obtain the corresponding prices: $p_A = \$115.20$ and $p_I = \$250$ per CPU.

APPLICATION

Bottled Water

Bottled water is the most dramatic recent example of *spurious product differentiation*, where the products do not significantly differ physically. Firms convince consumers that their products differ through marketing.

In a 2012 Gallup poll of U.S. consumers' top environmental fears, their greatest fear, held by 48% of respondents, was that their drinking water is polluted. Perhaps that helps to explain why the typical American consumed more than 29 gallons of bottled water in 2011.

If safety is their reason to buy bottled water, these consumers are being foolish. Not only does the U.S. Environmental Protection Agency set a stricter standard for tap water than the standard set by the Federal Drug Administration on bottled water, but a quarter of all bottled water is tap water according to the Natural Resources Defense Council.

PepsiCo's top-selling bottled water, Aquafina, has a colorful blue label and a logo showing the sun rising over the mountains. From that logo, consumers may guess that the water comes from some bubbling spring high in an unspoiled wilderness. If so, they're wrong. Pepsi finally admitted that its best-selling bottled water comes from the same place as tap water: public-water sources. However, Pepsi insists that it filters the water using a state-of-the-art "HydRO-7 purification system," implying that such filtering (which removes natural minerals) is desirable. Coca-Cola has also admitted that its Dasani bottled water comes from public water sources.

14.4   Stackelberg Oligopoly Model

In the Cournot model, both firms announce their output decisions simultaneously. In contrast, suppose that one of the firms, called the *leader*, can set its output before its rival, the *follower*, does. This type of situation where one firm acts before the other arises naturally if one firm enters a market before the other. Would the firm that acts first have an advantage?

To answer this question, the German economist Heinrich von Stackelberg showed how to modify the Cournot model. We examined the Stackelberg model in Chapter 13, where United and American Airlines could choose among only three possible output levels. Here, we consider the more general problem where the airlines firms are free to choose any output level they want.

How does the leader decide to set its output? The leader realizes that once it sets its output, the rival firm will use its Cournot best-response curve to select its best-response output. Thus, the leader predicts what the follower will do before the follower acts. Using this knowledge, the leader chooses its output level to "manipulate" the follower, thereby benefiting at the follower's expense.

Calculus Solution

We start by deriving the Stackelberg equilibrium for a general, linear model, and then we apply that analysis to the airlines example. We can use calculus to derive the Stackelberg equilibrium for a general linear inverse demand function, $p = a - bQ$, where two firms have identical marginal costs, m. Because Firm 1, the Stackelberg leader, chooses its output first, it knows that Firm 2, the follower, will choose its output using its best-response function. Setting the number of firms $n = 2$ in Equation 14.15, we know that Firm 2's best-response function, B_2, is

$$q_2 = B_2(q_1) = \frac{a - m}{2b} - \frac{1}{2}q_1. \tag{14.29}$$

The market price depends on the output of both firms, $p(q_1 + q_2)$. Consequently, the Stackelberg leader's profit is a function of its own and the follower's output: $\pi_1(q_1 + q_2) = p(q_1 + q_2)q_1 - mq_1$. By replacing the follower's output with the follower's best-response function so that the leader's profit depends only on its own output, we can write the leader's profit function as

$$\pi_1(q_1 + B_2(q_1)) = [p(q_1 + B_2(q_1)) - m]q_1$$
$$= [a - b(q_1 + B_2(q_1)) - m]q_1$$
$$= \left[a - b\left(q_1 + \frac{a - m}{2b} - \frac{1}{2}q_1\right) - m\right]q_1, \tag{14.30}$$

where we have used Equation 14.29 to obtain the last line.

The Stackelberg leader's objective is to choose q_1 so as to maximize its profit in Equation 14.30. The leader's first-order condition is derived by setting the derivative of its profit with respect to q_1 equal to zero: $a - 2bq_1 - (a - m)/2 + bq_1 - m = 0$. Solving this expression for q_1, we find that the profit-maximizing output of the leader is

$$q_1 = \frac{a - m}{2b}. \tag{14.31}$$

Substituting the expression for q_1 in Equation 14.31 into the follower's best-response function 14.29 gives the equilibrium output of the follower:

$$q_2 = \frac{a - m}{4b}.$$

Thus, given a linear demand curve and constant marginal cost, the leader produces twice as much as the follower.[15]

---

[15]Here, the leader produces the same quantity as a monopoly would, and the follower produces the same quantity as it would in the cartel equilibrium. These relationships are due to the linear demand curve and the constant marginal cost—they do not hold more generally.

We can use this analysis to ask what would happen in our airline example if American Airlines can act before United Airlines, so that American is a Stackelberg leader and United is a Stackelberg follower. Replacing the parameters in our linear analysis with the specific values for the airlines, $a = 339$, $b = 1$, $m = 147$, and $n = 2$, we find that American's output is $q_1 = (339 - 147)/2 = 96$, and United's output is $q_2 = (339 - 147)/4 = 48$.

Graphical Solution

We can illustrate this airline analysis with graphs. American, the Stackelberg leader, uses its residual demand curve to determine its profit-maximizing output. American knows that when it sets q_A, United will use its Cournot best-response function to pick its best-response q_U. Thus, American believes it faces a residual demand curve, D^r (panel a of Figure 14.4), that is the market demand curve, D (panel a), minus the output United will produce as summarized by United's best-response curve (panel b). For example, if American sets $q_A = 192$, United's best response is $q_U = 0$ (as United's best-response curve in panel b shows). As a result, the residual demand curve and the market demand curve are identical at $q_A = 192$ (panel a).

Similarly, if American set $q_A = 0$, United would choose $q_U = 96$, so the residual demand at $q_A = 0$ is 96 less than demand. The residual demand curve hits the vertical axis, where $q_A = 0$, at $p = \$243$, which is 96 units to the left of demand at that price. When $q_A = 96$, $q_U = 48$, so the residual demand at $q_A = 96$ is 48 units to the left of the demand.

American chooses its profit-maximizing output, $q_A = 96$, where its marginal revenue curve that corresponds to the residual demand curve, MR^r, equals its marginal cost, \$147. At $q_A = 96$, the price, which is the height of the residual demand curve, is \$195. Total demand at \$195 is $Q = 144$. At that price, United produces $q_U = Q - q_A = 48$, its best response to American's output of $q_A = 96$. Thus, as Figure 14.4 shows, the Stackelberg leader produces twice as much as the follower.

Why Moving Sequentially Is Essential

Why don't we get the Stackelberg equilibrium when both firms move simultaneously? Why doesn't American announce that it will produce the Stackelberg leader's output to induce United to produce the Stackelberg follower's output level? As we discussed in Chapter 13, the answer is that when the firms move simultaneously, United doesn't view American's warning that it will produce a large quantity as a *credible threat*.

If United believed that threat, it would indeed produce the Stackelberg follower's output level. But United doesn't believe the threat because it is not in American's best interest to produce that large a quantity of output. If American produced the leader's level of output and United produced the Cournot level, American's profit would be lower than if it too produced the Cournot level. Because American cannot be sure that United will believe its threat and reduce its output, American will produce the Cournot output level.

Indeed, each firm may make the same threat and announce that it wants to be the leader. Because neither firm can be sure that the other will be intimidated and produce the smaller quantity, both produce the Cournot output level. In contrast, when one firm moves first, its threat to produce a large quantity is credible because it has already *committed* to producing the larger quantity, thereby carrying out its threat.

Figure 14.4 Stackelberg Equilibrium

(a) The residual demand that the Stackelberg leader faces is the market demand minus the quantity produced by the follower, q_U, given the leader's quantity, q_A. The leader chooses $q_A = 96$ so that its marginal revenue, MR^r, equals its marginal cost. The total output, $Q = 144$, is the sum of the output of the two firms. (b) The quantity that the follower produces is its best response to the leader's output, as given by its Cournot best-response curve.

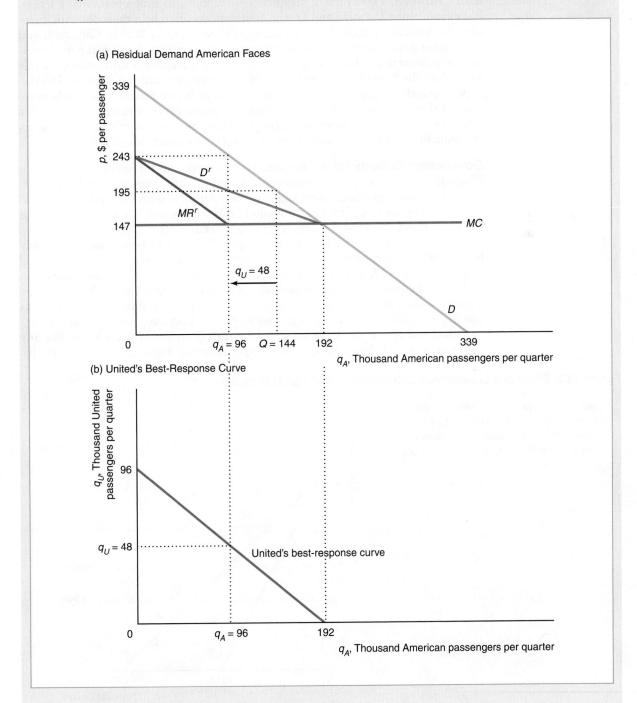

Strategic Trade Policy: An Application of the Stackelberg Model

Suppose that two identical firms in two different countries compete in a world market. Both firms act simultaneously, so neither firm can make itself the Stackelberg leader. However, a government may intervene to make its firm a Stackelberg leader. For example, the Japanese and French governments often help their domestic firms compete with international rivals; occasionally, so do U.S., British, Canadian, and many other governments. If only one government intervenes, it can make its domestic firm's threat to produce a large quantity of output credible, causing foreign rivals to produce the Stackelberg follower's level of output (Spencer and Brander, 1983).

We have already conducted a similar analysis in Solved Problem 14.1, where we showed that a firm with a lower marginal cost would produce more than its higher cost rival in a Nash-Cournot equilibrium. Thus, a government can subsidize its domestic firm to make it a more fearsome rival to the unsubsidized firm.

Government Subsidy for an Airline. By modifying our airline example, we can illustrate how one country's government can aid its firm. Suppose that United Airlines were owned by one country and American Airlines by another. Initially, United and American are in a Nash-Cournot equilibrium. Each firm has a marginal cost of $147 and flies 64 thousand passengers per quarter at a price of $211.

Now suppose that United's government gives United a $48-per-passenger subsidy but the other government doesn't help American. As a result, American's marginal cost remains at $147, while United's marginal cost after the subsidy drops to only $99.

The firms continue to act as in the Cournot model, but the playing field is no longer level. How does the Nash-Cournot equilibrium change? Your intuition probably tells you that United's output increases relative to that of American, as we now show.

United still acts at the same time as American does, so United behaves like any Cournot firm and determines its best-response curve. Figure 14.5 illustrates this

Figure 14.5 Effect of a Government Subsidy on United's Best Response

A government subsidy that lowers United's marginal cost from $MC^1 = \$147$ to $MC^2 = \$99$ causes United's best-response output to American's $q_A = 64$ to rise from $q_U = 64$ to 88.

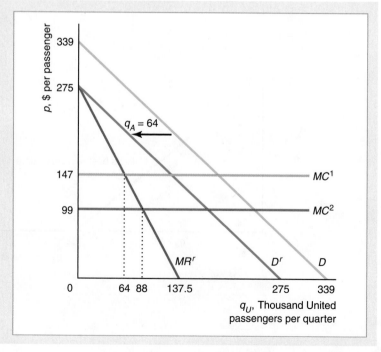

reasoning. United's residual demand, D^r, lies 64 units to the left of the market demand, D, if American produces 64. United's best response to any given American output is the output at which its corresponding marginal revenue curve, MR^r, equals its marginal cost. The subsidy does not affect United's MR^r curve, but it lowers its MC curve. The MR^r curve intersects the original marginal cost, $MC^1 = \$147$, at 64 and the new marginal cost, $MC^2 = \$99$, at 88. Thus, if we hold American's output constant at 64, United produces more as its marginal cost falls due to the subsidy.

Because this reasoning applies for any level of output American chooses, United's best-response curve in Figure 14.6 shifts outward as its after-subsidy marginal cost falls. As a result, the Nash-Cournot equilibrium shifts from the original e_1, at which both firms sold 64, to e_2, at which United sells 96 and American sells 48. Thus, the $48 subsidy to United causes it to sell the Stackelberg leader quantity and American to sell the Stackelberg follower quantity. The subsidy works by convincing American that United will produce large quantities of output.

Using the market demand Equation 14.1, we find that the market price drops from $211 to $195, benefiting consumers. United's profit increases from $4.1 million to $9.2 million, while American's profit falls to $2.3 million. Consequently, United Airlines and consumers gain and American Airlines and taxpayers lose from the drop in United's marginal cost.

This example illustrates that a government subsidy to one firm *can* lead to the same outcome as in a Stackelberg equilibrium. Would a government *want* to give the subsidy that leads to the Stackelberg outcome?

The answer depends on the government's objective. Suppose that the government is interested in maximizing its domestic firm's profit net of (not including) the government's subsidy. The subsidy is a transfer from some citizens (taxpayers) to others (the owners of United). We assume that the government does not care about

Figure 14.6 Effect of a Government Subsidy on a Nash-Cournot Equilibrium

If both airlines' marginal costs are $147, the Nash-Cournot equilibrium is e_1. If United's marginal cost falls to $99, its best-response function shifts outward. It now sells more tickets in response to any given American output than previously. At the new Nash-Cournot equilibrium, e_2, United sells $q_U = 96$, while American sells only $q_A = 48$.

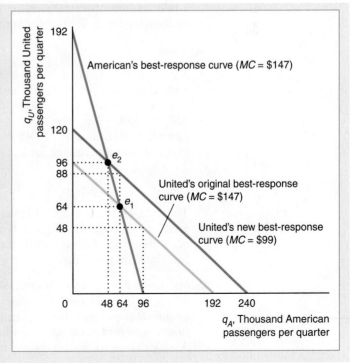

consumers—as is certainly true if they live in another country. Given this objective, the government maximizes its objective by setting the subsidy so as to achieve the Stackelberg equilibrium.

Table 14.3 shows the effects of various subsidies and a tax (a negative subsidy). If the subsidy is zero, we have the usual Nash-Cournot equilibrium. A $48-per-passenger subsidy leads to the same outcome as in the Stackelberg equilibrium and maximizes the government's welfare measure. At a larger subsidy, such as $60, United's profit rises, but by less than the cost of the subsidy to the government. Similarly, at smaller subsidies or taxes, welfare is also lower.

Table 14.3   Effects of a Subsidy Given to United Airlines

Subsidy, s	United			American	
	q_U	π_U	Welfare, $\pi_U - sq_U$	q_A	π_A
60	104	$10.8	$4.58	44	$1.9
48	96	**$9.2**	**$4.61**	48	$2.3
30	84	$7.1	$4.50	54	$2.9
0	64	$4.1	$4.10	64	$4.1
−30	44	$1.9	$3.30	74	$5.5

Notes: The subsidy is in dollars per passenger (and is a tax if negative). Output units are in thousands of passengers per quarter. Profits and welfare (defined as United's profits minus the subsidy) are in millions of dollars per quarter.

SOLVED PROBLEM 14.3

In our duopoly airline example, the government gives United a $48-per-passenger subsidy. Use calculus to show that the subsidy causes a parallel shift out of United's best-response curve. Assuming that only United is subsidized, use math to solve for the new equilibrium quantities.

Answer

1. *Set United's marginal revenue function equal to its subsidized marginal cost, and solve for United's best-response function.* United's marginal revenue with respect to its residual demand function is given by Equation 14.4: $MR_U = 339 - 2q_U - q_A$. Because United's original marginal cost was 147, its new marginal cost is $147 - 48 = 99$. Equating United's marginal revenue and marginal cost and solving for q_U, we find that United's best-response function is

$$q_U = 120 - \frac{1}{2}q_A. \tag{14.32}$$

This best-response function calls for United to provide more output for any given q_A than in the original best-response function, Equation 14.6, where $q_U = 96 - \frac{1}{2}q_A$. Because only the constants differ, these two best-response functions are parallel.

2. *Substitute for q_A from American's original best-response function into United's new best-response function and solve for United's new Nash-Cournot equilibrium quantity, then substitute that value into American's best-response function to find American's equilibrium quantity.* The subsidy does not affect American, so its best-response function remains the same, Equation 14.5:

$q_A = 96 - \frac{1}{2}q_U$. Substituting this expression for q_A into United's best-response function from Equation 14.32, we find that

$$q_U = 120 - \frac{1}{2}q_A = 120 - \frac{1}{2}(96 - \frac{1}{2}q_U) = 72 + \frac{1}{4}q_U. \qquad (14.33)$$

Solving Equation 14.33 for q_U, we find that $q_U = \frac{4}{3} \times 72 = 96$. Plugging this value into American's best-response function, we find that $q_A = 96 - (\frac{1}{2} \times 96) = 48$. Thus, compared to the original equilibrium where both firms produced 64, United produces more and American less in this new equilibrium.

Problems with Government Intervention. Thus, in theory, a government may want to subsidize its domestic firm to make it produce the same output as it would if it were a Stackelberg leader. However, if such subsidies are to work as desired, four conditions must hold:

1. The other government must not retaliate. (See the Challenge Solution.)
2. The government must be able to set its subsidy before the firms choose their output levels. The idea behind this intervention is that one firm cannot act before the other, but its government can act first.
3. The government's actions must be credible. If the foreign firm's country doesn't believe that the government will subsidize its domestic firm, the foreign firm produces the Cournot level. The foreign firm may not believe in the subsidies because governments have difficulty in committing to long-term policies.[16]
4. The government must know enough about how the firms behave to intervene appropriately. If it doesn't know the demand function and the costs of all firms or whether they are engaged in a Cournot game, the government may intervene inappropriately.

Comparison of Collusive, Nash-Cournot, Stackelberg, and Competitive Equilibria

The Nash-Cournot and Stackelberg equilibria price, quantities, and profits lie between those of the collusive and competitive equilibria. If the firms were to act as price takers, they would each produce where their residual demand curve intersects their marginal cost curve, so price would equal the marginal cost of $147. The price-taking equilibrium is $q_A = q_U = 96$. If American and United were to collude, they would maximize joint profits by producing the monopoly output, 96 units, at the monopoly price, and would charge $243 per passenger.

Thus, the competitive price, $147, is less than the Stackelberg price, $195, which is less than the Nash-Cournot price, $211, while is less than the collusive price, $243. Consumers, of course, prefer low prices. Consumer surplus is $18.4 million per quarter under competition, $10.4 million in the Stackelberg equilibrium, $8.2 million in the Nash-Cournot equilibrium, and only $4.6 million in the collusive outcome.

Panel a of Figure 14.7 shows the equilibrium quantities in the four models. The airlines could write a contract to collude by sharing the passengers in any

---

[16]For example, during the 1996 Republican presidential primaries, many candidates said that, if elected, they would reverse President Clinton's trade policies. The 2004 Democratic presidential candidates promised to change President George W. Bush's trade policies. The major Democratic presidential candidates in the 2008 election had conflicting views on optimal trade policies. Governor Romney, the 2012 Republican presidential candidate, said that he would reverse many of President Obama's trade policies.

combination such that the sum of the airlines' passengers equals the monopoly quantity: $q_A + q_U = 96$. We can rewrite this expression as

$$q_U = 96 - q_A. \tag{14.34}$$

Panel a shows the possible collusive output combinations in Equation 14.34 as a line labeled "Contract curve." In the figure, we assume that the collusive firms split the market equally so that $q_A = q_U = 48$. The quantities produced by the two firms are 192 (= 96 + 96) in the competitive equilibrium, 128 (= 64 + 64) in the Nash-Cournot equilibrium, 144 (= 96 + 48) in the Stackelberg equilibrium, and 96 in the collusive outcome.

The cartel profits are the highest-possible level of profits that the firms can earn. Panel b of Figure 14.7 shows the profit possibility frontier, which corresponds to the contract curve. At the upper left of the profit possibility frontier, United is a monopoly and earns the entire monopoly profit of approximately $9.2 million per quarter.[17] At the lower right, American earns the entire monopoly profit. At points in between, they split the profit. Where they split the profit equally, each earns approximately $4.6 million.

In contrast, if the firms act independently, each earns the Cournot profit of approximately $4.1 million. The Stackelberg leader earns more than the Cournot profit, $4.6 million, while the follower earns less, $2.3 million.

Welfare (the sum of consumer surplus and profit) is maximized at $18.4 million per quarter under competition. The deadweight loss is $1.2 million in the Stackelberg equilibrium, $2.0 in the Cournot equilibrium, and $4.6 million in the collusive outcome.

We showed that the Nash-Cournot equilibrium approaches the price-taking equilibrium as the number of firms grows. Similarly, we can show that the Stackelberg equilibrium approaches the price-taking equilibrium as the number of Stackelberg followers grows. As a result, the differences between the Cournot, Stackelberg, and price-taking market structures shrink as the number of firms grows.

APPLICATION

Deadweight Losses in the Food and Tobacco Industries

Bhuyan and Lopez (1998) and Bhuyan (2000) estimated the deadweight loss for various U.S. food and tobacco manufacturing oligopolies and monopolistically competitive markets. Most of these industries have deadweight losses that are a relatively small percentage of sales because their prices and quantities are close to competitive levels. However, a few less competitive industries, such as cereal and flour and grain mills, have deadweight losses that are a relatively large share of sales, as the last column of the table shows.

Industry	Loss, $ millions	Share of Sales, %
Cereal	2,192	33
Flour and grain mills	541	26
Poultry and eggs	1,183	8
Roasted coffee	440	7
Cigarettes	1,032	6
All food manufacturing	14,947	5

---

[17]Each firm's profit per passenger is price minus average cost, $p - AC$, so the firm's profit is $\pi = (p - AC)q$, where q is the number of passengers the firm flies. The monopoly price is $243 and the average cost is $147, so the monopoly profit is $\pi = (243 - 147) \times 96$ units per quarter = $9.216 million per quarter.

Figure 14.7 Duopoly Equilibria

(a) The intersection of the best-response curves determines the Nash-Cournot equilibrium. The possible cartel equilibria lie on the contract curve. If the firms act as price takers, each firm produces where its residual demand equals its marginal cost. The Stackelberg leader produces more and the follower produces less than does a firm in the Nash-Cournot equilibrium. (b) The highest possible profit for the two firms combined is given by the profit possibility frontier. It reflects all the possible collusive equilibria, including the one indicated where the firms split the market equally. All equilibria except collusive ones lie within the profit possibility frontier.

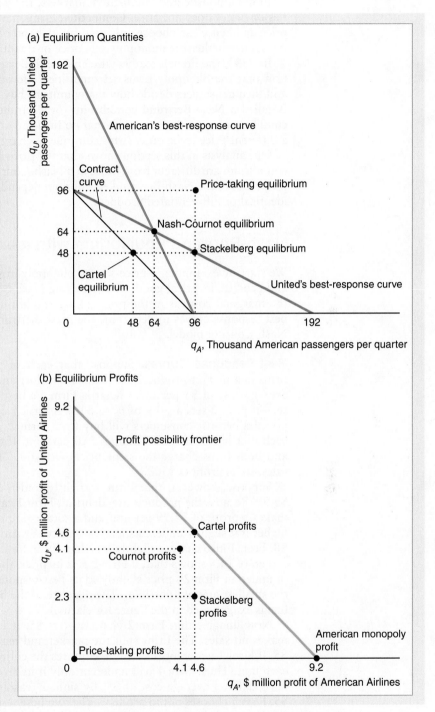

14.5 Bertrand Oligopoly Model

We have examined how oligopolistic firms set quantities to try to maximize their profits. However, many such firms set prices instead of quantities and allow consumers to decide how much to buy. The market equilibrium is different if firms set prices rather than quantities.

In monopolistic and competitive markets, the issue of whether firms set quantities or prices does not arise. Competitive firms have no choice: They cannot affect price and hence can choose only quantity (Chapter 8). The monopoly equilibrium is the same whether the monopoly sets price or quantity (Chapter 11).

In 1883, the French mathematician Joseph Bertrand rejected Cournot's assumption that the oligopoly firms set quantities. He argued that oligopolies set prices and then consumers decide how many units to buy. The resulting Nash equilibrium is called a **Nash-Bertrand equilibrium** (or **Bertrand equilibrium** or **Nash-in-prices equilibrium**): a set of prices such that no firm can obtain a higher profit by choosing a different price if the other firms continue to charge these prices.

Our analysis in this section shows that the price and quantity in a Nash-Bertrand equilibrium are different from those in a Nash-Cournot equilibrium. In addition, the properties of the Nash-Bertrand equilibrium depend on whether firms are producing identical or differentiated products.

Nash-Bertrand Equilibrium with Identical Products

We start by examining a price-setting oligopoly in which firms have identical costs and produce identical goods. The resulting Nash-Bertrand equilibrium price equals the marginal cost, as in the price-taking equilibrium. To show this result, we use best-response curves to determine the Nash-Bertrand equilibrium, as we did in the Nash-Cournot model.

Best-Response Curves. Suppose that each of the two price-setting oligopoly firms in a market produces an identical product and faces a constant marginal and average cost of $5 per unit. What is Firm 1's best response—what price should it set—if Firm 2 sets a price of $p_2 = \$10$? If Firm 1 charges more than $10, it makes no sales because consumers will buy from Firm 2. Firm 1 makes a profit of $5 on each unit it sells if it also charges $10 per unit. If the market demand is 200 units and both firms charge the same price, we would expect Firm 1 to make half the sales, so its profit is $500.

Suppose, however, that Firm 1 slightly undercuts its rival's price by charging $9.99. Because the products are identical, Firm 1 captures the entire market. Firm 1 makes a profit of $4.99 per unit and a total profit of $998. Thus, Firm 1's profit is higher if it slightly undercuts its rival's price. By similar reasoning, if Firm 2 charges $8, Firm 1 also charges slightly less than Firm 2.

Figure 14.8 shows that, if Firm 2 sets its price above $5, Firm 1's best response is to undercut Firm 2's price slightly so its best-response curve is above the 45° line by the smallest amount possible. (The distance of the best-response curve from the 45° line is exaggerated in the figure for clarity.)

Now imagine that Firm 2 charges $p_2 = \$5$. If Firm 1 charges more than $5, it makes no sales. The firms split the market and make zero profit if Firm 1 charges $5. If Firm 1 undercuts its rival, it captures the entire market, but it suffers a loss on each unit. Thus, Firm 1 will undercut only if its rival's price is higher than Firm 1's marginal and average cost of $5. By similar reasoning, if Firm 2 charges less than $5, Firm 1 chooses not to produce. The two best-response functions intersect only at e, where each firm charges $5. If its rival were to charge less than $5, a firm would choose not to produce.

It does not pay for either firm to change its price as long as the other charges $5, so e is a Nash-Bertrand equilibrium. In this equilibrium, each firm makes zero profit. Thus, *the Nash-Bertrand equilibrium when firms produce identical products is the*

Figure 14.8 Nash-Bertrand Equilibrium with Identical Products

With identical products and constant marginal and average costs of $5, Firm 1's best-response curve starts at $5 and then lies slightly above the 45° line. That is, Firm 1 undercuts its rival's price as long as its price remains above $5. The best-response curves intersect at *e*, the Bertrand or Nash equilibrium, where both firms charge $5.

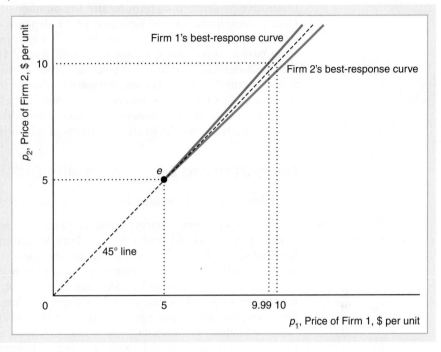

same as the price-taking, competitive equilibrium.[18] This result remains the same for larger numbers of firms.

Bertrand Versus Cournot. This Nash-Bertrand equilibrium differs substantially from the Nash-Cournot equilibrium. We can calculate the Nash-Cournot equilibrium price for firms with constant marginal costs of $5 per unit using Equation 14.11:

$$p = \frac{MC}{1 + 1/(n\varepsilon)} = \frac{\$5}{1 + 1/(n\varepsilon)}, \tag{14.35}$$

Where n is the number of firms and ε is the market demand elasticity. For example, if the market demand elasticity is $\varepsilon = -1$ and $n = 2$, the Nash-Cournot equilibrium price is $\$5/(1 - \frac{1}{2}) = \$10$, which is double the Nash-Bertrand equilibrium price.

When firms produce identical products and have a constant marginal cost, the Nash-Cournot model is more plausible than the Nash-Bertrand model. The Nash-Bertrand model—unlike the Nash-Cournot model—appears inconsistent with real oligopoly markets in at least two ways.

First, the Nash-Bertrand model's "competitive" equilibrium price is implausible. In a market with few firms, why would the firms compete so vigorously that they would make no profit, as in the Nash-Bertrand equilibrium? In contrast, the Nash-Cournot equilibrium price with a small number of firms lies between the competitive price and the monopoly price. Because oligopolies typically charge a higher price than competitive firms, the Nash-Cournot equilibrium is more plausible.

---

[18]This result depends heavily on the firms' facing a constant marginal cost. If firms face a binding capacity constraint so that the marginal cost eventually becomes large (infinite), the Nash-Bertrand equilibrium may be the same as the Nash-Cournot equilibrium (Kreps and Scheinkman, 1983).

Second, the Nash-Bertrand equilibrium price, which depends only on cost, is insensitive to demand conditions and the number of firms. In contrast, the Nash-Cournot equilibrium price, Equation 14.11, depends on demand conditions and the number of firms as well as on costs. In our last example, if the number of firms rises from two to three, the Cournot price falls from $10 to $5/(1 − $\frac{1}{3}$) = $7.50, but the Nash-Bertrand equilibrium price remains constant at $5. Again, the Cournot model is more plausible because we usually observe market price changing with the number of firms and demand conditions, not just with changes in costs. Thus, for both of these reasons, economists are much more likely to use the Cournot model than the Bertrand model to study markets in which firms produce identical goods.

Nash-Bertrand Equilibrium with Differentiated Products

Why don't they make mouse-flavored cat food? —Steven Wright

If most markets were characterized by firms producing homogeneous goods, the Bertrand model would probably have been forgotten. However, markets with differentiated goods—such as those for automobiles, stereos, computers, toothpaste, and spaghetti sauce—are extremely common, as is price setting by firms. In such markets, the Nash-Bertrand equilibrium is plausible, and the two problems of the homogeneous-goods Bertrand model disappear. That is, firms set prices above marginal cost, and prices are sensitive to demand conditions.

Indeed, many economists believe that price-setting models are more plausible than quantity-setting models when goods are differentiated. If products are differentiated and firms set prices, then consumers determine quantities. In contrast, if firms set quantities, it is not clear how the prices of the differentiated goods are determined in the market.

The main reason the differentiated-goods Bertrand model differs from the undifferentiated-goods version is that one firm can charge more than another for a differentiated product without losing all its sales. For example, Coke and Pepsi produce similar but not identical products; many consumers prefer one to the other.[19] If the price of Pepsi were to fall slightly relative to that of Coke, most consumers who prefer Coke to Pepsi would not switch. Thus, neither firm has to match its rival's price cut exactly to continue to sell cola.

Product differentiation allows a firm to charge a higher price because the differentiation causes its residual demand curve to become less elastic. That is, a given decrease in the price charged by a rival lowers the demand for this firm's product by *less*, the less substitutable the two goods. In contrast, if consumers view the goods as perfect substitutes, a small drop in the rival's price causes this firm to lose all its sales. For this reason, differentiation leads to higher equilibrium prices and profits in both the Bertrand and the Cournot models. As a result, a firm aggressively differentiates its products so as to raise its profit.[20]

---

[19]The critical issue is whether consumers believe products differ rather than whether the products physically differ because the consumers' beliefs affect their buying behavior. Although few consumers can reliably distinguish Coke from Pepsi in blind taste tests, many consumers strongly prefer buying one product over the other. I have run blind taste tests in my classes over the years involving literally thousands of students. Given a choice between Coke, Pepsi, and a generic cola, a very small fraction can consistently identify the products. However, people who do not regularly drink these products generally admit that they can't tell the difference. Indeed, relatively few of the regular cola drinkers can clearly distinguish among the brands.

[20]Chance that a British baby's first word is a brand name: 1 in 4.—*Harper's Index 2004.*

General Demand Functions. We can use calculus to determine the Nash-Bertrand equilibrium for a duopoly. We derive equilibrium for general demand functions, and then we present the solution for the cola market. In both analyses, we first determine the best-response functions for each firm and then solve these best-response functions simultaneously for the equilibrium prices for the two firms.

Each firm's demand function depends on its own price and the other firm's price. The demand function for Firm 1 is $q_1 = q_1(p_1, p_2)$ and that of Firm 2 is $q_2 = q_2(p_1, p_2)$. For simplicity, we assume that marginal cost for both firms is constant, m, and neither has a fixed cost.

Firm 1's objective is to set its price so as to maximize its profit,

$$\max_{p_1} \pi_1(p_1, p_2) = (p_1 - m)q_1(p_1, p_2), \tag{14.36}$$

where $(p_1 - m)$ is the profit per unit. Firm 1 views p_2 as a constant. Firm 1's first-order condition is the derivative of its profit with respect to p_1 set equal to zero:

$$\frac{\partial \pi_1}{\partial \pi_1} = q_1(p_1, p_2) + (p_1 - m)\frac{\partial q_1(p_1, p_2)}{\partial p_1} = 0. \tag{14.37}$$

Equation 14.37 contains the information in Firm 1's best-response function: $p_1 = B_1(p_2)$.

Similarly, we can derive Firm 2's best-response function. Solving the best-response functions, Equations 14.36 and 14.37, simultaneously, we obtain the Nash-Bertrand equilibrium prices: p_1 and p_2. We illustrate this procedure for Coke and Pepsi.

Cola Market. Because many consumers view Coke and Pepsi as imperfect substitutes, the demand for each good depends on both firms' prices. Gasmi, Laffont, and Vuong (1992) estimated the demand curve of Coke:[21]

$$q_C = 58 - 4p_C + 2p_P, \tag{14.38}$$

where q_C is the quantity of Coke demanded in tens of millions of cases (a case is 24 twelve-ounce cans) per quarter, p_C is the price of 10 cases of Coke, and p_P is the price of 10 cases of Pepsi. Partially differentiating Equation 14.38 with respect to p_C (that is, holding the price of Pepsi constant), we find that the change in quantity for every dollar change in price is $\partial q_C/\partial p_C = -4$, so a \$1-per-unit increase in the price of Coke causes the quantity of Coke demanded to fall by 4 units. Similarly, the demand for Coke rises by 2 units if the price of Pepsi rises by \$1, while the price of Coke remains constant: $\partial q_C/\partial p_P = 2$.

If Coke faces a constant marginal and average cost of m per unit, its profit is

$$\pi_C(p_C) = (p_C - m)q_C = (p_C - m)(58 - 4p_C + 2p_P). \tag{14.39}$$

To determine Coke's profit-maximizing price given that Pepsi's price is held constant, we set the partial derivative of the profit function, Equation 14.39, with respect to the price of Coke equal to zero,

$$\frac{\partial \pi_C}{\partial p_C} = q_C + (p_C - m)\frac{\partial q_C}{\partial p_C} = q_C - 4(p_C - m) = 0, \tag{14.40}$$

[21]Their estimated model allows the firms to set both prices and advertising. We assume that the firms' advertising is held constant. The Coke equation is Gasmi, Laffont, and Vuong's estimates (with slight rounding). The Pepsi demand equation reported below is their estimate rescaled so that the equilibrium prices of Coke and Pepsi are equal. Prices (to retailers) and costs are in real 1982 dollars per 10 cases.

and solve for p_C as a function of p_P and m to find Coke's best-response function:

$$p_C = 7.25 + 0.25p_P + 0.5m. \qquad (14.41)$$

Coke's best-response function tells us the price Coke charges that maximizes its profit as a function of the price Pepsi charges. Equation 14.41 shows that Coke's best-response price is 25¢ higher for every extra dollar that Pepsi charges and 50¢ higher for every extra dollar of Coke's marginal cost. Figure 14.9 plots Coke's best-response curve given that Coke's average and marginal cost of production is $5 per unit, so its best-response function is

$$p_C = 9.75 + 0.25p_P. \qquad (14.42)$$

If $p_P = \$13$, then Coke's best response is to set p_C at $13.

Pepsi's demand curve is

$$q_P = 63.2 - 4p_P + 1.6p_C. \qquad (14.43)$$

Using the same approach as we used for Coke, we find that Pepsi's best-response function (for $m = \$5$) is

$$p_P = 10.4 + 0.2p_C. \qquad (14.44)$$

Thus, neither firm's best-response curve in Figure 14.9 lies along a 45° line through the origin. The Bertrand best-response curves have different slopes than the Cournot best-response curves in Figure 14.3. The Cournot best-response curves—which plot relationships between quantities—slope downward, showing that a firm produces less the more it expects its rival to produce (as Figure 14.3 illustrates for identical goods, and Solved Problem 14.2 shows for differentiated goods). In Figure 14.9, the Bertrand best-response curves—which plot relationships between prices—slope upward, indicating that a firm charges a higher price the higher the price the firm expects its rival to charge.

The intersection of Coke's and Pepsi's best-response functions, Equations 14.42 and 14.44, determines the Nash equilibrium. By substituting Pepsi's best-response

Figure 14.9 Nash-Bertrand Equilibrium with Differentiated Products

If both firms have a constant marginal cost of $5, the best-response curves of Coke and Pepsi intersect at e_1, where each sets a price of $13 per unit. If Coke's marginal cost rises to $14.50, its best-response function shifts upward. In the new equilibrium, e_2, Coke charges a higher price, $18, than Pepsi, $14.

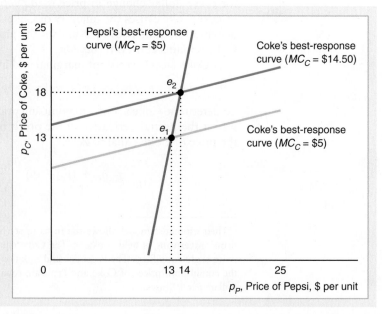

function, Equation 14.44, for p_P in Coke's best-response function, Equation 14.42, we find that

$$p_C = 9.75 + 0.25(10.4 + 0.2p_C).$$

The solution to this equation is that p_C— the equilibrium price of Coke—is $13. Substituting $p_C = \$13$ into Equation 14.44, we discover that the equilibrium price of Pepsi is also $13, as Figure 14.9 illustrates.

In this Nash-Bertrand equilibrium, each firm sets its best-response price *given the price the other firm is charging*. Neither firm wants to change its price because neither firm can increase its profit by doing so.

Product Differentiation and Welfare. We've seen that prices are likely to be higher when products are differentiated than when they are identical, all else the same. We also know that welfare falls as the gap between price and marginal cost rises. Does it follow that differentiating products lowers welfare? Not necessarily. Although differentiation leads to higher prices, which harm consumers, differentiation is desirable in its own right. Consumers value having a choice, and some may greatly prefer a new brand to existing ones.

One way to illustrate the importance of this second effect is to consider the value of introducing a new, differentiated product. This value reflects how much extra income consumers would require to be as well off without the good as with it.

APPLICATION

Welfare Gain from Greater Toilet Paper Variety

An article in the *Economist* asked, "Why does it cost more to wipe your bottom in Britain than in any other country in the European Union?" The answer given was that British consumers are "extremely fussy" in demanding a soft, luxurious texture—in contrast to barbarians elsewhere. As a consequence, they pay twice as much for toilet paper as the Germans and French, and nearly 2.5 times as much as Americans. (Indeed, British supermarkets reported that the share of luxury toilet paper sales spiked around Christmas 2009. Apparently during a major recession, Brits view luxury toilet paper as an appropriate present.)

Probably completely uninfluenced by this important cross-country research, Hausman and Leonard (2002) used U.S. data to measure the price effect and the extra consumer surplus from greater variety resulting from Kimberly-Clark's introduction of Kleenex Bath Tissue (KBT). Bath tissue products are divided into premium, economy, and private labels, with premium receiving more than 70% of revenue. Before KBT's entry, the major premium brands were Angel Soft, Charmin, Cottonelle, and Northern. ScotTissue was the leading economy brand.

Firms incur a sizable fixed cost from capital investments. The marginal cost depends primarily on the price of wood pulp, which varies cyclically. Because KBT was rolled out in various cities at different times, Hausman and Leonard could compare the effects of entry at various times and control for variations in cost and other factors.

The prices of all rival brands fell after KBT entered; the price of the leading brand, Charmin, dropped by 3.5%, while Cottonelle's price plummeted

8.2%. In contrast, the price of ScotTissue, an economy brand, decreased by only 0.6%.

Hausman and Leonard calculated that the additional consumer surplus due to extra variety was $33.4 million, or 3.5% of sales. When they included the gains due to lower prices, the total consumer surplus increase was $69.2 million, or 7.3% of sales. Thus, the gains to consumers were roughly equally divided between the price effect and the benefit from extra variety.

14.6 Monopolistic Competition

So far, we've concentrated on oligopolistic markets where the number of firms is fixed because of barriers to entry. We've seen that these firms in an oligopoly (such as the airlines in our example) may earn positive economic profits. We now consider firms in monopolistically competitive markets in which there are no barriers to entry, so firms enter the market until no more firms can enter profitably.

If both competitive and monopolistically competitive firms make zero economic profits, what distinguishes these two market structures? Competitive firms face horizontal residual demand curves and charge prices equal to marginal cost. In contrast, monopolistically competitive firms face downward-sloping residual demand curves and thus charge prices above marginal cost. Monopolistically competitive firms face downward-sloping residual demand curves because (unlike competitive firms) they have relatively few rivals or sell differentiated products.

The fewer monopolistically competitive firms, the less elastic the residual demand curve each firm faces. As we saw, the elasticity of demand for an individual Cournot firm is $n\varepsilon$, where n is the number of firms and ε is the market elasticity. Thus, the fewer the firms in a market, the less elastic the residual demand curve.

When monopolistically competitive firms benefit from economies of scale at high levels of output (the average cost curve is downward sloping), so that each firm is relatively large in comparison to market demand, there is room in the market for only a few firms. In the short run, if fixed costs are large and marginal costs are constant or diminishing, firms have economies of scale (Chapter 7) at all output levels, so there are relatively few firms in the market. In an extreme case with substantial enough economies of scale, the market may have room for only one firm: a natural monopoly (Chapter 11). The number of firms in equilibrium is smaller the greater the economies of scale and the farther to the left the market demand curve.

Monopolistically competitive firms also face downward-sloping residual demand curves if each firm differentiates its product so that at least some consumers believe that product is superior to other brands. If some consumers believe that Tide laundry detergent is better than Cheer and other brands, Tide won't lose all its sales even if Tide charges a slightly higher price. Thus, Tide faces a downward-sloping demand curve—not a horizontal one.

Monopolistically Competitive Equilibrium

In a monopolistically competitive market, each firm tries to maximize its profit, but each makes zero economic profit due to entry. Two conditions hold in a monopolistically competitive equilibrium: *marginal revenue equals marginal cost* because firms set output to maximize profit, and *price equals average cost* because firms enter until no further profitable entry is possible.

Figure 14.10 shows a monopolistically competitive market equilibrium. A typical monopolistically competitive firm faces a residual demand curve D^r. To maximize

---

Figure 14.10 Monopolistically Competitive Equilibrium

A monopolistically competitive firm, facing residual demand curve D^r, sets its output where its marginal revenue equals its marginal cost: $MR^r = MC$. Because firms can enter this market, the profit of the firm is driven to zero, so price equals the firm's average cost: $p = AC$.

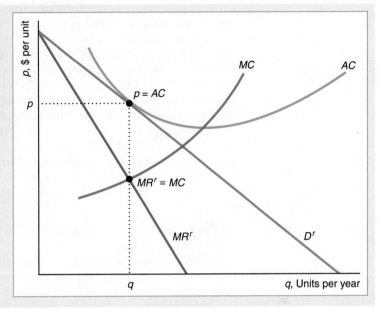

its profit, the firm sets its output, q, where its marginal revenue curve corresponding to the residual demand curve intersects its marginal cost curve: $MR^r = MC$. At that quantity, the firm's average cost curve, AC, is tangent to its residual demand curve. Because the height of the residual demand curve is the price, at the tangency point price equals average cost, $p = AC$, and the firm makes zero profit.

If the average cost were less than price at that quantity, firms would make positive profits and entrants would be attracted. If average cost were above price, firms would lose money, so firms would exit until the marginal firm was breaking even.

The smallest quantity at which the average cost curve reaches its minimum is referred to as *full capacity* or **minimum efficient scale**. The firm's full capacity or minimum efficient scale is the quantity at which the firm no longer benefits from economies of scale. Because a monopolistically competitive equilibrium occurs in the downward-sloping section of the average cost curve (where the average cost curve is tangent to the downward-sloping demand curve), a monopolistically competitive firm operates at less than full capacity in the long run.

Fixed Costs and the Number of Firms

The number of firms in a monopolistically competitive equilibrium depends on firms' costs. The larger each firm's fixed cost, the smaller the number of monopolistically competitive firms in the market equilibrium.

Although entry is free, if the fixed costs are high, few firms may enter. In the automobile industry, just to develop a new fender costs $8 to $10 million.[22] Developing a new pharmaceutical drug could cost more than $350 million.

[22]James B. Treece ("Sometimes, You Gotta Have Size," *Business Week*, Enterprise 1993:200–1) illustrates the importance of fixed costs on entry in the following anecdote: "In 1946, steel magnate Henry J. Kaiser boasted to a Detroit dinner gathering that two recent stock offerings had raised a huge $50 million to invest in his budding car company. Suddenly, a voice from the back of the room shot out: 'Give that man one white chip.'"

We can illustrate this relationship using the airline example, where we now modify our assumptions about entry and fixed costs. Recall that American and United are the only airlines providing service on the Chicago–Los Angeles route. Until now, we have assumed that a barrier to entry—such as an inability to obtain landing rights at both airports—prevented entry and that the firms had no fixed costs. If fixed cost is zero and marginal cost is constant at $147 per passenger, average cost is also constant at $147 per passenger. As we showed earlier, each firm in this oligopolistic market flies $q = 64$ thousand passengers per quarter at a price of $p = \$211$ and makes a profit of $4.1 million per quarter.

Now suppose that there are no barriers to entry and each airline incurs a fixed cost, F, due to airport fees, capital expenditure, or other factors.[23] Each firm's marginal cost remains $147 per passenger, but its average cost,

$$AC = 147 + \frac{F}{q},$$

falls as the number of passengers rises, as panels a and b of Figure 14.11 illustrate for $F = \$2.3$ million.

If there are only two firms in a monopolistically competitive market, what must the fixed costs be so that the two firms earn zero profit? We know that these firms each receive a profit of $4.1 million in the absence of fixed costs. As a result, the fixed cost must be $4.1 million per firm for the firms to earn zero profit. With this fixed cost, the monopolistically competitive price and quantity are the same as they are in the oligopolistic equilibrium, $q = 64$ and $p = \$211$, and the number of firms is the same, but now each firm's profit is zero.

Figure 14.11 Monopolistic Competition Among Airlines

(a) If each identical airline has a fixed cost of $2.3 million and there are two firms in the market, each firm flies $q = 64$ units (thousands of passengers) per quarter at a price of $p = \$211$ per passenger and makes a profit of $1.8 million. This profit attracts entry. (b) After a third firm enters, the residual demand curve shifts, so each firm flies $q = 48$ units at $p = \$195$ and makes zero profit, which is the monopolistically competitive equilibrium.

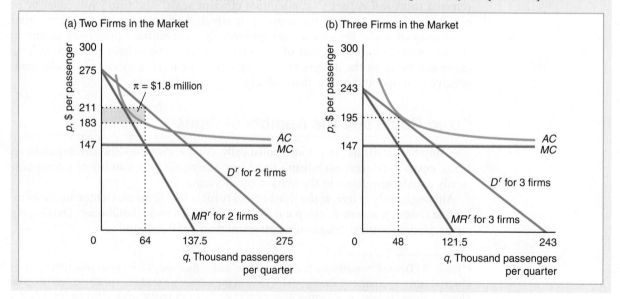

If the fixed cost is only $2.3 million and there are only two firms in the market, each firm makes a profit, as panel a shows. Each duopoly firm faces a residual demand curve (labeled "D^r for 2 firms"), which is the market demand minus its rival's Nash-Cournot equilibrium quantity, $q = 64$. Given this residual demand, each firm produces $q = 64$, which equates its marginal revenue, MR^r, and its marginal cost, MC. At $q = 64$, the firm's average cost is $AC = \$147 + (\$2.3 \text{ million})/(64 \text{ units}) \approx \$183$, so each firm makes a profit of $\pi = (p - AC)q \approx (\$211 - \$183) \times 64$ units per quarter $\approx \$1.8$ million per quarter.

This substantial economic profit attracts an entrant. The entry of a third firm causes the residual demand for any one firm to shift to the left in panel b. In the new equilibrium, each firm sets $q = 48$ and charges $p = \$195$. At this quantity, each firm's average cost is $195, so the firms break even. No other firms enter because if one did, the residual demand curve would shift even farther to the left and all the firms would lose money. Thus, if the fixed cost is $2.3 million, there are three firms in the monopolistically competitive equilibrium. This example illustrates a general result: *The lower the fixed costs, the more firms there are in the monopolistically competitive equilibrium.*

SOLVED PROBLEM 14.4

What is the monopolistically competitive airline equilibrium if each firm has a fixed cost of $3 million?

Answer

1. *Determine the number of firms.* We already know that the monopolistically competitive equilibrium has two firms if the fixed cost is $4.1 million and three firms if the fixed cost is $2.3 million. With a fixed cost of $3 million, if there are only two firms in the market, each makes a profit of $1.1 (= $4.1 − 3) million. If another firm enters, though, each firm's loss is −$0.7 (= $2.3 − 3) million. Thus, the monopolistically competitive equilibrium has two firms, each of which earns a positive profit that is too small to attract another firm. This outcome is a monopolistically competitive equilibrium because no other firm wants to enter.

2. *Determine the equilibrium quantities and prices.* We already know that each duopoly firm produces $q = 64$, so $Q = 128$ and $p = \$211$.

APPLICATION

Zoning Laws as a Barrier to Entry by Hotel Chains

U.S. local governments restrict land use through zoning. The difficulty of getting permission (generally from many agencies) to build a new commercial structure is a barrier to entry. Suzuki (forthcoming) examines the effect on Texas municipalities' zoning laws on chain hotels (such as Best Western, Holiday Inn, Quality Inn, Comfort Inn, La Quinta Inn, and Ramada).

According to his estimates, construction costs are large even in the absence of zoning regulations: Construction costs are $2.4 million for a new Best Western hotel and $4.5 million for a new La Quinta hotel. Going from a lenient to a stringent zoning policy increases a hotel's variable cost by 21% and its sunk entry cost by 19%. The average number of hotels in a small market falls from 2.3 under a lenient policy to 1.9 with a stringent policy due to the higher entry cost. As a consequence, there are 15% fewer rooms under a stringent policy, which increases the revenue per room by 7%. The change from the most lenient policy to the stringent policy decreases producer surplus by $1.5 million and consumer surplus by $1 million. Thus, more stringent zoning laws raise entry costs and thereby reduce the number of hotels and rooms, which causes the price to rise and lowers welfare.

At various times over the years, the United States has subsidized its aircraft manufacturer, Boeing, and various European countries have subsidized their aircraft manufacturer, Airbus. What happens if both firms are government subsidized?

To keep our answers to these questions as simple as possible, we assume that Airbus and Boeing compete in a Cournot model, they produce identical products with identical costs, and they face a linear demand curve. (Our analysis would be similar in a Cournot or Bertrand model with differentiated products.)

In Solved Problem 14.3, we showed that a government per-unit subsidy to one firm causes its marginal cost to fall and its best-response curve to shift out. If only one firm is subsidized, the subsidized firm produces more and the other firm less than they would in the absence of a subsidy.

If both governments give identical subsidies that lower each firm's marginal cost, then both firms' best-response curves shift out as the figure shows. The original, unsubsidized equilibrium, e_1, is determined by the intersection of the original best-response curves. The new, subsidized equilibrium, e_2, occurs where the new best-response curves intersect. Both firms produce more in the new equilibrium than in the original: $q_2 > q_1$. Thus, total equilibrium output increases, which causes the equilibrium price to fall.

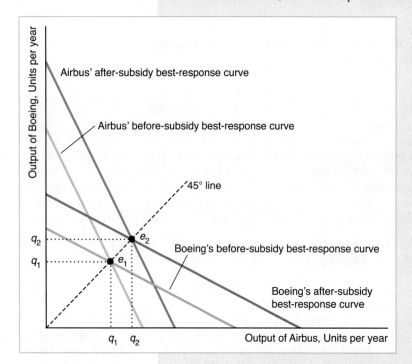

We can show these results mathematically, for the general linear model where the inverse demand function is $p = a - bQ$, and the marginal cost of each firm is m. A per-unit subsidy, s, reduces a firm's after-subsidy marginal cost to $m - s$. Thus, we can use the same equations we derived for the Cournot model for two firms ($n = 2$) where we replace the original marginal cost m by $m - s$. The subsidy changes the best-response function for Firm 1 from Equation 14.15 to

$$q_1 = \frac{a - m + s}{2b} - \frac{1}{2}q_2. \quad (14.45)$$

Similarly Firm 2's best-response function is the same as Equation 14.45 with the 1 and 2 subscripts reversed.

The equilibrium output ($q = q_1 = q_2$) expression, formerly Equation 14.16, becomes

$$q = \frac{a - m + s}{3b}. \quad (14.46)$$

Differentiating Equation 14.46 with respect to s, we find that the equilibrium output of each firm increases by $dq/ds = 1/(3b) > 0$. (In the American and

United Airlines example, a $1 subsidy would cause the equilibrium output to rise by a third of a unit, or about 333 passengers per quarter.)

Unlike the situation in which only one government subsidizes its firm, each subsidized firm increases its equilibrium output by the same amount so that the price falls. Each government is essentially subsidizing final consumers in other countries without giving its own firm a strategic advantage over its rival.

Each government's welfare function is the sum of its firm's profit including the subsidy minus the cost of the subsidy, which is the firm's profit ignoring the subsidy. Because the firms produce more than in the Nash-Cournot equilibrium, both firms earn less (ignoring the subsidies) so both countries are harmed. However, without the subsidy, its firm would be at a strategic disadvantage. Hence, both firms strongly lobby their governments for subsidies.

Many economists who analyze strategic trade policies strongly oppose them because they are difficult to implement and mean-spirited, "beggar thy neighbor" policies. If only one government intervenes, another country's firm is harmed. If both governments intervene, both countries may suffer. For these reasons, the World Trade Organization (WTO) has forbidden the use of all explicit export subsidies.

SUMMARY

1. **Market Structures.** Prices, profits, and quantities in a market equilibrium depend on the market's structure. Because profit-maximizing firms set marginal revenue equal to marginal cost, price is above marginal revenue—and hence marginal cost—only if firms face downward-sloping demand curves. In monopoly, oligopoly, and monopolistically competitive markets, firms face downward-sloping demand curves, in contrast to firms in a competitive market. Firms can earn positive profits when entry is blocked with a monopoly or an oligopoly, in contrast to the zero profits that competitive or monopolistically competitive firms earn with free entry. Oligopoly and monopolistically competitive firms, in contrast to competitive and monopoly firms, must pay attention to their rivals.

2. **Cartels.** If firms successfully collude, they produce the monopoly output and collectively earn the monopoly level of profit. Although their collective profits rise if all firms collude, each individual firm has an incentive to cheat on the cartel arrangement so as to raise its own profit even higher. For cartel prices to remain high, cartel members must be able to detect and prevent cheating, and noncartel firms must be unable to supply very much output. When antitrust laws or competition policies prevent firms from colluding, firms may try to merge if permitted by law.

3. **Cournot Oligopoly Model.** If oligopoly firms act independently, market output and firms' profits lie between the competitive and monopoly levels. In a Cournot model, each oligopoly firm sets its output simultaneously. In the Nash-Cournot equilibrium, each firm produces its best-response output—the output that maximizes its profit—given the output its rival produces. As the number of Cournot firms increases, the Nash-Cournot equilibrium price, quantity, and profits approach the price-taking levels.

4. **Stackelberg Oligopoly Model.** If one firm, the Stackelberg leader, chooses its output before its rivals, the Stackelberg followers, the leader produces more and earns a higher profit than each identical-cost follower firm. A government may subsidize a domestic oligopoly firm so that the firm produces the Stackelberg leader quantity, which it sells in an international market. For a given number of firms, the Stackelberg equilibrium output is less than the efficient (competitive market) level but exceeds that of the Nash-Cournot equilibrium, which exceeds that of the collusive equilibrium (which is the same as a monopoly produces). Correspondingly, the Stackelberg price is more than marginal cost but less than the Cournot price, which is less than the collusive or monopoly price. For a given number of firms, the Stackelberg equilibrium output exceeds that of the Nash-Cournot equilibrium, which is greater than that of the collusive or monopoly equilibrium. Correspondingly, the Stackelberg price is less than the Cournot price, which is less than the collusive or monopoly price, but greater than the competitive price.

5. Bertrand Oligopoly Model. In many oligopolistic or monopolistically competitive markets, firms set prices instead of quantities. If the product is homogeneous and firms set prices, the Nash-Bertrand equilibrium price equals marginal cost (which is lower than the Nash-Cournot equilibrium price). If the products are differentiated, the Nash-Bertrand equilibrium price is above marginal cost. Typically, the markup of price over marginal cost is greater the more the goods are differentiated.

6. Monopolistic Competition. In monopolistically competitive markets after all profitable entry occurs, there are few enough firms such that each firm faces a downward-sloping demand curve. Consequently, the firms charge prices above marginal cost. These markets are not perfectly competitive because there are relatively few firms—possibly because of high fixed costs or economies of scale that are large relative to market demand—or because the firms sell differentiated products.

EXERCISES

■ = *exercise is available on* MyEconLab; * = *answer appears at the back of this book;* **M** = *mathematical problem.*

1. Market Structures

1.1 Which market structure best describes (a) airplane manufacturing, (b) electricians in a small town, (c) farms that grow tomatoes, and (d) cable television in a city? Why?

2. Cartels

2.1 Many retail stores offer to match or beat the price offered by a rival store. Explain why firms that belong to a cartel might make this offer.

2.2 In an industry with inverse demand curve $p = 100 - 2Q$ there are four firms, each of which has a constant marginal cost given by $MC = 20$. If the firms form a profit-maximizing cartel and agree to operate subject to the constraint that each firm will produce the same output level, how much does each firm produce?

2.3 The European Union fined Sotheby's auction house more than €20 million for operating (along with rival auction house Christie's) a price-fixing cartel (see "The Art of Price Fixing" in MyEconLab, Chapter Resources, Chapter 14). The two auction houses were jointly setting the commission rates sellers must pay. Let r denote the jointly set auction commission rate, $D_i(r)$ represent the demand for auction house i's services by sellers of auctioned items, p denote the average price of auctioned items, F represent an auction house's fixed cost, and v denote its average variable cost of auctioning an object. At the agreed-upon commission rate r, the profit of an auction house i is $\pi_i = rpD_i(r) - [F + vD_i(r)]$.

  a. What is the sum of the profits of auction houses i and j?

  b. Characterize the commission rate that maximizes the sum of profits. That is, show that the commission rate that maximizes the sum of profits satisfies an equation that looks something like the monopoly's Lerner Index profit-maximizing condition, Equation 11.11.

  c. Do the auction houses have an incentive to cheat on their agreement? If Christie's does so while Sotheby's continues to charge r, what will happen to their individual and collective profits? **M**

3. Cournot Oligopoly

*3.1 What is the duopoly Nash-Cournot equilibrium if the market demand function is $Q = 1000 - 1000p$ and each firm's marginal cost is 28¢ per unit? **M**

3.2 In the initial Cournot oligopoly equilibrium, both firms have constant marginal costs, m, and no fixed costs, and there is a barrier to entry. Use calculus to show what happens to the best-response function of firms if both firms now face a fixed cost of F. **M**

3.3 According to Robert Guy Matthews, "Fixed Costs Chafe at Steel Mills," *Wall Street Journal*, June 10, 2009, stainless steel manufacturers are increasing prices even though the market demand curve had shifted to the left. In a letter to its customers, one of these companies announced that "Unlike mill increases announced in recent years, this is obviously not driven by increasing global demand, but rather by fixed costs being proportioned across significantly lower demand." If the firms are oligopolistic, produce a homogeneous good, face a linear market demand curve and have linear costs, and the market outcome is a Nash-Cournot equilibrium, does the firm's explanation as to why the market equilibrium price is rising make sense? (*Hint:* See Exercise 3.2.) What is a better explanation? **M**

3.4 In 2008, cruise ship lines announced they were increasing prices from $7 to $9 per person per day because of increased fuel costs. According to one analyst, fuel costs for Carnival Corporation's 84-ship fleet jumped $900 million to $2 billion in 2008 and its cost per passenger per day jumped from $10 to $33. Assuming that these firms are oligopolistic and the outcome is a Nash-Cournot equilibrium, why did prices rise less than in proportion to per-passenger-per-day cost? (*Hint*: Suppose that duopoly firms face a linear inverse market demand function $p = a - bQ$ and their marginal costs are m, solve for the equilibrium price, then show how the equilibrium price changes as m changes.) **M**

*3.5 In a Nash-Cournot equilibrium, each of the n firms faces a constant marginal cost m, the inverse market demand function is $p = a - bQ$, and the government assesses a specific tax of τ per unit. What is the incidence of this tax on consumers? **M**

*3.6 Your college is considering renting space in the student union to one or two commercial textbook stores. The rent the college can charge per square foot of space depends on the profit (before rent) of the firms and hence on whether there is a monopoly or a duopoly. Which number of stores is better for the college in terms of rent? Which is better for students? Why?

3.7 Connecticut sets a maximum fee that bail-bond businesses can charge for posting a given-size bond (Ayres and Waldfogel, 1994). The bail-bond fee is set at virtually the maximum amount allowed by law in cities with only one active firm (Plainville, 99%; Stamford, 99%; and Wallingford, 99%). The price is as high in cities with a duopoly (Ansonia, 99.6%; Meriden, 98%; and New London, 98%). In cities with three or more firms, however, the price falls well below the maximum permitted price. The fees are only 54% of the maximum in Norwalk (3 firms), 64% in New Haven (8 firms), and 78% in Bridgeport (10 firms). Give possible explanations for this pattern.

3.8 In 2005, the prices for 36 prescription painkillers shot up as much as 15% after Merck yanked its once-popular arthritis drug Vioxx from the market due to fears that it caused heart problems ("Prices Climb as Much as 15% for Some Painkillers," *Los Angeles Times*, June 3, 2005, C3). Can this product's exit be the cause of the price increases if the prices reflect a Nash-Cournot equilibrium? Explain.

3.9 Consider the Cournot model with n firms. The inverse linear market demand function is $p = a - bQ$. Each of the n identical firms has the same cost function $C(q_i) = Aq_i + \frac{1}{2}Bq_i^2$, where $a > A$. In terms of n, what is each firm's Nash equilibrium output and profit and the equilibrium price? As n gets very large (approaches infinity), does each firm's equilibrium profit approach zero? Why? **M**

3.10 The application "Deadweight Losses in the Food and Tobacco Industries" shows that the deadweight loss as a fraction of sales varies substantially across industries. One possible explanation is that the number of firms (degree of competition) varies across industries. Using Table 14.2 and other information from the chapter, show how the deadweight loss varies in the airline market as the number of firms increases from one to three. **M**

*3.11 The viatical settlement industry enables terminally ill consumers, typically HIV patients, to borrow against equity in their existing life insurance contracts to finance their consumption and medical expenses. The introduction and dissemination of effective anti-HIV medication in 1996 reduced AIDS mortality, extending patients' lives and hence delayed when the viatical settlement industry would receive the insurance payments. However, viatical settlement payments (what patients can borrow) fell more than can be explained by greater life expectancy. The number of viatical settlement firms dropped from 44 in 1995 to 24 in 2001. Sood et al. (2005) found that an increase in market power of viatical settlement firms reduced the value of life insurance holdings of HIV-positive persons by about $1 billion. When marginal cost rises and the number of firms falls, what happens to the Nash-Cournot equilibrium price? Use graphs or math to illustrate your answer. (*Hint*: If you use math, it may be helpful to assume that the market demand curve has a constant elasticity throughout.) **M**

*3.12 Why does differentiating its product allow an oligopoly to charge a higher price?

3.13 A duopoly faces an inverse market demand function of $p = 120 - Q$. Firm 1 has a constant marginal cost of 20. Firm 2's constant marginal cost is 40. Calculate the output of each firm, market output, and price if there is (a) a collusive equilibrium or (b) a Nash-Cournot equilibrium. (*Hint*: See Solved Problem 14.1.) **M**

3.14 Graph the best-response curve of the second firm in Solved Problem 14.1 if its marginal cost is m and if it is $m + x$. Add the first firm's best-response curve and show how the Nash-Cournot equilibrium changes as its marginal cost increases.

3.15 In 2012, Southwest Airlines reported that its "cost per available seat mile" was 13.0¢ compared to 13.8¢ for United Airlines. Assuming that Southwest and United compete on a single route, use a graph to show that their equilibrium quantities differ. (*Hint*: See Solved Problem 14.1.)

3.16 How would the Nash-Cournot equilibrium change in the airline example if United's marginal cost were $100 and American's were $200? (*Hint*: See Solved Problem 14.1.) **M**

*3.17 To examine the trade-off between efficiency and market power from a merger, consider a market with two firms that sell identical products. Firm 1 has a constant marginal cost of 1, and Firm 2 has a constant marginal cost of 2. The market demand is $Q = 15 - p$.

a. Solve for the Nash-Cournot equilibrium price, quantities, profits, consumer surplus, and deadweight loss. (*Hint*: See Solved Problem 14.1.)

b. If the firms merge and produce at the lower marginal cost, how do the equilibrium values change?

c. Discuss the change in efficiency (average cost of producing the output) and welfare—consumer surplus, producer surplus (or profit), and deadweight loss. **M**

3.18 The firms in a duopoly produce differentiated products. The inverse demand for Firm 1 is $p_1 = 52 - q_1 - 0.5q_2$. The inverse demand for Firm 2 is $p_2 = 40 - q_2 - 0.5q_1$. Each firm has a marginal cost of $m = 1$. Solve for the Nash-Cournot equilibrium quantities. (*Hint*: See Solved Problem 14.2.) **M**

*3.19 An incumbent firm, Firm 1, faces a potential entrant, Firm 2, that has a lower marginal cost. The market demand curve is $p = 120 - q_1 - q_2$. Firm 1 has a constant marginal cost of $20, while Firm 2's is $10.

a. What are the Nash-Cournot equilibrium price, quantities, and profits if there is no government intervention?

b. To block entry, the incumbent appeals to the government to require that the entrant incur extra costs. What happens to the Nash-Cournot equilibrium if the legal requirement causes the marginal cost of the second firm to rise to that of the first firm, $20?

c. Now suppose that the barrier leaves the marginal cost alone but imposes a fixed cost. What is the minimal fixed cost that will prevent entry? (*Hint*: See Solved Problem 14.3.) **M**

4. Stackelberg Oligopoly Model

*4.1 Duopoly quantity-setting firms face the market demand

$$p = 150 - q_1 - q_2.$$

Each firm has a marginal cost of $60 per unit.

a. What is the Nash-Cournot equilibrium?

b. What is the Stackelberg equilibrium when Firm 1 moves first? **M**

4.2 Determine the Stackelberg equilibrium with one leader firm and two follower firms if the market demand curve is linear and each firm faces a constant marginal cost, m, and no fixed cost. **M**

4.3 Show the effect of a subsidy on Firm 1's best-response function in Solved Problem 14.3 if the firm faces a general demand function $p(Q)$. **M**

4.4 Two firms, each in a different country, sell homogeneous output in a third country. Government 1 subsidizes its domestic firm by s per unit. The other government does not react. In the absence of government intervention, the market has a Nash-Cournot equilibrium. Suppose demand is linear, $p = 1 - q_1 - q_2$, and each firm's marginal and average costs of production are constant at m. Government 1 maximizes net national income (it does not care about transfers between the government and the firm, so it maximizes the firm's profit net of the transfers). Show that Government 1's optimal s results in its firm producing the Stackelberg leader quantity and the other firm producing the Stackelberg follower quantity in equilibrium. (*Hint*: See Solved Problem 14.3.) **M**

5. Bertrand Oligopoly Model

5.1 What happens to the homogeneous-good Nash-Bertrand equilibrium price if the number of firms increases? Why?

*5.2 Will price be lower if duopoly firms set price or if they set quantity? Under what conditions can you give a definitive answer to this question?

*5.3 Suppose that identical duopoly firms have constant marginal costs of $10 per unit. Firm 1 faces a demand function of $q_1 = 100 - 2p_1 + p_2$, where q_1 is Firm 1's output, p_1 is Firm 1's price, and p_2 is Firm 2's price. Similarly, the demand Firm 2 faces is $q_2 = 100 - 2p_2 + p_1$. Solve for the Nash-Bertrand equilibrium. **M**

5.4 Solve for the Nash-Bertrand equilibrium for the firms described in Exercise 5.3 if both firms have a marginal cost of $0 per unit. **M**

5.5 Solve for the Nash-Bertrand equilibrium for the firms described in Exercise 5.3 if Firm 1's marginal cost is $30 per unit and Firm 2's marginal cost is $10 per unit. **M**

5.6 In the Coke and Pepsi example, what is the effect of a specific tax, τ, on the equilibrium prices? (*Hint*: What does the tax do to the firm's marginal cost? You do not have to use math to provide a qualitative answer to this problem.)

5.7 At a busy intersection on Route 309 in Quakertown, Pennsylvania, the convenience store and gasoline station, Wawa, competes with the service and gasoline station, Fred's Sunoco. In the Nash-Bertrand equilibrium with product differentiation competition for gasoline sales, the demand for Wawa's gas is $q_W = 680 - 500p_W + 400p_S$, and the demand for Fred's gas is $q_W = 680 - 500p_S + 400p_W$. Assume that the marginal cost of each gallon of gasoline is $m = \$2$. The gasoline retailers simultaneously set their prices.

a. What is the Bertrand-Nash equilibrium?

b. Suppose that for each gallon of gasoline sold, Wawa earns a profit of 25¢ from its sale of salty snacks to its gasoline customers. Fred sells no products that are related to the consumption of his gasoline. What is the Nash equilibrium? (*Hint*: See Solved Problem 14.3.) **M**

5.8 In February 2005, the U.S. Federal Trade Commission (FTC) went to court to undo the January 2000 takeover of Highland Park Hospital by Evanston Northwestern Healthcare Corp. The FTC accused Evanston Northwestern of antitrust violations by using its post-merger market power in the Evanston hospital market to impose 40% to 60% price increases (Bernard Wysocki, Jr., "FTC Targets Hospital Merger in Antitrust Case," *Wall Street Journal*, January 17, 2005, A1). Hospitals, even within the same community, are geographically differentiated as well as possibly quality differentiated. Suppose that the demand for an appendectomy at Highland Park Hospital is a function of the price of the procedure at Highland Park and Evanston Northwestern Hospital: $q_H = 50 - 0.01p_H + 0.005p_N$. The comparable demand function at Evanston Northwestern is $q_N = 500 - 0.01p_N + 0.005p_H$. At each hospital, the fixed cost of the procedure is $20,000 and the marginal cost is $2,000.

a. Use the product-differentiated Bertrand model to analyze the prices the hospitals set before the merger. Find the Nash equilibrium prices of the procedure at the two hospitals.

b. After the merger, find the profit-maximizing monopoly prices of the procedure at each hospital. Include the effect of each hospital's price on the profit of the other hospital.

c. Does the merger result in increased prices? Explain. **M**

5.9 Firms in some industries with a small number of competitors earn normal economic profit. The *Wall Street Journal* (Gomes, Lee, "Competition Lives On in Just One PC Sector," March 17, 2003, B1) reports that the computer graphics chips industry is one such market. Two chip manufacturers, nVidia and ATI, "both face the prospect of razor-thin profits, largely on account of the other's existence."

a. Consider the Bertrand model in which each firm has a positive fixed and sunk cost and zero marginal cost. What are the Nash equilibrium prices? What are the Nash equilibrium profits?

b. Does this "razor-thin" profit result imply that the two manufacturers necessarily produce chips that are nearly perfect substitutes? Explain.

c. Assume that nVidia and ATI produce differentiated products and are Bertrand competitors. The demand for nVidia's chip is $q_V = a - bp_V + cp_A$; the demand for ATI's chip is $q_A = a - bp_A + cp_V$, where p_V is nVidia's price, p_A is ATI's price, and a, b, and c are coefficients of the demand function. Suppose each manufacturer's marginal cost is a constant, m. What are the values of a, b, and c for which the equilibrium profit of each chip manufacturer is zero? In answering this question, show that despite differentiated products, duopoly firms may earn zero economic profit. **M**

6. Monopolistic Competition

6.1 What is the effect of a government subsidy that reduces the fixed cost of each firm in an industry in a Cournot monopolistic competition equilibrium?

6.2 In the monopolistically competitive airlines model, what is the equilibrium if firms face no fixed costs?

6.3 In a monopolistically competitive market, the government applies a specific tax of $1 per unit of output. What happens to the profit of a typical firm in this market? Does the number of firms in the market change? Why?

6.4 Does an oligopoly or a monopolistically competitive firm have a supply curve? Why or why not? (*Hint*: See the discussion in Chapter 11 of whether a monopoly has a supply curve.)

*6.5 Show that a monopolistically competitive firm maximizes its profit where it is operating at less than *full capacity* or *minimum efficient scale*, which is the smallest quantity at which the average cost curve reaches its minimum (the bottom of a U-shaped average cost curve). The firm's minimum efficient scale is the quantity at which the firm no longer benefits from economies of scale.

6.6 Exercise 6.5 shows that a monopolistically competitive firm maximizes its profit where it is operating at less than full capacity. Does this result depend upon whether firms produce identical or differentiated products? Why?

6.7 In Solved Problem 14.4, what fixed cost would result in four firms operating in the monopolistically competitive equilibrium? What are the equilibrium quantities and prices?

7. Challenge

7.1 In the Challenge Solution's mathematical model, how much does Firm 1's best-response curve shift as the subsidy, s, increases?

7.2 Using the Challenge Solution's mathematical model, how much does Firm 1's profit (ignoring the subsidy) change as the subsidy, s, increases?

15

Factor Markets

Work is of two kinds: first, altering the position of matter at or near the earth's surface relative to other matter; second, telling other people to do so. —Bertrand Russell

For most of your childhood, your parents, teachers, or other adults urged you to go to college. However, during the recent recession, some people are no longer convinced that doing so is a good idea. A survey of Americans find that those who think college is a good investment has plummeted from 81% in 2008 to just 57% in 2012.

In the fall of 2011, 68% percent of high school graduates were enrolled in colleges or universities. However, only four out of ten young people earn two- or four-year college degrees now. Three out of ten adults over 25 years old have a bachelor's degree.

Going to college is expensive. In the 2011–2012 school year, half of all 18- to 24-year-old undergraduate students borrowed money to pay for college. Is going to college worth it?

This chapter examines factor markets, such as the markets for labor and capital. We want to answer questions such as Nokia faces when manufacturing cell phones: How many workers should Nokia hire? How much equipment does it need? Should it invest in a new factory? Its decisions depend on wages, the rental price of capital, and the interest rate, which the labor and capital factor markets determine.

We first look at factor markets, such as the market for labor. We look at *nondurable* services such as one hour of work by an engineer or a daily truck rental. Nondurable services are those consumed when they are purchased or soon thereafter.

Additional analytical complications arise when the input is *capital* or other *durable goods*: products that are usable for years. Firms use durable goods—such as manufacturing plants, machines, and trucks—to produce and distribute goods and services. Consumers spend one out of eight dollars on durable goods such as houses, cars, and refrigerators.

If a firm rents a durable good by the week, it faces a decision similar to its decision in buying a nondurable good or service. If the capital good must be bought or built rather than rented, the firm cannot apply this rule based on current costs and benefits alone. There are many types of specialized capital, such as custom-built factories or custom equipment, that a firm *cannot* rent.

We examine how purchases of durable goods or investments in college depend critically on the interest rate, which is also determined by the capital market. The interest rate also has a critical effect on how fast prices rise in natural resources markets, such as those for coal and oil.

In this chapter, we examine three main topics	1. **Factor Markets.** The intersection of the factor supply curve and the factor demand curve (which depends on firms' production functions and on the market price for output) determines the equilibrium quantity in a competitive factor market, which is greater quantity than in a noncompetitive factor market.
	2. **Capital Markets and Investing.** Investing money in a project pays if the return from that investment is greater than that from the best alternative.
	3. **Exhaustible Resources.** Scarcity, rising costs of extraction, and positive interest rates may cause the price of exhaustible resources such as coal and gold to rise exponentially over time.

15.1 Factor Markets

Virtually all firms rely on factor markets for at least some inputs, such as labor. The firms that buy factors may be competitive price takers or noncompetitive price setters, such as a monopsony firm. Competitive, monopolistically competitive, oligopolistic, and monopolistic firms sell factors.

We start with competitive factor markets. Factor markets are competitive when there are many small sellers and buyers. FloraHolland's daily flower auction in Amsterdam typifies such a competitive market with many sellers and buyers. The sellers supply inputs—flowers in bulk—to buyers, who sell outputs—trimmed flowers in vases and wrapped bouquets—at retail to final customers.

Our earlier analysis of the competitive supply curve applies to factor markets. Chapter 5 derives the supply curve of labor by examining how individuals' choices between labor and leisure depend on tastes and the wage rate. Chapter 8 determines the competitive supply curves of firms in general, including those that produce factors for other firms. Given that we know the supply curve, once we determine the factor's demand curve, we can analyze a competitive factor.

A firm chooses inputs so as to maximize its profit. We illustrate this decision for a firm that combines labor, L, and capital, K, to produce output, q, where its production function is $q = q(L, K)$.[1] Using the theory of the firm (Chapters 6 and 7), we show how the amount of each input that the firm demands depends on the prices of the factors and the price of the final output. We begin by considering the firm's short-run problem when the firm can adjust only labor because capital is fixed. We then examine its long-run problem when both inputs are variable.

A Firm's Short-Run Factor Demand Curve

In the short run, the firm's capital is fixed at $\overline{K}$ so the firm can increase its output only by using more labor. That is, the short-run production function might be written as $q = \widetilde{q}(L, \overline{K}) = q(L)$ to show that it is solely a function of labor.

---

[1]In Chapters 6 and 7, we wrote the production function as $q = f(L, K)$. Here, for notational simplicity, we write the function as $q(L, K)$.

The firm chooses how many workers to hire to maximize its profit. The firm is a price taker in the labor markets, so it can hire as many workers as it wants at the market wage, w. Thus, the firm's short-run cost is $C = wL + F$, where F is the fixed cost. The firm's revenue function is $R(q(L))$.

The firm's profit function is its revenue function minus its cost function. The firm's objective is to maximize its profit through its labor choice:

$$\max_{L} \pi = R(q(L)) - wL - F. \tag{15.1}$$

We use the chain rule to derive the firm's first-order condition for a profit maximum:[2]

$$\frac{d\pi}{dL} = \frac{dR}{dq}\frac{dq}{dL} - w = 0,$$

hence,

$$\frac{dR}{dq}\frac{dq}{dL} = w. \tag{15.2}$$

According to Equation 15.2, a profit-maximizing firm chooses L so that the additional revenue it receives from employing the last worker equals the wage it must pay for the last worker. The additional revenue from the last unit of labor, $(dR/dq)(dq/dL)$, is called the **marginal revenue product of labor** (MRP_L). That is, the firm's marginal benefit equals its marginal cost from one extra hour of work.

The marginal revenue product of labor is the marginal revenue from the last unit of output, $MR = dR/dq$, times the marginal product of labor, $MP_L = dq/dL$, which is the extra output produced by the last unit of labor (Chapter 6):

$$MRP_L = MR \times MP_L.$$

A Competitive Firm's Short-Run Factor Demand Curve. A competitive firm faces an infinitely elastic demand for its output at the market price, p, so its marginal revenue is p (Chapter 8), and its marginal revenue product of labor is

$$MRP_L = p\frac{dq}{dL} = pMP_L.$$

The marginal revenue product for a competitive firm is also called the *value of the marginal product* because the marginal revenue product equals the market price or value times the marginal product of labor, which is the market value of the extra output.

Thus, for a competitive firm, Equation 15.2 is

$$MRP_L = pMP_L = w. \tag{15.3}$$

Equation 15.3 is the firm's short-run labor demand function. It shows that the marginal revenue product of labor curve is the firm's demand curve for labor when capital is fixed. One interpretation of Equation 15.3 is that the MRP_L determines the maximum wage a firm is willing to pay to hire a given number of workers (or vice versa). Dividing both sides of Equation 15.3 by p, we find that the marginal product of labor equals the ratio of the wage to the output price: $MP_L = dq(L)/dL = w/p$.

[2]We assume that the second-order condition, $(dR/dq)(d^2q/dL^2) < 0$, holds and that the firm does not want to shut down.

Because the marginal product of labor is a function of labor, this expression can be restated so that the quantity of labor demanded by a competitive firm is a function of the wage-price ratio: $L = L(w/p)$.

We can illustrate these calculations using an estimated Cobb-Douglas production function for a Canadian thread mill (Baldwin and Gorecki, 1986): $q = L^{0.6}K^{0.2}$. If in the short run the firm's capital is fixed at $\overline{K} = 32$ units, its short-run production function is $q = L^{0.6}32^{0.2} = 2L^{0.6}$. The firm's marginal product of labor is $MP_L = d(2L^{0.6})/dL = 1.2L^{-0.4}$. As a result, Equation 15.3 becomes

$$MRP_L = 1.2pL^{-0.4} = w. \tag{15.4}$$

If the firm faces a price of $p = \$50$ per unit and a wage of $w = \$15$ an hour, Equation 15.4 becomes $MRP_L = 60L^{-0.4} = 15$, so the firm should employ $L = 32$ workers. More generally, when we solve Equation 15.4 for L in terms of p and w, the thread mill's demand for labor function is

$$L = \left(\frac{1}{1.2}\frac{w}{p}\right)^{1/(-0.4)} \approx 1.577\left(\frac{w}{p}\right)^{-2.5}. \tag{15.5}$$

Figure 15.1 plots the thread mill's MRP_L or labor demand curve when $p = \$50$. The wage line at $w = 15$ is the supply curve of labor that the firm faces. The firm can hire as many workers as it wants at a constant wage of $15. The marginal revenue product of labor curve, MRP_L, is the firm's demand curve for labor when other inputs are fixed. The MRP_L shows the maximum wage that a firm is willing to pay to hire a given number of workers. Thus, the intersection of the supply curve of labor facing the firm and the firm's demand curve for labor determines the profit-maximizing number of workers.

Effect of a Change in the Wage. What happens to the short-run demand for labor if the wage increases or decreases? The firm's labor demand curve is usually downward sloping because of the law of diminishing marginal returns (Chapter 6). The marginal product from extra workers, MP_L, of a firm with fixed capital eventually falls as the firm increases the amount of labor it uses. Because the marginal product of labor declines as more workers are hired, the marginal revenue product of labor (which equals a constant price times the marginal product of labor) or the demand curve must slope downward as well.

Figure 15.1 Short-Run Labor Demand of a Thread Mill

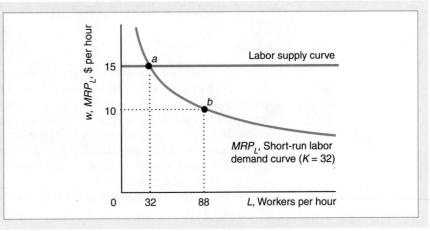

In the short run, capital is fixed at 32 units. If the market price is $50 per unit and the wage is $w = \$15$ per hour, a Canadian thread mill hires 32 workers at point a, where the labor supply curve intersects the mill's short-run labor demand curve. If the wage falls to $10, the mill hires 88 workers at point b.

According to Equation 15.3, the firm hires labor until the value of its marginal product of labor equals the wage: $pMP_L = w$. If w increases and p remains constant, the only way for the firm to maintain this equality is to adjust its labor force so as to cause its marginal product of labor to rise. If the firm operates where the production function exhibits diminishing marginal returns to labor, its marginal product of labor rises when it reduces its labor force. Thus, the firm's demand curve for labor is downward sloping.

We can confirm this reasoning using a formal comparative static analysis. Because Equation 15.3 is an identity, it must hold for all values of w; hence we can write the amount of labor demanded as an implicit function of the wage: $L(w)$. To show how labor demand varies with the wage, we differentiate Equation 15.3 with respect to w:

$$p \frac{dMP_L}{dL} \frac{dL}{dw} = 1.$$

Rearranging terms,

$$\frac{dL}{dw} = \frac{1}{p \dfrac{dMP_L}{dL}}. \tag{15.6}$$

Thus, if the firm is operating where the production function exhibits diminishing marginal product of labor, $dMP_L/dL = d^2q/dL^2 < 0$, $dL/dw < 0$, and the demand curve for labor slopes downward.

Figure 15.1 shows that the thread mill's short-run labor demand curve is downward sloping: The quantity of labor services demanded rises from 32 to 88 workers if the wage falls from \$15 to \$10. The reason the firm's demand curve is downward sloping is that its marginal product of labor, $MP_L = 1.2L^{-0.4}$, falls as the firm uses more labor: $dMP_L/dL = -0.48L^{-1.4} < 0$. Indeed, because this inequality holds for any L, the production function exhibits diminishing marginal product of labor at any quantity of labor, and hence the mill's labor demand curve slopes downward everywhere.

SOLVED PROBLEM 15.1

How does a competitive firm adjust its short-run demand for labor if the local government collects a specific tax of τ on each unit of output, where this tax does not affect other firms in the market because they are located in other communities?

Answer

1. *Give intuition.* Because the tax is applied to one competitive firm only, it does not affect p or w measurably. Because the specific tax lowers the after-tax price per unit that the firm receives, we can apply the same type of analysis that we would use to show the comparative statics effect of a change in the output price. For a given amount of labor, the marginal revenue product of labor falls from $pMP_L(L)$ to $(p - \tau)MP_L(L)$. The marginal revenue product of labor curve—the labor demand curve—shifts downward until it is only $(p - \tau)/p$ as high as the original labor demand curve at any quantity of labor, so the firm demands less labor at any given wage. We now use calculus to derive this result formally.

2. *Differentiate the profit-maximizing condition with respect to the tax.* The firm's profit-maximizing condition, Equation 15.3, is $(p - \tau)MP_L = w$ (which we evaluate at $\tau = 0$ before the tax is imposed). Given that this identity holds for all τ, the labor demanded is an implicit function of the tax: $L(\tau)$. Differentiating this identity with respect to τ, we find that

$$-MP_L + (p - \tau)\frac{\mathrm{d}MP_L}{\mathrm{d}L}\frac{\mathrm{d}L}{\mathrm{d}\tau} = 0,$$

where the right-hand side of the equation is zero because w does not vary with τ. Rearranging terms,

$$\frac{\mathrm{d}L}{\mathrm{d}\tau} = \frac{MP_L}{(p - \tau)\dfrac{\mathrm{d}MP_L}{\mathrm{d}L}}.$$

Because MP_L and $(p - \tau)$ are positive, the sign of this expression is the same as that of $\mathrm{d}MP_L/\mathrm{d}L$. Thus, if the production process exhibits diminishing marginal product of labor, the quantity of labor demanded falls with the tax: $\mathrm{d}L/\mathrm{d}\tau < 0$.

A Noncompetitive Firm's Short-Run Factor Demand Curve. Factor demand curves vary with market power. As we saw in Chapter 11, the marginal revenue of profit-maximizing Firm i, $MR = p(1 + 1/\varepsilon_i)$, is a function of the elasticity of demand, ε_i, facing the firm and of the market price, p. Thus, the firm's marginal revenue product of labor function is

$$MRP_L = p\left(1 + \frac{1}{\varepsilon_i}\right)MP_L.$$

The labor demand curve is $p \times MP_L$ for a competitive firm because it faces an infinitely elastic demand at the market price, so its marginal revenue equals the market price.

A monopoly operates in the elastic section of its downward-sloping market demand curve (Chapter 11), so its demand elasticity is less than -1 and finite: $-\infty < \varepsilon \leq -1$. As a result, at any given price, the monopoly's labor demand, $p(1 + 1/\varepsilon)MP_L$, lies below the labor demand curve, pMP_L, of a competitive firm with an identical marginal product of labor curve.

Figure 15.2 shows the short-run market labor demand curve for an actual competitive thread mill and the corresponding curve for a monopoly. In the short run, the thread mill's marginal product function is $MP_L = 1.2L^{-0.4}$. The labor demand is $p \times 1.2L^{-0.4}$ for a competitive firm and $p(1 + 1/\varepsilon) \times 1.2L^{-0.4}$ for a monopoly. In the figure, we assume that $\varepsilon = 2$.

A Cournot firm faces an elasticity of demand of $n\varepsilon$, where n is the number of identical firms and ε is the market elasticity of demand (Chapter 13). If the market has a constant elasticity demand curve with an elasticity of ε, the demand elasticity faced by a duopoly Cournot firm is twice that, 2ε, of a monopoly. Consequently, a Cournot duopoly firm's labor demand curve, $p[1 + 1/(2\varepsilon)]MP_L$, lies above that of a monopoly but below that of a competitive firm. In Figure 15.2, shows the short-run market labor demand curve for one of two identical Cournot thread mills is $p[1 + 1/(2\varepsilon)] \times 1.2L^{-0.4}$.

Figure 15.2 How Thread Mill Labor Demand Varies with Market Structure

For all profit-maximizing firms, the labor demand curve is the marginal revenue product of labor: $MRP_L = MR \times MP_L$. Because marginal revenue differs with market structure, so does the MRP_L. At a given wage, a competitive thread firm demands more workers than a Cournot duopoly firm, which demands more workers than a monopoly.

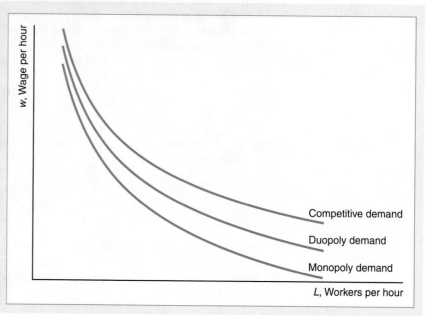

A Firm's Long-Run Factor Demand Curves

In the long run, the firm is free to vary all of its inputs. Thus, in the long run, if the wage of labor rises, the firm adjusts both labor and capital. As a result, the short-run marginal revenue product of labor curve that holds capital fixed is not the firm's long-run labor demand curve. The long-run labor demand curve takes account of changes in the firm's use of capital as the wage rises.

In the long run, the firm chooses both labor and capital so as to maximize its profit. If the firm is a price taker in these factor markets, then the firm's cost is $C = wL + rK$, where w is the wage and r is the rental cost of capital. Because the firm's production process is $q = q(L, K)$, its revenue function is $R(q(L, K))$.

The firm's profit function is its revenue function minus its costs. The firm's objective is to maximize its profit through its choice of inputs:

$$\max_{L, K} \pi = R(q(L, K)) - wL - rK. \tag{15.7}$$

The firm's first-order conditions for a profit maximum are

$$\frac{\partial \pi}{\partial L} = \frac{\partial R}{\partial q} \frac{\partial q}{\partial L} - w = 0,$$

$$\frac{\partial \pi}{\partial K} = \frac{\partial R}{\partial q} \frac{\partial q}{\partial K} - r = 0.$$

These first-order conditions are closely analogous to the short-run profit-maximizing condition. They show that the firm sets its marginal revenue product of labor equal to the wage and its marginal revenue product of capital equal to the rental price of capital:

$$MRP_L = MR \times MP_L = \frac{\partial R}{\partial q} \frac{\partial q}{\partial L} = w, \tag{15.8}$$

$$MRP_K = MR \times MP_K = \frac{\partial R}{\partial q}\frac{\partial q}{\partial K} = r. \tag{15.9}$$

A Competitive Firm's Long-Run Factor Demand Curve. Again, if the firm is competitive, $MR = p$, so Equations 15.8 and 15.9 can be written as

$$MRP_L = pMP_L = p\frac{\partial q}{\partial L} = w, \tag{15.10}$$

$$MRP_K = pMP_K = \frac{\partial q}{\partial K} = r. \tag{15.11}$$

That is, each input's factor price equals the value of its marginal product. Equations 15.10 and 15.11 are the competitive firm's long-run factor demand equations.

For example, if the production function is Cobb-Douglas, $q = AL^aK^b$, then Equations 15.10 and 15.11 are

$$paAL^{a-1}K^b = w,$$

$$pbAL^aK^{b-1} = r.$$

Solving these equations for L and K, we find that the factor demand functions are

$$L = \left(\frac{a}{w}\right)^{(1-b)/d}\left(\frac{b}{r}\right)^{b/d}(Ap)^{1/d}, \tag{15.12}$$

$$K = \left(\frac{a}{w}\right)^{a/d}\left(\frac{b}{r}\right)^{(1-a)/d}(Ap)^{1/d}, \tag{15.13}$$

where $d = 1 - a - b$.[3] By differentiating the input demand Equations 15.12 and 15.13, we can show that the demand for each factor decreases with respect to its own factor price, w or r, and increases with p. Given the parameters for the estimated Canadian thread mill production function, $a = 0.6$, $b = 0.2$, and $A = 1$, the long-run labor demand Equation 15.12 is $L = (0.6/w)^4(0.2/r)p^5$, and the long-run capital demand Equation 15.13 is $K = (0.6/w)^3(0.2/r)^2p^5$.

The shares of its total revenue that a competitive firm pays to labor and to capital do not vary with factor or output prices if the firm has a Cobb-Douglas production function, $q = AL^aK^b$. A competitive firm with a Cobb-Douglas production function pays its labor the value of its marginal product, $w = pMP_L = apAL^{a-1}K^b = apq/L$. As a result, the share of the firm's revenue that it pays to labor is $\omega_L = wL/(pq) = a$. Similarly, $\omega_K = rK/(pq) = b$. Thus, the payment shares to labor and to capital are fixed and independent of prices with a Cobb-Douglas production function.

Comparing Short-Run and Long-Run Labor Demand Curves. In both the short run and the long run, the labor demand curve is the marginal revenue product curve of labor. In the short run, the firm cannot vary capital, so the short-run MP_L curve and hence the short-run MRP_L curve are relatively steep. In the long run, when the firm can vary all inputs, its long-run MP_L curve and MRP_L curve are flatter.

Figure 15.3 illustrates this difference for the Canadian thread mill, where $p = \$50$ per unit and $r = \$5$ per hour. On the short-run labor demand curve where capital is

---

[3]If the Cobb-Douglas production function has constant returns to scale, $d = 0$, then Equations 15.12 and 15.13 are not helpful. The problem with constant returns to scale is that a competitive firm does not care how much it produces (and hence how many inputs it uses) as long as the market price and input prices are consistent with zero profit.

Figure 15.3 Labor Demand Curves of a Thread Mill

If the long-run market price is $50 per unit, the rental rate of capital services is $r = \$5$, and the wage is $w = \$15$ per hour, a Canadian thread mill hires 32 workers (and uses 32 units of capital) at point *a* on its long-run labor demand curve. In the short run, if capital is fixed at $\overline{K} = 32$, the firm still hires 32 workers per hour at point *a* on its short-run labor demand curve. If the wage drops to $10 and capital remains fixed at $\overline{K} = 32$, the firm would hire 88 workers, point *b* on the short-run labor demand curve. In the long run, however, it would increase its capital to $K = 108$ and hire 162 workers, point *c* on the long-run labor demand curve and on the short-run labor demand curve with $\overline{K} = 108$.

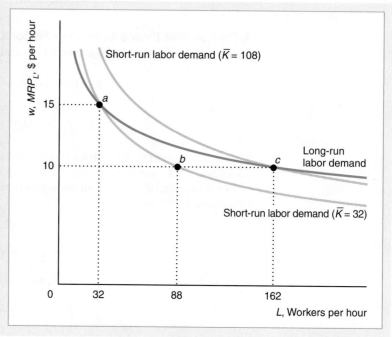

fixed at $\overline{K} = 32$ the firm hires 32 workers per hour at $w = \$15$. Using 32 workers and 32 units of capital is profit maximizing in the long run, so point *a* is also on the firm's long-run labor demand curve. The short-run labor demand curve is steeper than the long-run curve at point *a*.[4]

In the short run, if the wage fell to $10, the firm could not increase its capital, so it would hire 88 workers, point *b* on the short-run labor demand curve, where $\overline{K} = 32$. However, in the long run, the firm would employ more capital and even more labor (because it can sell as much output as it wants at the market price). It would hire 162 workers and use 108 units of capital, which is point *c* on both the long-run labor demand curve and the short-run labor demand curve for $\overline{K} = 108$.

Competitive Factor Markets

To determine the competitive equilibrium in a factor market, we aggregate the individual firms' demand curves to obtain the factor market demand curve, and then we determine where the factor market demand curve intersects the factor market supply curve.

A Factor Market Demand Curve. A factor market demand curve is the horizontal sum of the factor demand curves of the various firms that use the input. Determining a factor market demand curve is more difficult than deriving consumers' market

---

[4]If $p = \$50$, the Canadian thread mill's short-run labor demand equation is $L \approx 27,885.48w^{-2.5}$. In contrast, if $r = \$5$, its long-run labor demand equation is $L = 1,620,000w^{-4}$. At $w = \$15$, the two curves intersect at $L = 32$, as Figure 15.3 shows. At that point, the change in labor with respect to a change in the wage on the short-run labor demand curve is $dL/dw \approx -2.5(27,885.48)w^{-1.5} \approx -1,200$, and the corresponding derivative along the long-run curve is $dL/dw = -4(1,620,000) \times w^{-3} = -1,920$. Thus, the slope of the short-run labor demand curve, dw/dL, is steeper than that of the long-run curve.

demand for a final good. When horizontally summing the demand curves for individual consumers in Chapter 2, we were concerned with only a single market. However, inputs such as labor and capital are used in many output markets. Thus, to derive the labor market demand curve, we first determine the labor demand curve for each output market and then sum across output markets to obtain the factor market demand curve.

Earlier, we derived the factor demand of a competitive firm that took the output market price as given. However, the output market price depends on the factor's price. As the factor's price falls, each firm, taking the original market price as given, uses more of the factor to produce more output. This extra production by all the firms in the market causes the market price to fall. As the market price falls, each firm reduces its output and hence its demand for the input. Thus, a fall in an input price causes less of an increase in factor demand than would occur if the market price remained constant, as Figure 15.4 illustrates.

At the initial output market price of $9 per unit, the competitive firm's labor demand curve (panel a of Figure 15.4) is $MRP_L(p = \$9) = \$9 \times MP_L$. When the wage is $25 per hour, the firm hires 50 workers: point *a*. The 10 firms in the market (panel b) demand 500 hours of work: point *A* on the demand curve $D(p = \$9) = 100 \times \$9 \times MP_L$. If the wage falls to $10 while the market price

Figure 15.4 Firm and Market Demand for Labor

When the output price is $p = \$9$, the individual competitive firm's labor demand curve is $MRP_L(p = \$9)$. If $w = \$25$ per hour, the firm hires 50 workers, point *a* in panel a, and the 10 firms in the market demand 500 workers, point *A* on the labor demand curve $D(p = \$9)$ in panel b. When the wage falls to $10, each firm would

hire 90 workers, point *c*, if the market price stayed fixed at $9. The extra output, however, drives the price down to $7, so each firm hires 70 workers, point *b*. The market's demand for labor that takes price adjustments into account, D(price varies), goes through points *A* and *B*.

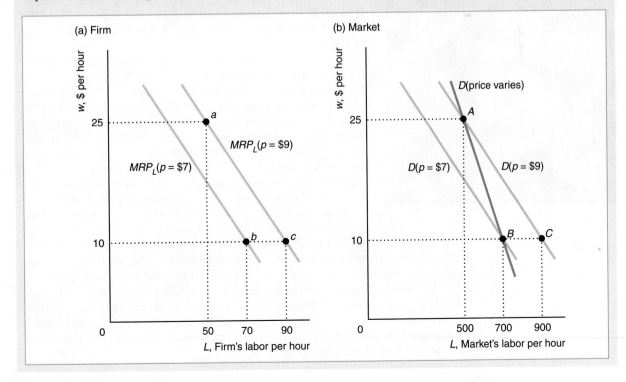

remains fixed at $9, each firm hires 90 workers, point *c*, and all the firms in the market would hire 900 workers, point *C*. However, the extra output drives the price down to $7, so each firm hires 70 workers, point *b*, and the firms collectively demand 700 workers, point *B*. The market labor demand curve for this output market that accounts for price adjustments, *D*(price varies), goes through points *A* and *B*. Thus, the market's demand for labor is steeper than it would be if output prices were fixed.

Competitive Factor Market Equilibrium. The intersection of the factor market demand curve and the factor market supply curve determines the competitive factor market equilibrium. We've just derived the factor market demand curve. There's nothing unusual about the factor market supply curve. The long-run factor supply curve for each firm is its marginal cost curve above the minimum of its average cost curve, and the factor market supply curve is the horizontal sum of the firms' supply curves. Because we've already analyzed competitive market equilibria for markets in general in Chapters 2, 8, and 9, there's no point in repeating the analysis. Been there. Done that.

Chapter 10 shows that factor prices are equalized across markets. For example, if wages were higher in one industry than in another, workers would shift from the low-wage industry to the high-wage industry until the wages were equalized.

APPLICATION

Black Death Raises Wages

The Black Death—bubonic plague—wiped out between a third and a half of the population of medieval Western Europe, resulting in a large increase in the real wage and sizable drops in the real rents on land and capital. Why?

The plague is characterized by large, dark lumps in the groin or armpits followed by livid black spots on the arms, thighs, and other parts of the body. In virtually all its victims, the Black Death led to a horrible demise within one to three days of onset.

In England, the plague struck in 1348–1349, 1360–1361, 1369, and 1375. According to one historian, the population fell from 3.76 million in 1348 to 3.13 million in 1348–1350, 2.75 million in 1360, 2.45 million in 1369, and 2.25 million in 1374.

In England, nominal wages rose in the second half of the fourteenth century compared to the first half: Thatchers earned 35% more, thatchers' helpers 105%, carpenters 40%, masons 48%, mowers 24%, oat threshers 73%, and oat reapers 61%. Adjusting for output price changes (at a medieval consumer price index), the average real wage rose by about 25%. In Pistoia, Italy, rents in kind on land fell by about 40%, and the rate of return on capital fell by about the same proportion.

Because the plague wiped out one-half to two-thirds of the labor force, labor became scarce relative to capital and land, which, of course, were unaffected by the disease. The scarcity of labor caused the marginal product of labor, MP_L, to rise: The remaining workers had lots of capital and land to use and hence were very productive. In competitive markets, workers are paid a wage equal to the value of their marginal product (marginal revenue product), $w = pMP_L$. If we rearrange this expression, the real wage (the wage relative to the price level), w/p, equals the marginal product of labor, $w/p = MP_L$. Hence, a large increase in the marginal product of labor causes a comparable increase in the real wage. Similarly, the fall in labor reduced the marginal products of capital and land, resulting in a drop in the real prices that these factors of production received.

SOLVED PROBLEM 15.2

For simplicity, suppose that medieval England was a single, large, price-taking firm that produced one type of output with a constant-returns-to-scale Cobb-Douglas production function, $q = L^{0.5}K^{0.5}$. Labor and capital have inelastic supply curves. That is, everyone, L, works and all capital, $K = 100$, is used. Suppose that the Black Death killed three-fourths of the workers, causing the number of workers to fall from L to $L^* = \frac{1}{4}L$. Show how much the wage, w, rose. Given that p is normalized to 1, calculate the changes in the factor prices.

Answer

1. *Show how output falls due to a reduction in labor.* When labor falls from L to $L^* = \frac{1}{4}L$, output falls from $Q = L^{0.5}K^{0.5}$ to $Q^* = (\frac{1}{4}L)^{0.5}K^{0.5} = \frac{1}{4}^{0.5}L^{0.5}K^{0.5} = \frac{1}{4}^{0.5}Q = \frac{1}{2}Q$. That is, when labor falls to one-fourth its original level, output falls less than in proportion to one-half its initial level.

2. *Given the effect of the plague on output, show how the marginal product of labor changed and hence how the real wage changed.* We know that the marginal product of labor for a Cobb-Douglas production function is $MP_L = \frac{1}{2}Q/L$. The output-to-labor ratio changes from Q/L to $Q^*/L^* = \frac{1}{2}Q/(\frac{1}{4}L) = 2Q/L > Q/L$. Consequently, the marginal product of labor rose from $MP_L = \frac{1}{2}Q/L$ to $MP_L^* = Q/L = 2MP_L$. The competitive labor demand equation is determined by equating the marginal product of labor to the real wage, $MP_L = w/p$. (We refer to w/p as the real wage because there is only one price, p.) For this equation to hold when the marginal product of labor rose, the real wage of labor, $w^*/p = MP_L^*$, had to rise in proportion to MP_L^*.

3. *Show the corresponding effect on capital.* Because output fell and capital remained the same, the marginal product of capital fell from $MP_K = \frac{1}{2}Q/K$ to $MP_K^* = \frac{1}{4}^{0.5} \times 0.5 \times Q/K = \frac{1}{4}MP_K$. Consequently, the real price of capital, $r^*/p = MP_K$, dropped.

4. *Calculate the changes in wages and the rental price of capital.* The initial output was $Q = L^{0.5}K^{0.5} = 100^{0.5}100^{0.5} = 100$. The marginal product of labor was $MP_L = \frac{1}{2}Q/L = \frac{1}{2}(100/100) = \frac{1}{2}$, so the real wage was $w/p = \frac{1}{2}$, given that $p = 1$. Similarly, the marginal product of capital was $MP_K = \frac{1}{2}Q/K = \frac{1}{2}$, and the real price of capital was $r/p = \frac{1}{2}$. After the plague, the labor force fell to $L^* = \frac{1}{4} \times 100 = 25$, and output dropped to $Q = 25^{0.5}100^{0.5} = 50$. Consequently, the marginal product of labor rose to $MP_L^* = \frac{1}{2}(50/25) = 1$, so the real wage rose to $w^*/p = 1$. Similarly, the marginal product of capital and the real price of capital fell to $MP_K^* = \frac{1}{2}(50/100) = \frac{1}{4} = r^*/p$. Thus, the real wage doubled and the real rental rate on capital dropped by half.

15.2 Capital Markets and Investing

If a firm rents a durable good by the week, it faces a decision similar to the one it encounters when buying a nondurable good or service. A firm demands workers' services (or other nondurable input) up to the point at which its *current* marginal cost (the wage) equals its *current* marginal benefit (the marginal revenue product of the workers' services). A firm that rents a durable good, such as a truck, by the week can use the same rule to decide how many trucks to rent per week. The firm rents trucks up to the point at which the *current* marginal rental cost equals its *current* marginal benefit—the marginal revenue product of the trucks.

If the capital good must be bought or built rather than rented, the firm cannot apply this rule based on current costs and benefits alone. (There are many types of specialized capital, such as a factory or a customized piece of equipment, that a firm *cannot* rent.) In deciding whether to build a factory that will last for many years, a firm must compare the *current* cost of the capital to the *future* higher profits it will make over time by using the plant.

Such comparisons may involve both *stocks* and *flows*. A **stock** is a quantity or value that is measured independently of time. Because a durable good lasts for many periods, its stock is discussed without reference to its use within a particular time period. We say that a firm owns "an apartment building *this* year" (not "an apartment building *per* year"). If a firm buys the apartment building for $5 million, we say that it has a capital stock worth $5 million today.

A **flow** is a quantity or value that is measured per unit of time. The consumption of nondurable goods, such as the number of ice-cream cones you eat per week, is a flow. Similarly, the stock of a durable good provides a flow of services. A firm's apartment building—its capital stock—provides a flow of housing services (apartments rented per month or year) to tenants. In exchange for these housing services, the firm receives a flow of rental payments from the tenants. If the capital good or *asset* provides a monetary flow, it is called a *financial asset*.

Does it pay for a firm to buy an apartment building? To answer this question, we need to extend our analysis in two ways. First, we must compare a flow of dollars in the future to a dollar today, which we do in this chapter. Second, we need to consider the role of uncertainty about the future (can the firm rent all the apartments each month?), which we discuss in Chapter 16.

We start by showing how we can use interest rates to compare money in the future to money today. Then, we show how we can use interest rates to compare streams of payments or streams of returns from investment over time to money today. Finally, we use these means of comparison to analyze how a firm chooses between two investments.

Interest Rates

Because virtually everyone values having a dollar today more than having a dollar in the future, you would not loan a bank a dollar today (that is, place money in a savings account) unless the bank agreed to pay back more than a dollar in the future. How much more you must be paid in the future is specified by an **interest rate:** the percentage more that must be repaid to borrow money for a fixed period of time.[5] In the following discussion, we assume that there is no inflation and concentrate on real interest rates.

If you invest a *present value* of PV dollars this year and the bank pays i percent interest per year, the bank will return a *future value* of $PV \times (1 + i)$ next year. If you leave your money in the bank for many years, you will earn interest in later

---

[5]For simplicity, we refer to *the* interest rate, but in most economies there are many interest rates. For example, a bank charges a higher interest rate to lend you money than the interest rate it pays you to borrow your money. (See "Usury" in MyEconLab's , Chapter Resources, Chapter 15 for a discussion of ancient people's opposition to paying interest, and current restrictions on Islamic banks.)

years on the interest paid in the earlier years, which is called *compounded interest*. Thus, if you deposit PV dollars in the bank today and allow the interest to compound for t years, the future value FV is

$$FV = PV \times (1 + i)^t. \tag{15.14}$$

Equivalently, we can ask what the *present value* is of an investment that pays FV next year. At an interest rate of i, the present value is $PV = FV/(1 + i)$. By rearranging Equation 15.14, we find that the amount of money that you would have to put in the bank today to get FV in t years at an interest rate of i is

$$PV = \frac{FV}{(1 + i)^t}. \tag{15.15}$$

Discount Rate

You may value future consumption more or less than other members of society do. If you knew you had two years to live, you would place less value on payments three or more years in the future than most other people would. We call an individual's personal "interest" rate that person's **discount rate**: a rate reflecting the relative value an individual places on future consumption compared to current consumption.

A person's willingness to borrow or lend depends on whether his or her discount rate is greater or less than the market interest rate. If your discount rate is nearly zero—you view current and future consumption as equally desirable—you would gladly lend money in exchange for a positive interest rate. Similarly, if your discount rate is high—current consumption is much more valuable to you than future consumption—you would be willing to borrow at a lower interest rate. In the following discussion, we assume for simplicity that an individual's discount rate is the same as the market interest rate unless we explicitly state otherwise.

Stream of Payments

Many people pay a certain amount each month over time for their purchases. These payments are flow measures—in contrast to a present value and a future value, which are stock measures. For example, a firm may pay for a new factory by making monthly mortgage payments. In deciding whether to purchase the factory, the firm compares the present value of the stock (the factory) to a flow of payments over time.

One way to evaluate this investment is to determine the present value of the stream of payments and compare this value directly to the present value of the factory. The present value of the stream of payments is the sum of the present value of each future payment. Thus, if the firm makes a *future payment* of f per year for t years at an interest rate of i, the present value (stock) of this flow of payments is

$$PV = f\left[\frac{1}{(1 + i)^1} + \frac{1}{(1 + i)^2} + \cdots + \frac{1}{(1 + i)^t}\right]. \tag{15.16}$$

If these payments must be made at the end of each year forever, the present value formula is easier to calculate than Equation 15.16. If the firm invests PV dollars into a bank account earning an interest rate of i, it receives interest or future payment of

$f = i \times PV$ at the end of each year. Dividing both sides of this expression by i, we find that to get a payment of f each year forever, the firm would have to put

$$PV = \frac{f}{i} \qquad (15.17)$$

in the bank.[6]

This payment-in-perpetuity formula, Equation 15.17, provides a good approximation of a payment for a large but finite number of years. At a 5% interest rate, the present value of a payment of $10 a year for 100 years, $198, is close to the present value of a permanent stream of payments, $200. At higher interest rates, this approximation is nearly perfect. At 10%, the present value of payments for 100 years is $99.9927 compared to $100 for perpetual payments. This approximation works better at high rates because $1 paid more than 50 or 100 years from now is essentially worthless today at high rates.

We just calculated the present value of a stream of payments. This type of computation can help a firm decide whether to buy something today that it will pay for over time. Alternatively, the firm may want to know the future value of a bank account if it invests f each year. At the end of t years, the account has

$$FV = f[1 + (1 + i)^1 + (1 + i)^2 + \cdots + (1 + i)^{t-1}]. \qquad (15.18)$$

APPLICATION

Saving for Retirement

If all goes well, you'll live long enough to retire. Will you live like royalty off your savings, or will you have to depend on Social Security to provide enough income so that you can avoid having to eat dog food to stay alive? (When I retire, I'm going to be a Velcro farmer.)

You almost certainly don't want to hear this now, but it isn't too early to think about saving for retirement. Thanks to the power of compounding (earning interest on interest), if you start saving when you're young, you don't have to save as much per year as you would if you start saving when you're middle aged.

Suppose that you plan to work full time from age 22 until you retire at 70 and that you can earn 7% on your retirement savings account. Let's consider two approaches:

1. **Early bird:** You save $3,000 a year for the first 15 years of your working life and then let your savings accumulate interest until you retire.

2. **Late bloomer:** After not saving for the first 15 years, you save $3,000 a year for the next 33 years until you retire.

Which scenario leads to a bigger retirement nest egg? To answer this question, we calculate the future value at retirement of each of these streams of investments.

---

[6]In Equation 15.16, if the number of periods is infinite, the present value is

$$PV = \frac{f}{1 + i} + \frac{f}{(1 + i)^2} + \frac{f}{(1 + i)^3} + \cdots .$$

We can factor $1/(1 + i)$ out of the right-hand side and rewrite the equation as

$$PV = \frac{1}{1 + i}\left[f + \frac{f}{1 + i} + \frac{f}{(1 + i)^2} + \frac{f}{(1 + i)^3} + \cdots \right] = \frac{1}{1 + i}(f + PV).$$

Rearranging terms, we obtain Equation 15.17.

The early bird adds $3,000 each year for 15 years into a retirement account. Using Equation 15.18, we calculate that the account has

$$\$3,000(1 + 1.07^1 + 1.07^2 + \cdots + 1.07^{14}) = \$75,387$$

at the end of 15 years. Leaving this amount in the retirement account for the next 33 years increases the fund about 9.3 times, to

$$\$75,387.07 \times 1.07^{33} = \$703,010.$$

The late bloomer makes no investments for 15 years and then invests $3,000 a year until retirement. Again using Equation 15.18, we calculate that the funds at retirement are

$$\$3,000(1 + 1.07 + 1.07^2 + \cdots + 1.07^{32}) = \$356,800.$$

Thus, even though the late bloomer contributes to the account for more than twice as long as the early bird, the late bloomer has saved only about half as much at retirement. Indeed, to have roughly the same amount at retirement as the early bird, the late bloomer would have to save nearly $6,000 a year for 33 years. (By the way, someone who saved $3,000 each year for 48 years would have $703,010 + $356,800 = $1,059,810 salted away by retirement.)

Investing

Frequently, firms must choose between two or more investments that have different streams of payments and streams of returns. MGM, a conglomerate, decides whether to produce a movie starring a muscle-bound hero who solves the pollution problem by beating up an evil capitalist, build a new hotel in Reno, buy a television studio, or put money in a long-term savings account.

For simplicity, we start by analyzing a firm's choice between two financial assets with no uncertainty and no inflation. In such a scenario, all assets must have the same rate of return, because no one would invest in any asset that had less than the highest available rate of return.

Just as you would not lend money to a bank unless it paid interest, a firm will not invest—tie up its funds for a while—in either a financial asset or a piece of capital unless it expects a payoff greater than its initial outlay. The *rate of return on an investment* is the payoff from that investment expressed as a percentage per time period. For example, a bond might pay a 5% rate of return per year.

One possible investment is to put $1 (or $1 million) in a bank and earn interest of i per year. For example, i might be 4%. The value of this investment next year is $1 + i$. A second possible investment is to buy an asset this year at $1 and sell it with certainty next year for FV, the future value of the asset. The firm is indifferent between these two investments only if $FV = 1 + i$.

We now consider more complex investments. As a general rule, a firm makes an investment if the expected return from the investment is greater than the opportunity cost (Chapter 7). The opportunity cost is the best alternative use of its money, which is what it would earn in the next best use of the money.

Thus, to decide whether to make an investment, the firm needs to compare the potential outlay of money to the firm's best alternative. One possibility is that its best alternative is to put the money that it would otherwise spend on this investment in an interest-bearing bank account. We consider two methods for making this comparison: the *net present value* approach and the *internal rate of return* approach.

Net Present Value Approach. A firm has to decide whether to buy a truck for $20,000. Because the opportunity cost is $20,000, the firm should make the investment only if the present value of expected future returns from the truck is greater than $20,000.

More generally, *a firm should make an investment only if the present value of the expected return exceeds the present value of the costs.* If R is the present value of the expected returns to an investment and C is the present value of the costs of the investment, the firm should make the investment if $R > C$.[7]

This rule is often restated in terms of the net present value, $NPV = R - C$, which is the difference between the present value of the returns, R, and the present value of the costs, C. *A firm should make an investment only if the net present value is positive*:

$$NPV = R - C > 0.$$

Assume that the initial year is $t = 0$, the firm's revenue in year t is R_t, and its cost in year t is C_t. If the last year in which either revenue or cost is nonzero is T, the net present value rule holds that the firm should invest if

$$NPV = R - C$$

$$= \left[R_0 + \frac{R_1}{(1 + i)^1} + \frac{R_2}{(1 + i)^2} + \cdots + \frac{R_T}{(1 + i)^T} \right]$$

$$- \left[C_0 + \frac{C_1}{(1 + i)^1} + \frac{C_2}{(1 + i)^2} + \cdots + \frac{C_T}{(1 + i)^T} \right] > 0.$$

Instead of comparing the present values of the returns and costs, we can examine whether the present value of the *cash flow* in each year (loosely, the annual *profit*), $\pi_t = R_t - C_t$, is positive. By rearranging the terms in the previous expression, we can rewrite the net present value rule as

$$NPV = (R_0 - C_0) + \frac{R_1 - C_1}{(1 + i)^1} + \frac{R_2 - C_2}{(1 + i)^2} + \cdots + \frac{R_T - C_T}{(1 + i)^T}$$

$$= \pi_0 + \frac{\pi_1}{(1 + i)^1} + \frac{\pi_2}{(1 + i)^2} + \cdots + \frac{\pi_T}{(1 + i)^T} > 0. \qquad (15.19)$$

This rule does not restrict the firm to making investments only where its cash flow is positive each year. For example, a firm buys a piece of equipment for $100 and spends the first year learning how to use it, so it makes no revenue from the machine and has a negative cash flow that year: $\pi_0 = -100$. The next year, its revenue is $350 and the machine's maintenance cost is $50, so its second year's cash flow is $\pi_1 = \$300$. At the end of that year, the machine wears out, so the annual cash flow from this investment is zero thereafter. Using Equation 15.19, the firm calculates the investment's net present value at $i = 5\%$ as

$$NPV = -100 + 300/1.05 \approx \$185.71.$$

Because this net present value is positive, the firm buys the equipment.

---

[7]This rule holds when future costs and returns are known with certainty and investments can be reversed but not delayed (Dixit and Pindyck, 1994).

SOLVED PROBLEM 15.3

In 2005, Lewis Wolff and his investment group bought the Oakland A's baseball team for $180 million. *Forbes* magazine estimated their net income in 2005 to be $5.9 million. If the new owners believed that they would continue to earn this annual profit (after adjusting for inflation), $f = \$5.9$ million, forever, was this investment more lucrative than putting the $180 million in a savings account that pays a real interest rate of $i = 3\%$?

Answer

Determine the net present value of the team. The net present value of buying the A's is positive if the present value of the expected returns, 5.9 million$/0.03 \approx \$196.7$ million, minus the present value of the cost, which is the purchase price of $180 million, is positive:

$$NPV = \$196.7 \text{ million} - \$180 \text{ million} = \$16.7 \text{ million} > 0.$$

Thus, it paid for the investors to buy the A's if their best alternative investment paid 3%.

Internal Rate of Return Approach. Whether the net present value of an investment is positive depends on the interest rate. In Solved Problem 15.3, the investors buy the baseball team, given an interest rate of 3%. However, if the interest rate were 10%, the net present value would be 5.9 million$/0.1 - \$180$ million $= -\$121$ million, and the investors would not buy the team.

At what discount rate (rate of return) is a firm indifferent between making an investment and not doing so? The **internal rate of return** (*irr*) is the discount rate such that the net present value of an investment is zero. Replacing the interest rate, i, in Equation 15.19 with *irr* and setting the *NPV* equal to zero, we implicitly determine the internal rate of return by solving

$$NPV = \pi_0 + \frac{\pi_1}{1 + irr} + \frac{\pi_2}{(1 + irr)^2} + \cdots + \frac{\pi_T}{(1 + irr)^T} = 0$$

for *irr*.

It is easier to calculate *irr* when the investment pays a steady stream of profit, f, forever and when the cost of the investment is *PV*. The investment's rate of return is found by rearranging Equation 15.17 and replacing i with *irr*:

$$irr = \frac{f}{PV}. \tag{15.20}$$

Instead of using the net present value rule, we can decide whether to invest by comparing the internal rate of return to the interest rate. If the firm is borrowing money to make the investment, *it pays for the firm to borrow to make the investment if the internal rate of return on that investment exceeds that of the next best alternative* (which we assume is the interest rate):[8]

$$irr > i.$$

---

[8]The net present value approach always works. The internal rate of return method is inapplicable if *irr* is not unique. In Solved Problem 15.4, *irr* is unique, and using this approach gives the same answer as the net present value approach.

SOLVED PROBLEM 15.4

A group of investors can buy the Oakland A's baseball team for $PV = \$180$ million. They expect an annual real flow of payments (profits) of $f = \$5.9$ million forever. If the interest rate is 3%, do they buy the team?

Answer

Determine the internal rate of return to this investment and compare it to the interest rate. Using Equation 15.20, we calculate that the internal rate of return from buying the A's is

$$irr = \frac{f}{PV} = \frac{\$5.9 \text{ million}}{\$180 \text{ million}} \approx 3.3\%.$$

Because this rate of return, 3.3%, is greater than the interest rate, 3%, the investors buy the team.

Durability

Many firms must decide how durable to make the products they sell or those they produce for their own use. Should they make long-lasting products at a relatively high cost or less durable goods at a lower cost?

Suppose that the company can vary the quality of a factor (a machine) that it uses in its own production process. If it needs exactly one machine, it must replace the machine when it wears out. Thus, *the firm should pick the durability level for the machine that minimizes the present discounted cost of having a machine forever.*

APPLICATION

Durability of Telephone Poles

Pacific Gas & Electric (PG&E), a western power utility, must decide how durable to make its 132 million wooden utility poles. The poles are a capital stock for PG&E, which uses them to provide a flow of services: supporting power and phone lines year after year. A wooden utility pole provides the same services each year for T years under normal use. After T years, the pole breaks and is replaced because it can't be repaired, but the flow of services must be maintained. Until recently, PG&E used poles with a life span of $T = 25$ years.

The constant marginal cost of manufacturing and installing the poles depends on how long they last, $m(T)$. For an additional cost, the firm can extend the life span of a pole by treating it with chemicals to prevent bug infestations and rot, reinforcing it with metal bands, varying its thickness, or using higher-quality materials. Because the marginal cost increases with the pole's expected life span, a pole that lasts 50 years costs more than one that lasts 25 years: $m(50) > m(25)$.

The replacement cost of a pole that lasts 25 years is $m(25) = \$1,500$. Thus, replacing all of PG&E's poles today would cost $198 billion—which is more than the cost of many giant power plants.

PG&E believes that it can save money by switching to a longer-lasting pole. The firm picks the duration, T, that minimizes its cost of maintaining its forest of poles. Because the utility keeps the same number of poles in place every year, after a pole wears out at T years, the firm incurs an expense of $m(T)$ to replace it. The present value of providing each pole is the cost of producing it today, $m(T)$, plus the discounted cost of producing another one in T years, $m(T)/(1 + i)^T$, plus the discounted cost of producing another one in $2T$ years, $m(T)/(1 + i)^{2T}$, and so on.

The table shows the present value of the cost of maintaining one pole for the next 100 years given that the utility faces an interest rate of 5%. Because the cost of producing a pole that lasts for 25 years is $m(25) = \$1,500$, the present value of the cost of providing a pole for the next 100 years is $2,112 (column 2). If the cost of a pole that lasts 50 years were $m(50) = \$1,943$ (column 4), the present value would be the same as that for the 25-year pole. If so, the utility would be indifferent between using poles that last 25 years and poles that last 50 years.

	25-Year Pole	50-Year Pole	
Marginal Cost, $m(T)$:	$1,500	$1,650	$1,943
Year			
0	$1,500	$1,650	$1,943
25	443	0	0
50	131	144	169
75	39	0	0
Present value of the cost of providing a pole for 100 years:	$2,112	$1,794	$2,112

Note: Due to rounding, column 2 does not add to the present value.

Thus, PG&E will not use 50-year poles if the extra cost is greater than $443 = \$1,943 - \$1,500$ but will use them if the difference in cost is less. The actual extra cost is less than $150, so $m(50) = \$1,650$. Thus, the present value of the cost of a 50-year pole is only about $1,794 (column 3 of the table). Because using the 50-year poles reduces the present value by $318, or about 15% per pole, the utility wants to use the longer-lasting poles. By so doing, PG&E cuts the present value of the cost of maintaining all its poles for 100 years by about $42 billion. Thus, the length of time one maintains a durable good depends on the alternatives and the rate of interest.

Time-Varying Discounting

Tomorrow: One of the greatest labor saving devices of today.

People want immediate gratification.[9] We want rewards now and costs delayed until later: "Rain, rain, go away; come again some other day; we want to go out and play; come again some other day."

Time Consistency. So far in this chapter, we have explained such impatience by assuming that people discount future costs or benefits by using *exponential discounting*, as in Equation 15.15: The present value is the future value divided by

---

[9]This section draws heavily on Rabin (1998), O'Donoghue and Rabin (1999), and Karp (2005).

$(1 + i)^t$, where t is the exponent and the discount rate, i, is constant over time. If people use this approach, their preferences are *time consistent*: They will discount an event that occurs a decade from the time they're asked by the same amount today as they will one year from now.

However, many of us indulge in immediate gratification in a manner that is inconsistent with our long-term preferences: Our "long-run self" disapproves of the lack of discipline of our "short-run self." Even though we plan today not to over-eat tomorrow, tomorrow we may overindulge. We have *present-biased preferences*: When considering the trade-off between two future moments, we put more weight on the earlier moment as it gets closer. For example, if you are offered $100 in 10 years or $200 in 10 years and a day, you will almost certainly choose the larger amount one day later. After all, what's the cost of waiting one extra day a decade from now? However, if you are offered $100 today or $200 tomorrow, you may choose the smaller amount today because an extra day is an appreciable delay when your planning horizon is short.

Behavioral Economics. One explanation that behavioral economists (see Chapter 11) give for procrastination and other time-inconsistent behavior is that people's personal discount rates are smaller in the far future than in the near future. For example, suppose you know that you can mow your lawn today in two hours, but if you wait until next week, it will take you two-and-a-quarter hours because the grass will be longer. Your displeasure (negative utility) from spending two hours mowing is -20 and from spending two-and-a-quarter hours mowing is -22.5. The present value of mowing next week is $-22.5/(1 + i)$, where i is your personal discount rate for a week. If today your discount rate is $i = 0.25$, then your present value of mowing in a week is $-22.5/1.25 = -18$, which is not as bad as -20, so you delay mowing. However, if you were asked six months in advance, your discount rate might be much smaller, say $i = 0.1$. At that interest rate, the present value is $-22.5/1.1 \approx -20.45$, which is worse than -20, so you would plan to mow on the first of the two dates. Thus, falling discount rates may explain this type of time-inconsistent behavior.

Falling Discount Rates and the Environment. A social discount rate that declines over time may be useful in planning for global warming or other future environmental disasters (Karp, 2005). Suppose that the harmful effects of greenhouse gases will not be felt for a century and that society used traditional, exponential discounting. We would be willing to invest at most 37¢ today to avoid a dollar's worth of damages in a century if society's constant discount rate is 1%, and only 1.8¢ if the discount rate is 4%. Thus, even a modest discount rate makes us callous toward our distant descendants: We are unwilling to incur even moderate costs today to avoid large damages far in the future.

One alternative is for society to use a declining discount rate, although doing so will make our decisions time inconsistent. Parents today may care more about their existing children than about their unborn grandchildren, and therefore may be willing to discount the welfare of their grandchildren significantly relative to that of their children. They probably have a smaller difference in their relative emotional attachment to the tenth future generation relative to the eleventh generation. If society agrees with such reasoning, our future social discount rate should be lower than our current rate. By reducing the discount rate over time, we are saying that the weights we place on the welfare of any two successive generations in the distant future are more similar than the weights on two successive generations in the near future.

APPLICATION

Falling Discount
Rates and
Self-Control

If people's discount rates fall over time, they have a *present bias* or a *self-control problem*, which means that they prefer immediate gratification to delayed gratification.[10] Several recent studies argue that governments should help people with this bias by providing self-control policies.

Shapiro (2004) finds that food stamp recipients' caloric intake declines by 10% to 15% over the food stamp month, implying that they prefer immediate consumption. With a constant discount rate, they would be more likely to spread their consumption evenly over the month. Governments can help people with a present bias by delivering food stamps at two-week intervals instead of once a month, as several states do with welfare payments.

Cigarette smokers often have inconsistent preferences with respect to smoking. Individuals with declining discount rates lack self-control and perpetually postpone quitting smoking. According to a 2011 Gallup survey, 78% of U.S. smokers would like to quit. Consequently, a smoker who wants to quit may support the government's impositions of control devices. Based on a survey in Taiwan, Kan (2007) finds that a smoker who intends to quit is more likely to support a smoking ban and a cigarette tax increase. In 2012, most (59%) New Zealand smokers supported more government action on tobacco, and nearly half (46%) supported banning sales of cigarettes in 10 years, provided effective nicotine substitutes were available.

In 2009, President Obama—a smoker who wanted to quit—signed a law bringing tobacco products under federal law for the first time. He said that this law, aimed at stopping children from starting to smoke, would have prevented him from taking up smoking. Perhaps the most striking evidence of smokers' mixed feelings is that Gruber and Mullainathan (2005) found that cigarette taxes make people with a propensity to smoke happier in both the United States and Canada.

Capital Markets, Interest Rates, and Investments

We've seen that an individual's decision about whether to make an investment depends on the market interest rate. The interest rate is determined in the capital market, where the interest rate is the price, the quantity supplied is the amount of funds loaned, and the quantity demanded is the amount of funds borrowed.

Because the capital market is competitive, the interest rate and the quantity of funds loaned and borrowed is determined by the intersection of the supply curve for funds and the demand curve for funds. Funds are demanded by individuals buying homes or paying for a college education, governments borrowing money to build roads or wage wars, and firms investing in new plants or equipment. The demand curve is downward sloping because more is borrowed as the interest rate falls.

The supply curve reflects loans made by individuals and firms. Many people, when their earnings are relatively high, save money in bank accounts and buy bonds (which they convert back to money for consumption when they retire or during lean times). Firms that have no alternative investments with higher returns may also lend money to banks or others. Higher interest rates induce greater savings by both groups, so the supply curve is upward sloping.

---

[10]In the famous marshmallow test, small children are offered one marshmallow now or a second one if they wait. See an excellent reenactment at **www.youtube.com/watch?v=6EjJsPylEOY**. Children who could delay gratification did better later in life: **www.newyorker.com/reporting/2009/05/18/090518fa_fact_lehrer**.

**SOLVED PROBLEM
15.5**

Suppose the government wants to borrow money to pay for fighting a war in a foreign land. Show that increased borrowing by the government—an increase in the government's demand for money at any given interest rate—raises the equilibrium interest rate, which discourages or *crowds out* private investment.

Answer

Using three side-by-side graphs, show how an outward shift of the government's demand curve affects the equilibrium interest rate and thereby reduces private investment. In the figure, panel a shows the private sector demand curve for funds, D_p, which are funds that private firms and individuals borrow to make investments. Panel b shows that the government sector demand curve shifts to the right from D_g^1 to D_g^2. As a result, in panel c, the total demand curve—the horizontal sum of the private and government demand curves—shifts from D^1 to D^2. Panel c also shows the supply curve of money, S.

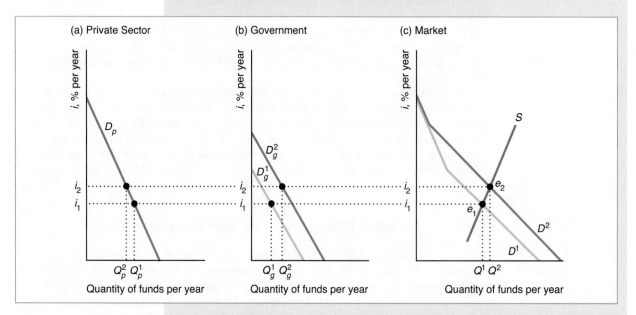

The initial equilibrium, e_1 in panel c, is determined by the intersection of the initial total demand for funds, D^1, and the supply curve, S, where the interest rate is i_1 and the quantity of funds borrowed is Q_1. After the government demand curve shifts out, the new equilibrium is e_2, where the interest rate is higher, $i_2 > i_1$, and more funds are borrowed, $Q_2 > Q_1$.

The higher market interest rate causes private investment to fall from Q_p^1 to Q_p^2 (panel a). That is, the government borrowing crowds out some private investment.

15.3   **Exhaustible Resources**

The meek shall inherit the earth, but not the mineral rights. —J. Paul Getty

Discounting plays an important role in decision making about how fast to consume oil, gold, copper, uranium, and other **exhaustible resources**: nonrenewable natural assets that cannot be increased, only depleted. An owner of an exhaustible resource decides when to extract and sell it so as to maximize the present value of the resource. Scarcity of the resource, mining costs, and market structure affect whether the price of such a resource rises or falls over time.

When to Sell an Exhaustible Resource

Suppose that you own a coal mine. In what year do you mine the coal, and in what year do you sell it to maximize its present value? To illustrate how to answer these questions, we assume that there is no inflation or uncertainty and that you can sell the coal only this year or next in a competitive market, that the interest rate is i, and that the cost of mining each pound of coal, m, stays constant over time.

Given the last two of these assumptions, the present value of mining a pound of coal is m if you mine this year and $m/(1 + i)$ if you mine next year. As a result, if you're going to sell the coal next year, you're better off mining it next year because you postpone incurring the cost of mining. You mine the coal this year only if you plan to sell it this year.

Now that you have a rule that tells you when to mine the coal—at the last possible moment—your remaining problem is when to sell it. That decision depends on how the price of a pound of coal changes from one year to the next. Suppose that you know that the price of coal will increase from p_1 this year to p_2 next year.

To decide in which year to sell, you compare the present value of selling today to that of selling next year. The present value of your profit per pound of coal is $p_1 - m$ if you sell your coal this year and $(p_2 - m)/(1 + i)$ if you sell it next year. Thus, to maximize the present value from selling your coal:

- *You sell all the coal this year* if the present value of selling this year is greater than the present value of selling next year: $p_1 - m > (p_2 - m)/(1 + i)$.
- *You sell all the coal next year* if $p_1 - m < (p_2 - m)/(1 + i)$.
- *You sell all the coal in either year* if $p_1 - m = (p_2 - m)/(1 + i)$.

The intuition behind these rules is that storing coal in the ground is like keeping money in the bank. You can sell a pound of coal today, netting $p_1 - m$, invest the money in the bank, and have $(p_1 - m)(1 + i)$ next year. Alternatively, you can keep the coal in the ground for a year and then sell it. If the amount you'll get next year, $p_2 - m$, is less than what you can earn from selling now and keeping the money in a bank, you sell the coal now. In contrast, if the price of coal is rising so rapidly that the coal will be worth more in the future than the wealth left in a bank, you leave your wealth in the mine.

Price of a Scarce Exhaustible Resource

This two-period analysis generalizes to many time periods (Hotelling, 1931). We use a multiperiod analysis to show how the price of an exhaustible resource changes over time.

The resource is sold both this year, year t, and next year, $t + 1$, only if the present value of a pound sold now is the same as the present value of a pound sold next year: $p_t - m = (p_{t+1} - m)/(1 + i)$, where the price is p_t in year t and is p_{t+1} in the following year. Using algebra to rearrange this equation, we obtain an expression that tells us how price changes from one year to the next:

$$p_{t+1} = p_t + i(p_t - m). \tag{15.21}$$

If you're willing to sell the coal in both years, the price next year must exceed the price this year by $i(p_t - m)$, which is the interest payment you'd receive if you sold a pound of coal this year and put the profit in a bank that paid interest at rate i.

The gap between the price and the constant marginal cost of mining grows over time, as Figure 15.5 shows. To see why, we subtract p_t from both sides of Equation 15.21 to obtain an expression for the change in the price from one year to the next:

$$\Delta p \equiv p_{t+1} - p_t = i(p_t - m).$$

This equation shows that the gap between this year's price and next year's price widens as your cash flow this year, $p_t - m$, increases. Thus, the price rises over time, and the gap between the price line and the flat marginal cost of mining line grows, as the figure illustrates.

Although we now understand how price changes over time, we need more information to determine the price in the first year and hence in each subsequent year. Suppose mine owners know that the government will ban the use of coal in year T (or that a superior substitute will become available that year). They want to price the coal so that all of it is sold by year T, because any resource that is unsold by then is worthless. The restriction that all the coal is used up by T and Equation 15.21 determine the price in the first year and the increase in the price thereafter.

Price in a Two-Period Example. To illustrate how the price is determined in each year, we assume that there are many identical competitive mines, that no more coal will be sold after the second year because of a government ban, and that the marginal cost of mining is zero in each period. Setting $m = 0$ in Equation 15.21, we learn that the price in the second year equals the price in the first year plus the interest rate times the first-year price:

$$p_2 = p_1 + (i \times p_1) = p_1(1 + i). \tag{15.22}$$

Thus, the price increases with the interest rate from the first year to the second year.

The mine owners face a resource constraint: They can't sell more coal than they have in their mines. The coal they sell in the first year, Q_1, plus the coal they sell in the second year, Q_2, equals the total amount of coal in the mines, Q. The mine

Figure 15.5 Price of an Exhaustible Resource

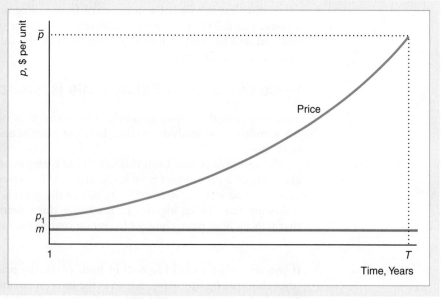

The price of an exhaustible resource in year $t + 1$ is higher than the price in year t by the interest rate times the difference between the price in year t and the marginal cost of mining, $i(p_t - m)$. Thus, the gap between the price line and the marginal cost line, $p_t - m$, grows exponentially with the interest rate.

owners want to sell all their coal within these two years because any coal they don't sell does them no good.

Suppose that the demand curve for coal is $Q_t = 200 - p_t$ in each year t. If the amount of coal in the ground is less than would be demanded at a zero price, the sum of the amount demanded in both years equals the total amount of coal in the ground:

$$Q_1 + Q_2 = (200 - p_1) + (200 - p_2) = Q.$$

Substituting the expression for p_2 from Equation 15.22 into this resource constraint to obtain $(200 - p_1) + [200 - p_1(1 + i)] = Q$ and rearranging terms, we find that

$$p_t = (400 - Q)/(2 + i). \tag{15.23}$$

Thus, the first-year price depends on the amount of coal in the ground and the interest rate.

If the mines initially contain $Q = 169$ pounds of coal, then p_1 is $110 at a 10% interest rate only $105 at a 20% interest rate, as Table 15.1 shows. At the lower interest rate, the difference between the first- and second-year prices is smaller ($11 versus $21), so relatively more of the original stock of coal is sold in the second year (47% versus 44%).

Rents. If coal is a scarce good, its competitive price is above the marginal cost of mining the coal ($m = 0$ in our example). How can we reconcile this result with our earlier finding that price equals marginal cost in a competitive market? The answer is that when coal is scarce, it earns a *rent*: a payment to the owner of an input beyond the minimum necessary for the input to be supplied (Chapter 9).

The owner of the coal need not be the same person who mines the coal. A miner could pay the owner for the right to take the coal out of the mine. After incurring the marginal cost of mining the coal, m, the miner earns $p_1 - m$. However, the owner of the mine charges that amount in rent for the right to mine this scarce resource, rather than giving any of this profit to the miner. Even if the owner of the coal and the miner are the same person, the amount beyond the marginal mining cost is a rent to scarcity.

If the coal were not scarce, no rent would be paid, and the price would equal the marginal cost of mining. Given the demand curve in the example, the most coal that anyone would buy in a year is 200 pounds, which is the amount demanded at a price of zero. If there are 400 pounds of coal in the ground initially—enough to provide 200 pounds in each year—the coal is not scarce, so the price of coal in both years is zero, as Table 15.1 illustrates.[11] As Figure 15.6 shows, the less coal in the ground initially, Q, the higher the initial price of coal.

Rising Prices. Thus, according to our theory, the price of an exhaustible resource rises if the resource (1) is scarce, (2) can be mined at a marginal cost that remains constant over time, and (3) is sold in a competitive market. The rate of increase in the price of old-growth redwood trees is predicted by this theory.

---

[11]Equation 15.23 holds only when coal is scarce: $Q \leq 400$. According to this equation, $p_1 = 0$ when $Q = 400$. If the quantity of coal in the ground is even greater, $Q > 400$, coal is not scarce—people don't want all the coal even if the price is zero—so the price in the first year equals the marginal mining cost of zero. That is, the price is not negative, as Equation 15.23 would imply if it held for quantities greater than 400.

Table 15.1   Price and Quantity of Coal Reflecting the Amount of Coal and the Interest Rate

	Q = 169		Q = 400
	i = 10%	i = 20%	Any i
$p_1 = (400 - Q)/(2 + i)$	$110	$105	$0
$p_2 = p_1(1 + i)$	$121	$126	$0
$\Delta p \equiv p_2 - p_1 = I \times p_1$	11	21	0
$Q_1 = 200 - p_1$	90	95	200
$Q_2 = 200 - p_2$	79	74	200
Share sold in Year 2	47%	44%	50%

Figure 15.6 First-Year Price in a Two-Period Model

In a two-period model, the price of coal in the first year, p_1, falls as the amount of coal in the ground initially, Q, increases. This figure is based on an interest rate of 10%.

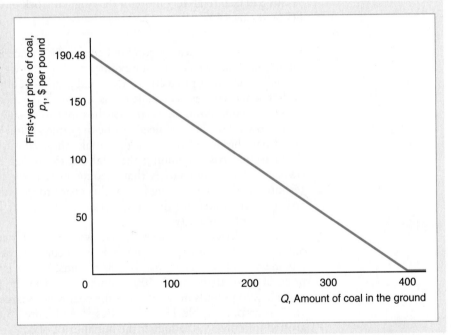

APPLICATION

Redwood Trees

Many of the majestic old-growth redwood trees in America's western forests are several hundred to several thousand years old. If a mature redwood is cut, young redwoods will not grow to a comparable size within our lifetimes. Thus, an old-growth redwood forest, like fossil fuels, is effectively a nonrenewable resource, even though new redwoods are being created (very slowly). In contrast, many other types of trees, such as those grown as Christmas trees, are quickly replenished and therefore are renewable resources like fish.

The exponential trend line on the graph shows that the real price of redwoods rose from 1953 to 1983 at an average rate of 8% a year. By the end of this period,

virtually no redwood trees were available for sale. The trees either had been harvested or were growing in protected forests. The last remaining privately owned stand was purchased by the U.S. government and the state of California from the Maxxam Corporation in 1996.

The unusually high prices observed in the late 1960s through the 1970s were in large part due to actions of the federal government, which used its power of eminent domain to buy, at the market price, a considerable fraction of all remaining old-growth redwoods for the Redwood National Park. The government bought 1.7 million million-board feet (MBF) in 1968 and 1.4 million MBF in 1978. The latter purchase represented about two-and-a-quarter years of cutting at previous rates. These two government purchases combined equaled 43% of private holdings in 1978 of about 7.3 million MBF. Thus, the government purchases were so large that they moved up the time of exhaustion of privately held redwoods by several years, causing the price to jump to the level it would have reached several years later.

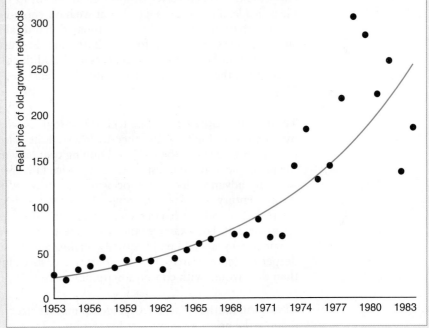

Why Price Might Not Rise

If any one of the three conditions we've been assuming—*scarcity, constant marginal mining costs,* and *competition*—is not met, the price of an exhaustible resource may remain steady or fall.[12] Most exhaustible resources, such as aluminum, coal, lead, natural gas, silver, and zinc, have had decades-long periods of falling or

---

[12]The following discussion of why prices of exhaustible resources might not rise and the accompanying examples are based on Berck and Roberts (1996) and additional data supplied by these authors. Their paper also shows that pollution controls and other environmental controls can keep resource prices from rising. Additional data are from Brown and Wolk (2000).

constant real prices. Indeed, the real price of each major mineral and metal is lower today than in 1948.

Abundance. As we've seen, the initial price is set at essentially the marginal cost of mining if the exhaustible resource is not scarce. The gap between the price and the marginal cost grows with the interest rate. If the good is so abundant that the initial gap is zero, the gap does not grow and the price stays constant at the marginal cost. Further, if the gap is initially very small, it has to grow for a long time before the increase becomes noticeable.

Because of abundance, the real prices for many exhaustible resources have remained relatively constant for decades. Moreover, the price falls when the discovery of a large deposit of the resource is announced.

The amount of a resource that can be profitably recovered using current technology is called a reserve. Known reserves of some resources are enormous; others are more limited.[13] We have enough silicon (from sand) and magnesium to last virtually forever at current rates of extraction. Bauxite (used to produce aluminum) reserves will last 130 years, mercury 48 years (but the rate at which it is used is plummeting), copper and tungsten 43 years, silver 22 years, tin 19 years, and lead 8 years (although identified lead resources suggest that we have enough for more than 300,000 years). The International Energy Agency estimated that total recoverable oil resources could sustain today's production for over 250 years. Because known reserves of aluminum (bauxite) will last for over a century and additional reserves are constantly being discovered, the real price of aluminum has remained virtually constant for the past 50 years.

Technical Progress. Steady technical progress over many years has reduced the marginal cost of mining and thereby lowered the price of many natural resources. A large enough drop in the marginal mining cost may more than offset the increase in the price due to the interest rate, so the price falls from one year to the next.[14]

Many advances in mining occurred in the years spanning the end of the nineteenth century and the beginning of the twentieth century. As a result of technical progress and discoveries of new supplies, the real prices of many exhaustible resources fell. For example, the real price of aluminum in 1945 was only 12% of the price 50 years earlier. Eventually, as mines play out, prospectors have to dig ever deeper to find resources, causing marginal costs to increase and prices to rise faster than they would with constant marginal costs.

Changing Market Power. Changes in market structure can result in either a rise or a fall in the price of an exhaustible resource. The real price of oil remained virtually constant from 1880 through 1972. But when the Organization of Petroleum Exporting Countries (OPEC) started to act as a cartel in 1973, the price of oil climbed rapidly. At its peak in 1981, the real price of oil was nearly five times higher than its nearly constant level during the period 1880–1972. When Iran and Iraq went to war in 1980, the OPEC cartel began to fall apart, and the real price of oil sank to traditional levels, where it remained through the 1990s. Since then, wars have caused the price to fluctuate substantially.

---

[13]Data are from **minerals.usgs.gov/minerals/pubs/mcs/2012/mcs2012.pdf**.

[14]When the marginal cost of mining is constant at m, Equation 15.21 shows that $p_{t+1} = p_t + i(p_t - m)$, so p_{t+1} must be above p_t. If we allow mining costs to vary from year to year, then $p_{t+1} = p_t + i(p_t - m_t) + (m_{t+1} - m_t)$. Thus, if the drop in the mining costs, $m_{t+1} - m_t$, is greater than $i(p_t - m_t)$, p_{t+1} is less than p_t.

CHALLENGE SOLUTION

Should You Go to College?

I have often thought that if there had been a good rap group around in those days, I would have chosen a career in music instead of politics. —Richard Nixon

Probably the most important human capital decision you've had to make was whether to attend college. If you opted to go to college solely for the purpose of increasing your lifetime earnings, have you made a good investment?

Let's look back at your last year of high school. During that year, you have to decide whether to invest in a college education or go directly into the job market. If you go straight into the job market, we assume that you work full time (35 hours or more a week) from age 18 until you retire at age 70.

If your motivation for attending college is to increase your lifetime earnings, you should start college upon finishing high school so that you can earn a higher salary for as long as possible. To keep the analysis relatively simple, we'll assume that you graduate from college in four years, during which time you do not work and you spend $20,000 a year on tuition and other schooling expenses such as books and fees, which is what the typical student paid for a year of college in 2012. When you graduate from college, you will work full time from age 22 to 70. Thus, the opportunity cost of a college education includes the tuition payments plus the four years of forgone earnings for someone with a high school diploma. The expected benefit is the stream of higher earnings in the future.

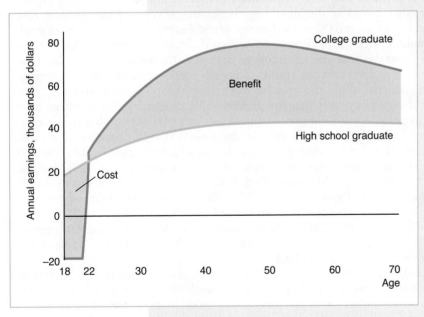

The figure shows how much the typical person earns with a high school diploma and with a college degree at each age.[15] At age 22, a typical college grad earns $29,335, and those with only a high school diploma earn $25,009. The college grad's earnings peak at 51 years of age, at $77,865. A high school grad's earnings also reach a maximum at 51 years, at $42,707.

If one stream of earnings is higher than the other at every age, we would pick the higher stream. Because these streams of earnings cross at age 22, we cannot use that simple approach to answer the question. One way to decide whether investing in a college education pays is to compare the present values at age 18 of the two earnings streams. The present values depend on the interest rate used, as the following table shows.

[15]The statistical analysis controls for age, education, and demographic characteristics but not innate ability. See Sources for Applications for information about the data. I thank Yann Panassie, a former student in my intermediate microeconomics course, for estimating this model. We assumed that wages increase at the same rate as inflation, so real earnings are constant over time. No adjustment is made for the greater incidence of unemployment among high school graduates, which was more than twice that of college graduates in 2012.

Discount Rate, %	Present Value, Thousands of 2009 Dollars	
	High School	College
0	2,007	3,225
2	1,196	1,823
4	779	1,103
6	547	708
8	410	476
10	323	332
10.42	309	309
12	264	238
14	223	174

If potential college students can borrow money at an interest rate of 0%, money in the future is worth as much as money today, so the present value equals the sum of earnings over time. According to the table, the sum of a college graduate's earnings (including the initial negative earnings) is $3.23 million (first row of the table), which is 61% more than the lifetime earnings of a high school grad, $2.01 million. Thus, it pays to go to college if the interest rate is 0%. The figure also illustrates that attending college pays at a 0% discount rate because the sum of the (negative) cost and (positive) benefit areas—the difference in earnings between going to college and going to work after high school—is positive.

The table demonstrates that the present value of earnings for a college grad equals that of a high school grad at an interest rate of 10.42%. That is, the average internal rate of return to the college education is 10.42%. Because the present value of earnings for a college grad exceeds that of a high school grad if the real interest rate at which they can borrow or invest is less than 10.42%, income maximizing people should go to college if the real interest rate is less than that rate.[16] According to **Payscale.com** for 2012, the average internal rate of return of going to college is higher for students at some schools than others: 11.2% at Harvey Mudd; 11.1% at the University of California, Berkeley (in state, 9.0% out of state); 10.7% at the Massachusetts Institute of Technology; 10.4% Harvard and Stanford; 9.8% at Lehigh; and 9.1% at Colgate.[17]

The decision whether to go to college is more complex for people for whom education has a consumption component. Somebody who loves school may go to college even if alternative investments pay more. Someone who hates going to school invests in a college education only if the financial rewards are much higher than those for alternative investments.

---

[16]The government-subsidized nominal interest rate on federal Stafford loans was 3.4% in 2011–2013. Some poor people who cannot borrow to pay for college at all—effectively, they face extremely high interest rates—do not go to college, unlike wealthier people with comparable abilities.

[17]For more schools, see **www.payscale.com/education/average-cost-for-college-ROI**. The Payscale's calculations, though similar to the one used in this Challenge Solution, differ in not controlling for individual characteristics and in several other ways.

SUMMARY

1. **Factor Markets.** Any firm maximizes its profit by choosing the quantity of a factor such that the marginal revenue product (*MRP*) of that factor—the marginal revenue times the marginal product of the factor—equals the factor price. The *MRP* is the firm's factor demand. A competitive firm's marginal revenue is the market price, so its *MRP* is the market price times the marginal product. The factor demand curves of a noncompetitive firm lie to the left of those of a competitive firm. The firm's long-run factor demand is usually flatter than its short-run demand because the firm can adjust more factors, and thus benefit from more flexibility. The market demand for a factor reflects how changes in factor prices affect output prices and hence output levels in product markets. The intersection of the market factor demand curve and the market factor supply curve determines the factor market equilibrium.

2. **Capital Markets and Investing.** Inflation aside, most people value money in the future less than money today. An interest rate reflects how much more people value a dollar today than a dollar in the future.

To compare a payment made in the future to one made today, we can express the future value in terms of current dollars—its present value—by discounting the future payment using the interest rate. Similarly, a flow of payments over time is related to the present or future value of these payments by the interest rate. A firm may choose between two options with different cash flows over time by picking the one with the higher present value. Similarly, a firm invests in a project if its net present value is positive or its internal rate of return is greater than the interest rate.

3. **Exhaustible Resources.** Nonrenewable resources such as coal, gold, and oil are depleted over time and cannot be replenished. If these resources are scarce, the marginal cost of mining them is constant or increasing, and the market structure remains unchanged, their prices rise rapidly over time because of positive interest rates. However, if the resources are abundant, the marginal cost of mining falls over time, or the market becomes more competitive, nonrenewable resource prices may remain constant or fall over time.

EXERCISES

■ = *exercise is available on* MyEconLab; * = *answer appears at the back of this book;* **M** = *mathematical problem.*

1. Factor Markets

1.1 What does a competitive firm's labor demand curve look like at quantities of labor such that the marginal product of labor is negative? Why?

*1.2 If a local government starts collecting an ad valorem tax of α on the revenue of a competitive firm (and all other firms are located outside this jurisdiction), what happens to the firm's demand curve for labor? (*Hint*: See Solved Problem 15.1.)

1.3 How does a fall in the rental price of capital affect a firm's demand for labor in the long run?

1.4 Oil companies, prompted by improvements in technology and increases in oil prices, are drilling in deeper and deeper water. Using a marginal revenue product and marginal cost diagram of drilling in deep water, show how improvements in drilling technology and increases in oil prices result in more deep-water drilling.

1.5 Georges, the owner of Maison d'Ail, earned his coveted Michelin star rating by smothering his dishes in freshly minced garlic. Georges knows that he can save labor costs by using less garlic, albeit with a reduction in quality. If Georges puts g garlic cloves in a dish, the dish's quality, z, is $z = 1/2g^{0.5}$. Georges always fills his restaurant to its capacity, 250 seats. He knows that he can raise the price of each dish by 40¢ for each unit increase in quality and continue to fill his restaurant. Jacqueline, who earns $10 per hour, minces Georges' garlic at a rate of 120 garlic cloves per hour.

a. What is Jacqueline's value of marginal revenue product?

b. How many hours per afternoon (while the kitchen prep work is being done) does Jacqueline work?

c. How many minced cloves of fresh garlic does Georges put in each dish? **M**

1.6 Show that the quantity of labor or capital that a firm demands decreases with a factor's own factor price and increases with the output price when the production function is Cobb-Douglas as in Equations 15.12 and 15.13. **M**

1.7 The estimated Cobb-Douglas production function for a U.S. tobacco products firm is $q = L^{0.2}K^{0.3}$ ("Returns to Scale in U.S. Manufacturing" application, Chapter 6). Derive the marginal revenue product of labor for this firm. **M**

*1.8 A competitive firm has a constant elasticity production function, $q = (L^\rho + K^\rho)^{1/\rho}$. What is its marginal revenue product of labor? $q = (L^\rho + K^\rho)^{1/\rho}$

1.9 Suppose that a firm's production function is $q = L + K$. Can it be a competitive firm? Why?

1.10 A monopoly with a Cobb-Douglas production function, $Q = (L^\rho + K^\rho)^{1/\rho}$, faces a constant elasticity demand curve. What is its marginal revenue product of labor? **M**

1.11 How does a monopoly's demand for labor shift if a second firm enters its output market and the result is a Cournot duopoly equilibrium?

1.12 Does a shift in the supply curve of labor have a greater effect on wages if the output market is competitive or if it is monopolistic? Explain.

1.13 What is a monopoly's demand for labor if it uses a fixed-proportions production function in which each unit of output takes one unit of labor and one unit of capital?

1.14 In Solved Problem 15.2, show how the results change if the share of workers killed by the Black Death was one-half.

1.15 An economic consultant explaining the effect on labor demand of increasing health care costs, interviewed for the *Wall Street Journal*'s Capital column (Wessel, David, "Health-Care Costs Blamed for Hiring Gap," March 11, 2004, A2), states, "Medical costs are rising more rapidly than anything else in the economy—more than prices, wages or profits. It isn't only current medical costs, but also the present value of the stream of endlessly high cost increases that retards hiring."

    a. Why does the present value of the stream of health care costs, and not just the current health care costs, affect a firm's decision whether to create a new position?

    b. Why should an employer discount future health care costs in deciding whether to create a new position? **M**

2. Capital Markets and Investing

*2.1 How does an individual with a zero discount rate compare current and future consumption? How does your answer change if the discount rate is infinite?

2.2 If you buy a car for $100 down and $100 a year for two more years, what is the present value of these payments at a 5% interest rate? If the interest rate is i? **M**

2.3 How much money do you have to put into a bank account that pays 10% interest compounded annually to receive annual payments of $200? **M**

2.4 Pacific Gas and Electric sent its customers a comparison showing that a person could save $80 per year in gas, water, and detergent expenses by replacing a traditional clothes washer with a new tumble-action washer. Suppose that the interest rate is 5%. You expect your current washer to die in five years. If the cost of a new tumble-action washer is $800, should you replace your washer now or in five years? Explain. **M**

2.5 You plan to buy a used refrigerator this year for $200 and to sell it when you graduate in two years. Assuming that you can get $100 for the refrigerator at that time, there is no inflation, and the interest rate is 5%, what is the true cost (your current outlay minus the resale value in current terms) of the refrigerator to you? **M**

2.6 You want to buy a room air conditioner. The price of one machine is $200. It costs $20 a year to operate. The price of another air conditioner is $300, but it costs only $10 a year to operate. Assuming that both machines last 10 years, which is a better deal? (Do you need to do extensive calculations to answer this question?) **M**

*2.7 Two different teams offer a professional basketball player contracts for playing this year. Both contracts are guaranteed, and payments will be made even if the athlete is injured and cannot play. Team A's contract would pay him $1 million today. Team B's contract would pay him $500,000 today and $2 million 10 years from now. Assuming that there is no inflation, that our pro is concerned only about which contract has the highest present value, and that his personal discount rate is 5%, which contract does he accept? Does your answer change if the discount rate is 20%? **M**

2.8 You are buying a new $20,000 car and have the option to pay for the car with a 0% loan or to receive $500 cash back at the time of the purchase. With the loan, you pay $5,000 down when you purchase the car and then make three $5,000 payments, one at the end of each year of the loan. You currently have $50,000 in your savings account.

    a. The rate of interest on your savings account is 4% and will remain so for the next three years. Which payment method should you choose?

    b. What interest rate, i, makes you indifferent between the two payment methods? **M**

2.9 Discussing the $350 price of a ticket for one of her concerts, Barbra Streisand said, "If you amortize the money over 28 years, it's $12.50 a year. So is it worth $12.50 a year to see me sing? To hear me sing live?"[18] Under what condition is it useful for an individual to apply Ms. Streisand's rule to decide whether to go to the concert? What do we know about the discount rate of a person who makes such a purchase?

2.10 If you spend $4 a day on a latte (in real dollars) for the rest of your life (essentially forever), what is your present discounted value at a 3% interest rate? **M**

2.11 At a 10% interest rate, do you prefer to buy a phone for $100 or to rent the same phone for $10 a year? Does your answer depend on how long you think the phone will last? **M**

*2.12 A firm is considering an investment in which its cash flow is $\pi_1 = \$1$ (million), $\pi_2 = -\$12$, $\pi_3 = \$20$, and $\pi_t = 0$ for all other t. The interest rate is 7%. Use the net present value rule to determine whether the firm should make the investment. Can the firm use the internal rate of return rule to make this decision? **M**

2.13 With the end of the Cold War, the U.S. government decided to *downsize* the military. Along with a pink slip, the government offered ex-military personnel their choice of $8,000 a year for 30 years or an immediate lump-sum payment of $50,000. The lump-sum option was chosen by 92% of enlisted personnel and 51% of officers (Warner and Pleeter, 2001). What is the break-even personal discount rate at which someone would be indifferent between the two options? What can you conclude about the personal discount rates of the enlisted personnel and officers? **M**

2.14 Dell Computer makes its suppliers wait 37 days on average to be paid for their goods; however, Dell is paid by its customers immediately. Thus, Dell earns interest on this *float*, the money that it is implicitly borrowing. If Dell can earn an annual interest rate of 4%, what is this float worth to Dell per dollar spent on inputs? **M**

2.15 Many retirement funds charge an administrative fee equal to 0.25% on managed assets. Suppose that Alexx and Spenser each invest $5,000 in the same stock this year. Alexx invests directly and earns 5% a year. Spenser uses a retirement fund and earns 4.75%. After 30 years, how much more will Alexx have than Spenser? **M**

*2.16 Your gas-guzzling car gets only 10 miles to the gallon and has no resale value, but you are sure that it will last five years. You know that you can always buy a used car for $8,000 that gets 20 miles to the gallon. A gallon of gas costs $2 and you drive

6,000 miles a year. If the interest rate is 5% and you are interested only in saving money, should you buy a car now rather than wait until your current car dies? Would you make the same decision if you faced a 10% interest rate? **M**

2.17 As discussed in Solved Problem 15.3, Lewis Wolff and his investment group bought the Oakland A's baseball team for $180 million in 2005. Reportedly, Hall-of-Famer Reggie Jackson offered $25 million more but was rebuffed (*Forbes*, 2005). How would the calculations in Solved Problem 15.3 change if the sales price had been $205 million? **M**

2.18 To virtually everyone's surprise, the Washington Nationals baseball team earned a pretax profit of $20 million in 2005, compared to a $10 million loss when the team was the Montreal Expos in 2004 (Heath, Thomas, "Nationals' Expected '05 Profit Is $20 Million," *Washington Post*, June 21, 2005, A1). Major League Baseball, which bought the franchise for $120 million in 2002, received eight bids of up to $400 million for the team. Reportedly, most baseball teams sell for between two and three times their revenue, so given that the Nationals' projected revenue was $129 million in 2005, an offer of $400 million would be typical. If the Nationals were expected to earn $20 million each year in the future, what is the internal rate of return on a $400 million investment for this club? (*Hint*: See Solved Problem 15.4.) **M**

2.19 If the government bars foreign lenders from loaning money to its citizens, how does the capital market equilibrium change?

2.20 In the figure in Solved Problem 15.5, suppose that the government's demand curve remains constant at D_g^1 but the government starts to tax private earnings, collecting 1% of all interest earnings. How does the capital market equilibrium change? What is the effect on private borrowers?

3. Exhaustible Resources

3.1 You can sell a barrel of oil today for p dollars. Assuming no inflation and no storage cost, how high would the price have to be next year for you to sell the oil next year rather than now? **M**

3.2 If all the coal in the ground, Q, is to be consumed in two years and the demand for coal is $Q_t = A(p_t)^{\varepsilon}$ in each year t where ε is a constant demand elasticity, what is the price of coal each year? **M**

3.3 Trees, wine, and cattle become more valuable over time and then possibly decrease in value. Draw a

---

[18]"In Other Words . . ." *San Francisco Chronicle*, January 1, 1995: Sunday Section, p. 3. She divided the $350 ticket price by 28 years to get $12.50 as the payment per year.

figure with present value on the vertical axis and years (age) on the horizontal axis and show this relationship. Show in what year the owner should "harvest" such a good assuming that there is no cost to harvesting. [*Hint*: If the good's present value is P_0 and we take that money and invest it at interest rate i (a small number such as 0.02 or 0.04), then its value in year t is $P_0(1 + i)^t$; or if we allow continuous compounding, $P_0 e^{it}$. Such a curve increases exponentially over time and looks like the curve labeled "Price" in Figure 15.5. Draw curves with different possible present values. Use those curves to choose the optimal harvest time.] How would your answer change if the interest rate were zero? Show in a figure. **M**

4. Challenge

4.1 If the interest rate is near zero, should an individual go to college, given the information in the figure in the Challenge Solution? State a simple rule for determining whether this individual should go to college in terms of the areas labeled "Benefit" and "Cost" in the figure.

4.2 At current interest rates, it pays for Bob to go to college if he graduates in four years. If it takes an extra year to graduate from college, does going to college still pay? Show how the figure in the Challenge Solution changes. Illustrate how the present value calculation changes using a formula and variables.

4.3 Which is worth more to you: (a) a $10,000 payment today or (b) a $1,000-per-year higher salary for as long as you work? At what interest rate would (a) be worth more to you than (b)? Does your answer depend on how many years you expect to work?

4.4 In 2012, the Clarkson Community Schools in Clarkson, Michigan paid its starting teachers $38,087 employees with a bachelor's degree and $41,802 with a master's degree. (For simplicity, assume that these salaries stay constant and do not increase with experience.) Suppose you know that you want to work for this school district and want to maximize your life-time earnings. To get a master's degree takes one extra year of schooling and costs $20,000. Should you get the master's if you cannot work during that year? Should you get your master's degree if you can work while studying for your master's? In your calculations, assume that you'll work for 40 years and then retire and consider interest rates of 3% and 10%. (*Hint*: You can get a reasonable approximation to the answer by assuming that you work forever and use Equation 15.17.)

Uncertainty

16

We must believe in luck. For how else can we explain the success of those we don't like? —Jean Cocteau

CHALLENGE

Flight Insurance

If flying is so safe, why do they call the airport the terminal?

Many folks fear flying. According to some estimates, 30% of Americans buy travel insurance that protects them against travel disruption and other dangers. However, many firms sell more limited flight insurance that covers you (or your heirs) against being maimed or killed while flying.

Travel Guard (TG) offers accidental death insurance for individual flights. If, just before I take my next regularly scheduled commercial flight, I pay TG $23 and I die on that flight, TG will pay my family $200,000. (Although TG offers much larger amounts of insurance, it seems a bad idea to make myself worth more to my family dead than alive.)

What are the chances of a given flight crashing? Given that probability, how reasonably priced is TG's insurance?

Life's a series of gambles. Will your plane crash? Will you receive Social Security benefits when you retire? Will you win the lottery tomorrow? Will your stock increase in value this year? In this chapter, we look at how uncertainty affects consumer choice (Chapters 3 through 5), such as how much insurance to buy, and investment decisions (Chapter 15).

Faced with uncertainty, consumers and firms consider the possible *outcomes* under various circumstances, or *states of nature*. Suppose that a regulator will approve or reject a new drug, so there are two states of nature: approve or reject. The outcome varies with these states of nature. The pharmaceutical firm's stock will be worth $100 per share if the drug is approved and only $75 if the drug is rejected.

We do not know with certainty what will happen in the future, but we may know that some outcomes are more likely than others. Often we can assign a probability to each possible outcome. For example, if we toss a coin, the probability of a head or of a tail is 50%. Quantifiable uncertainty is called **risk**: the situation in which the likelihood of each possible outcome is known or can be estimated, and no single possible outcome is certain to occur. All of the examples in this chapter concern quantifiable uncertainty.[1]

---

[1]Uncertainty is unquantifiable when we do not know enough to assign meaningful probabilities to different outcomes or if we do not even know what the possible outcomes are. If asked "Who will be the U.S. President in 20 years?" most of us do not even know the likely contenders, let alone the probabilities.

Consumers and firms behave differently as the degree of risk varies. Most people will buy more insurance or take additional preventive actions in riskier situations. Most of us will choose a riskier investment over a less risky one only if we expect a higher return from the riskier investment.

In this chapter, we examine five main topics

1. **Assessing Risk.** Probability, expected value, and variance are important concepts that are used to assess the degree of risk and the likely profit from a risky undertaking.

2. **Attitudes Toward Risk.** Whether people choose a risky option over a nonrisky option depends on their attitudes toward risk and on the expected payoffs of each option.

3. **Reducing Risk.** People try to reduce their overall risk by not making risky choices, taking actions to lower the likelihood of a disaster, combining offsetting risks, and insuring.

4. **Investing Under Uncertainty.** Whether people make an investment depends on the riskiness of the payoff, the expected return, their attitudes toward risk, the interest rate, and whether it is profitable to alter the likelihood of a good outcome.

5. **Behavioral Economics and Uncertainty.** Because some people do not choose among risky options the way that traditional economic theory predicts, some researchers have switched to new models that include psychological factors.

16.1 Assessing Risk

In America anyone can be president. That's one of the risks you take."
—Adlai Stevenson

Gregg, a promoter, is considering whether to schedule an outdoor concert on the Fourth of July. Booking the concert is a gamble: He stands to make a tidy profit if the weather is good, but he'll lose a substantial amount if it rains.

To analyze this decision, Gregg needs a way to describe and quantify risk. A particular *event*—such as holding an outdoor concert—has a number of possible *outcomes*—here, either it rains or it does not rain. When deciding whether to schedule the concert, Gregg quantifies how risky each outcome is using a *probability* and then uses these probabilities to determine what he can expect to earn.

Probability

A *probability* is a number between 0 and 1 that indicates the likelihood that a particular outcome will occur. If an outcome cannot occur, it has a probability of 0. If the outcome is sure to happen, it has a probability of 1. If there is one chance in four that it will rain on July 4, the probability of rain is $\frac{1}{4}$ or 25%.

These weather outcomes that it rains or does not rain are *mutually exclusive*: only one of these outcomes can occur. This list of outcomes is also *exhaustive* as no other outcomes are possible. If outcomes are mutually exclusive and exhaustive, exactly one of these outcomes will occur, and the probabilities sum to 100%.

How can Gregg estimate the probability of rain on July 4? Usually the best approach is to use the *frequency*, which tells us how often an uncertain event occurred in the past. Otherwise, one has to use a *subjective probability*, which is an estimate of the probability that may be based on other information, such as informal "best guesses" of experienced weather forecasters.

Frequency. The probability is the actual chance that an outcome will occur. Managers do not know the true probability so they have to estimate it.

Because Gregg (or the weather department) knows how often it rained on July 4 over many years, he can use that information to estimate the probability that it will rain this year. He calculates θ (theta), the frequency that it rained, by dividing n, the number of years that it rained on July 4, by N, the total number of years for which he has data:

$$\theta = \frac{n}{N}.$$

Then Gregg uses θ, the frequency, as his estimate of the true probability that it will rain this year.

Subjective Probability. Unfortunately, if an event occurs infrequently, we cannot use a frequency calculation to calculate a probability. For example, the disastrous magnitude 9.0 earthquake that struck Japan in 2011, with an accompanying tsunami and nuclear reactor crisis, was unprecedented in modern history.

We use whatever information we have to form a *subjective probability*, which is a best estimate of the likelihood that the outcome will occur—that is, our best, informed guess. The subjective probability can combine frequencies and all other available information—even information that is not based on scientific observation.

If Gregg is planning a concert months in advance, his best estimate of the probability of rain is based on the frequency of rain in the past. However, as the event approaches, a weather forecaster can give him a better estimate that takes into account atmospheric conditions and other information in addition to the historical frequency. Because the forecaster's probability estimate uses personal judgment in addition to an observed frequency, it is a subjective probability.[2]

Probability Distributions. A *probability distribution* relates the probability of occurrence to each possible outcome. Panel a of Figure 16.1 shows a probability distribution over five possible outcomes: zero to four days of rain per month in a relatively dry city. The probability that it rains no days during the month is 10%, as is the probability of exactly four days of rain. The chance of two rainy days is 40%, and the chance of one or three rainy days is 20% each. The probability that it rains five or more days in a month is 0%. These weather outcomes are mutually exclusive and exhaustive, so exactly one of these outcomes will occur, and the probabilities must sum to 100%. For simplicity in the following examples, we concentrate mainly on situations in which there are only two possible outcomes.

Expected Value

One of the common denominators I have found is that expectations rise above that which is expected. —George W. Bush

Gregg's earnings from his outdoor concert will depend on the weather. If it doesn't rain, his profit or value from the concert is $V = 15$ ($15,000). If it rains, he'll have to cancel the concert and he will lose the money, $V = -5$, that he must pay the band. Although Gregg does not know what the weather will be with certainty, he knows that the weather department forecasts a 50% chance of rain.

---

[2]When events are repeated, we can compare our subjective probabilities to observed frequencies. Our subjective probability that it rains 50% of the days in January can be compared to the frequency of rain in January during the recorded history. However if an event is not going to be repeated, it may not be possible to check whether our subjective probability is reasonable or accurate by comparing it to a frequency. We might believe that there's a 75% chance of dry weather tomorrow. If it does rain tomorrow, that doesn't mean we were wrong. Only if we believed that the probability of rain was 0% would observing rain tomorrow prove us wrong.

Figure 16.1 Probability Distribution

The probability distribution shows the probability of occurrence for each of the mutually exclusive outcomes. Panel a shows five possible mutually exclusive outcomes. The probability that it rains exactly two days per month is 40%. The probability that it rains more than four days per month is 0%. The probability distributions in panels a and b have the same expected value or mean. The variance is smaller in panel b, where the probability distribution is more concentrated around the mean than the distribution in panel a.

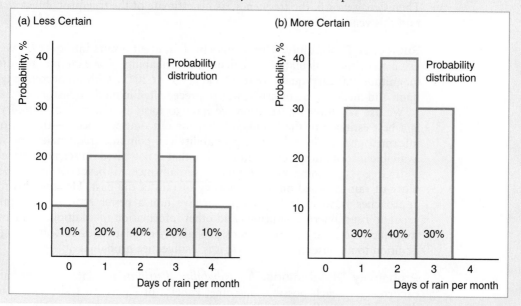

Gregg may use the *mean* or the *average* of the values from both outcomes as a summary statistic of the likely payoff from booking this concert. The amount Gregg expects to earn is called his *expected value* (here, his *expected profit*). The **expected value** is the weighted average of the values of each possible outcome, where the weights are the probability of each outcome. That is, the expected value, EV, is the sum of the product of the probability and the value of each outcome:[3]

$$EV = [Pr(\text{no rain} \times \text{Value(no rain)})] + [Pr(\text{rain}) \times \text{Value(rain)}]$$

$$= \left[\tfrac{1}{2} \times 15\right] + \left[\tfrac{1}{2} \times (-5)\right] = 5,$$

where Pr is the probability of an outcome, so $Pr(\text{rain})$ is the "probability that rain occurs."

The expected value is the amount Gregg would earn on average if the event were repeated many times. If he puts on such concerts on the same date over many years and the weather follows historical patterns, he will earn 15 at half of the concerts (those without rain), and he will get soaked for −5 at the other half of the concerts, when it rains. Thus, he'll earn an average of 5 per concert over a long period of time. More generally, if there are n possible outcomes—*states of nature*—with payoffs or values $V_i, i = 1, \ldots, n$, and associated probabilities θ_i, then the expected value is

$$EV = \sum_{i=1}^{n} \theta_i V_i. \tag{16.1}$$

---

[3]The expectation operator, E, tells us to take the weighted average of all possible values, where the weights are the probabilities that a particular value will be observed. If there are n possible outcomes, the value of outcome i is V_i, and the probability of that outcome is Pr_i, then the expected value is $EV = Pr_1 V_1 + Pr_2 V_2 + \cdots + Pr_n V_n$.

SOLVED PROBLEM 16.1

Suppose that Gregg could obtain perfect information so that he can accurately predict whether it will rain far enough before the concert that he could book the band only if needed. How much would he expect to earn, knowing that he will eventually have this perfect information? How much does he gain by having this perfect information?

Answer

1. *Determine how much Gregg would earn if he had perfect information in each state of nature.* If Gregg knew with certainty that it would rain at the time of the concert, he would not book the band, so he would make no loss or profit: $V = 0$. If Gregg knew that it would not rain, he would hold the concert and make 15.

2. *Determine how much Gregg would expect to earn before he learns with certainty what the weather will be.* Gregg knows that he'll make 15 with a 50% probability $\left(= \frac{1}{2}\right)$ and 0 with a 50% probability, so his expected value, given that he'll receive perfect information in time to act on it, is

$$\left(\tfrac{1}{2} \times 15\right) + \left(\tfrac{1}{2} \times 0\right) = 7.5.$$

3. *Calculate his gain from perfect information as the difference between his expected earnings with perfect information and his expected earnings with imperfect information.* Gregg's gain from perfect information is the difference between the expected earnings with perfect information, 7.5, and the expected earnings without perfect information, 5. Thus, Gregg expects to earn 2.50 ($= 7.50 - 5$) more with perfect information than with imperfect information.[4]

Variance and Standard Deviation

From the expected value, Gregg knows how much he is likely to earn on average if he books many similar concerts. However, he cannot tell from the expected value how risky the concert is. If Gregg's earnings are the same whether it rains or not, he faces no risk and the actual return that he receives is the expected value.[5] If there is risk, then the possible outcomes differ from one another.

We can measure the risk Gregg faces in various ways. The most common approach is to use a measure based on how much the values of the possible outcomes differ from the expected value, EV. If it does not rain, the *difference* between Gregg's actual earnings, 15, and his expected earnings, 5, is 10. The difference if it does rain is $-5 - 5 = -10$. Because there are two differences—one difference for each state of nature (possible outcome)—it is convenient to combine them in a single measure of risk.

One such measure of risk is the *variance*, which measures the spread of the probability distribution. For example, the probability distributions in the two panels in Figure 16.1 have the same means (two days of rain) but different variances. The variance in panel a, where the probability distribution ranges from zero to four days of rain per month, is greater than the variance in panel b, where the probability distribution ranges from one to three days of rain per month.

---

[4]This answer can be reached directly. Perfect weather information is valuable to Gregg because he can avoid hiring the band when it rains. (Having information has no value if it cannot be used.) The value of this information is his expected savings from not hiring the band when it rains: $\frac{1}{2} \times 5 = 2.50$.

[5]The Tappet brothers (the hosts of National Public Radio's *Car Talk*) offer a risk-free investment. Their Capital Depreciation Fund guarantees a 50% return. You send them $100 and they send you back $50.

Formally, the variance is the probability-weighted average of the squares of the differences between the observed outcome and the expected value. If there are n possible outcomes with an expected value of EV, the value of outcome i is V_i, and the probability of that outcome is θ_i, then the variance is

$$\text{Variance} = \sum_{i=1}^{n} \theta_i (V_i - \text{EV})^2. \tag{16.2}$$

The variance puts more weight on large deviations from the expected value than on smaller ones. Instead of describing risk using the variance, economists and businesspeople often report the *standard deviation*, which is the square root of the variance. The usual symbol for the standard deviation is σ (sigma), so the symbol for variance is σ^2.

Gregg faces the probability $\theta_1 = \frac{1}{2}$ if there is no rain and $\theta_2 = \frac{1}{2}$ if there is rain. The value of the concert is $V_1 = 15$ if there is no rain and $V_2 = -5$ if it rains, and EV $= 5$. Thus, the variance of the value that Gregg obtains from the outdoor concert is

$$
\begin{aligned}
\sigma^2 &= [\theta_1 \times (V_1 - \text{EV})^2] + [\theta_2 \times (V_2 - \text{EV})^2] \\
&= \left[\tfrac{1}{2} \times (15 - 5)^2\right] + \left[\tfrac{1}{2} \times (-5 - 5)^2\right] \\
&= \left[\tfrac{1}{2} \times (10)^2\right] + \left[\tfrac{1}{2} \times (-10)^2\right] = 100.
\end{aligned}
$$

Because the variance of the payoff from the outdoor concert is $\sigma^2 = 100$, the standard deviation is $\sigma = 10$.

Holding the expected value constant, the smaller the standard deviation or variance, the smaller the risk. Suppose that Gregg's expected value of profit is the same if he stages the concert indoors, but that the standard deviation of his profit is less. The indoor theater does not hold as many people as the outdoor venue, so the most that Gregg can earn if it does not rain is $10. Rain discourages attendance even at the indoor theater, so he just breaks even, earning $0. The expected value of the indoor concert, EV $= \left(\frac{1}{2} \times 10\right) + \left(\frac{1}{2} \times 0\right) = 5$, is the same as that of the outdoor concert. Staging the concert indoors involves less risk, however. The variance of his earnings from the indoor concert is

$$\sigma^2 = \left[\tfrac{1}{2} \times (10 - 5)^2\right] + \left[\tfrac{1}{2} \times (0 - 5)^2\right] = \left[\tfrac{1}{2} \times (5)^2\right] + \left[\tfrac{1}{2} \times (-5)^2\right] = 25,$$

which is only one-fourth of the variance if he holds the event outside.

16.2   Attitudes Toward Risk

Given the risks Gregg faces if he schedules a concert, will Gregg stage the concert? To answer this question, we need to know Gregg's attitude toward risk.

Although the indoor and outdoor concerts have the same expected value, the outdoor concert involves more risk. Gregg will earn more with good weather and lose more with bad weather by holding his concert outdoors. He'll book an outdoor concert only if he likes to gamble.

Even if he dislikes risk, Gregg may prefer a riskier option if it has a higher expected value. Suppose that he strikes a new agreement with the band by which he pays only if the weather is good and the concert is held. Gregg's expected value is $7.50, the variance is $56.25, and the standard deviation is $7.50.[6] By holding the concert outdoors instead of indoors, Gregg's expected value is higher ($7.50 instead

---

[6]The expected value is the same as in Solved Problem 16.1: $\left(\frac{1}{2} \times 15\right) + \left(\frac{1}{2} \times 0\right) = 7.5$. The variance is $\frac{1}{2} \times (15 - 7.5)^2 + \frac{1}{2} \times (0 - 7.5)^2 = 56.25$, so the standard deviation is 7.5.

of $5), and the standard deviation is higher ($7.50 instead of $5). He earns the same, $0, from both types of concerts in bad weather. In good weather, he earns more from the outdoor concert. Because he always does as well with an outdoor concert as with an indoor show, Gregg clearly prefers the riskier outdoor concert with its higher expected value.

If he dislikes risk, Gregg won't necessarily stage the concert with the higher expected value. Suppose that his choice is between the indoor concert and an outdoor concert from which he earns $100,015.50 if it doesn't rain and loses $100,005 if it rains. His expected value is greater with the outside concert, $5.25 instead of $5, but he faces much more risk. The standard deviation of the outdoor concert is $100,010.25 compared to $5. Gregg might reasonably opt for the indoor concert with the lower expected value if he dislikes risk. After all, he may be loath to risk losing $100,005 with a 50% probability.

Expected Utility Theory

We can formalize this type of reasoning by extending our model of utility maximization (Chapters 3 through 5) to show how people's taste for risk affects their choice among options (investments, career choices, consumption bundles) that differ in both value and risk. This approach is called expected utility theory. If people made choices to maximize expected value, they would always choose the option with the highest expected value regardless of the risks involved. However, most people care about risk in addition to the expected value. Indeed, most people are *risk averse*—they dislike risk—and will choose a bundle with higher risk only if its expected value is substantially higher than that of a less-risky bundle.

In Chapter 3, we described an individual's preferences over various bundles of goods using a utility function. John von Neumann and Oskar Morgenstern (1944) suggested an extension of this standard utility-maximizing model that includes risk.[7] They did so by treating utility as a cardinal measure rather than an ordinal measure (as we did in Chapters 3 through 5). In von Neumann's and Morgenstern's reformulation, a rational person maximizes *expected utility*. Expected utility, EU, is the probability-weighted average of the utility, $U(\cdot)$, from each possible outcome:

$$EU = \sum_{i=1}^{n}\theta_i U(V_i). \tag{16.3}$$

For example, Gregg's expected utility, EU, from the outdoor concert is

$$EU = [\theta_1 \times U(V_1)] + [\theta_2 \times U(V_2)] = \left[\tfrac{1}{2} \times U(15)\right] + \left[\tfrac{1}{2} \times U(-5)\right],$$

where his utility function, U, depends on his earnings. For example, $U(15)$ is the amount of utility Gregg gets from his earnings of 15. (People have preferences over the goods they consume. However, for simplicity we'll say that a person receives utility from earnings or wealth, which can be spent on consumption goods.)

In short, the expected utility calculation is similar to the expected value calculation. Both are weighted averages in which the weights are the probabilities that the state of nature will occur. The difference is that the expected value is the probability-weighted average of the monetary value, whereas the expected utility is the probability-weighted average of the utility from the monetary value.

[7]This approach to handling choice under uncertainty is the most commonly used method. Schoemaker (1982) discusses the logic underlying this approach, the evidence for it, and several variants. Machina (1989) discusses a number of alternative methods.

If we know how an individual's utility increases with wealth, we can determine how that person reacts to risky propositions. We can classify people in terms of their willingness to make a **fair bet**: a wager with an expected value of zero. An example of a fair bet is one in which you pay 1 if a flipped coin comes up heads and receive 1 if it comes up tails. Because you expect to win half the time and lose half the time, the expected value of this bet is zero:

$$\left[\tfrac{1}{2} \times (-1)\right] + \left[\tfrac{1}{2} \times 1\right] = 0.$$

In contrast, a bet in which you pay 2 if you lose the coin flip and receive 4 if you win is an unfair bet that favors you, with an expected value of

$$\left[\tfrac{1}{2} \times (-2)\right] + \left[\tfrac{1}{2} \times 4\right] = 1.$$

Someone who is unwilling to make a fair bet is **risk averse**. A person who is indifferent about making a fair bet is **risk neutral**. A person who is **risk preferring** will make a fair bet.

Risk Aversion

We can use our expected utility model to examine how Irma, who is risk averse, makes a choice under uncertainty. Figure 16.2 shows Irma's utility function. The utility function is concave to the wealth axis, indicating that Irma's utility rises with wealth but at a diminishing rate. Irma's utility from wealth W is $U(W)$. She has positive marginal utility from extra wealth, $dU(W)/dW > 0$; however, her utility increases with wealth at a diminishing rate, $d^2U(W)/dW^2 < 0$. That is, she has *diminishing marginal utility of wealth*: The extra pleasure she gets from each extra dollar of wealth is smaller than the pleasure she gets from the previous dollar. An individual whose utility function is concave to the wealth axis is risk averse, as we now illustrate.

Unwillingness to Take a Fair Bet. We can demonstrate that *a person whose utility function is concave picks the less-risky choice if both choices have the same expected value.* Suppose that Irma has an initial wealth of 40 and two options. One option is to do nothing and keep the 40, so her utility is $U(40) = 120$ (point *d* in Figure 16.2) with certainty.

Her other option is to buy a share (a unit of stock) in a start-up company. Her wealth will be 70 if the start-up is a big success and 10 otherwise. Irma's subjective probability is 50% that the firm will be a big success. Her expected value of wealth remains

$$40 = \left(\tfrac{1}{2} \times 10\right) + \left(\tfrac{1}{2} \times 70\right).$$

Thus, buying the stock is a fair bet because she has the same expected wealth whether she purchases the stock or not.

If Irma only cared about her expected value and didn't care about risk, she would be indifferent between buying the stock or not. However, because Irma is risk averse, Irma prefers not buying the stock because both options have the same expected wealth and buying the stock carries more risk.

We can show that her expected utility is lower if she buys the stock than if she does not. If she buys the stock, her utility if the stock does well is $U(70) = 140$,

Figure 16.2 Risk Aversion

Initially, Irma's wealth is 40, so her utility is $U(40) = 120$, point d. If she buys the stock and it's worth 70, her utility is $U(70) = 140$ at point c. If she buys the stock and it's worth only 10, she is at point a, where $U(10) = 70$. If her subjective probability that the stock will be worth 70 is 50%, the expected value of the stock is $40 = (0.5 \times 10) + (0.5 \times 70)$ and her expected utility from buying the stock is $0.5U(10) + 0.5U(70) = 105$, point b, which is the midpoint of the line between the good outcome, point c, and the bad outcome, point a. Thus, her expected utility from buying the stock, 105, is less than her utility from having a certain wealth of 40, $U(40) = 120$, so she does not buy the stock. In contrast, if Irma's subjective probability that the stock will be worth 70 is 90%, her expected utility from buying the stock is $0.1U(10) + 0.9U(70) = 133$, point f, which is more than her utility with a certain wealth of 40, $U(40) = 120$, d, so she buys the stock.

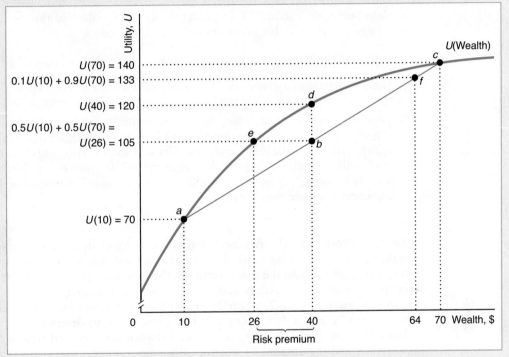

point c. If it doesn't do well, her utility is $U(10) = 70$, point a. Thus, her expected utility from buying the stock is

$$\left[\tfrac{1}{2} \times U(10)\right] + \left[\tfrac{1}{2} \times U(70)\right] = \left[\tfrac{1}{2} \times 70\right] + \left[\tfrac{1}{2} \times 140\right] = 105.$$

Figure 16.2 shows that her expected utility is point b, the midpoint of a line (called a *chord*) between a and c.[8]

Because Irma's utility function is concave, her utility from certain wealth, 120 at point d, is greater than her expected utility from the risky activity, 105 at point b. As a result, she does not buy the stock. Buying this stock, which is a fair bet, increases the risk she faces without changing her expected wealth.

A risk-averse person chooses a riskier option only if it has a sufficiently higher expected value. Given her wealth of $40, if Irma were much more confident that the stock would be valuable, her expected value would rise and she'd buy the stock, as Solved Problem 16.2 shows.

---

[8]The chord represents all the possible weighted averages of the utility at point a and the utility at point c. When the probabilities of the two outcomes are equal, the expected value is the midpoint.

SOLVED PROBLEM 16.2

Suppose that Irma's subjective probability is 90% that the stock will be valuable. What is her expected wealth if she buys the stock? What is her expected utility? Does she buy the stock?

Answer

1. *Calculate Irma's expected wealth.* Her expected value or wealth is 10% times her wealth if the stock bombs plus 90% times her wealth if the stock does well:

$$(0.1 \times 10) + (0.9 \times 70) = 64.$$

In Figure 16.2, 64 is the distance along the wealth axis corresponding to point f.

2. *Calculate Irma's expected utility.* Her expected utility is the probability-weighted average of her utility under the two outcomes:

$$[0.1 \times U(10)] + [0.9 \times U(70)] = [0.1 \times 70] + [0.9 \times 140] = 133.$$

Her expected utility is the height on the utility axis of point f. Point f is nine-tenths of the distance along the line connecting point a to point c.

3. *Compare Irma's expected utility to her certain utility if she does not buy.* Irma's expected utility from buying the stock, 133 (point f), is greater than her certain utility, 120 (point d), if she does not. Thus, if Irma is this confident that the stock will do well, she buys it. Although the risk is greater from buying than from not buying, her expected wealth is enough higher (64 instead of 40) that it's worth it to take the chance.

The Risk Premium. The **risk premium** is the amount that a risk-averse person would pay to avoid taking a risk. For example, an individual may buy insurance to avoid risk. Equivalently, the risk premium is the minimum extra compensation (premium) that a decision-maker would require to willingly incur a risk.

We can use Figure 16.2, where Irma owns the stock that has a 50% chance of being worth 70 and a 50% chance of being worth 10, to determine her risk premium. The risk premium is the difference between her expected wealth from the risky stock and the amount of wealth, called the *certainty equivalent*, that if held with certainty, would yield the same utility as this uncertain prospect.

Irma's expected wealth from holding the stock is 40. Her corresponding expected utility is 105. The certainty equivalent income is 26, because the utility Irma gets from having 26 with certainty is $U(26) = 105$, the same as her expected utility from owning the stock. She would therefore be willing to sell the stock for a price of 26. Thus, her risk premium, which is the difference between the expected value and the certainty equivalent, is $40 - 26 = 14$, as the figure shows.

SOLVED PROBLEM 16.3

Jen has a concave utility function of $U(W) = \sqrt{W}$. Her only major asset is shares in an Internet start-up company. Tomorrow she will learn her stock's value. She believes that it is worth \$144 with probability $\frac{2}{3}$ and \$225 with probability $\frac{1}{3}$. What is her expected utility? What risk premium, P, would she pay to avoid bearing this risk?

Answer

1. *Calculate Jen's expected wealth and her expected utility.* Her expected wealth is

$$EW = \left(\tfrac{2}{3} \times 144\right) + \left(\tfrac{1}{3} \times 225\right) = 96 + 75 = 171.$$

Her expected utility is

$$EU = \left[\tfrac{2}{3} \times U(144)\right] + \left[\tfrac{1}{3} \times U(225)\right]$$

$$= \left[\tfrac{2}{3} \times \sqrt{144}\right] + \left[\tfrac{1}{3} \times \sqrt{225}\right]$$

$$= \left[\tfrac{2}{3} \times 12\right] + \left[\tfrac{1}{3} \times 15\right] = 8 + 5 = 13.$$

2. *Solve for P such that her expected utility equals her utility from her expected wealth minus P.* Jen would pay up to an amount P to avoid bearing the risk, where $U(EW - P)$ equals her expected utility from the risky stock, EU. That is,

$$U(EW - P) = U(171 - P) = \sqrt{171 - P} = 13 = EU.$$

Squaring both sides, we find that $171 - P = 169$, or $P = 2$. That is, Jen would accept an offer for her stock today of $169 (or more), which reflects a risk premium of $2.

Risk Neutrality

Someone who is risk neutral has a constant marginal utility of wealth: Each extra dollar of wealth raises that person's utility by the same amount as the previous dollar. With constant marginal utility of wealth, the utility curve is a straight line in a utility and wealth graph. As a consequence, a risk-neutral person's utility depends only on wealth and not on risk.

Suppose that Irma is risk neutral and has the straight-line utility function in panel a of Figure 16.3. She would be indifferent between buying the stock and not buying it if her subjective probability is 50% that it will do well. Her expected utility from buying the stock is the average of her utility at points *a* (10) and *c* (70):

$$\left[\tfrac{1}{2} \times U(10)\right] + \left[\tfrac{1}{2} \times U(70)\right] = \left[\tfrac{1}{2} \times 70\right] + \left[\tfrac{1}{2} \times 140\right] = 105.$$

Her expected utility exactly equals her utility with certain wealth of 40 (point *b*) because the line connecting points *a* and *c* lies on the utility function and point *b* is the midpoint of that line.

Here, Irma is indifferent between buying and not buying the stock, a fair bet, because she doesn't care how much risk she faces. Because the expected wealth from both options is 40, she is indifferent between them.

In general, *a risk-neutral person chooses the option with the highest expected value because maximizing expected value maximizes utility*. A risk-neutral person chooses the riskier option if it has even a slightly higher expected value than the less risky option. Equivalently, the risk premium for a risk-neutral person is zero.

Risk Preference

An individual with an increasing marginal utility of wealth is risk preferring: that is, willing to take a fair bet. If Irma has the utility curve in panel b of Figure 16.3, she is risk preferring. Her expected utility from buying the stock, 105 at point *b*, is higher than her certain utility if she does not buy the stock, 82 at point *d*. Therefore, she buys the stock.

A risk-preferring person is willing to pay for the right to make a fair bet (a negative risk premium). As the figure shows, Irma's expected utility from buying the stock is the same as the utility from a certain wealth of 58. Given her initial wealth of 40, if you offer her the opportunity to buy the stock or offer to give her 18, she is indifferent. With any payment smaller than 18, she prefers to buy the stock.

Figure 16.3 Risk Neutrality and Risk Preference

(a) If Irma's utility curve is a straight line, she is risk neutral and is indifferent as to whether or not to make a fair bet. Her expected utility from buying the stock, 105 at *b*, is the same as from a certain wealth of 40 at *b*. (b) If Irma's utility curve is convex to the horizontal axis, Irma has increasing marginal utility to wealth and is risk preferring. She buys the stock because her expected utility from buying the stock, 105 at *b*, is higher than her utility from a certain wealth of 40, 82 at *d*.

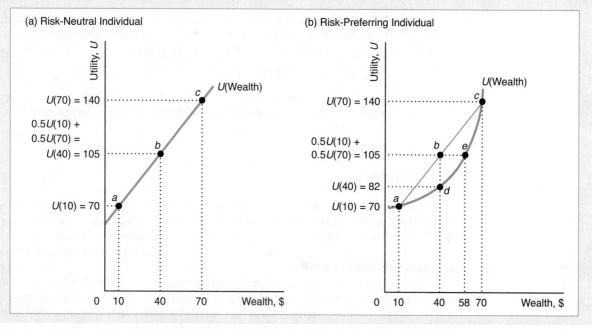

APPLICATION

Gambling

Horse sense is the thing a horse has which keeps it from betting on people.
—W. C. Fields

Most people say that they don't like bearing risk. Consistently, these consumers buy car, medical, and other insurance to protect against risks. But many of these same people gamble.

Christiansen Capital Advisors estimates that U.S. gambling industry revenues were $89 billion in 2009 and global Internet gambling was $24.5 billion in 2010. Over half of the countries in the world have lotteries. According to eLottery, worldwide sales were about $245 billion in 2010. One estimate puts global gambling at $400 billion in 2011.

Not only do many people gamble, but they make unfair bets, in which the expected value of the gamble is negative. That is, if they play the game repeatedly, they are likely to lose money in the long run. For example, the British government keeps half of the total amount bet on its lottery. Americans lose at least $50 billion or 7% of all legal bets. A casino has a *hold percentage*, the money on average that it retains as a percentage of the amount of chips its customers buy, which varies by game, from slightly over 20% for roulette wheels to 45% for the wheel of fortune.

Why do people take unfair bets? Some people gamble because they are risk preferring or because they have a compulsion to gamble. However, neither of these observations is likely to explain noncompulsive gambling by most people who exhibit risk-averse behavior in the other aspects of their lives (such as buying insurance).[9] Risk-averse people may make unfair bets because they get pleasure from participating in the game or they falsely believe that the gamble favors them.

The first explanation is that gambling provides entertainment as well as risk. Risk-averse people insure their property, such as their homes, because there is nothing enjoyable about bearing the risk of theft, flood, and fire. However, these same people may play poker or bet on horse races because they get enough pleasure from playing those games to put up with the financial risk and the expected loss.

Many people definitely like games of chance. One survey found that 65% of Americans say that they engage in games of chance, even when the games involve no money or only trivial sums.[10] That is, they play because they enjoy the games. The anticipation of possibly winning and the satisfaction and excitement arising from a win generate greater benefits than the negative feelings associated with a loss.

Instead or in addition, people may gamble because they make mistakes.[11] Either people do not know the true probabilities or cannot properly calculate expected values, so they do not realize that they are participating in an unfair bet.

Degree of Risk Aversion

Figures 16.2 and 16.3 illustrate that whether Irma is risk averse depends on the shape of her utility function over wealth, $U(W)$. Economists sometimes use quantitative measures of the curvature of the utility function to describe the degree of an individual's risk aversion.

Arrow-Pratt Measure of Risk Aversion. One of the most commonly used measures is the Arrow-Pratt measure of risk aversion (Pratt, 1964):

$$\rho(W) = \frac{d^2 U(W)/dW^2}{dU(W)/dW}. \qquad (16.4)$$

Because Irma's marginal utility of wealth is positive, $dU(W)/dW > 0$, $\rho(W)$ has the opposite sign of $d^2U(W)/dW^2$. Irma is risk averse if her utility function is

---

[9]Friedman and Savage (1948) suggest that some people are risk averse with respect to small gambles, and hence will buy insurance, but risk preferring for large ones, so they will gamble, such as by buying a lottery ticket.

[10]When I was an undergraduate at the University of Chicago, I lived in a dorm and saw overwhelming evidence that the "love of the game" is a powerful force. As the neighborhood provided few forms of entertainment, the dorm's denizens regularly watched the man from the vending company refill the candy machine with fresh candy. He took the old, stale, unpopular bars that remained unsold and placed them in the "mystery candy" bin. Thanks to our careful study of stocking techniques, we all knew that buying the mystery candy was not a fair bet—who would want unpopular, stale candy bars at the same price as a fresh, popular bar? Nonetheless, one of the dorm dwellers always bought the mystery candy. When asked why, he responded, "I love the excitement of not knowing what'll come out." Life was very boring indeed on the South Side of Chicago.

[11]Economists, who know how to calculate expected values and derive most of their excitement from economic models, are apparently less likely to gamble than others. A number of years ago, an association of economists met in Reno, Nevada. Reno hotels charge low room rates on the assumption that they'll make plenty from guests' gambling losses. However, the economists gambled so little that they were asked pointedly not to return.

concave to the horizontal axis, so she has diminishing marginal utility of wealth, $d^2U(W)/dW^2 < 0$. Thus, if she is risk averse, the Arrow-Pratt measure is positive.

If Irma has the concave utility function $U(W) = \ln W$, then $dU(W)/dW = 1/W$ and $d^2U(W)/dW^2 = -1/W^2$, so her Arrow-Pratt measure is $\rho(W) = 1/W > 0$. Her degree of risk aversion falls with wealth. In contrast, if she has an exponential utility function, $U(W) = -e^{-aW}$, where $a > 0$, her Arrow-Pratt measure is $\rho(W) = -(-a^2e^{-aW})/(ae^{-aW}) = a$, so her measure of risk aversion is constant over all possible values of wealth.

The Arrow-Pratt measure is zero if Irma is risk neutral. For example, if her utility function is $U(W) = aW$, then $dU(W)/dW = a$, $d^2U(W)/dW^2 = 0$, and her Arrow-Pratt risk aversion measure is $\rho(W) = -0/a = 0$. The Arrow-Pratt measure is negative if Irma is risk preferring.

Arrow-Pratt Measure and the Willingness to Gamble. We can show that the larger the Arrow-Pratt measure of risk aversion, the more small gambles that an individual will take. Suppose Ryan's house is currently worth W. He considers painting it bright orange, which he believes will lower its value by A with probability θ and raise it by B with probability $1 - \theta$. He will engage in this gamble if his expected utility is at least as high as his certain utility when he does not gamble: $\theta U(W - A) + (1 - \theta)U(W + B) > U(W)$. Let $B(A)$ show how large B must be for a given value of A such that Ryan's expected utility equals his certain utility:

$$\theta U(W - A) + (1 - \theta)U[W + B(A)] = U(W). \qquad (16.5)$$

From Equation 16.5, if $A = 0$, $B(0) = 0$. Given that A is initially 0, how much does B change as we slightly increase A? That is, how much does the house's value have to rise in the good state of nature to offset the drop in value in the bad state such that Ryan is willing to take the gamble on painting his house? To answer these questions, we differentiate Equation 16.5 with respect to A,

$$-\theta\frac{dU(W - A)}{dA} + (1 - \theta)\frac{dU(W + B(A))}{dA}\frac{dB(A)}{dA} = 0, \qquad (16.6)$$

and evaluate at $A = 0$:

$$-\theta\frac{dU(W)}{dA} + (1 - \theta)\frac{dU(W)}{dA}\frac{dB(0)}{dA} = 0,$$

Rearranging this last expression, we learn that

$$\frac{dB(0)}{dA} = \frac{\theta}{1 - \theta}. \qquad (16.7)$$

That is, Ryan will be willing to engage in this gamble if the increase in B in response to an increase in A equals the odds $\theta/(1 - \theta)$.

For a given θ, A, and B, Ryan is more likely to take this gamble, the less risk averse he is. How risk averse he is depends on the curvature of his utility function, which is reflected by the second derivative of his utility function. Differentiating the identity in Equation 16.6 again with respect to A and evaluating at $A = 0$, we discover that

$$\theta\frac{d^2U(W)}{dA^2} + (1 - \theta)\frac{d^2U(W)}{dA^2}\left[\frac{dB(0)}{dA}\right]^2 + (1 - \theta)\frac{dU(W)}{dA}\frac{d^2B(0)}{dA^2} = 0. \; (16.8)$$

Substituting Equation 16.7 into Equation 16.8, rearranging terms, and finally substituting in the definition from Equation 16.4, we obtain

$$\frac{d^2B(0)}{dA^2} = \frac{\theta}{(1-\theta)^2}\left[-\frac{d^2U(W)/dA^2}{dU(W)/dA}\right] = \frac{\theta}{(1-\theta)^2}\rho(W).$$

That is, $d^2B(0)/dA^2$ is proportional to the Arrow-Pratt risk-aversion measure. The larger d^2B/dA^2, the greater the rate that B must increase as A increases for Ryan to be willing to gamble. Thus, for a given θ, A, and B, he is more likely to take the gamble, the smaller his Arrow-Pratt measure.

SOLVED PROBLEM 16.4

Jen's utility function is $U(W) = W^{0.5}$, while Ryan's is $U(W) = W^{0.25}$. Use the Arrow-Pratt measure to show that Ryan is more risk averse. Next, suppose that each owns a home worth 100 (for simplicity) and is considering painting it orange. If each does so, there is a 50% probability that each house is worth 81 and a 50% probability that each is worth 121. Will either take this gamble?

Answer

1. *Calculate their Arrow-Pratt measures using Equation 16.4.* Differentiating Jen's utility function, $U(W) = W^{0.5}$, with respect to W, we find that $dU/dW = 0.5W^{-0.5}$. Differentiating again, we learn that $d^2U/dW^2 = -0.25W^{-1.5}$. Thus, her Arrow-Pratt risk measure is $\rho = -(d^2U/dW^2)/(dU/dW) = 0.25W^{-1.5}/0.5W^{-0.5} = 0.5/W$. Ryan's utility function is $U(W) = W^{0.25}$, so $dU/dW = 0.25W^{-0.75}$, $d^2U/dW^2 = -0.1875W^{-1.75}$, and his Arrow-Pratt risk measure is $\rho = 0.1875W^{-1.75}/0.25W^{-0.75} = 0.75/W$. Thus, Ryan is more risk averse than Jen.

2. *By comparing their expected utility with the gamble to their utility without the gamble, determine if either is willing to take the gamble.* Without the gamble, Jen's utility is $U(100) = 100^{0.5} = 10$. With the gamble, her expected utility is $0.5U(81) + 0.5U(121) = (0.5 \times 9) + (0.5 \times 11) = 10$. Consequently, she is (barely) willing to take the gamble. Ryan's certain utility is $U(100) = 100^{0.25} \approx 3.1623$. With the gamble, his expected utility is $0.5U(81) + 0.5U(121) \approx (0.5 \times 3) + (0.5 \times 3.3166) = 3.1583$, which is less than 3.1623, so he is unwilling to take the gamble. Thus, Jen will take this gamble, unlike Ryan, who is more risk averse.

16.3 Reducing Risk

If 75% of all accidents happen within 5 miles of home, why not move 10 miles away? —Steven Wright

Risk-averse people want to eliminate or reduce the risks they face. Risk-neutral people avoid unfair bets that are stacked against them, and even risk-preferring people avoid very unfair bets. Individuals can avoid optional risky activities, but often they can't escape risk altogether. Property owners, for instance, always face the possibility that their property will be damaged or stolen. However, they may be able to reduce the probability that bad events (such as earthquakes, tornadoes, fires, floods, and thefts) happen to them.

Individuals can avoid optional risky activities, but they can't escape risk altogether. Property owners, for instance, face the possibility that their property will be damaged or stolen or will burn down. They may be able to reduce the probability that bad states of nature occur, however.

Just Say No

The simplest way to avoid risk is to abstain from optional risky activities. No one forces you to bet on the lottery, work in a high-risk environment, or invest in a start-up biotech firm.

Even when you can't avoid risk altogether, you can take precautions to reduce the probability of bad states of nature happening or the magnitude of any loss that might occur. By maintaining your car as the manufacturer recommends, you reduce the probability that it will break down. By locking your apartment door, you lower the chance that your television will be stolen. Getting rid of the four-year-old collection of newspapers in your basement lessens the likelihood that your house will burn down.

APPLICATION	Harry Potter protects his young fans from traumatic injuries on weekends. Stephen Gwilym of the John Radcliffe Hospital in Oxford and his colleagues found that only half as many 7- to 15-year-old children came to the emergency department on the weekends immediately following the release of J. K. Rowling's books, compared to other summer weekends from 2003 to 2005. (Apparently, your mom was trying to maim you when she said, "Stop reading and go outside and play on this lovely summer day!")
Harry Potter's Magic	

Obtaining Information

Collecting accurate information before acting is one of the most important ways in which people can reduce risk and increase expected value and expected utility, as Solved Problem 16.1 illustrated. Armed with information, people may avoid making a risky choice, or may be able to take actions that reduce the probability of a disaster or the size of a loss.

Before buying a car or refrigerator, many people read *Consumer Reports* to determine how frequently a particular brand is likely to need repairs. By collecting such information before buying, they can reduce the likelihood of making a costly mistake.[12]

APPLICATION	Given Britain's notoriously changeable weather, predicting weather changes may save Tesco, the nation's largest grocery chain, substantial amounts of money by reducing costs and avoiding wasting food. If their stores stock up on meat and other barbecue items in anticipation of good weather, they are stuck with unsold food when it suddenly rains.
Weathering Bad Sales	

Tesco has its own weather team, which it hopes will better predict weather and determine the effects of weather conditions on consumers' demands. Tesco claims that its system is very accurate.

Tesco has developed its own software that shows how shopping patterns change "for every degree of temperature and every hour of sunshine." An increase of 18° generally triples sales of barbecue meat and increases demand for lettuce by 50%. In 2011, Tesco reported that during the first weekend of a hot spell, sales of hair removal cream increase by 1,400% as women wear short skirts and expose their legs. Using weather forecasts for 15 regions, orders from local depots are varied automatically during the day.

---

[12]See "Bond Ratings" in MyEconLab, Chapter Resources, Chapter 16 for a discussion of how the riskiness of bonds is reported.

Diversification

Although it may sound paradoxical, individuals and firms often reduce their overall risk by making many risky investments instead of only one. This practice is called *risk pooling* or *diversifying*. As your grandparents may have told you, "Don't put all your eggs in one basket."[13]

The extent to which diversification reduces risk depends on the degree to which various events are correlated over states of nature. The degree of correlation ranges from negatively correlated to uncorrelated to positively correlated.[14]

If two investments are positively correlated, one performs well when the other performs well. If two investments are negatively correlated, when one performs well, the other performs badly. If the performances of two investments move *independently*—do not move together predictably—their payoffs are uncorrelated.

Diversification can eliminate risk if two events are perfectly negatively correlated. Suppose that two firms are competing for a government contract and have an equal chance of winning. Because only one firm can win, the other must lose, so the two events are *perfectly negatively correlated*. You can buy a share of stock in either firm for $20. The stock of the firm that wins the contract will be worth $40, whereas the stock of the loser will be worth $10.

$$EV = \left(\tfrac{1}{2} \times 80\right) + \left(\tfrac{1}{2} \times 20\right) = 50$$

with a variance of

$$\sigma^2 = \left[\tfrac{1}{2} \times (80 - 50)^2\right] + \left[\tfrac{1}{2} \times (20 - 50)^2\right] = 900.$$

However, if you buy one share of each firm, your two shares will be worth 50 no matter which firm wins, and the variance is zero.

Diversification can reduce (but not eliminate) risk even when investments are not perfectly negatively correlated. Indeed, diversification reduces risk even if the two investments are uncorrelated or imperfectly positively correlated.

Now suppose that the two stocks' values are uncorrelated: Whether one firm wins a contract is independent of whether the other firm gets one. Each of the two firms has a 50% chance of receiving a government contract. The chance that each firm's share is worth 40 is $\tfrac{1}{4}$, the chance that one is worth 40 and the other is worth 10 is $\tfrac{1}{2}$, and the chance that each is worth 10 is $\tfrac{1}{4}$. If you buy one share of each firm, the expected value of these two shares is

$$EV = \left(\tfrac{1}{4} \times 80\right) + \left(\tfrac{1}{2} \times 50\right) + \left(\tfrac{1}{4} \times 20\right) = 50,$$

and the variance is

$$\sigma^2 = \left[\tfrac{1}{4} \times (80 - 50)^2\right] + \left[\tfrac{1}{2} \times (50 - 50)^2\right] + \left[\tfrac{1}{4} \times (20 - 50)^2\right] = 450.$$

---

[13]Unlike the supermarket manager who left all his baskets in one exit, where they were smashed by a car.

[14]A measure of the *correlation* between two random variables x and y is

$$\rho = E\left(\frac{x - \bar{x}}{\sigma_x} \frac{y - \bar{y}}{\sigma_y}\right),$$

where the $E(\cdot)$ means "take the expectation" of the term in parentheses, $\bar{x}$ and $\bar{y}$ are the means, and σ_x and σ_y are the standard deviations of x and y. This correlation can vary between -1 and 1. If $\rho = 1$ these random variables are perfectly positively correlated, if $\rho = -1$ they have a perfect negative correlation, and if $\rho = 0$ they are uncorrelated.

The expected value is the same as when buying two shares of one firm, but the variance is only half as large. Thus, diversification lowers risk when the values are uncorrelated.

Diversification can reduce risk even if the investments are positively correlated provided that the correlation is not perfect. However, *diversification does not reduce risk if two investments have a perfect positive correlation*. For example, if the government awards contracts only to both firms or to neither firm, the risks are perfectly positively correlated. The expected value of the stocks and the variance are the same whether you buy two shares of one firm or one share of each firm.

Because the stock price of any given firm is not perfectly correlated with the stock price of other firms, an investor or a manager can reduce risk by buying the stocks of many companies rather than the stock of just one firm. One way to effectively own shares in a number of companies at once is by buying shares in a *mutual fund* of stocks. A mutual fund share is issued by a company that buys stocks in many other companies. For example, a mutual fund may be based on the *Standard & Poor's Composite Index of 500 Stocks* (S&P 500), which is a value-weighted average of 500 large firms' stocks.[15]

However, a stock mutual fund has a *market-wide risk*, a risk that is common to the overall market, which arises because the prices of almost all stocks tend to rise when the economy is expanding and to fall when the economy is contracting. You cannot avoid the systematic risks associated with shifts in the economy that have a similar effect on most stocks even if you buy a diversified mutual stock fund.

APPLICATION

Employees' Failure to Diversify

Foolishly, many corporate employees fail to diversify their portfolios. Much of their wealth is tied up in their employer's stock. Managers and other corporate employees may receive stock bonuses, which they do not sell. For others, their employer matches their investment in the company's 401(k) retirement plans with company stock.[16] Others invest voluntarily as a sign of loyalty.

In 2007 at the beginning of the recent financial crisis, nearly two of every five 401(k) participants in large firms held 20% or more of their money in employer stock. About one-sixth of participants invested 50% or more in their company's equity. On average, these funds held 16% in company stock.

Is this practice a bad idea? Employees of the investment firm Bear Stearns owned one-third of the company's stock. Unfortunately for them, the firm faced bankruptcy in early 2008. Claiming that the firm was too big to be allowed to fail, the U.S. government bailed it out. Under the rescue plan, JPMorgan Chase offered $10 a share to buy Bear Stearns in 2008, which was only one-tenth of the stock's value in December 2007. Consequently, not only did many of these employees face losing their livelihoods, but also they lost most of their wealth.

If a Bear Stearns employee's 401(k) had $100,000 in a Standard & Poor's 500-stock index fund at the end of 2007, its value would have fallen to $90,760 by the end of the first quarter of 2008. However, if that employee shifted 16% into Bear Stearns stock, the investment would have fallen to $77,838. Even worse,

[15]The Calvert, Domini Social Investments, Pax World Funds, and at least 200 other funds have portfolios consisting of only socially responsible firms (by their criteria). An alternative, **www.vicefund.com,** invests in only sin stocks. Adding additional restrictions may lower the returns to mutual funds.

[16]A 401(k) plan is a retirement program run by a firm for its employees. By investing in a 401(k), employees can defer paying taxes on their investment returns until they start withdrawing funds after they reach 59.5 years.

if all the funds had been in Bear Stearns stock, the 401(k) would be worth only $10,000.

Consequently, many investment advisors recommend investing no more than 5% in employer stock. However, few employees have learned this lesson. Even by 2010, the average share of 401(k) funds invested in company stock was 14%.

Insurance

I detest life-insurance agents; they always argue that I shall some day die, which is not so. —Stephen Leacock

People and firms can also avoid or reduce risk by purchasing insurance. As we've seen, a risk-averse person is willing to pay money—a risk premium—to avoid risk. The demand for risk reduction is met by insurance companies, which bear the risk for anyone who buys an insurance policy. Many risk-averse individuals and firms buy insurance, leading to an industry of enormous size: Global insurance premiums exceeded $4.33 trillion in 2010.[17]

Determining the Amount of Insurance to Buy. Many individuals and firms buy insurance to shift some or all of the risk they face to an insurance company. A risk-averse person or firm pays a premium to the insurance company, and the insurance company transfers money to the policyholder if a bad outcome occurs, such as sickness, an accident, or property loss due to theft or fire.

Because Scott is risk averse, he wants to insure his home, which is worth 500. There is a 20% probability that his home will burn next year. If a fire occurs, the home will be worth nothing.

With no insurance, the expected value of his home is

$$EV = (0.2 \times 0) + (0.8 \times 500) = 400.$$

Scott faces a good deal of risk. The variance of the value of his home is

$$\sigma^2 = [0.2 \times (0 - 400)^2] + [0.8 \times (500 - 400)^2] = 10,000.$$

Suppose that an insurance company offers **fair insurance**: a contract between an insurer and a policyholder in which the expected value of the contract to the policyholder is zero. That is, the insurance is a fair bet. With fair insurance, for every $1 that Scott pays the insurance company, the *premium*, the insurance company will pay Scott $5 to cover the damage if the fire occurs, so that he has $1 less if the fire does not occur, but $4 (= 5 − 1) more if it does occur.

Because Scott is risk averse and the insurance is fair, he wants to *fully insure* by buying enough insurance to eliminate his risk altogether. That is, he wants to buy the amount of fair insurance that will leave him equally well off in both states of nature. That is, he pays a premium of x so that he has $500 - x$ if the fire does not occur, and has $4x$ if the fire occurs, such that $500 - x = 4x$, or $x = 100$.[18] If there is no fire he pays a premium of 100 and has a home worth 500 for a net value of 400. If a fire does occur, Scott pays 100 but receives 500 from the insurance company for a net value of 400. Thus, Scott's wealth is 400 in either case.

---

[17]According to Swiss Re, **www.plunkettresearch.com/insurance-risk-management-market-research/industry-overview** (viewed June 14, 2012).

[18]The expected value of Scott's insurance contract is $[0.8 \times (-100)] + [0.2 \times 400] = 0$, which shows that the insurance is fair.

Although Scott's expected value with full and fair insurance is the same as his expected value without insurance, the variance he faces drops from 10,000 without insurance to 0 with insurance. Scott is better off with full fair insurance because he has the same expected value and faces no risk. A risk averse person always wants full insurance if the insurance is fair.

Sometimes insurance companies put limits on the amount of insurance offered. For example, the insurance company could offer Scott fair insurance but only up to a maximum gross payment of, for example, 400 rather than 500. Given this limit, Scott would buy the maximum amount of fair insurance that he could.

SOLVED PROBLEM 16.5

The local government collects a property tax of 20 on Scott's home. If the tax is collected whether or not the home burns, how much fair insurance does Scott buy? If the tax is collected only if the home does not burn, how much fair insurance does Scott buy?

Answer

1. *Determine the after-tax expected value of the house without insurance.* If the tax is always collected, the house is worth $480 = 500 - 20$ if it does not burn and -20 if it does burn. Thus, the expected value of the house is

$$380 = [0.2 \times (-20)] + [0.8 \times 480].$$

If the tax is collected only if the fire does not occur, the expected value of the house is

$$384 = [0.2 \times 0] + [0.8 \times 480].$$

2. *Calculate the amount of fair insurance Scott buys if the tax is always collected.* Because Scott is risk averse, he wants to be fully insured so that the after-tax value of his home is the same in both states of nature. If the tax is always collected, Scott pays the insurance company 100. If no fire occurs, his net wealth is $500 - 100 - 20 = 380$. If a fire occurs, the insurance company pays 500, or a net payment of 400 above the cost of the insurance, and Scott pays 20 in taxes, leaving him with 380 once again. That is, he buys the same amount of insurance as he would without any taxes. The tax has no effect on his insurance decision because he owes the tax regardless of the state of nature.

3. *Calculate the amount of fair insurance Scott buys if the tax is collected only if there is no fire.* If the tax is collected only if no fire occurs, Scott pays the insurance company 96 and receives 480 if a fire occurs. If there is no fire, Scott's wealth is $500 - 96 - 20 = 384$. If a fire occurs, the insurance company pays 480, so Scott's wealth is $480 - 96 = 384$. Thus, he has the same after-tax wealth in both states of nature.

Comment: Because the tax system is partially insuring Scott by dropping the tax in the bad state of nature, he purchases less private insurance, 480, than the 500 he buys if the tax is collected in both states of nature.

Fairness and Insurance. We have been examining situations where the insurance is fair so that the customer's insurance contract has an expected value of zero. However, an insurance company could not stay in business if it offered fair insurance. With fair insurance, the insurance company's expected payments would equal the premiums that the insurance company collects. Because the insurance company has operating expenses, it loses money if it provides fair insurance. Thus, we expect that real-world insurance companies offer unfair insurance, charging a premium that exceeds the fair-insurance premium. Although a risk-averse consumer fully insures if offered fair insurance, they will buy less than full insurance if insurance is unfair.[19]

How much can insurance companies charge for insurance? A monopoly insurance company could charge an amount up to the risk premium a person is willing to pay to avoid risk. For example, in Figure 16.2, Irma would be willing to pay up to $14 for an insurance policy that would compensate her if her stock did not perform well. The more risk averse an individual is, the more a monopoly insurance company can charge. If there are many insurance companies competing for business, the price of an insurance policy is less than the maximum that risk-averse individuals are willing to pay—but still high enough that the firms can cover their operating expenses.

Insurance Only for Diversifiable Risks. Why is an insurance company willing to sell policies and take on risk? By pooling the risks of many people, the insurance company can lower its risk much below that of any individual. If the probability that one car is stolen is independent of whether other cars are stolen, the risk to an insurance company of insuring one person against car theft is much greater than the average risk of insuring many people.

However, if the risks from disasters to its policyholders are highly positively correlated, an insurance company is not well diversified just by holding many policies. A war affects all policyholders, so the outcomes that they face are perfectly correlated. Because wars are *nondiversifiable risks*, insurance companies normally do not offer policies insuring against wars.

APPLICATION

Limited Insurance for Natural Disasters

Losses from natural catastrophes have increased significantly in recent years (Kunreuther and Heal, 2012). Worldwide, the insurance industry shelled out $110 billion in 2011 due to record flooding and earthquake losses.

Insurance companies increasingly refuse to offer hurricane or earthquake insurance in many parts of the world because they are relatively nondiversifiable risks. When Nationwide Insurance Company announced that it was sharply curtailing sales of new policies along the Gulf of Mexico and the eastern seaboard from Texas to Maine, a company official explained, "Prudence requires us to diligently manage our exposure to catastrophic losses."

Insurers paid out $12.5 billion in claims to residential homeowners after the 1994 Los Angeles earthquake. Farmers Insurance Group reported that it paid out three times more for the Los Angeles earthquake than it had collected in earthquake premiums over the previous 30 years.

Japan's 2011 magnitude 9.0 earthquake and the associated tsunami was the most costly in history, with estimated losses other than from nuclear-related damage of more than $210 billion (with some estimates as high as $350 billion). However, the insurance industry paid only about $35 billion, or about 17%, because of Japan's low levels of earthquake insurance protection.

When private companies stop offering insurance, governments sometimes take their place. Since 2008, the U.S. government has provided flood insurance. It has

---

[19]As Solved Problem 16.5 shows, tax laws may offset the problem of unfair insurance, so that some insurance may be fair or more than fair after taxes.

insured over 5.6 million Americans against floods associated with hurricanes, tropical storms, heavy rains, and other conditions. However, Congress has not provided consistent funding for this program, which lapsed at least four times in 2010 alone. Thus, consumers may not be able to count on federal flood insurance always being available.

In some high-risk areas, state-run insurance pools—such as the Florida Joint Underwriting Association and the California Earthquake Authority—provide households with insurance. By the end of 2011, more than 35 government hurricane insurance programs provided 3.3 million households with insurance. Some hurricane insurance is more than fair—that is, the governments subsidize policyholders. However, the earthquake policies often set rates that are at least three times more expensive than previous private insurance.

16.4 Investing Under Uncertainty

Don't invest money with any brokerage firm in which one of the partners is named Frenchy. —Woody Allen

We now investigate how uncertainty affects the investment decision. In particular, we examine how attitudes toward risk affect individuals' willingness to invest, how people evaluate risky investments that last for many periods, and how investors pay to alter their probabilities of success.

In the following examples, the owner of a monopoly decides whether to open a new store. Because the firm is a monopoly, the owner's return from the investment does not depend on the actions of other firms. As a result, the owner faces no strategic considerations. The owner knows the cost of the investment but is unsure about how many people will patronize the new store; hence, the profits are uncertain.

How Investing Depends on Attitudes Toward Risk

We start by considering an investor who is only interested in the uncertain payoff for this year, so that we can ignore the problem of discounting the future profits. Whether the owner invests depends on how risk averse he or she is and on the risks involved.

We first consider the decision of Chris, a risk-neutral owner. Because she is risk neutral, she invests if the expected value of the firm rises due to the investment. Any action that increases her expected value must also increase her expected utility because she is indifferent to risk. In contrast in the next example, Ken is risk averse, so he might not make an investment that increases his firm's expected value if the investment is very risky. That is, maximizing expected value does not necessarily maximize his expected utility.

Risk-Neutral Investing. Chris, the risk-neutral owner of the monopoly, uses a *decision tree* (panel a of Figure 16.4) to decide whether to invest. The rectangle, called a *decision node*, indicates that she must make a decision about whether to invest or not. The circle, a *chance node*, denotes that a random process determines the outcome (consistent with the given probabilities). If Chris does not open the new store, she makes 0. If she opens the new store, she expects to make 200 with 80% probability and to lose 100 with 20% probability. The expected value from a new store (see the circle in panel a) is

$$EV = (0.8 \times 200) + [0.2 \times (-100)] = 140.$$

Because she is risk neutral, she prefers an expected value of 140 to a certain one of 0, so she invests. Thus, her expected value in the rectangle is 140.

Figure 16.4 Investment Decision Tree with Uncertainty

Chris and Ken, each the owner of a monopoly, must decide whether to invest in a new store. (a) The expected value of the investment is 140, so it pays for Chris, who is risk-neutral, to invest. (b) Ken is so risk averse that he does not invest even though the expected value of the investment is positive. His expected utility falls if he makes this risky investment.

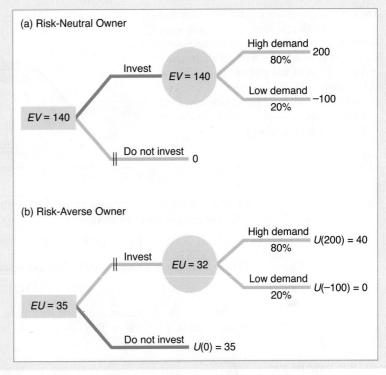

Risk-Averse Investing. We can compare Chris's decision to that of Ken, a risk-averse owner of a monopoly who faces the same investment decision. Ken invests in the new store if his expected utility from investing is greater than his certain utility from not investing. Panel b of Figure 16.4 shows the decision tree for a particular risk-averse utility function. The circle shows that Ken's expected utility from the investment is

$$EU = [0.2 \times U(-100)] + [0.8 \times U(200)]$$
$$= (0.2 \times 0) + (0.8 \times 40) = 32.$$

Ken's certain utility from not investing is $U(\$0) = 35$, which is greater than 32. Thus, Ken does not invest. As a result, his expected utility in the rectangle is 35 (his certain utility from not investing).

Investing with Uncertainty and Discounting

Now suppose that the uncertain returns or costs from an investment are spread out over time. In Chapter 15, we derived an investment rule by which we know future costs and returns with certainty. We concluded that an investment pays if its *net present value* (calculated by discounting the difference between the return and the cost in each future period) is positive.

How does this rule change if the returns are uncertain? A risk-neutral person chooses to invest if the *expected net present value* is positive. We calculate the expected net present value by discounting the difference between expected return and expected cost in each future period.

Sam is risk neutral. His decision tree, Figure 16.5, shows that his cost of investing is $C = \$25$ this year. Next year, he receives uncertain revenues from the investment

Figure 16.5 Investment Decision Tree with Uncertainty and Discounting

The risk-neutral owner invests if the expected net present value is positive. The expected value, *EV*, of the revenue from the investment next year is $110. With an interest rate of 10%, the expected present value, *EPV*, of the revenue is $100. The expected net present value, *ENPV*, is *EPV* = $100 minus the $25 cost of the investment this year, which is $75. The owner therefore invests.

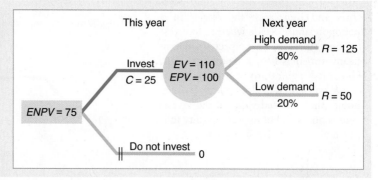

of $125 with 80% probability or $50 with 20% probability. Thus, the expected value of the revenues next year is

$$EV = (0.8 \times \$125) + (0.2 \times \$50) = \$110.$$

With a real interest rate of 10%, the expected present value of the revenues is

$$EPV = \$110/1.1 = \$100.$$

Subtracting the $25 cost incurred this year, Sam determines that his expected net present value is *ENPV* = $75. As a result, he invests.

SOLVED PROBLEM 16.6

We have been assuming that nature dictates the probabilities of various possible events. However, sometimes we can alter the probabilities at some expense. Gautam, who is risk neutral, is considering whether to invest in a new store, as the figure shows. After investing, he can increase the probability that demand will be high at the new store by advertising at a cost of $50 (thousand). If he makes the investment but does not advertise, he has a 40% probability of making 100 and a 60% probability of losing 100. Should he invest in the new store?

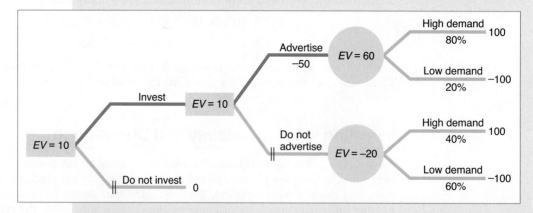

Answer

1. *Calculate the expected value of the investment and determine if it pays if Gautam does not advertise.* If Gautam makes the investment but does not advertise, the expected value of his investment is

$$[0.4 \times 100] + [0.6 \times (-100)] = -20.$$

> Thus, if he does not advertise, he expects to lose money if he makes this investment.
>
> 2. *Calculate the expected value of the investment and determine if it pays given that Gautam advertises.* With advertising, Gautam's expected value before paying for the advertisements is
>
> $$[0.8 \times 100] + [0.2 \times (-100)] = 60.$$
>
> Thus, his expected value after paying for the advertisements is 10 (= 60 − 50). As a result, he is better off investing and advertising than not investing at all or investing without advertising.

16.5 Behavioral Economics and Uncertainty

In the expected utility model, as in the standard utility model, we assume that people make rational choices (Chapter 3). However, many individuals make choices that are inconsistent with the predictions of the expected utility model. Economists and psychologists explain some of these departures from the predictions of the expected utility model using behavioral economics. Researchers have established that some people have difficulty determining probabilities or making probability calculations. Through experiments, they've shown that many people behave differently under certain circumstances than others. New theories have been developed to explain behavior that is inconsistent with expected utility theory.

Biased Assessment of Probabilities

People often have mistaken beliefs about the probability that an event will occur. These biases in estimating probabilities come from several sources, including false beliefs about causality and overconfidence.

Gambler's Fallacy. Many people fall victim to the *gambler's fallacy*: the false belief that past events affect current, independent outcomes.[20] For example, suppose that you flip a fair coin and it comes up heads six times in a row. What are the odds that you'll get a tail on the next flip? Because past flips do not affect this one, the chance of a tail remains 50%, yet many people believe that a head is much more likely because they're on a "run." Others hold the opposite but equally false view that the chance of a tail is high because a tail is "due."

Suppose that you have an urn with three black balls and two red ones. If you draw a ball without looking, your probability of getting a black ball is $\frac{3}{5} = 60\%$. If you replace the ball and draw again, the chance of a picking a black ball remains the same. However, if you draw a black ball and do not replace it, the probability of drawing a black ball again falls to $\frac{2}{4} = 50\%$. Thus, the belief that a tail is due after several heads are tossed in a row is analogous to falsely believing that you are drawing without replacement when you are actually drawing with replacement.

Overconfidence. Another common explanation for why some people engage in gambles that the rest of us avoid like the plague is that these gamblers are overconfident. For example, Golec and Tamarkin (1995) found that football bettors tend to

---

[20]The false belief that that one event affects another independent event is captured by the joke about a man who brings a bomb on board a plane whenever he flies because he believes that "The chance of having one bomb on a plane is very small, so the chance of having two bombs onboard is near zero!"

make low-probability bets because they greatly overestimate their probabilities of winning certain types of exotic football bets (an *exotic bet* depends on the outcome of more than one game). In a survey, gamblers estimated their chance of winning a particular bet at 45% when the objective probability was 20%.

Few groups exhibit more overconfidence than male high school athletes. Many U.S. high school basketball and football players believe they will get an athletic scholarship to attend college, but less than 5% receive one. Of this elite group, about 25% expect to become professional athletes, but only about 1.5% succeed. Of high school athletes, only 0.03% make it to the pros.[21]

APPLICATION

Biased Estimates

Do scare stories in newspapers, TV shows, and movies cause people to overestimate relatively rare events and underestimate relatively common ones? Newspapers are more likely to publish "man bites dog" stories than the more common "dog bites man" reports.[22]

If you have seen the movie *Jaws*, you can't help but think about sharks before wading into the ocean. In 2012, newspapers around the world reported that a mother saved her daughter from a shark attack off a Florida beach and an Australian man suffered a major gash in his leg from a shark. Do you worry about shark attacks? You really shouldn't.

Only seven people were killed by sharks in U.S. waters from 2002 through 2011—an average of 0.7 a year. (Worldwide, 51 were killed by sharks during this period, or 5.1 a year.) You're just as likely to die from beanbag chair suffocation, more than twice as likely to die from being crushed by a soda machine toppling on you, 10 times more likely to meet your maker in a roller skating accident, and 325 times more likely to die in a collision with a deer. A typical American's chance of dying from a shark attack is 1 in 3.7 million, 1 in 80,000 from lightning, 1 in 14,000 from sun or heat exposure, 1 in 218 from a fall, 1 in 84 from a car accident, 1 in 63 from flu, 1 in 38 from hospital infection, 1 in 24 from a stroke, 1 in 7 from cancer, and 1 in 5 from a heart attack.

When asked to estimate the probability of dying from various causes for the entire population, people overestimate the number of deaths from infrequent causes and underestimate those from more common causes (Benjamin et al., 2001). In contrast, when asked to estimate the number of deaths among their own age group, their estimates are almost completely unbiased. That is not to say that people know the true probabilities—only that their mistakes are not systematic. (However, you should know that, despite the widespread warnings issued every Christmas season, poinsettias are not poisonous.)

Violations of Expected Utility Theory

Over the years, economists and psychologists have shown that some people's choices vary with circumstances, which contradicts expected utility theory. One important class of violations arises because people change their choices in response to

---

[21]See Rossi and Armstrong (1989) and **www.ncaa.org/wps/wcm/connect/public/test/issues/recruiting/probability+of+going+pro** (viewed July 26, 2012).

[22]For example, Indian papers reported on a man bites snake story, noting that Neeranjan Bhaskar has eaten more than 4,000 snakes (*Calcutta Telegraph*, August 1, 2005) and the even stranger "Cobra Dies after Biting Priest of Snake Temple!" (*Express India*, July 11, 2005). In California, police reported that a python underwent emergency surgery after a man allegedly bit the creature twice (*San Francisco Chronicle*, September 2, 2011).

inessential changes in how choices are described or *framed*, even when the underlying probabilities and events do not change. Another class of violations arises because of a bias toward certainty.

Framing. Many people reverse their preferences when a problem is presented or *framed* in different but equivalent ways. Kahneman and Tversky (1981) posed the problem that the United States expects an unusual disease, such as avian flu, to kill 600 people. The government is considering two alternative programs to combat the disease. The "exact scientific estimates" of the consequences of these programs are

- If Program A is adopted, 200 people will be saved.
- If Program B is adopted, there is a one-third probability that 600 people will be saved and a two-thirds probability that no one will be saved.

When college students were asked to choose, 72% opted for the certain gains of Program A over the possibly larger but riskier gains of Program B.

A second group of students was asked to choose between an alternative pair of programs, and were told

- If Program C is adopted, 400 people will die.
- If Program D is adopted, there is a one-third probability that no one will die, and a two-thirds probability that 600 people will die.

When faced with this choice, 78% chose the larger but uncertain losses of Program D over the certain losses of Program C. These results are surprising if people maximize their expected utility: Program A is identical to Program C and Program B is the same as Program D in the sense that these pairs have identical expected outcomes. Thus, expected utility theory predicts consistent choices for the two pairs of programs.

In many similar experiments, researchers have repeatedly observed this pattern, called the *reflection effect*: attitudes toward risk are reversed (reflected) for gains versus losses. People are often risk averse when making choices involving gains, but they are often risk preferring when making choices involving losses.

Certainty Effect. Many people put excessive weight on outcomes that they consider to be certain relative to risky outcomes. This *certainty effect* (or *Allais effect*, named for the French economist who first noticed it) can be illustrated using an example from Kahneman and Tversky (1979). First, a group of subjects were asked to choose between two options:

- **Option A.** You receive $4,000 with probability 80% and $0 with probability 20%.
- **Option B.** You receive $3,000 with certainty.

The vast majority, 80%, chose the certain outcome, B.

Then, the subjects were given another set of options:

- **Option C.** You receive $4,000 with probability 20% and $0 with probability 80%.
- **Option D.** You receive $3,000 with probability 25% and $0 with probability 75%.

Now, 65% prefer C.

Kahneman and Tversky found that more than half the respondents violated expected utility theory by choosing B in the first experiment and C in the second one. If $U(0) = 0$, then choosing B over A implies that the expected utility from B is greater than the expected utility from A, so that $U(3,000) > 0.8U(4,000)$, or $U(3,000)/U(4,000) > 0.8$. Choosing C over D implies that $0.2U(4,000) > 0.25U(3,000)$, or $U(3,000)/U(4,000) < 0.8 \,(= 0.2/0.25)$. Thus, these choices are inconsistent with each other, and hence inconsistent with expected utility theory.

Expected utility theory is based on gambles with known probabilities, whereas most real-world situations involve unknown or subjective probabilities. Ellsberg (1961) pointed out that expected utility theory cannot account for an ambiguous situation where many people are reluctant to put substantial decision weight on any outcome. He illustrated the problem in a "paradox." There are two urns, each with 100 red and black balls. In the first urn, you know that there are 50 red and 50 black balls. In the second urn, you do not know the ratio of red to black balls. Most of us would agree that the known probability of drawing a red from the first urn equals the subjective probability of drawing a red from the second urn. Yet, most people would prefer to bet that a red ball will be drawn from the first urn than from the second urn.

Prospect Theory

Kahneman and Tversky's (1979) *prospect theory*, an alternative theory of decision making under uncertainty, can explain some of the choices people make that are inconsistent with expected utility theory. According to *prospect theory*, people are concerned about gains and losses—the changes in wealth—rather than the level of wealth, as in expected utility theory. People start with a reference point and consider lower outcomes as losses and higher ones as gains.

Comparing Expected Utility and Prospect Theories. We can illustrate the differences in the two theories by comparing how people would act under the two theories when facing the same situation. Both Muzhe and Rui have initial wealth W. They may choose a gamble where they get A dollars with probability θ or B dollars with probability $1 - \theta$. For example, A might be negative, reflecting a loss, and B might be a positive, indicating a gain.

Muzhe wants to maximize his expected utility. If he does not gamble, his utility is $U(W)$. To calculate his expected utility if he gambles, Muzhe uses the probabilities θ and $1 - \theta$ to weight the utilities from the two possible outcomes:

$$EU = \theta U(W + A) + (1 - \theta)U(W + B),$$

where $U(W + A)$ is the utility he gets from his after-gambling wealth if A occurs and $U(W + B)$ is the utility if he receives B. He chooses to gamble if his expected utility from gambling exceeds his certain utility from his initial wealth: $EU > U(W)$.

In contrast, Rui's decisions are consistent with prospect theory. Rui compares the gamble to her current reference point, which is her initial situation where she has W with certainty. The value she places on her reference point is $V(0)$, where 0 indicates that she has neither a gain nor a loss with this certain outcome. The negative value that she places on losing is $V(A)$, and the positive value from winning is $V(B)$.

To determine the value from taking the gamble, Rui does not calculate the expectation using the probabilities θ and $1 - \theta$, as she would with expected utility theory. Rather, she uses *decision weights* $w(\theta)$ and $w(1 - \theta)$, where the w function assigns a weight that differs the original probabilities. If people assign disproportionately high weights to rare events (see the application "Biased Estimates"), the weight $w(\theta)$ exceeds θ for low values of θ and is less for high values of θ.

Properties of Prospect Theory. To resolve various choice mysteries, the prospect theory value function, V, corresponds to an S-shaped curve, as in Figure 16.6. This

Figure 16.6 Prospect Theory Value Function

The prospect theory value function has an S shape. It passes through the reference point at the origin because gains and losses are measured relative to the initial condition. Because both sections of the curve are concave to the outcome axis, decision makers are less sensitive to a given change in the outcome for large gains or losses than for small ones. Because the curve is asymmetric with respect to gains and losses, people treat gains and losses differently. This S-curve shows a bigger impact to a loss than to a comparable size gain, reflecting loss aversion.

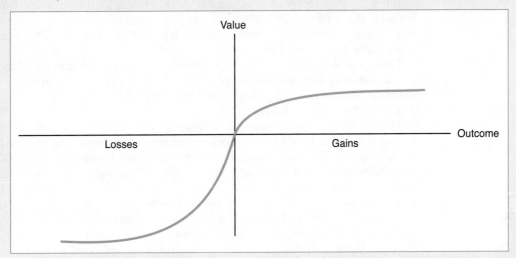

curve has three properties. First, the curve passes through the reference point at the origin, because gains and losses are determined relative to the initial situation where there is no gain or loss.

Second, both sections of the curve are concave to the horizontal, outcome axis. Because of this curvature, Rui is less sensitive to a given change in the outcome for large gains or losses than for small ones. For example, she cares more about whether she has a loss of $1 rather than $2 than she does about a loss of $1,001 rather than $1,002.

Third, the curve is asymmetric with respect to gains and losses. People treat gains and losses differently, in contrast to the predictions of expected utility theory. The S-curve in the figure shows that people suffer more from a loss than they benefit from a comparable size gain. That is, the value function reflects *loss aversion*: people dislike making losses more than they like making gains.

Given the subjective weights, valuations based on gains and losses, and the shape of the value curve, prospect theory can resolve some of the behavioral mysteries of choice under uncertainty. Because the S-shaped curve shows that people treat gains and losses differently, it can explain the reflection effect in the disease experiment described earlier in this section, where people make different choices when identical outcomes are stated in terms of lives saved instead of lives lost. It also provides an explanation as to why some people engage in unfair lotteries: They put heavier weight on rare events than the true probability used in expected utility theory.

Similarly, we could use a weighting function to resolve the Ellsberg paradox. For example, with the urn containing an unknown ratio of black and red balls, an individual might put 40% on getting a black ball, 40% on getting a red ball, and leave 20% to capture an unwillingness to take a gamble when faced with substantial ambiguity. Doing so reduces the expected value of the gamble relative to that of the initial, certain situation in which one does not gamble.

That airline that doesn't kill me makes me stronger.

We can now answer the Challenge questions. What are the chances of a given flight crashing? Given that probability, should I buy Travel Guard (TG) flight insurance for my next flight for which I pay them $23 and my family receives $200,000 if I die in an accident on that flight?

If θ is my probability of dying on a flight, my family's expected value from this bet with TG is $[\theta \times 200{,}000] - 23$. For this insurance to be fair, this expected this expected value must be zero, which is true if $\theta = 0.000115$. That is, one in every 8,696 passengers dies.

How great *is* the danger of being in a fatal commercial airline crash? According to the National Transportation Safety Board, there were no fatalities on scheduled U.S. commercial airline flights in 1993, 1998, 2002, 2007, 2008, 2010, and 2011 (and none through May 2012).

In 2001, the probability was much higher than any other year because of the 525 on-board deaths caused by the terrorist hijacking and crashes on September 11 and the subsequent sharp reduction in the number of flights. However, even in 2001, the probability was 0.00000077, or 1 in 1.4 million fliers—still much lower than the probability that makes TG's insurance a fair bet. For the decade 2002–2011, the probability was 0.00000002 risk of one fatality per 51 million fliers.

Suppose that the probability of a fatal accident per flight (rather than per passenger) is 0.00000088, the probability from 2002 through 2011. If I randomly choose a flight each day for 10 years, the probability of avoiding a fatal crash is 99.7%. After 100 years of flying every day, the probability drops to only 96.8%. Indeed, only by flying every day for about 2,150 years would the probability of a fatal accident reach 50%. (For most people, the greatest risk of an airplane trip is the drive to and from the airport. Twice as many people are killed in vehicle-deer collisions than in plane crashes.)

Given that my chance of dying in a fatal crash is $\theta = 0.00000002$ (the rate for the decade 2002–2011), the fair rate to pay for $200,000 of flight insurance is about 0.4¢. TG is offering to charge me 5,750 times more than the fair rate for this insurance.

I would have to be incredibly risk averse to be tempted by their kind offer. Even if I were that risk averse, I would be much better off buying general life insurance, which is much less expensive than flight insurance and covers accidental death from all types of accidents and diseases.

SUMMARY

1. **Assessing Risk.** A probability measures the likelihood that a particular state of nature occurs. People use historical frequencies to calculate probabilities. If they lack frequencies, people may form subjective estimates of a probability using other information. The expected value is the probability-weighted average of the values in each state of nature. One widely used measure of risk is the variance (or the standard deviation, which is the square root of the variance). The variance is the probability-weighted average of the squared difference between the value in each state of nature and the expected value.

2. **Attitudes Toward Risk.** Whether people choose a risky option over a nonrisky one depends on their attitudes toward risk and the expected payoffs of the various options. Most people are *risk averse*. They choose a riskier option only if its expected value is sufficiently higher than that of a less risky option. *Risk-neutral* people choose the option with the highest rate of return because they do not care about risk. *Risk-preferring* people may choose the riskier option even if it has a lower rate of return because they like risk. They will give up some expected return to take on more risk. A utility function reflects a person's

attitude toward risk. People pick the option with the highest expected utility. Expected utility is the probability-weighted average of the utility from the outcomes in the various states of nature. The larger an individual's Arrow-Pratt measure of risk aversion, the less likely that person will take a small gamble.

3. **Reducing Risk.** People reduce their risk in several ways. They can avoid some risks, and take actions to lower the probabilities of bad events. They might act to reduce the harm from bad events. Investors make better choices if they have more information. Unless returns to the different investments are perfectly positively correlated, diversification reduces risk. Insurance companies diversify by pooling risks across many individuals.

Insurance is fair if the expected return to the policy-holder is zero: the expected payout equals the premium paid. Risk-averse people fully insure if they are offered fair insurance. Because insurance companies must earn enough income to cover their costs, they offer insurance that is unfair. Risk averse people often buy unfair insurance, but they buy less than full insurance. When buying unfair insurance, policy-holders exchange the risk of a large loss for the certainty of a smaller loss (paying the premium).

4. **Investing Under Uncertainty.** Whether an individual invests depends on the uncertainty of the payoff, the expected return, the individual's attitudes toward risk, the interest rate, and the cost of altering the likelihood of a good outcome. An investment pays for risk-neutral people if the expected net present value is positive. Risk-averse people invest only if investing raises their expected utilities. Thus, risk-averse people make risky investments if those investments pay higher rates of return than do safer investments. If an investment takes place over time, a risk-neutral investor invests if the expected net present value is positive. People pay to alter the probabilities of various outcomes from an investment if doing so raises their expected utility.

5. **Behavioral Economics and Uncertainty.** Some people's actions in uncertain situations are inconsistent with expected utility theory. Their choices may be due to biased estimates of probabilities or different objectives than maximizing expected utility. Prospect theory explains some of these puzzling choices. Under this theory, people may care more about losses than gains and weight outcomes differently than with the probabilities used in expected utility theory.

EXERCISES

■ = *exercise is available on* MyEconLab; * = *answer appears at the back of this book;* **M** = *mathematical problem.*

1. Assessing Risk

1.1 In a neighborhood with 1,000 houses, 5 catch fire (but are not damaged by high winds), 7 are damaged by high winds (but do not catch fire), and the rest are unharmed during a one-year period. What is the probability that a house is harmed by fire or high winds? **M**

*1.2 Asa buys a painting. There is a 20% probability that the artist will become famous and the painting will be worth $1,000. There is a 10% probability that the painting will be destroyed by fire or another disaster and become worthless. If the painting is not destroyed and the artist does not become famous, it will be worth $500. What is the expected value of the painting? **M**

*1.3 By next year, your stock has a 25% chance of being worth $400 and a 75% probability of being worth $200. What are the expected value and the variance?

1.4 The EZ Construction Company is offered a $20,000 contract to build a new deck for a house. The company's profit if they do not have to sink piers (vertical supports) down to bedrock will be $4,000. However, if they have to sink the piers, they

will lose $1,000. The probability they will have to put in the piers is 25%. What is the expected value of this contract? Now, EZ learns that it can obtain a seismic study of the property that would specify whether piers have to be sunk before EZ must accept or reject this contract. By how much would the seismic study increase EZ's expected value? What is the most that it will pay for such a study? (*Hint:* See Solved Problem 16.1.) **M**

1.5 What is the difference—if any—between an individual gambling at a casino and gambling by buying a stock? What is the difference for society?

*1.6 To discourage people from breaking the traffic laws, society can increase the probability that someone exceeding the speed limit will be caught and punished, or it can increase the size of the fine for speeding. Explain why either method can be used to discourage speeding. Which approach is a government likely to prefer, and why?

1.7 Suppose that most people will not speed if the expected fine is at least $500. The actual fine for speeding is $800. How high must the probability of being caught and convicted be to discourage speeding? **M**

2. Attitudes Toward Risk

2.1 Guojun offers to bet Kristin that if a six-sided die comes up with one or two dots showing, he will pay her $3, but if it comes up with any other number of dots, she'll owe him $2. Is that a fair bet for Kristin? **M**

2.2 Jen's utility function with respect to wealth is $U(W) = \sqrt{W}$. Plot her utility function. Use your figure and calculus to show that Jen is risk averse. (*Hint:* You can also use calculus to see if she is risk averse by determining the sign of the second derivative of the utility function.) **M**

*2.3 Jen, in Exercise 2.2, may buy Stock A or Stock B. Stock A has a 50% chance of being worth $100 and 50% of being worth $200. Stock B's value is $50 with a change of a half or $250 with a probability of 50%. Show that the two stocks have an equal expected value but different variances. Show that Jen prefers Stock A to Stock B because her expected utility is higher with Stock A. **M**

2.4 Suppose that an individual is risk averse and has to choose between $100 with certainty and a risky option with two equally likely outcomes: $100 - x$ and $100 + x$. Use a graph (or math) to show that this person's risk premium is smaller, the smaller x is (the less variable the gamble is).

*2.5 Given the information in Solved Problem 16.2, Irma prefers to buy the stock. Show graphically how high her certain wealth would have to be for her to choose not to buy the stock.

2.6 In Solved Problem 16.3, what is Jen's risk premium if her utility function were $\ln(W)$? **M**

*2.7 Hugo has a concave utility function of $U(W) = W^{0.5}$. His only asset is shares in an Internet start-up company. Tomorrow he will learn the stock's value. He believes that it is worth $144 with probability $\frac{2}{3}$ and $225 with probability $\frac{1}{3}$. What is his expected utility? What risk premium would he pay to avoid bearing this risk? (*Hint:* See Solved Problem 16.3.) **M**

2.8 Mary's utility function is $U(W) = W^{0.33}$, where W is wealth. Is she risk averse? Mary has an initial wealth of $27,000. How much of a risk premium would she require to participate in a gamble that has a 50% probability of raising her wealth to $29,791 and a 50% probability of lowering her wealth to $24,389? (*Hint:* See Solved Problem 16.3 and the discussion of the risk premium in Figure 16.2.) **M**

2.9 Would risk-neutral people ever buy insurance that was not fair (that was biased against them)? Explain.

2.10 Lisa just inherited a vineyard from a distant relative. In good years (when there is no rain or frost during harvest season), she earns $100,000 from the sale of grapes from the vineyard. If the weather is poor, she loses $20,000. Lisa's estimate of the probability of good weather is 60%.

a. Calculate the expected value and the variance of Lisa's income from the vineyard.

b. Lisa is risk averse. Ethan, a grape buyer, offers Lisa a guaranteed payment of $70,000 each year in exchange for her entire harvest. Will Lisa accept this offer? Explain.

c. Why might Ethan make such an offer?

2.11 Joanna is considering three possible jobs. The following table shows the possible incomes she might get in each job.

	Outcome A		Outcome B	
	Probability	Earnings	Probability	Earnings
Job 1	0.5	20	0.5	40
Job 2	0.3	15	0.7	45
Job 3	1	30		

For each job, calculate the expected value, the variance and the standard deviation. If Joanna is averse to risk (as measured by variance), what can you predict about her job choice? What if she is risk neutral?

2.12 Suppose that Irma's utility function with respect to wealth is $U(W) = 100 + 100W - W^2$. Show that for $W < 10$, Irma's Arrow-Pratt risk-aversion measure increases with her wealth. (*Hint:* See Solved Problem 16.4.) **M**

2.13 Carolyn and Sanjay are neighbors. Each owns a car valued at $10,000. Neither has comprehensive insurance (which covers losses due to theft). Carolyn's wealth, including the value of her car is $80,000. Sanjay's wealth, including the value of his car is $20,000. Carolyn and Sanjay have identical utility of wealth functions, $U(W) = W^{0.4}$. Carolyn and Sanjay can park their cars on the street or rent space in a garage. In their neighborhood, there is a 50% probability that a street-parked car will be stolen during the year. A garage-parked car will not be stolen.

a. What is the largest amount that Carolyn is willing to pay to park her car in a garage? What is the maximum amount that Sanjay is willing to pay?

b. Compare Carolyn's willingness-to-pay to Sanjay's. Why do they differ? Include a comparison of their Arrow-Pratt measures of risk aversion. (*Hint*: See Solved Problem 16.4.) **M**

3. Reducing Risk

3.1 Lori, who is risk averse, has two pieces of jewelry, each worth $1,000. She plans to send them to her sister's firm in Thailand to be sold there. She is concerned about the safety of shipping them. She believes that the probability that any box shipped will not reach its destination is θ. Is her expected utility higher if she sends the articles together or in two separate shipments? **M**

3.2 Helen, the owner of Dubrow Labs, worries about the firm being sued for botched results from blood tests. If it isn't sued, the firm expects to earn a profit of 100, but if it is successfully sued, its profit will be 10. Helen believes that the probability of a successful suit is 5%. If fair insurance is available and Helen is risk averse, how much insurance will she buy? (*Hint*: You may only be able to express your answer as an inequality.) **M**

3.3 Jill possesses $160,000 worth of valuables. She faces a 0.2 probability of a burglary, where she would lose jewelry worth $70,000. She can buy an insurance policy for $15,000 that would fully reimburse the $70,000. Her utility function is $U(X) = 4X^{0.5}$.

   a. What is the actuarially fair price for the insurance policy?

   b. Should she buy this insurance policy?

   c. What is the most that she is willing to pay for an insurance policy that fully covers it against loss? **M**

3.4 An insurance agent (interviewed in Jonathan Clements, "Dare to Live Dangerously: Passing on Some Insurance Can Pay Off," *Wall Street Journal*, July 23, 2005, D1) states, "On paper, it never makes sense to have a policy with low deductibles or carry collision on an old car." But the agent notes that raising deductibles and dropping collision coverage can be a tough decision for people with a low income or little savings. Collision insurance is the coverage on a policyholder's own car for accidents where another driver is not at fault.

   a. Suppose that the loss is $4,000 if an old car is in an accident. During the six-month coverage period, the probability that the insured person is found at fault in an accident is $\frac{1}{36}$. Suppose that the price of the coverage is $150. Should a wealthy person purchase the coverage? Should a poor person purchase the coverage? Do your answers depend on the policyholder's degree of risk aversion? Does the policyholder's degree of risk aversion depend on his or her wealth?

   b. The agent advises wealthy people not to purchase insurance to protect against possible small losses. Why? **M**

3.5 After Hurricane Katrina in 2005, the government offered subsidies to people whose houses were destroyed. How does the expectation that subsidies will be offered again for future major disasters affect the probability that risk-averse people will buy insurance and the amount they buy? Use a utility function for a risk-averse person to illustrate your answer. (*Hint*: See Solved Problem 16.5.)

4. Investing Under Uncertainty

*4.1 Andy and Kim live together. Andy may invest $10,000 (possibly by taking on an extra job to earn the additional money) in Kim's MBA education this year. This investment will raise the current value of Kim's earnings by $24,000. If they stay together, they will share the benefit from the additional earnings. However, the probability is $\frac{1}{2}$ that they will split up in the future. If they were married and then split, Andy would get half of Kim's additional earnings. If they were living together without any legal ties and they split, then Andy would get nothing. Suppose that Andy is risk neutral. Will Andy invest in Kim's education? Does your answer depend on the couple's legal status? **M**

4.2 Use a decision tree to illustrate how a risk-neutral plaintiff in a lawsuit decides whether to settle a claim or go to trial. The defendants offer $50,000 to settle now. If the plaintiff does not settle, the plaintiff believes that the probability of winning at trial is 60%. If the plaintiff wins, the amount awarded is x. How large can x be before the plaintiff refuses to settle? How does the plaintiff's attitude toward risk affect this decision? **M**

4.3 Use a decision tree to illustrate how a kidney patient would decide whether to have a transplant operation. The patient currently uses a dialysis machine, which lowers her utility. If the operation is successful, her utility will return to its level before the onset of her kidney disease. However, there is a 5% probability that she will die if she has the operation. (If it will help, make up utility numbers to illustrate your answer.)

4.4 Robert Green repeatedly and painstakingly applied herbicides to kill weeds that would harm his beet crops in 2007. However, in 2008, he planted beets genetically engineered to withstand Monsanto's Roundup herbicide. Roundup destroys weeds but leaves the crop unharmed, thereby saving a farmer thousands of dollars in tractor fuel and labor (Andrew Pollack, "Round 2 for Biotech Beets," *New*

York Times, November 27, 2007). However, this policy is risky. In the past when beet breeders announced they were going to use Roundup-resistant seeds, sugar-using food companies like Hershey and Mars objected, fearing consumer resistance. Now, though, sensing that consumer concerns have subsided, many processors have cleared their growers to plant the Roundup-resistant beets. A Kellogg spokeswoman said her company was willing to use such beets, but Hershey and Mars declined to comment. Thus, a farmer like Mr. Green faces risks by switching to Roundup Ready beets. Use a decision tree to illustrate the analysis that a farmer in this situation needs to do.

4.5 In Solved Problem 16.6, advertising increases the probability of high demand to 80%. What is the minimum probability of high demand resulting from advertising such that Gautam decides to invest and advertise? **M**

5. Behavioral Economics and Uncertainty

5.1 Before reading the rest of this exercise, answer the following two questions about your preferences:

a. You are given $5,000 and offered a choice between receiving an extra $2,500 with certainty or flipping a coin and getting $5,000 more if heads or $0 if tails. Which option do you prefer?

b. You are given $10,000 if you will make the following choice: return $2,500 or flip a coin and return $5,000 if heads and $0 if tails. Which option do you prefer?

Most people choose the sure $2,500 in the first case but flip the coin in the second. Explain why this behavior is not consistent. What do you conclude about how people make decisions concerning uncertain events? **M**

5.2 What are the major differences between expected utility theory and prospect theory?

5.3 Draw an individual's utility curve to illustrate that the person is risk-averse with respect to a loss but is risk-preferring with respect to a gain.

5.4 Evan is risk-seeking with respect to gains and risk-averse with respect to losses. Louisa is risk-seeking with respect to losses and risk-averse with respect to gains. Illustrate both utility functions. Which person's attitudes toward risk are consistent with prospect theory?

5.5 Is someone who acts as described in prospect theory always more likely or less likely to take a gamble than someone who acts as described by expected utility theory? Why? Are there conditions (such as on the weights) where you can answer this question definitively?

6. Flight Insurance

6.1 Using information in the Challenge Solution, show how to calculate the price of fair insurance if the probability of being in a crash were as high as the frequency in 2001, 0.00000077? Use a graph to illustrate why a risk-averse person might buy unfair insurance. Show on the graph the risk premium that the person would be willing to pay.

Property Rights, Externalities, Rivalry, and Exclusion

17

There's so much pollution in the air now that if it weren't for our lungs there'd be no place to put it all. —Robert Orben

Does free trade pollute the earth? That's what protestors in many countries allege. For years, these protesters have disrupted meetings of the World Trade Organization (WTO), which promotes free trade among its 153 member countries. The WTO forbids member countries from passing laws that unreasonably block trade, including environmental policies. The environmental protesters argue that when rich countries with relatively strong pollution laws import from poor countries without controls, world pollution rises. Even a country that only cares about its own welfare wants to know the answer to the question: Does exporting benefit a country if it does not regulate its domestic pollution?

In this chapter, we show that if a **property right**—an exclusive privilege to use an asset—is not clearly assigned, a market failure is likely. By owning this book, you have a property right to read it and to stop others from reading or taking it. But many goods have incomplete or unclear property rights.

Unclearly defined property rights may cause *externalities*, which occur when someone's consumption or production activities help or harm someone else outside of a market. An externality occurs when a manufacturing plant spews pollution, harming neighboring firms and individuals. When people lack a property right to clean air, factories, drivers, and others pollute the air rather than incur the cost of reducing their pollution.

Indeed, if no one holds a property right for a good or a bad (like pollution), it is unlikely to have a price. If you had a property right to be free from noise pollution, you could use the courts to stop your neighbor from playing loud music. Or you could sell your right, permitting your neighbor to play the music. If you did not have this property right, no one would be willing to pay you a positive price for it.

A Some of the most important bad externalities arise as a by-product of production (such as water pollution from manufacturing) and consumption (such as congestion or air pollution from driving). A competitive market produces more pollution than a market that is optimally regulated by the government, but a monopoly may not create as much of a pollution problem as a competitive market. Clearly defined property rights may reduce externality problems.

Market failures due to externalities also occur if a good lacks exclusion. A good has *exclusion* if its owner has clearly defined property rights and can prevent others from consuming it. You have a legal right to stop anyone from eating your apple. However, a country's national defense cannot protect some citizens without protecting all citizens.

597

Market failures may also occur if a good lacks *rivalry*, where only one person can consume it, such as an apple. National defense lacks rivalry because my consumption does not prevent you from consuming it.

We look at three types of markets that lack exclusion or rivalry or both. An *open-access common property* is a resource, such as an ocean fishery, where *exclusion* of potential users is impossible. A *club good*, such as a swimming pool, is a good or service that allows for exclusion but is *nonrival*: One person's consumption does not use up the good, and others can also consume it (at least until capacity is reached). A *public good*, such as national defense, is both nonexclusive and nonrival. Goods that lack exclusion or rivalry may not have a market or the market undersupplies these goods.

When such market failures arise, government intervention may raise welfare. A government may regulate an externality such as pollution directly, or indirectly control an externality through taxation or laws that make polluters liable for the damage they cause. Similarly, a government may provide a public good.

In this chapter, we examine six main topics	
	1. **Externalities.** By-products of consumption and production may benefit or harm others.
	2. **The Inefficiency of Competition with Externalities.** A competitive market produces too much of a harmful externality.
	3. **Regulating Externalities.** Overproduction of pollution and other externalities can be prevented through taxation or regulation.
	4. **Market Structure and Externalities.** With a harmful externality, a noncompetitive market equilibrium may be closer to the socially optimal level than that of a competitive equilibrium.
	5. **Allocating Property Rights to Reduce Externalities.** Clearly assigning property rights allows exchanges that reduce or eliminate externality problems.
	6. **Rivalry and Exclusion.** If goods lack rivalry or exclusion, competitive markets suffer from a market failure.

17.1 Externalities

Tragedy is when I cut my finger. Comedy is when you walk into an open sewer and die. —Mel Brooks

An **externality** occurs when a person's well-being or a firm's production capability is directly affected by the actions of other consumers or firms rather than indirectly through changes in prices. A firm whose production process generates fumes that harm its neighbors is creating an externality for which there is no market. In contrast, the firm is not causing an externality when it harms a rival by selling extra output that lowers the market price.

Externalities may either help or harm others. An externality that harms others is called a *negative externality*. For example, a chemical plant spoils a lake's beauty when it dumps its waste products into the water and in so doing harms a firm that rents boats for use on that waterway. In Sydney, government officials played loud Barry Manilow music to drive away late-night revelers from a suburban park—and in the process drove local residents out of their minds.

A *positive externality* benefits others.[1] By installing attractive shrubs and sculptures around its store, a firm provides a positive externality to its neighbors.

---
[1]See the Application "Positive Externality: The Superstar Effect" in MyEconLab, Chapter Resources, Chapter 17.

A single action may confer positive externalities on some people and negative externalities on others. Some people think that their wind chimes are pleasing to their neighbors, but anyone with an ounce of sense would realize that those chimes are annoying! It was reported that the efforts to clean the air in Los Angeles, while enabling people to breathe more easily, caused radiation levels to increase much faster than if the air had remained dirty.

APPLICATION

Spam: A Negative
Externality

In 2011, 79% of global email was *spam*: unsolicited bulk email messages. Spam inflicts a major negative externality on businesses and individuals. A spammer targets gullible people who respond to the spam message. However, the spam is a negative externality for the vast majority of recipients who hate it and incur the cost of buying spam filters and wasting time reading and removing it. According to a study of the cost at a German university, spam inflicted working time losses of 1,200 minutes or 2.5 days per employee (Caliendo, et al., 2012). Spam-victim firms may also suffer substantial costs to clear computers of virus infections and repair their reputations from spammers' false use of their firms' names.[2] Yahoo! researchers, Rao and Reiley (2012), concluded that society loses $100 for every $1 of profit to a spammer, a rate that is "at least 100 times higher than that of automobile pollution."

17.2 The Inefficiency of Competition with Externalities

I shot an arrow in the air and it stuck.

Competitive firms and consumers do not have to pay for the harms of their negative externalities, so they create excessive amounts. Similarly, because producers are not compensated for the benefits of a positive externality, too little of these externalities is produced.

To illustrate why externalities lead to nonoptimal production, we examine a competitive market in which paper mills produce paper and by-products of the production process—such as air and water pollution—that harm people who live nearby. We'll call the pollution *gunk*. Each ton of paper produced increases the amount of gunk by one unit, and the only way to decrease the volume of gunk is to reduce the amount of paper manufactured. No less-polluting technologies are available, and it is not possible to locate plants where the gunk bothers no one.

Paper firms do not have to pay for the harm from the pollution they cause. As a result, each firm's **private cost**—the cost of production only, not including externalities—includes its direct costs of labor, energy, and wood pulp but not the indirect costs of the harm from gunk. The true **social cost** is the private cost plus the cost of the harms from externalities.

Supply-and-Demand Analysis

The paper industry is the major industrial source of water pollution. We use a supply-and-demand diagram for the paper market in Figure 17.1 to illustrate that a competitive market produces excessive pollution because each firm's private cost is less

---

[2]Much of the world's spam comes from *botnets*, which are collections of Internet-connected computers that have been surreptitiously taken over by the spammers. Before Microsoft used court orders to shut it down in 2011, the Rustock botnet sent 44 billion spam messages. According to **commtouch** .com, spammers sent 150 billion emails daily in 2011 before Rustock was stopped, whereas "only" 94 billion spam emails polluted the Internet daily in early 2012.

Figure 17.1   Welfare Effects of Pollution in a Competitive Market

The competitive equilibrium, e_c, is determined by the intersection of the demand curve and the competitive supply or private marginal cost curve, MC^p, which ignores the cost of pollution. The social optimum, e_s, is at the intersection of the demand curve and the social marginal cost curve, $MC^s = MC^p + MC^g$, where MC^g is the marginal cost of the pollution (gunk). Private producer surplus is based on the MC^p curve, and social producer surplus is based on the MC^s curve.

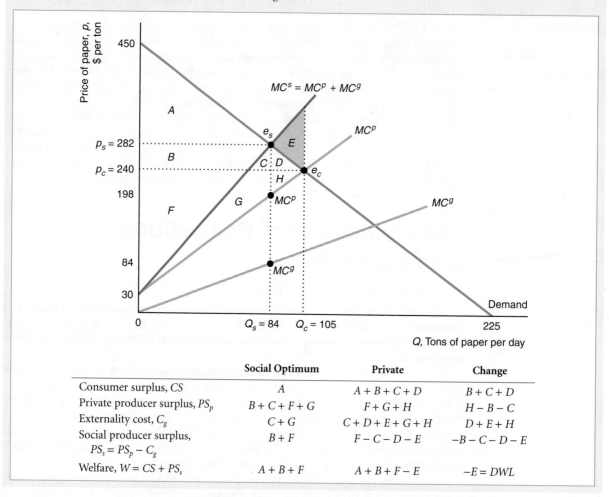

	Social Optimum	Private	Change
Consumer surplus, CS	A	$A + B + C + D$	$B + C + D$
Private producer surplus, PS_p	$B + C + F + G$	$F + G + H$	$H - B - C$
Externality cost, C_g	$C + G$	$C + D + E + G + H$	$D + E + H$
Social producer surplus, $PS_s = PS_p - C_g$	$B + F$	$F - C - D - E$	$-B - C - D - E$
Welfare, $W = CS + PS_s$	$A + B + F$	$A + B + F - E$	$-E = DWL$

than the social cost. In the competitive equilibrium, a firm considers only its private costs when making decisions and ignores the harms of the pollution externality it inflicts on others. The market supply curve is the aggregate private marginal cost curve, MC^p, which is the horizontal sum of the private marginal cost curves of each of the paper manufacturing plants.

The competitive equilibrium, e_c, is determined by the intersection of the market demand curve and the inverse market supply curve for paper. The inverse market demand function in the figure is $p = 450 - 2Q$. The inverse market supply function—the sum of the private marginal cost curves of the individual firms—is $MC^p = 30 + 2Q$. Equating these functions and solving (or looking at the figure), we find that the competitive equilibrium quantity is $Q_c = 105$ tons per day, and the competitive equilibrium price is $p_c = \$240$ per ton.

The firms' *private producer surplus* is the producer surplus of the paper mills based on their *private marginal cost* curve: the area $F + G + H$, which is below the market price and above MC^p up to the competitive equilibrium quantity, 105. The competitive equilibrium maximizes the sum of consumer surplus and private producer surplus (Chapter 9). If there were no externality, the sum of consumer surplus and private producer surplus would equal welfare, so competition would maximize welfare.

Because of the pollution externality, however, the competitive equilibrium does *not* maximize welfare. Competitive firms produce too much gunk because they do not have to pay for the harm it causes. This *market failure* (Chapter 9) results from competitive forces that equalize the price and *private marginal cost* rather than *social marginal cost*, which includes both the private costs of production and the externality damage.

For a given amount of paper production, the full cost of one more ton of paper to society, the *social marginal cost* (MC^s), is the cost to the paper firms of manufacturing one more ton of paper plus the additional externality damage to people in the community from producing this last ton of paper. Thus, the height of the social marginal cost curve, MC^s, at any given quantity equals the vertical sum of the height of the MC^p curve (the private marginal cost of producing another ton of paper) plus the height of the marginal externality damages curve, $MC^g = Q$ (the marginal harm from the gunk) at that quantity: $MC^s(Q) = MC^p(Q) + MC^g(Q) = (30 + 2Q) + Q = 30 + 3Q$.

The social marginal cost curve intersects the demand curve at the socially optimal quantity, $Q_s = 84$, and price $p_s = 282$. At smaller quantities, the price—the value consumers place on the last unit of the good sold—is higher than the full social marginal cost. There, the gain to consumers of paper exceeds the cost of producing an extra unit of output (and hence an extra unit of gunk). At larger quantities, the price is below the social marginal cost, so the gain to consumers is less than the cost of producing an extra unit.

Welfare is the sum of consumer surplus and *social producer surplus*, which is based on the *social marginal cost* curve rather than the *private marginal cost* curve. *Welfare is maximized where price equals social marginal cost.* At the social optimum, e_s, welfare equals $A + B + F$: the area between the demand curve and the MC^s curve up to the optimal quantity, 84 tons of paper.

Welfare at the competitive equilibrium, e_c, is lower: $A + B + F - E$, the area between the demand curve and the MC^s curve up to 105 tons of paper. The area between these curves from 84 to 105, $-E$, is a deadweight loss because the social cost exceeds the value that consumers place on the last 21 tons of paper. *A deadweight loss results because the competitive market equates price with private marginal cost instead of with social marginal cost.*

Welfare is higher at the social optimum than at the competitive equilibrium because the gain from reducing pollution from the competitive to the socially optimal level more than offsets the loss to consumers and paper producers. The cost of the pollution to people who live near the factories is the area under the MC^g curve between zero and the quantity produced. By construction, this area is the same as the area between the MC^p and the MC^s curves. The total damage from the gunk is $-C - D - E - G - H$ at the competitive equilibrium and only $-C - G$ at the social optimum. Consequently, the extra pollution damage from producing the competitive output rather than the socially optimal quantity is $-D - E - H$.

The main beneficiaries from producing at the competitive output level rather than at the socially optimal level are the paper buyers, who pay \$240 rather than \$282 for a ton of paper. Their consumer surplus rises from A to $A + B + C + D$. The corresponding change in private producer surplus is $H - B - C$, which is negative in this figure.

The figure illustrates two main results with respect to negative externalities. First, *a competitive market produces excessive negative externalities.* Because the price of the pollution to the firms is zero, which is less than the marginal cost that the last unit of pollution imposes on society, an unregulated competitive market produces more pollution than is socially optimal. Second, *the optimal amount of pollution is greater than zero.* Even though pollution is harmful and we'd like to have none of it, we cannot wipe it out without eliminating virtually all production and consumption. Making paper, dishwashers, and televisions creates air and water pollution. Agricultural fertilizers pollute the water supply, and people pollute the air by driving by your home.

Cost-Benefit Analysis

We've used a supply-and-demand analysis to show that a competitive market produces excessive pollution because the price of output equals the marginal private cost rather than the marginal social cost. By using a cost-benefit analysis, we obtain another interpretation of the pollution problem in terms of the marginal cost and benefit of the pollution itself.

Let $H = \overline{G} - G$ be the amount that gunk, G, is reduced from the competitive level, $\overline{G}$. Let $B(H)$ be the benefit to society of reducing the units of gunk produced by H, and $C(H)$ be the associated social cost due to the forgone consumption of the good so as to reduce gunk. Society wants to maximize welfare, which is defined as the benefit net of the cost: $W = B(H) - C(H)$. To find the optimal amount of gunk to remove to maximize this measure of welfare, we set the derivative of welfare with respect to H equal to zero:

$$\frac{dW(H)}{dH} = \frac{dB(H)}{dH} - \frac{dC(H)}{dH} = 0.$$

Thus, welfare is maximized when marginal benefit, $dB(H)/dH$, equals marginal cost, $dC(H)/dH$.

In the cost-benefit diagram, panel a of Figure 17.2 (which corresponds to Figure 17.1), the quantity on the horizontal axis starts at the competitive level, 105 tons, and *decreases to the right.* That is, H is zero at the origin of the axis and increases as G diminishes. Thus, a movement to the right indicates a reduction in paper and gunk.

The benefit of reducing output is the reduced damage from gunk. At any given quantity, the height of the benefit curve in panel a is the difference between the pollution harm at that quantity and the harm at the competitive quantity. The cost of reducing output is that the consumer surplus and private producer surplus fall. The height of the cost curve at a given quantity is the sum of consumer surplus and private producer surplus at that quantity minus the corresponding value at the competitive quantity.

If society reduced output to 63 tons, the quantity at which the total benefit equals the total cost, society would be no better off than it is in the competitive equilibrium. To maximize welfare, we want to set output at 84 tons, the quantity at which the gap between the total benefit and total cost is greatest. At that quantity, the slope of the benefit curve, the marginal benefit, *MB*, equals the slope of the cost curve, the marginal cost, *MC*, as panel b of the figure shows.[3] Thus, *welfare is maximized by reducing output and pollution until the marginal benefit from less pollution equals the marginal cost of less output.*

---

[3]The marginal cost curve, *MC*, in Figure 17.2 reflects the social cost of removing the last unit of paper, whereas the social marginal cost curve, *MC^s* in Figure 17.1 captures the extra cost to society from providing the last unit of paper, which includes the cost from one more unit of gunk.

Figure 17.2 Cost-Benefit Analysis of Pollution

(a) The benefit curve reflects the reduction in harm from pollution as the amount of gunk falls from the competitive level. The cost of reducing the amount of gunk is the fall in output, which reduces consumer surplus and private producer surplus. Welfare is maximized at 84 tons of paper and 84 units of gunk, the quantities at which the difference between the benefit and cost curves, the net benefit, is greatest. (b) The net benefit is maximized where the marginal benefit, *MB*, which is the slope of the benefit curve, equals the marginal cost, *MC*, the slope of the cost curve.

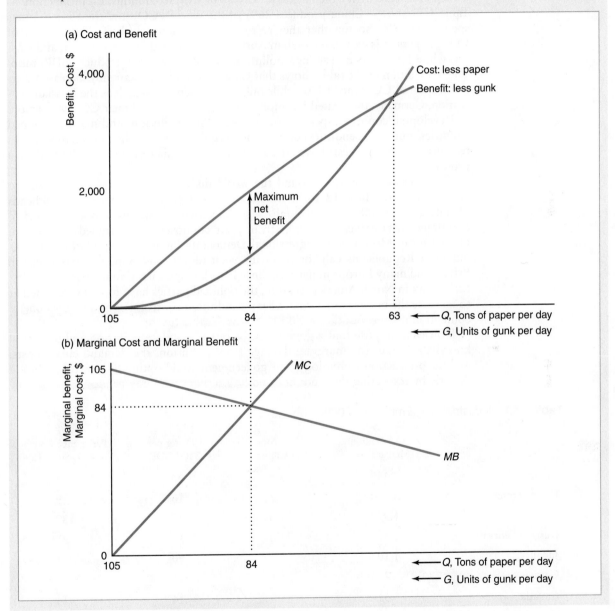

17.3 Regulating Externalities

Because competitive markets produce excessive negative externalities, government intervention may increase welfare. In 1952, London suffered from a thick "pea souper" fog—pollution so dense that people had trouble finding their way home—that killed an estimated 4,000 to 12,000 people. Those dark days prompted the British government to pass the first Clean Air Act in 1956. The United States passed a Clean Air Act in 1970.

Now virtually the entire world is concerned about pollution. Carbon dioxide (CO_2), which is primarily produced by burning fossil fuels, is a major contributor to global warming, damages marine life, and causes additional damage. China and the United States are by far the largest producers of CO_2 from industrial production, as Table 17.1 shows. China produces 26% of the world's CO_2 and the United States spews out 18%, so together they're responsible for nearly half. The amount of CO_2 per person is extremely high in Australia, the United States, Canada, and Russia, while Japan has a very high pollution to gross domestic product (GDP) ratio. The last column of the table shows that China and India substantially increased their production of CO_2 since 1990, while only a few countries—such as the Russian Federation, Germany, the United Kingdom, and France—reduced their CO_2 production.

Developing countries spend little on controlling pollution, and many developed countries' public expenditures on pollution regulation have fallen in recent years. In response, various protests have erupted. China and India now face regular pollution protests.

Nonetheless, politicians around the world disagree about how and whether to control pollution. In 2012 at the United Nations (UN) Rio+20 meeting, 120 heads of state and 50,000 environmentalists, social activists, and business leaders met to encourage sustainable, green growth in poor countries. They argued and accomplished little. Most U.S. Congressional Democrats favor stiffer pollution controls but most Republicans call for removing such regulations. Similar fights occur in Britain and many European nations. Since British Columbia, Canada passed the first carbon tax in North America in 2008, the political parties have fought over whether to increase the tax or eliminate it. Clearly, pollution control will be a major bone of contention throughout the world for the foreseeable future.

However, suppose that a government wants to regulate pollution and it has full knowledge about the marginal damage from pollution, the demand curve, costs, and the production technology. The government could optimally control pollution directly by restricting the amount of pollution that firms may produce or by taxing

Table 17.1   Industrial CO_2 Emissions, 2009

	CO_2, Million Metric Tons	CO_2 Tons per Capita	CO_2 kg per $100 GDP	Percentage Change in CO_2 Since 1990
China	7,687	5.8	26	212
United States	5,300	17.2	16	9
India	1,979	1.6	37	187
Russian Federation	1,574	11.0	12	−26[a]
Japan	1,101	8.7	90	1
Germany	735	8.9	27	−21[b]
Canada	514	15.3	14	14
United Kingdom	475	7.7	10	−17
Mexico	446	4.0	19	42
Australia	400	18.3	28	39
France	363	5.8	17[c]	−9

[a]Since 1992; [b]Since 1991; [c]In 2008.

Source: CO_2 emissions in metric tons (CDIAC): **mdgs.un.org/unsd/mdg/Data.aspx** (viewed August 2, 2012).

them for the pollution they create. A limit on the amount of air or water pollution that may be released is an *emissions standard*. A tax on air pollution is an *emissions fee*, and a tax on discharges into the air or waterways is an *effluent charge*.

Frequently, however, a government controls pollution indirectly, through quantity restrictions or taxes on outputs or inputs. Whether the government restricts or taxes outputs or inputs may depend on the nature of the production process. It is generally better to regulate pollution directly than to regulate output, because direct regulation of pollution encourages firms to adopt efficient, new technologies to control pollution (a possibility we ignore in our example).

Emissions Standard

We can use the paper mill example in Figure 17.1 to illustrate how a government may use an emissions standard to reduce pollution. Here, the government can achieve the social optimum by forcing the paper mills to produce no more than 84 units of paper per day. (Because, in this example, output and pollution move together—are perfectly correlated—regulating either reduces pollution in the same way.)

Unfortunately, the government usually does not know enough to regulate optimally. To set quantity restrictions on output optimally, the government must know how the marginal social cost curve, the demand for paper curve, and pollution vary with output. The ease with which the government can monitor output and pollution may determine whether it sets an output restriction or a pollution standard.

Even if the government knows enough to set the optimal regulation, it must enforce this regulation to achieve the desired outcome. The U.S. Environmental Protection Agency (EPA) tightened its ozone standard to 0.075 parts per million in 2008. As of 2012, 36 areas were marginally out of compliance with this rule, three moderately, three severely, and two extremely (the Los Angeles-South Coast Air Basin and the San Joaquin Valley, California).[4]

APPLICATION

Reducing Pulp and Paper Mill Pollution

Pulp and paper mills are major sources of air and water pollution. For simplicity in our example, we assumed that pollution is emitted in fixed ratio to output and controlled by reducing output. However, firms can also choose less-polluting technologies, use additional pollution-controlling capital, and take other actions to lower the amount of pollution per unit of output (Gray and Shimshack, 2011).

These regulations reduce pollution. For example, a 10% increase in pollution-reducing capital in U.S. paper plants reduced air pollution per unit of paper by 6.9% (Shadbegian and Gray, 2003). Each dollar spent on extra capital stock provided an annual return of about 75¢ in pollution reduction benefits. In the year following an additional fine for not meeting pollution standards at a paper plant, water pollution discharges fell by 7% (Shimshack and Ward, 2005).

---

[4]See www.epa.gov/epahome/commsearch.htm or www.scorecard.org for details on the environmental risks in your area.

Emissions Fee

The government may impose costs on polluters by taxing their output or the amount of pollution produced. (Similarly, a law could make a polluter legally liable for damages.) In our paper mill example, taxing output works as well as taxing the pollution directly because the relationship between output and pollution is fixed. However, if firms can vary the output-pollution relationship by varying inputs or adding pollution-control devices, then the government should tax pollution.

In our paper mill example, if the government knows the marginal cost of the gunk, MC^g, it can set the output tax equal to this marginal cost curve, $t(Q) = MC^g$, so that the tax varies with output, Q. Figure 17.3 illustrates the manufacturers' after-tax marginal cost, $MC^s = MC^p + t(Q)$.

The output tax causes a manufacturer to **internalize the externality**: to bear the cost of the harm that one inflicts on others (or to capture the benefit that one provides to others). The after-tax private marginal cost or supply curve is the same as the social marginal cost curve. As a result, the after-tax competitive equilibrium is the social optimum.

Usually, the government sets a specific tax rather than a tax that varies with the amount of pollution, as MC^g does. As Solved Problem 17.1 shows, applying an appropriate specific tax results in the socially optimal level of production.

Figure 17.3 Taxes to Control Pollution

Placing a tax on firms equal to the harm from the gunk, $t(Q) = MC^g$, causes them to internalize the externality, so their private marginal cost is the same as the social marginal cost, MC^s. As a result, the competitive after-tax equilibrium is the same as the social optimum, e_s. Alternatively, applying a specific tax of $\tau = \$84$ per ton of paper, which is the marginal harm from the gunk at $Q_s = 84$, also results in the social optimum.

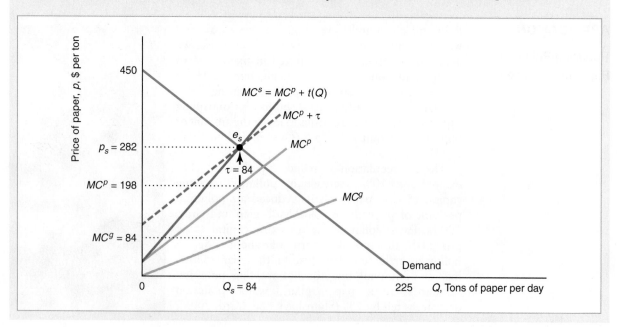

SOLVED PROBLEM 17.1

For the market with pollution in Figure 17.1, what constant, specific tax, τ, on output could the government set to maximize welfare?

Answer

Set the specific tax equal to the marginal harm of pollution at the socially optimal quantity. At the socially optimal quantity, $Q_s = 84$, the marginal harm from the gunk is $84, as Figure 17.3 shows. If the specific tax is $\tau = \$84$, the after-tax private marginal cost (the after-tax competitive supply curve), $MC_p + \tau$, equals the social marginal cost at the socially optimal quantity. Consequently, the after-tax competitive supply curve intersects the demand curve at the socially optimal quantity. By paying this specific tax, the firms internalize the cost of the externality at the social optimum. All that is required for optimal production is that the tax equals the marginal cost of pollution at the optimum quantity; the tax need not equal the marginal cost of pollution at other quantities.

APPLICATION

Why Tax Drivers

Driving causes many externalities including pollution, congestion, and accidents. Taking into account pollution from producing fuel and driving, Hill et al. (2009) estimated that burning one gallon of gasoline (including all downstream effects) causes a carbon dioxide-related climate change cost of 37¢ and a health-related cost of conventional pollutants associated with fine particulate matter of 34¢.

Edlin and Karaca-Mandic (2006) measured the accident externality from additional cars by the increase in the cost of insurance. These externalities are big in states with a high concentration of traffic but not in states with low densities. In California, with many cars per mile, an extra driver raises the total statewide insurance costs of other drivers by between $1,725 and $3,239 per year, and a 1% increase in driving raises insurance costs 3.3% to 5.4%. While the state could build more roads to lower traffic density and hence accidents, it's cheaper to tax the externality. A tax equal to the marginal externality cost would raise $66 billion annually in California—more than the $57 billion raised by all existing state taxes—and over $220 billion nationally.

An alternative to a tax per driver is a tax per mile or gallon of gas. Each 10% increase in the gasoline tax results in a 0.6% decrease in the traffic fatality rate (Grabowski and Morrissey, 2006).

Vehicles are inefficiently heavy because owners of heavier cars ignore the greater risk of death that they impose on other drivers and pedestrians in accidents (Anderson and Auffhammer, 2011). Raising the weight of a vehicle by 1,000 pounds increases the chance of a fatality by 47% if that car hits someone. The higher externality risk due to the greater weight of vehicles since 1989 is 27¢ per gallon of gasoline and the total fatality externality roughly equals a gas tax of $1.08 per gallon.

To reduce the consumption of fuel to reduce pollution and accidents, governments have taxed gasoline and cars and carbon. As of 2012, the Netherlands is debating introducing a prorated distance tax that is more clearly targeted at preventing congestion and accidents.

Benefits Versus Costs from Controlling Pollution

The Clean Air Act of 1970 and the Clean Air Act Amendments of 1990 cleansed U.S. air. Between 1980 and 2010, the national average of sulfur dioxide (SO_2) plummeted 83%, carbon monoxide (CO) fell 82%, nitrogen dioxide (NO_2) tumbled 52%, and ozone dropped 28%. From 1990 to 2010, particulate matter (PM10) in the air fell 38%.[5]

The EPA believes that the CAA saves over 160,000 lives a year; avoids more than 100,000 hospital visits; prevents millions of cases of respiratory problems; and saves 13 million lost workdays. The EPA (2011) estimated the costs of complying with the Clean Air Act were $53 billion, but the benefits were $1.3 trillion in 2010: Benefits outweighed costs by nearly 25 to 1.

APPLICATION

Protecting Babies

Some policy changes raise benefits and *lower* costs. E-ZPass reduces congestion and pollution and increases babies' health. The E-ZPass, an electronic toll collection system on toll ways in New Jersey, Pennsylvania, and 12 other states, allows vehicles to pay a toll without stopping at a toll booth. It lowers the cost of collecting tolls.

Idling cars waiting to pay a toll create extra pollution and waste drivers' time. E-ZPass reduces delays at toll plazas by 85% and lowers NO_2 emissions from traffic by about 6.8%. Introducing E-ZPass reduced premature births by 11% and led to 12% fewer low birth-weight babies of mothers who lived within 2 kilometers (km) of a toll plaza relative to those who lived 2 to 10 km from a toll plaza (Currie and Walker, 2011).[6]

Emissions Fees Versus Standards Under Uncertainty

To control pollution, the United States is more likely to use standards and the European Union is more likely to use taxes. Is it better to tax emissions or to set standards? With full information, a government can induce a firm to produce efficiently by setting either a fee or a standard optimally. However, if the government is uncertain about the cost of pollution abatement, which approach is better depends on the shape of the marginal benefit and marginal cost curves for abating pollution (Weitzman, 1974).

Figure 17.4 shows the government's knowledge about the shape and location of the marginal benefit (*MB*) curve of reducing gunk, a pollutant, and the marginal cost (*MC*) of abating it. We assume that the government knows the *MB* curve, which the figure shows, but is uncertain about the *MC* curve. It believes that it is equally likely that the true marginal cost of abatement curve is MC^1 or MC^2.

To start our analysis, we ask how the government would regulate if it were certain that the *MC* curve equaled the expected marginal cost of abatement curve in the figure, to set an emissions standard, *s*, on emissions (gunk) or an emissions fee, *f*, per unit. The government would set an emissions standard at $s = 100$ units or an emissions fee at $f = \$70$ per unit, which are determined by the intersection of the *MB* and the expected *MC* curves.

---

[5]According to **www.epa.gov/air/airtrends** (viewed August 1, 2012).

[6]Knittel et al. (2011) found that lowering the amount of particulate matter by one unit (during their sample, the average was 29 micrograms per cubic meter of air) saves 18 lives per 100,000 births: a decrease in the infant mortality rate of about 6%.

Figure 17.4 Fees Versus Standards Under Uncertainty

The government knows the marginal benefit curve but is uncertain about the marginal cost curve from abating gunk. If the government uses the expected marginal cost curve to set a fee of $70 or a standard of 100, the deadweight loss from the fee will be smaller than the deadweight loss from the standard regardless of whether the actual marginal cost curve is MC^1 or MC^2.

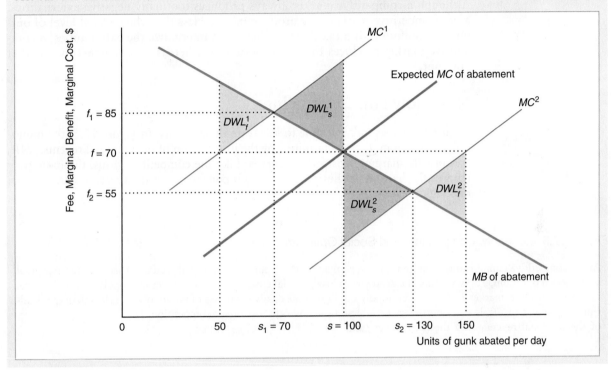

Although either regulation would be optimal in a world of certainty, these regulations are not optimal if the actual marginal cost curve is higher or lower than the expected curve. For example, if the true marginal cost of abatement curve is MC^1, which is higher than the expected marginal cost curve, the optimal standard is $s_1 = 70$ and the optimal fee is $f_1 = \$85$. Thus, if the government uses the expected MC curve, it sets the emissions standard too high and the fee too low. In this example, the deadweight loss from too high an emissions standard, DWL_s^1, is greater than the deadweight loss from too low a fee, DWL_f^1, as the figure illustrates.

If the true marginal cost is less than expected, MC^2, the government has set the standard too low and the fee too high. Again, the deadweight loss from the wrong standard, DWL_s^2 is greater than that from the wrong fee, DWL_f^2. Consequently, given how this figure is drawn, if the government is uncertain about the marginal cost curve, it should use the fee.

However, if we redraw the figure with a much steeper marginal benefit curve, the deadweight loss from the fee will be greater than that from the standard. Thus, whether it is optimal to use fees or standards depends on the government's degree of uncertainty and the shape of the marginal benefit and marginal cost curves.

17.4   Market Structure and Externalities

Two of the main results concerning competitive markets and negative externalities—too much pollution is produced and a tax equal to the marginal social cost of the externality solves the problem—do not hold for other market structures. Although a competitive market always produces too many negative externalities, a noncompetitive market may produce more or less than the optimal level of output and pollution. If a tax is set so that firms internalize the externalities, a competitive market produces the social optimum, whereas a noncompetitive market does not.

Monopoly and Externalities

We use the paper mill example to illustrate these results. In Figure 17.5, the monopoly equilibrium, e_m, is determined by the intersection of the marginal revenue, MR, and private marginal cost, MC^p, curves. Like the competitive firms, the monopoly ignores the harm its pollution causes, so it considers just its direct, private costs in making decisions.

Figure 17.5 Monopoly, Competition, and Social Optimum with Pollution

At the competitive equilibrium, e_c, more is produced than at the social optimum, e_s. As a result, the deadweight loss in the competitive market is D. The monopoly equilibrium, e_m, quantity, 70, is determined by the intersection of the marginal revenue and the private marginal cost, MC^p, curves. The social welfare (based on the marginal social cost, MC^s, curve) under monopoly is $A + B$. Here, the deadweight loss of monopoly, C, is less than the deadweight loss under competition, D.

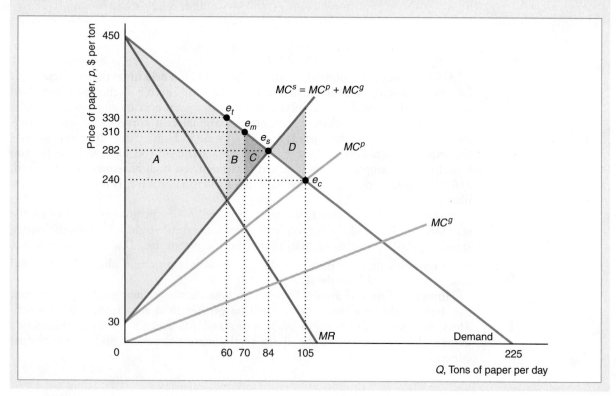

Output is only 70 tons in the monopoly equilibrium, e_m, which is less than the 84 tons at the social optimum, e_s.[7] Thus, this figure illustrates that *the monopoly outcome may be less than the social optimum even with an externality*.

Although the competitive market with an externality always produces more output than the social optimum, a monopoly may produce more than, the same as, or less than the social optimum. The reason that a monopoly may produce too little or too much is that it faces two offsetting effects. The monopoly tends to produce too little output because it sets its price above its marginal cost. However, the monopoly tends to produce too much output because its decisions depend on its private marginal cost instead of the social marginal cost.

Which effect dominates depends on the elasticity of demand for the output and on the extent of the marginal damage the pollution causes. If the demand curve is very elastic, the monopoly markup is small. As a result, the monopoly equilibrium is close to the competitive equilibrium, e_c, and is greater than the social optimum, e_s. If extra pollution causes little additional harm—when MC^g is close to zero at the equilibrium—the social marginal cost essentially equals the private marginal cost, and the monopoly produces less than the social optimum.

Monopoly Versus Competitive Welfare with Externalities

In the absence of externalities, welfare is greater under competition than under an unregulated monopoly (Chapter 11). However, with an externality, welfare may be greater with a monopoly than with competition.[8]

If both monopoly and competitive outputs are greater than the social optimum, welfare must be greater under monopoly because the competitive output is larger than the monopoly output. If the monopoly produces less than the social optimum, we must check which distortion is greater: the monopoly's producing too little or the competitive market's producing too much.

Welfare is lower at the monopoly equilibrium, area $A + B$, than at the social optimum, $A + B + C$, in Figure 17.5. The deadweight loss of monopoly, C, results from the monopoly's producing less output than is socially optimal.

In the figure, the deadweight loss from monopoly, C, is less than the deadweight loss from competition, D, so welfare is greater under monopoly. The monopoly produces only slightly too little output, whereas competition produces excessive output—and hence far too much gunk.

SOLVED PROBLEM 17.2

In Figure 17.5, what is the effect on output, price, and welfare of taxing the monopoly an amount equal to the marginal harm of the externality?

Answer

1. *Show how the monopoly equilibrium shifts if the firm is taxed.* A tax equal to the marginal cost of the pollution causes the monopoly to internalize the

---

[7]Given that the inverse demand function is $p = 450 - 2Q$, the monopoly's revenue function is $R = 450Q - 2Q^2$, so its marginal revenue function is $MR = 450 - 4Q$. If the monopoly is unregulated, its equilibrium is found by equating its marginal revenue function and its private marginal cost function, $MC^p = 30 + 2Q$, and solving: $Q_m = 70$ and (using the inverse demand function) $p_m = 310$.

[8]Pennsylvania and North Carolina use state-owned monopolies to sell liquor. By charging high prices, they may reduce the externalities created by alcohol consumption, such as drunk driving.

externality and to view the social marginal cost as its private cost. The intersection of the marginal revenue, *MR*, curve and the social marginal cost, *MC*^{s}, curve determines the taxed-monopoly equilibrium, e_t. The tax causes the equilibrium quantity to fall from 70 to 60 and the equilibrium price to rise from $310 to $330.

2. *Determine how this shift affects the deadweight loss of monopoly.* The sum of consumer and producer surplus is only *A* after the tax, compared to *A* + *B* before the tax. Thus, welfare falls. The difference between *A* and welfare at the social optimum, *A* + *B* + *C* is −(*B* + *C*), which is the deadweight loss from the taxed monopoly. The tax exacerbates the monopoly's tendency to produce too little output. The deadweight loss increases from *C* to *B* + *C*. The monopoly produced too little before the tax; the taxed monopoly produces even less.

Taxing Externalities in Noncompetitive Markets

Many people argue that the government should tax firms an amount equal to the marginal harm of pollution because such a tax achieves the social optimum in a competitive market. Solved Problem 17.2 shows that such a tax may lower welfare if applied to a monopoly. The tax definitely lowers welfare if the untaxed monopoly produces less than the social optimum. If the untaxed monopoly was originally producing more than the social optimum, a tax may cause welfare to increase.

If the government has enough information to determine the social optimum, it can force either a monopolized or a competitive market to produce the social optimum. If the social optimum is greater than the unregulated monopoly output, however, the government has to subsidize (rather than tax) the monopoly to get it to produce as much output as is desired.

In short, trying to solve a negative externality problem is more complex in a noncompetitive market than it is in a competitive market. To achieve a social optimum in a competitive market, the government only has to reduce the externality, possibly by decreasing output. In a noncompetitive market, the government must eliminate problems arising from both externalities *and* the exercise of market power. Thus, the government needs more information to regulate a noncompetitive market optimally and may require more tools, such as a subsidy. To the degree that the problems arising from market power and pollution are offsetting, however, the failure to regulate a noncompetitive market is less harmful than the failure to regulate a competitive market.

17.5   Allocating Property Rights to Reduce Externalities

Instead of controlling externalities directly through emissions fees and emissions standards, the government may take an indirect approach by assigning a *property right*: an exclusive privilege to use an asset. If no one holds a property right for a good or a bad, the good or bad is unlikely to have a price. If you had a property right that assured you of the right to be free from air pollution, you could go to court to stop a nearby factory from polluting the air. Or you could sell your right, permitting the factory to pollute. If you did not have this property right, no one would be willing to pay you a positive price for it. Because of this lack of a price, a polluter's private marginal cost of production is less than the full social marginal cost.

Coase Theorem

According to the Coase Theorem (Coase, 1960), a polluter and its victim can achieve the optimal levels of pollution if property rights are clearly defined and they can practically bargain. Coase's Theorem is not a practical solution to most pollution problems. Rather, it demonstrates that a lack of clearly defined property rights is the root of the externality problem.

To illustrate the Coase Theorem, we consider two adjacent firms, Alice's Auto Body Shop and Theodore's Tea House. The noise from the auto body shop hurts the tea house's business, as Table 17.2 illustrates. As the auto body shop works on more cars per hour, its profit increases, but the resulting extra noise reduces the tea house's profit. The last column shows the total profit of the two firms. Having the auto body shop work on one car at a time maximizes their joint profit: the socially optimal solution.

No Property Rights. Initially, rights are not clearly defined. Alice won't negotiate with Theodore. After all, why would she reduce her output and the associated noise, if Theodore has no legal right to be free of noise? Why would Theodore pay Alice to reduce the noise if he harbors the hope that the courts will eventually declare that he has a right to be free from noise pollution? Thus, Alice's shop works on two cars per hour, which maximizes her profit at 400. The resulting excessive pollution drives Theodore out of business, so their joint profit is 400.

Property Right to Be Free of Pollution. Now, suppose that the courts grant Theodore the right to silence. He can force Alice to shut down, so that he makes 400 and their joint profit is 400. However, if Alice works on one car, her gain is 300, while Theodore's loss is 200. They should be able to reach an agreement where he pays her between 200 and 300 for the right to work on one car. As a result, they maximize their joint profit at 500.

Why doesn't Alice buy the rights to work on two cars instead of one? Her gain of 100 from working on the second car is less than Theodore's loss of 200, so they cannot reach a deal to let her work on the second car.

Property Right to Pollute. Alternatively, suppose that the court says that Alice has the right to make as much noise as she wants. Unless Theodore pays her to reduce the noise, he has to shut down. The gain to Theodore of 200 from Alice working on one rather than two cars is greater than the 100 loss to Alice. They should be able to reach a deal in which Theodore pays Alice between 100 and 200, she works on only one car, and they maximize their joint profit at 500.

Table 17.2 Daily Profits Vary with Production and Noise

Auto Body Shop's Output, Cars per Hour	Profits, $		
	Auto Body Shop	Tea House	Total
0	0	400	400
1	300	200	500
2	400	0	400

Summary. This example illustrates the three key results of the Coase Theorem:

1. If property rights are not clearly assigned, one firm pollutes excessively and joint profit is not maximized.
2. Clearly assigning property rights results in the social optimum, maximizing joint profit, regardless of who gets the rights.
3. However, who gets the property rights affects how they split the joint profit. Because the property rights are valuable, the party with the property rights is compensated by the other party.

Problems with the Coase Approach. To achieve the socially optimal outcome, the two sides must bargain successfully with each other. However, the parties may not be able to bargain successfully for at least three important reasons.

First, if transaction costs are very high, it might not pay for the two sides to meet. For example, if a manufacturing plant pollutes the air, thousands or even millions of people may be affected. The cost of getting all of them together to bargain is prohibitive.

Second, if firms engage in strategic bargaining behavior, an agreement may not be reached. For instance, if one party says, "Give me everything I want" and will not budge, reaching an agreement may be impossible.

Third, if either side lacks information about the costs or benefits of reducing pollution, the outcome is likely not to be optimal. It is difficult to know how much to offer the other party and to reach an agreement if you do not know how the polluting activity affects the other party.

For these reasons, Coasian bargaining is likely to occur in relatively few situations. Where bargaining cannot occur, the allocation of property rights affects the amount of pollution.

APPLICATION

Buying a Town

By stating that the James Gavin American Electric Power was violating the Clean Air Act by polluting Cheshire, Ohio, the Environmental Protection Agency (EPA) effectively gave Cheshire's residents the right to be free from pollution. To avoid the higher cost of litigation and installing new equipment and other actions to reduce pollution at its plant, the company bought the town for $20 million, inducing the residents to pack up and leave.

Markets for Pollution

If high transaction costs preclude bargaining, society may be able to overcome this problem by using a market, which facilitates exchanges between individuals. Starting in the early 1980s, the U.S. federal government, some state governments, and many governments around the world introduced a cap-and-trade system. Under a *cap-and-trade* system, the government distributes a fixed number of permits that allow firms to produce a specified amount of pollution. These permits not only create a property right to pollute, but they also limit or cap the total amount of pollution. These permits can then be traded in a market, often by means of an auction. Firms that do not use all their permits sell them to other firms that want to pollute more—much as sinners bought indulgences in the Middle Ages.

Firms whose products are worth a lot relative to the harm from pollution they create buy rights from firms that make less valuable products. Suppose that the cost in terms of forgone output from eliminating each ton of pollution is $200 at one firm and $300 at another. If the government reduces the permits it gives to each firm so that each must reduce its pollution by 1 ton, the total cost is $500. With tradable permits, the first firm can reduce its pollution by 2 tons and sell one permit to the second firm, so the total social cost is only $400. The trading maximizes the value of the output for a given amount of pollution damage, thus increasing efficiency.

If the government knew enough, it could assign the optimal amount of pollution to each firm, and trading would be unnecessary. By using a market, the government does not have to collect this type of detailed information to achieve efficiency. It only has to decide how much total pollution to allow.

APPLICATION U.S. Cap and Trade Programs	The Acid Rain Program under the 1990 U.S. Clean Air Act was designed to reduce 10 million tons of sulfur dioxide (SO_2) and 2 million tons of nitrogen oxides (NO_x), the primary components of acid rain. It reduced the SO_2 in 2010 level to only 30% of that in 1990.

Under the law, the EPA issues SO_2 permits, each of which allows a firm to produce 1 ton of emissions of SO_2 annually, equal to the aggregate emission cap. A firm that exceeds its pollution limit is fined $2,000 per ton of emissions above its allowance. At the end of a year, if a company's emissions are less than its allowance, it may sell the remaining allowance to another firm, thus providing the firm with an incentive to reduce emissions.

The EPA holds an annual spot auction for permits that may be used in the current year and an advanced auction for permits effective in seven years. Anyone can purchase allowances. Recently, environmental groups, such as the Acid Rain Retirement Fund, the University of Tampa Environmental Protection Coalition, University of Tampa Environmental Protection Coalition, and Bates College Environmental Economics classes purchased permits and withheld them from firms to reduce pollution further. (You can see the outcome of the 2012 auctions at **www.epa.gov/airmarkets/trading/2012/12summary. html**.)

According to some estimates, pollution reduction under this market program costs about a quarter to a third less than it would cost if permits were not tradable—a savings on the order of $225 to $375 million per year. Moreover, the EPA calculated the Acid Rain Program's annual benefits in 2010 at approximately $340 billion (in 2012 dollars), at an annual cost of about $8 billion, or a 40-to-1 benefit-to-cost ratio.

17.6 Rivalry and Exclusion

Until now, we've focused on *private goods*, which have the properties of rivalry and exclusion. A good is **rival** if only one person can consume the good. If Jane eats an orange, that orange is gone. **Exclusion** means that others can be prevented from consuming the good. If Jane owns an orange, she can easily prevent others from consuming that orange by, for example, locking it in her home. Thus, an orange is subject to rivalry and exclusion.

If a good lacks rivalry, everyone can consume the same good, such as clean air or national defense. If a market charges a positive price for that good, there is a market failure because the marginal cost of providing the good to one more person is zero.

If the good lacks exclusion, such as clean air, no one can be stopped from consuming it because no one has an exclusive property right to the good. Consequently, a market failure may occur as when people who don't have to pay for the good overexploit it, as when they pollute the air. If the market failure is severe, as it often is for open-access common resources and for public goods, governments may play an important role in provision or control of the good. For example, governments usually pay for streetlights.

We can classify goods by whether they exhibit rivalry and exclusion. Table 17.3 outlines the four possibilities: private good (which have rivalry and exclusion); open-access common property (rivalry, no exclusion); club good (no rivalry, exclusion); and public good (no rivalry, no exclusion).

Open-Access Common Property

An **open-access common property** is a resource that is nonexclusive but rival, such as an open-access fishery. Everyone has free access and an equal right to exploit this resource.

Many fisheries have common access such that anyone can fish and no one has a property right to a fish until it is caught. Each fisher wants to land a fish before others do to gain the property right to that fish, which is rival. The lack of clearly defined property rights leads to overfishing. Fishers have an incentive to catch more fish than they would if the fishery were private property.

Suppose instead that each fisher owns a private lake. No externality occurs because the property rights are clearly defined. Each owner is careful not to overfish in any one year to maintain the stock (or number) of fish in the future.[9]

In contrast, most ocean fisheries are open-access common property. Like polluting manufacturers, ocean fishers look only at their private costs. In calculating these costs, fishers include the cost of boats, other equipment, a crew, and supplies. They do not include the cost that they impose on future generations by decreasing the stock of fish today, which reduces the number of fish in the sea next year. The fewer fish there are, the harder it is to catch any, so reducing the population today raises the cost of catching fish in the future. As a result, fishers do not forgo fishing now to leave fish for the future.

The social cost of catching a fish is the private cost plus the *externality cost* from reduced current and future populations of fish. Thus, the market failure arising from open-access common property can be viewed as a special type of negative externality.

Other important examples of open-access common property are petroleum, water, and other fluids and gases that are often extracted from a *common pool*. Owners of wells drawing from a common pool compete to remove the substance most rapidly, thereby gaining ownership of the good. This competition creates an externality by lowering fluid pressure, which makes further pumping more difficult.

Table 17.3   Rivalry and Exclusion

	Exclusion	*No Exclusion*
Rivalry	*Private good*: apple, pencil, computer, car	*Open-access common property*: fishery, freeway, park
No Rivalry	*Club good*: cable television, concert, tennis club	*Public good*: national defense, clean air, lighthouse

---

[9]"There's a fine line between fishing and standing on the shore looking like an idiot." —Steven Wright

Iraq justified its invasion of Kuwait, which led to the Persian Gulf War in 1991, on the grounds that Kuwait was overexploiting common pools of oil underlying both countries. In 2011, the State of Alaska proposed leasing land next to the federal Alaska National Wildlife Reserve (ANWR), which would allow the leasing companies to drill and potentially drain oil from ANWR.[10]

If many people try to access a single Web site at one time, congestion may slow traffic to a crawl. In addition, email messages can be sent freely, even though they may impose handling costs on recipients, leading to excessive amounts of unwanted or junk email, a negative externality.

If you own a car, you have a property right to drive that car but public roads and freeways are common property. But because you lack an exclusive property right to the highway on which you drive, you cannot exclude others from driving on the highway and must share it with them. Each driver, however, claims a temporary property right in a portion of the highway by occupying it, thereby preventing others from occupying the same space. Competition for space on the highway leads to congestion, a negative externality that slows every driver.

To prevent overuse of a common resource, a government can clearly define property rights, restrict access, or tax users. Many developing countries over the past century have broken up open-access, common agricultural land into smaller private farms with clearly defined property rights. Governments frequently grant access to a resource on a first-come, first-served basis, such as at some popular national parks.

Alternatively, the government can impose a tax or fee to use the resource. Only those people who value the resource most gain access. Governments often charge an entrance fee to a park or a museum. Tolls are commonly used on highways and bridges. By applying a tax or fee equal to the externality harm that each individual imposes on others (such as the value of increased congestion on a highway), the government forces each person to internalize the externality.

APPLICATION

For Whom the Bridge Tolls

The toll to cross the Bay Bridge from Oakland into San Francisco rose in 2010 from $4 to $6 during weekday rush hours (5:00 to 10:00 A.M. and 3:00 to 7:00 P.M.), and using the formerly free carpool lanes now cost $2.50. The new carpool toll reduced traffic in carpool lanes by 30% compared to the previous year. Overall traffic was down roughly 9% during the first few days after the toll changed. The effect on the Bay Bridge's traffic flow during the busiest hours was dramatic: rush hour traffic moved twice as quickly as in the previous year. The managers of the bridge were delighted by the substantially increased toll revenue and decreased congestion.

Club Goods

A **club good** is a good that is nonrival but is subject to exclusion, such as swimming clubs or golf clubs. These clubs exclude people who do not pay membership fees, but the services they provide, swimming or golfing, are nonrival. An extra person can swim or golf without reducing the enjoyment of others until these facilities become congested as capacity is reached.

However, the most significant club goods are not offered through actual clubs. An important example is cable television. Any available channels can be provided to additional consumers at almost no additional cost (provided they have the cable in

---

[10]Taylor, Phil, "Alaska Unveils Plan to 'Drain' Federal Crude from ANWR," *E&ENews*, June 30, 2011.

place). The service lacks rivalry as adding one more viewer for a given channel in no way impairs the viewing experience of other viewers (and the marginal cost is nearly zero). However, people can be easily excluded. Only people who pay for the service receive the signal and can view the channel. Extra consumers can subscribe to cable television channels almost without limit.

Because club goods are nonrival, the goods can be provided to additional consumers at (virtually) zero marginal cost. Admitting one more person to hear a concert harms no one as long as the concert hall is not full. If a positive price is charged for admission, there is a market failure because the price exceeds the marginal cost of providing the good. If there are empty seats because no additional person will pay the ticket price of $50, but if there are potential consumers willing to pay $30 for those seats, then failing to admit those people leads to a deadweight loss.

One of the most important examples of a good without rivalry but with exclusion is computer software, such as Microsoft Word. Software is nonrival. At almost no extra cost, Microsoft can provide a copy of the software program to another consumer. When Microsoft charges a (high) positive price, there is a market failure in which too few units are sold.

Although club goods create a market failure, government intervention is rare because it is difficult for the government to help. As with regulation, an attempt to eliminate deadweight loss by forcing Microsoft to charge a price equal to its zero marginal cost would be self-defeating as the service would not be produced and even more total surplus would be lost. A government could cap the price of Microsoft Word at average cost, which would reduce but would not eliminate the deadweight loss.

Public Goods

A **public good** is nonrival and nonexclusive. Clean air is a public good. One person's enjoyment of clean air does not stop other people from enjoying clean air as well, so clean air is nonrival. In addition, if we clean up the air, we cannot prevent others who live nearby from benefiting, so clean air is nonexclusive.

A public good is a special type of externality. If a firm reduces the amount of pollution it produces, thereby cleaning the air, it provides a nonpriced benefit to its neighbors: a positive externality.

Free Riding. Unfortunately, markets undersupply public goods due to a lack of clearly defined property rights. Because people who do not pay for the good cannot be excluded from consuming it, the provider of a public good cannot exercise property rights over the services provided by the public good. This problem is often described as the **free rider problem**: a situation in which people benefit from the actions of others without paying. That is, they want to benefit from a positive externality. Consequently, it is very difficult for firms to profitably provide a public good because few people want to pay for the good no matter how valuable it is to them.

We use two examples to illustrate the free rider problem. In both, two stores in a mall decide whether to pay for guard service to protect their merchandise. Guards patrolling the mall provide a service without rivalry: Both stores in the mall are simultaneously protected. In the first example, the stores make a discrete choice whether to hire a guard or not because extra guards provide no extra protection. In the second example, the number of guards to hire is a continuous variable.

To determine whether to hire a guard, a shoe store and a television store play a game. Each decides whether to hire one guard or none. A guard costs 10 per hour. The benefit to each store is 8 per hour. Because the collective benefit, 16, is greater than the cost of hiring a guard, the optimal solution is to hire a guard.

However, if the stores act independently, they do not achieve the optimal solution. Table 17.4 shows two games. In panel a, each store acts independently and pays 10 to hire a guard on its own or does not hire a guard. If both stores decide to hire a guard, two guards are hired, but the benefit is still only 8 per store.

In panel b, the stores split the cost of a guard if both firms agree to hire one. If only one firm wants to hire the guard, it must bear the full cost.

In each of these games, the Nash equilibrium is for neither store to hire a guard because of free riding. Each store has a dominant strategy. Regardless of what the other store does, each store is always as well off or better off not to hire a guard. For example, in panel a, each store's payoff is −2 if it hires a guard but 0 (if the other firm does not hire) or 8 (if the other firm hires) if it does not hire, so its dominant strategy is not to hire. The nonoptimal outcome occurs for the same reason as in other prisoners' dilemma games (Chapter 13): When the stores act independently, they don't do what is best for them collectively.

We now turn to another mall where additional guards increase the firms' protection. To illustrate why public goods are underprovided by markets, we examine why the demand curve for a public good is different from that for a private good. The social marginal benefit of a private good is the same as the marginal benefit to the individual who consumes that good. The market demand or social marginal benefit curve for private goods is the *horizontal* sum of the demand curves of each individual (Chapter 2).

In contrast, the social marginal benefit of a public good is the sum of the marginal benefit to each person who consumes the good. Because a public good lacks rivalry, many people can get pleasure from the same unit of output. Consequently, the *social demand curve* or *willingness-to-pay curve* for a public good is the *vertical* sum of the demand curves of each individual.

Table 17.4   Private Payments for a Public Good

(a) *Stores Decide Independently Whether to Hire a Guard*

		Television Store	
		Hire	Do Not Hire
Shoe Store	Hire	−2, −2	−2, 8
	Do Not Hire	8, −2	0, 0

(b) *Stores Voting to Hire a Guard Split the Cost*

		Television Store	
		Hire	Do Not Hire
Shoe Store	Hire	3, 3	−2, 8
	Do Not Hire	8, −2	0, 0

We illustrate this vertical summing by deriving the demand for guard services by stores in a mall that want to discourage theft. Each store's demand for guards reflects its marginal benefit from a reduction in thefts due to the guards. The demand curve for the electronics store, which stands to lose a lot if thieves strike, is D^1 in Figure 17.6. The ice-cream parlor, which is at less risk from a theft, demands fewer guards at any given price, D^2.

Because a guard patrolling the mall protects both stores at once, the marginal benefit to society of an additional guard is the sum of the benefit to each store. The social marginal benefit of a fifth guard, 10, is the sum of the marginal benefit to the television store, 8 (the height of D^1 at five guards per hour), and the marginal benefit to the ice-cream store, 2 (the height of D^2 at five guards per hour). Thus, the social demand is the vertical sum of the individual demand curves.

A competitive market supplies as many guards as the stores want at 10 per hour per guard. At that price, the ice-cream store would not hire any guards on its own. The television store would hire four. If the stores act independently, four guards are hired at the private equilibrium, e_p. The sum of the marginal benefit to the two stores from four guards is 13, which is greater than the marginal cost of an additional guard, 10. If a fifth guard is hired, the social marginal benefit, 10, equals the marginal cost of the last guard. Therefore, the social equilibrium, e_2, has five guards.

The ice-cream store can get guard services without paying because the guard service is a public good. Acting alone, the television store hires fewer guards than are socially optimal because it ignores the positive externality provided to the ice-cream store, which the television store does not capture. Thus, the competitive market for guard services provides too little of this public good.

Figure 17.6 Inadequate Provision of a Public Good

Security guards protect both tenants of the mall. If each guard costs $10 per hour, the electronics store, with demand D^1, is willing to hire four guards per hour. The ice-cream parlor, with demand D^2, is not willing to hire any guards. Thus if everyone acts independently, the equilibrium is e_p. The social demand for this public good is the vertical sum of the individual demand curves, D. Thus, the social optimum is e_s, at which five guards are hired.

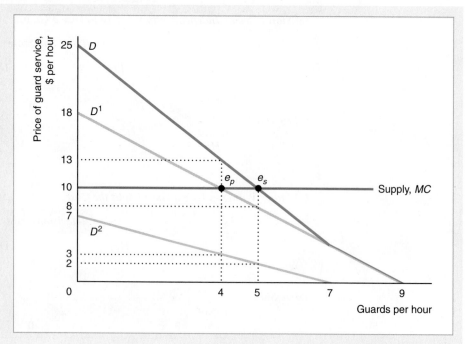

In more extreme cases, no public good is provided because nonpurchasers cannot be stopped from consuming the good. Usually, if the government does not provide a nonexclusive public good, no one provides it.

APPLICATION

Radiohead's Public Good Experiment

In 2007, the British rock band Radiohead sold its album *In Rainbows* by offering its fans a digital download without copy restriction software off the Internet at a price chosen by each fan for a three-month period. By so doing, the band faced a problem similar to that of society for a public good: Fans knew that the album could be theirs regardless of what they paid, so individuals were tempted to pay substantially less than their valuations of the album or the price of comparable albums.

The band did not release official figures about digital sales. According to comScore's estimates, 38% of fans paid an average of $6, while the rest paid nothing. Thus, many fans chose to free ride. After the initial three months, the band removed the digital version from the Internet and issued a traditional CD version with a list price of $13.98. The band chose not to repeat this experiment with their 2011 album, *The King of Limbs*.

Optimal Provision of a Public Good. To illustrate how to determine the socially optimal level of a public good, we use an example of a society consisting of two people. Individual i's utility, $U_i(G, P_i)$, is a function of a public good, G, and that person's consumption of a private good, P_i. Each has an income, Y_i, which can be used to pay for a unit of either good at a price of $1 per unit. Thus, Individual i, buys G_i amount of the public good and $P_i = Y_i - G_i$ of the private good. Thus, $U_i(G, P_i) = U_i(G_1 + G_2, Y_i - G_i)$.

We use the Pareto concept to evaluate society's optimal policy (Chapter 10). Any reallocation that increases one person's utility while holding the other person's utility constant is Pareto superior. Thus, to allocate resources efficiently, society chooses G_1 and G_2 to maximize Person 1's utility while holding Person 2's utility at a given level, $\overline{U}_2$ (or vice versa). The corresponding Lagrangian expression is

$$\mathcal{L} = U_1(G_1 + G_2, Y_1 - G_1) + \lambda[U_2(G_1 + G_2, Y_2 - G_2) - \overline{U}_2], \quad (17.1)$$

where λ is the Lagrangian multiplier. The first-order conditions are

$$\frac{\partial \mathcal{L}}{\partial G_1} = \frac{\partial U_1}{\partial G}\frac{dG}{dG_1} + \frac{\partial U_1}{\partial P_1}\frac{dP_1}{dG_1} + \lambda\frac{\partial U_2}{\partial G}\frac{dG}{dG_1} = \frac{\partial U_1}{\partial G} - \frac{\partial U_1}{\partial P_1} + \lambda\frac{\partial U_2}{\partial G} = 0, \quad (17.2)$$

and

$$\frac{\partial \mathcal{L}}{\partial G_2} = \frac{\partial U_1}{\partial G}\frac{dG}{dG_2} + \lambda\left(\frac{\partial U_2}{\partial G}\frac{dG}{dG_2} + \frac{\partial U_2}{\partial P_2}\frac{dP_2}{dG_2}\right)$$

$$= \frac{\partial U_1}{\partial G} + \lambda\left(\frac{\partial U_2}{\partial G} - \frac{\partial U_2}{\partial P_2}\right) = 0. \quad (17.3)$$

By subtracting Equation 17.3 from Equation 17.2, we learn that $\partial U_1 / \partial P_1 = \lambda \partial U_2 / \partial P_2$. Dividing Equation 17.2 by $\partial U_1 / \partial P_1$ and substituting $\lambda \partial U_2 / \partial P_2$ for $\partial U_1 / \partial P_1$ in the second term, we find that

$$\frac{\partial U_1 / \partial G}{\partial U_1 / \partial P_1} + \frac{\partial U_2 / \partial G}{\partial U_2 / \partial P_2} = 1, \tag{17.4}$$

or

$$MRS_1 + MRS_2 = 1. \tag{17.5}$$

That is, the sum of the marginal rates of substitution of all the members of society equals one.

In Chapter 3, we learned that an individual chooses a bundle of two goods to equate the consumer's marginal rate of substitution between the goods with the marginal rate of transformation in the market. Here, the marginal rate of transformation between the public good and a private good is one: You can trade one unit of the public good for one unit of the private good. With a public good, instead of equating one person's marginal rate of substitution with the marginal rate of transformation, we equate the sum of the marginal rates of substitution for the two people with the marginal rate of transformation. Because both people suffer if one person contributes less to the public good, society's marginal rate of substitution must reflect how much of the public good all members of society are willing to give up for one more unit of the private good.

For example, suppose that the individuals have Cobb-Douglas utility functions, $U_i(G, P_i) = a_i \ln G + \ln P_i$. The marginal utilities are $\partial U_i / \partial G = a_i / G$ and $\partial U_i / \partial P_i = 1/P_i$. Substituting these expression into Equation 17.4, we obtain $a_1 P_1 / G + a_2 P_2 / G = 1$, or

$$G = a_1 P_1 + a_2 P_2. \tag{17.6}$$

We know that the two individuals can each allocate Y_i to the goods, so the total constraint on this society is

$$P_1 + P_2 + G = Y_1 + Y_2. \tag{17.7}$$

We have two equations, Equations (17.6) and (17.7), to determine three values, P_1, P_2, G.[11] Thus, these equations restrict the optimal set of allocations, but there are an infinite number of combinations of G, P_1, and P_2 that are consistent with these equations.

**SOLVED PROBLEM
17.3**

What is the optimal level of the public good if the utility functions are quasilinear, $U_i(G, P_i) = a_i \ln G + P_i$?

Answer

Rewrite the optimality Equation 17.4 using these specific utility functions and solve for G. The marginal utilities are $\partial U_i / \partial G = a_i / G$ and $\partial U_i / \partial P_i = 1$. Thus, Equation 17.4 becomes $a_1 / G + a_2 / G = 1$, or

$$G = a_1 + a_2. \tag{17.8}$$

Thus, we have determined a unique G that is optimal if society has adequate resources so that this G does not violate Equation 17.7. That is, $G \leq Y_1 + Y_2$.

---

[11]Or, substituting Equation 17.6 into Equation 17.7, we have $(1 + a_1)P_1 + (1 + a_2)P_2 = Y_1 + Y_2$, so we have one equation to determine $P_1 + P_2$ (with G determined residually) for given Y_1 and Y_2.

Reducing Free Riding

Unfortunately, individuals rarely contribute the optimal amounts toward a public good. One solution to the free riding problem is for the government to provide it. Governments provide public defense, roads, and many other public goods.

Alternatively, governmental or other collective actions can reduce free riding. Methods that may be used include social pressure, mergers, privatization, and compulsion.

Social pressure may reduce or eliminate free riding, especially for a small group. Such pressure may cause most firms in a mall to contribute "voluntarily" to hire security guards. The firms may cooperate in a repeated prisoners' dilemma game, especially if there are relatively few firms.

A direct way to eliminate free riding by firms is for them to *merge* into a single firm and thereby internalize the positive externality. The sum of the benefit to the individual stores equals the benefit to the single firm, so an optimal decision is made to hire guards.

If the independent stores sign a contract that commits them to share the cost of the guards, they achieve the practical advantage from a merger. However, the question remains as to why they would agree to sign the contract, given the prisoners' dilemma problem (Chapter 13).

Finally, coercion may solve the free riding problem. The government may use mandatory taxes to pay for roads or national defense. Similarly, the owner of a mall may require tenants to sign a rental contract that requires them to pay "taxes" to provide security.

Valuing Public Goods

To ensure that a nonexclusive public good is provided, a government usually produces it or compels others to do so. Issues faced by a government when it provides such a public good include whether to provide it at all and, if so, how much of the good to provide. When grappling with these questions, the government needs to know the cost—usually the easy part—and the value of the public good to many individuals—the hard part.

Through surveys or voting results, the government may try to determine the value that consumers place on the public good. A major problem with these methods is that most people do not know how much a public good is worth to them. How much would you pay to maintain the National Archives? How much does reducing air pollution improve your health? How much better do you sleep at night knowing that the Army stands ready to protect you?

Even if people know how much they value a public good, they have an incentive to lie on a survey. Those who highly value the good and want the government to provide it may exaggerate its value. Similarly, people who place a low value on it may report *too low* a value—possibly even a negative one—to discourage government action.

Rather than relying on surveys, a government may ask its citizens to vote on public goods. Suppose that a separate, majority-rule vote is held on whether to install a traffic signal—a public good—at each of several street corners. If a signal is installed, all voters are taxed equally to pay for it. An individual will vote to install a signal if the value of the signal to that voter is at least as much as the tax that each voter must pay for the signal.

Whether the majority votes for the signal depends on the preferences of the *median voter*: the voter with respect to whom half the populace values the project less and half values the project more. If the median voter wants to install a signal, then at least half the voters agree, so the vote carries. Similarly, if the median voter is against the project, at least half the voters are against it, so the vote fails.

It is *efficient* to install the signal if the value of the signal to society is at least as great as its cost. Does majority voting result in efficiency? The following examples illustrate that efficiency is not ensured.

Each signal costs $300 to install. There are three voters, so each individual votes for the signal only if that person thinks that the signal is worth at least $100, which is the tax each person pays if the signal is installed. Table 17.5 shows the value that each voter places on installing a signal at each of three intersections.

For each of the proposed signals, Hayley is the median voter, so her views "determine" the outcome. If Hayley, the median voter, likes the signal, then she and Asa, a majority, vote for it. Otherwise, Nancy and Hayley vote against it. The majority favors installing a signal at corners *A* and *C* and is against doing so at corner *B*. It would be efficient to install the signal at corner *A*, where the social value is $300, and at corner *B*, where the social value is $375, because each value equals or exceeds the cost of $300.

At corner *A*, the citizens vote for the signal, and that outcome is efficient. The other two votes lead to inefficient outcomes. No signal is installed at corner *B*, where society values the signal at more than $300, but a signal is installed at corner *C*, where voters value the signal at less than $300.

The problem with yes-no votes is that they ignore the intensity of preferences. A voter indicates only whether or not the project is worth more or less than a certain amount. Thus, such majority voting fails to value the public good fully and hence does not guarantee that the public good is efficiently provided.[12]

Table 17.5 Voting on $300 Traffic Signals

Signal Location	Value to Each Voter, $			Value to Society, $	Outcome of Vote*
	Nancy	Hayley	Asa		
Corner *A*	50	100	150	300	Yes
Corner *B*	50	75	250	375	No
Corner *C*	50	100	110	260	Yes

*An individual votes to install a signal at a particular corner if and only if that person thinks the signal is worth at least $100, the tax that the individual must pay if the signal is installed.

APPLICATION

What's Their Beef?

Under U.S. federal law, agricultural producers can force all industry members to contribute to public goods if the majority of firms agrees. Under the Beef Promotion and Research Act, all beef producers must pay a $1-per-head fee on cattle sold in the United States. The $80 million raised by this fee annually finances research, educational programs on mad cow disease, and collective advertising such as its original "Beef: It's What's for Dinner" campaign and its 2012 campaign, "Stay Home. Grill Out." Supporters of this collective advertising estimate that producers receive $5.67 in additional marginal revenue for every dollar they contribute.

[12]Although voting does not reveal how much a public good is worth, Tideman and Tullock (1976) and other economists have devised taxing methods that can sometimes induce people to reveal their true valuations. However, these methods are rarely used.

CHALLENGE SOLUTION	In the Challenge at the beginning of the chapter, we asked whether free trade benefits a country if it does not regulate its domestic pollution. This issue is increasingly important as nations move toward free trade and trade expands.

Trade and Pollution

The United States has signed free-trade agreements (FTA) that eliminate or reduce tariffs and quotas and liberalize rules on foreign investment to increase trade with Australia, Bahrain, Canada, Chile, Costa Rica, El Salvador, Guatemala, Honduras, Israel, Jordan, Mexico, Morocco, Nicaragua, Peru, Singapore, South Korea, and other countries. As of May 2012, FTA countries accounted for 46% of U.S. exports and 35% of imports.

Liberalized trade has expanded trade. Trade was 28% of the U.S. gross domestic product (GDP) in 2008–2010, compared to only 10% in 1970. The GDP share of trade is even greater in many other countries: 30% in the European Union, 31% in Japan, 48% in India, 55% in China, 59% in Mexico and in the United Kingdom, and 63% in Canada.

Everyone can gain from free trade if losers are compensated and if domestic markets are perfectly competitive and not distorted by taxes, tariffs, or pollution (Chapters 9 and 10). Business and jobs lost in one sector from free trade are more than offset by gains in other sectors. However, if an economy has at least two market distortions, correcting one of them may either increase or decrease welfare.[13] For example, if a country bars trade and has uncontrolled pollution, then allowing free trade without controlling pollution may not increase welfare.

What are the welfare effects of permitting trade if a country's polluting export industry is unregulated? To analyze this question, we couple the trade model from Chapter 9 with the pollution model from this chapter.

Suppose that the country's paper industry is a price taker on the world paper market. The world price is p_w. Panel a of the figure shows the gain to trade in the usual case where there is no pollution or it is optimally regulated by the government. The domestic supply curve, S, is upward sloping, but the home country can import as much as it wants at the world price, p_w. In the free-trade equilibrium, e_1, the equilibrium quantity is Q_1 and the equilibrium price is the world price, p_w. With a ban on imports, the equilibrium is e_2, quantity falls to Q_2, and price rises to p_2. Consequently, the deadweight loss from the ban is area D. (See the discussion of Figure 9.8 for a more thorough analysis.)

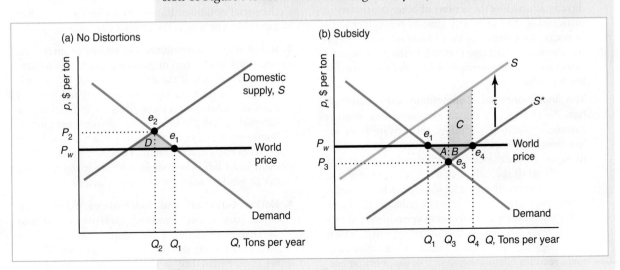

[13]In the economics literature, this result is referred to as the *Theory of the Second Best*.

In panel b, we include pollution in the analysis. The supply curve S^* is the sum of the firms' private marginal cost curves where the firms do not bear the cost of the pollution (and similar to curve MC^p in Figure 17.1). If the government imposes a specific tax, τ, that equals the marginal cost of the pollution per ton of paper, then the firms internalize the cost of pollution, and the resulting supply curve is S (similar to MC^s in Figure 17.1).

If the government does not tax or otherwise regulate pollution, the private supply curve S^* lies below the social supply curve, which results in excess domestic production. If trade is banned, the equilibrium is e_3, with a larger quantity, Q_3, than in the original free-trade equilibrium and a lower consumer price, p_3. Because the true marginal cost (the height of the S curve at Q_3) is above the consumer price, there is deadweight loss.

If free trade is permitted, the Theory of the Second Best tells us that welfare does not necessarily rise, because the country still has the pollution distortion. The free-trade equilibrium is e_4. Firms sell all their quantity, Q_4, at the world price, with Q_1 going to domestic consumers and $Q_4 - Q_1$ to consumers elsewhere. The private gain to trade—ignoring the government's cost of providing the subsidy—is area $A + B$. However, the expansion of domestic output increases society's cost due to excess pollution from producing Q_4 rather than Q_3, which is area $B + C$. The height of this area is the distance between the two supply curves, which is the marginal and average costs of the pollution damage (τ), and the length is the extra output sold ($Q_4 - Q_3$). Thus, if area C is greater than area A, there is a net welfare loss from permitting trade. In this diagram, C is greater than A, so allowing trade lowers welfare if pollution is not taxed.

Should the country prohibit free trade? No, the country should allow free trade and regulate pollution to maximize welfare.

SUMMARY

1. **Externalities.** An externality occurs when a consumer's well-being or a firm's production capabilities are directly affected by the actions of other consumers or firms rather than indirectly affected through changes in prices. An externality that harms others is a negative externality, and one that helps others is a positive externality. Some externalities benefit one group and harm another.

2. **The Inefficiency of Competition with Externalities.** Because producers do not pay for a negative externality such as pollution, the private costs are less than the social costs. Consequently, competitive markets produce more negative externalities than are optimal. If the only way to cut externalities is to decrease output, the optimal solution is to set output where the marginal benefit from reducing the externality equals the marginal cost to consumers and producers from less output. It is usually optimal to have some negative externalities, because eliminating all of them requires eliminating desirable outputs and consumption activities as well. If the government has sufficient information about demand, production cost, and the harm from the externality, it can use taxes or quotas to force the competitive market to produce the social optimum. It may tax or limit the negative externality, or it may tax or limit output.

3. **Regulating Externalities.** Governments may use emissions fees (taxes) or emissions standards to control externalities. If the government has full knowledge, it can set a fee equal to the marginal harm of the externality that causes firms to internalize the externality and produce the socially optimal output. Similarly, the government can set a standard that achieves the social optimum. However, if the government lacks full information, whether it should use a tax or fee depends on a number of factors.

4. **Market Structure and Externalities.** Although a competitive market produces excessive output and negative externalities, a noncompetitive market may produce more or less than the optimal level. With a negative externality, a noncompetitive equilibrium may be closer than a competitive equilibrium to the social optimum. Although a fee equal to the marginal

social harm of a negative externality results in the social optimum when applied to a competitive market, such a fee may lower welfare when applied to a noncompetitive market.

5. **Allocating Property Rights to Reduce Externalities.** Externalities arise because property rights are not clearly defined. According to the Coase Theorem, allocating property rights to either of two parties results in an efficient outcome if the parties can bargain. However, the assignment of the property rights affects income distribution because the rights are valuable. Unfortunately, bargaining is usually not practical, especially when many people are involved. In such cases, using markets for permits to produce externalities may overcome the externality problem.

6. **Rivalry and Exclusion.** Private goods are subject to rivalry—if one person consumes a unit of the good it cannot be consumed by others—and to exclusion—others can be stopped from consuming the good.

Some goods lack one or both of these properties. Open-access common property, such as a fishery, is nonexclusive, but is subject to rivalry. This lack of exclusion causes overfishing because users of the fishery do not take into account the costs they impose on others (forgone fish) when they go fishing. A club good is nonrival but exclusive. For example, a swimming club lacks rivalry up to capacity but can exclude nonmembers. A market failure occurs if a positive price is charged for such a good while there is still extra capacity, because the marginal cost of providing the good to one more person is zero, which is less than the price. A public good such as public defense is both nonrival and nonexclusive. The lack of exclusion causes a freerider problem in a market: People use the good without paying for it. Therefore, potential suppliers of such goods are not adequately compensated and underprovide the good. Because private markets tend to underprovide nonprivate goods, governments often produce or subsidize such goods.

EXERCISES

■ = *exercise is available on* MyEconLab; * = *answer appears at the back of this book;* **M** = *mathematical problem.*

1. Externalities

1.1 According to a study in the *New England Journal of Medicine*, your friendships or "social networks" are more likely than your genes to make you obese (Jennifer Levitz, "Can Your Friends Make You Fat?" *Wall Street Journal*, July 26, 2007, D1). If it is true that people who have overweight friends are more likely to be overweight all else the same, is that an example of a negative externality? Why? (*Hints*: Is this relationship a causal one, or do heavier people choose heavier friends? Also, people with thinner friends may be thinner.)

1.2 When *Star Wars Episode III*: *Revenge of the Sith* opened at 12:01 A.M., Thursday, May 19, 2005, the most fanatical *Star Wars* fans paid $50 million for tickets to stay up until 3:00 to 4:00 A.M. Businesses around the country, especially those tied to high-tech industries, suffered reduced productivity due to absent (suffering from Darth Vader flu) or groggy workers on Thursday and Friday. By one estimate, fan loyalty cost U.S. employers as much as $627 million (Josie Roberts, *Pittsburgh Tribune-Review*, May 19, 2005). Is this productivity loss an example of a negative externality? Explain.

1.3 In 2009, when the world was worried about the danger of the H1N1 influenza virus (swine flu), Representative Rosa DeLauro and Senator Edward Kennedy proposed the Healthy Families Act in Congress to guarantee paid sick days to all workers (Ellen Wu, and Rajiv Bhatia, "A Case for Paid Sick Days," *San Francisco Chronicle*, May 15, 2009). Although the Centers for Disease Control and Prevention urges ill people to stay home from work or school to keep from infecting others, many workers—especially those who do not receive paid sick days—ignore this advice. Evaluate the efficiency and welfare implications of the proposed law taking account of externalities.

1.4 Other sports teams benefit financially from playing a team with a superstar whom fans want to see. Do such positive externalities lower social welfare? If not, why not? If so, what could the teams do to solve that problem?

1.5 According to the digital media company Captivate Network, employees viewing the 2012 Olympics instead of working caused a $1.38 billion loss in productivity for U.S. companies. Is this productivity loss an example of a negative externality? Explain.

2. The Inefficiency of Competition with Externalities

2.1 Why isn't zero pollution the best solution for society? Can there be too little pollution? Why or why not?

2.2 In Figure 17.1, explain why area $D + E + H$ is the externality cost difference between the social optimum and the private equilibrium.

2.3 Let $H = \overline{G} - G$ be the amount that gunk, G, is reduced from the competitive level, $\overline{G}$. The benefit of reducing gunk is $B(H) = AH^{\alpha}$. The cost is $C(H) = H^{\beta}$. If the benefit is increasing but at a diminishing rate as H increases, and the cost is rising at an increasing rate, what are the possible ranges of values for A, α, and B? **M**

2.4 Applying the model in Exercise 2.3, use calculus to determine the optimal level of H. **M**

3. Regulating Externalities

3.1 Australia required that incandescent light bulbs be phased out by 2010 in favor of the more fuel-efficient compact fluorescent bulbs. Ireland's ban started in 2009, and the United States started phasing out incandescent bulbs in 2012. These restrictions were designed to reduce carbon and global warming. What alternative approaches could be used to achieve the same goals? What are the advantages and disadvantages of a ban relative to the alternatives?

3.2 Markowitz (2012) found that limiting the number of liquor stores reduces crime. To maximize welfare taking into account the harms associated with alcohol sales, how should a regulatory agency set the number of liquor licenses? Should the profit maximizing owner of a liquor store lobby for or against tighter restrictions on licenses?

3.3 In 1998, the National Highway Traffic Safety Administration distributed the film *Without Helmet Laws, We All Pay the Price*. Two reasons for this title are that some injured motorcyclists are treated at public expense (Medicaid) and that the dependents of those killed in accidents receive public assistance.

   a. Does the purchase of a motorcycle by an individual who does not wear a helmet create a negative externality? Explain.

   b. If so, how should government set a no-helmet tax that would lead to a socially desirable level of motorcycle sales?

*3.4 In the paper mill example in this chapter, what are the optimal emissions fee and the optimal tax on output (assuming that only one fee or tax is applied)?

3.5 In Figure 17.1, could the government use a price ceiling or a price floor to achieve the optimal level of production?

3.6 In Figure 17.3, the government may optimally regulate the paper market by taxing output. Given that the output tax remains constant, what are the welfare implications of a technological change

that drives down the private marginal cost of production?

*3.7 Suppose that the inverse demand curve for paper is $p = 200 - Q$, the private marginal cost (unregulated competitive market supply) is $MC^p = 80 + Q$, and the marginal harm from gunk is $MC^g = Q$.

   a. What is the unregulated competitive equilibrium?

   b. What is the social optimum?

   c. What specific tax (per unit of output of gunk) results in the social optimum? (*Hint*: See Solved Problem 17.1.) **M**

3.8 Connecticut announced that commercial fleet operators would get a tax break if they converted vehicles from ozone-producing gasoline to what the state said were cleaner fuels such as natural gas and electricity. For every dollar spent on the conversion of their fleets or building alternative fueling stations, operators could deduct 50¢ from their corporate tax. Is this approach likely to be a cost-effective way to control pollution?

3.9 If global warming occurs, output of three of the major U.S. cash crops could decline by as much as 80% according to Roberts and Schenkler (2010). Crop yields increase on days when the temperature rises above 50°, but fall precipitously on days when it is above 86°. Given this relationship between agricultural output and temperature, what would be the government's optimal policy if it can predictably control pollution and hence temperature (and this agricultural effect is the only externality from global warming)? Can you use either a tax or an emissions standard to achieve your optimal policy? How does your policy recommendation change if the government is uncertain about its ability to control pollution and temperature or there are other externalities?

*3.10 Suppose that the government knows the marginal cost, MC, curve of reducing pollution but is uncertain about the marginal benefit, MB, curve. With equal probability, the government faces a relatively high or a relatively low MB curve, so its expected MB curve is the same as the one in Figure 17.4. Should the government use an emissions fee or an emissions standard to maximize expected welfare? Explain. (*Hint*: Use an analysis similar to that employed in Figure 17.4.)

4. Market Structure and Externalities

4.1 Suppose that the only way to reduce pollution from paper production is to reduce output. The government imposes a tax on the monopoly producer that is equal to the marginal harm from the pollution. Show that the tax may raise welfare. (*Hint*: See Solved Problem 17.2.)

4.2 In the following, use the model in Exercise 3.7.

a. What is the unregulated monopoly equilibrium?

b. How could you optimally regulate the monopoly? What is the resulting (socially optimal) equilibrium? (*Hint*: See Solved Problem 17.2.) **M**

5. Allocating Property Rights to Reduce Externalities

5.1 List three specific examples where Coasian bargaining may result in the social optimum.

5.2 Analyze the following statement. Is garbage a positive or a negative externality? Why is a market solution practical here?

Since the turn of the twentieth century, hog farmers in New Jersey fed Philadelphia garbage to their pigs. Philadelphia saved $3 million a year and reduced its garbage mound by allowing New Jersey farmers to pick up leftover food scraps for their porcine recyclers. The city paid $1.9 million to the New Jersey pig farmers for picking up the waste each year, which was about $79 a ton. Otherwise, the city would have had to pay $125 a ton for curbside recycling of the same food waste.

5.3 To the dismay of business travelers, airlines discretely cater to families with young children who fly first class (Rosman, Katherine, "Frequent Criers," *Wall Street Journal*, May 20, 2005, W1). Suppose a family's value is $4,500 from traveling in first class and $1,500 from traveling in coach. The total price of first-class tickets for the family is $4,000. Thus, the family's net value of traveling in first class is $500 = $4,500 − $4,000. Because the total price of coach tickets for the family is $1,200, the family's net value of traveling in coach is $300 = $1,500 − $1,200. A seasoned and weary business traveler who prefers to travel first class observes that a family is about to purchase first-class tickets. The business traveler quickly considers whether to offer to pay the family to fly in coach instead.

a. Suppose that the business traveler knows the value that the family places on coach and first-class travel. What is the minimum price that the traveler can offer the family not to travel in first class?

b. Suppose the business traveler values peace and quiet at $600. Will the business traveler and family reach a mutually agreeable price for the family to move to coach?

c. If instead the business traveler values peace and quiet at $200, can the business traveler and family reach a mutually agreeable price for the family to move to coach?

6. Rivalry and Exclusion

6.1 List three examples of goods that do not fit neatly into the categories in Table 17.3 because they are not strictly rivalrous or exclusive.

6.2 Are heavily used bridges, such as the Bay Bridge, Brooklyn Bridge, and Golden Gate Bridge, commons? If so, what can be done to mitigate externality problems?

6.3 Are broadcast TV and cable TV public goods? Is exclusion possible? If either is a public good, why is it privately provided?

6.4 To prevent overfishing, could one set a tax on fish or on boats? Explain and illustrate with a graph.

6.5 There are 240 automobile drivers per minute who are considering using the E-ZPass lanes of the Interstate 78 toll bridge over the Delaware River that connects Easton, Pennsylvania, and Phillipsburg, New Jersey. With that many autos, and a 5 mph speed restriction through the E-ZPass sensors, there is congestion. We can divide the drivers of these cars into groups A, B, C, and D. Each group has 60 drivers. Each driver in Group i has the following value of crossing the bridge: v_i if 60 or fewer autos cross, $v_i - 1$ if between 61 and 120 autos cross, $v_i - 2$ if between 121 and 180 autos cross, and $v_i - 3$ if more than 180 autos cross. Suppose $v_A = \$4$, $v_B = \$3$, $v_C = \$2$ and $v_D = \$1$. The marginal cost of crossing the bridge, not including the marginal cost of congestion, is zero.

a. If the price of crossing equals a driver's marginal private cost—the price in a competitive market—how many cars per minute will cross? Which groups will cross?

b. In the social optimum, which groups of drivers will cross? That is, which collection of groups crossing will maximize the sum of the drivers' utilities? **M**

6.6 You and your roommate have a stack of dirty dishes in the sink. Either of you would wash the dishes if the decision were up to you; however, neither will do it, in the expectation (hope?) that the other will deal with the mess. Explain how this example illustrates the problem of public goods and free riding.

6.7 Do publishers sell the optimal number of intermediate microeconomics textbooks? Discuss in terms of public goods, rivalry, and exclusion.

6.8 Vaccinations help protect the unvaccinated from disease. Boulier et al. (2007) find that the marginal externality effect can be greater than one case of illness prevented among the unvaccinated. Is vaccination a public good? If so, what might the government do to protect society optimally?

*6.9 According to the "What's Their Beef?" application, collective generic advertising produces $5.67 in additional marginal revenue for every dollar contributed by producers. Is the industry advertising optimally (see Chapter 12)? Explain.

6.10 Guards patrolling a mall protect the mall's two stores. The electronics store's demand curve for guards is greater at all prices than that of the ice-cream parlor. The marginal cost of a guard is $10 per hour. Use a diagram to show the equilibrium, and compare that to the socially optimal equilibrium. Now suppose that the mall's owner will provide a subsidy of s per-hour-per-guard. Show in your graph the optimal s that leads to the socially optimal outcome for the two stores.

6.11 Two tenants of a mall are protected by the guard service, q. The number of guards per hour demanded by the electronics store is $q_1 = a_1 + b_1 p$, where p is the price of one hour of guard services. The ice-cream store's demand is $q_2 = a_2 + b_2 p$. What is the social demand for this service? **M**

6.12 In the analysis of the optimal level of a public good, suppose that each person's utility function is quasilinear: $U_i(G) + P_i$. Show that the optimal G is unique and independent of P_1 and P_2 if society has adequate resources. (*Hint*: See Solved Problem 17.3.) **M**

6.13 Anna and Bess are assigned to write a joint paper within a 24-hour period about the Pareto optimal provision of public goods. Let A denote the number of hours that Anna contributes to the project and B the number of hours that Bess contributes. The numeric grade that Anna and Bess earn is a function, $23 \ln(A + B)$, of the total number of hours that they contribute to the project. If Anna contributes t_A, then she has $(24 - A)$ hours in the day for leisure. Anna's utility function is $U_A = 23 \ln(A + B) + \ln(24 - A)$; and Bess's utility function is $U_B = 23 \ln(A + B) + \ln(24 - B)$. If they choose the hours to contribute simultaneously and independently, what is the Nash equilibrium number of hours that each will provide? What is the number of hours each should contribute to the project that maximizes the sum of their utilities? **M**

7. Challenge

*7.1 Redraw panel b of the Challenge Solution figure to show that it is possible for trade to increase welfare even when pollution is not taxed or otherwise regulated.

*7.2 In the Challenge Solution, where there is no pollution as in panel a of the figure, how do we know that winners from trade can compensate losers and still have enough left over to benefit themselves?

Asymmetric Information

18

The buyer needs a hundred eyes, the seller not one.
—George Herbert (1651)

In part because of the differing amounts that firms invest in safety, jobs in some firms are more dangerous than in others. In 2010, the BP's Deepwater Horizon oil rig explosion in the Gulf of Mexico killed 11 workers, Massey Energy's West Virginia mine explosion slayed 29 coal miners, and 33 Chilean miners were trapped half a mile underground for 69 days in another mine disaster. In 2011, Fukushima Daiichi's decision to send workers with inadequate protection to deal with a nuclear crisis in its critically damaged power plant met with worldwide condemnation.

Rational people who fear danger agree to work in dangerous jobs only if those jobs pay a sufficiently higher wage than less-risky alternative jobs.[1] Workers receive such *compensating wage differentials* in industries and occupations that government statistics show are relatively risky.

Injury rates vary dramatically by industry. According to 2012 U.S. government statistics, the financial services industry averages 1.3 fatal injuries per 100,000 workers each year, while the construction rate is 9.8, the police rate is 18.1, and the mining rate is 19.8. Some occupations are particularly dangerous. Fishing has a fatal injury rate of 152.9 per 100,000 workers; logging, 93.5; agriculture, 42.5; and truck driving, 23.0. On the other hand, safe occupations include sales, 2.0, and educational services, 0.9 (although students sometimes risk dying of boredom).[2]

However, if workers are unaware of the greater risks at certain firms within an industry, they may not receive compensating wage differentials from more dangerous employers within that industry. Workers are likely to have a sense of the risks associated with an industry: Everyone knows that mining is relatively risky—but they do not know which mining companies are particularly risky until a major accident occurs. For example, in the past decade, 54 coal miners have been killed in Massey mines, a much higher rate than at other firms' mines, yet there's no evidence that these workers received higher pay than workers at other mining firms.[3]

---

[1] In 2012, Redhook Brewery started selling a special beer in memory of an employee who was killed when a keg exploded, with the proceeds going to his family (**boston.cbslocal.com**, July 20, 2012).

[2] Government statistics also tell us that males have an accident rate, 6.0, that is an order of magnitude greater than females, 0.7. Some of this difference is due to different occupations and some to different attitudes toward risk. How many women die after saying, "Hey! Watch this!"?

[3] The U.S. Mine Safety and Health Administration issued Massey 124 safety-related citations in 2010 prior to the April 2010 accident at Massey's Upper Big Branch mine in West Virginia that killed 29 workers. Massey had 515 violations in 2009. Mine Safety and Health Administration safety officials concluded in 2011 that the 2010 explosion that took 29 lives could have been prevented by Massey. Justice Department officials brought a criminal indictment against the former head of safety at the mine.

631

The recent U.S. disasters resulted in renewed calls by unions for greater U.S. government intervention to protect workers, such as the Miner Safety and Health Act of 2010. Firms strongly opposed such proposals.

One justification often given for government intervention is that firms have more information than workers do about job safety at their plants. Prospective employees often do not know the injury rates at individual firms but may know the *average* injury rate over an entire industry, in part because such data are reported by governments. Does such a situation cause firms to underinvest in safety? Can government intervention overcome such safety problems?

So far, we've examined models in which everyone is equally knowledgeable or equally ignorant: They have *symmetric information*. In the competitive model, everyone knows the relevant facts. In the uncertainty models in Chapter 16, the companies that sell insurance and the people who buy it are equally uncertain about future events. In contrast, in this chapter's models, people have **asymmetric information**: One party to a transaction has relevant information that another party does not have. For example, the seller knows the quality of a product and the buyer does not.

We concentrate on two types of asymmetric information: *hidden characteristics* and *hidden actions*. A **hidden characteristic** is a fact about a person or thing that is known to one party but unknown to others. For example, the owner of a property may possess extensive information about the mineral composition of the land that is unknown to a mining company that is considering buying the land.

A **hidden action** occurs when one party to a transaction cannot observe important *actions* taken by another party. An example is a firm's manager using a company jet for personal use without the owners' knowledge.

The more-informed party may exploit the less-informed party. That is, the informed party may engage in **opportunistic behavior**: taking advantage of someone when circumstances permit. Such *opportunistic behavior* due to asymmetric information leads to market failures, and destroys many desirable properties of competitive markets. In a competitive market in which everyone has full information, consumers can buy whatever quality good they want at its marginal cost. In contrast, when firms have information that consumers lack—when information is asymmetric—firms may sell only the lowest-quality good, the price may be above marginal cost, or other problems may occur.

If consumers do not know the quality of a good they are considering buying, some firms may try to sell them a dud at the price of a superior good. However, knowing that the chance of buying schlock is high, consumers may be unwilling to pay much for goods of unknown quality. As a result, firms that make high-quality products may not be able to sell them at prices anywhere near their cost of production. In other words, *bad products drive good products out of the market*. The market failure is that the market for a good-quality product is reduced or eliminated, even though (knowledgeable) consumers value the high-quality product at more than the cost of producing it.

If consumers (unlike sellers) do not know how prices vary across firms, *firms may gain market power and set prices above marginal cost*. Suppose that you go to Store A to buy a television set. If you know that Store B is charging $499 for the same TV, you are willing to pay Store A at most $499 (or perhaps a little more to avoid having to go to Store B). *Knowledge is power*. However, if you don't know Store B's price for that TV, Store A might charge you much more than $499. *Ignorance costs*.

Market failures due to asymmetric information can be eliminated if consumers can inexpensively determine the quality of a product or learn the prices that various stores charge. In many markets, however, obtaining this information is prohibitively expensive.

In this chapter, we examine five main topics	1. **Problems Due to Asymmetric Information.** Informed people take advantage of uninformed people. 2. **Responses to Adverse Selection.** To reduce the harms from adverse selection—an informed person's benefiting from trading with an uninformed person who does not know about a characteristic of the informed person—government actions or contracts between involved parties may be used to prevent opportunistic behavior, or the information asymmetry may be reduced or eliminated. 3. **How Ignorance About Quality Drives Out High-Quality Goods.** If consumers cannot distinguish between good and bad products before purchase, it is possible that only bad products will be sold. 4. **Market Power from Price Ignorance.** Firms gain market power from consumers' about the price that each firm charges. 5. **Problems Arising from Ignorance When Hiring.** Attempts to eliminate information asymmetries in hiring may raise or lower social welfare.

18.1   Problems Due to Asymmetric Information

When both parties to a transaction have equally limited information, neither has an advantage. If a roadside vendor sells a box of oranges to a passing motorist and neither knows the quality of the oranges, neither has an advantage because both are operating with equal uncertainty.

In contrast, asymmetric information leads to problems of *opportunism*, whereby the informed person benefits at the expense of the person with less information. If only the vendor knows that the oranges are of low quality, the vendor may allege that the oranges are of high quality and charge a premium price for them.

The two major types of opportunistic behavior are *adverse selection* and *moral hazard*. **Adverse selection** occurs when one party to a transaction possesses information about a hidden characteristic that is unknown to other parties and takes economic advantage of this information. Adverse selection causes low-quality products to be over-represented in transactions. Some or all of the parties to a transaction characterized by adverse selection are worse off than they would be if the information were symmetric.

For example, people who buy life insurance policies are better informed about their own health than insurance companies are. If an insurance company offers to insure people against death for 10 years at a fixed rate, a disproportionately large share of unhealthy people buy this policy. Because of this adverse selection, the insurance company pays on more policies than it would if healthy and unhealthy people bought the policy in proportion to their share in the population.

Adverse selection creates a market failure by reducing the size of a market or eliminating it, preventing desirable transactions. Insurance companies charge higher rates for insurance due to adverse selection or choose not to offer insurance. Very few older people, even healthy ones, buy term life insurance, because the rates are extremely high due to adverse selection. The higher cost of a parental leave benefit due to adverse selection may discourage firms from offering the benefit. That decision hurts both employees who are new parents, who lose the benefit, and firms, which cannot offer a benefit that would otherwise allow them to pay a lower wage.

Moral hazard is opportunism characterized by an informed person's taking advantage of a less-informed person through an *unobserved action*. An employee may *shirk*—fail to fulfill job responsibilities—if not monitored by the employer. Similarly, insured people may take unobserved actions—engage in risky behaviors—that increase the probability of large claims against insurance companies, or they may fail to take reasonable precautions that would reduce the likelihood of such claims. An insured homeowner may ignore fire hazards such as piles of old newspapers. Some insured motorists drive more recklessly than they would if they were uninsured. Moral hazards such as shirking, failure to take care, and reckless behavior reduce output or increase accidents, which are market failures that harm society.

The distinction between adverse selection and moral hazard—between unobserved characteristics and unobserved actions—is not always clear. A life insurance company may face unusually high risks if it insures George and Marge, who, unknown to the company, are skydivers. George will skydive whether or not he has life insurance. Knowing the risks of skydiving, he's more likely to buy life insurance than others. His unobserved characteristic—his love of plunging toward the earth at high speed—leads to adverse selection. Marge will skydive only if she has life insurance. Her unobserved action is a moral hazard for the insurance company.

This chapter focuses on adverse selection and unobserved characteristics. We identify the problems that arise from adverse selection and discuss how they can sometimes be solved. Chapter 19 concentrates on moral hazard problems due to unobserved actions and the use of contracts to deal with them.

18.2 Responses to Adverse Selection

The two main methods for solving adverse selection problems are to restrict opportunistic behavior and to equalize information. Responses to adverse selection problems increase welfare in some markets, but they may do more harm than good in others.

Controlling Opportunistic Behavior Through Universal Coverage

Health insurance markets have adverse selection because low-risk consumers do not buy insurance at prices that reflect the average risk. Such adverse selection can be eliminated by providing insurance to everyone or by mandating that everyone buy insurance. Canada, the United Kingdom, and many other countries provide basic health insurance to all residents, financed by a combination of mandatory premiums and taxes. In 2012, the U.S. Supreme Court confirmed the constitutionality of the "individual mandate" in the 2010 Patient Protection and Affordable Care Act, which requires virtually all Americans to have health care coverage.

Similarly, firms often provide mandatory health insurance as a benefit to all employees, rather than paying them a higher wage and allowing them to decide whether to buy such insurance on their own. By doing so, firms reduce adverse selection problems for their insurance carriers: Both healthy and unhealthy people are covered. As a result, firms can buy medical insurance for their workers at a lower cost per person than workers could obtain on their own.

Equalizing Information

Either informed or uninformed parties can eliminate information asymmetries. **Screening** is an action taken by an uninformed person to determine the information possessed by informed people. For example, a buyer may test-drive (screen) several used cars to determine which one starts and handles the best. **Signaling** is an action taken by an informed person to send information to a less-informed person. A firm may send a signal—such as by widely distributing a favorable report on its product by an independent testing agency—to try to convince buyers that its product is of high quality. In some markets, government agencies or nonprofit organizations such as Consumers Union also provide consumers with information.

Screening. Uninformed people may eliminate their disadvantage by screening to gather information on the hidden characteristics of informed people. Life insurance companies reduce adverse selection problems by requiring medical exams. Based on this information, a firm may decide not to insure high-risk individuals or to charge them a higher premium as compensation for the extra risk.

It is costly to collect information on the health of a person or whether that individual has dangerous habits such as smoking, drinking, or skydiving. As a result, insurance companies collect information only up to the point at which the marginal benefit from the extra information they gather equals the marginal cost of obtaining it. Over time, insurance companies have increasingly concluded that it pays to collect information about whether individuals exercise, have a family history of dying young, or engage in potentially life-threatening activities.

APPLICATION

Risky Hobbies

To reduce the risk of adverse selection, life insurance companies no longer rely solely on information about age and general health in determining risk. Now, they also investigate individuals' smoking and drinking habits, occupations, and even their hobbies. For example, in 2011, people who scuba dive to 100 feet or more typically pay $5 more for every $1,000 of life insurance. If they dive deeper than 150 feet, insurance companies usually deny them coverage.

Steve Potter, a 40-year-old managing director at an executive recruiting firm, prepared to climb Mount Everest by buying a $2 million life insurance policy. His firm took out an additional $1 million on his life. Although Prudential Insurance Company of America would offer a typical healthy 40-year-old a $1 million policy for $1,000, the company wanted $6,000 to cover the adventurous Mr. Potter.

Signaling. An informed party may signal the uninformed party to eliminate adverse selection. Potential employees who know their own abilities use a variety of signals to impress a possible employer who does not know their abilities. For a job interview, serious candidates arrive on time, dress appropriately, refrain from chewing gum, document their training and achievements, and prove their employment longevity at other firms. Similarly, an applicant for life insurance could have a physical examination and then present an insurance company with a written statement from the doctor to signal the applicant's good health.

Only people who believe they can show that they are better than others want to send a signal. Moreover, signaling solves an information problem only if the signals are accurate. For example, if it is easy for people to find an unscrupulous doctor who will report falsely that they are in good health, insurance companies won't rely on such signals. Here, screening may work better, and the insurance firms may require that potential customers get a checkup from a designated doctor.

18.3   How Ignorance About Quality Drives Out High-Quality Goods

We now examine markets in which asymmetric information causes major problems due to adverse selection. In most of these situations, buyers know less than sellers do.

Consumers often have trouble determining the quality of goods and services. Most people don't know how to judge the abilities of a professional such as a doctor, lawyer, plumber, electrician, or economist. Many of us have no reliable information about whether the foods we eat are safe or whether it's safer to fly in a Boeing 747 or an Airbus 380.

Consumer ignorance about quality leads to a less-efficient use of resources than would occur if everyone were perfectly informed. In this section, we first examine how limited consumer information leads to adverse selection. We demonstrate that adverse selection occurs whether or not a seller can alter the quality of the good. We then consider how to ameliorate—though not necessarily eliminate—the adverse selection problem.

Lemons Market with Fixed Quality

Anagram for General Motors: or great lemons.

When buyers cannot judge a product's quality before purchasing it, low-quality products—lemons—may drive high-quality products out of the market (Akerlof, 1970). This situation is common in used-car markets: Owners of lemons are more likely than owners of high-quality vehicles to sell their cars, creating an adverse selection problem.

Cars that appear to be identical often differ in quality. A lemon is cursed. It has a variety of insidious problems that the new owner learns about only after driving it for a while. In contrast, the seller of a used car knows from experience whether it's a lemon. We assume that the seller cannot practically alter the quality of the used car.

All potential buyers are willing to pay $4,000 for a lemon and $8,000 for a good used car: The demand curve for lemons, D^L, is horizontal at $4,000 in panel a of Figure 18.1, and the demand curve for good cars, D^G, is horizontal at $8,000 in panel b.

Although the number of potential buyers is virtually unlimited, only 1,000 owners of lemons and 1,000 owners of good cars are willing to sell. The *reservation price* of lemon

Figure 18.1 Markets for Lemons and Good Cars

If everyone has full information, the equilibrium in the lemons market is *e* (1,000 cars sold for $4,000 each), and the equilibrium in the good-car market is *E* (1,000 cars sold for $8,000 each). If buyers can't tell quality before buying but assume that equal numbers of the two types of cars are for sale, their demand in both markets is D^*, which is horizontal at $6,000. If the good car owners' reservation price is $5,000, the supply curve for good cars is S^1, and 1,000 good cars (point *F*) and 1,000 lemons (point *f*) sell for $6,000 each. If their reservation price is $7,000, the supply curve is S^2. No good cars are sold; 1,000 lemons sell for $4,000 each (point *e*).

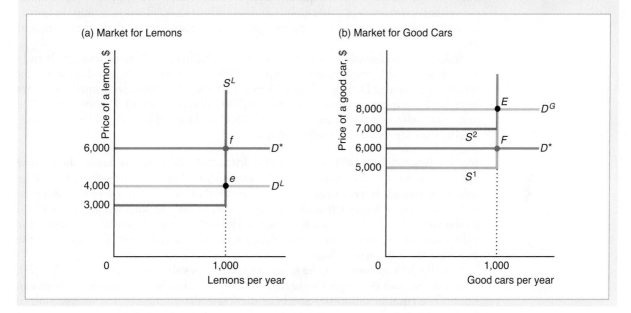

owners—the lowest price at which they will sell their cars—is $3,000. Consequently, the supply curve for lemons, S^L in panel a, is horizontal at $3,000 up to 1,000 cars, where it becomes vertical (no more cars are for sale at any price). The reservation price of owners of high-quality used cars is *v*, which is less than $8,000. Panel b shows two possible values of *v*. If *v* = $5,000, the supply curve for good cars, S^1, is horizontal at $5,000 up to 1,000 cars and then becomes vertical. If *v* = $7,000, the supply curve is S^2.

Market Equilibrium with Symmetric Information. If sellers and buyers know the quality of all the used cars before any sales take place (they have full, symmetric information), all 2,000 cars are sold, and the good cars sell for more than the lemons. In panel a of Figure 18.1, the intersection of the lemons demand curve D^L and the lemons supply curve S^L determines the equilibrium at *e* in the lemons market, where 1,000 lemons sell for $4,000 each. Regardless of whether the supply curve for good cars is S^1 or S^2 in panel b, the equilibrium in the good-car market is *E*, where 1,000 good cars sell for $8,000 each.

This market is efficient because the goods go to the people who value them the most. All current owners, who value the cars less than the potential buyers, sell their cars.

More generally, all buyers and sellers may have symmetric information by being equally informed or equally uninformed. *All the cars are sold if everyone has the same information.* It does not matter whether they all have full information or all lack information—it's the equality of information that matters. However, *the amount of information they have affects the price at which the cars sell.* With full information, good cars sell for $8,000 and lemons sell for $4,000.

If information is symmetric because buyers and sellers are equally ignorant (neither group knows if a car is good or a lemon), all cars sell for the same price. A buyer has an equal chance of buying a lemon or a good car. The expected value of a used car is $\left(\frac{1}{2} \times \$4,000\right) + \left(\frac{1}{2} \times \$8,000\right) = \$6,000$.

Suppose buyers and sellers are risk neutral (Chapter 16). Buyers would pay $6,000 for a car of unknown quality. Because sellers cannot distinguish between the cars either, sellers accept this amount and sell all the cars.[4] Thus, this market is efficient because the cars go to people who value them more than their original owners.

Sellers of good-quality cars are implicitly subsidizing sellers of lemons. If only lemons were sold, they would sell for $4,000. The presence of good-quality cars raises the price received by sellers of lemons to $6,000. Similarly, if only good cars were sold, their owners would obtain $8,000. The presence of lemons lowers the price that sellers of good cars receive to $6,000. Thus, effectively, sellers of good-quality cars are subsidizing sellers of lemons.

Market Equilibrium with Asymmetric Information. If sellers know the quality but buyers do not, the market may be inefficient: Better-quality cars may not be sold even though buyers value good cars more than sellers do. There are two possible equilibria: All cars sell at the average price, or only lemons sell at a price equal to the value that buyers place on lemons. The equilibrium depends on whether the value that the owners of good cars place on their cars, v, is greater or less than the expected value of buyers, $6,000.

Initially, let's assume that the sellers of good cars value their cars at $v = \$5,000$, which is less than the buyers' expected value of the cars, $6,000, so transactions can occur. The equilibrium in the good-car market is determined by the intersection of S^1 and D^* at point F, where 1,000 good cars sell for $6,000. Similarly, owners of lemons, who value their cars at only $3,000, are very happy to sell them for $6,000. The new equilibrium in the lemons market is f.

Thus, all cars sell at the same price. Consequently, *asymmetric information does not cause an efficiency problem, but it does have equity implications.* Sellers of lemons benefit and sellers of good cars suffer from consumers' inability to distinguish quality. Consumers who buy the good cars get a bargain, and buyers of lemons are left with a sour taste in their mouths.

Now suppose that the sellers of good cars place a value of $v = \$7,000$ on their cars and thus are unwilling to sell them for $6,000. As a result, the *lemons drive good cars out of the market.* Buyers realize that they can buy only lemons at any price less than $7,000. Consequently, in equilibrium, the 1,000 lemons sell for the expected (and actual) price of $4,000, and no good cars change hands. This equilibrium is inefficient because high-quality cars remain in the hands of people who value them less than potential buyers do.

In summary, if buyers have less information about product quality than sellers do, the result might be a lemons problem in which high-quality cars do not sell, even though potential buyers value the cars more than their current owners do. If so, the asymmetric information causes a competitive market to lose its desirable efficiency and welfare properties. However, if the information is symmetric, the lemons

---

[4]Risk-neutral sellers place an expected value of $\left(\frac{1}{2} \times \$3,000\right) + \frac{1}{2}v = \$1,500 + \frac{1}{2}v$ on a car of unknown quality. If $v = 7,000$, this expected value is $1,500 + $3,500 = $5,000. If $v = \$5,000$ this expected value is only $4,000. In either case, sellers would be happy to sell their cars for $6,000.

problem does not occur. That is, if buyers and sellers of used cars know the quality of the cars, each car sells for its true value in a perfectly competitive market. Moreover, if, as with new cars, neither buyers nor sellers can identify lemons, both good cars and lemons sell at a price equal to the expected value rather than at their (unknown) true values.

SOLVED PROBLEM 18.1	Suppose that everyone in our used-car example is risk neutral; potential car buyers value lemons at \$4,000 and good used cars at \$8,000; the reservation price of lemon owners is \$3,000; and the reservation price of owners of high-quality used cars is \$7,000. The share of current owners who have lemons is θ. (In our previous example, the share was $\theta = \frac{1}{2} = 1,000/[1,000 + 1,000]$). For what values of θ do all the potential sellers sell their used cars? Describe the equilibrium.

Answer

1. *Determine how much buyers are willing to pay if all cars are sold.* Because buyers are risk neutral, if they believe that the probability of getting a lemon is θ, the most they are willing to pay for a car of unknown quality is

$$p = [\$8,000 \times (1 - \theta)] + (\$4,000 \times \theta) = \$8,000 - (\$4,000 \times \theta). \qquad (18.1)$$

For example, $p = \$6,000$ if $\theta = \frac{1}{2}$ and $p = \$7,000$ if $\theta = \frac{1}{4}$.

2. *Solve for the values of θ such that all the cars are sold, and describe the equilibrium.* All owners will sell if the market price equals or exceeds their reservation price, \$7,000. Using Equation 18.1, we know that the market (equilibrium) price is \$7,000 or more if a quarter or fewer of the used cars are lemons, $\theta \leq \frac{1}{4}$. Thus, for $\theta \leq \frac{1}{4}$, all the cars are sold at the price given in Equation 18.1.

Lemons Market with Variable Quality

Most firms can adjust their product's quality. If consumers cannot identify high-quality goods before purchase, they pay the same for all goods regardless of quality. Because the price that firms receive for top-quality goods is the same they receive for low-quality items, they do not produce top-quality goods. Such an outcome is inefficient if consumers are willing to pay sufficiently more for top-quality goods.

SOLVED PROBLEM 18.2	It costs \$10 to produce a low-quality wallet and \$20 to produce a high-quality wallet. Consumers cannot distinguish between the products before purchase, do not make repeat purchases, and value the wallets at the cost of production. The five firms in the market produce 100 wallets each. Each firm produces only high-quality or only low-quality wallets. Consumers pay the expected value of a wallet. Do any of the firms produce high-quality wallets?

Answer

Show that it does not pay for one firm to make high-quality wallets if the other firms make low-quality wallets due to asymmetric information. If all five firms make low-quality wallets, consumers pay $10 per wallet. If one firm makes high-quality wallets and all the others make low-quality wallets, the expected value per wallet to consumers is

$$\left(\$10 \times \tfrac{4}{5}\right) + \left(\$20 \times \tfrac{1}{5}\right) = \$12.$$

Thus, if one firm raises the quality of its product, all firms benefit because the wallets sell for $12 instead of $10. The high-quality firm receives only a fraction of the total benefit from raising quality. It gets $2 extra per high-quality wallet sold, which is less than the extra $10 it costs to make the better wallet. The other $8 is shared by the other firms. Because the high-quality firm incurs all the expenses of raising quality, $10 extra per wallet, and reaps only a fraction, $2, of the benefits, it opts not to produce high-quality wallets. Therefore, *due to asymmetric information, the firms do not produce high-quality goods even though consumers are willing to pay for the extra quality.*

Limiting Lemons

In some markets, it is possible to avoid adverse selection problems that stem from consumer ignorance. Laws might provide protection against being sold a lemon, consumers might screen by collecting the information themselves, the government or another third party might supply reliable information, or sellers might send credible signals.

Laws to Prevent Opportunism. In many countries, product liability laws protect consumers from being stuck with nonfunctional or dangerous products. Moreover, many U.S. state supreme courts have concluded that products are sold with an implicit understanding that they will safely perform their intended functions. If they do not, consumers can sue the seller even in the absence of product liability laws. If consumers can rely on explicit or implicit product liability laws to force a manufacturer to compensate consumers for defective products, they do not need to worry about adverse selection. However, the transaction costs of going to court are very high.

Consumer Screening. Consumers can avoid the lemons problem if they can screen: obtain reliable information about quality. If the benefit of getting this information is greater than the cost, consumers obtain the information, and markets function smoothly. However, if the cost exceeds the benefit, consumers do not gather the information, and the market is inefficient.

Consumers buy information from experts or infer product quality from sellers' reputations. For many goods, consumers can buy reliable information from *objective experts*. For example, customers can pay to have a mechanic appraise a used car. If the mechanic can reliably determine whether the car is a lemon, the information asymmetry is eliminated.

In some markets, consumers learn of a firm's *reputation* from other consumers or from observation. Consumers can avoid the adverse selection problem by buying only from firms with reputations for providing high-quality goods. Consumers know that a used-car firm that wants repeat business has a strong incentive to sell non-defective products.

Generally, in markets in which the same consumers and firms trade regularly, it's easy to establish a reputation. In markets in which consumers buy a good only once, such as in tourist areas, firms cannot establish good reputations as readily.

APPLICATION

Changing a Firm's Name

A firm's good name is one of its most valuable assets. If the firm has sold high-quality goods or provided superior service in the past, then its reputation serves as a signal to consumers that they can expect the same excellence in the future.

But what if the firm's goods or services have been below par? Then the firm's name becomes poison to consumers. The firm can spend a great deal of money trying to improve its reputation. However, a less expensive approach is to change the firm's name: No reputation is better than a bad one. In a more extreme case, the firm may exit the market. For example, Cabral and Hortacsu (2010) reported that eBay sellers are likely to stop selling after receiving their first negative feedback.

McDevitt (2011) found that the more complaints that the Better Business Bureau received about a plumbing firm in Illinois, the more likely the firm was to change its name or exit the industry. Firms that advertised extensively were more likely to change their names than to exit. Finally, all else the same, firms in smaller cities outside of Chicago were 49% less likely to change their names than firms within metro Chicago. Presumably, it is more difficult to shake a bad reputation in a small town than in a large city.[5]

Third-Party Comparisons. Some nonprofit consumer groups and for-profit firms publish expert comparisons of brands. If this information is credible, it helps reduce adverse selection by enabling consumers to avoid buying low-quality goods.

If an outside organization is to provide believable information, it must convince consumers that it is trustworthy. Consumers Union, which publishes the product evaluation guide *Consumer Reports*, seeks to establish its credibility by refusing advertising or other payments from firms.

Unfortunately, expert information is undersupplied because information is a *public good* (nonrivalrous and only sometimes exclusive—see Chapter 17). Consumers Union does not capture the full value of its information through sales of *Consumer Reports* because magazine buyers lend their copies to friends, libraries stock it, and newspapers report on its findings. As a result, Consumers Union conducts less research than is socially optimal.

Standards and Certification. The government, consumer groups, industry groups, and others provide information based on a **standard**: a metric or scale for evaluating the quality of a particular product. For example, the R-value of insulation—a standard—tells how effectively insulation works. Consumers learn about a brand's quality through **certification**: a report that a particular product meets or exceeds a given standard.

Many industry groups set their own standards and hire an outside group or firm, such as Underwriters' Laboratories (UL) or Factory Mutual Engineering Corporation (FMEC), to certify that their products meet specified standards. For example, setting standards for screw threads ensures that screws work properly in all products, regardless of the brand.

When standard and certification programs inexpensively and completely inform consumers about the relative quality of all goods in a market and do not restrict the goods available, the programs are socially desirable. However, some of these

[5]Because when a shady operator loses its reputation, it can simply change its name, some have called for making name changes more difficult. The U.S. Government Accountability Office found that at least 9% of motor coach carriers that were ordered "out of service" by the Federal Motor Carrier Safety Administration for violating safety standards merely changed their names, undermining the effectiveness of such regulatory bodies.

programs have harmful effects. Standard and certification programs that provide degraded information, for instance, may mislead consumers. For example, many standards use only a high- or low-quality rating, even though quality varies continuously. Such standards encourage manufacturers to produce either the lowest-possible quality good (with the lowest cost of production) or a good with the minimum quality level necessary to obtain the top rating.

If standard and certification programs restrict salable goods and services to those that are certified, such programs may also have anticompetitive effects. Many governments license only professionals and craftspeople who meet minimum standards (Chapter 2). People without a license are not allowed to practice their occupation or profession.

The restrictions raise the average quality in the industry by eliminating low-quality goods and services. They drive up prices to consumers for two reasons: The number of service providers is reduced because the restrictions eliminate some potential suppliers, and consumers are unable to obtain lower-quality and less-expensive goods or services (see the Application "Occupational Licensing" in Chapter 2). As a result, welfare may go up or down, depending on whether the increased-quality effect or the higher-price effect dominates. Whether such restrictions can be set properly and cost-effectively by government agencies is widely debated.

Signaling by Firms. Producers of high-quality goods often try to signal consumers that their products are superior to their rivals' goods. If consumers believe these signals, the firms can charge higher prices for their goods. But for signals to be effective, they must be credible.

Firms use brand names as a signal of quality. For example, some firms like Dole brand their produce, while rivals sell their produce without labels. Shoppers may rely on this signal and choose only fruits and vegetables with brand labels. Presumably, a firm uses a brand name to enable buyers to identify its product only if the item's quality is better than that of a typical unbranded product.

Some firms provide guarantees or warranties as signals to convince consumers that their products are of high quality. Consumer durables such as cars and refrigerators almost always come with guarantees or warranties.

Signals prevent the adverse selection problem only when consumers view them as credible (only high-quality firms find their use profitable). Smart consumers may place little confidence in unsubstantiated claims by firms. Would you believe that a used car runs well just because an ad tells you so? Legally enforceable guarantees and warranties are more credible than advertising alone.

Signaling will not prevent an adverse selection problem if it is unprofitable for high-quality firms to signal or if both high- and low-quality firms send the same signal, thus making the signal worthless to consumers. For example, both low-quality and high-quality fruit and vegetable firms can use trademarks in tourist areas, where there are few repeat purchases. Similarly, all firms may provide guarantees for inexpensive goods, but transaction costs are usually too high for consumers to take advantage of guarantees.

APPLICATION

Adverse Selection on eBay Motors

Because consumers can't see a good before buying it over the Internet, it's easy for a shady seller to misrepresent its quality. In the worst-case lemons-market scenario, low-quality goods drive out high-quality ones. We'd expect adverse selection to be particularly bad on eBay Motors, the largest used car marketplace in the United States, where nearly 50,000 cars are sold each month. Three-quarters of the cars are sold to out-of-state buyers, so most people cannot examine the car before bidding.

Sellers' reputations and warranties are of limited help. Although eBay posts reviews from past customers, most sellers have limited records except for dealers, who sell only 30% of the cars. Usually only dealers offer warranties, and then on only some cars.

However, enforceable contracts and sellers' signals reduce adverse selection on eBay Motors. The disclosures on eBay's Web page create an enforceable contract. If the car doesn't live up to the claims, buyers can refuse to pay on delivery. In addition, outright lies are frauds and may be prosecuted. (In contrast, in most private sales between individuals, buyers do not have an enforceable contract.)

Each Web page contains some standard, mandatory information such as car make, model, and mileage. But most sellers signal by voluntarily disclosing additional information ("the car has no rust, scratches, or dents") and posting photos, graphics, and videos. The typical eBay Web page has 17 photos.

Sellers disclose more information for high-quality cars than for lemons. All else the same, a seller who posts 10 photos rather than 9 sells a car for 1.54% more, about $171 on average (Lewis, 2011).

While the contract rights and voluntary positing of information reduce adverse selection, they do not eliminate it. The cost of posting information limits how much is disclosed. In addition to eBay's fees for positing additional photos and other information, which are relatively low (15¢ for additional photos, 75¢ for a larger picture, $5 for a bold title), sellers incur substantial opportunity costs for their time. Those dealers who buy professional software, which lowers their marginal cost of posting photos, post 10 more photos on average than dealers who don't. Given the high payoff to extra photos, sellers must view their marginal costs as substantial.

18.4 Market Power from Price Ignorance

We've seen that consumer ignorance about quality can keep high-quality goods out of markets. We now illustrate that consumer ignorance about price variation across firms gives firms market power. As a result, firms have an incentive to make it difficult for consumers to collect pricing information. Because of this incentive, some stores won't quote prices over the phone.

In this section, we examine why asymmetric pricing information leads to noncompetitive pricing in a market that would otherwise be competitive. Suppose that many stores in a town sell the same good. If consumers have *full information* about prices, all stores charge the full-information competitive price, p^*. If one store were to raise its price above p^*, the store would lose all its business. Each store faces a residual demand curve that is horizontal at the going market price and has no market power.

In contrast, if consumers have *limited information* about the price that firms charge for a product, one store can charge more than others and not lose all its customers. Customers who do not know that the product is available for less elsewhere buy from the high-price store.[6] Thus, each store faces a downward-sloping residual demand curve and has some market power.

---

[6]A grave example concerns the ripping-off of the dying and their relatives. A cremation arranged through a memorial society—which typically charges a nominal enrollment fee of $10 to $25—often costs half or less than the same service when it is arranged through a mortuary (**articles.moneycentral .msn.com/RetirementandWills/PlanYourEstate/HowToPlanAFuneral.aspx?page=all**, September 18, 2007). Consumers who know about memorial societies—which get competitive bids from mortuaries—can obtain a relatively low price.

Tourist-Trap Model

We now show that, if there is a single price in such a market, it is higher than p^*. Suppose you arrive in a small town in California near the site of the discovery of gold. Souvenir shops crowd the street. Wandering by one of them, you see that it sells the town's distinctive snowy: a plastic ball filled with water and imitation snow featuring a model of the Donner party. You decide that you must buy at least one of these tasteful souvenirs—perhaps more if the price is low enough. Your bus is leaving soon, so you can't check the price at each shop to find the lowest price. Moreover, determining which shop has the lowest price won't be useful to you in the future because you do not intend to return anytime soon.

Let's assume that you and other tourists have a guidebook that reports how many souvenir shops charge each possible price for the snowy, but it does not provide the price at any particular shop.[7] There are many tourists in your position, each with an identical demand function.

It costs each tourist c in time and expenses to visit a shop to check the price or buy a snowy. Thus, if the price is p, the cost of buying a snowy at the first shop you visit is $p + c$. If you go to two souvenir shops before buying at the second shop, the cost of the snowy is $p + 2c$.

When Price Is Not Competitive. Will all souvenir shops charge the same price? If so, what is it? We start by considering whether each shop charges the full-information, competitive price, p^*.

The full-information, competitive price is the equilibrium price only if no firm has an incentive to charge a different price. No firm would charge less than p^*, which equals marginal cost, because it would lose money on each sale.

However, a shop could gain by charging a higher price than p^*, so p^* is *not* an equilibrium price. If all other shops charge p^*, a shop can profitably charge $p_1 = p^* + \varepsilon$, where ε, a small positive number, is the shop's price markup. Suppose that you walk into this shop and learn that it sells the snowy for p_1. You know from your guidebook that all the other souvenir shops charge only p^*. You say to yourself, "How unfortunate [or other words to that effect]! I've wandered into the only expensive shop in town." Annoyed, you consider going elsewhere. Nonetheless, you do not go to another shop if this first shop's markup, $\varepsilon = p_1 - p^*$, is less than c, the cost of going to another shop.

As a result, it pays for this shop to raise its price by an amount that is just slightly less than the cost of an additional search, thereby deviating from the proposed equilibrium where all other shops charge p^*. Thus, *if consumers have limited information about price, an equilibrium in which all firms charge the full-information, competitive price is impossible.*

Monopoly Price. We've seen that the market price cannot be lower than or equal to the full-information, competitive price. Can there be an equilibrium in which all stores charge the same price and that price is higher than the competitive price? In particular, can we have an equilibrium when all shops charge $p_1 = p^* + \varepsilon$? No, because shops would deviate from this proposed equilibrium for the same reason that they deviated from charging the competitive price. A shop can profitably raise its price to $p_2 = p_1 + \varepsilon = p^* + 2\varepsilon$. Again, it does not pay for a tourist who is unlucky enough to enter that shop to go to another shop as long as $\varepsilon < c$. Thus, p_1 is not the equilibrium price. By repeating this reasoning, we can reject other possible equilibrium prices that are above p^* and less than the monopoly price, p_m.

---

[7]We make this assumption about the guidebook to keep the presentation as simple as possible. This assumption is not necessary to obtain the following result.

However, the monopoly price may be an equilibrium price. No firm wants to raise its price above the monopoly level because its profit would fall due to reduced sales. When tourists learn the price at a particular souvenir shop, they decide how many snowies to buy. If the price is set too high, the shop's lost sales more than off-set the higher price, so its profit falls. Thus, although the shop can charge a higher price without losing all its sales, it chooses not to do so.

The only remaining question is whether a shop would like to charge a lower price than p_m if all other shops charge that price. If not, p_m is an equilibrium price.

Should a shop reduce its price below p_m by less than c? If it does so, it does not pay for consumers to search for this low-price firm. The shop makes less on each sale, so its profits must fall. Thus, a shop should not deviate by charging a price that is only slightly less than p_m.

Does it pay for a shop to drop its price below p_m by more than c? If there are few shops, consumers may search for this low-price shop. Although the shop makes less per sale than the high-price shops, its profits may be higher because of greater sales volume. If there are many shops, however, consumers do not search for the low-price shop because their chances of finding it are low. As a result, when the presence of a large number of shops makes searching for a low-price shop impractical, no firm lowers its price, so p_m is the equilibrium price. Thus, *when consumers have asymmetric information and when search costs and the number of firms are large, the only possible single-price equilibrium is at the monopoly price.*

If the single-price equilibrium at p_m can be broken by a firm charging a low price, there is no single-price equilibrium. Either there is no equilibrium or there is an equilibrium in which prices vary across shops (see Stiglitz, 1979, or Carlton and Perloff, 2005). Multiple-price equilibria are common.

SOLVED PROBLEM 18.3

Initially, there are many souvenir shops, each of which charges p_m (because consumers do not know the shops' prices), and buyers' search costs are c. If the government pays for half of consumers' search costs, can there be a single-price equilibrium at a price less than p_m?

Answer

Show that the argument we used to reject a single-price equilibrium at any price except the monopoly price does not depend on the size of the search cost. If all other stores charge any single price p, where $p^* \leq p < p_m$, a firm profits from raising its price. As long as it raises its price by no more than $c/2$ (the new cost of search to a consumer), unlucky consumers who stop at this deviant store will not search further. This profitable deviation shows that the proposed single-price equilibrium is not an equilibrium. Again, the only possible single-price equilibrium is at p_m.[8]

Advertising and Prices

The U.S. Federal Trade Commission (FTC), a consumer protection agency, opposes groups that want to forbid price advertising; the FTC argues that advertising about price benefits consumers. If a firm informs consumers about its unusually low price,

---

[8]If the search cost is low enough, however, the single-price equilibrium at p_m can be broken profitably by charging a low price so that only a multiple-price equilibrium is possible. If the search cost falls to zero, consumers have full information, so the only possible equilibrium is at the full-information, competitive price.

it may be able to gain enough additional customers to more than offset its loss from the lower price. If low-price stores advertise their prices and attract many customers, they can break the monopoly-price equilibrium that occurs when consumers must search store by store for low prices. The more successful the advertising, the larger these stores grow and the lower the average price in the market. If enough consumers become informed, all stores may charge the low price. Thus, without advertising, no store may find it profitable to charge low prices, but with advertising, all stores may charge low prices.

18.5   Problems Arising from Ignorance When Hiring

Asymmetric information is frequently a problem in labor markets. Prospective employees may have less information about working conditions than firms do. Firms may have less information about potential employees' abilities than potential workers do.

Information asymmetries in labor markets lower welfare below the full-information level. Workers may signal and firms may screen to reduce the asymmetry in information about workers' abilities. Signaling and screening may raise or lower welfare, as we now consider.

Cheap Talk

Honesty is the best policy—when there is money in it. —Mark Twain

We now consider situations in which workers have more information about their ability than firms do. We look first at inexpensive signals sent by workers, then at expensive signals sent by workers, and finally at screening by firms.

When an informed person voluntarily provides information to an uninformed person, the informed person engages in **cheap talk**: unsubstantiated claims or statements (see Farrell and Rabin, 1996). People use cheap talk to distinguish themselves or their attributes at low cost. Even though informed people may lie when it suits them, it is often in their and everyone else's best interest for them to tell the truth. Nothing stops me from advertising that I have a chimpanzee for sale, but doing so serves no purpose if I actually want to sell a refrigerator. One advantage of cheap talk, if it is effective, is that it is a less-expensive method of signaling ability to a potential employer than paying to have that ability tested.

Suppose that a firm plans to hire Cyndi to do one of two jobs. The demanding job requires someone with high ability. The undemanding job can be performed better by someone with low ability because the job bores more able people, who then work poorly.

Cyndi knows whether her ability level is high or low, but the firm is unsure, initially thinking that either level is equally likely. Panel a of Table 18.1 shows the payoffs to Cyndi and the firm under various possibilities.[9] If Cyndi has high ability, she enjoys the demanding job: Her payoff is 3. If she has low ability, she finds the demanding job too stressful—her payoff is only 1—but she can handle the

---

[9]Previously, we used a 2×2 matrix to show a simultaneous-move game, in which both parties choose an action simultaneously. In contrast, in Table 18.2, only the firm can make a move. Cyndi does not take an action, because she cannot choose her ability level.

Table 18.1   Employee-Employer Payoffs

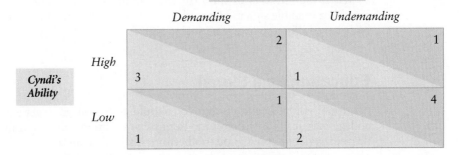

(a) When Cheap Talk Works

		Job That the Firm Gives to Cyndi	
		Demanding	Undemanding
Cyndi's Ability	High	3 / 2	1 / 1
	Low	1 / 1	2 / 4

(b) When Cheap Talk Fails

		Job That the Firm Gives to Cyndi	
		Demanding	Undemanding
Cyndi's Ability	High	3 / 2	1 / 1
	Low	3 / 1	2 / 4

undemanding job. The payoff to the firm is greater if Cyndi is properly matched to the job: She is given the demanding job if she has high ability and the undemanding job if she has low ability.

We can view this example as a two-stage game. In the first stage, Cyndi tells the firm something. In the second stage, the firm decides which job she gets.

Cyndi could make many possible statements about her ability. For simplicity, though, we assume that she says either, "My ability is high" or "My ability is low." This two-stage game has an equilibrium in which Cyndi tells the truth and the firm, believing her, assigns her to the appropriate job. If she claims to have high ability, the firm gives her the demanding job.

If the firm reacts to her cheap talk in this manner, Cyndi has no incentive to lie. If she does, the firm would make a mistake, and a mistake would be bad for both parties. Cyndi and the firm want the same outcome, so cheap talk works.

In many other situations, however, cheap talk does not work. Given the payoffs in panel b, Cyndi and the firm do not want the same outcome. The firm still wants Cyndi in the demanding job if she has high ability and in the undemanding job otherwise. But Cyndi wants the demanding job regardless of her ability, so she claims to have high ability regardless of the truth. Knowing her incentives, the firm views her statement as meaningless—it does not change the firm's view that her ability is equally likely to be high or low.

Given that belief, the firm gives her the undemanding job, for which its expected payoff is higher. The firm's expected payoff is $\left(\frac{1}{2} \times 1\right) + \left(\frac{1}{2} \times 4\right) = 2.5$ if it gives her the undemanding job and $\left(\frac{1}{2} \times 2\right) + \left(\frac{1}{2} \times 1\right) = 1.5$ if it assigns her to the demanding job. Thus, given the firm's asymmetric information, the outcome is inefficient if Cyndi has high ability.

When the interests of the firm and the individual diverge, cheap talk does not provide a credible signal. Here, an individual has to send a more expensive signal to be believed. We now examine such a signal.

Education as a Signal

No doubt you've been told that you should go to college to get a good job. Going to college may result in a better job because you obtain valuable training. Or, a college degree may land you a good job because it signals your ability to employers. If high-ability people are more likely to go to college than low-ability people, schooling signals ability to employers (Spence, 1974).

To illustrate how such signaling works, we'll make the extreme assumptions that graduating from an appropriate school serves as the signal and that schooling provides no useful training to firms (Stiglitz, 1975). High-ability workers are θ share of the workforce, and low-ability workers are $1 - \theta$ share. For a firm, the value of output produced by a high-ability worker is worth w_h, and that of a low-ability worker is w_l (over their careers). If competitive employers knew workers' ability levels, they would pay this value of the marginal product to each worker, so a high-ability worker receives w_h and a low-ability worker earns w_l.

However, suppose that employers cannot directly determine a worker's skill level. For example, when production is a group effort—such as in an assembly line—a firm cannot determine the productivity of a single employee.

Two types of equilibria are possible, depending on whether employers can distinguish high-ability workers from others. If employers have no way of distinguishing workers, the outcome is a **pooling equilibrium**: Dissimilar people are treated (paid) alike or behave alike. Employers pay all workers the average wage:

$$\overline{w} = \theta w_h + (1 - \theta)w_l. \tag{18.2}$$

Risk-neutral, competitive firms expect to break even because they underpay high-ability people by enough to offset the losses from overpaying low-ability workers.

We assume that high-ability individuals can get a degree by spending c to attend a school, but low-ability people cannot graduate from the school (or that the cost of doing so is prohibitively high). If high-ability people graduate and low-ability people do not, a degree is a signal of ability to employers. Given such a clear signal, the outcome is a **separating equilibrium**: One type of people takes actions (such as sending a signal) that allow them to be differentiated from other types of people. Here, a successful signal causes high-ability workers to receive w_h, and others to receive w_l, so wages vary with ability.

We now examine whether a pooling or a separating equilibrium is possible. We consider whether anyone would want to change behavior in an equilibrium. If no one wants to change, the equilibrium is feasible.

Separating Equilibrium. In a separating equilibrium, high-ability people pay c to get a degree and are employed at a wage of w_h, while low-ability individuals do not get a degree and work at a wage of w_l. The low-ability people have no choice, because they can't get a degree. High-ability individuals have the option of not going to school. Without a degree, however, they are viewed as having low ability once they are hired, so they receive w_l. If they go to school, their net earnings are $w_h - c$.

Thus, it pays for a high-ability person to go to school if $w_h - c > w_l$. Rearranging terms in this expression, we find that a high-ability person chooses to get a degree if

$$w_h - w_l > c. \tag{18.3}$$

Equation 18.3 says that the benefit from graduating, the extra pay $w_h - w_p$, exceeds the cost of schooling, c. If Equation 18.3 holds, no worker wants to change behavior, so a separating equilibrium is feasible.

Suppose that $c = \$15{,}000$ and that high-ability workers are twice as productive as others: $w_h = \$40{,}000$ and $w_l = \$20{,}000$. Here, the benefit to a high-ability worker from graduating, $w_h - w_l = \$20{,}000$, exceeds the cost by \$5,000. Thus, no one wants to change behavior in this separating equilibrium.

Pooling Equilibrium. In a pooling equilibrium, all workers are paid the average wage from Equation 18.2, $\overline{w}$. Again, because low-ability people cannot graduate, they have no choice. A high-ability person must choose whether or not to go to school. Without a degree, that individual is paid the average wage. With a degree, the worker is paid w_h. It does not pay for the high-ability person to graduate if the benefit from graduating, the extra pay $w_h - \overline{w}$, is less than the cost of schooling:

$$w_h - \overline{w} < c. \tag{18.4}$$

If Equation 18.4 holds, no worker wants to change behavior, so a pooling equilibrium persists.

For example, if $w_h = \$40{,}000$, $w_l = \$20{,}000$, and $\theta = \frac{1}{2}$, then

$$\overline{w} = \left(\tfrac{1}{2} \times \$40{,}000\right) + \left(\tfrac{1}{2} \times \$20{,}000\right) = \$30{,}000.$$

If the cost of going to school is $c = \$15{,}000$, the benefit to a high-ability person from graduating, $w_h - \overline{w} = \$10{,}000$, is less than the cost, so a high-ability individual does not want to go to school. As a result, there is a pooling equilibrium.

SOLVED PROBLEM 18.4

If $c = \$15{,}000$, $w_h = \$40{,}000$, and $w_l = \$20{,}000$, for what values of θ is a pooling equilibrium possible?

Answer

1. *Determine the values of θ for which it pays for a high-ability person to go to school.* From Equation 18.4, we know that a high-ability individual does not go to school if $w_h - \overline{w} < c$. Using Equation 18.2, we substitute for $\overline{w}$ in Equation 18.4 and rearrange terms to find that high-ability people do not go to school if $w_h - [\theta w_h + (1 - \theta)w_l] < c$, or

$$\theta > 1 - \frac{c}{w_h - w_l}. \tag{18.5}$$

If almost everyone has high ability, so θ is large, a high-ability person does not go to school. The intuition is that, as the share of high-ability workers, θ, gets large (close to 1), the average wage approaches w_h (Equation 18.2), so there is little benefit, $w_h - \overline{w}$, in going to school.

2. *Solve for the possible values of θ for the specific parameters.* If we substitute $c = \$15{,}000$, $w_h = \$40{,}000$, and $w_l = \$20{,}000$ into Equation 18.5, we find that high-ability people do not go to school—that is, a pooling equilibrium is possible—when $\theta > \frac{1}{4}$.

Unique Equilibrium or Multiple Equilibria. Depending on differences in abilities, the cost of schooling, and the share of high-ability workers, only one type of equilibrium may be possible or both may be possible. In the following examples, using Figure 18.2, $w_h = \$40,000$ and $w_l = \$20,000$.

Only a pooling equilibrium is possible if schooling is very costly: $c > w_h - w_l = \$20,000$, so Equation 18.3 does not hold. The horizontal line in Figure 18.2 shows where $c = w_h - w_l = \$20,000$. Only a pooling equilibrium is feasible above that line, $c > \$20,000$, because it is not worthwhile for high-ability workers to go to school.

Equation 18.5 shows that, if there are few high-ability people (relative to the cost and earnings differential), only a separating equilibrium is possible. The figure shows a sloped line where $\theta = 1 - c/(w_h - w_l)$. Below that line, $\theta < 1 - c/(w_h - w_l)$, relatively few people have high ability, so the average wage, $\overline{w}$, is low. A pooling equilibrium is not possible because high-ability workers would want to signal. Thus, below this line, only a separating equilibrium is possible. Above this line, Equation 18.5 holds, so a pooling equilibrium is possible. (The answer to Solved Problem 18.3 shows that no one wants to change behavior in a pooling equilibrium if $c = \$15,000$ and $\theta > \frac{1}{4}$, which are points to the right of x in the figure, such as y.)

Below the horizontal line where the cost of signaling is less than $\$20,000$ and above the sloped line where there are relatively many high-ability workers, either equilibrium may occur. For example at y, where $c = \$15,000$ and $\theta = \frac{1}{2}$, Equations

Figure 18.2 Pooling and Separating Equilibria

If firms know workers' abilities, high-ability workers are paid $w_h = \$40,000$ and low-ability workers get $w_l = \$20,000$. The type of equilibrium depends on the cost of schooling, c, and on the share of high-ability workers, θ. If $c > \$20,000$, only a pooling equilibrium, in which everyone gets the average wage, is possible. If there are relatively few high-ability people, $\theta < 1 - c/\$20,000$, only a separating equilibrium is possible. Between the horizontal and sloped lines, either type of equilibrium may occur.

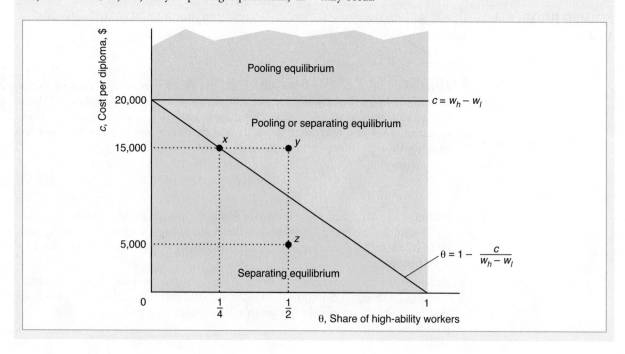

18.3 and 18.4 (or, equivalently, Equation 18.5) hold, so both a separating equilibrium and a pooling equilibrium are possible. In the pooling equilibrium, no one wants to change behavior, so that equilibrium is possible. Similarly, no one wants to change behavior in a separating equilibrium.

A government could ensure that one or the other of these equilibria occurs. It can achieve a pooling equilibrium by banning schooling (and other possible signals). Alternatively, the government can create a separating equilibrium by subsidizing schooling for some high-ability people. Once some individuals start to signal, so that firms pay either a low or a high wage (not a pooling wage), it is worthwhile for other high-ability people to signal.

Efficiency. In our example of a separating equilibrium, high-ability people get an otherwise useless education solely to show that they differ from low-ability people. An education is privately useful to the high-ability workers if it serves as a signal that gets them higher net pay. In our extreme example, education is socially inefficient because it is costly and provides no useful training.

Signaling changes the distribution of wages. Without signaling, everyone receives the average wage. With signaling, high-ability workers earn more than low-ability workers. Nonetheless, the total amount that firms pay is the same, so firms make zero expected profits in both equilibria.[10] Moreover, everyone is employed in both the pooling and screening equilibria, so total output is the same.

Nonetheless, everyone may be worse off in a separating equilibrium. At point y in Figure 18.2 ($w_h = \$40,000$, $w_l = \$20,000$, $c = \$15,000$, and $\theta = \frac{1}{2}$), either a pooling equilibrium or a separating equilibrium is possible. In the pooling equilibrium, each worker is paid $\overline{w} = \$30,000$ and there is no wasteful signaling. In the separating equilibrium, high-ability workers make $w_h - c = \$25,000$ and low-ability workers make $w_l = \$20,000$.

High-ability people earn less in the separating equilibrium, $\$25,000$, than they would in the pooling equilibrium, $\$30,000$. Nonetheless, if anyone signals, all the other high-ability workers want to send a signal to prevent their wage from falling to that of a low-ability worker. High-ability workers net an extra $[w_h - c] - w_l = \$25,000 - \$20,000 = \$5,000$. The reason socially undesirable signaling happens is that the private return to signaling, $\$5,000$, exceeds the net social return to signaling. The gross social return to the signal is zero because the signal changes only the distribution of wages. The net social return is negative because the signal is costly.

This inefficient expenditure on education is due to asymmetric information and the desire of high-ability workers to signal their ability. The government can increase total social wealth by banning wasteful signaling (eliminating schooling). Both low-ability and high-ability people benefit from such a ban.

In other cases, however, high-ability people do not want a ban. At point z (where $\theta = \frac{1}{2}$ and $c = \$5,000$), only a separating equilibrium is possible without government intervention. In this equilibrium, high-ability workers earn $w_h - c = \$35,000$ and low-ability workers make $w_l = \$20,000$. If the government bans signaling, both types of workers earn $\$30,000$ in the resulting pooling equilibrium, so high-ability workers are harmed, losing $\$5,000$ each. Thus, although the ban raises efficiency by eliminating wasteful signaling, high-ability workers oppose the ban.

In this example, efficiency can always be increased by banning signaling because signaling is unproductive. However, some signaling is socially efficient because it

---

[10]Firms pay high-ability workers more than they pay low-ability workers in a separating equilibrium, but the average amount they pay per worker is $\overline{w}$, the same as in a pooling equilibrium.

increases total output. Education may raise output because its signal results in a better matching of workers and jobs or because it provides useful training and serves as a signal. Also, education may make people better citizens. In conclusion, *total social output falls with signaling if signaling is socially unproductive but may rise with signaling if signaling also raises productivity or serves some other desirable purpose.*

Empirical evidence on the importance of signaling is mixed. For example, Tyler, Murnane, and Willett (2000) find that, for the least-skilled high school dropouts, passing the General Educational Development (GED) credential (the equivalent of a high school diploma) increases white dropouts' earnings by 10% to 19% but does not have a statistically significant effect on nonwhite dropouts.

Screening in Hiring

Firms screen prospective workers in many ways. An employer may hire someone based on a characteristic that the employer believes is correlated with ability, such as how a person dresses or speaks. Or a firm may use a test. Further, some employers engage in statistical discrimination, believing that an individual's gender, race, religion, or ethnicity is a proxy for ability.

Interviews and Tests. Most societies accept the use of interviews and tests by potential employers. Firms commonly assess abilities using interviews and tests. If such screening devices are accurate, firms benefit by selecting superior workers and assigning them to appropriate tasks. However, as with signaling, these costly activities are inefficient if they do not increase output. In the United States, the use of hiring tests may be challenged and rejected by the courts if the employer cannot demonstrate that the tests accurately measure skills or abilities required on the job.

Statistical Discrimination. If employers think that people of a certain age, gender, race, religion, or ethnicity have higher ability than others on average, they may engage in statistical discrimination (Aigner and Cain, 1977) and hire only people with that characteristic. Employers may engage in this practice even if they know that the correlation between these factors and ability is imperfect.[11]

Figure 18.3 illustrates one employer's belief that members of Race 1 have, on average, lower ability than members of Race 2: Much of the distribution curve for Race 2 lies to the right of the curve for Race 1. Nonetheless, the figure also shows that the employer believes that the highest-skilled members of Race 1 have higher ability than the lowest-skilled members of Race 2: Part of the Race 1 curve lies to the right of part of the Race 2 curve. Still, because the employer believes that a group characteristic, race, is an (imperfect) indicator of individual ability, the employer hires only people of Race 2 if enough of them are available.

The employer may claim not to be prejudiced but to be concerned only with maximizing profit. Nonetheless, this employer's actions harm members of Race 1 as much as they would if they were due to racial hatred.

Even though ability distributions are identical across races, eliminating statistical discrimination is difficult. If all employers share the belief that members of Race 1 have such low ability that it is not worth hiring them, people of that race are never hired, so employers never learn that their beliefs are incorrect. Here, false beliefs can persist indefinitely. Such discrimination lowers social output by preventing skilled members of Race 1 from performing certain jobs.

---

[11]Other common sources of employment discrimination are prejudice (Becker, 1971) and the exercise of monopsony power (Madden, 1973).

Figure 18.3 Statistical Discrimination

This figure shows the beliefs of an employer who thinks that people of Race 1 have less ability on average than people of Race 2. This employer hires only people of Race 2 even though the employer believes that some members of Race 1 have greater ability than some members of Race 2. Because this employer never employs members of Race 1, the employer may never learn that workers of both races have equal ability.

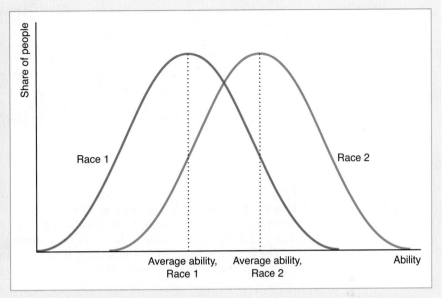

However, statistical discrimination may be based on true differences between groups. For example, insurance companies offer lower auto insurance rates to young women than to young men because young men are more likely, *on average*, to have an accident. The companies report that this practice lowers their costs of providing insurance by reducing moral hazard. Nonetheless, this practice penalizes young men who are unusually safe drivers, and benefits young women who are unusually reckless drivers.

CHALLENGE SOLUTION

Dying to Work

In the Challenge at the beginning of the chapter, we asked whether a firm under-invests in safety if the firm knows how dangerous a job is but potential employees do not. Can the government intervene to improve this situation?

Consider an industry with two firms that are simultaneously deciding whether to make costly safety investments such as sprinkler systems in a plant or escape tunnels in a mine. Unlike the firms, potential employees do not know how safe it is to work at each firm. They know only how risky it is to work in this industry. If only Firm 1 invests, workers do not know that safety has improved at Firm 1's plant only. Because the government's accident statistics for the industry fall, workers realize that it is safer to work in the industry, so both firms pay lower wages.

The profit table shows how the firms' profits depend on their safety investments. Firm 1 has a dominant strategy (Chapter 13). If Firm 2 invests (compare profits in the cells in the right column), Firm 1's *no investment* strategy has a higher profit, 250, than its *investment* strategy, 225. Similarly, if Firm 2 does not invest (compare the cells in the left column), Firm 1's profit is higher if it doesn't invest, 200, than if it does. Thus, not investing is its dominant strategy and investing is the dominated strategy, as is indicated by the horizontal red line through the investing strategy. Because the game is symmetric, Firm 2's dominant strategy is not to invest.

The pair of dominant strategies where neither firm invests (the upper-left cell) is the Nash equilibrium. Both firms receive an equilibrium profit of 200. If both firms invest in safety (the lower-right cell), each earns 225, which is more than they earn in the Nash equilibrium. However, the pair of strategies where both firms invest is not an equilibrium, because each firm can increase its profit from 225 to 250 by not investing if the other firm invests.

The firms are engaged in a prisoners' dilemma game. *Because each firm bears the full cost of its safety investments but derives only some of the benefits, the firms underinvest in safety.*

This prisoners' dilemma outcome results because workers do not know which firm is safer. If workers know how safe each firm is, a firm that invests in safety could hire at a lower wage than one that does not. Because that changes the profits, firms are more likely to invest in safety. Thus, if the government or a union collects and provides workers with firm-specific safety information, the firms might opt to invest. However, they will collect and provide this information, only if their cost of doing so is sufficiently low.

SUMMARY

1. **Problems Due to Asymmetric Information.** Asymmetric information causes market failures when informed parties engage in opportunistic behavior at the expense of uninformed parties. The resulting failures include the elimination of markets and pricing above marginal cost. Two types of problems arise from opportunism: adverse selection and moral hazard. Adverse selection is opportunism whereby only informed parties who have an unobserved characteristic that allows them to benefit from a deal accept it, to the detriment of less-informed parties. In moral hazard, an informed party takes advantage of a less-informed party through an unobserved action.

2. **Responses to Adverse Selection.** Avoiding adverse selection problems requires restricting the opportunistic behavior or eliminating the information asymmetry. To prevent the opportunism that occurs when information is asymmetric, governments may intervene in markets, or the people involved may write contracts that restrict the behavior of informed people. To eliminate or reduce information asymmetries, uninformed people screen to determine the information of informed people, informed people send signals to uninformed people, or third parties such as the government provide information.

3. **How Ignorance About Quality Drives Out High-Quality Goods.** If consumers cannot distinguish between good and bad products before a purchase, bad products may drive good products out of the market. This lemons problem is due to adverse selection. Approaches to reducing the lemons problem include laws limiting opportunism; consumer screening (such as by using experts or relying on firms' reputations); the provision of information by third parties such as government agencies and consumer groups; and signaling by firms (including establishing brand names and providing guarantees or warranties).

4. **Market Power from Price Ignorance.** If consumers do not know how prices vary across firms, a firm can raise its price without losing all its customers. As a consequence, consumers' ignorance about price creates market power. In a market that would be competitive with full information, consumer ignorance about price may lead to a monopoly price or a distribution of prices.

5. **Problems Arising from Ignorance When Hiring.** Companies use signaling and screening to try to eliminate information asymmetries in hiring. Where prospective employees and firms share common interests—such as assigning the right worker to the right task—everyone benefits from eliminating the information asymmetry by having informed job candidates honestly tell the firms—through cheap talk—about their abilities. When the two parties do not share common interests, cheap talk does not work.

Potential employees may inform employers about their abilities by using an expensive signal such as a college degree. An unproductive signal (as when education serves only as a signal and provides no training) may be privately beneficial but socially harmful. A productive signal (as when education provides training or leads to greater output due to more appropriate job assignments) may be privately and socially beneficial. Firms may also screen. Job interviews, objective tests, and other screening devices that lead to a better matching of workers and jobs may be socially beneficial. However, screening by statistical discrimination harms the discriminated-against groups. Employers who discriminate based on a particular group characteristic may never learn that their discrimination is based on false beliefs because they never test these beliefs.

EXERCISES

■ = *exercise is available on* MyEconLab; * = *answer appears at the back of this book;* **M** = *mathematical problem.*

1. Problems Due to Asymmetric Information

1.1 According to a 2007 study by the Federal Trade Commission, 4.8 million U.S. consumers were victims of weight-loss fraud, ranging from a tea that promised to help people shed pounds to fraudulent clinical trials and fat-dissolving injections. Do these frauds illustrate adverse selection or moral hazard?

*1.2 California set up its own earthquake insurance program for homeowners. The rates vary by zip code, depending on the proximity of the nearest fault line. However, critics claim that the people who set the rates ignored soil type. Some houses rest on bedrock; others sit on unstable soil. What are the implications of such rate setting?

*1.3 A firm spends a great deal of money in advertising to inform consumers of the brand name of its mushrooms. Should consumers conclude that its mushrooms are likely to be of higher quality than unbranded mushrooms? Why or why not?

1.4 A grocery advertises a low price on its milk as a "loss leader" to induce customers to shop there. It finds that some people buy only milk there and do their other grocery shopping elsewhere. Is that an example of adverse selection or moral hazard?

1.5 While self-employed workers have the option to purchase private health insurance, many—especially younger—workers do not, due to adverse selection. Suppose that half the population is healthy and the other half is unhealthy. The cost of getting sick is $1,000 for healthy people and $10,000 for unhealthy people. In a given year, any one person (regardless of health) either becomes sick or does not become sick. The probability that any one person gets sick is 0.4. Each person's utility of wealth function is $U(Y) = Y^{0.5}$, where Y is the person's wealth. Each worker's initial wealth is $30,000. Although each person knows whether he or she is healthy, the insurance company does not have this information. The insurance company offers complete, actuarially fair insurance. Because the insurance company cannot determine whether a person is healthy or not, it must offer each person the same coverage at the same price. The only costs to the company are the medical expenses of the coverage. Under these conditions, the insurance company covers all the medical expenses of its policyholders, and its expected profit is zero.

a. If everyone purchases insurance, what is the price of the insurance?

b. At the price you determined in part a, do healthy people purchase the optimal amount of insurance?

c. If only unhealthy people purchase insurance, what is the price?

d. At the price you determined in part c, do unhealthy people purchase the optimal amount of insurance?

e. Given that each person has the option to purchase insurance, which type actually purchases insurance? What is the price of the insurance? Discuss the adverse selection problem. **M**

2. Responses to Adverse Selection

2.1 Some states prohibit insurance companies from using car owners' home addresses to set auto insurance rates. Why do insurance companies use home addresses? What are the efficiency and equity implications of forbidding such practices?

2.2 You want to determine whether there is a lemons problem in the market for single-engine airplanes. Can you use any of the following information to help answer this question? If so, how?

a. Repair rates for original-owner planes versus planes that have been resold,

b. The fraction of planes resold in each year after purchase.

2.3 According to Edelman (2011), the widely used online "trust" authorities issue certifications without adequate verification, giving rise to adverse selection. Edelman finds that TRUSTe certified sites are more than twice as likely to be untrustworthy as uncertified sites. Explain why.

3. How Ignorance About Quality Drives Out High-Quality Goods

3.1 If you buy a new car and try to sell it in the first year—indeed, in the first few days after you buy it—the price that you get is substantially less than the original price. Use your knowledge about signaling and Akerlof's lemons model to explain this much-lower price.

3.2 Use Akerlof's lemons model to explain why restaurants that cater to tourists are likely to serve low-quality meals. Tourists will not return to the area, and they have no information about the relative quality of the food at various restaurants, but they can determine the relative price by looking at menus posted outside each restaurant.

*3.3 Many potential buyers value high-quality used cars at the full-information market price of p_1 and lemons at p_2. A limited number of potential sellers value high-quality cars at $v_1 \leq p_1$ and lemons at $v_2 \leq p_2$. Everyone is risk neutral. The share of lemons among all the used cars that might potentially be sold is θ. Under what conditions are all the cars sold? When are only lemons sold? Are there any conditions under which no cars are sold? (*Hint:* See Solved Problem 18.1.) **M**

3.4 Suppose that the buyers in Exercise 3.3 incur a transaction cost of $200 to purchase a car. This

transaction cost is the value of their time to find a car. What is the equilibrium? Is it possible that no cars are sold? **M**

3.5 Suppose that everyone in the used-car example in the text is risk neutral, potential car buyers value lemons at $2,000 and good used cars at $10,000, the reservation price of lemon owners is $1,500, and the reservation price of owners of high-quality used cars is $8,000. The share of current owners who have lemons is θ. For what values of θ do all the potential sellers sell their used cars? Describe the equilibrium.(*Hint:* See Solved Problem 18.1.) **M**

3.6 It costs $12 to produce a low-quality electric stapler and $16 to produce a high-quality stapler. Consumers cannot distinguish good staplers from poor staplers when they make their purchases. Four firms produce staplers. Consumers value staplers at their cost of production and are risk neutral. Will any of the four firms be able to produce high quality staplers without making losses? What happens if consumers are willing to pay $36 for high quality staplers? (*Hint:* See Solved Problem 18.2.) **M**

3.7 In the world of French haute cuisine, a three-star rating from the Michelin Red Guide is a widely accepted indicator of gastronomic excellence. French consumers consider Gault Milleau, another restaurant guide, to be less authoritative than the Michelin guide because Gault Milleau, unlike Michelin, accepts advertising and its critics accept free meals (Echikson, William, "Wish upon a Star," *Wall Street Journal*, February 28, 2003, A8).

a. Why are guides' ratings important to restaurant owners and chefs? Discuss the effect of a restaurant's rating on the demand for the restaurant.

b. Why do advertising and free meals taint the credibility of Gault Milleau? Discuss the moral hazard problem of Gault Milleau's ratings.

c. If advertising and free meals taint the credibility of Gault Milleau, why does the guide accept advertising and free meals?

3.8 Many wineries in the Napa Valley region of California enjoy strong reputations for producing high-quality wines and want to protect those reputations. Fred T. Franzia, the owner of Bronco Wine Co., sold Napa-brand wines that do not contain Napa grapes (Flynn, Julia, "In Napa Valley, Winemaker's Brands Divide an Industry," *Wall Street Journal*, February 22, 2005, A1). Other Napa wineries sued Mr. Franzia, contending that his wines, made from lower-quality grapes, damaged the reputation of the Napa wines. Suppose that the wine market has

2,000 wineries, and each sells one bottle of wine. Half, 1,000, have Napa grapes that they can turn into wine, and half have Central Valley grapes. The marginal opportunity cost of selling a Napa wine is $20, and the marginal opportunity cost of selling a Central Valley wine is $5. A large number of risk-neutral consumers with identical tastes are willing to buy an unlimited number of bottles at their expected valuations. Each consumer values a wine made from Napa grapes at $25 and a wine made from Central Valley grapes at $10. By looking at the bottles, consumers cannot distinguish between the Napa and the Central Valley wines.

a. If all of the wineries choose to sell wine, what is a consumer's expected value of the wine? If only the wineries with Central Valley grapes sell wine, what is a consumer's expected value of the wine?

b. What is the market equilibrium price? In the market equilibrium, which wineries choose to sell wine?

c. Suppose that wine bottles clearly label where the grapes are grown. What are the equilibrium price and quantity of Napa wine? What are the equilibrium price and quantity of wine made from Central Valley grapes?

d. Does the market equilibrium exhibit a lemons problem? If so, does clearly labeling the origin of the grapes solve the lemons problem? **M**

4. Market Power from Price Ignorance

*4.1 In Solved Problem 18.3, if the vast majority of all consumers knows the true prices at all stores and only a few shoppers have to incur a search cost to learn the prices, would the equilibrium be single-price at the monopoly level, p_m?

4.2 Sometimes a firm sells the same product under two brand names. For example, the Chevy Tahoe and the GMC Yukon are virtually twins (although the Yukon sells for $490 more than the Tahoe). Give an asymmetric information explanation as to why the firm might use pairs of brand names and why one product might sell for more than the other.

5. Problems Arising from Ignorance When Hiring

5.1 In the education signaling model, suppose that firms can pay c^* to have a worker's ability determined by a test. Does it pay for a firm to make this expenditure?

5.2 Some universities do not give letter grades. One rationale is that eliminating the letter-grade system reduces pressure on students, thus enabling them to learn more. Does this policy help or hurt students? (*Hint*: Consider the role grades play in educating and signaling.)

5.3 Some firms are willing to hire only high school graduates. Based on past experience or statistical evidence, these companies believe that, on average, high school graduates perform better than nongraduates. How does this hiring behavior compare to statistical discrimination by employers on the basis of race or gender? Discuss the equity and efficiency implications of this practice.

5.4 Suppose that you are given w_h, w_l, and θ in the education signaling model. For what value of c are both a pooling equilibrium and a separating equilibrium possible? For what value of c are both types of equilibria possible, and do high-ability workers have higher net earnings in a separating equilibrium than in a pooling equilibrium? (*Hint*: See Solved Problem 18.4.) **M**

5.5 Education is a continuous variable, where e_h is the years of schooling of a high-ability worker and e_l is the years of schooling of a low-ability worker. The cost per period of education for these types of workers is c_h and c_l, respectively, where $c_l > c_h$. The wages they receive if employers can tell them apart are w_h and w_l. Under what conditions is a separating equilibrium possible? How much education will each type of worker get? (*Hint*: See Solved Problem 18.4.) **M**

5.6 In Exercise 5.5, under what conditions is a pooling equilibrium possible? (*Hint*: See Solved Problem 18.4.) **M**

5.7 In Exercises 5.5 and 5.6, describe the equilibrium if $c_l \leq c_h$. (*Hint*: See Solved Problem 18.4.) **M**

5.8 When is statistical discrimination privately inefficient? When is it socially inefficient? Does it always harm members of the discriminated-against group? Explain.

6. Challenge

6.1 What is the minimum fine that the government could levy on firms that do not invest in safety that would lead to a Nash equilibrium in which both firms invest?

19

Contracts and Moral Hazards

The contracts of at least 33 major league baseball players have incentive clauses providing a bonus if that player is named the Most Valuable Player in a Division Series. Unfortunately, no such award is given for a Division Series.[1]

By 2014, the 2010 U.S. Patient Protection and Affordable Care Act will provide medical insurance to 32 million previously uninsured Americans. Society benefits by shifting risk from these previously uncovered, risk-averse people to risk-neutral insurance companies (Chapter 16). However, many analysts argue that extending insurance coverage will result in more people being subjected to *moral hazard*, which occurs if an informed person takes advantage of a less-informed person. Doctors may exploit patients and insurance companies, such as by ordering unnecessary tests. Similarly, patients may use the medical system excessively, driving up costs to everyone.

Schmitz (2012) found that, in Germany, low users of medical services with private supplementary insurance visit doctors on average 2.2 more times a year than those without this insurance. Finkelstein et al. (2011) reported that people with insurance in Oregon had a 2.1 percentage point greater probability of a hospital admission (30% more). Kawalski (2012) examined an employer-sponsored health insurance for a large U.S. firm and estimated that the average deadweight losses from moral hazard substantially outweighed the average welfare gains from risk protection.

Does medical insurance lead to a moral hazard problem and inefficiency for doctors and patients? The Application "Selfless or Selfish Doctors?" addresses whether insurance encourages doctors to act opportunistically. In the Challenge Solution, we investigate why medical insurance induces patients to make more visits to doctors, and whether adding high deductibles to medical insurance is socially preferable to complete coverage.

A dentist caps your tooth, not because you need it, but because he wants to purchase a new flat-screen TV. An employee cruises the Internet for jokes instead of working when the boss is not watching. A driver of a rental car takes it off the highway, risking ruining its suspension.

Each of these examples illustrates an inefficient use of resources due to a *moral hazard*, where an informed person takes advantage of a less-informed person, often through an *unobserved action* (Chapter 18). In this chapter, we examine how to design contracts that *eliminate inefficiencies* due to moral hazard problems *without shifting risk to people who hate bearing risk*—or contracts that at least reach a good compromise between these two goals.

[1]Tom FitzGerald, "Top of the Sixth," *San Francisco Chronicle*, January 31, 1997, C6.

For example, insurance companies face a trade-off between reducing moral hazards and increasing the risk of insurance buyers. Because an insurance company pools risks, it acts as though it is risk neutral (Chapter 16). The firm offers insurance contracts to risk-averse homeowners so that they can reduce their exposure to risk. If homeowners can buy full insurance so that they will suffer no loss if a fire occurs, some of them fail to take reasonable precautions. For example, they might store flammable liquids and old newspapers, increasing the chance of a catastrophic fire.

A contract that avoids this moral hazard problem specifies that the insurance company will not pay in the event of a fire if the company can show that a policyholder was negligent by storing flammable materials in the home. If this approach is impractical, however, the insurance company might offer a contract that provides incomplete insurance, covering only a fraction of the damage from a fire. The less complete the coverage, the greater the incentive for policyholders to avoid dangerous activities but the greater the risk that risk-averse homeowners must bear.

To illustrate methods of controlling moral hazards and the trade-off between moral hazards and risk, in this chapter, we focus on contracts between a principal—such as an employer—and an agent—such as an employee. The *principal* contracts with the *agent* to take some *action* that benefits the principal. Until now, we have assumed that firms can produce efficiently. However, if a principal cannot practically monitor an agent constantly, the agent may steal, **shirk**—a moral hazard in which agents do not provide all the services they are paid to provide—or engage in other opportunistic behavior that lowers productivity.

Opportunistic behavior by an informed agent harms a less-informed principal. Sometimes the losses are so great that both parties would be better off if each had full information and if opportunistic behavior were impossible.

In this chapter, we examine six main topics	1. **Principal-Agent Problem.** How an uninformed principal contracts with an informed agent determines whether moral hazards occur and how risks are shared.
	2. **Production Efficiency.** The agent's output depends on the type of contract used and the ability of the principal to monitor the agent's actions.
	3. **Trade-Off Between Efficiency in Production and in Risk Bearing.** A principal and an agent may agree to a contract that does not eliminate moral hazards or optimally share risk but strikes a balance between these two objectives.
	4. **Monitoring to Reduce Moral Hazard.** Employees work harder if an employer monitors their behavior and makes it worthwhile for them to keep from being fired.
	5. **Contract Choice.** By observing which type of contract an agent picks when offered a choice, a principal may obtain enough information to reduce moral hazards.
	6. **Checks on Principals.** To avoid moral hazard, an employer may agree to contractual commitments that make it in the employer's best interest to tell employees the truth.

19.1 Principal-Agent Problem

If you contract with people whose actions you cannot observe or evaluate, they may take advantage of you. If you pay someone by the hour to prepare your tax return, you do not know whether that person worked all the hours billed. If you retain a lawyer to represent you in a suit arising from an accident, you do not know whether the settlement that the lawyer recommends is in your best interest or the lawyer's.

Of course, many people behave honorably even if they have opportunities to exploit others. Also many people honestly believe that they are putting in a full day's work even when they are not working as hard as they might. Paul, the *principal*, hires Amy, the *agent*, to manage his ice-cream store. Paul pays Amy an hourly wage. She works every hour she is supposed to, even though Paul rarely checks on her. Nonetheless, Amy may not be spending her time as effectively as possible. She politely (but impersonally) asks everyone who enters the shop, "May I help you?" However, if she were to receive an appropriate financial incentive—say, a share of the shop's profit—she would memorize the names of her customers, greet them enthusiastically by name when they enter the store, and devise incentives for customers, such as frequent shopper discounts to increase sales.

A Model

We can describe many principal-agent interactions using a model in which the output or profit from this relationship and the risk borne by the two parties depend on the actions of the agent and the state of nature.

In a typical principal-agent relationship, the principal owns some property, such as a firm, or has a property right such as the right to sue for damages from an injury. The principal hires or contracts with an agent to take some action a that increases the value of his property or that produces profit, π, from using his property.

The principal and the agent need each other. If Paul hires Amy to run his ice-cream shop, Amy needs Paul's shop, and Paul needs Amy's efforts to sell ice cream. The profit from the ice cream sold, π, depends on the number of hours, a, that Amy works. The profit may also depend on the outcome of θ, which represents the *state of nature*:

$$\pi = \pi(a, \theta).$$

For example, profit may depend on whether the ice-cream machine breaks, $\theta = 1$, or does not break, $\theta = 0$. Or it may depend on whether it is a hot day, $\theta =$ the temperature.

In extreme cases, the profit function depends only on the agent's actions or only on the state of nature. At one extreme, profit depends only on the agent's action, $\pi = \pi(a)$, if there is only one state of nature: no uncertainty due to random events. In our example, the profit function has this form if demand does not vary with weather and if the ice-cream machine is reliable.

At the other extreme, profit depends only on the state of nature, $\pi = \pi(\theta)$, such as in an insurance market in which profit or value depends only on the state of nature and not on the actions of an agent. For instance, a couple buys insurance against rain on their wedding day. The value they place on their outdoor wedding ceremony is $\pi(\theta)$, which depends only on the weather, θ, because no actions are involved.

Types of Contracts

A verbal contract isn't worth the paper it's written on. —Samuel Goldwyn

When a formal market exists, the principal may deal impersonally with an anonymous agent by buying a good or service of known quality at the market price, so that opportunism cannot occur. We focus on transactions outside of formal markets where a principal and an agent agree on a customized contract that is designed to reduce opportunism.

A contract between a principal and an agent determines how the outcome of their partnership (such as the profit or output) is split between them. Three common types of contracts are fixed-fee, hire, and contingent contracts.

In a *fixed-fee contract*, the payment to the agent, F, is independent of the agent's actions, a, the state of nature, θ, or the outcome, π. The principal keeps the *residual profit*, $\theta(a, \theta) - F$. Alternatively, the principal may get a fixed amount and the agent may receive the residual profit. For example, the agent may pay a fixed rent for the right to use the principal's property.[2]

In a *hire contract*, the payment to the agent depends on the agent's actions as they are observed by the principal. Two common types of hire contracts pay employees an *hourly rate*—a wage per hour—or a *piece rate*—a payment per unit of output produced. If w is the wage per hour (or the price per piece of output) and Amy works a hours (or produces a units of output), then Paul pays Amy wa and keeps the residual profit $\pi(a, \theta) - wa$.

In a *contingent contract*, the payoff to each person depends on the state of nature, which may not be known to the parties at the time they write the contract. For example, Penn agrees to pay Alexis a higher amount to fix his roof if it is raining than if it is not.

One type of contingent contract is a *splitting* or *sharing contract*, where the payoff to each person is a fraction of the total profit (which is observable). Alain sells Pamela's house for her for $\pi(a, \theta)$ and receives a commission of 7% on the sales price. He receives $0.07\pi(a, \theta)$, and she keeps $0.93\pi(a, \theta)$.

Efficiency

The type of contract selected depends on what the parties can observe. A principal is more likely to use a hire contract if the principal can easily monitor the agent's actions. A contingent contract may be chosen if the state of nature can be observed after the work is completed. A fixed-fee contract does not depend on observing anything, so it can be used anytime.

Ideally, the principal and agent agree to an **efficient contract**: an agreement with provisions that ensure that no party can be made better off without harming the other party. Using an efficient contract results in *efficiency in production* and *efficiency in risk sharing*.

Efficiency in production requires that the principal's and agent's combined value (profits, payoffs) is maximized. We say that production is efficient if Amy manages Paul's firm so that the sum of their profits cannot be increased. In our examples, the moral hazard hurts the principal more than it helps the agent, so total profit falls. Thus, achieving efficiency in production requires preventing the moral hazard.

Efficiency in risk bearing requires that risk sharing is optimal in that the person who least minds facing risk—the risk-neutral or less-risk-averse person—bears more of the risk. In Chapter 16, we saw that risk-averse people are willing to pay a risk premium to avoid risk, whereas risk-neutral people do not care if they face fair risk or not. Suppose that Arlene is risk averse and is willing to pay a risk premium of $100 to avoid a particular risk. Peter is risk neutral and would bear the risk without a premium. Arlene and Peter can strike a deal whereby Peter agrees to bear *all* of Arlene's risk in exchange for a payment of between $0 and $100.[3]

If everyone has full information—there is no uncertainty and no asymmetric information—efficiency can be achieved. The principal contracts with the agent to

---

[2]Jefferson Hope says in the Sherlock Holmes mystery *A Study in Scarlet*, "I applied at a cab-owner's office, and soon got employment. I was to bring a certain sum a week to the owner, and whatever was over that I might keep for myself."

[3]For simplicity, we concentrate on situations in which one party is risk averse and the other is risk neutral. Generally, if both parties are risk averse, with one more risk averse than the other, both can be made better off if the less-risk-averse person bears more but not all of the risk.

perform a task for some specified reward and observes whether the agent completes the task properly before paying, so no moral hazard problem arises. Production inefficiency is more likely when either the agent has more information than the principal or both parties are uncertain about the state of nature.

If the agent has more information than the principal and there is no risk because there is only one state of nature, contracts can achieve efficiency in production by conveying adequate information to the principal. Alternatively, incentives in the contract may discourage the informed person from engaging in opportunistic behavior. The contracts do not have to address efficiency in risk bearing because there is no risk.

Given that they face both asymmetric information and risk, the parties try to contract to achieve efficiency in production and efficiency in risk bearing. Often, however, both objectives cannot be achieved, so the parties must trade-off between them.

APPLICATION

Selfless or Selfish Doctors?

Patients (principals) rely on doctors (agents) for good medical advice. Do doctors act selflessly in their patient's best interests, or do they take advantage of their superior knowledge to exploit patients or the companies that insure them?

Lu (2011) conducted an experiment to investigate doctors' behavior at top Beijing hospitals, in which the doctors were unaware that they were part of an experiment. In the experiment, a doctor knew whether a patient had insurance. The doctor also knew if the patient planned to buy any prescribed drugs at the hospital, where the doctor received a share of the patient's payment, or at an outside drugstore, where the doctors received no compensation from the prescriptions. Many doctors were asked to recommend treatment for a particular patient under these four possibilities: insurance and buy at the hospital, insurance and buy elsewhere, no insurance and buy at the hospital, and no insurance and buy elsewhere.

If a doctor is concerned about a patient's overall well-being and takes the patient's ability to pay into account, the doctor may prescribe more for patients with insurance, even if the doctor does not receive compensation for extra prescriptions. If *the doctor is primarily interested in earning as much as possible,* the doctor is likely to prescribe excessively for patients who are insured and who buy the drugs at the hospital. This excessive prescribing is a hidden action that creates a moral hazard.

Lu (2011) found that doctors prescribed similarly whether or not a patient had insurance if the doctors received no compensation for prescriptions. However, if the doctors were compensated for prescriptions, they prescribed drugs that cost 43% more on average for insured patients than for uninsured patients. Moreover, many of these extra, very expensive drugs were unjustified by the patient's medical condition. Thus, these doctors appeared to be largely motivated by self-interest rather than concern for their patients.

19.2 Production Efficiency

We start by examining situations with no risk due to random events, so that total profit, $\pi(a)$, is solely a function of the agent's action, a. Production efficiency is achieved by maximizing total or joint profit: the sum of the principal's and the agent's individual profits.

Efficient Contract

To be efficient and to maximize joint profit, the contract that a principal offers to an agent must have two properties. First, the contract must provide a large enough payoff that the *agent is willing to participate* in the contract. We know that the principal's payoff is adequate to ensure the principal's participation because the principal offers the contract.

Second, the contract must be **incentive compatible**: It provides inducements such that the agent wants to perform the assigned task rather than engage in opportunistic behavior. That is, it is in the agent's best interest to act to maximize joint profit. If the contract is not incentive compatible so the agent tries to maximize personal profit rather than joint profit, efficiency is achieved only if the principal monitors the agent and forces the agent to maximize joint profit.

We use an example to illustrate why only some types of contracts lead to efficiency. Paula, the principal, owns a store called Buy-A-Duck (located near a canal) that sells wooden duck carvings. Arthur, the agent, manages the store. Paula and Arthur's joint profit is

$$\pi(a) = R(a) - ma, \tag{19.1}$$

where $R(a)$ is the sales revenue from selling a carvings, and ma is the cost of the carvings. Arthur has a constant marginal cost m to obtain and sell each duck, including the amount he pays a local carver and the opportunity value (best alternative use) of his time.

Because Arthur bears the full marginal cost of selling one more carving, he wants to sell the joint-profit-maximizing output only if he also gets the full marginal benefit from selling one more duck. To determine the joint-profit-maximizing solution, we can ask what Arthur would do if he owned the shop and received all the profit, giving him an incentive to maximize total profit.

How many ducks, a, must Arthur sell to maximize the parties' joint profit, Equation 19.1? To obtain the first-order condition to maximize profit, we set the derivative of Equation 19.1 with respect to a equal to zero:

$$\frac{d\pi}{da} = \frac{dR(a)}{da} - m = 0. \tag{19.2}$$

According to Equation 19.2, joint profit is maximized by choosing the number of ducks such that marginal revenue, $dR(a)/da$, equals marginal cost, m.

Suppose the marginal cost is $m = 12$. The inverse demand function is $p = 24 - \frac{1}{2}a$ so that the revenue function is $(R)a = 24a - \frac{1}{2}a^2$. The marginal revenue function is $MR(a) = dR(a)/da = 24 - a$. Substituting the marginal revenue function and the marginal cost into Equation 19.2, we find that $MR = 24 - a = 12 = m = MC$, or $a = 12$. Panel a of Figure 19.1 illustrates this result: The marginal revenue curve, MR, intersects the marginal cost curve, $MC = m = \$12$, at the equilibrium point e. Panel b shows that total profit, π, reaches a maximum of \$72 at point E.

Which types of contracts lead to production efficiency? To answer this question, we first examine which contracts yield that outcome when both parties have full information and then consider which contracts bring the desired result when the principal is relatively uninformed. It is important to remember that we are considering a special case: Contracts that work here may not work in some other settings, whereas contracts that do not work here may be effective elsewhere.

Full Information

Suppose that both Paula and Arthur have full information. Each knows the actions Arthur takes—the number of carvings sold—and the effect of those actions on profit. Because she has full information, Paula can dictate exactly what Arthur is to do. Are there incentive-compatible contracts that do not require such monitoring and supervision? To answer this question, we consider four kinds of contracts: a fixed-fee rental contract, a hire contract, and two types of contingent contracts.

Figure 19.1 Maximizing Joint Profit When the Agent Gets the Residual Profit

(a) If the agent, Arthur, gets all the joint profit, π, he maximizes his profit by selling 12 carvings at *e*, where the marginal revenue curve intersects his marginal cost curve: *MR* = *MC* = 12. If he pays the principal, Paula, a fixed rent of $48, he maximizes his profit by selling 12 carvings. (A fixed rent does not affect either his marginal revenue or his marginal cost.) (b) Joint profit at 12 carvings is $72, point *E*. If Arthur pays a rent of $48 to Paula, Arthur's profit is π − $48. By selling 12 carvings and maximizing joint profit, Arthur also maximizes his profit.

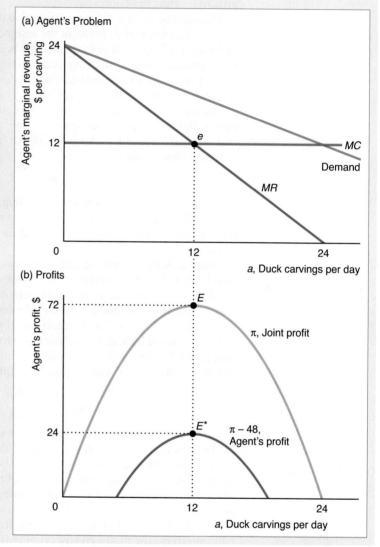

Fixed-Fee Rental Contract. If Arthur contracts to rent the store from Paula for a fixed fee, *F*, joint profit is maximized. Arthur earns a residual profit equal to the joint profit minus the fixed rent he pays Paula, π(*a*) − *F*. Because the amount that Paula makes is fixed, Arthur gets the entire marginal profit from selling one more duck. As a consequence, the amount, *a*, that maximizes Arthur's profit,

$$\pi(a) - F = R(a) - ma - F, \tag{19.3}$$

also maximizes joint profit, π(*a*). To show this result, we note that his first-order condition based on Equation 19.3,

$$\frac{d[\pi(a) - F]}{da} = \frac{dR(a)}{da} - m - \frac{dF}{da} = \frac{dR(a)}{da} - m = 0, \tag{19.4}$$

is identical to the first-order condition in Equation 19.2.

In Figure 19.1, Arthur pays Paula *F* = $48 rent. This fixed payment does not affect his marginal cost. As a result, he maximizes his profit after paying the rent,

$\pi - \$48$, by equating his marginal revenue to his marginal cost: $MR = MC = 12$ at point e in panel a.

Because Arthur pays the same fixed rent no matter how many units he sells, his profit curve in panel b lies \$48 below the joint-profit curve at every quantity. As a result, Arthur's net-profit curve peaks (at point E^*) at the same quantity, 12, where the joint-profit curve peaks (at E). Thus, the fixed-fee rental contract is incentive compatible. Arthur participates in this contract because he earns \$24 after paying the rent and for the carvings.

Hire Contract. Now suppose that Paula contracts to pay Arthur for each carving he sells. If she pays him \$12 per carving, Arthur just breaks even on each sale. He is indifferent between participating and not. Even if he chooses to participate, he does not sell the joint-profit-maximizing number of carvings unless Paula supervises him. If she does supervise him, she instructs him to sell 12 carvings, and she gets all the joint profit of \$72.

For Arthur to want to participate and to sell carvings without supervision, he must receive more than \$12 per carving. If Paula pays Arthur \$14 per carving, for example, he makes a profit of \$2 per carving. He now has an incentive to sell as many carvings as he can (even if the price is less than the cost of the carving), which does not maximize joint profit, so this contract is not incentive compatible.

Even if Paula can control how many carvings Arthur sells, joint profit is not maximized. Paula keeps the revenue minus what she pays Arthur, \$14 times the number of carvings, $R(a) - 14a$. Thus, her objective differs from the joint-profit-maximizing objective,

$$p(a) = R(a) - 12a.$$

Joint profit is maximized when marginal revenue equals the marginal cost of \$12. Because Paula's marginal cost, \$14, is larger, she directs Arthur to sell fewer than the optimal number of carvings. Paula maximizes $R - 14a = \left(29a - \frac{1}{2}a^2\right) - 14a = 10a - \frac{1}{2}a^2$. Given her first-order condition, where the derivative of Paula's profit with respect to a equals zero, $10 - a = 0$, she maximizes her profit by selling 10 carvings. Joint profit is only \$70 at 10 carvings, compared to \$72 at the optimal 12 carvings.

Revenue-Sharing Contract. If Paula and Arthur use a *contingent contract* whereby they share the *revenue*, joint profit is not maximized. Suppose that Arthur receives three-quarters of the revenue, $\frac{3}{4}R$, and Paula gets the rest, $\frac{1}{4}R$. Panel a of Figure 19.2 shows the marginal revenue that Arthur obtains from selling an extra carving, $MR^* = \frac{3}{4}$. He maximizes his profit at \$24 by selling eight carvings, for which $MR^* = MC$ at e^*. Paula gets the remaining profit of \$40, which is the difference between their total profit from selling eight ducks per day, $\pi = \$64$, and Arthur's profit.

Thus, their joint profit in panel b at $a = 8$ is \$64, which is \$8 less than the maximum possible profit of \$72 (point E). Arthur has an incentive to sell fewer than the optimal number of ducks because he bears the full marginal cost of each carving he sells, \$12, but gets only three-quarters of the marginal revenue.

Even if Paula controls how many carvings are sold, joint profit is not maximized. Because the amount she makes, $\frac{1}{4}R$, depends only on revenue and not on the cost of obtaining the carvings, she wants the revenue-maximizing quantity sold. Revenue is maximized where marginal revenue is zero at $a = 24$ (panel a). Arthur would not participate if the contract granted him only three-quarters of the revenue but required him to sell 24 carvings, because he would lose money.

Figure 19.2 Why Revenue Sharing Reduces Agent's Efforts

(a) Joint profit is maximized at 12 carvings, where $MR = MC = 12$ at equilibrium point e. If Arthur gets three-quarters of the revenue and Paula gets the rest, Arthur maximizes his profit by selling 8 carvings per day, where his new marginal revenue curve, $MR^* = \frac{3}{4}MR$, equals his marginal cost at point e^*. (b) Joint profit reaches a maximum of $72 at E, where they sell 12 carvings per day. If they split the revenue, Arthur sells 8 duck carvings per day and gets $24 at E^*, and Paula receives the residual, $40 (= $64 − $24).

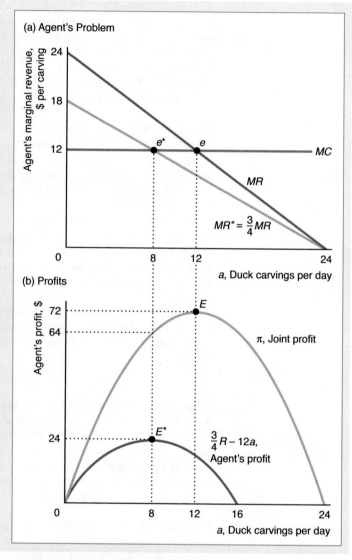

SOLVED PROBLEM 19.1

Use calculus to show that, if Arthur receives three-quarters of the revenue, $\frac{3}{4}R$, and Paula gets the rest, he does not sell the joint-profit-maximizing quantity.

Answer

1. *Write Arthur's profit function, calculate his first-order condition, and solve for his profit-maximizing output.* Arthur's profit is $\frac{3}{4}R(a) - 12a = \frac{3}{4}\left(24a - \frac{1}{2}a^2\right) - 12a$. To maximize his profit, he needs to choose a such that his marginal profit with respect to a equals zero: $\frac{3}{4}dR(a)/da - 12 = \frac{3}{4}(24 - a) = 0$. Thus, the output that maximizes his profit is $a = 8$.

2. *Compare this solution to the joint-profit-maximizing output.* We know that the joint profit is maximized at 72, where $a = 12$. With revenue sharing, $a = 8$ and joint profits are only 64.

Comment: Arthur produces too little output because he bears the full marginal cost, 12, but earns only three-quarters of the marginal benefit (marginal revenue), $\frac{3}{4}(24 - a)$ from the joint-profit-maximizing problem, $24 - a$.

Profit-Sharing Contract. Paula and Arthur may use a contingent contract by which they divide the economic profit π. If they can agree that the true marginal and average cost is $12 per carving (which includes Arthur's opportunity cost of time), the contract is incentive compatible. Only by maximizing total profit can Arthur maximize his share of profit.

As Figure 19.3 shows, Arthur receives one-third of the joint profit and chooses to produce the level of output, $a = 12$, that maximizes joint profit. Arthur's share is $\frac{1}{3}\pi = \frac{1}{3}(R - C) = \frac{1}{3}R - \frac{1}{3}C$, where R is revenue and C is cost. He maximizes his profit where $d\left[\frac{1}{3}\pi(a)\right]/da = \frac{1}{3}MR - \frac{1}{3}MC = 0$, or $\frac{1}{3}MR = \frac{1}{3}MC$. Although he receives only one-third of the marginal revenue, he bears only one-third of the marginal cost. Dividing both sides of the equation by $\frac{1}{3}$, we find that this condition is the same as the one for maximizing total profit: $MR = MC$. Arthur earns $24, so he is willing to participate.

The second column of Table 19.1 summarizes our analysis. Whether efficiency in production is achieved depends on the type of contract that the principal and the agent use. If the principal has full information (knows the agent's actions), the principal achieves production efficiency without having to supervise by using one of the incentive-compatible contracts: fixed-fee rental or profit-sharing.

Asymmetric Information

Now suppose that the principal, Paula, has less information than the agent, Arthur. She cannot observe the number of carvings he sells or the revenue. As Table 19.1 shows, with asymmetric information, only the fixed rent contract results in production efficiency and no moral hazard problem. All the other contracts result in inefficiency, and Arthur has an opportunity to take advantage of Paula.

Figure 19.3 Why Profit Sharing Is Efficient

If the agent, Arthur, gets one-third of the joint profit, he maximizes his profit, $\frac{1}{3}\pi$, by maximizing joint profit, π.

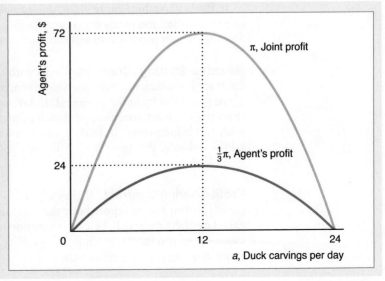

Table 19.1 Production Efficiency and Moral Hazard Problems for Buy-A-Duck

	Full Information	Asymmetric Information	
Contract	Production Efficiency	Production Efficiency	Moral Hazard Problem
Fixed-fee rental contract			
Rent (to principal)	Yes	Yes	No
Hire contract, per unit pay			
Pay equals marginal cost	No[a]	No[b]	Yes
Pay is greater than marginal cost	No[c]	No	Yes
Contingent contract			
Share revenue	No	No[b]	Yes
Share profit	Yes	No[b]	Yes

[a]The agent may not participate and has no incentive to sell the optimal number of carvings. Efficiency can be achieved only if the principal supervises.
[b]Unless the agent steals all the revenue (or profit) from an extra sale, inefficiency results.
[c]The agent sells too many or the principal directs the agent to sell too few carvings.

Fixed-Fee Rental Contract. Arthur pays Paula the fixed rent that she is due because Paula would know if she were paid less. Arthur receives the residual profit, joint profit minus the fixed rent, so he wants to sell the joint-profit-maximizing number of carvings.

Hire Contract. If Paula offers to pay Arthur the actual marginal cost of $12 per carving and he is honest, he may refuse to participate in the contract because he makes no profit. Even if he participates, he has no incentive to sell the optimal number of carvings.

If he is dishonest, he may underreport sales and pocket some of the extra revenue. Unless he can steal all the extra revenue from an additional sale, he sells less than the joint-profit-maximizing quantity.

If Paula pays him more than the actual marginal cost per carving, he has an incentive to sell too many carvings, whether or not he steals. If he also steals, he has an even greater incentive to sell too many carvings.

Revenue-Sharing Contract. Even with full information, the revenue-sharing contract is inefficient. Asymmetric information adds a moral hazard problem: The agent may steal from the principal. If Arthur can steal a larger share of the revenues than the contract specifies, he has less of an incentive to undersell than he does with full information. Indeed, if the agent can steal all the extra revenue from an additional sale, the agent acts efficiently to maximize joint profit, all of which the agent keeps.

Profit-Sharing Contract. If they use a contingent contract and split the economic profit, Arthur has to report both the revenue and the cost to Paula so that they can calculate their shares. If he can overreport cost or underreport revenue, he has an incentive to produce a nonoptimal quantity. Only if Arthur can appropriate all the profit does he produce efficiently.

APPLICATION

Contracts and
Productivity in
Agriculture

In agriculture, landowners (principals) contract with farmers (agents) to work their land. Farmers may work on their own land (the principal and agent are the same person), work on land rented from a landowner (fixed-fee rental contract), work as employees for a time rate or piece rate (hire contract), or sharecrop (contingent contract). A sharecropper splits the crop with the landowner at the end of the growing season.[4]

According to theory, farmers' willingness to work hard depends on the type of contract used. Farmers who keep all the marginal profit from additional work—those who own the land or rent it for a fixed fee—work hard and maximize (joint) profit. Sharecroppers, who bear the full marginal cost of working an extra hour and receive only a fraction of the extra revenue, put in too little effort. Hired farmworkers who are paid by the hour may shirk—not work hard—unless they are closely supervised.

Foster and Rosenzweig (1994) tested these predictions about contract type and agent effort using data on Philippine farmers. They could not directly monitor the work effort (any more than most landowners could). Rather, they ingeniously measured the effort indirectly. They contended that the harder people work, the more they eat and the more they use up body mass (defined as weight divided by height squared), holding calorie intake constant.

Foster and Rosenzweig estimated the effect of each compensation method on body mass and consumption, adjusting for gender, age, activity type, and other factors. They found that people who work for themselves or are paid by the piece use up 10% more body mass, holding calorie consumption constant, than time-rate workers and 13% more than sharecroppers. Foster and Rosenzweig also discovered that piece-rate workers (who are paid according to how much they produce) consume 25% more calories per day and that farm owners consume 16% more than time-rate workers.

19.3 Trade-Off Between Efficiency in Production and in Risk Bearing

Writing an efficient contract is difficult if the agent knows more than the principal, the principal never learns the truth, and both face risk. Usually, a contract does not achieve efficiency in production and in risk bearing. Contract clauses that increase production efficiency may reduce efficiency in risk bearing, and vice versa. If these goals are incompatible, the parties may write imperfect contracts that compromise between the two objectives. To illustrate the trade-offs involved, we consider a common situation in which it is difficult to achieve efficiency: contracting with an expert such as a lawyer.

Pam, the principal, is injured in a traffic accident and is a plaintiff in a lawsuit. Alfredo, the agent, is her lawyer. Pam faces uncertainty due to risk and to asymmetric information. The jury award at the conclusion of the trial, $\pi(a, \theta)$, depends on a,

---

[4]If a farmer is someone who is outstanding in his field, a sharecropper is someone who is outstanding in someone else's field.

Table 19.2   Efficiency of Client-Lawyer Contracts

Type of Contract	Fixed Fee to Lawyer	Fixed Payment to Client	Lawyer Paid by the Hour	Contingent Contract
Lawyer's payoff	F	$\pi(a, \theta) - F$	wa	$\alpha\pi(a, \theta)$
Client's payoff	$\pi(a, \theta) - F$	F	$\pi(a, \theta) - wa$	$(1 - \alpha)\pi(a, \theta)$
Production efficiency?	No*	Yes	No*	No*
Who bears risk?	Client	Lawyer	Client	Shared

*Production efficiency is possible if the client can monitor and enforce optimal effort by the lawyer.

the number of hours Alfredo works before the trial, and θ, the state of nature: the unknown attitudes of jury members. All else the same, the more time Alfredo spends on the case, a, the larger the expected π. Pam never learns the jury's attitude, θ, so she cannot accurately judge Alfredo's efforts even after the trial. For example, if she loses the case, she won't know whether she lost because Alfredo didn't work hard (low a) or because the jury disliked her (bad θ).

Contracts and Efficiency

How hard Alfredo works depends on his attitude toward risk and his knowledge of the payoff for his trial preparations. For any hour that he does not devote to Pam's case, Alfredo can work on other cases. The most lucrative of these forgone opportunities is his marginal cost of working on Pam's case.

Who benefits from Alfredo's extra work depends on his contract with Pam. If Alfredo is risk neutral and gets the entire marginal benefit from any extra work, he sets his expected marginal benefit equal to his marginal cost, works the optimal number of hours, and maximizes the expected joint payoff.

The choice of various possible contracts between Pam and Alfredo affects whether efficiency in production or in risk bearing is achieved. They choose among fixed-fee, hire (hourly wage), and contingent contracts. Table 19.2 summarizes the outcomes under each of these contracts.

Lawyer Gets a Fixed Fee. If Pam pays Alfredo a fixed fee, F, he gets paid the same amount no matter how much he works. Thus, he has little incentive to work hard on this case, and his production is inefficient.[5] Production efficiency can be achieved only if Pam can monitor Alfredo and force him to act optimally. However, most individual plaintiffs cannot monitor a lawyer and therefore cannot determine whether the lawyer is behaving appropriately.

Whether the fixed-fee contract leads to efficiency in risk bearing depends on the attitudes toward risk on the part of the principal and agent. Alfredo gets F regardless, so he bears no risk. Pam bears all the risk: Her net payoff $\pi(a, \theta) - F$ varies with the unknown state of nature, θ.

A lawyer who handles many similar cases may be less risk averse than an individual client whose financial future depends on a single case. If Alfredo has had many cases like Pam's and if Pam's future rests on the outcome of this suit, their choice of this type of contract leads to inefficiency in both production and risk bearing. Not only is Alfredo not working hard enough, but Pam bears the risk, even though she is more risk averse than Alfredo.

---

[5]His main incentive to work hard (other than honesty) is to establish a reputation as a good lawyer so as to attract future clients. For simplicity, we will ignore this effect, because it applies for all types of contracts.

In contrast, if Alfredo is a self-employed lawyer working on a major case for Pam, who runs a large insurance company with many similar cases, Alfredo is risk averse and Pam is risk neutral. Here, having the principal bear all the risk is efficient. If the insurance company can monitor Alfredo's behavior, it is even possible to achieve production efficiency. Indeed, many insurance companies employ lawyers in this manner.

SOLVED PROBLEM 19.2	Alfredo, the lawyer, pays Pam, the client, a *fixed payment*, F, for the right to try the case and collect the entire verdict less the payment to Pam, $\pi(a, \theta) - F$. Does such a contract lead to efficiency? Are the parties willing to sign such a contract?

Answer

1. *Show that Alfredo has an incentive to put in the optimal number of hours.* Alfredo works until his marginal cost—the opportunity cost of his time—equals the marginal benefit—the extra amount he gets if he wins at trial. Because he has already paid Pam, all extra amounts earned at trial go to Alfredo. Therefore, Alfredo has an incentive to put in the optimal number of hours.

2. *Show that whether there is efficiency in risk bearing depends on the parties' attitudes toward risk.* Alfredo bears all the risk related to the outcome of the trial. Thus, if he's risk neutral and Pam is risk averse, this contract results in efficient risk bearing, but not otherwise.

3. *Explain why the parties are hesitant to sign the contract because of asymmetric information and moral hazard.* No matter how risk averse Pam is, she may hesitate to agree to this contract. Because she is not an expert on the law, she cannot easily predict the jury's likely verdict. Thus, she does not know how large a fixed fee she should insist on receiving. There is no practical way in which Alfredo's superior information about the likely outcome of the trial can be credibly revealed to her. She suspects that it is in his best interest to tell her that the likely payout is lower than he truly believes. Similarly, Alfredo may be hesitant to offer Pam a fixed fee. How well they do in court depends on the merits of her case. At least initially, Alfredo does not know how good a case she has. Initially, she has an incentive to try to convince him that the case is very strong.

Lawyer Is Hired by the Hour. If Pam pays Alfredo a wage of w per hour for the a hours that he works, Alfredo could bill her for more hours than he actually worked unless she can monitor him.[6] Even if Pam could observe how many hours he works, she would not know whether Alfredo worked effectively and whether the work was necessary. Thus it would be difficult, if not impossible, for Pam to monitor Alfredo's work.

Pam bears all the risk. Alfredo's earnings, wa, are determined before the outcome is known. Pam's return $\pi(a, \theta) - wa$ varies with the state of nature and is unknown before the verdict.

Fee Is Contingent. Some lawyers offer plaintiffs a contract whereby the lawyer works for "free"—receiving no hourly payment—in exchange for splitting the compensation awarded in court or in a pre-trial settlement. The lawyer receives a **contingent fee**: a payment that is a share of the award in a court case (usually after legal expenses are deducted) if the client wins and nothing if the client loses. If the

---

[6]A lawyer dies in an accident and goes to heaven. A host of angels greet him with a banner that reads, "Welcome Oldest Man!" The lawyer is puzzled: "Why do you think I'm the oldest man? I was only 47 when I died." One of the angels replies, "You can't fool us; you were at least 152 when you died. We saw the hours you billed!"

lawyer's share of the award is β and the jury awards $\pi(a, \theta)$, the lawyer receives $\beta\pi(a, \theta)$ and the principal gets $(1 - \beta)\pi(a, \theta)$. This approach is attractive to many plaintiffs because they cannot monitor how hard the lawyer works and are unable or unwilling to make payments before the trial is completed.

How they split the award affects the amount of risk each bears. If Alfredo gets one-quarter of the award, $\beta = \frac{1}{4}$, and Pam gets three-quarters, Pam bears more risk than Alfredo does. Suppose that the award is either 0 or 40 with equal probability. Alfredo receives either 0 or 10, so his average award is 5. His variance (Chapter 16) is $\sigma_a^2 = \frac{1}{2}(0 - 5)^2 + \frac{1}{2}(10 - 5)^2 = 25$. Pam makes either 0 or 30, so her average award is 15 and her variance is $\sigma_p^2 = \frac{1}{2}(0 - 15)^2 + \frac{1}{2}(30 - 15)^2 = 225$. Thus, the variance in Pam's payoff is greater than Alfredo's.

Whether splitting the risk in this way is desirable depends on how risk averse each party is. If one is risk neutral and the other is risk averse, it is efficient for the risk-neutral person to bear all the risk. If they are equally risk averse, a splitting rule in which $\beta = \frac{1}{2}$ and they face equal risk may be optimal.[7]

A sharing contract encourages shirking: Alfredo is likely to put in too little effort. He bears the full cost of his labors—the forgone use of his time—but gets only β share of the returns from this effort. Thus, this contract results in production inefficiency and may or may not lead to inefficient risk bearing.

Choosing the Best Contract

Which contract is best depends on the parties' attitudes toward risk, the degree of risk, the difficulty in monitoring, and other factors. If Alfredo is risk neutral, they can achieve both efficiency goals if Alfredo charges Pam a fixed fee. He has the incentive to put in the optimal amount of work and does not mind bearing the risk.

However, if Alfredo is risk averse and Pam is risk neutral, they may not be able to achieve both objectives. Contracts that provide Alfredo a fixed fee or a wage rate allocate all the risk to Pam and lead to inefficiency in production because Alfredo has too little incentive to work hard.

Often when the parties find that they cannot achieve both objectives, they choose a contract that attains neither goal. For example, they may use a contingent contract that fails to achieve efficiency in production and may not achieve efficiency in risk bearing. The contingent contract strikes a compromise between the two goals. Alfredo has more of an incentive to work if he splits the payoff than if he receives a fixed fee. He is less likely to work excessive hours with the contingent fee than if he were paid by the hour. Moreover, neither party has to bear all the risk—they share it under the contingent contract.

Lawyers usually work for a fixed fee only if the task or case is very simple, such as writing a will or handling an uncontested divorce. The client has some idea of whether the work is done satisfactorily, so monitoring is relatively easy and little risk is involved.

In riskier situations, the other types of contracts are more common. When the lawyer is relatively risk averse or when the principal is very concerned that the lawyer works hard, an hourly wage may be used.

Contingent fee arrangements are particularly common for plaintiffs' lawyers who specialize in auto accidents, medical malpractice, and product liability. Because these plaintiffs' lawyers can typically pool risks across clients, they are less concerned than their clients are about risk. As a consequence, these attorneys are willing to accept contingent fees (and might agree to pay a fixed fee to the plaintiff). Moreover, accident victims often lack the resources to pay for a lawyer's time before winning at trial, so they often prefer contingent contracts.

---

[7]If Pam and Alfredo split the award equally and each receives either 0 or 20 with equal probability, each has a variance of $\frac{1}{2}(0 - 10)^2 + \frac{1}{2}(20 - 10)^2 = 100$.

Ice Cube, Jackson Browne, Jay-Z, the Eagles, Madonna, Pearl Jam, Prince, and Radiohead are no longer signing traditional contracts with major-label recording companies. Many have their own labels. Justin Timberlake's label dates back to 2007, while Justin Bieber started his own label in 2012.

Traditional contracts obligate the artist to deliver a specific number of albums. The record company gives a cash advance and retains the lion's share (often 90%) of the revenue. The artist receives a share (usually less than $2 a copy) only after the advance is paid back to the company. The record company owns the master recordings of the music and pays to produce, promote, and distribute the album.

Now these stars are forgoing the upfront payments. Each artist bears the recording and promotional cost and retains ownership of the album, leaving only distribution to one of the major labels. The artist can license the music to whichever major label offers the biggest share of sales instead of being contractually tied to one label. Consequently, the artists receive a larger share of revenue than in the past, but the artist incurs more of the costs, as well as much more of the risk.

Ice Cube chose to "bet on himself" and take the risk on his CD *Laugh Now, Cry Later*. EMI made and distributed the album, but Ice Cube paid for the recordings and, with his managers, oversaw most of the U.S. marketing. In 2007, the Eagles released their first album in nearly 30 years exclusively through Wal-Mart. Pearl Jam sold its *Pearl Jam* album through a "partnership" agreement with Sony BMG's J Records, where the label received a percentage of sales for distribution and other services it provided.

When Jackson Browne's contract with Warner Music Group Corporation's Elektra Records expired, he financed an album, *Solo Acoustic Vol. 1*, and licensed it to a Warner unit that distributes for independent record companies. It sold more copies than his last studio album for Elektra. Mr. Browne earned 7 to 10 times as much per copy sold under the new arrangement than under his previous contract.

Greg Johnson broke with EMI and released an album, *Secret Weapon*, in 2010 by asking fans to contribute to the recording and marketing costs before it was released. In return, fans could pre-purchase a signed copy of the album and receive it one week ahead of commercial release under his label, JMA.

Thus, these new relationships between artists and record companies are changing production incentives and risk sharing. Because the artist bears more of the production and promotion costs and much more of the risk, only successful, wealthy artists are likely to use this new approach. However, as a consequence of using this new type of contract, some artists are releasing more albums because their incentives to produce have increased. And some of these artists are earning substantial returns for bearing the extra costs and risks.

19.4 Monitoring to Reduce Moral Hazard

When a firm cannot pay workers in proportion to the work they do (a piece rate) or share the firm's profit with the workers, the firm usually pays fixed-fee salaries or hourly wages, which may lead to employees shirking.[8] A firm can reduce such shirking by intensively supervising or monitoring workers. Monitoring eliminates the asymmetric information problem: Both the employee and the employer know how

---

[8]Shearer (2004) found that when tree planters were randomly assigned piece-rate pay or fixed hourly wages, they were 19% more productive when paid by the piece. See MyEconLab, Chapter Resources, Chapter 19, "Payments Linked to Production or Profit," for more details about alternative compensation methods.

hard the employee works. If the cost of monitoring workers is low enough, it pays to prevent shirking by carefully monitoring and firing employees who do not work hard.

Firms experiment with various means of lowering the cost of monitoring. Requiring employees to punch a time clock or recording employees' work efforts by installing video cameras are examples of firms' attempts to use capital to monitor job performance. By using assembly lines that force employees to work at a set pace, employers can control employees' work rate.

According to a survey by the American Management Association, nearly two-thirds of employers record employees' voice mail, email, and phone calls; review employee computer files; or videotape workers. A quarter of the firms that use surveillance don't tell their employees. The most common types of surveillance are tallying outgoing phone calls and recording their duration (37%), videotaping the workplace (16%), storing and reviewing emails (15%), storing and reviewing computer files (14%), and taping and reviewing phone conversations (10%). Monitoring and surveillance are most common in the financial sector, in which 81% of firms use these techniques. Rather than watching all employees all the time, companies usually monitor selected workers randomly.

For some jobs, however, monitoring is counterproductive or not cost effective. Monitoring may lower employees' morale, reducing productivity. Several years ago, Northwest Airlines removed the doors from bathroom stalls to prevent workers from slacking off there. When new management changed this policy (and made many other changes as well), productivity increased.

It is usually impractical for firms to monitor how hard salespeople work if they spend most of their time away from the main office. As telecommuting increases, monitoring workers may become increasingly difficult.

When direct monitoring is very costly, firms may use various financial incentives, which we consider in the next section, to reduce the amount of monitoring that is necessary. Each of these incentives—bonding, deferred payments, and efficiency (unusually high) wages—acts as a *hostage* for good behavior (Williamson, 1983). Workers who are caught shirking or engaging in other undesirable acts not only lose their jobs but also give up the hostage. The more valuable the hostage, the less monitoring is necessary to deter bad behavior.

Bonding

One way to ensure agents behave well is to require that they deposit funds guaranteeing their good behavior, just as a landlord requires tenants to post security deposits to ensure that they will not damage an apartment. Typically, the agent posts (leaves) this bond with the principal or another party, such as an insurance company, before starting the job.

Many couriers who transport valuable shipments (such as jewels) or guards who protect them post bonds against theft and other moral hazards. Similarly, bonds prevent employees from quitting immediately after receiving costly training (Salop and Salop, 1976). Most of the other approaches that we will examine for controlling shirking can be viewed as forms of bonding.

Bonding to Prevent Shirking. Some employers require a worker to post a bond that is forfeited if the employee is discovered shirking. For example, a professional athlete faces a specified fine (the equivalent of a bond) for skipping a meeting or game. The higher the bond, the less frequently the employer needs to monitor to prevent shirking.

Let G be the value that a worker puts on taking it easy on the job. If a worker's only potential punishment for shirking is dismissal if caught, some workers will shirk.

Shirking is less likely if the worker must post a bond of B that is forfeited if the employee is caught not working. Given the firm's level of monitoring, the probability that a worker is caught is θ. Thus, a worker who shirks expects to lose θB.[9] A risk-neutral worker chooses not to shirk if the certain gain from shirking, G, is less than or equal to the expected penalty, θB, from forfeiting the bond if caught: $G \leq B$. Thus, the minimum bond that discourages shirking is

$$B = \frac{G}{\theta}. \tag{19.5}$$

Equation 19.5 shows that the bond must be larger, the higher the value that the employee places on shirking and the lower the probability that the worker will be caught.

Thus, the larger the bond, the less monitoring is necessary to prevent shirking. Suppose that a worker places a value of $G = \$1,000$ a year on shirking. A bond that is large enough to discourage shirking is $\$1,000$ if the probability of the worker's being caught is 100%, $\$2,000$ at 50%, $\$5,000$ at 20%, $\$10,000$ at 10%, and $\$20,000$ at 5%.

SOLVED PROBLEM 19.3	Workers post bonds of B that are forfeited if they are caught stealing (but no other punishment is imposed). Each extra unit of monitoring, M, raises the probability that a firm catches a worker who steals, θ, by 5%. A unit of M costs $\$10$. A worker can steal a piece of equipment and resell it for its full value of G dollars. What is the optimal M that the firm uses if it believes that workers are risk neutral? In particular, if $B = \$5,000$ and $G = \$500$, what is the optimal M?

Answer

1. *Determine how many units of monitoring are necessary to deter stealing.* The least amount of monitoring that deters stealing is the amount at which a worker's gain from stealing equals the worker's expected loss if caught. A worker is just deterred from stealing when the gain, G, equals the expected penalty, θB. Thus, the worker is deterred when the probability of being caught is $\theta = G/B$. The number of units of monitoring effort is $M = \theta/0.05$, because each extra unit of monitoring raises θ by 5%.

2. *Determine whether monitoring is cost effective.* It pays for the firm to pay for M units of monitoring only if the expected benefit to the firm is greater than the cost of monitoring, $\$10 \times M$. The expected benefit if stealing is prevented is G, so monitoring pays if $G > \$10 \times M$, or $G/M > \$10$.

3. *Solve for the optimal monitoring in the special case.* The optimal level of monitoring is

$$M = \frac{\theta}{0.05} = \frac{G/B}{0.05} = \frac{500/5,000}{0.05} = \frac{0.1}{0.05} = 2.$$

It pays to engage in this level of monitoring because $G/M = \$500/2 = \$250 > \$10$.

---

[9]The expected penalty is $\theta B + (1 - \theta)0 = \theta B$, where the first term on the left-hand side is the probability of being caught times the fine of B and the second term is the probability of not being caught and facing no fine.

Problems with Bonding. Employers like the bond-posting solution because it reduces the amount of employee monitoring that is necessary to discourage moral hazards such as shirking and theft. Nonetheless, firms use explicit bonding only occasionally to prevent stealing, and they rarely use it to prevent shirking.

Having an agent post a bond has two major problems. First, an unscrupulous employer might falsely accuse an employee of stealing. Employees who fear such employer opportunism are unwilling to post a bond. To avoid this problem, the firm may develop a reputation for not behaving in this manner or to make the grounds for forfeiture of the bond objective and verifiable by others.

Second, workers may not have enough wealth to post them. In our example, if the worker could steal $10,000, and if the probability of being caught were only 5%, shirking would be deterred only if a risk-neutral worker posted a bond of at least $200,000.

Consequently, bonds are more common in contracts between firms than between an employer and employees. Construction contractors sometimes post bonds to guarantee that they will satisfactorily finish their work by a given date. It is easy to verify whether the contract has been completed on time, and firms may post a bond more easily than employees.

Deferred Payments

Effectively, firms can post bonds for their employees through the use of deferred payments. For example, a firm pays new workers a low wage for some initial period of employment. Over time, workers who are caught shirking are fired, and those who remain are paid higher wages. Pensions are another form of deferred wages that reward only hard workers who stay with the firm until their retirement. Deferred payments function like bonds. They raise the cost of being fired, so less monitoring is necessary to deter shirking.

Workers care about the present value (Chapter 15) of their earnings stream over their lifetime. A firm may offer its workers one of two wage payment schemes. In the first, the firm pays w per year for each year that the worker is employed by the firm. In the second arrangement, the starting wage is less than w but rises over the years to a wage that exceeds w.

If hard workers can borrow against future earnings, those who work for one company their entire careers are indifferent between the two wage payment schemes if those plans have identical present values. However, the firm prefers the deferred payment method because employees work harder to avoid being fired and losing the high future earnings.

Reducing shirking results in greater output. If the employer and the employee share the extra output through higher profit and lifetime earnings, both prefer the deferred-payment scheme that lowers incentives to shirk.

A drawback of the deferred-payment approach is that employers may engage in opportunistic behavior. For example, an employer might fire nonshirking senior workers to avoid paying their higher wages, and then replace them with less expensive junior workers. However, if the firm can establish a reputation for not firing senior workers unjustifiably, the deferred-payment system can help prevent shirking.

Efficiency Wages

As we've seen, the use of bonds and deferred payments discourages shirking by raising an employee's cost of losing a job. An alternative is for the firm to pay an **efficiency wage**: an unusually high wage that a firm pays workers as an incentive to avoid shirking.[10] If a worker who is fired for shirking can immediately go to another firm and earn the same wage, the worker risks nothing by shirking. However, if the firm pays each worker an efficiency wage w, which is more than the wage $\underline{w}$ that an employee would earn elsewhere after being fired for shirking, it discourages shirking.[11] The less frequently the firm monitors workers, the greater the wage differential must be between w and $\underline{w}$ to prevent shirking.

An efficiency wage acts like a bond to prevent shirking. A risk-neutral worker decides whether to shirk by comparing the expected loss of earnings from getting fired to the value, G, that the worker places on shirking. An employee who never shirks is not fired and earns the efficiency wage, w. A fired worker goes elsewhere and earns the lower wage, $\underline{w}$. Consequently, a shirking worker expects to lose $\theta(w - \underline{w})$, where θ is the probability that a shirking worker is caught and fired and where the term in parentheses is the lost earnings from being fired. Thus, the expected value to a shirking employee is $\theta\underline{w} + (1 - \theta)w + G$, where $\theta\underline{w}$ is the probability of being caught shirking, θ, times earnings elsewhere if caught and fired; $(1 - \theta)w$ is the probability of not being caught times the efficiency wage; and G is the value that a worker derives from shirking.

The worker chooses not to shirk if the efficiency wage, w, exceeds the expected return from shirking: $w \geq \theta\underline{w} + (1 - \theta)w + G$. Subtracting the first two right-hand side terms from both sides of the equation, we find that a worker does not shirk if the expected loss from being fired, $\theta(w - \underline{w})$, is greater than or equal to the gain from shirking, G:

$$\theta(w - \underline{w}) \geq G. \tag{19.6}$$

The smallest amount by which w can exceed $\underline{w}$ and prevent shirking is determined when Equation 19.6 holds with equality, $\theta(w - \underline{w}) = G$, or

$$w - \underline{w} = \frac{G}{\theta}. \tag{19.7}$$

The extra earnings, $w - \underline{w}$, in Equation 19.7 serve the same function as the bond, B, in Equation 19.5 in discouraging bad behavior.

Suppose that the value of the pleasure that a worker gets from not working hard is $G = \$1,000$, and the wage elsewhere is $\underline{w} = \$20,000$ a year. If the probability that a shirking worker is caught is $\theta = 20\%$, then the efficiency wage must be at least $w = \$25,000$ to prevent shirking. With greater monitoring, so that θ is 50%, the minimum w that prevents shirking is $\$22,000$. From the possible pairs of monitoring levels and efficiency wages that deter shirking, the firm picks the combination that minimizes its labor cost.

After-the-Fact Monitoring

So far, we've concentrated on monitoring by employers checking for bad behavior as it occurs. If shirking or other bad behavior is detected after the fact, the offending employee is fired or otherwise disciplined. If payment occurs after the

---

[10]The discussion of efficiency wages is based on Yellen (1984), Stiglitz (1987), and especially Shapiro and Stiglitz (1984).

[11]There are other explanations for why efficiency wages lead to higher productivity. Some economists claim that in less-developed countries, employers pay an efficiency wage—more than they need to hire workers—to ensure that workers can afford to eat well enough that they can work hard. Other economists (Akerlof, 1982) and management experts contend that the higher wage acts like a gift, making workers feel beholden or loyal to the firm, so that little or no monitoring is needed.

principal checks for bad behavior, after-the-fact monitoring discourages bad behavior.[12]

Often detecting bad behavior as it occurs is difficult, but detecting it after the fact is relatively easy. For example, after an employer finds that the quality of an employee's work is substandard, the employer can force the employee to correct it or refuse to pay.

Insurance firms try to avoid extreme moral hazard by offering contracts that do not cover spectacularly reckless, stupid, or malicious behavior. An auto insurance company will not pay damages for a traffic accident if the insured driver was drunk at the time. A home insurance company disallows claims due to an explosion that resulted from an illegal activity such as making methamphetamine on the premises and claims by arsonists who torch their own property. Life insurance companies may refuse to pay benefits to the family of someone who commits suicide soon after buying the policy (as in the play *Death of a Salesman*).

APPLICATION

The Mortgage Market Meltdown

During the mortgage market meltdown that started in 2007, many mortgage holders defaulted on their loans and their homes went into foreclosure, and the lender took ownership. The problem was particularly bad in California, where, even by July 2012, one in every 325 housing units had a foreclosure filing (more than twice the national average).

There are at least four important reasons (in addition to fraud) for the housing crisis. First, many mortgage-initiating firms failed to require down payments for subprime loans. In the San Francisco Bay Area, 69% of families whose owner-occupied homes were in foreclosure had put down 0% at the time of purchase, and only 10% made the traditional 20% down payment in the first nine months of 2007.

Second, firms loaned to speculators who were more likely to walk away from a loan than would someone who lived in the mortgaged house. Speculators were a serious problem in Miami and Las Vegas. In Las Vegas during the first half of 2007, absentee investors owned 74% of single-family homes in foreclosure. (Nationally, nonowner-occupied homes accounted for 13% of prime defaults and 11% of subprime defaults.)

Third, mortgages used adjustable rates that started very low and increased rapidly over time. Because the implications of these escalator clauses were not made clear to borrowers, many poor people suddenly found themselves unable to make their mortgage payments.

Fourth, many mortgage-originating firms such as banks failed to check borrowers' creditworthiness properly. Of the properties repossessed in the San Francisco Bay Area, one in six was owned by people who had two or more past foreclosures, and some had five or more.

Thus, mortgage-originating firms did not take a number of obvious actions to mitigate adverse selection and moral problems such as large down payments, tight loan caps, and high enough interest rates to cover the risk of default. As a consequence, many borrowers defaulted on their loans and lenders hemorrhaged money.

---

[12]Learning about a moral hazard after it occurs is too late if the wrongdoer cannot be punished at that time. Although it's upsetting to find that you've been victimized, there may be nothing you can do beyond trying to prevent the situation from happening again.

SOLVED PROBLEM 19.4

An S&L can make one of two types of loans. It can lend money on home mortgages, where it has a 75% probability of earning $100 million and a 25% probability of earning $80 million. Alternatively, it can lend money to oil speculators, where it has a 25% probability of earning $400 million and a 75% probability of losing $160 million (due to loan defaults by the speculators). Bernie, the manager of the S&L who will make the lending decision, receives 1% of the firm's earnings. He believes that if the S&L loses money, he can walk away from his job without repercussions, although without compensation. Bernie and the shareholders of the company are risk neutral. Which decision would Bernie make if all he cares about is maximizing his personal expected earnings? Which investment would the stockholders prefer?

Answer

1. *Determine the S&L's expected return on the two investments.* If the S&L makes home mortgage loans, its expected return is

$$(0.75 \times 100) + (0.25 \times 80) = 95$$

million dollars. Alternatively, if it loans to the oil speculators, its expected return is

$$(0.25 \times 400) + [0.75 \times (-160)] = -20$$

million dollars, an expected loss.

2. *Compare the S&L manager's expected profits on the two investments.* Bernie expects to earn 1% of $95 million, or $950,000, from investing in mortgages. His take from investing in oil is 1% of $400 million, or $4 million, with a probability of 25% and no compensation with a probability of 75%. Thus, he expects to earn

$$(0.25 \times 4) + (0.75 \times 0) = 1$$

million dollars from investing in oil. Because he is risk neutral and does not care a whit about anyone else, he invests in oil.

3. *Compare the shareholders' expected profits on the two investments.* The shareholders expect to receive 99% of the profit from the mortgages, or $0.99 \times \$95$ million = $94.05 million. With the oil loans, they earn 99% of the $400 million, or $396 million, if the investment is good, and bear the full loss in the case of defaults, $160 million, so their expected profit (loss) is

$$(0.25 \times 396) + [0.75 \times (-160)] = -21$$

million dollars. Thus, the shareholders would prefer that the S&L invest in mortgages.

Comment: Given that the manager has the wrong incentives (and no integrity), he makes the investment that is not in the shareholders' interest. One solution to the problem of their diverging interests is to change the manager's compensation package.

19.5 Contract Choice

By offering an agent a choice of contracts, the principal may obtain enough information to prevent agent opportunism. Firms want to avoid hiring workers who shirk. Employers know that not all workers shirk, even when given an opportunity to do so. So rather than focusing on stopping lazy workers from shirking, an employer may concentrate on hiring only industrious people. With this approach, the firm seeks to avoid *moral hazard* by preventing *adverse selection*, where lazy employees falsely assert that they are hardworking.

The firm makes potential job candidates select between two contracts in which payment depends on how hard they work. Suppose that a firm wants to hire a salesperson to run its Cleveland office and that the potential employees are risk neutral. A hardworking salesperson sells $100,000 worth of goods a year, but a lazy one sells only $60,000 worth (see Table 19.3). A hard worker can earn $30,000 from other firms, so the firm considers using a contingent contract that pays a salesperson a 30% commission on sales.

If the firm succeeds in hiring a hard worker, the salesperson makes $100,000 \times 0.30 = \$30,000$. The firm's share of sales is $70,000. If the firm has no costs of production but maintaining this branch office costs the firm $50,000 a year, the firm's profit is $20,000. If the firm hires a lazy salesperson under the same contract, the salesperson makes $18,000, the firm's share of sales is $42,000, and the firm loses $8,000 after paying for the office.

To determine if potential employees are hardworking, the firm offers each a choice of contracts:

- Contingent contract: no salary and 30% of sales,
- Fixed-fee contract: annual salary of $25,000, regardless of sales.

A prospective employee who doesn't mind hard work would earn $5,000 more by choosing the contingent contract. In contrast, a lazy candidate would make $7,000 more from a salary than from commissions. If an applicant chooses the fixed-fee contract, the firm knows that the person does not intend to work hard and decides not to hire that person.

The firm learns what it needs to know by offering this contract choice as long as the lazy applicant does not pretend to be a hard worker and chooses the contingent

Table 19.3 Firm's Spreadsheet

	Contingent Contract (30% of Sales), $	Fixed-Fee Contract ($25,000 Salary), $
Hard Worker		
Sales	100,000	100,000
− Salesperson's pay	−30,000	−25,000
= Firm's net revenue	70,000	75,000
− Office expenses	−50,000	−50,000
= Firm's profit	20,000	25,000
Lazy Worker		
Sales	60,000	60,000
− Salesperson's pay	−18,000	−25,000
= Firm's net revenue	42,000	35,000
− Office expenses	−50,000	−50,000
= Firm's profit	−8,000	−15,000

contract. Under the contingent contract, the lazy person makes only $18,000, but that offer may dominate others available in the market. If this pair of contracts fails to sort workers, the firm may try different pairs. If all these choices fail to sort the potential employees, the firm must use other means to prevent shirking.

19.6 Checks on Principals

Because employers (principals) often pay employees (agents) after work is completed, employers have many opportunities to exploit workers. For example, a dishonest employer can underpay after falsely claiming that a worker took time off or that some of the worker's output was substandard. Employers who provide bonuses can underreport the firm's output or profit.

Efficient contracts prevent or reduce such moral hazard problems. Requiring a firm to post a bond can be an effective method of deterring the firm's opportunistic behavior. For example, a firm may post bonds to ensure that it has the means of paying current wages and future pensions.

A firm cannot act opportunistically if information is symmetric because it reveals relevant information to employees. An employer can provide access to such information by allowing employee representatives to sit on the company board so as to monitor the firm's behavior. To induce workers to agree to profit sharing, a firm may provide workers with information about the company's profit by allowing them (or an independent auditor) to check its accounts. A firm may argue that its stock closely mirrors its profit and suggest that the known stock price be used for incentive payments.

Firms may rely on a good reputation. For instance, a firm may publicize that it does not make a practice of firing senior employees to avoid paying pensions. The better the firm's reputation, the more likely workers are to accept a deferred payment scheme, which deters shirking.

When these approaches are infeasible, a firm may use less efficient contracts such as one that bases employee payments on easily observed revenues rather than less reliable profit reports. The next application discusses a particularly damaging but common type of inefficient contract.

APPLICATION

Layoffs Versus
Pay Cuts

During recessions and depressions, demand for most firms' products fall. Many firms respond by laying off workers and reducing production rather than by lowering wages and keeping everyone employed. From the second quarter in 2002 through the second quarter in 2012, the average real U.S. weekly earnings fluctuated in a narrow band from $333 to $345. In contrast, the U.S. unemployment rate over this period started at 5.8% in 2002, rose to 6.3% in 2003, dropped to 4.5% in 2007, rose to 9.6% in mid-2010, and then dropped to 8.2% in 2012.

If both sides agreed to it, a wage reduction policy would benefit firms and workers alike. Collectively, workers would earn more than they would if they were laid off. Because the firm's costs would fall, it could sell more during the downturn than it otherwise could, so its profit would be higher than it would be if there were layoffs. Firms that provide relatively low wages and then share profits with employees achieve this type of wage flexibility.

Why then are wage reductions less common than layoffs? A major explanation involves asymmetric information: Unlike the firm, workers don't know whether the firm is actually facing a downturn, so they refuse to cut wages. They fear that the firm will falsely claim that economic conditions are bad to justify a wage cut. Workers believe that if the firm has to lay off workers—an action that hurts the firm as well as the workers—the firm is more likely to be telling the truth about economic conditions.[13]

We illustrate this reasoning in the following matrix, which shows the payoffs if wages are reduced during downturns. The value of output produced by each worker is $21 during good times and $15 during bad times. The lower left of each cell is the amount the firm pays workers. The firm pays employees $12 per hour if it reports that economic conditions are good and $8 if it says that conditions are bad. The amount the firm keeps is in the upper right of each cell. If economic conditions are bad, the firm earns more by reporting these bad conditions, $7, than it earns if it says that conditions are good, $3. Similarly, if conditions are good, the firm earns more if it claims that conditions are bad, $13, than if it says that they are good, $9. Thus, regardless of the true state, the firm benefits by always claiming that conditions are bad.

Wage Cut

		Firm's Claim About Conditions	
		Bad	Good
Actual Conditions	Bad	8 / 7	12 / 3
	Good	8 / 13	12 / 9

To shield themselves from such systematic lying, employees may insist that the firm lay off workers whenever it says that conditions are bad. This requirement provides the firm with an incentive to report the true conditions. In the next matrix, the firm must lay off workers for half of each period if it announces that times are bad, causing the value of output to fall by one-third. Because they now work only half the time, workers earn only half as much, $6, as they earn during good times, $12. If conditions are bad, the firm makes more by telling the truth, $4, than by claiming that conditions are good, $3. In good times, the firm makes more by announcing that conditions are good, $9, than by claiming that they are bad, $8. Thus, the firm reports conditions truthfully.

Worker Layoff (for half of any period the firm claims is bad)

		Firm's Claim About Conditions	
		Bad	Good
Actual Conditions	Bad	6 / 4	12 / 3
	Good	6 / 8	12 / 9

---

[13]In 2010, after several years of recession (which proves that the downturn was real), layoffs were increasingly replaced with pay cuts, especially by state and local government employers. Similarly, Sub-Zero, which makes refrigerators and other appliances, told its workers it might close one or more factories and lay off 500 employees unless they accepted a 20% cut in wages and benefits.

With the wage-cut contract in which the firm always says that conditions are bad, workers earn $8 regardless of actual conditions. If economic conditions are good half the time, the firm earns an average of $10 = $\left(\frac{1}{2} \times \$7\right) + \left(\frac{1}{2} \times \$13\right)$. Under the contract that requires layoffs, the workers earn an average of $9 = $\left(\frac{1}{2} \times \$6\right) + \left(\frac{1}{2} \times \$12\right)$ and the firm earns an average of $6.50 = $\left(\frac{1}{2} \times \$4\right) + \left(\frac{1}{2} \times \$9\right)$.

Therefore, the firm prefers the wage-cut contract and the workers favor the layoff contract. However, if the workers could observe actual conditions, both parties would prefer the wage-cut contract. Workers would earn an average of $10 = $\left(\frac{1}{2} \times \$8\right) + \left(\frac{1}{2} \times \$12\right)$, and the firm would make $8 = $\left(\frac{1}{2} \times \$7\right) + \left(\frac{1}{2} \times \$9\right)$. With the layoff contract, total payoffs are lower because of lost production. Thus, socially inefficient layoffs may be used because of the need to keep relatively well-informed firms honest.

CHALLENGE SOLUTION

Health Insurance

The Challenge at the beginning of the chapter asks whether medical insurance creates a moral hazard and whether insurance policies with deductibles are socially preferable to complete coverage. To illustrate the basic ideas, we consider Gary's demand for medical services—visits to his doctor—which depends on his health.

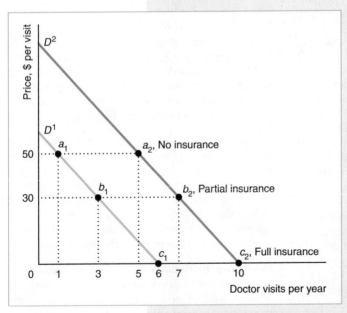

Half the time his health is good, so he only wants preventive care and his demand curve is D^1 on the graph. When he's not feeling well, his demand curve is D^2. Without medical insurance, he pays $50 a visit. Because Gary is risk averse, he wants to buy medical insurance. With full insurance, Gary pays a fixed fee at the beginning of the year, and the insurance company pays the entire cost. Alternatively, with a contingent contract, Gary pays a smaller premium at the beginning of the year, and the insurance company covers only $20 per visit and Gary pays the remaining $30. How likely is a moral hazard problem to occur with each of these contracts? What is Gary's risk (variance of his medical costs) with each of the three types of insurance?

We start by describing the moral hazard associated with each contract. If Gary's health is good, he increases from one visit, a_1, with no insurance (where he pays $50 a visit) to six visits, c_1, with full insurance (where he pays nothing per visit). Similarly, if his health is poor, he increases his visits from five, a_2, to ten, c_2. Thus, regardless of his health, he makes five extra visits a year with full insurance. These extra visits are the moral hazard. With a contingent contract whereby Gary pays $30 a visit, the moral hazard is less because he makes only two extra visits instead of five: the difference between the number of visits at b_1 and a_1 and between b_2 and a_2.

Partially offsetting the harm from the moral hazard problem, the insurance reduces Gary's risk, which is desirable because he is risk averse. Without insurance, his expected number of doctor visits is $\left(\frac{1}{2} \times 1\right) + \left(\frac{1}{2} \times 5\right) = 3$, so his average annual medical cost is $150. Thus, the variance of his medical expenses without insurance is

$$\sigma_n^2 = \tfrac{1}{2}[(1 \times \$50) - \$150]^2 + \tfrac{1}{2}[(5 \times 50) - \$150]^2 = \$10,000.$$

If he has full insurance, he makes a single fixed payment each year, so his payments do not vary with his health: His variance is $\sigma_f^2 = 0$. With partial insurance, he averages five visits with an average cost of $150, so his variance is

$$\sigma_p^2 = \tfrac{1}{2}[(3 \times \$30) - \$150]^2 + \tfrac{1}{2}[(7 \times 30) - \$150]^2 = \$3,600.$$

Thus, $\sigma_n^2 > \sigma_p^2 > \sigma_f^2$.

Because Gary is risk averse, efficiency in risk bearing requires that the risk-neutral insurance company bear all the risk, as with full insurance. However, full insurance leads to a moral hazard. Without insurance, there is no moral hazard but Gary bears all the risk. A contingent contract—such as an insurance policy with a deductible—is a compromise where both the moral hazard and the degree of risk lie between the extremes. If the moral hazard problem cannot be eliminated directly, it may make sense to provide partial insurance with a deductible.

SUMMARY

1. **Principal-Agent Problem.** A principal contracts with an agent to perform some task. The size of their joint profit depends on any assets that the principal contributes, the actions of the agent, and the state of nature. If the principal cannot observe the agent's actions, the agent may engage in opportunistic behavior. This moral hazard reduces the joint profit. An efficient contract leads to efficiency in production (joint profit is maximized by eliminating moral hazards) and efficiency in risk bearing (the less-risk-averse party bears more of the risk). Three common types of contracts are fixed-fee contracts, whereby one party pays the other a fixed fee and the other keeps the rest of the profits; hire contracts, in which the principal pays the agent a wage or pays by the piece of output produced; and contingent contracts, wherein the payoffs vary with the amount of output produced or in some other way. Because a contract that reduces the moral hazard may increase the risk for a relatively risk-averse person, a contract is chosen to achieve the best trade-off between the twin goals of efficiency in production and efficiency in risk bearing.

2. **Production Efficiency.** Whether efficiency in production is achieved depends on the type of contract that the principal and the agent use and on the degree to which their information is asymmetric. For the agent in our example to put forth the optimal level of effort, the agent must get the full marginal profit from that effort or the principal must monitor the agent. When the parties have full information, an agent with

a fixed-fee rental or profit-sharing contract gets the entire marginal profit and produces optimally without being monitored. If the principal cannot monitor the agent or does not observe profit and cost, only a fixed-fee rental contract prevents moral hazard problems and achieves production efficiency.

3. **Trade-Off Between Efficiency in Production and in Risk Bearing.** A principal and an agent may agree to a contract that strikes a balance between reducing moral hazards and allocating risk optimally. Contracts that eliminate moral hazards require the agent to bear the risk. If the agent is more risk averse than the principal, the parties may trade off a reduction in production efficiency to lower risk for the agent.

4. **Monitoring to Reduce Moral Hazard.** Because of asymmetric information, an employer must normally monitor workers' efforts to prevent shirking. Less monitoring is necessary as the employee's interest in keeping the job increases. The employer may require the employee to post a large bond that is forfeited if the employee is caught shirking, stealing, or otherwise misbehaving. If an employee cannot afford to post a bond, the employer may use deferred payments or efficiency wages—unusually high wages—to make it worthwhile for the employee to keep the job. Employers may also be able to prevent shirking by engaging in after-the-fact monitoring. However, such monitoring works only if bad behavior can be punished after the fact.

5. **Contract Choice.** A principal may be able to prevent moral hazard problems from adverse selection by observing choices made by potential agents. For example, an employer may present potential employees with a choice of contracts, prompting hard-working job applicants to choose a contract that compensates the worker for working hard and lazy candidates to choose a different contract that provides a guaranteed salary.

6. **Checks on Principals.** Often both agents and principals can engage in opportunistic behavior. If a firm must reveal its actions to its employees, it is less likely to be able to take advantage of the employees. To convey information, an employer may let employees participate in decision-making meetings or audit the company's books. Alternatively, an employer may make commitments so that it is in the employer's best interest to tell employees the truth. These commitments, such as laying off workers rather than reducing wages during downturns, may reduce moral hazards but lead to nonoptimal production.

EXERCISES

■ = *exercise is available on* MyEconLab; * = *answer appears at the back of this book;* **M** = *mathematical problem.*

1. Principal-Agent Problem

1.1 California provides earthquake insurance. Because the state agency in charge has few staff members, it pays private insurance carriers to handle claims for earthquake damage. These insurance firms receive 9% of each approved claim. Is this compensation scheme likely to lead to opportunistic behavior by insurance companies? Explain. What would be a better way to handle the compensation?

*1.2 Some sellers offer to buy back a good later at some prespecified price. Why would a firm make such a commitment?

*1.3 A promoter arranges for various restaurants to set up booths to sell Cajun-Creole food at a fair. Appropriate music and other entertainment are provided. Customers can buy food using only "Cajun Cash," which is scrip that has the same denominations as actual cash and is sold by the fair promoter. Why aren't the food booths allowed to sell food directly for cash?

1.4 A flyer from one of the world's largest brokers says, "Most personal investment managers base their fees on a percentage of assets managed. We believe this is in your best interest because your manager is paid for investment management, not solely on the basis of trading commissions charged to your account. You can be assured your manager's investment decisions are guided by one primary goal—increasing your assets." Is this policy in a customer's best interest? Why or why not?

1.5 A study by Jean Mitchell found that urologists in group practices that profit from tests for prostate cancer order more of them than doctors who send samples to independent laboratories. Doctors' groups that perform their own lab work bill Medicare for analyzing 72% more prostate tissue samples per biopsy and detect fewer cases of cancer than doctors who use outside labs (Weaver, Christopher, "Prostate-Test Fees Challenged," *Wall Street Journal*, April 9, 2012). Explain these results. Do these results necessarily demonstrate moral hazard or is there another possible explanation?

1.6 In 2012, a California environmental group found that 14 plum and ginger candies imported from Asia contained 4 to 96 times the level of lead allowed under California law (Lee, Stephanie M., "Lead Found in Asian Candies," *San Francisco Chronicle*, August 14, 2012). Some observers predicted that U.S. consumers would face significant price increases if U.S. law were changed to require third-party testing by manufacturers and sellers. Suppose instead that candies could be reliably labeled "tested" or "untested," and untested candy sold at a discount. Would consumers buy cheaper, untested goods or would they fear a moral hazard problem? Discuss.

2. Production Efficiency

*2.1 When I was in graduate school, I shared an apartment with a fellow who was madly in love with a woman who lived in another city. They agreed to split the costs of their long-distance phone calls equally, regardless of who placed the calls. (In those days, long-distance calls were expensive and billed separately from general phone service.) What was the implication of this fee-sharing arrangement on their total phone bill? Why?

*2.2 Zhihua and Pu are partners in a store in which they do all the work. They split the store's business profit equally (ignoring the opportunity cost of their own time in calculating this profit). Does their business profit-sharing contract give them an incentive to maximize their joint economic profit if neither can force the other to work? (*Hint*: Imagine Zhihua's thought process late one Saturday night when he is alone in the store, debating whether to keep the store open a little later or go out on the town. See Solved Problem 19.1.)

2.3 In Solved Problem 19.1, does joint profit increase, decrease, or remain the same as the share of revenue going to Arthur increases?

*2.4 In the duck-carving example with full information (summarized in the second column of Table 19.1), is a contract efficient if it requires Paula to give Arthur a fixed-fee salary of $168 and leaves all the decisions to Arthur? If so, why? If not, are there additional steps that Paula can take to ensure that Arthur sells the optimal number of carvings?

2.5 In the duck-carving example with limited information (summarized in the third and fourth columns of Table 19.1), is a fixed-fee contract efficient? If so, why? If not, are there additional steps that Paula can take to ensure efficiency?

2.6 The author of a science fiction novel is paid a royalty of β share of the revenue from sales, where the revenue is $R = pq$, p is the competitive market price for novels, and q is the number of copies of this book sold. The publisher's cost of printing and distributing the book is $C(q)$. Determine the equilibrium, and compare it to the outcome that maximizes the sum of the payment to the author plus the firm's profit. Answer using both math and a graph. **M**

2.7 Suppose now that the publisher in Exercise 2.6 faces a downward-sloping demand curve. The revenue is $R(Q)$, and the publisher's cost of printing and distributing the book is $C(Q)$. Compare the equilibria for the following compensation methods in which the author receives the same total compensation from each method:

a. The author is paid a lump sum, $\mathscr{L}$.

b. The author is paid α share of the revenue.

c. The author receives a lump-sum payment and a share of the revenue.

Why do you think that authors are usually paid a share of the revenue? (*Hint*: See Solved Problem 19.1.) **M**

2.8 John manages Rachel's used CD music store. To provide John with the incentive to sell CDs, Rachel offers him 50% of the store's profit. John has the opportunity to misrepresent sales by fraudulently recording sales that actually did not take place. Let t represent his fraudulent profit. John's expected earnings from reporting the fraudulent profit is $0.5t$. Rachel tries to detect such fraud and either detects

all or none of it. The probability that Rachel detects the entire fraud is $t/(1 + t)$ and the probability that Rachel does not detect the fraud is $1 - t/(1 + t)$. Hence, Rachel's probability of detecting fraud is zero if John reports no fraudulent profit, increases with the amount of fraudulent profit he reports, and approaches 1 as the amount of fraud approaches infinity. If Rachel detects the fraud, then $x > 0.5$ is the fine that John pays Rachel per dollar of fraud. John's expected fine of reporting fraudulent profit t is $t^2x/(1 + t)$. In choosing the level of fraud, John's objective is to maximize his expected earnings from the fraud, $0.5t$, less his expected fine, $t^2x/(1 + t)$. As a function of x, what is John's optimal fraudulent profit? (*Hint*: check the second-order condition.) Show that $\partial t/\partial x < 0$. Also show that as $x \to \infty$, John's optimal reported fraudulent profit goes to zero. (*Hint*: See Solved Problem 19.1.) **M**

2.9 In the National Basketball Association (NBA), the owners share revenue but not costs. Suppose that one team, the L.A. Clippers, sells only general-admission seats to a home game with the visiting Philadelphia 76ers (Sixers). The inverse demand for the Clippers-Sixers tickets is $p = 100 - 0.004Q$. The Clippers' cost function of selling Q tickets and running the franchise is $C(Q) = 10Q$.

a. Find the Clippers' profit-maximizing number of tickets sold and the price if the Clippers must give 50% of their revenue to the Sixers. At the maximum, what are the Clippers' profit and the Sixers' share of the revenues?

b. Instead, suppose that the Sixers set the Clippers' ticket price based on the same revenue-sharing rule. What price will the Sixers set, how many tickets are sold, and what revenue payment will the Sixers receive? Explain why your answers to parts a and b differ.

c. Now suppose that the Clippers must share their profit rather than their revenue. The Clippers keep 45% of their profit and share 55% with the Sixers. The Clippers set the price. Find the Clippers' profit-maximizing price and determine how many tickets the team sells and its share of the profit.

d. Compare your answers to parts a and c using marginal revenue and marginal cost in your explanation. (*Hint*: See Solved Problem 19.1.) **M**

2.10 Book retailers can return unsold copies to publishers. Effectively, retailers pay for the books they order only after they sell them. Dowell's Books believes that it will sell, with $\frac{1}{2}$ probability each, either zero or one copy of *The Fool's Handbook of Macroeconomics*. The bookstore also believes that it will sell, with $\frac{1}{2}$ probability each, either zero or one copy of *The Genius' Handbook of Microeconomics*. The retail price of each book is $100. Suppose that the marginal cost of manufacturing another copy of a book is $24. The publisher's value of a returned copy is $0. The *Microeconomics* publisher charges a $52 wholesale price and offers a full refund if an unsold book is returned. While the *Macroeconomics* publisher charges a low $42 wholesale price, it pays a retailer only $32 if it returns an unsold book. Dowell's places an order for one copy of each title. When the two books arrive, Dowell's has space to shelve only one. Which title does Dowell's return? Comment on how Dowell's decision about which title to return depends on the books' wholesale prices and on the compensation from the publishers for returned unsold books. **M**

3. Trade-Off Between Efficiency in Production and in Risk Bearing

3.1 Traditionally, doctors have been paid on a fee-for-service basis. Now doctors are increasingly paid on a capitated basis: They get paid for treating a patient for a year, regardless of how much treatment is required. In this arrangement, doctors form a group and sign a capitation contract whereby they take turns seeing a given patient. What are the implications of this change in compensation for moral hazards and for risk bearing?

3.2 Padma has the rights to any treasure on the sunken ship the *Golden Calf*. Aaron is a diver who specializes in marine salvage. If Padma is risk averse and Aaron is risk neutral, does paying Aaron a fixed fee result in efficiency in risk bearing and production? Does your answer turn on how predictable the value of the sunken treasure is? Would another compensation scheme be more efficient? (*Hint*: See Solved Problem 19.2.)

3.3 Fourteen states have laws that limit whether a franchisor (such as McDonald's) can terminate a franchise agreement. Franchisees (such as firms that run individual McDonald's outlets) typically pay the franchisor a fixed fee or a share of revenues. What effects do such laws have on production efficiency and risk bearing? (*Hint*: See Solved Problem 19.2.)

3.4 Louisa is an avid cyclist who is currently working on her business degree. She normally rides an $800 bike to class. If Louisa locks her bike carefully—locks both wheels—the chance of theft for the term is 5%, but this careful locking procedure is time consuming. If she is less careful—just quickly locks the frame to a bike rack—the chance of theft is 20%. Louisa is risk averse and is considering buying theft insurance for her bike. There are two types of insurance. With full insurance, Louisa pays the premium and gets the full $800 value of the bike if it is stolen. Alternatively, with partial insurance, Louisa receives only 75% of the bike's value, $600, if the bike is stolen. Which contract is more likely to induce moral hazard problems? To break even on consumers like Louisa, what price would the risk-neutral insurance company have to charge for full insurance? If we observe Louisa buying partial insurance what can we say about the trade-off between moral hazard and efficient risk-bearing.

4. Monitoring to Reduce Moral Hazard

4.1 Many law firms consist of partners who share profits. On being made a partner, a lawyer must post a bond, a large payment to the firm that will be forfeited on bad behavior. Why?

*4.2 In Solved Problem 19.3, a firm calculates the optimal level of monitoring to prevent stealing. If $G = \$500$ and $\theta = 20\%$, what is the minimum bond that deters stealing? **M**

4.3 In Exercise 4.2, suppose that, for each extra $1,000 of bonding the firm requires a worker to post, the firm must pay that worker $10 more per period to get the worker to work for the firm. What is the minimum bond that deters stealing? (*Hint*: See Solved Problem 19.3.) **M**

4.4 Starting in 2008, Medicare would not cover the cost of a surgeon leaving an instrument in a patient, giving a patient transfusions of the wrong blood type, certain types of hospital-acquired infections, or other "preventable" mistakes (Liz Marlantes, "Medicare Won't Cover Hospital Mistakes: New Rules Aimed at Promoting Better Hospital Care and Safety," *ABC News*, August 19, 2007). Hospitals will have to cover these costs and cannot bill the patient. These changes are designed to provide hospitals with a stronger incentive to prevent those mistakes, particularly infections. The Centers for Disease Control and Prevention estimates that 2 million patients are annually infected in hospitals, costing society more than $27 billion. Nearly 100,000 of those infections are fatal. Many of these infections could be prevented if hospitals more rigorously follow basic infection control procedures, including having doctors and nurses wash their hands between every patient treatment. Is Medicare's policy designed to deal with adverse selection or moral hazard? Is it likely to help? Explain.

4.5 When rental cars are sold on the used car market they are sold for lower prices than cars of the same model and year that were owned by individuals. Does this price difference reflect adverse selection or moral hazard? Could car rental companies reduce this problem by carefully inspecting rental cars for damage when renters return such cars? Why do car companies normally do only a cursory inspection?

4.6 In 2012, Hewlett-Packard Co. announced that its new chief executive, Meg Whitman, would receive a salary of $1 and about $16.1 million in stock options, which are valuable if the stock does well (**marketwatch.com**, February 3, 2012). How would you feel about this compensation package if you were a shareholder? What are the implications for moral hazard, efficiency, and risk sharing? (*Hint*: See Solved Problem 19.4.)

4.7 Adrienne, a manager of a large firm, must decide whether to launch a new product or make a minor change to an existing product. The new product has a 30% chance of being a big success and generating profits of $20 million, a 40% chance of being fairly successful and generating profits of $5 million, and a 30% chance of being a costly failure and losing $10 million. Making minor changes in the old product would generate profits of $10 million for sure. Adrienne's contract gives her a bonus of 10% of any profits above $8 million arising from this decision. If Adrienne is risk neutral and cares

only about her own income, what is her decision? Should shareholders be happy with this compensation contract? Is there a contract that would be better for both Adrienne and the shareholders? (*Hint*: See Solved Problem 19.4.) **M**

5. Contract Choice

5.1 List some necessary conditions for a firm to be able to sort potential employees by providing them with a choice of contracts.

6. Checks on Principals

6.1 In the Application "Layoffs Versus Pay Cuts," the firm either uses a pay cut or layoffs. Can you derive a superior approach that benefits both the firm and the workers? (*Hint*: Suppose that the firm's profit or some other variable is observable.)

7. Challenge

7.1 A health insurance company tries to prevent the moral hazard of "excessive" dentist visits by limiting the number of compensated visits that a patient can make in a year. How does such a restriction affect moral hazard and risk bearing? Show in a graph.

Calculus Appendix

In mathematics you don't understand things. You just get used to them.
—John von Neumann

This appendix reviews the basic tools from calculus and mathematics that we use throughout this book.[1] It emphasizes unconstrained and constrained maximization.

A.1 Functions

A *function* associates each member of a set with a single member of another set. In this section, we first examine *functions of a single variable* and then discuss *functions of several variables*.

Functions of a Single Variable

Suppose that we are interested in a variable x that is a member or an element of a set X. For example, the set X may be the nonnegative real numbers. A function f associates elements of the set X with elements of a set Y, which may be the same set as X. The function f is a *mapping* from X to Y, which we denote by $f: X \rightarrow Y$. The set X is the *domain* of the function f, while Y is the *range* of the function. In applying the mapping from an element of X to Y, we write $y = f(x)$.

We concentrate on real-number functions. Frequently, these functions map from the set of real numbers ($X = \mathbb{R}$) into the same set of real numbers ($Y = \mathbb{R}$). However, sometimes we consider functions with a domain that is an *interval* within the real numbers. For example, we might study a function that maps the numbers between zero and one. Such intervals are written as $[0, 1]$ if the interval includes zero and one, or as $(0, 1)$ if the endpoints of the interval are not included in the set. One can also use a parenthesis and a bracket, writing $(0, 1]$ for the interval of real numbers that are strictly greater than zero but less than or equal to one. By writing that $x \in (0, 1]$, we mean that the variable x can take on only a value that is greater than zero and less than or equal to one.

Some examples of functions of a single variable include the

- *Identity function*: $f(x) = x$ for all $x \in X$.
- *Zero function*: $f(x) = 0$ for all $x \in X$.
- *Square root function*: $f(x) = \sqrt{x}$ for all $x \geq 0$.
- *Hyperbolic function*: $f(x) = 1/x$, which is not defined when $x = 0$.

[1] Ethan Ligon is the co-author of this appendix.

These examples are called *explicit* functions because we can write them in the form $y = f(x)$. Some functions are *implicit* mappings between X and Y and are written in the form $g(x, y) = 0$. For example, $x^2 + y^2 - 1 = 0$ implicitly defines y in terms of x. We can always express an explicit function f in implicit form by defining $g(x, y) = y - f(x)$. However, it is not possible to express every implicit function explicitly. For example, the implicit function $g(x, y) = ay^5 + by^4 + cy^3 + dy^2 + ey + x = 0$ cannot generally be rewritten so that y is a closed-form expression of the variable x and the parameters a, b, c, d, and e.

Functions of Several Variables

A function may depend on more than one variable. An example of such a function is $y = f(x_1, x_2)$, where $x \in X_1$ and $x_2 \in X_2$. Then the domain of the function is written as $X = X_1 \times X_2$, where the symbol $\times$ when applied to sets means to take all possible combinations of elements of the two sets. For example, the set $X = [0, 1] \times [0, 1]$ contains all the pairs of real numbers between zero and one, inclusive. The function f associates elements of the domain, the set $X = X_1 \times X_2$, with elements of the range, the set Y. That is, f is a mapping from X to Y, which may be denoted either by f: $X \to Y$ or by f: $X_1 \times X_2 \to Y$.

An example of mapping from a pair of variables to a single variable is the well-known measure of physical fitness, the *body mass index* (BMI), which is a function of weight (in kilograms) and height (in meters):

$$\text{BMI} = \frac{\text{weight}}{(\text{height})^2}.$$

If we let the variable z measure the BMI, w reflect the weight, and h denote the height, we can write this function more compactly as

$$z = f(w, h) = \frac{w}{h^2}.$$

Other examples of functions of two or more variables are the

- *Cobb-Douglas function with two variables*: $y = f(K, L) = 3L^{0.33}K^{0.66}$.
- *Cobb-Douglas function with two variables and two parameters*: $y = f(K, L) = AL^{\alpha}K^{1-\alpha}$, where A and α are parameters rather than variables—they represent unknown numbers rather than quantities that can change. The previous example is a special case, where $A = 3$ and $\alpha = \frac{1}{3}$.
- *Cobb-Douglas function with n variables*: $y = f(x_1, x_2, x_3, \ldots, x_n) = Ax_1^{\alpha_1}x_2^{\alpha_2} \ldots x_n^{\alpha_n}$.

A.2 Properties of Functions

We make extensive use of several key properties that functions may possess. In this section, we start by discussing the main properties that we use, which are *monotonicity* (the graph of a function always goes up or always goes down), *continuity* (there are no breaks in the graph of the function), *concavity* and *convexity* (the function consistently curves upward or downward), and *homogeneity* (the function "scales" up or down consistently). After reviewing these properties, we list three properties of the logarithmic function that we use repeatedly.

Monotonicity

A monotonic function is one that is either always *increasing* or always *decreasing*. For example, the identity function, $f(x) = x$, is monotonically increasing. That is, as x increases, so does the value of the function $f(x)$. Some functions are monotonic only under certain conditions. For example, the function $f(x) = 1/x$ is monotonically decreasing when x is positive. The function $f(x) = x^2$ isn't monotonic; it is decreasing when x is negative and increasing when x is positive.

Continuity

A function exhibits the property of *continuity* if a graph of the function has no jumps or breaks. A function can be continuous *at a point* if there are no jumps or breaks very near the point; if the function is continuous at all points, we say that the function is continuous. A sufficient condition for a function to be continuous at a point a is

$$\lim_{x \to a} f(x) = f(a),$$

which indicates that the limit of the function $f(x)$ as x approaches a is $f(a)$.[2]

Concavity and Convexity

Economists make extensive use of the properties of concavity and convexity. We say that the function f is *concave* over a region A if the graph of the function $f(x)$ never goes below the line drawn between *any* pair of points in A. For example, in panel a of Figure A.1, we evaluate a function f with a domain X. Within this domain, we choose a subset A, and we evaluate f at two points x and x' within this subset A. This procedure gives us two points in the range of f, $f(x)$ and $f(x')$. The line connecting the points $(x, f(x))$ and $(x', f(x'))$ is below $f(x)$ for all x between x and x'.

This "never below the line" test reflects the intuition of concavity for functions of a single variable. But for functions of multiple variables and for testing the concavity of a function that we cannot easily draw, we have a better test. To illustrate this approach, we examine the concavity of a function of a pair of variables (x, y) that maps $f: X \times Y \to Z$. Again, let A be a subset of the domain of f, $X \times Y$, and choose two points from the domain, (x, y) and (x', y'). The function f is concave over A if, for any value of θ such that $0 < \theta < 1$ and for any pair (x, y) and (x', y') in A,

$$f(\theta x + [1 - \theta]x', \theta y + [1 - \theta]y') \ge \theta f(x, y) + [1 - \theta]f(x', y'). \quad \text{(A.1)}$$

Equation A.1 is an extension of our "never below the line" test. If we let θ vary between zero and one, we can trace out all the values of the function f evaluated at points in A on the left-hand side of the inequality, while varying θ on the right-hand side of the expression traces out a line segment connecting the function f evaluated at (x, y) and at (x', y'). Thus, this expression says that the function lies above the connecting line.

---

[2]If an infinite sequence tends toward some particular value as we progress through that sequence, that value is the limit of the sequence. For example, in the sequence $\left\{ 1, \frac{1}{2}, \frac{1}{3}, \frac{1}{4}, \ldots \right\}$ the nth element in the sequence equals $1/n$, where n is a positive whole number. As n gets larger, the value of $1/n$ tends to zero, so the limit of this sequence is zero (even though zero is not an element of the sequence).

Figure A.1 Concave and Convex Functions

Some functions are convex, some concave, and some neither. (a) This function is convex because a straight line drawn between any two points never goes above the curve. (b) This function is concave because a straight line drawn between two points never goes below the curve. (c) This function violates both of these conditions and thus is neither convex nor concave.

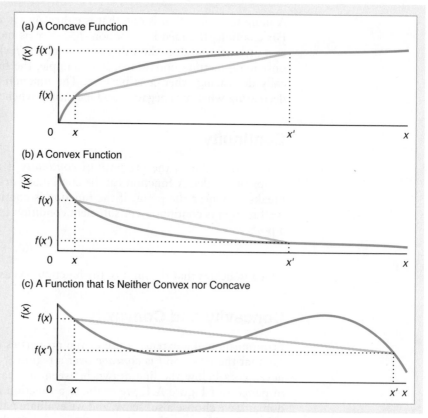

Sometimes a distinction is drawn between a function that is *weakly concave* or *strictly concave*. A *weakly concave* function f satisfies the requirement in Equation A.1, while a *strictly concave* function satisfies a replacement condition:

$$f(\theta x + [1 - \theta]x', \theta y + [1 - \theta]y') > \theta f(x, y) + [1 - \theta]f(x', y').$$

A function is *convex* over a region A if the opposite of the concavity condition holds. That is, the function never goes *above* a line connecting points on the function, as panel b of Figure A.1 illustrates. The mathematical requirement is the same as the requirement for concavity with the inequality reversed: The function f is *weakly convex* over A if, for any value of θ such that $0 < \theta < 1$ and for any (x, y) and (x', y') in A,

$$f(\theta x + [1 - \theta]x', \theta y + [1 - \theta]y') \le \theta f(x, y) + [1 - \theta]f(x', y').$$

The function is *strictly convex* if this expression holds with a strict inequality.

The function $f(x) = x^2$ is strictly convex. To demonstrate this convexity, we pick any two points on the real line x and x', and check that

$$f(\theta x + [1 - \theta]x') < \theta f(x) + [1 - \theta]f(x')$$

holds for this function. We substitute the actual function into this expression:

$$(\theta x + [1 - \theta]x')^2 < \theta x^2 + [1 - \theta](x')^2.$$

Rearranging terms,

$$\theta^2 x^2 + [1 - \theta]^2(x')^2 + 2\theta[1 - \theta]xx' < \theta x^2 + [1 - \theta](x')^2,$$

$$\theta[1 - \theta]x^2 + \theta[1 - \theta](x')^2 - 2\theta[1 - \theta]xx' > 0,$$

$$x^2 + (x')^2 - 2xx' = (x - x')^2 > 0. \;.$$

Thus, this function is strictly convex.

In panel c of Figure A.1, the function x^3 is not concave or convex over the domain of real numbers: It is concave over the negative real numbers and convex over the positive real numbers. Finally, the Cobb-Douglas function $f(K, L) = AL^\alpha K^\beta$, where L and K are nonnegative real numbers, is concave if $\alpha + \beta \le 1$.

Homogeneous Functions

A function $f(x_1, x_2, \ldots, x_n)$ is said to be *homogeneous* of degree γ if

$$f(ax_1, ax_2, \ldots, ax_n) = a^\gamma f(x_1, x_2, \ldots, x_n)$$

for any constant $a > 0$. For example, suppose that f is a production function and the set $\{x_i\}$ consists of inputs to production. Given a particular set of inputs $(x_1, x_2, \ldots, x_n)$, the production function tells us how much output, $q = f(x_1, x_2, \ldots, x_n)$, the firm can produce. What happens to q if we double all the inputs so that $a = 2$? If for any set of inputs, output always doubles, then the production function is homogeneous of degree one. If output does not change at all, then it is homogeneous of degree zero. If it always quadruples, it is homogeneous of degree two, and so on. Some other examples are

- The function $f(x) = 1$ is homogeneous of degree zero because doubling x leaves $f(x)$ unchanged.
- The square root function $f(x_1, x_2) = \sqrt{x_1 + x_2}$ is homogeneous of degree one-half because doubling x_1 and x_2 causes the function to change to $\sqrt{2x_1 + 2x_2} = \sqrt{2}\sqrt{x_1 + x_2} = 2^{0.5}\sqrt{x_1 + x_2}$.
- The function $f(x_1, x_2) = \sqrt{x_1 x_2}$ is homogeneous of degree one because $\sqrt{(2x_1)(2x_2)} = 2\sqrt{x_1 x_2}$.
- The Cobb-Douglas function $f(L, K) = AL^\alpha K^\beta$ is homogeneous of degree $\alpha + \beta$ because $A(2L)^\alpha(2K)^\beta = 2^{\alpha+\beta}AL^\alpha K^\beta$.
- The functions $f(x) = x + 1$ and $f(x_1, x_2) = x_1 + \sqrt{x_2}$ are not homogeneous of any degree.

Special Properties of Logarithmic Functions

Logarithms are wonderful, logarithms are fine.
Once you learn the rules of logs, you'll think they are sublime.

We use the logarithmic function repeatedly in this textbook because it has a number of desirable properties. For example, we can convert some multiplication problems into addition problems by using the logarithmic function. We always use the natural logarithm (or natural log) function of x, which we write as $\ln(x)$, where $x = e^{\ln(x)}$ for $x > 0$.

The key properties of logarithms that we use are

- The log of a product is equal to a sum of logs: $\ln(xz) = \ln(x) + \ln(z)$.
- The log of a number to a power is equal to the power times the log of the number: $\ln(x^b) = b \ln(x)$.
- It follows from this previous rule that the log of the reciprocal of x equals the negative of the log of x: $\ln(1/x) = \ln(x^{-1}) = -\ln(x)$.

A.3 Derivatives

We want a way to summarize how a function changes as its argument changes. One such measure is the slope. However, we generally use an alternative measure, the *derivative*, which is essentially the slope at a particular point. We illustrate the distinction between these two measures using a function of a single variable, $f: \mathbb{R} \to \mathbb{R}$.

The usual definition of a *slope* is "rise over run"—that is, the change in the value of a function when moving from point x_1 to another point x_2:

$$\text{Slope} = \frac{\text{rise}}{\text{run}} = \frac{f(x_2) - f(x_1)}{x_2 - x_1}.$$

This definition of a slope depends on comparing the function at *two* different points, x_1 and x_2. However, typically we want the slope of f at a point.

To determine the slope at a point, we first implicitly define the difference, h, between these points as $x_2 = x_1 + h$. Substituting this expression into our formula for the slope gives us

$$\frac{f(x_2) - f(x_1)}{x_2 - x_1} = \frac{f(x_1 + h) - f + (x_1)}{h}.$$

The derivative of a real-value function $f: \mathbb{R} \to \mathbb{R}$ at a point x in $\mathbb{R}$ is

$$\frac{df(x)}{dx} = \lim_{h \to 0} \frac{f(x + h) - f(x)}{h}. \tag{A.2}$$

In the text of this book, we use two different notational conventions to denote the derivative of a function. Here and in most places in the text, we write the derivative using the notation $df(x)/dx$. Sometimes for notational simplicity, we omit explicit reference to the argument of f, writing the derivative of f at x as df/dx where no ambiguity results.

The derivative has a graphical interpretation. The slope of a function between two points is equal to the slope of a straight line connecting those two points. The slope of such a straight line can be computed using the rise-over-run formula. In Figure A.2, the

Figure A.2 Derivative and Slope

The slope of a function between x_1 and x_2 is equal to the slope (= rise over run) of a straight line connecting the two points $b = (x_1, f(x_1))$ and $(x_2, f(x_2))$. If we fix one of the points, b, and move the other point closer, then the run ($h = x_2 - x_1$) grows smaller and smaller. If the derivative exists, the rise, $f(x_2) - f(x_1) = f(x_1 + h) - f(x_1)$, will eventually get smaller as well, but typically at a different rate than the run. The limiting value of this slope is the derivative, which equals the slope of a line tangent to the function at b.

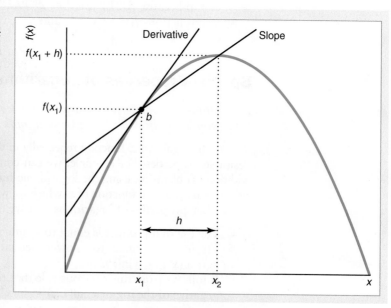

slope of a function between x_1 and x_2 is equal to the slope of a straight line connecting the two points $b = (x_1, f(x_1))$ and $(x_2, f(x_2))$. Now fix one of the points, b, and move the other point ever closer so that the run ($h = x_2 - x_1$) gets smaller and smaller. If the derivative exists, the rise, $f(x_2) - f(x_1) = f(x_1 + h) - f(x_1)$, will eventually get smaller and smaller as well, but typically at a different rate than the run. The limiting value of the ratio of the rise to the run will be the slope of an infinitesimally short line—the slope of the function at a point. The limiting value of this slope is the derivative, which equals the slope of a line tangent to the function at b.

If $df(x)/dx$ is positive, the function is *increasing* at x. That is, as x increases slightly, the function evaluated at x also increases. Similarly, if $df(x)/dx$ is negative, the function is *decreasing* at x.

One problem with using derivatives instead of slopes is that in some circumstances, the derivative of a function may not be defined because the limit given in Equation A.2 does not exist. Discontinuous functions do not have derivatives at any point of discontinuity. For example, the derivative of the function $1/x$ does not exist at $x = 0$. The derivative also fails to exist for a continuous function at a kink, such as at $x = 0$ for the function $|x|$.

Rules for Calculating Derivatives

This book repeatedly uses a few rules for calculating the derivatives of functions.

- *The addition rule*: If a function $f: \mathbb{R} \to \mathbb{R}$ can be written as the sum of two other functions, so that $f(x) = g(x) + h(x)$, then

$$\frac{df(x)}{dx} = \frac{dg(x)}{dx} + \frac{dh(x)}{dx}.$$

In words, this expression says that the derivative of the sum is equal to the sum of the derivatives.

- *The product rule*: If a function $f: \mathbb{R} \to \mathbb{R}$ can be written as the product of two other functions, so that $f(x) = g(x)h(x)$ where g and h are both differentiable at x, then

$$\frac{df(x)}{dx} = \frac{dg(x)}{dx}h(x) + g(x)\frac{dh(x)}{dx}.$$

An important special case occurs when $g(x)$ is a constant, say, b. Then $dg(x)/dx = 0$, so the product rule yields the result that $dbh(x)/dx = bdh(x)/dx$.

- *The power rule*: If $f(x) = ax^b$, then the derivative of f at x, provided that the derivative exists, is

$$\frac{df(x)}{dx} = abx^{b-1}.$$

For example, using the power rule, we can show that $d(bx^2)/dx = 2bx$. Applying this result and the product rule, we can determine the derivative $d(bx^3)/dx$:

$$\frac{dbx^3}{dx} = x\frac{dbx^2}{dx} + \frac{dx}{dx}bx^2 = x(2bx) + bx^2 = 3bx^2.$$

Continuing in this vein using the product rule repeatedly, we learn that in general, $dbx^n/dx = nbx^{n-1}$.

- *The polynomial rule*: A polynomial function is a function that takes the form

$$f(x) = b_0 + b_1x + b_2x^2 + \ldots + b_nx^n,$$

where n is a nonnegative whole number. The *order* of the polynomial is the largest exponent, n. Using the power rule repeatedly (as we just showed), the derivative of the polynomial $f(x)$ is

$$\frac{df(x)}{dx} = b_1 + 2b_2x + \ldots + nb_nx^{n-1}.$$

- *The reciprocal rule*: Using the power rule and the product rule, we can show that the derivative of the reciprocal of a function, $1/f(x)$, is

$$\frac{d[1/f(x)]}{dx} = -\frac{\dfrac{df(x)}{dx}}{[f(x)]^2}.$$

- *The quotient rule*: Using the reciprocal rule and the product rule, we can show that if $f(x) = g(x)/h(x)$, then

$$\frac{d[g(x)/h(x)]}{dx} = \frac{h(x)\dfrac{dg(x)}{dx} - g(x)\dfrac{dh(x)}{dx}}{[h(x)]^2}.$$

- *The chain rule*: We can compute the derivatives of functions such as $f(x) = g(h(x))$ by using all the previous rules,

$$\frac{df(x)}{dx} = \frac{dg(h(x))}{dx} = \frac{dg(h(x))}{dh(x)}\frac{dh(x)}{dx},$$

provided that h is differentiable at x and that g is differentiable at $h(x)$. As an example, let $h(x) = x^2$, and $g(z) = 2 + z^2$ so that $f(x) = g(h(x)) = 2 + x^4$. By direct differentiation, we know that $df(x)/dx = 4x^3$. We can derive the same result using the chain rule. First, we use the power rule to show that $dg(z)/dz = 2z$ and that $dh(x)/dx = 2x$. Second, we substitute $h(x)$ for z in the expression for $dg(z)/dz$, which gives us $dg(h(x))/dh(x)$, and apply the chain rule to obtain

$$\frac{dg(h(x))}{dx} = \frac{d[2 + h(x)]}{dh(x)}\frac{dh(x)}{dx} = (2x^2) \times (2x) = 4x^3.$$

- *The exponential rule*: For any differentiable function $g(x)$,

$$\frac{de^{g(x)}}{dx} = \frac{dg(x)}{dx} \cdot e^{g(x)}.$$

An important special case of this rule is that

$$\frac{dae^{bx}}{dx} = abe^{bx}.$$

- *The exponent rule*: An exponential function is one that can be written in the form $f(x) = a^x$, where a number a is raised to the power x. One can use the properties of logarithms together with the exponential rule and the chain rule to show that

$$\frac{da^x}{dx} = \frac{de^{\ln(a)x}}{dx} = \ln(a)a^x.$$

- *The logarithm rule*: The derivative of the function $\ln(x)$ is

$$\frac{d\ln(x)}{dx} = \frac{1}{x}.$$

Higher-Order Derivatives

If the derivative exists everywhere in the domain, we say that the function is *continuously differentiable*. For example, the function $f(x) = 1/x$ on the domain $(0, 1]$ is a continuously differentiable function. We can use the power rule to show that the ordinary derivative is

$$\frac{d[1/x]}{dx} = \frac{d[x^{-1}]}{dx} = -\frac{1}{x^2}.$$

This derivative is itself continuously differentiable on $(0, 1]$. Accordingly, we can use the power rule to differentiate this derivative a second time:

$$\frac{d[-1/x^2]}{dx} = \frac{d[-x^{-2}]}{dx} = \frac{2}{x^3}.$$

Rather than referring to this result as the "derivative of the derivative of $f(x)$," we call it the *second derivative of* $f(x)$, which we write as $d^2f(x)/dx^2$.

Higher-order derivatives are defined similarly. The derivative of the derivative of the derivative of $f(x)$, called the third derivative of $f(x)$, is written $d^3f(x)/dx^3$. In general, the nth order derivative of $f(x)$ is $d^nf(x)/dx^n$.

Partial Derivatives

When using a function of more than one variable, we want to know how the value of the function varies as we change one variable while holding the others constant. Consider a function of two real variables, $f: \mathbb{R}^2 \rightarrow \mathbb{R}$. The slope of this function at a point is a little more complicated to define than the slope of a function with a single argument, because the slope of the function at a point now depends on direction. For example, let

$$f(N, E) = N^2 - E^2 + 1.$$

The variable names are chosen to evoke a map, where N reflects the latitude and E denotes the longitude. The value of the function f evaluated at a point on this map can then be thought of as corresponding to the altitude (height). Figure A.3 shows the surface and contour lines of this function.

This function takes the value of zero at the origin but changes in quite different ways as one moves away from the origin, depending on the direction of the move. If one were to move directly to the northeast, then N and E would increase at the same rate (hence their squares do, too). Thus, if one moves directly to the northeast (or southwest), the altitude does not change. In the figure, the curves in the (N, E) plane are contour lines of the surface above the plane. The curves show that if E increases at the same rate as N, the elevation remains constant.

However, if one begins at the origin and heads directly north, then N increases while E remains fixed. One's altitude increases in this direction. If, on the other hand, one heads directly east, E increases while N remains fixed, and one heads downhill (after traveling E units, one attains an altitude of $1 - E^2$).

Going *just* north or *just* east gets at the idea behind the *partial derivative*: The idea is to vary the value of one variable while holding all the other variables fixed. This procedure also gives us an easy algorithm for computing the partial derivative of f with respect to, say, N: Just pretend that E is a constant, and compute the *ordinary* derivative. Thus, we have the partial derivative of f with respect to N,

$$\frac{\partial f(N, E)}{\partial N} = \frac{\partial (N^2 - E^2)}{\partial N} = \frac{\partial N^2}{\partial N} = 2N,$$

Figure A.3 Illustration of Partial Derivatives

The figure shows the surface and contour lines of the function $f(N, E) = N^2 - E^2 + 1$. If we move only in the N direction, the elevation rises at an increasing rate, whereas if we move only in the E direction, the elevation falls at the same increasing rate. The curves in the (N, E) plane are contour lines of the surface above the plane. The curves show that if E increases at the same rate as N, the elevation remains constant.

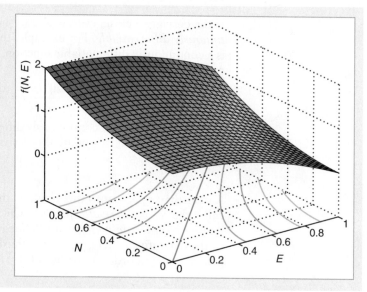

and the partial derivative of f with respect to E,

$$\frac{\partial f(N, E)}{\partial E} = \frac{\partial(N^2 - E^2)}{\partial E} = -\frac{\partial E^2}{\partial E} = -2E.$$

In the special case in which f is a function of only a single variable, the partial derivative is exactly the same as the ordinary derivative:

$$\frac{\partial f(x)}{\partial x} = \frac{df(x)}{dx}.$$

In the general case in which the function $f: \mathbb{R}^m \to \mathbb{R}$ depends on several variables, one can think of the partial derivative of f with respect to, say, the first variable as measuring the *direct* effect of a change in the first variable on the value of the function, while neglecting the effects that a change in this variable might have on *other* variables that might influence the value of $f(x)$. Just as the ordinary derivative of an ordinary derivative is called a second (ordinary) derivative, there are also higher-order partial derivatives. For example, the partial derivative of $g(x_1, x_2)$ with respect to x_1 is written as $\partial g(x_1, x_2)/\partial x_1$; the *second* partial derivative of $g(x_1, x_2)$ with respect to x_1 is written as $\partial^2 g(x_1, x_2)/\partial x_1^2$, while the second partial derivative of $g(x_1, x_2)$ with respect to x_2 is written as $\partial^2 g(x_1, x_2)/\partial x_2^2$.

We can derive second-order (or higher-order) derivatives that involve the repeated differentiation of the function with respect to more than one variable. For example, if we differentiate the partial derivative of our function $g(x_1, x_2)$ with respect to x_1, $\partial g(x_1, x_2)/\partial x_1$, with respect to x_2, we obtain the cross-partial derivative, $\partial^2 g(x_1, x_2)/(\partial x_1 \partial x_2)$. The order of differentiation doesn't matter for the functions we usually study. According to Young's Theorem, $\partial^2 f/(\partial x_1 \partial x_2) = \partial^2 f/(\partial x_2 \partial x_1)$ if the cross-partial derivatives $\partial^2 f/(\partial x_1 \partial x_2)$ and $\partial^2 f/(\partial x_2 \partial x_1)$ exist and are continuous. Similarly, $\partial^5 g(x_1, x_2)/\partial x_1^2 \partial x_2^3$ indicates partial differentiation of g with respect to x_1 twice and with respect to x_2 thrice, thus yielding a fifth-order partial derivative.

Euler's Homogeneous Function Theorem

A function $f: \mathbb{R}^n \to \mathbb{R}$ is *homogeneous* of degree γ if

$$f(tx_1, tx_2, \ldots, tx_n) = t^\gamma f(x_1, \ldots, x_n)$$

holds for all possible values of $x_1, x_2, \ldots, x_n$ and constant scalar t. That is, multiplying each of the arguments of the function by t increases the value of the function by t^γ. The degree need not be an integer. For example, the Cobb-Douglas function $Ax_1^{\alpha_1}x_2^{\alpha_2} \ldots x_n^{\alpha_n}$ is homogeneous of degree $\alpha_1 + \alpha_2 + \ldots + \alpha_n$, where each α_i may be a fraction. Such a function satisfies Euler's homogeneous function theorem

$$\sum_{i=1}^n x_i \frac{\partial f(x_1, \ldots, x_n)}{\partial x_i} = \gamma f(x_1, \ldots, x_n).$$

A.4 Maximum and Minimum

Most microeconomic analysis concerns finding the maximum or minimum of a function. For example, a consumer chooses a bundle of goods to maximize utility, or a firm chooses inputs to minimize cost.

The problems of finding a maximum and finding a minimum may sound as though they are very different, but they are similar mathematically. We think of the problems of finding either *maxima* or *minima* as special cases of the more general problem of finding *extrema*.

Local Extrema

Mathematicians and economists are sometimes interested in the *local* properties of a function, or, equivalently, the properties of a function within the *neighborhood* of a point x. A local property is one that holds within a neighborhood of x—that is, within some positive (but possibly very small) distance $\varepsilon > 0$ from the point x. For example, a function has a local maximum at x^* if there exists an $\varepsilon > 0$ such that $f(x^*) \geq f(x)$ for all $x \in (x^* - \varepsilon, x^* + \varepsilon)$—that is, in the neighborhood of x^*.

A *local* extremum of a function $f(x)$ is either a local minimum or a local maximum of the function f. If we move from the local extremum at x by an amount less than ε, the value of the function becomes less extreme. Figure A.4 graphs the function $f(x) = x \sin(6\pi x)$, which has many peaks and troughs. All the local extrema are indicated with bullets. Points a, b, and c are local maxima, while points d, e, and f are local minima. All these local maxima and local minima together compose the set of local extrema. Point a is a local maximum because if we either increase or decrease x just a little, the value of $f(x)$ decreases. Similarly, d is a local minimum because if we either increase or decrease x slightly, the value of $f(x)$ increases.

Global Extrema

The *global maximum* (usually called the *maximum*) is the largest local maximum, and the *global minimum* (or *minimum*) is the smallest local minimum. In Figure A.4, the global maximum is point c and the global minimum is point f. If there are two local maxima that are both equally large and larger than all other points, we would say that there are *two* global maxima.

Existence of Extrema

In economics, we often want to know if a function has a maximum or a minimum in the relevant domain. For example, we might examine whether there is a minimum for a function $f: [0, 1] \to \mathbb{R}$; that is, f takes values from the interval between zero and one (inclusive) and maps them into the real line.

Not all such functions have a maximum or a minimum. Continuity of a function is a *sufficient* condition for the existence of both a maximum and a minimum. This result is a consequence of the *Extreme Value Theorem*: If the function f is continuous and defined on the closed interval $[a, b]$, there is at least one c in $[a, b]$ such that $f(c) \geq f(x)$ for all x in $[a, b]$, and there is at least one d in $[a, b]$ such that $f(d) \leq f(x)$ for all x in $[a, b]$. Functions that are not continuous *might* have minima and maxima—but there's no guarantee.

Figure A.5 illustrates several possibilities. Panel a shows a continuous function, $y = f(x) = 24x - 75x^2 + 50x^3$, with a single minimum and a single (local and global) maximum in $[0, 1]$. In panel b, the continuous function $y = f(x) = 1$ has an infinite number of maxima and minima in $[0, 1]$. In panel c, the discontinuity in the function

$$y = \begin{cases} 24x - 75x^2 + 50x^3, & x < 0.8 \\ 24x - 75x^2 + 50x^3, & x > 0.8 \end{cases}$$

is shown as a hollow circle. Because of this missing point, there is a unique maximum, but there isn't a global minimum within $[0, 1]$. Finally, the discontinuous function plotted in panel d,

$$y = \begin{cases} 0, & x < 0.8 \\ 1, & x \geq 0.8, \end{cases}$$

has an infinite number of maxima and minima in $[0, 1]$.

Uniqueness of Extrema

As panels b and d of Figure A.5 illustrate, even when a function has global maxima or global minima, there may be more than one maximum or minimum. We want to determine when the function will have a unique solution. There is a unique global maximum if the function f is strictly concave, and a unique global minimum if f is strictly convex. For example, in panel a of Figure A.5, when x is less than about 0.46, where the curve hits the horizontal axis, the function is concave, so there is a single global maximum. However, to the right of this point, the function is convex and has a single global minimum.

Figure A.4 Illustration of Local and Global Extrema

The bullets indicate the local extrema. Point c is the global maximum, and point f is the global minimum.

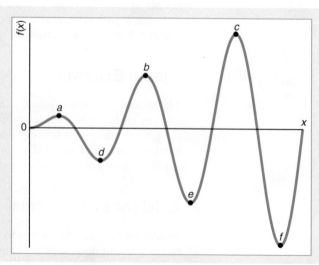

Figure A.5 Illustration of the Extreme Value Theorem

According to the Extreme Value Theorem, if a function is continuous and defined on the closed interval, it contains at least one minimum and at least one maximum. (a) This continuous function has a maximum at point *a* and a minimum at point *b*. (b) This continuous function has an infinite number of maxima and minima that equal one.

(c) This function is discontinuous at the point marked with a hollow point, so the theorem cannot be used to draw inferences about the existence of minima and maxima. For the domain (0, 1], the function has a maximum, but no minimum. (d) This discontinuous function has infinite maxima and minima.

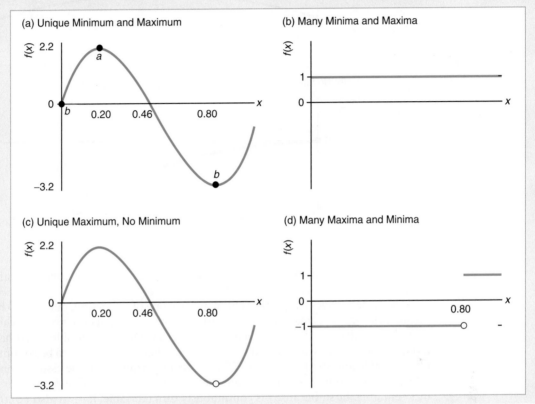

Interior Extrema

Often in the text, we care whether the maximum or minimum is located in the interior of the range of x or at one of the end points. To illustrate this distinction, we consider the function $f(x) = -(x - \frac{1}{2})^2/2$, where x lies within [0, 1], as panel a of Figure A.6 shows. This function has a maximum at point *a* where $x^* = 0.5$, which we call an *interior* maximum because $x^* \in (0, 1)$ and it is not on the edge of the domain [0, 1]. That is, x^* is not zero or one. In contrast, in panel b, because the maximum of the function $g(x) = -x^2/2$ is zero at point *a*, which is on the edge or *corner* of the domain [0, 1], the maximum of this function is *not* interior.

A.5   Finding the Extrema of a Function

Because it is not always practical to plot functions and look for extrema, we use calculus to find local extrema. The key insight is that for functions that are continuously differentiable, the *slope* of the function at any interior minimum or maximum

Figure A.6 Interior Extrema

In panel a, the maximum, point *a*, occurs at $x = 0.5$, which lies in the interior of the interval $[0, 1]$. In panel b, the maximum at *a* is at the corner— not in the interior of the domain.

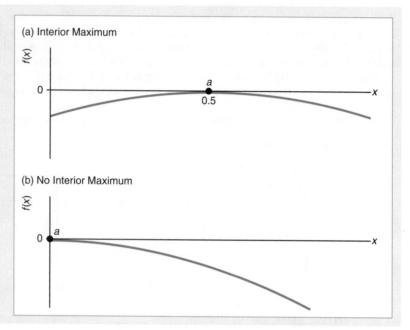

is zero. Figure A.7 illustrates that the slope of the graph at every interior local mini- mum or maximum is zero.

Because derivatives can be thought of as the slope of a function, one way to find all the interior local extrema of a continuously differentiable function is to find where the partial derivatives of the function equal zero. Let's begin with a problem that has only a single independent variable and $f: [0, 1] \rightarrow \mathbb{R}$, where *f* is assumed to be continuously differentiable and strictly concave. What is the importance of these assumptions?

There are two important consequences of our assumption that *f* is continuously differentiable. First, because *f* is continuously differentiable, it must also be continu- ous, so we know that it has a maximum. Second, because it is continuously differ- entiable, we know that its derivative exists, and hence we can use this derivative to determine the local extrema.

Because *f* is assumed to be strictly concave, we know that it has a unique global maximum. Thus, if we find a point *x* where $df(x)/dx = 0$, it follows that this point *x* is the unique global maximum of the function *f* over the interval $[0, 1]$.

The usual way to write the problem of finding a maximum of a function $f(x)$ is

$$\max_{x} f(x),$$

where *max* is called the *max operator*, the variable *x* that appears below the max operator is the *choice variable*, and *f* is the function to be maximized and is called the *objective function*.

Any x^* in $[0, 1]$ that solves $df(x^*)/dx = 0$ is a point at which the function $f(x)$ has a local maximum. The equation $df(x)/dx = 0$, in which we set the first-order derivative equal to zero, is called the *first-order condition*. The x^* that solves this equation, $df(x^*)/dx$, is called a *critical value*. Given our assumptions that *f* is con- tinuously differentiable and concave, we know that x^* is a unique global maximum.

So far, we've assumed that *f* is concave, as in panel a of Figure A.7. In practice, we need to check whether the function is concave. For example, if we falsely assume

Figure A.7 Extrema and the First-Order Condition (F.O.C.)

If a function is continuously differentiable and concave, it must have a unique maximum. Further, if the F.O.C. has a solution (that is, the function has a point where its slope is zero), the F.O.C. characterizes the unique maximum. (a) This function is continuously differentiable and concave, so the F.O.C. identifies a unique maximum (at point *a*). (b) The function is continuously differentiable, so it has at least one maximum, but the function is not concave, so the maximum may not be unique (indeed, there are two maxima at the end points). The function is convex, so the F.O.C. characterizes a minimum. (c) The function is continuously differentiable, so it possesses a maximum in the interval [0, 1]. However, at point *a* where the F.O.C. holds, the function is neither concave nor convex, so *a* is neither a minimum nor a maximum—it is a saddle point. (d) The function is concave, so this maximum will be unique. However, the F.O.C. does not have a solution in the interval [0, 1]—there is no place where the function has a slope equal to zero—so the unique maximum is not characterized by the F.O.C.

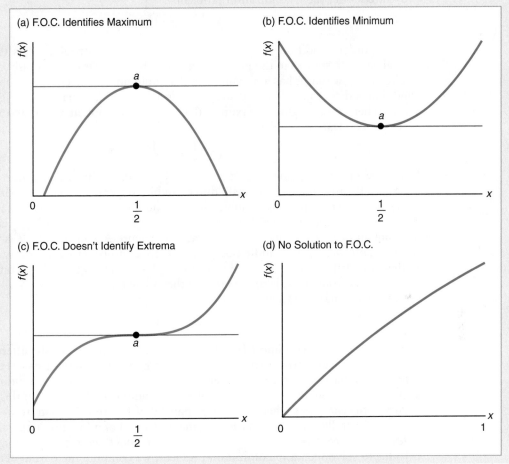

that the function is concave and it is convex, we may find a minimum rather than a maximum, as in panel b.

If $f(x^*)$ is at least twice-differentiable in a neighborhood of x^*, we can use the *second-order condition* to determine whether the function is concave in that neighborhood. The second-order condition for concavity is that the second derivative of $f(x^*)$ is negative, $d^2f(x^*)/dx^2 < 0$. If this condition holds, we know that the x^* that the first-order condition identified is a unique maximum in this neighborhood of x^*. In contrast, if the second derivative is positive, we know that the function is convex in this neighborhood and that we have found a minimum.

Examples

We can illustrate this approach using several examples where f: $[0, 1] \to \mathbb{R}$. Our first maximization problem is

$$\max_x -\tfrac{1}{2}\left(x - \tfrac{1}{2}\right)^2.$$

The first-order condition is $df(x)/dx = \tfrac{1}{2} - x = 0$, so $x^* = \tfrac{1}{2}$, as panel a of Figure A.7 shows. The second-order condition is $d^2f(x^*)/dx^2 = -1 < 0$, so $\tfrac{1}{2}$ is a maximum. One can demonstrate that this function f is continuously differentiable and concave throughout the domain, so $f\left(\tfrac{1}{2}\right) = 0$, point a, is the global maximum of this function.

Now consider the maximization problem

$$\max_x \tfrac{1}{2}\left(x - \tfrac{1}{2}\right)^2.$$

The first-order condition is $df(x)/dx = x - \tfrac{1}{2} = 0$, so this problem has the same critical value, $x = \tfrac{1}{2}$, as in the previous example. Because f is continuously differentiable, we know that it has a maximum and a minimum on $[0, 1]$. The second-order condition is $d^2f\left(\tfrac{1}{2}\right)/dx^2 = 1 > 0$ so $x^* = \tfrac{1}{2}$ is a minimum, as panel b of Figure A.7 shows. There are two global maxima, which are not interior, at $x = 0$ and $x = 1$.

The maximization problem

$$\max_x \tfrac{1}{3}\left(x - \tfrac{1}{2}\right)^3$$

has a first-order condition $df(x)/dx = \left(x - \tfrac{1}{2}\right)^2 = 0$, so the critical value is again at $x = \tfrac{1}{2}$. Because f is continuously differentiable, we know it has a maximum on $[0, 1]$, but as in the previous example, the maximum is not interior; instead, it occurs at $x = 1$. This function is neither concave nor convex at $x = \tfrac{1}{2}$, so $x^* = \tfrac{1}{2}$ is neither a minimum nor a maximum of f, as panel c of Figure A.7 illustrates. It is called a *saddle point*. We have a saddle point when the second-order condition is zero, as in this case: $d^2f\left(\tfrac{1}{2}\right)/dx^2 = 2\left(x - \tfrac{1}{2}\right) = 2\left(\tfrac{1}{2} - \tfrac{1}{2}\right) = 0$. The sign of the second derivative changes from one side to the other of the saddle point.

Finally, the maximization problem

$$\max_x \ln(x + 1)$$

yields the first-order condition $1/(x + 1) = 0$. Here, f is continuously differentiable and strictly concave, so we know that a unique global maximum exists. However, there is no value of x in the $[0, 1]$ interval that solves the first-order condition. Consequently, we know that the unique global maximum is *not* interior (in this case, it occurs at the end point where $x = 1$), as panel d of Figure A.7 illustrates.

More generally, we may want to find the maximum of a function of several variables, and hence several choice variables appear under the max operator. To use calculus to solve such a maximization problem, we compute the partial derivatives of the objective function with respect to each of the choice variables and then set these equal to zero. These equations, in which the first-order partial derivatives are set equal to zero, are called the *first-order conditions*.

For example, let g: $[0, 1] \times [0, 1] \to \mathbb{R}$, and assume that g is continuously differentiable and strictly concave. Then we know, as we did for f, that g has a unique global maximum. Accordingly, we can write the problem as

$$\max_{x_1, x_2} g(x_1, x_2),$$

which yields the pair of first-order conditions

$$\frac{\partial g(x_1, x_2)}{\partial x_1} = 0, \tag{A.3}$$

$$\frac{\partial g(x_1, x_2)}{\partial x_2} = 0. \tag{A.4}$$

The solution to Equations A.3 and A.4 determines where the global maximum of g is located, if a solution exists. If a solution to these equations does not exist, then the maximum must lie on the boundary of the choice set $[0, 1] \times [0, 1]$, so either x_1 or x_2 (or both) must be equal to either zero or one at the maximum.

Indirect Objective Functions and the Envelope Theorem

Economic problems generally involve choice variables that are under the control of a person or a firm, such as how much of a good to buy or produce. Economic problems may also depend on *exogenous* parameters that influence the decision maker's behavior but are not under the decision maker's direct control, such as the price at which the good can be bought or sold. We can add these exogenous parameters to the formulation of a maximization problem.

To illustrate this approach, we examine a function g: $[0, 1] \times [0, 1] \times \mathbb{R} \to \mathbb{R}$. We write this function and its arguments as $g(x_1, x_2, z)$, where the variables x_1 and x_2 are choice variables and z is an exogenous parameter. We assume that g is continuously differentiable in all three of its arguments and is strictly concave in the first two (the choice variables). Consequently, g has a unique global maximum (even if g is not concave in the exogenous parameters).

The decision maker's problem of choosing x_1 and x_2 to maximize g given z is written as

$$\max_{x_1, x_2} g(x_1, x_2, z).$$

The first-order conditions are

$$\frac{\partial g(x_1, x_2, z)}{\partial x_1} = 0 \quad \text{and} \quad \frac{\partial g(x_1, x_2, z)}{\partial x_2} = 0,$$

so the optimal choice of x_1 and x_2 typically depends on the value of z. Accordingly, the values of x_1 and x_2 that solve the optimization problem for a given z may be written as $x_1^*(z)$ and $x_2^*(z)$.

Given a solution to the maximization problem, the value of g at the maximum is $g(x_1^*(z), x_2^*(z), z)$ Given some value z, the act of maximization determines the optimal values of x_1^* and x_2^*. Accordingly, we may sometimes write the maximum as

$$V(z) = g(x_1^*(z), x_2^*(z), z) = \max_{x_1, x_2} g(x_1, x_2, z).$$

The function $V(z)$ is called the *value function* because it tells us what the value of z is to the decision maker. It is also called the *indirect objective function*, in contrast to $g(x_1, x_2, z)$, which is the *direct objective function*.

A natural question to ask is how the value function changes when z changes. At first glance, this problem is very complicated because (as we have seen) a change in z has a direct effect on the value of $g(x_1, x_2, z)$ and it *also* causes the decision maker to change x_1 and x_2 in ways that may be complicated. However, at least for *small* changes in z, an important shortcut to solving this problem exists. The *Envelope Theorem* tells us that the direct effect of small changes in z matter but that the indirect effects do not. That is, according to the Envelope Theorem, the solution to our particular problem is

$$\frac{\partial V(z)}{\partial z} = \frac{\partial g(x_1, x_2, z)}{\partial z}. \tag{A.5}$$

We offer another, more general statement of this theorem below when we discuss the solutions to constrained maximization problems, and offer a constructive proof.

Comparative Statics

Not only do we want to know how a change in the exogenous parameter affects the value function, but we also want to know how this change in the exogenous parameter, z, affects the choice variables, x_1 and x_2. We can use our first-order conditions to answer this question because the first-order conditions show how the optimal choice of x_1 and x_2 depends on z. In our example, the first-order conditions are

$$\frac{\partial g\,(x_1^*(z),\, x_2^*(z),\, z)}{\partial x_1(z)} = 0 \quad \text{and} \quad \frac{\partial g\,(x_1^*(z),\, x_2^*(z),\, z)}{\partial x_2(z)} = 0.$$

Provided that the function g is twice continuously differentiable, we can then compute the derivatives of each of these first-order conditions with respect to the exogenous parameter:

$$\frac{\partial^2 g}{\partial x_1^2}\frac{dx_1^*(z)}{dz} + \frac{\partial^2 g}{\partial x_1 \partial x_2}\frac{dx_2^*(z)}{\partial z} + \frac{\partial g}{\partial z} = 0, \tag{A.6}$$

$$\frac{\partial^2 g}{\partial x_1 \partial x_2}\frac{dx_1^*(x)}{dz} + \frac{\partial^2 g}{\partial x_2^2}\frac{dx_2^*(z)}{dz} + \frac{\partial g}{\partial z} = 0, \tag{A.7}$$

where we omit the arguments to the function g for notational simplicity.

By treating the derivatives $dx_1^*(z)/dz$ and $dx_2^*(z)/dz$ as variables in the pair of linear Equations A.6 and A.7 and the partial derivatives of g as coefficients, we can solve this system of equations to determine how the maximizing choice of x_1 and x_2 changes for small changes in z. That is, we can solve for $dx_1^*(z)/dz$ and $dx_2^*(z)/dz$.

A.6   Maximizing with Equality Constraints

Most questions in microeconomics involve maximizing or minimizing an objective function subject to one or more *constraints*. For example, consumers maximize their well-being subject to a budget constraint. A firm chooses the cost-minimizing bundle of inputs subject to a feasibility constraint that summarizes which combinations of inputs can produce a given amount of output.

There are two commonly used approaches to solving problems with equality constraints mathematically: the substitution method and Lagrange's method. To illustrate these two approaches, we consider the problem of maximizing the function $g(x_1, x_2)$ subject to the constraint that $h(x_1, x_2) = z$, where z is an exogenous parameter. We write the constraint in implicit function form as $z - h(x_1, x_2) = 0$. This *constrained* maximization problem is written

$$\max_{x_1,\, x_2} g(x_1, x_2)$$

$$\text{s.t. } z - h(x_1, x_2) = 0. \tag{A.8}$$

Conceptually, we need to find the set of all those x_1 and x_2 that satisfy the constraint $z - h(x_1, x_2) = 0$, and from only this set, we need to choose those values of x_1 and x_2 that maximize $g(x_1, x_2)$.

Substitution Method

Sometimes we can solve a constrained maximization problem by substituting the constraint into the objective so that the problem becomes an unconstrained problem. We can rewrite the constraint as $x_1 = r(x_2, z)$. Because this solution for x_1 as a function of x_2 contains the information in the constraint, we can substitute it into our objective function and rewrite the problem as an unconstrained maximum:

$$\max_{x_2} g(r(x_2, z), x_2).$$

Because we wrote x_1 as a function of x_2, the unconstrained maximization problem has only one choice variable, x_2.

As with any unconstrained maximum problem, we use the first-order condition,

$$\frac{\partial g(r(x_2, z), x_2)}{\partial x_1} \frac{\partial r(x_2, z)}{\partial x_2} + \frac{\partial g(r(x_2, z), x_2)}{\partial x_2} = 0, \qquad (A.9)$$

to find the critical value of the choice variable x_2. We solve the first-order equation, Equation A.9, for x_2^*, substitute this solution for x_2 into $x_1 = r(x_2, z)$ to obtain $x_1^* = r(x_2^*, z)$, and then substitute x_1^* and x_2^* into the objective function to determine the maximum.

The following example illustrates this approach, where the objective function is $g(x_1, x_2) = x_1 x_2$ and the constraint is $z - h(x_1, x_2) = z - x_1 - x_2$, so the constrained maximization problem is

$$\max_{x_1, x_2} \ln(x_1 x_2)$$
$$\text{s.t. } z - x_1 - x_2 = 0. \qquad (A.10)$$

Using the constraint to solve for x_1 in terms of x_2, we find that $x_1 = r(x_2, z) = z - x_2$. Substituting this function into the objective function, we obtain the corresponding unconstrained maximization problem:

$$\max_{x_2} \ln((z - x_2) x_2) = \ln(z - x_2) + \ln(x_2).$$

Because the first-order condition is $-1/(z - x_2) + 1/x_2 = 0$, the solution of the first-order condition is $x_2^* = 0.5z$. Substituting this expression into the formula for x_1, we find that $x_1^* = z - 0.5z = 0.5z$. Evaluating the objective function at the maximizing values x_1^* and x_2^*, we find that $g(x_1^*, x_2^*) = \ln(0.25z^2)$.

The problem with using this method is that writing x_1 as a function of x_2 and z may be very difficult. If we have many constraints, this approach will usually be infeasible or impractical.

Lagrange's Method

Joseph Louis Lagrange developed an alternative method to solving a constrained maximization problem that works for a wider variety of problems than the substitution method does. As with the substitution method, Lagrange's method (or the Lagrangian method) converts a constrained maximization problem into an unconstrained maximization problem.

Solving a General Problem. The first step of Lagrange's method is to write the *Lagrangian function*, which is the sum of the original objective function, $g(x_1, x_2)$, and the left-hand side of the constraint, $z - h(x_1, x_2) = 0$, multiplied by a constant, λ, called the Lagrangian *multiplier*:

$$\mathcal{L}(x_1, x_2, \lambda; z) = g(x_1, x_2) + \lambda[z - h(x_1, x_2)]. \qquad (A.11)$$

If $\lambda = 0$ or the constraint holds, the Lagrangian function is identical to the original objective function.

The second step is to find the critical values of the (unconstrained) Lagrangian function, Equation A.11, where the choice variables are the original ones and λ:

$$\mathcal{L}(x_1, x_2, \lambda; z) = g(x_1, x_2) + \lambda[z - h(x_1, x_2)]. \tag{A.12}$$

To do so, we use the first-order conditions:

$$\frac{\partial \mathcal{L}(x_1, x_2, \lambda; z)}{\partial x_1} = \frac{\partial g(x_1, x_2)}{\partial x_1} - \lambda \frac{\partial h(x_1, x_2)}{\partial x_1} = 0, \tag{A.13}$$

$$\frac{\partial \mathcal{L}(x_1, x_2, \lambda; z)}{\partial x_2} = \frac{\partial g(x_1, x_2)}{\partial x_2} - \lambda \frac{\partial h(x_1, x_2)}{\partial x_2} = 0, \tag{A.14}$$

$$\frac{\partial \mathcal{L}(x_1, x_2, \lambda; z)}{\lambda} = z - h(x_1, x_2) = 0. \tag{A.15}$$

We simultaneously solve the first-order conditions, Equations A.13, A.14, and A.15, for the critical values of $x_1^*(z)$, $x_2^*(z)$ and $\lambda^*(z)$. Then, we substitute $x_1^*(z)$ and $x_2^*(z)$ into the original objective function to determine the maximum value, $g(x_1^*(z), x_2^*(z))$.

The key result of Lagrange's method is that the solution to this unconstrained problem, Equation A.12, also satisfies the original constrained problem, Equation A.8. Lagrange's method can be generalized to handle problems with more choice variables and more constraints. For each constraint, we need an additional Lagrange multiplier.

An Example. To illustrate this method, we return to the problem A.10, where $g(x_1, x_2) = \ln(x_1 x_2)$ and the constraint is $z - h(x_1, x_2) = z - x_1 - x_2$. The Lagrangian is

$$\mathcal{L}(x_1, x_2, z, \lambda) = \ln(x_1 x_2) + \lambda(z - x_1 - x_2).$$

The first-order conditions are

$$1/x_2 = \lambda, \quad 1/x_1 = \lambda \quad \text{and} \quad z - x_1 - x_2 = 0.$$

Solving these first-order conditions simultaneously, we find that

$$x_1^*(z) = 0.5z, \quad x_2^*(z) = 0.5z, \quad \text{and} \quad \lambda^*(z) = 2/z.$$

Because this solution is the same as the one we obtained using the substitution method, the maximum value of our original objective function is also the same: $g(x_1^*(z), x_2^*(z)) = \ln(0.25z^2)$.

Interpreting the Lagrange Multiplier. The Lagrange multiplier not only helps us convert a constrained maximization problem to an unconstrained problem but also provides additional information that is often valuable in economic problems. The value of λ that solves the first-order conditions can be interpreted as the (marginal) cost of the constraint.

The change in the original objective function with respect to a change in z is

$$\frac{dg(x_1^*, x_2^*)}{dz} = \frac{\partial g}{\partial x_1} \frac{dx_1^*}{dz} + \frac{\partial g}{\partial x_2} \frac{dx_2^*}{dz}.$$

By substituting the first-order conditions for the original choice variables, Equations A.13 and A.14, into this expression, we obtain

$$\frac{dg(x_1^*, x_2^*)}{dz} = \lambda^* \frac{\partial h}{\partial x_1} \frac{dx_1^*}{dz} + \lambda^* \frac{\partial h}{\partial x_2} \frac{dx_2^*}{dz}. \tag{A.16}$$

Differentiating the first-order condition for the Lagrange multiplier, Equation A.15, we have the additional result that

$$\frac{\partial h}{\partial x_1}\frac{dx_1^*}{dz} + \frac{\partial h}{\partial x_2}\frac{sx_2^*}{dz} = 1. \tag{A.17}$$

Substituting Equation A.17 into Equation A.16, we find that

$$\frac{dg(x_1^*, x_2^*)}{dz} = \lambda^*. \tag{A.18}$$

Equation A.18 shows that the critical value of the Lagrange multiplier reflects the sensitivity of the original objective function to a change in the exogenous parameter, z. In our last example, a small increase in z changes the value of the objective function by a factor of $\lambda = 2/z$. The Lagrange multiplier shows the value of relaxing the constraint slightly.

A.7 Maximizing with Inequality Constraints

The method of solving constrained extremum problems devised by Lagrange is appropriate if the constraints hold with strict equality. This method works even when the constraint need not hold with equality in general, as long as we know that it *will* hold with equality at the solution to the problem. For example, even if Lisa, who would always like to consume more goods, doesn't *have* to spend all of her money, we know that she will. However, if we do not know whether a constraint will be satisfied with equality, we need new tools.

Figure A.8 illustrates the distinction between an unconstrained maximum and a maximum for a concave objective function $f(x)$ subject to an inequality constraint. The unconstrained function reaches a maximum at its peak, point a, where a line tangent to the curve is horizontal. That is, the first-order condition requires that $df(x)/dx = 0$.

Figure A.8 Constrained and Unconstrained Maxima

In the absence of constraints, the maximum occurs at point a. However, if the choice variable, x, is constrained to be less than or equal to z (that is, it lies to the left of the constraint line), the constrained maximum is point b, where the line tangent to the curve at the constrained maximum is upward sloping.

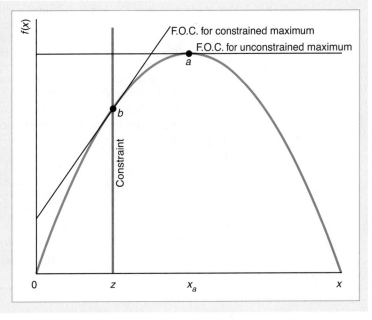

If x is constrained to be less than or equal to z, $x \leq z$, then point b in the figure is the constrained maximum. It occurs where the vertical constraint line at z intersects the function. There the line tangent to the function, or first-order condition, is upward sloping, so $df(x)/dx > 0$.

An inequality constraint need not bind. If z is so large that it exceeds the x corresponding to point a, x_a, then the inequality constraint does not bind and the maximum remains at a, where the unconstrained-maximum first-order condition holds. We can solve these types of problems mathematically by using the Kuhn-Tucker method, named after its inventors, Harold Kuhn and Albert Tucker. We start by applying the method to a specific example and then use it on a general problem.

An Illustration of the Kuhn-Tucker Method

The Kuhn-Tucker approach closely resembles the Lagrange approach except that it permits the use of inequality ("greater-than-or-equal-to") constraints as well as equality constraints. To illustrate this method, we consider the problem of trying to maximize an objective function $a\ln(x_1) + b\ln(x_2)$, where a and b are positive, subject to the inequality constraints that $z - p_1 x_1 - p_2 x_2 \geq 0$ *and* $x_1 \geq 0$, where p_1, p_2, and z are all positive. It is possible that these constraints could hold with equality. For example, it is possible that the solution to this problem involves setting x_1 equal to zero. We write this problem as

$$\max_{x_1, x_2} a \ln(x_1 + 1) + b \ln(x_2)$$
$$\text{s.t. } z - p_1 x_1 - p_2 x_2 \geq 0, \qquad x_1 \geq 0. \qquad (A.19)$$

The collection of all the constraints on choice variables implicitly defines a set of "feasible" values for the choice variables. In the present example, the set of feasible values is defined by $\{(x_1, x_2) \mid z - p_1 x_1 - p_2 x_2 \geq 0 \text{ and } x_1 \geq 0\}$, called the *constraint set*.

We now formulate the Lagrangian function (the function is still named after Lagrange rather than after Kuhn and Tucker) by choosing some additional variables to multiply times the left-hand side of the constraints, and then adding these to the objective function,

$$\mathcal{L}(x_1, x_2; \lambda, \mu) = \ln(x_1 + 1) + \ln(x_2) + \lambda(y - p_1 x_1 - p_2 x_2) + \mu x_1,$$

where λ and μ are called the *Kuhn-Tucker multipliers* (or often simply *multipliers*).

Kuhn and Tucker showed that we can characterize the solution to problem A.19 using four conditions (two sets of two conditions each). The first two equations are the first-order conditions that are obtained by setting the partial derivatives of the Lagrangian function with respect to the original choice variables, x_1 and x_2, equal to zero:

$$\frac{\partial \mathcal{L}}{\partial x_1} = \frac{a}{x_1 + 1} - p_1 \lambda + \mu = 0, \qquad (A.20)$$

$$\frac{\partial \mathcal{L}}{\partial x_2} = \frac{b}{x_2} - p_2 \lambda = 0. \qquad (A.21)$$

The next two conditions, called *complementary slackness conditions*, state that the product of each multiplier and the left-hand side of the corresponding constraint equals zero:

$$\lambda(y - p_1 x_1 - p_2 x_2) = 0, \tag{A.22}$$

$$\mu x_1 = 0. \tag{A.23}$$

That is, either the constraint holds with equality or the multiplier is zero.

To find the solution to the problem A.19, we solve Equations A.20–A.23 in several steps. Combining the first-order conditions in Equations A.20 and A.21 with the complementary slackness conditions in Equations A.22 and A.23 gives us a system of equations that characterize any local extrema for the problem, provided that both objective function and constraints are all continuously differentiable in the choice variables.

Rearranging Equation A.21, we find that $\lambda = b/(p_2 x_2)$, so because b and p_2 are positive, λ is strictly positive: $\lambda > 0$. Combining this result with the first-order condition for x_1, Equation A.22, we find that the first constraint holds with equality: $z - p_1 x_1 - p_2 x_2 = 0$. Moreover, by substituting this expression for λ into the first-order condition for x_2, Equation A.21, we obtain

$$\frac{a}{x_1 + 1} + \mu = b\frac{p_1}{p_2 x_2}.$$

Multiplying both sides of this expression by $(x_1 + 1)$ yields

$$a + \mu x_1 + \mu = b(x_1 + 1)\frac{p_1}{p_2 x_2}.$$

However, $\mu x_1 = 0$ from Equation A.23, so we know that

$$(a + \mu)p_2 x_2 = bp_1(x_1 + 1). \tag{A.24}$$

Now we have two cases to consider. Either x_1 or μ must be zero if Equation A.23 is to be satisfied. If $\mu = 0$ and we substitute that value into Equation A.24, we find that

$$x_2 = \frac{p_1}{p_2}\frac{b}{a}(x + 1).$$

Substituting this expression into the complementary slackness condition for the first constraint, Equation A.22, and remembering that $\lambda > 0$, we find that

$$x_2 = \frac{b}{a + b}\frac{z}{p_2} \quad \text{and} \quad x_1 = \frac{a}{a + b}\frac{z}{p_1} - 1. \tag{A.25}$$

Now instead suppose that $x_1 = 0$, so Equation A.24 becomes

$$x_2 = \frac{p_1}{p_2}\frac{b}{a + \mu}.$$

Remembering that $\lambda > 0$ and substituting this expression into the complementary slackness condition for the first constraint, Equation A.22, we find that $\mu = p_1(b/y) - a$ and $x_2 = y/p_2$.

Thus we have two possible solutions. Either

$$x_1 = \frac{a}{a+b}\frac{z}{p_1} - 1, \qquad x_2 = \frac{b}{a+b}\frac{z}{p_2}, \qquad \text{and} \qquad \mu = 0; \qquad \text{or} \quad \text{(A.26)}$$

$$x_1 = 0, \qquad x_2 = \frac{z}{p_2}, \qquad \text{and} \qquad \mu = p_1\frac{b}{z} - a. \qquad \text{(A.27)}$$

This multiplicity of possible solutions, Equations A.26 and A.27, does *not* mean that both solve the maximization problem. Only one of these possible answers solves the maximization problem, and which one is the solution depends on the values of the parameters a, b, p_1, p_2, and y. There are several ways to check which is correct, conditional on these values. One way in this example is to substitute the actual values of a, b, y, and p_1 into the expression for x_1 in Equation A.25 and check whether it is positive. If not, $x_1 = 0$.

Conditions for Existence and Uniqueness. Although the Kuhn-Tucker method gives us a general means of *formulating* problems of finding constrained extrema, there is no guarantee that a solution to the Kuhn-Tucker formulation exists. Even if a solution does exist, there is no guarantee that it is unique.

In Section A.4, we summarized the sufficient conditions that guarantee the existence and uniqueness of solutions to *unconstrained* extrema problems. Now we would like some simple conditions guaranteeing both the existence and the uniqueness of a solution to the Kuhn-Tucker formulation of a *constrained* extremum problem.

We want to specify these conditions for a general Kuhn-Tucker problem with n choice variables $x_1, x_2, \ldots, x_n$, where we want to maximize an objective function $f: \mathbb{R}^n \to \mathbb{R}$ subject to m constraints, $g_j(x_1, x_2, \ldots, x_n) \geq 0$, for $j = 1, 2, \ldots, m$:

$$\max_{x_1, x_2, \ldots, x_n} f(x_1, x_2, \ldots, x_n)$$

$$\text{s.t. } g_j(x_1, x_2, \ldots, x_n) \geq 0, \qquad \text{for} \qquad j = 1, 2, \ldots, m. \qquad \text{(A.28)}$$

The *Slater condition* guarantees the existence of a solution to problem A.28. The Slater condition requires that the solution to the maximization problem is not determined entirely by the constraints for any of the choice variables: There exists a point $(x_1, x_2, \ldots, x_n)$ such that $g_j(x_1, x_2, \ldots, x_n) > 0$ for all $j = 1, 2, \ldots, m$. Because this condition holds with a strict inequality, the constraint set has a non-empty interior.

A local maximum exists if the objective function and constraints are continuously differentiable and if the Slater condition is satisfied. If $(x_1^*, \ldots, x_n^*)$ is a local maximum of the problem A.28, it is also global maximum if f is weakly concave and if g_j is weakly convex for all $j = 1, \ldots, m$. However, there could be more than one global maximum.

Sufficient conditions for a local maximum $(x_1^*, \ldots, x_n^*)$ to the problem A.28 to be a unique global maximum are that f is weakly concave; g_j is weakly convex for all $j = 1, 2, \ldots, m$; and one of two alternative conditions holds:

1. The objective function f is strictly concave; or
2. At least one of the constraints $g_j(x_1^*, \ldots, x_n^*) = 0$ and is strictly convex at $g_j(x_1^*, \ldots, x_n^*)$.

The Envelope Theorem. We can state and prove a version of the Envelope Theorem that holds for constrained extremum problems. To facilitate this discussion, we use our previous formulation of the Kuhn-Tucker problem, but we explicitly add an exogenous parameter z so that z can have a direct effect on the objective function as well as a direct effect on any of the constraints g_j,[3]

$$V(z) = \max_{x_1, x_2, \ldots, x_n} f(x_1, x_2, \ldots, x_n, z)$$

$$\text{s.t. } g_j(x_1, x_2, \ldots, x_n, z) \geq 0, \quad \text{for } j = 1, 2, \ldots, m, \quad (A.29)$$

where $V(z)$ is the maximized value of the objective function. The equivalent Lagrangian problem is

$$V(z) = \max_{x_1, x_2, \ldots, x_n} f(x_1, x_2, \ldots, x_n, z) + \sum_{j=1}^{m} \lambda_j g_j(x_1, x_2, \ldots, x_n, z), \quad (A.30)$$

where $\lambda_1, \lambda_2, \ldots, \lambda_m$ are the Kuhn-Tucker multipliers.

The first-order conditions are

$$\frac{\partial f}{\partial x_i} + \sum_{j=1}^{m} \lambda_j \frac{\partial g_j}{\partial x_i} = 0, \quad \text{for} \quad i = 1, \ldots, n \quad \text{and} \quad j = 1, \ldots, m, \quad (A.31)$$

and the complementary slackness conditions are

$$\lambda_j g(x_1, \ldots, x_n, z) = 0, \quad \text{for} \quad j = 1, \ldots, m. \quad (A.32)$$

The *Envelope Theorem* states that, if the constraints $g_j(x_1, x_2, \ldots, x_n, z)$ satisfy the Slater condition and if $x_i(z)$, $i = 1, 2, \ldots, n$, solve the first-order conditions, Equation A.31, and complementary slackness conditions, Equation A.32, then

$$\frac{\partial V(z)}{\partial z} = \frac{\partial f(x_1, \ldots, x_n, z)}{\partial z} + \sum_{j=1}^{m} \lambda_j \frac{\partial g_j}{\partial z}.$$

Proof. The value function $V(z) = f(x_1(z), \ldots, x_n(z), z) + \sum_{j=1}^{m} \lambda_j g_j(x_1, \ldots, x_n, z)$. Differentiating this expression with respect to z yields

$$\frac{\partial V(z)}{\partial z} = \frac{\partial f(x_1, \ldots, x_n, z)}{\partial z} + \sum_{i=1}^{n} \left[\frac{\partial f(x_1, \ldots, x_n, z)}{\partial x_i} \frac{\partial x_i(z)}{\partial z} \right.$$

$$\left. + \sum_{j=1}^{m} \lambda_j \frac{\partial g_j(x_1, \ldots, x_n, z)}{\partial x_i} \frac{\partial x_i(z)}{\partial z} \right]$$

$$+ \sum_{j=1}^{m} \left[\frac{\partial \lambda_j(z)}{\partial z} g_j(x_1, \ldots, x_n, z) + \lambda_j(z) \frac{\partial g_j(x_1, \ldots, x_n, z)}{\partial z} \right].$$

Collecting terms, we can rewrite this equation as

$$\frac{\partial V(z)}{\partial z} = \frac{\partial f(x_1, \ldots, x_n, z)}{\partial z}$$

$$+ \sum_{j=1}^{m} \left[\frac{\partial \lambda_j(z)}{\partial z} g_j(x_1, \ldots, x_n, z) + \lambda_j(z) \frac{\partial g_j(x_1, \ldots, x_n, z)}{\partial z} \right]$$

$$+ \sum_{i=1}^{n} \left[\frac{\partial f(x_1, \ldots, x_n, z)}{\partial x_i} \frac{\partial x_i(z)}{\partial z} + \sum_{j=1}^{m} \lambda_j \frac{\partial g_j(x_1, \ldots, x_n, z)}{\partial x_i} \right] \frac{\partial x_i(z)}{\partial z}. \quad (A.33)$$

---

[3]We could have added any finite number of such exogenous parameters; however, one is enough for our purposes.

Using Equation A.31, the last bracketed expression in Equation A.33 equals zero. If we can show that the $\sum (\partial \lambda_j / \partial z) g_j$ expression in the other bracketed term is zero, we have proved the theorem. We know by the complementary slackness conditions that $\lambda_j g_j(x_1, x_2, \ldots, x_n, z) = 0$. If $g_j(x_1, x_2, \ldots, x_n, z) = 0$, then $(\partial \lambda_j / \partial z) g_j(x_1, x_2, \ldots, x_m) = 0$. Alternatively, if $g_j(x_1, x_2, \ldots, x_n, z) > 0$, so that $\lambda_j = 0$, the Slater condition implies that $\partial \lambda_j(z) / \partial z = 0$, thus proving the theorem.

Comparative Statics. The method of comparative statics can often be applied when one is solving a problem with inequality constraints, but the matter is complicated by the need to keep track of which inequality constraints are binding. Let's return to our earlier problem A.19, where the Lagrangian function is $\mathscr{L} = a \ln(x_1 + 1) + b \ln(x_2) + \lambda(y - p_1 x_1 - p_2 x_2) + \mu x_1$ and has first-order conditions

$$\frac{a}{x_1 + 1} - \lambda p_1 + \mu = 0 \quad \text{and} \quad \frac{b}{x_2} - \lambda p_2 = 0,$$

and associated complementary slackness conditions

$$\lambda(y - p_1 x_1 - p_2 x_2) = 0, \tag{A.34}$$

$$\mu x_1 = 0. \tag{A.35}$$

These complementary slackness conditions complicate the comparative statics analysis. If a constraint is clearly binding, we don't have a problem, because we know how it affects the solution. Unfortunately, we do not always know if a constraint binds.

In this example, we may be confident that the first constraint binds, so we know that $\lambda > 0$. Consequently, we can divide both sides of Equation A.34 by λ to eliminate it from the complementary slackness conditions. However, we do not know whether the constraint $x_1 \geq 0$ is binding without knowing the actual parameters.

In one approach, we initially assume that all the constraints *are* binding, and then use this assumption to substitute the constraints into the first-order conditions and solve them. Here we assume that the constraint, Equation A.35, holds, $x_1 = 0$. Consequently, using Equation A.27, $x_2 = y/p_2$. Substituting these solutions into the first-order conditions, we have

$$a - \lambda p_1 + \mu = 0 \quad \text{and} \quad \frac{b}{y} - \lambda = 0,$$

or solving for μ and λ,

$$\mu = \frac{b}{y} p_1 - a \quad \text{and} \quad \lambda = b/y.$$

Consequently, we've potentially solved the entire system, with proposed solutions for x_1, x_2, and both the multipliers. However, our initial assumption that $x_1 = 0$ implies that $\mu > 0$ or that $(b/y)p_1 > a$. This last inequality is exactly what we need to check. If it's satisfied, then we have the correct solution that we're at a *corner*. If it's not, then the maximum is in the interior and not at a corner, and the constraint $x_1 \geq 0$ does not bind. If it's not binding, then $\mu = 0$. Now we can go back and plug this condition into the first-order conditions, and solve. Given either set of these solutions, we can examine the effect of a change in a parameter.

Recipe for Finding the Constrained Extrema of a Function

The following is a step-by-step set of practical instructions for solving a constrained extrema problem. The focus of this section is very much on the mechanics of *how* rather than on the issues of *why*.

1. *Make the problem a maximization problem.* If the problem is to minimize $f(x_1, x_2, \ldots, x_n)$ subject to constraints, we can convert it into a maximization problem by maximizing *minus* the function subject to the same constraints.

2. *Rewrite any constraints so that they take the form of "greater than or equal to zero."* Here's a brief field guide to constraints and how to deal with them:

   a. *Greater than or equal to*: If the constraint is initially stated in the form of $g(x_1, x_2) \geq f(x_1, x_2)$, subtract the term $f(x_1, x_2)$ from both sides to obtain $g(x_1, x_2) - f(x_1, x_2) \geq 0$.

   b. *Less than or equal to*: Given an initial constraint of $g(x_1, x_2) \leq f(x_1, x_2)$, multiply both sides by -1, making it a greater-than-or-equal-to problem, and use the method in (a): $f(x_1, x_2) - g(x_1, x_2) \geq 0$.

   c. *Strictly greater than or strictly less than*: If your constraint is $g(x_1, x_2) > f(x_1, x_2)$ or $g(x_1, x_2) < f(x_1, x_2)$, you're in trouble! If this constraint has any effect on the problem, it will be to make it so that no solution exists. (Consider the problem of minimizing x such that $x > 0$ to see why this is a problem.) You have to reformulate your problem.

   d. *Equal to*: If it seems that the constraint truly has to hold with equality, put yourself in the shoes of the firm's manager, who is doing the maximizing. If the firm could somehow challenge the natural order of things and violate the constraint, would the firm prefer a "less-than-or-equal-to" constraint or a "greater-than-or-equal-to" constraint? For example, a firm facing a constraint that required output q to be equal to a function $f(x)$ of inputs x would, if the firm could violate the laws of nature, prefer that output was greater than production, or that $q \geq f(x)$. Let's give the firm the opposite of what it would want, imposing the constraint $q \leq f(x)$. Multiply both sides by -1 and then move the terms on the right-hand side to the left to get a "greater-than-or-equal-to-zero" constraint: $f(x) - q \geq 0$. Think again about whether the constraint *really* has to be an equality constraint—in this case, could the firm throw some output away? If the answer is yes, then you're done. Otherwise, add *another* "greater-than-or-equal-to" constraint but with the opposite sign. So, in the example of our firm, we would have both constraints:

$$f(x) - q \geq 0, \tag{A.36}$$

$$q - f(x) \geq 0. \tag{A.37}$$

   You can verify that these two inequality constraints imply a single equality constraint.

   Now you've got all your constraints formulated in the "greater-than-or-equal-to" form. Take a moment to be sure you haven't neglected any. Are there some choice variables that can't be negative? If so, add a nonnegativity constraint requiring them to be greater than or equal to zero.

3. *Construct the Lagrangian function.* Assign a multiplier to each of your constraints (it's traditional to use Greek letters for these multipliers), which you multiply times the left-hand side of the corresponding constraint, and add the products to the objective function you formulated in the first step.

4. *Partially differentiate the Lagrangian function.* Beginning with the first of your choice variables, partially differentiate the Lagrangian function with respect to this variable. Repeat for each of the remaining choice variables. Set each of these expressions equal to zero, yielding a collection of first-order conditions.

5. *List the complementary slackness conditions.* Take each of the products of the "greater-than-or-equal-to" constraints with their corresponding multipliers and set them equal to zero, yielding the complementary slackness conditions.

6. *Solve the system of equations.* Simultaneously solve the collection of first-order conditions and the complementary slackness conditions to find the critical values. The set of values of the choice variables that satisfy this system solve the constrained maximization problem.[4]

A.8 Duality

There's a close connection between constrained maxima and minima called *duality*. The following proposition makes this connection: Let λ be a scalar greater than zero. If there exists a solution $x^*(z)$ to the *primal* problem

$$V(z) = \max_x f(x, z) + \lambda(C(z) - g(x, z)), \tag{A.38}$$

then $x^*(z)$ also solves the *dual* problem

$$C(z) = \min_x g(x, z) + \frac{1}{\lambda}(V(z) - f(x, z)). \tag{A.39}$$

Proof. We need to show that the maximization problem A.38 is equivalent to the minimization problem A.39 when $\lambda > 0$. Because a solution $x^*(z)$ exists, the function $V(z)$ exists. Subtracting $V(z)$ from both sides of Equation A.38 yields

$$0 = \max_x [f(x, z) - V(z)] + \lambda(C(z) - g(x, z)).$$

Then subtracting $\lambda C(z)$ from both sides gives us

$$-\lambda C(z) = \max_x [f(x, z) - V(z)] - \lambda g(x, z).$$

Multiplying both sides by -1 transforms the max operator into the min operator,

$$\lambda C(z) = \min_x [V(z) - f(x, z)] + \lambda g(x, z),$$

and dividing both sides by the positive constant λ yields the result in Equation A.39.

This result implies that when we solve a primal constrained maximization problem *and the constraint binds*, then a dual representation of the problem also exists. To see why, consider the constrained problem

$$\max_x f(x, z)$$

$$\text{s.t. } g(x, z) \leq C(z)$$

For example, a firm could face this problem when it is maximizing output $f(x, z)$ subject to keeping its cost $g(x, z)$ below some critical level $C(z)$. The Lagrangian function corresponding to this problem is $\mathscr{L}(x, z) = f(x, z) + \lambda(C(z) - g(x, z))$. The result implies that if the maximizing choice of x given z (which in our example maximizes output subject to keeping cost below some limit) makes the constraint bind, then this same choice also solves the *dual* problem of minimizing $g(x, z)$ subject to satisfying the constraint $f(x, z) \geq V(z)$ [or, in our example, minimizing costs subject to keeping output above $V(z)$]. Further, the value of the multiplier in the dual problem will be the reciprocal of the value of the multiplier in the primal problem.

This result does not rely on the differentiability or shape of the functions f and g, only on the existence of a solution to the primal maximization problem. However, if the solution to the primal problem satisfies its associated first-order conditions and the constraint is binding, then the same first-order conditions will characterize the dual problem.

---

[4]We sometimes may be unable to find an explicit solution to these sets of equations, even if a solution exists. In such cases, we can use numerical techniques to find solutions (see Judd, 1998), or we can employ the method of comparative statics to try to understand the character of the solution.

Regression Appendix

Economists use a *regression* to estimate economic relationships such as demand curves and supply curves. A regression analysis allows us to answer three questions:

1. How can we best fit an economic relationship to actual data?
2. How confident are we in our results?
3. How can we determine the effect of a change in one variable on another if many other variables are changing at the same time?

Estimating Economic Relations

We use a demand curve example to illustrate how regressions can answer these questions. The points in Figure B.1 show eight years of data on Nancy's annual purchases of candy bars, q, and the prices, p, she paid.[1] For example, in the year when candy bars cost 20¢, Nancy bought q_2 candy bars.

Because we assume that Nancy's tastes and income did not change during this period, we write her demand for candy bars as a function of the price of candy bars and unobservable random effects. We believe that her demand curve is linear and want to estimate the demand function:

$$q = a + bp + e,$$

where a and b are the coefficients we want to determine and e is an error term. This *error term* captures random effects that are not otherwise reflected in our function. For instance, in one year, Nancy took an economics course that raised her anxiety level, causing her to eat more candy bars than usual, resulting in a relatively large positive error term for that year.

The data points in the figure exhibit a generally downward-sloping relationship between quantity and price, but the points do not lie strictly on a line because of the error terms. There are many possible ways in which we could draw a line through these data points.

The way we fit the line in the figure is to use the standard criterion that our estimates *minimize the sum of squared residuals*, where a residual, $e = q - \hat{q}$, is the difference between an actual quantity, q, and the fitted or predicted quantity on the

---

[1] We use a lowercase q for the quantity demanded for an individual instead of the uppercase Q that we use for a market. Notice that we violated the rule economists usually follow of putting quantity on the horizontal axis and price on the vertical axis. We are now looking at this relationship as statisticians who put the independent or explanatory variable, price, on the horizontal axis and the dependent variable, quantity, on the vertical axis.

Figure B.1

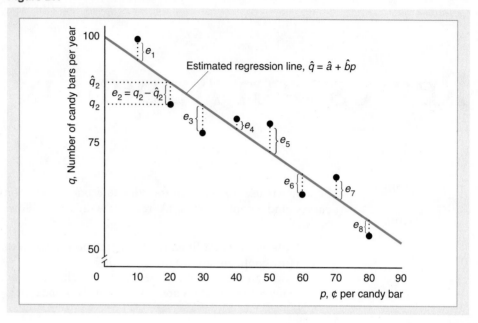

estimated line, $\hat{q}$. That is, we choose estimated coefficients $\hat{a}$ and $\hat{b}$ so that the estimated quantities from the regression line,

$$\hat{q} = \hat{a} + \hat{b}p,$$

make the sum of the squared residuals, $e_1^2 + e_2^2 + \ldots + e_8^2$, as small as possible. By summing the square of the residuals instead of the residuals themselves, we treat the effects of a positive or negative error symmetrically and give greater weight to large errors than to small ones.[2] In the figure, the regression line is

$$\hat{q} = 99.4 - 0.49p,$$

where $\hat{a} = 99.4$ is the intercept of the estimated line and $\hat{b} = -0.49$ is the slope of the line.

Confidence in Our Estimates

Because the data reflect random errors, so do the estimated coefficients. Our estimate of Nancy's demand curve depends on the *sample* of data we use. If we were to use data from a different set of years, our estimates, $\hat{a}$ and $\hat{b}$ of the true coefficients, a and b, would differ.

   If we had many estimates of the true parameter based on many samples, the estimates would be distributed around the true coefficient. These estimates are *unbiased* in the sense that the average of the estimates would equal the true coefficients.

---

[2]Using calculus, we can derive the $\hat{a}$ and $\hat{b}$ that minimize the sum of squared residuals. The estimate of the slope coefficient is a weighted average of the observed quantities, $\hat{b} = \sum_i w_i q_i$, where $w_i = (p_i - \bar{p})/\sum_i (p_i - \bar{p})^2$, $\bar{p}$ is the average of the observed prices, and $\sum_i$ indicates the sum over each observation i. The estimate of the intercept, $\hat{a}$, is the average of the observed quantities.

Computer programs that calculate regression lines report a *standard error* for each coefficient, which is an estimate of the dispersion of the estimated coefficients around the true coefficient. In our example, a computer program reports

$$\hat{q} = 99.4 - 0.49p,$$
$$(3.99)\ (0.08)$$

where below each estimated coefficient is its estimated standard error between parentheses.

The smaller the estimated standard error, the more precise the estimate, and the more likely it is to be close to the true value. As a rough rule of thumb, there is a 95% probability that the interval that is within two standard errors of the estimated coefficient contains the true coefficient.[3] Using this rule, the *confidence interval* for the slope coefficient, $\hat{b}$, ranges from $-0.49 - (2 \times 0.08) = -0.65$ to $-0.49 + (2 \times 0.08) = -0.33$. If zero were to lie within the confidence interval for $\hat{b}$, we would conclude that we cannot reject the hypothesis that the price has no effect on the quantity demanded. In our case, however, the entire confidence interval contains negative values, so we are reasonably sure that the higher the price, the less Nancy demands.

Multiple Regression

We can also estimate relationships involving more than one explanatory variable using a *multiple regression*. For example, Moschini and Meilke (1992) estimate a pork demand function, Equation 2.2, in which the quantity demanded is a function of income, Y, and the prices of pork, p, beef, p_b, and chicken, p_c:

$$Q = 171 - 20p + 20p_b + 3p_c + 2Y.$$

The multiple regression is able to separate the effects of the various explanatory variables. The coefficient 20 on the p variable indicates that an increase in the price of pork by $1 per kg lowers the quantity demanded by 20 million kg per year, holding the effects of the other prices and income constant.

---

[3]The confidence interval is the coefficient plus or minus 1.96 times its standard error for large samples (at least hundreds of observations) in which the coefficients are normally distributed. For smaller samples, the confidence interval tends to be larger.

Answers to Selected Problems

I know the answer! The answer lies within the heart of all mankind! The answer is twelve? I think I'm in the wrong building. —Charles Schultz

Chapter 2

1.1 The demand curve for pork is $Q = 171 - 20p + 20p_b + 3p_c + 2Y$. As a result, $\partial Q/\partial Y = 2$. A \$100 increase in income causes the quantity demanded to increase by 0.2 million kg per year.

1.2 To solve this problem, we first rewrite the inverse demand functions as demand functions and then add them together. The total demand function is $Q = Q_1 + Q_2 = (120 - p) + (60 - \frac{1}{2}p) = 180 - 1.5p$.

2.3 In the figure, the no-quota total supply curve, S in panel c, is the horizontal sum of the U.S. domestic supply curve, S^d, and the no-quota foreign supply curve, S^f. At prices less than $\bar{p}$, foreign suppliers want to supply quantities less than the quota, $\bar{Q}$. As a result, the foreign supply curve under the quota, $\bar{S}^f$, is the same as the no-quota foreign supply curve,

S^f, for prices less than $\bar{p}$. At prices above $\bar{p}$, foreign suppliers want to supply more but are limited to $\bar{Q}$. Thus, the foreign supply curve with a quota, $\bar{S}^f$ is vertical at $\bar{Q}$ for prices above $\bar{p}$. The total supply curve with the quota, $\bar{S}$, is the horizontal sum of S^d and $\bar{S}^f$ At any price above $\bar{p}$, the total supply equals the quota plus the domestic supply. For example at p^*, the domestic supply is Q_d^* and the foreign supply is $\bar{Q}_f$, so the total supply is $Q_d^* + \bar{Q}_f$. Above $\bar{p}, \bar{S}$ is the domestic supply curve shifted $\bar{Q}$ units to the right. As a result, the portion of $\bar{S}$ above $\bar{p}$ has the same slope as S^d. At prices less than or equal to $\bar{p}$ the same quantity is supplied with and without the quota, so $\bar{S}$ is the same as S. At prices above $\bar{p}$, less is supplied with the quota than without one, so $\bar{S}$ is steeper than S, indicating that a given increase in price raises the quantity supplied by less with a quota than without one.

For Chapter 2, Exercise 2.3

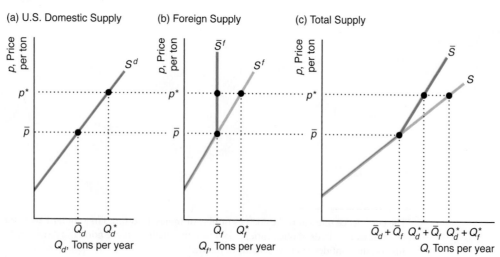

(a) U.S. Domestic Supply (b) Foreign Supply (c) Total Supply

3.1 The statement "Talk is cheap because supply exceeds demand" makes sense if we interpret it to mean that the *quantity* of talk *supplied* exceeds the *quantity demanded* at a price of zero. Imagine a downward-sloping demand curve that hits the horizontal, quantity axis to the left of where the upward-sloping supply curve hits the axis. (The correct aphorism is "Talk is cheap until you hire a lawyer.")

3.3 Equating the right-hand sides of the tomato supply and demand functions and using algebra, we find that $\ln p = 3.2 + 0.2 \ln p_t$. We then set $p_t = 110$, solve for $\ln p$, and exponentiate $\ln p$ to obtain the equilibrium price, $p \approx \$62.80$ per ton. Substituting p into the supply curve and exponentiating, we determine the equilibrium quantity, $Q \approx 11.91$ million short tons per year.

4.3 To determine the equilibrium price, we equate the right-hand sides of the supply function, $Q = 20 + 3p - 20r$, and the demand function, $Q = 220 - 2p$, to obtain $20 + 3p - 20r = 220 - 2p$. Using algebra, we can rewrite the equilibrium price equation as $p = 40 + 4r$. Substituting this expression into the demand function, we learn that the equilibrium quantity is $Q = 220 - 2(40 + 4r)$, or $Q = 140 - 8r$. By differentiating our two equilibrium conditions with respect to r, we obtain our comparative statics results: $dp/dr = 4$ and $dQ/dr = -8$.

4.7 The graph reproduces the no-quota total American supply curve of steel, S, and the total supply curve under the quota, $\bar{S}$, which we derived in the answer to Exercise 2.3. At a price below $\bar{p}$, the two supply curves are identical because the quota is not binding: It is greater than the quantity foreign firms want to supply. Above $\bar{p}$, $\bar{S}$ lies to the left of S. Suppose that the American demand is relatively *low* at any given price so that the demand curve, D^l, intersects both the supply curves at a price below $\bar{p}$. The equilibria

both before and after the quota is imposed are at e_1, where the equilibrium price, p_1, is less than $\bar{p}$. Thus, if the demand curve lies near enough to the origin that the quota is not binding, the quota has no effect on the equilibrium. With a relatively *high* demand curve, D^h, the quota affects the equilibrium. The no-quota equilibrium is e_2, where D^h intersects the no-quota total supply curve, S. After the quota is imposed, the equilibrium is e_3, where D^h intersects the total supply curve with the quota, $\bar{S}$. The quota raises the price of steel in the United States from p_2 to p_3 and reduces the quantity from Q_2 to Q_3.

5.8 The elasticity of demand is $(dQ/dp)(p/Q) = (-9.5$ thousand metric tons per year per cent$) \times (45\cent/1{,}275$ thousand metric tons per year$) \approx -0.34$. That is, for every 1% fall in the price, a third of a percent more coconut oil is demanded. The cross-price elasticity of demand for coconut oil with respect to the price of palm oil is $(dQ/dp_p)(p_p/Q) = 16.2 \times (31/1{,}275) \approx 0.39$.

6.4 We showed that, in a competitive market, the effect of a specific tax is the same whether it is placed on suppliers or demanders. Thus, if the market for milk is competitive, consumers will pay the same price in equilibrium regardless of whether the government taxes consumers or stores.

6.8 Differentiating quantity, $Q(p(\tau))$, with respect to τ, we learn that the change in quantity as the tax changes is $(dQ/dp)(dp/d\tau)$. Multiplying and dividing this expression by p/Q, we find that the change in quantity as the tax changes is $\varepsilon(Q/p)(dp/d\tau)$. Thus, the closer ε is to zero, the less the quantity falls, all else the same.

Because $R = p(\tau)Q(p(\tau))$, an increase in the tax rate changes revenues by

$$\frac{dR}{d\tau} = \frac{dp}{d\tau}Q + p\frac{dQ}{dp}\frac{dp}{d\tau},$$

using the chain rule. Using algebra, we can rewrite this expression as

$$\frac{dR}{d\tau} = \frac{dp}{d\tau}\left(Q + p\frac{dQ}{dp}\right) = \frac{dp}{d\tau}Q\left(1 + \frac{dQ}{dp}\frac{p}{Q}\right) = \frac{dp}{d\tau}Q(1 + \varepsilon).$$

Thus, the effect of a change in τ on R depends on the elasticity of demand, ε. Revenue rises with the tax if demand is inelastic ($-1 < \varepsilon < 0$) and falls if demand is elastic ($\varepsilon < -1$).

7.3 A usury law is a price ceiling, which causes the quantity that firms want to supply to fall.

7.4 We can determine how the total wage payment, $W = wL(w)$, varies with respect to w by differentiating. We then use algebra to express this result in terms of an elasticity:

$$\frac{dW}{dw} = L + w\frac{dL}{dw} = L\left(1 + \frac{dL}{dw}\frac{w}{L}\right) = L(1 + \varepsilon),$$

For Chapter 2, Exercise 4.7

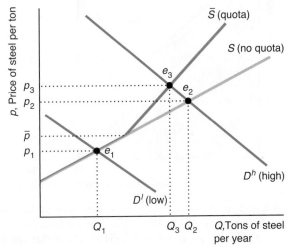

where ε is the elasticity of demand of labor. The sign of dW/dw is the same as that of $1 + \varepsilon$. Thus, total labor payment decreases as the minimum wage forces up the wage if labor demand is elastic, $\varepsilon < -1$, and increases if labor demand is inelastic, $\varepsilon > -1$.

9.2 Shifts of both the U.S. supply and U.S. demand curves affected the U.S. equilibrium. U.S. beef consumers' fear of mad cow disease caused their demand curve in the figure to shift slightly to the left from D^1 to D^2. In the short run, total U.S. production was essentially unchanged. Because of the ban on exports, beef that would have been sold in Japan and elsewhere was sold in the United States, causing the U.S. supply curve to shift to the right from S^1 to S^2. As a result, the U.S. equilibrium changed from e_1 (where S^1 intersects D^1) to e_2 (where S^2 intersects D^2). The U.S. price fell 15% from p_1 to $p_2 = 0.85p_1$, while the quantity rose 43% from Q_1 to $Q_2 = 1.43Q_1$. *Comment*: Depending on exactly how the U.S. supply and demand curves had shifted, it would have been possible for the U.S. price and quantity to have both fallen. For example, if D^2 had shifted far enough left, it could have intersected S^2 to the left of Q_1, and the equilibrium quantity would have fallen.

For Chapter 2, Exercise 9.2

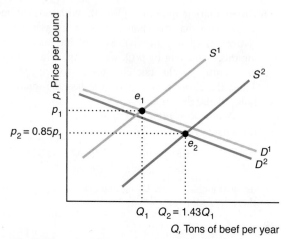

Chapter 3

1.5 If the neutral product is on the vertical axis, the indifference curves are parallel vertical lines.

2.2 Sofia's indifference curves are right angles (as in panel b of Figure 3.5). Her utility function is $U = \min(H, W)$, where *min* means the minimum of the two arguments, H is the number of units of hot dogs, and W is the number of units of whipped cream.

2.4 If we apply the transformation function $F(x) = x^\rho$ to the original utility function, we obtain the new utility function $V(q_1, q_2) = F(U(q_1, q_2)) = [(q_1^\rho +$

$q_2^\rho)^{1/\rho}]^\rho = q_1^\rho + q_2^\rho$, which has the same preference properties as does the original function.

2.5 Given the original utility function, U, the consumer's marginal rate of substitution is $-U_1/U_2$. If $V(q_1, q_2) = F(U(q_1, q_2))$, the new marginal rate of substitution is $-V_1/V_2 = -[(dF/dU)U_1]/[(dF/dU)U_2] = -U_1/U_2$, which is the same as originally.

2.6 By differentiating we know that
$$U_1 = a(aq_1^\rho + [1 - a]q_2^\rho)^{(1-\rho)/\rho}q_1^{\rho-1} \text{ and}$$
$$U_2 = [1 - a](aq_1^\rho + [1 - a]q_2^\rho)^{(1-\rho)/\rho}q_2^{\rho-1}.$$
Thus, $MRS = -U_1/U_2 = -[(1 - a)/a](q_1/q_2)^{\rho-1}$.

3.1 Suppose that Dale purchases two goods at prices p_1 and p_2. If her original income is Y, the intercept of the budget line on the Good 1 axis (where the consumer buys only Good 1) is Y/p_1. Similarly, the intercept is Y/p_2 on the Good 2 axis. A 50% income tax lowers income to half its original level, $Y/2$. As a result, the budget line shifts inward toward the origin. The intercepts on the Good 1 and Good 2 axes are $Y/(2p_1)$ and $Y/(2p_2)$, respectively. The opportunity set shrinks by the area between the original budget line and the new line.

3.3 In the figure, the consumer can afford to buy up to 12 thousand gallons of water a week if not constrained. The opportunity set, area A and B, is bounded by the axes and the budget line. A vertical line at 10 thousand on the water axis indicates the quota. The new opportunity set, area A, is bounded by the axes, the budget line, and the quota line. Because of the rationing, the consumer loses part of the original opportunity set: the triangle B to the right of the 10-thousand-gallons quota line. The consumer has fewer opportunities because of rationing.

For Chapter 3, Exercise 3.3

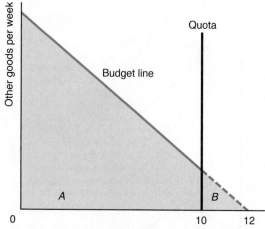

4.3 Andy's marginal utility of apples divided by the price of apples is $3/2 = 1.5$. The marginal utility for kumquats is $5/4 = 1.2$. That is, a dollar spent on apples gives him more extra utils than a dollar spent on kumquats. Thus, Andy maximizes his utility by spending all his money on apples and buying $40/2 = 20$ pounds of apples.

4.14 David's marginal utility of q_1 is 1 and his marginal utility of q_2 is 2. The slope of David's indifference curve is $-U_1/U_2 = -\frac{1}{2}$. Because the marginal utility from one extra unit of $q_2 = 2$ is twice that from one extra unit of q_1, if the price of q_2 is less than twice that of q_1, David buys only $q_2 = Y/p_2$, where Y is his income and p_2 is the price. If the price of q_2 is more than twice that of q_1, David buys only q_1. If the price of q_2 is exactly twice as much as that of q_1, he is indifferent between buying any bundle along his budget line.

4.15 Vasco determines his optimal bundle by equating the ratios of each good's marginal utility to its price.
 a. At the original prices, this condition is $U_1/10 = 2q_1q_2 = 2q_1^2 = U_2/5$. Thus, by dividing both sides of the middle equality by $2q_1$, we know that his optimal bundle has the property that $q_1 = q_2$. His budget constraint is $90 = 10q_1 + 5q_2$. Substituting q_2 for q_1, we find that $15q_2 = 90$, or $q_2 = 6 = q_1$.
 b. At the new price, the optimum condition requires that $U_1/10 = 2q_1q_2 = 2q_1^2 = U_2/10$, or $2q_2 = q_1$. By substituting this condition into his budget constraint, $90 = 10q_1 + 10q_2$, and solving, we learn that $q_2 = 3$ and $q_1 = 6$. Thus, as the price of chickens doubles, he cuts his consumption of chicken in half but does not change how many slabs of ribs he eats.

6.2 Change the labels on the figure in the Challenge Solution to illustrate the answer to this question: When the price in Canada is relative low, the motorist buys gasoline in Canada, and vice versa.

Chapter 4

1.7 The figure shows that the price-consumption curve is horizontal. The demand for CDs depends only on income and the own price, $q_1 = 0.6Y/p_1$.

2.2 Guerdon's utility function is $U(q_1, q_2) = \min(0.5q_1, q_2)$. To maximize his utility, he always picks a bundle at the corner of his right-angle indifference curves. That is, he chooses only combinations of the two goods such that $0.5q_1 = q_2$. Using that expression to substitute for q_2 in his budget constraint, we find that

$$Y = p_1q_1 + p_2q_2 = p_1q_1 + p_2q_1/2 = (p_1 + 0.5p_2)q_1.$$

Thus, his demand curve for bananas is $q_1 = Y/(p_1 + 0.5p_2)$. The graph of this demand curve is downward sloping and convex to the origin (similar to the Cobb-Douglas demand curve in panel a of Figure 4.1).

For Chapter 4, Exercise 1.7

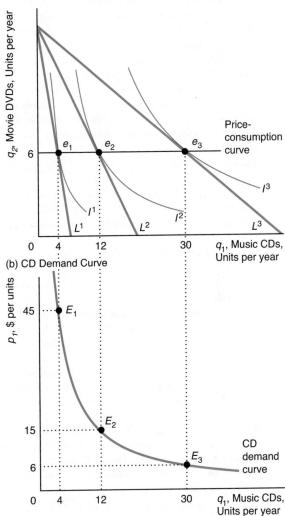

(a) Indifference Curves and Budget Constraints

(b) CD Demand Curve

2.4 Barbara's demand for CDs is $q_1 = 0.6Y/p_1$. Consequently, her Engel curve is a straight line with a slope of $dq_1/dY = 0.6/p_1$.

3.2 An opera performance must be a normal good for Don because he views the only other good he buys as an inferior good. To show this result in a graph, draw a figure similar to Figure 4.4, but relabel the vertical "Housing" axis as "Opera performances." Don's equilibrium will be in the upper-left quadrant at a point like a in Figure 4.4.

3.5 On a graph show I^f, the budget line at the factory store, and L^o, the budget constraint at the outlet store. At the factory store, the consumer maximum occurs at e_f on indifference curve I^f. Suppose that we increase the income of a consumer who shops at the outlet store to Y^* so that the resulting budget line L^* is tangent to the indifference curve I^f. The consumer would buy Bundle e^*. That is, the pure substitution effect (the movement from e_f to e^*) causes the consumer to buy relatively more firsts. The total effect (the movement from e_f to e_o) reflects both the substitution effect (firsts are now relatively less expensive) and the income effect (the consumer is worse off after paying for shipping). The income effect is small if (as seems reasonable) the budget share of plates is small. An ad valorem tax has qualitatively the same effect as a specific tax because both taxes raise the relative price of firsts to seconds.

3.7 We can determine the optimal bundle, e_1, at the original prices $p_1 = p_2 = 1$ by using the demand equation from Table 4.1: $q_1 = 4(p_2/p_1)^2 = 4$ and $q_2 = Y/p_2 - 4(p_2/p_1) = 10 - 4 = 6$. This optimal bundle is on an indifference curve where $U = 4(4)^{0.5} + 6 = 14$.

At the new bundle, e_2, where $p_1 = 2$ and $p_2 = 1$, $q_1 = 4(1/2)^2 = 1$, and $q_2 = 10 - 4(1) = 8$. This optimal bundle is on an indifference curve where $U = 4(1)^{0.5} + 8 = 12$.

To determine e^*, we want to stay on the original indifference curve. We know that the tangency condition will give the same q_1 as at e_2 because q_1 depends on only the relative prices, so $q_1 = 1$. The question is what Y will compensate Phillip for the higher price so that he can stay on the original indifference curve. Because $q_2 = Y - 4(1/2) = Y - 4$, the utility is $U = 1 + (Y - 4) = Y - 3$. So the Y that results in $U = 14$ is $Y = 17$. Thus, the substitution effect is -3 (based on the movement from e_1 to e^*) and the income effect is 0 (the movement from e^* to e_2), so the total effect is -3 (movement from e_1 to e_2).

3.9 At Sylvia's optimal bundle, $q_1 = jq_2$ (see Chapter 3). Otherwise, she could reduce her expenditure on one of the goods and attain the same level of utility. Because at the optimal bundle $\overline{U} = \min(q_1, jq_2)$, the Hicksian demands are $q_1 = H_1(p_1, p_2, \overline{U}) = \overline{U}$ and $q_2 = H_2(p_1, p_2, \overline{U}) = \overline{U}/j$. The expenditure function is $E = p_1 q_1 + p_2 q_2 = p_1 \overline{U} + p_2 \overline{U}/j = (p_1 + p_2/j)\overline{U}$.

4.1 The CPI accurately reflects the true cost of living because Alix does not substitute between the goods as the relative prices change.

Chapter 5

1.1 At a price of 30, the quantity demanded is 30, so the consumer surplus is $\frac{1}{2}(30 \times 30) = 450$, because the demand curve is linear.

1.4 Hong and Wolak (2008) estimate that Area A is $215 million and area B is $118 (= 333 - 215)$

million (as you should have shown in your figure in the answer to Exercise 1.3).

a. Given that the demand function is $Q = Xp^{-1.6}$, the revenue function is $R(p) = pQ = Xp^{-0.6}$. Thus, the change in revenue, $-\$215$ million, equals $R(39) - R(37) = X(39)^{-0.6} - X(37)^{-0.6} \approx -0.00356X$. Solving $-0.00356X = -215$, we find that $X \approx 60,353$.

b. We follow the process in Solved Problem 5.1

$$\Delta CS = -\int_{37}^{39} 60,353p^{-1.6}dp_1 = \frac{60,353}{0.6}p^{-0.6}\Big|_{37}^{39}$$
$$\approx 100,588(39^{-0.6} - 37^{-0.6})$$
$$\approx 100,588 \times (-0.00356) \approx -358.$$

This total consumer surplus loss is larger than the one estimated by Hong and Wolak (2008) because they used a different demand function. Given this total consumer surplus loss, area B is $146 (= 358 - 215)$ million.

2.2 Because the good is inferior, the compensated demand curves cut the uncompensated demand curve, D, from below as the figure shows. Consequently, $|CV| = A$, $|\Delta CS| = A + B$, $|EV| = A + B + C$. $|CV| < |\Delta CS| < |EV|$.

For Chapter 5, Exercise 2.2

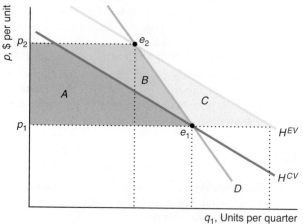

3.4 The two demand curves cross at e_1 in the diagram. The price elasticity of demand, $\varepsilon = (dQ/dp)(p/Q)$, equals 1 over the slope of the demand curve, dp/dQ, times the ratio of the price to the quantity. Thus, at e_1 where both demand curves have the same price, p_1, and the same quantity, Q_1, the steeper the demand curve, the lower the elasticity of demand. If the price rises from p_1 to p_2, the consumer surplus falls from $A + C$ to A with the relatively elastic demand curve (a loss of C) and from $A + B + C + D$ to $A + B$ (a loss of $C + D$) with the relatively inelastic demand curve.

For Chapter 5, Exercise 3.4

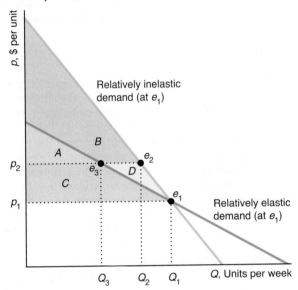

Julia chooses to work eight hours a day and to consume $Y_2 = 8w$ goods, at e_2. (She will not choose to work fewer than eight hours. For her to do so, her indifference curve I^2 would have to be tangent to the downward-sloping section of the new budget constraint. However, such an indifference curve would have to cross the original indifference curve, I^1, which is impossible: see Chapter 3.) Thus, forcing Julia to restrict her hours lowers her utility: I^2 must be below I^1. *Comment*: When I was in college, I was offered a summer job in California. My employer said, "You're lucky you're a male." He claimed that, to protect women (and children) from overwork, an archaic law required him to pay women, but not men, double overtime after eight hours of work. As a result, he offered overtime work only to his male employees. Such clearly discriminatory rules and behavior are now prohibited. Today, however, both females and males must be paid higher overtime wages—typically 1.5 times as much as the usual wage. Consequently, many employers do not let employees work overtime.

For Chapter 5, Problem 5.11

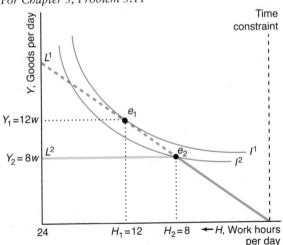

5.8 The proposed tax system exempts an individual's first $10,000 of income. Suppose that a flat 10% rate is charged on the remaining income. Someone who earns $20,000 has an average tax rate of 5%, whereas someone who earns $40,000 has an average tax rate of 7.5%, so this tax system is progressive.

5.10 As the marginal tax rate on income increases, people substitute away from work due to the pure substitution effect. However, the income effect can be either positive or negative, so the net effect of a tax increase is ambiguous. Also, because wage rates differ across countries, the initial level of income differs, again adding to the theoretical ambiguity. If we know that people work less as the marginal tax rate increases, we can infer that the substitution effect and the income effect go in the same direction or that the substitution effect is larger. However, Prescott's (2004) evidence alone about hours worked and marginal tax rates does not allow us to draw such an inference because U.S. and European workers may have different tastes and face different wages.

5.11 The figure shows Julia's original consumer equilibrium: Originally, Julia's budget constraint was a straight line, L^1 with a slope of $-w$, which was tangent to her indifference curve I^1 at e_1, so she worked 12 hours a day and consumed $Y_1 = 12w$ goods. The maximum-hours restriction creates a kink in Julia's new budget constraint, L^2. This constraint is the same as L^1 up to eight hours of work, and is horizontal at $Y = 8w$ for more hours of work. The highest indifference curve that touches this constraint is I^2. Because of the restriction on the hours she can work,

6.2 Parents who do not receive subsidies prefer that poor parents receive lump-sum payments rather than a subsidized hourly rate for child care. If the supply curve for child-care services is upward sloping, by shifting the demand curve farther to the right, the price subsidy raises the price of child-care for these other parents.

6.3 The government could give a smaller lump-sum subsidy that shifts the L^{LS} curve down so that it is parallel to the original curve but tangent to indifference curve I^2. This tangency point is to the left of e_2, so the parents would use fewer hours of child care than with the original lump-sum payment.

Chapter 6

3.1 One worker produces one unit of output, two workers produce two units of output, and n workers produce n units of output. Thus, the total product of labor equals the number of workers: $q = L$. The total product of labor curve is a straight line with a slope of 1. Because we are told that each extra worker produces one more unit of output, we know that the marginal product of labor, dq/dL, is 1. By dividing both sides of the production function, $q = L$, by L, we find that the average product of labor, q/L, is 1.

3.4 (a) Given that the production function is $q = L^{0.75}K^{0.25}$, the average product of labor, holding capital fixed at $\overline{K}$, is $AP_L = q/L = L^{-0.25}\overline{K}^{0.25} = (\overline{K}/L)^{0.25}$. (b) The marginal product of labor is $MP_L = dq/dL = \frac{3}{4}(\overline{K}/L)^{0.25}$. (c) At $\overline{K} = 16$, $AP_L = 2L^{0.25}$ and $MP_L = 1.5L^{0.25}$.

4.4 The isoquant looks like the "right angle" ones in panel b of Figure 6.3 because the firm cannot substitute between discs and machines but must use them in equal proportions: one disc and one hour of machine services.

4.8 Using Equation 6.8, we know that the marginal rate of technical substitution is $MRTS = -MP_L/MP_K = -\frac{2}{3}$.

4.9 The isoquant for $q = 10$ is a straight line that hits the B axis at 10 and the G axis at 20. The marginal product of B is $MP_B = \partial q/\partial B = 1$ everywhere along the isoquant. Similarly, $MP_G = 0.5$. Given that B is on the horizontal axis, $MRTS = -MP_B/MP_G = -1/0.5 = -2$.

5.4 This production function is a Cobb-Douglas production function. Even though it has three inputs instead of two, the same logic applies. Thus, we can calculate the returns to scale as the sum of the exponents: $\gamma = 0.27 + 0.16 + 0.61 = 1.04$. That is, it has (nearly) constant returns to scale. The marginal product of material is

$$\partial q/\partial M = 0.61L^{0.27}K^{0.16}M^{-0.39} = 0.61q/M.$$

6.4 The marginal product of labor of Firm 1 is only 90% of the marginal product of labor of Firm 2 for a particular level of inputs. Using calculus, we find that the MP_L of Firm 1 is $\partial q_1/\partial L = 0.9\,\partial f(L, K)/\partial L = 0.9\,\partial q_2/\partial L$.

7.2 We do not have enough information to answer this question. If we assume that Japanese and American firms have identical production functions and produce using the same ratio of factors during good times, Japanese firms will have a lower average product of labor during recessions because they are less likely to lay off workers. However, it is not clear how Japanese and American firms expand output during good times: Do they hire the same number of extra workers? As a result, we cannot predict which country has the higher average product of labor.

Chapter 7

1.3 If the plane cannot be resold, its purchase price is a sunk cost, which is unaffected by the number of times the plane is flown. Consequently, the average cost per flight falls with the number of flights, but the total cost of owning and operating the plane rises because of extra consumption of gasoline and maintenance. Thus, the more frequently someone has a reason to fly, the more likely that flying one's own plane costs less per flight than a ticket on a commercial airline. However, by making extra ("unnecessary") trips, Mr. Agassi raises his total cost of owning and operating the airplane.

2.5 The total cost of building a 1-cubic-foot crate is $6. It costs four times as much to build an 8-cubic-foot crate, $24. In general, as the height of a cube increases, the total cost of building it rises with the square of the height, but the volume increases with the cube of the height. Thus, the cost per unit of volume falls.

2.12 Because the franchise tax is a lump-sum tax that does not vary with output, the more the firm produces, the less tax it pays per unit, $\mathcal{L}/q$. The firm's after-tax average cost, AC^a, is the sum of its before-tax average cost, AC^b, and its average tax payment per unit, $\mathcal{L}/q$. Because the franchise tax does not vary with output, it does not affect the marginal cost curve. The marginal cost curve crosses both average cost curves from below at their minimum points. The quantity, q_a, at which the after-tax average cost curve reaches its minimum, is larger than the quantity q_b at which the before-tax average cost curve achieves a minimum.

For Chapter 7, Exercise 2.12

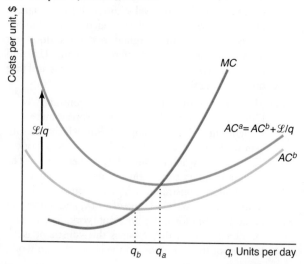

3.1 Let w be the cost of a unit of L and r be the cost of a unit of K. Because the two inputs are perfect substitutes in the production process, the firm uses only the less expensive of the two inputs. Therefore, the long-run cost function is $C(q) = wq$ if $w \le r$; otherwise, it is $C(q) = rq$.

3.2 According to Equation 7.11, if the firm were minimizing its cost, the extra output it gets from the last dollar spent on labor, $MP_L/w = 50/200 = 0.25$, should equal the extra output it derives from the last dollar spent on capital, $MP_K/r = 200/1,000 = 0.2$. Thus, the firm is not minimizing its costs. It would save money if it used relatively less capital and more labor, from which it gets more extra output from the last dollar spent.

3.4 You produce your output, exam points, using as inputs the time spent on Question 1, t_1, and the time spent on Question 2, t_2. If you have diminishing marginal returns to extra time on each problem, your isoquants have the usual shapes: They curve away from the origin. You face a constraint that you may spend no more than 60 minutes on the two questions: $60 = t_1 + t_2$. The slope of the 60-minute isocost curve is -1: For every extra minute you spend on Question 1, you have one less minute to spend on Question 2. To maximize your test score, given that you can spend no more than 60 minutes on the exam, you want to pick the highest isoquant that is tangent to your 60-minute isocost curve. At the tangency, the slope of your isocost curve, -1, equals the slope of your isoquant, $-MP_1/MP_2$. That is, your score on the exam is maximized when $MP_1 = MP_2$, where the last minute spent on Question 1 would increase your score by as much as spending it on Question 2 would. Therefore, you've allocated your time on the exam wisely if you are indifferent as to which question to work on during the last minute of the exam.

3.6 From the information given and assuming that there are no economies of scale in shipping baseballs, it appears that balls are produced using a constant returns to scale, fixed-proportion production function. The corresponding cost function is $C(q) = (w + s + m)q$, where w is the wage for the time period it takes to stitch one ball, s is the cost of shipping one ball, and m is the price of all material to produce one ball. Because the cost of all inputs other than labor and transportation are the same everywhere, the cost difference between Georgia and Costa Rica depends on $w + s$ in both locations. As firms choose to produce in Costa Rica, the extra shipping cost must be less than the labor savings in Costa Rica.

4.2 The average cost of producing one unit is α (regardless of the value of β). If $\beta = 0$, the average cost does not change with volume. If learning by doing

increases with volume, $\beta < 0$, so the average cost falls with volume. Here, the average cost falls exponentially (a smooth curve that asymptotically approaches the quantity axis).

6.1 If $-w/r$ is the same as the slope of the line segment connecting the wafer-handling stepper and the stepper technologies, then the isocost will lie on that line segment, and the firm will be indifferent between using either of the two technologies (or any combination of the two). In all the isocost lines in the figure, the cost of capital is the same, and the wage varies. The wage such that the firm is indifferent lies between the relatively high wage on the C^2 isocost line and the lower wage on the C^3 isocost line.

6.3 The firm chooses its optimal labor-capital ratio using Equation 7.11: $MP_L/w = MP_K/r$. That is, $\frac{1}{2}q/(wL) = \frac{1}{2}q/(rK)$, or $L/K = r/w$. In the United States where $w = r = 10$, the optimal $L/K = 1$, or $L = K$. The firm produces where $q = 100 = L^{0.5}K^{0.5} = K^{0.5}K^{0.5} = K$. Thus, $q = K = L = 100$. The cost is $C = wL + rK = 10 \times 100 + 10 \times 100 = 2,000$. At its Asian plant, the optimal input ratio is $L^*/K^* = 1.1r/(w/1.1) = 11/(10/1.1) = 1.21$. That is, $L^* = 1.21K^*$. Thus, $q = (1.21K^*)^{0.5}(K^*)^{0.5} = 1.1K^*$. So $K^* = 100/1.1$ and $L^* = 110$. The cost is $C^* = [(10/1.1) \times 110] + [11 \times (100/1.1)] = 2,000$. That is, the firm will use a different factor ratio in Asia, but the cost will be the same. If the firm could not substitute toward the less expensive input, its cost in Asia would be $C^{**} = [(10/1.1) \times 100] + [11 \times 100] = 2,009.09$.

Chapter 8

2.3 How much the firm produces and whether it shuts down in the short run depend only on the firm's variable costs. (The firm picks its output level so that its marginal cost—which depends only on variable costs—equals the market price, and it shuts down only if market price is less than its minimum average variable cost.) Learning that the amount spent on the plant was greater than previously believed should not change the output level that the manager chooses. The change in the bookkeeper's valuation of the historical amount spent on the plant may affect the firm's short-run business profit but does not affect the firm's true economic profit. The economic profit is based on opportunity costs—the amount for which the firm could rent the plant to someone else—and not on historical payments.

2.5 The first-order condition to maximize profit is the derivative of the profit function with respect to q set equal to zero: $120 - 40 - 20q = 0$. Thus, profit is maximized where $q = 4$, so that $R(4) = 120 \times 4 = 480$, $VC(4) = (40 \times 4) + (10 \times 16) = 320$, $\pi(4) = R(4) - VC(4) - F = 480 - 320 - 200 = -40$. The firm should operate in the short run because its revenue exceeds its variable cost: $480 > 320$.

3.9 Some farmers did not pick apples so as to avoid incurring the variable cost of harvesting apples. These farmers left open the question of whether they would harvest in the future if the price rose above the shutdown level. Other, more pessimistic farmers did not expect the price to rise anytime soon, so they bulldozed their trees, leaving the market for good. (Most farmers planted alternative apples such as Granny Smith and Gala, which are more popular with the public and sell at a price above the minimum average variable cost.)

3.11 The competitive firm's marginal cost function is found by differentiating its cost function with respect to quantity: $MC(q) = dC(q)/dq = b + 2cq + 3dq^2$. The firm's necessary profit-maximizing condition is $p = MC = b + 2cq + 3dq^2$. We can use the quadratic formula to solve this equation for q for a specific price to determine its profit-maximizing output.

3.13 Suppose that a U-shaped marginal cost curve cuts a competitive firm's demand curve (price line) from above at q_1 and from below at q_2. By increasing output to $q_1 + 1$, the firm earns extra profit because the last unit sells for price p, which is greater than the marginal cost of that last unit. Indeed, the price exceeds the marginal cost of all units between q_1 and q_2, so it is more profitable to produce q_2 than q_1. Thus, the firm should either produce q_2 or shut down (if it is making a loss at q_2). We can derive this result using calculus. The second-order condition for a competitive firm requires that marginal cost cut the demand line from below at q^*, the profit-maximizing quantity: $dMC(q^*)/dq > 0$.

4.2 The shutdown notice reduces the firm's flexibility, which matters in an uncertain market. If conditions suddenly change, the firm may have to operate at a loss for six months before it can shut down. This potential extra expense of shutting down may discourage some firms from entering the market initially.

4.5 To derive the expression for the elasticity of the residual or excess supply curve in Equation 8.17, we differentiate the residual supply curve, Equation 8.16, $S^r(p) = S(p) - D^o(p)$, with respect to p to obtain

$$\frac{dS^r}{dp} = \frac{dS}{dp} - \frac{dD^o}{dp}.$$

Let $Q_r = S^r(p)$, $Q = S(p)$, and $Q_o = D(p)$. We multiply both sides of the differentiated expression by p/Q_r, and for convenience, we also multiply

the second term by $Q/Q = 1$ and the last term by $Q_o/Q_o = 1$:

$$\frac{dS^r}{dp}\frac{p}{Q_r} = \frac{dS}{dp}\frac{p}{Q_r}\frac{Q}{Q} - \frac{dD^o}{dp}\frac{p}{Q_r}\frac{Q_o}{Q_o}.$$

We can rewrite this expression as Equation 8.17 by noting that $\eta_r = (dS^r/dp)(p/Q_r)$ is the residual supply elasticity, $\eta = (dS/dp)(p/Q)$ is the market supply elasticity, $\varepsilon_o = (dD^o/dp)(p/Q_o)$ is the demand elasticity of the other countries, and $\theta = Q_r/Q$ is the residual country's share of the world's output (hence $1 - \theta = Q_o/Q$ is the share of the rest of the world). If there are n countries with equal outputs, then $1/\theta = n$, so this equation can be rewritten as $\eta_r = n\eta - (n - 1)\varepsilon_o$.

4.6 a. The incidence of the federal specific tax is shared equally between consumers and firms, whereas firms bear virtually none of the incidence of the state tax (they pass the tax on to consumers).

b. From Chapter 2, we know that the incidence of a tax that falls on consumers in a competitive market is approximately $\eta/(\eta - \varepsilon)$. Although the national elasticity of supply may be a relatively small number, the residual supply elasticity facing a particular state is very large. Using the analysis about residual supply curves, we can infer that the supply curve to a particular state is likely to be nearly horizontal—nearly perfectly elastic. For example, if the price in Maine rises even slightly relative to the price in Vermont, suppliers in Vermont will be willing to shift their entire supply to Maine. Thus, we expect the nearly full incidence to fall on consumers from a state tax but less from a federal tax, consistent with the empirical evidence.

c. If all 50 states were identical, we could write the residual elasticity of supply, Equation 8.17, as $\eta_r = 50\eta - 49\varepsilon_o$. Given this equation, the residual supply elasticity to one state is at least 50 times larger than the national elasticity of supply, $\eta_r \geq 50\eta$, because $\varepsilon_o < 0$, so the $-49\varepsilon_o$ term is positive and increases the residual supply elasticity.

5.5 Because the clinics are operating at minimum average cost, a lump-sum tax that causes the minimum average cost to rise by 10% would cause the market price of abortions to rise by 10%. Based on the estimated price elasticity of between -0.70 and -0.99, the number of abortions would fall to between 7% and 10%. A lump-sum tax shifts upward the average cost curve but does not affect the marginal cost curve. Consequently, the market supply curve, which is horizontal and the minimum of the average cost curve, shifts up in parallel.

5.6 Each competitive firm wants to choose its output q to maximize its after-tax profit: $\pi = pq - C(q) - \mathcal{L}$.

Its necessary condition to maximize profit is that price equals marginal cost: $p - dC(q)/dq = 0$. Industry supply is determined by entry, which occurs until profits are driven to zero (we ignore the problem of fractional firms and treat the number of firms, n, as a continuous variable): $pq - [C(q) + \mathcal{L}] = 0$. In equilibrium, each firm produces the same output, q, so market output is $Q = nq$, and the market inverse demand function is $p = p(Q) = p(nq)$. By substituting the market inverse demand function into the necessary and sufficient condition, we determine the market equilibrium (n^*, q^*) by the two conditions:

$$p(n^*q^*) - dC(q^*)/dq = 0,$$
$$p(n^*q^*)q^* - [C(q^*) + \mathcal{L}] = 0.$$

For notational simplicity, we henceforth leave off the asterisks. To determine how the equilibrium is affected by an increase in the lump-sum tax, we evaluate the comparative statics at $\mathcal{L} = 0$. We totally differentiate our two equilibrium equations with respect to the two endogenous variables, n and q, and the exogenous variable, $\mathcal{L}$:

$$dq(n[dp(nq)/dQ] - d^2C(q)/dq^2)$$
$$+ dn(q[dp(nq)/dQ]) + d\mathcal{L}(0) = 0,$$
$$dq(n[qdp(nq)/dQ] + p(nq) - dC/dq)$$
$$+ dn(q^2[dp(nq)/dQ]) - d\mathcal{L} = 0.$$

We can write these equations in matrix form (noting that $p - dC/dq = 0$ from the necessary condition) as

$$\begin{vmatrix} n\dfrac{dp}{dQ} - \dfrac{d^2C}{dq^2} & q\dfrac{dp}{dQ} \\ nq\dfrac{dp}{dQ} & q^2\dfrac{dp}{dQ} \end{vmatrix} \begin{bmatrix} dq \\ dn \end{bmatrix} = \begin{bmatrix} 0 \\ 1 \end{bmatrix} d\mathcal{L}.$$

There are several ways to solve these equations. One is to use Cramer's rule. Define

$$D = \begin{vmatrix} n\dfrac{dp}{dQ} - \dfrac{d^2C}{dq^2} & q\dfrac{dp}{dQ} \\ nq\dfrac{dp}{dQ} & q^2\dfrac{dp}{dQ} \end{vmatrix}$$

$$= \left(n\dfrac{dp}{dQ} - \dfrac{d^2C}{dq^2}\right)q^2\dfrac{dp}{dQ} - q\dfrac{dp}{dQ}\left(nq\dfrac{dp}{dQ}\right)$$

$$= -\dfrac{d^2C}{dq^2}q^2\dfrac{dp}{dQ} > 0,$$

where the inequality follows from each firm's sufficient condition. Using Cramer's rule:

$$\dfrac{dq}{d\mathcal{L}} = \dfrac{\begin{vmatrix} 0 & q\dfrac{dp}{dQ} \\ 1 & q^2\dfrac{dp}{dQ} \end{vmatrix}}{D} = \dfrac{-q\dfrac{dp}{dQ}}{D} > 0,$$

$$\dfrac{dn}{d\mathcal{L}} = \dfrac{\begin{vmatrix} n\dfrac{dp}{dQ} - \dfrac{d^2C}{dq^2} & 0 \\ nq\dfrac{dp}{dQ} & 1 \end{vmatrix}}{D} = \dfrac{n\dfrac{dp}{dQ} - \dfrac{d^2C}{dq^2}}{D} < 0.$$

The change in price is

$$\dfrac{dp(nq)}{d\mathcal{L}} = \dfrac{dp}{dQ}\left[q\dfrac{dn}{dl} + n\dfrac{dq}{dl}\right]$$

$$= \dfrac{dp}{dQ}\left[\dfrac{\left(n\dfrac{dp}{dQ} - \dfrac{d^2C}{dq^2}\right)q}{D} - \dfrac{nq\dfrac{dp}{dQ}}{D}\right]$$

$$= \dfrac{dp}{dQ}\left(\dfrac{-\dfrac{d^2C}{dq^2}q}{D}\right) > 0.$$

Chapter 9

5.5 The specific subsidy shifts the supply curve, S in the figure, down by $s = 11¢$, to the curve labeled $S - 11¢$. Consequently, the equilibrium shifts from e_1 to e_2, so the quantity sold increases (from 1.25 to 1.34 billion rose stems per year), the price that consumers pay falls (from 30¢ to 28¢ per stem), and the amount that suppliers receive, including the subsidy, rises (from 30¢ to 39¢), so that the differential between what the consumers pay and what the producers receive is 11¢. Consumers and producers of roses are delighted to be subsidized by other members of society. Because the price to customers drops, consumer surplus rises from $A + B$ to $A + B + D + E$. Because firms receive more per stem after the subsidy, producer surplus rises from $D + G$ to $B + C + D + G$ (the area under the price they receive and above the original supply curve). Because the government pays a subsidy of 11¢ per stem for each stem sold, the government's expenditures go from zero to the rectangle $B + C + D + E + F$. Thus, the new welfare is the sum of the new consumer surplus and producer surplus minus the government's expenses. Welfare falls from $A + B + D + G$ to $A + B + D + G - F$. The deadweight loss, this drop in welfare $\Delta W = -F$, results from producing too much: The marginal cost to producers of the last stem, 39¢, exceeds the marginal benefit to consumers, 28¢.

5.7 If the tax is based on *economic* profit, the tax has no long-run effect because the firms make zero economic profit. If the tax is based on *business* profit

For Chapter 9, Problem 5.5

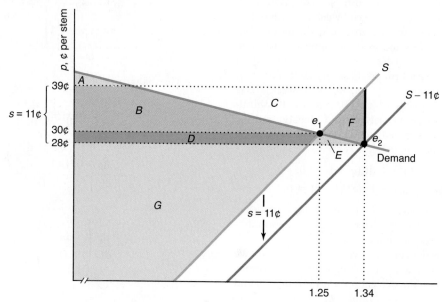

and business profit is greater than economic profit, the profit tax raises firms' after-tax costs and results in fewer firms in the market. The exact effect of the tax depends on why business profit is less than economic profit. For example, if the government ignores opportunity labor cost but includes all capital cost in computing profit, firms will substitute toward labor and away from capital.

5.8 The Challenge Solution in Chapter 8 shows the long-run effect of a lump-sum tax in a competitive market. Consumer surplus falls by more than tax revenue increases, and producer surplus remains zero, so welfare falls.

5.10 a. The initial equilibrium is determined by equating the quantity demanded to the quantity supplied: $100 - 10p = 10p$. That is, the equilibrium is $p = 5$ and $Q = 50$. At the support price, the quantity supplied is $Q_s = 60$. The market clearing price was $p = 4$. The deficiency payment was $D = (p - p)Q_s = (6 - 4)60 = 120$.

   b. Consumer surplus rises from $CS_1 = \frac{1}{2}(10 - 5)$ $50 = 125$ to $CS_2 = \frac{1}{2}(10 - 4)60 = 180$. Producer surplus rises from $PS_1 = \frac{1}{2}(5 - 0)50 = 125$ to $PS_2 = \frac{1}{2} \times (6 - 0)60 = 180$. Welfare falls from $CS_1 + PS_1 = 125 + 125 = 250$ to $CS_2 + PS_2 - D = 180 + 180 - 120 = 240$. Thus, the deadweight loss is 10.

6.5 Without the tariff, the U.S. supply curve of oil is horizontal at a price of \$14.70 (S^1 in Figure 9.9), and the equilibrium is determined by the intersection of this horizontal supply curve with the demand curve. With a new, small tariff of τ, the U.S. supply curve is horizontal at \$14.70 + τ, and the new equilibrium quantity is determined by substituting $p = 14.70 + \tau$ into the demand function: $Q = 35.41(14.70 + \tau)p^{-0.37}$. Evaluated at $\tau = 0$, the equilibrium quantity remains at 13.1. The deadweight loss is the area to the right of the domestic supply curve and to the left of the demand curve between \$14.70 and \$14.70 + τ (area $C + D + E$ in Figure 9.9) minus the tariff revenues (area D):

$$DWL = \int_{14.70}^{14.70+\tau} [D(p) - S(p)]dp - \tau[D(p + \tau) - S(p + \tau)]$$

$$= \int_{14.70}^{14.70+\tau} [3.54p^{-0.67} - 3.35p^{0.33}]dp$$

$$-\tau[3.54(p + \tau)^{-0.67} - 3.35(p + \tau)^{0.33}].$$

To see how a change in τ affects welfare, we differentiate DWL with respect to τ:

$$\frac{dDWL}{d\tau} = \frac{d}{d\tau}\left\{ \int_{14.70}^{14.70+\tau} [D(p) - S(p)]dp \right.$$

$$\left. - \tau[D(14.70 + \tau) - S(14.70 + \tau)] \right\}$$

$$= [D(14.70 + \tau) - S(14.70 + \tau)] - [D(14.70 + \tau)$$

$$-S(14.70 + \tau)] - \tau\left[\frac{dD(14.70 + \tau)}{d\tau} - \frac{dS(14.70 + \tau)}{d\tau}\right]$$

$$= -\tau\left[\frac{dD(14.70 + \tau)}{d\tau} - \frac{dS(14.70 + \tau)}{d\tau}\right].$$

If we evaluate this expression at $\tau = 0$, we find that $dDWL/d\tau = 0$. In short, applying a small tariff to the free-trade equilibrium has a negligible effect on quantity and deadweight loss. Only if the tariff is larger—as in Figure 9.9—do we see a measurable effect.

Chapter 10

1.7 A subsidy is a negative tax. Thus, we can use the same analysis that we used in Solved Problem 10.1 to answer this question by reversing the signs of the effects.

4.1 If you draw the convex production possibility frontier on Figure 10.5, you will see that it lies strictly inside the concave production possibility frontier. Thus, more output can be obtained if Jane and Denise use the concave frontier. That is, each should specialize in producing the good for which she has a comparative advantage.

4.2 As Chapter 4 shows, the slope of the budget constraint facing an individual equals the negative of that person's wage. Panel a of the figure illustrates that Pat's budget constraint is steeper than Chris's because Pat's wage is larger than Chris's. Panel b shows their combined budget constraint after they marry. Before they marry, each spends some time in the marketplace earning money and other time at home cooking, cleaning, and consuming leisure. After they marry, one of them can specialize in earning money and the other at working at home. If they are both equally skilled at household work (or if Chris is better), then Pat has a comparative advantage (see Figure 10.5) in working in the marketplace, and Chris has a comparative advantage in working at home. Of course, if both enjoy consuming leisure, they may not fully specialize. As an example, suppose that, before they got married, Chris and Pat each spent 10 hours a day in sleep and leisure activities, 5 hours working in the marketplace, and 9 hours working at home. Because Chris earns $10 an hour and Pat earns $20 an hour, they collectively earned $150 a day and worked 18 hours a day at home. After they marry, they can benefit from specialization. If Chris works entirely at home and Pat works 10 hours in the marketplace and the rest at home, they collectively earn $200 a day (a one-third increase) and still have 18 hours of work at home. If they do not need to spend as much time working at home because of economies of scale, one or both could work more hours in the marketplace, and they will have even greater disposable income.

Chapter 11

1.4 For a general linear inverse demand function, $p(Q) = a - bQ$, $dQ/dp = -1/b$, so the elasticity is $\varepsilon = -p/(bQ)$. The demand curve hits the horizontal (quantity) axis at a/b. At half that quantity (the midpoint of the demand curve), the quantity is $a/(2b)$, and the price is $a/2$. Thus, the elasticity of demand is $\varepsilon = -p/(bQ) = -(a/2)/[ab/(2b)] = -1$ at the midpoint of any linear demand curve. As the chapter shows, a monopoly will not operate in the inelastic section of its demand curve, so a monopoly will not operate in the right half of its linear demand curve.

2.2 Amazon's Lerner Index was $(p - MC)/p = (359 - 159)/359 \approx 0.557$. Using Equation 11.11, we know that $(p - MC)/p \approx 0.557 = -1/\varepsilon$, so $\varepsilon \approx -1.795$.

For Chapter 10, Exercise 4.2

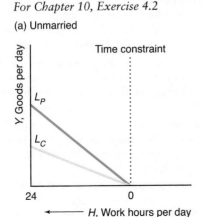

(a) Unmarried

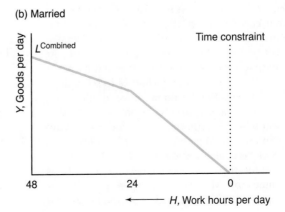

(b) Married

2.4 Given that Apple's marginal cost was constant, its average variable cost equaled its marginal cost, $200. Its average fixed cost was its fixed cost divided by the quantity produced, $736/Q$. Thus, its average cost was $AC = 200 + 736/Q$. Because the inverse demand function was $p = 600 - 25Q$, Apple's revenue function was $R = 600Q - 25Q^2$, so $MR = dR/dQ = 600 - 50Q$. Apple maximized its profit where $MR = 600 - 50Q = 200 = MC$. Solving this equation for the profit-maximizing output, we find that $Q = 8$ million units. By substituting this quantity into the inverse demand equation, we determine that the profit-maximizing price was $p = \$400$ per unit, as the figure shows. The firm's profit was $\pi = (p - AC)Q = [400 - (200 + 736/8)]8 = \$864$ million. Apple's Lerner Index was $(p - MC)/p = [400 - 200]/400 = \frac{1}{2}$. According to Equation 11.11, a profit-maximizing monopoly operates where $(p - MC)/p = -1/\varepsilon$. Combining that equation with the Lerner Index from the previous step, we learn that $\frac{1}{2} = -1/\varepsilon$, or $\varepsilon = -2$.

3.4 A tax on economic profit (of less than 100%) has no effect on a firm's profit-maximizing behavior. Suppose the government's share of the profit is β. Then the firm wants to maximize its after-tax profit, which is $(1 - \gamma)\pi$. However, whatever choice of Q (or p) maximizes π will also maximize $(1 - \gamma)\pi$. Figure 19.3 gives a graphical example where $\gamma = \frac{1}{3}$. Consequently, the tribe's behavior is unaffected by a change in the share that the government receives. We can also answer this problem using calculus. The before-tax profit is $\pi_B = R(Q) - C(Q)$, and the after-tax profit is $\pi_A = (1 - \gamma)[R(Q) - C(Q)]$. For both, the first-order condition is marginal revenue equals marginal cost: $dR(Q)/dQ = dC(Q)/dQ$.

4.1 Yes. The demand curve could cut the average cost curve only in its downward-sloping section. Consequently, the average cost is strictly downward sloping in the relevant region.

6.1 Given the demand curve is $p = 10 - Q$, its marginal revenue curve is $MR = 10 - 2Q$. Thus, the output that maximizes the monopoly's profit is determined by $MR = 10 - 2Q = 2 = MC$, or $Q^* = 4$. At that output level, its price is $p^* = 6$ and its profit is $\pi^* = 16$. If the monopoly chooses to sell 8 units in the first period (it has no incentive to sell more), its price is $2 and it makes no profit. Given that the firm sells 8 units in the first period, its demand curve in the second period is $p = 10 - Q/\beta$, so its marginal revenue function is $MR = 10 - 2Q/\beta$. The output that leads to its maximum profit is determined by $MR = 10 - 2Q/\beta = 2 = MC$, or its output is 4β. Thus, its price is $6 and its profit is

16β. It pays for the firm to set a low price in the first period if the lost profit, 16, is less than the extra profit in the second period, which is $16(\beta - 1)$. Thus, it pays to set a low price in the first period if $16 < 16(\beta - 1)$, or $2 < \beta$.

7.6 If a firm has a monopoly in the output market and is a monopsony in the labor market, its profit is $\pi = p(Q(L))Q(L) - w(L)L$, where $Q(L)$ is the production function, $p(Q)Q$ is its revenue, and $w(L)L$—the wage times the number of workers—is its cost of production. The firm maximizes its profit by setting the derivative of profit with respect to labor equal to zero (if the second-order condition holds):

$$\left(p + Q(L)\frac{dp}{dQ}\right)\frac{dQ}{dL} - w(L) - \frac{dw}{dL}L = 0.$$

Rearranging terms in the first-order condition, we find that the maximization condition is that the marginal revenue product of labor,

$$MRP_L = MR \times MPL = \left(p + Q(L)\frac{dp}{dQ}\right)\frac{dQ}{dL}$$
$$= p\left(1 + \frac{1}{\varepsilon}\right)\frac{dQ}{dL},$$

equals the marginal expenditure,

$$ME = w(L) + \frac{dw}{dL}L = w(L)\left(1 + \frac{L}{w}\frac{dw}{dL}\right)$$
$$= w(L)\left(1 + \frac{1}{\eta}\right),$$

where ε is the elasticity of demand in the output market and η is the supply elasticity of labor.

Chapter 12

1.3 This policy allows the firm to maximize its profit by price discriminating if people who put a lower value on their time (so are willing to drive to the store and transport their purchases themselves) have a higher elasticity of demand than people who want to order by phone and have the goods delivered.

1.4 The colleges may be providing scholarships as a form of charity, or they may be price discriminating by lowering the final price for less wealthy families (who presumably have higher elasticities of demand).

3.5 See MyEconLab, Chapter Resources, Chapter 12, "Aibo," for more details. The two marginal revenue curves are $MR_J = 3,500 - Q_J$ and $MR_A = 4,500 - 2Q_A$. Equating the marginal revenues with the marginal cost of $500, we find that $Q_J = 3,000$ and $Q_A = 2,000$. Substituting these quantities into the inverse demand curves, we learn that $p_J = \$2,000$ and $p_A = \$2,500$. As the chapter shows, the elasticities of demand are $\varepsilon_J = p/(MC - p) = 2,000/(500 - 2,000) = -\frac{4}{3}$ and $\varepsilon_A = 2,500/(500 - 2,500) = -\frac{5}{4}$. Using Equation 12.9, we find that

$$\frac{p_J}{p_A} = \frac{2,000}{2,500} = 0.8 = \frac{1 + 1/\left(-\frac{5}{4}\right)}{1 + 1/\left(-\frac{4}{3}\right)} = \frac{1 + 1/\varepsilon_A}{1 + 1/\varepsilon_J}.$$

The profit in Japan is $(p_J - m)Q_J = (\$2,000 - \$500) \times 3,000 = \$4.5$ million, and the U.S. profit is \$4 million. The deadweight loss is greater in Japan, \$2.25 million $\left(= \frac{1}{2} \times \$1,500 \times 3,000 \right)$, than in the United States, \$2 million $\left(= \frac{1}{2} \times \$2,000 \times 2,000 \right)$.

3.6 By differentiating, we find that the American marginal revenue function is $MR_A = 100 - 2Q_A$, and the Japanese one is $MR_J = 80 - 4Q_J$. To determine how many units to sell in the United States, the monopoly sets its American marginal revenue equal to its marginal cost, $MR_A = 100 - 2Q_A = 20$, and solves for the optimal quantity, $Q_A = 40$ units. Similarly, because $MR_J = 80 - 4Q_J = 20$, the optimal quantity is $Q_J = 15$ units in Japan. Substituting $Q_A = 40$ into the American demand function, we find that $p_A = 100 - 40 = \$60$. Similarly, substituting $Q_J = 15$ units into the Japanese demand function, we learn that $p_J = 80 - (2 \times 15) = \$50$. Thus, the price-discriminating monopoly charges 20% more in the United States than in Japan. We can also show this result using elasticities. Because $dQ_A/dp_A = -1$ the elasticity of demand is $\varepsilon_A = -p_A/Q_A$ in the United States and $\varepsilon_J = -\frac{1}{2}p_J/Q_J$ in Japan. In the equilibrium, $\varepsilon_A = -60/40 = -3/2$ and $\varepsilon_J = -50/(2 \times 15) = -5/3$. As Equation 12.9 shows, the ratio of the prices depends on the relative elasticities of demand: $p_A/p_J = 60/50 = (1 + 1/\varepsilon_J)/(1 + 1/\varepsilon_A) = (1 - 3/5)/(1 - 2/3) = 6/5$.

3.8 From the problem, we know that the profit-maximizing Chinese price is $p = 3$ and that the quantity is $Q = 0.1$ (million). The marginal cost is $m = 1$. Using Equation 11.11, $(p_C - m)/p_C = (3 - 1)/3 = -1/\varepsilon_C$, so $\varepsilon_C = -3/2$. If the Chinese inverse demand curve is $p = a - bQ$, then the corresponding marginal revenue curve is $MR = a - 2bQ$. Warner maximizes its profit where $MR = a - 2bQ = m = 1$, so its optimal $Q = (a - 1)/(2b)$. Substituting this expression into the inverse demand curve, we find that its optimal $p = (a + 1)/2 = 3$, or $a = 5$. Substituting that result into the output equation, we have $Q = (5 - 1)/(2b) = 0.1$ (million). Thus, $b = 20$, the inverse demand function is $p = 5 - 20Q$, and the marginal revenue function is $MR = 5 - 40Q$. Using this information, you can draw a figure similar to Figure 12.3.

3.11 If a monopoly manufacturer can price discriminate, its price is $p_i = m/(1 + 1/\varepsilon_i)$ in Country i, $i = 1, 2$. If the monopoly cannot price discriminate, it charges everyone the same price. Its total demand is $Q = Q_1 + Q_2 = n_1 p^{\varepsilon_1} + n_2 p^{\varepsilon_2}$. Differentiating with respect to p, we obtain $dQ/dp = \varepsilon_1 Q_1/p + \varepsilon_2 Q_2/p$. Multiplying through by p/Q, we learn that the weighted sum of the two groups' elasticities is $\varepsilon = s_1\varepsilon_1 + s_2\varepsilon_2$, where $s_i = Q_i/Q$. Thus, a profit-maximizing, single-price monopoly charges $\underline{p} = m/(1 + 1/\varepsilon)$.

Chapter 13

1.1 The payoff matrix in this prisoners' dilemma game is

		Duncan	
		Squeal	Silent
Larry	Squeal	-2 / -2	-5 / 0
	Silent	0 / -5	-1 / -1

If Duncan stays silent, Larry gets 0 if he squeals and -1 (a year in jail) if he stays silent. If Duncan confesses, Larry gets -2 if he squeals and -5 if he does not. Thus, Larry is better off squealing in either case, so squealing is his dominant strategy. By the same reasoning, squealing is also Duncan's dominant strategy. As a result, the Nash equilibrium is for both to confess.

1.3 No strategies are dominant, so we use the best-response approach to determine the pure-strategy Nash equilibria. First, identify each firm's best responses given each of the other firms' strategies (as we did in Solved Problem 13.1). This game has two Nash equilibria: (a) Firm 1 medium and Firm 2 low, and (b) Firm 1 low and Firm 2 medium.

1.8 Let the probability that a firm sets a low price be θ_1 for Firm 1 and θ_2 for Firm 2. If the firms choose their prices independently, then $\theta_1\theta_2$ is the probability that both set a low price, $(1 - \theta_1)(1 - \theta_2)$ is the probability that both set a high price, $\theta_1(1 - \theta_2)$ is the probability that Firm 1 prices low and Firm 2 prices high, and $(1 - \theta_1)\theta_2$ is the probability that Firm 1 prices high and Firm 2 prices low. Firm 2's expected payoff is $E(\pi_2) = 2\theta_1\theta_2 + (0)\theta_1(1 - \theta_2) + (1 - \theta_1)\theta_2 + 6(1 - \theta_1)(1 - \theta_2) = (6 - 6\theta_1) - (5 - 7\theta_1)\theta_2$. Similarly, Firm 1's expected payoff is $E(\pi_1) = (0)\theta_1\theta_2 + 7\theta_1(1 - \theta_2) + 2(1 - \theta_1)\theta_2 + 6(1 - \theta_1)(1 - \theta_2) = (6 - 4\theta_2) - (1 - 3\theta_2)\theta_1$. Each firm forms a belief about its rival's behavior. For example, suppose that Firm 1 believes that Firm 2 will choose a low price with a probability $\hat{\theta}_2$. If $\hat{\theta}_2$ is less than $\frac{1}{3}$ (Firm 2 is relatively unlikely to choose a low price), it pays for Firm 1 to choose the low price because the second term in $E(\pi_1)$, $(1 - 3\hat{\theta}_2)\theta_1$, is positive, so as θ_1 increases, $E(\pi_1)$ increases. Because the highest possible θ_1 is 1, Firm 1 chooses the low price with certainty. Similarly, if Firm 1 believes $\hat{\theta}_2$ is greater than $\frac{1}{3}$, it sets a high price with certainty ($\theta_1 = 0$). If Firm 2 believes that Firm 1 thinks $\hat{\theta}_2$ is slightly below $\frac{1}{3}$, Firm 2 believes that Firm 1 will choose a low price with certainty, and hence Firm 2 will also choose a low price. That outcome, $\theta_2 = 1$, however, is not consistent with Firm 1's expectation that $\hat{\theta}_2$ is a fraction. Indeed, it is only rational for Firm 2 to believe that Firm 1 believes Firm 2 will use a mixed strategy if Firm 1's belief about Firm 2 makes Firm 1 unpredictable. That is, Firm 1 uses a mixed strategy only if it is *indifferent* between setting a high or a low price. It is indifferent only if it believes $\hat{\theta}_2$ is exactly $\frac{1}{3}$. By similar reasoning, Firm 2 will use a mixed strategy only if its belief is that Firm 1 chooses a low price with probability $\hat{\theta}_1 = \frac{5}{7}$. Thus, the only possible Nash equilibrium is $\theta_2 = \frac{5}{7}$ and $\theta_2 = \frac{1}{3}$

1.9 We start by checking for dominant strategies. Given the payoff matrix, Toyota always does at least as well by entering the market. If GM enters, Toyota earns 10 by entering and 0 by staying out of the market. If GM does not enter, Toyota earns 250 if it enters and 0 otherwise. Thus, entering is Toyota's dominant strategy. GM does not have a dominant strategy. It wants to enter if Toyota does not enter (earning 200 rather than 0), and it wants to stay out if Toyota enters (earning 0 rather than −40). Because GM knows that Toyota will enter (entering is Toyota's dominant strategy), GM stays out. Toyota's entering and GM's not entering is a Nash equilibrium. Given the other firm's strategy, neither firm wants to change its strategy. Next, we examine how the subsidy affects the payoff matrix and

dominant strategies. The subsidy does not affect Toyota's payoff, so Toyota still has a dominant strategy: It enters the market. With the subsidy, GM's payoff if it enters increases by 50: GM earns 10 if both enter and 250 if it enters and Toyota does not. With the subsidy, entering is a dominant strategy for GM. Thus, both firms' entering is a Nash equilibrium.

2.3 If the airline game is known to end in five periods, the equilibrium is the same as the one-period equilibrium. If the game is played indefinitely but one or both firms care only about current profit, then the equilibrium is the one-period one because future punishments and rewards are irrelevant to it.

2.9 The game tree illustrates why the incumbent may install the robotic arms to discourage entry even though its total cost rises. If the incumbent fears that a rival is poised to enter, it invests to discourage entry. The incumbent can invest in equipment that lowers its marginal cost. With the lowered marginal cost, it is credible that the incumbent will produce larger quantities of output, which discourages entry. The incumbent's monopoly (no-entry) profit drops from $900 to $500 if it makes the investment because the investment raises its total cost. If the incumbent doesn't buy the robotic arms, the rival enters because it makes $300 by entering and nothing if it stays out of the market. With entry, the incumbent's profit is $400. With the investment, the rival loses $36 if it enters, so it stays out of the market, losing nothing. (If the rival were to enter, the incumbent would earn $132.) Because of the investment, the incumbent earns $500. Nonetheless, earning $500 is better than earning $400, so the incumbent invests.

2.10 The incumbent firm has a *first-mover advantage*, as the game tree illustrates. Moving first allows the incumbent or leader firm to *commit* to producing a relatively large quantity. If the incumbent does not make a commitment before its rival enters, entry occurs and the incumbent earns a relatively low

For Chapter 13, Exercise 2.9

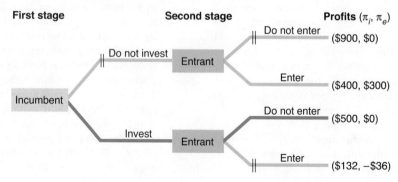

For Chapter 13, Exercise 2.10

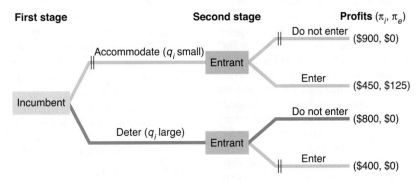

For Chapter 13, Exercise 2.11

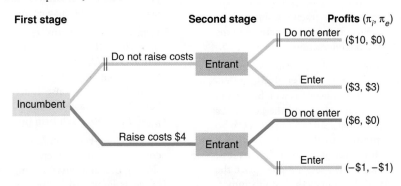

profit. By committing to produce such a large output level that the potential entrant decides not to enter because it cannot make a positive profit, the incumbent's commitment discourages entry. Moving backward in time (moving to the left in the diagram), we examine the incumbent's choice. If the incumbent commits to the small quantity, its rival enters and the incumbent earns $450. If the incumbent commits to the larger quantity, its rival does not enter and the incumbent earns $800. Clearly, the incumbent should commit to the larger quantity because it earns a larger profit and the potential entrant chooses to stay out of the market. Their chosen paths are identified by the darker blue in the figure.

2.11 It is worth more to the monopoly to keep the potential entrant out than it is worth to the potential entrant to enter, as the figure shows. Before the pollution-control device requirement, the entrant would pay up to $3 to enter, whereas the incumbent would pay up to $\pi_i - \pi_d = \$7$ to exclude the potential entrant. The incumbent's profit is $6 if entry does not occur, and its loss is $1 if entry occurs. Because the new firm would lose $1 if it enters, it does not enter. Thus, the incumbent has an incentive to raise costs by $4 to both firms. The incumbent's profit is $6 if it raises costs rather than $3 if it does not.

Chapter 14

3.1 The inverse demand curve is $p = 1 - 0.001Q$. The first firm's profit is $\pi_1 = [1 - 0.001(q_1 + q_2)]q_1 - 0.28q_1$. Its first-order condition is $d\pi_1/dq_1 = 1 - 0.001(2q_1 + q_2) - 0.28 = 0$. If we rearrange the terms, the first firm's best-response function is $q_1 = 360 - \frac{1}{2}q_2$. Similarly, the second firm's best-response function is $q_2 = 360 - \frac{1}{2}q_1$ By substituting one of these best-response functions into the other, we learn that the Nash-Cournot equilibrium occurs at $q_1 = q_2 = 240$, so the equilibrium price is 52¢.

3.5 Given that the firm's after-tax marginal cost is $m + \tau$, the Nash-Cournot equilibrium price is

$$p = (a + n[m + \tau])/(n + 1),$$

using Equation 14.17. Thus, the consumer incidence of the tax is $dp/d\tau = n/(n + 1) < 1 (= 100\%)$.

3.6 The monopoly will make more profit than the duopoly will, so the monopoly is willing to pay the college more rent. Although granting monopoly rights may be attractive to the college in terms of higher rent, students will suffer (lose consumer surplus) because of the higher textbook prices.

3.11 One approach is to show that a rise in marginal cost or a fall in the number of firms tends to cause the price to rise. The Challenge Solution shows the effect of a decrease in marginal cost due to a subsidy (the opposite effect). The section titled "The Cournot Equilibrium with Many Firms" shows that a decrease in the number of firms causes market power (the markup of price over marginal cost) to increase. The two effects reinforce each other. Suppose that the market demand curve has a constant elasticity of ε. We can rewrite Equation 14.10 as $p = m/[1 + 1/(n\varepsilon)] = m\mu$, where $\mu = 1/[1 + 1/(n\varepsilon)]$ is the markup factor. Suppose that marginal cost increases to $(1 + a)m$ and that the drop in the number of firms causes the markup factor to rise to $(1 + b)\mu$; then the change in price is $[(1 + a)m \times (1 + b)\mu] - m\mu = (a + b + ab)m\mu$. That is, price increases by the fractional increase in the marginal cost, a, plus the fractional increase in the markup factor, b, plus the interaction of the two, ab.

3.12 By differentiating its product, a firm makes the residual demand curve it faces less elastic everywhere. For example, no consumer will buy from that firm if its rival charges less and the goods are homogeneous. In contrast, some consumers who prefer this firm's product to that of its rival will still buy from this firm even if its rival charges less. As the chapter shows, a firm sets a higher price the lower the elasticity of demand at the equilibrium.

3.17 You can solve this problem using calculus or the formulas in Solved Problem 14.1.
 a. Using Equations 14.21 and 14.22 for the duopoly, $q_1 = (15 - 1 + 1)/3 = 5$, $q_2 = (15 - 1 - 2)/3 = 4$, $p_d = 6$, $\pi_1 = (6 - 1)5 = 25$, $\pi_2 = (6 - 2)4 = 16$. Total output is $Q_d = 5 + 4 = 9$. Total profit is $\pi_d = 25 + 16 = 41$. Consumer surplus is $CS_d = \frac{1}{2}(15 - 6)9 = 81/2 = 40.5$. At the efficient price (equal to marginal cost of 1), the output is 14. The deadweight loss is $DWL_d = \frac{1}{2}(6 - 1)(14 - 9) = 25/2 = 12.5$.
 b. The monopoly equates its marginal revenue and (its lowest) marginal cost: $MR = 15 - 2Q_m = 1 = MC$. Thus, $Q_m = 7$, $p_m = 8$, $\pi_m = (8 - 1)7 = 49$. Consumer surplus is $CS_m = \frac{1}{2}(15 - 8)7 = 49/2 = 24.5$. The deadweight loss is $DWL_m = \frac{1}{2}(8 - 1)(14 - 7) = 49/2 = 24.5$.
 c. The average cost of production for the duopoly is $[(5 \times 1) + (4 \times 2)]/(5 + 4) = 1.44$, whereas the average cost of production for the monopoly is 1. The increase in market power effect swamps the efficiency gain, so consumer surplus falls while deadweight loss nearly doubles.

3.19 a. The Nash-Cournot equilibrium in the absence of government intervention is $q_1 = 30$, $q_2 = 40$, $p = 50$, $\pi_1 = 900$, and $\pi_2 = 1,600$.

 b. The Nash-Cournot equilibrium is now $q_1 = 33.3$, $q_2 = 33.3$, $p = 53.3$, $\pi_1 = 1,108.9$, and $\pi_2 = 1,108.9$.
 c. Because Firm 2's profit was 1,600 in part a, a fixed cost slightly greater than 1,600 will prevent entry.

4.1 a. Using Equation 14.16, the Nash-Cournot equilibrium quantity is $q_i = (a - m)/(nb) = (150 - 60)/3 = 30$, so $Q = 60$, and $p = 90$.
 b. In the Stackelberg equilibrium (Equations 14.31 and 14.32) if Firm 1 moves first, then $q_1 = (a - m)/(2b) = (150 - 60)/2 = 45$, $q_2 = (a - m)/(4b) = (150 - 60)/4 = 22.5$, $Q = 67.5$, and $p = 82.5$.

5.2 Given that the duopolies produce identical goods, the equilibrium price is lower if the duopolies set price rather than quantity. If the goods are heterogeneous, we cannot answer this question definitively.

5.3 Firm 1 wants to maximize its profit: $\pi_1 = (p_1 - 10) q_1 = (p_1 - 10)(100 - 2p_1 + p_2)$. Its first-order condition is $d\pi_1/dp_1 = 100 - 4p_1 + p_2 + 20 = 0$, so its best-response function is $p_1 = 30 + \frac{1}{4}p_2$. Similarly, Firm 2's best-response function is $p_2 = 30 + \frac{1}{4}p_1$. Solving, the Nash-Bertrand equilibrium prices are $p_1 = p_2 = 40$. Each firm produces 60 units.

6.5 In the long-run equilibrium, a monopolistically competitive firm operates where its downward sloping demand curve is tangent to its average cost curve as Figure 14.9 illustrates. Because its demand curve is downward sloping, its average cost curve must also be downward sloping in the equilibrium. Thus, the firm chooses to operate at less than full capacity in equilibrium.

Chapter 15

1.2 Before the tax, the competitive firm's labor demand was $p \times MP_L$. After the tax, the firm's effective price is $(1 - \alpha)p$, so its labor demand becomes $(1 - \alpha)p \times MP_L$.

1.8 The competitive firm's marginal revenue of labor is $MRP_L = pMP_L = p(L^\rho + K^\rho)^{1/\rho - 1}L^{\rho - 1}$.

2.1 An individual with a zero discount rate views current and future consumption as equally attractive. An individual with an infinite discount rate cares only about current consumption and puts no value on future consumption.

2.7 Because the first contract is paid immediately, its present value equals the contract payment of $1 million. Our pro can use Equation 15.15 and a calculator to determine the present value of the second contract (or hire you to do the job for him). The present value of a $2 million payment 10 years from now is $\$2,000,000/(1.05)^{10} \approx \$1,227,827$ at 5%

and $2,000,000/(1.2)^{10} \approx \$323,011$ at 20%. Consequently, the present values are as shown in the table.

Payment	Present Value at 5%	Present Value at 20%
$500,000 today	$50,000	$500,000
$2 million in 10 years	$1,227,827	$323,011
Total	$1,727,827	$823,011

Thus, at 5%, he should accept Contract B, with a present value of $1,727,827, which is much greater than the present value of Contract A, $1 million. At 20%, he should sign Contract A.

2.12 Solving for *irr*, we find that *irr* equals 1 or 9. This approach fails to give us a unique solution, so we should use the *NPV* approach instead. The $NPV = 1 - 12/1.07 + 20/1.07^2 \approx 7.254$, which is positive, so that the firm should invest.

2.16 Currently, you are buying 600 gallons of gas at a cost of $1,200 per year. With a more gas-efficient car, you would spend only $600 per year, saving $600 per year in gas payments. If we assume that these payments are made at the end of each year, the present value of these savings for five years is $2,580 at a 5% annual interest rate and $2,280 at 10%. The present value of the amount you must spend to buy the car in five years is $6,240 at 5% and $4,960 at 10%. Thus, the present value of the additional cost of buying now rather than later is $1,760 (= $8,000 − $6,240) at 5% and $3,040 at 10%. The benefit from buying now is the present value of the reduced gas payments. The cost is the present value of the additional cost of buying the car sooner rather than later. At 5%, the benefit is $2,580 and the cost is $1,760, so you should buy now. However, at 10%, the benefit, $2,280, is less than the cost, $3,040, so you should buy later.

Chapter 16

1.2 Assuming that the painting is not insured against fire, its expected value is

$(0.2 \times \$1,000) + (0.1 \times \$0) + (0.7 \times \$500) = \$550.$

1.3 The expected value of the stock is $(0.25 \times 400) + (0.75 \times 200) = 250$. The variance is $(0.25 \times [400 - 250]^2) + (0.75 \times [200 - 250]^2) = 7,500$.

1.6 The expected punishment for violating traffic laws is θV, where θ is the probability of being caught and fined and V is the fine. If people care only about the expected punishment (that is, there's no additional psychological pain from the experience), increasing the expected punishment by increasing θ or V works equally well in discouraging bad behavior. The government prefers to increase the fine, V, which is costless, rather than to raise θ, which is costly because doing so requires extra police, district attorneys, and courts.

2.3 The expected value for Stock A, $(0.5 \times 100) + (0.5 \times 200) = 150$, is the same as for Stock B, $(0.5 \times 50) + (0.5 \times 250) = 150$. However, the variance of Stock A, $(0.5 \times [100 - 150]^2) + (0.5 \times [200 - 150]^2) = 2,500$, is less than that of Stock B, $(0.5 \times [50 - 150]^2) + (0.5 \times [250 - 150]^2) = 10,000$. Consequently, Jen's expected utility from Stock A, $(0.5 \times 100^{0.5}) + (0.5 \times 200^{0.5}) \approx 12.07$, is greater than from Stock B, $(0.5 \times 50^{0.5}) + (0.5 \times 250^{0.5}) \approx 11.44$, so she prefers Stock A.

2.5 As Figure 16.2 shows, Irma's expected utility of 133 at point f (where her expected wealth is $64) is the same as her utility from a certain wealth of Y.

2.7 Hugo's expected wealth is $EW = \left(\frac{2}{3} \times 144\right) + \left(\frac{1}{3} \times 225\right) = 96 + 75 = 171$. His expected utility is

$$EU = \left[\frac{2}{3} \times U(144)\right] + \left[\frac{1}{3} \times U(225)\right]$$
$$= \left[\frac{2}{3} \times \sqrt{144}\right] + \left[\frac{1}{3} \times \sqrt{225}\right]$$
$$= \left[\frac{2}{3} \times 12\right] + \left[\frac{1}{3} \times 15\right] = 13.$$

He would pay up to an amount P to avoid bearing the risk, where $U(EW - P)$ equals his expected utility from the risky stock, EU. That is, $U(EW - P) = U(171 - P) = \sqrt{171 - P} = 13 = EU$. Squaring both sides, we find that that $171 - P = 169$, or $P = 2$. That is, Hugo would accept an offer for his stock today of $169 (or more), which reflects a risk premium of $2.

4.1 If they were married, Andy would receive half the potential earnings whether they stayed married or not. As a result, Andy will receive $12,000 in present-value terms from Kim's additional earnings. Because the returns to the investment exceed the cost, Andy will make this investment (unless a better investment is available). However, if they stay unmarried and split, Andy's expected return on the investment is the probability of their staying together, 1/2, times Kim's half of the returns if they stay together, $12,000. Thus, Andy's expected return on the investment, $6,000, is less than the cost of the education, so Andy is unwilling to make that investment (regardless of other investment opportunities).

Chapter 17

3.4 As Figure 17.3 shows, a specific tax of $84 per ton of output or per unit of emissions (gunk) leads to the social optimum.

3.7 a. Setting the inverse demand function, $p = 450 - 2Q$, equal to the private marginal cost, $MC^p = 30 + 2Q$, we find that the unregulated equilibrium quantity is $Q_p = (450 - 30) \div (2 + 2) = 105$. The equilibrium price is $p_p = 450 - (2 \times 105) = 240$.

   b. Setting the inverse demand function, $p = 450 - 2Q$, equal to the new social marginal cost, $MC^s = 30 + 3Q$, we find that the socially optimal quantity is $Q_s = (450 - 30)/(2 + 3) = 84$. The socially optimal price is $p_s = 450 - (2 \times 84) = 282$.

   c. Adding a specific tax τ, the private marginal cost becomes $MC^p = 30 + 2Q$, so the equilibrium quantity is $Q = (450 - 30 - \tau)/4$. Setting that equal to $Q_s = 282$ and solving, we find that $\tau = 84$.

3.10 As the figure shows, the government uses its expected marginal benefit curve to set a standard at S or a fee at f. If the true marginal benefit curve is MB^1, the optimal standard is S_1 and the optimal fee is f_1. The deadweight loss from setting either the fee or the standard too high is the same, DWL_1. Similarly, if the true marginal benefit curve is MB^2, both the fee and the standard are set too low, but both have the same deadweight loss, DWL_2. Thus, the deadweight loss from a mistaken belief about the marginal benefit does not depend on whether the government uses a fee or a standard. When the government sets an emissions fee or standard, the amount of gunk actually produced depends only on the marginal cost of abatement and not on the marginal benefit. Because the fee and standard lead to the same level of abatement at e, they cause the same deadweight loss.

6.9 No. The marginal benefit of advertising exceeds the marginal cost.

7.1 There are several ways to demonstrate that welfare can go up despite the pollution. For example, one could redraw panel b with flatter supply curves so that area C became smaller than A (area A remains unchanged). Similarly, if the marginal pollution harm is very small, then we are very close to the no-distortion case, so that welfare will increase.

7.2 See Figure 9.7 (which corresponds to panel a). Going from no trade to free trade, consumers gain areas B and C, while domestic firms lose B. Thus, if consumers give firms an amount between B and $B + C$, both groups will be better off than with no trade.

Chapter 18

1.2 Because insurance costs do not vary with soil type, buying insurance is unattractive for houses on good soil and relatively attractive for houses on bad soil. These incentives create a moral hazard problem: Relatively more homeowners with houses on poor soil buy insurance, so the state insurance agency will face disproportionately many bad outcomes in the next earthquake.

1.3 Brand names allow consumers to identify a particular company's product in the future. If a mushroom company expects to remain in business over time, it would be foolish for it to brand its product if its mushrooms are of inferior quality. (Just ask Babar's grandfather.) Thus, all else the same, we would expect branded mushrooms to be of higher quality than unbranded ones.

3.3 Because buyers are risk neutral, if they believe that the probability of getting a lemon is θ, the most they are willing to pay for a car of unknown quality is $p = p_1(1 - \theta) + p_2\theta$. If p is greater than both v_1 and v_2, all cars are sold. If $v_1 > p > v_2$, only lemons are sold. If p is less than both v_1 and v_2, no cars are sold. However, we know that $v_2 < p_2$ and that $p_2 < p$, so owners of lemons are certainly willing to sell them. (If sellers bear a transaction cost of c and $p < v_2 + c$, no cars are sold.)

4.1 If almost all consumers know the true prices, and all but one firm charges the full-information competitive price, then it does not pay for a firm to set a high price. It gains a little from charging ignorant consumers the high price, but it sells to no informed

For Chapter 17, Exercise 3.10

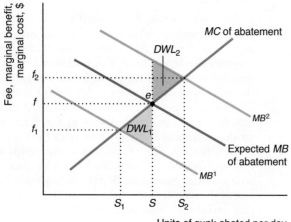

Units of gunk abated per day

customer. Thus, the full-information competitive price is charged in this market.

Chapter 19

1.2 By making this commitment, a company may be trying to assure customers who cannot judge how quickly a product will deteriorate that the product is durable enough to maintain at least a certain value in the future. The firm is trying to eliminate asymmetric information to increase the demand for its product.

1.3 Presumably, the promoter collects a percentage of the revenue of each restaurant. If customers can pay cash, the restaurants may not report the total amount of food they sell. The scrip makes such opportunistic behavior difficult.

2.1 This agreement led to very long conversations. Whichever of them was enjoying the call more apparently figured that he or she would get the full marginal benefit of one more minute of talking while having to pay only half the marginal cost. From this experience, I learned not to open our phone bill so as to avoid being shocked by the amount due (back in an era when long-distance phone calls were expensive).

2.2 A partner who works an extra hour bears the full opportunity cost of this extra hour but gets only half the marginal benefit from the extra business profit. The opportunity cost of extra time spent at the store is the partner's best alternative use of time. A partner could earn money working for someone else or use the time to have fun. Because a partner bears the full marginal cost but gets only half the marginal benefit (the extra business profit) from an extra hour of work, each partner works only up to the point at which the marginal cost equals half the marginal benefit. Thus, each has an incentive to put in less effort than the level that maximizes their joint profit, where the marginal cost equals the marginal benefit.

2.4 If Paula pays Arthur a fixed-fee salary of $168, Arthur has no incentive to buy any carvings for resale, given that the $12 per carving cost comes out of his pocket. Thus, Arthur sells no carvings if he receives a fixed salary and can sell as many or as few carvings as he wants. The contract is not incentive compatible. For Arthur to behave efficiently, this fixed-fee contract must be modified. For example, the contract could specify that Arthur gets a salary of $168 and that he must obtain and sell 12 carvings. Paula must monitor his behavior. (Paula's residual profit is the joint profit minus $168, so she gets the marginal profit from each additional sale and wants to sell the joint-profit-maximizing number of carvings.) Arthur makes $24 = $168 − $144, so he is willing to participate. Joint profit is maximized at $72, and Paula gets the maximum possible residual profit of $48.

4.2 The minimum bond that deters stealing is $2,500.

Definitions

I hate definitions.   —Benjamin Disraeli

adverse selection: occurs when one party to a transaction possesses information about a hidden characteristic that is unknown to other parties and takes economic advantage of this information. (18)

asymmetric information: the situation in which one party to a transaction has relevant information that another party does not have. (18)

auction: a sale in which a good or service is sold to the highest bidder. (13)

average cost (*AC*): the total cost divided by the units of output produced: $AC = C/q$. (7)

average fixed cost (*AFC*): the fixed cost divided by the units of output produced: $AFC = F/q$. (7)

average product of labor (*AP_L*): the ratio of output, q, to the number of workers, L, used to produce that output: $AP_L = q/L$. (6)

average variable cost (*AVC*): the variable cost divided by the units of output produced: $AVC = VC/q$. (7)

backward induction: a process in which we first determine the best response by the last player to move, next determine the best response for the player who made the next-to-last move, and then repeat the process until we reach the first move of the game. (13)

bad: something for which less is preferred to more, such as pollution. (3)

bandwagon effect: the situation in which a person places greater value on a good as more and more other people possess it. (11)

barrier to entry: an explicit restriction or a cost that applies only to potential new firms—existing firms are not subject to the restriction or do not bear the cost. (9)

behavioral economics: adds insights from psychology and empirical research on human cognition and emotional biases to the rational economic model to better predict economic decision making. (3)

Bertrand equilibrium (*Nash-Bertrand equilibrium* or *Nash-in-prices equilibrium*): a set of prices such that no firm can obtain a higher profit by choosing a different price if the other firms continue to charge these prices. (14)

best response: the strategy that maximizes a player's payoff given its beliefs about its rivals' strategies. (13)

bounded rationality: a person's limited capacity to anticipate, solve complex problems, and enumerate all options. (3)

budget line (*budget constraint*): the bundles of goods that can be bought if a consumer's entire budget is spent on those goods at given prices. (3)

bundling (*package tie-in sale*): a type of tie-in sale in which two goods are combined so that customers cannot buy either good separately. (12)

cartel: a group of firms that explicitly agree (collude) to coordinate their activities. (14)

certification: a report that a particular product meets or exceeds a given standard. (18)

cheap talk: unsubstantiated claims or statements. (18)

club good: a commodity that is nonrival but is subject to exclusion. (17)

collude: coordinate actions such as setting prices or quantities among firms. (14)

common knowledge: a piece of information known by all players, and it is known by all players to be known by all players, and it is known to be known to be known, and so forth. (13)

comparative advantage: the ability to produce a good at a lower opportunity cost than someone else. (10)

comparative statics: the method economists use to analyze how variables controlled by consumers and firms react to a change in *environmental variables* (also called *exogenous variables*) that they do not control. (2)

compensating variation (*CV*): the amount of money one would have to give a consumer to offset completely the harm from a price increase. (5)

complete information: the situation where the payoff function is common knowledge among all players. (13)

constant returns to scale (*CRS*): the property of a production function whereby when all inputs are increased by a certain percentage, output increases by that same percentage. (6)

consumer surplus (*CS*): the monetary difference between the maximum amount that a consumer is willing to pay for the quantity of the good purchased and what the good actually costs. (5)

contingent fee: a payment to a lawyer that is a share of the award in a court case (usually after legal expenses are deducted) if the client wins and nothing if the client loses. (19)

contract curve: the set of all Pareto-efficient bundles. (10)

cost (*total cost, C*): the sum of a firm's variable cost and fixed cost: $C = VC + F$. (7)

Cournot equilibrium (*Nash-Cournot equilibrium* or *Nash-in-quantities equilibrium*): a set of quantities chosen by firms such that, holding the quantities of all other firms constant, no firm can obtain a higher profit by choosing a different quantity. (14)

credible threat: an announcement that a firm will use a strategy harmful to its rivals that the rivals believe is rational in the sense that it is in the firm's best interest to use it. (13)

cross-price elasticity of demand: the percentage change in the quantity demanded in response to a given percentage change in the price of another good. (2)

deadweight loss (*DWL*): the net reduction in welfare from a loss of surplus by one group that is not offset by a gain to another group. (9)

decreasing returns to scale (*DRS*): the property of a production function whereby output rises less than in proportion to an equal percentage increase in all inputs. (6)

demand curve: a plot of the demand function that shows the quantity demanded at each possible price, holding constant the other factors that influence purchases. (2)

demand function: the correspondence between the quantity demanded, price, and other factors that influence purchases. (2)

discount rate: a rate reflecting the relative value an individual places on future consumption compared to current consumption. (15)

diseconomies of scale: the property of a cost function whereby the average cost of production rises when output increases. (7)

dominant strategy: a strategy that produces a higher payoff than any other strategy the player can use for every possible combination of its rivals' strategies. (13)

duopoly: an oligopoly with two (*duo*) firms. (14)

durable good: a product that is usable for a long period, typically for many years. (7)

dynamic game: a game in which players move either sequentially or repeatedly. (13)

economic cost (*opportunity cost*): the value of the best alternative use of a resource. (7)

economic profit: revenue minus opportunity (economic) cost. (8)

economically efficient: minimizing the cost of producing a specified amount of output. (7)

economies of scale: the property of a cost function whereby the average cost of production falls as output expands. (7)

economies of scope: a situation in which it is less expensive to produce goods jointly than separately. (7)

efficiency in production: a situation in which the principal's and the agent's combined value (profits, payoffs) is maximized. (19)

efficiency in risk bearing: a situation in which risk sharing is optimal in that the person who least minds facing risk—the risk-neutral or less-risk-averse person—bears more of the risk. (19)

efficiency wage: an unusually high wage that a firm pays workers as an incentive to avoid shirking. (19)

efficient contract: an agreement with provisions that ensure that no party can be made better off without harming the other party. (19)

efficient production (*technological efficiency*): a situation in which the current level of output cannot be produced with fewer inputs, given existing knowledge about technology and how to organize production. (6)

elasticity: the percentage change in one variable in response to a given percentage change in another variable, holding other relevant variables constant. (2)

elasticity of substitution (σ): the percentage change in the capital-labor ratio divided by the percentage change in the *MRTS*. (6)

endowment: an initial allocation of goods. (10)

endowment effect: the condition that occurs when people place a higher value on a good if they own it than they do if they are considering buying it. (3)

Engel curve: the relationship between the quantity demanded of a single good and income, holding prices constant. (4)

equilibrium: a situation in which no participant wants to change its behavior. (2)

equivalent variation (*EV*): the amount of money one would have to take from a consumer to harm the consumer by as much as the price increase. (5)

essential facility: a scarce resource that rivals need to use to survive. (11)

excess demand: the amount by which the quantity demanded exceeds the quantity supplied at a specified price. (2)

excess supply: the amount by which the quantity supplied is greater than the quantity demanded at a specified price. (2)

exclusion: a situation whereby others can be prevented from consuming a good. (17)

exhaustible resources: nonrenewable natural assets that cannot be increased, only depleted. (15)

expansion path: the cost-minimizing combination of labor and capital for each output level. (7)

expected value: the weighted average of the values of each possible outcome, where the weights are the probability of each outcome. (16)

expenditure function: the relationship showing the minimal expenditures necessary to achieve a specific utility level for a given set of prices. (3)

extensive form: a representation of a game that specifies the *n* players, the sequence in which they make their moves, the actions they can take at each move, the information that each player has about players' previous moves, and the payoff function over all possible strategies. (13)

externality: an event in which a person's well-being or a firm's production capability is directly affected by the actions of other consumers or firms rather than indirectly through changes in prices. (17)

fair bet: a wager with an expected value of zero. (16)

fair insurance: a bet between an insurer and a policyholder in which the value of the bet to the policyholder is zero. (16)

firm: an organization that converts *inputs* such as labor, materials, and capital into *outputs*, the goods and services that it sells. (6)

fixed cost (*F*): a production expense that does not vary with the level of output. (7)

fixed input: a factor of production that cannot be varied practically in the short run. (6)

flow: a quantity or value that is measured per unit of time. (15)

free rider problem: a situation whereby people benefit from the actions of others without paying. (17)

game: a competition between players (such as individuals or firms) in which players use strategies. (13)

game theory: a set of tools that economists and others use to analyze players' strategic decision-making. (13)

general-equilibrium analysis: the study of how equilibrium is determined in all markets simultaneously. (10)

Giffen good: a commodity for which a decrease in its price causes the quantity demanded to fall. (4)

good: a commodity for which more is preferred to less, at least at some levels of consumption. (3)

group price discrimination (*third-degree price discrimination*): a situation in which a firm charges different groups of customers different prices but charges a given customer the same price for every unit sold. (12)

hidden action: a situation in which one party to a transaction cannot observe important actions taken by another party. (18)

hidden characteristic: a fact about a person or thing that is known to one party but unknown to others. (18)

incentive compatible: a condition in which a contract provides inducements such that the agent wants to perform the assigned task rather than engage in opportunistic behavior. (19)

incidence of a tax on consumers: the share of the tax that falls on consumers. (2)

income effect: the change in the quantity of a good a consumer demands because of a change in income, holding prices constant. (4)

income elasticity of demand (*income elasticity*): the percentage change in the quantity demanded in response to a given percentage change in income. (2)

increasing returns to scale (*IRS*): the property of a production function whereby output rises more than in proportion to an equal increase in all inputs. (6)

indifference curve: the set of all bundles of goods that a consumer views as being equally desirable. (3)

indifference map (*preference map*): a complete set of indifference curves that summarize a consumer's tastes. (3)

inferior good: a commodity of which less is demanded as income rises. (4)

interest rate: the percentage more that must be repaid to borrow money for a fixed period of time. (15)

internal rate of return (*irr*): the discount rate such that the net present value of an investment is zero. (15)

internalize the externality: to bear the cost of the harm that one inflicts on others (or to capture the benefit that one provides to others). (17)

isocost line: a plot of all the combinations of inputs that require the same (*iso*) total expenditure (*cost*). (7)

isoquant: a curve that shows the efficient combinations of labor and capital that can produce a single (*iso*) level of output (*quan*tity). (6)

Law of Demand: consumers demand more of a good the lower its price, holding constant tastes, the prices of other goods, and other factors that influence the amount they consume. (2)

learning by doing: the productive skills and knowledge of better ways to produce that workers and managers gain from experience. (7)

learning curve: the relationship between average costs and cumulative output. (7)

Lerner Index (*price markup*): the ratio of the difference between price and marginal cost to the price: $(p - MC)/p$. (11)

limited liability: a condition whereby the personal assets of corporate owners cannot be taken to pay a corporation's debts even if it goes into bankruptcy. (6)

long run: a long enough period of time that all inputs can be varied. (6)

marginal cost (*MC*): the amount by which a firm's cost changes if it produces one more unit of output: $MC = \Delta C/\Delta q$. (7)

marginal product of labor (MP_L): the change in total output resulting from using an extra unit of labor, holding other factors (capital) constant. (6)

marginal profit: the change in the profit a firm gets from selling one more unit of output. (8)

marginal rate of substitution (*MRS*): the maximum amount of one good that a consumer will sacrifice (trade) to obtain one more unit of another good. (3)

marginal rate of technical substitution (*MRTS*): how many units of capital a firm can replace with an extra unit of labor while holding output constant. (6)

marginal rate of transformation (*MRT*): the trade-off the market imposes on the consumer in terms of the amount of one good the consumer must give up to obtain more of the other good. (3)

marginal revenue (*MR*): the change in revenue a firm gets from selling one more unit of output. (8)

marginal revenue product of labor (MRP_L): the additional revenue from the last unit of labor. (15)

marginal utility: the extra utility that a consumer gets from consuming the last unit of a good. (3)

market: an exchange mechanism that allows buyers to trade with sellers. (1)

market failure: inefficient production or consumption, often because a price exceeds marginal cost. (9)

market power: the ability of a firm to charge a price above marginal cost and earn a positive profit. (11)

market structure: the number of firms in the market, the ease with which firms can enter and leave the market, and the ability of firms to differentiate their products from those of their rivals. (8)

microeconomics: the study of how individuals and firms make themselves as well off as possible in a world of scarcity, and the consequences of those individual decisions for markets and the entire economy. (1)

minimum efficient scale (*full capacity*): the smallest quantity at which the average cost curve reaches its minimum. (14)

mixed strategy: a strategy in which the player chooses among possible actions according to probabilities the player assigns. (13)

model: a description of the relationship between two or more economic variables. (1)

monopolistic competition: a market structure in which firms have market power but no additional firm can enter and earn a positive profit. (14)

monopoly: the only supplier of a good for which there is no close substitute. (11)

monopsony: the only buyer of a good in a market. (11)

moral hazard: opportunism characterized by an informed person's taking advantage of a less-informed person through an *unobserved action*. (18)

Nash equilibrium: a set of strategies such that, when all other players use these strategies, no player can obtain a higher payoff by choosing a different strategy. (13)

Nash-Bertrand equilibrium (*Bertrand equilibrium* or *Nash-in-prices equilibrium*): a set of prices chosen by firms such that no firm can obtain a higher profit by choosing a different price if the other firms continue to charge these prices. (14)

Nash-Cournot equilibrium (*Cournot equilibrium* or *Nash-in-quantities equilibrium*): a set of quantities chosen by firms such that, holding the quantities of all other firms constant, no firm can obtain a higher profit by choosing a different quantity. (14)

natural monopoly: a situation in which one firm can produce the total output of the market at lower cost than several firms could. (11)

network externality: the situation where one person's demand for a good depends on the consumption of the good by others. (11)

nonlinear price discrimination (*second-degree price discrimination*): the situation in which a firm charges a different price for large quantities than for small quantities, but all customers who buy a given quantity pay the same price. (12)

nonuniform pricing: the practice of charging consumers different prices for the same product or charging a single customer a price that depends on the number of units purchased. (12)

normal form: a representation of a static game of complete information, which specifies the players in the game, their possible strategies, and the payoff function that specifies the players' payoffs for each combination of strategies. (13)

normal good: a commodity of which more is demanded as income rises. (4)

normative statement: a conclusion as to whether something is good or bad. (1)

oligopoly: a small group of firms in a market with substantial barriers to entry. (14)

open-access common property: resources to which everyone has free access and an equal right to exploit. (17)

opportunistic behavior: taking advantage of someone when circumstances permit. (18)

opportunity cost (*economic cost*): the value of the best alternative use of a resource. (7)

opportunity set: all the bundles a consumer can buy, including all the bundles inside the budget constraint and on the budget constraint. (3)

Pareto efficient: describing an allocation of goods and services such that any possible reallocation would harm at least one person. (10)

Pareto improvement: a change, such as a reallocation, that helps at least one person without harming anyone else. (10)

Pareto principle: the belief that society should favor a change that benefits some people without harming anyone else. (10)

partial-equilibrium analysis: an examination of equilibrium and changes in equilibrium in one market in isolation. (10)

patent: an exclusive right granted to the inventor to sell a new and useful product, process, substance, or design for a fixed time. (11)

payoffs (of a game): players' valuations of the outcome of the game, such as profits for firms or utilities for individuals. (13)

perfect competition: a market structure in which buyers and sellers are price takers. (8)

perfect complements: goods that a consumer is interested in consuming only in fixed proportions. (3)

perfect price discrimination (*first-degree price discrimination*): the situation in which a firm sells each unit at the maximum amount each customer is willing to pay, so prices differ across customers, and a given customer may pay more for some units than for others. (12)

perfect substitutes: goods that a consumer is completely indifferent as to which to consume. (3)

pooling equilibrium: an equilibrium in which dissimilar people are treated (paid) alike or behave alike. (18)

positive statement: a testable hypothesis about cause and effect. (1)

price discrimination: charging consumers different prices for the same good based on individual characteristics of consumers, membership in an identifiable subgroup of consumers, or on the quantity purchased by the consumers. (12)

price elasticity of demand (*demand elasticity* or *elasticity of demand*): the percentage change in the quantity demanded in response to a given percentage change in the price at a particular point on the demand curve. (2)

price elasticity of supply (*supply elasticity*): the percentage change in the quantity supplied in response to a given percentage change in the price. (2)

prisoners' dilemma: a game in which all players have dominant strategies that lead to a profit (or another payoff) that is inferior to what they could achieve if they cooperated and pursued alternative strategies. (13)

private cost: the cost of production only, not including externalities. (17)

producer surplus (*PS*): the difference between the amount for which a good sells and the minimum amount necessary for the seller to be willing to produce the good. (9)

production function: the relationship between the quantities of inputs used and the *maximum* quantity of output that can be produced, given current knowledge about technology and organization. (6)

production possibility frontier: the maximum amount of outputs that can be produced from a fixed amount of input. (7)

profit (π): the difference between a firm's revenue, R, which is what it earns from selling a good, and its cost, C, which is what it pays for labor, materials, and other inputs: $\pi = R - C$. (6)

property right: an exclusive privilege to use an asset. (17)

public good: a commodity or service whose consumption by one person does not preclude others from also consuming it. (17)

pure strategy: strategy in which each player chooses a single action. (13)

quantity demanded: the amount of a good that consumers are willing to buy at a given price during a specified period (such as a day or a year), holding constant the other factors that influence purchases. (2)

quantity supplied: the amount of a good that firms *want* to sell during a given time period at a given price, holding constant other factors that influence firms' supply decisions, such as costs and government actions. (2)

quota: a limit that a government sets on the quantity of a foreign-produced good that may be imported. (2)

rent seeking: efforts and expenditures to gain a rent or a profit from government actions. (9)

rent: a payment to the owner of an input beyond the minimum necessary for the factor to be supplied. (9)

requirement tie-in sale: a type of nonuniform pricing in which customers who buy one product from a firm are required to make all their purchases of another product from that firm. (12)

reservation price: the maximum amount a person is willing to pay for a unit of output. (12)

residual demand curve: the market demand that is not met by other sellers at any given price. (8)

residual supply curve: the quantity that the market supplies that is not consumed by other demanders at any given price. (8)

risk: the situation in which the likelihood of each possible outcome is known or can be estimated, and no single possible outcome is certain to occur. (16)

risk averse: unwilling to make a fair bet. (16)

risk neutral: indifferent about making a fair bet. (16)

risk preferring: willing to make a fair bet. (16)

risk premium: the amount that a risk-averse person would pay to avoid taking a risk. (16)

rival: a situation in which only one person can consume a good. (17)

rules of the game: regulations that determine the timing of players' moves (such as whether one player moves first), the various actions that are possible at a particular point in the game, and possibly other specific aspects of how the game is played. (13)

screening: an action taken by an uninformed person to determine the information possessed by informed people. (18)

separating equilibrium: an equilibrium in which one type of people takes actions (such as sending a signal) that allows them to be differentiated from other types of people. (18)

shirk: a moral hazard in which agents do not provide all the services they are paid to provide. (19)

short run: a period of time so brief that at least one factor of production cannot be varied practically. (6)

shortage: a persistent excess demand. (2)

signaling: an action taken by an informed person to send information to a less-informed person. (18)

snob effect: the situation in which a person places greater value on a good as fewer and fewer people possess it. (11)

social cost: the private cost plus the cost of the harms from externalities. (17)

standard: a metric or scale for evaluating the quality of a particular product. (18)

static game: a game in which each player acts only once and the players act simultaneously (or, at least, each player acts without knowing rivals' actions). (13)

stock: a quantity or value that is measured independently of time. (15)

strategy: a battle plan that specifies the actions or moves that a player will make conditional on the information available at each move and for any possible contingency. (13)

subgame perfect Nash equilibrium: the situation in which players' strategies are a Nash equilibrium in every subgame. (13)

substitution effect: the change in the quantity of a good that a consumer demands when the good's price rises, holding other prices and the consumer's utility constant. (4)

sunk cost: a past expenditure that cannot be recovered. (7)

supply curve: the quantity supplied at each possible price, holding constant the other factors that influence firms' supply decisions. (2)

supply function: the correspondence between the quantity supplied, price, and other factors that influence the number of units offered for sale. (2)

tariff (*duty*): a tax only on imported goods. (9)

technical progress: an advance in knowledge that allows more output to be produced with the same level of inputs. (6)

technological efficiency (*efficient production*): property of a production function such that the current level of output cannot be produced with fewer inputs, given existing knowledge about technology and how to organize production. (6)

tie-in sale: a type of nonuniform pricing in which customers can buy one product or service only if they agree to purchase another as well. (12)

total cost (C): the sum of a firm's variable cost and fixed cost: $C = VC + F$. (7)

total product of labor: the amount of output (or *total product*) that a given amount of labor can produce holding the quantity of other inputs fixed. (6)

transaction costs: the expenses, over and above the price of the product, of finding a trading partner and making a trade for the product. (2)

two-part pricing: a pricing system in which the firm charges each consumer a lump-sum *access fee* (or price) for the right to buy as many units of the good as the consumer wants at a per-unit *price*. (12)

uniform pricing: charging the same price for every unit sold of a particular good. (12)

utility: a set of numerical values that reflect the relative rankings of various bundles of goods. (3)

utility function: the relationship between utility measures and every possible bundle of goods. (3)

variable cost (VC): a production expense that changes with the quantity of output produced. (7)

variable input: a factor of production whose quantity the firm can change readily during the relevant period. (6)

winner's curse: auction winner's bid exceeds the common-value item's value. (13)

References

Abelson, Peter, "The High Cost of Taxi Regulation, with Special Reference to Sydney," *Agenda*, 17(2), 2010: 41–70.

Adelaja, Adesoji O., "Price Changes, Supply Elasticities, Industry Organization, and Dairy Output Distribution," *American Journal of Agricultural Economics*, 73(1), February 1991: 89–102.

Aigner, Dennis J., and Glen G. Cain, "Statistical Theories of Discrimination in Labor Markets," *Industrial and Labor Relations Review*, 30(2), January 1977: 175–187.

Akerlof, George A., "The Market for 'Lemons': Quality Uncertainty and the Market Mechanism," *Quarterly Journal of Economics*, 84(3), August 1970: 488–500.

Akerlof, George A., "Labor Contacts as Partial Gift Exchanges," *Quarterly Journal of Economics*, 97(4), November 1982: 543–569.

Alexander, Donald L., "Major League Baseball," *Journal of Sports Economics*, 2(4), November 2001: 341–355.

Altonji, Joseph G., and Ernesto Villanueva, "The Marginal Propensity to Spend on Adult Children," *B.E. Journal of Economic Analysis & Policy*, Advances, 7(1), 2007, Article 14.

Anderson, Keith B., and Michael R. Metzger, *Petroleum Tariffs as a Source of Government Revenues*. Washington, D.C.: Bureau of Economics, Federal Trade Commission, 1991.

Anderson, Michael, and Maximilian Auffhammer, "Pounds That Kill: The External Costs of Vehicle Weight," NBER Working Paper, 2011.

Arrow, Kenneth, *Social Choice and Individual Values*. New York: Wiley, 1951.

Asai, Sumiko, "Scale Economies and Scope Economies in the Japanese Broadcasting Market," *Information Economics and Policy*, 18(3), April 2006: 321–331.

Auffhammer, Maximilian, and Ryan Kellogg, "Clearing the Air? The Effects of Gasoline Content Regulation on Air Quality," *American Economic Review*, 101(6), October 2011: 2687–2722.

Ayres, Ian, and Joel Waldfogel, "A Market Test for Race Discrimination in Bail Setting," *Stanford Law Review*, 46(5), May 1994: 987–1047.

Baldwin, John R., and Paul K. Gorecki, *The Role of Scale in Canada/U.S. Productivity Differences in the Manufacturing Sector, 1970–1979*. Toronto: University of Toronto Press, 1986.

Balistreri, Edward J., Christine A. McDaniel, and Eina Vivian Wong, "An Estimation of US Industry-Level Capital-Labor Substitution Elasticities: Support for Cobb-Douglas," *North American Journal of Economics and Finance*, 14(3), December 2003: 343–356.

Bapna, Ravi, Wolfgang Jank, and Galit Shmueli, "Consumer Surplus in Online Auctions," *Information Systems Research*, 19(4), December 2008: 400–416.

Barrett, Sean D., "Regulatory Capture, Property Rights and Taxi Deregulation: A Case Study," *Economic Affairs*, 23(4), 2003: 34–40.

Basker, Emek, "Raising the Barcode Scanner: Technology and Productivity in the Retail Sector," *American Economic Journal: Applied Economics*, 4(3), July 2012: 1–27.

Battalio, Raymond, John H. Kagel, and Carl Kogut, "Experimental Confirmation of the Existence of a Giffen Good," *American Economic Review*, 81(3), September 1991: 961–970.

Bauer, Thomas K., and Christoph M. Schmidt, "WTP vs. WTA: Christmas Presents and the Endowment Effect," Institute for the Study of Labor Working Paper, 2008.

Beatty, Timothy K.M., and Charlotte Tuttle, "Expenditure Responses to Increase in In-Kind Transfers," University of Minnesota Working Paper, 2012.

Becker, Gary S., *The Economics of Discrimination*, 2nd ed. Chicago: University of Chicago Press, 1971.

Benjamin, Daniel K., William R. Dougan, and David Buschena, *Journal of Risk and Uncertainty*, 22(1), January 2001: 35–57.

Berck, Peter, and Michael Roberts, "Natural Resource Prices: Will They Ever Turn Up?" *Journal of Environmental Economics and Management*, 31(1), July 1996: 65–78.

Besley, Timothy J., and Harvey S. Rosen, "Sales Taxes and Prices: An Empirical Analysis," *National Tax Journal*, 52(2), June 1999: 157–178.

Bezman, Trisha L., and Craig A. Depken II, "Influences on Software Piracy: Evidence from the Various United States," *Economic Letters*, 90(3), March 2006: 356–361.

Bhuyan, Sanjib, "Corporate Political Activities and Oligopoly Welfare Loss," *Review of Industrial Organization*, 17(4), December 2000: 411–426.

Bhuyan, Sanjib, and Rigoberto A. Lopez, "What Determines Welfare Losses from Oligopoly Power in the Food and Tobacco Industries?" *Agricultural and Resource Economics Review*, 27(2), October 1998: 258–265.

Bils, Mark, "Do Higher Prices for New Goods Reflect Quality Growth or Inflation?" *Quarterly Journal of Economics*, 124(2), May 2009: 637–675.

Blanciforti, Laura Ann, "The Almost Ideal Demand System Incorporating Habits: An Analysis of Expenditures on Food and Aggregate Commodity Groups," Ph.D. thesis, U.C. Davis, 1982.

Blau, David, and Edral Tekin, "The Determinants and Consequence of Child Care Subsidy Receipt by Low-Income Families," in Bruce Mery and Greg Duncan, *The Incentives of Government Programs and the Well-Being of Families*, Joint Center for Poverty Research, 2001.

Borenstein, Severin, James Bushnell, and Matthew Lewis, "Market Power in California's Gasoline Market," University of California Energy Institute, CSEM WP 132, May 2004, **www.ucei.berkeley.edu/PDF/csemwp132.pdf.**

Borenstein, Severin, and Nancy L. Rose, "Competition and Price Dispersion in the U.S. Airline Industry," *Journal of Political Economy*, 102(4), August 1994: 653–683.

Borjas, George J., "The Labor Demand Curve Is Downward Sloping: Reexamining the Impact of Immigration on the Labor Market," *Quarterly Journal of Economics*, 118(4), November 2003: 1335–1374.

Boroski, John W., and Gerard C. S. Mildner, "An Economic Analysis of Taxicab Regulation in Portland, Oregon," Cascade Policy Institute, **www.cascadepolicy.org**, 1998.

Boskin, Michael J., Ellen R. Dulberger, Robert J. Gordon, Zvi Griliches, and Dale W. Jorgenson, "The CPI Commission: Findings and Recommendations," *American Economic Review*, 87(2), May 1997: 78–93.

Boskin, Michael J., and Dale W. Jorgenson, "Implications of Overstating Inflation for Indexing Government Programs and Understanding Economic Progress," *American Economic Review*, 87(2), May 1997: 89–93.

Boulier, Bryan L., Tejwant S. Datta, and Robert S. Goldfarb, "Vaccination Externalities," *The B.E. Journal of Economic Analysis & Policy*, 7(1, Contributions), 2007: Article 23.

Bradbury, Hinton, and Karen Ross, "The Effects of Novelty and Choice Materials on the Intransitivity of Preferences of Children and Adults," *Annals of Operations Research*, 23(1–4), June 1990: 141–159.

Brand, Keith, Gautam Gowrisankaranz, Aviv Nevo, Robert Town, "Mergers When Prices Are Negotiated: Evidence from the Hospital Industry," University of Arizona Working Paper, 2012.

Brander, James A., and M. Scott Taylor, "The Simple Economics of Easter Island: A Ricardo-Malthus Model of Renewable Resource Use," *American Economic Review*, 88(1), March 1998: 119–138.

Brander, James A., and Anming Zhang, "Market Conduct in the Airline Industry: An Empirical Investigation," *Rand Journal of Economics*, 21(4), Winter 1990: 567–583.

Brown, Jennifer, Justine Hastings, Erin T. Mansur, and Sofia B. Villas-Boas, "Reformulating Competition? Gasoline Content Regulation and Wholesale Gasoline Prices," *Journal of Environmental Economics and Management*, 55(1), January 2008: 1–19.

Brown, Jennifer, and John Morgan, "Reputation in Online Auctions: The Market for Trust," *California Management Review*, 49(1), Fall 2006: 61–81.

Brown, Jennifer, and John Morgan, "How Much Is a Dollar Worth? Tipping versus Equilibrium Coexistence on Competing Online Auction Sites," *Journal of Political Economy*, 117(4), August 2010: 668–700.

Brown, Stephen P. A., and Daniel Wolk, "Natural Resource Scarcity and Technological Change," *Economic and Financial Review* (Federal Reserve Bank of Dallas), First Quarter 2000: 2–13.

Brownlee, Oswald, and George Perry, "The Effects of the 1965 Federal Excise Tax Reductions on Prices," *National Tax Journal*, 20(3), September 1967: 235–249.

Brunk, Gregory G., "A Test of the Friedman-Savage Gambling Model," *Quarterly Journal of Economics*, 96(2), May 1981: 341–348.

Bucks, Brian K., Arthur B. Kennickell, Traci L. Mach, and Kevin B. Moore, "Changes in U.S. Family Finances from 2004 to 2007: Evidence from the Survey of Consumer Finances," *Federal Reserve Bulletin*, 2009, **www.federalreserve.gov/pubs/bulletin/2009/pdf/scf09.pdf.**

Busch, Susan H., Mireia Jofre-Bonet, Tracy Falba, and Jody Sindelar, "Burning a Hole in the Budget: Tobacco Spending and Its Crowd-out of Other Goods," *Applied Health Economics and Policy*, 3(4), 2004: 263–272.

Buschena, David E., and Jeffrey M. Perloff, "The Creation of Dominant Firm Market Power in the Coconut Oil Export Market," *American Journal of Agricultural Economics*, 73(4), November 1991: 1000–1008.

Cabral, Luis, and Ali Hortacsu, "The Dynamics of Seller Reputation: Evidence from eBay," *Journal of Industrial Economics*, 58(1), March, 2010: 54–78.

Caliendo, Marco, Michel Clement, Dominki Papies, and Sabine Scheel-Koeinig, "The Cost Impact of Spam Filters: Measuring the Effect of Information System Technologies in Organizations," *Information Systems Research*, 2012 (online).

Camerer, Colin F., George Lowenstein, and Matthew Rabin, eds., *Advances in Behavioral Economics*. New York: Russell Sage Foundation, 2004.

Card, David, and Alan B. Krueger, *Myth and Measurement: The New Economics of the Minimum Wage*, Princeton, N.J.: Princeton University Press, 1995.

Carlton, Dennis W., and Jeffrey M. Perloff, *Modern Industrial Organization*, 4th ed. Reading, Mass.: Addison Wesley Longman, 2005.

Carpenter, Christopher, and Carlos Dobkin, "The Effect of Alcohol Consumption on Mortality: Regression Discontinuity Evidence from the Minimum Drinking Age," *American Economic Journal: Applied Economics*, 1(1), January 2009: 165–182.

Chetty, Raj, Adam Looney, and Kory Kroft, "Salience and Taxation: Theory and Evidence," *American Economic Review*, 99(4), September 2009: 1145–1177.

Chouinard, Hayley H., David Davis, Jeffrey T. LaFrance, and Jeffrey M. Perloff, "The Effects of a Fat Tax on Dairy Products," *Forum for Health Economics & Policy*, 10(2, 2), 2007.

Chouinard, Hayley, and Jeffrey M. Perloff, "Incidence of Federal and State Gasoline Taxes," *Economic Letters*, 83(1), April 2004: 55–60.

Coase, Ronald H., "The Problem of Social Cost," *Journal of Law and Economics*, 3, October 1960: 1–44.

Cohen, Jeffrey P., and Paul, Catherine Morrison, "Scale and Scope Economies for Drug Abuse Treatment Costs: Evidence for Washington State," *Applied Economics*, 43(30), January 2011: 4827–4834.

Cohen, Wesley M., Richard R. Nelson, John P. Walsh, "Protecting Their Intellectual Assets: Appropriability Conditions and Why U.S. Manufacturing Firms Patent (or Not)," NBER Working Paper, 2000.

Colman, Gregory J., and Dahlia K. Remler, "Vertical Equity Consequences of Very High Cigarette Tax Increases: If the Poor Are the Ones Smoking, How Could Cigarette Tax Increases Be Progressive?" *Journal of Policy Analysis and Management*, 27(2), Spring 2008: 376–400.

Crawford, David, John Del Roccili, and Richard Voith, "Comments on Proposed Tax Reforms," Econsult Corporation, June 9, 2004.

Cummins, J. David, Mary A. Weiss, Xiaoying Xie, Hongmin Zi, "Economies of Scope in Financial Services: A DEA Efficiency Analysis of the US Insurance Industry," *Journal of Banking & Finance*, 34(7), July 2010: 1525–1539.

Currie, Janet, and Reed Walker, "Traffic Congestion and Infant Health: Evidence from E-ZPass," *American Economic Journal: Applied Economics*, 3(1), January 2011: 65–90.

Currie, Janet, and Firouz Gahvari, "Transfers in Cash and In-Kind: Theory Meets the Data," *Journal of Economic Literature*, 46(2), June 2008: 333–383.

Cutler, David M., Edward L. Glaeser, and Jesse M. Shapiro, "Why Have Americans Become More Obese?" *Journal of Economic Perspectives*, 17(3), Summer 2003: 93–118.

Dafny, Leemore, "Estimation and Identification of Merger Effects: An Application to Hospital Mergers," *Journal of Law and Economics*, 52(3), August 2009: 523–550.

Davies, James B., Susanna Sandström, Anthony Shorrocks, and Edward N. Wolff, "Estimating the Level and Distribution of Global Household Wealth," World Institute for Development Economic Research Working Paper, 2007.

Davis, Lucas W., and Lutz Kilian, "The Allocative Cost of Price Ceilings in the U.S. Residential Market for Natural Gas," *Journal of Political Economics*, 119(2), April 2011: 212–241.

Davis, Lucas W., and Erich Muehlegger, "Do Americans Consume Too Little Natural Gas? An Empirical Test of Marginal Cost Pricing," *Rand Journal of Economics*, 41(4), Winter, 2010: 791–810.

Deacon, Robert T., and Jon Sonstelie, "The Welfare Costs of Rationing by Waiting," *Economic Inquiry*, 27(2), April 1989: 179–196.

Dean, David, et al., *The Internet Economy in the G-20*, Boston Consulting Group, 2012, **www.bcgperspectives.com/Images/Internet_Economy_G20_tcm80-100409.pdf**.

de Melo, Jaime, and David Tarr, *A General Equilibrium Analysis of U.S. Foreign Trade Policy*. Cambridge, Mass.: MIT Press, 1992.

Delipalla, Sophia, and Michael Keen, "The Comparison Between Ad Valorem and Specific Taxation Under Imperfect Competition," *Journal of Public Economics*, 49(3), December 1992: 351–367.

Delipalla, Sophia, and Owen O'Donnell, "Estimating Tax Incidence, Market Power and Market Conduct: The European Cigarette Industry," *International Journal of Industrial Organization*, 19(6), May 2001: 885–908.

DellaVigna, Stefano, "Psychology and Economics: Evidence from the Field," *Journal of Economic Literature*, 47(2), June 2009: 315–372.

Diewert, W. Edwin, and Alice O. Nakamura, eds., *Essays in Index Number Theory*, Vol. 1. New York: North Holland, 1993.

Dixit, Avinash K., and Robert S. Pindyck, *Investment Under Uncertainty*. Princeton, N.J.: Princeton University Press, 1994.

Duffy-Deno, Kevin T., "Business Demand for Broadband Access Capacity," *Journal of Regulatory Economics*, 24(3), 2003: 359–372.

Duncan, Denvil, and Klara Sabirianova Peter, "Does Labor Supply Respond to a Flat Tax? Evidence from the Russian Tax Reform," IZA Discussion Paper, 2009.

Dunham, Wayne R., "Moral Hazard and the Market for Used Automobiles," *Review of Industrial Organization*, 23(1), August 2003: 65–83.

Eastwood, David B., and John A. Craven, "Food Demand and Savings in a Complete, Extended, Linear Expenditure System," *American Journal of Agricultural Economics*, 63(3), August 1981: 544–549.

Economides, Nicholas, "The Economics of Networks," *International Journal of Industrial Organization*, 14(6), October 1996: 673–699.

Econsult Corporation, *Choosing the Best Mix of Taxes for Philadelphia: An Econometric Analysis of the Impacts of Tax Rates on Tax Bases, Tax Revenue, and the Private Economy*, Report to the Philadelphia Tax Reform Commission, 2003.

Edelman, Benjamin, "Adverse Selection in Online 'Trust' Certifications and Search Results," *Electronic Commerce Research and Applications*, 10(1), January-February, 2011: 17–25.

Edlin, Aaron S., and Pinar Karaca-Mandic, "The Accident Externality from Driving," *Journal of Political Economy*, 114(5), October 2006: 931–955.

Einav, Liran, Dan Knoepfle, Jonathan D. Levin, and Neel Sundaresan, "Sales Taxes and Internet Commerce," NBER Working Paper, 2012.

Ellsberg, Daniel, "Risk, Ambiguity, and the Savage Axioms," *Quarterly Journal of Economics*, 75(4), November 1961: 643–669.

Environmental Protection Agency, *The Benefits and Costs of the Clean Air Act from 1990 to 2020*, **www.epa.gov/oar/sect812/feb11/fullreport.pdf**, 2011.

Epstein, Andrew J., "Do Cardiac Surgery Report Cards Reduce Mortality? Assessing the Evidence," *Medical Care Research and Review*, 63(4), August 2006: 403–426.

Espey, Molly, "Gasoline Demand Revisited: An International Meta-analysis of Elasticities," *Energy Economics*, 20(3), 1998: 273–295.

Evers, Michiel, Ruud De Mooij, and Daniel Van Vuuren, "The Wage Elasticity of Labour Supply: A Synthesis of Empirical Estimates," *De Economist*, 156(1), March 2008: 25–43.

Farrell, Joseph, and Matthew Rabin, "Cheap Talk," *Journal of Economic Perspectives*, 10(3), Summer 1996: 103–118.

Farsi, Mehdi, Aurelio Fetz, and Massimo Filippini, "Economies of Scale and Scope in Multi-Utilities," *Energy Journal*, 29 (4), 2008: 123–143.

Fasciano, Nancy, Daryl Hall, and Harold Beebout, eds., *New Directions in Food Stamp Policy Research*. Alexandria, Va.: U.S. Department of Agriculture, Food and Nutrition Service, 1993.

Finkelstein, Amy, et al., "The Oregon Health Insurance Experiment: Evidence from the First Year," NBER working paper, 2011.

Fisher, Franklin M., "The Social Cost of Monopoly and Regulation: Posner Reconsidered," *Journal of Political Economy*, 93(2), April 1985: 410–416.

Flath, David, "Industrial Concentration, Price-cost Margins, and Innovation," *Japan and the World Economy*, 23(2), March 2011: 129–139.

Foster, Andrew D., and Mark R. Rosenzweig, "A Test for Moral Hazard in the Labor Market: Contractual Arrangements, Effort, and Health," *Review of Economics and Statistics*, 76(2), May 1994: 213–227.

Friedlaender, Ann F., Clifford Winston, and Kung Wang, "Costs, Technology, and Productivity in the U.S. Automobile Industry," *Bell Journal of Economics and Management Science*, 14(1), Spring 1983: 1–20.

Friedman, Milton, and Leonard J. Savage, "The Utility Analysis of Choices Involving Risk," *Journal of Political Economy*, 56(4), August 1948: 279–304.

Furnham, Adrian, "Understanding the Meaning of Tax: Young Peoples' Knowledge of the Principles of Taxation," *Journal of Socio-Economics*, 34(5), October 2005: 703–713.

Garratt, Rod, Mark Walker, and John Wooders, "Behavior in Second-Price Auctions by Highly Experienced eBay Buyers and Sellers," *Experimental Economics*, 15(1), March 2012: 44–57.

Garrett, Thomas A., "An International Comparison and Analysis of Lotteries and the Distribution of Lottery Expenditures," *International Review of Applied Economics*, 15(20), April 2001: 213–227.

Gasmi, Farid, Jean-Jacques Laffont, and Quang H. Vuong, "Econometric Analysis of Collusive Behavior in a Soft-Drink Market," *Journal of Economics and Management Strategy*, 1(2), Summer 1992: 277–311.

Goldfarb, Avi, and Catherine E. Tucker, "Search Engine Advertising: Pricing Ads to Context," Working Paper, University of Toronto, May 2008.

Golec, Joseph, and Maurry Tamarkin, "Do Bettors Prefer Long Shots Because They Are Risk Lovers, or Are They Just Overconfident?" *Journal of Risk and Uncertainty*, 11(1), July 1995: 51–64.

Grabowski, David C., and Michael A. Morrisey, "Do Higher Gasoline Taxes Save Lives?" *Economics Letters*, 90(1), January 2006: 51–55.

Grafton, R. Quentin, and Michael B. Ward, "Prices Versus Rationing: Marshallian Surplus and Mandatory Water Restrictions," *Economic Record*, 84(S1), September 2008: S57–S65.

Gray, Wayne B., and Jay P. Shimshack, The Effectiveness of Environmental Monitoring and Enforcement: A Review of the Empirical Evidence, *Review of Environmental Economics and Policy*, 5(1), Winter 2011: 123.

Green, Richard, Richard Howitt, and Carlo Russo, "Estimation of Supply and Demand Elasticities of California Commodities," manuscript, May 2005.

Growitsch, Christian, and Heike Wetzel, "Testing for Economies of Scope in European Railways: An Efficiency Analysis," *Journal of Transport Economics and Policy*, 43(1), January 2009: 1–24.

Gruber, Jonathan H., and Sendhil Mullainathan, "Do Cigarette Taxes Make Smokers Happier," *Advances in Economic Analysis & Policy*, 5(1), 2005: article 4.

Gruber, Jonathan, Anihdya Sen, and Mark Stabile, "Estimating Price Elasticities When There Is Smuggling: The Sensitivity of Smoking to Price in Canada," *Journal of Health Economics* 22(5), September 2003: 821–842.

Guinnane, Timothy W., "The Historical Fertility Transition: A Guide for Economists," *Journal of Economic Literature*, 49(3), September 2011: 589–614.

Haas-Wilson, Deborah, and Garmon, Christopher, "Hospital Mergers and Competitive Effects: Two Retrospective Analyses," *International Journal of the Economics of Business*, 18(1), February 2011: 37–41.

Hall, Robert E., and David M. Lilien, "Efficient Wage Bargains Under Uncertain Supply and Demand," *American Economic Review*, 69(5), December 1979: 868–879.

Hamilton, Stephen F., "The Comparative Efficiency of Ad Valorem and Specific Taxes Under Monopoly and Monopsony," *Economics Letters*, 63(2), May 1999: 235–238.

Hanson, Andrew, and Ryan Sullivan, "The Incidence of Tobacco Taxation: Evidence from Geographic Micro-Level Data," *National Tax Journal*, 62(4), December 2009: 677–698.

Harkness, Joseph, and Sandra Newman, "The Interactive Effects of Housing Assistance and Food Stamps on Food Spending," *Journal of Housing Economics*, 12(3), September 2003: 224–249.

Hausman, Jerry, "Valuation of New Goods Under Perfect and Imperfect Competition," in T. Bresnahan and R. Gordon, eds., *The Economics of New Goods*, National Bureau of Economic Research Studies in Income and Wealth, Chicago: University of Chicago Press 58, 1997: 209–237.

Hausman, Jerry A., and Gregory K. Leonard, "The Competitive Effects of a New Product Introduction: A Case Study," *Journal of Industrial Economics*, 50(3), September 2002: 237–263.

Hay, George A., and Daniel Kelley, "An Empirical Survey of Price-Fixing Conspiracies," *Journal of Law and Economics*, 17(1), April 1974: 13–38.

Henderson, Jason, "FAQs about Mad Cow Disease and Its Impacts," *The Main Street Economist*, December 2003.

Herod, Roger, "Analyzing the Metrics of Global Mobility Programs," *International HR Journal*, Summer 2008: 9–15.

Heston, Alan, Robert Summers, and Bettina Aten, Penn World Table Version 6.2, Center for International Comparisons of Production, Income and Prices at the University of Pennsylvania, September 2006: **pwt.econ.upenn.edu/php_site/pwt62/pwt62_form.php**.

Highhouse, Scott, Michael J. Zickar, and Maya Yankelevich, "Would You Work If You Won the Lottery? Tracking Changes in the American Work Ethic," *Journal of Applied Psychology*, 95(2), March 2010: 349–357.

Hill, Jason, S. Polasky, E. Nelson, D. Tilman, H. Huo, L. Ludwig, J. Neumann, H. Zheng, and D. Bonta, "Climate Change and Health Costs of Air Emissions from Biofuels and Gasoline." *Proceedings of the National Academy of Sciences*, 106(6), February 2009: 2077–2082.

Ho, Jason Y.C., Tirtha Dhar, and Charles B. Weinberg, "Playoff Payoff: Super Bowl Advertising for Movies," *International Journal of Research in Marketing*, 26(3), September 2009: 168–179.

Holt, Matthew, "A Multimarket Bounded Price Variation Model Under Rational Expectations: Corn and Soybeans in the United States," *American Journal of Agricultural Economics*, 74(1), February 1992: 10–20.

Hong, Seung-Hyun, and Frank A. Wolak, "Relative Prices and Electronic Substitution: Changes in Household-Level Demand for Postal Delivery Services from 1986 to 2004," *Journal of Econometrics*, 145(1–2), July 2008: 226–242.

Hotelling, Harold, "The Economics of Exhaustible Resources," *Journal of Political Economy*, 39(2), April 1931: 137–175.

Hoynes, Hilary W., and Diane Whitmore Schanzenbach, "Consumption Responses to In-Kind Transfers: Evidence from the Introduction of the Food Stamp Program," *American Economic Journal: Applied Economics*, 1(4), October 2009: 109–139.

Hsieh, Wen-Jen, "Test of Variable Output and Scale Elasticities for 20 U.S. Manufacturing Industries," *Applied Economics Letters*, 2(8), August 1995: 284–287.

Hummels, David, and Alexandre Skiba, "Shipping the Good Apples Out? An Empirical Confirmation of the Alchian-Allen Conjecture," *Journal of Political Economy*, 112(6), December 2004: 1384–1402.

Ida, Takanori, and Tetsuya Kuwahara, "Yardstick Cost Comparison and Economies of Scale and Scope in Japan's Electric Power Industry," *Asian Economic Journal*, 18(4), December 2004: 423–438.

Imbens, Guido W., Donald B. Rubin, and Bruce I. Sacerdote, "Estimating the Effect of Unearned Income on Labor Earnings, Savings, and Consumption: Evidence from a Survey of Lottery Players," *American Economic Review*, 91(4), September 2001: 778–794.

Irwin, Douglas A., "The Welfare Cost of Autarky: Evidence from the Jeffersonian Trade Embargo, 1807–09," *Review of International Economics*, 13(4), September 2005: 631–645.

Irwin, Douglas A., and Nina Pavcnik, "Airbus versus Boeing Revisited: International Competition in the Aircraft Market," *Journal of International Economics*, 64(2), December 2004: 223–245.

Ito, Harumi, and Darin Lee, "Assessing the Impact of the September 11 Terrorist Attacks on U.S. Airline Demand," *Journal of Economics and Business*, 57(1), January-February 2005: 75–95.

Jacobson, Michael F., and Kelly D. Brownell, "Small Taxes on Soft Drinks and Snack Foods to Promote Health," *American Journal of Public Health*, 90(6), June 2000: 854–857.

Jakopin, Nejc M., and Andreas Klein, "First-mover and Incumbency Advantages in Mobile Telecommunications," *Journal of Business Research*, 65(3), March 2012: 362–370.

Jensen, Robert T., and Nolan H. Miller, "Giffen Behavior and Subsistence Consumption," *American Economic Review*, 98(4), September 2008: 1553–1577.

Jetter, Karen M., James A. Chalfant, and David A. Sumner, "Does 5-a-Day Pay?" *AIC Issues Brief*, No. 27, August 2004.

Jha, Prabhat, and Frank J. Chaloupka, "The Economics of Global Tobacco Control," *BMJ*, **bmj.com**, 321, August 2000: 358–361.

Johnson, Ronald N., and Charles J. Romeo, "The Impact of Self-Service Bans in the Retail Gasoline Market," *Review of Economics and Statistics*, 82(4), November 2000: 625–633.

Kahneman, Daniel, Jack L. Knetsch, and Richard H. Thaler, "Experimental Tests of the Endowment Effect and the Coase Theorem," *Journal of Political Economy*, 98(6), December 1990: 1325–1348.

Kahneman, Daniel, and Amos Tversky, "Prospect Theory: An Analysis of Decision under Risk," *Econometrica*, 47(2), March, 1979: 313–327.

Kaiser, Ulrich, and Julian Wright, "Price Structure in Two-Sided Markets: Evidence from the Magazine Industry," *International Journal of Industrial Organization*, 24(1), January 2006: 1–28.

Kan, Kamhon, "Cigarette Smoking and Self-Control, *Journal of Health Economics*, 26(1), January 2007: 61–81.

Karp, Larry, "Global Warming and Hyperbolic Discounting," *Journal of Public Economics*, 89(2–3), February 2005: 261–282.

Katz, Michael L., and Carl Shapiro, "Systems Competition and Network Effects," *Journal of Economic Perspectives*, 8(2), 1994: 93–115.

Keane, Michael P., "Labor Supply and Taxes: A Survey," *Journal of Economic Literature*, 49(4), December 2011: 961–1075.

Keeler, Theodore E., Teh-Wei Hu, Paul G. Barnett, and Willard G. Manning, "Taxation, Regulation, and Addiction: A Demand Function for Cigarettes Based on Time-Series Evidence," *Journal of Health Economics*, 12(1), April 1993: 1–18.

Keeler, Theodore E., Teh-Wei Hu, Michael Ong, and Hai-Yen Sung, "The U.S. National Tobacco Settlement: The Effects of Advertising and Price Changes on Cigarette Consumption," *Applied Economics*, 36(15), August 2004: 1623–1629.

Kellogg, Ryan, "Learning by Drilling: Inter-Firm Learning and Relationship Persistence in the Texas Oilpatch," *Quarterly Journal of Economics* 126(4), November, 2011: 1961–2004.

Kennickell, Arthur B., "Ponds and Streams: Wealth and Income in the U.S., 1989 to 2007," Federal Reserve Board, 2009.

Kennickell, Arthur B., "Tossed and Turned: Wealth Dynamics of U.S. Households 2007–2009," Federal Reserve Board, 2011.

Kim, DaeHwan, and J. Paul Leigh, "Are Meals at Full-Service and Fast-Food Restaurants Normal or Inferior?" *Population Health Management*, 14(6), December 2011: 307–315.

Kim, H. Youn, "Economies of Scale and Scope in Multiproduct Firms: Evidence from U.S. Railroads," *Applied Economics*, 19(6), June 1987: 733–741.

Kim, Jin-Woo, *When Are Super Bowl Advertisings Super?* University of Texas at Arlington Ph.D. dissertation, 2011.

Klein, Lawrence R., "The Use of the Input–Output Tables to Estimate the Productivity of IT," *Journal of Policy Modeling*, 25(5), July 2003: 471–475.

Kleiner, Morris M., and Alan B. Krueger, "The Prevalence and Effects of Occupational Licensing," *British Journal of Industrial Relations*, 48(4), December 2010: forthcoming.

Klemperer, Paul, *Auctions: Theory and Practice*. Princeton, N.J.: Princeton University Press, 2004.

Knetsch, Jack L., "Preferences and Nonreversibility of Indifference Curves," *Journal of Economic Behavior and Organization*, 1992, 17(1): 131–139.

Knittel, Christopher R., Douglas L. Miller, and Nicholas J. Sanders, "Caution, Drivers! Children Present: Traffic, Pollution, and Infant Health," NBER working paper, 2011.

Knittel, Christopher R., and Victor Stango, "Celebrity Endorsements, Firm Value and Reputation Risk: Evidence from the Tiger Woods Scandal," Massachusetts Institute of Technology working paper, 2012.

Kong, Clement, Wing Chow, Michael Ka, and Yiu Fung, "Efficiencies and Scope Economies of Chinese Airports in Moving Passengers and Cargo," *Journal of Air Transport Management* 15(6), November 2009: 324–329.

Kotchen, Matthew J., and Nicholas E. Burger, "Should We Drill in the Arctic National Wildlife Refuge? An Economic Perspective," NBER Working Paper, 2007.

Kowalski, Amanda E., "Estimating the Tradeoff Between Risk Protection and Moral Hazard with a Nonlinear Budget Set Model of Health Insurance, NBER Working Paper, 2012.

Kreps, David M., and Jose A. Scheinkman, "Quantity Precommitment and Bertrand Competition Yield Cournot Outcomes," *Bell Journal of Economics*, 14(2), Autumn 1983: 326–337.

Kuhn, Peter J., Peter Kooreman, Adriaan R. Soetevent, and Arie Kapteyn, "The Own and Social Effects of an Unexpected Income Shock: Evidence from the Dutch Postcode Lottery,"

American Economic Review, 101(5), August 2011: 2226–2247.

Kunreuther, Howard, and Geoffrey Heal, "Managing Catastrophic Risk," National Bureau of Economic Research, 2012.

Kuroda, Sachiko, and Isamu Yamamoto, "Estimating Frisch Labor Supply Elasticity in Japan," *Journal of Japanese International Economies*, 22(4), December 2008: 566–585.

Labonne, Julien, and Robert S. Chase, "So You Want to Quit Smoking: Have You Tried a Mobile Phone?" World Bank Policy Research Working Paper No. 4657, June 2008.

Lee, Young Han, and Ulrike Malmendier, "The Bidder's Curse," *American Economic Review*, 101(2), April 2011: 749–787.

Levin, Richard C., Alvin K. Klevorick, Richard R. Nelson, and Sidney G. Winter, "Appropriating the Returns from Industrial Research and Development," *Brookings Papers on Economic Activity*, 3 (Special Issue on Microeconomics), 1987: 783–820.

Levy, Douglas E., and Ellen Meara, "The Effect of the 1998 Master Settlement Agreement on Prenatal Smoking," *Journal of Health Economics*, 25(2), March 2006: 276–294.

Lewis, Gregory, "Asymmetric Information, Adverse Selection and Online Disclosure: The Case of eBay Motors," *American Economic Review*, 101(4), June, 2011: 1535–1546.

Lewit, Eugene M., and Douglas Coate, "The Potential for Using Excise Taxes to Reduce Smoking," *Journal of Health Economics*, 1(2), January 1982: 121–145.

Li, Shanjun, Roger von Haefen, and Christopher Timmins, "How Do Gasoline Prices Affect Fleet Fuel Economy?" *American Economic Journal: Economic Policy*, 1(2), August 2009: 113–137.

Liebenstein, Harvey, "Bandwagon, Snob, and Veblen Effects in the Theory of Consumers' Demand," *Quarterly Journal of Economics*, 64(2), May 1950: 183–207.

Lipsey, R. G., and Kelvin Lancaster, "The General Theory of Second Best," *Review of Economic Studies*, 24(1), October 1956: 11–32.

List, John A., "Does Market Experience Eliminate Market Anomalies?" *Quarterly Journal of Economics*, 118(1), February 2003: 41–71.

Lopez, Rigoberto A., and Emilio Pagoulatos, "Rent Seeking and the Welfare Cost of Trade Barriers," *Public Choice*, 79(1–2), April 1994: 149–160.

Lu, Fangwen, "Insurance Coverage and Agency Problems in Doctor Prescriptions: Evidence from a Field Experiment in China," in *Experiments on Health and Education in Developing Economies*, University of California, Berkeley Ph.D. dissertation, 2011.

Luchansky, Matthew S., and James Monks, "Supply and Demand Elasticities in the U.S. Ethanol Fuel Market," *Energy Economics*, 31(3), May 2009: 403–410.

MacAvoy, Paul W., "Tacit Collusion Under Regulation in the Pricing of Interstate Long-Distance Services," *Journal of Economics and Management Strategy*, 4(2), Summer 1995: 147–185.

MacAvoy, Paul W., *The Natural Gas Market*, New Haven: Yale University Press, 2000.

MacCrimmon, Kenneth R., and M. Toda, "The Experimental Determination of Indifference Curves," *Review of Economic Studies*, 56(3), July 1969: 433–451.

Machina, Mark, "Dynamic Consistency and Non-Expected Utility Models of Choice Under Uncertainty," *Journal of Economic Literature*, 27(4), December 1989: 1622–1668.

MacKie-Mason, Jeffrey K., and Robert S. Pindyck, "Cartel Theory and Cartel Experience in International Minerals Markets," in R. L. Gordon, H. D. Jacoby, and M. B. Zimmerman, eds., *Energy: Markets and Regulation: Essays in Honor of M. A. Adelman*. Cambridge, Mass.: MIT Press, 1986.

Madden, Janice F., *The Economics of Sex Discrimination*. Lexington, Mass.: Heath, 1973.

Madrian, Brigitte C., and Dennis F. Shea, "The Power of Suggestion: Inertia in 401(k) Participation and Savings Behavior," *Quarterly Journal of Economics*, 116(4), November 2001: 1149–1187.

Madrian, Brigitte C., and Dennis F. Shea, "The Power of Suggestion: Inertia in 401(k) Participation and Savings Behavior: Erratum," *Quarterly Journal of Economics*, 117(1), February 2002: 377.

Markowitz, Sara, et al., "Estimating the Relationship Between Alcohol Policies and Criminal Violence and Victimization," NBER working paper, 2012.

Marks, Steven V., "A Reassessment of Empirical Evidence on the U.S. Sugar Program," in S. V. Marks and K. Maskus, eds., *The Economics and Politics of World Sugar Policy*. Ann Arbor: University of Michigan Press, 1993.

McDevitt, Ryan C., "Names and Reputations: An Empirical Analysis," *American Economic Journal: Microeconomics*, 3(3), August, 2011: 193–209.

Medoff, Marshall H., "A Pooled Time-Series Analysis of Abortion Demand," *Population Research and Policy Review*, 16(6), December 1997: 597–605.

Moschini, Giancarlo, and Karl D. Meilke, "Production Subsidy and Countervailing Duties in Vertically Related Markets: The Hog-Pork Case Between Canada and the United States," *American Journal of Agricultural Economics*, 74(4), November 1992: 951–961.

Nash, John F., "Equilibrium Points in *n*-Person Games," *Proceedings of the National Academy of Sciences*, 36, 1950: 48–49.

Nash, John F., "Non-Cooperative Games," *Annals of Mathematics*, 54(2), July 1951: 286–295.

O'Donoghue, Ted, and Matthew Rabin, "Doing It Now or Later," *American Economic Review*, 89(1), March 1999: 103–124.

OECD (Organization for Economic Cooperation and Development), *Agricultural Policies In OECD Countries*, 2009.

Oxfam, *Dumping Without Borders*, Oxfam Briefing Paper 50, 2003.

Paltsev, Sergey, et al., "Assessment of U.S. Cap-and-Trade Proposals," NBER Working Paper, 2007.

Panzar, John C., and Robert D. Willig, "Economies of Scale in Multi-Output Production," *Quarterly Journal of Economics*, 91(3), August 1977: 481–493.

Panzar, John C., and Robert D. Willig, "Economies of Scope," *American Economic Review*, 71(2), May 1981: 268–272.

Paszkiewicz, Laura. "From AFDC to TANF: Have the New Public Assistance Laws Affected Consumer Spending of Recipients?" Bureau of Labor Statistics, *Consumer Expenditure Survey Anthology*, 2005, **www.bls.gov/cex/csxanthol05.htm.**

Perloff, Jeffrey M., and Ximing Wu, "Tax Incidence Varies Across the Price Distribution," *Economic Letters*, 96(1), July 2007: 116–119.

Perry, Martin K., "Forward Integration by Alcoa: 1888–1930," *Journal of Industrial Economics*, 29(1), September 1980: 37–53.

Plott, Charles R., and Kathryn Zeiler, "The Willingness to Pay— Willingness to Accept Gap, the 'Endowment Effect,' Subject Misconceptions, and Experimental Procedures for Eliciting Values," *American Economic Review*, 95(3), June 2005: 530–545.

Pollak, Robert A., *The Theory of the Cost-of-Living Index*. New York: Oxford University Press, 1989.

Posner, Richard A., "The Social Cost of Monopoly and Regulation," *Journal of Political Economy*, 83(4), August 1975: 807–827.

Pratt, John W. "Risk Aversion in the Small and in the Large," *Econometrica*, 32(1–2), January/April 1964: 122–136.

Prescott, Edward C., "Why Do Americans Work So Much More Than Europeans?" *Federal Reserve Bank of Minneapolis Quarterly Review*, 28(1), July 2004: 2–13.

Prince, Jeffrey T., "Repeat Purchase amid Rapid Quality Improvement: Structural Estimation of Demand for Personal Computers," *Journal of Economics & Management Strategy*, 17(1), Spring 2008: 1–33.

Rabin, Matthew, "Psychology and Economics," *Journal of Economic Literature*, 36(1), March 1998: 11–46.

Rao, Justin M., and David H. Reiley, "The Economics of Spam: Strategic Games, Market Institutions and Externalities," *Journal of Economic Perspectives*, Fall 2012 (forthcoming).

Rawls, John, *A Theory of Justice*. New York: Oxford University Press, 1971.

Richards, Timothy J., and Luis Padilla, "Promotion and Fast Food Demand," *American Journal of Agricultural Economics*, 91(1), February 2009: 168–183.

Roberts, Mark J., and Larry Samuelson, "An Empirical Analysis of Dynamic Nonprice Competition in an Oligopolistic Industry," *Rand Journal of Economics*, 19(2), Summer 1988: 200–220.

Roberts, Michael J., and Wolfram Schlenker, "Identifying Supply and Demand Elasticities of Agricultural Commodities: Implications for the US Ethanol Mandate," NBER Working Paper, 2010.

Robidoux, Benoît, and John Lester, "Econometric Estimates of Scale Economies in Canadian Manufacturing," Working Paper No. 88–4, Canadian Department of Finance, 1988.

Robidoux, Benoît, and John Lester, "Econometric Estimates of Scale Economies in Canadian Manufacturing," *Applied Economics*, 24(1), January 1992: 113–122.

Rohlfs, Jeffrey H., "A Theory of Interdependent Demand for a Communications Service," *Bell Journal of Economics and Management Science*, 5(1), Spring 1974: 16–37.

Rohlfs, Jeffrey H., *Bandwagon Effects in High-Technology Industries*. Cambridge, Mass.: MIT Press, 2001.

Rosenberg, Howard R., "Many Fewer Steps for Pickers—A Leap for Harvestkind? Emerging Change in Strawberry Harvest Technology," *Choices*, 1st Quarter 2004: 5–11.

Rossi, Robert J., and Terry Armstrong, *Studies of intercollegiate athletics*. Palo Alto, CA: Center for the Study of Athletics, American Institutes for Research, 1989.

Rousseas, S. W., and A. G. Hart, "Experimental Verification of a Composite Indifference Map," *Journal of Political Economy*, 59(4), August 1951: 288–318.

Ruffin, R. J., "Cournot Oligopoly and Competitive Behavior," *Review of Economic Studies*, 38(116), October 1971: 493–502.

Salgado, Hugo, "A Dynamic Firm Conduct and Market Power: The Computer Processing Market under Learning-by-doing," U.C. Berkeley Ph.D. Dissertation, Chapter 2, 2008.

Salop, Joanne, and Steven C. Salop, "Self-Selection and Turnover in the Labor Market," *Quarterly Journal of Economics*, 90(4), November 1976: 619–627.

Salop, Steven C., "Practices That (Credibly) Facilitate Oligopoly Coordination," in Joseph E. Stiglitz and G. Frank Mathewson, eds., *New Developments in the Analysis of Market Structure*. Cambridge, Mass.: MIT Press, 1986.

Salvo, Alberto, and Cristian Hsuh, "Build It, But Will They Come? Evidence from Consumer Choice Between Gasoline and Sugarcane Ethanol," working paper, 2012.

Samuelson, Paul A., *Foundations of Economic Analysis*. Cambridge, Mass.: Harvard University Press, 1947.

Schaller Consulting, *The New York City Taxicab Fact Book*, 2006, **www.schallerconsult.com**.

Scherer, F. M., "An Early Application of the Average Total Cost Concept," *Journal of Economic Literature*, 39(3), September 2001: 897–901.

Schmalensee, Richard, Paul L. Joskow, A. Denny Ellerman, Juan Pablo Montero, and Elizabeth M. Bailey, "An Interim Evaluation of Sulfur Dioxide Emissions Trading," *Journal of Economic Perspectives*, 12(3), Summer 1998: 53–68.

Schmitz, Hendrik, "More Health Care Utilization with More Insurance Coverage? Evidence from a Latent Class Model with German Data," *Applied Economics*, 44(34), December 2012: 4455–4468.

Schoemaker, Paul J. H., "The Expected Utility Model: Its Variants, Purposes, Evidence and Limitation," *Journal of Economic Literature*, 20(2), June 1982: 529–563.

Shadbegian, Ronald J., and Wayne B. Gray, "What Determines Environmental Performance at Paper Mills? The Roles of Abatement Spending, Regulation and Efficiency," *Topics in Economic Analysis and Policy*, 3(1), 2003.

Shapiro, Carl, and Joseph E. Stiglitz, "Equilibrium Unemployment as a Worker Discipline Device," *American Economic Review*, 74(3), June 1984: 434–444.

Shapiro, Carl, and Hal R. Varian, *Information Rules: A Strategic Guide to the Network Economy*. Boston: Harvard Business School Press, 1999.

Shapiro, Jesse M., "Is There a Daily Discount Rate? Evidence from the Food Stamp Nutrition Cycle," *Journal of Public Economics*, 89(2–3), February 2004: 303–325.

Shearer, Bruce, "Piece Rates, Fixed Wages and Incentives: Evidence from a Field Experiment," *Review of Economic Studies*, 71(2), April 2004: 513–534.

Shiller, Ben, and Joel Waldfogel, "Music for a Song: An Empirical Look at Uniform Song Pricing and Its Alternatives," NBER Working Paper, 2009.

Shimshack, Jay, and Michael B. Ward, Regulator Reputation, Enforcement, and Environmental Compliance, *Journal of Environmental Economics and Management*, 50(3), November 2005: 519–540.

Skeath, Susan E., and Gregory A. Trandel, "A Pareto Comparison of Ad Valorem and Unit Taxes in Noncompetitive Environments," *Journal of Public Economics*, 53(1), January 1994: 53–71.

Slade, Margaret E., "Product Rivalry with Multiple Strategic Weapons: An Analysis of Price and Advertising Competition," *Journal of Economics and Management Strategy*," 4(3), Fall 1995: 224–276.

Sood, Neeraj, Abby Alpert, and Jay Bhattacharya, "Technology, Monopoly, and the Decline of the Viatical Settlements Industry," NBER Working Paper 11164, March 2005, **www.nber.org/papers/w11164**.

Spence, A. Michael, *Market Signaling*. Cambridge, Mass.: Harvard University Press, 1974.

Spencer, Barbara J., and James A. Brander, "International R&D Rivalry and Industrial Strategy," *Review of Economic Studies*, 50(4), October 1983: 707–722.

Stevenson, Betsey, and Justin Wolfers, "Economic Growth and Subjective Well-Being: Reassessing the Easterlin Paradox," *Brookings Papers on Economic Activity*, Spring 2008: 1–87.

Stiglitz, Joseph E., "The Theory of 'Screening,' Education, and the Distribution of Income," *American Economic Review*, 65(3), June 1975: 283–300.

Stiglitz, Joseph E., "Equilibrium in Product Markets with Imperfect Information," *American Economic Review*, 69(2), May 1979: 339–345.

Stiglitz, Joseph E., "The Causes and Consequences of the Dependence of Quality on Price," *Journal of Economic Literature*, 25(1), March 1987: 1–48.

Suzuki, Junichi, "Land Use Regulation as a Barrier to Entry: Evidence from the Texas Lodging Industry," *International Economic Review*, forthcoming.

Swinton, John R., and Christopher R. Thomas, "Using Empirical Point Elasticities to Teach Tax Incidence," *Journal of Economic Education*, 32(4), Fall 2001: 356–368.

Tian, Weiming, and Guang Hua Wan, "Technical Efficiency and Its Determinants in China's Grain Production," *Journal of Productivity Analysis* 13(2), 2000: 159–174.

Tenn, Steven, "The Price Effects of Hospital Mergers: A Case Study of the Sutter–Summit Transaction," *International Journal of the Economics of Business*, 18(1), February 2011: 65–82.

Tideman, T. Nicholaus, and Gordon Tullock, "A New and Superior Process for Making Social Choices," *Journal of Political Economy*, 84(6), December 1976: 1145–1159.

Trabandt, Mathias, and Harald Uhlig, "How Far Are We From the Slippery Slope? The Laffer Curve Revisited," NBER Working Paper, 2011.

Tullock, G., "The Welfare Cost of Tariffs, Monopolies, and Theft," *Western Economic Journal*, 5(3), June 1967: 224–232.

Tversky, Amos, and Daniel Kahneman, "The Framing of Decisions and the Psychology of Choice," *Science*, 211(4481), January, 1981: 453–458.

Tyler, John H., Richard J. Murnane, and John B. Willett, "Estimating the Labor Market Signaling Value of the GED," *Quarterly Journal of Economics*, 115(2), May 2000: 431–468.

Urban, Glen L., Theresa Carter, and Steven Gaskin, "Market Share Rewards to Pioneering Brands: An Empirical Analysis and Strategic Implications," *Management Science*, 32(6), June 1986: 645–659.

Usero, Belén, and Zulima Fernández, "First Come, First Served: How Market and Non-market Actions Influence Pioneer Market Share," Journal of Business Research 62(11), November 2009: 1139–1145.

Varian, Hal R., "Measuring the Deadweight Cost of DUP and Rent-Seeking Activities," *Economics and Politics*, 1(1), Spring 1989: 81–95.

Veracierto, Marcelo, "Firing Costs and Business Cycle Fluctuations," *International Economic Review*, 49(1), February 2008: 1–39.

Villegas, Daniel J., "The Impact of Usury Ceilings on Consumer Credit," *Southern Economic Journal*, 56(1), July 1989: 126–141.

Viscusi, W. Kip, *Employment Hazards*. Cambridge, MA: Harvard University Press, 1979.

von Neumann, John, and Oskar Morgenstern, *Theory of Games and Economic Behavior*. Princeton, N.J.: Princeton University Press, 1944.

Waldfogel, Joel, "The Deadweight Loss of Christmas," *American Economic Review*, 83(5), December 1993: 1328–1336.

Waldfogel, Joel, "Does Consumer Irrationality Trump Consumer Sovereignty?" *Review of Economics and Statistics*, 87(4), November 2005: 691–696.

Waldfogel, Joel, *Scroogenomics*. Princeton University Press, 2009.

Warner, John T., and Saul Pleeter, "The Personal Discount Rate: Evidence from Military Downsizing Programs," *American Economic Review*, 91(1), March 2001: 33–53.

Weiher, Jesse C., Robin C. Sickles, and Jeffrey M. Perloff, "Market Power in the U.S. Airline Industry," in D. J. Slottje, ed., *Economic Issues in Measuring Market Power, Contributions to Economic Analysis*, Vol. 255. Elsevier 2002.

Weinstein, Arnold A., "Transitivity of Preferences: A Comparison Among Age Groups," *Journal of Political Economy*, 76(2), March/April 1968: 307–311.

Weitzman, Martin L., "Prices vs. Quantities," *Review of Economic Studies*, 41(4), October 1974: 477–491.

Wellington, Donald C., "The Mark of the Plague," *Rivista Internazionale di Scienze Economiche e Commerciali*, 37(8), August 1990: 673–684.

Whitmore, Diane, "What Are Food Stamps Worth?" Princeton University Working Paper #468, July 2002, **www.irs.princeton.edu/pubs/pdfs/468.pdf**.

Williamson, Oliver E., "Credible Commitments: Using Hostages to Support Exchange," *American Economic Review*, 73(4), September 1983: 519–540.

Willig, Robert D., "Consumer's Surplus without Apology," *American Economic Review*, 66(4), September 1976: 589–597.

Yatchew, A., "Scale Economies in Electricity Distribution: A Semiparametric Analysis," *Journal of Applied Econometrics*, 15(2), March/April 2000: 187–210.

Yellen, Janet L., "Efficiency Wage Models of Unemployment," *American Economic Review*, 74(2), May 1984: 200–205.

Sources for Applications and Challenges

Chapter 1

Twinkie Tax: Jacobson and Brownell (2000); Bartlett, Bruce, "The Big Food Tax," *National Review Online*, April 3, 2002; Lemieux, Pierre, "It's the Fat Police," *National Post*, April 6, 2002; Tobler, Helen, "Call for Tax War on Obesity," *Australian IT*, August 16, 2002; "Soda Pop to Be Banned in L.A. Schools," **CBSNEWS.com**, August 28, 2002; Chouinard et al. (2007); "'Fat tax' proposed for obese in Britain," **sify.com/news/fat-tax-proposed-for-obese-in-britain-news-national-jegmLFabedd.html**, February 25, 2008; **www.upi.com/Top_News/US/2012/05/02/Chicago-considers-soft-drink-tax/UPI-86561335967080**, May 2, 2012.

Income Threshold Model and China: "Next in Line: Chinese Consumers," *Economist*, 326 (7795), January 23, 1993: 66–67; Pelline, Jeff, "U.S. Businesses Pour into China," *San Francisco Chronicle*, May 17, 1994: B1–B2; *China Statistical Yearbook* (Beijing: China Statistical Publishing House, 2000); **www.uschina.org/info/forecast/2007/foreign-investment.html**; Wei, Jiang, "FDI Doubles Despite Tax Concerns," *China Daily*, February 19, 2008; Bradsher, Keith, "With First Car, a New Life in China," *New York Times*, April 24, 2008; **www.worldometers.info/cars** (viewed May 6, 2012).

Chapter 2

Quantities and Prices of Genetically Modified Foods: Dick Ahlstrom, "Use of GM Foods Inevitable in EU—Expert," *Irish Times*, July 18, 2008; Bobby Jordan, "GM Surprise in the Cereal Box," *The Times*, August 3, 2008; "Genetically Modified Food Is Almost Everywhere," **English.vietnamnet.vn**, April 21, 2010; David Cronin, "Advantage GM in Europe," **www.ipsnews.net/ news.asp?idnews=51472**, May 18, 2010; **redgreenandblue.org/2011/03/23/is-europes-ban-on-monsantos-gmo-crops-illegal**; **www.guardian.co.uk/environment/2012/feb/08/industry-claims-rise-gm-crops**.

Aggregating the Demand for Broadband Service: Duffy-Deno (2003).

Occupational Licensing: Kleiner and Krueger (2010); **http://admissions.calbar.ca.gov/Examinations/Statistics.aspx** (viewed May 5, 2012); **http://www.ncbex.org/assets/media_files/Statistics/2011Statistics.pdf** (viewed May 5, 2012).

Oil Drilling in the Arctic National Wildlife Refuge: Lee, Dwight, "To Drill or Not to Drill: Let the Environmentalists Decide," *The Independent Review*, Fall 2001, pp. 217–226; Energy Information Administration, "The Effects of Alaska Oil and Natural Gas Provisions of H.R. 4 and S. 1776 on U.S. Energy Markets," February 2002; United States Geological Survey, "Arctic National Wildlife Refuge, 1002 Area, Petroleum Assessment, 1998, Including Economic Analysis," **pubs.usgs.gov/fs/fs-0028-01/fs-0028-01.pdf**; "Oil Companies Could Benefit from Alaska Drilling," VNU Business Media, Inc., November 22, 2004; Borenstein, Severin, "ANWR Oil and the Price of Gasoline," U.C. Energy Institute, *Energy Notes*, 3(2), June 2005.

Subsidizing Ethanol: Luchansky and Monks (2009); **www.biofuelsdigest.com/blog2/2010/01/07/ethanol-subsidies-are-82-per-barrel-of-replaced-gasoline-says-incendiary-baker-institute-report** (June 21, 2010); **www.motherjones.com/transition/inter.php?dest=http://www.motherjones.com/kevin-drum/2012/01/ethanol-subsidies-not-gone-just-hidden-little-better** (May 11, 2012).

Price Controls Kill: "Smuggling Results in Sugar Shortages in Zimbabwe," *Harare*, April 21, 2002; "Construction Industry Faces Bleak Future," *Zimbabwe Standard*, May 5, 2002; "Makoni Admits Price Controls to Blame for Thriving Black Market," *The Daily News*, May 10, 2002; "Zim Slaps Price Control on Food," News24, **finance24.com**, June 4, 2005; Jongwe, Fanuel, "Watchdog Unlikely to Get Teeth into Zimbabwe Inflation," *Business Report*, November 13, 2006, **www.busrep.co.za/index.php?fArticleId$=$3534401**; Kotchen and Burger (2007); **tonto.eia.doe.gov/dnav/pet/hist/wtotworldw.htm** (October 25, 2007); "Zimbabwe Arrests Over Price Curbs," *Al Jazeera*, July 9, 2007, **english.aljazeera.net/NR/exeres/81D1350D-2D57-40C9-871F-EC95C875D5FC.htm**; **www.theaustralian.news.com.au/story/0,25197,23351335-2703,00.html** (March 11, 2008); **www.monstersandcritics.com/news/business/news/printer_1419238.php**, July 24, 2008; Latham, Brian, "Zimbabwe abandons price controls, promotes currency trading," January 29, 2009, **www.tradeafricablog.com/2009/01/zimbabwe-abandons-price-controls.html**; Marawanyika, Godfrey, "Mugabe Defends Sale of Foreign Firms to Locals," **www.google.com/hostednews/afp/article/ALeqM5jK-PanDRNzEjTbmWRZ48AgI9KesNw**, February 27, 2010.

Chapter 3

Why Americans Buy E-books and Germans Do Not: www.publishersweekly.com/binary-data/ARTICLE_ATTACHMENT/file/000/000/522-1.pdf, 2011; Wishenbart, Rüdiger, *The Global eBook Market*, February 2012; Biba, Paul, "Publishing Business Conference: International Trends in Ebook Consumption," www.teleread.com, March 20, 2012; Wiener, Aaron, "We Read Best on Paper, Cultural Resistance Hobbles German E-Book Market," www.spiegel.de, April 13, 2012.

You Can't Have Too Much Money: *Business Week*, February 28, 2005, p. 13; Stevenson and Wolfers (2008); "Annual Happiness Index Again Finds One-Third of Americans Very Happy," www.digitaljournal.com, June 22, 2011; latimesblogs.latimes.com/world_now/2012/04/happiness-world-bhutan-meeting-denmark.html, April 2, 2012.

***MRS* Between Recorded Tracks and Live Music:** We estimated the Cobb-Douglas utility function using budget share information from *The Student Experience Report, 2007*, National Union of Students. Budget allocations between live and recorded music are from the 2008 survey of the *Music Experience and Behaviour in Young People* produced by the British Music Rights and the University of Hertfordshire.

Indifference Curves Between Food and Clothing: Eastwood and Craven (1981).

Utility Maximization for Recorded Tracks and Live Music: See sources for "*MRS* Between Recorded Tracks and Live Music" above.

How You Ask the Question Matters: Madrian and Shea (2001, 2002); aon.mediaroom.com/index.php?s=43&item=2285, May 24, 2011; www.arielinvestments.com/401k-Study-2012 (May 13, 2012).

Chapter 4

Paying Workers to Relocate: Katherine Rosman, "Expat Life Gets Less Cushy," *Wall Street Journal*, October 26, 2007; Barbara Worthington, "FYI: Relocation," www.hreonline.com/HRE/story.jsp?storyId=69921696, February 1, 2008; www.orcworldwide.com/news/080212.php (February 12, 2008); Grace W. Weinstein, "The Good and Bad of Moving Overseas," *Financial Times*, May 24 2008; www.mercer.com/referencecontent.htm?idContent=1312800 (July 21, 2008); Jane M. Von Bergen, "More U.S. Workers Getting Global Assignments," *Philadelphia Inquirer*, July 31, 2008; Herod (2008); www.lib.umich.edu/govdocs/steccpi.html (August 2008); www.mercer.com/summary.htm?idContent=1351425 (July 7, 2009); www.expatistan.com/cost-of-living/comparison/seattle/london (June, 2011); www.citymayors.com/economics/expensive_cities2.html, August 18, 2011; www.kpmgcareers.com (May 19, 2012).

Quitting Smoking: Busch et al. (2004); Levy and Meara (2006); Colman and Remler (2008); Labonne and Chase (2008); www.who.int/tobacco/mpower/tobacco_facts/en/index.html (viewed July 22, 2009); www.ash.org (2012); tobaccofreekids.org (2012); ash.org/cigtaxfacts.html (2012); www.cdc.gov (2012).

Fast-Food Engel Curve: Kim and Leigh (2011).

Shipping the Good Stuff Away: Hummels and Skiba (2004).

Fixing the CPI Substitution Bias: Hausman (1997); "Who's Afraid of the Big Bad Deficit?" *Economist*, 336(7934), September 30, 1995: 25–26; Uchitelle, Louis, "Balancing Quantity, Quality and Inflation," *New York Times*, December 18, 1996: C1, C6; Marshall, Jonathan, "Figuring Inflation Is a Truly Tough Job," *San Francisco Chronicle*, December 9, 1996: C1, C2; Boskin et al. (1997); *Statistical Abstract of the United States* (Washington, D.C.: U.S. Bureau of the Census, 1999); White, Alan G., "Measurement Biases in Consumer Price Indexes," *International Statistical Review*, 67(3), December 1999: 301–325; Boskin and Jorgenson (1997); symposium in *Journal of Economic Perspectives*, Winter 1998; www.bls.gov/cpi/home.htm (2010); www.post-office-jobs.com/Postal-Jobs/compensation.html (viewed August 20, 2009); www.bls.gov/news.release/empsit.t14.htm (2010); www.simplyhired.com/a/salary/search/q-usps (2010).

Chapter 5

Child-Care Subsidies: Blau and Tekin (2001); Elena Cherney, "Giving Day-Care Cash to Stay-at-Home Parents Sounds Like Politics to Some Canadians," *Wall Street Journal*, July 3, 2006: A2; Tekin (2007); clasp.org/WelfarePolicy/pdf/map100907us.pdf (2007); Currie and Gahvari (2008); nccic.acf.hhs.gov/categories/index.cfm?categoryId=2\# (viewed May 26, 2009); U.S. Department of Health Services, "Child Care and Development Fund," www.acf.hhs.gov/programs/ccb/ccdf/factsheet.htm (viewed May 26, 2012); www.hss.gov.yk.ca/pdf/childcaresubsidy_en.pdf, February 2012.

Willingness to Pay and Consumer Surplus on eBay: www.eBay.com (2009), Bapna et al. (2008).

Compensating Variation, and Equivalent Variation for the Internet: Dean (2012); Kidner, Sarah, "What Would you Give Up for the Net?" conversation.which.co.uk/technology/what-would-you-give-up-for-internet-chocolate-coffee-sex, March 22, 2012.

Water Quota: Grafton and Ward (2008).

Food Stamps Versus Cash: Whitmore (2002); "U.S. Converting Food Stamps into Debit-Card Benefits," *Chattanooga Times Free Press*, June 23, 2004; U.S. Department of Agriculture, *Characteristics of Food Stamp Households: Fiscal Year 2007*, September 2008; www.fns.usda.gov/FSP/faqs.htm (viewed August 31, 2009); Hoynes and Schanzenbach (2009); Andrews, Margaret, and David Smallwood, "What's Behind the Rise in SNAP Participation?" *Amber Waves*, March 2012; Beatty and Tuttle (2012).

Working After Winning the Lottery: Imbens et al. (2001); Kuhn et al. (2011).

Chapter 6

Labor Productivity During Recessions: Hsieh (1995); Tom Abate, "Licorice Company Looks to Weather the Storm," *San Francisco Chronicle*, September 28, 2008; Veracierto (2008); Timothy Aeppel, and Justin Lahart, "Lean Factories Find It Hard to Cut Jobs Even in a Slump," *Wall Street Journal*, March 9, 2009; "Union City Licorice Factory Workers Accept Contract, End Strike," CBS San Francisco, January 11, 2012.

Malthus and the Green Revolution: Norman Borlaug, "Nobel Lecture," www.nobelprize.org, December 11, 1970;

Easterbrook, Gregg, "Forgotten Benefactor of Humanity," *Atlantic Monthly*, February 1997; Brander and Taylor (1998); Alan Barkema, "Ag Biotech," *The Main Street Economist*, October 2000; "Biotechnology and the Green Revolution: Interview with Norman Borlaug," www.actionBioscience .org, November 2002; United Nations, *Millennium Development Goals Report*, New York, 2008; www.ers.usda .gov/Data/AgProductivity (May 16, 2012); www.fao.org/ NEWS/2000/000704-e.htm (viewed May 17, 2012); www.wfp.org/hunger/stats (viewed June 11, 2012).

A Semiconductor Integrated Circuit Isoquant: Nile Hatch, personal communications; Roy Mallory, personal communications; "PC Processor War Rages On," Deutsche Presse-Agentur, September 1, 2002.

Returns to Scale in U.S. Manufacturing: Hsieh (1995).

U.S. Electric Generation Efficiency: Fabrizio et al. (2007).

Tata Nano's Technical and Organizational Innovations: "Engineering the Nano," The Times of India, January 11, 2008; Reuters, "How Green Is My Low-cost Car? India Revs Up Debate," June 19, 2008, www.enn.com/sci-tech/ article/37437; John Hagel and John Seely Brown, "Learning from Tata's Nano," February 27, 2008, www.businessweek .com/print/innovate/content/feb2008/id20080227_377233 .htm; Gerard J. Tellis, "A Lesson for Detroit: Tata Nano," *San Francisco Chronicle*, March 31, 2009; "Tata Nano: Not Only a Product Revolution, but also a Breakthrough in Product Distribution," www.automotive-business-review .com/comment/tata_nano_not_only_a_product_revolution_ but_also_a_breakthrough_in_product_distribution_070509?, May 7, 2009; www.tatanano.inservices.tatamotors.com/ tatamotors/index.php?option=com_content&task=view&id= 184&Itemid=210&limit=1&limitstart=0 (viewed September 6, 2009); articles.economictimes.indiatimes.com/2011-05- 10/news/29528296_1_nano-sales-tata-nano-nisheeth-mehta, May 10, 2011; "LCVs, Nano push Tata Motors May Sales Up 4%," Moneycontrol.com, June 1, 2012.

Chapter 7

Technology Choice at Home Versus Abroad: Industrial College of the Armed Forces, *Spring 2008 Industry Study Final Report, Electronics Industry*, www.ndu.edu/icaf/ industry/reports/2008/pdf/icaf-is-report-electronics-ay08 .pdf; www.epi.org/content.cfm/bp219 (November 22, 2008); www.sia-online.org (viewed June 15, 2012); Hookway, James, Patrick Barta, and Dana Mattioli, "China's Wage Hikes Ripple Across Asia," *Wall Street Journal*, March 13, 2012.

The Opportunity Cost of an MBA: Edmonston, Peter, "In Tough Times, M.B.A. Applications May Be an Economic Indicator," *New York Times*, October 7, 2008; "Profile of GMAT Candidates, 2005–06 to 2009–10," www.gmac.com (view June 18, 2011). *2011 Application Trend Survey*, www.gmac.com (viewed June 11, 2012).

Short-Run Cost Curves for a Japanese Beer Manufacturer: Flath (2011).

Small Is Beautiful: "Print me a Stradivarius," www.economist .com/node/18114327, February 10, 2011; Symes, Mark D., et al. "Integrated 3D-printed Reactionware for Chemical Synthesis and Analysis," *Nature Chemistry*, www.nature.com/ nchem/journal/v4/n5/pdf/nchem.1313.pdf, April 2012.

Choosing an Inkjet or Laser Printer: www.amazon.com (viewed June 15, 2012).

Learning by Drilling: Kellogg (2009).

Economies of Scope: Friedlaender et al. (1983); Kim (1987); Ida and Kuwahara (2004); Asai (2006); Farsi et al. (2008).

Chapter 8

The Rising Cost of Keeping On Truckin': "About Interstate Trucking Authority," www.ehow.com/about_4739672_ interstate-trucking-authority.html (viewed June 2012); www.fmcsa.dot.gov/rules-regulations/rules-regulations.htm (viewed June 2012); www.dotauthority.com/ucr.htm?gclid= CKma5tebnqQCFSFZiAodN2bunA (viewed June 2012); Gattuso, James L., "Truckers Don't Need Mandated Recorders," *Freemont Tribune*, May 29, 2012.

Oil, Oil Sands, and Oil Shale Shutdowns: Salpukas, Agis, "Low Prices Have Sapped Little Oil Producers," *New York Times*, April 3, 1999:B1, B4; Collier, Robert, "Oil's Dirty Future," *San Francisco Chronicle*, May 22, 2005:A1, A14, A15; Collier, Robert, "Coaxing Oil from Huge U.S. Shale Deposits," *San Francisco Chronicle*, September 4, 2006:A1; Birger, Jon, "Oil Shale May Finally Have Its Moment," *Fortune*, November 1, 2007; Kohler, Judith, "Energy Firms Cautious on Oil Shale," OCRegister, November 3, 2007; Geman, Ben, "Canada Warns U.S. Against Using Energy Law to Bar Fuel from Oil Sands," Greenwire, February 28, 2008; "Scraping Bottom," *National Geographic Magazine*, March 2009; www.bloomberg.com/energy (viewed June 17, 2012).

The Size of Ethanol Processing Plants: futures .tradingcharts.com/chart/AC (viewed June 18, 2012); www.ethanolrfa.org/pages/statistics (viewed June 18, 2012).

U.S. Fast-Food Firms Entry in Russia: Kramer, Andrew E., "Russia Becomes a Magnet for U.S. Fast-Food Chains," New York Times, August 3, 2011.

Upward-Sloping Long-Run Supply Curve for Cotton: International Cotton Advisory Committee, *Survey of the Cost of Production of Raw Cotton*, September 1992:5; *Cotton: World Statistics*, April 1993:4–5. The figure shows the supply of the major producing countries for which we have cost information. The only large producers for whom cost data are missing are India and China.

Reformulated Gasoline Supply Curves: Borenstein et al. (2004); David R. Baker, "Rules Fuel Patchwork Quilt of Gas Blends Nationwide," *San Francisco Chronicle*, June 19, 2005: B1, B3; Brown et al. (2008); Ronald D. White, "Refinery Work Boosts Gasoline Prices in California," *Los Angeles Times*, September 9, 2009; David R. Baker, "Why Californians Are Paying Even More for Gas," *San Francisco Chronicle*, September 23, 2009, p. A1; Auffhammer and Kellogg (2011); tonto.eia.doe.gov/dnav/pet/pet_pnp_cap1_dcu_ nus_a.htm (viewed June 17, 2012).

Chapter 9

Licensing Taxis: Marshall, Jonathan, "Cab Companies Hauled into Court," *San Francisco Chronicle*, July 1, 1993: A1, A11; Epstein, Edward, "S.F. Tax Deal Rejected by Board of Supervisors," *San Francisco Chronicle*, April 13, 1999: A16; Boroski and Mildner (1998); Barrett (2003); Berdik, Chris,

"Fare Game," *Boston Globe*, 42(9) September 2004:98–105; Kim, Hansu, "Taxi Medallions—Why Give S.F. Assets Away?" *San Francisco Chronicle*, March 29, 2005:B7; Schaller Consulting (2006); "Better than Gold," **www.upi .com/Business_News/2009/08/06/Better-than-gold-A-cab-medallion/UPI-87711249585126/print/**, August 6, 2009; Abelson (2010): **blogs.reuters.com/felix-salmon/2011/10/21/ why-taxi-medallions-cost-1-million** (viewed June 23, 2012); Horwitz, Jeff, and Chris Cumming, "Taken for a Ride," **Slate.com**, June 6, 2012; **www.nyc.gov/html/tlc/downloads/ pdf/corporate_accessible.pdf** (viewed June 23, 2012).

Tiger Woods' Rents: **www.guardian.co.uk/sport/2009/ dec/15/tiger-woods-timeline-golf-turmoil**; Knittel and Stango (January 2012).

The Deadweight Loss of Christmas Presents: Waldfogel (1993, 2005, 2009); Herring, Hubert B., "Help! What Do We Do With All This Stuff? Regift, of Course," *New York Times*, December 26, 2004: 3.2; "Gift Card Appeal Remains Strong and Continues to Grow," May 20, 2008; Bauer and Schmidt (2008); Mitchell, Eve, "Cashing In," *Oakland Tribune*, June 12, 2011, C1; Farfan, Barbara, "2011 U.S. Christmas Holiday Retail Data, Statistics, Results, Numbers Roundup Complete U.S. Retail Industry Christmas Holiday Shopping Year-Over-Year Results," **About.com**, December 29, 2011; Helft, Miguel, Meet the Anti-Groupon, *CNNMoney*, April 30, 2012.

How Big Are Farm Subsidies and Who Gets Them?: *Agricultural Policies Monitoring and Evaluations 2011*, Organization for Economic Cooperation and Development, 2012 (preliminary); **www.oecd.org** (viewed June 27, 2012).

The Social Cost of a Natural Gas Price Ceiling: MacAvoy (2000); Davis and Kilian (2011).

Chapter 10

Anti-Price Gouging Laws: Davis (2008); Carden (2008); Michael Giberson, "Predictable consequences of anti-price gouging laws," **knowledgeproblem.com/2009/06/01/ predictable-consequences-of-anti-price-gouging-laws**, June 1, 2009; "Bill Allows Gas Price Increase in Emergency," **www.ajc.com**, March 22, 2010; "Price Gouging Law Goes into Effect Following State of Emergency Declaration," **www.neworleans.com**, April 29, 2010; Goble, Keith, "Rhode Island Imposes Price-gouging Protections," **landlinemag.com**, June 25, 2012.

Partial-Equilibrium Versus Multimarket Equilibrium Analysis in Corn and Soy Markets: Holt (1992).

Urban Flight: Econsult (2003); Crawford et al. (2004); **www .phila.gov/revenue/wage_tax.html** (viewed July 1, 2012).

The Wealth and Income of the 1%: Nasar, Sylvia, "The Rich Get Richer, but Never the Same Way Twice," *New York Times*, August 16, 1992: 3; Davies et al. (2007); Bucks et al. (2009); Kennickell (2009); **www.joshuakennon.com/ how-much-money-does-it-take-to-be-in-the-top-1-of-wealth-and-net-worth-in-the-united-states**, September 16, 2011; Allegretto, Sylvia, "The State of Working America's Wealth," EPI Briefing Paper, March 23, 2011; Kennickell (2009, 2011); Saez, Emmanuel, "Striking it Richer: The Evolution of Top Incomes in the United States (Updated with 2009 and

2010 estimates)," University of California Department of Economics, March 2, 2012; Mishel, Lawrence, and Natalie Sabadish, "CEO Pay and the Top 1%," EPI Issue Brief, May 2, 2012; **www.aflcio.org/Corporate-Watch/CEO-Pay-and-the-99/Trends-in-CEO-Pay** (viewed July 1, 2012).

Chapter 11

Pricing Apple's iPad: Albanesius, Chloe, "iSuppli: iPad Could Produce Profits for Apple," **pcmag.com**, February 10, 2010; Reisinger, Don, "IDC: Apple iPad Secures 87 Percent Market Share," **cnet.com**, January 18, 2011; Reisinger, Don, "Study: iPad Tallies 89 Percent of Table Traffic," **cnet.com**, January 24, 2011; Wortham, Jenna, "So Far Rivals Can't Beat iPad's Price," *New York Times*, March 6, 2011; **www.abiresearch .com/press/3919-iPad+Remains+Dominant+in+1Q%E2%80 %992012+While+Kindle+Fire+Fizzles**, June 4, 2012. In Solved Problem 11.2, the marginal cost estimate (slightly rounded) is from iSuppli. I assumed that the company's gross profit margin for 2010 of about 40% (**forbes.com**) held for the iPad and used that to calculate the fixed cost. I derived the linear demand curve by assuming Apple maximizes short-run profit using the information on price, marginal cost, and quantity.

Cable Cars and Profit Maximization: Gordon, Rachel, "A Fare Too Steep?" *San Francisco Chronicle*, September 12, 2006: B-1; **bart.gov** (viewed July 9, 2012); Gordon, Rachel, "Cable Car Fares Rising a Buck to $6 on July 1," *San Francisco Chronicle*, June 7, 2011; "Cable Car Fares," *SFMTA*, 2012, **www.sfmta.com/cms/mfares/fareinfo.htm#cable** (viewed on June 4, 2012).

Botox Patent Monopoly: Weiss, Mike, "For S.F. Doctor, Drug Botox Becomes a Real Eye-Opener," *San Francisco Chronicle*, April 14, 2002: A1, A19; Abelson, Reed, "F.D.A. Approves Allergan Drug for Fighting Wrinkles," *New York Times*, April 16, 2002; Tramer, Harriet, "Docs Detecting How to Boost Botox Profitability," *Crain's Cleveland Business*, March 7, 2005: 17; Singer, Natasha, "Botox Plus: New Mixes for Plumping and Padding," *New York Times*, July 14, 2005; "The No-Knife Eye Lift," **magazines.ivillage.com/ goodhousekeeping/archive/0,284598,00.html**, 2005; Singer, Natasha, "So Botox Isn't Just Skin Deep," *New York Times*, April 12, 2009; "Nice News for Allergan–Analyst Blog," **community.nasdaq.com/News/2012-06/nice-news-for-allergan-analyst-blog.aspx?storyid=152408**, June 29, 2012.

Natural Gas Regulation: Davis and Muehlegger (2009).

Critical Mass and eBay: Steiner, Ina, "Yahoo Closes Australian Auction Site," **auctionbytes.com**, August 7, 2003; Brown and Morgan (2006, 2009); Barrett, John, "MySpace Is a Natural Monopoly," **ecommercetimes.com**, January 17, 2007; Ou, Carol Xiaojuan, and Robert M. Davison, "Why eBay Lost to TaoBao in China: The Global Advantage," *Communications of the ACM*, 52(1), January 2009: 145–148.

Chapter 12

Sale Price: Perloff and Wu (2007); Datko, Karen, "My Ketchup Taste Test: It's an Upset!" **msn.com**, January 14, 2011; Smithers, Rebecca, "Heinz Left Playing Tomato Catch-Up after Ketchup Tasting Trouncing," *The Guardian*,

May 25, 2011; Newman, Andrew Adam, "Ketchup Moves Upmarket, with a Balsamic Tinge," *New York Times*, October 25, 2011; www.heinz.com/our-company/press-room/trivia.aspx (viewed July 9, 2012).

Disneyland Pricing: "Couple Tries for Year of Daily Disneyland Visits," *San Francisco Chronicle*, July 3, 2012; www.disneyland.com (viewed July 9, 2012).

Preventing Resale of Designer Bags: Eric Wilson, "Retailers Limit Purchases of Designer Handbags," *New York Times*, January 10, 2008; www.prada.com, www.gucci.com, www.saksfifthavenue.com (viewed, July 10, 2009 and July 9, 2012).

Botox Revisited: See the sources for the Chapter 11 application "Botox Patent Monopoly."

Google Uses Bidding for Ads to Price Discriminate: Goldfarb and Tucker (2008).

Smuggling Prescription Drugs into the United States: Colliver, Victoria, "U.S. Drug Prices 81% Higher than in 7 Western Nations," *San Francisco Chronicle*, October 29, 2004: C1, C6; Ridgeway, James, "Congress vs. Big Pharma: Let the Games Begin," *Mother Jones*, December 14, 2006; Frederick, Jim, "New Senate Move to Allow Importation Draws Condemnation of Retail Pharmacy," www.drugstorenews.com/print.aspx?id=119855, October 21, 2009; www.decisionresources.com/Products-and-Services/Report.aspx?r=spech40709 (November 1, 2009); "Statins Cost 4 Times More in U.S. Than in U.K.," www.modernmedicine.com, January 10, 2012.

Buying Discounts: Borenstein and Rose (1994); "Wortham, Jenna, "Coupons You Don't Clip, Sent to Your Cellphone," *New York Times*, August 29, 2009; "Up Front," *Consumer Reports*, September 2009:7; Musick, Carmen, "Computer Technology Fueling Coupon Trend," October 31, 2009, www.timesnews.net/print_article.php?id= 9018027; www.santella.com/Trends.htm (viewed May 28, 2012); "Groupon and the Online Deal Revolution," emarketer.com, June 7, 2011; "Coupon Trends," *JPS*, March 2, 2012, www.santella.com/Trends.htm (viewed on June 16, 2012); *NCH Annual Coupon Facts*, nchmarketing.com, 2012.

Pricing iTunes: Shiller and Waldfogel (2011).

IBM: *IBM v. United States*, 298 U.S. 131 (1936).

Available for a Song: Shiller and Waldfogel (2009).

Super Bowl Commercials: Ho et al. (2009), Kim (2011); "Cost of Average Super Bowl Commercial? $3.5M," *USA Today*, January 3, 2012; Adegoke, Yinka, "Super Bowl Advertisers Seek Buzz on Social Media," *Reuters*, January 29, 2012; Terlep, Sharon, and Suzanne Vranica, "GM to Forgo Costly Super Bowl Ads," *Wall Street Journal*, May 18, 2012.

Chapter 13

Intel and AMD's Advertising Strategies: Salgado (2008).

Strategic Advertising: "50 Years Ago...," *Consumer Reports*, January 1986; Roberts and Samuelson (1988); Gasmi et al. (1992); Elliott, Stuart, "Advertising," *New York Times*, April 28, 1994: C7; Slade (1995); Richards and Padilla (2009); www.kantarmedia.com/sites/default/files/press/Kantar_Media_2011__Q4_US_Ad_Spend.pdf, March 12, 2012.

Tough Love: Choroszewicz, Marta, and Pascal Wolff, "Population and Social Conditions," *Eurostat*, 50/2010; Goudreau, Jenna, "Nearly 60% of Parents Provide Financial Support to Adult Children," forbes.com, May 20, 2011; Fagan, Kevin, "Boomerang Kids Moving Back Home with Parents," San Francisco Chronicle, October 16, 2011; Parker, Kim, "The Boomerang Generation," Pew Research Center, March 15, 2012; www.britishinsurance.com/insurance-news/2nd-july—financial-support.aspx, July 2, 2012.

First Mover Advantages and Disadvantages: The cost estimates are based on an iSuppli "teardown" analysis: McGrath, Dylan, "'Teardown' Finds Toshiba Taking a Loss on HD DVD Player,"*EE Times*, June 23, 2006; Urban et al. (1986); McGrath, Dylan, "Analyst Predicts Stalemate in Next-Gen DVD War," *EE Times*, June 23, 2006; Usero and Fernández (2009); Jakopin and Klein (2012).

Bidders' Curse: Lee and Malmendier (2011); Garratt et al. (2012).

GM's Ultimatum: Schoenberger, Robert, "GM Sends Ultimatums to All Its 6000 US dealers," *Cleveland Plain Dealer*, June 2, 2009; and "GM Dealers Sue to Keep Doors Open," *Toronto Star*, November 27, 2009; Kurnovich, Janet, "GM Canada Sued For $750 Million by Former Dealers," insurance-car.co, May 17, 2011.

Chapter 14

Government Aircraft Subsidies: Irwin and Pavcnik (2004); Brand, Constant, "EU, Washington Resume Battle Over Boeing," *San Francisco Chronicle*, May 31, 2005; www.google.com/hostednews/afp/article/ALeqM5huKmlnkxMn60qKQUBMK-nx5kUPlw (December 18, 2009); Heilpin, John, "WTO: Boeing Got $5B In Illegal Subsidies," March 12, 2012; Fishman, Charles, "U.S. Bottled Water Sales Are Booming (Again) Despite Opposition," newswatch.nationalgeographic.com, May 17, 2012; www.manufacturing.net/news/2012/03/wto-boeing-got-5b-in-illegal-subsidies. (viewed on June 10, 2012.

Catwalk Cartel: Sherman, William, "Catwalk Rocked by Legal Catfight," *Daily News*, March 14, 2004; St. John, Warren, "Behind the Catwalk, Suspicion and Suits," *New York Times*, April 18, 2004:sec. 9: 1, 12; Chandler, Neil, "Models in GBP 28m Wage Battle," *Daily Star*, June 6, 2004: 8; *Carolyn Fears et al. v. Wilhelmina Model Agency, Inc., et al.*, 02 Civ. 4911 (HB), United States District Court for the Southern District of New York, 2004 U.S. Dist. Lexis 4502; 2004–1 Trade Cas. (CCH) P74,351, March 23, 2004; graphics8.nytimes.com/packages/pdf/national/20071126Fears.pdf (July 5, 2007); "Singapore: Competition Commission Fines Modeling Agencies for Price Fixing," conventuslaw.com, December 8, 2011.

Market Power Versus Efficiency in Hospital Mergers: Town et al. (2006); Dafny (2009).

Air Ticket Prices and Rivalry: Weiher et al. (2002).

Bottled Water: Lazarus, David, "How Water Bottlers Tap Into All Sorts of Sources," *San Francisco Chronicle*, January 19, 2007; Tong, Vinnee, "What's in that Bottle?" suntimes.com, July 28, 2007; Cowherd, Kevin, "Bottled-Water Labeling: A Source of Irritation," baltimoresun.com, August 1,

2007; www.myspringwater.com/ SpringWaterInformation/ LeadingWaterBrands.aspx?CMP=KNC-SRCH_MSW_WTR (2007); www.worldwater.org/data20082009/Table20 .pdf (December 23, 2009); Alsever, Jennifer, "Bottled Water Sales Dry Up; Industry Asks 'Why?'" www.msnbc.msn.com/ id/34451973/ns/business-going_green, December 18, 2009; www.gallup.com/poll/153875/worry-water-air-pollution-historical-lows.aspx (viewed July 16, 2012).

Deadweight Losses in the Food and Tobacco Industries: Bhuyan and Lopez (1998); Bhuyan (2000).

Welfare Gain from Greater Toilet Paper Variety: "Going Soft?" *The Economist*, March 4, 2000:59; Hausman and Leonard (2002); www.upi.com/Odd_ News/2009/12/21/Brits-buying-top-end-TP-for-holidays/ UPI-84811261428817.

Zoning Laws as a Barrier to Entry by Hotel Chains: Suzuki (forthcoming).

Chapter 15

Should You Go to College?: Pérez-Peña, Richard, "U.S. Bachelor Degree Rate Passes Milestone," *New York Times*, February 23, 2012; www.bls.gov/news.release/hsgec.htm, April 19, 2012; Linn, Allison, "Fewer people See College as Good Financial Investment," lifeinc.today.msnbc.msn.com, July 17, 2012; *How American Pays for College*, SallieMae, 2012. The statistical analysis is based on annual earnings (wages or self-employment) data from the 2009 U.S. *Current Population Survey* (Miriam King, Steven Ruggles, J. Trent Alexander, Sarah Flood, Katie Genadek, Matthew B. Schroeder, Brandon Trampe, and Rebecca Vick. *Integrated Public Use Microdata Series, Current Population Survey: Version 3.0*. Minneapolis: University of Minnesota, 2010).

Black Death Raises Wages: Wellington (1990); www .history-magazine.com/black.html; www.historylearningsite .co.uk/black_death_of_1348-to-1350.htm; www.bric .postech.ac.kr/science/97now/00_11now/001127a.html.

Saving for Retirement: Author's calculations.

Durability of Telephone Poles: Marshall, Jonathan, "PG&E Cultivates Its Forest," *San Francisco Chronicle*, May 5, 1995:D1.

Falling Discount Rates and Self-Control: Shapiro (2004); Kan (2007); Gruber and Mullainathan (2005); Zeleny, Jeff, "Occasional Smoker, 47, Signs Tobacco Bill," *New York Times*, June 23, 2009; www.gallup.com/poll/1717/ Tobacco-Smoking.aspx (view July 22, 2012); aspire2025 .org.nz/2012/05/22/article-support-for-a-tobacco-endgame, May 22, 2012.

Redwood Trees: Berck, Peter, and William R. Bentley, "Hotelling's Theory, Enhancement, and the Taking of the Redwood National Park," *American Journal of Agricultural Economics*, 79(2), May 1997: 287–298; Berck, Peter, personal communications.

Chapter 16

Flight Insurance: www.worldtravelcenter.com (viewed July 26, 2012); www.ntsb.gov/data/table3_2012.html and www .ntsb.gov/data/table6_2012.html (viewed July 26, 2012).

Gambling: Friedman and Savage (1948); Brunk (1981); Gurdon, Meghan Cox, "British Accuse Their Lottery of Robbing the Poor to Give to the Rich," *San Francisco Chronicle*, November 25, 1995: D1; Coll, Steve, "Chances Are Brits Have Bet on It," *San Francisco Examiner*, July 10, 1994:4; Pollack, Andrew, "In the Gaming Industry, the House Can Have Bad Luck, Too," *New York Times*, July 25, 1999: Business, 4; Garrett (2001); Walton, Marsha, "The Business of Gambling," CNN.com, July 6, 2005; grossannualwager.com/Primary Navigation/Online Data Store/internet_gambling_data.htm (December 2009); www .americangaming.org/Industry/factsheets/statistics_detail .cfv?id=7 (December 2009); www.elottery.com/markets.html (December 2009); www.elottery.com/markets.html (viewed July 26, 2012); www.gbgc.com/2012/02/2011-global-gambling-revenues-passed-us-400-billion (viewed July 26, 2012).

Harry Potter's Magic: Gardner, Amanda, "Harry Potter Books Keep Kids Safe," www.healthday.com, December 22, 2005; "Harry Potter and the Injury-Free Children," *San Francisco Chronicle*, December 27, 2005: A2.

Weathering Bad Sales: Werdigier, Julia, "Tesco, British Grocer, Uses Weather to Predict Sales," *New York Times*, September 2, 2009; Cohen, Tamara, "Here Is the Shopping Forecast: How Supermarkets Use Weather Predictions to Decide What to Stock," www.dailymail.co.uk, August 16, 2011.

Employees' Failure to Diversify: Lim, Paul J., "Don't Paint Nest Eggs in Company Colors," *New York Times*, March 30, 2008; Mincer, Jilian, "Company-Stock Ownership Down Amid Fears," *Financial Advisor*, financialadviserblog .dowjones.com/blog/stay-ahead-of-your-clients/company-stock-ownership-down-amid-fears (viewed April 1, 2012).

Limited Insurance for Natural Disasters: Joseph B. Treaster, "Insurer Plans to Curb Sales Along Coasts," *New York Times*, October 10, 1996; Joseph B. Treaster, "Why Insurers Shrink from Earthquake Risk," *New York Times*, November 21, 1999; Paul Vitello, "Home Insurers Canceling in East," *New York Times*, October 16, 2007, Pielke et al. (2008); "Tropical Storm Bonnie Dissipates; Still No Plan from Congress on Flood Insurance," www.insurancenewsnet.com/ article.aspx?id=210913&type=newswires, July 28, 2010; Bandel, Carolyn, "Swiss Re Says 2011 Natural Disasters Cost Insurers \$110 Billion," www.bloomberg.com, March 28, 2012; Lehmann, Evan, "State Insurance Programs Continue to Grow Amid Hurricane Lull," *ClimateWire*, July 12, 2012; Kunreuther and Heal (2012).

Biased Estimates: Benjamin et al. (2001); "What Should You Really Be Afraid of? Mortality Risks," www.findarticles .com/p/articles/mi_m0GER/is_2002_Fall/ai_93135768. (viewed June 26, 2012); Hu, Arthur, "Death Spectrum," April 11, 2011, www.arthurhu.com/index/health/death .htm#deathrank (viewed July 26, 2012); International Shark Attack File, *Ichthyology*, www.flmnh.ufl.edu/fish/sharks/ isaf/graphs.htm (viewed on July 26, 2012).

Chapter 17

Trade and Pollution: Tideman and Tullock (1976); wto.org (viewed August 1, 2012); www.trade.gov (viewed August 1, 2012).

Spam: A Negative Externality: Henderson, Nicole, "Symantec Report Finds Spam Accounts for 73 Percent of June Email," *Web Host Industry Review*, June 28, 2011; Caliendo, Marco, et al. (2012); Musil, Steven, "Experts Take Down Grum Spam Botnet, World's Third Largest," net.csnet.com, July 18, 2012; Magnier, Mark, "India Tops List of Spam Email Spewers," *Los Angeles Times*, July 21, 2012; *April 2012 Internet Threats Trend Report*, commtouch.com (viewed July 29, 2012).

Reducing Pulp and Paper Mill Pollution: Shadbegian and Gray (2003); Shimshack and Ward (2005); Gray, and Shimshack (2011).

Why Tax Drivers: Levitt and Porter (2001); Grabowski and Morrisey (2006), Edlin and Karaca-Mandic (2006), Anderson (2008); Hill et al. (2009); "Dutch Road Tax Inflames Debate in Neighboring Germany," *Deutsche Welle*, November 16, 2009, www.dw-world.de/dw/article/0,,4896686,00.html; cesifo-group.de/portal/pls/portal/docs/1/1192818.PDF (viewed August 1, 2012); Anderson and Auffhammer (2011).

Protecting Babies: Currie and Walker (2011); Knittel et al. (2011).

Buying a Town: Seelye, Katharine Q., "Utility Buys Town It Choked, Lock, Stock and Blue Plume," *New York Times*, May 13, 2002; "Cheshire Ohio," *Abandoned*, www.abandonedonline.net/neighborhoods/cheshire-ohio (viewed on August 1, 2012).

U.S. Cap and Trade Programs: Burtraw, Dallas, "Trading Emissions to Clean the Air: Exchanges Few but Savings Many," *Resources*, 122, Winter 1996: 3–6; Passell, Peter, "For Utilities, New Clean-Air Plan," *New York Times*, November 18, 1994: C1, C6; Passell, Peter, "Economic Scene," *New York Times*, January 4, 1996: C2; Rensberger, Boyce, "Clean Air Sale," *Washington Post*, August 8, 1999: W7; Schmalensee et al. (1998); EPA (2011); www.epa.gov/airmarkets/trading/2012/12spotbids.html, 2012; www.epa.gov/airtrends/sulfur.html (viewed August 1, 2012).

For Whom the Bridge Tolls: Michael Cabanatuan "New Tolls Don't Gum Up Bay Bridge Commute," *San Francisco Chronicle*, July 2, 2010; Will Kane, "Bay Area Bridge Tolls Take a Toll on Commuters," *San Francisco Chronicle*, July 29, 2010.

Radiohead's "Public Good" Experiment: Jeff Leads, "Radiohead to Let Fans Decide What to Pay for Its New Album," *New York Times*, October 2, 2007; Eliot Van Buskirk, "Estimates: Radiohead Made Up to $10 Million on Initial Album Sales," blog.wired.com/music/2007/10/estimates-radio.html, October 19, 2007; David Jenison, "Radiohead Fans Still Not Over the *Rainbow*," www.eonline.com, January 9, 2008; Perry, Andrew, "Radiohead's King of Limbs Is Wet Weekend Mood Music," *The Telegraph*, February 25, 2011.

What's Their Beef?: Holland, Gina, "Top Court Considers Challenge to Beef Ads," *San Francisco Chronicle*, December 9, 2004:C1, C4; www.extension.iastate.edu/agdm/articles/ mceowen/McEowJuly05.htm; www.beefboard.org/promotion/checpromotion.asp (December 2009; August 2012).

Chapter 18

Dying to Work: Viscusi (1979); Dick Meister, "Safety First!" www.truth-out.org/safety-first61799, July 28, 2010; Kris Alingod, "Massey to Resume Operations in West Virginia Mine Despite Deaths," allheadlinenews.com, July 29, 2010; osha.gov (August 2010); Mauriello, Tracie, and Len Boselovic, "Historic Fine Issued for Mine Disaster," *Pittsburgh Post-Gazette*, December 7, 2011, www.post-gazette.com/pg/11341/1195085-455.stm.

Risky Hobbies: Cropper, Carol Marie, "Risk Takers Pay Dearly: It's the Danger of Living Fearlessly," *New York Times*, April 2, 1995: sec. 3:11; McIntyre, Douglas, "The 7 Deadly Hobbies: Pastimes Your Insurer Hates," dailyfinance.com, October 4, 2011.

Changing a Firm's Name: Cabral, and Hortacsu (2010); McDevitt (2011).

Adverse Selection on eBay: Lewis (2011); pages.ebay.com/help/sell/motorfees.html (viewed August 10, 2012).

Chapter 19

Health Insurance: Finkelstein et al. (2011); Kawalski (2012); Schmitz (2012).

Selfless or Selfish Doctors?: Lu (2011).

Contracts and Productivity in Agriculture: Foster and Rosenzweig (1994).

Music Contracts: Changing Their Tunes: Smith, Ethan, "Bands on the Run," July 14, 2006, p. W8; www.adweek.com/aw/magazine/article_display.jsp?vnu_content_id=1003686015, December 24, 2007; entertainment.howstuffworks.com/recording-contract.htm, 2008; www.contactmusic.com/news.nsf/story/leto-reached-out-to-de-havilland-over-emi-lawsuit_1124108 (November 30, 2009); www.spin.com/articles/jay-z-leaves-def-jam-his-own-label, May 22, 2009; www.billboard.com/bbcom/news/article_display.jsp?vnu_content_id=1003591100#/bbcom/news/article_display.jsp?vnu_content_id=1003591100 (viewed August 16, 2012); masterclasslady.com/2012/02/16/canadian-carly-rae-jepson-signed-by-justin-bieber, February 16, 2012.

The Mortgage Meltdown: riginatortimes.com/content/templates/default.aspx?a=2724&template=print-article.htm, December 27, 2007; Erin McCormick and Carolyn Said, "Investors Own about One-Fifth of Bay Area Homes in Foreclosure," *San Francisco Chronicle*, December 16, 2007; Adams et al. (2009); www.realtytrac.com/content/foreclosure-market-report/july-2012-us-foreclosure-market-report-7332 (viewed August 16, 2012).

Layoffs Versus Pay Cuts: Hall and Lilien (1979); www.bls.gov (August 2010); Steven Greenhouse, "More Workers Face Pay Cuts, Not Furloughs," *New York Times*, August 3, 2010.

Index

Credits